THE
CAMBRIDGE
ECONOMIC HISTORY

GENERAL EDITORS: M. POSTAN, Professor Emeritus of Economic History in the University of Cambridge; D. C. COLEMAN, Professor of Economic History in the University of Cambridge; and PETER MATHIAS, Chichele Professor of Economic History in the University of Oxford

VOLUME V

THE
CAMBRIDGE
ECONOMIC HISTORY
OF EUROPE

VOLUME V

THE ECONOMIC ORGANIZATION
OF EARLY MODERN EUROPE

EDITED BY

E. E. RICH

Sometime Vere Harmsworth Professor
of Imperial and Naval History in the
University of Cambridge, and
Sometime Master of St Catharine's
College

AND

C. H. WILSON

Professor of Modern History in
the University of Cambridge, and
Professor of History and Civilization
in the European University Institute
at Florence

CAMBRIDGE UNIVERSITY PRESS

CAMBRIDGE

LONDON . NEW YORK . MELBOURNE

1977

Published by the Syndics of the Cambridge University Press
The Pitt Building, Trumpington Street, Cambridge CB2 1RP
Bentley House, 200 Euston Road, London NW1 2DB
32 East 57th Street, New York, NY 10022, USA
296 Beaconsfield Parade, Middle Park, Melbourne 3206, Australia

Printed in Great Britain at the
University Press, Cambridge

Library of Congress Cataloguing in Publication Data (Revised)

Main entry under title:

The Cambridge economic history of Europe from the decline
of the Roman empire.

Includes bibliographies and indexes.
Vol. 2 planned by Sir John Clapham and Eileen Power,
edited by M. Postan and E. E. Rich.
CONTENTS. – v. 1. The agrarian life of the middle ages.
– v. 2. Trade and industry in the middle ages. [etc.]
1. Europe – Economic conditions. 2. Europe – History.
I. Clapham, Sir John Harold, 1873–1946, ed. II. Power,
Eileen Edna, 1889–1940, joint ed.
HC240.C3   330.94   41–3509

ISBN 0 521 08710 4

CONTENTS

List of Illustrations　　　　　　　　　　　　　　　*page* ix

Preface　　　　　　　　　　　　　　　　　　　　xi

CHAPTER I

The Historical Study of Economic Growth and Decline in Early Modern History

By C. H. WILSON, Professor of Modern History in the University of Cambridge, and Professor of History and Civilization in the European University Institute at Florence

I　The Ends and Means of Economic History: Some Changing Concepts　　　　　　　　　　　　　　　　　I
II　Some Case Studies　　　　　　　　　　　　　　21
III　The Limitations of Historical Analysis　　　　　35

CHAPTER II

Agriculture in the Vital Revolution

By B. H. SLICHER VAN BATH, Emeritus Professor of Economic History in the Agricultural University of Wageningen

I　General Characteristics of the Period　　　　　42
II　Agrarian Production　　　　　　　　　　　　57
III　Receipts and Expenditure in Farming Husbandry　104
IV　Landownership　　　　　　　　　　　　　　109
V　Serfdom in Central and Eastern Europe　　　　113
VI　Social Stratification, Prices and Population　　123

CHAPTER III

The European Fisheries in Early Modern History

By A. R. MICHELL, Lecturer in Economic History, University of Hull

I　Sources for the History of Fishing　　　　　　134
II　Natural Fluctuations　　　　　　　　　　　　135

III The Different Structures of Fishing *page* 140
IV The Herring Fishery 142
V The Cod Fishery 155
VI Pilchard and Mackerel Fisheries 166
VII The Whale Fishery 168
VIII Markets and the Consumption of Fish 172
IX Fishing in the Economy and the Government Response 178
X The Eighteenth-Century Problem 182
XI Conclusion 184

CHAPTER IV

The Changing Patterns of Trade

By KRISTOF GLAMANN, Professor of History, University of Copenhagen

I The Ship and the Plough 185
II Demand and Consumption 195
III Areas and Trade Flows 205
IV The Market and its Organization 265

CHAPTER V

Monetary, Credit and Banking Systems

By HERMAN VAN DER WEE, Professor of Social and Economic History, Catholic University of Louvain

I Money and Credit in the Local Economy 290
II The World of Trade and Finance 306
III The Financing of the Mercantilist State 358
IV Conclusion 391

CHAPTER VI

The Nature of Enterprise

By BARRY SUPPLE, Professor of Economic and Social History,
University of Sussex

I	The Framework of Enterprise	page 394
II	International Enterprise in Trade and Finance	407
III	Industrial Enterprise	424
IV	Corporate Enterprise	436
V	Aristocracy and Enterprise	447
VI	Nations and Enterprise	451
VII	Conclusion	459

CHAPTER VII

The Organization of Industrial Production

By HERMANN KELLENBENZ, Professor of Economic History,
Friedrich-Alexander University, Erlangen-Nuremberg

I	The Sixteenth-Century Prospect	462
II	Definition	462
III	Location	462
IV	Organization	464
V	Technological Progress	472
VI	Investment Costs and Financing	478
VII	The Role of Government	480
VIII	Private Entrepreneurship and the Labour Force	484
IX	Production	488
X	Industrial Production: Expansion and Crisis	543
XI	Conclusion	547

CHAPTER VIII

Government and Society

By BETTY BEHRENS, Fellow Emerita, Clare Hall, University of Cambridge

I The Military-Bureaucratic Monarchies and the *Société d'Ordres* *page* 549
II The Monarchs and their Nobility 561
III Mercantilism and the Bourgeoisie 573
IV The Social and Political Gospels of the German and French Enlightenments 588
V The Physiocrats and the Peasants 604

Bibliographies

Editors' Note 621
Chapter I, p. 623; Chapter II, p. 626; Chapter III, p. 644;
Chapter IV, p. 645; Chapter V, p. 651; Chapter VI,
p. 669; Chapter VII, p. 672; Chapter VIII, p. 676

Index 681

ILLUSTRATIONS

1 Population/number of households in the province of Overijssel *page* 130
2 Major herring fishing grounds, with principal fish caught in various parts of Europe 136
3 Annual fluctuations in Dutch herrings passing through the Sound, 1600–49 137
4 The fishing banks from Cape Cod to Labrador 156
5 Herring passing through the Sound 165
6 Shipments of fish by one Dieppe commission merchant, 1729 167
7 Centres of metal production 490–1
8 Centres of textile production 512–13

PREFACE

This volume of the *Cambridge Economic History of Europe* and its predecessor (1967) were conceived and planned as a whole. As the Editor's Preface to volume IV explained, the emphasis of that volume was upon what he called the 'formative influences' – social, technological, environmental, intellectual – which helped to shape the early modern economy. The emphasis of volume V is upon the organization of production, agricultural and manufacturing, of the processes of commercial distribution and exchange, of money, credit, banking and the varied and complex modes of payment, and upon certain social aspects of the early modern economy.

No one can regret the delay in publishing this volume, and *a fortiori* the reasons for it, more than the Editors. Contributions have been delayed by the illness and withdrawal of some contributors, and the premature death of another, David Joslin. The volume might still have appeared earlier if we had been prepared to scrap our plan and replace it by a pot-pourri of impromptu essays. We nevertheless decided to adhere to our original scheme, even though the search for contributors able and willing to help us replace the contributions thus lost was necessarily slow and difficult. We can only offer our gratitude to those who have stepped into the vacant places, and hardly less, to those others who endured with great patience the long delay which separated the writing of their chapters from the satisfaction of seeing them in print. Regrettably, it has not proved possible for those earlier contributors (especially Professor Supple) to revise their chapters in the light of more recent scholarship.

Cambridge   C.H.W.
1976

CHAPTER I

The Historical Study of Economic Growth and Decline in Early Modern History

I. *The Ends and Means of Economic History: Some Changing Concepts*

RECENT DECADES have seen important changes in the objectives, techniques and methodologies of economic history. As a confluence of two different streams of thought and practice – that of the economic theorists on the one hand and that of the general or political historians on the other – economic history often meandered uncertainly in its course, urged sometimes more by one tributary, sometimes more by the other. Each national 'school' reflected the characteristics of its diverse ancestry, but in all the traditional pull of 'institutional' history was strong. The habit of proceeding by the more or less disparate analysis of celebrated institutions already familiar through their political importance – gilds, companies, colonial trading organizations, public banks, etc. – went hand in hand with an adumbration of the macro-economy of this or that state, again vaguely familiar (if only in outline) from the earlier study of the political history of the different nations. To be sure, this latter varied in interest and influence with the actual history of the individual state. It assumed a lower profile in a country like the Netherlands with its obstinate traditions of local municipal autonomy and provincial federation than it did in the economic history of modern Germany, where late but swift and revolutionary industrial-ization was reflected in the strong political and strategic orientations of the school of Gustav Schmoller and the 'historical economists'. At the same time the strength of the German tradition of idealist philosophy was also vividly reflected in the socio-economic analysis of German historians like Max Weber, Werner Sombart and Artur Spiethoff: hence the 'ideal types' of the first, the 'systems' of the second and the isolation by the third of *Gestalt* theory – 'the closest possible approxi-mation [of theory] to observable reality'.[1]

German economic history differed, in turn, from French, which reflected the strength of the positivist tradition in French philosophy since Comte but shared the same emphasis on inductive argument.

[1] 'Pure theory and economic gestalt theory: ideal types and real types', by A. Spiethoff, translated by Dr Fritz Redlich, printed in *Enterprise and Secular Change*, ed. by F. C. Lane and J. C. Riemersma (Homewood, Illinois, 1953).

Theory was to be the child of empirical data in the social sciences. This passionate ambition to achieve an objective reality, the concept that the observer must place himself entirely outside the situation which he studies, was characteristic of Emile Durkheim's studies of suicide or the division of labour and of François Simiand's study of price and wage fluctuations. Quantitative measurement was vital to the method (though it did not constitute the whole of it), and French socio-economic history down to the work of Marc Bloch, Ernest Labrousse, Georges Lefebvre and the modern school of the *Annales* pays continuing tribute to the strength of a deeply-rooted French tradition.

Central to Marc Bloch's highly personal version of the tradition was his emphasis on the 'understanding' of history: for this it was essential that the necessary work of specialists should be linked by others intent on seeking out these underlying 'causes' of historical change and developing 'differences' which were embedded in the various social structures. This was the vital and suggestive function of comparative history, which would identify both similarities and differences between institutions at different times and in different places.

Quite other were the ideas of Eli Heckscher, the distinguished Swedish historian. Trained as an economist and powerfully influenced by classical economic theory, Heckscher could not accept the idea of an underlying antipathy between theory and history evident in so much economic historical writing. As a theorist he held passionately that since 'the economic problem must be *fundamentally* the same in all ages',[1] economic theory – by which he meant principally classical theories of supply and demand – must be the historians' principal tool for selecting and explaining the facts of economic history. Heckscher stopped short of claiming that 'the real economic meaning of what has happened' would in every case be made clear by a wave of the theorist's wand; but he did believe that without a basic theoretical training (in classical economics) the student would stand helpless when confronted by the problems of this kind of history.

Heckscher's *tour de force*, his great study of *Mercantilism*, vindicated in part his claims for 'theory'; it also revealed the hazards of its historical application to conditions very different from those in which it was conceived. Perhaps it also dismissed too lightly the distinction between theory and reality which Archdeacon William Cunningham had cannily made in the introduction to his great three-volume study *The Growth of English Industry and Commerce* many years earlier:[2]

[1] 'A plea for theory in economic history', by Eli Heckscher, *Economic History* (supplement to the *Economic Journal*), 1 (1926–9), 525–34.
[2] W. Cunningham, *The Growth of English Industry and Commerce* (5th edition, Cambridge, 1922), I, 21–2.

The science [of Political Economy]...is hypothetical and claims to trace the action of economic forces in a well-defined sphere of life, and to show what always tends to happen in so far as they have free play...But with Economic History it is different: the very sphere we are about to study is conditioned by the political circumstances which have extended or diminished the area over which the English government and the English race have held sway at different times...History must trace out the conscious efforts...to develop the resources and expand the commerce of the realm.[1]

Sir John Clapham, first incumben of the new Chair of Economic History at Cambridge, took up where Cunningham had left off. But Clapham was a liberal where Cunningham was a nationalist. He was also a statistician. Clapham's article on 'Economic History as a Discipline' in the *Encyclopaedia of the Social Sciences*[2] set out the problems and opportunities of the new kinds of economic history made possible by statistical records, shrewdly narrowing the claims of theory which, he thought, too often handed over the history of important social problems (like prices and wages) to inductive economists who were historians only by accident. In a few brisk and penetrating paragraphs, Clapham identified the weakness of that kind of economic history which merely took over the conventional divisions of general history. Equally, however, he summed up the failings of such methods as those of the German historians who, he believed, had emphasized the importance of 'stages' of development in history too strongly and dogmatically and without adequate attention to the simple set of criteria he then set forth:

Every economic historian should...have acquired what may be called the statistical sense, the habit of asking in relation to any institution, policy, group or movement the questions: how large? how long? how often? how representative? The requirement seems obvious but a good deal of the older politico-institutional economic history was less useful than it might have been through neglect of it.

To this statistical sense of quantity must be added the sense of size in spatial terms: the economic historian must be something of a geographer.

It may be said that these are the views of a working craftsman in history rather than those of a philosopher; that they reflect the age of the Blue Book of which Clapham remains the acknowledged master, but that economic history is not all Victoriana. There is some truth in such criticisms, especially the last one, as is proved by such contemporary studies as Georges Duby's *Early Growth of the European Economy* (1974) with its rich and vivid use of sociological, archaeological and anthropological evidence. Yet in large measure the wisdom of Clap-

[1] *Ibid.*   [2] *Encyclopaedia of the Social Sciences*, v (New York, 1930), 327-30.

ham's words has not only survived the passage of time but heralds and describes much (not all) of that recent development of economic history labelled – a trifle presumptuously, for the title suggests an ignorance of the quantitative sophistication of Clapham's own monumental works – the 'new economic history'.

Clapham was not content with devising a practical approach to the *technical* problems of economic history: he also attacked with earthy vigour the emptiness of economic theory itself – a shelf lined with empty boxes, as he called them, abstractions devoid of any real content. Clapham's successor as Professor of Economic History at Cambridge has delineated sharply the problems of re-incorporating these economic abstractions into their environment, from which they had originally been removed for ease of analysis and manipulation. 'This work of re-incorporation', Professor Postan has written, 'can best be done by students whose job it is to deal with real facts and with social situations in their entirety' – in other words, by those historians and sociologists appropriate to the task of attempting to fill the voids in history which correspond to the voids in economic and social theory.[1]

Comprehensive attempts to explain history in terms of theory have not been killed off easily. Sir John Hicks has braved the critics of both professions with *A Theory of Economic History* (1969), and Douglass North and R. P. Thomas have followed with their *Rise of the Western World: A New Economic History* (1973). Both works have been criticized by historians for being too loosely related to actual historical occurrences. And to this perennial complaint of the practising historian faced with attempted comprehensive interpretations is now added another, from E. L. Jones: 'what now seems necessary is not so much to achieve a union of economic history with economics but its reunion with history'.[2] The inference is a fair one. Moreover, it helps to explain a current change in the nature of the continuing controversy over the relationship between economic history and economic theory: a change that may be characterized as a move away from exogenous and towards endogenous theory. As the social element in economic history grows (e.g. via the investigation of demographic and family structure) the manipulative character of history as a social science is increasingly emphasized. Purely exogenous theory has invariably proved either too general or wholly irrelevant to the needs of the working historian. Its logical modes will continue to be a useful source of working hypothesis; but his greater need is for working tools, and it is this which is

---

[1] M. M. Postan, 'Sir John Clapham: the economic historian', *University of Leeds Review*, XVII: 1 (May 1974).

[2] E. L. Jones, 'Institutional determinism and the rise of the western world', *Economic Enquiry*, XII: 1 (March 1974), 121.

creating new, empirical, statistical methods which are emerging endogenously from the stuff of history itself.

The feature most characteristic of economic historiography in the last quarter-century has been a growing degree of integration between component parts which formerly stood in a semi-independent relationship to one another. This semi-independence was in part a consequence of the unresolved problems of the relationship between history and economic theory already remarked upon; in part, of the technical weakness of the social elements in the study of economic history and, in consequence, of the willingness of historians to suppose that the different economic institutions concerned with agrarian, mercantile, industrial, financial and other activity could be treated satisfactorily as free-standing phenomena. It followed that while the older economic history produced many institutional studies of enduring value, on, e.g., manorial organization, gilds, companies, colonial trading organizations, industrial invention, technology, etc., it remained weak where the social or abstract components of history were concerned. Population movements, their causes and consequences, prices, salaries, wages and profits were often treated only in the most nominal fashion. A widely read textbook like the *Economic History of England* by E. Lipson or H. O. Meredith's study of the same title treats population movement only *en passant*. L. Dechesne's *Histoire Économique et Sociale de la Belgique* (1932), like many other European studies of the period, sets out a few basic data of population growth but does not attempt to relate them to other phenomena of change. Taxation long occupied the centre of the stage for political historians. It suffered an equally long neglect at the hands of economic historians and is even now only beginning to be the object of serious attention once more.

In spite of its often high descriptive merits, this older type of institutional history was little regarded by economists. If for them it seemed too loosely constructed to conform to the canons of logical analysis, to students brought up in the political tradition it seemed – *pace* the socialist enthusiasm of a Tawney, the laissez-faire passion of an Unwin, or the convictions of an anti-laissez-faire believer like William Cunningham – history *manqué*. Economic history seemed to describe too much and to explain too little; hence the attractions of Marxian analysis for those who felt this lack of explanatory power. Marxist doctrine at least seemed to provide a set of explanatory links between the disparate institutions which made up the various national economies at any given moment in time. The difficulties emerged only when objective research exposed the problems of fitting the awkward facts of history back into the preordained historical framework of Marxist thought. In consequence, many an enthusiast was compelled to face the dilemma: to abandon the framework, to keep it so loose or broad that it lacked anything but semantic significance, or to risk a confrontation between fact and theory.

The relatively recent shift of interest towards a closer integration of the elements in socio-economic history has not eliminated the schools of Marxist, Manchester or *dirigiste* thought from economic history altogether. It has, however, much reduced the importance of the older debate on the relationship of 'external' theory to history and to some extent has shifted the focus of the practising historian away from these older doctrinal influences on the interpretation of events. To the fore have come the studies of population movements and of *conjoncture*; of total demographic growth, stagnation or decline; birth, death and marriage ratios; the influence of the occupational structure of society, life expectation, etc.; of fluctuations in prices, incomes and their relationship to population movements: in short, social as well as economic, non-economic as well as economic influences upon creation and distribution of wealth. It was especially those historians who studied pre-industrial, agrarian and largely rural societies where yields were low and economic growth was limited by 'internal' obstacles (technological ignorance, the blind forces of custom and conservatism) and checked by external disaster (bad harvests, murrains, plagues, storm and flood) who were most deeply struck by the close relationship between the growth or decline of human numbers and the progress or regress of the economy. It is no accident that the extension and refinement of this type of socio-economic analysis should have come from scholars like M. M. Postan and B. H. Slicher van Bath, whose original enquiries were centred upon the flux of pre-industrial society.

The logical development of the basic links between demography and conjuncture leads the student ineluctably back into examination of the social structure and social stratification. The accumulation of global numbers, prices and incomes is not enough. For society is not uniform in its activity: it comprises both producers and consumers, and they are neither wholly identical nor wholly different. Even the small peasant farmers who formed numerically the largest group in the agrarian society of early modern history were buyers as well as sellers, often producing insufficient for their own needs, sometimes producing a surplus. What they produced is therefore also critical to an understanding of their role in the early economy. Were they limited to a largely static role in a monoculture based on cereals? Or were they capable of diversifying their production, spreading their risks and earning a modest competence for the purchase of non-essential but desirable goods on the market? On the answer to this (as we shall see) was to depend the answer to the fundamental question – to grow or not to grow?

Very early in the revolution of thinking that has come to fruition in this type of history, François Simiand encountered the problem that bedevils this as it bedevils all systems of historical interpretation that strive after totality. In the attempt to eliminate unscientific methods and to quantify to the maximum the treatment of his enquiries, Simiand nevertheless found himself compelled to recognize the existence of accidental happenings exogenous to his theory and method which exercised an undeniable influence on the course of events. One was the effect of the growth of the supply of money on price levels. It was not impossible to bring the fiduciary issue of money by the state into an unbroken circle of linked phenomena satisfactory to minds dominated by economic logic. The discovery of America, the development and export of its wealth of precious metal to Europe, remained a more obstinate problem. Was the great inflation of the sixteenth century an exception to the rule increasingly seen as the natural law governing economic change? Did economic science, in the shape of quantity theory, here help to explain a departure from the norm of 'internal' explanation? Or could the 'price revolution', after all, be explained by the demographic growth that preceded and accompanied it? Or are we oversimplifying a problem that can be solved only in terms of a large population, greater demand *and* a larger monetary supply? Similar historiographical propensities may be seen at work elsewhere, illustrating the growing tendency to revert to internal explanations of socio-economic phenomena in history at the expense of exogenous, and less logically explicable, causes.

Demographic history supplies several examples. For a century and more the Malthusian conviction persisted that eighteenth-century population growth owed much to a system of outdoor poor relief (the so-called 'Speenhamland' system) which put a premium on large families and more births. This explanation, a mixture of direct observation and economic logic, held sway for a long time. It was a Cambridge historian, Talbot Griffiths, in a Trinity College fellowship thesis which surely had as great an impact upon historical thinking on an important issue as any of its kind had ever enjoyed, who reversed the Malthusian doctrine and placed the onus (or credit) for the upturn in population squarely on the fall in the death-rate; this was attributed to causes such as advances in medical knowledge and treatment. The heresy was not to last long. Steadily the birth-rate was brought back into the picture as economic logic regained its hold on the historical process; for economists abhor exogeny as nature abhors a vacuum. Yet if economic historians quickly deserted the theory that accidental medical discovery or even hospital development could have reduced mortality in the eighteenth century, there was still enough evidence to hold many of them to the opinion that the expulsion of the black rat by the brown played a direct and vital part in putting a term to the plague, at least in its bubonic form. Was this a decisive victory for the exogenous factor? Not at all: other historians were not slow to advance the hypothesis that vulnerability to plague was more important than the virulence of the plague itself. And vulnerability or resistance to this, as to other diseases, was directly related to malnutrition or otherwise. Demography was back in the unbroken circle of economic causation.

A problem of quite different character – the phenomenon of early industrialization in Britain – has nevertheless also evoked a similar concern with demographic and agrarian change. The early signs of industrial growth in Britain (as illustrated e.g. by the export statistics constructed by T. S. Ashton and Elizabeth Schumpeter) preceded any marked signs of population growth. This knowledge seemed likely to prolong the hypothesis that industrialization was export-led, given the substantial rise in export figures. That some of it was orientated towards export (especially colonial) demand seems true. Equally evidently, a rising proportion went to satisfying rising domestic demand; and this can only have come by way of increased purchasing power within sections of a still predominantly rural society. Without placing too much weight on the statistics, it seems that we may accept the general impression of substantially increased arable production and higher values of stock-farming, wool and hides, etc. as reliable evidence that agricultural wealth was indeed rising in the late seventeenth century. As to the set-back that undoubtedly occurred between the 1730s and 1750s, it seems likely that this was more serious on the Midland clays than elsewhere. East Anglia and the west and north of Britain saw a fairly steady rise in well-being which was subsumed in general progress as the pace of manufacturing, agricultural and demographic change all quickened into sustained movement after the 1760s. To this under-pinning of domestic demand by social and economic change must be added the steady spread of a network of internal linkages of mutual supply and demand (including the vital and still insufficiently appreci-ated link of water transport) within the industrial sector itself. In Britain two scholars in particular, T. S. Ashton and J. D. Chambers, helped to unfold the implications of these linkages for a full understanding of the eighteenth-century economy as a whole.

Behind the workings of demographic forces, their details often still obscure, historians have recently discerned a series of broad movements. The first chapter of volume IV of this *History*, by Professor Helleiner, described the remarkable rise in population that marked a period beginning in the late fifteenth century, continuing through the sixteenth century and falling away only in the seventeenth century. The next chapter in the demographic story, described by Professor Michael Flinn as 'the stabilisation of mortality' in pre-industrial Europe, provides further new evidence of the factors exogenous to the strictly *economic* processes of change which explain the end of the demographic crisis.[1] His phrase derives from the discovery (which adds a fresh dimension to the account of demographic fluctuations provided in Professor Helleiner's chapter, written in the 1960s) that the high death-rate which prevented European populations from achieving steady, uninterrupted total growth was not itself steady or uniform. The recorded 'rates' used by historians often merely averaged out over the decades an incidence of mortality which in reality varied from relatively low rates to disastrously high 'crisis' rates. This critical 'bunching' of deaths resulted from a sudden concatenation of disasters – war, deaths in action, the accompanying destruction and ravaging of the civilian population, and outbreaks of disease (typhus especially) which followed in the wake of the destruction. Even more important were the famines which struck hard and often – as in 1598, 1602, 1623, 1667, the 1690s, the 1720s and the 1740s. These mortality crises when deaths soared to quite abnormal heights were characteristic of the age. Compared with its mean average of 337 annual deaths in the previous and succeeding quinquennia, Basle, in 1667, suffered 1,626 deaths, an excess of 1,289 or 382 per cent. These 'famine crises' persisted long after western Europe had seen the last of the plague, at any rate in its truly horrific forms, in the latter part of the seventeenth century. England apparently suffered less devastating harvest failures than Scandinavia or France, yet even in England mortality was still very high in the bad harvest years of the 1720s and the 1740s.

The 'famine crises' did not vanish from history in the twinkling of an eye. Sir John Clapham once wrote: 'If the nineteenth century had done nothing else, it would deserve credit for having first reduced and then, it may fairly be said, removed the age-long dread of famine from the peasants and people of Western Europe.'[2] More recently, historians have pushed back the 'famine frontier', at least in some areas of the west. The French historians Goubert and Meuvret have designated the 1740s as the time when the great subsistence crises which had devastated French history through the centuries finally began to tail away. The same was true in other places too. Somewhere between the late seventeenth and the late eighteenth centuries, with variations from country to country, harvest failures lost their earlier, lethal power.

[1] See M. W. Flinn, 'The stabilisation of mortality in pre-industrial western Europe', in *The Journal of European Economic History*, III: 2 (1974), 285–318.

[2] J. H. Clapham, *The Economic Development of France and Germany 1815–1914* (3rd ed., 1928), p. 402.

Many factors contributed to this fundamental amelioration in the condition of humanity. One arose from a direct response of peoples to the threat of starvation. People migrated from the poor to less poor areas, alleviating food shortages in countries like Ireland, Scotland, Poland and Spain. Improvements and additions to Europe's transport resources may possibly have made such migration marginally easier. Operated with great entrepreneurial skill, they certainly worked powerfully (*via* the Dutch and other mercantile fleets carrying grain from the Baltic) to cushion the effects of population increase on sixteenth- and seventeenth-century Europe, not only in the countries along the Atlantic seaboard but elsewhere too. In France and Switzerland, evidence accumulates that human skill and conscious forethought were also taking a hand in dealing with famine crises. Grain reserves were built up against misfortune; surpluses transferred from the better-provided to less-provided regions. More varied and sometimes more heavily yielding crops like potatoes, maize and rice reduced the risks inherent in monocultural agriculture.

As remarked earlier, it has not been fashionable in recent years to treat improved medicine as a very significant or direct influence in reducing mortality. While this is doubtless a justifiable verdict on medical therapy, preventive medicine may well have been more effective. Recent studies by Professor Carlo Cipolla have suggested that the stricter enforcement of quarantine regulations may have helped to check the spread of epidemics from country to country. Thus, in one way and another, the massive differences between region and region that had existed earlier were slowly somewhat reduced, prosperous and healthy regions protected against poverty-stricken or contaminated neighbours, poor regions assisted by reduced price differentials between good and bad harvest years.

The study of the various elements in the *conjoncture*, prices and wages in particular, has a long history. In England it goes back to the six-volume *History of Prices* by Thomas Tooke and William Newmarch published between 1838 and 1857, and to the works of J. E. Thorold Rogers, a classical scholar, philosopher and Tractarian priest of progressive social opinions whose appointment to the Tooke Chair of Statistics in the University of London enabled him to concentrate for the rest of his life on the study of economic problems, especially the collection and analysis of series of prices and wages. Rogers's main work was his six-volume *History of Agriculture and Prices* published from 1866 to 1887 and executed in the spirit of Tooke's own ideas. The scientific study of price history was continued on an international scale at the close of the nineteenth century by Georg Wiebe, whose gleanings of European prices were designed to prove the existence of a *Preis-*

revolution in the sixteenth century. François Simiand followed with his skilful research into French price history. Numerous additions have been made in their wake in different countries by the authors working under the aegis of the International Committee under Sir William Beveridge – Hauser, Elsas, Posthumus, Pribram, Hamilton, and Beveridge himself. The result was to reveal the rich complexity of price history. In the Netherlands, for example, it showed, as the Dutch editor, N. W. Posthumus, remarked, how increments of precious metal and successive doses of price inflation were not only absorbed and reconciled in the rising Dutch economy but probably represented an important element in its progress. They had 'a decisive favourable influence on our economy, thanks to the equilibrium established between productivity and the amount of money in circulation'.[1] In spite of serious lacunae, then, the history of prices and wages has received intensive scientific treatment of great value to historical analysts dealing with broad economic movements. It reached an important milestone with the publication of the essay by Henry Phelps Brown and Sheila Hopkins on seven centuries of prices of consumables and wages in England: here was a study which was a unique example of the cooperation of the techniques of economist, statistician and historian to which Clapham attached so much value.

More typical of the chequered history of economic historiography was the attempt by the American historian E. J. Hamilton to explain the decline of the Spanish (and inferentially the rise of the English) economy by a comparison of their responses to the impact of American silver. He suggested that down to about 1580 the influx of treasure had created a great 'profit inflation' in Spain, only to be followed by inevitable decline as wages caught up with and overtook prices. Profits thereupon turned into losses. Hamilton's thesis was enlarged upon generously by J. M. Keynes, whose great authority gave it much prestige: not, however, in the eyes of Hamilton's American colleague J. U. Nef, who attacked it vigorously in a paper delivered to the Anglo-American Historians' Conference in 1936. If the origins of modern capitalism were to be sought in rising prices and low labour costs, why did France (which suffered both) lag so far and so long behind? The controversy is now a classic and, like the classics, is dead; but it illustrates several features of historiographical development still worth a comment. First, one must note the poverty of historical evidence regarding *profits*. The evidence as to prices and wages might, as Nef showed, be debatable: the evidence of profits (which was what counted for the *producer*) was virtually non-existent. Profit margins

[1] N. W. Posthumus, *Inquiry into the History of Prices in Holland*, 2 vols. (Leiden, 1971), II, p. lxv.

were obtained by subtracting general wage costs from general prices – a method as likely to achieve reliable results as the attempt to calculate manufacturing profits from the statistics of the input of raw materials. No problem presents greater difficulties in the early modern period than the accurate calculation of gross (let alone net) profits. For the agricultural sector, the task is bedevilled by the poverty of evidence for the vast majority of peasant, small and medium farmers. Even for the noble and gentry owners of large or sizeable estates, the problems remain enormous, as Lawrence Stone's studies of the sixteenth- and seventeenth-century aristocracy have shown. The manufacturing sector presents equally intractable problems. As Professor Kellenbenz shows in his survey of European manufacturers in the same period (chapter VII, pp. 495–526 below), the most striking phenomenon of this pre-industrial age throughout all European countries was the growing control of many manufacturing processes by mercantile capital, though it fluctuated from place to place and industry to industry: in terms of textile organization, the putting-out process; in mining, large-scale capital investment in plant; and in brewing, the buildings, plant and equipment. The quintessential characteristic of the larger part of this type of investment, designed to meet the need for working capital, was its mobility. As Professor Supple has shown in his study of the early seventeenth-century English economy in crisis and change, entrepreneurs shifted their liquid resources swiftly and without warning to meet the exigencies of market demand. *Pace* the critics of industrial capitalism, who have seen it as capricious in its attitudes to humanity and negligent in its sense of social responsibility, its record compares well with that of its mercantile-capitalistic predecessor. And for a very obvious reason: in the period of full industrial capitalism the ownership of fixed capital demands, in the name of self-interest if for no higher reason, utmost effort to obtain a return on that more or less immovable investment to which business prosperity and probably familial sentiment are both attached. The merchant capitalist who controlled a large part of the manufactures of early modern Europe was a much more mobile, transient and elusive figure than his successors.[1] Business enterprise on any scale was as often as not a matter for partnership, and many partnerships were made up of groups which changed with disconcerting frequency. The calculation of real profit can never be easy; before fixed capital in great volume became a normal feature of manufacturing industry, it is far more speculative. Little wonder that historians have often been tempted to take the easy way out and assume that the trend of profits could be identified with those of production or

[1] See below, pp. 426, 460.

turnover; and if these were not available for the individual business or farm unit or industry, then some vague identity between the fortunes of the individual enterprise and the supposed national economic trend would have to do.

The temptations and pressures to execute such rough justice on the social or economic past are easily understood: but they do not lessen the errors that result from such haphazard methods. Historians have often read back into earlier history the experience of later periods when large national or even international markets, closely integrated by efficient, powered transport systems, responded more or less uniformly to pervasive commercial and technological influences and the injection of massive doses of capital. Such anachronisms have distorted the true nature of early economics. We are all too familiar with the smudging of history that has followed from rough and ready assumptions that period *A* was one of national prosperity in, say, textiles, and that period *B* was one of decline. Regional differences, the difference between one *branch* of the textile industry and another, are blurred or ignored. Attempts to use general mechanisms (such as the rate of interest) to explain growth or decline failed to notice that within the total economy superficially similar industries were experiencing quite different fates. In the early eighteenth century Devon serges declined as Norfolk 'stuffs' rose: by the mid-century, the Norfolk industry was in decline as the star of its Yorkshire rival rose. The 'new draperies' of England prospered while those of Holland declined. Equally important is the study of fluctuations in the prices of necessities – food and clothing especially – as they affected the production and consumption of less necessary and (in the last analysis) luxury goods. T. S. Ashton made important pioneering forays into this territory, hitherto largely unexplored for centuries earlier than the nineteenth, where the effects of the fall in prices in the period in and after the 1870s were plain to see.

The impact of price changes on the structure of eighteenth-century farming in England has received careful attention. But how much the proliferation of manufactures in the years between the Restoration and the industrialization of the late eighteenth century owed to the levelling off and even the fall in the general price level of necessities remains an unsolved problem, as do similar situations in the other European countries for which Professor Kellenbenz provides detailed evidence in chapter VII of this volume.

In short, the study of prices, wages, and profits provides an endless series of problems in the social development of early modern society, comprising saving, investment, private and public borrowing, and the consequences of all these on production and consumption. To assess the interaction of such variables we are likely to have to rely on data which an economist would dismiss as flimsy and unreliable. There must remain a large area of history where the historian has to rely on his general 'feel' of the times and use his intuition as well as his techniques of exact measurement.

Even more speculative is the area of social and (in the broadest sense) cultural history into which the economic historian is led by demographic and price history. It is well over half a century since R. H. Tawney tried to use the differential of rents and prices in Tudor England as a pivot on which a complex of social theories was supposed to turn – the social climbing of freeholders and customary tenants with security of tenure; the operations of sharp commercial intruders taking advantage of rustic ignorance and aristocratic insouciance or boneheadedness; the disintegrating impact of capitalism on an ossified medieval social structure based on commuted labour services rapidly depreciating to nothing while prices and profits rose by equivalent stages. Professor Stone is still pursuing the lines of development suggested by Tawney regarding the destiny of the Elizabethan aristocracy. Professor Trevor-Roper's theme of a 'declining gentry' driven to penury and political and religious dissent emerges at intervals in the historiography of almost every European country affected by the price revolution of the sixteenth century. Here the historian's problem is to refine and adjust the sweeping generalizations of the pioneers. But the more socio-cultural the exploration becomes, the more likely is it that refinement will need to give way to complete reformation. Thus that bold chapter in ideal-type historiography, the Weber–Tawney thesis that linked the Protestant ethic with the emergence of capitalism, has become a positive hindrance to thought and is probably better dispensed with. In the light of present knowledge of the social and occupational structure of the Calvinist congregations of France, the Low Countries, England and New England, it is increasingly hard to envisage a Calvinist ethic designed to suit a rising bourgeois class 'conscious of the contrast between its own standards and those of a laxer world, proud of its vocation as the standard bearer of the economic virtues'.[1] It is some years since Sir George Clark remarked how little attention Calvin in fact gave to the central problem of usury – two pages in the whole twenty or more printed volumes of his works. About as long since, Gustaf Renier recalled, in his account of Gisbert Voetius, *doyen* of the Utrecht strict Counter-Remonstrants and hammer of the great merchant rulers of the Dutch Republic (for the greater part *libertins*), how this grim Calvinist prophet ousted from his congregation a God-fearing woman who had the misfortune to be married to the employee of a pawnbroker and therefore a usurer. With the flux of time Calvinism

[1] R. H. Tawney, *Religion and the Rise of Capitalism* (1926), p. 111.

might become politically revolutionary: socially it was medieval. Professor Le Roy Ladurie's enumeration of the members of Calvinist congregations in Languedoc confirms that they were largely urban artisans. At Montpellier in 1560, for example, 69 per cent of a Huguenot community of 561 persons were artisans. Representatives of professions (15.4 per cent) and trade (4.5 per cent) were included, but wherever they can be identified the majority were craftsmen and town labourers. Proportionately, the 'merchants' and 'capitalists' were a small element in this predominantly urban Protestantism: of rural Protestants we hear little until much later. The same appears to have been equally true in East Anglia and the Netherlands.

The simple counting of heads is far from being the whole of socio-economic history. Yet without the evidence or the techniques to interpret such quantitative evidence as may exist, wholly erroneous theories may be constructed, as the Weberian and post-Marxist theories of fifty years ago were. Of itself quantification solves few of those problems of causality in social history after which the student will continue to seek. If the 'Protestant ethic' grows dim, the problem of the psychology of oppressed minorities remains. Did they take to business (as they so often did) because they were moved by complex and cryptic motives of a psychological or sociological nature, or simply because they were excluded from other means of earning a living? David Ogg suggested that the economic dominance of Dissenters in post-1660 England should be explained in this latter way. Is the same true of the *conversos* and crypto-Jews so prominent in the life of Seville and other Spanish cities? Theology explains nothing of their social role: racial aptitudes *per se* little more. If Ruth Pike is right, their prodigies of fortune-building and 'miracles of social mobility'[1] seem to be only temporary manifestations, agonized attempts to escape from tortured anxiety into a safe haven of social and political security promised by hidalgo privilege. Much remains to be done in exploring the complex relationships between the growing literacy of urban, mercantile society with its counting-houses, its need for men who could read, write and count, and the growing demand for forms of religion that provided some opportunity for lay participation, as Protestantism did.

Do economic causes explain the hysterical violence of religious antagonisms in the sixteenth and seventeenth centuries? Karol Gorski has suggested that fatigue and undernourishment may help to induce panics amongst men as they do in animals. Yet there he pauses in his analogy: the problems of the relationship between the spiritual and material culture are, he concludes, insoluble. All we know is that above

[1] Ruth Pike, *Aristocrats and Traders: Sevillian Society in the Sixteenth Century* (New York, 1972), p. 100.

the provision of a basic diet, men sought other forms of satisfaction –
such as comfort or weapons against their fears, and enrichment of the
natural environment by the genius of artists, architects and musicians.
Charms were contrived against the devil, sorcerers and witches.
Strangers and aliens like Jews were socially quarantined and victimized.
Yet a world of fear and antidotes to fear was also a world of fashions,
songs and stories to while away the winter's night; amusements and
games to keep men at home and away from the brothels and ale-houses.
The more deeply we explore these aspects of social history, the less
relevant the supposedly 'basic' economic explanations seem to become.
Activities of leisure, spirituality, intellect and culture take on a life of
their own. Men might often riot and plague authority for simple
economic reasons, as English peasants, masons and carpenters in the
seventeenth century concerted their protests against enclosure of
common land, against the greedy stranger who threatened their grazing
rights, their right to collect firewood in the forest or catch fish and fowl
round the meres and fens. The chronic unemployment, underemployment and poverty that afflicted every society in early modern history
certainly contributed to the risks of disorders and increasing violence by
thieves and vagabonds. But in many other instances social violence does
not seem to have borne much relationship to the general level of
wealth or poverty. The Dutch Republic (the society which probably
enjoyed the highest average standards of living) was as subject to the
assassination of its governors as France. Spain, much poorer than France,
suffered chronically from brigandage but had fewer outbreaks of social
violence than France. The Massacre of St Bartholomew was not an
isolated incident. The third quarter of the sixteenth century saw many
similar, if smaller-scale, specifically 'religious' massacres. Doubtless
some socio-economic factors were at work. Yet the troubles invariably
blew up on holy days, clustering around religious processions or heresy
trials. Protestants would desecrate or pollute religious objects to slake
their hatreds and demonstrate the fraudulence of their opponents'
magic. Roman Catholics would attack Calvinists as devils and embodi-
ments of anti-Christ. Such manifestations were fundamentally ritual-
istic, rooted in fear, hatred and revenge. They stemmed not from
economic grievances but from the clash of creeds as organizing concepts
of human emotions. It is important to distinguish between those
disorders which were economically inspired and those which were not.
The economic writ does not run through all history.

Early modern history – the 'age of the modern state' – has traditionally been for economic historians the age of the mercantilist state and
economy. The concept of 'mercantilism', a complex of ideas and
policies designed to achieve national power and, ostensibly, wealth, has

long been a source of controversy amongst historians. Recent trends in
the study of economic history have, on the one hand, tended to favour
some of the authors of the concept and conceded favourable results to its
practice. Professor Le Roy Ladurie has sited Colbert in a period of
general economic recession in rural and agrarian society, yet sees his
encouragement of 'the industrial morality' as a shaft of light and hope
piercing the contemporary gloom and heralding the diversification of
economic activities so desperately needed if France was to escape from
the 'scissors' mechanism of demographic growth and productive
stagnation which had for centuries rendered material improvement at
best intermittent, at worst impossible. Criticisms which rest on the
failure of the sixteenth century to equip itself with the men or the skills
to make government work, lose some of their force when applied to
the next two centuries. France, Germany, England and some Italian
cities at least could claim considerable expertise in certain areas of
government administration. France and Switzerland took increasingly
effective steps to deal with contagious diseases and famine. Some of this
'preventive' apparatus (often neglected in the historical treatment of
medicine, which has laid undue emphasis on the therapeutic aspects of
the problem) was copied from the centuries-old experience of the
Italian cities and states, where quarantine regulations and the compulsory possession of health passes for travellers and goods had long been
enforced to some effect.

That mercantilism had its specific successes is difficult to deny: it
is equally difficult to accept as they stand the sweeping generalizations
drawn from economic, monetary and investment theory adduced by
Keynes to explain and justify e.g. the mercantilist concentration of
attention on the balance of payments. One tends rather to turn to the
insistence on human and social capacity to organize economic life as a
central feature of the new doctrines that emerge everywhere in varying
forms in the sixteenth and seventeenth centuries. These were the inner
dynamic that kept alive the faith of powers and government in economic *dirigisme* in spite of its repeated failures and demonstrably wasteful
losses. In our own time M. Monnet has pointed out that the immediate
success or failure of any particular exercise in planning is less important
than the instinct to believe that targets themselves are of great importance. We must not press the analogy to the point of anachronism, but
it is worth remarking that for good or for ill, along the Atlantic
seaboard of Europe, ambitions for material gain were steadily increasing
in these centuries as the belief in the sanctity of poverty ebbed and as
examples of the individual and social rewards of industry multiplied.
These changes did not escape the notice of statesmen, their administrators and businessmen. Their varied interests and motives were reflected

in the vast output of memoirs, books and pamphlets which form the classic corpus of 'mercantilist' literature. Nor did the state always need to be equipped with an expert technocracy to achieve substantial economic and social gains. The newly-forged United Provinces were hardly a 'state' in the sense in which the word is used of the centralized princely states of its day. There was a specific lack of 'mercantilist' apparatus or legislation comparable to that which was multiplying in France or England. There was, however, a recognition of some basic social facts which was equally important; this manifested itself in shrewd common sense and needed no elaborate apparatus of administration or enforcement. The semi-laissez-faire of the Dutch Republic (a loose federation of urban economies) was based on an empirical, self-interested faith in the economic and social merits of toleration and freedom of thought and expression; hardly less on the policy (in which such beliefs found special expression) of free immigration into the newly-founded Republic, which brought to the new 'state' vital increments of manufacturing, mercantile and financial skill, a network of personal business relationships and a vast addition of capital and ships. They came from the southern Netherlands, Spain, Portugal, France, Germany and England. Without them the progress of the Dutch would have been slower and smaller.

To a necessary extent, the economic history of early modern Europe continues to be studied in the context of the national economies. In one respect – the analysis of domestic demand, especially for foods and other necessities of life – this form of macro-economic history is even more firmly entrenched than it was in the days when (as a matter of evidential convenience) the progress of trade and industry tended often to be measured in terms of *exports*. A mutation in historiography has taken place somewhat similar to the actual changes in policy and thought of the eighteenth century, when the dominant concepts of the balance of trade, underpinned by policies concentrating on an export drive, gave way to a strong reaction (at least in western Europe) led by the Physiocrats. David Hume and Adam Smith extrapolated their ideas, pouring out on Colbertism and the mercantile system all the scorn and ridicule of their variegated repertoire of logic and rhetoric. The underlying distrust and contempt for the merchant and his business, passed down from antiquity to the Middle Ages and onwards to the Christian Socialists and Marxists, have never been wholly dispersed. In spite of all the efforts of the propagandists of France to dilute the rigours of *dérogation*, prejudice against the active participation of the landed nobility in trade remained strong. The aristocratic, intellectual, French paternity of the *Wealth of Nations* comes through strongly in the author's social attitudes: a contempt for the merchant ethos was at least one belief that Adam Smith shared with Colbert.

This strong reaction against what seemed the excessive mercantilist preoccupation with trade and industry and the undervaluing of land and agriculture went hand in hand with the rising tide of international-ism mirrored in Hume's famous declaration: 'not only as a man but as a British subject' he would 'pray for the flourishing commerce of Germany, Spain, Italy and even France itself'. In somewhat similar fashion but more than a century later, the Victorian export of capital was to evoke the strong radical, anti-imperial reaction of the 1900s, with its swing back to the needs of the domestic economy and society, a cyclical reaction renewed from time to time down to our own day.

Recent trends in economic historiography may be seen as something of an intellectual analogue to these long swings of historical actuality. To call the product 'new' history would be dangerous as well as presumptuous. No history (*pace* the claims of recent exponents of the 'new' economic history) can claim to be 'new' without risking well-grounded suspicions that it is not history at all. Every kind of history worth the name inherits a legacy of methods and intuitions from earlier practitioners of the craft, none the less real and indispensable for being unspecific and unrecorded. The new *element* in demographic and con-junctural history derives partly from its use of new material, partly from its use of new techniques. Sometimes it will continue to use the frame-work of national economies as the boundaries of its working area, but increasingly its exponents see the scope of their work as either more local or more universal. Demographic movements often appear as a universal groundswell due to some far distant occurrence, or as an undercurrent on at least a continental scale which may without warning boil up into more or less violent local disturbances. Their investigators therefore need to work on an international scale, and they and their researches are increasingly linked together internationally at many points. In some-what different ways, the historians who investigate 'conjunctural' situations find that even if there are no clear laws governing the be-haviour of wages, prices, profits, money etc. (since it is the essence of the matter that no 'conjuncture' ever repeats itself), certain tendencies recur and are recognizable to the historian whose vision is broad or long enough to discern the underlying similarities. European historians, for example, are perhaps less aware than their North American colleagues of the *social* importance of monetary policy, because in the United States (as nowhere else) the relationship between easy money and agri-cultural debt on the one hand and hard money and the supply of credit on the other became a conflict between one distinct region in the west and another in the east. Yet the controversy itself is potentially universal and timeless. In this relatively little-known area, the Belgian historian Professor R. van Uytven has recently demonstrated how powerfully the alternating policies of revaluation and devaluation (sound and easy money, deflation and inflation) operated to polarize and align support and opposition to the policies of e.g. Charles V or Philip II in the Netherlands in the sixteenth century. Sound money had the support of landowners and the *rentier* classes. Easy money was favoured by traders and exporters who saw in deflation and a cheaper currency a boost for overseas trade. Sound money worked against them but favoured other traders and manufacturers whose business lay in the supply of luxuries to the wealthy *rentiers* (as most landowners were). These in turn were encouraged to spend more freely by the higher value of their rent rolls. Wage earners suffered (often in apparent silence) price rises by devaluation that might halve the real value of their unadjusted earnings. The nobility were less docile. Philip of Cleves, leader of the Flemish rebellion against the Archduke Maximilian, tried to win the states and towns of Flanders over to his side by arguing that the Archduke's repeated debasements of the coinage had injured the *rentiers* and men of substance and at the same time had raised the cost of living for everybody.

The evidence demonstrates not only how monetary policy which alters relative income values can help to explain political alignments which are otherwise inexplicable, but also how, over a period of time, a single element in the conjuncture can profoundly alter the economic and social structure of a whole area. (Polish historians have similarly concluded that the devaluation of the Polish currency in the seventeenth century, by reducing the value of exports, added to the forces pressing the peasantry down into serfdom.) Neither Maximilian's monetary policy nor Philip of Cleves's arguments bow political history off the stage, any more than William Jennings Bryan's 'Cross of Gold' speech dispenses us from any further study of American radical politics. Professor van Uytven's analysis merely shows, without pressing the case too far, the added dimension which conjunctural analysis can bring to the interpretation of certain historical episodes and events. As he says, in summing up the course of monetary policy in the sixteenth century, it is not simply coincidental that the Netherlands nobility rebelled against Philip II, who had repeatedly devalued the currency, and not against his father, who had stood fairly consistently throughout his reign for a policy of stable currency.

In recent economic historiography it is the village, or region, or continent – E. A. Wrigley's Colyton, Pierre Goubert's Beauvais, Le Roy Ladurie's Languedoc, Fernand Braudel's Mediterranean – which has tended to become the 'sites' most appropriate to the techniques and objectives of historians trying to fit together the diverse elements in particular socio-economic historical situations (perhaps also this approach is most acceptable to the tastes of a generation which – in the west at least – often equates the 'nation' with what currently seems least creditable in its history).

At certain points, nevertheless, the new techniques have already been used to help explain the growth or decline of *national* economies – very successfully in the case of the Dutch Republic, the economic prodigy of Europe from the 1590s, and of seventeenth-century France; partially in the case of Spain, which rapidly passed from the apex of its power in the third quarter of the sixteenth century into economic stagnation and decay by the early seventeenth century.

II.   *Some Case Studies*

The original plan for volumes IV and V envisaged a broad division of labour between the two. Volume IV explored what might be called the wider context – social, geographical, scientific, demographic – of expansion in the early modern world. Volume V was to be devoted to the actual processes of production, exchange, consumption etc. Broadly, this plan has been followed, with some modifications that seemed desirable in the light of research in the years between the planning and publication of this volume. The history of agrarian development is fully examined in chapter II of this volume by B. H. Slicher van Bath. The industrial, commercial and social development of continental Europe is dealt with in the chapters by Professor Glamann, Professor Kellenbenz and Miss Behrens. Since these chapters were completed, important studies have appeared which relate to the linked processes of change – agrarian, demographic, commercial and industrial – in France, the Netherlands and Spain. These merit a special mention.

Until late in the sixteenth century there is little positive evidence to differentiate the agrarian economy of the northern Netherlands provinces from that of many other areas, at least in respect of 'growth points'. When the Eighty Years War began in 1568, the Dutch were still experiencing the chronic crises, the mingled effects of food shortages, famine and general poverty familiar to all the peasant economies of Europe. In one of these, France, Le Roy Ladurie, in his masterly study of the peasantry of Languedoc, has traced the long-term fluctuations of demographic and agricultural growth and contraction. Demographic expansion in the 1530s and 1540s followed a vigorous expansion of production but by the seventeenth century had clearly outrun the capacity of the economy to support any further increase in numbers. The comparative standstill of economy and society was relieved somewhat towards the end of the century; then followed the depression of the 1730s and 1740s, shared by large areas of Europe. Only after this can the signs of a long and sustained period of true growth be discerned. Throughout this long struggle the ever-present forces of population growth found themselves constricted and checked by the relative stagnation of the rural economy. Only by the middle of the eighteenth century does the French peasant economy begin to diversify its production for the market, adding specialized crops – notably the grape and olive – to cereals.

The sombre and often bloody chronicles of French social history contrast strongly with those of the new Republic in the Netherlands. Here, from the 1590s until the mid seventeenth century, a new type of international exchange economy arose, highly urbanized, dependent to an unprecedented extent on imported food and raw materials, yet providing its society, including a dominant middle-class element as well as a large body of urban workers and rural peasantry, with an unusually high standard of living. New financial institutions – banks, public and private; stock, produce and shipping exchanges; new ship-building techniques and new commercial methods – raised the productivity of labour and capital. Here was growth – true growth, which a recent historian of Netherlands development, Jan de Vries has carefully distinguished from the 'expansion' which had earlier manifested itself in many ways in sixteenth-century Europe. Evidence of that expansion was to be seen in land reclamation, new city walls, harbours and ports and in the expansion of Europe and Europeans into other areas and continents. Yet, as we have seen in France, true improvements in the quality and quantity of the factors of production – land, labour and capital – had in the past been at best fitful and sporadic. Recurrent scarcities of grain brought falls in real income; the division of holdings by the peasantry reduced the productivity of labour. There seemed to be a ruthlessly predetermined process by which these occasional bursts of economic activity were checked and progress ground to a halt. Unemployment, underemployment, high mortality, famine and plague followed ineluctably. Expansion of this fluctuating and treacherous kind there was in plenty, but, as Dr de Vries has said, 'a more elusive phenomenon was growth'.[1] It was in the northern Netherlands provinces, formerly poor relations of their more affluent southern neighbours, that a new and genuine form of growth was to be found in the next century. Why and how did this happen? For long the accepted view was that the dynamic thrust came from *urban* development, *urban* trade.

[1] J. de Vries, *The Dutch Rural Economy in the Golden Age 1500-1700* (Yale University Press, 1974), p. 119.

In a classic formulation by Henri Pirenne, urban economic life spread 'an infection [to the countryside] which raised the peasant from his age-long torpor'. The work of Professor B. H. Slicher van Bath and his assistants at the Wageningen Agricultural University, carried forward by Dr de Vries, has modified this explanation in some respects vital for the historian and for the specialists in development economics. In the new analysis the impulses to change do not emanate exclusively from urban initiatives: they emanate also from the internal transformation of *rural* society and economy, in a mutual relationship between town and country.

These recent and intensive studies of the Netherlands make them an appropriate starting-point for a survey of the processes of economic growth and decline in early modern Europe.

In the province of Holland especially, a 'new country' had been slowly reclaimed. Unlike the provinces to the south, unlike the countries to the west and south, Holland was not dominated by a landed nobility; its agriculture, unlike that of the 'manorial' areas of Europe, was not cramped within any Procrustean bed of cooperative farming or intermingled ownership of strips. Peasant ownership, even before 1500, was widespread. Population was not yet exceptionally dense but urbanization was unusually high. In the next two centuries and a half it became higher, underpinned by high rural birth-rates. Relatively short-distance local migration (with some qualitatively very important immigration from the south after the mid sixteenth century) helped to swell urban numbers and vitalize economic activity. But cities were, here as elsewhere, killers as well as employers of men. Dutch cities, like others of the time, had constantly to be replenished and fortified against continuing high rates of urban mortality by further immigration. While transport, foreign trade and technology were all involved in this process, the sustained economic progress of the seventeenth century – down to the 1670s at least – would have been impossible without a revolution in the peasant *agriculture* of the northern Netherlands. Far earlier than in other areas of Europe, peasant producers were able to specialize in growing a wide range of commercial crops. A class of independent farmers came into being, prosperous on the profits of larger farms, on larger and healthier herds of stock, on higher yields of milk, cheese, hay, clover, wheat, barley, oats, oil-bearing seeds, flax, rape, hemp, madder, hops, tobacco etc. All these products of more efficient labour, better drainage and the generous application of manure were sold in the town markets. Cabbages, beans and roots, bulbs and flowers were incorporated in an ever-richer pattern of efficient horti-cultural–agricultural production. Those members of the rural population who became surplus to the needs of the farm emigrated to the town or became absorbed in activities ancillary (but vitally necessary) to developing agriculture: dyke, polder or canal construction and repair, ironmongery, smithy work, transport or harbour work in all its forms.

Sea, river and canal transport was essential if the developing mutual relationship between rural improvement and urban growth was not to be checked by shortages: hence one stimulus to the growth of an exceptionally large and efficient carrying fleet based on the *fluitschip*, a (usually) unarmed sea-going barge, cheap to build and run. From the late sixteenth century, this enabled the new state to import an increasing proportion of its basic food, first from the Baltic and later from France, England and the southern Netherlands. The records of imports suggest that by the mid-seventeenth century foreign grain supplied over half of the million inhabitants of the provinces of Holland, Utrecht, Friesland and Groningen with their food. Imported grain not only fed the people and supplied the raw materials of the intensive brewing and distilling industries of the Republic: it released capital, land and resources which enabled the Netherlands to concentrate on the production of the specialized crops (enumerated earlier) which yielded much higher profit margins than bread grains. Land, labour and capital could thus be more intensively employed.

Inland transport made an almost equally vital contribution. By the early seventeenth century, much of the canal network which, along with rivers and roads, linked the northern provinces into a tightly-knit economic whole (contrasting oddly with the political decentralization of the area), came into being to serve the needs of transport for heavy bulk cargoes, peat and manure especially. Peat was the primary fuel of a country which had limited supplies of local timber and no coal. Urban domestic use and the needs of rising industries like textiles, sugar-refining, brewing etc. created the need for a steady flow of peat from the main areas of exploration (between Ij and the Maas) to the towns. Conversely, night-soil was shipped regularly back from town to country. In the mid-eighteenth century eleven special *vuilnisvaarders* (manure barges) were busy shipping to the countryside the night-soil of Leiden alone. The new rotation systems and heavy manuring helped to achieve the uniquely high yields of Dutch cereal farming. Manure was also especially crucial to specialized crops like hemp.

Thus some six or seven decades of vigorous investment of many kinds equipped Dutch rural society to make its contribution, unique in the Europe of its day, to nearly sustained growth. Other factors also contributed. One was the uniquely high rate of literacy, which struck Guicciardini and other foreign observers: by 1660 it had reached levels that varied between 40 and 60 per cent. Standards of clothing and diet for the common people were similarly in advance of those in other parts of Europe, except possibly England.

Yet, as early as the 1670s, again in 1730 and in 1750–1, observers remarked uneasily that not all was well. Again, the analysis of Dutch economic 'decline' has been both broadened and refined. An economy which had risen on a combination of international and local demands (especially those consequent upon the rising population and its demand in the sixteenth century) felt the effects of a general European levelling off and even decline in numbers by the mid seventeenth century. As a middleman in European and world markets the Dutch merchant could be regarded as benefactor or intruder: mercantilist aspirations ensured that he was frequently cast in the latter role by the second half of the seventeenth century. Just because they were uniquely progressive, the Dutch were the prime targets for English, French, and later Prussian and Spanish aggressive mercantilism. The indicators show a levelling off of maritime expansion after 1650; textile output at Leiden, the largest single concentration of the industry in Europe, reached its peak between 1654 and 1667, thereafter falling victim to cost-cutting rivalry from the industries of East Anglia, Devon and Yorkshire, as well as of France and even Poland. But the crisis was not limited to trade or industry. There were signs of demographic exhaustion. Fertility fell as the age of marriage of women seemed to rise. More celibates, more resort to prostitution and perhaps some form of birth control may also have contributed to a fall in the size of families.

Behind all these lay less palpable, less measurable influences. The Republic remained small. It had protested violently, sensibly and understandably against Spain's proposal to use the Netherlands as a treasure-chest for her crusades against heretic and infidel. Yet (like the English of the Interregnum) the Dutch discovered that it was hardly less costly to run their own state, with the daunting problems of defending its frontiers, its shipping and trade, in a world of continuous war, than it was to sustain Imperial Spain. Remorselessly, the tide of debt and taxation went on rising. The Dutch, it seemed, had staved off the Tenth Penny only to be hoist by their own petard in the shape of the *accijns* (excise). The heavy incidence of indirect taxation struck almost every observer of Dutch economic affairs as the seventeenth century went on. Basically, the Republic, from a population half as large as that of England and one-sixth of that of France, extracted a public revenue larger than that of England and a third of that raised by France. The result? '. . . a man cannot eat a dish of meat in an ordinary [inn] but that one way and another he shall pay 19 excises out of it. This is not more strange than true': thus Sir George Downing from The Hague in January 1658/9. His comment was repeated scores of times by others.

The effects on manufacturing costs were serious. As early as 1651 an anonymous English writer reckoned that labour costs in the English cloth industry were about half 'what the Hollander pays, by reason of their high rate of Houses and Victuals to which all labourers' wages are proportioned'.

But indirect taxes were not the only ones. If total population numbers were small, land was scarce and costly to reclaim, drain and maintain. Hence very high rates of drainage and land taxes. By the eighteenth century these burdens were bearing hard on the profits of landownership. So much so that by 1700 much land lay abandoned or was handed over to provincial governments because the owners could not afford to pay their taxes. Contemporaneously with such urban and rural troubles came the end to demographic growth: it was to remain stagnant until the nineteenth century. Possible causes have already been mentioned. To these the continuing problem of high urban mortality may be added: 'We see', wrote a Dutch demographer three quarters of a century ago, 'that the cities of earlier times can be likened to the Minotaur, which gobbled up the children of the Greeks, and that hygiene was the Theseus which disarmed the monster. Athens (to stay with this image) was the countryside which sent each year its hecatombs to the cities.'[1] It has been calculated that the Dutch cities of the eighteenth century needed some two and a half thousand immigrants a year simply to maintain their size. Hence the steady drain of people from the countryside.

Yet the condition of the Republic after the Golden Age had passed cannot correctly be described (as it often has been) as petrifaction caused by total economic collapse and moral decay. Even this so-called 'Periwig Period', when French, English and other 'alien' influences are sometimes held to have withered the tough fibre of the Dutch people, was not as decadent, economically or morally, as it is sometimes painted. The bright colours of the preceding age were dimmed; the canvas woefully faded but not uniformly faded. The image is patchy, spotty, uneven, but still, like the curate's egg, good in parts; a state of which Adam Smith could still remark that it was the wealthiest in Europe. Its overseas trade and shipping, though fallen somewhat below the high-water mark of 1648, were still impressive. Its fisheries likewise. The condition of its industries was uneven. The textiles of Leiden, especially the *Nieuwe Draperijen* by which the refugees from Hondschoote from the 1560s onwards had revivified a decayed city, were in poor shape after the 1670s; by 1750 they had virtually disappeared. The once great

[1] J. H. F. Kohlbrugge, 'Over den invloed der steden op hare bewoners en op de bewoners van het land', *De Economist* LVI (1907), 372–93, quoted by de Vries, *The Dutch Rural Economy*, p. 117.

Haarlem linen-bleaching industry suffered a similar fate. Here, as later with pottery and ceramics at Delft and elsewhere, high-cost, labour-intensive Dutch industry could not compete with its English rivals. But on the other hand, the more capital-intensive manufactures, which felt the effects of high labour costs less sharply, did better: brewing, distilling, sugar-boiling, paper-making, printing etc. remained more prosperous.

If industry's fate was variable, banking and finance positively throve on the abundance of capital still seeking remunerative employment. Throughout the seventeenth century the Dutch had thrown out a wide network of world trade. In one way or another its products had left a residue in the form of vast savings held by banks, charitable institutions, magistrates and individuals. Lacking adequate outlets through domestic investment,[1] these were channelled systematically and skilfully into the rising debts of a variety of European governments in the eighteenth century – the states of Scandinavia, Germany and the Austrian Empire, Russia, Spain, Portugal, Sardinia, France, but above all England, where the Dutch investors' decisions were large enough to be an important consideration with successive First Lords of the Treasury. After the Fourth Dutch War (1780–3) much money was diverted to France and North America. But the once widely-held belief that the Revolutionary and Napoleonic periods (disastrous though they certainly were to the Dutch economy) destroyed these reserves of foreign investment has been shown to be much exaggerated. On the whole these skilfully invested savings and profits brought home large and regular dividends. The specialist bankers like Pels, Muilman, Clifford, de Smeth, Hogguer Horneca, and Hope, each operating in his own area of expertise, benefitted an army of investing clients whose capital they managed.

With an impressive history of technological development, scientific knowledge and observation and keen commercial acumen behind them, why did the Dutch not press on to the last logical phase of development – full-scale industrialization? The question is not simply one asked by historians in retrospect; it was widely canvassed by Dutch publicists in the late eighteenth century. It admits of many answers: the domestic market was small, overseas markets were increasingly protected, Dutch costs were high, capitalists could reap high and easy rewards from portfolio investments abroad. The traditional tunes of a mercantile society never became transposed into an industrial key, at least until the later nineteenth century. Thus much upper- and middle-class comfort was compatible with increasing unemployment and social distress for

[1] See the perceptive comment by a Dutch observer in 1774, quoted in my *Anglo-Dutch Commerce and Finance in the Eighteenth Century* (1941), p. 188.

others (though this was also a feature of the age in Europe, not excluding England). The gap between the decayed traditional manufactures and the newer types of mass-produced products now appearing in England was not to be closed. At all points in society, from top to bottom, structural and mental lesions existed which made it impossible to convert the old economy into new forms. Yet, in decline as in growth, the critical importance of the agrarian sector remains. A transformed rural economy, long overshadowed by the commerce and industry of the towns in the Golden Age, survived to provide the basis for nineteenth-century development, long after the urban glories of that age, the Amsterdam staple market and its related activities, had disappeared.

For this continuation of the specialized peasant economy a price had to be paid. The progressive, diversified character of Dutch peasant agriculture made it an independent, commercial economic activity, not merely a static or backward means of eking out a livelihood in the face of constant threats from natural hazards. It was an occupation technologically as resourceful and exacting as the trade or manufacture to which it was closely assimilated. Dutch eighteenth-century agriculture remained advanced, and criticisms that it failed to adopt inventions (some of dubious value in Dutch conditions) ignore the fact that it was not primarily concerned with cereal production. Urban manufactures, on the other hand, were being rendered uncompetitive by the rise of rural industries in the quite different social and technical context of England and, to a lesser extent, of other European countries.[1] The attraction of the towns ensured that in the Netherlands no permanent class of rural poor arose to provide the labour force which operated the spreading cottage industries of other countries – the outwork weavers and spinners of England, for example, who characterized English industry in the pre-industrial age and opened the way to full industrialization. It may be (as Professor de Vries suggests) that the very economic progress which had lifted the Netherlands above her contemporaries and neighbours in the sixteenth and seventeenth centuries had created insuperable institutional obstacles to full industrialization in the eighteenth.

At the other end of the spectrum of economic development from the Dutch Republic was Spain. Thanks to the pioneer work of Hamilton, historians possess a remarkable foundation on which to base further studies of Spain's rise and decline in terms of monetary supplies and policy. Indeed, the curve representing the tide of American silver that began to find its way to Spain in a growing surge from the 1530s, its climax of the 1590s and its ineluctable ebbing away to the relative trickle of the mid-century has proved too seductive to those who sought (as always) a simple answer to a complicated question. For Hamilton,

---

[1] See de Vries, *The Dutch Rural Economy*, pp. 234-5.

economics and politics were interrelated, but 'the loss of economic strength appears to have been more largely a cause than a result of political decline'.[1] His basic explanation was that industry was 'geared to the influx of silver', and that this created the illusion of prosperity, a mirage drawing princes and people into endless wars on all fronts. Protestant heretics in the Netherlands, England and France, Ottoman Turks to the East, Erasmians, Protestants, Moriscoes and Jews at home – all became the objects against which one crusade after another was launched, by land and sea, without regard to expense of blood or treasure. Thus while Hamilton recognized that the economic consequences of war itself were disastrous, the prime mover urging on the whole cavalcade to disaster seemed to be silver, or perhaps, more even than silver, the illusion of bottomless prosperity and indomitable power conjured up by the silver influx. Thus the explanation of Spanish decline, from the peaks of the mid sixteenth to the troughs of the mid seventeenth century, lies, to this way of thinking, in the realm of monetary supply.

Other historians, including most of those of earlier generations of political historians, thought differently. With Robert Watson, whose *History of the Reign of Philip III* was published in 1783, they would have declared that Spanish power 'corresponded not with her inclination' – in plain words, politically and militarily, Spain had bitten off more than she could chew. Hence the material and moral decline pictured by Jaime Vicens Vives: the crushing burden of taxation which caused a steady exodus of people from Castile, reducing parts of Spain to virtual desert; the expulsion of the Moriscoes which left hundreds of villages empty in Valencia and Aragon; widespread undernourishment that left the victims exposed to disease; the so-called hidalgo mentality, the contempt for manual work, and a proliferation of priests, monks, bandits, vagabonds and thieves; the destitution, the agricultural decline, both arable and animal; the fall of the traditional industrial and mercantile cities of Castile – Burgos, Toledo, Segovia, Valladolid etc. – some of which had lost up to half their population of 1580 by 1650; finally, the collapse of the currency from 1599 to 1630, when the owners of the largest supplies of treasure the world had ever seen found themselves reduced to minting a copper coinage. Except for the uneasy interlude from 1627 to 1634, when the government attempted a wholesale deflation, the seventeenth-century crisis was mirrored in protracted, uncontrollable and disastrous inflation.

If economists and their remedies were any cure for economic ills, Spain would have been passing rich. Bullionists and restrictionists (advocates of Spain-first policies designed to keep bullion at home)

[1] E. J. Hamilton, 'The Decline of Spain', *Economic History Review*, VIII (1938).

fought endless battles against mercantilists proper, i.e. writers like Luis Ortiz whose *Memorial against the Flight of Money from this Realm* (1558) resembled, both in diagnosis and cure, the later ideas of the Neapolitan Antonio Serra, Thomas Mun in England, or Bodin and Jean Éon in France. They were, that is to say, balance-of-payments men wedded to programmes of government-stimulated industrial growth, using prohibitions on raw material exports and manufactured imports, bounties and subsidies for shipbuilding and strategic industries. The *arbitristas* did not lack either imagination or constructive intelligence. They only lacked the power to make the slightest impact on the apathy of government or the immobility of the bureaucracy. Herein lies the frightening aspect of their total failure to assert the minutest control of mind over circumstantial matter.

In Spanish history, as in the history of other national economies, recent enquiry has worked towards remedying the imbalance between the external and internal factors which combined to create Spain's economic problems in the late sixteenth and seventeenth centuries. Writing as recently as 1961, Professor Elliot could declare: 'Little more is known now than was known fifty years ago about Spanish forms of land tenure and cultivation, or about population changes, or about the varying fortunes of the different regions or social groups in the peninsula.'[1] Fifteen years later, we know a little more about some of these aspects of the evolution of Spanish economy and society; much still remains obscure.

The chronology and mechanism of the great inflation in Europe as a whole has been illuminated by Ingrid Hammerström's analysis, which has shown that prices in many areas of western Europe began to rise *before* the effects of Spanish-American silver could have been felt. Silver of European provenance, debasement and, above all, rising aggregate demand must be added to increased monetary supply by way of explanation. The needs of governments for war and luxury, large armies and navies, more splendid courts, conspicuous consumption by the nobility and gentry, and the luxury of life on great estates and in urban palaces all went to swell demand for textiles and metals, labour and services. These new demands on agricultural and industrial production could be matched only by increasing output; but when the demographic curve turned down, and with it the supply of labour, higher prices necessarily followed. If demand could be matched only by increased imports (and such was the case in Spain) the result must be, in the end, the same: the treasure of the Indies flowed in only to flow out again in settlement of an unavoidable deficit on the balance of payments (shrewdly detected by the *arbitristas*).

[1] J. H. Elliott, 'The Decline of Spain', *Past and Present*, no. 20 (1961).

When the neo-mercantilists of the eighteenth century looked back on their country's history, it was to see a Golden Age followed by a long decadence. The neo-mercantilist Geronymo de Uztariz remarked in the 1730s that in the century following the Spanish settlement of America, some two thousand million dollars of silver had reached Spain. In the next century and a quarter, and until 1724, another fifteen hundred million had arrived – in all a total of over three and a half thousand million dollars. Yet by 1724 only a hundred million dollars remained in Spain. Silver and gold, Uztariz calculated, had been lost to Spain at a rate of fifteen million dollars a year. All this was the consequence of Spain's persistent deficit of payments with the outside world. It could be righted only by the restoration and modernization of the once-great industries and trades of cities like Seville, Segovia, Toledo, Valladolid etc. This would demand the removal of that inflated and ill-conceived muddle that was the Spanish system of taxation, the encouragement of labour by the common people, greater sea power, an efficient merchant fleet and a rational, national, economic policy aimed at enlarging Spanish trade and industry. Uztariz's essay was burnt by the public hangman. Yet these were the dreams which the Enlightened Despots later tried to realize. Their achievements were limited, but in so far as they had any results they may have depended as much on the general demographic upswing experienced in the second half of the eighteenth century as on the various encouragements and rewards given to enterprise.

More detailed research into the seventeenth-century 'decline' (e.g. in and around Toledo) amply confirms the opinions of Fernand Braudel, Jaime Vicens Vives, Jean Vilar, B. Bennassar and others, that beneath the outward symptoms of the sickness of Spanish economy and society lay deeper organic causes, of which demographic decline was perhaps the most serious.

By 1620, Toledo, once the most important city of Castile, was deserted, its manufactures ruined, its houses shuttered and empty. The surrounding countryside was bleak and depopulated. By 1646 the city's population had fallen to less than half its 1571 figure of over 12,000. Was this the result of the great plague of 1594? Or, as some thought, of the irresistible attractions of Madrid after it became the seat of the Court in 1607? Or did the causes antedate both these events? Michael Weisser has collected important evidence showing that serious food shortages had begun to show themselves in earlier decades. These resulted partly from soil exhaustion, partly from a shift from food-growing to sheep-farming as the needs of the cloth industry grew. The result was that harvests fell behind population trends. Population, in turn, was exposed to famine; commercial farming and trade declined; the reversion to subsistence farming became apparent as agricultural techniques proved incapable of meeting the combined demands of subsistence *and* industrial production. The *millones* tax, imposed first in 1590 but raised by 1626 to four times its original amount, was government's contribution to a crisis already beyond solution. We need only turn to the staggering costs of the war in the Netherlands revealed in N. G. Parker's account of *The Army of Flanders and the Spanish Road* to see how Pelion was piled upon Ossa, while Olympus remained notably unscaled.

The history of those provinces of the Southern Netherlands which had returned to 'Spanish obedience' after 1579 is no less complex than that of Spain itself. Fallen from their former unique international predominance they might be; but once their appalling crisis of the late sixteenth century was passed, they managed to retrieve more of their prosperity than has often been allowed. Belgian historians – van Houtte, Verlinden, Stols and others – have shown in recent years how the old commercial and industrial skills survived, emerging to recreate a modest local and Hispano-Netherlandish economy; a society which, even though subject to awkward social divisions and pockets of great poverty in the once-great ports and cities, could claim a profitable place in the material and cultural world of the seventeenth and eighteenth centuries.

Especially complex is the problem of Italy. In his succinct essay on the economic decline of Italy, Carlo Cipolla begins by limiting himself to the centre and north of Italy. Here, in 1600 and for nearly a century afterwards, we may see what was still one of the most highly developed economies and societies of the early modern world, still sustaining a rich and vital civilization that remained the model for European art, architecture and literature. The studies of Braudel, Cipolla, Sella, Lane, Pullan and others have rectified the misconceptions of earlier generations regarding the impact of the Cape route on Italian trade, especially that of Venice. Not only did Venetian trade survive: it enjoyed a spectacular recovery in the middle decades of the sixteenth century. Then, as trading conditions became more difficult (owing largely to war), Venetian entrepreneurs once again demonstrated their imaginative flexibility by seizing the initiative temporarily lost by Milan, Turin, Pavia, Florence, Como and other traditionally manufacturing cities ravaged by war. The second half of the sixteenth century therefore saw the Venetian cloth industry rise from almost nothing to become the major industry of its kind in all Italy, with an output of 28,000 cloths a year. Cloth, with other manufactures for which Venice was famous – shipbuilding, printing, glass, ceramics, sugar-refining, silk manufacture – maintained the city in prosperity until well into the next century. Then, after about 1620, as rival industries recovered, the textile industries of Venice slowly faded away to a mere trickle of output by the end of the century. Yet once again, the versatility and re-source of the Venetians showed themselves. Their capital was transferred once more, this time into agriculture, for the prices of foodstuffs and raw materials fell less than those of manufactured goods. True, some of the investment in the Veneto was recreational or prestigious, but the fact that these large estates were managed by bailiffs or leased out to peasants does not necessarily mean that farming standards were low: on the contrary.

The decline of the economy within the great quadrilateral formed by Milan, Genoa, Florence and Venice was largely a commercial or industrial decline. In Venice, Domenico Sella has pinpointed the causes – the inability of Venetian manufacturers to compete with Dutch or English rivals either on price or attractiveness; the constraints imposed on productivity and design by the power of the artisan guilds; the operation of monopolies and rings, which raised raw material costs; and an irrational and burdensome fiscal system, which raised raw material costs and damaged manufactured exports. As against the experience of some of her competitors, Venice had to pay the price for a relatively well-paid labour force. Its size was restricted by plague in the 1570s and afterwards; the city never again reached the size of 170,000 inhabitants attained in 1563. Workers were accordingly in a relatively strong bargaining position in an island site limited in space.

Of all the great urban economies, Venice was probably the most tenacious, though all the rest shared its problems in some degree. Thus the decline of an urban trade and industry once unchallenged in its commercial and technological primacy was general. Yet, relatively highly urbanized as north Italy was, was this the whole story? How far was urban decline offset by increased agricultural investment, diversification of crops or higher productivity in the countryside?

Here the answer is uncertain. Vast differences between one region and another in matters of land tenure, estate management and social conditions and relations make generalization exceedingly difficult. Aldo de Maddalena has shown that in northern and central Italy – the south was always a different story – the ratios of crop yields to seed sown, though not as high as in the Low Countries or England, were in some cases respectably near (for Piedmont and the Romagna, for example) and certainly a great deal higher then those of large areas of Germany, central and eastern Europe, or Spain. Piedmont, Tuscany, Milan, Mantua and the Veneto could show many examples of well-managed estates and intelligent, rational division of function between landlord, tenant farmer and peasantry. New crops were introduced. Rice, 'the corn of the marshes', improved the crop cycle and offered increasing yields as cultivating methods improved. In the sixteenth century the rice-yield ratio was seven to nine times the seed sown; by the eighteenth century it was fifteen to eighteen times as much. Maize, a heavily yielding crop, was introduced from the mid-sixteenth century. Animals generally remained small and, by later standards, poor in quality: but milk yields recorded in Lombardy were well above general European averages: by the eighteenth century – if the tenuous figures can be relied on – they surpassed all except those of Friesland.

Plainly, some Italian agriculture was well managed by contemporary standards, a fact borne out by estate accounts collected by de Maddalena for properties in Lombardy and Piedmont. But were there enough swallows to make a summer? The answer must remain in suspense until more evidence is available. And as against the evidence quoted for particular estates and areas, we should not overlook Professor Cipolla's belief that Italian development was moving counter to what ought, ideally, to have happened. Landownership was being concentrated among smaller numbers of 'feudal' proprietors; *mezzadria* was increasing; large areas of Italy once 'developed' were becoming 'underdeveloped', i.e. importing manufactures and services and exporting primary products. In the second half of the seventeenth century, agriculture itself suffered, especially in those coastal areas which demanded regular attention to drainage, and in regions like the Romagna and southern Italy which were plagued by political troubles. Even Lombardy and the Po Valley suffered a serious fall in population which took many decades to repair. Moreover the political character of Italy, especially in the south, communicated itself to the countryside so that 'improvement' often took on a neo-feudal aspect. Finally, it was unlucky that the shift from trade and industry to agriculture took place just as Europe was about to experience a widespread fall in crop yields – a phenomenon as yet little understood but certainly socially and economically burdensome, as Aldo de Maddalena has shown.

Thus, a picture diverse and complex but by no means hopeless. Compared with Spain, Italy was progressive. Compared with these fragmented economies, early modern England was advanced and, more important, stable and balanced in its more unified though still regionalized economy. As Professor Fisher has written, the achievement of the Tudor economy was to absorb successfully a considerable rise in population 'without running into a Malthusian crisis of mass starvation and mass unemployment'.[1] Certainly the harvest remained critical to the fortunes of the community, and not only of the agrarian community, as Professor Supple has shown in his study of seventeenth-century crisis and change in England. A gentleman landowner in North Lincolnshire could write early in the seventeenth century, after three

[1] F. J. Fisher, *Economic History Review* (February, 1975), p. 119.

wet summers, that his tenants had given up farming and left their farms on his lands, that utmost poverty and unemployment were to be seen everywhere.

Dog's flesh is a dainty dish and found upon search in many houses, also such horse flesh as hath lain long in a deke [ditch] for hounds. And the other day one stole a sheep who for mere hunger tore a leg out and did eat it raw. All that is most certainly true and yet the great time of scarcity is not yet come.[1]

Yet Sir William Pelham's cries echo in one's ears not because they are typical but because they are atypical. The note of anxiety was often sounded in rural England in the seventeenth century. *Crisis* was rare. Burgeoning trade (colonial trade included) and diversifying industry grew, but they went hand-in-hand with an agriculture slowly progressing through empirical innovation, scientific knowledge (spread by institutions such as the Royal Society and by individual enthusiasts) and imitation of the Flemish and Dutch. Opportunities and improvements in water transport were second only to those of the Netherlands.

III.   *The Limitations of Historical Analysis*

Was it accidental that the countries in which the commercial and industrial revolutions were enacted were those in which for two or three hundred years agrarian yields, methods, products and profits had edged ahead of those elsewhere? Did trade and industry utilize capital accumulated from their higher standards of agrarian performance? Or did similar results follow in countryside as in town from the growing freedom of the *entrepreneur*, growing literacy, growing rationality? Or was it a combination of both, as a comparison with eastern Europe might suggest? For here Jablonskis and Radziwills, Junkers and Magyar lords could make great private fortunes from the land; yet no general commercial, much less industrial, revolution followed.

The 'rise of the Western World' in early modern history was not a uniform curve easily traced. It included the steady decline of northern Italy, from whose earlier triumphs many economic skills and techniques were derived; the spectacular rise and equally spectacular decline of Spain; and, perhaps most significant of all, the swift ascent of the politically fragmented and economically ill-endowed Dutch Republic to a degree of economic maturity unprecedented in the world. Yet, in its turn, by 1700 this economic prodigy seemed to have run out of initiative and to have stabilized at a level of development beyond which it was unable to progress.

[1] Quoted by Joan Thirsk in *English Peasant Farming* (London, 1957), p. 192.

As previous pages have indicated, recent research has travelled a considerable way beyond the institutional and traditional explanations offered for these differential rates of progress in Europe. In attempting to define 'growth' and 'decline', Carlo Cipolla has pointed out that 'decline' is not simply the opposite of 'growth', for (logically at least) there is no limit to growth whereas there are limits beyond which decline cannot go. He concludes that by 'decline' we mean the *relative* decline of a national economy, usually its failure to maintain economic primacy relative to other states, rather than *absolute* decline. He has also analysed the signs and portents that seem to characterize such decline. Common to all seem to be rising public expenditure, rising taxation, rising prices, falling productivity, falling inventiveness, decreasing ability to initiate, even to accept, change. Innovation gives way to conservatism, adventurousness to stuffiness. More people think in terms of 'rights', fewer in terms of 'duties'. Hedonism or idleness replaces the will to work. Spending replaces saving. These tensions and failures are reflected in the unchecked growth of public sectors of economies, in balance-of-payments deficits. In the private sector different social groups jostle to shift economic sacrifices on to each other. Public spirit dwindles and disappears as the social struggle grows more acute. 'Cooperation among people and social groups fades away, a sense of alienation from the commonwealth develops, and with it group and class selfishness.'[1]

If we look more closely into the domestic economies themselves, we see the internal shifts of advantage and disadvantage that accompanied their general movements *in toto*. As the studies of Toledo, Leiden, Venice and other declining centres of former industrial and commercial greatness have shown, the recession in such *individual* cases could prove irreversible, the marginal shift of economic emphasis leaving large pockets of population with their living standards permanently impaired.

The search for clear, total explanations of such socio-economic processes of development and decline continues. Naturally enough: what enquiring mind, faced with the extraordinary evidence of industrial inventiveness provided in Professor Kellenbenz's survey of European manufacture, can fail to ask why England should have inaugurated the move into an era of continuous and rapid socio-economic development, commonly called industrial revolution?[2] Equally clearly, no explanation is forthcoming. Every attempt to formulate universally applicable rules only makes it more clear that every situation has its own peculiar 'mix' of developmental factors, positive and negative. Not only is it impossible to conceive a 'social'

[1] Carlo Cipolla, *The Economic Decline of Empires* (London, 1970), p. 13.
[2] See below, ch. VII.

equivalent of DNA for the body politic; it is also immediately apparent that such attempted formulae do not rest upon the scientific evidence ideally *necessary* to achieve scientifically watertight answers, but only on the evidence on hand to suggest working hypotheses. For a large part, this evidence consists of the disparate efforts of research scholars with regard to particular areas and problems. The only possible conclusion is that the synthesizer of their results should comport himself modestly, remembering that his pretence to universal answers hangs upon a precarious thread largely spun from provisional answers to random questions.

In recent decades there has been a growing realization among economic historians of the limitations on the utility of abstract principles and exogenous theory. Little beyond the simplest applications of the economist's abstractions is really of much help, and even these can easily be pressed to a point in any particular enquiry when they become misleading. Thus to explain the entire agricultural field arrangements of medieval and post-medieval England by, e.g., reference to the calculated 'avoidance of risk' is not merely to overlook the existence of vital (and abundant) exceptions to the conventional 'strip' system, but also to attribute to a society bound by institutional and mental conservatism the ability to change its fundamental economic arrangements by the exercise of rational economic faculties. Here the basic instincts of the historian, *qua* historian, for the 'feel' of an historical situation must be balanced against the abstract logic of the economist.

In such situations – and they recur regularly – the historian can only proceed *per gradus et non per saltus et sensim et pedetentim et non sine sensu*, constructing such theoretical and statistical methods as may seem appropriate to the case, sharpening what Clapham called the statistical 'sense', testing his hypotheses as he goes along by reference to the evidence – all the evidence he may be able to muster, direct and contingent. He will not place upon a single explanatory cause or theory more than it will bear, having regard to the historical facts known and systematically analysed. This does not mean that he will not need to 'quantify'. Quantities need not destroy the historian's sense of the human quality of history any more than an exact knowledge and application of systems of notation, counterpoint or harmony need destroy the musicality of music. Indeed, without them no music could exist: with them, an infinite variety of forms may flourish. The fallacy of some of the protagonists of quantification in current historiographical controversy lies in the narrow, philistine (and false) conceptions of what constitutes history and historical explanation, and in a failure to judge how far quantities can contribute to its understanding.

M. M. Postan warned us many years ago that the historian's contribution to new knowledge in the social sciences must be 'small and
uncertain'.[1] The historian must therefore jettison not merely single
causes but the temptation to treat as *sens uniques* what in reality are
two-way tracks: e.g. sixteenth-century inflation, which had social and
economic consequences in Spain quite different from those in Holland
and England. He must also be prepared to investigate with an open
mind those widely held opinions of contemporaries which may seem
to a modern mind to be merely superstitious substitutes for properly
analytical attitudes. Such was the custom, in declining societies and
economies like seventeenth-century Spain or eighteenth-century
Holland (or twentieth-century Britain), of resorting to 'explanations'
of the current malaise couched in terms of failing energy and decaying
moral fibre. The tragic aspect of all those situations is precisely that they
were not simply the result of the dislocation of one or two major
factors which could have been relatively easily corrected by economic
and sociological knowledge. They were, on the contrary, situations so
complex and daunting as to defy rational analysis. Thus rationality
turned to the baffled despair of seventeenth-century Spaniards or
bewildered would-be reformers of the 'Periwig Period' of Holland,
who looked on helplessly while every *nostrum* proved to be equally and
hopelessly impotent. Perhaps those who equated economic decline
with a total collapse of psychological morale were not, after all, wholly
without justification.

As Carlo Cipolla has concluded in his *Economic Decline of Empires*, the
case of each economy is unique. The historian's task remains the same:
to unravel and analyse the interlocking social components of success or
failure. They include those geographical, geological and climatic
characteristics which are always basic to socio-economic development.
This does not necessarily mean that favourable endowment is a *sine qua
non* of development; it may simply mean that special ingenuity has to
be employed (as in the Netherlands) to avoid the consequences of poor
natural endowment and turn evil into good. Similarly, demographic
growth is in itself no guarantee against disaster. When growth is
maximum rather than optimum it may prove merely temporary –
ultimately a recipe for catastrophe. Yet in general (and only in general),
natural endowment and conditions favourable to demographic growth
were often among the preconditions of that agricultural health which
is itself usually the necessary precursor of commercial and industrial
development. In the ages before powered transport, limitations on
market expansion and therefore on the growth of the exchange
economy left societies heavily dependent on natural or contrived forms

[1] M. M. Postan, *The Historical Method in Social Science* (Cambridge, 1939), p. 35.

of water-borne transport. Sea, river and canal transport were no longer limited to their role of carrying e.g. foodstuffs (as the triremes, quadriremes and quinquiremes had carried corn from Africa to Rome). By 1600 Dutch shipbuilding, textile manufacture, sugar-refining, brewing and distilling etc. were wholly dependent on supplies brought by water transport. Ships, barges and lighters must be seen as a genuine factor of *production* in the industrial development of the maritime economies. To such basic factors must be added operational industrial techniques developed largely by empirical method, but also by the scientific thought and experiment which characterized especially, but not exclusively, the lively commercial and industrial societies of northern Italy and the Netherlands.

Finally, there is the whole spectrum of conscious policy-making by governments, whether absolutist, princely or more or less 'representative'. Historians of the recent post-liberal, 'post-political' age of historiography have tended to fight shy of attributing as much importance as their predecessors did (usually for ill rather than for good) to fiscal factors. Orthodox economic thought made light of such things, regarding 'policy' as the fly on the chariot wheel. This attitude has changed in recent times. Historians of Spain and the Netherlands have recently emphasized the problems created by excessive government spending and the taxation it brought in its train: yet so far this important field of enquiry has been worked only at the surface and much still remains to be done. Similarly the approach to the claims of 'mercantilism' to be a positive dynamic force in economic growth has been cautious, in spite of a measure of rehabilitation of mercantilist ideas and the passing of the rigid hostility of classical theory towards all forms of economic 'interventionism'. Professor J. R. Hale has depicted the governments of renaissance Europe as being paralysed by economic and statistical ignorance and an almost total lack of skilled, experienced economic administrators. *Ergo* economic 'policy' must have rested upon guesswork, much of it wrong.[1] Professor E. L. Jones has recently suggested a less pejorative view, asking whether the essence of the question is not whether 'excellent arrangements' for inducing growth were devised, 'but that age-old impediments on the inherent propensity to truck and barter' (i.e. tolls, tariffs, guilds, debasements, forced loans, confiscations, monopolies, settlement laws, sumptuary legislation etc.) were stripped away.[2] Yet were these in themselves not *positive* as well as *negative* acts of policy, especially as we pass into the seventeenth century? And what of the verdicts of L. A. Harper and Ralph Davis, whose

[1] J. R. Hale, *Renaissance Europe 1480–1520* (London, 1971), p. 162.
[2] E. L. Jones, 'Institutional determinism and the rise of the western world', *Economic Enquiry*, XII: 1 (March 1974), 121.

careful and detailed research has led them on balance to favour the claims of, e.g., the Navigation Acts to be a positive factor in English maritime growth? Or D. C. Coleman's conclusion that protective tariffs were an indispensable element in e.g. the growth of the English paper industry? The same might be argued of a whole range of manufactures in 'developing' countries (like France, England and later Prussia) where a policy of import substitution could only be furthered by deliberate protective action.

By no means all government policy with a significant bearing on the probability of future growth or stagnation demanded sophisticated economic knowledge or comprehensive administrative expertise. The contrast between liberal Dutch or English immigration policy and Spanish or French expulsions was of the greatest economic importance. But it did not derive so much from economic expertise or economic ignorance as from the contrasting priorities accorded to material welfare or religious orthodoxy. Expert administration hardly came into the question.

The importance of migration in ages when technological knowledge was virtually identical with the person and skill of the artisan has been remarked earlier. It is the best part of a century ago since William Cunningham called the attention of English scholars to this fact of their own history.[1] Manufactured articles could be exported, even occasionally imitated, but the only safe and reliable way to transplant technology in the pre-industrial world was to transplant the men in whose heads and hands the secrets of technology were carried. If the debate still continues on the degree of loss suffered by Spain or France by the expulsion of Morisco or Huguenot, no one has ever disputed the enormous and decisive gains won by the northern Netherlands, England and Prussia from the immigration of skilled and resourceful Flemings, Walloons and Huguenots from the sixteenth to the eighteenth centuries: and if the first illustrated the folly of intolerant rulers, the latter equally certainly represented the intelligence of a conscious policy that equated greater tolerance with greater prosperity.

If the once-fashionable problem of the so-called 'Protestant ethic' has been in large measure disposed of, the wider problem of identifying the general and particular conditions that favoured or obstructed economic development remains. Some of these can be quantified, even if only approximately, as Gregory King tried to do in his comparison of tax rates in England, Holland and France in his tables for 1695. The Dutch, he calculated, enjoyed *per capita* incomes higher than those of the French or English. But they suffered crippling rates of tax on these incomes: more than twice those of their larger neighbours. Only very

[1] Cunningham, *Alien Immigrants to England* (first published 1897; second edition, with Introduction by Charles Wilson, 1969).

high tax rates could compensate the government of the Dutch Republic (even given its aspiration towards pacific, neutral policies and its modest expenditure on government itself) for a relatively diminutive population. Other conditions cannot, by their very nature, be measured; yet it would be rash to exclude from the economic historian's purview those 'qualities of life' that derived from the nature of government and law.[1] Professor Lance Davis once observed that the task of the new, more rigorously econometric history was to concentrate on small, well-formulated questions, where, even if 'we may not learn much, we may be sure what we do learn'.[2] Yet history is not merely a cellular structure of small, well-formulated problems awaiting the analysis of the econometrists. Larger, more elusive problems remain, and some will continue to believe that, of all the specialist varieties of historian, the economic historian is the one who should derive most intellectual benefit from attending to H. A. L. Fisher's famous injunction to historians to 'use large maps'. It would be a cramped and distorted history which did not take account of the need of man (even economic man) for a degree of predictability and security in his everyday affairs. The benefits conferred by the Tudor peace in England, by absolutist and Colbertist economic management in France, by the patrician regard for utmost commercial convenience and by opportunist policies of toleration and neutrality in the Dutch Republic – none of these was absolute or undiluted. Their claims to favour material improvement have to be balanced in each case against their costs: but to calculate costs calls for the exploration of a whole area of social enquiry that lies somewhere between economic history proper and the world of politics and culture. One of the changes of *ethos* most influential (and least quantifiable) during the period covered by this volume was the spread of secular attitudes, amongst them the belief that material improvement, the economic gain of states and individuals, was not only morally permissible but was in itself the major duty of governments and peoples alike.

[1] Charles Wilson, 'Taxation and the decline of empires', in *Economic History and the Historian* (London, 1969), p. 120.

[2] Quoted by E. L. Jones, 'Institutional determinism', p. 118.

CHAPTER II

Agriculture in the Vital Revolution

I.   *General Characteristics of the Period*

HISTORIOGRAPHY

BEFORE THE Second World War agrarian history was invariably treated either as a legal or as a technically agricultural study. The first method concerned itself with the legal status of the various groups (freemen, *ministeriales*, villeins, etc.) and the laws pertaining to villeinage and common land (*Marken*). In Austria and Germany Dopsch and von Below fiercely debated the subject of land tenure in Germanic times; in England, successive generations of scholars tackled with untiring vigour the problems of the manorial system.

The legal approach had a number of disadvantages. The field of research was almost entirely limited to the Middle Ages. The economic aspects of the manorial system and of the use of common land were ignored. No account was taken of the fact that history is concerned with what was once a living reality, people of flesh and blood. Marc Bloch's somewhat disdainful comment is applicable to these legal historians: 'ces érudits pour qui le paysan d'autrefois ne semble avoir existé qu'afin de fournir l'occasion de plaisantes dissertations juridiques'. The basic objection to this legally orientated agrarian history is that it starts with extensive chapters on the Germanic and Carolingian periods, continues until the end of villeinage after 1300, and comes to an end about 1500.

The agricultural line of investigation generally confines itself to the history of crops, crop rotation systems, breeds of cattle or agricultural implements and machines. This kind of technical history often provides little more than a collection of unrelated facts. Except for the atypical phenomena of the so-called 'Agricultural Revolution' in eastern England, they refer almost exclusively to the nineteenth and twentieth centuries. Little attention is normally paid to the interrelationship between events and often there is no attempt to offer a rationale.

The split between these two approaches – the legal towards the Middle Ages and the agricultural towards the nineteenth and twentieth centuries – accounts for the almost universal gap in research on the period from 1500 to 1800, centuries of no further interest to the legal historian and too early for the agriculturalist.

It is only during the last forty years or so that agrarian history has been studied from an economic and sociological point of view. The possibility of an economic approach was opened up by the publication of sources from the archives showing prices of agricultural products. In 1932 studies by Simiand and Labrousse clearly indicated the extraordinary impact of price fluctuations in agricultural products, especially grain, on the entire economic structure of previous centuries. During the same year Usher demonstrated that it was possible to establish a secular trend based on quantitative data. Fundamental factors in the secular trend are, according to Usher: 'changes in the mass of population, changes in the distribution and density of population and changes in the standard of living expressed in the per capita consumption of the population'. He added: 'It is important to observe also that the historian is concerned with the rate of change in these quantitative factors.'

In 1935 Usher's ideas were taken up in books by Abel, Madame Griziotti-Kretschmann and soeur Kerhuel. Of these three, Abel's work is the most important since it shows the link between demographic facts and prices, particularly of grain and meat. Historians had already produced a variety of demographic facts or long lists of prices and wages, but there had been no systematic correlation of the two. Prior to Abel, the emphasis had been mostly on the short fluctuations in trade after 1800, since the population factor in the shorter fluctuations during this period was relatively unimportant. Abel, however, in his book *Agrarkrisen und Agrarkonjunktur in Mitteleuropa vom 13. bis zum 19. Jahrhundert* (1935, rev. ed. 1966) studied price trends over a period of many centuries, where the increase or decrease of population could not possibly be ignored, particularly in a pre-industrial, predominantly agrarian society.

Abel's work remained little known among historians until after the Second World War, when the late medieval crisis and the depression of the seventeenth century became common themes in international writings. At the same time theories of economic growth were gaining ground. With this change in outlook, historians came to regard agriculture as part of the general economy and to attempt to take developments in agriculture into the purview of general economic history. Interest shifted to a wide range of interconnected factors: population, agriculture, monetary matters, prices, market ratios, feeding and social conditions. Because the processes governing these interdependent factors are highly complex, there can be no question of simple causal explanations.

This macro-economic historical research has gone hand in hand with micro-economic studies in which the profitability of one or more farms has been examined. Such research reminds us to some extent of the books on farm husbandry published at the end of the eighteenth and the beginning of the nineteenth century, the studies by William Marshall,

Arthur Young, von Schwerz and von Thünen. These authors, however, were primarily interested in the farming of their day. They wanted to acquire a better understanding of it in order to raise the standard of farming by agricultural improvements. The research undertaken by a number of Professor J. E. C. Conrad's students at Halle was purely historical. But the dissertations from this school, appearing c. 1900, were ignored by historians until they were used by Riemann for his study on arable farming and animal husbandry in pre-industrial Germany (1953). In England, accounts and diaries of peasants and gentlemen-farmers, and – for the Middle Ages – accounts of abbeys and other religious institutions, were studied, particularly after the work of Thorold Rogers (1866–1902) had been published.

Social agrarian history is concerned with such matters as the social stratification of rural society in groups and classes, the occupational structure, the characteristics of the progressive farmers, the composition of the farming household, relationships between farmers and their workers, the spreading of knowledge and of innovations, education, literacy and human adaptability.

PRE-INDUSTRIAL SOCIETY: AGRICULTURE, POPULATION AND PRICES

Chronologically, the material of this chapter is bounded by L. Genicot's contribution, 'Crisis: from the Middle Ages to Modern Times' in volume I of this series, and by F. Dovring's chapter, 'The Transformation of European agriculture', in part II, of volume VI. Thematically it follows K. F. Helleiner, 'The Population of Europe from the Black Death to the Eve of the Vital Revolution' and F. P. Braudel and F. Spooner, 'Prices in Europe from 1450 to 1750', both in volume IV.

The economic and social evolution of rural, pre-industrial society and even the technical development of agriculture cannot be understood without a knowledge of the history of prices and population. The main difference between the accompanying chapters and this one is that since agriculture is the main theme here, the subject is approached from another angle, and the problems of population and prices appear in a different light. Our interest in population is focused on the number of people or farmsteads that grew the crops, in other words the *producers*, *vis-à-vis* the consumers, i.e. the total population minus the infants. Prices of farm produce are of particular interest, with special emphasis on the price ratio between different agrarian products, as well as on the ratio between farm and industrial prices (PA/PI) and the ratio between food prices and wages (PA/W).

Any account of the factors influencing the production and consumption of agrarian goods in our pre-industrial society is hampered by the lack of any basic theory in the writings on the period. One frequently encounters incomplete explanations, half-truths and at times quite erroneous interpretations. The foundations of pre-industrial society have not been thought out systematically, and only a greater theoretical knowledge can show the limitations of that society. This theoretical *lacuna* cannot possibly be filled within the scope of this chapter; we can only touch on a number of characteristic phenomena. A beginning in this field has recently been made by Henning in his book on farmers, receipts, and expenditure during the eighteenth century, especially in eastern Germany (*Dienste und Abgaben der Bauern im 18. Jahrhundert*, 1969).

During the period from 1500 to 1800, almost everywhere in Europe more than half the working population was still employed in agriculture. Yet even before 1800 there were areas where people earned their living in industry, trade, shipping and fishing, as well as in agriculture – Holland and Flanders probably offer examples of this kind of non-agrarian structure, but we have no precise facts about them. However, even in a province like Overijssel, somewhat off the beaten track of the great trade routes, only 46 per cent of the working population was active in agriculture, according to the population census of 1795.

On the other hand, even where pre-industrial life was no longer based on agriculture, it remained a very important factor. Industry itself was mainly concerned with the processing of agricultural produce, e.g. the textile industry which used flax and wool as raw materials. The same applies to breweries, distilleries, oil mills, flour mills, bakeries and rope-works, to the manufacture of dyes for the cloth industry and to the processing of tobacco. The importance of grain in trade and commerce is shown by the cargoes passing through the Danish Sound: about 50 per cent of the Dutch ships passing westwards through the Sound during the seventeenth century were carrying grain.

The rich bourgeoisie of the towns also had interests in agriculture since a sizeable part of their property consisted of land and farm holdings, and land remained an attractive means of investing the capital earned in commerce, in industry or in official functions. Between 30 and over 50 per cent of the property owned by the bourgeoisie in the Overijssel towns in the mid eighteenth century consisted of land and farm holdings.

So even apparently non-agricultural aspects of the pre-industrial economy were closely linked to rural activities. Agriculture remained the dominant factor in the economy as a whole.

Before 1800, moreover, farming in most parts of Europe was heavily biased in favour of corn production. During the sixteenth and seventeenth centuries the cultivation of buckwheat became more general in western and central Europe, and rice and maize were introduced into southern Europe, but these did not alter the tradition of single-crop cultivation in many regions. This change did not occur until potatoes came to be grown in large quantities on the fields.

The production of corn offered the farmer an opportunity of consuming part of what he produced, sometimes even the whole of it, and it was unusual for the total yield of the harvest to be sent to market. Individual productivity was limited both by lack of technical development and by the restricted energy available from the human labour force and the tractive power of horses, mules, donkeys, oxen and at times cows. Each worker, therefore, could cover only a very limited acreage, so that individual productivity was low and never rose above a certain maximum. Agricultural productivity was obviously geared to total numbers of farm workers and vice versa.

Productivity was not the same on all farms; small farms were much less efficient than large ones. In Brunswick in 1685, a 'normal' family holding (47 acres of arable) meant one adult male worker for every 20¼ acres, but on the small farms there was one worker to 7 acres. In the same region during the eighteenth century on the farms of the *Ackerleute*, we find one adult male worker on 14–23 acres; on the smaller farms of the *Halbspänner*, one worker on 10–16 acres and on those of the cottagers, one worker on 5–8 acres. The labour force on the small-holdings was therefore three to five times as large as that on the family farms: they had in fact an over-capacity of labour. Sometimes this was utilized by the intensive cultivation of specialized crops, like flax and potatoes, at other times by cottage industry. The smallholdings suffered from an excess not only of manpower but also of animal power; the smallholders mostly used a pair of horses or oxen for ploughing and other fieldwork.

The quantities produced on each farm varied greatly from year to year and from this fluctuating production a 'fixed' amount had to be reserved for seed for the coming year and for feeding the household. If production is expressed as a ratio between the seed sown and the quantity harvested – the yield ratio – then it is obvious that a reduction of the total yield with one unit of seed is much more serious where the ratio is low than where it is high: if the harvest yields four times the amount of seed sown, 25 per cent of the harvest will have to be reserved for seed the next year, whereas, if the production is sixteen times the amount sown, only 6–7 per cent will have to be reserved. Again, the acreage which must be reserved for the production of seed is much larger when the yield is low than when it is high, so that a rise in yield ratios has a cumulative effect, since more ground can be used for other purposes.

The amount of food consumed in the farm household is largely determined by the number of members of the family and employees. The amount actually marketed therefore varies also according to the ratio between producers and consumers on the farm, as well as being directly related to the acreage. This in turn is related to the total number of producers.

The fact that after deduction of the 'fixed' amounts for seed and for domestic use, only a varying portion of the harvest reached the market each year, meant that market prices were affected by these fluctuations in supply. Sharp price fluctuations are characteristic of grain prices from the sixteenth to the eighteenth century.

In the long term, the population factor has a bearing on supply as well as on demand. We have already seen that low individual productivity affects the relationship between the total population and the gross marketed yield. Supply affects the price of grain. On the other hand, demand is determined by the number of consumers not supplying their own needs by home production. This number of consumers also varies in direct relation to the total population. Not surprisingly, the secular trend shows broadly comparable fluctuations in both population and grain prices.

The gross value of the agricultural yield is calculated by multiplying the amount marketed – which is the total yield *minus* the amount needed for seed, home consumption and cattle food – by the current market price. From this must be deducted rent, tithes, taxes, other dues and wages for regular and casual labour. Where payments are made in kind, these quantities can be deducted from the total yield; wages paid in kind are usually consumed directly. Similarly, the lessor or tithe-owner may take his rent or tithe by marketing the goods in kind.

Farms producing for the market have to cope with sharp annual fluctuations in yields as well as in prices; dues, taxes and wages are far less variable, except for those types of rent and tithe which are paid in kind. The annual fluctuations in yields and prices and the changes over a longer period affect the different farms in different ways. When yields are falling, the number of farmers who provide for themselves will decrease; when yields are increasing, the number of these farmers will rise. The increased demand from the producer in times of scarcity and the increased supply when harvests were plentiful, resulting in sharply accentuated price fluctuations, were particularly characteristic of an economy whose production and consumption were largely self-contained, without either import or export of large quantities of corn. Opinions differ as to whether consumption, that is the amount eaten annually by one individual, is fixed or variable. If it is a variable it lies within certain known limits: the maximum is determined by the capacity of the human stomach; the minimum is the amount just sufficient to stay alive. When the quantity of food is reduced, there will be a decrease in productivity in agriculture because of the decline in human energy, since human labour is one of the principal production factors.

The number of persons in a household is an important factor affecting the spending of wages or income. The consumption of one individual may be variable to some extent, but there is much less possibility of variability in the number of persons in a household. The only way to lower the number of persons in a household is by reducing the number of servants or by sending the growing children to work on other farms or in the town. Much will depend on whether a household relies on more or less fixed wages, whether the income is irregular or whether the income fluctuates with agrarian prices or harvests. A feature of wages is that, even over a long period, they tend to alter only slightly. Since corn and bread were an important part of the staple diet in the period 1500–1800, the marked fluctuations in the price of grain resulted in a varying expenditure on them. There was thus an incompatibility between the 'fixed' wage and the variable amounts spent on the most important items of food. Obviously the amount that is left to be spent on other needs is also subject to great variations. The people whose income goes up or down with the agrarian yields (lessors and tithe-owners who receive goods in kind) and people whose income goes up or down with agrarian prices (lessors receiving rents), do not suffer the disadvantages of a 'fixed' wage. These people might, however, be affected in the other ways they spend their agrarian income, and this of course also applies to the farmers producing for the market.

The development in agrarian productivity may be calculated in various ways. It can be calculated on the basis of the total area of cultivated land: the arable acreage and the acreage available for grain. Or we can compare the number of producers and the number of consumers. Another favoured method is to take the number of people or farms required to produce food for one non-agrarian person or one non-agrarian family. We can also compare the quantities produced and consumed at different times, but here import and export must be taken into account. And finally we can compare the monetary values of the year by year yield, bearing in mind the fluctuating market prices.

It has frequently been pointed out that some factors bearing on production and consumption are constant or liable to little variation; others are subject to fairly marked fluctuation. In various combinations of factors this could produce problems, as for instance the instability of the harvests *vis-à-vis* the limited productivity per worker, and the more stable quantities of seed for sowing and food consumed by the farm household. As against the varying net income of the farms, we have the 'fixed' quantities of food, seed, dues, rates, wages and sometimes rents. The set wage is supposed to feed a fixed number of members of the family, whose consumption is bounded by certain limits, yet this food, consisting largely of bread and corn was particularly subject to the price fluctuations in grain. This is typical of the conflict situations prevailing in pre-industrial society.

There is, moreover, another important point; some factors, like yield ratios, grain prices and the net income of farms, show marked fluctuations over shorter periods and yet over a longer period remain constant. This is true, for instance, of yield ratios in eastern European countries, which show little change between 1500 and 1750.[1] Several other factors, on the other hand, can be shown to remain more or less constant over a short period but display a certain variability when reviewed over a longer period. There are therefore four possibilities:

	Short run		*Long run*	
1.	Constant	1.	Constant	(c c)
2.	Fluctuating	2.	Constant	(f c)
3.	Constant	3.	Variable	(c v)
4.	Fluctuating	4.	Variable	(f v)

On examination of 73 factors affecting agrarian production (exogenous factors such as weather conditions, politics, government measures and wars *excluded*), 55 of them appear to be constant over a short period and 18 appear to be fluctuating. This indicates the rigidity of agriculture which does not adapt itself readily in the short term. Things are different over a longer period. Here we find 13 constant factors against 60 variable ones. Those factors showing little change between 1500 and 1800 include: the seed required per area unit, the yield ratios in eastern Europe, the area tillable by one worker, individual home consumption, the milk yield of cows, the live and dead weight of cattle, the weight of a sheep's skin, the wine crop per area unit, the olive harvest per area unit, farm buildings, agricultural implements and tools, field systems (except for England and Scandinavia) and the time needed to accomplish special agricultural tasks. In the analysis of consumption there are, in the short run 8 constant as against 12 fluctuating factors; over a longer period there are 18 variables and only 2 constants (the amount consumed per typical family and per individual).

[1] See yield ratios, pp. 79 *et seq.* below, and esp. Table 7, p. 81.

Table 1. *Constant and variable factors in the short and long term*

Short term	Long term	Production	Consumption
		number of factors	
Constant	Constant (c c)	13	2
Fluctuating	Constant (f c)	—	—
Constant	Variable (c v)	42	6
Fluctuating	Variable (f v)	18	12
Total number of factors		73	20

On examination of the factors in respect of acreage, numbers of people and animals, quantities and amounts of money, the acreage appears to be very constant in the short term but variable in the long run; the numbers of people and animals are all variable in the long run, and partly constant in the short run; quantities are subject to little change, as we have seen already, but there is considerable fluctuation in amounts of money. Population and prices are variable in the long run; prices fluctuate considerably over a short period, population less so.

Prices, representing the balance between supply and demand, are negotiated on the market. There are three kinds of markets for agricultural produce: the local, the interregional and the international market. It is only in the local markets that the familiar negative correlation between crops and prices is encountered: large crops meant low prices, small crops meant high prices. Many historians, unaware of the difference between the local markets on the one side and the interregional or international markets on the other side, assume that this negative correlation applies to the latter too.

The areas of production and consumption for the interregional and international markets expand and contract according to the price ratios between the different regions or countries. A large price differential causes expansion: the area supplying the market increases; the consumption area expands. A small price differential causes contraction: the marketing areas of production and consumption will be smaller. The cost of interregional and international grain transport is not very flexible as a rule. Since the cereal trade is concerned with fluctuating price differentials, 'fixed' transport costs will operate against transportation when the price gap decreases.

Where price fluctuations operate we have to distinguish between the short and the long term. They affect the production and consumption of farm products in different ways. Yield–price ratios can move in four directions:

(1) Yields increase, prices decrease (negative correlation);

(2) Yields increase, prices increase (sixteenth century and second half of the eighteenth century);

(3) Yields decrease, prices increase (negative correlation);

(4) Yields decrease, prices decrease (seventeenth and eighteenth century).

The negative correlation occurs especially in short-term fluctuations. These ratios apply particularly to the local market. Without sufficient outlets to increase the area of consumption, over-production can be just as disastrous for the farmers as a bad harvest. The second and fourth trends occur in fluctuations over a longer period (the secular trend). The cause will be found outside agriculture, among such factors as population shifts, the quantity of money and the velocity of circulation of money, or such unpredictable factors as war, disaster, epidemics, weather conditions, etc.

If it is assumed that a relation exists between yields, grain prices and population, then this means that there should be some connection between (1) the amount of the crops marketed, (2) the ratio between grain prices on the one side and the prices of other goods and wages on the other side, and (3) consumers' demand. The relationship between these factors will, however, be more complicated if an interregional or international market has been formed.

A number of frequently recurring phenomena have been observed in the trends in grain prices.

(1) There is a correlation in the fluctuations of all grain prices.

(2) By comparison, the prices of the cheaper grains display sharper fluctuations than those of the more expensive grains. In times of scarcity the consumer turns to the cheaper cereals, whereas in times of plenty there is little demand for the cheaper grains.

(3) Grain prices go up in the course of the agrarian year: prices are lowest immediately after the harvest; the highest prices occur in the spring and early summer.

(4) In the absence of import and export there will be a relatively steep price-increase in times of scarcity; if there is a grain surplus prices will fall rapidly (Gregory King's law, with Jevon's and Bouniatian's formulae).

(5) A correlation may exist between grain prices and the price of land and rents. This correlation may be disturbed by population pressures, causing the demand for land and tenant farms to rise disproportionately. The demand may also increase in some countries where landownership is a status symbol, sought after by the socially ambitious.

(6) In addition to the daily, seasonal and annual fluctuations in the prices of grain, variations also occur over longer periods, of which the secular trend is of great importance.

(7) In the course of the eighteenth and nineteenth centuries the amplitude of fluctuations in grain prices narrowed as a result of improved seed, research in plant diseases, better manuring and the possibility of importing grain from non-European countries.

We can also trace a pattern in the relationship between grain prices and the prices of other goods and wages.

(1) When the indices of grain prices are compared with those of livestock and dairy products such as meat, butter and cheese, and also with industrial crops, the range of the former is shown to be much wider than that of either of the latter two.

(2) When the indices of the prices of agrarian products are compared with those of non-agrarian products, the range of the former is again wider than that of the latter. During a boom, agrarian prices rise to a higher peak; during a slump, agrarian prices fall lower.

(3) During a boom, the wage index generally tended in former ages to lag behind the rising price indices of goods, in particular behind those of grain. During a recession, the wage index fell more slowly than the price index. Rising grain prices therefore meant a decline in real wages, while falling grain prices indicated an increase in the real wage.

(4) When there is a fall in real wages as a result of a large supply of labour, the real wages of the skilled labourer will show a less marked decrease than those of the unskilled labourer; conversely, with the rise of real wages resulting from a labour shortage, the wages of skilled labour will show a relatively smaller increase than the wages of unskilled labour.

These points are of course only valid in general terms; exceptions are always possible. During the sixteenth century, in the region of ox-breeding and ox trade in Schleswig Holstein, there was a relatively far greater increase in the price of bullocks than in the price of rye. After 1620 the price of bullocks fell much more rapidly than that of rye. Schleswig Holstein and Jutland had concentrated during the sixteenth century on this particular branch of animal husbandry which was much more sensitive to market conditions through its dependence on the economic situation of the area of consumption (the western German and Dutch towns).

Wine-growing is exceptional in that heavy cropping means good quality. The cost of the storage vats used to be relatively high compared with the price of wine. As a result, after an abundant harvest of good quality grapes, the vats containing older wine of inferior quality were emptied to provide storage for the new.

A study of the available material on prices and wages indicates that, in the ratio between the prices of grain and of other commodities and wages, grain was unfavourably placed at the end of the Middle Ages (fourteenth and part of the fifteenth century); it was strong from the late fifteenth to the early or mid seventeenth century, weak again in the seventeenth and first half of the eighteenth century, and finally favourably placed after 1750. The periods of high grain prices were those of agricultural expansion (increase of arable land, improvements in agriculture); the periods of low grain prices were those of agricultural regression (decrease of arable land, only few improvements in agriculture). It should be kept in mind, however, that the term 'agricultural' is used here in a limited sense and refers only to grain growing. Though not strictly accurate, this identification of grain growing with general farming is justified by the primacy of grain in agriculture throughout our period.

When speaking of crisis or depression in the seventeenth century, we are in fact referring to the grain crisis, i.e. a period characterized by an unfavourable ratio between grain on the one hand and other goods and wages on the other. This by no means precludes prosperity in other sectors of economic life, as in the flourishing breweries, distilleries, textile and tobacco industries during this period.

The transition from boom to depression, and the reverse, is rarely clearly defined. Nor does a depression affect all countries at the same time. It is rather a question of adverse situations arising in different areas at different times from different causes, which may eventually lead to a crisis. The trend may spread from one area to the next. Urbanized areas with a diversified economy are more resilient than those which produce hardly anything but raw materials. Worst hit would be those areas with the most restricted economies: regions growing nothing but grain or those confined entirely to cattle-rearing. During the seventeenth and eighteenth centuries the plight of the Baltic states was identical with that of the developing countries whose only source of income is raw materials, e.g. Latin America and Africa in the nineteenth and twentieth centuries. More favourably placed were the areas which, during a period of agrarian regression, could move from grain production to cattle breeding, or to the growing of commercial crops, wine-growing or the planting of olive groves. During periods of agricultural expansion, cereal-farming would be preferred.

On the whole, grain prices fluctuate more strongly than the prices of other products and wages. Over a shorter period wages do not vary as much as grain prices, and wage-earners are at a disadvantage when grain prices go up, while the farmer whose income is based on grain prices is in serious trouble when they fall, since his liabilities in rents, taxes, mortgage interests and the like remain steady.

Clearly it is not the grain prices themselves which provide the determinant factor, but the *ratio* between grain prices on the one hand

and wages with earnings on the other. A change in these ratios does not affect all groups or classes in the same way, since what means profit to some means a loss to others. Precisely because the various social groups react differently, we ought to investigate the relative importance of each of these groups and the way in which they react to economic change. The significance of social stratification is often overlooked by those historians who are simply concerned with the correlation between the size of harvest, grain prices and population figures.

Periods of agricultural expansion are found to coincide with rises in population, while periods of agricultural regression are marked by a levelling or decline in population (see pp. 55–6, Table 2). It is not easy to tell which of the two comes first, the rise in production or that in population, since a reinforcing secondary effect has to be taken into account. Increased productivity enables a farmer and his family to subsist on a smaller farm, and the subsequent distribution of the land leads to more marriages at an earlier age and consequently to a higher birth-rate. Furthermore, better grain yields provide better labour prospects in agriculture and in the non-agrarian industries linked to it.

A reinforcing secondary effect also contributes to the decline in population, and this decline partly accounts for the economic depression at the end of the Middle Ages and in the seventeenth century. The economic depression in turn resulted in the postponement of marriages and in a larger number of bachelors, thereby leading to a further stagnation or reduction in the birth-rate.

AGRICULTURAL EXPANSION AND REGRESSION

It is possible to list the agricultural, economic and social phenomena occurring in times of agricultural expansion and regression. This provides a schematic representation, consisting of a simple grouping of empirical facts, which should be viewed as a tool for research rather than as a dogma. Circumstances can be typical of a certain period without applying to each and every place and time. There will be deviations from the general pattern and there are regional exceptions. This does not invalidate the survey; it merely means that an important deviation has been traced which deserves closer scrutiny. Some of the phenomena listed are linked to a definite economic situation. However, they are symptoms of more general causes, which may be demographic, monetary, politico-economic or just political. The phenomena and the transformations of agricultural society cannot be ascribed to one single cause.

Table 2.   *Scheme of circumstances which accompany periods of agricultural expansion and of agricultural regression*

Periods of expansion	Periods of regression
1 End 15th century–1600 or 1650	1 Early 14th century–end 15th century
2 After 1750	2 1600 or 1650–1750

Feature of agricultural expansion	*Feature of agricultural regression*
Grain prices rise in relation to the prices of other wares and to wages; terms of trade favourable to grain.	Grain prices fall in relation to the prices of other wares and to wages; terms of trade unfavourable to grain.

Economic and social phenomena	*Economic and social phenomena*
1	1 The period of agricultural regression is not an overall crisis. It affects only grain and does not preclude prosperity in other sectors of the economy.
2	2 No sudden crisis in the transition from expansion to regression; no crisis affecting all countries at the same time; producing and exporting countries are affected earlier and more severely than importing countries; contrast between farming areas and industrialized or trading areas; regression unfavourable to grain-exporting countries (Baltic countries), favourable to grain-importing countries (Holland).
3	3 Sharp fluctuations in grain prices.
4 Reduction in real wages.	4 Increase in real wages.
5 The wages of skilled workers are relatively high compared with those for unskilled labour.	5 The wages for unskilled labour are relatively high compared with those for skilled labour.
6 Increase of land rents.	6 Reduction of land rents.
7 Advantageous to landed farmers.	7 Disadvantageous to landed farmers.
8 Increasing differentiation in the social stratification of the rural population; multiplication of lower social groups.	8 Number of social groups contracts.
9 Increase in the number of small farmers.	9 Decrease in the number of small farmers.
10 Creation of a landless rural proletariat.	10
11 Occasionally, shift from industry to agriculture.	11 Creation of rural industry, particularly textiles.
12	12 Grain used for industrial purposes: breweries, distilleries, starch manufacture, etc.

Table 2 (*cont.*)

Agricultural phenomena		*Agricultural phenomena*	
13	Clearing of land for arable farming, land reclamation, new polders and peateries.	13	The tillable land surface shrinks and lies fallow, villages are abandoned (*Wüstungen*), floods.
14		14	Erosion, shifting sands.
15	Improvement of yield ratios.	15	Lowering of yield ratios.
16	Shift from cattle raising to arable farming; hay and pasture fields used for crop-growing.	16	Shift from arable farming to livestock-breeding; arable fields used as meadows and hay fields.
17		17	Increased fodder production for livestock.
18		18	Increased production of cheap cereals (barley, oats, buckwheat).
19		19	Increased growing of work-consuming and industrial crops (flax, hops, colza, madder, etc.).
20	Decrease of vineyards.	20	Increase of vineyards.
21		21	More sheep raising, greater production of wool.
22	Good manuring, purchase of dung; marling.	22	No manure is bought for the cornfields; no marling.
23	Introduction of new tools (ploughing equipment, farming machines); new special equipment for grain cultivation; the purpose of the new tools is to increase output (ploughs, machines for making furrows).	23	Few new tools are introduced (ploughs, farming tools); new special tools for processing dairy produce and stocking hay; the new equipment aims at quick handling of the production (churning).
24	The individual farm grows smaller.	24	The farm increases in size.
25	The plots allotted become smaller.	25	
26	New books on agriculture.	26	The old books on agriculture are reprinted.

It has already been pointed out that the phenomena listed in Table 2 will not necessarily all occur during one period of agrarian expansion or regression. It is quite feasible, for instance, during an agrarian regression, that despite the low grain prices farmers will not go over to the production of other commodities or to cattle-rearing. In order to maintain his income the farmer may concentrate on more intensive cereal-cropping, for instance by using a better system of crop rotation or by more manuring. In this way yield will increase and, despite the lower prices, his income will remain more or less constant. The years of crises after 1929 showed us the disastrous effect this kind of policy has on market prices. Increased production caused prices to fall even more than they would otherwise have done. An instance of more intensive corn-cropping during the period of agrarian regression in the second half of the seventeenth century, can be found on farms near Maastricht, where the farmers went over to more intensive systems of grain cultivation and began growing vetch and other fodder crops. There was a rapid rise in yields per acre between 1660 and 1700. Better quality grains were also produced, such as wheat; and much more barley was grown for the breweries.

II.   *Agrarian Production*

EXOGENOUS FACTORS

External factors which might seriously affect agrarian production include weather conditions and plant and animal diseases. Weather conditions obviously have a considerable bearing on annual yields. If we mean by climate the 'average weather conditions over a period of thirty years', we could ask whether changes in climate have affected production over a longer period of time.

The relationship between plant growth and weather conditions is more complicated than is generally assumed in historical literature. There are three factors of importance to the growth of plants: temperature, precipitation and intensity of light. Each of these factors is required in varying degrees throughout the eight phases of growth of a wheat plant, and too much or too little at any time can be detrimental. The ideal weather conditions for wheat in the temperature zone could be listed as follows:

1	End of September	Fairly moist
2	October, November to 20 December	Fairly dry, not too mild
3	21 December to end of February	Fairly dry, a little snow, never more than 10 °C of frost, no hard winds
4	March	No frost after the grain has resumed its growth
5	April	Sunny, slight rainfall at regular intervals
6	May to 15 June	Warm, no heat-wave, a little rain
7	16 June to 10 July	Cool, cloudy, no rain while the grain is in flower
8	End of July, August to beginning of September	Dry, warm and sunny, no heat-wave

A negative correlation has been found to exist between the amount of precipitation during the period from 10 June to 20 July and the number of grains of corn, whereas there is a positive correlation between the percentage of sunshine during the period between 20 March and 10 May and the number of grains of corn.

Other cereals react in more or less the same way as wheat. Rye and barley may be grown in colder areas since they are more winter-proof than wheat. For barley, which has a short period of growth, a cold spring and a wet summer are harmful. Oats need a longer period of growth, and although oats do not like late night frosts, they can be grown in very damp areas. The potato requires cool and moist climate; the notorious potato blight thrives in warm, damp weather and little intensity of light.

Since the vine is a perennial, the effects of climatic conditions on it are much more complicated than on cereals. A good wine harvest will follow when:

(1) the summer of the preceding year was warm, so that there are numerous buds;

(2) the autumn is mild enough for the ripening of the shoots;

(3) there is no severe frost during the winter and the spring;

(4) the summer and early autumn are warm to allow the fruit to ripen. The quality of the wine improves in relation to the intensity of the light.

Where intensive heat might cause corn to wither, these weather conditions are exactly right for the quantity as well as the quality of wine, whereas rainy summers produce small yields of poor quality. It takes five years for a vineyard to produce a full yield, and since it will be exhausted after twenty-five years, weather conditions during the productive period are of great importance.

The olive tree needs twenty years before it produces a full yield. In Languedoc the trees were only productive every two years because of a shortage of manure. The olive tree is very susceptible to frost and the severe winters of 1565 and 1573, those in the period from 1690 to 1700 and especially the winter of 1709 caused heavy damage to the cultivation of olives in the south of France.

Studies of grass show a positive correlation between temperature and raw-protein content, and between the degree of light intensity and the raw-cellulose content. In hay, a variation in starch content seems to be largely dependent on the amount of rain and sunshine during the period between April and the end of July. A dry summer with much sunshine produces a high starch content; wet summers produce a large yield of roughage but of indifferent quality, with a poor starch content. The starch content in turn influences the milk yield during the winter. The milk yields are also directly affected by the weather; very hot summers or extensive rain in the autumn will adversely affect milk production.

In general, the shorter the period of growth, the higher the variability of yield, as for instance in buckwheat. Seed plants, in particular papilionaceous plants, which are sensitive during the time of flowering, are usually more risky than bulbous and tuberous plants.

The following grades of cropping variability can be distinguished:

(1) high risk: mangels, linseed, horse beans and peas;

(2) medium risk: cole-seed, winter and spring wheat, winter barley and flax fibre;

(3) low risk: early potatoes, summer barley, clover and oats;

(4) virtually safe: hay, potatoes and rye.

Although most areas were already growing summer barley, oats and rye – crops that involved relatively little risk – the introduction of the potato, offering a new crop with little risk, was obviously of great importance.

The stability of the yield also depended on soil conditions. Yields fluctuated least of all on loess, the soil of the earliest permanent settlements in Europe. Light clay soils were cultivated at a somewhat greater risk; heavy clay or sandy soil at considerable risk. Hence even within a small area yields could vary greatly where there was a wide diversity of soil structures.

It is therefore clear that in order to study the correlation between yields and weather or climate in the past, we require a much more detailed knowledge of weather and soil conditions than is usually available. Such indications as cold winters or wet summers mean very little by themselves.

Research has shown that in the cultivation of grain in the temperate zone, yields were much more susceptible to precipitation than to temperature. There is thought to be a correlation between precipitation in the autumn and winter months and the degree of acidity of the soil. A high precipitation results in rising acidity and lower yields. In the past, the continuous cultivation of corn in the same fields must of itself have produced a high level of acidity, and heavy rainfall would only increase this. Too much precipitation also reduces the calcium, phosphates and nitrogen in the soil, thereby impoverishing the harvest. In particular, variations in nitrogen content of the soil must have added greatly to the wide fluctuations in yields. Nowadays the influence of these factors has been largely levelled out by much more extensive manuring and by the use of fertilizers.

That all these factors at one time or another played their part is apparent from the harvests of forty-odd manors belonging to the bishop of Winchester. According to the data published in an article by J. Titow, during the period between 1211 and 1350 the harvests were very good when the preceding summer and autumn had been very dry, the winter cold or normal and the summer also dry. Wet or very wet autumns and wet winters were followed by bad harvests. After cold winters the harvests were usually good, unless the winter had been preceded by a wet autumn. It also appears from eighteenth-century data that severe winters like those of 1784/5 and that of 1785/6, with, respectively, 89 and 112 days of frost in London, followed by dry, warm summers, produced good harvests.

Over a period of years the yields of different types of cereal within an area of the same precipitation display similar fluctuations. This is because different cereals react in similar ways to soil fertility, which varies according to the precipitation accumulated in the soil over a longer period. Today, yields of wheat and rye are one and a half times as high in dry years as in wet years, and peas, which are so susceptible to moisture, give in dry years three times the yield of wet years.

In the past, maximum yields could be from three to almost five times the minimum yields. Taking the 'normal' yield as 100, minimal and maximal yields between 1500 and 1800 were on average as given in Table 3, although there were poorer and also richer harvests.

Table 3.   *Minimum and maximum grain yields between 1500 and 1800*

Grain	Minimum	Maximum	Maximum/Minimum
Wheat	40–80	120–40, 150–90	4·75
Rye	50 or 60–80	120–70	3·50
Barley	40–70	110–50	3·75
Oats	50–90	110–40, 150–70	3·40

It is obvious from the marked fluctuations of yields that prior to the nineteenth century corn was much more subject to changing weather conditions than it is now, when better quality seed, artificial fertilizing, phytopathological research, weed killing, improved implements and rotation of crops achieve much more constant yields.

Taking the harvests ranging between 85 and 115 per cent of the average harvest as normal, in accordance with general practice, and denoting those above 115 per cent as good harvests and those below 85 per cent as bad ones, then about half the harvests prior to 1800 appear to have been normal, one quarter bad and one quarter good. On an average, therefore, there was a risk of a bad harvest every four years, with disastrous consequences in areas with poor transport facilities where people relied to a great extent on the local market.

Considering the weather conditions over a longer period, Europe can be divided into four climatic zones.

(1) Northern Europe, where the temperature is particularly important for plant growth. In the north, preference is given to the growing of

spring corn, since the growing of winter cereals would require too early a start with preparations for sowing.

(2) The area bordering on the Mediterranean, where plant growth is very dependent on the amount of precipitation. Here they concentrate on winter cereals, since the amount of precipitation in spring is too small for spring sowing.

(3) The Russian steppe region, where precipitation is also of great importance.

(4) The temperate zone in western Europe, where precipitation as well as temperature are important factors for plant growth. In this zone, harvests are adversely affected by too much precipitation and by low summer temperatures with not enough sunshine.

Western Europe and the Mediterranean region are climatological opposites in that 'wet' years produce good harvests in southern Europe and bad crops in western Europe; conversely 'dry' years are favourable to the west and unfavourable to the south. France is the only country embracing both regions; as a result, it comprises two areas of different economic and agricultural development, illustrated by the historical studies of Goubert on the Beauvaisis in the north and of Le Roy Ladurie on the Languedoc in the south. Only when price differentials were considerable was it profitable to transport grain from one region to the other. At the end of the sixteenth century, grain was shipped from western Europe to the Mediterranean in cases of shortages of grain in those regions.

Although the earliest instrumental readings are faulty, it has been established that since 1770 the temperatures recorded at the different European observatories show a roughly analogous pattern. In the amount of rainfall, however, there appear to be considerable regional differences. This is very significant since, as we have seen, the yields in western Europe are more dependent on rainfall than on temperature. The harvests will therefore show considerable regional variability, except for harvests coming after a severe winter and a late spring, since temperature is far less localized.

Available historical material confirms regional variability. There is a close similarity in the yields of neighbouring estates with more or less similar weather conditions. There is mutual agreement between the yield ratios of wheat on the Polish estates Rzgów-Gospodarz, Wiskitno and Dłutów (1564–9) and between the Schleswig-Holstein estates Cismar and Körnick (1648–53). The yield ratios of rye show very close agreement on twelve Polish estates (1564–9): all show a rise in 1567 and a fall in 1568. The same similarity is found on five Esthonian estates (1681–5), on the Swedish estates Skarhult and Rydboholm (1724–78) and on the Schleswig Holstein estates Bürau, Oppendorf and Schönhorst (1728–81).

No international congruence can be found, at any rate with the material available, nor in fact should we expect it, seeing that climatic conditions vary extensively over long distances. There is a marked discrepancy between yield ratios of wheat at Bürau (Schleswig-Holstein) and at Fontmorigny (France) in 1728–45. Figures for yield ratios of rye on the Swedish estates Skarhult and Rydboholm (1724–78) on the one hand, and for the three Schleswig-Holstein estates (1728–81) on the other, disagree in every respect. There is a similar disagreement between the yield ratios of rye at Kuckau and Deutschbaselitz in Lusatia (1779–99) and at Löfstad in Sweden (1768–97). In the early nineteenth century Björno in Sweden (1803–20), Kuckau in Lusatia (1800–20) and Pfeddersheim in the Palatinate (1803–12) each show different trends.

On the strength of instrumental readings an attempt has been made to establish a certain periodicity in climatic changes. In the case of precipitation, however, periodicity is out of the question because of the divergence of readings at the various observation posts. After prolonged attempts, the majority of scholars now incline to the view that it is impossible to establish periodicity for temperature too. In the past the so-called 'period-hunters' often have used uncritical methods to determine periodicity. There does not appear to be any association with the sunspot cycles of roughly 11, $22\frac{1}{2}$, 37, 83 and 300 years. Manley posits fluctuations with an irregular duration of 22 ± 10 years (12–32 years). During this period the average annual temperature fluctuates by one degree Fahrenheit. In longer periods of 100 to 300 years the difference is two degrees Fahrenheit. For the growing of cereals in the temperate zone, fluctuations of this order are of little significance, but they will affect the cultivation of grain under unfavourable conditions, as in the Alps and in northern Europe.

Several methods have been adopted to try and fill the gap in available historical evidence prior to the time of instrumental recordings. A variety of data about the weather in the past has been collected from chronicles; further information has been gleaned on the contraction and expansion of glaciers, the freezing of harbours and lakes, the annual tree rings, the dates of grape harvests and cherry blossom. All these facts, however, can only be used with respect to the particular area they covered. Under influence of the 'period-hunters' there has been a tendency to accumulate all the facts and then draw hasty conclusions. The necessity for caution is illustrated by our evidence of the severity of the winters. The correlation coefficient between the winters in England and Germany is low; the same applies to the winters of England and Russia. The period of cold winters between 1530 and 1700 is more pronounced in England and Russia than in northern Germany. We can trace a period of cool summers, high rainfall and snow between 1691 and 1700 in England, Sweden, the French mountains and the western Alps, but not in central Europe.

Research in annual tree rings has shown that these rings sometimes indicate temperature, sometimes precipitation. The well-known sequoias in California show precipitation; the trees in Scotland and Norway summer temperatures; in the annual rings in Hessen and Bavaria it is easier to trace precipitation than temperature. Like cereals, the annual rings show an irregular zigzag curve. Here, too, it has proved impossible to discover any correspondence with the sunspot period.

An irregular oscillating curve can also be traced from the dates on which grape-picking was started. These dates give an indication of summer temperatures, since early picking follows warm summers with much sunshine, and late picking comes after damp and cool summers. Grape-picking data are not of much use for comparison with the cereal harvests, since the grain yield is determined not so much by summer temperature as by precipitation during the preceding autumn and winter. Moreover, the late summer and early autumn months are important for the maturing of the grape and by then the grain has already been taken in.

A study of climate prior to the introduction of instrumental records shows that changes did occur. Investigations comparing periods of fifty years' duration have shown that the winters between 1551 and 1600 and those between 1651 and 1700 were generally colder than in the other periods of those centuries. The many severe winters during the period between 1540 (1590) and 1850 (1860) are sometimes referred to as the little Ice Age. In northern Sweden there are clear indications that grain-growing decreased in the middle of the seventeenth century, probably because of the decrease in temperature in those regions.

It might be asked to what extent a change in the climate was responsible for the slight fall in yield ratios during the seventeenth century in most of the European countries, a fact assumed from the currently available data. In fact at that time the climate was very variable. Between 1591 and 1650 there were relatively cold winters and wet, cool summers; between 1651 and 1680 there were very cold winters and warm summers; between 1681 and 1740 there were mild winters. It seems more likely that the fall in yield ratios can be attributed to economic factors. In this particular period there was not only a fall in yields per acre but also a decrease in acreage. This must have brought about a considerable fall in total grain production. If all other factors had remained constant, *ceteris paribus*, grain prices during this period should have shown a tendency to rise. In fact, in most countries they showed a tendency to fall. The implication is that changes must have taken place which affected demand. We know that for many reasons the population decreased in the seventeenth century in many countries and remained constant elsewhere. The fall in yield ratios could be explained by the fact that the farmers transferred their manure to relatively lucrative commercial crops instead of to grains.

The effect of weather conditions on grain price must be assessed against the knowledge that production was largely affected by precipitation, which shows considerable regional variation, so that yields, too, show great regional differences. Weather conditions, therefore, can only affect prices in regional or local markets, where there is a negative correlation between production and prices. As soon as the grain trade expands over a larger area, however, regional fluctuations in production will cancel each other out and price differences will disappear. But when fluctuations in production are the result of weather conditions in which temperature plays an important part – as in hard and long winters – prices will show a sharp increase, since the pressure of demand from all directions will force them up.

On interregional and international markets there is no question of a negative correlation between prices and production. Many writers ignore this fact when they take international market prices as indicative of harvest yields, as was done by Ashton, Gould and Heckscher. For Sweden, Heckscher attempted to trace a connection between the estimated yields during the period 1680–1780 and the marriage and mortality rates there. A later Swedish study by Brolin proved that these so-called yields were really reconstructed from the grain prices in Uppsala during that period. There is certainly a striking correlation between the prices in Uppsala and those in Amsterdam, which is not surprising, since Sweden before 1800 could not produce enough grain to supply its own needs and had to import grain from the Baltic countries. These prices, therefore, were those of the international market and they certainly did not reflect Swedish production.

It is impossible to correlate climatological changes and prices. The period of severe winters in the first half of the sixteenth century did not affect the trend in grain prices, which had already started to rise during the fifteenth century. The agricultural regression with its low grain prices began for most countries as early as the first half of the seventeenth century. Yet the first half of the eighteenth century was a period of mild winters and abundant harvests. During the years between 1690 and 1810 there were twelve very severe winters. Six of them were followed by high grain prices; yet after the other six hard winters, prices even went down.

Historians are too often inclined to enumerate a series of severe winters, bad harvests or even abundant harvests in order to 'explain' changes in the secular trend. But they fail to clarify why it is that this kind of incidental occurrence should have such a lasting effect. Nor is there any agreement among historians on whether it is the periods with abundant harvests or those with poor harvests that can be termed 'favourable'. They work on the assumption of the negative correlation between production and prices on the local market: abundant harvests produce low prices, poor harvests are followed by high prices. But during the periods of the secular trend this cannot apply, because of the emergence of the population factor. Moreover, they lose sight of the fact that the relationship of grain prices *vis-à-vis* other prices and wages is really of essential importance. And finally, they forget that changes in the price ratios affect different groups of consumers in different ways, according to their income, spending patterns and diet.

There are several other external factors which affect agrarian production. During the nineteenth century the potato crops in many countries were attacked by potato blight (*phytophthora infestans*), the grapes suffered from *phylloxera*, and cotton from the boll weevil Before 1800, plant diseases and pests were probably more localized. Harvests on the fields and grain in granaries suffered from locusts, rats and mice, but mostly these were local or regional plagues.

The cattle plague, which affected Europe repeatedly during the eighteenth century, was particularly virulent. The first attack, in 1709, came from Asia along the Caspian Sea to European Russia, and spread from there to most European continental countries; England was scarcely affected. The disease raged until 1720. A second wave in the wake of the War of the Austrian Succession was first recorded in Hungary in 1740, it reached its peak during 1744 and 1745 but continued to flare up until 1765. The same year saw the third and last attack, spreading from the eastern Balkans, with peaks in 1769 and 1770. If the records are reliable, it appears that between 60 and over 80 per cent of the cattle in the affected areas died. Some part of the blame for these disastrous figures can possibly be attributed to the over-grazing of fields, which resulted in starvation. During the eighteenth century there was a preference for cattle-breeding, since the prices of cattle and dairy produce were relatively better than those of grains.

The people were powerless in the face of the disease, and looked upon it as a punishment from God. The authorities in the various afflicted countries issued a stream of regulations, in particular an embargo on cattle from contaminated areas. The only effective weapon, recommended by the Italian doctor Giovanni Lancisi, was the immediate slaughter of all infected animals. In 1714 this method was used in England and during the third plague in the Austrian Netherlands and in the south of France. In 1754 inoculation was introduced in England.

Later this achieved good results when applied to the calves of those cows which had survived the plague. The necessity to combat this disease was one of the factors responsible for the establishment of the first veterinary school, in Lyons in 1762.

The losses suffered by the farmers were vast, but the authorities and landowners sustained losses too, since the farmers were unable to pay either taxes or rents. In those areas of Friesland and Holland where pasture predominated, livestock was very rapidly replenished because prices of dairy produce had also risen. Sheep-farming, however increased as well. But in predominantly arable regions with sandy or light clay soil pasturage tended to be put under the plough; in these areas there was a much slower replacement of livestock since cattle were only of secondary importance.

GENERAL FACTORS AFFECTING PRODUCTION

Many factors have a bearing on production: the acreage available and the way in which it was used, whether for cropping or for livestock, for vineyards or olive groves, for horticulture or fruit-growing; the range of crops, the farming intensity (and reduction in fallowing), crop rotation and yields, the number of heads of livestock, the weight of the cattle, the milk-yield, the weight of the sheepskins, the yield of wine and olives, manuring, agricultural tools and implements, working time and the amount of work per hour or per day, the investment of capital and, finally, the competence and mentality of the farmers. Changes occurred in most of these factors between 1500 and 1800, and there is a striking difference between the *degree* of changes during periods of agricultural expansion and those during agricultural regression. This is due to the fact that, since corn figured so prominently in agriculture as a whole, it was always directly dependent on the ratio between grain prices and those of other products.

RECLAMATIONS AND DESERTED FIELDS

In many countries the area under cultivation increased again during the second half of the fifteenth century. This new period of expansion came to an end in some countries at the end of the sixteenth century; in others it continued till *c.* 1660. There can be no doubt that the demand for increased acreage was prompted by favourable trends in agrarian prices as compared with those of other commodities and wages. The reversal in price ratios after 1450 was associated with an almost universal increase in population and with a growing concentration in the towns and cities of the Netherlands, Rhineland, southern Germany, northern

Italy, Paris, London, Marseilles, Rome, Naples and other large cities.

The extent of reclamation after 1450 is by no means on a par with the very large-scale spread of settlements between the eleventh and fourteenth centuries. In these centuries there was feverish activity in land clearance among landowners, monasteries and individual farmers; vast new regions were opened up. During the sixteenth and the seventeenth centuries, operations on this scale moved to America and southern and eastern Russia. There was still a considerable amount of wasteland in Europe, but it was generally of an inferior quality and could not be profitably exploited with the implements and knowledge available at the time. It was not until the invention of artificial fertilizers in the n neteenth century that progress could be made here.

Part of the reclamation during the fifteenth and the sixteenth centuries was the recovery of ground that had been abandoned during the agricultural depression and the decline in population after 1300. Records in Germany, for instance, show that especially in central and southern Germany arable land that had become part of the *Wüstungen* was brought back into cultivation, but the abandoned hamlets remained uninhabited because the people preferred to continue living in larger villages, perhaps for reasons of safety.

In those areas where a *Feldgraswirtschaft* (temporary cultivation) or an 'infield–outfield' system was used, the ground was reclaimed almost imperceptibly. During the fourteenth century, part of the arable acreage had reverted to waste, thereby becoming common land once more, until *c.* 1450 when its cultivation was taken in hand again. Changing circumstances allowed great flexibility between ploughing and animal husbandry on the common land, and although this is a form of an extensive farming system, it had the advantage of being easily adaptable.

In the Alps human settlements did not re-establish themselves on the high-altitude slopes where they had been before 1300; because of climatic changes in the Alpine region, they remained on a lower level. The spread of the glaciers dates from 1540, indicating colder and longer winters and more snow.

In addition to recovering abandoned farmland, the reclamation work of the sixteenth and seventeenth centuries was particularly concerned with polders and irrigation. There was of course nothing new in this, but the scale of operations was now much larger than before. The draining of marshes and the reclamation of land won from the sea were capital-intensive enterprises. Contractors, backed by a combined force of financiers and technical experts, embarked on reclamation schemes of a highly speculative nature. In the Middle Ages polders in the Low

Countries had already been made with the cooperation of the citizens of neighbouring towns, but it was quite novel for individuals to aspire to quick fortunes in this fashion. Sometimes they were lucky, but more often the problems arising during the operation multiplied to such an extent that the work came to a halt halfway through. Sometimes the contractor was an adventurer who underestimated the technical difficulties, but more often there was not enough capital at the start and anyway the invested capital was usually unexpectedly slow to show a yield.

The technical experts involved in polder-making and drainage in Europe came almost invariably from Zealand, Holland, Friesland and Flanders, men like Vermuyden working in the English Fenland, Jérome de Comans in the Midi, Jan van Ens in the Provence, and Adriaen Boot in Mexico; Dutch dyke-masters worked also in the neighbourhood of Ferrara.[1] In the battle against water in their own country these people had gained invaluable experience. Sometimes the capital, too, was supplied by Dutch money-lenders or business houses, as in France (Jan Hoeufft), in England (Jacob Cats, the van Valckenburghs, Constantijn Huygens and others), in northern Germany (Willem van den Hove) and in the peat-marsh reclamations in the north-eastern parts of the Netherlands (e.g. the Wildervanck and Trip families).

In the Mediterranean region, the sixteenth century saw the emergence of monocultures, large enterprises for the exclusive growing of, e.g. grain, vines, olives, cotton and sugar cane, in Andalusia, Morocco, Naples, Bulgaria, Thrace, Corfu, Sicily, Crete and Cyprus. Like the paddy-fields planted in the Po Valley from the end of the fifteenth century, the 'monocultures' were often owned by rich townsmen. In these ventures and in those for the reclamation of marshland and the making of polders, we find the first instances of capitalist enterprise on a large scale in agriculture.

During the seventeenth century efforts to open up new land came to an end in most of the European countries. Once again the records show deserted villages, land left to waste and dikes breached, just as in the later Middle Ages. The Thirty Years War caused vast devastation in Bohemia, Germany, Poland and Burgundy. Poland was particularly affected by the Swedish War which lasted from 1655 till 1660, and central Europe was the battlefield of the war against the Turks. But even in countries that were less affected, like Italy and Spain, the people complained of abandoned villages and farms, e.g. in the Campagna, south of Rome, in Tuscany and in the diocese of Salamanca.

[1] See C. Wilson, *The Dutch Republic* (London, 1969), pp. 79–88, esp. the map, pp. 80–1.

Just as in the later Middle Ages, strong signs of land erosion appeared during the second half of the seventeenth century and the whole of the eighteenth century. Complaints about it came from Saxony, Thuringia, Franconia, Bavaria, Lorraine and Champagne. One writer thought erosion to have been due to the bare fallow in the three-course rotation. When, at the end of the eighteenth century, fodder crops were grown during the fallow year, erosion died away.

After 1660, drainage and reclamation in the Netherlands and East Friesland (Germany) continued only on a very limited scale. Historical studies in France, Spain, Italy, Greece, Germany, England and Poland have revealed that the number of deserted villages in the seventeenth century was not as large as that in the later Middle Ages, since the seventeenth-century agricultural regression as a whole was less pronounced.[1] Nevertheless the shrinkage of arable acreage was a general European phenomenon and the wars, coupled with a flare-up of the plague during the seventeenth century, cannot have been the only cause for this. In nearly all European countries we find a complete reversal of price ratios, adversely affecting agricultural products in general, and cereals in particular. As we saw earlier, a shrinkage of acreage, accompanied by a fall in prices, can only be explained by a decrease in population, and this is in fact confirmed by the demographic data so far available.

In the German lands, so badly devastated in the Thirty Years War, an improvement was already noticeable during the last twenty years of the seventeenth century; elsewhere land reclamation was not resumed until the second half of the eighteenth century. This applies particularly to the Dutch provinces, the Austrian Netherlands, France, Prussia, Schleswig Holstein and England.

The close connection between agricultural prices and polder-making shows up very clearly in Table 4. Regarding the period 1565–1589 the fact must be taken into account that most drainage undertakings were stopped by the Eighty Years War, which involved the provinces where these activities were centred. The conditions of war prevented the reclamation of new land. It stands out clearly that after 1664 the great period of polder-making had come to an end, at exactly the same time that the price of corn was going down and the general economic situation was deteriorating. The average area drained annually remained small till 1765; it was pointless to invest in increasing the area of cultivation as long as farming remained so depressed. When, after 1755, cereal prices began to rise once more and prospects brightened, men immediately returned to draining the land: a clear example of the direct

[1] See various articles in *Villages désertés et histoire économique, XIe–XVIIIe siècle* (1965).

Table 4. *Indices of area of land gained in the Netherlands by polders, compared to price indices of wheat, 1501–1864*

Period	Average area of land gained by polders per annum (in hectares)	Indices of area of polder-making (1715–39 = 100)	Indices of prices of wheat, at Amsterdam (1721–45 = 100, Königsberg wheat)	Period	Indices of international prices of wheat (1721–45 = 100)	
					Min.	Max.
1540–64	1,474	346·0	—	1501–50	41·4 –	78·8
1565–89	321	75·3	95·5¹	1551–1600	133·2 –	180·4
1590–1614	1,448	339·9	—			
1615–39	1,783	418·5	146·6	1601–50	124·2 –	176·8
1640–64	1,163	273·0	135·8			
1665–89	493	115·7	101·4	1651–1700	98·9 –	151·2
1690–1714	501	117·6	124·4			
1715–39	426	100·0	88·7	1701–50	99·1 –	114·0
1740–64	404	94·8	113·0			
1765–89	717	168·3	142·2	1751–1800	123·3 –	154·3
1790–1814	634	148·8	250·0			
1815–39	684	160·6	189·6	1801–50	169·9 –	220·5
1840–64	1,568	368·0	209·9			

¹ Zealand wheat, 1575–89.

link between agricultural prices and agricultural activity, which is confirmed by the similar development of the reclamations in East Friesland (Germany) and of the peat marsh reclamations in the north-eastern parts of the Netherlands.

CROP ROTATION

It was possible to increase production without opening up new ground by decreasing the area that was periodically left fallow; if a two-year rotation was used, half the arable acreage was left fallow; with a three-year rotation, one third. It was necessary to fallow and plough in order to restore fertility to the soil, exhausted by successive grain crops. By growing fodder-plants and pulses on the fallow fields, nitrogen could be added to the soil. Even in the Middle Ages this kind of intensive farming was practised in the Rhineland near Cologne (1277) and in Flanders (1278). Another advantage of this method was that the growing of fodder-plants enabled the farmer to keep more livestock, so that there was more manure available for the arable.

Stall-feeding was already in use. The livestock would be kept in the sheds for nearly the whole year and fed on fodder-plants, linseed and rapeseed cakes, and the manure was stored in the mucking-shed. As these more intensive agricultural methods had long been known and were certainly not new to the so-called 'agricultural revolution' of the eighteenth century, we might well ask why they were only applied in some areas. Those who were keen to bring eighteenth- and nineteenth-century agriculture up-to-date tended to attribute this lack of initiative to traditionalism and ignorance among farmers who were conservative by nature. This, however, does the farmers an injustice. Where intensive farming was profitable it had already been practised in the late Middle Ages, but it was confined to the neighbourhood of populous areas, where *débouchés* and reasonable prices were guaranteed.

During the period from the sixteenth to the eighteenth century agriculture was not on the same level everywhere in Europe; small areas of intensive farming were scattered everywhere: in Flanders, Brabant, Zealand, Holland, Friesland, the Rhineland, Nassau, the Palatinate, Baden, in the surroundings of towns such as Erfurt, Würzburg and Augsburg, in French Flanders, Artois, Alsace, Provence, Languedoc, Catalonia, the Po Valley, Norfolk, Suffolk, Essex and the environs of London. It is not clear whether the situation in 1800 differed greatly from that in 1500. Some areas of intensive farming in Germany suffered badly as a result of the Thirty Years War; but on the other hand, the position had certainly improved in England, in some of the Dutch provinces and, during the eighteenth century, in northern Germany.

Much has been made of an agricultural revolution supposed to have taken place during the eighteenth century, comparable with the Industrial Revolution. But closer inspection clearly shows that agriculture during that period did not undergo great revolutionary changes. Though there was some expansion locally and regionally in areas where intensive farming systems had been used for a long time, the actual rate of development did not increase until the nineteenth and twentieth centuries and then, of course, on a much wider scale.

During the seventeenth and eighteenth centuries the following systems of tillage could be found side by side.

(1) Temporary cultivation (*Feldgraswirtschaft*), still used in Scotland, Ireland, Sweden and elsewhere.

(2) The infield–outfield system, e.g. in Scotland and Namur.

(3) Continuous rye cultivation, e.g. in the eastern Netherlands and western Germany.

(4) Two-course rotation, in southern France, England, etc.

(5) Three-course rotation with a two-year fallow, e.g. in Andalusia.

(6) Free three-course rotation with a one-year fallow, without *Flurzwang* (i.e. the husbandman was free to choose what crop he would grow). In general use.

(7) Regulated three-course rotation with a one-year fallow, with *Flurzwang* (with stipulation of the crops to be grown and common grazing of the livestock on the stubble). In general use.

(8) A rotation of four, five, six or more courses, usually in combination with the cultivation of pulses on the fields, e.g. in England, the Netherlands and Alsace.

(9) Convertible husbandry, in which the land was cultivated for several years and then turned over to pasture for a period, as in Flanders, Groningen, England, Alsace and Schleswig Holstein.

(10) Rotation of crops with fodder-crops as catch-crops (stubble-crops), in the *Meijerij* of den Bosch (Netherlands) and other places.

(11) A rotation of crops with fodder crops in the fallow year, e.g. in Flanders and Norfolk.

This list is arranged according to an increasing intensity of land use or a decreasing amount of fallow.

A change-over to a more intensive use of land depended not only on soil conditions but also on whether the returns would cover the additional labour and capital costs, and on adequate transport facilities with a marketing centre. Conditions of war or economic setback could bring about a reversal from intensive to less intensive methods. Chronologically speaking, therefore, agricultural development did not follow a straight course by any means. During the fifteenth and sixteenth centuries, farmers on fertile soil in northern Germany used a tillage system with fallowing every four, five, six or eight years; during the eighteenth century the same regions, devastated and depopulated after the Thirty Years War, used a system of three-course rotation.

The application of a more intensive tillage-system does not necessarily imply increased corn production. The convertible husbandry in Schleswig Holstein during the eighteenth century bears this out. Here the grain yield ratio (the average of wheat, rye and barley, taken together) rose from an average of 5·0 between 1600 and 1699 to 6·7 between 1700 and 1799. Under the old three-course rotation, grain was grown for two out of every three years; under the convertible husbandry of the eighteenth century corn was sown only in five out of eleven. The higher yields could not entirely compensate for the reduced period of cultivation, and so the total annual production of corn showed a slight fall. The advantage of the new system was that for five years the land could be used as pasture for the cattle and there was only one unproductive year of fallow every eleven years, whereas the three-course system involved four years of fallow every twelve years.

Two systems of tillage made a name for themselves in the eighteenth century: the 'Norfolk system', a feature of the 'new husbandry' in England, and the 'convertible husbandry' of Schleswig Holstein, Denmark and Mecklenburg. The Norfolk system was based on a method applied in the 'Land van Waas' between Antwerp and Ghent in Flanders about 1650. It was here that the Englishman, Sir Richard Weston, encountered the following system: flax, immediately succeeded by turnips; in about April of the following year, oats were sown and then clover undersown which, sprouting only after the oats harvest, provided pasture till Christmas. Subsequently, clover was grown for four or five years. Judged by the standard of the times, the yields from this naturally poorish soil were extraordinarily high. In the Norfolk system, wheat and barley crops alternated with the growing of fodder-turnips and clover. The cultivation of fodder-crops, either as after-crops when the corn had been harvested or during the fallow, had already been known during the Middle Ages. There are thirteenth- and fourteenth-century accounts mentioning the cultivation of vetch near Doornik in Flanders in 1278 and near Maastricht in 1382; in the fifteenth century spurrey (Maaseik, 1426) and fodder-turnips (Messelbroek near Aalst, 1404, and Rooigem near Ghent, 1446) were grown. Albertus Magnus mentions the cultivation of clover on the fields in his *Historia Naturalis* (mid thirteenth century). We know from several sources that clover was grown during the sixteenth century in Italy (Brescia, 1550–60), Brabant (1566) and Holland (Schagen, 1599). In this respect the Norfolk system offered nothing new. The fact that the 'new husbandry' throve during the eighteenth century in England and later on in several other countries is also due to many other factors, such as marling, enclosures, long leases, and the size of holdings. The marked increase in corn prices during the second half of the eighteenth century and the beginning of the nineteenth century made it profitable to introduce this kind of intensive tillage system. The knowledge of increasing production by these methods had existed for a long time, but economic conditions had not been sufficiently favourable to apply the system on a large scale.

The convertible husbandry of northern Germany and Denmark closely resembled a system used in Flanders as early as the fourteenth century, in which two years of corn were followed by one year fallow and three or six years of pasture. During the seventeenth century, clover was often substituted for grass in Flanders. In northern Germany and Denmark a rotation of five years of corn, five years of pasture and one year of fallow came to be used.

ADAPTATION TO CHANGES IN ECONOMIC CONDITIONS

Land use is affected by fluctuations in the correlation between grain prices and the prices of dairy products. During a period of agricultural regression when grain prices are relatively low compared with the prices of meat, butter, cheese and wool, arable land is sometimes turned over to pasture. Conversely, at a time of agricultural expansion pasture may be ploughed and sown with grain. Of the various systems of tillage discussed above, two facilitate changes of this nature: under the *Feldgraswirtschaft* system, wasteland, the natural pasture for cattle, can be partly cultivated or, under less favourable circumstances, allowed to revert to waste. Under convertible husbandry, pasture periods could be extended or even made permanent, or else grass could be replaced by clover, thus providing permanently arable land. Both systems have the advantage of being adaptable to changes in the economic situation. Under other systems, a switch between animal husbandry and arable farming presented problems, involving soil conditions, the parcelling of land, the size of the farm and the buildings available. For livestock more capital was required; there was also a difference of mentality between the arable and the cattle farmer. A change to another type of farming could be promoted by government measures, as in the Spanish Netherlands in the 'Land van Herve' (between Liège and Aachen), where, from the first half of the sixteenth century, export embargoes on grain kept grain prices low in an area that had previously exported grain. As a result many farmers took up livestock. The same shift can be seen in England after 1673 when a bounty promoted the growing of corn at a time when grain prices compared unfavourably with those of dairy products. The Nine Years War (1688–97) and the War of the Spanish Succession (1702–13) by cutting off grain imports created a situation that favoured cereal farming in southern France.

For any change-over between grazing and arable, prices have to move in a certain direction over a considerable period. Apart from convertible husbandry and *Feldgraswirtschaft*, agriculture is not a little inflexible in this respect. The change-over in the 'Land van Herve' in Belgium illustrates the problems that faced farmers who were tied by the size and shape of the holdings allotted to them. The land belonging to each holding was scattered, and an acreage whose high fertility had made it adequate for arable farming was now too small for livestock.

We have records of thirty-four changes from arable land to pasturage and twenty-three changes from meadows to arable land from the fourteenth century to the beginning of the nineteenth century as shown in Table 5.

Governments often deplored a shift from arable farming to stock-raising since they were afraid that the nation's grain supplies would be jeopardized. They aimed at the greatest possible degree of national self-sufficiency, since imports were vulnerable in wartime, and they feared also a drain on national monetary resources via the balance of payments. The only exception to this general rule was the Dutch Republic, which had relied on imported corn since the end of the Middle Ages.

In the wine-growing regions similar changes from arable land to vineyards and vice versa have been recorded; in many cases these changes were connected with the price differentials between corn and wine. We find that when grain and bread prices were low, the demand for wine and beer increased, and when grain prices were relatively high, consumption of wine and beer went down. This is related to the spending patterns of certain sectors of the population, the townspeople and others who did not work on the land and those who received a fixed income or wage.

Here, too, there were obstacles in the way of a change-over from arable farming to wine growing: the vineyards were usually very small, *métayage* was quite common, and wine growing provided employment for many other people such as coopers, carters and shippers. Many regions grew wine for local or regional consumption, and here price differentials were quite different from those in areas where wine was grown for a much wider market. In this respect the surroundings of Bordeaux, a typical wine-exporting area, differed greatly from those of Languedoc where the substantial exporting of wine did not take place until much later.

There are twenty-four recorded change-overs from arable farming to wine-growing and vice versa, as shown in Table 6.

Table 5.   *Change from arable farming to cattle-raising and back again, before 1825*

Arable land to meadow	Meadow to arable land
14th–15th centuries	
England: Yorkshire, Lincolnshire, Midlands	
Germany	
Austria: Vorarlberg, Tyrol	
Italy: Lombardy, Campagna near Rome	
France: Thiérache	
Belgium: Brabant	
Norway	
	1550–1650
	England: Leicestershire, Fenland
	Germany: East Friesland
	Netherlands: Friesland, Gelderland
	Norway
	Spain
1650–1750	*1660–1750*
England: Midlands, Kent, Surrey	England: East Anglia, Wiltshire
Ireland	
Germany: Schwerin, Allgäu	
Austria: Vorarlberg, Bregenzerwald	
Switzerland: Emmental, Pays d'Enhaut, Gruyères	
France: Savoy, Jura, Burgundy, Thiérache, Pays d'Auge, Bessin, Cotentin	
Belgium: 'Land van Herve'	
Spain: Castile	
	About 1700
	France: Landes, Périgord
	1750–1820
	England: Lincolnshire, Warwickshire
	Ireland
	Germany: Silesia, East Friesland
	France: Thiérache, French Flanders, Burgundy
	Netherlands: Friesland, Groningen
	Sweden
	Spain
1823	
England: Counties in southern England, Midlands	
Ireland	

Table 6. *Change from arable farming to wine-growing and back again, before 1825*

Arable land to vineyards	Vineyards to arable land
Fourteenth–fifteenth centuries	
Germany: Harz	
Belgium: Brabant, Limburg	
Early sixteenth century	*Sixteenth century*
Germany: Upper Rhine, surroundings of Stuttgart	Switzerland: Hallwil
	France: Maine, surroundings of Paris, Languedoc, Langlade, surroundings of Nîmes
	Germany: Würzburg (since 1550 or 1580)
1630–1771	
Switzerland: Wallis, Hallwil, Zürich-Canton	
France: Landes, Périgord, Sète, Montpellier, Langlade, Burgundy, Loire Valley, Alsace	
Spain: Castile	

Another means of compensating for relatively low grain prices was to increase the cultivation of industrial crops like flax, hemp, hops, oil seeds, woad, madder, weld and saffron. Periods of agricultural regression are marked by the emergence of many new industries, not only in the towns, which had had to absorb part of the rural population, but also in the countryside. In the late Middle Ages and during the seventeenth century the textile industry flourished, particularly in the country: for instance, throughout the seventeenth century and the early eighteenth century in Ireland, Scotland, Maine (France), Flanders, Twente (Dutch Republic), Westphalia, the surroundings of Münster, Saxony and Silesia. Generally the situation developed according to the same pattern: the area became relatively over-populated, with an increase in the number of the poor, who provided the labour force for weaving and spinning. The output of the cottage industries was bought and exported by wealthy merchants. Socially, great differences grew between the merchants and the weavers and spinners. Very often the merchants did not belong to the original population; they were immigrants, sometimes members of a different denomination.

In many cases this rural industry was the foundation on which the nineteenth-century factory system was built, though the development was not always straightforward. During the second half of the eighteenth century, when there was a relative increase in grain prices, some of the industries disappeared from certain rural areas which reverted to arable farming again. This occurred in some villages in Twente (the Netherlands), in the surroundings of Oudenaarde in Flanders and in parts of Scotland.

During the seventeenth and eighteenth centuries, grain production and demand were affected by the cultivation of food-crops which could replace corn, such as rice, maize, buckwheat and potatoes. In many cases we know when these crops were first introduced into a particular country; it is much more difficult to determine when they became an important part of the total diet of the people. In the case of potatoes this process must have been very rapid. Around 1750 potatoes were scarcely known in some countries of Europe, but thirty or forty years later they had become part of the staple diet, eaten twice a day. Producers as well as consumers showed a remarkable adaptability which completely belies the usual ascription of conservatism to farming folk. Between 1710 and 1740 grain consumption fell by 10 per cent in Flanders and Brabant, but the great change occurred after 1740, when grain consumption fell again, this time by nearly 30 per cent, and went down to 62·5 per cent of the figure for the beginning of the eighteenth century.

The potato yield per acre was 10·5 times as high as the wheat yield and 9·6 times as high as the rye yield. This higher yield compensates for the lower calorific value of potatoes, which is only 20 per cent of an equal quantity of wheat and 23 per cent of an equal quantity of rye. An acre of potatoes will feed between 2·1 and 2·3 times as many people as an acre of wheat and rye respectively, but three times more manure is required.

In some areas it was not corn but pulses that potatoes replaced. For human consumption too, potatoes replaced not only cereals but beans, peas and carrots. During the Middle Ages the hot meal was likely to consist of a stew of pulses, cabbage, turnips or carrots, a few herbs and some meat; later on potatoes might be substituted for other vegetables.

From the records it appears that rice was first cultivated on a large scale in northern Italy in the second half of the seventeenth century. During the eighteenth century and particularly after 1730, large quantities of rice were shipped from North America to Europe. Maize became an important food in Italy after 1630, a year of plague and starvation, and the cultivation of maize brought about a noticeable improvement in the diet of the Portuguese population during the second half of the seventeenth century. By the middle of the eighteenth century maize was also an important item in Spanish cereal farming. The cultivation of buckwheat in the Low Countries and western

Germany probably increased rapidly during the second half of the seventeenth and the beginning of the eighteenth century.

Since maize and buckwheat were eaten by the poorer sections of the community, we would expect the consumption of these crops to have increased during periods of rising grain prices – i.e. the sixteenth and the latter half of the eighteenth centuries. Higher grain prices cause the greatest demand for the cheapest product, and the price of this product will show the greatest relative increases. This applied to the increasing consumption of potatoes in several European countries during the second half of the eighteenth century. In Ireland, however, the potato had been introduced earlier, during the period of low grain prices. Here the peasants grew potatoes for domestic consumption, and the grain crop was sold in an attempt to keep down the cost of home consumption while economic conditions were unfavourable to them. During the seventeenth century, farmers in other countries may very well have kept their own cost of living down by growing and eating buckwheat and maize.

YIELD RATIOS

Grain yields could obviously be increased by enlarging the acreage as well as by heavier cropping. In any research into the quantities of the yields in the past, the interpretation of the data in the sources is always complicated by the difficulty of expressing crop yields in terms of modern unitary measurements. Apart from the great diversity of local weights and measures, there is the difficulty of converting old standards into modern ones. This can be overcome by expressing the harvests in terms of the amount of seed sown, in other words by employing yield ratios, which is consistent with the methods previously used for calculating the harvests. The source documents will often state that the crop was four or five times the amount of the seed. The size of the harvest was designated in this way because it was the amount of seed and crop rather than the acreage which were the important factors under conditions prevailing in the past. Of course, this does not preclude other methods of calculating agricultural productivity. In France, special attention is drawn to the absolute figures of the quantities harvested and to the tithes which are recorded in the tithe-registers, but international and interregional comparison becomes rather difficult on the base of these data. Added to this, in many regions the tithes were not always the tenth part of the yields; in the calculations made on the basis of the total yields, it is mostly taken for granted that the acreage sown with the various crops had remained unchanged.[1]

[1] For a discussion of the difficulties in calculating yields on the basis of tithes, see the article by A. L. Head-Koenig and B. Veyrassat-Herren, 'La production agricole

During recent years much research has been done and many data published, especially in Poland, Russia and Hungary. The picture of eastern and central Europe is somewhat clearer now, but for the rest of Europe material is unevenly distributed, both chronologically and geographically, so that the interpretation of the figures demands great care. Over 27,000 yield ratios are available of which almost 24,400 relate to the four principal grains: wheat, rye, barley and oats. As 8,900 yield ratios belong to the medieval period, there still remain 15,500 for the period from 1500 to 1820.

Wheat, rye and barley show identical stages of development in all countries, but oats were often sown on infertile, marshy soil and the yields were low. The pattern of development of this crop deviates somewhat from that of the three other cereals. For a general impression it is better to leave out oats and use only the mean yield ratio of wheat, rye and barley together; 12,080 yield ratios of these three cereals are known. A general analysis of the yield ratios shows that at the end of the eighteenth century the mean level varied strongly over four zones of production in Europe: a temperate North Sea zone (England and the Low Countries), a south and western European zone (France, Spain and Italy), a central and northern European zone (Germany, Switzerland and Scandinavia), and lastly an eastern European zone (Russia, Poland, Czechoslovakia and Hungary).

There were, however, some exceptions. Very high yields were reached in Sicily during the period 1650–99; the figures for Germany are inflated by the higher yields in Schleswig Holstein after 1700; and good harvests on model farms in Switzerland and the Rhineland, together with the high level of agriculture in East Friesland (Germany), give a high average for central Europe during the period 1800–20. We have figures of low yields in Languedoc (1550–99), in Denmark and Sweden (1600–49) and in Russia after 1800.

When we exclude these excessively high and low yield ratios which were produced under special circumstances, we still have 9,586 yield ratios left. The average yield ratios of the three grains together (wheat, rye and barley) over fifty-year periods in the four zones of production are shown in Table 7. The figures clearly show that there was a decrease in yield ratios in Europe going from west to east. Western Europe has always had better results than central and eastern Europe. Everywhere we find a rise after 1750, which goes from 10 per cent in the west to 25–30 per cent in the east. The figures for Zone II remain on the same level during the whole period because there was not much change in France between 1500 and 1800. A fall in yield ratios can be detected

du plateau suisse aux XVIIᵉ et XVIIIᵉ siècles', *Schweizerische Zeitschrift für Geschichte*, XX (1970).

Table 7. *Average yield ratios of wheat, rye and barley together,*
1500–1820

Periods	Zone I[a]		Zone II		Zone III		Zone IV	
	N[b]	YR	N	YR	N	YR	N	YR
1500–49	15	7·4	16	6·7	32	4·0	36	3·9
1550–99	17	7·3	—	—	87	4·4	1531	4·3
1600–49	55	6·7	—	—	142	4·5	823	4·0
1650–99	25	9·3	12	6·2	120	4·1	1112	3·8
1700–49	—	—	125	6·3	32	4·1	820	3·5
1750–99	506	10·1	181	7·0	578	5·1	2777	4·7
1800–20	157	11·1	192	6·2	195	5·4	—	—

[a] Zone I: England, the Low Countries; zone II: France, Spain, Italy; zone III: Germany, Switzerland, Scandinavia; zone IV: Russia, Poland, Czechoslovakia, Hungary.
[b] N = number; YR = yield ratio.

between 1600 and 1749, not so pronounced in western and central Europe (8 to 9 per cent), but quite marked in eastern Europe (19 per cent). We find this decline in nearly all countries, with the exception of Hungary. The decrease was greater in barley and oats than in wheat and rye yield ratios.

The improvement between 1500 and 1820 was most pronounced in England and the Low Countries. In Flanders, Brabant, Holland, Zealand and Friesland this is not surprising because since the Middle Ages they had maintained a continuous tradition of agricultural improvement. The much-improved figures in England would suggest an agrarian revolution if historical research in the last twenty years had not refuted such a sudden growth in development. During the period of England's apprenticeship (1603–1763), a great deal of knowledge and experience was derived from the Low Countries and on this the English farmers continued to build independently during the eighteenth century.

The importance of improvements in agriculture is clearly illustrated by the figures for Schleswig Holstein. During the seventeenth century, the average yield ratios of wheat, rye and barley, taken together, were 5·0 for Schleswig Holstein and 4·0 for the rest of Germany. After 1700 there is a striking difference: the ratio rose to 6·7 in Schleswig Holstein and to 4·9 in the rest of Germany. As we have already seen, there had been a large-scale conversion to the convertible husbandry system in Schleswig Holstein.

Production could be increased not only by adopting a different tillage system but also by sowing in drills. Possibly this was already being done in the Middle Ages, but it was only after 1800 that it became a more general practice. Another method of achieving the same result was to chance an early-autumn sowing of winter corn, despite the risk of frost. At the beginning of the nineteenth century the application of this method in East Friesland caused the yield ratio to rise from 10·0 to 11·0.

The general rise in yield ratios in the different countries was never achieved suddenly but was preceded by a protracted period of sporadic improvement by some few farmers, during which the vast majority took much longer to emulate the few. Yield ratios can only rise when more money is invested in cereal growing, i.e. in the form of additional labour, heavier manuring, better implements, more draught animals, a better crop rotation and, most important of all perhaps, a spirit of enterprise in the farmer. In a subsequent section on fertilization, the obvious connection between high yields and heavy dressing will be discussed.

Farms with high cereal yields, copious manuring and 'modern' management could only exist in densely populated areas and in times of relatively high grain prices. Economic factors determine whether high yield ratios will be obtained on a given farm or in a particular district. Figures show that as early as the fourteenth and fifteenth centuries it was possible to attain yield ratios that were not regarded as normal, even in the most advanced western European countries, until about 1800. From this it can be concluded that from the fourteenth century onwards it was *possible* to obtain yield ratios exceeding 10·0. Hence the absence of any rise in the yield ratios was not due to lack of technical skill but rather to unfavourable economic conditions.

A simultaneous rise in the yield ratios and an increase in the population can be seen in England during the thirteenth century, in England and the Low Countries during the sixteenth century, in England in the second half of the eighteenth and the beginning of the nineteenth centuries and in the countries of Germany during the eighteenth century. But as soon as we try to make further investigations, we find that either the demographic data or the yield ratios are lacking.

A fall in the yield ratios occurred not only between 1600 and 1749, as we have seen, but also earlier, during the Middle Ages: between 1300 and 1349 and between 1400 and 1499. These were periods of agrarian regression. Generally speaking, the fluctuations in yield ratios show fairly close agreement with the movements of cereal prices in the secular trend. Here we have a positive and not a negative correlation, as we should have expected. We have already explained that the rise and fall in cereal prices in the long run, therefore, must be mainly attributed to demographic and monetary causes.

GRAIN PRODUCTION AND CONSUMPTION

There are no national statistics on land utilization for this period. All we have are Gregory King's estimates for England and Wales at the end of the seventeenth century and Wyczański's calculations of corn production and consumption in Poland during the second half of the sixteenth century. According to King the acreage in England was divided as follows: 9 million acres of arable, 2 million acres of fallow, 12 million acres of pasture and meadows, 6 million acres of woods, parks, forests and commons. King estimates the average corn yield at 11 bushels per acre and the total annual corn yield in England at 70 million bushels or approximately 1,780,000 tons. But at his estimated yield per acre, the entire corn harvest could have been grown on 6·4 million acres, the remaining arable acreage being available for the growing of other crops. The actual proportion of arable to fallow land was, however, probably less favourable than in his estimates. It is reasonable to assume that one third of the arable land was fallow, since more intensive cultivation existed side by side with an extensive two-course rotation or an infield–outfield system. Making the above adjustments to King, we might assume that the land was divided up roughly as follows: 6·4 million acres of corn, 3·7 million acres of fallow, 0·9 million acres of other crops, a total of 11·0 million acres of arable and fallow.

With the aid of King's figures it is possible to draw up a balance of the total corn production and consumption, though we should bear in mind that it can be no more than a global estimate. Assuming that at the end of the seventeenth century the total English corn yield was 1,780,000 tons, and a yield ratio averaging 7·5, about a seventh of the production would have to be reserved for next year's seed, or about 250,000 tons.

Total consumption can be calculated by multiplying population figures by average individual grain consumption. Helleiner quotes the estimate for the population of England and Wales at 5·2 million at the end of the seventeenth century (*C.E.H.E.*, IV, 69). We have, unfortunately, no such certainty about the annual *per capita* consumption. Authorities give widely divergent figures for human consumption, varying between a minimum of 118·5 kilograms of grain and a maximum of 520 kilograms of grain (see Table 8).

We have fairly extensive figures for the consumption of corn in Flanders and Brabant (as given in Table 9). During the eighteenth century there was a clear drop in corn consumption, most likely because of the increase in the consumption of potatoes.

The consumption of corn thus varied widely in different countries, depending on the consumption of other products. The low figures in

Table 8.   *Annual grain consumption per capita in kilograms,*
fifteenth century to the end of the eighteenth century

Region	Period	Annual grain consumption, in kilograms
Antwerp	15th and 16th cents.	200
Languedoc	c. 1480	392
Padua	1554–5	236–53
Hitsum, Friesland	1569–3	153–91
Languedoc	1580–90	490
Valladolid	16th century	158
Hanover	1750	240
Schaumburg-Lippe	1772	243
Holland	1798	118·5
Near Orléans	18th century	200–300, mostly 250
Burgundy	18th century	520
France	c. 1700	212–40
—	1750–60	220–75
—	1775–80	235–75
—	1789–90	216–75
East Prussia	1750–1800	460 (persons above 12 years)
Wandlacken (G.)	1758	320 (persons above 12 years)
		160 (children under 12 years)
Prussia	End 18th century	160
Germany	End 18th century	250

Table 9.   *Annual per capita consumption of wheat or rye in Flanders*
and Brabant, in kilograms, 1557–1791

Period	Amount of corn, expressed in terms of wheat or rye, consumed per person annually (including beer consumption), in kilograms		
	Wheat	Rye	
1557–1601	260	243	
1648–1692	267	250	
1693	298	279	
(1694)	(344)	(322)	Quota determined by the government
1710	277	259	
1740	248	232	
(1758–1759)	(158)	(148)	For the army
1781	174	162	
1791	173	162	

Holland in 1798, with a population of 828,532, can be explained by a
fairly high consumption of cheese, butter, milk, meat, fish and eggs.
Since a high consumption of corn indicates an unbalanced diet, it can
reasonably be associated with a lower standard of living. If we estimate
the annual consumption in England at 240 kilograms per head, we are

probably erring on the generous side, in view of the high consumption of meat in England. At the end of the seventeenth century, therefore, 1,248,000 tons of corn would have been consumed annually in England. At the beginning of the seventeenth century, production fell short of the home demand; there was surplus until after 1660, but by the beginning of the eighteenth century, England was exporting an average of 35,000 tons of corn a year.

At the end of the seventeenth century England's grain balance was as follows:

Consumption	1,248,000 tons
Seed	250,000 tons
Export	35,000 tons
Stock-feeding and industrial use	247,000 tons
Total	1,780,000 tons

The last item in this account, the figure for stock-feeding and industrial use, is merely a closing entry. It is obvious that the export figure is still low, 1·8–2·1 per cent of the total gross corn-yield. Yet within half a century exports claimed no less than 4 per cent of the annual yield.

We have no figures for corn supplies in England at the end of the eighteenth century, though it is possible to make some assessment of the problem at the time. During the second half of the eighteenth century there had been a sharp rise in the population of England and Wales, and by 1800 this reached 9·6 million. We can assume that the corn consumption of this population was 2,304,000 tons. The mean yield ratio had risen from 7·5 between 1600 and 1699, to 9·5 between 1750 and 1820. Total production may have been as much as one and a half times what it was at the end of the seventeenth century – it was now 2,670,000 tons. The amount reserved for seed did not change very much.

Consumption	2,304,000 tons
Seed	280,000 tons
Stock-feeding and industrial use	86,000 tons
Total	2,670,000 tons

A closer look at the index figures reveals that the population increased at a much greater rate than the yield ratios:

	Indices of population	Indices of yield ratios
End of the seventeenth century	100	100
1800	185	127

The margin between the production and consumption of corn had become very much narrower, and the increase in population could not be entirely catered for by improved methods of agriculture. We know that during this period many meadows were put down to crops and new ground was put to the plough, though this was generally less fertile; so the erstwhile grain-exporting country finally had to resort to the import of corn. Malthus's concern about population growth was therefore not unfounded.

Estimated figures are now available for the production and consumption of corn in Poland during the second half of the sixteenth century. These are of importance in relation to the large-scale export to western Europe during the sixteenth and seventeenth centuries. The annual

Table 10. *Polish grain production, 1560–1570*

Type of grain	Annual production in tons excluding seed	Yield ratio	Annual production in tons including seed
Wheat	172,577	4·6	220,515
Rye	597,424	4·0	796,564
Barley	140,595	4·8	177,595
Oats	457,885	3·8	621,415
Total	1,368,481		1,816,089

yields there are shown in Table 10. We can see that total production was higher than in England and the population was probably smaller, though assessments of this vary considerably. Wyczański, whose study provides most of the figures, estimates the total population of the 'Crown territories' at 2·4–2·6 million, and he assumes that the annual consumption per head was 219 kilograms. The population figure is likely to have been higher, however, and we must assume a consumption of 240 kilograms. Wyczański's figures nevertheless indicate a large surplus of corn which was used for cattle feed and for industrial purposes and, since 74,600 tons were exported, he arrives at this final calculation:

Table 11

Consumption	527,800 tons
Seed	451,100 tons
Export	74,600 tons
Stock-feeding and industrial use	762,600 tons
Total	1,816,100 tons

More detailed information can be gained from the figures for rye which topped the exports. They are given to the nearest 100 tons.

Table 12

	(Tons)	(Percentages)
Domestic consumption of rural population	414,900	52
Consumption of town population	112,900	14
Export[1]	74,600	9
Seed	199,100	25
Total	801,500	100
Imports into southern Poland	6,000	
Polish production	795,500	

Of the total rye production therefore 187,500 tons (112,900 plus 74,600) were marketed, which amounts to 23 per cent of the gross production or 31 per cent of the net production of rye (from which seed has been deducted). The population must also have consumed the entire wheat harvest and almost half the barley crop.

Polish rye exports reached a peak during the first half of the seventeenth century (1600–49) when the average annual export amounted to 137,000 tons. During the second half of the seventeenth century it went down to 111,600 tons. The highest export was 290,000 tons in 1619. These figures refer to the amount of rye that was shipped from the Polish ports through the Danish Sound to Amsterdam. It is doubtful, however, whether the increase in export was a result of an increase in total production. It is true that the yield ratio for barley during the first half of the seventeenth century showed a slight rise, but those for wheat, rye and oats fell a little:

Polish yield ratios	Wheat	Rye	Barley	Oats
1550–99	4·7	4·0	4·8	3·7
1600–49	4·2	3·5	5·1	3·3

The acreage may have been increased, but there may also have been a change in consumption habits. Exports of rye increased perhaps because the Polish population preferred the less expensive cereals and in particular buckwheat grown on the sandy soils, if the experience in the Netherlands is any guide to the supposed change in consumption habits.

Assuming that rye consumption during the first half of the seventeenth century was the same as during the latter half of the sixteenth century and also assuming that only rye was exported – though in fact exports now included 10 per cent wheat – then the export figures for rye, in percentages of the total corn production and of the gross and net figures for rye production, were:

[1] During the period 1560–70, only rye was exported.

Period	Percentage of the total gross production of corn	Percentage of the gross production of rye	Percentage of the net production of rye
End of the sixteenth century	4·1	9·3	12·3
1600–49, mean	7·6	17·1	22·8
1600–49, maximum	15·9	36·2	48·1

The figures show clearly that the exports of corn must have had a considerable effect on market relations and prices in Poland, and an even greater effect on production.

Grain movements on this scale affected not only the producing areas but also the consuming areas. Belgian historians have estimated the corn consumption in the Low Countries and have assessed the significance of imports between 1562 and 1569. According to them the population of the Low Countries should have been 2·5 million. This is on the low side, as the United Provinces, in the North, already had a population of 1·2–1·3 million, and the density in the south was certainly greater than in the north. Annual consumption was at least 600,000 tons (240 kilograms per head), with an import of 100,000 tons. The estimates of the Polish export in these years show, as we have seen, only 74,000 tons, but the Low Countries also imported grain from northern France, northern Germany, the Rhineland and Alsace. The production of the Low Countries may have been 500,000 tons, to which must be added the amounts needed for seed, cattle food and industrial use. So imports accounted for 16·7 per cent of the total consumption. If we assume a higher per capita consumption of 300 kilograms, the imports would account for 13·3 per cent of a total consumption of 750,000 tons, and home production must have been considerably more than 650,000 tons.

During the first half of the seventeenth century the population of the northern provinces was 1·7 million, representing a consumption of 408,000 tons. An annual average of 137,000 tons was imported from the Baltic countries alone, but there were other sources of supply. But since some of this imported corn was re-exported, it is hard to calculate the import percentages on the basis of the total consumption. The vital importance of imports is nevertheless clear.

Throughout the greater part of Europe, low yields of corn made it necessary to put down most of the arable acreage to corn in order to provide sufficient to feed the population. This can even be seen from the proportion of corn-crop acreage to the total arable acreage in England, where yields were higher than those in most other European countries.

Only those parts of the Low Countries (especially in the west and north) where yields were even higher than in England, may have constituted an exception to this general rule.

From the data available on individual farms in England, Germany, northern France and the Low Countries, it appears that between 50 and 70 per cent or more of the arable land was put down to corn growing. But from the later Middle Ages onward, pulses played an important part in central England and in parts of the Low Countries. Statistics for individual farms may, however, give a somewhat distorted picture of the *total* production of agricultural crops. The material is gathered from farm accounts and we only have those of the larger farms. A large farm could produce corn in sufficient quantities for supplying the market, but in some areas smaller farms concentrated on the growing of crops requiring more intensive labour. There are indications that crops like flax, hemp, rapeseed, cole, dye-producing plants and vines were generally grown on small farms, where such intensive labour could be provided.

ANIMAL HUSBANDRY

In stock-farming production can be improved by increasing the number of stock and by raising the quality of the product in the form of better live or dead weights, better milk yields, heavier sheepskins or better-quality wool. Statistics for the gross holdings of livestock in the period prior to 1800 are scarce. There are Gregory King's estimates for England and Wales: 4·5 million cattle, 11 million sheep and 2 million pigs at the end of the seventeenth century. This amounts to between one third and one half of the present numbers. At that time the human population was one eighth of the present figure.

For some other regions we have the figures given in Table 11. The ratio between horses and cattle is mostly 1:4 or 1:6, with the exception of the bishopric of Ratzeburg and Champagne which had relatively more horses, and of western Finland, where horses were not so common. The number of pigs depended on the existence of forests in the area. In many French provinces the number of pigs decreased between 1500 and 1800 as a consequence of deforestation; it rose again after potatoes came into use as pig food. The number of sheep also tended to decline as a result of the clearing of moorland.

Livestock could not be increased beyond certain limits because of the poor quality of meadows and grassland. Cattle often grazed on common land and wasteland, which consisted of poor-quality grass overgrown with weeds and wild shoots. Land was often marshy because of bad drainage. In order to avoid over-grazing, the farmer was commonly restricted to a quota of animals allowed to graze on this land.

Table 13. *Number of horses, cattle, pigs and sheep in various
countries, sixteenth century to nineteenth century*

Region	Year	Horses	Cattle	Pigs	Sheep
Overijssel[a]	1602	12,146	54,000	10,914	40,987
Overijssel[b]	1800–44	11,992	72,683	19,531	32,921
Ratzeburg	1630	4,254	3,116	3,859	2,625
County of					
Burgundy[c]	1688	50,208	203,361	54,152	112,523
Western Finland[c]	1719	9,918	75,633	?	53,845
Champagne[c]	1732	153,666	213,480	96,845	713,015

[a] Horses older than two years; also 6,346 bee hives.
[b] Horses in 1844, cattle in 1800, pigs in 1812 and sheep in 1844.
[c] Oxen and bulls: Burgundy, 60,293; western Finland, 14,824; Champagne 37,782; goats: Burgundy, 37,145.

The amount of dung produced by stock in the stables during the winter was insufficient for an adequate manuring of the arable land. If the arable acreage is increased by reclamation – and in most cases land with the best soil is chosen – there is a decreased acreage of poor-quality land left for grazing, whereas ideally the livestock ought to have been proportionately *increased* after reclamation in order to provide the larger amount of manure needed. This, however, can only be done when and where the area of wasteland is still extensive. Where regulations on the use of wasteland, beginning with the twelfth and thirteenth centuries were issued – as in Germany and the Netherlands, by the *Marken* communities – we can assume that from that time on there was a conflict of interests between arable and stock-farming. This conflict could only be resolved by the cultivation of fodder-crops, and in some countries this was started as early as the thirteenth century.

Wherever arable farming predominated, livestock as such was of secondary importance. What mattered most to the arable farmer were the production of manure and the pulling power of the horses, oxen and cows. The production of cheese, butter, milk, meat, skins and wool for the market and for home consumption was of no great consequence. From the sixteenth century onwards controversy raged in agricultural writings between advocates and opponents of keeping more livestock on arable farms. The calculations usually showed a deficit in stock farming since the value of the manure produced by the stock and the pulling power provided by it were not normally taken into account.

In districts where stock-farming predominated the situation was entirely different. Here we should distinguish between two different types of animal husbandry: the *extensive* system with large areas of grazing, where stock was kept for the production of skins, meat and wool, and the *intensive* system in which the emphasis might be on the production of cheese, butter and later on milk from the cattle, as well as on wool, meat and in some cases cheese and milk from the sheep. This meant maintaining a high density of grazing in meadows separated by gates, ditches or natural hedges.

Originally, extensive stock-farming predominated in large areas of Europe, with a preference for sheep and goats rather than cows. The reclamations in western Europe before 1300 resulted in an increase in arable land and a shift of emphasis to horses and cows. There is a close correlation between this agricultural trend and the population increase at that time in certain areas of western and southern Europe. Extensive stock-farming still persisted at about 1500 in the outlying countries: western and northern England, Scotland, Scandinavia, Poland, Russia, Hungary, the Balkan countries and Spain. These countries could be described as fringe areas (the frontier) surrounding the centre, which consisted of western and southern Europe; or, in terms of von Thünen's concentric circles, as the outer ring with the most extensive form of agriculture.

Characteristic of these outer areas was 'transhumance': the movement of cattle to and fro between summer and winter pasturage, sometimes covering enormous distances; and, from the fifteenth century onwards, large-scale movements of cattle from these fringe areas to the central areas of consumption. This long-distance cattle dealing reached its peak during the second half of the sixteenth century and the first half of the seventeenth. After that, it declined sharply. The herds were driven from Scotland and Wales to eastern England; from Schleswig Holstein, Jutland, the Danish Islands and Skåne to the German Hansa towns, Flanders, Brabant and Holland, or from Ribe (Jutland) by boat to Holland; and from Hungary, the Balkan countries and Poland to southern and central Germany.

Before being sold, the animals were kept for a while in the vicinity of the market and given supplementary feeding so as to compensate for the loss of weight incurred during the long trek. The importance of this commerce is clearly demonstrated by the figures for the Jutland ox trade. At the beginning of the seventeenth century the annual export of oxen was worth 30,000 kilograms of silver. We can estimate the importance of this by comparing it with the value of corn shipped through the Danish Sound to the west at the same period, which was 55,000 kilograms of silver.

This long-distance cattle trade was profitable so long as there was a considerable difference between the price in the area of production and that in the area of consumption. The long journeys were full of hazards which claimed their victims. There was a general loss of weight, complicated provisions had to be made along the routes and toll was levied in many places. It is therefore not surprising that this long-haul cattle trade was a temporary phenomenon, closely bound up with positively favourable circumstances.

Where the choice lay (at the centre, as it were, of the von Thünen concentric rings) between extending livestock production or opening up more arable land, cattle production could be increased not only by importing cattle from the extensive 'fringe' areas but also by improving the dead weight of stock, the yield of wool from the sheep and the milk yield. Meat production could also be increased by slaughtering younger animals.

It is impossible to be sure, on the basis of the available material, whether production was indeed increased between 1500 and 1800. There are some data on the live and dead weight of cows, calves, oxen, pigs and sheep, on the milk and butter yield of cows (either daily or over the whole lactation period) and on the weight of sheepskins. But the available figures refer to different periods and to widely dispersed areas.

Subject to many reservations, the average live weight of cows can be estimated at 225–325 kilograms and of oxen at 300–400 kilograms. The total milk yield per period of lactation varied between 600 and 1100 litres. Sheepskins weighed between 0·6 and 0·8 kilograms; the live weight of pigs varied between 50 and 60 kilograms and sheep between 20 and 30 kilograms.

Changes may well have occurred in total meat consumption. At the end of the Middle Ages a good deal of meat is supposed to have been eaten in Germany, relatively much more per person than during the eighteenth century. Meat consumption largely depended on how much was left in the household budget after provision had been made for bread and corn, so that the demand for bread and corn was much steadier than the demand for meat. There may also have been changes in the kind of meat that was eaten. During the fifteenth and sixteenth centuries there was a preference for beef; later, in the eighteenth and nineteenth centuries, pork became popular, when it was possible to feed the pigs with potatoes and therefore pork became cheaper. During the eighteenth century, mutton became the national diet in England. This was the result of concentrating on the production of meat rather than wool, but it should be remembered that it was (and still remains) a largely English phenomenon.

The demand for meat was satisfied not only by increasing the number of cattle or through their gain in weight, but also by killing them at an earlier age. The average age of the stock fell rapidly. This was very evident, e.g. in Schmatzfeld (Harz): in 1750 there were 24 cattle of five years or over, by 1760 this number had fallen to 9 and in 1770 there was not a single five-year-old beast among the stock. In 1740 there were still 3 three-year-old sows, in 1750 not one. Prior to 1750 there were cows on the farm that had attained the venerable age of sixteen. On a large farm at Liesheim (East Prussia) in 1740 the age of the horses varied from between three and twenty years, of the twelve horses, eight were thirteen years or older. The cows at Bartenstein in the same region were also three to twenty years old; and of 177 cows, 67 were ten years or older. The age at which the cows first calved was late. In Wernigerode in the sixteenth century, six-, seven- and eight-year-olds still counted as belonging to the young stock, as did four-year-old sheep and three-year-old pigs.

The effect of the new methods used by English stock-breeders like Robert Bakewell, Sir Thomas Gresley, Wester, Fowler, the Culley brothers, the Colling brothers and others, during the eighteenth century was not really felt until the nineteenth century, when stock-farmers' requirements changed completely. Originally sheep had been kept for wool and dung; oxen, with their strongly developed withers, for traction; the pigs with their heavy heads and sturdy forelegs, were supposed to forage for their own food in the woods. In order to increase the usable weight of the carcase, more attention was now paid through breeding to the development of the fleshy hind quarters. The gains of the past two hundred years are derived much more from the increase in the amount of *edible* meat than from an increase in the *total* weight. Skins have become thinner, bones lighter.

The pulling power and working rate of the horses, oxen and some-times cows that were used as draught animals remained much the same between 1500 and 1800, when a horse could pull a load of 200 to 300 kilograms. The amount of land which could be ploughed or harrowed was dictated by the speed of the draught animals and this remained the same between 1500 and 1800. Consequently, shortening the hours of labour was impossible for work in which draught animals were used. A change-over from oxen to horses could have accelerated the work, but horses were more expensive to feed. For this reason horses were profitable in districts where the weather was very change-able and jobs might have to be finished in the short periods when conditions were favourable. Yet there are some areas of arable farming where there was an over-abundance of horses on the farms, e.g. in the Low countries, Denmark, northern Germany and Alsace. Since there are no indications that the horses were bred for selling, they must have been used on the farm itself, perhaps for carting of manure.

MANURING

In spite of the fundamental importance of manure production to the arable farm, little material dealing with this subject is found in historical documents. Some fairly trustworthy information was noted down concerning the manure produced on the Ostra estates (Saxony) from 1740 to 1825 and in Bersdorf (Silesia) from 1772 to 1870. In Ostra in 1740 5,900 kilograms of manure per adult beast were produced. The quantity rose to 8,800 kilograms in 1760; in Bersdorf in 1772–4 the annual production was 4,025 kilograms per fully grown head of cattle. At the end of the eighteenth century, an annual yield of 3,000–4,000 kilograms of manure per adult beast was considered normal in Germany and Switzerland. This is the figure for a winter stabling period of about 120 days. If the herd was kept stabled throughout the whole year, the annual production rose to 10,000 kilograms per beast, as we can see at Ostra, Bersdorf and in Switzerland. The stalls could only be used in this way when fodder-crops began to be cultivated. Nearly always, however, this was accompanied by the extension of the arable area at the expense of pasture, of which less was now needed for cattle. The remaining grass-land had to be specially manured, whereas formerly the cattle had fulfilled that task as they grazed. Thus it is doubtful whether, seen as a whole, any more manure was available per unit area than before. The advantage of stall-feeding through the whole year was that the total arable acreage could be extended.

Manure was applied in two different ways: a heavy dressing of 28,000 to 36,000 kilograms per acre, as in Artois (1336/7), Hitsum (Friesland, c. 1570), the Palatinate (c. 1800), Vianen, Steenwijk, Etten and Houten (the Netherlands, c. 1800); and a lighter dressing of 8,000 to 15,200 kilograms per acre, which was applied during the eighteenth century in Switzerland, Silesia, the Harz, and on a farm near Lille (France). The different quantities depend on the incidence of harvests: lighter dressing would often serve for two harvests, heavy dressing would normally last for a succession of six crops, which in the two-course rotation meant that each piece of land would be manured only once in twelve years. The latter was the case in Harwell. In general the total quantity of manure amounted to 4,000–5,600 kilograms per acre per crop, regardless of whether a heavy or a lighter dressing was applied.

In the absence of fodder crops, between $2\frac{1}{2}$ and $3\frac{3}{4}$ acres of grassland were needed for the summer and winter feeding of a fully grown cow. For the adequate manuring of $7\frac{1}{2}$ acres of arable land – 5 acres of which were cultivated each year – 6 head of cattle were required with 15–$22\frac{1}{2}$ acres of grassland. This proportion of arable to grassland is consistent with the distribution reported on the Frisian farm of Rienck Hemmema during the sixteenth century: it had 21 acres of arable and 42 acres of grassland, and its livestock consisted of 14–16 cattle. As a fairly intensive system of tillage was used, whereby only one-sixth or one-seventh part of the land lay fallow each year, the farm needed some 21 cows for manure. Hence the farmer had to buy a fairly large amount of manure from the neighbouring town of Franeker. If he had been using the three-course system, 17 head of cattle would have been sufficient. The purchase of extra manure enabled him to use the more intensive system of tillage.

A connection between manuring and corn yields is demonstrated by figures from the English farmholding of Robert Loder at Harwell near Oxford at the beginning of the seventeenth century. Over a period of years the east field on this farm was given a heavier dressing than the west field; the average yield ratio for wheat on the east field was 15·5, and for barley 8·0. The yield ratios on the west field were considerably lower during this period: for wheat 7·8 and for barley 5·8. After some years Loder decided to give the west field the same dressing as the east field with the result that the yields increased noticeably: the yield ratio for wheat on the west field went up to 14·1, and for barley to 7·9, thereby equalizing the yields from both fields. There could scarcely be clearer proof of the importance of manuring.

A secondary consequence of heavy dressing could be the greater risk of 'laying' the corn; to avoid this, the cultivation of oleiferous plants had to be inserted in the crop rotation, as was done at the end of the eighteenth century.

The purchase of additional manure to increase the corn yield was profitable only in times of high grain prices. On the other hand, some industrial crops that were grown as a preferable alternative to low-priced corn often required fairly heavy feeding too – e.g. flax, hops and tobacco. It was therefore tempting for the farmers either to starve their corn for the sake of these industrial crops, or to sell their manure to other farmers who were willing to pay a good price for it.

The sale of manure could indeed prove a profitable business. During the seventeenth and eighteenth centuries, governments as well as landlords were frequently apprehensive about the threat to corn offered by the industrial crops and their heavy demands on manure. Regulations were issued against the sale and export of manure, especially to foreign countries. In the Low Countries, for instance, the law prohibited the transport to other provinces of certain manures, such as pigeon manure, of importance for the growing of tobacco. Reductions in the quantity or quality of manuring were probably responsible for the slight fall in the yield ratios of cereals between 1600 and 1750 in most of the countries of Europe for which we have evidence.

IMPLEMENTS AND TOOLS

Implements and tools were in general use to save labour, but labour shortage was never the major problem in Europe that it was in North America, where it was a constant source of anxiety. European farms were often small, suffering from a surplus of labour rather than from a shortage. Indeed in the rural areas there was a good deal of concealed unemployment, sometimes absorbed by cottage industries. The farmer did not count his own labour or that of the members of his family in terms of costs, and whenever production was low he tried to make ends meet by working harder or by growing crops that required more intensive labour.

Further agricultural progress in Europe was hampered mainly by low individual productivity, small yields, the poor weight of the livestock and poor milk yields. The main effort was directed towards increasing production by, e.g., deeper ploughing, improved sowing and better threshing. Secondary problems arose when production went up so much that the increased harvest could no longer be threshed by old-established methods. A similar problem occurred when milk flowed more abundantly, so that the farmer's wife and daughters could not turn it all into cheese and butter. It was under these circumstances that threshing machines and improved butter churns came into use.

The introduction of new farm implements was impeded in many European countries by the small size of holdings and the adoption of differing systems of tillage. Most of the new agricultural implements of the eighteenth and nineteenth centuries were used in corn cultivation, but this monoculture of cereals was frequently interrupted by the introduction of fodder-crops, pulses, potatoes, and an ever-increasing variety of crops. The early machines could only be used on open, flat terrain where the plots were not separated from one another, and where the ground was more or less free of stones. In western European countries the small size of many farms, the diversity of the soil, the terrain and the crops discouraged the introduction of these machines.

Until 1800 there were no mechanical sources of energy for farming. There were only human labour and draught animals, chiefly horses and oxen. Water and windmills had been in use for a long time, but only for drainage and the manufacture of agricultural products. For arable farming, mobile machines were needed and these were only to arrive in the shape of the steam engine and the tractor. There was still no means of transporting energy over longer distances. Before 1800, therefore, the energy available in agriculture was directly proportionate to the number of local workers and beasts of burden. Yet an increase in the number of workers did not always lead to a corresponding rise in production. The acreage of the farm and the number of workers were closely interrelated, and particularly on the smaller farms it was hard to achieve the ideal balance. Besides, there were those on the farm who could contribute little or nothing to the work – the sick, the aged, the simple-minded. The number of non-productive inhabitants of a farm could be surprisingly high.

In general, the market prices of agricultural products must have influenced farmers in the purchase of improved tools or new machinery. There is, however, no agreement among economists and historians as to the conditions which induced farmers to purchase new machinery and tools. According to Simiand and Bublot, farmers would take this step during periods of agricultural recession. Kondratieff and Mousnier, on the contrary, believe that farmers used periods of expansion for introducing innovations. According to the first analysis the farmer would want to lower his production costs because of the low prices and relatively high level of real wages. In the latter case the farmer would treat the higher prices as yielding a bonus profit (even though this may not have been justified since his costs may also have gone up). In the absence of a sound accounting system the farmer would equate high prices with large profits and would attempt to increase profits even more by purchasing new tools, since during these conditions of expansion he could convert more funds into innovations. Profits were large, real wages were relatively low and rents did not, as a rule, go up as much as grain prices.

On the whole the evidence favours the view that it was especially during times of expansion that farmers embarked on innovations, and that this was also when most agricultural inventions made their appearance. This shows once again that what mattered to the farmer was not the saving of labour but the increase in production. Labour he could usually command in abundance.

It is difficult to calculate how much labour was saved by the new and improved machinery, because the data are scant and incomplete. For example, the speed of threshing is sometimes recorded in bushels per day, without stating the kind of grain. But it made a great difference whether it was wheat, barley or oats that was threshed. Another problem is the duration of the working day. In the medieval English documents, the 'time for the job' is reckoned in work days, which were probably only part-days, from sunrise until noon. But in other sources a day would mean the full period from sunrise to sunset.

Few improvements in working time occurred between the Middle Ages and the Industrial Revolution. The energy potential of humans and animals did not increase. The horses or oxen pulling the plough did not walk any faster in 1750 than in 1250. In Hallwil (Switzerland) and in

Brunswick during the seventeenth century the farmers could plough
0·9–1·2 acres in a day. In England it took the same time to plough 1·0
acre with oxen or 1·25 to 1·50 acres with horses. In Russia during the
eighteenth century a plough with four horses could work 2·5 acres a
day. With one horse 1·25 acres could be ploughed. Some progress was
made in England in the eighteenth century through the introduction of
the lighter Norfolk plough, with which 1·5 to 2·0 acres could be broken
up in a day. The working day was long, and as the ploughing season
advanced the draught animals grew progressively weaker. It was easy
to plough over 1·0 acre a day with oxen at the beginning of the season,
but after two or three weeks their rate dwindled to barely 0·5 acre.

In the Baltic states two horses could harrow 2·5 acres a day, but in the
greater part of Russia four horses were needed to do the same work. In
eighteenth-century Norfolk, where sickles were used, it still took 1·4–
2·0 man-days for the reaping, binding and shocking of one acre with
wheat. In eastern Germany, one man with a sickle could reap 0·3–0·6
acres of wheat in one day (1·7–3·3 man-days for one acre); with a
scythe he could do 0·9–1·25 acres (0·8–1·1 man-days). In Russia two
reapers could harvest one acre with rye or 2·5 acres with barley or
oats in a day. Generally, two weeks were barely enough for three men
to reap over an area of 30 acres. The ordinary family farm, without
hired help, seldom had the use of more than three grown men for the
harvest. The area that could be sown with cereals on a family farm
depended to a great extent on how much family labour was available at
harvest time.

In 1613, on Robert Loder's farm at Harwell, 3·5 bushels of wheat and
10·5 bushels of barley were threshed by flail per man-day. Threshing
was winter work for the small farmer, but for the big farmer it was an
expensive business, because of the high cost of wages. If the corn was
trodden out by animals, instead of being flailed, much greater quantities
could be dealt with. With three horses, 23·4–30·0 bushels of grain
could be worked in this way, but the losses of grain were larger. At the
end of the eighteenth century in France, the aid of a threshing machine
made it possible to deal with 13·75–26·5 bushels of wheat per day.
Even the first, still imperfect machines brought the time needed for the
work down to a quarter or an eighth of the time formerly required by
threshing with flails. In haymaking in Russia two men could mow
1,920–2,880 kilograms a day.

Agricultural implements and tools were usually made of wood
(since iron was costly), so that only the vital parts were made of iron or
were protected by iron plates. This meant, for instance, that the milk
churn, invented during the seventeenth century, often had intricate
pinions of wood, and it was not possible to improve the design of these

and other tools until high grade iron could be produced cheaply. In this respect agriculture relied completely on developments in the iron industry.

By comparison with the total inventory of a farm, the value of the implements and tools was low: from the few figures available, we see that it was not more than 3–4 per cent during the seventeenth century. From a number of farm inventories in Sussex it is evident that a change occurred during the eighteenth century, when the value of implements rose to 9 per cent of the total inventory.

During the agrarian expansion of the sixteenth century agricultural invention, experiment and improvement were all active. There were many designs of a new implement that sowed corn in drills, thereby using less seed while maintaining the yield. The corn was generally sown much too closely, but this was the only way of stifling the rank growth of weeds, which otherwise resulted from thinner sowing. Not until the advent of the horse-drawn hoe in the eighteenth century was it possible to kill the weeds between the rows. The designs of Camillo Tarello, Tadeo Cavalini, Joseph Locatelli and John Worlidge played an important part in the later development of sowing machinery but they did not contribute to practical improvement in their own day.

The recession in farming during the seventeenth and the early eighteenth centuries scarcely favoured a spirit of enterprise towards inventions and improvements. Ploughs with a small foot instead of the wheel carriage had already been in use in England since the thirteenth century and in Zealand since the fourteenth century. In the regions where both types of ploughs – with foot and with wheel-carriage – were found, the farmers in the long run preferred the foot-ploughs as they were lighter and required fewer horses or oxen. In Brabant and Flanders the foot was replaced by a single wheel during the sixteenth century. Ploughs with iron mouldboards with a concave surface were another important advance. These ploughs required little tractive power, the soil in the furrow being completely turned over and crumbled. There is some evidence that such ploughs were in use in the Austrian Netherlands in the eighteenth century. This 'Brabant plough' is regarded as the prototype of the modern plough, which was perfected in England and the United States.

In Holland and Friesland, various kinds of milk-churns were invented and cheese presses came into use, probably as a result of increasing milk yields. Earthenware and copper dishes replaced the earlier wooden vessels in the process of skimming the milk.

Dutchmen introduced from China the winnowing mill which was brought over to Europe and greatly improved the separation of the corn from the chaff. Threshing blocks (conical blocks revolving round an axle, and pulled by horses), which had been known even in the Middle Ages, were found in the sixteenth century in Italy and in the eighteenth century over a wide area: Seeland (Denmark), Sweden, the northern parts of the Netherlands, southwest France and Austria.

The agrarian expansion after 1750 produced numerous inventions of importance to agriculture, but as a rule they were not applied until the nineteenth century.

ADVANCE IN MENTAL OUTLOOK AND KNOWLEDGE

New methods and technical devices obviously appealed to farmers of more than ordinarily progressive outlook. These were the ones who obtained better results than other farmers in their production of grain, and their milk and meat yields, produced for the market and therefore had to balance cost and profit. In planning their production they took into account the price ratios of agricultural produce and the changes affecting them. They were motivated by rational considerations of profit. Their relations with their farmhands were less paternalistic and more businesslike. During the harvest season they employed day-labourers, and their personnel would change frequently because they wanted to save on wages.

From bookkeeping accounts, personal diaries and reports – our chief sources for production analyses – we find that this kind of progressive attitude existed as early as the fourteenth century, e.g. in Artois. Later on, farmers like Rienck Hemmema and Dirck Jansz are found in Friesland (sixteenth and seventeenth centuries), and Robert Loder in England (seventeenth century) – in general, the more educated and cultured farmers. Hemmema studied for some years at the university of Louvain, and his brother was an eminent scholar in Roman Law.

How far, in practice, could the 'progressive' farmer adapt his techniques to changing conditions and avail himself of improvements? Farms differ widely in the extent to which they can adapt themselves to a change in market conditions. Sometimes they are held back by soil conditions or climate, sometimes by the way the farm is situated and the distribution of its fields. Farms situated near towns, or those that have good transport facilities, will adapt themselves more readily than farms in remote areas. Smaller farms often stand a better chance than larger ones, in which much more capital is invested in buildings and implements. A farm worked by the owner will adapt to changes in the market more easily than a farm held on lease, where restraints on changing the system of tillage and the cultivation of new crops hamper general development.

Adjustment to changed market conditions is not, therefore, simply a matter of the farmer's attitude. A number of factors lie more or less beyond his control. It was impossible, e.g., for one individual to convert an open-field system into enclosures; the cooperation of at least part of the village community was essential. Sometimes, however, we can clearly detect a close relationship between the production scheme of the farmer and the relative price fluctuations of farm products. The effect of the secular trend on the shift from arable farming to animal husbandry, wine-growing or the cultivation of industrial crops, and vice versa, has already been considered. But apart from the secular trend there were annual price fluctuations. Farmers whose policy was influenced by these were sensitive to the market conditions which prevailed in the area of consumption of their products. In their planning they were led by the price ratios of agricultural products during the previous year. This kind of policy, whereby the acreage sown to corn varied according to the relative prices of the various cereals, is clearly illustrated in the accounts of the two Frisian farmers Rienck Hemmema and Dirck Jansz. Hemmema's accounts for the harvests of 1569/70 – 1572/3 demonstrate that he changed the acreage sown with barley, wheat, oats and pulse in accordance with the price ratios of the previous harvest year. His policy here is unmistakable, because the price fluctuations in those years were considerable. On one occasion, when the price of rye was very high, he actually sold his entire rye stocks, which, since he did not grow any rye himself, he had bought for feeding his farm servants.

Dirck Jansz, whose accounts between the years 1601 and 1608 have been preserved, closely followed the price fluctuations in the cultivation of wheat, oats and beans. Robert Loder grew only barley and wheat for the market, so that he did not have much latitude for adapting himself to price changes. But even his accounts show evidence that he based his cropping on price fluctuations.

The capitalistic outlook and profit motive of such men also found its expression in more rational relationships between them and their servants, in which there was no question of a protective, patriarchal attitude. Increasingly businesslike, they might not always be efficient, for they faced many other difficulties which did not improve the work of the farm. Feeding was poor, and, in Hemmema's case particularly, wages were on the low side. Small wonder that his workers were constantly leaving, compelling him to take on new farmhands and girls in May every year.

Masters continually complained that work was done badly and that the workers had no sense of discipline, so that they sometimes had to sack a worker halfway through the season. Loder will complain that he is being robbed. In their dealings with labour they bear the marks of employers who regard the workers' wages as an unnecessary expense.

It was cheaper to give them board and lodging in 'dear years' than to pay them wages, but it was better still to keep as few workers as possible.

The 'progressive' farmers were a small minority. They could read and write. They even commanded a rudimentary knowledge of bookkeeping. Loder was probably the first farmer to be aware that he was losing interest on the capital invested in seed and cattle. He also took account of his own labour, his wife's and that of his female staff, and entered it on the debit side of his accounts.

In most cases, however, the farmers could neither read nor write. Only fairly recently has an extensive study of literacy among the rural population been undertaken. In the middle of the eighteenth century in a not very prosperous province like Overijssel, 20–25 per cent of the farmers could not sign their name. Things were rather better along the coast of this province, where literacy was about 10 per cent. In the more prosperous western and northern provinces of the Netherlands the situation was also probably much better.

During the sixteenth century, 90 per cent of the rural workers and 65 per cent of the more wealthy farmers in Languedoc were unable to write. Of these, 10 per cent could write their names, and 25 per cent only their initials. There was a marked distinction in this respect between the rural and urban population. A third of the townsmen could write their names, a third only their initials, while the others could not write at all. By the end of the seventeenth century in France, there was a considerable difference between the areas north and south of the line Avranches–Geneva. To the south only 10–15 per cent of those signing marriage contracts could write their names, whereas to the north the percentage was 33–40 per cent. It is estimated that throughout France at the end of the seventeenth century an average of 20 per cent of the population could write, and by the end of the eighteenth century 37 per cent. These averages, of course, obscure the fact that the percentages varied widely between town and country and between men and women. Illiteracy among women was between 15 and 20 per cent higher than among men.

Recent historical research is inconclusive about the bearing that the educational background of the farmer may have had on intensive systems of agriculture and progressive farming. One gets the impression nevertheless, that in the Low countries such a causal connection does exist. Does this also apply to other areas, like the east of England, the Palatinate, Alsace, the Po Valley, Catalonia? Agricultural theory was rarely intended for farmers; writers addressed themselves to the land-owners, who exercised a kind of supervision over their property. The farmers may of course have learned from the landowners, and this is probably what happened in England, where the large landowners lived in the country and took a keen interest in farming. Normally, however, in France, the Low Countries and eastern Europe, the owner avoided direct contact with the farmer by appointing a steward or (in France) a notary.

In almost all European countries agricultural societies flourished during the eighteenth century. Among the oldest and most well known are: The Society of Improvers in the Knowledge of Agriculture, founded at Edinburgh in 1723, the Society of Dublin (1736), the Physikalische (Naturforschende) Gesellschaft at Zürich from the year 1747, the Italian Accademia dei Georgofili at Florence, 1753, the Société d'agriculture, du commerce et des arts, at Rennes, 1757, the Ökonomische und gemeinnützige Gesellschaft des Kantons Bern, 1759 and the Société libre d'économie de Saint-Petersbourg, 1765. As the agricultural societies consisted mainly of landowners, it is easy to ridicule the members of these learned societies for their lack of practical knowledge of farming, yet they deserve credit for offering prizes for books and articles on agriculture, in which a number of problems came to the attention of a larger public. For the first time, too, experiments on a large scale were conducted, experimental farms were set up, official enquiries were held, and sets of agricultural tools and implements were collected, tested and compared. Members travelled in their own country and abroad for the purpose of studying agriculture. It was a time of general surveys and stock-taking, a time of general interest in agriculture. In the latter half of the eighteenth century the foundations were laid for the scientific development of agriculture during the nineteenth century.

Book-learning contributed little to intensive farming in the Low Countries, since agriculture there had already reached a high standard before it came to be written about. Our knowledge of agriculture in Flanders, Brabant and Holland is largely based on the reports of foreign farming experts who came to visit and observe these countries. The high degree of agricultural development in such areas must be attributed to the high density of the population, which necessitated the most intensive use of small plots of ground. The shift to intensive cultivation was not made for gain but out of necessity. This is clearly shown in a treatise by a French writer on Flemish farming in 1776. After pointing out that the soil in these parts was, on the whole, of poorer quality than in some French departments, he attributed the superior results of Flemish farming to heavy manuring and the diligence and thrift of the peasants. 'They say, with good reason, that the Flemish farmer, in order to live, haggles over everything and turns everything to profit.' More than a century earlier, Sir Richard Weston on his travels through the 'Land van Waas' in Flanders had been similarly impressed by the fact that this infertile soil, which in its natural state produced only broom and heather, could yield such good crops.

The high standard of development in these areas, then, was not founded on theories but on practical experience gained in the hard school of local and demanding conditions. Practical experience is often thought of as knowledge handed down from one generation to the next, but in this type of farming, sharply focussed on the market, there was no room for a traditional attitude of mind. The farmers had to possess a high degree of adaptability and inventiveness if they were to wrest a living with a narrow profit margin out of an unpromising soil.

In general, the rate of adjustment varied according to circumstances or factors which affected production. These could be influenced by the following.

(1) Short- or long-term trends. One can distinguish between a policy of adjustment to the annual fluctuations of market prices, and the ploughing of grassland for crops according to the secular trend.

(2) The general economic situation in agriculture: agrarian expansion or regression.

(3) The special circumstances in certain areas, such as soil conditions, the climate, and situation in relation to centres of population, transport and communications.

(4) The mentality of the farmer.

III.   *Receipts and Expenditure in Farming Husbandry*

It would be fascinating to know exactly what a typical farmer's receipts and expenses consisted of, and how much income remained as net profit. But although records, accounts, and calculations from many countries have been preserved, the question remains hard to answer. It is almost impossible to compare information from existing accounts because farms differed so widely in nature and size. Moreover, book-keeping was generally still very primitive.

In Germany, the farmer's income fluctuated between 14·8 and 53·4 per cent of the gross annual takings. For some farms in the Low Countries, the percentage varied between 16·5 and 27·6 per cent. In France, the rule-of-thumb principle was that one-third of the proceeds went to the owner, one-third to the tenant and the remaining third was absorbed in farming costs. On a small farm near Verona the average interest on the capital invested was: 1727–37, 8·1 per cent; 1738–48, 8·9 per cent; 1749–59, 11·5 per cent; 1760–71, 15·4 per cent.

In discussing the farmer's income and the interest calculated from the capital invested in the business, we are already in the realm of pure money economy. In this respect, however, the period between 1500 and 1800 is a time of transition from the traditional payment in kind or in services towards modern thinking in terms of money. Originally assessments were made on yield totals and the obligatory contributions were expressed as a proportion of the harvest yields. Tithes are one clear example of this; but there were other charges like the frequently occurring 'shared lease' (a quarter, third or half of the yield), and other annual benefits in kind. Since the harvests were subject to wide annual fluctuations, it was fortunate that rents, tithes and other charges fluctuated to the same extent. But the farmer had to cope with the fact that the amounts allocated for seed, and for his own consumption, were fixed, or at any rate varied to a much smaller extent. The advantage was that at least the farmer shared the risk of a bad harvest with the lessor, the tithe-holder and the other persons entitled to payments in kind.

A system whereby rents were fixed in terms of either goods in kind or money could only be introduced when yields remained more or less constant. Thus it was possible to give reasonable estimates of future harvests. When yields were assessed in terms of money, yield totals and market prices both fluctuated, though because of the negative correlation between prices and yields these fluctuations tended to level out in the local market. At a later stage, with the advent of interregional and international markets, this negative correlation disappeared, and, with it, the tendency towards levelling.

Where the farmer paid a fixed rent either in kind or in money, annual harvests would fluctuate, but his major expenses were fixed: rents, seed for the coming year and the feeding of the household. In this situation all the risk was borne by the farmer, and his annual earnings would show great variations.

During the early Middle Ages the farmer's payments were nearly always in kind; money payments were the exception. During the later Middle Ages, monetary payments became more common. Sometimes the market value of the produce was handed over, instead of the produce itself; in this case the amount of money varied each year according to market prices. When dues were small, a standard value was attached to the produce, and these values remained constant for centuries. Because of the steady depreciation of money, especially during the sixteenth century, these conversions were prejudicial to those who were entitled to the dues but advantageous to the farmers. The transition from settlements in kind to money payments was by no means straightforward. Especially during the depression in the seventeenth century, when money was scarce in many countries, transactions frequently reverted to payments in kind.

During the Middle Ages, farmers were obliged not only to pay dues but also to perform specific tasks. Between 1500 and 1800 residual traces of these services still remained in several western European countries; and even during the second half of the seventeenth century, when real wages were relatively high, there is evidence in France, Germany and the eastern Netherlands of a revival of these services, when owners attempted to re-introduce services that had long gone by default. We shall return later to the changing patterns in the rendering of dues and services in central and eastern Europe.

During the early stages of tenurial systems, leases were drawn up for long periods – one to three generations. Gradually the terms were reduced, until untied land might be leased for as little as one year at a time. Sometimes there was a connection between the period of the lease and the tillage system employed so that a lease of three years, or a multiple of three, would operate with the three-course system. But this was by no means a universal custom. In some regions farmers on fiefs and former villeins owed a fee only when a new farmer took possession of the fief or entered into tenancy. Usually this system was advantageous for the farmers, but it could become detrimental during periods of epidemics when tenants succeeded each other very rapidly.

The terms of the leases concluded for a period of years were influenced by the market values of farm produce and by the demand for land. There might be a connection between these two, but this is certainly not self-evident. The demand for land was governed by four factors.

(1) Land was sought for its potential yield of farm produce, in which case there is a correlation between the market prices of those goods and the value of land.

(2) Land was looked upon as an investment, by merchants and industrialists who had accumulated wealth and who chose farming as one of a strictly limited number of investment possibilities.

(3) Land was seen as a commodity for speculation, offering a quick return. This was frequently the motivation for reclamation projects and polder-making.

(4) Land was regarded as a means of acquiring social status. In several countries, e.g. England and France, it was possible to scale the social heights through the acquisition of land, and a large number of middle-class families won aristocratic titles in this way.

The landlord's economic position varied with changes in the secular trend. In Languedoc, the fifteenth century was a golden age for the wage-earner because of high real wages; the sixteenth century was favourable to the farmers because of the relatively rapid rise of the prices of agricultural produce; the seventeenth was the lessors' heyday because of the rapidly rising values of land and leasehold. But after 1665, when the economic depression between 1650 and 1750 began to make itself felt, the lessors' situation deteriorated. Many other areas of western Europe followed roughly the same pattern between the fifteenth and the seventeenth centuries.

During the depression between 1650 and 1750, when monetary yields were low, many owners, especially in the Netherlands, France and Belgium, took to running the farms themselves, or let them out on half-share leases, in which the lessor and lessee shared the yields. The landlord would supply the seed, the implements and in some cases the livestock; sometimes he would even anticipate the harvest and supply the tenant with food, thereby reducing the tenant to complete dependence on him. Occasionally middlemen would act between owners and lessors. Even in the Middle Ages this had happened in northern Italy. In the sixteenth century, sub-leasing was introduced in France. Initially only ecclesiastical property was concerned, but during the eighteenth century stewards administered Crown lands and noblemen's estates. Notaries, merchants, villagers with an eye to business – innkeepers, smiths and bakers – would act as sub-lessors. There were even sub-leasing companies. The system was widespread in Berry, Burgundy, and around Nevers and Bourbon. In Scotland and in the Hebrides, large tracts of land were given on favourable terms to the *tacksmen*, cadets of the chieftain's family, who exercised immediate control over the occupiers of the subdivisions of such areas.

Besides the landowner, there were often other persons or institutions who were entitled to part of the produce. As a rule, the quantities to be contributed were extremely small: a chicken, a few pounds of butter, one or two bushels of corn, a pound of beans, some flax, some beeswax. These goods had to be delivered annually to churches, monasteries, parsons and so on. Then there were the tithes, which, though originally intended to maintain the church and the incumbent, had often over the years fallen into secular hands. The total sum of all these obligations might well amount to more than the entire rent, so that the rights of the original owner were completely eclipsed by the aggregates of other parties. A French historian, de Saint Jacob, speaks of 'un droit terrien que des siècles avaient compliqué en superposant les formes les plus variés du statut de la terre et de l'homme'. In his opinion, tenure counted for more than ownership: 'On *tient* les biens de diverses façons: toute une gamme de modalités s'étendent sur la possession de la terre.'

Taxes constituted a heavy burden on agriculture. Growing interference by public authorities and the many costly wars – especially during the seventeenth century – caused a sharp rise in financial demands by governments, just at a time when the economic situation was least favourable, especially in agriculture. In most countries, agriculture was still the most important source of income, so that farm-land and produce were naturally the chief sources of tax levies. Despite the depression from which agriculture was suffering most severely, land taxation, both direct and indirect, was increased, since in pursuance of mercantilist policies governments went to the greatest pains to protect industry and trade. Complaints of excessive taxation came above all from France (at the time of Louis XIV) and from the Netherlands, where taxation increased after the 1672 war. Unequal tax assessment especially caused much resentment. Some countries granted complete or partial exemption for the nobility and clergy. Elsewhere, tax assess-ment was in the hands of titled landowners who made sure that their own peasants paid a smaller contribution.

Wars were catastrophic. Armies lived off the countryside and made little distinction between friend and foe. Looting and levying were the order of the day, villages were burned to the ground, livestock stolen and the peasants' sons and workers forcibly recruited. The worst of these catastrophes was the Thirty Years War in central Europe.

The farmer had to deal with local authorities as well as the national state. In many countries, seignorial rights inherited from the Middle Ages still existed. Though jurisdiction had generally passed entirely or partly out of control of the territorial lords – in the Netherlands they had no jurisdiction at all, and in France they no longer had criminal jurisdiction – they still possessed a great deal of authority in the village community: rights of tolls and ferries, of hunting over common land and forests, rights of weights and measures, of the wine press, the oven and the mill, rights of pre-emption when land was sold, and the control of the open fields. In France, after the Edict of 1667, the lord received one-third of the common land as his property (*triage*). In the seventeenth century, the lords made a great effort to extend their seignorial rights. This was probably due to a deterioration in the economic situation, but it inevitably led to stubborn resistance from the farmers. There were endless court cases, sometimes leading to violent revolts, equally violently suppressed. Nevertheless, peasant revolts in western Europe, such as those against enclosures in England, and the French resistance to tax-collectors and seignorial rights were less extensive and less violent than in central and eastern Europe. In France, Austria and southern Germany, motives were not limited to politics and economics: religious controversies also entered in. We find peasant uprisings in Switzerland (1652–3), in Bavaria and Austria (sixteenth to the eighteenth centuries), and in France, especially during the seventeenth century in Normandy, Boulogne, Béarn, Bigorre, Guyenne, Brittany, Languedoc and the Cévennes.

IV. *Landownership*

In many countries earnest attempts have been made by historians to determine how much land was owned by different social groups. These investigations to determine how the land was distributed among the five groups – Crown, nobility, clergy, townspeople and peasantry – have been marred either by the false perspective of modern concepts of ownership or by the temptation to base quantitative estimates on criteria of heterogeneous character.

All such investigations start from the modern, fairly clearly defined, concept of ownership; but, as we have seen earlier, ownership prior to 1800 was a much more complex matter than it is now. Who *owns* the feudal holdings, for which payment is only made at times of transfer or succession? The feudal lord or the vassal? Who *owns* the goods, on which only a small tribute is demanded? There were all kinds of intricate tenurial relations: e.g. tenant-farmers, who were themselves owners of estates which they in turn let out on lease. Parents leased their own farm to their children. The question of sub-letting has already been mentioned.

Historians investigating the distribution of landownership have often displayed a certain bias in favour of the farmer's being the owner of his holding. The owner-occupier is considered socially superior to the tenant-farmer. We nearly always find owner-occupiers predominant, however, where the soil is of inferior quality. The densely populated and more fertile regions were farmed by tenants more prosperous than the poorer sort of owner-occupier. There was a higher proportion of landowners among the smallholders and the cottars than among the large farmers. Landownership and wealth were far from always going hand in hand. And where do we place the owner-occupier so burdened by debt that the annual interest he has to pay is higher than the tenant-farmer's rent?

Problems also arise in respect of quantitative estimates of landownership among the five groups. The following criteria can be used for estimating the amount of land owned.

(1) The number of farms, irrespective of their size or their value.

(2) The acreage: here the problem is whether only the strictly agricultural acreage should be taken into account, or whether woods, moors and marshes should be included. In the case of estates belonging to the Crown, the nobility or the Church, the amount of strictly agricultural land was often small, because the estates included large areas of this less productive land for hunting or game preserves.

(3) The value: calculations can be based on the purchase price, the rent or the assessment for land-tax.

Calculations based on such differing criteria can lead to widely divergent results. The choice of criteria, however, is often limited by the nature of the available material.

The results of these investigations have shown that local conditions varied considerably. There might be a number of villages close to each other where landownership was almost equally distributed among the five groups; elsewhere the nobility or the Church predominated.

Nine villages in the surroundings of Orléans during the eighteenth century show the following diversity: property of the nobility, between 11·2 and 73·2 per cent; property of the Church, between 0 and 21·2 per cent; property of townspeople, between 1·4 and 32·6 per cent; property of farmers, between 18·8 and 78·4 per cent.

Some historians see a connection between the introduction of new agricultural methods and the commercialization of agriculture on the one side, and ownership by townspeople on the other, since the latter are supposed to have been the advocates of modernization. This may have applied less to the continent than to England, where the townsman often settled on his own estate and actively concerned himself with the running of it. In the Netherlands, where the townspeople were generally commercially minded, they were much more interested in new polders and reclamation than in the pursuit of existing farming activities. The landlord, who lived in the town, cared little about how the tenant worked the farm as long as his rent was paid on time. Leasehold contracts did, nevertheless, contain regulations against over-cropping and exhaustion of the soil, and at the end of the tenure the tenant was expected to hand over the farm in the same condition as he had received it.

A variety of causes brought substantial changes in the distribution of land among the five groups. After the Reformation the land owned by the Church in Protestant countries became secularized. In central Europe, the devastations and depopulation of the Thirty Years War caused a complete change in the distribution of ownership; similar changes occurred in England during the Civil War and in France after the French Revolution; enclosures in England started a process of change that lasted for many centuries.

In some Protestant countries the sale of Church property by the State was carried out at great speed because of the State's need for ready money. The result was that it was not always easy to find buyers since the market was flooded. Elsewhere (as in the Netherlands) these estates remained in the hands of the authorities for hundreds of years, the income being used to provide salaries for ministers and teachers, for the upkeep of churches and for poor relief. It used to be said that the English Parliament sold the land for a price far below the real value, as a favour to certain families, but closer study has shown that there is no foundation for this allegation. In England the Great Rebellion brought about considerable changes in landownership. After 1642, £3½ million worth of Crown lands and £2½ million of Church land were sold, and the estates of more than 700 Royalists, worth £1 million, were confiscated.

In Germany the Thirty Years War had caused a serious depopulation of rural areas. In order to bring the affected farms back into cultivation, the large landowners merged the deserted farms and estates, and sometimes those still occupied as well, into extensive properties, taking the management into their own hands. During the eighteenth century, when grain prices began to rise, this policy of driving out the smallholders continued (the so-called *Bauernlegen*), but the character of farming changed because the new large landowners concentrated on commercial exploitation. One or two of the princes took action to protect farmers against this policy. In the German countries beyond the Elbe not all the large estates consisted of land taken from the small farmers. In 1800 the total acreage of the *Gutsbesitz* in the Mittelmark (Brandenburg), comprised land derived from:

Table 14

	(Percentages)
The colonization period in the Middle Ages	26·2
Wasteland in the Middle Ages (*Wüstungen*)	27·7
Bauernlegen of the seventeenth century	18·7
Land deserted during the Thirty Years War (*Wüstungen*)	18·2
Bauernlegen in the eighteenth century	5·5
Eighteenth-century reclamations	2·1
Unknown	1·6
Total	100·0

The percentage for eighteenth-century *Bauernlegen* is low in this part of Germany, where there was an active policy of protecting the small farmers.

In England, the system of enclosures first appeared in the Middle Ages. The term is used in several senses.

(1) The consolidation of arable plots, formerly distributed over the open fields, into compact blocks, linked together and surrounded by hedges or fences and gates.

(2) The shift from arable to grassland.

(3) The expansion of estates by large owners who combined several farmsteads and removed the farmhouses on them ('engrossing').

(4) The occupation of commons by large landowners who restricted or entirely denied the rights of other farmers.

All four processes led to the partial or complete disintegration of the open fields and the emancipation of the individual farmer from the control of the community.

If by enclosures we mean any one of these four extended senses of the term, they are not only typical of England. During the eighteenth century, large landowners in Burgundy surrounded their estates with railings and incurred the indignant opposition of the farmers in the process. In the German lands the *Bauernlegen* were enclosures in the third sense of the word.

In England, enclosures were fiercely opposed by the peasants, and during the Middle Ages and in the sixteenth century the government's policy was to protect the farmers against the powerful landowners. A change came about during the eighteenth century when enclosures might be authorized by Act of Parliament. Whenever a sufficient number of people in a district – most of them large landowners – requested permission to proceed with enclosure, an investigating Commission was set up. In many cases, the small landowners informed the Commission of their disapproval, but their objections had no effect if 80 per cent of the area was owned by supporters of the petition. If the Commission's findings were favourable, the enclosure of the area in question was authorized by Act of Parliament. Local landowners bore the cost of the enclosure scheme, the surveyor's expenses, fencing and the Commission's expenses. This might prove a heavy burden for the small landowners, especially since the cost of fencing per acre was higher for small plots than for larger ones. During the period 1702–60, 338,177 acres were enclosed by Act of Parliament, and after 1760 the process continued at a higher rate until 1815.

Contemporary sources (and many later historians, e.g. the Hammonds, Lord Ernle, Hasbach, Mantoux, Trevelyan, Levy and Slater) claimed that the decisions made favoured the large landowner; that Commissions were biased and that powerful landowners put pressure on smaller ones. Enclosures were, and still are, blamed for the disappearance of small farms and for the loss to the small farmers and peasants of the commons they had of right previously used for grazing. As a result (it is argued) they were forced to decrease the numbers of their livestock, which meant less manure for their arable land. In the end they were compelled to sell their farms to the large landowners and find work in industry. Other historians (e.g. Ashton, Clapham, Tate, Hunt, Chambers and Mingay) have shown that this is exaggerated. The small landowners' opposition to enclosure was by no means general; the

Commissions accomplished their tasks reasonably well; between 1793 and 1815 the number of small farms rose rather than fell and enclosures resulted in greater intensity of labour. The rural population were not driven into industry; they went of their own free will, attracted by higher wages and anyway labour was in good supply because of population increase.

In France, the peasants were ostensibly better off, if the distribution of landownership is any guide. In several provinces, the farmers either owned a substantial part of the land or paid only a very low annual rent (the *censiers*). The individual farmer's acreage was often small and badly split up. Before 1789 the farmers' problems were not caused by the distribution of landownership but by the small size of farms and also by seignorial rights. With the rise in grain prices in the second half of the eighteenth century the situation became critical, particularly for those farms that produced insufficient for their own family needs.

The seigneur of the village derived a substantial income from his seignorial rights, even where he owned no land. Even so, this often proved insufficient to meet the rising cost of living, so that lords unearthed all sorts of long-forgotten and defunct rights, to the great indignation of the population. This feudal revival caused a great deal of bad blood until the night of 4 August 1789, when all seignorial and manorial rights were abolished by the National Assembly. During the French Revolution the possessions of the clergy and of the *émigrés* were confiscated. Some of the revolutionaries wanted to distribute free the confiscated properties among the small farmers and those who owned no land at all, but the government was badly in need of money and sold them. The possessions of the aristocracy were largely bought by nominees or relatives of the *émigrés*. Church property was bought by wealthy citizens and by the larger farmers, who also benefited from the distribution of common land. As a consequence, in the country at large, the gap widened between *laboureurs* and *manoeuvriers*.

V. *Serfdom in Central and Eastern Europe*

Eastern and western Europe moved in contrary directions in the trend to or from political and economic freedom or serfdom in the period between 1200 and 1800. In western Europe, to the west of the river Elbe, the manorial system, feudal relations between lords and peasants, and medieval villeinage disappeared between the twelfth and the sixteenth centuries. After 1500, and in many countries some centuries earlier, the rural population was free to move, and to buy and sell land. The peasants were free in marriage, free to inherit, and to own land or use it under different types of tenancy: leasehold, copyhold, half-share lease or feudal vassalage. They paid rents in money or kind, or they paid dues when they took possession of the farm or inherited the property. In most countries the dissolution of the manorial system started in the twelfth or thirteenth century and was completed by the sixteenth century.

On the other side, in the trans-Elbian regions of eastern and central Europe, where the rural population during the Middle Ages had perhaps enjoyed *more* freedom than the peasants in western Europe, the situation deteriorated after the early fifteenth century. A process of increasing serfdom set in, culminating during the second half of the eighteenth century in Russia, where people were bought and sold like cattle, enjoying virtually no rights. Their heritage comprised only obligations, and freedom was almost unknown. According to an eighteenth-century ordinance the serfs had to give tacit obedience to their masters in everything that was not contrary to the laws of the land. Their condition was not so much serfdom as pure slavery.

The problem of the underlying causes of this particular revival of serfdom in central and eastern Europe has long engaged the attention of historians. Their answers vary according to which countries were involved: eastern Germany, Austria, Hungary, Bohemia, Poland or Russia. Their answers vary, too, according to their viewpoints: whether they are Marxists or non-Marxists, German or Slav historians.

The question is whether there were any factors common to all these countries which would explain, at least in some measure, the increase of serfdom in central and eastern Europe. Allowance must of course be made for varying political circumstances. Serfdom in Austria was not the same as in Bohemia, Hungary, Poland or Russia. But however the systems of serfdom may have differed, they all shared a development entirely contrary to the process of steady emancipation in western Europe.

The characteristics of central and eastern European serfdom emerge more clearly when it is compared with medieval villeinage in western Europe. There are similarities and differences. They were similar in legal status, since both villeins and serfs were tied to the soil or the farm, in which they both had hereditary rights. In fact they enjoyed more security than a modern leaseholder who has rented the farm for a term of years. In both systems, in villeinage as in serfdom, we find obligatory payments, mostly in kind – the Russian *obrok* – the entry dues, the payments for marriage and death, and the purchase price of freedom.

The greatest differences between villeinage and serfdom appeared in the exploitation of the demesne or *réserve*. In those western European countries where villeinage existed in all its aspects, there were relatively few manors each with a large demesne, farmed by the landlord with labour services rendered by the villeins. Generally, the farms belonging to a manor were dispersed over a number of villages, and other owners also had farms in these villages. Sometimes farms were so widely scattered that many of the farms and their villeins were too remote from the manor to use the labour of the villeins on the demesne. In central and eastern Europe (mostly in eastern Germany, Poland and Bohemia), it was not uncommon for whole villages to belong to one landlord; in other places, although scattered, isolated farms might also belong to one man. In Russia the fields of the estate were interspersed with the peasants' plots. Large landownership did not always include large concerns.[1]

The manorial system, using villeins for the tillage of the demesne, was most widespread in western Europe during the Merovingian and Carolingian periods. In trans-Elbian Europe, this type of service increased during the sixteenth century and became an important part of the whole system (*barshchina* in Russia). Serfs were compelled to render services on three or five days, sometimes even six or seven days a week. These services consisted of ploughing, sowing, harrowing and harvesting on the arable of the demesne, further threshing, haymaking, and carrying produce to the manors or to the export harbours (e.g. in Poland). Where labour for six or seven days a week was exacted, the work could sometimes be done by a son of the peasant; otherwise the serf was obliged to feed and pay an extra hand to work almost exclusively on the demesne of the lord. In this way, the labour costs of cultivating the demesne were transferred to the farming serfs. Similarly, they had to bear the costs of cart-horses, oxen, carts, agricultural implements and tools, all of which had to be supplied by the serfs working on the demesne. Thus the running costs of the demesne for the lord were reduced to the absolute minimum, in a way unheard of in western Europe. In central and eastern Germany another kind of service was known, the *Gesindezwangsdienst*, first mentioned in 1534 in Brandenburg. All the children of the serfs could be compelled to work as domestics in the house of the lord for one to four years. The *Gesindezwangsdienst* was an extra burden over and above the 'normal' agricultural services.

In practice, a limit to the extension of the demesne was imposed by the ratio between the size of the demesne and the number of serfs. Since the serfs had to raise their own food from their own land as well as work in the fields of the demesne, a balance necessarily had to be

[1] Cf. M. Confino: 'grands domaines... mais n'étaient certainement pas de grandes exploitations', in *Domaines et seigneurs en Russie vers la fin du XVIIIᵉ siecle* (1963), p. 117.

struck between the size of the demesne's fields and those farmed by the serfs for their own use.

It is difficult to estimate how much the lords saved by farming their own demesnes. In Poland the revenue from a demesne equivalent to two to four farms was said to be worth as much to the lord as a village with ten to fifteen farms cultivated by peasants who paid him in money or in kind.

In western as well as in central and eastern Europe the seignorial lords enjoyed valuable economic monopolies. They might be seised of seignorial rights over watermills, windmills, fisheries, bakery ovens, the sale of wine, beer and liquors, the trade in oxen, etc. Fisheries were an important source of revenue for lords in Bohemia; as were the ox trade in Hungary, the sale of wine in Austria and Hungary, and the profits of breweries and distilleries in Poland. Bohemian and Hungarian landowners made much of these dues in the sixteenth century, and in the eighteenth century many Polish lords received larger revenues from beer and liquor monopolies than from farming their demesnes, since grain prices were particularly low in that period.

In western European countries, by the end of the sixteenth century, central governments had frequently taken over many of the legal and administrative functions of the local lords. In central and eastern Europe, state governments, whether voluntarily or under coercion from the nobility, disclaimed all responsibility for jurisdiction and administration, especially during the seventeenth and eighteenth centuries. The serfs were deprived and defenceless, wholly at the mercy of the landed proprietors who were also their judges. In some countries, the landlords were also responsible for the collection of taxes and the drafting of soldiers into the army, as in Russia.

So far only the contrasts between east and west have been stressed. This, however, oversimplifies a much more complex reality. Remnants of the manorial system survived in many regions of western Europe from the sixteenth to the eighteenth centuries. Villeinage existed, e.g., in Germany and the Low Countries until the French Revolution or the French occupation that followed it. But we should not underrate the prestige of these villeins. In the eastern Netherlands the largest farms in the eighteenth century were those of the villeins, since it was prohibited to divide them by inheritance. As a result, the villeins were sometimes the wealthiest men in the village, and their annual obligations were lower than those of the ordinary peasants, since they were subject to heavy payments only at death, marriage or acceptance of the farm. On the other hand, in France, Germany and the Netherlands, the landed gentry enjoyed economic monopolies (mills, tolls, ferries) and other rights, such as hunting, which could be a heavy burden on the rural population.

The other side of the coin was represented by those freeholders and peasants who lived quite well in central and eastern Europe. Farmers enjoying a greater degree of freedom could be found on the frontiers of Hungary and the Ukraine, in the mountains of Transylvania and in inhospitable regions like northern Russia and Siberia.

In some central and eastern European areas, e.g. the lands of the Habsburg monarchy, Prussia and Saxony, governments, or rather princes, took an interest in the social and legal status of the peasants. Sometimes their motive was humanitarian, but as often as not their concern was for the peasants as taxpayers and potential soldiers for the army. To this end legislation was introduced to protect the serfs from tyrannical landlords. Already by a law of 1597 labour services in Upper Austria had been limited to two weeks a year, though this did not prevent other services being increased between 1710 and 1720. The so-called *Robot-patente* of 1680 and 1738 limited the services of the serfs in Bohemia, Moravia and Silesia to a maximum of three days a week, while on Crown and State lands in Bohemia and Moravia services were completely abolished in 1781 and 1783. Frederic II of Prussia legislated against the expulsion of peasants by landlords seeking to enlarge their demesnes. In 1749 he prohibited *Bauernlegen* and in 1759 the sale of landless serfs. Since any policy of peasant protection was directed against the nobility, it could only be carried out by strong governments.

In countries where the nobility were strong, as they were in Mecklenburg, Upper Lusatia and Swedish Pomerania, the serfs were entirely at the mercy of the noblemen. In Mecklenburg, even the expulsion of peasants was legally permitted in 1755. The policy of the princes to protect the peasants had nevertheless started a process that was to end in the abolition of serfdom in the whole of central and eastern Europe during the nineteenth century.

The river Elbe marks the rough demarcation line in Germany between freedom and serfdom, although to the west of the Elbe, in the Altmark of Brandenburg, the eastern German *Gutsbesitz* also existed.

The rise of serfdom was a long process of gradual erosion, not a sudden destruction of old liberties. It is very difficult to mark any date or year as an exact starting point. In some countries serfdom developed out of medieval conditions. In the Slav countries the original population had been unfree to some extent during the early Middle Ages. When Christianity spread to Russia the Church acquired large estates which it farmed itself, as in Byzantium. Such an estate is first mentioned in 1146. Later, the nobility too started farming their large landed properties, and there are some indications that the same thing happened in Poland. It is not known to what extent these estates disappeared during the wars and the domination by the Tartars in the thirteenth and fourteenth centuries. Probably there are some connections with the demesnes worked by serf labour in the later Middle Ages.

In the fourteenth or fifteenth century demesnes with serf labour are to be found throughout central and eastern Europe possibly as early as the fourteenth century in eastern Germany, Poland and Russia, certainly in the Land of the Teutonic Knights after their defeat by the Polish armies at Tannenberg in 1410, in Hungary after the Peasants' War of 1514 and the conquest of part of the country by the Ottoman Empire in 1526, and in Bohemia about 1500.

Originally the domanial services were not particularly heavy: in the fourteenth century in Poland, fifteen days a year were required, the same as in Upper Austria after 1597. In 1421 in Poland they were extended to one day a week. This became the rule in Russia too at the end of the fifteenth century and in Hungary after 1514. During the sixteenth century services were further increased to three days a week in Poland and Russia. In Hungary at the end of the sixteenth century there was no fixed limit. In Russia they were increased from five to seven days a week in the eighteenth century, except in those few provinces where they had been fixed at three or four days a week.

Serfdom was at its height in most of these countries during the sixteenth and seventeenth centuries: in chronological order, in the Land of the Teutonic Knights after 1526, in Russia during the second half of the sixteenth century under the reign of Tsar Ivan IV, especially between 1570 and 1580; in Hungary and Wallachia at the end of the sixteenth century; in Bohemia after the Battle of the White Mountain in 1620; in Moldavia after 1621, in Moravia in 1628, in many eastern German countries during and after the Thirty Years War, in Poland after that war and the war against Sweden (1655–60), in Estonia after the wars at the end of the seventeenth century. In eastern Prussia the position of the serfs deteriorated again after the plague at the beginning of the eighteenth century, and the condition of Russian serfs became worse than ever after 1762 and especially after 1775.

There is no single satisfactory explanation for this protracted growth of the demesnes and the accompanying deterioration in social conditions. We can, however, make a distinction between the economic, demographic, political and institutional aspects of the problem, and several historians have examined more than one of these aspects.

From an economic standpoint the consumer market and grain prices are the two most important factors. German and Polish historians have emphasized the significance of the export of grain to western Europe. It has been argued that Holland and England profited from the economic weakness of the countries in eastern Europe. This foreign market theory has been applied to eastern Germany, Poland and, less convincingly to Bohemia. There were grain exports from Wallachia and Moldavia to the large consumer market at Constantinople. Some historians even consider the theory of the export market as offering a general explanation of the whole phenomenon of serfdom: everywhere serfdom is seen as a consequence of the foreign demand of grain. But even in Poland, grain was only exported from certain regions bordering on the Vistula which were well situated for transport. Another weakness of the foreign market theory is that some of the countries with domanial serfdom during these centuries (like Russia, Hungary and Bohemia) did not export grain at all. In these areas, the *domestic* market is held to be the explanation, e.g. in eastern Germany, Upper Lusatia, Silesia, Russia and Bohemia.

Market theories, foreign or domestic, cannot, however, completely account for the demesne system. From the sixteenth to the eighteenth century, the demesnes in some countries produced largely for their own needs alone, that is for the landlords and their many servants. Such was the case in Russia and Hungary, and the Hungarian historian Pach has given a convincing explanation of this phenomenon. In the territorial expansion of the demesnes, more and more serfs became involved; as a result of their impoverishment, the domestic market weakened, while the large estates became more and more self-sufficient. Monetary economy gave way to natural economy. The whole process tended towards economic, technical and cultural stagnation. Is this conclusion not inconsistent with the pursuit of gain by the landlords? We should not forget, however, that the general trend of the economy was depressed; in this situation a small group of large landowners seized the opportunity to make great profits at the cost of the common good.

Some historians consider the markets themselves less important than the prices fetched in them. The secular trend in the relations between grain prices and the prices of other goods must also have had its influence on the development of the demesne system. Every prolonged rise in grain prices must have spurred on the landlords to increase their profits by expanding their demesnes. During the fifteenth and sixteenth centuries this must have been the intention of the landlords in eastern Germany, Bohemia, and after 1530, in Upper Lusatia; during the second half of the eighteenth century it occurred in eastern Germany and Russia. The theory of the relation between the origin and expansion of serfdom and prevailing prices has also been generalized by some historians, who associated the increase in demesne farming with the depreciation of money.

Conversely, an economic regression might also prompt landlords to enlarge their properties and to make greater demands on the serfs. Lower grain prices would compel owners to produce more grain in order to maintain their former revenues. At the same time, wages fell relatively less, so that real wages rose. To economize on labour costs, landlords demanded more services, for services were cheap labour, if often ineffective labour. The evolution of the serfdom system has thus been attributed to the decrease in grain prices and economic regression in eastern Germany (1650–90), in Russia during the fourteenth and fifteenth centuries and after 1550, and in Hungary during the seventeenth century.

Other scholars have been less interested in markets and prices than in labour. After periods of war and epidemics which caused serious depopulation, there was inevitably a shortage of labour to work the fields deserted by the peasants. The shortage of labourers obliged the landowners to increase the services of the remaining serfs. Hence an exodus from the countryside, which could be prevented only by tying the serfs to the land.

Depopulation has been offered as the explanation of increasing serfdom in Russia during the thirteenth century and after 1550, in Hungary after 1526, in eastern Germany after the Thirty Years War, in Estonia at the end of the seventeenth century, and in eastern Prussia again, after the plague at the beginning of the eighteenth century.

Many historians have attributed the increase of serfdom in trans-Elbian Europe to war, and it cannot be denied that some of the wars left a fearful aftermath, especially the Thirty Years War and the war against Sweden in Poland (1655–60). But a whole series of lesser wars is also blamed for the exacerbation of serfdom: the defeat of the Teutonic Knights in 1410 at Tannenberg and the Peasants' War in 1525 in the Land of the Teutonic Knights, the Peasants' War of 1514 and the conquest of Hungary by the Ottoman Empire, especially the war between Austria and the Turks in 1593–1606, the end of the Hussite War in 1534 and the Battle of the White Mountain in 1620 in Bohemia, the wars in Russia in the latter half of the sixteenth century (1558–82) and in the beginning of the seventeenth century (1605–13); the Thirty Years War in eastern Germany and Poland, the war against the Swedes in Poland, and finally the wars at the end of the seventeenth century in Estonia.

Changes in institutions or internal policy may also have affected the growth of the demesne system: e.g., the emergence of the *pomestye* – the smaller demesnes given to vassals who were more dependent on the tsar than the old nobility – during the second half of the sixteenth century, the collapse of the central government after 1490 in Hungary, and the behaviour of the new nobility (mostly of foreign origin) placed in power by the Habsburg monarchs after 1620 in Bohemia.

Most historians, however, tend to emphasize the significance of the increase in the power of the nobility, their juridical function and their commercial motivation, as causes of the growth of serfdom. This trend was accompanied by a weakening of the central government in Poland, Hungary, Mecklenburg, Upper Lusatia and Swedish Pomerania; though the demesne system sometimes gained ground also during the reigns of strong monarchs, as in Bohemia after 1620, in Hungary under Leopold I, and in Russia under Peter I and Catherine II.

Internal politics may even have been relatively uninfluential, as they were in Hungary during the sixteenth century, when the country was split up into three parts: the west under the Habsburgs, the south under the Ottoman Empire, and the east remaining independent. Despite the different types of government, the demesne system, still in its infancy at that time in Hungary, evolved along similar lines in all three regions, with the Habsburg region taking the initiative. We have another example of this in the Swedish territories in northern Germany after 1648, when the demesnes of Swedish Pomerania show the same pattern of growth as those of the other surrounding trans-Elbian countries. In the cis-Elbian bishopric of Verden, also under Swedish rule, the land was farmed under conditions similar to those in other western German countries.

To demonstrate the complexity of the demesne question still further, it may be noted that all the foregoing arguments to explain the rise of serfdom have also been adduced to account for the end of villeinage in the western European countries during the late Middle Ages. These arguments include, for instance, the rise of grain prices during the thirteenth and early fourteenth centuries, the prosperity of the towns and the expansion of the markets, the new settlements and the population increase, and, on the other side, the long period of depression after 1350 with low grain prices and the shortage of manpower caused by epidemics and wars.

In the preceding observations some basic facts have been overlooked. The countries where the demesne system throve were *grain-producing* areas. Nearly all the large estates employing considerable numbers of serfs grew corn either for the market or for auto-consumption. The countries of eastern and central Europe at that time were overwhelmingly rural; agriculture was basic to their survival. Yet in all these countries grain yields were low, particularly so between 1600 and 1750, for the most part because of the effects of war and the inefficiency of the demesne system with its forced labour. The yields of rye were no higher than 3·7 times the seed sown. Yields generally were markedly lower than in western Europe at that time, lower even than in southern Europe and western Germany. This means that in eastern and central

Europe – a rural society with low grain yields – the gross national product must have been low too. It is uncertain if the acreage of corn crops remained the same, but production per acre had decreased after the sixteenth century to the same low level as during the Middle Ages. On the other hand, the commitments of the governments had increased. The foreign policy of the states of eastern Europe led to wars against economically more advanced countries, for which higher yields from taxation were needed.

In societies with low grain yields, a fixed ratio exists between the rural and non-rural population. The growth of the latter was restricted to certain limits; otherwise its growth would have been at the expense of the producers themselves, i.e. the peasants. In the non-rural sectors of the population, the number of nobles and clergy had also increased, and the whole situation indicates that the balance between the rural and non-rural populations had been upset.

Some trade and industry certainly existed in eastern Europe, although it was often in foreign hands. Most of the towns were small, and a real urban middle class did not exist. The result was that in Hungary and Poland, for instance, the stagnation in economic life reduced the towns more and more to the level of rural communities. This did not inhibit the governments of central and eastern Europe, who chose to pursue seventeenth- and eighteenth-century policies with the resources of the twelfth and thirteenth centuries. To make the situation still worse, there was virtually no productive investment; indeed, opportunities for increasing production were few and far between. The princes spent their revenues on armies, on the building of palaces and on large royal households. Many a wealthy nobleman followed their example, living with a large retinue in magnificent castles and country seats, while many of the lower aristocracy scarcely owned the means to exist. From all sides rose a chorus of complaints about the debts of the noblemen and farmers.

Opportunities for lowering the cost of cultivating grain were limited. There was little latitude in the proportion of the yield needed for re-sowing, implements and tools were crude and in any case generally belonged to the serfs. In the demesne system the lords could shed the cost of labour on to the serfs, and did so. For the farmers this meant a reduction in their standard of living to an unprecedented level of penury. The revolutionary effects of the oppression of the rural population were plain to see. This was a period of frequent peasant wars and revolts in the whole of central and eastern Europe, and especially in Russia, Bohemia, Austria, Poland, Silesia and Lusatia. The most important of these were the risings of Stepan Razin (1670–1) and Yemelyan Pugachyov (1773–5) in Russia. Both were violently crushed.

In western Europe too there were vast areas of poverty, where the standard of life was not very different from that in central and eastern Europe. But throughout this period in the west these were always offset by scattered pockets of highly developed and diversified farming. Such areas of high productivity, some of medieval origin, others in densely populated regions, were completely lacking from the scene of central and eastern Europe.

VI. *Social Stratification, Prices and Population*

During the last twenty years, important research has been done into the fields of historical demography and of the secular economic fluctuations between 1200 and 1800. Attempts have been made to relate the population increase between 1500 and 1620 (1650) and after 1750 to the rise in prices, which happened almost simultaneously. Equally, historians have paid attention to the relation between the population decrease or standstill between 1620 (1650) and 1750 and the fall in prices. There has, however, been no agreement among scholars on the effect of these fluctuations in population and price ratios on the various groups of the population. According to some historians, with the farmers in mind, those periods with relatively high grain prices were favourable; others have thought the periods with relatively low grain prices better on account of the high real wages of the wage earners. The divergence of opinion is largely a consequence of insufficient research into the social structure of the pre-industrial society.

The effects of short-term fluctuations in prices differ from the effects of long-term changes in price ratios. The population – or at any rate the poorer sections of it – could only react passively to sudden disruptions such as bad harvests and the high prices which accompanied them; faced with starvation, they simply had to make the best of it by eating whatever was edible. Changes in price ratios over a longer period could lead to structural changes, in production for instance, through the application of new techniques, the investment of capital or the employment of more or fewer workers. In the consumer sector, alterations in price ratios could result in changes in the spending pattern and diet, with the attendant risks of malnutrition. Changes in the producer and consumer sectors would cause a shift among the different groups, affecting their numerical relationships to one another and their economic and social positions. An increase or decrease in the total population will not of course result in a proportional change throughout the various groups, but there will be a shift between the different groups, relatively as well as absolutely, since the existing balance between them has been disturbed.

Because not all producers react in the same way to changes in price ratios and population, criteria must be found for classifying persons or farms which do respond in a similar way, in order to arrive at a social stratification of producers. Similarly, consumers will have to be divided into groups according to their patterns of behaviour under changing conditions. There will be people or families whose income and expenditure on food will be similar. A social stratification of consumers is therefore also essential. The social stratification of producers is by no means the same as that of consumers, since the former comprise a much smaller group than the latter – the number of consumers consisting of virtually the entire population, with the exception of babies. Moreover, so far from being identical, the producers' and consumers' interests often clash. And, of course, we are still left with the problem that many producers consume part of their own production.

So far, historical writing has given comparatively little attention to this stratification and to the widely differing reactions of these varying groups. It has often been assumed that all farmers or, in the case of consumers, the entire population reacted in the same way. It has not been appreciated that there are two quite different categories (producers and consumers), and that the criteria applied to producers are not at all the same as those that should be applied to consumers.

When we study the effects of price fluctuations and population on the various groups of the rural population, we can observe that an increase in the prices of the most important foodstuffs in relation to the prices of other goods and wages favours those family holdings which send part of their production to the market each year. If they pay their workers in wages, they profit even more, while this trend is less favourable if payment is made in kind. What applies to wages also applies to the payment of rents and other dues, in money or in kind. Family holdings which can only produce just enough for their own needs neither gain nor lose from price increases. A relative increase in price adversely affects farms not producing enough for their own needs and those marketing products which are not foodstuffs. Conversely, a relative fall in prices favours those farms which do not produce enough foodstuffs for the market; farms producing for the market are at a disadvantage. A line dividing favourable from unfavourable economic factors runs right through the farming community. The most important distinction is between the extent of the farmer's selling and buying on the open market. Farms that manage to be self-supporting are in a neutral buffer zone.

In view of the small scope for technical development and capital investment between 1500 and 1800, a growth of population would result in an increased number of smallholdings and cottages, but not of large farms. In general, an increase in the rural population will cause a downward trend on the social ladder. The number of people affected by the market situation will grow and the non-agrarian population will increase at a faster rate than the total population, because there are too few opportunities in agriculture. When a rise in the mortality rate brings down the population, the small farmers are the more vulnerable because of malnutrition. On the larger farms under these circumstances, many relatives would tend to remain on one farm (*Familienhöfe*, patriarchal families, three-generation households); or several brothers, married or single, would stay together (*affrèrements, frérêches*). These large households appeared especially in areas with poor soil conditions, during periods of decrease in population and during periods of relatively high wages, since labour costs could be reduced by offering the members of the household board and lodging but no wages. We find these *Familienhöfe* and *frérêches* during the later Middle Ages and in the seventeenth century, e.g. in Languedoc, Burgundy, Switzerland and Austria. In Russia, households on farms became larger between 1678 and 1715, a trend caused by a new tax on houses in 1679.

When we turn to the study of the influence of fluctuations in price ratios and in population on consumer groups, we find that a relative increase in the prices of food as against other goods and wages will adversely affect almost all consumer groups, and in particular the non-agrarian consumers. This kind of price trend, however, has advantages for the farmers who produce for their own consumption as well as for the market, since, from their point of view, their role of producer is more important than that of consumer. The situation is also profitable for those who receive payment in kind from the farm and then sell it on the market, and for such people as lessors who are paid in money, if such payments are linked to the market prices. But those who receive a fixed income from farming are at a disadvantage when prices go up. A relative fall in prices is favourable for most consumer groups. Changes in price ratios will not affect the groups who neither produce for the market nor appear as buyers.

A growth of population will result in an increase in the number of non-agrarian consumers, and especially those whose income does not meet the cost of the essential foodstuffs. It will also lead to an increase in the number of subsistence farmers, agrarian consumers who can only just produce sufficient for their own needs. A decrease in population will affect groups who are not able (or only just able) to provide for their own needs.

It will now be clear why a primary consideration is the extent to which farms produce essential food for the market or have to buy food there themselves. Between the two extremes are farms that are able to produce just enough to supply their own needs. For the purpose of social stratification it should be important to know just where this 'neutral zone' lies. The question is – what is the minimum acreage needed for the production of foodstuffs for an average household, mostly estimated at five persons? The minimum-sized family farm, however, is not an absolute figure which applies everywhere and under all circumstances. Its size depends e.g. on the fertility of the soil, the crops under cultivation, the rotation system, the mentality and adaptability of the farmer, the prices of farm produce, the obligations in the form of rents, tithes, rates and other dues. A further difficulty is that the food, especially of the small farmers, consisted not only of cereals but also of beans, peas, carrots, cabbage, turnips etc.

In Flanders during the seventeenth century, an average household of five persons could live on 2 acres of wheat or $1\frac{3}{4}$ acres of rye. Elsewhere in the seventeenth century, in Overijssel, for instance, the smallholdings, usually worked by the owners themselves, consisted of $2\frac{1}{2}$ to $3\frac{1}{2}$ acres of arable land. The larger, more usual, family farms had between 10 and $12\frac{1}{2}$ acres of arable land, but these were generally tenant farms. From their yields, payment had to be made for rent – usually a quarter of the harvest – tithes, government taxes and sometimes other dues. In Auvergne the minimum acreage for a lowland farm was $7\frac{1}{2}$ acres; for a farm in the mountains, $12\frac{1}{2}$ acres. In Russia, 10 acres was considered a minimum arable acreage, but there the takings had to cover all kinds of dues.

The quantities which were produced on the larger farms for the market vary according to the acreage of the arable land and the circumstances of the harvest, so that it is impossible to give exact figures or percentages. It is estimated that in the western European countries, about half the yield reached the market, as compared with 20–25 per cent in the eastern European countries. The yield ratios being lower here, a higher percentage had to be reserved for seed. The degree of auto-consumption was still high. In 1570 the Castilian farmers consumed about half of the national production.

In many areas a traditional classification of the rural population divides it into two or three groups, mostly according to the size of the holdings:

1. Peasants owning at least one pair of horses or draught-oxen.
2. Peasants possessing no horses, with only the strength of their arms to help them: smallholders, cottars and day-labourers.

Marc Bloch and Soboul use this classification (*laboureurs* on the one hand, and *manoeuvriers* or *brassiers*, on the other). Génicot inserts for

Table 15.   *Landownership in Hallwil, Switzerland, 1693*

Description	Percentage
Families without any arable land	19·8
Families with holdings of 0·25–7·5 acres	59·2
Families with holdings of more than 7·5 acres	21·0

Namur an intermediate group: the peasants with one horse, past its best, a single cow or a heifer. In Saint-Martin-de-la-Mer (Auxois) in 1442, the population is classified into: *laboureurs*, who have four oxen, *demi-laboureurs*, who have two oxen or cows, and *manoeuvriers*, who have no draught-animals. The peasants of Saxony could be divided into three classes: farmers, *Gärtner* and *Häusler*. The *Gärtner* had smallholdings never larger than a ¼ farm, with a few cattle and sometimes no horse. The *Häusler* had little or no land; they were day-labourers who occasionally followed some home industry as well. In Bohemia we find during the eighteenth century: *Ganzbauer*, with holdings from 30 to 60 acres, *Häusler* (cottars here) and *Inleute*, the servants or day-labourers. In Brunswick were four classes: *Ackerhöfe* or *volle Meierhöfe*, *Halbspänner-höfe* or *Halbmeierhöfe* (half-farms), *Grosskothöfe* (larger cottars) and *Kleinkothöfe* (smaller cottars). In other regions different terms were in use, but nearly everywhere we meet the classification into two to four groups. This distribution applies to England, France, Belgium, eastern Netherlands, Alsace, Switzerland, Saxony, eastern Germany, Silesia and Poland. One can assume that the large farmers and those with a 'normal' family business produced for the market. The smallholders will in general have been subsistent farmers; the workers in the rural home industries and some of the day-labourers will have been largely dependent on the market for their provisions.

For some regions it is possible to illustrate the influence that a rise in population had on the distribution of the various groups in rural society; everywhere we can observe a deterioration of the situation of the poorer groups. In Hallwil (Switzerland) a distinction was made between *Hofbauern*, who ran large or medium-sized farms, and *Tauner*, who were smallholders, day-labourers and artisans, with little or no land. The *Tauner* probably first emerged during the pre-1300 increase of population. During the sixteenth and seventeenth centuries, when the population trebled within 130 years, the *Tauner* class increased with great rapidity. Many younger sons of farmers also merged into this group. In 1693 only one rural family in five had a farm capable of producing enough grain for its own consumption. The distribution of land to families was as shown in Table 15.

The smallholders with less than 7·5 acres eked out their living by secondary occupations, such as vine growing, carting and cattle trading.

Table 16. *Landownership in Lespignan, Languedoc*

| | 1492 | | 1607 | |
Size	Number of farms	Acreage of arable land	Number of farms	Acreage of arable land
66 acres or larger	5	1,112·4	12	1,624·8
12–24 acres	59	1,659·0	44	1,239·6
Smaller than 12 acres	39	219·0	115	498·6
Total	103	2,990·4	171	3,363·0

In Lespignan (Languedoc) we see a decrease of the middle groups and an increase of the large farms and of the cottars during the period between 1492 and 1607 – as shown in Table 16. Holdings of less than 20 *setérées* (12 acres) could scarcely produce food enough for two adult persons.

In Argelliers, northwest of Montpellier, on very unfertile soil, 54 acres were necessary for the subsistence of the peasant and his family. Here the small farms with an average acreage of 10 acres increased from 3 in 1531 to 34 in 1664.

In middle and eastern Germany the *Gärtner* (smallholders) are already mentioned in the thirteenth century. The population increase after the end of the fifteenth century led to a sharp rise in their number; the *Häusler* (cottars) grew in many regions during the seventeenth and eighteenth centuries, as may be seen in Table 17.

Saxony possessed in 1750 85 per cent more inhabitants than in 1550. The numbers of farms and smallholdings at these two dates were:

	1550	1750
Farms	43,150	42,787
Smallholdings and cottages	4,000	36,700

The number of farms in Saxony had remained almost the same since the colonization period of the twelfth and thirteenth centuries. The increase of population had led in particular to a great rise in the number of cottars and day-labourers, especially in the mountainous regions; they found their employment in mining, timber-felling, sheep-farming and textiles. The areas where there were most cottars in 1750 became in the nineteenth century the industrial districts.

An increase of population and a corresponding rise in the number of cottars and day-labourers was also evident in the eighteenth century in the bishoprics of Osnabrück and Münster, as well as in Brunswick, in Flanders, in Burgundy and in Sweden.

Table 17. *Rural stratification in middle and eastern German areas,*
1374–1807 (in percentages)

Region	Year	Farmers (*Bauern*)	Smallholders (*Gärtner*)	Cottars (*Häusler*)
Marienstern	1374	88·6	11·4	—
	1777	30·5	14·5	54·9
Hoyerswerda	1568	78·4	12·7	8·9
	1620	61·4	15·7	22·9
	1777	55·7	14·1	30·2
Königsbrück	1560	81·3	18·7	—
	1670	59·0	35·1	5·9
	1750	58·0	27·0	15·0
	1777	47·4	21·4	31·2
	1807	54·9	12·3	32·8
52 small villages in	1700	66·1	13·2	20·7
Swedish Pomerania[a]	1760	28·4	1·5	70·1

[a] Increase of population in Swedish Pomerania between 1700 and 1760 was 76·6 per cent.

Development over a wider area can best be illustrated by figures from the province of Overijssel. It can be ascertained from the tax registers that in 1602 the composition of the agricultural population was as follows.

Farmers	3,718	with two or more horses, size of farm greater than 6 acres
Cottars	2,336	with one or no horse, size of farm less than 6 acres
Total	6,054	listed in tax registers

Judging by the 1795 census, with regard to the occupation followed and the number of cattle kept, the population of that year was composed of:

Farmers	4,614	with four or more cattle and some servants
Cottars	3,429	with fewer than four cattle and no servants
Casual labourers	1,803	without cattle
Total	9,846	heads of family employed in agriculture

The indices for the population growth in Overijssel between 1602 and 1795 are as given in Table 18.

The indices in Table 18 show that the agricultural population did not

Table 18.   *Population in Overijssel, 1602/1675–1795*

	Year	Indices	Year	Indices
Total population	1675	100	1795	217·6
Non-agricultural population	1675	100	1795	291·2
Agricultural population	1602	100	1795	162·6
Farmers on family-sized farms	1602	100	1795	124·1
Cottars on smallholdings	1602	100	1795	146·9
Cottars and day-labourers	1602	100	1795	224·0

Note. The population figure for 1675 is not likely to have been very different from that for 1602. In 1602 the number of day-labourers was still very small, so that the index of day-labourers without cottars in 1795 is excessively high.

A schematic survey of changes in the province of Overijssel between 1700 and 1795 is given in Fig. 1, below.

grow as rapidly as the total population, so that a proportion of the increase between 1602 and 1795 had to find jobs in the non-agricultural sectors. In 1602, farmers still formed the largest group of the agricultural population (61·4 per cent), but by 1795 they were less than half (46·9 per cent), while the cottars had maintained their relative numbers (38·6 per cent of the agricultural population in 1602, 34·8 per cent in 1795). Owing to the steep rise in population, there was insufficient living space for large numbers of country dwellers, even as cottars. A large group of day-labourers developed, amounting to 18·3 per cent of the entire agricultural population in 1795, some settling in arable districts, but the large majority in stock-farming areas.

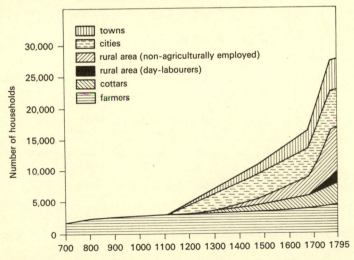

Fig. 1. Population/number of households in the province of Overijssel.

A comparison of the population growth between 1602 and 1795 with the increase of arable acreage and grassland and the number of horses, pigs and sheep is shown in Table 19:

Table 19. *Increase of arable acreage and grassland and the number of horses, pigs and sheep in Overijssel, 1602–1749/1844*[*]

(Index: 1602 = 100)

	Year	Indices
Agricultural population	1795	162·6
Acreage of arable land	{ 1749	106·4
	1812	135·6
Acreage of pasture	{ 1749	104·2
	1812	223·3
Number of horses	1812	100·4
Number of pigs	1812	179·0
Number of sheep	1844	80·6

[*] Numbers of cows and oxen in 1602 are not known.

It is obvious from these indices that the increase in the acreage of arable land and pasture during the period 1602–1795 lagged a long way behind the growth of the agricultural population. Farms therefore became smaller and cottar holdings more numerous. The fact that the number of horses remained practically unchanged also indicates that there were not many more medium-sized farms than in 1602. Pig-keeping is characteristic of cottar-farming; we therefore see a great increase in the number of pigs. The decline in the number of sheep was due to the decrease of wasteland during the first half of the nineteenth century.

The rapid growth of the rural *non-agricultural* population includes a striking variety of occupations. In the Low Countries, the emergence of non-agricultural occupations probably dates back to the Middle Ages. Elsewhere the eighteenth century saw a rising demand for artisans to do jobs once done by the farmer himself – carpentry, plastering, roofing etc. Since the farmer no longer had to be the Jack-of-all-Trades, he could specialize in agriculture. It is by no means surprising, then, that in areas of very intensive systems of agriculture the non-agricultural trades had also progressed most rapidly.

From a study of the occupational structure of rural districts during the second half of the eighteenth century in Overijssel and the Veluwe, it appears that out of a total of 21,664 householders of the rural working population, 63·3 per cent were active in agriculture and 36·7 per cent in non-agricultural occupations (industry, trade, transport, finance and social services). Some occupations were common to all sizeable villages:

innkeeper, tailor, carpenter and tradesman; agricultural trades like those of the miller, blacksmith and cartwright and village trades like those of the weaver, roofer, baker and brewer. Less common were such regional occupations as plasterer, surgeon, clog-maker and cooper. Only rarely do we come across the so-called urban occupations of painter, glazier, midwife, apothecary, barber, clockmaker and butcher. Each *kerkdorp* (literally 'church-village', as distinct from hamlets or isolated farms) had a minister, a verger and in most cases a schoolmaster.

Medical care was still on an insignificant scale: in 1795 there was in the province of Overijssel one doctor per 4,000 and one midwife per 8,000 inhabitants. The situation was worse in the rural areas because the doctors and midwives were concentrated in the towns. The same rural deficiency characterized spiritual care and education: one Protestant minister per 1,600, one Roman Catholic priest per 4,300 and one teacher per 900 inhabitants.

The combination of agricultural and other occupations by one man is less widespread than is sometimes thought. It has been argued that the frequent combination of farming with other occupations makes it impossible to separate agrarian and non-agrarian occupations. In Overijssel and the Veluwe there were only 247 instances of mixed occupations (1·1 per cent). In Overijssel the textile industry was already quite separate from agriculture by 1795. In 1675 most of the weavers and spinners still lived on the farms, but around 1725, when the population was rapidly increasing, the majority of the weavers lived in the *kerkdorpen* under very poor conditions.

As the expansion of arable land and the livestock population did not keep pace with the growth of the population, Overijssel became dependent on cereals imported from other areas to supply not only the towns with food, but also the villages and the rural districts. There was insufficient corn and animal proteins available to the population, and this had an adverse effect on the health of the poorer sections. The cottage weavers of Almelo were said to be weak and lacking in energy. Conditions were aggravated by the poor housing in towns and rural areas where people lived in turf huts, sheds, bakehouses and pigsties. Many new 'houses' had a surface area of 4 by 4·5 yards, the height being under 2 yards. House-building also lagged behind the increase in population. During the second half of the eighteenth century the growth came to an end. The population suffered from epidemics and famine, especially after 1770. Overijssel offers a picture – common enough in eighteenth-century Europe – of growth of population in an agrarian society without sufficient development of economic resources.

CHAPTER III

The European Fisheries in Early Modern History

THE FISHERMAN'S CATCH – the 'harvest of the seas' – was subject to unique conditions quite different from those which governed the harvest on land. In many ways it resembled the reward of the hunter rather than that of the farmer; unlike the farm land of Europe, the areas of the great fisheries were subject to occupation, not by tenure depending on law or custom, but by the skill of the fisherman backed, if need be, by force. Their product was subject to natural fluctuations even more complex than those affecting the grain harvest. Commercial fishing required capital equipment – boats, nets and fish houses and salting houses on shore; it also required skills which ordinary seamen did not possess. It was therefore subject to many of the pressures felt by early modern industry. Moreover, being basically a maritime industry, dealing with a highly perishable product, it needed intimate links with shipping and merchant interests.

This chapter concentrates on elucidating the general relationships and constraints which moulded the fishing industry and the fish trade, and the general fortunes of the cod and herring industries, rather than technical considerations (nets, ship design etc.), important though these were. *A priori*, one might have expected a rapid expansion of this source of food during the sixteenth and seventeenth centuries as a response to population pressure, expanding urban markets, the growth of new marketing techniques, and a symbiotic relationship between the mercantile economy and the fishing industry. In so far as these failed to materialize to their fullest extent, the reasons lay in formidable constraints which hindered the development of the fishing industry. They may be summarized as follows.

The pre-industrial economy was as badly equipped to handle a glut as a scarcity. Agricultural and fish prices behaved according to Gregory King's law, which meant that a ten per cent surplus would lower the price by 30 per cent, and a 10 per cent scarcity would raise the price by 30 per cent. Thus a fisherman would be badly hit by a glut, and might even do well out of a degree of scarcity. In all respects the fisherman was particularly vulnerable; the size of his catch was quite unpredictable because of complex natural fluctuations; throughout most of Europe he was a poor man, largely at the mercy of the merchant who could afford to advance money for the fitting out of ships, and pay the high cost of preserving the fish. Even more serious, the fishing fleet was particularly vulnerable to attack in times of war. Its location was predictable; while at work the boats were more or less stationary; they were not designed to be defended; and because of numbers and the need to spread out while fishing, they were difficult to convoy effectively. It is hardly necessary to reiterate Sir George Clark's observation that there were only four years of peace in the seventeenth century to bring home the problems facing the fishermen.

I.   *Sources for the History of Fishing*

One reason why the definitive history of European fishing has yet to be written is that quantitative records concerning fishing pre-1750 are few. The most accessible and widely drawn-on sources, the panegyrics of the English pamphleteers praising the Dutch herring fishery, are usually demonstrably false, even when they claim (as do John Keymor and Sir William Monson) to be based on the consultation of original records, very few of the writers having had any first-hand knowledge of fishing. English contemporary estimates of the size, profits and other attributes of the Dutch fishing fleet have been convincingly disproved by Dr H. Kranenburgh.[1]

It is rarely possible to build up any long-term series of either the total number of ships at work, or more important, the total catch. Some of the best series are reproduced at the end of this chapter. From about the middle of the eighteenth century a larger range of figures becomes available. Unfortunately this coincides with a turning point in the history of European fisheries, which once more begin to grow after a long period of decline or at least stagnation. Post-1760 data bear little relevance to the period 1500–1750 and rightly belong to the history of nineteenth-century pre-steam fishing. Thus the history of early modern fishing has to be built up precariously like a jigsaw puzzle from many scattered sources. Dr Kranenburgh's history of the sea fisheries of Holland, E. Dardel's book on the French herring fishery[2] and Ch. de la Morandière's mammoth *Histoire de la Pêche Française de la Morue dans L'Amèrique Septentrionale, des origines à 1789*, are all distinguished works of this nature. The structure of the fish trade requires even more investigation. The English customs records and the Danish Sound tolls are invaluable for tracing the movements of processed fish, but they often raise as many problems as they solve. Intensive work in Spanish archives would probably yield useful information on the Newfoundland

---

[1] H. A. H. Kranenburgh, *De Zeevisscherij van Holland in den Tijd Republiek* (Amsterdam, 1946), pp. 25–43.
[2] E. Dardel, *La Pêche Harenguière en France* (Paris, 1941).

fisheries' produce arriving in that country. Basically, this chapter rests not only on a summary of published work, but on archival material throughout western Europe.

Scarcity of reliable information makes the resolution of the first problem, the growth of the fisheries in the sixteenth century, insoluble in absolute terms. Even where numbers of ships involved can be compared, their size and the average yield are normally lost. Generally, the fisheries of Europe did grow during this period, but two important fisheries defy this trend. The first is the Scania herring fishery: the reported catches from this fishery are so large as to raise suspicions amounting to disbelief. Nevertheless the virtual extinction of this source of herrings offsets the increase in output of the Low Country herring fishery. In terms of numbers of ships involved, this latter industry may already have been as large by the mid sixteenth century as it was in the seventeenth century. The second problem is that of the English fisheries. Compared with the other European fisheries, the English fisheries were slow to expand. Not until the later 1570s can one say confidently that the English fishing fleets surpassed pre-Reformation levels. The one great area of new endeavour was in North America, but it is possible that the total catch of the English North Seas and Iceland cod fisheries was larger than that of the English Newfoundland fisheries. One thing seems clear; the total yield of the European fisheries did not expand as fast as the average European rate of population expansion.

II. *Natural Fluctuations*

Every type of fishery is subject to enormous fluctuations in the catch: and for many obvious reasons. Storms may prevent the fishermen from putting to sea, or from fishing when they reach the fishing grounds. Winds and fluctuating temperatures add to the natural hazards, not just during the fishing period itself, but during the whole life cycle of the fish. Unfavourable conditions, whether climatic or relating to the fishes' food supply or predators at the time of incubation, could result (as in the case of the North Sea herring) in a bad season three or four years later. There were also long-term cycles and fluctuations. The decline of the Baltic herring fishery in the fifteenth century is a well known, though inadequately investigated, case. The history of climate is still a relatively new topic of research, and the sources for the quantitative history of fishing are so sparse that no precise correlation between long-term climatic changes and the fishing industry during this period can seriously be established.

Fluctuations were most pronounced amongst those sections of the

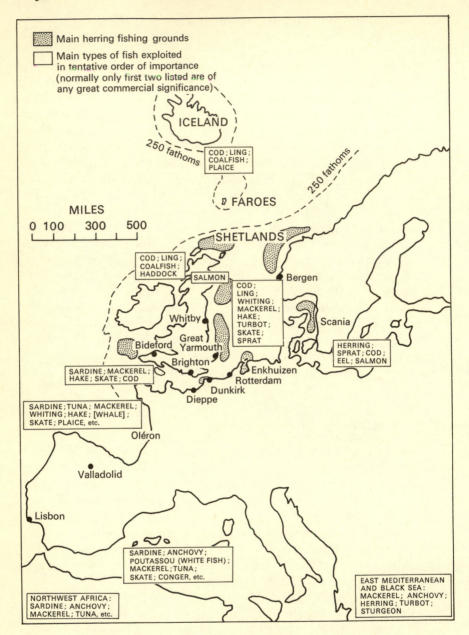

Fig. 2. Major herring fishing grounds, with principal fish caught in various parts of Europe.

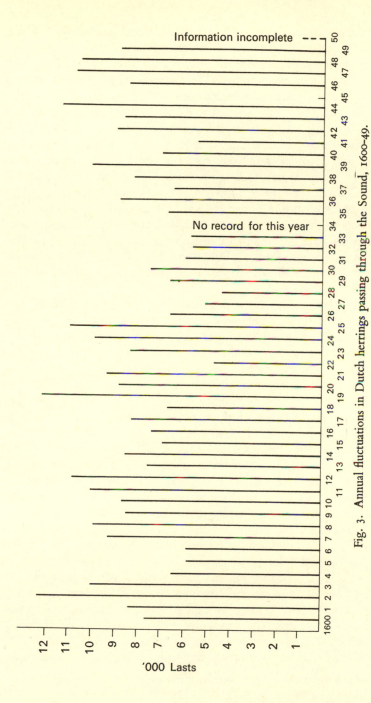

Fig. 3. Annual fluctuations in Dutch herrings passing through the Sound, 1600–49.

industry dependent on *pelagic* species of fish. These include the herring, the mackerel, and the pilchard or sardine. Such fish are caught on a seasonal basis, normally during the spawning season when they appear off the breeding grounds in innumerable shoals. 'Il y a des années ou la sardine [pilchard] abonde et d'autres que l'on n'en pêche que tres peu', the Intendant of Bourneuf reported to the French fishery commissioner in 1717. The same was true of the mackerel; in some years 25,000–30,000 *livres* worth might be taken, 'mais il y a aussy d'autres ou il s'en pêche tres peu'. Similar statements could have been made of any other fishing. The attempts of the English Fishery Company to establish a commercial herring fishery on the Isle of Lewis were frustrated first by the fact that they caught 'more than they had Caske and Hopes for' and in subsequent years because the fish did not come in the quantity and quality expected. Even at Yarmouth, the most prolific of herring fishing grounds where English, Dutch and French fleets were at work, there were periods such as 1610–20 when fish were scarce and of poor quality.[1]

Fishing for *demersal* species such as cod, ling and other white fish was similarly unpredictable. These species fed on the sea-bed and were normally caught by individually-baited hooks on long lines. Naturally it was not possible to observe these fish from the surface, they did not swim in shoals, and the seasons were more flexible, largely depending on whether the weather was suitable for fishing; but the catch depended on whether cod was naturally abundant that year or not, in any given area. The evidence for the English Newfoundland fishery after 1676 suggests that the white fish industry was no more likely to control its catch than the *pelagic* fisheries were. If the shoals of herring or mackerel or pilchards did not appear there was nowhere else to look for them. If one cod fishing ground off the Newfoundland banks, Iceland or the Dogger seemed unprofitable, there were usually others within reasonable reach. Unpredictability was equally the hall-mark of fishing for larger species such as the migratory shoals of tuna in the Mediterranean and Atlantic, and also that aquatic mammal, the whale. The English company fishing off Spitzbergen declared in 1654 that there were 'more losing than gaining voyages made', their profit depending on the fact that every three or four years the whales appeared in great shoals.

These fluctuations created considerable, though not insoluble, problems. The price of different species of fish could show considerable fluctuations at all stages from fisherman to consumer. Those fishing grounds where harvests were most unpredictable were least exploited.

---

[1] Gotthiff Hempel has postulated a regime affecting Swedish herring of 30–60 years of good catches followed by 50–80 bad years (the last good season ending in 1906). Much longer cycles up to 500 years have also been suggested.

The most secure were those industries not dependent on one fishing ground. The Dutch were able to exploit three herring-fishing seasons, the first between June and July around the Orkneys, Shetlands and north of Scotland, during August from Dunbar in Scotland to York-shire, and from the end of September until November off Yarmouth. Contemporaries believed that the Dutch followed the same shoal that annually set out from the Arctic, performed a complete circumnavigation of the British Isles and so home for the next year. In reality the itinerary was not nearly so strenuous. Recent research has shown that these seasons are made up by entirely different populations of fish moving in complicated and mutually contradictory directions. The Yarmouth season was made up of two merging fish populations, one moving coastally and the other shorewards. These facts gave the three main seasons entirely different characteristics. Between 1715 and 1730 Enkhuizen busses achieved large catches from their first fishing voyage, but only a mediocre catch from the second, between 20 and 50 per cent less than the first. From 1731 this situation was entirely altered. The second fishing became prolific, and the first began to yield less.

The Yarmouth deepwater fishermen spent the spring and summer fishing for cod in the North Sea or off Iceland before joining in the herring season. The East Anglian coastal fishermen followed an entirely different pattern, fishing for cod, whiting and flat fish during the winter and spring until the mackerel season in June–July, then for hake from the feast of St Bartholomew until Michaelmas, when they took part in the herring fishery. The fishermen of Barking in Essex, using a trawl net (universally condemned along the western littoral as destroying the fish stocks, yet apparently able to survive despite ordinances to the con-trary), annually migrated up the East Anglian coast. The fishermen of the south coast of England from Brighton eastwards made two ventures into the North Sea, in early summer for cod, and in autumn for herring as well as benefiting from local fishing off the Kent and Sussex coast. The French fishermen of Dieppe were divided into deepwater and coastal fishermen. The 'grands Pescheurs' made four voyages a year: two for herring, once to Yarmouth in the autumn, and in the Channel in the winter, and two for mackerel, once off Ireland in the spring, and once within the Channel off the coast of Normandy. Some of the smaller fishermen did not stop fishing for white and flat fish with lines all the year round; the larger ones stopped for the Channel herring and mackerel fisheries. Each fishing port along the coasts of Europe had its distinctive fishing patterns, each differing slightly from its neighbour, each attempting to evolve a fishing year which lasted as long as possible, taking in as many different species of fish as possible. The only excep-tions to this rule were the Newfoundland fishing boats of the West

Country in England, and the various fishing ports of France which were tied to one voyage a year in search of white fish; the whale fishing fleets; and the inshore fishermen. The latter caught everything they possibly could, with a variety of nets and lines; they survived because, as a general rule, conditions which harmed one species normally proved beneficial to another.

One more problem calls for comment. The fishing industry throughout Europe, with the exception of the Dutch herring buss fishery, was marked by a distinct lack of vertical or horizontal integration. The fisherman was poor, and for each different season he needed different equipment. Herring nets needed smaller meshes than mackerel nets, hake nets were different yet again. Contemporary English estimates put the cost of a fleet of herring nets at 66 per cent of the cost of the rest of the boat. English probate inventories put the value of herring nets at around 20 per cent of many fishermen's movable wealth. Nets were highly vulnerable in storms. In 1715, for instance, a quarter of Yarmouth's town fishing boats lost their nets. Probably the Dieppe coastal fishermen who did not stop for the herring and mackerel season were too poor to own suitable nets. Lines for cod fishing on the other hand cost almost nothing. 'One can truly say that the best trade in Europe', a Frenchman commented in the seventeenth century, 'is to go and fish cod because it costs nothing to have the aforesaid cod, except the effort of fishing and selling.'[1]

III. *The Different Structures of Fishing*

In most ranges of economic activity in Europe there is evidence of a dual economy. Donald Coleman has pointed this out in relation to the cloth industry, and further investigation would shed light on its action in many other spheres. Nowhere is this more true than in the fishing industry. Along the shores of Europe from the Black Sea to Iceland there were subsistence fishermen, a sort of sea-going peasantry, often part-time farmers, fishing first and foremost for their own needs, and only then selling any surplus, or else like the Shetland fishermen using their surplus to buy grain and other foodstuffs. Since many of these communities were in remote areas far from centres of population, whether in Norway, the west coast of Scotland and Ireland, or Brittany, and since most types of fish decay rapidly without preservation, these communities remained almost totally outside the market economy. If enterprising merchants sought them out, they could buy their fish at a fraction of the price at the main fishing ports. At the end of the seven-

[1] Quoted in Braudel, *Capitalism and Material Life 1400–1800* (London, 1967), p. 149.

teenth century, according to John Spreull, Yarmouth North Sea cod fishermen found that they could fill their boats more quickly by buying from the Scots fishermen than by fishing themselves:

I went aboard and saw the Fish, and informed myself of the Master, whence he came with his Loading, who told me he had been at the Norts fishing; concealing the place and magnifying his Fish as caught in some far Countrie, yet when I spent some time with him he told he went with a Ballast Vessel having onlie Provisions to his Companie and some money, straight to Colkenie [in Scotland] where he bought his Salt, and so from that verie place bargain'd with the Fishers for all the Cod they could catch, and so went round our Coast be North Aberdeen till his loading was obtained, which he purchased for a small Price as any conversing in Fishing may conceive, by what we buy the dryed Ling and Cod on our Coast or at Leith, I suppose he peyed not above 1.2 ster. d. per piece. . .and see'd some of the largest sold and retailed at 2sh 6d per piece.[1]

It is clear from this remark and from other abundant evidence that along most fishing coasts, fresh fish and dried whitefish were usually cheap, even at Leith, the outport for Edinburgh. It seems probable that this class of subsistence fishermen merged imperceptibly with the majority of coastal fishermen who might hope to sell rather than consume the bulk of their catch. This includes not only fishermen using small boats, but fishermen who never left the shore, setting stationary nets, 'parcs' and other devices, around the low water mark, particularly along estuaries. Such a style of fishing was particularly common along the coasts of Picardy, Normandy and Brittany. This class included another very important category of fishermen, the freshwater fishers, working with nets, eel sets and even boats. The records of Norwich market, to take but one example, show that in the sixteenth century, although this city of 15,000 was very well supplied with sea food from Yarmouth, enormous quantities of freshwater fish such as roach, which few Englishmen would look at twice today, found a ready sale. Thorold Rogers's researches amply confirm this conclusion. Fish from all these sources were cheap wherever they were close to their point of capture, and they supplemented many a poor man's diet. Wherever this supply of cheap fish was available, fresh fish was a widely consumed commodity. It had to be sold quickly before it decayed beyond the long-suffering endurance of the seventeenth-century palate. This in practice introduced quite a large tolerance. Fish condemned by the Fishmongers' Company in London as unfit for human consumption appears to have found a ready sale at smaller towns lower down the Thames. Unfortunately, by its very nature this section

[1] J. Spreull, *An accompt current betwixt Scotland and England ballanced together with a few remarks* (Edinburgh, 1705; repr. Glasgow, 1881), p. 68.

of the industry, which was most closely linked to the problem of food supply for the bulk of the population, and may in quantity of fish caught rival some of the more famous branches of the industry, has left very little in the way of quantitative records. The sale was by cash on market stalls, on the seashore or hawked by itinerant fish-pedlars, or even the fisherman's wife, in a trade which leaves no written trace. It is therefore on the third and fourth categories of fishing that the bulk of the attention must be focused.

The third category, after subsistence fishermen, and coastal fishermen catering for local markets, grew out of the seasonal nature of some species. During a herring, or mackerel, or sprat, or pilchard season, far more fish were landed than could be absorbed by the local market. It therefore required the intervention of merchants to preserve and transport these catches. These seasons most closely resembled fairs in economic form. At Aberdovey in Wales in 1566 there were only three houses, but during the herring-fishing season 'there is a wonderfull greate resorte of fyshers assembled from all places within this Realme with Shippes, Boottes and Vessells'.[1] In the Shetlands Hanseatic merchants set up their booths to buy locally caught ling and cod, while local men set up stalls to service the needs of Dutch fishermen in June–August, a fair which became vital to the local economy. During its era of importance the Scania herring fair was a much more significant example of this type, and throughout this period the Yarmouth 'free fair' was the most important event within this category. 'What a huge multitude of people from all parts of England, France, Holland and Zealand do resort hither!', Camden exclaimed. Finally in the fourth category comes the most advanced form of fishing – one which was totally market-oriented, and mounted on a firm commercial basis. At the top of this order of economic development was the Dutch buss herring fishery, followed by the French and English and Irish herring fisheries, the Newfoundland fishery, the Iceland fishery and the whale fishery.

IV. *The Herring Fishery*

The crucial determinant of this fishery was that if urgent steps were not taken to preserve herring within 24–48 hours, spoilage would take place, making it unacceptable to all but the poorest in the community. Since the main fishing grounds were close to the British Isles, the French, Dutch and other continental nations who might take part in this fishery, had to do all fish-curing and barrelling on board ship. The native

[1] P.R.O. SP.12/38/30.

English, Scottish and Irish industry could survive with minute boats, landing each night's catch at a convenient port, and leave all the curing, barrelling etc. to be done on shore. The English pamphleteers, over-awed by the fact that the Dutch were forced to use boats of up to 80 tons burden, when the English were using craft of 2–15 tons, mistook practical necessity for economic virtue.[1] The great nineteenth-century British herring fishery was after all built on the basis of small boats and curing on shore. This is not to say that the ingenious Dutch did not advance far beyond economic necessity; the real question of interest is a comparison between the Dutch buss fishery and that of the French, Spanish Netherlanders, Hamburgers and East Frieslanders.

(1) THE ENGLISH HERRING INDUSTRY

Leaving aside the minor fisheries off Aberdovey and Plymouth and eastern Channel ports, two herring seasons remain. The first and least significant was that off the North Yorkshire coast dominated by the tiny fishing hamlets and villages from Hartlepool to Bridlington. This was conducted by 'five-man cobbles', a type of boat which hardly changed until the twentieth century, with side keels for beaching on the shore and probably not more than 6 tons in size. The port books record almost no herring shipments from this coast and it must be assumed that the catch was small, and was consumed locally. These fishermen brought their small craft to the second season off Yarmouth and Lowestoft, where their boats mingled with the East Anglian coast boats of a similar size, Yarmouth town boats of 8–15 tons and those of the Channel fishing ports from Thanet to Brighton which were on average rather larger, reaching 24 tons in the seventeenth century. They mixed, too, with the smaller coastal fishermen from the Dutch, French and, to a lesser extent, Spanish Netherlands fishing villages. These foreign boats, comprised of 'swoard pinks, holland toads, crab skuits, walnut shells and great and small yeuers', were too small to take part in the buss fishery, curing on board, and therefore landed their catch fresh or rough salted, selling their fish to the Yarmouth townsmen, who then for the most part smoked them, to produce the 'red herring' or *bokking* as distinct from the salt or white herring which was produced on board Dutch busses.[2]

At its height, around 1600, this fishery attracted (according to Yarmouth records) nearly 500–600 small boats. This number decreased after the early 1600s, 'the Seas being grown fruitless and barren' as one ecclesiastic observed in 1627 (characteristically anachronistic, since by

---

[1] All dimensions are understood to be tons or lasts burden.
[2] T. Gentleman, *England's Way to Win Wealth* (London, 1614), p. 26.

Table 20. *Great Yarmouth Fishing Fleet*[a]

Year	Herring boats	Mackerel boats	1st North Sea voyage	2nd North Sea voyage	Iceland boats
1581	99	n.a.	n.a.	n.a.	n.a.
1582	n.a.	n.a.	47	59	n.a.
1583	—	—	—	—	—
1584	116	n.a.	n.a.	n.a.	n.a.
1585	n.a.	n.a.	46	57	n.a.
1592	97	n.a.	n.a.	n.a.	n.a.
1593	107	47	31	n.a.	n.a.
1594	111	37	30	n.a.	10
1595	111	41	43	51	19
1596	98	34	34	27	27
1597	113	36	32	—	35
1598	98	39	38	51	39
1599	115	27	32	32	27
1600	104	32	40	42	21
1601	104	51	46	49	25
1602	113	49	61	74	26
1603	119	41	65	71	15
1604	120	41	57	72	6
1605	114	39	69	81	5
1606	109	36	82	87	—
1607	108	36	75	85	11
1608	100	n.a.	80	91	17
1609	95	37	83	95	13
1610	92	32	85	87	20
1611	84	23	83	90	17
1612	86	32	84	100	17
1613	83	31	88	90	18
1614	82	28	92	105	22
1615	68	30	95	119	24
1616	68	39	100	125	20
1617	63	25	126	109	13
1618	46	19	116	144	18
1619	49	20	108	94	n.a.
1620	41	19	87	96	31
1621	46	17	82	64	29
1622	44	12	85	59	23
1623	46	12	79	76	36
1624	45	n.a.	86	81	43
1625	46	n.a.	87	n.a.	n.a.
1626	40	4	58	20	34
1627	n.a.	7	77	49	49
1628	85	6	69	21	19

[a] SOURCE: Great Yarmouth Corporation MSS 27/1–4. These figures only include fishing boats wintering in Yarmouth harbour and paying a dole, i.e. making a profit.

Table 20 (*cont.*)

Year	Herring boats	Mackerel boats	1st North Sea voyage	2nd North Sea voyage	Iceland boats
1629	124	12	83	75	32
1630	103	14	97	70	50
1631	113	15	110	110	48
1632	99	14	141	122	51
1633	103	8	145	131	44
1634	91	7	160	120	63
1635	88	7	158	138	43
1636	78	7	145	142	48
1637	83	8	149	161	39
1638	86	9	156	144	50
1639	92	6	150	145	35
1640	89	5	154	140	36
1641	89	n.a.	157	154	25
1642	87	6	159	153	23
1643	82	8	49	131	25
1644	77	5	182	182	3
1645	78	6	136	97	10
1646	76	7	127	119	20
1647	76	6	139	136	25
1648	74	4	160	155	33
1649	80	4	122	91	17
1650	75	4	132	96	39
1651	68	5	102	20	34
1652	53	5	81	23	18
1653	55	4	31	11	20
1654	162	4	60	37	15
1655	44	4	81	67	21
1656	33	n.a.	46	3	15
1657	n.a.	4	42	11	31
1658	n.a.	n.a.	n.a.	n.a.	n.a.
1659	45	n.a.	n.a.	n.a.	n.a.
1660	46	1	23	17	57
1661	40	n.a.	25	26	23
1662	n.a.	2	18	10	20
1663	n.a.	n.a.	n.a.	n.a.	n.a.
1664	n.a.	n.a.	n.a.	n.a.	n.a.
1665	n.a.	n.a.	n.a.	n.a.	n.a.
1666	30	n.a.	n.a.	n.a.	n.a.
1667	47	n.a.	6	n.a.	13
1668	56	6	20	15	17
1669	64	9	24	19	27
1670	60	11	28	22	36
1671	77	13	42	25	40
1672	76	9	26	10	8
1673	68	16	12	5	17
1674	86	14	32	26	27
1675	102	12	48	48	32

Table 20 (*cont.*)

Year	Herring boats	Mackerel boats	1st North Sea voyage	2nd North Sea voyage	Iceland boats
1676	102	6	51	31	21
1677	105	8	45	40	13
1678	96	12	23	140	12
1679	87	11	50	27	23
1680	92	16	50	42	14
1681	n.a.	10	43	36	10
1682	84	n.a.	n.a.	n.a.	n.a.
1683	81	8	40	26	15
1684	63	7	33	31	15
1685	44	8	25	20	15
1686	49	5	5	11	12
1687	49	5	21	15	12
1688	46	5	21	15	12
1689	51	3	n.a.	30	6
1690	41	n.a.	8	1	All taken
1691	22	7	2	2	2
1692	15	4	3	3	3
1693	16	2	7	3	4
1694	19	5	9	0	3
1695	16	4	8	3	2
1696	14	5	1	3	4
1697	18	4	2	0	3
1698	24	6	16	12	4
1699	32	6	16	1	2
1700	10	7	15	4	2
1701	19	5	2	1	1
1702	10	5	1	0	1
1703	9	9	3	0	0
1704	3	n.a.	0	0	1
1705	7	6	0	0	1
1706	4	7	0	0	1
1707	9	8	3	0	0
1708	9	7	3	3	2
1709	13	7	3	0	1
1710	13	12	13	0	0
1711	18	12	1	0	1
1712	17	15	2	6	2
1713	21	17	9	7	5
1714	22	13	7	3	1

then the seas were recovering their bounty off Yarmouth).[1] Another peak was reached after 1670, though an increase in the size rather than number of boats took place, the total only reaching 300, and then shortly after 1720 another period of relative dearth began. The approxi-

[1] G. Hakewill, *An Apologie or Declaration of the Power and Providence of God in the Government of the World* (London, 1627), pp. 21–2.

mate quantity of herrings cured and packed during these periods (those consumed fresh cannot be estimated but, given the rapid spoilage rate, are unlikely to be more than 100 lasts) are as follows (lasts): 1598–1604, 3,000;[1] 1619–37, 1,500; 1660s, 3,500; 1678–88, 3,800; 1689–1711, 2,000; 1712–20, 4,000. It should be emphasized that the early seventeenth-century peak was achieved with the assistance of fishermen from the Low Countries (mainly from Zealand) and French fishing boats. This was true through most of the sixteenth century (hostilities permitting). From the 1630s the English fisheries began to rely more on their own resources, first through Charles I's hostile attitude towards Dutch fishing in general, followed by the three Dutch wars. In 1665 legislation was passed forbidding the landing of fresh fish by foreign vessels, though this was only intermittently observed on the East Anglian coast.

(2) THE SCOTTISH HERRING FISHERY

Herring were caught virtually right round the Scottish coast at one time of the year or another, most of them in shallow inshore waters, and always by very small boats. The Orkneys were visited by Danish and Hanseatic merchants during July in the sixteenth century with the intention of buying fish, but the quantities sold were quite small. Most of the fish was consumed locally with the minimum of preservation, and only the major east coast ports from Dundee to Dunbar and the Clyde ports in the west dealt with large quantities of herring on a mercantile basis. Aberdeen, although an important centre for the export of salmon, played very little part in the trade in herring.

Fishing was a far more important component in the Scottish economy than in the English. Lythe estimates that before 1625 fish products represented 20 per cent of Scottish exports by value, and in the 1630s and after the 1690s the percentage was probably higher. Such evidence as survives suggests that consumption of fish in the northern kingdom was much higher than in England, and that export figures represent a lower percentage of the catch than in East Anglia. In the 1590s the eastern ports were exporting between 200 and 250 lasts, and the Clyde between 400 and 500. Most of the exports of the east coast ports were sent to the Baltic, and from 1600 onwards an average of 300 lasts passed through the Sound, rising to over 400 after 1620, but tailing off in the 1640s and not consistently rising above 200 until 1696. Once

[1] These figures, based on P.R.O. E.190 series, represent modal catches rather than arithmetical means which in view of the violent fluctuations from year to year give a rather distorted picture. In 1629, for instance, there was an exceptionally good catch probably equalling those of the 1598–1604 period.

peace was restored exports rose to well over 1,000 lasts, and actually exceeded the very much diminished quantities of Dutch herrings passing into the Baltic. After 1731 conditions changed again and the Scottish exports shrank to a relatively minor level.

The produce of the western ports is less easy to trace. This was almost entirely marketed in the Atlantic coast ports of France. At the end of the seventeenth century two contemporaries spoke confidently of 2,500–3,000 lasts leaving the Clyde in peace time. Like many pamphlet sources these should be regarded as gross exaggerations. None of the few surviving port books (all pre-1681) show more than 100 lasts leaving this coast. Besides which, the edict of Louis XIV which forbade the import of foreign fish, and the French wars, must have effectively destroyed this trade.

(3) THE DUTCH 'GROOTE VISSCHERIJ'

The Dutch herring fishery represents a truly remarkable achievement. In a sense the herring buss represents a pre-industrial factory ship, of a sort only recently reintroduced into fishing. Pamphleteers represent the buss as being between 30 and 100 lasts, but all the records indicate that it settled down at an optimum economic size of around 30 lasts (in the sixteenth century busses up to 46 lasts did exist). On board this ship were skilled gippers (removers of the intestines), curers and fishermen, with enough salt, food and barrels to stay at sea for six to eight weeks. Strict regulations surrounded the Dutch manufacture of white herrings, controlling quality of salt, fish etc. To check the quality, all herrings were repacked when they were brought back to shore in Holland. This *Groote Visscherij* was closely watched over by a collegiate organization representing the five major Holland fishing ports: Brill, Rotterdam, Schiedam, Delft and Enkhuizen. Representatives of these five towns enacted all fishery legislation relating to the herring industry. This organization effectively came into being at a meeting arranged by William of Orange in 1575, and became officially established under the statutes of 1580–2.

The Low Countries' herring fishery was already well established at this date, though it was more evenly spread throughout the country. In 1562 there were said to be 700 'begroot' fishing boats of which 400 belonged to Holland, 200 to Zealand and 100 to Flanders. It was to be a standing tradition at Dunkirk that the port had possessed 200 fishing boats at this date, a fleet rapidly eroded into extinction during the next two decades. The Yarmouth records confirm that a very large number of Dunkirk boats were landing fish during the free fair in the middle of the century. Kranenburgh estimates that there were about 450 busses at work from Holland and Friesland at the turn of the seventeenth cen-

tury. Recent research confirms this view, though it should be pointed
out that the estimate excludes any Zealand ships. The Zealand fishing
industry suffered severely during the war with Spain, being nearest to
the privateering bases of Dunkirk and, after 1601, Ostend. Veere and Zie-
riekzee were probably the only towns to have busses at work after 1600.

Dr Kranenburgh's estimate must therefore be revised upwards by
about 20–30 busses. On the basis of salt taxes he puts the total catch at
around 18,000 lasts in 1599. Kranenburgh believes that the number of
ships at work rose to 500 in the 1630s. The only series available for this
period, for Schiedam, does not confirm this. While there were 50–60
busses at work in the period 1600–25, there were only 20–5 sailing in
the 1630s. Nevertheless the quantities of Dutch herring passing through
the Sound in the 1640s were equal to those of the period 1599–1612.
Fig. 3 sets out the quantities recorded as passing through the Sound.
Kranenburgh's estimate for the mean total catch in the 1640s is 20,000
lasts. Historians remembering the pamphleteers' claim of 1,000–2,000
ships bringing in 100,000–300,000 lasts have been loath to accept these
estimates, especially as it means a downward correction of other
estimates such as the 50,000 lasts alleged to have been caught in 1537 off
Scania, the last peak year of the Baltic herring fishery. Nevertheless all
the documentary evidence that survives supports these low estimates.
Perhaps Dr Kranenburgh is unduly pessimistic about the average catch;
he certainly omits the Zealand fishery, and may overestimate the
truthfulness of the records, but any adjustment will still keep the total
average Dutch catch at below 25,000 lasts per annum. In the 1660s this
total had fallen below 16,000, and it continued to fall until by the 1720s
there were no more than 200–50 busses at work bringing in around
8,000 lasts. Only four times after 1654 did the quantity of herrings
passing through the Sound exceed 4,000 lasts. After 1714, as has already
been stated, the Scottish exports overtook the Dutch.

The causes of this decline are complex and will be examined in more
detail later. One simple contributor was the fact that by this date hardly
any busses were making three voyages a year. Despite the usual descriptions of the three-voyage character of the industry it appears that if one
of the three voyages was bringing in a small catch it was omitted, and
similarly if the first two voyages brought in bumper catches, the third
attracted fewer participants.

The use of *ventjagers* has similarly sometimes been misunderstood.
These were fast ships which bought packed herrings at sea in exchange
for supplies during the early part of the first voyage. They then raced
home to attempt to exploit the high prices reigning until herrings came
in in considerable amounts. The College of the *Groote Visscherij*
regarded them with the utmost suspicion and did everything within its

Table 21.   *The Delftshaven Fishing Fleet, 1633–1750*

Note particularly the variation in mean last per buss from year to year.

Year	Herring jagers	Herring busses	Total catch (lasts)	Mean catch/ buss
1633	—	85	2,559	30·1
1634–8	—	—	—	—
1639	—	61	2,516	41·2
1640–1	—	—	—	—
1642	—	67	2,754	41·1
1643	—	64	2,129½	33·2
1644	6	63	2,580	40·9
1645	—	68	2,764	40·6
1646	—	61	2,117	34·7
1647	—	64	3,012	47
1648	—	61	2,581	42·3
1649	—	62	2,973	47·9
1650	—	70	3,262	46·6
1651	—	72	3,035	42·1
1652	5	69	1,538	22·2
1653	—	34	1,194	35·1
1654	8	64	3,267	51
1655	—	43	2,083	48·4
1656	5	45	1,593½	35·4
1657	9	46	1,822	39·6
1658	13	49	2,111	43
1659	—	46	1,874	40·7
1660	8	47	2,222	47·2
1661	8	50	2,115½	42·3
1662	8	45	1,838	40·8
1663	—	45	1,465	32·5
1664	—	48	1,703½	35·4
1665–6	—	—	—	—
1667	—	32	824½	25·75
1668	4	39	2,029½	52
1669–78	—	—	—	—
1679	3	40	1,242	31·05
1680	4	46	1,851½	40·2
1681	—	51	2,001	39·2
1682	—	53	1,608	30·3
1683	3	45	1,709½	37·9
1684	3	47	1,420	30·2
1685	6	43	2,503½	58·2
1686	4	46	1,743	37·83
1687	—	42	867½	20·6
1688	7	37	968	26·1
1689	—	26	736	28·3
1690	—	28	880½	31·4
1691	—	26	627	24·5

Table 21 (*cont.*)

Year	Herring jagers	Herring busses	Total catch (lasts)	Mean catch/ buss
1692	1	17	659½	28·7
1693	—	20	744	37·2
1694	—	27	899½	33·2
1695	—	23	792½	39·4
1696	—	26	500½	19·2
1697	—	17	327½	19·2
1698	—	28	1,089	38·8
1699	3	35	1,460	41·7
1700	1	44	1,663½	37·7
1701	—	29	542	18·6
1702	—	19	390	20·5
1703	—	25	120	4·8
1704	—	8	238½	29·8
1705	—	10	121	12·1
1706	—	6	122	20·3
1707	—	13	233	17·92
1708	—	19	429½	22·60
1709	—	19	628½	33
1710	—	17	409	24·0
1711	—	17	391½	23·29
1712	—	14	270	19·2
1713	—	18	735½	40·9
1714	—	17	686½	40·4
1715	—	16	871	54·4
1716	—	18	663½	36·9
1717	—	19	975	51·3
1718	—	17	913½	53·7
1719	—	19	843	44·3
1720	—	14	315½	22·5
1721	—	16	537½	33·5
1722	—	17	727½	42·8
1723	—	19	715½	37·6
1724	—	19	520	27·3
1725	—	17	828½	48·7
1726	—	18	978	54·3
1727	—	18	697	38·7
1728	—	18	441½	24·5
1729	—	18	450½	25
1730	—	16	577	36
1731	—	16	495	30·9
1732	—	17	615½	36·2
1733	—	15	622½	41·5
1734	—	14	673½	48·1
1735	—	13	808½	62·1
1736	—	15	702	46·8
1737	—	9	521	57·8
1738	—	10	490½	49

Table 21 (cont.)

Year	Herring jagers	Herring busses	Total catch (lasts)	Mean catch/ buss
1739	—	13	489½	37·6
1740	—	16	404½	25·3
1741	—	17	486	28·5
1742	—	18	351	19·5
1743	—	14	332	23·7
1744	—	14	321	22·4
1745	—	12	468	39
1746	—	12	689	57·4
1747	—	11	318½	28·9
1748	—	11	234½	21·2
1749	—	11	300	27·2
1750	—	12	173½	14·4

SOURCE: H. Watjen, 'Zur Statistik der hollandischen Heringfischerei im 17. u. 18. Jahrhundert', *Hansische Geschichtsblätter* (1910).

power to restrict them. The main fear was that these ships might make for foreign ports without repacking and thus bring the name of Dutch herrings into bad repute. They were only permitted to operate during July, and although some infringement doubtless occurred it should be remembered that the College provided the convoying warships which could also police the fishing grounds. In 1668 *ventjagers* brought back only 1·75 per cent of the total catch, in 1669 only 4·75 per cent, and in other years for which records survive a similarly low proportion.

Although the collegiate structure was based on five important fishing ports, significant numbers of busses came from the smaller coastal villages and towns, particularly Egmont, Wijk-op-Zee, Maerchen, the island of Texel and Venkuysen. During the seventeenth century there was a considerable restructuring of the industry. The number of busses sailing from Enkhuizen and other north Holland ports increased, while those from Brill and Delftshaven steadily declined. On the other hand Vlaandingen, still an important fishing port today, showed a sharp rise from 7 busses in 1693 to over 70 in 1699.

The real Dutch achievement was not in building large ships, but in achieving a consistent quality in their product. Nothing was more difficult in the pre-industrial world than ensuring a standardized product prepared on board 500 different boats. Yarmouth attempted to copy this process of curing exactly by using Dutch fishermen, immigrants driven out by Alba's persecution. Although the town attempted to supervise the production precisely with English and Dutch wardens, in the end the necessary continuous vigilance proved too much, and the attempt lapsed in the early seventeenth century. The known quality of the Dutch product commanded a superior price in every market in Europe. In 1575 the Dutch herrings sold at £24 10s per last at Rouen, and the Yarmouth copy, then in its prime, was sold at £20 12s per last, which was considered a tremendous achievement.

The Dutch therefore had a built-in advantage when it came to competition. It was true that the capital outlay involved was much higher than in the simple English, Scottish and coastal fisherman's enterprise, but capital was readily available, and at a low rate of interest, in Holland. Alongside this one can compare the problems of the English attempts to set up fishery companies working on the Dutch model. The English began with the notion that the only place to establish their base was either Stornoway on the Isle of Lewis or the Orkneys. Thus, on top of the formidable problems of raising enough capital at English rates of interest, an exaggerated notion of the Dutch profits and a lack of expertise, the project imposed the additional burden of setting up a base *de novo*, bringing in labour, materials, salt, timber etc., which would normally have been readily available at a Dutch or English east coast port. In practice, the first fishery company during the reign of Charles I (and the scheme which came closest to fruition) compounded its difficulties yet further by dividing its limited means, in that it maintained a base at Stornoway in the face of firm indigenous opposition, while at the same time using other busses based on Yarmouth.

When the English had finally scraped together enough white herring to sell, they faced implacable competition from the Dutch who, it was alleged, were prepared to sell below cost for a short period to drive the English off the market. The implication that emerges, and will be investigated later, is that despite the demographic problem of Europe, the demand for herring was limited, and in normal years the Dutch could hope to match production to demand.

In addition to the buss fishery, the Dutch coastal fishermen caught herring off Yarmouth (as already mentioned), off their own coast, and particularly in the Zuider Zee which had its own species of herring. Estimates for this latter catch have been put in the region of 600–700 lasts, most of which was processed by smoking as *bokking*.

(4) THE FRENCH HERRING FISHERY

The centre of the herring fishery in France was Dieppe, seconded (to a decreasing extent as the seventeenth century wore on) by Calais and Boulogne. The most important voyage consistently exploited was to Yarmouth, followed by the Channel fishing off Boulogne which began to fail after 1686. At various times the French fishing fleet also exploited the northeast coast fishery. The primary problem was that the French were peculiarly vulnerable in times of war with England, Holland, or Spain. This made the first half of the sixteenth century (to 1569) particularly difficult, likewise the years after 1672. In the 1550s the French fishing fleet, estimated at 250 boats, was mistaken for an invasion fleet heading for the east coast of England. The biggest boats were in the region of 35 lasts, of comparable size to the Dutch. Like the Dutch, the French curing had to be done on board ship. Numbers fluctuated widely, Dieppe seeing anything from 34 (1715) to 120 (1694) ships set out for Yarmouth. The average after 1650 was probably in the region of 60, with 40 from all the other ports along the Pas de Calais, Picardy and Normandy coast. Inadequate data prevent any serious estimates before this date but logic would point towards a larger number. During the years 1715–23 the mean landing at Dieppe (where most of the French catch was landed) was 7,877 lasts. More than half this total was in fresh herring caught in the Channel. The average catch per boat was spread over a range and distribution curve comparable to that of the Dutch. As fishermen the French were in no way inferior to the Dutch; the problems began with the quality of the curing of the herrings, and the close and suspicious watch kept on the French salt trade. It was a tradition at Yarmouth that the making of Leghorn red herring (as the herrings specially prepared for the Mediterranean were called) was first invented at Calais. If so, the French industry may have been more productive in the sixteenth century than later. During the seventeenth century few if any herrings were exported far beyond the frontiers of France.

(5) OTHER HERRING FISHERIES

Once the Scania fishery had declined, the most important remaining area for herring fishing was probably off the Norwegian coast. Fishing was carried out by the local inhabitants from small boats. Herring shoals were not present in commercial quantities throughout the whole period. In later times they have sometimes disappeared for up to forty years. Clearly they were present in the 1580s, when large quantities were carried into the Baltic, and it is agreed that 1699–1784 mark out years when the shoals were present. But absence of Norwegian fish from Baltic markets is no guarantee that the shoals were absent. The practice was for only a small part of the catch to be handled commercially, and for the farmers only to take sufficient herrings to satisfy their own requirements and to obtain money and necessaries. The farmers/ fishermen were forced to take their own herrings to Bergen to be salted, by which time they were often so rotten 'ordinary Poles and Muscovites' could not stomach them. Faced with superior Dutch competition the Norwegians could only rely on years of low Dutch catches to stimulate any great demand for the Norwegian product in the Baltic. From 1753 the Danish government began to regulate the fishery to improve its quality, and Bergen citizens began to erect salting houses on the coast. In the same decade the Swedish seas began to recover their bounty and there was a tremendous revival in Swedish herring.

Dutch competition was also responsible for the failure of the East Friesland and Hamburg fisheries which were attempted on the buss principle in the late sixteenth century. The Dutch were alleged to have swamped the market and undercut the prices of the Emden and Hamburg fishermen. More ambitious was the attempt to set up a buss fishery based on Bruges in the 1660s. Encouraged by the grant of freedom to fish in English waters from Charles II, and by the new shipping canal to Zeebrugge completed in 1666, the citizens of Bruges built a fleet of 50 busses and proceeded to fish in the Dutch manner. The attempt appears to have petered out in the unsettled economic conditions of the later seventeenth century. Minute quantities of Bruges herring entered the Baltic between 1664 and 1676; thereafter whatever herring fishing was done only served the internal markets.

In total the catch of all the European herring fisheries amounted to rather less than 50,000 lasts, a catch comparable to the output of Holland or Yarmouth and Lowestoft in the first decade of the twentieth century. Considering the resources available and the much smaller market this seems a very creditable achievement.

V.   *The Cod Fishery*

The other fisheries of major international importance were for cod off Newfoundland and in the Icelandic and North Seas. Much attention has been given to the former, but very little to the latter. For the fishing industry the voyage of John Cabot in 1497 was of more direct importance than that of Columbus. By December 1497 word had already reached Italy that the 'sea there is swarming with fish, which can be taken not only with the net but in baskets let down with a stone... [the English] say that they could bring so many fish that this kingdom [England] would have no further need of Iceland, from which place there comes a very great quantity of fish called stockfish'.[1] Equally important was the fact that the voyage was made by Bristol and West Countrymen who were least able to exploit the North and Icelandic Seas. By 1522 the English 'New found Isle landes flete' was large enough to warrant a warship to convoy it home.

[1] H. P. Biggar, *Precursors of Jacques Cartier 1497–1534* (Ottawa, 1911), p. 20.

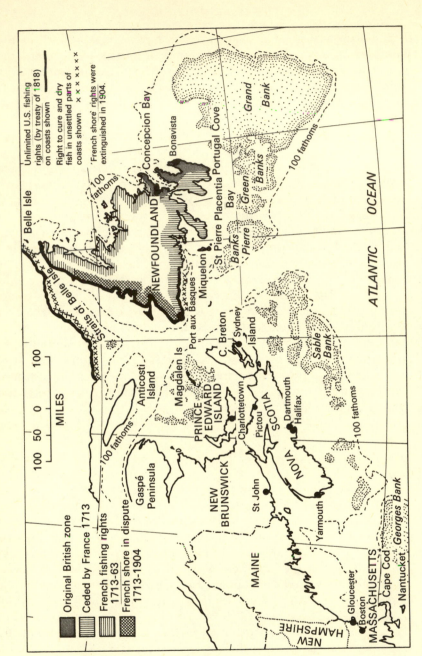

Fig. 4. The fishing banks from Cape Cod to Labrador.

But there is every reason to suppose that the Portuguese were the first to exploit this fishery to the full. According to Hakluyt, an English ship saw 50 Spanish, Portuguese and French ships at work in 1517. By 1550 it was claimed that Aviero alone sent more than 150 ships to Newfoundland. The Spanish mentioned were presumably Basque fishermen, while the French probably came from Normandy or Brittany. The structure, financing and trade of the Newfoundland fishery was even more complicated than that of any other. At present we lack detailed evidence to give a statistical corroboration of many of the statements which could allow a proper comparison of the relative importance of the Newfoundland trade to different countries. The following outline may be modified by research on Iberian sources which could provide some important statistical series.

(1) THE PORTUGUESE AND SPANISH FISHERIES

The Iberian peninsula proved throughout the early modern period to be one of the best markets for cod, particularly dried cod, which was lightly salted and then wind dried, for varying lengths of time, a form of preservation to which the cod was ideally suited because of its low fat content, and which was cheaper than full salting. This fish was variously known as stockfish, poor John, Haberdine or *merluche*. Fish consumption appears to have been exceptionally high, even for a Catholic country that was forced more and more to import a large percentage of its food supply. Hamilton notes that fish prices rose more rapidly than other foodstuffs. It was natural that, during the heyday of Iberian commerce in the first half of the sixteenth century, Basque and Portuguese fishermen should seek out an increasing supply of this commodity. Despite its early start, the Portuguese fishery declined rather than increased after 1550, so that in 1578, three years before the union with Spain, Anthony Parkhurst, who appears to have been as reliable as any contemporary observer, put the Portuguese ships at 'not lightly above 50 saile'. At the same time the Spaniards were 'above 100 saile'. Both nationalities dried their catch at home in the manner of English Iceland fishermen.

The decline of the Spanish fishery can be directly attributed to the hostilities with England, followed by the decay of the Basque ports in the early seventeenth century. The English inflicted upon the Newfoundland fisheries a degree of disruption similar to that which the Dunkirkers laid upon the North Sea fisheries. As early as 1517 John Rastell's expedition to fish at Newfoundland broke up because the crew thought piracy more profitable. Even before the war with Spain during 1582–5, English sailors made heavy depredations on Spanish and

Portuguese fishermen, and for the next two years the Basque fleet was not permitted to sail. The French also attacked the Spanish when an opportunity presented itself. Once the Iberian fleet had been reduced, the rivalry became intense between the French and the English. These continual hostilities, which were mirrored in those existing in the Spitzbergen whale fishery, put the Newfoundland cod fishery in an entirely different category from nearly every other fishery.

(2) THE FRENCH NEWFOUNDLAND FISHERY

In 1578, the French Newfoundland fleet was three times the size of the English with over 150 ships against the English 50. The average size of boat is almost impossible to calculate. The majority of boats of all nationalities were in the region of 50–60 tons, though some French boats may have been as small as 40 tons (about the smallest economically possible), though even at this date ships of 200 tons could be found. Obviously, in view of the dangers of attack, larger boats had an advantage beyond economic considerations. The character of the Newfoundland trade in the seventeenth and eighteenth centuries was such as to make the size of ships involved less a mark of sophistication than in any other fishery. In the case of *la pêche sédentaire* (dried fish) the large ship used to cross the Atlantic was laid up for the season and small boats were used to spread the area of line fishing.

Cod fishing was a tedious and unselective business. Lines of great length with individually baited hooks were trailed in the sea, sometimes using floats to spread the area (in the North Sea), sometimes (as at Newfoundland) using additional boats. The basic principle was used along all the coastal waters of Europe as well as at Iceland and Newfoundland. It had the advantage that very little specialist equipment was needed. Any ship could be used. During the Commonwealth period English warships convoying Iceland fishermen were unofficially catching such large quantities of cod that the fishermen became afraid their market would be spoilt. The Newfoundland fishery was not dependent on purpose-built ships (as was the case of buss fishing) and in time of war the ships could be used for other purposes.

More significant was the development of the 'sack ship'. This was largely confined to the English fishery. The sack ship brought out supplies of salt, food etc. to the fishermen, purchased the cod and took it directly to its market in southern Europe. Thus the fisherman was no longer limited by the capacity of his ship. It meant too that settlers in Newfoundland could also take part in the fishing industry and never leave their islands.

From the mid sixteenth century the French predominated in fishing.

They were the first to settle in Newfoundland and neighbouring lands. But they did not match the English in bellicose spirit, and from the seizure of St John's by Sir Humphrey Gilbert in 1583 to the capture of Quebec by Wolfe in 1759, the French were gradually pushed out of the areas which the English considered best for fishing. During the period 1550–1650 some important structural changes came over the industry. In the sixteenth century Rouen, La Rochelle and Bordeaux were the vital centres of the French Newfoundland fleet. Increasingly these ports became sources of finance for the main fishing ports of Le Havre, Honfleur, St Malo, Nantes and Sables d'Olonne, which according to the survey of 1664 provided 71 per cent of the 352 ships involved. The second change was the increasing specialization in either dried fish (sometimes referred to as *la pêche sedentaire*) or green or salted and gutted cod (*la pêche errante*). The ships from Brittany and the Basque country specialized in the former, those from Olonne and Normandy in the latter. In 1664 there were 132 ships fishing for dried cod, and 120 for green cod, the specialization of the other 100 is unknown. The French dried their fish on shore at Newfoundland, or Canada, while the green cod were gutted on board ship in the manner of the buss fishery. It therefore followed that the latter required more specialized equipment, skilled workmen, and more salt. The former was more suited to those poorer ports where less capital was available.

Instances of symbiosis can be found. Large cod were highly unsuitable for drying, whereas small cod were a nuisance to salt and gut. Denys, writing in 1672, states that Basque and Normandy fishermen fishing in the same area used to exchange fish at the rate of two small for one large, since the Normandy fishermen had no sale for dried cod in Paris, and the Basques no sale of salt in the south. How common this practice was it is impossible to say. The French, unlike the English, tended to spread out widely in Newfoundland, other islands and on the mainland. The French Newfoundland fishery probably reached its peak around 1688 when the fleet numbered around 400. From then on wars with the English destroyed the viability of the French enterprise. Several settlements were captured including the important bases of Acadia and Plaisance. Not until 1748 did the French industry now based on Labrador and L'Isle Royale attain its former height, only to be decimated shortly afterwards by the Seven Years War.

The French industry suffered greatly from dispersion. The ships came from ports as far apart as St Valery-en-Caux and St Jean de Luz. They spread out over the vast area from Labrador to the southernmost of the Grand Banks without any real coordination, presenting easy targets for the more united English. More surprisingly, it was not until after 1750 that they adopted the multi-hook line, although this practice was well established in French coastal waters. Each line was hand-held until the fish was taken.

(3) THE ENGLISH FISHERY

It was not until the 1570s that the English seriously exploited the New-foundland seas, in four years the number of ships rising from 30 to 50. These ships all came from West Country ports, mainly from Dart-mouth, Plymouth, Bideford and Barnstaple. Up to this date there is every indication that Newfoundland fish were imported from French ports. The total number of ships at work in the first half of the seven-teenth century is difficult to calculate. Most of the numerous contem-porary estimates are probably inaccurate. One, in the State Papers for 1629, puts the number of ships involved from ports from Southampton to Bristol at 300 per year; a pamphleteer of 1622 speaks of 26,700 tons of shipping involved, which would amount to at least 267 ships at the same time as Innis and Judah gloomily conclude, 'The 50 vessels which had sailed from the West Country to New England [to fish] in 1524 had dwindled to 15 in 1637.'[1] Probably the total fleet between 1615 and 1640 was in the region of 200–300 ships, of which the four above-mentioned ports supplied about 70 per cent. This represents the peak of the fishing fleet, since thereafter the sack ships combined with New-foundland boats tended to diminish the number of fishing boats making the annual voyage. In 1677, 103 fishing ships sailed from the West Country, and from London, Exeter and other ports 89 sack ships.

Commentators have neglected to answer the question of technique in the case of the English fishery. Certainly they were using multi-hook lines before the French, but whether they did so from the beginning is impossible to state at the present time. Certainly the comparison with the Iceland fishery would be more explicable if hand-held single hook lines were in use in the seventeenth century (see below, p. 166).

During the second half of the seventeenth century the growth of the Newfoundland colony was a matter of considerable controversy. It was claimed that labour was lured from the West Country to settle in New-foundland, and that between them Newfoundland and New England had more or less engrossed or were likely to engross the trade. The removal of all settlers from the Island was seriously debated in govern-ment circles. The outbreak of hostilities with the French, followed by

---

[1] H. A. Innis, *The Cod Fisheries*, p. 80. Curiously Innis does not estimate the total fleet as C. B. Judah does (*The North American Fisheries and British Policy to 1713* (Urbana, 1933), p. 157), leaving this statement to stand as though it related to all the Newfoundland fisheries.

the exceptionally hard winter of 1713–14, upset the normal fish distribution pattern so that very low yields were obtained in the following years. This resulted in the virtual withdrawal of the West Country from the fishing side of the trade. Newfoundland and the other planters' boats which had numbered little more than 300 in 1677 had risen to an average of 1,118 between 1736 and 1739. Increasingly the West Country ports became concerned with the trading side. Almost exclusively the end product was dried fish, not green or salt cod.

Figures for French landings before 1760 are virtually non-existent, and it is therefore impossible to make any useful comparison between the English and French fisheries in terms of efficiency. By the 1670s when detailed English figures first become available the two industries vary so greatly in structure that it is impossible to hazard an estimate of the French catch on the basis of the number of ships employed, the more so since yield per boat could vary by as much as 100 per cent from fishing ground to fishing ground. Table 22 gives the figures for the English catch. In addition some cod was reduced to produce 'train oil' (see p. 171, on whaling).

(4) THE ICELAND AND NORTH SEA FISHERY

Very rarely before the eighteenth century did any Newfoundland cod find its way into northwest Europe, or even on to the London market in appreciable quantities. Newfoundland fish dominated Europe south of Normandy, including the western parts of the British Isles, but its main markets were in southern Europe and later in the West Indies and North America. London was already supplied by the East Anglian cod fishery, and stockfish imported via the Hanse network. These cod fisheries have not received a great deal of attention from historians in the way that the Newfoundland fisheries have. In part this is because most of the English catch was consumed at home with only minor trade with north France. The Scandinavian catch appears to have been consumed more and more within the Northern countries as Newfoundland fish drove Icelandic stockfish off the market. But ling and cod caught off Shetland and handled by the Hanse were imported into Germany. By and large historians have been interested in fishing industries that stimulated trade and attracted comparatively large investments, not those which have quietly fed the growing populations of sixteenth- and seventeenth-century Europe. For this reason the English Newfoundland industry has attracted more attention than the French, the herring industry more than the cod fishery.

Carus-Wilson writes as though the English Iceland trade died in the

Table 22. *English Returns for the Newfoundland Trade, 1615–1731*

Year	Total	Fishing	'Sack'	American[a]	Tonnage	Boats[b]	Inhab. boats	Total	Catch quintals	Train oil tons
(1615)	250	n.a.	n.a.	n.a.	(15,000)	n.a.	n.a.	n.a.	(300,000)	—
1675	172	n.a.	n.a.	n.a.	13,106	688	277	965	n.a.	—
1676	212	126	86	—	n.a.	894	206	1,190	219,443	1,063
1677	231	109	112	—	16,949	892	337	1,229	221,220	1,382
1677[c]	102	n.a.	n.a.	n.a.	n.a.	n.a.	n.a.	1,836	550,800	n.a.
1679	n.a.	n.a.	138	n.a.	n.a.	n.a.	n.a.	n.a.	159,059[d]	n.a.
1680	198	99	99	—	17,428	793	361	1,153	201,250	412
1681	172	151	21	—	n.a.	806	361	1,167	(83,240)	n.a.
1682	87	32	55	—	n.a.	183	299	482	(76,830)	n.a.
1684	110	43	67	—	n.a.	294	304	598	115,420	n.a.
1691	n.a.	n.a.	88	—	n.a.	n.a.	275	n.a.	104,450	325
1692	n.a.	n.a.	54	—	n.a.	92	274	n.a.	95,900	624
1693	96	59	37	—	n.a.	92	92	303	129,050	2,737
1694	70	40	30	—	n.a.	n.a.	n.a.	1,000	100,000	1,000
1698	252	n.a.	n.a.	—	24,318	532	397	929	215,922	n.a.
1699	236	n.a.	n.a.	—	n.a.	920	467	1,387	n.a.	n.a.
1700	220	171	49	—	n.a.	890	674	1,564	n.a.	n.a.
1701	121	75	46	—	(7,991)	435	558	993	216,320	1,049
1702	41	16	25	—	(1,330)	44	206	637	82,140	366
1703	63	23	40	—	n.a.	44	·214	258	75,000	300¼
1704	(65)	23	42	20	(2,400)	n.a.	n.a.	n.a.	(68,000)	97
1705	60	20	20		—	100	160	260	78,000	455
1706	83	46	37	16	n.a.	136	368	504	106,270	537
1707	116	70	30	15	n.a.	236	217	453	120,682	412
1708	97	49	33	15	10,995	170	356	536	135,934	772
1709	97	35	57	5	9,770	130	258	388	90,364	503

Year										
1710	93	49	26	18	(5,748)	204	314	518	139,528	535
1711	127	62	55	10	(6,880)	261	346	607	120,546	729
1712	103	66	17	20	(8,000)	268	389	568	64,430	666
1713	106	46	40	20	(5,520)	357	288	645	104,750	325
1714	150	85	45	20	(8,000)	500	500	1,000	115,000	520
1715	188	108	38	42	(11,925)	573	468	1,041	98,856	1,029
1716	147	86	30	31	(8,070)	503	408	911	88,469	320
1717	166	89	33	44	(7,530)	389	402	791	113,990	417
1718	156	95	35	26	(7,902)	511	393	904	100,823	1,574
1719	119	69	28	22	9,835	333	341	674	94,599	393
1720	151			36	12,210			617	80,220	590½
1722	143			—	12,240			679	107,880	696½
1723	**221**			—	17,554			966	139,756	801
1724	195			23	15,253			677	109,530	654
1725	158			12	13,118			637	120,998	1,698
1726	167			18	11,770			735	174,670	861
1727	185			15	16,126			1,008	207,530	1,117
1729	190			42	12,880			705	170,220	1,234½
1730	269			56	19,240			984	250,040	1,314½
1731	182			24	14,680			840	181,350	1,009

SOURCE: P.R.O. C.O. 390/6.

( ) = fishing boats only.

[a] No figures for American ships from New England are returned before 1705 although documentary evidence suggests they were present, in small numbers.

[b] This figure includes bye-boats: boats and men fishing independently from the other fishermen but carried out by the West Country fishermen as passengers.

[c] English estimate of French catch.

[d] Sack ships only.

face of Danish regulation in the fifteenth century.[1] In fact it continued in a healthy fashion for nearly 250 years. In 1528 149 ships from ports along the coast from London to Boston sailed to Iceland, while a further 222 from ports as far apart as Hastings and Whitby put out for the North Sea fishing grounds, and 78 more to fish for cod in Scottish waters. Of these ships, 62 or 13 per cent came from Yarmouth. By the beginning of the seventeenth century Yarmouth was setting out 120 ships, and at the zenith of the English cod fisheries in the 1630s about 200 ships, or about half the English total. The 1650s marked the end of the great era of the English cod fisheries, the total of the Yarmouth fleet being about 70 in the 1670s, falling to under 30 in the eighteenth century. The other ports appear to have followed this trend with a somewhat sharper rate of decline.

Outside Scandinavia, England was the most important cod-fishing nation in the North and Icelandic Seas. The French ports from Dieppe northwards sent a few ships to fish for cod in the North Seas, and at one time Dunkirk had a thriving Iceland fishery, which perished like its herring fishery in the troubles of the sixteenth century. Occasional French and Basque ships were also at work off Iceland. The Dutch inshore fishermen sailed into the North Sea to fish for cod off the Dogger Banks, and tried to invade the Iceland waters. Sometimes they hired Yarmouth fishing boats to do their work for them. Attempts were also made by Dieppe fishermen to persuade Yarmouth fishermen to show them the methods of fishing in the North Sea with the drogue sail in the early seventeenth century. By the later seventeenth century Dutch and French fishermen were regularly seen off Iceland. More cod was caught by the Icelanders and Norwegians using small boats, and wind-drying the catch, in the same way as the Shetland Islanders who fished off their coast. The Hanse did their best to prevent any trade being conducted directly with Iceland and to a large extent were successful in steering all stockfish through the great staple at Bergen. No complete estimate of the size of this important trade can at present be made. Fig. 5 compares the quantities of herring and other fish recorded in the Sound Toll registers. The bulk of this was cod coming from Bergen. At first sight it might appear that the amount of herring vastly outweighs the amount of cod. There is no doubt that herring was more plentiful and more popular in the Baltic than anywhere else in Europe, but it must be remembered that a last is a unit of volume, not weight, and therefore in terms of tons of fish the role of cod is more important than the table suggests.[2]

[1] E. Carus-Wilson, 'The Iceland Trade', in E. Power and M. M. Postan (eds.), *Studies in English Trade* (London, 1933), p. 182.
[2] The chief problem preventing accurate calculations is that it is never clear in the records whether quintals and other measures are those of processed or unprocessed

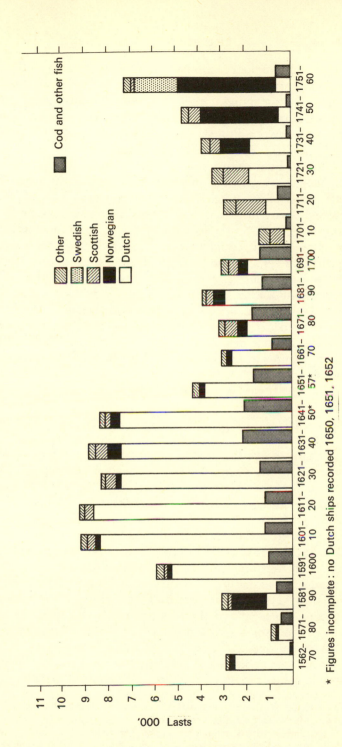

Fig. 5. Herring passing through the Sound.

* Figures incomplete: no Dutch ships recorded 1650, 1651, 1652

Only the roughest comparison can be made between the yield of the English North Seas and Iceland fishery and that of Newfoundland waters. The surviving figures for the seventeenth and eighteenth century are printed in Table 22. These show the yield fluctuating widely from under 20,000 quintals (quintal = cwt) to 219,443 quintals, out of all proportion to the number of boats employed. During the 1620s a catch of 300,000 quintals may have been possible. Estimates for the East Anglian fishery are more difficult to form, but on the basis of the average yield per boat, the total catch during the 1620s and 1630s must have equalled if not surpassed that of the England Newfoundland fishery. Since the North Sea boats were under 30 tons and the Iceland barks about 50 tons, it could be argued that during the first half of the seventeenth century the Newfoundland fisheries were less productive per ton of shipping employed. But this is merely a way of stating the obvious; in the pre-industrial world productivity was not directly related to investment; investment was determined by the conditions necessary to carry on the trade. A study of the European fisheries repeats this lesson again and again. The total cod catch of Europe may have amounted to 140,000 tons of unprocessed fish, nearly a third of the English white fish catch in 1900.

VI.   *Pilchard and Mackerel Fisheries*

Pilchard and sardine are the same basic species, *Sardina pilchardus*, and occur off western England, Ireland, western France, Portugal, Spain, Italy and Morocco. It is closely related to the herring, occurring seasonally in large shoals, though more prone to periods of dearth. Salted pilchards were exported from both England and Ireland to France, Iberia and the Mediterranean. At official valuations the English pilchard export industry came to rival and overtake the herring industry after 1714. Throughout the period under discussion, the pilchard played the same role in the West Country as the herring did in the East Anglian economy, save that there was no Dutch competition with this fish. In Brittany, Portugal and the Mediterranean this species played a vital part in the fishing economy, making up the bulk of the catch of southern Europe.

The mackerel belongs to a different group from the herring and sardine. It is more closely related to the tuna, but behaves very like the

---

fish. A stockfish will only weigh 20 per cent of its weight when caught, a dried fish anything between 35 and 50 per cent of its weight when caught, a salt fish more. A last contained 1,000 cod; but at an average weight 1,000 cod would weigh nearer four tons than two. I have assumed that all weights stated refer to processed fish.

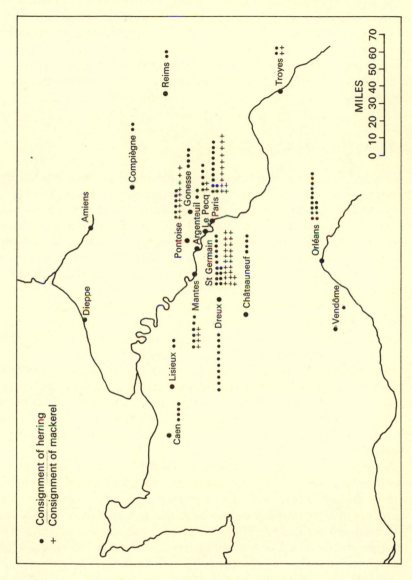

Fig. 6. Shipments of fish by one Dieppe commission merchant, 1729.

herring, and similar nets are used to catch it. Mackerel proved extremely hard to preserve, and the English hardly bothered to try, all mackerel being consumed fresh. There are more references to stinking mackerel in English literature than to any other fish! The French managed to pickle it by using a great deal of salt and sold it over a wide area of France, though less widely than the herring. Both fisheries used small inshore boats, though the French used their herring ships to fish for mackerel further afield.

VII. *The Whale Fishery*

This industry suffered from some of the problems which faced the Newfoundland fishery. It took the sailors a long way from their home ports, and the production of blubber and dissection of the whales made it essential to establish shore bases. As in Newfoundland these bases were sited on uninhabited islands on the basis of first come, first served. There was always the temptation for a stronger latecomer to use force.

The first whale fishermen were the French and Spanish Basques. Having virtually fished the Biscay whale to extinction the Basques went further afield into the Arctic Circle early in the sixteenth century. The area around Newfoundland is said to have attracted over 30 boats in the 1570s, but by the turn of the century it was widely accepted that Spitzbergen (confusingly referred to as Greenland) was the ideal base for whale fishing. The Basques were followed by two equally arrogant maritime peoples who first hired 'Biscayners' as guides and instructors and then rapidly eliminated any rivals, finally turning on one another and on themselves. The English may have been able to harass the French and Spanish in Newfoundland, but at Spitzbergen they were outmatched by the Dutch.

A comparison of the two nations' whale fishery exhibits some of the classic weaknesses of the two economies. Originally Spitzbergen fell within the monopoly area of the English Muscovy Company. The members of this company lacked both the capital and apparently the will to develop this branch of their trade. Initially the running was made by interlopers. The first company expedition in 1608 met a Hull and a London ship at Spitzbergen; in 1611 both the Company's ships were lost and the crews were rescued by interlopers. In 1622 the Muscovy Company auctioned off the whale fishery to a separate concern which began to try to take a tougher line with interlopers. This Company was by this time waging a war on two fronts, against interlopers from Hull, Yarmouth and a citizen of London holding a patent to supply Scotland with whale oil, and against the Dutch who were

Table 23. *Statistics of Dutch Whaling, 1670–1760*

Years	Vessels sailed to 'Greenland' (Spitzbergen)	Whales caught off 'Greenland'	Vessels sailed to Davis Straits	Whales caught in Davis Straits
1670	148	792		
1671	155	630½		
1672, 1673, 1674	The Greenland trade in these years was forbidden.			
1675	148	881½		
1676	145	808⅔		
1677	149	686		
1678	110	1,118¾		
1679	126	831		
1680	148	1,373		
1681	172	889		
1682	186	1,470		
1683	242	1,343		
1684	246	1,185		
1685	212	1,383¼		
1686	189	639		
1687	194	617		
1688	214	345		
1689	163	243		
1690	117	818½		
1691	2	(Sailed from Hamburg and Bremen, whaling being prohibited throughout the Republic.)		
1692	32	62		
1693	89	175		
1694	62	156¼		
1695	96	201		
1696	100	380		
1697	111	1,274½		
1698	140	1,488½		
1699	151	775½		
1700	173	907		
1701	207	2,071¾		
1702	225	697¾		
1703	208	646½		
1704	130	651½		
1705	157	1,664½		
1706	149	452½		
1707	131	128		
1708	121	525⅓		
1709	127	190½		
1710	137	62		
1711	117	630½		
1712	108	370½		
1713	94	256		

Table 23 (*cont.*)

Years	Vessels sailed to 'Greenland' (Spitzbergen)	Whales caught off 'Greenland'	Vessels sailed to Davis Straits	Whales caught in Davis Straits
1714	108	1,234		
1715	134	696½		
1716	153	519		
1717	180	391		
1718	194	281¾		
1719	182	308		
1719–28	1,504	3,439	748	1,251
1729–38	858	2,198	975	1,929
1737	88	149	106	355
1738	74	113	112	360
1739	58	51¾	133	676½
1740	—	—	—	—
1741	—	—	—	—
1742	48	50	125	508½
1743	49	74½	137	850½
1744	39	182½	148	1,311
1745	31	206½	153	362½
1746	40	341	130	820
1747	37	135¼	128	820
1748	—	—	93	217
1749	116	470$\frac{7}{11}$	41	206
1750	112	533½	46	62½
1751	117	264$\frac{11}{12}$	45	65½
1752	117	438¾	42	107½
1753	118	539½	48	100
1754	135	654$\frac{11}{12}$	36	18
1755	152	685½	29	31
1756	160	529½	26	39
1757	159	413½	20	10
1758	151	—	7	—
1759	133	425	22	39
1760	139	376½	15	78

SOURCE: A. Beaujon, *History of the Dutch Sea Fisheries* (London, 1883), Appendix B, pp. 583–4.

mounting much larger enterprises under the auspices of the Noordsche Compagnie, which was virtually open to all comers. At the end of the Civil Wars, chartered company and interlopers came to an agreement to provide 12 ships of which just over half were London-based. In the same year the Dutch sent 70 ships, convoyed by 3 men-of-war. Twenty-five years earlier English ships had probably outnumbered the Dutch. By 1670, according to Zordrager, there were 148 Dutch ships whereas the English trade had almost completely collapsed. In an effort to revive it the trade was made free in 1672, but to no avail, and it was not until the second half of the eighteenth century that the English again became important whale fishermen. The Dutch fishery was hampered by the fact that during wartime the sailors were needed by the States' men-of-war. Some ships sailed from Emden and Hamburg in 1691, but by and large the whale industry was hampered by the war; average sailings during the 1690s fell to 90 per year as against 197 in the previous decade, which in terms of the Greenland voyage was the statistical peak. In the 1720s whaling voyages to the Davis Straits became an important branch of the industry, though it was only temporarily in the 1740s that this area took first place.

Meanwhile the English industry floundered. Neither the abolition of monopoly in 1672, nor the abolition of customs duties solved the problem. The re-imposition of a temporary monopoly with a new joint-stock company served no better. The English could no longer draw on native experienced men, only the last voyage of the Company promised a profit, and this single ship was caught by the ice on its homeward voyage. In 1707 the trade became free, but again to no avail. In 1720 a 'Company to revive the Greenland whale fishery' was formed with a capital of £2m (that of the 1690s had a capital of only £82,000). This was mainly a financial enterprise born of the financial bubble. Curiously it was the South Seas Company that seriously began the revival of English whaling. It was reckoned that three whales per ship would make a profit, but the Company only averaged one per ship. Between 1725 and 1732 the Company managed to make a loss of £177,782. In 1733 the first Bounty Act was passed granting 20s per ton on shipping employed. This was not sufficient encouragement, and it was not until 1749 when this bounty was doubled that the number of English whalers began to average double figures.

The whale fishery had little connection with the demand for food. Only the whale fishermen and coast dwellers dealing with stranded whales ever ate whale meat. The blubber was needed for 'train oil', which was used in the manufacture of soap, for burning in lamps etc., and the bone for a wide variety of items mainly connected with clothing. The course of the whale fishery should therefore reflect the industrial rather than the demographic history of Europe. The failure of the English to achieve self-sufficiency (let alone a surplus) of whale products at the height of their mercantile supremacy, while the Dutch maintained their position despite general economic decline, is interesting. The German maritime towns and the Danes managed to maintain whaling fleets which were larger than the English. More than the question of monopoly, and probably more than the ability to survive years of financial loss, the key factor was skill in fishing and local knowledge, whether fishing for herrings, cod or whales. Fishing was a

traditional industry in which knowledge was handed down from generation to generation, and only slowly acquired by newcomers. The
Frisians took thirty years to become as expert as the Basques at whale
fishing. In every branch of fishing new techniques were hard to im-
plant. Even in the twentieth century some sardine fishermen of Portugal still fish with equipment probably first evolved in pre-historic
times.

The most successful Anglo-Saxon whalers were those off New
England who used Indians to teach them how to catch whales from
small boats. This industry lasted a hundred successful years before the
rise of Nantucket and the building of large ocean-going whalers in the
eighteenth century.

VIII.   *Markets and the Consumption of Fish*

Fish consumption varied widely from country to country, from
class to class, and from region to region. Dietary history is still not well
enough established to be certain how representative the figures given
in Tables 24 and 25 are, but they do illustrate some of the variations in
diet, and the relative importance of fish. These figures do not, of course,
give any indication of what sort of fish was consumed by different
classes, nor what proportion was fresh or locally caught fish. Estimates
for fish consumption at Valladolid in the sixteenth century emphasize
the importance of local fisheries, rather than the long-distance fish
trade. Unfortunately it is impossible to estimate the scale of coastal
fisheries, even in relatively well-documented cases. All that is possible
is to indicate that the inshore fishermen of Europe and not the commercial fisheries for herring and cod may well have produced a sizeable
proportion of the continent's fish. There were also coastal fisheries producing shell fish, large quantities of which were carried to major urban
centres.

Fishing suffered from the pre-industrial problem of bad communications and distribution. Ideally a cheap food for mass consumption, the
problems of rapid deterioration meant that only close to the sea shore
could cheap fish be widely consumed. Once salting and barrelling and
transport costs were taken into account, preserved fish became a commodity which the poorest sections of the community could not afford.
As Thomas Nashe observed at Yarmouth, 'The poore sort make it
three parts of there sustenance; with it for his dinner, the patchedest
Leather piltche laboraths may dine like a Spanish Duke, when the
niggardliest mouse of biefe will cost him sixpence.'[1] An exceptionally

[1] T. Nashe, *Nashes Lenten Stuffe* (1599; repr. Oxford, 1958), p. 179.

Table 24. *Consumption of fish in the sixteenth and
seventeenth centuries*

Grammes per day

Upper class	Italy	Poland	Sweden
Bread	1017	1056	1026
Meat	297	169	235
Fish	27	30	266
Poor			
Bread	968	962	
Meat	145	20	
Fish	28	4	

SOURCE: A. Wyczański, 'Consommation Alimentaire en Italie', *Mélanges en
l'honneur de Fernand Braudel. Histoire économique du monde méditerranéen 1450–1650*
(Toulouse, 1973).

Table 25. *Consumption of fish in Sweden, 1573*

Calories per day

	Agric. servants	Royal court	Counts	Sweden 1912–13
Bread	2,370	2,870	4,195	1,795
Meat	540	945	935	577
Fish	370	450	325	58

SOURCE: E. F. Heckscher, *An Economic History of Sweden* (Cambridge, Mass., 1954),
p. 69.

good catch could lead to a great increase in the consumption of herrings
by the poor. 'Twelve herrings a penny make many a full belly', the
town clerk of Norwich wrote cheerfully in 1665 when herrings were
half their normal price. Efforts were made to keep costs down; in the
sixteenth century red herrings were often transported by the cade (half-
barrel), packed in straw, both along the English coast and to Holland.
On the other hand mackerel, which needed so much salt to preserve it,
was almost entirely eaten fresh along the east coast, aided by the fact
that the mackerel season came at a time of year when all sorts of provisions were at their dearest.

A further complication was that (as already observed) though the
fishermen were prepared to sell their fresh fish cheaply enough, the
fish merchants were anxious to make as much profit as possible. At
Dieppe herring had to pass through two sets of middlemen before it
was dispatched to the Paris market. The fishermen sold to the hostmen
who had a monopoly on all fish sales. The hostmen after curing and

packing as necessary were then required to sell the herring to a further group of commission merchants who actually transported them to Paris or other towns. At Paris and Rouen duties on incoming fish were also high. In fact, by raising the tariff on fish to 38 per cent of the price of the merchandise in 1640, Rouen appears to have eliminated itself as the most important herring mart in France. In the opinion of E. Dardel, both producer and consumer lost by this practice. The commission merchants were able to impose their own price on the Dieppe hosts, 'and as a consequence, regiment the conditions of existence of the maritime population' while manipulating the Paris market through their 'magasins' at Poissy, St Germain en Laye, Pontoise and Pecq.[1] A further disadvantage was that the Parisian merchants, having no interest in the production, frequently preferred Dutch herrings which were universally recognized as being of superior quality to the French. The fishermen/host relationship was prevalent along the north coast of France even in insignificant fishing ports like Etaples. In England it survived long after the hosting system for foreign merchants had faded away. Vestiges can be seen at Brighton, the Cinque Ports and Lowestoft, while at Yarmouth it was carefully manipulated.

In France the native fisherman of Dieppe was as subject to hosting as the visitor from St Valéry en Caux. At Yarmouth the town fisherman was free from interference, selling to whomever he liked. But his freedom was less real in practice since a far higher percentage of herrings landed at Dieppe was already cured, whereas at Yarmouth the curing was still to be done at the first point of sale, and therefore there was only a limited opportunity to look for a buyer. Local regulations also ensured that the 'peddars' (the hawkers who would walk through Norfolk and Suffolk selling fresh herrings) were free to buy at will. All other herrings landed during the fishing season were sold to freemen acting as hosts. Unlike their unfortunate Dieppe counterparts the Yarmouth merchants were in a position to dictate terms to the London merchants when disputes arose. Moreover in such a dispute Yarmouth could rely on government support in a way the French citizens could not.

Surprisingly, the position regarding the Dutch herring trade is less clear. The minute regulations of the colleges were aimed at quality of production, not monopoly of sales, and there seems every reason to believe that the Dutch trade in herrings was conducted on an entirely free basis. Certainly the financing of the voyage was on a much superior basis. At least throughout the seventeenth century most busses were run as joint-stock companies, with an ongoing 'bank' and periodic calls on the partners as necessary. English pamphleteers believed that shares in

[1] E. Dardel, *La Pêche Harenguière en France*, pp. 108–11.

busses were sometimes bought for widows and orphans, and while this
may be an exaggeration, there was no reason why individuals from
outside the fishing industry should not have invested in busses. This
gave the Dutch industry a great advantage over the English and French
fisheries where fishing-boat ownership frequently rested with the
poorer sections of the maritime community. Conditions of free trade
may well have been a contributory reason for the Dutch ability to sell
at what seemed to the English and French to be ridiculous prices in
times of competition. Expectation of a low rate of interest and the joint-
stock system of finance allowed the Dutch to sell at a loss if the market
dictated. In 1700 a French observer believed that the Dutch were over-
fishing for their market, despite the fact that they had sold at a loss the
year before even in the Mediterranean area. This was in marked contradiction to the general pattern along the coasts of Europe, where a good
season meant that more boats would set out the following year, and
conversely in the case of a bad year. Such a practice was still observable
in the early nineteenth century. As a result the financial structure of
the Dutch herring industry enabled it to operate with less violent
fluctuations in the number of boats fishing than any other fishing
industry.

It is normally assumed, particularly by English writers, that the
Reformation struck a considerable blow at the fishing industries of
Europe. This view needs considerable qualification. We need to distinguish between the demand for fish as a basic element in the diet, the
artificially stimulated demand for fish on fast days, during Lent etc.,
and the demand of monastic buyers as an important class of consumer.
In the first case, in countries where fish was an important part of the
diet, such as Holland, Norway, Scotland, Iberia and the coastal regions
of Europe from Trondheim to Constantinople, and likewise the coast
of North America, the Reformation (where it occurred) appears to
have had a relatively minor effect. In England it may have reduced the
number of fishing boats so that fresh fish sold as a 'by-gone' alongside
a diminishing market for processed fish was reduced. Elsewhere it
seems to have had a relatively minor impact, probably hitting freshwater fishing (where the yield was lower) hardest. Even here, and even
in England, freshwater fish supplied from Surrey ponds and rivers were
an important part of the London fish market in the seventeenth century, and eighteenth-century prints of the Thames in the Richmond
area frequently show boats fishing with seine nets, while in Czechoslovakia fishing could make up over 50 per cent of the landowner's
revenue.

The artificial demand for fish, stimulated by fish days and the observance of Lent, was chiefly effective in towns, in inns, and in the houses

of the well-to-do, since the poor could hardly afford meat at the best of times. This was the sector of the market which could afford preserved fish, and which therefore most acutely affected the most highly commercialized fishing fleets. The English experience between 1540 and 1563 was certainly grim, but was not apparently shared by other parts of Protestant Europe. This was of course a time of unique economic dislocation in England, occurring simultaneously with severe navigational difficulties at Yarmouth, and possibly coinciding with a period when the herring shoals were smaller or less predictable than usual. It was also the time when the Scania industry finally faded into insignificance. The fishermen and local fishmerchants of England were more interested in the liberty, granted in 1563 and subsequently renewed, to export fish duty free than in the enforcement of fish days. On the other hand fish days and the enforcement of Lent appealed to the self interest of the London Fishmongers Company, and the fishmongers in other significant cities and towns. But the English fishermen had clearly come to rely on the enforcement of Lent by the middle of the seventeenth century. This is particularly true of the North Sea and Icelandic fishermen, since it would appear that cod, particularly dried cod which was wind dried on the coasts at small towns like Wells, Cromer, Southwold and Aldeburgh, was most affected, dried cod being the cheapest sort of preserved fish. The erosion of English cod fishing fleets in the North and Icelandic Seas after the last enforced Lent of the 1660s was particularly rapid. The English were too well supplied with cereals to turn to fish save in the direst emergency; there was, for instance, a big leap in fish prices in the 1590s. England, though an important fishing nation, was not an important consumer of fish.

The Dutch fisheries survived without any of the paraphernalia of state fish days; so did the Norwegian coastal industry. James I thought it worth instituting a fish day on Wednesdays, Fridays and Saturdays in 1610 'as in all other well governed commonwealths', but this appears to have been a personal whim of that king who, with the earl of Northampton, was actively preparing the first abortive buss fishery scheme.

The importance of monastic houses in raising the demand for fish is indisputable. Monasteries and convents presented a rich and steady demand for processed fish, which the English irrevocably lost at their dissolution, but since these houses had also done their best to provide themselves with fish ponds, the loss was less than it might otherwise have been. Compensatory markets were sought in the monastic houses of Catholic Europe. It is one of the ironies of history that red herrings prepared at Yarmouth, one of the most puritanical of towns, were almost certainly enjoyed by the Pope and College of Cardinals in Italy! On the other hand, widespread exemption from fish fasts was allowed in Spanish hospitals while Italians allowed themselves chicken instead of fish.

The Sound tolls show a continued demand for fish within the Baltic. In the first two decades of the seventeenth century the Dutch were exporting up to 12,000 lasts of herring per annum. There may have been a certain element of 'dumping' in this. The period 1604 to 1632 is the one during which most concern was shown by the fishery colleges about *ventjagers* and others spoiling the market, throwing it 'so much under foot that neither fisherman nor dealer can make a profit from it'. The Baltic was the only market large enough to absorb such quantities of herring, a mere fraction of which would have upset the more delicately adjusted French and Italian markets. The absorption capacity of the Baltic is something of a mystery. Presumably the fish was exchanged for grain, and the real profit was made on the return trade; fish prices in Poland and Baltic ports would well repay study. Certainly there was in other areas a great deal of substitution between types of fish, and one would anticipate repercussions on the limited local fisheries. The Dutch dominated the supply of sea fish to Hamburg, the Rhineland, and the Spanish Netherlands (which because of continual warfare was never able to establish permanently a strong fishing industry during the years 1560–1714), though Hanseatic stockfish was also important in this area.

France was an important market for the fish of many nations until Louis XIV began to interfere with the import of salted fish. France never produced enough fish to satisfy its own population. The erratic fortunes of the French fisheries, harassed as they were by war, allowed East Anglian cod into north France, Dutch salt herring and Yarmouth red herring into Rouen and the Seine basin; in the Atlantic coast ports Dutch, English, Scottish, Irish and north French herring competed, while English and Irish pilchards competed with the native product. On the other hand, France produced sufficient Newfoundland cod and sardines to export to Iberia and compete with native, English, Irish and to a lesser extent Dutch produce. Iberia and the Mediterranean were more favourably disposed towards dried and smoked fish than to salt fish. At Newfoundland the French, Basque and Normandy fishermen exchanged large and small fish so that each group had the sort best suited for their own product.

In many ways the collapse of the Iberian Newfoundland fisheries in the second half of the sixteenth century and the relative infecundity of the Atlantic and western Mediterranean proved the salvation of the English Newfoundland fisheries and the south French fishermen. In a petition to the Cortes of 1558 it was alleged that all the fish consumed in Castile came from the Galician ports. By 1600 foreign fish was predominating. The need to eat fish as a basic foodstuff, where all types of food had to be imported, is underlined in the accounts of charitable institutions by those frequent shifts from one sort of fish to another which made Hamilton's price indices so difficult to construct. Without the continuing high demand for fish in Spain, and of course the growing market for New England and Newfoundland fish in the West Indies, it is difficult to see how the western European participation in the North American fisheries could have avoided the fate of the North Sea and Icelandic fisheries in the eighteenth century.

Like Spain, Italy provided a good market for foreign fish. The discovery of the Leghorn market for Yarmouth red herrings in the 1570s probably did more good than all Cecil's fish days. Even so, by the mid seventeenth century there were ominous signs of a glut of red herrings at Leghorn and Venice. The problem even for the Dutch was that while potentially there was an unlimited demand for fish in the Mediterranean, actual demand showed such price elasticity that at the price which the north European merchants demanded there was only a limited number of takers; hence a widespread feeling that the market needed to be very carefully managed to get the best price.

IX. *Fishing in the Economy and the Government Response*

Approaching European fisheries from an English point of view tends to distort perspectives. No European government took as much interest in fishing as the English except the States of Holland. But the Dutch attitude was purely pragmatic. Fishing was a vital part of the economy of the province of Holland and West Friesland and the States took an interest in its smooth day-to-day running. English intervention was always posed in terms of 'the maintenance of Our navie and Shipping, (a principal strength of this Land)'.[1] The primary motive was therefore strategic rather than economic. This picture is further confused by a large body of economic literature written by all comers from Sir Walter Raleigh onwards, pointing out the enormous benefits the Dutch reaped from their fisheries and describing how easy it would be to build a comparable fishing fleet and capture this important trade. The strategic and economic importance of the fisheries became an accepted truism for all English statesmen. 'Men are all fond of a fishery', the author of *Considerations on the East India Trade* (Anon., London,

[1] The preamble of the Proclamation of Lent.

1701) complained bitterly in the best contemporary critique of this belief.

In Elizabeth's reign the fisheries were seen as a nursery for seamen, which also in certain cases provided useful shipping. In James I's reign there emerges the more mercantilist notion that the Dutch were reaping enormous economic benefit from fishing close to the British Isles, and that therefore the English should wrest this trade from them by building up their own fishing fleet, and by taxing the Dutch busses. James himself appears to have been passionately attached to this idea, and Charles actually used his ship money fleet to tax the Dutch fleet. The fisheries were a contributory *casus belli* in the First and Second Dutch wars. One of Admiral Blake's three major directives when the first war began in 1652 was to destroy the Dutch fishing fleet assembling in Scottish waters. The theory that east coast fishermen were all potential naval recruits received a hard knock during the Cromwellian wars when captains earnestly begged the commissioners of the navy to send them sailors and not fishermen. After the Restoration one hears very little about this idea, except from economic pamphleteers repeating the nostrums of their predecessors. The 1665 session of Parliament passed a bill forbidding the import of fresh fish into England as a limited measure of protection (a measure promoted by fishing boat owners in the country and tacked onto the bill forbidding the import of Irish cattle). At the same time an excise drawback on beer consumed during the fishing season was granted to certain favoured towns (notably Yarmouth) and later a drawback was given on the excise on salt used for exported herrings, the fishing bounty so roundly condemned by Adam Smith and recently by R. H. Barback.[1] The unequal terms of this bounty aided the pilchard industry, but came close to crippling the herring industry. Fishing was never viewed as a vital element in the English food supply, though if one takes the proclamations for the enforcement of Lent at face value, there was an intention to keep down the price of flesh and remove the temptation to slaughter livestock. Some perceptive pamphleteers, particularly in Elizabeth's reign, saw the fisheries as a solution for the relief of the poor, preservation of the rich, reformation of rogues and idle persons and the wealth of thousands that know not how to live.[2] Robert Hitchcock, who got a 'poor law' fisheries scheme into Parliament in 1580, saw it as a solution to social unrest. 'Having nothing, they [the poor] are desperate; but having some little goods, they will die before they lose it.'

Certainly fishing propagandists were keen to point out the backward

[1] R. H. Barback, 'The Political Economy of Fisheries: From Nationalism to Internationalism', *Yorkshire Bulletin of Economic and Social Research*, 19 (1967), 71–84.

[2] R. Hitchcock, *A Political Plat for the honour of the Prince* (London, 1580).

and forward linkages of the fishing industry. One encyclopaedic enthusiast with first-hand knowledge listed 'Anchorsmiths, Bakers, Ballastmen, Basketmakers, Blacksmiths, Brewers, Butchers, Carpenters, Caulkers, Clap Board Splitters, Compass Makers, Coopers, Duck weavers, Hemp dressers, Hook makers, Mariners, Mast Makers, Net Makers, Net Tanners, Plumbers, Pulley Makers, Pump Makers, Rope Makers, Sail Makers, Sawyers, Ship Chandlers, Ship Wrights, Tallow Chandlers, Thread and Twine Spinners.'[1] Certainly Yarmouth merchants were employing coopers as far away as King's Lynn to make barrels against the herring season. All the ships' carpenters were employed on preparing the Icelandic and North Seas fleet in February and March.

If these backward linkages were important in the regional economy of coastal East Anglia, how much more important must it have been in Holland! It was, for instance, reckoned that 2,500 people were kept permanently employed in making nets for the herring fishery. Along the infertile coast of north Holland a large number of people were engaged in some aspect of the fisheries, and although Rotterdam and Delft clearly had diverse economies, Delftshaven, Schiedam, Enkhuizen, Vlaardingen and many smaller towns were heavily dependent on fishing. Johan de Witt went as far as to estimate that 450,000 persons were employed in fishing or subsidiary occupations. It is highly improbable that this is a realistic figure when the total population in Holland and West Friesland in 1622 was around 671,675, but the proportion of the population involved with fishing at least tangentially must have been unique in Europe. Fresh fish could reach every part of these provinces; fish consumption was probably as high as anywhere in Europe and herring was known as 'the poor man's steak'. This was a valuable asset in a province which was not intrinsically self-supporting. The first herrings of the season were rushed inland by carts which raced one another to get to the market first.

Clearly in France, Germany, Iberia and Italy fishing was much less important in the economy as a whole. In France it was tied to the coastal regions where it was a vital element, and a seventeenth-century writer claimed that a million people were dependent on fishing, but in maritime towns like Bremen and Hamburg most fish appears to have been imported. The one vital backward linkage not so far mentioned was with the salt industry. Salt was one of the important bulk commodities shipped round Europe. At the prompting of the Fishery Colleges the Dutch States enforced the use of Spanish or Portuguese salt. Originally in the fourteenth century when the Dutch method of preserving was invented, traditionally by William Beukelsz, local salt

[1] J. Puckle, *England's Path to Wealth and Honour* (London, 2nd ed., 1700), p. 30.

obtained by burning peat was used. From the second half of the sixteenth century the use of salt-on-salt[1] of Iberian origin was rigorously enforced, and salt shipments formed an important part in the return trade from the south. In the years of seizure of Dutch ships, as in 1585, 1595 and 1598, French bay salt from Bourgneuf may have been tolerated, but through most of the Eighty Years War Dutch ships continued to load salt in Portugal for the fisheries. The Dutch 'bay fleet' supplied salt for the inshore fisheries and the Baltic. Salt was even re-exported to England for fishery purposes, particularly during the war with Spain.

The English were usually content to use French salt for most fisheries and Newcastle or Scottish salt for the cod trade. During the 1630s the English salt monopolists seriously hampered the English fisheries by obtaining an embargo on the import of foreign salt. The French were similarly hampered by the minute regulations designed to see that no fishery salt was fraudulently used for domestic purposes to evade the *gabelle*. Nineteenth-century writers like Beaujon believed that the meticulous regulation of the Dutch fisheries, in which the States were continually interfering to regulate quality, supply and convoying, brought about the ultimate decline of the Dutch industry. The Dutch also paid excise on salt and *lastgeld* on their catch. Compared with this the English fisheries were particularly free, but this does not seem to have been adequate compensation for the Dutch ability to raise capital at a low rate of interest and their willingness to accept a low rate of profit.

The French fishery was entirely unregulated by the government until Colbert turned his attention to it. The fish caught by French fishermen was subject to a tax on landing, and many Frenchmen felt this made their product uncompetitive with the Dutch. They were also subject to local tolls. Colbert was anxious to develop the fisheries, but lacked the navy to ensure that they were protected in convoy as the Dutch and (after 1650) the English fisheries were. His efforts therefore remained largely exhortatory until Louis attacked the Dutch fish importers with a ban on salt fish. The French continued to toy with this legislation until well into the eighteenth century. By this time they had, alone amongst the European nations, a fishery commissioner.

Mention of convoys brings one back to the all-important problem of fishing under wartime conditions. Along the western coast of Europe there was a tradition of a *trêves pêcheur*: this was a practice of excluding either coastal fishermen or all fishing boats from the sphere of hostilities. This medieval notion took a heavy battering during the eras of warfare from the sixteenth century onwards. The Spanish government was ready enough to sell licences for the protection of French or Dutch

---

[1] A process by which salt was added to sea water and refined a second time.

boats, so that in the peak year of 1598 no fewer than 879 Dutch boats bought licences. Because of this the fishermen of Zealand refused to pay *lastgeld* on the catch after 1597, on the grounds that the *lastgeld* was intended to pay for their protection, whereas they were buying *that* from the Spaniards. Unlike the States of Holland, the States of Zealand never thereafter levied *lastgeld*. Even in the 1670s licences between the three countries continued to be issued intermittently. Three factors led to the demise of the system. The Dunkirkers and Ostenders protested that it discouraged them from privateering since they could not tell before taking a fishing boat whether it had a licence or not; protagonists of *Realpolitik* (like Vauban) argued that since the Dutch had the most boats any licence system could only favour the Dutch; and finally the English refused to have anything to do with the system. Despite requests from fishing ports in England and on the continent, no official truces were ever negotiated, though simple bilateral truces such as those between Dover and Calais during the 1690s were not unknown. With increasing English belligerence this system seems to have finally died during the later seventeenth century. One of the most serious blows the Dutch sustained was the burning of 100 busses in Bressay Sound in 1703 by the French.

One last instance of government interference is worthy of mention. This was the attitude of the king of Denmark to Iceland. The Danes and the Hanse were determined to keep Iceland to themselves, and prevent any trade with the outside world. Persistent imports of wadmal cloth and falcons into East Anglia by fishing boats belies the efficiency of this scheme, but by and large it prevented any sale of stockfish by Icelanders except to the Hanse who took it to their last great staple, Bergen. This policy did, however, make the Iceland fishing grounds rather more dangerous, since any ship driven into port by weather or accident was technically liable to seizure.

X.   *The Eighteenth-Century Problem*

The yield of the European fisheries was certainly considerably less after 1689 than before. The causes are complex. The probability of natural changes should seriously be considered. Fish populations were singularly sensitive to micro-changes in temperature. The 1680s form a climatic turning point in terms of date of the vine harvest and glacial recession. Fish of all species may well have been less plentiful in the traditional fishing grounds. But even if this is so, the growing relative abundance of other foodstuffs must also play an important part. Merchants in the Newfoundland trade complained that Lent was less well observed in Catholic countries, but the chances are that this resulted from a combination of smaller populations and a relative increase in food. Most fish prices certainly fell, in common with those of many other foodstuffs, after 1650. In France certain species, mainly freshwater fish but including turbot, held their price. Over most of Europe fishermen and fish merchants were confronted with lower prices and probably lower catches. North Sea cod fishermen at Lowestoft complained early in the eighteenth century that they could not see how previous generations made their trade pay. At Calais the traditional shoals of herring ceased to appear after 1689. Enkhuizen herring buss accounts of the 1720s show the consistent unprofitability of the trade as the Dutch industry became caught in a vicious downward spiral of declining home and overseas demand and lower profitability.

With this recession came a change in structure of the industry, at least in England. All along the coasts of Europe fishermen were traditionally paid by dividing the catch or the profits into lots, often called 'doles', and distributing them amongst the crew on a pre-arranged basis. In France this practice continued into the twentieth century. Early in the eighteenth century in East Anglia 'doles' were replaced by money wages with bonuses, a distinct move towards a more capitalistic mode of production. Probably the contraction of the industry was most acute in the wealthiest countries, Holland and England, particularly the latter where coastal fishing as an occupation diminished. The contraction of the Dutch herring industry to less than 40 per cent of its former size must have been a considerable factor in Holland's decline.

Against this gloomy picture must be set the experience of Scotland between 1700 and 1730. The Scots' production of herrings and possibly salmon increased rapidly. Dutch exports were completely eclipsed by Scots in the Baltic. This remarkable resurgence has largely gone unexplained. Was it that the Scots escaped the destruction of capital in the wars of the second half of the seventeenth century which clearly weighed so heavily on the Dutch and destroyed the English cod fleet? Were the Scottish fishing grounds suddenly more prolific? Did the post-1726 bounty stimulate the industry in a way Adam Smith believed could not happen? Or was declining domestic demand matched by increasing mercantilist ability in a booming Scottish economy? The experience of Norway during this period suggests that it was largely a question of more prolific shoals of herring and the absence of Dutch competition. One important fact cannot escape the notice of the economic historian. Throughout Europe fishing industries began to exhibit a new virility in the second half of the eighteenth century. The Iberian market began to consume more fish, even from the Shetlands which had never previously exported southwards. This new vitality coincided with a general upswing in population, and a rise in grain prices. Once again a growing population would stimulate the fishing industry. But even in these more favourable circumstances the fishermen were still subject to the unpredictability of the seas.

XI.   *Conclusion*

The position of fishing in the European economy changed substantially during the early modern period. Growth in other sectors overshadowed the considerable achievements of the fishermen. By the later 1630s the value of Dutch colonial goods imported into the Baltic had come to exceed the value of herring imports. English ports like Yarmouth which had been totally dependent on fishing in the sixteenth century developed other profitable trades. Yet while research has tended to trim contemporary estimates of the size of the fisheries, the early seventeenth-century Dutch industry remained of a very respectable size compared with nineteenth-century fishing fleets.

The most important area in which fishing was actually stimulating economic growth was in the New World. The importance of the Newfoundland and New England fisheries in the development of Canada and northeast America can hardly be overestimated, even if the total catch was not superior to that of other cod fisheries. Finally reference has been made continually to long-distance trade in fish. The fisheries were an important part of the international economy, providing outlying parts of Europe and America with produce to exchange for manufactures and imported food and drink. In the most advanced economy in Europe – Holland – fishing provided one of the principal pillars on which rested a complex if precarious prosperity. Anyone tempted to construct a counterfactual model of the early modern economy without fishing would find the whole maritime economy of western Europe and North America altered out of all recognition.

CHAPTER IV

The Changing Patterns of Trade[1]

I.   *The Ship and the Plough*

Nature indeed furnishes us with the bare necessaries of life, but traffic gives us a great variety of what is useful, and at the same time supplies us with everything that is convenient and ornamental. For these reasons there are not more useful members in a commonwealth than merchants. They knit mankind together in a mutual intercourse of good offices, distribute the gifts of nature, find work for the poor, add wealth to the rich, and magnificence to the great.

The words are Addison's. He goes on:

Our ships are laden with spices and oils and wines; our rooms are filled with pyramids of china, and adorned with workmanship of Japan; our morning's draught comes to us from the remotest corners of the earth; we repair our bodies by the drugs of America and repose ourselves under Indian canopies.

Thus splendidly did trade present itself to the eyes of an English Secretary of State at the beginning of the eighteenth century. Such an assessment, as is well known, is by no means unique in the era with which the following pages are concerned, i.e. the period from about 1500 to 1750. There are countless examples of the contemporary glorification of trade, especially foreign trade, which was regarded as the chief, and by some as the only, means of securing the national prosperity. Foreign trade was the great wheel setting the machinery of society into motion – to use a metaphor which often appears in the economic literature of the period. Trade was the driving force of the nation. The ship, for obvious reasons, was often chosen as the symbol of this dynamic.

At first glance the idea of a close causal connection between foreign trade and the prosperity of modern nation-states does not, perhaps, carry a great deal of conviction. Early modern Europe was for the most part agrarian, and measured by the standards of a later age the nations were small and poor. European cities, apart from a dozen or so capitals, had the character of large provincial towns, whose function was usually to act as the local market for foodstuffs and raw materials. Production

[1] I should like to express my gratitude to E. G. French who in spite of his own literary engagements kindly took upon himself the tedious task of doing the translation of the present paper, and to Yrsa Larsen who carefully and patiently typed the early drafts as well as the final version of my contribution. They have both furnished me with valuable comments and suggestions.

units were generally small and transport links tenuous. Districts frequently produced and sold the same commodities as did their neighbouring districts. A considerable proportion of day-to-day business took place without the aid of money, by barter or some such means; and indeed most of the inhabitants were so heavily occupied in the struggle for their daily bread that they had scarcely formulated any Addisonian ideas about the beneficent traces left on the English morning table by world trade and the division of labour. Stated in economic terms: their demand was inelastic. Replacement of clothes and household utensils was slow, and housebuilding was based largely upon local materials and labour. The market was limited by low *per capita* income and high transport costs. The latter were determined by the structure of the communications network and the slowness of transport. Nature offered resistance: the spatial factor is central to the understanding of the character of trade. Innumerable local tariff and other fiscal barriers had to be overcome in order that a commodity might reach its destination. Safety was no less important a factor in transport. All this, together with the countless trials to which sixteenth- and seventeenth-century populations were exposed in the form of wars, epidemics, harvest failures and other natural catastrophes, seems to indicate that the European economy should be considered as a series of disparate localities and regions in which it is not political frontiers but geographical, climatic, demographic and cultural conditions that determine production and the exchange of goods generated by it.

Viewed in this light it is isolation, not interaction, that leaps to the eye. Where international or interregional exchanges of goods occur, they do so by virtue of a marginal or peripheral demand, often emanating from the towns, from the upper social strata of the population, and from the most important instruments of political institutions, viz. the courts, the armies and the navies. The situation may be illustrated by an analogy with the problems of the underdeveloped countries of today, inasmuch as in the early modern period we can distinguish between a large traditional sector on the one hand, self-sufficient and based upon agriculture, primitive and static, and a smaller sector on the other, modern and dynamic, governed strategically by trade and industry, in which agriculture becomes directly involved in an innovatory process only in the zones surrounding the towns.

It was one of the favourite notions of the time that the sum of prosperity was constant. Men were convinced that anyone who tried to secure a larger slice of the cake could only succeed at the expense of his neighbour. This belief indeed was grounded in experience in the large static sector. The majority of the population was quite literally dependent upon the amount of corn that was harvested. The market was not

without importance, of course. Professor Kula has stated that in
Poland the general level of prices varied inversely with the volume of
the national product, and that in that sense the market exercised a
moderating influence upon economic life. Harvests varied less in
monetary terms than they did physically. However, the situation was
quite simple viewed from the standpoint of the individual peasant or
townsman. It was reflected in public supply policy through the regulation in many places of the prices of basic food commodities. The weight
of bread and strength of beverages were varied in accordance with what
was called the 'circumstances of the times'. This meant that the daily
loaf, which the poor man in the town bought from the baker because
in his dwelling-place he did not enjoy access to an oven for baking his
bread himself, dwindled when poor crops brought scarcity in their
train and increased in weight when harvest improved.

The harvest was society's heartbeat. Oscillations could be violent in
the short term, but long-term changes were modest. There are still
only a few studies of productivity in early modern Europe to draw
upon, but those that are available seem to confirm and explain the in-
grained contemporary belief about the constancy of prosperity. Professor Le Roy Ladurie has characterized the peasant world of France
and Belgium over the long span of years from the fifteenth to the
nineteenth century as a universe in which production was stable,
whether measured by sowings or by area. He describes it as a Malthusian universe in which peasant-proprietors, tenant farmers and day-
labourers, living by manual work, automatically became poorer as the
population increased. Yields per acre were invariable. An increased
number of hands meant fewer working days or hours per individual.
Unemployment and undernourishment were the consequence, not to
mention greater dependence upon landowners and moneylenders.
Indeed, broadly speaking, agricultural production in many parts of
Europe was quite simply proportional to the area under cultivation. So
was the value of land. To sell a piece of land and use the proceeds for
improving what was left is a conception that belongs to a later age.

The output of farm produce served in the first instance to meet the
requirements of the farmer and his family. The surplus was sold on the
market and the proceeds used for defraying rents, taxes and other
expenses and for sundry purchases. If the farmer paid his dues and taxes
in kind then it was the recipients who marketed the fruits of the soil.
What quantity reached the market in one form or another is not a
matter about which a great deal is known, but we can guess that over
the European continent as a whole the quantities involved were marginal. In general terms it may be assumed that even if the producers
were dependent upon market sales of their products, in many places

where subsistence economics prevailed, the extent to which the market influenced the use of resources for production, or the volume and pattern of production, was limited. Variations from region to region were probably wide, however, for the proximity of towns was a particularly crucial factor. The correlation between production and price was negative on the local and regional markets. Large harvests meant low prices and small harvests high ones. The market contracted and expanded accordingly.

Conditions on the international markets were more complex. If one examines, as Professor Wyczański has done, the relationships between Polish corn production and the world market of Amsterdam, one finds that the level of exports from Danzig to the Netherlands was dictated in the short run by production in Poland, i.e. by the size of the harvest. The immediate effect of exports was neither a shortage of corn nor a decrease of corn consumption at home, still less any reduction of sowings. Actual surplus was what determined the exports of the following year. This applies to the micro-economic plane. But in the long run and on the macro-economic plane it was demand that fixed the level. The price situation was the important factor here. Demand on the international market was made up of large geographical components. Demand on the Amsterdam market, for example, can be broken down into demand from the Netherlands, France and southern Europe. Here too the market expanded as prices rose (since it could then absorb the transport costs of longer distances) and contracted as they fell, but political and monetary factors entered into the reckoning as well. In market conditions of such complexity there was, as Professor Slicher van Bath has pointed out, no direct relationship between price and size of harvest in those regions where the international price prevailed. But in the longer term, international demand could occasion changes in the extent of the cultivated area and in the proportions of the various crops. The considerations set forth here apply principally to arable products. But the products of animal husbandry were more deliberately intended for the market, and in the pastoral zones around the towns cash trading was more highly developed.

Productivity of course is different from, and more than, the ratio between sowings and crop yields. There are regions and periods outside the agricultural sector where productivity undoubtedly improved quite substantially. This is true of the mining industry, for instance, in consequence of technological innovations, of cloth manufacturing as a result of the division of labour and the advantages of large-scale production, and of parts of the service sector as the outcome of better organization and greater knowledge.

If we take a commodity important in international trade, such as copper, for example, we find wide fluctuations of output stemming partly from technical conditions – copper-mining experienced a number of bottlenecks during the sixteenth, seventeenth and eighteenth centuries – and partly from the extension of the industry to new geographical areas. Copper was produced in various parts of Europe during the fifteenth and sixteenth centuries, but three principal regions stand out as suppliers of most of the copper circulating in international trade. These were the eastern Alpine area (the Tyrol), the so-called Upper Hungary region (around Neusohl or Banska Bystrica in Slovakia) and the region around Mansfeld in Thuringia. The aggregate output of these three regions was at a high level in the first half of the sixteenth century, running at between 4,500 and 5,000 tons annually. A remarkable decline then occurred in the second half of the century. By about 1620 the central European mines were producing altogether no more than about 2,000 tons annually. However, a new producer appeared on the scene in the seventeenth century – Sweden. Swedish production quintupled in the first two decades of the seventeenth century, and during the Thirty Years War, Sweden became the greatest copper producer in Europe. Its production reached a peak of 3,000 tons annually around 1650. The level continued high until 1690, in fact, when a severe drop occurred. The growth of the production figures, however, does not itself reflect any corresponding increase of productivity, and looking at Europe as a whole it must be said that despite the considerable fluctuations and shifts of supply there seems to have been a kind of ceiling on aggregate European copper production, which scarcely ever exceeded an annual rate of 6,000 tons.

It is possible that similar results would be shown by other fields of production outside the agricultural sector. Professor Cipolla has essayed some discussion of productivity in the Middle Ages and during the Renaissance. His conclusion is that, except for brief periods and in very narrow sectors, the productivity of the economic system as a whole made only very limited progress.

Slowly and sedately did the ploughs furrow the European acres and only reluctantly did nature yield her bounty. The privileged members of society made similar resistance to the *ordo oeconomicus*. Measured against a secular yardstick, the average tended to be held constant by the basic elements in the household of man and nature.

If now we turn our attention to the symptoms of the dynamic forces of the period, it is evident that interaction between the various regions and zones becomes more frequent and that many markets grow vigorously in their geographical extent. When we look at the trend of prices we can see that in terms of the analysis by Braudel and Spooner in the previous volume of this work a degree of unity is discernible despite all the divergences. To be sure, the conductor is absent now and then, and the orchestra plays in many keys – the two scholars afore-mentioned call it a regime of imperfect control – but the unity waxes stronger as the centuries unfold. This applies particularly to intercourse by sea. Regions linked by water are more apt to evolve as part of the same development than are those linked by land; and indeed this is another feature cutting across national differences. The corn trade offers many examples of this. We are dealing with an epoch when inter-national trade is often cheaper and more convenient than internal trade, with the result that specialization between countries is often attained earlier than specialization between the different localities of individual countries. The development of sea-routes, described elsewhere in this volume, is very striking, not to say revolutionary. To the coastwise is now added an ocean-going exchange of commodities. An inter-continental trade of regular character emerges for the first time in the history of mankind. This means that in a number of fields, European trade can no longer be treated in isolation but has to be viewed in a more or less global context. The linking up of Europe and the two Americas in particular has far-reaching consequences for the economies of both continents. These new features, which attracted much contem-porary attention, were not the least contributors to making this the epoch of trade *par excellence*.

It was not only around the sea-routes that international trade flou-rished, however. As a result of his studies of the growth of Antwerp, Professor van der Wee has drawn attention to the motor function per-formed by the transcontinental route between Flanders and south Germany–Italy in the sixteenth century. He has stressed the connection of commercial growth with technology and organizational improve-ments in the land-transport sector. Falling transport costs furthered interregional specialization, which again stimulated trade along this European overland north–south axis. Hidden reserves – whether of labour or in the form of unexploited mineral wealth – were released, and a rise of incomes followed both directly and indirectly. Those directly involved were merchants, carriers, textile workers and mine workers. Indirectly the rings of increased activity spread outwards to owners of vehicles and pack-animals, to saddlers and harness-makers, to innkeepers, hostlers and grooms, to market traders and workers, and further again to the producers of tools and machines, to millwrights and to workers in a number of foodstuffs industries such as bakeries, breweries and slaughterhouses. Along this axis, some of the transit-trade products found their way into new towns which were centres at once of production and consumption. The growth of the towns stimu-lated the demand for foodstuffs from the zones around them, where wastelands and marshes were brought under the plough and where polyculture was frequently replaced by one or another form of monoculture. Growing centres of consumption attracted long-distance imports of comestibles as well, especially cattle from northern, eastern and central Europe. Increased demand for basic and auxiliary raw materials such as wool, flax and dyestuffs is also perceptible.

In Van der Wee's model, maritime expansion is secondary and supportive, not primary and determinant. When transcontinental growth was succeeded early in the seventeenth century by stagnation and decline, some of the slack was taken up by the vigorous expansion of the northwest European colonial trade, which triggered off income effects and exercised a stimulating influence in the regions around the Channel and the North Sea, where new transfers of resources from the traditional to the expansive sector came about.

Growth was not so buoyant, however, as to outweigh continental stagnation and the decay of the Mediterranean world. For in the first place, part of the Dutch–English expansion represented a simple take-over of corresponding Spanish and Portuguese activity; and secondly, colonial activity in the Indies generated only a very limited dynamic income effect in the places overseas. Expansion in the West Indies was dominated by the plantation culture based upon negro slave-labour. Fossilization occurred rapidly and income became concentrated into a few hands, where it produced no widespread effect on demand. Nor was the pirate economy which emerged in certain coastal regions and in the islands of the Caribbean Sea particularly productive of growth, based as it was upon primitive barter and trading transactions. There are ships and ships. Men-of-war, whether flying the black flag or not, were sterile instruments of trade and prosperity compared with heavily-laden corn barges or other coastal vessels with coal and bricks, casks of wine or salt and dried fish in their holds. European activity in the East Indies was still more limited in its income effects. The point has been discussed by Professor T. Raychaudhuri in relation to seventeenth-century India.

Dr Faber's great analysis of Friesland through 300 years furnishes a recent example of the evolution of a region in the northwest European area of development. Friesland lay on the margin of the area of development. It remained securely founded on agriculture and did not have any very sensitive industries linked to foreign markets. Farming predominated and was the great stabilizing factor. The social stability of the region was correspondingly great. Nevertheless we can perceive an economic and social differentiation taking place over the 300 years, notably in the non-agrarian sector, where towns were growing and with them a class of retail traders. Over the area as a whole a middle class and a working class were emerging, and a degree of disintegration of the peasantry was taking place involving farmers both large and small. What is interesting in the present context is the secular trend observable in Friesland. The sixteenth and the first half of the seventeenth century are characterized by population growth, rising prices, large-scale land reclamation, intensification of agriculture, an increase in peat-cutting, advances in shipping, trade and handicrafts, and a growth of urban populations with a strengthening of the middle class. The picture changes about 1650 and is now characterized by slump and stagnation. The number of inhabitants falls; price levels are depressed; land reclamation activity is drastically reduced; farming becomes more extensive; peat manufacturing is checked; so is shipping through the Sound and to Norway; foreign trade dwindles; a number of craft industries decline. The social structure shows signs of rigidity with a tendency towards oligarchy. A renewed upward trend manifests itself in the second half of the eighteenth century, with rising population figures and prices, new activity in agriculture, especially in the pastoral sector, i.e. cattle-raising. Peat-cutting expands, trade via the Sound and elsewhere increases, and the oligarchy loses ground relatively to prosperous urban dwellers and farmers.

There are certain features of the economic system which help to explain the role played by merchants in the dynamics of the age. Outside the agrarian sector, the system was characterized by the relatively moderate importance of fixed capital, the correspondingly large role played by circulating capital, and an enormous need for liquid funds. One of the most important consumers of circulating capital was the labour force, which represented a high proportion of production costs. Rapid turnover in mercantile trading meant that cash could be relatively easily directed wherever expectations were large. The merchant occupied a strategic position. Despite the degree of government interest encompassing him in some places, he was in fact inhibited but little by official regulations, and he had close contact with a large number of possible investment fields. Moreover, the nation's general supply of money, i.e. the monetary system, rested basically upon the flow of precious metals, one of whose determinants was the state of foreign trade. If the supply of ready money fell off, much disquiet resulted. Large parts of Europe suffered during this era under a badly-functioning bimetallist system which was placed under heavy strain from time to time by the operations of money speculators. This was not the least of the reasons why foreign trade became an important factor in the national economy as a whole, and the merchant something of a key figure. The declared aim of governments was to secure for themselves the largest possible share of international trade, and in such a manner as to bring about a favourable trade balance and a net import of bullion and precious metals. The decisive impulses – especially in the short term, which was what always concerned statesmen and businessmen most – came most frequently from elsewhere. Professor Supple has demonstrated convincingly how this applies to England in the first half of the seventeenth century.

If one wished to devise a more prosaic counterpart to Joseph Addison's eloquent exposition of the system of trade, one might say that trade embraces the buying and selling activity intermediate between producer and consumer and undertaken with a view to profit, or income. The activity involves an investment of capital, and one of the factors conditioning its continuance is the return on this capital. Furthermore, trade involves the (geographical) transfer of a series of objects or services. This transfer takes time. The transaction is carried out with the aid of a number of instruments, is arranged by one or more persons, and is accompanied by an accounting in one form or another. It is not necessary for goods to be physically moved for business to take place, but they usually are. The nature of the objects traded makes it possible to separate true commodity trade, with which we shall concern ourselves below in some degree, and trade in money, land, securities etc., which we shall leave aside. The commodity trade can be analysed from various angles: by type of commodity (colonial goods, corn, textiles, metals and other articles); by function in production (raw materials, finished and part-finished goods) and consumption (luxury articles *versus* necessaries); by value (total and relative); by volume, which is related to the transport capacity required for conveyance and the routes (by sea or by land) and distances traversed. A distinction, determined by the scope of business and the nature of the process involved, can be drawn between wholesale trade, retail trade and peddling. In foreign trade it is wholesale business that is paramount.

Most accounts of European commercial history in this epoch have given foreign or long-distance trade pride of place, especially the more conspicuous sectors of it, i.e. seaborne and intercontinental trade. This is understandable, but it has produced a certain lack of balance, which has meant for instance that less spectacular trades figuring among the most important of the age by volume, value and distance (e.g. the trade in cattle) have been overlooked. Another difficulty has arisen in the actual demarcation of the subject 'foreign trade'. Foreign to whom? In order partially to overcome this difficulty, an attempt is made below to deal with the subject in a more organic context. Trade can be broken down into a number of circles or regions ranging geographically all the way from local trade to traffic between continents and socially from the production and consumption of farmers and labourers to lords and princes. Thus, a brief discussion of demand and consumption is required for this purpose. The same applies to some extent to discussion of the market and its organization. Furthermore, we have tried, by devoting a little attention to commodity-flows, to offer an account which is more balanced from the geographical standpoint and which takes due note of the various 'compartments' of European trade. In most trades we can distinguish between a permanent and regular trade, and a casual and variable trade. The structural changes lurking behind the shifting trends of supply and demand are of special interest in an account whose chief emphasis will rest upon the regular trades and their trends. Viewed in this light, commercial history can act as a mirror in which to glimpse the production and consumption patterns wherein the peoples of former days passed their lives, the good times and the bad times and the times between.

The relevant sections of this and earlier volumes may be consulted concerning the organization of trade and various of its instruments. A considerable number of the more technical problems relating to trade routes, ports and transport equipment (ships, vehicles etc.) are also discussed elsewhere. The same applies to commercial and tariff policy and its relation to governments and other interest groups. Lack of information, moreover, means that there are many interesting questions at which it has been possible only to glance in passing. One of the most important problems of the age – whether trade balances were active or passive – belongs to this category. The same applies to the problem of the terms of trade, on which a mere few preliminary studies have been made. The difficulties are associated to some extent with the fragmentary character of commercial statistical data. Many of the quantifiable data in the field of commercial statistics are attended with serious defects. We know that alongside the legitimate trade of this epoch there existed, so it would seem, an extensive illegitimate trade in the form of smuggling and contraband traffic. There was also 'precarious trade', so-called, which is the secret trade under neutral colour between merchants of nations at war, as well as apparently extensive privateering and piracy. Finally, any numerically minded reader disappointed by the absence from the following pages of tables and other statistical apparatus may seek consolation in some of the works listed in the bibliography, especially those of recent date, which contain the data on which the statements and evaluations embodied in the text are founded.

II.   *Demand and Consumption*

'Consumption is the sole end and purpose of all production.' The dictum is Adam Smith's. Others have added that trade is the ingenious mechanism or gearing whereby the reciprocal action between consumption and production is established. Above we have attempted to discuss production in general terms. We shall now glance at consumption, with a view to discovering, if possible, other features of interest to an analysis of some of the fundamental conditions of European trade in the period 1500–1750.

If we are to start by characterizing consumption in very broad terms, it should be emphasized that the dominant factor in the lives of the majority of people was their daily bread. 'He who eats well, lives well' is an ancient rustic adage worth remembering. Man toiled that he might eat. And he ate that he might toil. A Hungarian saying which has its counterparts elsewhere runs: 'He labours well who has a full belly', and to this one added: 'As long as I eat, so must I labour.' 'Heavy' food was appropriate to strenuous manual work, 'light' food to light work. Children were punished by being sent to bed on an empty stomach. Eating made one handsome. A thin wife brought disgrace to a peasant. But of a plump wife it was said that 'a man will love her and not begrudge the food she eats'. Men too ought to be stout. That this ideal was not confined to the rustic world is plain from a glance at the magnificent amplitude of the human frame so abundantly depicted by Renaissance painters. It was the quality rather than the quantity of fare that changed as living standards rose: it became more complex and dainty but not really lighter in terms of calories. Fifty different ways of preparing pork are described by the agriculturist Heresbach in the work *Rei rusticae libri quattor* (1570). Eli Heckscher remarked of the changes in the diet of the Swedish aristocracy from the sixteenth to the seventeenth centuries that these did not involve a quantitative increase in food and drink for the simple reason that this would have been virtually a physical impossibility.

'Give us this day our daily bread' was a prayer meaningful to all, including even those able to look out over a well-laden table as they prayed. Hunger is a feature not easily captured in historical statistics but none the less real for that. Alongside war and sickness, it was one of the acknowledged evils of existence in early modern Europe. Times could change so easily. Supplies could be cut off by war, a town enervated by siege, a port closed to the outside world for months by ice. Or a crop failure could bring famine stalking in its wake. The constant pressure of resources of foodstuffs upon mortality curves is one of the fundamental features of the demography of the period. Hunger not only visited the towns, which were always dependent upon supplies from outside. It also ravaged the countryside, which was far from being a nutritionally homogeneous region but embraced a wide range of possibilities, from the abundance produced by rich arable soils to the meagre yields of forest, fell and coastal tracts. It was difficult to bring succour to a starving rural population gripped by merciless winter, especially in time of war, because of its dispersion and the tenuousness of communications. In some parts of Europe, starvation was deeply implanted in the body social. Professor Goubert's great study of conditions in Beauvais in the seventeenth century has led him to divide the population of France into two broad categories: those who had enough to eat and those who did not. Other regions of Europe featured similar conditions of rural wretchedness, which prompts some reflection on the great crises of disease and subsistence in the late Middle Ages.

According to the Christian concept that stamped western civilization for hundreds of years, the fruits of the soil are a gift, and food is a loan, from God. Conversely, failure of the harvest was viewed as God's punishment. In his struggle for food, therefore, man should not only work but pray. Humility in regard to food was reflected in religious rites. The tale of the feeding in the desert – truly a miracle! – was heard with devotion. The concept of the meal as a fellowship between men grew to that of a fellowship between God and man. Sacrifice and communion became blended. Religious dietary prohibitions, together with otheri ngredients, difficult to define but none the less real, such as prestige, fashion and authority, form part and parcel of the standards of consumption of family and class, of region and nation.

Patterns of consumption are generally not an individual matter, and to discover them is therefore of some relevance in a historical account. Moreover, since they change only very slowly – and this is especially true of patterns of food consumption – they are indispensable to any study of the basic structures of a society. The features determined by religion were the governing factor of some of the rhythms of trade, on both the local and the international plane. Some of the seasons of local trade were established by the demand for food for the festivals. In northern regions of Europe, Christmas was the most important in this respect. The role of the Lenten fast in long-distance trade is well known. It triggered demand for particular foodstuffs at particular times of year. Dried fish from Iceland and salt cod from Newfoundland found vast markets in the Catholic countries of central Europe and the Mediterranean. Sacramental wine for monasteries and churches furnishes another example.

The merchant with his sacks of corn and meal could come as an angel of mercy, relieving the sufferings of the hungry. But he could be regarded also as a fiend, coolly speculating upon empty stomachs and withholding his stocks until he judged his profit to have reached the optimum. Innumerable local, regional and national prohibitions upon engrossing and forestalling testify to the vigour of the forces against which the authorities had to struggle in their supply policy. The merchant indeed was not alone in exploiting situations of heavy demand. The endeavours of local rulers to cash in on scarcity often lurk behind the caprices of the corn trade. They could do this by imposing embargoes on export or transit traffic, by extraordinary dues and licensing requirements, and by other devices. Braudel and Spooner point out that the disparities between European wheat-price series diminish with time, and that after the beginning of the eighteenth century these curves are plainly on the point of merging; and they enquire whether this means that a particular type of merchant capitalism, pivoting upon price differences, is about to disappear. Did these merchants, by over-exploiting these differences, create a system of communications that in the end eliminated their profits? A further question might be asked: was the sting thus taken out of the famine-years so much feared by earlier generations? It seems likely that in some cases years of scarcity and high prices had a stimulating effect on long-distance trade. A period of dearth in Amsterdam, for example, gave the impulse to a large-scale Baltic trade, which subsequently continued in being. Shortage of bread grains in northern Italy in the early 1590s generated a northwest European traffic in corn to the Mediterranean, thereby establishing a connection that became permanent, although based on other commodities once the corn crisis had ended.

The demand for food was many-faceted. There is no abundance of budgets for this period to base ourselves on, but useful knowledge can be obtained in other ways, notably by studying diet, which until recently was an ethnological specialism of no great interest to the economic historian, a state of affairs for which the latter was probably most to blame. Here again, the absence of quantifiable data does not necessarily preclude the historian from informing himself about a number of basic features of the social structure, although he will be unable to measure their importance relative to one another. It is a general principle of pre-industrial economies that they based themselves on local crops. One took what was available. Not infrequently indeed, this ecological adaptation led to considerable dietary imbalance. There are regions of Europe with inhabitants of decided porridge-eating, vegetable-eating, meat-eating, fish-eating and game-eating propensities. On closer scrutiny, these imbalances may cloak distinctive features of trade. For example, good sales outlets in nearby markets may lead to butter, churned and sold in the town, becoming a luxury of rare occurrence on the farmer's own table in a milk-producing region. Many specialities of the European trade in comestibles were in fact reserved for foreigners and not consumed by the producers themselves. These specialities, dubbed with many local names, did indeed abound. They are evidence of an extensive interchange of goods, as may be seen, for instance, from a comparative study of price-currents, market lists and production catalogues. The two great alcoholic beverages, beer and wine, travelled far and wide, on the strength of their local reputations, from such points of departure as Alicante and Tinto, Bordeaux and Nantes, Hamburg, Bremen and Danzig. Local history amply demonstrates that this specialization, generating an interchange of commodities, extends right down to the level of individual provinces. The products of local bakeries, breweries and cheese-factories were in demand in wider or narrower circles, depending upon such factors as perishability. They might be quite insignificant products, such as Skåne mustard, Halland kale and Småland cheese-cakes, all of which were seasonal provincial specialities traded from region to region in Sweden.

When the smallest local units, the parishes, are examined, more than one dietary culture, each with its own demand, can be discerned in one and the same parish. In simple terms, there is poor man's fare and rich man's fare. The lines of distinction can be drawn across the middle of the table. At a wedding feast, for example, the priest had wine to his meal – a consumer article available in Nordic countries only through imports from abroad – while the farmers drank aquavit, which could be furnished from the production of the local town. The cottagers and day-labourers, out in the barn, were given ale with their food – a beverage manufactured on the farm itself. Another and even more telling example of the social hierarchy of eating may be cited from a Swedish farm of the eighteenth century. It concerns the consumption of one of northern Europe's humblest yet greatest articles of trade, the salt herring. Three herrings perform in this everyday drama. The first of them goes to the *paterfamilias*, the second to the chief farmhand and the third to the kitchen maid. The head of the household divides his herring into three portions: the centre cut he takes for himself, giving his wife the head and the eldest child the tail. The farmhand's herring is divided into three also. He retains the centre cut and passes the upper and lower cuts to the second farmhand and farmer's boy, respectively. The kitchen maid carves up her herring and apportions it between herself and the rest of the family.

Of course nothing can be deduced from this and similar examples as to the proportions in which demand is distributed between the various products; still less can elasticity of demand and other quantitative concepts of interest in the modern consumer economy be calculated. The examples merely illustrate the composite character of demand and enumerate some of its elements. By doing this they may also serve to break down the concept of trade into a number of circles and regions, socially and geographically.

Food was the reward of labour and payment for services. Kings and governors accepted food as dues and used it as a means of payment. If there was a surplus, it had to be disposed of through trade. Priests and local persons of authority received food as perquisites for special services. These might be connected with weddings or funerals, or they could simply be the parish clerk's tot of aquavit for reading out the letter of a student son to his illiterate parents. To servants, the reputation enjoyed by a farm or burgher establishment for good food and decent clothing could be quite as decisive as the actual cash stipend. The pride of a household was its stock of food, whether in the shape of the smoked articles hanging from the ceiling, the salt food in barrels and kegs, or the jars of olive oil, raisins, dried fruits and spices. One took food on journeys. It was the custom at feasts, especially among the peasantry, for the guests to supply some of the dishes, so that the occasion became a Dutch treat. Distinct epochs can be discerned in the history of meals: a baroque period, in which excess was cultivated, and a rococo, when delicacy was the aim. Two new beverages, tea and coffee, took their place during the latter period alongside wine, beer and aquavit, and the consumption of animal foodstuffs fell off.

Now and then rulers became worried over the intemperance of ordinary folk's consumption, especially at festivals and on family occasions. They promulgated ordinances without number in their endeavours to regulate and limit gluttony. Princes and their counsellors, however, seldom set their subjects a worthy example: rather the reverse. Royal banquets and feasts were veritable orgies of eating and drinking. The vast capacity of the elaborately appointed kitchen and pantry regions, the brew-houses and wine-cellars of European castles and manor-houses, are testimony to the central role of meal-times in daily life. Bills of fare and instructions to chefs and cellarers tell the same story. The household accounts of great farms, houses and courts reveal at once that there was no question of simply taking what was immediately to hand. Consumption needs were met by large-scale purchases of articles generally supplied from distant places. The same applies to the victualling of armies and navies. These centres of consumption, along with the towns and mining districts, played a particularly important role in the long-distance trade in foodstuffs.

Professor Ingomar Bog has drawn attention to the enormous demand generated by the military campaigns of the Turkish wars. At a conservative estimate, there were 65 campaigns between 1526 and 1718. The campaign of 1689, to cite a single instance, involved a victualling requirement of 260,000 cwt of corn, a massive demand orientated largely towards the upper German market and which left its mark both locally and regionally. Bog argues that demand evoked by the Turkish wars constitutes one of the chief reasons why the agrarian depression came to an end more swiftly in Germany than in other regions of Europe. Another example of military demand is furnished by the victualling of the British Navy at the end of the seventeenth century, when over 20,000 men were committed to sea service – a figure comparable to the contemporary populations of cities such as Bristol and Norwich. Over 2,000 oxen were slaughtered annually in the first half of the seventeenth century to supply the needs of the Dutch East India Company's Amsterdam-based ships: Jutland cattle were preferred because of their fine-fibred flesh, which was suitable for salting down, palatable to the taste, and of good keeping qualities.

The perishability of comestibles set limits upon their transport, but the number of food commodities capable of withstanding carriage over quite considerable distances both by land and by water is surprisingly large. They include most cereal grains, many dried fruits, most types of salt or dried fish, the majority of wines and the stronger varieties of beer, virtually all spices, and such articles as salt and sugar. Even such a delicacy as caviare could be transported as ship's cargo from Russia to the Mediterranean via western Europe. The radius of movement for most commodities was shorter. However, one exception to this was meat, which, in the guise of oxen on the hoof, transported itself over the long and weary miles from the stockbreeder's sheds to the place of final fattening for slaughter and processing in the pots and roasting-hearths of the consumer. Hungarian and Danish cattle were driven over the widely ramified European network of cattle-trails to the great consumer centres of northern Italy (notably Venice), central Europe (where the lion's share was bought by Vienna, Munich and Frankfurt) and the lowlands of the northwest (where Hamburg, Amsterdam and Antwerp were major purchasers).

It has already been remarked that some fundamental long-term modifications of consumption must have taken place during our period; but although various contributions to the history of consumption have appeared in recent years, the ground is still too scantily covered for generalizations to be attempted. Whereas the demand for corn is fairly inelastic in relation to population numbers, demand for meat is to be regarded as elastic. It varies according to income. It has been argued that rising real wages in the late Middle Ages resulted in increased meat consumption, and Professor Wilhelm Abel has calculated that it amounted in the case of Germany to 199 kg per head of population annually. On this line of reasoning the lower real wages of the sixteenth century ought to be reflected in a lower average figure, but growing urbanization may have offset some of the decline in consumption. Scholliers's studies of the consumption of an Antwerp mason family in the late sixteenth century show that bread absorbed just under 50 per cent of living costs, while meat accounted for a good 22 per cent. Heavy consumption of bread and meat was accompanied by ale and wine consumption on a similarly substantial scale, a factor which may have something to do with dietary imbalance, since fare that is principally albuminous requires large quantities of these beverages. Consumption of beef and pigmeat moved downwards in northern Europe during the seventeenth and eighteenth centuries. On the other hand a slow rise in consumption of dairy products, cheese, milk and butter, is especially noticeable in the eighteenth century. But consumption of vegetables undergoes fewer changes, though even within this category some adjustments occurred.

The point has been made that in southern Europe maize, which was introduced in Portugal in the sixteenth and Spain in the early seventeenth century, occupied a more important place than before in the consumption of the people. The same trend is observable in Italy after about 1630. Italian production of rice – and therefore its consumption, since exports are of minor importance – was on the increase all through the seventeenth century. These new food commodities, in conjunction with stagnation both of population numbers and of the general economy, contributed to the subduing of the once so buoyant south European demand for Baltic corn, which had been the prime mover in establishing the seaborne trade between north and south. Expanded cultivation and consumption of buckwheat in western and central Europe in the seventeenth century may be mentioned as another example of a shift in the plant-food sector in which the effects are transmitted through trade.

In the beverages sector, consumption of beer diminished considerably during the period, and the formerly extensive trade in strong varieties of beer was reduced accordingly, with corresponding repercussions on the trade of the north German towns in this commodity, so important in the Middle Ages. The reasons for the decrease of beer consumption are not easy to discover. Some part of it may be laid to the account of competition from the new beverages, coffee and tea, which were becoming great articles of commerce. The emergence of aquavit on to the scene may be partly to blame. This was consumed as an accompaniment to beer, the beer being primed with aquavit; above all, as is well known, the eighteenth century was the age of gin and the century of alcoholism. The combination was not fortuitous. It was a productive association, with beer the subordinate factor. Beer was required in the manufacture of aquavit for charging the mash: the beer used for this purpose was less than fully fermented and so produced vigorous fermentation in the aquavit. At the same time aquavit manufacture yielded a by-product in the shape of the mash or dregs, which constituted an indispensable supplement to the winter fodder of cattle, which otherwise, under the primitive agricultural system, would have consisted only of straw and meadow hay. Straw dipped in dregs stimulated the productivity of milch cows. In Copenhagen, for instance, as in other European cities, a considerable number of cows was kept within the city walls, and it was reckoned that 'braendevin (aquavit) cows', fed on mash, yielded 20 litres of milk a day compared with the modest 6 litres produced by a well-cared-for country cow. Thus aquavit was one of the links in a production chain which now and then was housed under the same roof, with beer one by-product and milk another. Neither part furnished the basis for a trade over distances or of a volume comparable to the strong beer varieties of the sixteenth century.

It has already been remarked that the market played a part in determining the pattern of consumption. A favourable seller's market could affect diet and bring it into imbalance. It must be added, however, that the market itself provided other consumable goods in exchange. It was where the farmer obtained his salt, his spices and other merchandise. And the impact of trade routes upon diet in the broader context is discernible in the overseas products, such as spices and sugar, which penetrated and as it were created a need, first among the better-off echelons of society and in the towns (which were identical with the market places for these commodities), then spreading out in widening social and geographical circles while simultaneously becoming cheaper.

It is also a well-known fact that people who change their place of residence change their habits. Their clothes change first, then their speech, and finally their eating habits. Urbanization changes consumption, and thus the pattern of demand which it is the function of trade to meet. Demand for utensils and other details associated with mealtimes also changes with urbanization. It is a long jump from the common bowl of porridge in the low-ceilinged cottage of the peasant, where the diner serves himself spoon in hand and the ale tankard passes round the table, to the Addisonian high society banquet with ingredients from far and near, with glassware, porcelain, knives and forks; and there are countless transitional stages depending upon time and place.

The demand for mealtime utensils is a variegated one, both for utensils used in the preparation of the meal and for those used in its consumption.

Such utensils circulated in local and regional trade especially, and were carried by pedlars, most notably those trading in Nuremburg smallware. A shift can be detected away from utensils fabricated from copper and towards those manufactured from iron. A cheapening of the prices of iron products was partly responsible for this, but so too was the fact that iron pots and pans were easier to clean and did not taint the taste of the food. This shift can be observed in the trade in these two important categories of goods. The circulation of crockery and porcelain expanded very markedly in the eighteenth century following upon the introduction into the European market of large quantities of Chinese wares. Our collections today are dominated by the spectacular pieces, such as commissioned sets of dinnerware, fine bowls and centre-pieces. However, a study of the imports of the East India companies reveals that it was the less-regarded everyday (and ultimately broken) articles such as kitchen basins and plates that counted. They formed a supplement to local earthenware products, attained a wider circulation in trade than the latter and also gave an impetus to the embryo European crockery- and porcelain-manufacturing industry.

Food, clothing, and shelter constitute a trinity. Whether clothing or shelter occupies the second place in the budget is difficult to say: it depends mainly upon place of residence, i.e. on whether we are concerned with a rural or urban budget. However, there is one similarity between clothing and food that makes it expedient to deal with them in succession, *viz.* the fact that being more 'consumable' than shelter they both constitute a function of current consumption.

As with food so also with textiles: one availed oneself of what was to hand. Local populations clothed themselves with what was available. Almost everywhere in Europe there was local manufacturing of textiles covering most of the requirements of local consumption, especially in rural areas. Despite the high degree of self-sufficiency, however, it is possible here too to descry local specialities, i.e. local techniques and local patterns often circulated by itinerant merchants, who might be hucksters peddling lace, jerseys, table-linen and such items. It is also clear that despite local manufacturing of textiles, local supplies were inadequate both qualitatively and quantitatively. The need for supplementary sources of supply was met primarily by the trade in the products of the more advanced textile centres. These were situated in Italy, Flanders, Brabant, Holland, England, Ireland and Silesia, and outside Europe in India, China and Japan, all depending upon which member of the variegated family of textiles was in question.

Many of the finer fabrics were regarded as luxury articles, which was not to say that the importance of these articles consisted solely in their capacity to satisfy the demand of a class of affluent individuals.

'Conspicuous consumption' was already a familiar concept. The propaganda value of appearing in imposing garb was great and could enlarge the prestige and influence of a royal house. The heavy 'state' dresses of brocade or velvet and silk, trimmed with gold, silver and precious stones, worn by princes and potentates of the sixteenth century, could be obtained by most countries and courts of Europe only through imports. Nevertheless it was not this high-quality cloth that made up the greatest share of the total European cloth trade. Ordinary cloth or broadcloth predominated in terms of value. In some parts of Europe this cloth weighed quite heavily in import statistics, especially in the non-textile-manufacturing countries. More than a third of imports into Sweden in the sixteenth century consisted of cloth. As has been pointed out by Professor Hildebrand, the historical significance of Swedish sixteenth-century foreign trade in textiles, and the real reason for the interest taken by the authorities in imports of such goods, derived from considerations quite different from the demand for such imports by the middle classes and the peasantry. Imported broadcloth had the advantage over the domestic product that it was not merely more durable and elegant but also that the qualities were comparatively uniform. The buyer would have a reasonably good idea what quality to expect. These advantages helped to bring about the use of imported broadcloth in medieval and early modern Sweden by both military men and others. It was not uncommon either that wages were paid, in part at least, in cloth. When Gustav Vasa and his successors built up stronger and better organized armed forces this became even more important. Mercenaries had a traditional claim to be supplied with broadcloth. There were important considerations of prestige involved in the provision of parade-dress. It was impossible, as Gustav Vasa is said to have put it, to avoid acting in conformity with 'other potentates, emperors, kings and princes, so that we Swedes are no more swines and goats than they'.

The lower orders of society, too, demanded textiles which could not be supplied from local production. In Russia in the period from the fifteenth to the seventeenth centuries, for example, only boyars and rich merchants dressed in Flemish or English cloth, while the middle classes made do with cheaper wares imported from Bohemia. The efforts made later in the eighteenth century to promote textile manufacturing in Russia had in view the supplanting of Bohemian imports. Even those on the lowest rung of the social ladder might in some instances be attired in cloths originating from abroad. The Silesian linen industry, which sold its products only locally at first, found a market, thanks to its low prices, in the European plantations of North and South America where there were Indian and negro slaves to be clothed. The

Indian textile industry did the same thing in the seventeenth and eighteenth centuries. Guinees, as they were called, were cheap cottons for use as loincloths and were in demand by the slave traders of the west and east coasts of Africa. They were brought to Europe by the East India companies and sold in Amsterdam and London to companies and merchants engaged in the West India trade. Large quantities of cheap Indian cloth were sold in Europe as well in the second half of the seventeenth century, not only for clothing, especially underclothing, handkerchiefs and the like, but also for such domestic uses as bed-spreads, curtains and so on.

III.   Areas and Trade Flows

One way of establishing a bird's eye view of European trade is to approach it geographically, viewing it by regions, districts or 'com-partments' (an aspect which German scholarship in particular has cultivated since the days of von Thünen). Another is to analyse trade in terms of commodities. This approach affords other opportunities for comparative appraisals of production and marketing conditions, brings to light the links between regions or 'compartments', and provides an opening for a more detailed assessment of the forces underlying the changes in trade. An attempt will be made below to employ both approaches, which are complementary to each other. Some regions generated more trade than others. Both the historian, Bruno Kuske, and the economist, François Perroux, have been somewhat attracted by the concept of 'the dominant area' or 'a dominant economy', i.e. an area or region upon which other districts orientate themselves. Price history offers a number of examples of regional components spatially related to a principal market and so do entrepreneurial studies on movements and the diffusion of technology.

During the period a notable shift occurs away from the dominance of the Italian regions in the sixteenth century and towards the assump-tion of that role by northwestern Europe in the seventeenth century. The shift took place over the heads, as it were, of the two nations of the Iberian peninsula, although commercial activity of global scope was conducted from both Lisbon and Seville. Nevertheless, neither Portu-gal nor Spain managed to develop as a dominant economy. Neither their raw materials basis nor their social structures were adequate, with the result that their trade evolved for the most part into the character of transit trade. The German region, or the southern part of it at least, orientated itself chiefly towards the Italian region; later in the seven-teenth century much of Germany, especially the north, became very heavily orientated towards the Netherlands. The east European 'compartment', too, orientated itself increasingly towards the Netherlands; the social consequences of this have engaged much of the attention of east European historians. The topic leads on to the problem of the trade balances of the various regions, to which we shall revert later.

The demarcation of regions is not without its problems, despite the aid to be obtained from geography, but for a rough breakdown we can look first at some of the classical regions of maritime trade – i.e. the Mediterranean basin, the Baltic, the Atlantic coast and the overseas areas – then deal with some of the continental regions where transport is by river or overland routes. In regard to trade flows, descriptions and analyses will embrace a selection of commodities which, both by volume and by value, are of significance in the overall picture of European trade, in the hope thereby of both raising and illuminating some of the most important problems.

The Mediterranean basin is the classic trading region of Europe, and the conditions prevailing there during early modern history have been the subject of intensive study. Credit for this is due especially to the pioneering work of Professor Braudel, in the wake of which a whole series of specialized studies has appeared. The region forms a world in itself, but linked to the eastward with the orient and to the north and west with central and western Europe respectively. The basin can be divided into a number of major reservoirs of trade: these are, from east to west, the Levantine Sea, the Aegean Sea, the Adriatic, the Tyrrhenian Sea and the Gulf of Lyons. Vast urban concentrations of population meet the eye: Constantinople and Cairo in the east, both immense cities by European standards; the rich plain of Lombardy with the important manufacturing centres of Florence and Milan and the great maritime powers of Venice and Genoa, which were also the home ports of large merchant fleets; next the region of southern France, with dense concentrations of population dotted here and there and a lively traffic up the Rhône valley via Marseilles; and finally Andalusia, furthest to the west and one of the richest regions of the Mediterranean, whose trade burst out of the basin in the sixteenth century and leapt across to the New World, establishing the navigation from Seville to America.

It was principally foodstuffs that entered into the Mediterranean trade. Bulk goods such as corn, salt, salt victuals, oil and wine made the greatest demands upon shipping space. But cheese, dried grapes and sugar were also included in the maritime trade flow of the basin. The Nile valley furnished sustenance for the populations of Cairo and Alexandria and yielded a surplus for export. The same service was performed for Constantinople by the fertile regions of the Black Sea coast. The Syrian trading cities were concerned chiefly with local deliveries. In the western part of the basin, however, local supplies of grain often failed, so that the securing of shipments from elsewhere was here an almost continuous and at times pressing problem. Sicily was the most important granary. Another corn district was Apulia, whose output went to the supplying of Naples and other places. Sicily, together with Istria, was also one of the most important salt producers and a supplier of tuna-fish, which were caught during the season in considerable numbers in the waters surrounding the island. The Mediterranean was relatively poor in fish otherwise. Salt fish was always in demand, and the Italian and Spanish towns were notable importers of fish caught and salted down in the Atlantic. The Portuguese were leaders in these fisheries and in this trade. Southern Italy and southern Spain furnished the bulk of the olive oil traded, while Cyprus and Crete produced wines that were in demand everywhere. Some of the sugar traded came from there and some from Sicily and Andalusia.

The richest of the many branches of the trade in comestibles was of course the celebrated spice trade. Spices entered the Mediterranean world via a long chain of commercial exchanges extending from south and southeast Asia to Alexandria and Tripoli, thanks to the initiative and activity of the Italian cities. Venice was one of the principal centres of this trade. Spices were distributed from that city to northern Italy, across the Alps to southern and central Germany, by sea to Marseilles and France, to the Spanish cities and through the Straits of Gibraltar to western and northern Europe.

Many of the raw materials in Mediterranean trade demanded a great deal of shipping space too. The Italian cloth industry was based on fine Spanish wool exported via Malaga, Alicante and Cartagena to Genoa, Leghorn and Venice. Raw silk, which was produced in many places, was also traded far and wide. One of its most important distribution centres was Messina. Skins went as ship's cargo from Algeria to Italy, while Spain, which was a large producer of skins, used up the whole of its production itself in its celebrated leather-working industries, which also took in supplies from elsewhere. Among minerals, copper, tin and lead were ancient articles of trade. Copper in particular became one of the most important objects of long-distance trade by virtue of the increasing use of bronze cannon. It came mainly from south Germany overland to Venice, continuing thence in the Mediterranean trade to the east, west and south. Supplies of lead and tin came from outside as well, England being the chief source of supply. The Mediterranean region itself produced a mineral in international demand, *viz.* alum, which was indispensable to the textile industry.

Alongside food commodities and raw materials, the various manufactures of the Mediterranean cities found widespread markets: Italian textiles, Venetian glassware, Italian and Spanish leather goods, to mention only a few, were in demand inside as well as outside the area. So were the elaborate varieties of costly oriental commodities such as Chinese and Persian silks, Indian calicoes and precious stones.

It was the Italian city-states particularly that represented in the sixteenth century the dynamic element in the Mediterranean region and which established the link between it and the world beyond. The Italian merchant houses of the Renaissance were pioneers everywhere, not only in transport itself but in the methods by which trade was organized, recorded and financed. There is much evidence to confirm this; to mention just one example: Francesco Datini, of Prato, merchant in wool, an extraordinarily large part of whose archives has survived (his records having been studied by the Prato Institute under the direction of Professor Melis). The commercial empire of the Italians covered a wide area, ranging from the Levant to central and western Europe, whither their connections reached out either overland via the German cities or via Lyons, or by sea to the Iberian peninsula and around it to London, Bruges and Antwerp. The links functioned in the opposite direction as well. The Fuggers, the greatest mercantile dynasty of the sixteenth century, were particularly active in the trade from south Germany and Hungary to Venice and beyond into the Mediterranean region: their operations were based upon the export of copper and silver, and the import of spices, notably pepper. Evidence of the south German influence in Venice is furnished by *Fondaco dei Tedeschi*, which served as a market place, entrepôt and hotel for German merchants (recently forming the subject of renewed and detailed research by the French historian Ph. Braunstein). There were very close business links between Italy and the Iberian peninsula too, as Professor Ruiz-Martin, for instance, has demonstrated (on the basis of another example of information about the Mediterranean world, the house of Felipe Ruiz).

The Mediterranean basin showed itself during the course of the second half of the sixteenth century to be increasingly dependent upon supplies from the world outside. This was especially true of the corn supply. Shortage began in the west and extended eastwards until at last Constantinople was affected. One of the causes of this worsening shortage – which in fact affected the whole area – was a general increase in population. This is the context in which shipments of corn were obtained from sources not previously resorted to, *viz.* the northwest European and Baltic regions. English and Dutch ships – notably the latter – were engaged in this traffic, which also embraced the supply of salt herring from the North Sea as well as increasing quantities of skins imported into Spain and Italy from Poland, Russia and the New

World. At the same time the old spice trade with the Levant via the Italian cities was beginning seriously to feel the effects of competition from the new Cape route towards the end of the sixteenth century. The massive exertions of the new west European East India companies, especially the Dutch, brought the Venetian paramountcy to an end around the turn of the century. The northwest European trading nations penetrated further and further into the basin, bringing with them new articles of trade, such as fabrics for the Levant market, with the result that the Mediterranean ceased to be a world of its own. The economic power-centre had shifted northwestwards into Europe.

The Atlantic coast from the Straits of Gibraltar to the Channel can also be regarded as one of Europe's ancient and important trading 'compartments' which, with its many coastal harbours and river estuaries, was the scene of a port-to-port trade of a variety and volume capable of bearing comparison with that of the Mediterranean, and which indeed was intimately linked with the latter, as it was with northern Europe too.

As with the Mediterranean region, the Atlantic coastal trade was mostly of bulk character, comprising everyday commodities such as corn, oil, salt, wine and wool. The dominance of salt is noticeable in the traffic between the Atlantic and north European regions, the connection being so close that it is almost meaningless to make a distinction between the two regions; cf. Professor Virginia Rau's and Professor Pierre Jeannin's studies of this important article. France and Portugal were the two rival suppliers of sea salt: the consumers were the lands around the North Sea and the Baltic. The trade was complemented by a flow of corn in the opposite direction to offset the increasing dearth of bread grains in Portugal and Spain. These two commodities, in fact, occupied a key position in the international maritime traffic of the sixteenth century. Their bulk character explains why their prices were very much bound up with the actual transport costs. It is also symptomatic that for a long time a ship's carrying capacity was measured simply by stating the number of lasts of corn and salt it could hold. Salt was the most voluminous commodity in the west- and eastbound navigation through the Sound, and the customs officers at Elsinore classified the shipping trade into the Baltic in two main groups: ships in ballast and salt ships from France, Portugal and Spain.

It was the merchants of the northern region who were the most heavily engaged in the exchange of goods between the coasts of the Atlantic and northern Europe. At the beginning the Hanseatics and the Dutch were particularly active, and later on Dutch cargo traffic wholly dominated this navigation. The Scandinavian nations adopted it as one of the principal aims of their mercantilist policy to employ tariffs and subsidies in order to attract some of the salt trade into their own ships, but not until the end of the seventeenth century were the Dutch forced to concede a share of the freight market to Scandinavian as well as English and Scottish shipowners. Russia, too, emerged as an active trader in salt in the eighteenth century, and as its traffic with the Mediterranean grew another salt route was established from southern to northern Europe. Lisbon and Danzig were the chief termini of the Atlantic–north European traffic, and it is a matter for wonderment that the exchange of goods between the two areas became a Dutch speciality; but as stated below in the section on corn, part of the reason was that country's intermediate geographical position, which permitted business to be done with both trade terminals in one and the same trading season.

It was from bases in the Atlantic coastal region that the most spectacular trade of the age was conducted: the transoceanic trade, with its two long arms reaching out to Asia and to the Americas. The Iberian peoples were the pioneers. The Portuguese had been driving westwards, southwards and northwards into the Atlantic since the Middle Ages in a mixed effort of exploration, fishing and colonization. The desire for trade fuelled the machine too, especially along the African coast. The movement culminated in 1496 in the opening of the southern sea route to the Indies round the Cape of Good Hope, and contact was established with the New World shortly afterwards. The Portuguese monopoly of transoceanic traffic to the east endured for the best part of a hundred years. Then a number of countries in the north European sector emerged as competitors: Holland, England, France and Denmark–Norway. The Dutch trade attained particularly imposing dimensions in the seventeenth century, extending over the whole of maritime Asia, from Japan in the east and via Formosa to various stations in southeast Asia, with Batavia on Java as the Asiatic headquarters, and thence onwards over India, Ceylon, Persia and Arabia to South Africa in the west.

A universal feature of European trade with the Orient was its decided bias towards imports. It was not undertaken primarily in order to secure new sales outlets for European products, although the English company in particular did at first repose great hopes in the Indies as a market for English cloth. One engaged in the business in order to obtain those prized commodities which, though condemned as luxury by the pedants of the time, pleased the palate and decorated the body. The only 'commodity', apart from weapons and ammunition, that could find a market was bullion. The changes in European demand are reflected in the pattern of imports. In the sixteenth century, spices were paramount, especially pepper, but the range of merchandise became more varied as the seventeenth century progressed, and spices lost ground in step with the modification of eating habits in Europe, where the formerly massive consumption of meat – in the processing of which many of the spices had been used – was on the wane. East Indian textiles succeeded spices as the dominant group of commodities imported into Europe. These were accounting for over 40 per cent of the Dutch East India Company's imports around 1700. Later on, in the 1720s and 1730s, coffee and tea (especially the latter) came very much into demand, being responsible for about a quarter of the Dutch company's imports around 1740. Prices fell as import figures rose. Tea ceased to be an expensive drug on the chemist's shelves and became a popular drink.

With the tea trade a new chapter began in the history of the European trade with Asia. The older traffics were characterized by steadily rising protection costs, with a most complicated process of collection involved in procuring the return cargoes destined for Europe, many of which could be obtained only by active participation in the Asian country trade: tea cargoes, on the other hand, were mostly obtained by sailing direct to Canton, in China, where the imperial officials fixed the conditions under which the Europeans traded. All European nations enjoyed free admission, which in itself rendered the old companies' monopoly of navigation east of the Cape of Good Hope illusory. The direct trade to China encouraged interloping. New European trading partners of Canton appeared on the scene: Ostend, Hamburg, Copenhagen and Gothenburg. From the point of view of the small European countries this trade had the great advantage of not being burdened with the usual expensive colonial overheads. The arrival of new participants in the trade intensified the competition. The benefits soon emerged in the form of higher turnover with lower returns, and of rapid transport. European trade with Asia was thus split into two halves: traditional, slow and expensive *versus* direct, swift and cheap.

The Atlantic oceanic trade differed from the Asiatic first and foremost by virtue of the colonization taking place in the New World, which ranged from the colony of settlement established by the English and the French in North America, via the plantation type of colony that emerged in the southern states of North America, the West Indian islands and Portuguese Brazil, to the mixed forms of colonization in the Spanish colonies of Mexico and Peru. Only in the less hospitable regions of South America, where the conditions of geography and demography made white settlement on a major scale impossible, was a factory system established reminiscent of that in Asia. The acquisition of land and its exploitation by local or imported labour marked the intercourse between the Old World and the New. The mining of the

New World's deposits of precious metals, and the flow of precious metals from the Spanish-owned mines of Central America to Seville and Cadiz, whence the American treasure was distributed to the rest of Europe, had profound repercussions upon the European economy. This flow was supplemented later on by the Brazilian gold which found its way into circulation via Lisbon.

Of greater bulk in the traffic between the New World and the Old, and just as vital from the purely commercial standpoint, were Brazil wood, sugar, tobacco and cotton. The cod fisheries of Newfoundland and the fur trade of North America added further commodities greedy of shipping space to the international circulation. Sugar and tobacco, like tea, made the leap during the seventeenth century from the exclusive luxury price level down to the mass consumption level. These two articles became the foundation of the entrepôt trade which developed in the second half of the seventeenth century in Holland and England, where the re-export of colonial goods accounted for a steadily increasing proportion of foreign trade.

Exports from Europe to the two Americas were very varied and reflected the needs of the colonial communities. They ranged from cloth, household articles and implements, to wine and other consumer goods. Towards the end of the period especially, the demand for manufactured products of every kind for the fast-growing North American colonies was of great importance to England, whose foreign trade around 1700 was for the first time in hundreds of years losing its one-sided dependence on cloth exports and becoming based upon a broad-spectrum supply traffic to the colonies and a re-export trade in colonial goods.

Then there was the exporting of human beings across the Atlantic. The transfer of manual labour swiftly embodied itself in the system as a dominant feature of the traffic. Portugal, a slave-owning country before she became a colonial power, led the way. Negro slavery spread with sugar cultivation, from Portugal to the Atlantic islands and on to Brazil and the New World. The slave trade from Africa to Brazil and the West Indies became one of the cornerstones of the Atlantic trading system, which reached its apogee in the seventeenth and eighteenth centuries. One of the components of the system comprised the various forms of triangular trade such as that between Europe, Africa and the West Indies, or between the North American colonies, Africa and the West Indies, or – without slaves – between northern Europe, North America and southern Europe. In the last-mentioned case, manufactured articles were exchanged for fish, meat, timber and corn, which in turn were exchanged for wine and southern fruits. The supplying of the New World with negro labour became a trade that in the latter part of our period was marked by fierce international rivalry. This was the principal reason why, in the seventeenth century, eight European nations were engaged in a race for territory in West Africa. A particularly intense competition developed over the *asiento*, *viz.* the monopoly of the supply of labour to the Spanish colonies. This had been in Portuguese and French hands up to the Treaty of Utrecht; the British habit of sending more shiploads of *other* merchandise than the treaty permitted turned the *asiento* into an instrument by which Britain extended its influence in Spanish America to such a degree that it might be regarded as an English rather than a Spanish trading colony.

There were various links between the two great ocean trades mentioned above. Metals knew no frontiers and flowed all around the globe – some of them via the back door, as it were, *viz.* from Acapulco on the Pacific coast to Manila in the Philippines, whence they merged into the Asian circulation. It is easy to indulge in exaggerated talk of a world economy and global business cycles in the period 1500 to 1750. Nevertheless it cannot be denied that in the throbbing of the pulse of economic life both within and beyond Europe, it becomes increasingly possible to detect rhythms which echo or reproduce themselves over long distances. The great influx of silver and gold from the Americas extended to Asia from Europe, and the price revolution accompanied it. Dr Aziza Hasan, the Indian historian, has recently adduced interesting statistical evidence of this. By means of a tabulation of the surviving coins by years he has constructed currency-output curves and currency-in-circulation curves for northern India during the Moghul period. A comparison with the import of American treasure into Spain has revealed a degree of correlation which strongly suggests that the silver influx into Europe extended to India during the late sixteenth and early seventeenth centuries. Dr Hasan has also substantiated the view that some of the price changes in India were largely due to the influx of silver from Europe, although his information on this point is much more fragmentary.

A number of globetrotters are to be found among commodities as well. One example is furnished by the Indian textile articles known as *guinees*, named after Guinea in Africa, where they were used as cheap loincloths for negro slaves. Cowries, the mussel shells brought up from the blue waters of the Indian Ocean off the Maldives and accepted as currency in parts of Africa, were an article in demand in the African slave trade. Amsterdam was the chief market for them, the Dutch East India Company being the main supplier and the West India companies and others trading with Africa and the Americas the principal buyers. Nor was there any want of projects for merging the East and West Indies trade; interloping individuals especially, dreaming of evading the monopolies of the great companies, were attracted by such schemes. Most of the plans remained on paper, however, and the few attempts made to put them into practice were shortlived.

Overseas and European articles were offered in competition with one another in the principal market places of Europe: sugar from Java, Bengal, Madeira, Sao Tomé, Brazil, the West Indies and the Mediterranean region; tobacco grown in tropical, sub-tropical and temperate climates; Chinese, Persian and Italian silk; Japanese, Hungarian, Swedish and West Indian copper; Asian spices *versus* American; coffee from Mocca, Java and the West Indies. Business and prices at selected places display numerous instances of uniform fluctuation. Examples of good observation posts from which to view the state of international trade are furnished by sailings through the Sound to and from the Baltic, by the traffic to and from the New World by way of Seville, and by statistics from Lisbon or from Manila in the Philippines. However, the best barometer of all is provided by the prices on the commodity exchanges of Amsterdam. The annual prices of colonial goods in this, the most important market place of Europe, are probably the closest we can get to a global trade cycle. The European price-currents do reflect a regular traffic, moving along an elaborate network of trade routes and collected into a European redistribution system of which Antwerp, Amsterdam, London and Hamburg were some of the most important centres. An embryonic international division of labour had been established – or, as an English economist, Dudley North, wrote in 1691: 'The Whole World as to Trade, is but as one Nation or People, and therein Nations are as Persons.'

The Baltic has been called a Mediterranean in miniature, and some of the geographical components of each are indeed reminiscent of the other. However, the Baltic region is less self-contained than the Mediterranean. It is set in the context of a vaster north European area extending from the northern coast of the Netherlands via the North Sea, Cattegat and Belt to the Baltic Sea. We can distinguish between two trades in this area: a seaborne and an overland trade, both in bulk goods for daily use. The first includes grain, salt and salt fish, woollen cloth and furs, together with such commodities as timber and other forest products, e.g. potash, pitch and tar, and also flax and hemp, iron and copper. The salt and cloth, and from about the middle of the sixteenth century herring too, moved from west to east, while the other goods travelled in the opposite direction. The second trade embraced but a single commodity, though one possessing the extraordinary capacity of being able, so to speak, to transport itself – oxen, which moved from north to south.

The Baltic itself was the granary of northern Europe. It was also, at the beginning of the sixteenth century, the chief northern source of another vital food, namely salt herring. The principal fisheries were those of Skanör, at the southern tip of Sweden, and off the island of Rügen. The salt used came either from Lüneburg in northern Germany, supplied by way of Hamburg or Lübeck, or from the Biscay coast of France. In the course of the first half of the century the herring fisheries declined, mainly because the herring were disappearing from the Baltic; to replace them, large-scale herring fisheries developed on the Dogger Bank and elsewhere in the North Sea. Two groups of port towns competed in the seaborne trade of northern Europe, those of the North German Hanse and those of the Netherlands. Hanseatic traders had in the Middle Ages predominated in the Baltic trade and in the trade to Scandinavia and Iceland, as well as on the North Sea, but changes in trade routes and trade relations tended to favour the Dutch at German expense. The sea route from the North Sea around the Skaw and through the Sound into the Baltic was pioneered by the Dutch and soon came to surpass the old overland route from Hamburg to Lübeck. The Danish Sound Toll Register shows Dutch ships already forming a majority of the vessels passing the Sound in the 1490s. The proportion increased steadily in the next century and a half. However, Lübeck held a central position in the Baltic trade for most of the sixteenth century, as has been illustrated by Pierre Jeannin in an analysis of shipping traffic around 1580. Amsterdam's supremacy was particularly important in the corn trade, the city becoming in fact the principal grain market for the whole of Europe. The corn trade and the fisheries comprised the core of the impressive Dutch commercial empire of the seventeenth century. In the carriage of both bulk and general cargoes they were unrivalled. At the end of the seventeenth century the whole carrying trade between France and northern Europe and most of the corresponding English trade were in Dutch hands. Not until the eighteenth century were the English able seriously to challenge the Dutch in the trade of northern Europe.

The Dutch were not the only competitors of the Hanseatics, however. The transcontinental trade also curtailed the activities of the Hanse towns in the west, where the old staple place of Bruges was overtaken by Antwerp in the same way as their eastern operations were abridged by the Fuggers' shipments of copper from central Europe via Poland and the Baltic to Antwerp. The Nordic countries too joined in the effort to make inroads into the Hanseatic trade. So did English merchants. Finally, the new trade routes created tensions within the Hanseatic League itself. The merchants of Danzig and the other eastern Hanse ports found it advantageous to cooperate with the Dutch. The Wendish towns headed by Lübeck found themselves isolated. Hamburg went its own way and became a great city. It is symptomatic that in 1611 the English Merchant Adventurers fixed their German head-quarters at Hamburg, where they remained until the nineteenth century. Thus it is an exaggeration to imagine the Hanse towns as being in decay. They lost terrain relatively to the Dutch dynamo in the west, but some of them were able to adapt themselves to draw advantages from the new pattern of trade in northern Europe.

The overland trade in oxen in the north European region extended from northern Jutland, the Danish islands and Skåne (Scania) down through the Duchies of Schleswig Holstein to the Elbe, where the principal market for cattle was situated and whence cattle were dis-tributed to the north German towns, especially Lübeck and Hamburg, to the Rhine cities as far as Cologne, and to the Dutch towns, especially Amsterdam. As also in the case of corn, the background to this trade, the volume of which can be seen from the surviving customs ledgers, is to be found in the demand emanating from the growing populations of western Europe, especially the Netherlands. Population numbers in the Netherlands doubled in the period 1500–1650, and of this increase a substantial proportion occurred in the towns, which in the province of Holland itself accounted for no less than half of the total population. The densest concentration of population in Europe outside of northern Italy was in this northwestern corner. Part of the food supply of these towns, in fact, came to consist of Polish corn and Danish cattle. This trading relationship became of the highest importance, both economic-ally and socially, to the countries concerned.

Stagnating west European population numbers in the second half of the seventeenth century in conjunction with increased output of farm produce in western Europe – England among others became a net exporter of corn – caused the demand for both corn and cattle to fall. The south European demand for corn was decreasing too in the second half of the seventeenth century. This reduction of shipments, especially of corn, had a crucial impact on the economic life of the Dutch com-mercial republic, where the decline was not offset by progress in other branches of trade. The trade of Holland still played a vital role in inter-national business up to 1730. Then it ebbed away. Dutch commercial capital moved into government bonds and other safe securities. The dynamic centre crossed to the other side of the Channel.

It has been suggested above that any clear-cut division of trade into sea and land compartments is something of an abstraction. In the real world, land and sea traffic were intermingled. Rivers were especially important as feeder-routes to the sea ports. Some of the European production regions, moreover, were geographically on such a scale and so located that their products were marketed via diverse outlets, and not all the trade routes have left an equally good trail of statistics. One example that may be cited is the east European (Russian) production regions, whose products (flax, hemp, tallow, wax, skins and furs) found their way overseas to western Europe via the Baltic ports, and after the middle of the sixteenth century via the Arctic Ocean (Archangel) and overland to central Europe, Persia and Siberia. It has recently been stressed too (by Mirslaw Hoch) that, until a number of regional analyses have been made, the concept of compartments will remain a fluid one. Thus, in the European context the central European region sub-divides into not only eastern and western but also northern and southern districts.

If notwithstanding these reservations one were to attempt to view the great continental European trading compartment in perspective from east to west, one might follow Professor Kellenbenz in pointing out the north–south lines, created by nature, which break up the compartments and very broadly speaking correspond to the political divisions of early modern Europe. The first of these lines consists of the river systems of the Volga, Don and Dvina, the second of the Dnieper, Bug and Dniester, the third of the Duna, Memel and Vistula, and the fourth of the Oder, Weser and Rhine. Only the Danube flows in a west–east direction. A number of commercial routes connect up these 'compartments': examples are the routes over Novgorod and Pskov, the southern route through Plotzk to Vilnius and Kaunas, and also the routes via Smolensk and Kiev respectively. The west European routes were connected to the Polish 'compartment's' links with Moldavia and Wallachia and to the Siebengebirge. Such commercial centres as Warsaw, Crakow, Lemberg (Lwow) and Chemnitz were situated along these lines. Furthermore, a network of routes ran westwards from the Polish 'compartment'; one of the most important of them, the celebrated *Hohe Landstrasse*, led via Silesia and Saxony to Thuringia, passing through Leipzig and Erfurt and terminating at Frankfurt. Breslau (Wroclaw) in Silesia was a nodal point of two diagonals. The old *Bernsteinstrasse* from the south to the Baltic here met the route running from Flanders via Liegnitz, Breslau and Crakow to Lemberg and Kiev and on to the Black Sea. The German 'compartment' indeed was penetrated by a network of land routes and rivers. The Danube and the Rhine stand out as the most important arteries of trade. The Fuggers' principal seat of Augsburg, Regensburg and – greatest of all in its number of inhabitants – Nuremberg organized the transit trade between the Mediterranean and important parts of continental Europe. In the year 1500 the so-called 'great trading company of Regensburg' had offices in Vienna, in Budapest, in Berne and Geneva, at Lyons, Avignon and Marseilles, in Milan and Genoa, in Barcelona and Valencia, at Antwerp

and in Cologne and Nuremberg. The central European towns themselves represented consumption and production units of significance in
the international exchange of goods; for example, they attracted large
supplies of cattle and other foodstuffs from Hungary and Poland. On
the production side it was metal and metal goods that furnished the
basis of large-scale trade in the central European 'compartment'.

An economic expansion based on central European silver production
was already under way in the second half of the fifteenth century. It was
orientated from south Germany towards the Netherlands, especially
Brabant, and it continued into the sixteenth century, though now with
copper as the driving force. Sales of the latter became concentrated
more and more at Antwerp, whose rise rested upon a commercial
alliance between that metal and silver from both the Old and the New
Worlds as well as spices arriving via Portugal. A number of other
commodities followed – cloth, linen, canvas, hops, and corn – and were
drawn into international business. Overland traffic expanded, the
Netherlands and northern Italy being the two terminal areas. This
trading axis was dominated around the middle of the sixteenth century
by large firms and their transactions. The combination of transcontinental trade and maritime expansion stamped sixteenth-century
merchant capitalism, centred on Antwerp, as described and analysed by
Professor van der Wee. South German merchant houses, the factors of
the Portuguese crown, English Merchant Adventurers, Italian and
Hanseatic merchants and Netherlanders themselves were the active
entrepreneurs of the brief but hectic epoch that ended so dramatically
with the conquest of the city by Parma in 1585 and the blockade of the
Scheldt by the Dutch. The expansion had already changed its character
by that time: transcontinental trade was losing ground to maritime;
business at the Brabant fairs was declining in the middle thirty years of
the century; in Germany the economy was being ravaged by the
religious wars; and in northern Italy competition was beginning to be felt
from the Dutch and English trade offensive in the Mediterranean basin.

The southeast European 'compartment' perhaps illustrates the difficulties of the geographical classification better than any other, partly
because of its size and diversity and partly because, with the Ottoman
empire's growth, the political boundaries cut across the geography.
Although there is at no time any question of the boundaries cutting the
trade routes, nevertheless they do weaken them and cause the routes to
be modified. In southeastern Europe the circle in a sense is closed,
inasmuch as we are back at the Mediterranean, to which part of the area
belongs.

The Italian cities, notably Ragusa, were here instrumental in the
region's commercial intercourse with the outside world. We find

Ragusa merchants at many places in southeastern Europe in the sixteenth century: Sofia, Varna, Belgrade, Hermannstadt (Sibiu), Alba Julia, Temesvar and Ofen, Salonika and Istanbul. Ragusa's neutrality during the naval wars in the Mediterranean contributed to this position. English cloth was imported via Ragusa (especially into Serbia and Bulgaria) as also were silk, spices, sugar and olive oil. The Turkish region exported wool, skins and cattle, wax, honey and (especially from Macedonia, Greece and Thrace) considerable quantities of corn. The English Levant Company became a factor after the end of the sixteenth century in the seaborne commercial intercourse with southeastern Europe, especially with the Rumanian principalities of Moldavia and Wallachia, which with their economic and political semi-autonomy enjoyed a somewhat privileged position in the Ottoman political system (cf. the work of Paul Cernovodeanu). The trade routes across and along the rivers crisscrossed the region. Two main routes can be distinguished: the ancient Thracian way via Belgrade, and the route via Wallachia, where Hermannstadt (Sibiu) and Kronstadt (Brasov) were important commercial centres.

Bucharest was an important commercial centre too. The northward connection to the Polish 'compartment' went either along the Moldau via Lemberg (Lwow), Jaroslaw and Crakow or via Chemnitz-Lublin. Greek, Italian and Jewish merchants often used these routes. The connections from Crakow to Poland were also lively from Siebengebirge, which was under Ottoman rule, from Slovakia and Upper Hungary. Copper from the great mines of Neusohl (Banska Bystrica) was one of the products carried along this route to the Baltic. Cattle were exported in large numbers from the Hungarian region to both northern Italy and central Europe; however, the Turkish embargo of 1568 put a halt to this export traffic. A mixed bag of commodities – English cloth, textiles from Poland, Silesia, Bohemia and Moravia, salt, fish and lead – flowed in the opposite direction. The Habsburg Danube regions were distinctly transit regions, in which a motley throng of merchants operated, including many Serbs, Greeks and Armenians. Vienna enjoyed a special role as the procurer of luxury articles for southeastern Europe's nobility and prosperous burghers. It was the court that set the tone.

(1) THE CORN TRADE

The importance of corn in the development of European trade in our period can scarcely be overstated. It was a commodity fundamental to the standard of life of the people. Wheat and rye constituted the principal ingredients of the daily bread. In northern Europe, barley also formed the basic ingredient in the brewing of beer; and in that part of

Europe beer was as important an item of everyday fare as bread, in rather the same way as wine was in southern Europe. Finally, oats was a food for humans and beasts alike. In an age when the horse was indispensable as a draught and riding animal, both in the peaceful everyday round and in time of war, the supply of oats must have been as vital as that of the other cereal grains. Everywhere there was movement of corn from producer to consumer, over distances long or short – even if only down the road to the mill and back. Locally it was carried into the towns from the countryside round about in wagons and sacks, along the coast or by river in smacks and barges. Its uniformity made it a commodity well suited for being transported, but it was heavy, so that over longer distances it was best carried by water. We do encounter isolated examples, it is true, of long-range overland trade in corn: Dr Achilles, for instance, found in his study of corn prices and corn trade connections in the European region during the sixteenth and seventeenth centuries an intensive traffic between Augsburg and Würzburg. Even the distance between these two cities, however, was probably too great for transport to pay for itself at a single bound. The trade probably took the form of barter by stages with a resultant levelling-out of prices rather than of a direct supply traffic. It was a general rule that however coveted a commodity corn was, it could not absorb heavy transport costs. Corn therefore traversed relatively short distances overland. A celebrated example of the cost-inflationary effects of land transport is furnished by the computations of corn prices and transport costs made by a Venetian secretary of state, Marc Ottoborn. When he was in Poland in 1590-1, trying to secure the supply of bread grain, he worked out that grain bought in Cracow would quadruple in price by the time it had been conveyed to Venice overland. Only dire need and a full purse would justify transport by such means.

Professor Braudel has remarked, in his classic work *La Méditerranée et le monde méditerranéen à l'époque de Philippe II*, that the study of the corn trade is tantamount to a study of one of the weaknesses of the economies of the Mediterranean lands, *viz.* their shortage of bread grains. This deficiency is associated with structural economic changes. Vine and olive cultivation, handicrafts and manufactures were favoured at the expense of corn. Population growth was a factor as well, inasmuch as there were some regions where population outstripped the immediate resources. The corn trade was subject to very severe fluctuations, and corn prices oscillated more wildly than any other commodity prices. The trade was characterized by its capriciousness, stemming not only from see-sawing harvests that could transform grain-exporting regions into importing regions, but also from speculation and the often arbitrary regulations and exactions imposed by the government. No effective adjustment ever emerged despite the continual movement of corn between regions of surplus and deficit. Periods of famine and high prices were not avoided.

The supply situation in southern Europe worsened during the sixteenth century, especially in the towns, which were the corn trade's biggest customers. Deterioration began in the west, in Portugal; next Spain was affected, then Italy. Portugal, having been an exporter of corn in the Middle Ages (to places as far afield as England), shifted the emphasis of its agriculture from corn to the olive and vine, but offset this by establishing corn cultivation in its areas of overseas expansion, *viz*. Morocco, Madeira and the Azores. These new sources, however, were insufficient to meet the nation's requirements. Portugal became increasingly dependent upon supplies from external sources – from Andalusia, Castile and Sicily, and from Flanders in the north, where the trade with Bruges and subsequently with Antwerp was well established. All this happened in the first half of the century.

In the second half, Spain too ran into a supply crisis that was especially acute in the 1560s and 1570s. Andalusia, formerly a corn exporter, now had to import foreign supplies in order to meet its own consumption requirements. Italy suffered a corn crisis as well around mid-century, the causes being somewhat obscure. Here recourse was had to shipments from the Turkish markets. Considerable quantities of corn were sent westwards from the staple places of the Levant: it is true that a Turkish export embargo was promulgated in 1555, but deliveries continued until the middle of the 1560s, when the flow was stemmed by a series of misfortunes in Turkey, especially poor harvests and an outbreak of plague. The situation in Italy was improving at the same time. The big cities of Rome, Genoa, Florence and Venice solved their immediate supply problems with aid from other parts of Italy, *viz*. Apulia and Sicily, which now were able to resume grain deliveries. In the case of Venice, imports from Dalmatia and Albania played a part too. This 'Italian' market situation lasted until 1590. Then the picture changed. A series of crop failures beginning in 1586 exerted an undermining influence. The situation became desperate in 1590 and 1591. The rains were torrential, and northern Italy was threatened with food shortage. The Grand Duke of Tuscany established contact with Danzig to the north. Venice did the same, and the first big shipments arrived in 1590–3. Leghorn, a week's voyage from Gibraltar, was the port selected to receive large consignments in the succeeding years – whole flotillas of grain-ships from Danzig, Holland and England.

A new phase then opened. Of course there had been shipments of corn from northwestern Europe to the Italian cities on previous occasions – for example to Genoa as early as the middle of the fifteenth century, to Venice from Flanders in 1527, to Rome in 1530, and so on – but it was only in consequence of the harvest failures of 1586 and after that deliveries became large-scale and regular. How long the crisis in Italy lasted is difficult to say. Consignments from the north did dwindle after 1608. Sicily, which seems to have suffered a brief period of corn shortage at the beginning of the new century, had not yet played out its role as Italy's most important granary. Corn from northern Europe probably continued to flow for the first twenty or thirty years of the seventeenth century, but other commodities replaced it as the foundation of commercial intercourse – chiefly the new English and Dutch fabrics, which surpassed the Italian cloths on the Levant market in the 1630s.

In northwestern Europe too, especially in the densely populated province of Flanders, we find a demand for corn, generated particularly in the towns, setting shipments in motion and determining their rhythm, at least partly. A number of important changes associated with the weakening position of the Hanse towns were in progress in the north European trading 'compartment' towards the end of the fifteenth century, and growing numbers of merchants from Holland, Zeeland and Brabant were entering the east Baltic trade in corn. Lübeck's monopoly of east–west through traffic via the overland Lübeck–Hamburg link was broken by sailings from the new seaports, which took the northwards route around the Skaw, through the Sound and into the Baltic Sea. Amsterdam and Antwerp were the Netherlands cities that profited most from the corn trade. In 1501, Amsterdam obtained from Philip the Fair the right to free trade in grain. Antwerp was granted a similar privilege by an ordinance of 1521. However, it was not only deliveries from the east that were of importance to the transit trade in corn which was being built up in a number of Netherlands cities from the early sixteenth century onwards; corn from the west as well, from the Beauce, Valois, Picardy, Artois and French Flanders, had a role, and the Antwerp market was also supplied with corn from Haspengouw (the large rural area of east central Belgium containing the regions of the present-day provinces of Brabant, Limburg, Liège and Namur).

In the first two decades of the sixteenth century, Antwerp felt the competition of nearby Ghent, which had been an important grain staple for a long time. But the city managed to extricate itself. Both Hanseatic sources and the business ledgers of the Fuggers testify to the maritime contacts between Danzig and Stettin on the one hand and Antwerp on the other in the first quarter of the sixteenth century. Both the Hanseatic, Antwerp, and Walcheren merchants were engaged in this traffic. Documentary evidence also shows that corn was being exported from Antwerp to England, Spain and Italy in these decades, and that at the beginning of the 1530s the question whether Antwerp or Amsterdam was the more favourable corn market of the Baltic trade was still one to deliberate over. However, it was the Amsterdam market that later on gained dominance over the whole Netherlands area. It is no exaggeration to say that in the seventeenth and eighteenth centuries, the celebrated corn exchange of the Dutch metropolis fixed the grain prices of Europe.

Baltic shipping and trade, especially the corn trade, became the life blood of the economy of the northern Netherlands. The ups and downs of the Baltic corn trade determined the rhythm of economic life of the Netherlands community. The main axis lay between the two cities of Amsterdam and Danzig. The study by Dr Achilles cited above is based upon the hypothesis that parallelism of corn-price curves between two places or regions constitutes evidence of the price-forming effects of trade and thus of a regular commercial link between them. Dr Achilles further concludes that the correlation coefficients between Amsterdam and Danzig are the clearest of all the sixteenth- and seventeenth-century European sea and land connections analysed. The study also shows that the sea route between the two cities was ten or twelve times as long as the longest overland route for which a causal connection has been discovered, *viz.* the trade between Paris and Angers. In other words, a grain trade exploiting cheap maritime freight-rates influenced prices much further afield than did a similar trade by land. A survey of price levels in the various regions of Europe (made by Abel and Achilles, who analysed the grain prices of 14 European towns and provinces from 1551 to 1600) paints a compelling picture of the east–west orientation of the trade. It shows a price-differential between Amsterdam and Danzig of 53 per cent, and this is the *raison d'être* of the trade between the two regions. This presupposes that the resistances to transport were capable of being overcome and that the costs involved would not swallow up the price-differential, and such was indeed the case. The best quantitative evidence of the regularity and intensity attained by the corn trade between Danzig and Amsterdam is furnished by the Sound Toll Registers.[1] It is worth noting too that Danzig, in company with the other great trading centres of Antwerp, Middelburg, Rouen and Seville, figures in the oldest known official list of Amsterdam exchange rates.

Demand in the Netherlands was undoubtedly linked with population growth and the distribution of population between town and country. Professor Slicher van Bath and his colleagues have estimated that the population of the Netherlands doubled in the period 1500–1650

[1] See p. 226 below.

and that a substantial share of this increase occurred among the inhabitants of cities. The area was the most densely populated in Europe north of the Alps. According to Father Mols, urban inhabitants accounted for 35 per cent of the total in Brabant, 29 per cent in Hennegau, 40–5 per cent in Flanders and no less than 52 per cent in the province of Holland. Industrialization went hand in hand with this urbanizing process, and included notably not only the manufacture of cloth but also – in Holland – the production of oil and soap. The large-scale demands thus generated were more than the local food marts could satisfy. A whole succession of years of high prices and food scarcity, so characteristic of the region, testifies to this.

It was a combination of circumstances that gave the Dutch, and especially Amsterdam, so central a position in the supply trade. The political factors must not be forgotten. The boycott of Flanders by the Hanseatics in 1451–6 benefited the Dutch towns generally and Amsterdam in particular. So did the war between Prussia and Poland of 1454–66, which afforded both Danzig and Amsterdam an opportunity of fishing in troubled waters and establishing a trading link outside the channels authorized by the Hanseatic league and notably the Wendish part of it. The struggle between the Hanseatic league and England in 1469–74, too, a result of which was that the once very vigorous English traffic with the Baltic dwindled to nothing, was turned to advantage by Dutch merchants. The endeavours of the Scandinavian countries to beat back the Hanse towns produced similar favourable openings, and so did the south German commercial offensive in the region.

Amsterdam and Danzig resembled one another in a number of ways. Danzig, tucked away behind the peninsula of Hel, could boast a site well protected from the open sea and not dissimilar from that of Amsterdam. The city functioned as the economic centre for a considerable hinterland, and foreign trade featured prominently in its early history. The trade of the two towns was complementary from the purely commodity standpoint, though this did not preclude periods of strained relations between them, occasioned in part by the fact that Danzig's active trade westwards was diminishing in step with the expansion of Dutch traffic to the Baltic. Like Amsterdam, and more especially the towns in its vicinity such as Zaandam, Danzig had a sizeable shipbuilding industry. But it lacked any other industries apart from the sort of crafts directly associated with shipbuilding and trade.

It has to be admitted that, regarded overall, the great corn-exporting period in Poland produced very limited economic effects. It was mainly Danzig and the landowning class who benefited, not the peasantry or the provincial towns. Matters were otherwise in Holland and Amsterdam, where the effects of the corn trade spread like ripples in a pond.

Three-quarters of the Baltic corn was re-exported, which generated increased business. Among the effects directly induced were the building of ships and lighters in large numbers and intensive building activity in the city, where more than three-quarters of the warehouses were devoted to corn. Many people found employment in looking after the corn. It required regular tossing during storage, for instance, in order to prevent germination and spontaneous combustion. Then there was the work of loading and unloading as well as the sewing of sacks. A string of minor industries was linked indirectly with the corn trade, including for example the supply of ballast wares such as flagstones, tiles and bricks. There were also the manifold branches of the service sector.

The volume of trade carried on the river Vistula in the sixteenth and seventeenth centuries was probably much larger than Poland's overland foreign commerce. There were relatively few obstacles to river traffic, which extended over a whole network of rivers with the Vistula as the main trunk route. This meant that corn and timber belonging geographically to other regions were conveyed along the Vistula. Thus a link was established at Augustow, via the river Narew, with the vast forested tracts along the Niemen. Similarly, the river Bug provided a connection with the Pripet forests. The corn of the Warta region could be shipped via Ner and Bzura to the Vistula, and at Wloclawek (Leslau) there were still connections in the seventeenth century from the Vistula via its tributaries and across Lake Goplo with the fertile black-earth region of Kujaw. Surviving fragments of customs registers from Wloclawek, Weissenberg and other places, enable an impression to be formed of the extent of the region from which shipments of corn were attracted. The Leslau registers show that most of the corn cleared through customs came from Masovia and Plotzk, while some also came from Brest, Rawa, Lublin, Sandomierz and Belz. Lithuania, Ruthenia and Cracow, on the other hand, lay on the periphery of the despatching region. Cardinal Commendon, who visited Poland in 1563–4 and while there travelled on the Vistula, mentioned that Podolia was sparsely populated and ascribed this to the fact that the inhabitants were unable to convey their corn to the Vistula. Most of the corn exported originated from areas immediately adjacent to the lower course of the Vistula, i.e. north of Leslau. The interruptions to which traffic was subject on the river Oder, the Vistula's nearest rival, contributed to the high levels attained by trade on the Vistula and exports via Danzig in the sixteenth and seventeenth centuries. Wrangles between Stettin and Frankfurt over the Warta trade from Poland led to the Oder's being closed by the former city in 1562; the closure was made permanent in 1573, and only towards the end of the seventeenth century did regular navigation again become possible on the Oder.

Sources of widely differing characters are available on which to base a quantitative assessment of the corn trade between the Baltic and western Europe. There are customs registers for a number of ports in both the east and the west. Some of these go back to the sixteenth century. Dutch notarial archives begin to furnish valuable information at about this time concerning the chartering of ships to the Baltic, and a limited quantity of merchants' records have survived with detailed shipowners' accounts, such as those of the Delft merchant van Adrichem, whose activities fall within the second half of the sixteenth century, or of two Amsterdam merchants, Symon Reyersz and Reyer Dircsz, whose trading books for Danzig cover the years 1485–8. To these sources representing only fragments of the very wide-ranging Baltic trade should be added the imposing registers of the Sound with detailed information, ship by ship, over a period of more than 300 years. A number of scholars have attempted to determine the value of this important source of international trade history by means of confrontations with units common to the other sources. Examples are Dr Huhnhäuser's confrontation of the Sound Toll Registers with the Rostock Toll Registers, Professor S. van Brakel's enquiry into the Dutch ships' and shipmasters' home ports, Professor Astrid Friis's comparisons with the English port books, and Professor Aksel E. Christensen's thorough study entitled *Dutch Trade to the Baltic around 1600*, in which three main sources are correlated and evaluated, *viz.* the charter parties in the Dutch notarial archives, the archives of Claes Adriaensz van Adrichem, the Delft merchant mentioned above, and the Sound Toll Registers themselves. These discussions, inevitably, have raised questions of principle concerning the monumental edition of the Sound Toll Registers, published by Nina Bang and Knud Korst and covering the period 1497–1783, of which two volumes were devoted to the shipping lists and five to the transport of goods with the year 1660 as the dividing date.

We shall not go into these problems of criticism here. Nina Bang began the work of publication in the belief that the Registers reflected accurately the development of the traffic on this important European trade route. She thought that a sound basis for historical conclusions could be obtained by simply reading off the figures from the tables. Subsequent criticism has revealed many gaps and defects, however, and shown that the present edition can be safely used only in limited applications. Nevertheless there is no reason to abandon the Sound Toll Registers. In terms of continuity and scope they are still unique and ought to constitute a prime source for the commercial historian even though they cannot be employed in their raw state. For many purposes the primary material does require to be processed. Modern data-processing techniques offer the opportunity of laying new foundations in this way, and a start has been made on the unpublished portion of the registers, though the material for our period is still only available in Bang and Korst's edition.

The tables show more than 400,000 entries into and exits from the Sound during the years 1497–1660, while the total for the second half comprised by the edition, the years 1661–1783, was over 520,000 entries. Nearly 60 per cent of the entries in the first half were ships from the seven United Provinces of the Netherlands, while in the second half the Dutch percentage was only 35·5. As regards corn, the total volume of rye and wheat amounted to 4·6 million lasts over the first period, comprising nearly 4 million of rye and 0·6 million of wheat. During the second (and longer) period, 4·7 million lasts passed the Sound, i.e. 3·3 million of rye and 1·4 million of wheat. Shipments of rye thus fell off absolutely and relatively, while those of wheat increased. When considering the ratio of rye to wheat, some allowance should be made for the interest which merchants had in declaring their cargoes as rye, on which the tariff was lower. The Dutch carried 76·5 per cent of the rye and 77·5 per cent of the wheat in the first period; the figures were 71 and 70 per cent respectively in the second period. We can therefore conclude that the Dutch managed to maintain their position in the Baltic grain trade right down to 1720.

The Sound Toll statistics further reveal Danzig to have been by far the most important of the exporting ports. In the first period 70 per cent of rye and 63·5 per cent of wheat came from Danzig. Lagging far behind were Königsberg, Riga and Livonia-Esthonia as suppliers of rye and Stettin as a supplier of wheat. In the second period Danzig lost much ground as a supplier of rye – its share dropped to 42·2 per cent – but it held and even improved its position as a supplier of wheat with just on 70 per cent. Königsberg improved its share of both commodities. A shift towards the eastern Baltic seems to have occurred in the course of the eighteenth century.

It is only from 1669 onwards that the tables contain information about the destinations of the corn cargoes. Indirectly, however, it may be inferred that the lion's share went to the Netherlands both before and after 1669. Professor Christensen has established from his study that Baltic corn totally dominated the Amsterdam market and that there are no grounds for attaching much weight to Dutch complaints that the east–west flow of corn was by-passing Amsterdam. It is true that direct movement of corn from the north German Hanse towns to the Iberian peninsula and Italy did take place and that some through-transits, for example from Portugal to the Baltic and back, also occurred, but analyses of the amounts passing the Sound and of imports and exports at Amsterdam make it plain that these through-transits did not signify a great deal in quantitative terms. The complaints made are expressive of a latent fear among the Dutch merchants, but Amsterdam's central role in the European corn trade was not shaken. There is further evidence too of the importance of Baltic corn on the Amsterdam market in the shape of the corn-exchange quotations, in which Baltic rye and wheat types predominated.

Axel E. Christensen's analysis of east–west corn shipments through the Sound from the middle of the sixteenth to the end of the seventeenth century discloses a generally steady volume of traffic. In the long run the Netherlands–Baltic trade was thus characterized by a high degree of stability and fixity. But there are some violent year-to-year fluctuations in the shorter term. These are normally the immediate outcome of interaction between the oscillating harvest yields of east and west, but in certain years they are caused by wars and other political factors. Thus particularly high exports from Danzig coincide with crop failures in western Europe, e.g. in 1562, 1565, 1586 and all through the 1590s, when shortages in the Mediterranean countries exerted a strong pull. Examples of low points are furnished by the bad years of 1557, when the Polish king was besieging the city, the severe depression of the 1620s associated with the Swedish-Polish war and the Swedish blockade of Danzig in 1626–9. The slump of the 1620s is the more dramatic of the two and partakes of the character of both a corn crisis and a Danzig crisis. It falls into two parts, and is preceded by four years (1618–21) during which enormous quantities of corn were exported. Poor harvests in the Baltic region in 1622–4 occasioned the first significant drop in the quantities exported. Matters improved in 1625–6, but there was a further fall in 1627–30, this time with an almost total standstill on exports in consequence of the Swedish blockade of the Vistula estuary.

As is well known, the Swedes brought more and more territories of the Baltic and its grain-producing hinterland under their dominion in the 1620s. Danzig itself was never conquered, but when Gustavus Adolphus moved his army into west Prussia, the city's trade came under Swedish control in such matters as tax imposts. Substantial sectors of the Baltic corn trade fell into Swedish hands or came under Swedish export-licensing regulation. In this atmosphere the idea of establishing a Swedish state monopoly came up. Axel Oxenstierna mooted it as early as 1623. Any such monopoly would also have to embrace exports of Russian corn that went via Archangel. This route was of recent date. Professor Attman has shown that the Russian trading regions were closely interlocked. Russia did not itself have harbours on the Baltic, but its corn used to pass through Riga and Königsberg and so into the Baltic market. Geographically, the supplying region for these cities extended up the rivers into Russia, to districts which also supplied Archangel. The trade could therefore be switched from the one region to the other. Analysis of corn consignments through the Sound reveals strikingly that shipments from Riga and Königsberg fall as those via Archangel and the White Sea route rise, and vice versa. Swedish monopoly planning would therefore have to take account of the new northern trade route as well. Gustavus Adolphus sounded the tsar in 1627 about the possibility of buying corn from Russia, and did in fact receive permission to make limited purchases. Negotiations were renewed in 1629, and it is evident that Königsberg and Danzig too were interested in the Swedish plans, one of whose purposes was to maintain price-levels in Amsterdam by restricting the supply. Despite such a restriction being introduced, prices in the Dutch metropolis began to fall after 1630.

This episode raises the question of the extent to which prices in Amsterdam were determined by deliveries from the east. In other words, was it supply in the east or demand in the west that was the decisive factor? The harvest in Poland or the economic situation in Holland and western Europe? Price analyses made by Dr Achilles have led him to conclude that it was not always the crop yields in the Danzig hinterland that determined corn prices in Amsterdam. If the harvest failed in Spain or France the price-bulge could travel from west to east. The increase in demand was felt first in the Netherlands and was then transmitted eastwards. Supply and demand met on the Amsterdam corn exchange.

It must be stressed too that Baltic grain was not the sole determinant of supply at Amsterdam. Large quantities of grain were still produced in western Europe. How large a surplus was available for export is not known as precisely as in the case of the Baltic, but whatever surplus there was mostly went to Amsterdam. France exported grain to Holland regularly from the 1630s. The grain-producing provinces of France were situated nearer to the Dutch market than to regions of France that were simultaneously suffering from a shortage of grain. Exports of grain to Amsterdam took place from Hamburg too, and England became a grain-exporting nation again in the second half of the seventeenth century. A substantial share of English exports went to the great corn exchange on the other side of the Channel and North Sea.

Some contemporaries asserted that Baltic corn was not in fact indispensable to western Europe, even though in times of scarcity long distances were covered – as far as to Archangel on the White Sea – in order to fetch it. Johann Köstner, a Danzig merchant, wrote a brief treatise in 1660 on the causes of the declining corn trade from Danzig. In it he pointed out that when the war of 1656–60 between Sweden and

Poland cut off Danzig's exports for no less than five years, Holland had managed with corn from elsewhere, and he believed that peace in Germany would cause deliveries from the east to lose their significance. Only a bad harvest in the west or very low prices in the east would make exports a paying proposition. This line of argument, coupled with the failure of Sweden's monopoly policy of the 1620s, could lead one to conclude that it was prices in Amsterdam that determined in what volume and at what price grain could be exported from Danzig, while the Amsterdam prices in turn were themselves decided for the most part by harvest yields and market conditions in western Europe as a whole.

There are other indications that there was a turning point about 1650 in the great east–west grain trade. The long phase of expansion was about to come to an end. An analysis of the volume of trade and of Amsterdam prices (such as that conducted by Professor Pierre Jeannin) shows that the cyclical fluctuations of the traffic through the Sound after the middle of the seventeenth century differ from those before it. There are more fluctuations after 1650 than before, and the curves are more turbulent. While the cyclical contractions of western demand before 1650 were unable to bring about a lasting reduction of the volume of corn imported, and massive rises in imports from the Baltic in certain years were unable to break Amsterdam price-levels either, the situation changes after 1650.

The new conjuncture is conditioned not so much by the political conflicts of which the subsequent period shows such a profusion – the Anglo-Dutch war, the war between Holland and France, and the Great Northern War – as by more profound changes both in the east and in the west. The second Swedish–Polish war of 1650–60 was a turning-point for Danzig. It dealt a lasting blow to the Vistula river-trade. Corn exports in the next half-century succeeded only rarely in reaching the 50,000–60,000 lasts annually that had been the normal exports of the preceding period. The campaign of Charles X went on, with its ravagings and requisitions. The devastation inflicted on town and country alike bears comparison with that of the worst-hit areas of Germany during the Thirty Years War. On top of this, southern and western Europe were apparently becoming self-sufficient in bread grains. Maize, which was introduced in Portugal in the sixteenth century and in Spain at the beginning of the seventeenth, began to feature in the second half of the seventeenth century as an ordinary article of the people's diet. Rice production in Italy was rising in the seventeenth century, and here too increased cultivation of maize is observable after the plague and famine of 1630. These new foodstuffs in conjunction with stagnating economies and population in most of the former corn-importing regions contributed to a slackening of demand in southern Europe.

But there is also plenty of evidence of increased production of food-stuffs in western Europe in the second half of the seventeenth century, coinciding with a general stagnation of population. Dr Faber has drawn attention to the increased cultivation of buckwheat in western and central Europe in the seventeenth century. Evidence of the entry of this species of grain into the international corn trade is provided by the appearance of Brabantine buckwheat in the Amsterdam price-lists for the first time in 1669. Cultivation of buckwheat gained favour in Brunswick after the end of the Thirty Years War. Despite sagging corn prices (in some places perhaps because of them), many districts of western Europe showed increased corn production in the second half of the seventeenth century. Protectionist agricultural legislation in England, after 1660, exemplified in such devices as export bounties, fostered an export trade in corn that continued right down to the middle of the eighteenth century. On the other hand, the history of agriculture also shows examples of falling grain prices occasioning a switch from grain cultivation to animal husbandry and the cultivation of industrial crops. Demographic data point to a stagnation of the population growth, but much data undeniably is lacking. This reservation having been made, we may infer by way of conclusion that the general conditions in western and southern Europe must have led to a decline in demand for grain from the Baltic. Against such a background, the interruptions of the Vistula trade consequent upon the wars of 1655–60 were especially fateful for Danzig and Poland.

The final question to be asked is what the east–west corn-supply trade really signified quantitatively in relation to the aggregate demand for corn. Precise calculations are quite impossible. By taking the annual transit-trade figures, which were around 68,500 lasts in the first half of the seventeenth century, converting them to pounds and correlating them with the estimated average grain consumption of western Europe, Dr Faber arrives at the conclusion that Baltic grain supplies were equivalent to the annual consumption of about ¾ million people. In relation to aggregate population numbers in western and southern Europe, this figure is unimpressive. It may be objected that international business ought not to be viewed in relation to total populations but only to the regions in which the international trade arteries ran, which means chiefly the urbanized areas. On the other hand every town had a hinterland and a local trade that included grain. Even Amsterdam had a local corn exchange (*de korenbeurs op het Water*) alongside its celebrated international corn exchange and a local trade with *het binnenland* (the hinterland), consisting of the Rhine, Flanders, northern France, England

– it is difficult to say where the boundary lies and supplies become international rather than local in character, unless a purely political yardstick is applied and the distinction is drawn at the frontiers, which is not a very satisfactory proceeding.

The local and international traffic in corn are inextricably interwoven. It would be wrong in the case of a commodity like corn to think in terms of a dual economy with two mutually distinct sectors. If this argument is sound and supplies from the Baltic were indeed marginal in relation to total demand and total supply, then it follows that relatively slight fluctuations of supply or demand will have been capable of producing relatively large changes in the Baltic corn trade. The decline of the corn trade in the second half of the seventeenth century, which in the long term came to affect the whole economy of Holland, may therefore be regarded as having been caused by a relatively slight decrease of (total) demand coinciding with a slight increase of corn production in southern and western Europe.

This marginal conception is perhaps specially applicable to the relationship between Baltic corn and demand in southern Europe. This demand was for wheat, and wheat alone. As already noted, the proportion of wheat in aggregate grain shipments through the Sound is not large, even though some inaccuracy must be allowed for in the customs declarations. The quantity involved in the period prior to 1660 amounts altogether to 13 per cent of the total consignments of grain. These fluctuate, being more important in some years than in others. It is also clear that south European demand was a key factor in the establishment of Dutch traffic with the Mediterranean, and that this speculative trade in grain had other important effects, e.g. upon the organization of trade. But if the quantities are viewed in a long-term perspective and in relation to the number of mouths there were to feed, they are in fact small. They could bring relief to particular regions in years of famine. The traffic was not, however, capable of forming the basis of a long-term continuous flow of goods. It became the function of other commodities to nourish and extend the link thus created between north and south.

(2) THE CATTLE TRADE

Cattle, by virtue of the fact that they transported themselves, formed an exception to the general rule that bulky and heavy goods could be profitably conveyed over longer distances only by sea. The ancient network of drove-roads spanned continental Europe. Some minor shipments did take place by sea, it is true,[1] but for the most part this singular trade, which has been somewhat neglected by historians of

[1] See below, p. 237.

international commerce, was of a distinctly landward character, ranging over distances that gave it international stature by the standards of the age. The trade attained its zenith somewhere between the fifteenth and early seventeenth centuries. Professor Abel has attempted a comparison of the value of grain exports from the Baltic with that of contemporaneous exports of cattle from Denmark (including the duchies of Schleswig Holstein and Skåne) in the period 1601–20. He concludes the annual average value of grain transported was equivalent to that 55,000 kg of silver, while the figure for cattle was 30,000 kg. It was true of cattle as of grain that the merchandise moved towards the markets where prices were high, i.e. on towards the urbanized regions. This is evident, for instance, from Abel's compilation of prices of pigmeat and beef in fifteen European cities in the period 1551–1600. The production of cattle was not dependent upon the vagaries of the weather to the same extent as grain production, and prices were accordingly far more stable. In most places, princes and noble landowners asserted that the rearing of cattle for export was their special privilege. They claimed the right of pre-emption over the peasants' young bullocks, thus enabling prices to be held down and the lord's own profit increased correspondingly. Trading, on the other hand, was often under the control of middle-class merchants and engrossers. The actual rearing of stock was carried on far from the towns and other consuming centres. The animals lost weight during the migration (the drove), and had to be fattened in the vicinity of the place of consumption. There is therefore a clear geographical distinction between the stock-rearing areas on the one hand and the fattening areas on the other.

The typical stock-rearing zones lay beyond the so-called 'corn-growing zones'. In the north the stock-rearing region extended from Jutland across the Danish islands to Skåne and thence eastwards to Poland, Bohemia and Hungary, with parts of Russia and Rumania adjoining. The east and south European 'compartment' supplied chiefly northern Italy and south and central Germany, while the north European 'compartment' delivered cattle to the cities of northwest Europe.

To be more specific, the stock-rearing region meeting the consumption requirements of south and central Germany was situated east of the line Breslau–Prague–Vienna and included notably Poland and Hungary. The territories of Brandenburg-Prussia too – Pomerania particularly – had a surplus of cattle for export, but this was a traffic of the seventeenth and eighteenth centuries. The Polish stock-breeding region was extensive. It included Reussenland, as it was called, the district around Lwow (Lemberg) whence the westward droves via Cracow and Breslau set off; but Lwow was also the assembly point for droves from the principality of Moldavia, which was both a corn and a cattle area. The importance of Moldavia as a supplier of cattle to central Europe waned with the expansion of the Turkish dominions, however, for large supplies of corn and cattle were now absorbed in victualling Turkish troops and supplying Constantinople.

The west Ukrainian province of Podolia, ruled since 1430 by Poland, also had an important role as a stock-rearing region for cattle destined for the westward traffic. The Crimea, on the other hand, was situated on the margin of the 'compartment' from which the cattle were drawn. The largest of the east European stock-rearing regions was probably Hungary. It is true that some of the animals which came from Hungary to central Europe were transit oxen from Wallachia and Moldavia; most of them, however, were reared in Hungary itself, where there were periods in the fifteenth and sixteenth centuries when oxen were in fact that country's paramount export article and a considerable source of income, especially for the nobility. Gy. Ember, the Hungarian historian, has attempted a computation of the exports for 1542. It shows that more than 93 per cent by value of all exports consisted of animals on the hoof, 87 per cent being accounted for by oxen alone. A geographical breakdown of the markets shows oxen to have constituted 83 per cent of exports to Austria and no less than 99·7 per cent of exports to the German lands. A third export outlet for Hungarian oxen was northern Italy, especially Venice. Hungarian exports encountered a number of serious difficulties in the sixteenth century. The Turkish wars brought interruptions of the trade; so did cattle-plague, particularly the severe outbreaks of 1518 and 1549–59. The epidemic of 1518 was regarded in Nuremberg as something of a catastrophe for Germany. It was believed that the whole of Germany's meat supply was now cut off. The flow of cattle from Hungary, however, was by no means brought to a lasting halt. Upper Germany and northern Italy were still being supplied from there in the eighteenth century. But the difficulties occurring in the sixteenth century did lead to increased supplies being brought to central Europe from Silesia and Poland.

The fattening regions were situated in immediate proximity to the centres of consumption, in an inner 'pastoral zone' consisting of flood plains and tracts of meadow. The North Sea marshes and Friesland furnish an example of such a fattening zone that was important to the towns of north Germany and Holland. The two zones were connected by the so-called drove-roads, along which the droves were conducted. They followed special trails, where possible through sparsely-populated districts so that traffic on the ordinary commercial routes should not be blocked by the slow-moving herds, which covered about two to four miles a day and had to rest on every third day. There was no point in forcing the pace, since the cattle would then lose too much meat and fat. The cattle passed through a series of intermediate stations at intervals during the droves, which were often long and might extend to more than a thousand kilometres. The intermediate stations were identical in many cases with the customs posts, where the droves were registered and tolls were paid. A considerable number of people accompanied the animals. In northern Europe there was normally one drover to every twenty oxen, together with a 'forager', often the son of the merchant, who sought out accommodation at inns and overnight space and hay for the animals, which spent the night in the open air. Numbers of lodging-houses sprang up along the drove-roads to serve the needs of animals and men.

The cattle were sold at some market near the fattening district, e.g. the famous cattle market at the small town of Buttstädt in Thuringia (north of Weimar), where fairs were held three times a year (on the feasts of St John, St Michael and All Saints). As many as 16,000–20,000 head of livestock used to change hands here. The cattle sold came from Poland, Brandenburg and Pomerania. The buyers came to Buttstädt from all over central and west Germany. Another celebrated market was that of Wedel, west of Hamburg. Here Danish exporters met buyers from Germany and the Netherlands at the great spring fair, which lasted from the middle of March to the middle of April. Most of the cattle traded at this fair came from Jutland. They would set off from there in February. The journey from Vendsyssel to the Elbe took about thirty days. The animals were scarcely more than skin and bone by the time they reached Wedel – which was known, appropriately enough, as 'the lean market'. However, a summer's grazing on Dutch or German meadows was sufficient to prepare them for slaughter. There was an autumn fair at Wedel too, for the droves of cattle from the duchy of Schleswig. These were cattle ready for slaughter.

We are especially well-informed about the cattle trade of the north-west European coastal area, thanks to a copious mass of surviving customs data, of which use has been made in a monograph by Dr Wiese. Cattle brought from the kingdom of Denmark passed through no fewer than five customs barriers in the duchy of Schleswig, the last two of which, *viz.* Gottorp (at the city of Schleswig) and Rendsborg, were the most important, since duty was paid there on each individual head of cattle. With the exception of the Sound Toll Registers, no surviving series of customs registers from the kingdom of Denmark is anything like as complete as the Gottorp and Rendsborg registers. The proceeds of the tolls were shared between the Danish king and the duke of Schleswig, so that the registers were entered up in duplicate – and sometimes, since in certain years there were two dukes of Schleswig, in triplicate. The entries were made with great care, and a particularly valuable feature is that even oxen which were passed through duty-free are registered as well. Oxen raised in the Danish 'compartment' were mainly of importance in supplying the Netherlands and the cities of north Germany, notably Hamburg and Lübeck. Some shipments went further south, however, to Cologne; Frankfurt was on the margin and was supplied for the most part from the east and southeast European regions.

Examination of the secular fluctuations in the transport of cattle as revealed in the aforementioned customs records discloses an upward trend from 1483 to about 1560. The figures rise from just on 13,000 animals a year in transit to over 40,000. The trend remained almost stationary for the next two decades, and then after the 1570s the export figures fell off to low points of 26,000 in 1579 and only 19,000 in 1583. The explanation of this decline may well lie in the political and econo-mic condition of the Netherlands. A Danish ordinance of 1583 dealing with the trade in stall oxen makes reference to the tumults and dis-turbances going on in the Netherlands, which were threatening to ruin the cattle trade. The Dutch buyers were absent from the Elbe market during these years. The depression was over by 1596, however, and now began the high-noon of the cattle trade. In practically every year up to 1625, the customs records at Gottorp–Rendsborg show duty levied on over 30,000 cattle; in some years there were over 40,000 animals and in one year (1612) no fewer than 52,350. Fragments of a customs register of 1618 give reason to believe that exports in that year were higher still.

How long the boom lasted is an open question. Dr Wiese believes that it ebbed away during the 1620s, since the devastations of the Thirty Years War and the Danish king's participation in it from 1625 to 1628 would have weakened both demand and supply; for instance, deliveries from Jutland were interrupted during Wallenstein's cam-paign in that peninsula. On this point Wiese draws attention to a Danish ordinance of 1620 with a provision entitling the commonalty to stall their cattle on the farms of the nobles. Wiese sees in this a move towards a 'livery system', whereby the nobility sought to evade the risk of a failure of trade overseas while retaining the services involved in the stalling of cattle. Alternatively, however, one may agree with Pro-fessor Ladewig Pedersen in construing the ordinance of 1620 as a manifestation of a liquidity crisis connected with the Danish king's calling-in of loans to the nobles and intensified by poor harvests in the early 1620s. Viewed in this light it does resolve the immediate diffi-culties but tells us little about subsequent events. Nor is there any strong indication that the demand of cities such as Hamburg and Amsterdam went into a lasting decline in the 1620s.

Once the access routes to foreign markets had been reopened, exporting was resumed at a relatively high rate estimated at between 30,000 and 40,000 head of cattle annually. The only contemporary statistics to survive in Denmark are from the year 1640–1. They indicate an aggregate export (based on the customs registers at all the points of export) amounting to more than 37,500 head. It may be noted too that while for fiscal reasons the export of cattle was confined to the overland route through the duchy of Schleswig until the beginning of the seventeenth century, a liberalization permitting transport by sea took place during the period 1615–23, to the profit of both the eastern Danish provinces and of the ports on the west coast of Jutland. The traffic from Ribe to Holland was an important feature here, accounting for about 7,000 oxen in 1640–1. Its significance is reflected also in the fact that Danish warships convoyed the cattle fleets to Holland from time to time.

In the early 1640s, complaints began to be heard from the Danish nobility about the difficulties involved in raising and marketing cattle. The first reference to the failure of the Elbe market is to be found in a petition of 1647. The occasion for the petition was a report on cattle production and trade. It was proposed that the Elbe market should be transferred to Ribe, whence it would be possible to transport the oxen direct to Holland by sea, or – if the market failed – to drive them home again. A curtailment of the production of stalled oxen by one third over a period of two years was also mooted. Finally, regrets were expressed over the encroachments of the other two estates upon the monopoly claimed by the nobility in regard to the stalling of export cattle, and in 1639 the nobility succeeded in obtaining a direct embargo on the exporting of cattle stalled by the peasants.

The background to this tightening-up was undoubtedly the deterioration of market conditions in the aftermath of the Thirty Years War. Prices on the Elbe market were falling. One merchant after another forsook the cattle-export trade, once the almost exclusive preserve of Danish businessmen. Evidence that market conditions had changed is furnished by a surviving business ledger belonging to Steffen Rode, a big merchant, which shows that during the eleven years from 1639 to 1649 he incurred losses totalling 19,000 rix-dollars on the exporting of cattle. When prices fell, the stalling of cattle was no longer remunerative, especially on the landed estates. Other forms of agricultural production, such as milk, enabled the larger ones to weather the storm better. Market outlets for butter, cheese and similar commodities were increasing, for instance among the expanding naval fleets of the west European maritime powers. The conversion of Danish farming from beef-cattle production to dairying was an exceedingly slow process, however, and it did not resolve the difficulties at a stroke.

The decline of the cattle trade was felt most severely in the Danish islands, while Jutland and Skåne appear to have survived it better. Cattle production and trade continued to play a prominent role in these regions. The golden age was over, but exports of oxen did continue. About 20,000 animals a year was the normal figure overland in the second half of the seventeenth century, though there were numerous interruptions and temporary depressions because of war. Thus, exports were completely broken off from 1658 to 1660 during the Danish-Swedish war, and the Anglo-Dutch war of 1665–7 and Louis XIV's war of aggression left their impress in the form of disappointing Netherlands purchases on the Elbe market. The Great Northern War created difficulties at the beginning of the eighteenth century. So did outbreaks of cattle-plague in 1713 and 1745. It used to be thought that the raising of the Danish export toll in 1718, and the Dutch reprisal in the shape of a heavy import duty upon Danish oxen, must have occasioned a sudden drop in exports. Dr Wiese's analysis does not bear out this supposition. On the contrary, the export figures of the 1720s were rather higher than in the immediately preceding period. It was not until 1734 that a noticeable decline set in.

The heyday of the cattle trade coincided with the golden age of the nobility. This is evidenced by the many examples in Hungary, Poland and Denmark, of large incomes from cattle being lavishly dispensed upon the building of stately homes and the maintenance of great households and a high standard of living. The trade was a firm component of the base on which the rule of the aristocracy rested. But cattle furnished the livelihoods of the peasants too, and the customs levies swelled the treasuries of princes. Professor Astrid Friis believed that in the case of Denmark, the swift growth of cattle exports brought foreign currency into the country in such quantities that the monetary structure recovered rapidly from the civil war of 1533–6 and so was able subsequently to finance Denmark's participation in the Seven Years War of the North in 1563–70. Last but not least, merchants made their profits out of this long-distance trade.

Scrutiny of the separate elements of the north European cattle trade discloses that the animals changed hands at least four times before reaching the urban consumer: from the farmer who undertook the actual rearing (a three- or four-year process, on farms whose capacity was often limited to 2–4 head of cattle), to the lord, who had a monopoly of stalling (duration: one winter; capacity: several hundred head), to the merchant, who organized the drove of a month or more with herds numbering twenty, forty or as many as several hundred head of livestock, to the engrosser or slaughterer, who arranged for fattening-up prior to delivery of the beasts to the slaughterhouse in the autumn.

It is difficult to determine for certain what levels of profit it was possible to make from the actual trading of cattle, for the data available from the different stages of the trade never relate to the same drove, and it is known that the cattle could vary in quality a great deal. The business ledger of Steffen Rode cited above shows that the costs involved in the drove amounted to 25–30 per cent of the purchase price, i.e. the price at which the dealer bought the cattle from the farmer or the landlord. There are isolated instances in the early sixteenth century where the costs were even bigger, reaching as high as 46 per cent. The cost of transport by sea greatly exceeded that by land. In Steffen Rode's case, the costs entailed in conveying cattle from Copenhagen to Holland by the maritime route amounted to about 72 per cent. Although a fall in freight rates did occur during the seventeenth century, transport of cattle by sea remained an expensive business.

Dr Wiese has attempted, by comparing the prices of grass-fed, stall, lean and fat cattle respectively, to estimate what share of the final price to the consumer accrued to each of the various cattle-trade interests in the period 1550–1650. His conclusions must, as he himself says, be treated with great caution, but they suggest that 29·2 per cent of the price to the consumer was accounted for by the rearing process, 18·6 per cent by stalling, 25·3 per cent by pure trading transactions and 26·9 per cent by the engrosser. The values involved in the trading transactions fluctuate a great deal, especially at the beginning of the period, when the figures are low and at one point (the decade 1571–80) even negative, which can hardly be correct. Dr Wiese believes that the cattle trade between Denmark and the Elbe market was not notably lucrative in the second half of the sixteenth century. About 75 per cent of Danish–Schleswig exports in these years went on beyond the Elbe to Oldenburg, Friesland and the Netherlands, where prices may have been better. After 1600, when the cattle trade enjoyed its biggest boom, the price statistics indicate higher profits – there is a succession of years when selling prices are continuously almost double the buying prices – but towards the end of the period under review prices were sagging again, which accords with the information furnished by Steffen Rode's business ledger, where direct losses on the transport of cattle to the Elbe market are being recorded towards the end. The fact that the trade nonetheless continued suggests either that our price-statistics are not reliable or that the market was not a self-regulating one with demand, cost of supply, and prices all reached by mutual interaction. The small farmer, who had a need for ready cash at intervals to pay for necessaries beyond the scope of subsistence housekeeping or for taxes, produced and sold his livestock without much insight into such rational calculations as production costs or export and market prices. Only to a limited extent is it true to say that the market influenced the manner in which resources were utilized in production or the volume and pattern of production.

The Danish nobility scarcely ever appeared in the customs registers as exporters of cattle. It was merchants who conducted the actual trade, some of the most important of them being from Flensburg. Only a few German or Dutch exporters can be traced before about 1630, but after that date foreign engrossers became more prominent. Towards the middle of the century the customs registers at Toldsted (a third customs post on the road south) record about fifty Danish merchants together with seventeen Germans and thirty-two Dutchmen. Foreign engrossers account for more than half the total in the second half of the century. Dutch exporters were already coming to Denmark during the wars of 1625–9 and 1643–5. A merchant in Gothenburg is acting as a factor for Dutch cattle engrossers in 1629, and from that time on the exporting of cattle from Skåne direct to Holland by sea begins to achieve some importance. The brisk and continuous Dutch demand brought the Dutch engrossers to the doors of the Danish byres, so to speak, and may have compensated somewhat for the failing German demand.

(3) THE COPPER TRADE

Several features make metals an interesting subject for study. Central European mining of metallic ores is one of the fields in which capital formation and new organizational forms were most clearly observable. Serious social conflicts were enacted around the industries connected with the winning and smelting of the ores, and metals played an important role in international trade. Copper figured prominently among them. Innumerable attempts were made to cartelize the trade in it. Copper occupied an intermediate position between the true coinage metals – the so-called precious metals, gold and silver – and the cheaper metals. By royal privilege, a prince could redeem gold and silver at a price determined by himself. This right was bound up with the right of coinage itself. Copper was not a true coinage metal in medieval times, and for this reason the prince might refrain from exercising that right of pre-emption which in principle he asserted to be reserved to himself even in the case of copper. During the course of the sixteenth century, however, princes were extending their insistence upon the royal right of pre-emption to the baser metals, including copper, which now began to find employment as a coinage metal at the same time as it was becoming of high strategic significance by virtue of its use in cannon-founding. Furthermore, copper ore often occurred in association with other ores, which means that in some instances copper was the primary objective in mining the ore while in others it was a by-product. Thus, Dr Westermann has demonstrated recently that copper accounted for only 40 per cent of the output of the Thuringian metal-mining companies in the period 1460–1560, the other 60 per cent consisting of silver. Any interpretation of the production and trade of the region in that period must accordingly be made in the light of conditions on the European silver market. The Hungarian region (the Neusohl workings), on the other hand, provides an example of production that was dominated by the mining of copper.

Irrespective of whether the montane princes availed themselves of their right of pre-emption or not, they received revenues in copper by way of taxes in kind, such as tithes and tolls, and often operated copper-mines as well. If they could not or would not use the copper themselves, then they had to dispose of it either by selling it or by entrusting its sale to merchants. In the sixteenth century, merchants took a notable part in the smelting of copper from the ore. This took place at the foundries and associated with it was the refining of the various qualities (refined copper, bar copper, copper wire etc.), which became in turn the raw materials of subsequent processes such as the casting of bronze, the manufacture of brass, and wire-drawing. The technical properties of the copper constituted an important factor in determining the prices of the various types. The production of some regions was heavily specialized: e.g. Eislebener copper was best suited for making wire and brass. A copper dealer not involved in the refining of the ore was an exception in the sixteenth century. However, there are numerous examples in the next century of copper dealers without any vertical links with the production and refining of the various copper types, though in this century too most of the trade in copper is rooted, if not in the actual mining of the ore, then in the next stages of the production process.

The interest of the princely power was soon reinforced by – and soon at variance with – that of the merchants. On a number of occasions – often at some critical juncture when the need for money was most acute – the right to collect future revenues of metal, whether in the shape of tolls, tithes, pre-emption or forced deliveries, was handed over to capitalist financiers in return for large credits or advances in ready cash. In fact copper became in this way a key to much of the great-power politics of Europe. In the sixteenth century the emperor Maximilian and his successors financed their wars by means of central European copper and silver. The Swedish king did likewise in the seventeenth century. Gustavus Adolphus, the champion of Protestantism, sold copper to Catholic Spain via middlemen in Amsterdam – by no means the only example of trade cutting across the religious boundaries that were so strictly drawn in that age. Thus, despite prohibitions without number, a substantial share of Hungarian copper production reached Turkey, the principal antagonist of Christendom.

The 'copper purchase', as it was called, could mean that a fair proportion of the output of an area might fall into relatively few hands. Merchants were not always interested in becoming deeply involved in the production process, but from time to time they found themselves forced to do so, as for instance when a prince could not repay his loans and the creditors accordingly had to foreclose. This happened to the Fuggers. Once involved in production, it could be difficult to disengage again. In the depressed trade conditions of the latter half of the sixteenth century, the Fuggers were unable to find anyone willing to buy their copperworks and mines in the Tyrol.

As is stated elsewhere in this section three main production regions in central Europe stand out as important in international trade – the east Alpine district, the upper Hungarian district and the Mansfeldt district of Thuringia. Sweden, whose production was on a notable scale in the seventeenth century, may be added to the list as well. The supply of raw copper was inelastic in the short run. The fluctuations of output, which could be severe, were usually produced by technical or natural causes, and it proved difficult to regulate the market through output at the mines. But it was at the next stage that attempts at regulation were made. Considerable changes, especially of the geographical kind, did take place on the supply side in the long run.

Copper made heavy demands on transport capacity, whether by sea or by land, and this function was usually entrusted to independent entrepreneurs not associated with the international copper trade. An example of copper's demand for transport is furnished by the carriage of Hungarian copper from Neusohl to the smelting works at Hohenkirchen, whence the Nuremberg, Frankfurt, and other markets were supplied. An annual production of 11,000 centner (1 centner = approx. 1 hundredweight) required 220 four-in-hand wagons with a payload of 0·8 tons each, which covered the distance of 800 kilometres between the two places (i.e. a round trip of 1,600 kilometres) three times a year, a journey of between 68 and 82 days depending upon wind, weather and the condition of the roads.

Copper was in demand for many purposes: for coinage and cast-bronze cannon, for countless articles in industry, handicrafts and the household, for the vats used in brewing and distilling, cooking and boiling, as a roofing material, in shipbuilding, for a variety of instruments, for kitchen pots and pans, and for sundry decorative purposes (bells, church doors, bronze statues, fitments and so on). It was also used in making jewellery and trinkets, particularly to meet the needs of the less well-off. Copper was the poor man's gold. Demand did not remain constant. Bronze cannon-founding flourished from the middle of the fifteenth century to the beginning of the seventeenth. This was the era of the new nation-states with their armies, their fleets and their wars which, coupled with geographical expansion, all added to the demand for cannon, copper and tin. Cast-bronze artillery reached a high state of perfection, especially the German and Flemish pieces, in which there was an extensive trade, while the Italian and French products went for local use. Nevertheless bronze cannon lost ground during the seventeenth century to the new and cheaper, though heavier and less perfect, cast-iron pieces in which England and Sweden were specialists. The Swedish entrepreneur Louis de Geer declared in 1644 that iron cannon could be procured for the war fleet at one-third the price of bronze cannon, and a survey of the Swedish navy's armament in 1658 shows that there were as many iron cannon as bronze. In the subsequent decades iron cannon, now improved to such an extent as to stand comparison with the older ordnance even from the technical standpoint, gained ground everywhere. Naturally this development was bound to affect the demand for copper. But in other fields, too, iron was advancing at the expense of copper, especially among household articles; iron pots and pans were cheaper and cleaner, and, unlike copper, they did not transmit any taste to the food. The increased use of brass afforded some compensation for these changes, but the output of brass was hardly of such proportions as to offset what had been lost to iron elsewhere.

The use of copper for coining was an excellent example of a once-for-all demand. Once the circulation was fully supplied with copper coin, it could only absorb further copper to cover wear and tear or any extra need for currency generated by commercial expansion. To exceed these limits was to court inflation. This is precisely what a number of countries, especially Spain, did. Several countries bought substantial quantities of copper exclusively for minting, but the demand was uneven and indeed probably constituted the demand-side factor most responsible for the ups and downs of the trade cycle. Other short-term fluctuations of demand were induced by business conditions in industries like sugar-refining, brewing, the manufacture of saltpetre, and of course the armaments programmes associated with wars.

Copper sought the nearest route to the sea. This meant that Venice was a principal sales outlet for the Tyrolean and Hungarian portions of the central European output. Despite the ups and downs, the city retained this position right up to the beginning of the seventeenth century. From Venice, copper was traded eastwards to the Levant and thence to India (for it was one of the few commodities with which Europe was able to pay for its imports of spices), and westwards to

Majorca and Malaga, the centres of redistribution to Spain and Portugal, whence copper entered into the trade with Africa and the New World. Some of the central European production, however, flowed northwards and westwards, too. While Venice remained the chief market and south Germany the subsidiary market for Tyrolean production, in the early decades of the sixteenth century Hungarian copper was already finding its way via Danzig to Antwerp or via the river Oder to Stettin and thence via Hamburg and Lübeck to the Netherlands. In 1508 the Portuguese factory at Antwerp was founded as a branch of the Casa da India, and the Portuguese king bought up considerable quantities of copper each year through his factors. The Antwerp market was of great consequence as an outlet for Hungarian production until the 1570s. Thereafter it was Hamburg that rose to prominence. Germany as a whole constituted an important market for copper, notably that supplied by Mansfeldt, with cities like Nuremberg, Aachen (the seat of the largest brass industry in Europe) and Frankfurt acting as the main centres. The biggest buyers of Swedish copper in the sixteenth century were in Lübeck. Later on they were in Hamburg and Amsterdam. Dutch demand was stimulated not only by general business activity but also by the development after 1600 of a considerable copper-working industry in the towns of the Netherlands.

It was the European market that fixed the production and marketing conditions. As has already been indicated, it was difficult to adjust the output of copper at short notice, and so it was in the marketing of semi-manufactured products that endeavours to regulate supply and demand manifested themselves, especially in periods of over-production. These endeavours ranged from monopoly schemes to oligopolistic arrangements. A notorious early one is ascribed to Jakob Fugger, who contracted with the Emperor Maximilian in 1490 to purchase the whole output of the Tyrol and followed this up by entering the Hungarian field in 1494. A syndicate was formed in 1498 between Fugger and his nearest rivals in the copper trade, three Augsburg merchant houses. However, Fugger broke the agreement by bringing Hungarian copper on to the Venetian market at dumping prices and, although in so doing he incurred losses himself by virtue of his one-third holding in the Augsburg syndicate, the coup succeeded. His competitors withdrew, and the first European copper monopoly was established. Thereafter the Hungarian share of the output was channelled to the Netherlands and the Tyrolean to Venice. The monopoly was short-lived, although business conditions as a whole were good during the first half of the sixteenth century. At intervals, however, the market showed signs of saturation. This was the case in the 1520s, for example, when the Thuringian copper dealers got into difficulties, partly because the

Peasant Wars and their requisitions weakened demand on the markets of Nuremberg and Frankfurt while simultaneously the brisk demand for silver was automatically bringing increased quantities of copper with it. A surprising offer of Swedish copper on the Netherlands market increased the uncertainties, and so did the Fuggers' dispositions in Hungary. This was the setting for the bankruptcies of the succeeding years and the efforts to concentrate production in the Mansfeldt district. Cartel agreements were established from 1531 to 1534 and again from 1537 to 1540. The Fuggers' interest in the Hungarian Neusohl workings ceased in 1546, and after some years of state operation these mines were transferred to other Augsburg houses. Hungarian production was drastically restricted in the 1570s, and that of the other chief suppliers was falling too in these decades.

The business climate took a turn for the better again during the 1590s. Prices on the Netherlands market doubled between 1599 and 1610 as a result of a general increase in demand. Exports overseas were expanding, as was copper coinage, especially in Spain with its intensified use of *vellon* money, the three main periods of minting there being 1599–1606, 1617–19 and 1621–6. The demand of the European munitions industry for copper was probably also a factor to be taken into account, as was the fast-growing demand of the new copper industry in the Netherlands itself, an industry founded by German (especially Aachen) and Dutch entrepreneurs in the first decade of the seventeenth century.

In this period of booming business, Amsterdam succeeded in establishing itself as a major copper staple, thanks mainly to supplies from Sweden, whose production formerly had been disposed of at the medieval staple towns of Lübeck and Hamburg. Swedish production increased fivefold during the first two decades of the century and, as the Thirty Years War proceeded, Sweden became the biggest supplier of copper in Europe. Between 1616 and 1619 Swedish exports were largely channelled towards the Netherlands as a result of the alliance with the States-General established in 1614. Extensive Dutch loans had been granted to Sweden on condition repayment was effected in copper. The sale of the copper was left in private hands, and as the quantities in question were very substantial, various Dutch groups competed for the supplies with a view to securing a controlling influence over the Dutch copper market. The Swedes countered these manoeuvres in 1619 by setting up the Swedish Copper Company. They redirected their exports towards the old Hanseatic markets, but in 1626 found themselves in serious financial difficulties. Copper prices were now showing a tendency to fall.

Gustavus Adolphus had tried to ward off the effects of the declining market by introducing a bimetallic standard of silver and copper, the system of *vellon* money permitting him to restrict exports of Swedish copper without reducing production. His policy failed, however. Sweden did not enjoy a monopolistic position, and as its war finances rested largely on copper, the fall in prices meant a serious threat to its liquidity. By granting new loans to be repaid in copper, Dutch investors, especially the Trip firm, whose activities have been studied by Professor Klein, succeeded in re-establishing the Amsterdam copper staple. The fall in prices may have been connected with the cessation of the third period of Spanish *vellon* mintings. It may also have been due, as contemporary sources believed, to growing competition from iron utensils. The high level of copper prices during the first quarter of the seventeenth century may have occasioned a shifting of demand from copper to iron. But it is worth noting that the Swedish entrepreneur Louis de Geer expressed in a letter of 1633 the opinion that the first fall in copper prices in Amsterdam was due to the Dutch East India Company which, attracted by the prevailing high prices, had begun to import overseas copper.

Copper was being produced in many parts of the world outside Europe in the early modern age. We find it both in the New World and in Asia. Japan was the most important of the Asian regions. That country had one of the biggest mining industries in the world, and her production of copper outstripped all other commodities and became the great staple of Japanese export. This is attested by the Dutch traders of the time, who have left us frequent evidence of the pre-eminence of copper in the cargoes of their southern-bound vessels and of the huge profits which they derived from resale in the markets of Tonkin, Malacca, and numerous other places in Asia.

The Dutch East India Company had obtained permission from the Shogun in 1608 to trade in Japan, and after 1623 it had a monopoly over its European rivals in the Japan trade. The company became instrumental in linking the European and Asian copper markets together. We first find the idea of sending Japanese copper to the Netherlands being ventilated in 1620. In February of that year, Jan Pietersz: Coen, the famous governor-general, wrote to the Dutch factory at Firando asking for 'a sample of copper for the Netherlands'; and at the same time Mijnheer Specz, who was Dutch resident at Firando, suggested that an attempt should be made to send coarse and fine copper as ballast to Holland; this in his opinion would be not only profitable but practical, as the ships needed a heavy loading to ensure a safe passage. The small quantity of copper ordered by Coen was shipped to Europe in April 1621 aboard the 'Leyden'. The Company's directors had the copper tested by a coppersmith in Amsterdam, but his findings disappointed their expectations. The wastage of the trial consignment was too great, and the quality was not high enough to convince the directors that further imports would pay. A letter dated April 1622 cancelled Japanese copper as a return commodity until further notice. The factors at Firando, however, were still optimistic, and varying quantities were shipped to Europe during the years that followed, although the European management of the Company recommended the Batavian government to send Japanese copper to Persia instead. In 1624 the directors took a more serious interest in the matter, some of the consignments having been sold at a satisfactory profit in Amsterdam. They ordered between 200,000 and 300,000 Dutch lbs in annual shipments to the Netherlands, and they sent out a plate of copper as a model together with instructions for the assaying. How far these orders were carried into effect cannot be decided with full accuracy, as the invoices are not extant from all the returning ships, but it does appear that about 123,000 Dutch lbs of copper were shipped to the Netherlands in February 1626 and more than 300,000 lbs in November 1627 and January 1628.

In his letter mentioned above, de Geer stated that the copper from Japan in 1626 went to Aix in France. One of the agents of the Swedish Crown in Amsterdam, Conrad von Falkenberg, reported that the quality of the Japanese copper was excellent, whereas de Geer told his associates that the new copper was not as good as Swedish copper; nevertheless it had begun to find a ready market in Amsterdam, and this was one of the causes of the lower price. It is difficult to determine the quantitative significance of Dutch imports of Japanese copper compared with Swedish copper on the Amsterdam market. It is certain, however, that the presence of Japanese copper on the Amsterdam market in these years influenced Swedish commercial policy. De Geer argued how necessary it was for Sweden to have large quantities of copper as a resource with which she might threaten the Dutch to beat down the price and so keep them from importing too much. The essential thing was to let sleeping dogs lie. It also gives food for thought to learn that one of the members of the Trip family firm was a director of the Dutch East India Company, and that in 1626 and 1627 he bought the whole import of Japanese copper from the Company. The Trips were among Europe's leading merchants in arms, and they were notable also for their activities in the copper trade. The decision of the directors of the Dutch East India Company in 1624 to order copper from Japan could be interpreted as a manoeuvre inspired by the Trip firm in order to soften up the Swedes by undercutting them on the European market and thereby to bring them back into the Dutch fold.

The first act of Japanese copper on the European stage turned out to be a brief one, mainly because of difficulties that arose for the Dutch in

Japan during the years 1628–33 and the Japanese embargo laid on copper in 1638. The embargo was motivated by the fact that copper was war material, and it lasted until 1645. During this period copper was ordered from the Netherlands for the Dutch factories in India. But the resumption of exports from Japan caused the copper bars to pour out again, and by 31 December 1646 the Batavian government was writing to the Directors in the Netherlands that it no longer had any use for European copper. The first cargoes of Japanese copper bars were sent to Europe in 1649, the next lot in 1651. Then followed an interval of four years with no consignments, at the end of which the directors for the first time entered Japanese copper in their special lists of the most wanted import commodities. This was in November 1655, and on that occasion the directors stated that the price of copper in Holland had risen from 36 fl. to 56 fl. per 100 Dutch lb. They asked the Batavian government to ship to Europe as much copper as could be spared from the Asian trade. A period of more than 20 years followed in which supplies to the Netherlands were continuous and large.

Japanese copper must have been an important element in the offers on the European market in these years. When the imports were at their peak, i.e. in 1672–5, they equalled one third to one half of the estimated Swedish exports. Accordingly, Japanese copper made its début in the famous Amsterdam price-lists in 1669 – together with Norwegian copper – and continued to figure there until 1688.

It is evident that the European demand stimulated the Dutch Company's exports from Japan, but besides the impulse derived from the rising prices of copper in Europe, the Company's interest in Japanese copper may also have been strengthened to some degree by a simultaneous heavy fall in the prices of East India sugar, which was another commodity used for ballast. When the directors asked in 1655 for copper in homeward-bound ships, they ordered the Batavian government not to send more sugar than necessary, but only to ship what could not be sold on the Asian markets. Part of the Company's ballast capacity was being switched from sugar to copper. The heavy imports to Europe in the 1660s and 1670s did not change the Company's main principle that copper from Japan was regarded throughout as a commodity primarily for its Asian factories, especially the factories in India. Shipments to Europe remained a secondary affair. The Japanese embargo on silver and the rising prices of Japanese gold coins caused the Dutch Company to try its hand at the third coinage metal, copper, in the areas in which Japanese silver and gold had previously been sold, i.e. on the Coromandel coast, in Bengal, Surat, Ceylon and Persia. At many of these places the prices of Japanese copper were higher than in the Netherlands, and the commodity accounted for a much greater share of the local trade and of profits. Whereas Japanese copper at the Company's sales in the Netherlands represented almost 6–8 per cent of the total receipts from the auctions, it contributed proportionately much more to the provision of cash for the Company at the Indian factories. Of a range of commodities including forty different items in Surat, only cloves yielded a greater profit to the Company than copper. The position of Japanese copper was further consolidated on the Asian markets during the decades that followed.

On the Dutch side, as has been remarked, the Trip family was notable for its activity in the copper trade in the first half of the seventeenth century. Around 1632 the Swedish Crown was in debt to Elias Trip to the tune of about a million guilders. By threatening to sell off the Swedish stocks of copper in Amsterdam and thus make Sweden bankrupt, Trip tried repeatedly to secure for himself a veritable monopoly, as for instance in 1634, when the Dutch and German copper merchants combined to form a company in which the Trip influence preponderated. The Swedish government, however, refused to have any dealings with them. In the following year, two copper companies were established to divide the market, one of them Dutch-Hanseatic, the other Swedish. The Trip family again dominated the Dutch-Hanseatic enterprise. This collaboration lasted until 1639. These repeated attempts to gain control of the marketing of the entire Swedish copper production (which dominated the market after the outbreak of the Thirty Years War, when central European production was plagued by extensive disturbances) show that in the seventeenth century too, the copper trade was too large a mouthful for any single group or merchant house to swallow.

(4) THE TEXTILE TRADE

The history of textile production and trade has been dominated by interest in woollen goods, chiefly cloth. That this has been one of the classical fields of study for English scholars is a natural consequence of the fact that scarcely any country in Europe was as dependent upon the textile trade as England in the fifteenth, sixteenth and part of the seventeenth centuries. Accordingly it may be pertinent to point out that Europe did manufacture other textiles besides wool and that commerce on a considerable scale developed outside the confines of the classical cloth routes and markets. While the manufacture of woollen fabrics was largely a speciality of the towns, the production of linen and canvas articles was predominantly a rural craft. We find early on a substantial trade in linen goods alongside that in woollens, notably from south Germany to the Mediterranean countries, where even the Italian cities purchased linen. In the sixteenth century, north German linen also penetrated into Spain and thence to the New World. The Spanish market remained one of the chief outlets for the European linen industry in the seventeenth and eighteenth centuries, its favours being courted by linens from Silesia, Saxony and Bohemia as well as Ireland.

A characteristic feature of the European textile trade is the expansion of the market both socially and geographically, and the continuous development of lighter and more variegated fabrics. This is attested by the enormous influx in the seventeenth and eighteenth centuries of Asian textiles, notably non-woollen fabrics, in a great variety of types differentiated by size, quality, texture and colour. They included silks and cotton, both finished and semi-finished. The art of calico-printing spread with this trade to Europe.

Fashion came to play a vital role in production and trade. Dr Chaudhuri has rightly remarked of the English East India Company's imports of calicoes in the first half of the seventeenth century that the market was very broad and consumption very elastic. The English Company, under the stimulus of a rapid expansion in demand for calicoes in the European markets, began to stake heavily on these imports from the early 1620s. But detailed knowledge of this new market is lacking. Was it a change in consumer taste alone that evoked such intense interest? Or were Indian textiles more competitive in price than the corresponding European products? Some of the imports were re-exported to continental Europe and the Mediterranean. The finer varieties of Indian cloths had been particularly prized as articles of clothing in north Africa and the Levant since ancient times. The European market for silk and linen goods, moreover, was expanding vigorously towards the end of the seventeenth century and in the first half of the eighteenth; this is true, for instance, of the English home market, as Professor John has observed.

The second half of the seventeenth century was probably the heyday of Asian textiles in Europe. Professor Khan points to the years 1665–80 as the period when the English Company changed its commercial policy. It turned from raw materials and coarse textiles to finished, finer-quality commodities. 'We resolve to drive our trade through', wrote the London directors in 1683 to their officials in India, 'especially in silks and calicoes.' The last decades of the century were characterized by 'the Indian craze', the forerunner and counterpart of the later Chinese fashion in the eighteenth century. John Cary, in his *A Discourse concerning the East India Trade*, dated the new wave in the 1680s:

It was scarce thought about twenty years since that we should ever see calicoes, the ornaments of our greatest gallants (for such they are whether we call them Muslins, Shades or anything else) when they were then rarely used [he wrote in 1699], but now few think themselves well dressed till they are made up in calicoes, both men and women, calico shirts, neck-cloths, cuffs, pocket-handkerchiefs for the former, head-dresses, nightrolls, hoods, sleeves, aprons, gowns, petticoats and what not for the latter, besides India stockings for both sexes.

The Dutch Company, too, staked heavily on textiles during this period. It was a race for procuring novelties. The English Company's directors wrote in 1681:

Know this for a constant and general rule, that in all flowered silks you change the fashion and flower as much as you can every year, for English ladies and they say the French and other Europeans will give twice as much for a new thing not seen in Europe before, though worse, than they will give for a better silk of the same fashion worn the former years.

The companies watchfully analysed their competitors' returns. The English Company sent samples procured from Holland in orders for its servants in India. The tendency was towards finer textiles. The Indian silks replaced the Chinese ones, and above all Bengal emerged as the country of unexpected possibilities. In fact, the new trade in textiles fundamentally changed the composition of the companies' imports to Europe. In 1697 the Dutch East India Company imported goods from Asia to the purchasing value of 5·4 million guilders, all collected from the Company's elaborate chain of factories from Japan to Mocha in Yemen. Of this total, Bengal contributed no less than one-third, half of which were Bengal silks and cotton goods.

Competition between the English and Dutch companies was very intense around 1700, and especially so in textile imports. The position of the English Company was weakened by the opposition to its monopoly at home, which led to the establishment of rival companies, and by growing pressure from the local woollen and silk industries, which wanted imports of Indian textiles banned. Dramatic scenes preceded the passing in 1700 of the act prohibiting printed calicoes, when weavers' wives invaded the House of Commons threatening those members who had voted against the bill. A mob of 3,000 weavers assembled to attack Child's mansion, and East India House was also assailed and the Company's treasure nearly seized. However, the law did not prohibit the importing of semi-manufactures, and the subsequent years witnessed a brisk growth of imports of plain cottons for the rapidly-established European calico-printing works. Another act had to be passed in 1720 forbidding the use of any calicoes in England. None of these statutes, however, was able to slow down the flourishing English trade in Asian textiles, most of which were re-exported; and in fact the English trade managed to surpass that of the Dutch rival.

After the favours of fashion had fallen on Bengali silks in the 1680s and (especially) the 1690s, Chinese fabrics appear to have won increased ground after 1700. The English Company, which in general attached greater weight than did the Dutch to direct sailings in the China trade – a tradition carried on later by the Ostend company – had a better starting position. The abolition of the English Company's monopoly of the Indies trade opened India to interloping, which drove prices up and made the trade less profitable. On top of this, the uneasy condition of India after the death of Aurangzeb in 1707 began to influence production and quality in many of the textile districts.

The directors of the Dutch Company wrote in 1716 that it was a unanimous complaint among Dutch merchants who had been dealing in India fabrics for many years that the Company's auction goods had become poorer in quality year by year and more expensive to buy. Matters had reached a stage where there were now qualities of manufactured goods which the company bought in India at prices almost as high as or even higher than the prices at which the English were selling the same commodity in Europe. Bengal particularly was in the limelight. These complaints continued to be heard in later years, often with the additional observation that Dutch merchants were increasingly meeting their needs by purchasing Asian textiles abroad, especially in London, because their own company's imports were not up-to-date. The fragmentary trade statistics seem to substantiate these allegations.

The anxieties facing East India House are not unique in the history of the European textile trade. Few areas, in fact are so filled with drama – which is clear when we turn our attention to woollen goods and the European production thereof. The European textile industry experienced profound changes between about 1550 and 1650. The chief of these was that the production of pure 'woollens', evolved during the late Middle Ages, ran into great difficulties. Certainly this commodity did not vanish, but it did find itself being supplemented and to a large extent replaced by vigorous new manufactures, different in character, organization and technology. Again a trend can be discerned away from the heavier and in favour of the cheaper materials, lighter in both weight and colour, customarily embraced under the common denomination of the New Draperies. Technically, less wool was used in making these materials and it was of the combed long variety, not carded short. No fulling was necessary, they could be handled more easily in the dye-vat, and more semi-skilled labour was used in their production. In brief: the manufacturing process was shorter and yielded a finished product that was cheaper – in transport costs as well.

This new technique originated in the south Netherlands, in the region around Ypres, whence it spread northwards and westwards during the 1560s. Both political and economic forces were involved.

Professor Posthumus has unearthed data from his wide range of sources to show how Leiden became what was probably the largest single production centre of this new industry in northwestern Europe. The city had a population of 12,000 in 1581; by 1620 the figure had risen to 43,000 and by 1660 to 72,000, while its output of cloth grew from almost nil to 97,000 pieces in 1620 and 118,000 in 1660. England, especially eastern England, benefited too from the migration of this new textile manufacture. As many as one third to one half of the inhabitants of towns like Norwich and Colchester were of Netherlands origin, and even though not all of them were engaged in the New Draperies, which were located predominantly in the villages, this manufacture was vital also to the growth of the towns from where the new products were traded. The English differentiated between the manufacture of 'stuffs' and 'mixtures'. Stuffs were worsteds in which both warp and weft consisted of combed wool. Mixtures were fabrics in which the weft was carded yarn of either cotton or silk, while the warp consisted of combed yarn. In both categories the pattern of the weave could still be seen in the finished product.

Comparison of the product-ranges of the Dutch and English manufacturing regions respectively shows them to be similar in the beginning; but by degrees the paths followed in the two regions diverged under influences such as competition for markets. Professor Wilson has demonstrated that a form of international division of labour gradually emerged between the two chief producers of textiles. The questions of costs and access to raw materials played a part in this process no doubt. English cost-levels were lower than Dutch, one reason being that English production was still based chiefly in the countryside, while Dutch was more concentrated in the towns. Price- and wage-levels in Holland were increasing all through the seventeenth and eighteenth centuries, partly because of rising taxation of foodstuffs. As well as this, the powerful Dutch mercantile interest, especially that of Amsterdam, opposed any protection of the Leiden cloth manufacture. Amsterdam imported considerable quantities of Devonshire cloth from Exeter and Topsham in the seventeenth century, and also exported substantial amounts of German linen products bleached in Haarlem and sold in export markets under the name of 'Dutch linen'. Add to this the increased severity of English legislation during the seventeenth century against the exportation of English and Scottish raw wool, and the most important of the conditions under which the Leiden cloth industry developed have been stated. In these circumstances Leiden gradually came to concentrate on the production of finished articles, which were relatively expensive because of the numerous processing stages involved, using Spanish wool as the raw material. One group of these articles was *lakens*, which became a great Dutch export commodity, being sold in the Mediterranean, the Levant, Africa and the West Indies. But the English market was closed to *lakens*. In the worsted group, Leiden had success with the so-called *greinen*, or camlet. The manufacture of this article began around 1630, when a group of Walloon cloth-makers discovered how to blend camel-hair (or Turkish yarn), or goat-hair if desired, into the wool. Later on, camel-hair was also mixed with silk. The result was a comparatively light material used particularly for men's clothes and sold in France, the Levant and many other places. In the other worsted categories, however, England was clearly the leader, being more successful than its Dutch rival in the selling of cheaper cloths with a narrow profit margin.

The emergence of the New Draperies in the south Netherlands in itself constituted a way out of the depression under which local textile industries of the region had suffered during the first half of the sixteenth century, when English dominance in the traditional woollen cloth – an article which literally went all over Europe by land and water – had been overwhelming. English woollen exports had risen by two-thirds during the first half of the sixteenth century, the increase having been particularly pronounced from the beginning of the 1530s to the beginning of the 1550s and London's export of cloth lying well above the national average. English competition had brought adversity upon the traditional cloth manufacture of Flanders and of other areas in the Low Countries so that, in the 1540s particularly, cloth-making had ceased in many places. The collapse of the Antwerp market in the 1550s and the decline of this entrepôt marked a turning-point in London's export trade in traditional cloth. The third quarter of the sixteenth century saw a severe contraction.

As an ever-growing portion of the English cloth export had been funnelled through London, the difficulties assumed national dimensions. Restrictionism revived, the rivalry between the Merchant Adventurers and the Hanse flared up, and attempts were made in every conceivable manner to find new markets. The drive to sell English textiles abroad inspired a good many of the famous trading ventures of the Elizabethan Age, from the search for northeast and northwest passages to China to the foundation of the East India Company in 1600. With the opening of the seventeenth century, a further fall in the export of traditional cloth from London occurred. In the early 1620s there is a real slump in this particular trade. The factors of the London merchants reported that a cause of slack markets for English textiles was the making of cloth in Hungary and Silesia. The widespread insecurity and economic breakdown that followed the wars of the early seventeenth century both in the Baltic area and in central Europe favoured the cheaper native industries. There was a growing supply of inexpensive local wool. Moreover, increasing quantities of Spanish wool were reaching the principal manufacturing centres of Europe. For long in demand in Flanders (where Bruges was its main port of entry), wool from Spain was now being sent to Italy, France, the Netherlands and Germany, and it even found a market in England. At the same time a qualitative change was taking place in the English wool supply – possibly as a result of enclosures, since the main influence on the nature of wool is the pasturage itself. The new wool was more suited to lighter and thinner kinds of textiles.

Although the English outports in the long run lost ground to London their decline was not a steady one but subject to fluctuations. During the 1550s exports via the outports tended to be more stable than the faltering London exports. The decline in cloth exports also temporarily meant a relative recovery of the wool exports, which in some cases was to the advantage of the outports. In the early seventeenth century we have similar examples of short intervals during which the outports fared better than the metropolis. Many of the southwestern ports, exporting cloth to France, Spain and the Atlantic islands, benefited from the cessation of the hostilities with Spain in 1604. In the Londoners' years of depression, 1620–4, some of the West Country ports, as well as Hull and Newcastle on the east coast, managed fairly well, the great crisis for these ports being the late 1620s. In the 1630s the cloth trade of Hull shifted from the Baltic to the Netherlands, this outport thus forcing its way into a market previously dominated by London merchants.

Both the English and the Dutch made considerable advances in the Mediterranean cloth trade in the seventeenth century at the expense of the Italian, and to some extent French, textiles. The great Italian cloth-producing cities – Milan, Florence, Como – lost ground as the century proceeded. Even the Italian silk industry was hit by the crisis, although the Italian cities did preserve their market for luxury wares such as gold brocades, silks, satins and velvets. Venice struggled longest against the tide, still maintaining in the 1640s a relatively considerable output of textiles, though a decline set in thereafter. The foreign competition from the north was too stiff. The Levantine market wanted light, cheap fabrics. The level of costs and the rigidity of the system of production were hindrances. The Venetian cloth industry, one of the oldest and most brilliant in Europe, was mainly based on Spanish wool. The supply of the latter was monopolized, and the price of the finished product rose. To the north, the French industry, centred upon Rouen, had made successful attempts to market lighter fabrics in the Levant, but the religious wars undermined the French success. Not until the last quarter of the seventeenth century did France return to the Levantine market with excellent fabrics from the textile towns of southern France.

Leghorn, the port of Pisa and under the rule of the grand dukes of Tuscany, had been made a free port in 1593. It became the favourite port of the English and Dutch and a centre of Mediterranean commerce. It also became the gateway to the Italian market, for not only did the northern textiles displace Italian in the Levant, they actually competed with them successfully at home. Leghorn soon became a flourishing city of cosmopolitan character, with Italian, Dutch, English, Armenian, Persian and even Indian residents, as well as – last but not least – a large and wealthy Jewish community, mainly of Spanish and Portuguese origin. It has been said that it was primarily Leghorn and the Mediterranean market that first helped to rescue the English economy from the disastrous consequences of the decline of the old industry.

(5) THE BALANCE OF TRADE

It is impossible, in our present state of knowledge, to compose any systematic account of the way in which trade between the various regions balanced at different times. The question was important, and engaged much contemporary attention. As is well known, a good deal of the mercantilist literature, especially the English, was devoted to it. The balance of trade was one of the hot potatoes of the English debate, as is clearly to be seen, for instance, if one analyses Thomas Mun's *England's Treasure by Forraign Trade*, which bears the significant sub-title *The Balance of our Forraign Trade is the Rule of our Treasure*. There were, however, two areas of international trade in the sixteenth and seventeenth centuries which particularly interested contemporaries and have subsequently also attracted the notice of scholars. These were the Asiatic and Baltic areas, both of which enjoyed large export surpluses over a very long span of time. These surpluses must have been offset somehow or other. The problem of how this was done has not really been resolved, but by now sufficient light has been shed on it to enable some of the outlines to be sketched in. It is true of both areas that a closer understanding of the trade-balance problem can be attained by dividing them into regions or countries. Their identities need to be specified in detail.

This is obvious at once as far as the Asiatic area is concerned. It is evident that after the establishment of the Asiatic trade with the founding of the East India companies, equalization of trade balances was effected by exports of precious metals from Europe. The companies were primarily importing concerns, and it was clear early on that Europe had little to offer the Asiatic countries from its production of finished goods, semi-manufactures and raw materials, either because of the uncompetitiveness of European products in price and quality or because of the inability or disinclination of Asiatic countries to acquire European products apart from certain special categories, e.g. of weaponry and mechanical instruments. Some of the precious metals (both bullion and coin) for settling the European import trade came from Europe itself, but most came from Africa and the New World, thus giving the traffic a global character.

Adam Smith in 1776 remarked of the forces setting in motion this flow of precious metals from the European to the Asian continent that 'in the East Indies, particularly in China and Indostan, the values of the precious metals, when the Europeans first began to trade to those countries, was much higher than in Europe'. Smith believed that this factor was still operative at the end of the eighteenth century: 'There is scarce any commodity which brings a better price there; or which, in proportion to the quantity of labour and commodities which it costs in Europe, will purchase more or command a greater quantity of labour and commodities in India.' Smith added that it was advantageous to carry silver rather than gold to Asia 'because in China, and the greater part of the other markets of India, the proportion between fine silver and fine gold is but as ten, or at most as twelve, to one; whereas in Europe it is as fourteen or fifteen to one'. This applied to the traffic across the Pacific Ocean, from Acapulco to Manila, as well: 'The silver of the new continent seems in this manner to be one of the principal commodities by which the commerce between the two extremities of the old one is carried on, and it is by means of it, in a great measure, that those distant parts of the world are connected with one another.'

Closer observation of the vast Asiatic trading area in which the East India companies transacted business and found return cargoes for Europe discloses many indications that the values of gold and silver were at first almost unrelated in many parts of Asia, and subject to great disparities, but from the latter half of the sixteenth century new ratios of a 'modern' character were establishing themselves. This may be taken as reflecting the fact that areas formerly isolated were now taking part in or being influenced by foreign trade – which does not, however, amount to saying that it was European activity alone that produced this result. It is an over-simplification to believe that the flow of metals from America (and Africa) via Europe to Asia, or from America to Asia across the Pacific Ocean, was a one-way traffic. There were numerous producers of precious metals within the Asiatic area, and settlements of trade surpluses and deficits took place with their aid.

The biggest producer was undoubtedly Japan. There was also pro-duction of gold and silver in China, in Tonkin, in Sumatra and in

India. In Japan, the history of mining was marked by the sudden opening of gold and silver mines throughout the country about the middle
of the sixteenth century, and by a great increase in the production of
gold and silver from about this time to the middle of the seventeenth
century. Then the output declined, and instead of gold and silver the
mining of copper showed a sudden rise and became of paramount importance, as has been noted elsewhere. At its peak, Japan's output of
precious metals may have paralleled the production figures of the New
World. Through the commercial intercourse of Asian and European
merchants with Japan, these precious metals came to play an important
role in the offsetting of the trade balances of individual regions of
maritime Asia. They influenced European shipments to Asia too, not
only in their amount but also in their composition, for, rightly considered and over time, conditions were not as simple as in Adam Smith's
day, when silver was supreme.

The activity of the Dutch East India Company in the seventeenth and
eighteenth centuries throws an interesting light on these questions, particularly since the Company straddled the whole Asian scene, as it were,
and at the same time had had a monopoly among Europeans of the
trade with Japan since 1639. The history of the Company contains
periods when its participation in the inter-Asiatic trade furnished it
with a considerable proportion – between one third and one half – of
the requisite precious metals. The flow of silver from Japan was a vital
factor down to 1668. In that year the Japanese government issued a
decree prohibiting the exporting of silver. The officials of the Dutch
Company then turned their attention towards Japanese gold coins, the
so-called *koubangs*. The Company had secured permission to export
koubangs as early as 1665. The Dutch had previously obtained gold
coins from China via Formosa, but the loss of Formosa as a consequence
of Koxinga's conquest of the island in 1662 put an end to this trade.
Great discoveries of gold were made in Japan towards the end of the
1660s, and the Dutch were able to acquire large quantities for export.
An export boom in gold developed in the years around 1670. Then the
Japanese raised the price, and the export figures slowed down. There
was a temporary ban on the export of gold in 1685–6, the Japanese
government fearing that exports would cause a shortage of their currency. Exports were resumed afterwards, however, though on a more
modest scale, partly because of the debasements of 1696 and 1720.

The Dutch Company's interest in gold from Japan had its counterpart in a desire to have gold sent out from Europe. This manifested
itself, for instance, in the requests emanating from the Batavia government at the beginning of the 1660s for shipments, which were motivated by the fact that gold could be exchanged at a more favourable

rate than silver, notably in India generally and the Coromandel coast in particular. Professor Raychaudhuri has remarked that the demand for precious metals in India was neither uniform nor in any way unlimited. Silver and silver coins were the most affected by price fluctuations, whereas the position with regard to gold and gold coins was somewhat different. These were the only commodities almost universally in demand, though the prices varied considerably from region to region and were subject to fluctuations.

It is evident, moreover, that the Indian states' policy with regard to coinage exercised a considerable influence on the demand for the two metals. Coromandel was basically a gold-standard area, while Bengal had a silver (or mixed silver–copper) standard. At intervals the picture varied, however, as for instance with the revival of silver in Golconda (Coromandel) in 1656, when the minting of silver coins was resumed to cover the increased tribute payable to the Mogul. Conversely, in the 1660s the Mogul emperor wanted his tribute to be paid in gold pagodas, which immediately created a demand for gold.

The considerable interest evinced by the Dutch and other European companies during the 1660s and 1670s in the Coromandel area generated an increased need for gold coins. The East India Company's shipments of precious metals from England to India do in fact show a strikingly high percentage of gold in the years 1662–80. The European companies staked heavily in Bengal from the 1680s, and demand for silver increased correspondingly. The Dutch Company now became more dependent on supplies of silver coin and bullion from the Netherlands. Exports of the latter rose during the 1680s and 1690s from 2·4 million to 3·6 million guilders annually, and in 1700 they attained a temporary peak of 5·1 million guilders. The figures went still higher in the eighteenth century. Average exports of silver in the first thirty years were never less than 3 million guilders. Another peak period occurred in 1722–8, when 6·8–7·9 million guilders annually were being sent to Asia.

The Dutch Company's records show also that a stream of precious metals flowed overland from Europe to Asia as well. It debouched into Persia and northwest India, where Gamron, Gujarat and Surat were places at which both silver rix-dollars (including German) and gold ducats, obtained via Poland and Russia, could be procured through Armenian and other merchants. Thus, in 1697–8 the Dutch factory at Gamron sent for 980,000 guilders' worth of goods and money for Surat and Ceylon. Of these exports, 88·5 per cent consisted of European gold ducats. Jean Baptiste Tavernier mentioned the same thing in *Les six voyages* (1678). The Dutch example illustrates too the need for caution in seeking to explain all the flows of precious metals in terms of the silver–gold ratio alone. The ratio argument appears in the sources and features in economic theory (even before Adam Smith), but in many situations and at many places there was in fact no choice: one had to manage as best one could. This applied to the Coromandel coast, for example, at the close of the seventeenth century and for long periods during the eighteenth.

Amsterdam was the European market *par excellence* for precious metals during the seventeenth century and much of the eighteenth. This was where the East India companies generally found their supplies. The 'negotiating money' of the Netherlands was a concept embracing both silver coins (including the ducatoon, which was intended only for export) and gold coins, chiefly the gold ducat. Thanks to Professor van Dillen, much is known about this market, which took on the character more or less of a staple for precious metals during the course of the seventeenth century. Silver from America and gold from Africa (later from Brazil) arrived here for such purposes as paying for corn deliveries to the Mediterranean and defraying the costs of Spanish and other armies in the south Netherlands. It came via many routes: mule-trains carried the Spanish silver from Seville to Barcelona, whence it was shipped to Genoa and then onwards by horse and cart under armed escort through Germany to the Netherlands. Or it might go by silver ship to the Flemish ports, running the gauntlet of the Channel privateers on the way. It could also be conveyed overland through France. When the north Netherlands finally achieved recognition, the Amsterdam silver fleet took care of the transport. Between thirty and fifty ships a year were engaged in the business (though their cargoes did include other commodities as well). The Dutch poet Vondel wrote with pride in 1655 of the new town hall of Amsterdam, whose south wing contained the cellars of the discount bank, declaring that the whole of Peru and its silver could be held within it! Other flows of silver, much more modest in scale, reached the city too. For example, when the Danish king effected settlements with his factor in Amsterdam, one of the methods he employed was to hand over quantities of coin in sacks and chests from the customs revenues of Norway north of the Dovre or from the mines of Kongsberg.

This metal market dated from the 1630s and lasted through the first half of the eighteenth century. Contemporaries cited it as an example of the value of free movement of money. Many of the writers of the day regarded it as a misfortune if a country was forced to ban the export of bullion and coin. The English East India Company, too, satisfied its requirements of precious metals for export on the Amsterdam market, especially after 1695. Dr Chaudhuri, who has analysed the Company's exports of precious metals in the period 1660–1720, has shown that the

Company found its sources of supply of silver in south European (Cadiz and Lisbon) and west European (Amsterdam) countries, and that this supply was conditioned by such factors as the Company's extensive re-export trade and England's balance of trade with the world at large.

Trade balances, capital movements and the ups and downs of the European currencies all affected the availability and prices of precious metals for the east; and the demand of the companies for these metals itself attained such dimensions, especially towards the end of the seventeenth century and in the first half of the eighteenth, that it affected the prices of gold and silver. Sir Isaac Newton's observation of 1717 is well known: 'When ships are leaving for the East Indies the demand for silver for exportation raises the price to 5s. 6d. or 5s. 8d. per ounce or above.' Further exemplification can be cited from elsewhere, e.g. the Danish Asiatic Company's silver purchases in the 1740s and 1750s, which influenced Danish exchange rates. The Danish example also testifies to Amsterdam's leading role. That city, indeed, held the key to the European international payments system, of which the transfers of precious metals constituted an important feature. This did not mean that many deficits could not be settled without transfers. The position held by Amsterdam was the very factor that enabled a chain of settlements to be effected by multilateral offsets using bills of exchange. A large share of western Europe's trade was financed via Amsterdam; and this applied to England's too. A broad stream of payments – in the form of both bills and ready cash – flowed across the Channel in both directions between England and Holland. Amsterdam enjoyed a key position in the financing and settlement of Baltic trade as well.

The Baltic area too has been progressively broken down and analysed by regions as the debate about trade balances has unfolded. A number of interesting studies have been published, especially in recent years; Polish scholars, for example, have contributed a great deal to this differentiating process (A. Mączak, H. Samsonowicz, M. Małowist, Maria Bogucka, M. Hroch). The almost classical discussion of the character of English–Baltic trade (C. Wilson, Eli Heckscher, J. M. Price, J. Sperling, S.-E. Åström) has had a similar effect. The most recent recapitulation of the problem comes from the pen of Professor A. Attman, himself an *Altmeister* of the subject with his studies of the role of the Russian market in sixteenth-century Baltic politics.

For western Europe, the Baltic was the world beyond the Sound. If with A. E. Christensen we seek to draw up from the Sound Toll Registers a transit balance of Baltic trade as a whole, the feature that stands out is that the flow westwards through the Sound was far larger than that in the opposite direction. This is so whether the traffic is measured by volume or by value of goods. The value of exports from the Baltic was, roughly speaking, double that of imports. For the latter part of the sixteenth century and the first half of the seventeenth, the value of imports was 30 per cent, and of exports 70 per cent, of all goods passing through the Sound. The export surplus from the Baltic was thus 40 per cent of the total. That a portion of this balance was offset by the import into the Baltic area of precious metals in the form of ready money is established beyond all doubt, although such trans-actions were not usually entered in the customs registers. Dutch com-mercial correspondence from the latter half of the sixteenth century mentions the large quantities of ready money which were constantly being brought into the Baltic. Part of the flow of precious metals from the New World went this way eastwards. The problem, however, is how much. The deficit in the transit balance could have been made good through imports to the Baltic area by some other route than via the Sound. What commercial and balance-of-trade relationship does the area have with the continent and the Arctic trade route via Arch-angel? What do the trade balances of individual countries look like, and what adjustments between them over time are perhaps concealed behind the grand total aforementioned?

Professor Attman has attempted in his most recent work a collation of balance estimates for eastern Europe. The source-material is frag-mentary. Some of the balances relate only to individual years (Viborg 1558, 1640; Riga 1632, 1683; Königsberg 1641); others cover a rather broader span of time (Narva 1583–8, 1595–8, 1605–8; Smolensk 1673–9; Danzig 1583, 1634, 1640–9); others yet again embrace a single body of merchants (the trade of the Russians in Reval 1606–12; and in Riga 1677, 1679, 1680; England's trade in Narva and Archangel 1699–1700). All these estimates are to the same effect: the export surplus from eastern Europe was usually between 30 per cent and 40 per cent. The only exceptions were Viborg in 1558, Narva in 1605–8, Königsberg in 1641, and Danzig in 1640–9, which showed somewhat lower export surpluses. In Attman's words, 'it can therefore be established generally that exports from the Baltic ports during the latter part of the sixteenth century and the first half of the seventeenth century were roughly twice as large as the imports there. This relationship corresponds very closely to that which A. E. Christensen had calculated from the Sound's cus-toms accounts for the Baltic trade.'

Turning next to overland trade, the source-material is more flimsy, and the conclusions must be taken with the appropriate degree of reservation. The general trade-balance situation across the frontiers between east and west seems to suggest that there was an active east European balance during that same period of 1500–1650. Thus, the customs registers at Smolensk indicate that the balance must have been equalized by payments in precious metals. Smolensk was, incidentally, a centre of the foreign money trade. In the case of Poland the situation is more complicated. Here, precious metals were exported across the frontiers with Russia and Turkey, but Poland's trade balance across the German frontier was probably favourable. Customs registers for Poznań and Ostrzeszów, along the routes to Leipzig and Breslau, point to this conclusion. The overall opinion of present researchers is that Poland's aggregate trade balance was active too. As far as Hungary is concerned, the investigations of Professors Gy. Ember and Zs. P. Pach point to a very active balance developing during the sixteenth century, based on exports westwards of oxen and copper. Professor Pach believes that Bohemia had an active balance as well in the sixteenth century.

The foregoing account of trade relations overland covers the period up to the middle of the seventeenth century. Then we seem to reach a turning-point. On the Hungarian side a noticeable decline started at this time in both the oxen and the copper trades, with the result, it must be supposed, that the trade balance became negative. Conditions changed for Poland as well. Thus, the Thirty Years War brought grave impediments to the westward export of cattle from the Polish-Lithuanian region. The Polish towns lost ground to the markets of Breslau, Frankfurt and Leipzig. The Leipzig fairs particularly became of importance to the trade between Russia and Poland on the one hand and central and western Europe on the other. Competition from American furs, too, damaged Russian trade, which had had a monopoly of furs until the end of the seventeenth century. The Leipzig market shows around 1750 that east European trade came out with a negative balance, but it would be indefensible – bearing in mind the great changes in conditions that had taken place by this time – to conclude from this that by around 1650 the balance of overland trade had already become a negative one. As far as concerns the conditions of trade between the Russian market and central Europe in particular, Professor Attman believes that a negative balance does not seem to have established itself until political and economic conditions altered around the year 1700.

If we now turn our attention again to the commercial intercourse channelled via the Baltic Sea, the years around 1660 reveal themselves as a turning-point here too. Holland had been the dominant nation in this trade until about the middle of the seventeenth century. A relative decline now set in, primarily in consequence of competition from England, which had had a favourable trade balance with the Baltic until the 1630s but which now entered a period of growing deficits for which increased English imports of naval stores and iron were partly responsible. A further factor contributing to Holland's decline was the decreased imports of grain, especially from Danzig. It can be expressed in this way: after the middle of the seventeenth century the deficit items in the Baltic balance were being divided between Holland and England.

While it had long been customary to pay for the export surplus with Dutch silver rix-dollars or gold ducats, business practice was moving towards the greater use of bills of exchange, which had been an instrument of the Baltic trade all through the seventeenth century. The English deficit was being settled increasingly by bills of exchange drawn on Amsterdam, and only to a small extent by bullion from England. The middle of the seventeenth century forms a turning-point on the bill market too. The old inflexible system of non-negotiable foreign bills was gradually superseded by a modern system featuring a greater element of negotiability. Amsterdam bills were in the last resort paid through the medium of bullion exports from Holland to the Baltic. However, in certain special regions of the Baltic – particularly the Russian market – settlement by means of bullion exports continued until the eighteenth century, while the situation in the Poland–Lithuania region and Sweden was mixed. Leipzig, too, came by degrees to play an important role as a clearing centre for bill-of-exchange dealings in settlement of maritime trade transactions.

The system here outlined is probably not unconnected with the shortage of precious metals that was a feature of the second half of the seventeenth century, when imports of silver from America were dwindling and the mining of gold in Africa was also falling off. In this period and in the first half of the eighteenth century there are a number of years with pronounced silver crises, and the ratio between silver and gold is fluctuating as well. The vigorous demand for silver for the East Indies, mentioned above, was also partly responsible for there no longer being the same sources of supply available as formerly. The mining of gold began in Brazil from 1690, as is well known, and this led to Dutch silver *negotiepennigen* (ducatoons and rix-dollars) becoming dearer. When Brazilian production increased sharply in the 1740s, the rise in the price of silver was reinforced. Gold fell, resulting in the spectacle of gold ducats from eastern Europe, which had formed part of the balance-material, actually flowing back to the Netherlands in large quantities.

IV. *The Market and its Organization*

'Krieg, Handel und Piraterie. Dreieinig sind sie, nicht zu trennen' is a poetic dictum containing a germ of truth, and one in which Frederic C. Lane and Alexander Gerschenkron have recently taken an interest. The attitude of the state to trade was coloured by it. Vital questions were often at issue, concerning the nation's supply of a range of commodities which, for many countries and in many situations, were articles of necessity, even if not every nation regarded them at all times as 'strategic' or had to obtain them from external sources. Most of these articles were bulky goods demanding vast transport capacity: salt, hops and corn, saltpetre and gunpowder, timber and wood products, tar, pitch and hemp, or metals, weapons and cloth.

The nation's supply of these goods was therefore a matter which no responsible government could shirk, and the solicitude of the state concerning the inflow of coin and bullion, access to foreign credits and the trading rights of the towns was bound up with it. Although it is tempting and worth trying to use the scanty statistics of the time and combine them with more theoretical reflections about comparative commercial differences as an explanation of trade flows and routes, it must be kept clearly in mind that an acquaintance with the political arithmetic of the age and the prevailing geographical and climatic patterns will often explain more than will deliberations about terms of trade and marginal utility. The rational theories of the nineteenth and twentieth centuries, influenced by the international specialization of production, are of limited value in an epoch when resources could be transferred only with difficulty, and technology placed a ceiling on their exploitation. Total trade was thought of as finite in its dimensions, and the aim of commercial policy was to secure for the particular nation or city concerned as large a share of the total as possible. It was a national concern. The motive force was fuelled from the same sources as the instinct of self-preservation.

From the fiscal standpoint, moreover, trade provided revenues which no sovereign could or would afford to do without. Another characteristic feature of early modern Europe – also the object of recent interest on the part of scholars – is the state's almost chronic shortage of tax revenues. The taxation of land and incomes was fraught with great difficulties both of collection and of a political nature. Foreign trade, on the other hand, was a more suitable object. It worked with money, and could therefore be taxed in money. Its practitioners maintained relationships with foreign countries depending on the state's support, and the state might claim something in return. As well as this, taxes imposed on foreign trade could be passed on in part to the foreigner. Admittedly this might bring retaliation, but the more important foreign trade became as a national activity, the more intense became relations between the state and the merchants. Finally, foreign trade was generally canalized geographically in such a manner as to render the control and collection of dues at selected points a relatively simple matter. Frontiers and crossing-points were well defined.

The Sound Tolls exemplify this. These tolls, which tapped the largest of the northwest European trade arteries for imposts upon ships and merchandise, developed originally from the medieval dues associated with the market of Skanör, in southern Sweden. By the time we are concerned with them, they had become a transit due, nominally to cover the maintenance of the lighthouses and buoys necessary for ensuring the safety of vessels on passage through the difficult waters of the Cattegat but in reality one of the most important sources of revenue of the Danish Crown. These tolls were conveyed by special transports over the short distance from Kronborg to Frederiksborg Castle, where the money-grille and the built-in chute down which the coins, after having been counted in the king's own chamber, rolled down to the treasury in the vaults beneath the castle could serve as an illustration for the nursery rhyme from *Mother Goose*: 'The King was in his Counting House counting out his money.' The tolls went into the so-called *Partikulaerkasse* ('Privy Purse'). The political and administrative history of the latter (on which incidentally, little research has been done) embraces the whole of the complicated power-game involving foreign trade and the national finances.

The state of affairs outlined above is reflected most clearly, perhaps, in the regulation of the market. A market is generally understood as a regularly-recurring assembly of sellers and buyers in a fixed locality and for a fixed period for purposes of trade. The seller may be identical with the producer and the buyer with the consumer, but this is not a necessary condition. Many combinations and intermediate forms are conceivable and indeed may be encountered in practice. Regulation grew out of the crown prerogatives associated with the possession of territory, one of which was the right to impose taxes upon land, upon passage and upon trade in the name of commercial peace, i.e. law and order for all at the emporium itself, safe passage along the associated trade routes by land and by water, and maintenance of channels, harbours, roads, bridges, passes and so on. Provincial towns and markets frequently grew up on crown land, where they received the best protection, and the notion soon developed that the establishment of markets and provincial towns was a royal prerogative. In the Middle Ages the princely power tended in its charter policy to show special favour to the towns as places of business, whether local or longer-range, but a number of important marts elsewhere than in provincial towns and capital cities did survive for a long time.

The number of markets is legion. They range from the daily market of entirely local character through weekly markets, where farmers and craftsmen from the neighbouring countryside brought their wares to the market-place, to the sort of markets that were held in the spring and autumn and were often timed to coincide with church festivals. The annual markets, which, as already stated, might also be held outside the towns, were the most important ones from the standpoint of international trade. At these, foreign merchants would buy up a major region's output of farm produce and also supply the peasants and burghers with imports. It was from annual markets that international trade fairs developed – a coveted form of market which enjoyed the favours of governments since they attracted large-scale trade into their territories.

The cattle market at Wedel, outside Hamburg, was an example of a rural trading-place which blossomed and flourished twice a year in conjunction with the cattle drives from north to south. People, animals, vehicles: the throng milled about everywhere – in the market-place itself, in farmyards and cowsheds, on the streets. Low German, High German, Dane, Friesian and Netherlander all mingled together. Over all loomed *Roland*, the emblem of the market court of justice, beneath which the court assembled for adjudication upon disputes. A bargain was concluded when buyer and seller had noted its outcome on their slates. If it concerned a small number of cattle, settlement was effected in cash. Settlement for large lots, on the other hand, would be made via a German factor, who would be reimbursed by the purchaser in ready cash or drafts. The particular importance of the Wedel market to Hamburg (aside from its function as a source of supply) derived from the circulation of money. Good faith was the rule in the transactions themselves. The bargain would be sealed with a drink in one of the thirty inns fringing the market place. People mostly traded in the morning and made their settlements in the afternoon. It was often ready cash that passed from hand to hand, sewn in terry-cloth or linen pouches with the amount shown on the outside. The rich lowland farmers buying cattle for fattening, or selling the fatstock later in the year, left their purses in the inn, where the landlord looked after them in a wooden chest in his bedroom. The farmer would collect his purse from here whenever he wanted it. Nobody doubted that its contents would be intact. Once the great event was over, Wedel went back to sleep. The lean cattle were driven off to be fattened up nearer to the towns. The drovers who had come from the north with the cattle trekked back again with small quantities of portable merchandise in their knapsacks – boots, notebooks, perhaps a few reading-books – for sale to Jutland farmers. The merchant for his part would stow his money in an iron-bound chest and carry it off northwards on horseback – hopefully avoiding the thieves and bandits lying in ambush in the trackless wastes between the inns – there to settle up with the farmers. In Wedel the summer ran its course as if nothing had happened. Not until the autumn did activity revive in preparation for the November market. Then the whole scene was repeated.

The concept of the staple has played an important part in the debate about the rise of the market towns and trade routes of Europe. The older literature of commercial history, more particularly, is deeply concerned with staple policy, the analysis of which has been largely founded upon documents of a chiefly constitutional or legal character, and centring mainly on the Middle Ages, the great era of the genesis of towns. However, the problem of the staple is important in the early modern period too. It presents itself in relation to both the rise of the great new emporia and to the decline of already-established commercial centres. The debate of recent years has focused particularly upon the place of Amsterdam as Europe's leading international trading mart of the seventeenth century. How is the phenomenal growth of this metropolis to be assessed in relation to the policies applied and to the organization of the market? It is no less important that some of the devices and approaches employed in staple policy in the era after 1500 are transferred from the local and regional to the national plane.

What is really connoted by the term the staple – or entrepôt, as it was also called – is simply that a particular trade or certain commodities are directed through a specific town or trading centre. Who does the directing and whither it is orientated depends upon time and place. A multiplicity of different interests – at times coinciding, at times conflicting – lurks behind staple policy. The staple may be established chiefly from the desire to lead a transit trade through a particular place (with compulsory transhipment of the merchandise in transit), or there may be an avowed import or export interest which determines (directs) the choice of the point of entry and exit. There may be a mixture of influences at work in many cases. A staple once established may be self-reinforcing: merchants will come to where the goods are; contracts are concluded and transactions recorded; trend-setting prices are established here; the whole commercial organization expands, and so does the credit system; insurance institutions and other risk-reducing agencies appear; and a whole range of secondary effects benefit the economic life of the locality. A compulsory canalization of trade, on the other hand, may well produce negative effects, especially if the transit trade remains in outside hands. The trade will then be of a decidedly passive nature viewed from the standpoint of the local community, and the secondary effects will therefore be limited. The hinterland may stagnate and a sustained staple policy, either fashioned upon narrow local considerations or dictated from outside, may prevent associated places from exploiting the opportunities presented by economic booms or structural changes. Geographical situation is presumably not without influence in determining whether a staple policy will have positive or negative results. On the whole, maritime staples seem to be more viable and more profitable to the nation than landward ones.

Direction can be the expression of what one may call producer-interests. The concept of the staple embraces also the choosing by mercantile organizations and companies of places abroad at which they desired to concentrate sales and to which members were tied by the general regulations of the guild. An example of this may be cited from the history of the English cloth trade. The great textile region of Flanders in the fifteenth century wanted English wool for raw material, but not English fabrics. Antwerp was the first city of the region to admit the English cloth, with the result that it became in the first half of the sixteenth century the 'market city' *par excellence* on the continent for the merchants of London. Through Antwerp, English cloth found its way to Germany and parts of southern Europe, to Italy and to the Levant. But the English merchants did not confine themselves to Antwerp: they were active also in Middelburg and Bergen-op-Zoom. When Antwerp lost its place as the chief market soon after the middle of the sixteenth century and the Netherlands prohibited all imports of English fabrics and other woollen goods in 1563, the Merchant Adventurers were strong enough to do without Flemish commercial and financial support. There were already staples at Danzig, Bordeaux and Lisbon. In 1564 Emden was secured. The fairs at Frankfurt were visited from there. Even Nuremberg was reached. The Hanse towns capitulated. Hamburg accorded such favourable terms to the Merchant Adventurers in 1567 that they transferred the staple thither. It is true that pressure from the other Hanse towns forced Hamburg in 1578 to refuse the renewal of the Englishmen's privileges – Emden and Stade then became the preferred places – but Hamburg did renew the agreement with England in 1611, and the Merchant Adventurers returned to the Elbe port, which was exceedingly well situated geographically for exporting to central Germany via Frankfurt and also for exporting overland to Italy.

The export offensive inspired awe, but it also created bitterness, especially among the German merchants, who spoke of the Englishmen's pride and arrogance. The English merchants in cloth did not need to travel from town to town to find their outlets: they were able to compel their customers to visit the few places selected by them as staples in order to tighten their grip on the market. The customers were allowed to view the cloth on certain days of the week (usually Mondays, Wednesdays and Fridays) known as show days (*tooneeltage* in Dutch). On the other weekdays it was only permitted to conclude transactions in respect of cloth already viewed. This seller's market is also reflected in the conditions of sale and in the assertion of the nationality principle, by which English merchants were prohibited from handing their goods on commission to merchants of foreign nationality.

The system of exporting used is well known: the merchants, each trading on his own account and at his own risk, were incorporated in regulated companies, assigned to particular markets, which drew up jointly-agreed rules for the transport and sale of their wares. The oldest of the companies, the Merchant Adventurers, had its region defined in 1564 as the tract between the Somme and the Skaw, with Hamburg as the main emporium. The Baltic region was reserved in 1579 for the Eastland Company, with Danzig, Königsberg and Elbing as the staple towns. The trade with Russia was assigned in 1555 to the Russian and Muscovy Company, with Archangel as the staple. A Levant Company was established in 1562, its sphere of operation being defined in a charter dated 1605 as comprising the Adriatic Sea and eastern Mediterranean, with Constantinople, Smyrna and Aleppo as the staples.

The principle embodied in many municipal charters, to the effect that sole rights in the trade of the town and in the purchase and onward conveyance of the products of the hinterland were vested in its citizens, implied a kind of right of staple on a small scale. It was an attempt to make the town a staple for internal trade. Efforts were made too to protect the inhabitants of regions or countries against outside merchants by forbidding the latter to purchase goods outside the towns or to furnish credit to farmers. Municipal charters were intended to promote trade in the towns and to secure supplies of merchandise for their inhabitants. The hope was that under cover of this protection a local or national merchant class would emerge. It looked excellent on paper, but often turned out less well in practice. Strong producer interests asserted themselves in many places, securing rights, sanctioned by usage, to conduct trade themselves both at home and abroad. The farmers of the vicinity sold their produce on market days, and merchants from elsewhere operated freely at the annual markets. More important – and annoying, from the standpoint of the towns – was the trade carried on by the nobility and the larger farmers on their own account. Attempts were made in many places to restrict this to a volume sufficient for the consumption needs only of the household itself, but the corn and cattle-producing regions of Europe offer many examples of active trade on a substantial scale being carried on by the nobility. This producer interest developed so sturdily in some places that it disregarded the national merchant element, attempting over the head of the latter to channel exports via a strong staple.

The Baltic region shows several examples of this very thing. One of the most notable of them is the relationship between the Polish nobility and the city of Danzig during the great corn trade epoch. Danzig had liberated itself more and more during the fifteenth century, both from the influence of Lübeck and from the Teutonic Order of Knights, with the result that the city came under Polish suzerainty. In 1457 Casimir IV accorded the city staple rights and various commercial and political privileges, giving its merchants (who were both of local and foreign-immigrant, especially German and Dutch, origin) wide access to the Polish hinterland. Danzig soon outstripped Elbing, Culm and Thorn, and came to account for the export of most of the goods brought down to the sea along the great Vistula river-system, especially corn and timber, but also potash, pitch and tar. In the reverse direction, it was via Danzig that the Polish hinterland was supplied with salt, cloth and other west European goods. While most of the river trade was still in the hands of farmers and urban merchants in the fifteenth century, the Polish nobles on the great estates, encouraged by flourishing economic conditions, were beginning to evince interest in the selling of corn to western Europe via Danzig. The merchants became agents of the noble landed proprietors, who even placed foreign merchants in the towns. Maximilian Transylvanus, the envoy of the emperor Charles V, remarked that thanks to the corn exports of the Polish and Prussian nobility, Danzig had become the most powerful city in the Baltic.

The extent to which the producer interests sought dominance is illustrated by the notorious resolution of the Polish diet in 1565 barring Polish merchants from exporting Polish goods and importing goods from abroad. The law was never put into effect, and the Danzig merchants still survived. The largest of them acquired estates and so profited in a double sense from the prosperity of the corn trade. But it was the merchants and artisans of the other Polish towns who suffered from the alliance between Danzig and the great landed interest. Rising corn prices brought higher living costs at home, especially in the provincial towns, while increased imports of western industrial and handicraft products created difficulties for native manufacturers. The introduction of villeinage, the abolition of peasant land and its consolidation under the estates pauperized the peasantry, which in its turn had the effect of retarding the progress of the provincial towns.

The fiscal interest of the king or prince in controlling trade by trying to direct it through the towns has already been noted. The prince might himself lend backing to the urban market by channelling his own trade to it, disposing there either of taxes and dues received in kind or else of the Crown's own production. On other occasions the prince might prefer to sell directly abroad, over the heads of capital city, provincial towns and the nation's mercantile class, being forced into this position by the strength of foreign buyers and his own financial weakness.

It was often simply the fluctuating opportunities of obtaining loans that determined the choice of staple. The various staples of the Swedish Crown trade illustrate this. The Swedish kings received copper as royalties in kind from the *bergsmän* (small producers who mined and smelted their own ore). In addition they bought copper to use in settling their indebtedness abroad, and they also manufactured copper themselves. The copper trade, which had been chiefly the concern of the *bergsmän* and copper exporters in the Middle Ages, gradually became of crucial importance to the royal finances. The role of copper steadily increased during the sixteenth century, both in the efforts to liberate Sweden from the Lübeck trading monopoly by establishing direct commercial intercourse with the Netherlands and western Europe and in the endeavour to control the exchange of goods between western Europe and Russia via the Baltic Sea – two constant themes of Swedish foreign policy. The market in Stockholm was the Crown's preferred point of sale, but experiments were made with other outlets and methods of disposal, and major contracts disposing of large consignments were concluded from time to time with foreign merchants. An attempt was made at one stage under Gustav Vasa to establish a direct connection with western Europe via Lödöse, on the Swedish Cattegat coast, but this project suffered from the serious defect that the carriage overland to Lödöse made the metal so much dearer that it was unable to compete with goods conveyed to Stockholm by sea via the Sound. The king tried to form a trading company in the late 1540s to sell raw and sheet copper to England, the Netherlands and Portugal, and to carry refined copper to eastern Europe. This plan too came to nothing.

In the 1570s, when Swedish copper production was increasing rapidly, the Crown attempted to establish a trading monopoly in order to regulate supply and maintain prices. A decree of 1580 arrogated to the Crown the right to purchase the products of the *bergsmän* and introduced a system of export licences to prevent the export of copper not originating from crown stocks. This supply monopoly was renewed in 1582 and 1585 but had to be abandoned in 1588, partly because international price-levels were sagging despite all efforts and partly because the *bergsmän* were dissatisfied. In lifting the monopoly the Crown imposed a special toll upon future trade by way of compensation. The economic outlook changed again in the 1590s, bringing a much increased demand for Swedish copper. Liberation from Lübeck as the principal market was then at last achieved. Amsterdam now moved into first place, with Hamburg and Lübeck as joint runners-up. The later history of Swedish copper exports (dealt with in more detail elsewhere) shows that the Crown deliberately sought to gain advantage by playing off these markets against each other.

It seems probable from the foregoing that while some degree of unity might be achieved between the various staple-policy interests as far as the import side was concerned (i.e. in regard to supplies, trade and fiscal questions), it was often much more difficult to harmonize them on the export side. Here the general level of development of the country was the crucial factor determining how active or passive a role it could adopt in the international exchange of goods via its staples. Politics alone did not decide the matter. What may loosely be termed general economic forces played a part. A little more light may be shed on this by examining the phenomenon of Amsterdam, which developed into a *rendez-vous général des peuples commerçants* during the course of the sixteenth and seventeenth centuries, apparently without any major effort in the shape of a policy on the part of the government.

Actually Amsterdam did not lack a policy entirely. One of the factors responsible for the commanding position later attained by the city was probably the protectionist line it adopted in its shipping policy in the second half of the fifteenth century. It was laid down in 1471 and 1473 that all shipmasters coming from the Baltic who were citizens of Amsterdam were to arrive at the city via Marsdiep, Vlie or one of the other sea-gates. This applied also where a ship was owned by Amsterdam citizens in partnership with a foreign shipmaster. The regulation, which is an embryonic navigation law, was aimed against Lübeck and against the direct traffic from the Baltic to Flanders, meaning mostly to Bruges. There was a kind of counterpart to it in the rule of the Hanseatic League compelling its members to use Bruges as their staple. This navigation law signalled a stiffening of the competition for hegemony over the staple commodities from the Baltic Sea. On the whole, the attitude of the government towards the Amsterdam market was a passive one in the sixteenth and seventeenth centuries, and Holland is often cited as an example of a liberal commercial policy in an otherwise protectionist or mercantilistic epoch. As Professor Klein has remarked, however, it is not difficult to conceive of a passive attitude exercising an influence of the same decisive character as an 'active' government policy, inasmuch as government policy is in a sense never neutral in the economic process. And this passive attitude was exactly the right one to chime in with the growth of the staple in Amsterdam.

The situation around the middle of the seventeenth century is illuminating in this respect. Amsterdam feared at this time the competition of both Hamburg and Dunkirk, especially in the corn trade. France was striving energetically to draw international trade towards Dunkirk, whose harbour was being deepened and enlarged and whose military installations were being strengthened. The location of the town in terms of transport geography was excellent for links with the densely populated provinces of Flanders and Brabant, which figured among the Amsterdam corn trade's most important market outlets. Dunkirk acquired the status of a free port. Business transacted at Amsterdam, on the other hand, laboured under such encumbrances as import and export tolls, which indeed were increased in 1651, partly for fiscal reasons (naval wars cost money) and partly in consequence of the demands of Zeeland agriculture for increased import tolls on corn, designed to protect the home product, which was suffering from the low corn prices of these years. The increased duties, especially the higher export toll, gave cause for much concern. The corn ships from Holstein and the Baltic began to by-pass the Amsterdam staple and sail direct from producer to consumer instead. The export toll was abolished in 1681, but the import toll was retained, although eased in practice. *Laissez faire* was resumed. Dunkirk remained a source of anxiety for some time yet – until 1713, in fact, when France was compelled by England, which was also irritated by the free port and its occasional character of a freebooting port, to relinquish the city as a staple.

On the face of it we find no immediate indication that the city of Amsterdam was to become the focal point of the supply trade between the Baltic and western Europe. There were other towns in the region whose initial position can be regarded as equally favourable. Amsterdam shipping enjoyed no predominance over that of other towns of Holland and Zeeland in the late Middle Ages. A number of the latter were active in international trade – not only the trade with the Baltic but also the trade westwards with Flanders and France, whence salt, wine and other commodities were collected. They achieved too some prominence in the herring industry, whose fishing grounds had been shifting since the beginning of the fifteenth century from the waters south of Skåne to the North Sea. The most important Dutch exports of the late Middle Ages were cloth and beer, the former being manufactured from English wool and the latter brewed from hops, one of the specialities of the region. Herring, salt, wine, lamp-oil and soap were exported as well. Competition was primarily with the Hanse towns, whose traditional route from Novgorod to Lübeck, overland to Hamburg and thence by sea to Bruges, in Flanders, was outflanked by the establishment of a direct shipping-route (the *ummeland* traffic, as it was known) around the Skaw. English and Dutch merchants were both involved in this new traffic.

The Hanseatic League's boycott of Flanders in 1451–6 helped the Dutch towns, and so did the war between Prussia and Poland, in the course of which commercial links became established outside the channels authorized by the Hanseatic League, especially in the Wendish sector. Particular use was made of the *Klippehäfen* (interlopers' ports), where both gentry and peasantry offered their produce for sale, and of the two *Gross-schäffereien* (general magazines) at Königsberg and Marienburg belonging to the Teutonic Order. The struggle between the Hanseatic League and England in 1469–74 resulted in the dwindling to nothing of the once-thriving English traffic with the Baltic, greatly to the profit of the trade of Dutch towns. The Dutch profited also from the efforts of Scandinavian countries to liberate themselves from the Hanseatic hegemony. And a final beneficial development was that the south German merchant houses, notably the Fuggers, became active in western Europe during the last decade of the fifteenth century, paying particular attention to Antwerp. This confronted the Hanse towns, and especially Lübeck, with serious competition in the shape of such developments as the sending of Hungarian copper westwards to Antwerp either via Krakow and Danzig or via Hamburg. The trans-continental trade between Flanders and Italy reduced the Hanseatic League's trade in western Europe, where the League's old staple at Bruges was eclipsed by Antwerp. The later blow to Antwerp represented by the closure of the Scheldt served as a further preparation for the growth of the Dutch towns.

Another aspect is worth mentioning while discussing the factors responsible for the success of the Dutch towns as carriers of an ever-growing share of Europe's trade, especially that along the west–east axis between Lisbon and Danzig. Lisbon was one of the principal suppliers of salt and spices, and Danzig of bread grain. The geographical positions of the two commercial centres at each end of the route in relation to the seasonal fluctuations of the markets probably hold part of the explanation of the function of Dutch middlemen. The new season's crop arrived on the Danzig corn market each year almost simultaneously with the arrival at Lisbon of the 'new' spices from the east. However, the spices were too late for the last fleet from Lisbon to the Baltic. The Netherlands, on the other hand, was in an exceptionally favourable position to gain control of this intermediate trade. It was possible for both Lisbon spices and Polish corn to reach the Netherlands before the onset of winter. This central location was excellent for

exploiting the markets at the two termini, while the merchants of the
terminal stations were too far apart to be able to make their dispositions
on the basis of information received from the other end. The central
location also permitted a quicker turnover of trading capital.

The Dutch themselves never doubted for a moment that Baltic shipping and trade were vital to the economic growth of the northern
Netherlands. They called the trade 'the mother trade' or even 'the soul
of trade', and the corn trade in particular was characterized as 'the
source and root of all other trades in these lands'. Such scanty knowledge as we have about the Amsterdam trade at the beginning of our
period seems to confirm this. By the year 1500, the Baltic navigation
predominates over the Rhine trade, the trade with Flanders and
northern France, trade with western France and with England and
Scandinavia. And we observe right from the start one feature which is
characteristic of the subsequent period, *viz.* the fact that the number of
outward freights (many of them in ballast) is lower than the number of
return freights. The route taken by Baltic traffic was either from
Amsterdam to the Baltic and back or from Amsterdam to one of the
western trading stations (Brouage for instance) and thence direct to the
Baltic, and back to Amsterdam.

When the corn trade is scrutinized in detail it is not difficult to trace
the movement of the corn from a number of local markets via a
regional or national staple to the great Dutch-operated world market
located in Amsterdam. The picture is one of a hierarchy of markets
linked like vats to the central reservoir of the market of Amsterdam,
with its imposing array of granaries and its celebrated corn exchange.
Whereas trade at the lower levels outside the metropolis was intermittent (being conducted at seasonal markets or fairs) the frequency of
dealings in the great Amsterdam market place was such that merchants
could conduct business every day. The Italian historian Guicciardini
described it as a permanent fair.

Dr van der Kooy has described the mechanism of this market system.
In his view the central market place had to be on the coast, for the sea
routes were crucial to the establishment of bulk-carrying connections
between the markets. On the landward side the staples spread out a
network of forwarding centres. The central market place itself offered
every conceivable facility: bank, giro, insurance, storage, harbourage,
knowledge of commodities, facilities for processing raw materials and
semi-manufactures, market expertise, packing facilities and so on. It was
the clearing house for the other market places all over the world. The
system fed on itself and generated capital. But just why Amsterdam
became the centre of this great spider's web is not really explained by
van der Kooy. He takes refuge in a complex of 'natural, ethical and

fortuitous causes' and stresses the distinction between three market functions: imports, storage and exports. He has three different groups of merchants who were handling these three functions. Imports were in the hands of 'sea traders', who specialized in geographical regions and covered between them practically the whole world. The storage function was conducted by the 'merchants at second hand'. These specialized in the various categories of goods and performed a key function in the system, since their storage facilities acted as a buffer or shock absorber when supply and/or demand were not in balance. The third group of merchants on the Amsterdam market comprised the 'export dealers', who, as the name implies, were responsible for the distribution of the goods all over the world.

Van der Kooy's account has not won the undisputed acceptance of later scholars. It has been rightly pointed out that organizational relationships on the Dutch staple market in its seventeenth-century heyday were not as sharply defined as he assumes. On the contrary, importing, exporting and storage were often handled by one and the same firm or one and the same individual. It is particularly true of the great merchants that they might be engaged in all three fields of activity. Nor is geographical or commodity specialization a feature characteristic of the seventeenth century. This in fact is a phenomenon which made its appearance later with the maturing of the staple in the eighteenth century, so that it cannot be used to explain the emergence and growth of the staple. But it is useful to distinguish between the three functions cited and (in company with Professor Klein, who recently launched a positive critique against van der Kooy's model of the staple) to enquire in what manner they were in point of fact carried out, if not by specialized merchants.

Klein attempts to supplement van der Kooy with a number of more dynamic comments in which he endeavours to combine van der Kooy's ideas about the price-equalizing effect of the development of storage facilities with his own observations concerning the monopolistic tendencies of the Netherlands market. Whereas the older literature generally regarded monopolies by implication as injurious, Klein has invoked Schumpeter's theory of monopoly to argue that monopolizing tendencies in certain circumstances may have served productive purposes viewed from the standpoint of social economies. That clear monopoly tendencies did manifest themselves in respect of a number of commodities on the Netherlands market has been demonstrated in the past by such scholars as N. W. Posthumus on the basis of the behaviour of commodity prices on the Bourse. Posthumus's data, however, suffer from the weakness that they stem particularly from the more recent, more mature phase of the Amsterdam market, i.e. the second half of the seventeenth century and the eighteenth century. Attempts at monopolization were more characteristic of the supply side, where irregularity and unpredictability were greatest, while the selling of goods exhibited less marked fluctuations. The monopoly tendency is strong in certain groups of commodities. Examples are furnished by the copper trade and the spice trade.

Much ingenuity was employed in establishing monopolies. We find both horizontal and vertical combinations; we find also single firms so strong at times as to be able by assembling large stocks to hold their competitors at bay. We find monopolies created with the support of the authorities both at home and abroad – what might be termed a juridical monopoly. The great trading companies, enjoying sole rights in the shipping traffic with areas overseas, may be cited as examples. We find, finally, monopolies created by employing the credit weapon to bind foreign supplies to a sole delivery outlet. The monopolies were usually short-lived but the tendency persisted. These monopolistic practices diminished the risks and thus also the costs of transactions, which in a market with large and to some extent unpredictable fluctuations, especially abroad, gave both purchasers and sellers the opportunity to carry out a planned transaction at the planned time. The conditions of trade became more precise and the risk of ruinous price fluctuations smaller. Klein has expressed this by saying that the market became more 'transparent'. It is beyond dispute that there is an interaction between the rationally calculating entrepreneur and the form of market we find at the Amsterdam staple in the seventeenth century.

Whether the comparison is made within or beyond Europe, there is a striking difference between, on the one hand, the permanent market based upon storage (both physical and in the shape of the capital tied up in stocks) and other markets based upon facilities, and, on the other, the smaller, sporadic markets furnished with little in the way of ancillary services (especially credit). Attention was drawn to this difference years ago by another Dutch scholar, Dr van Leur, in his studies (which were influenced by the sociologist Max Weber) of the Asian market places around the year 1600. He elevated the pedlar, continually moving from place to place with his small stock of goods, to the status of a central figure in this market mechanism. The existence of a few merchants with considerable resources of capital did not disturb van Leur, who classified this special phenomenon as 'political capitalism' in contrast to 'modern capitalism'. In van Leur's view the market structure was characterized by its lack of cohesion and by the very large number of markets, 'as many as there were towns and ports'.

A Danish scholar, Dr Steensgaard, illustrated this point recently, in the course of an interesting study of the structural crisis in the European-

Asian trade in the early seventeenth century, by examining in detail the fate that overtook Hormuz, at the mouth of the Persian Gulf. In doing so he has developed van Leur's observations a stage further, combining them with Professor Lane's theory of protection costs and Professor van Klaveren's theory of corruption. Protection was an essential cost item for the pre-industrial producer and merchant, both within and beyond Europe, just as the exercise of power was an important source of income and formed the basis of redistribution of the available supply of goods. This applies not merely to the formal users of power, i.e. governments, but also to their local representatives. Protection costs normally exceeded transport costs in the pedlar trade. It is Steensgaard's thesis that the west European companies were able to defeat the caravan trade in the Middle East simply because they 'internalized' protection costs. This involved an expropriation of the tribute formerly paid to the local rulers and thus lower and more predictable protection costs.

Taken in conjunction with the quasi-monopolistic position of the companies on the European market, where the establishment of storage facilities made it possible to pursue a stable price policy around an optimal profit point, this meant in the long run a more economic use of scarce resources than before. Where the 'transparency' of the pedlar market was poor and the short-run elasticity of supply very weak and therefore characterized by wide price fluctuations, improved cohesion between market, consumer, and producer was established through the new, capitalistic organizational form. The companies used scarce resources more economically than did the older institutions by virtue of their innovative characteristics. Colour is lent to this hypothesis – Steensgaard believes – by the long-term trends of known producer and consumer prices for the relevant commodities.

Although the above discussion of the defects and advantages of the two market structures or systems contains a number of basically correct observations, the 'model' does not permit of universal, unconditional application. Much depends upon place and perspective. What is true of conditions at Hormuz is not necessarily the case elsewhere. Falling prices of raw and retail articles over a long period do not necessarily originate in the organization of trade and its better utilization of scarce resources. Two circumstances can be cited that weaken the general applicability of the model.

The first of these is van Leur's overemphasis on the peddling character of Asian trade. Asian trade is very wide-ranging and embraces many variations. It includes trade both in luxury articles and in bulk cargoes. Both travelling and established merchants were engaged in it. Numerous local studies touching upon this very topic of maritime trade have appeared, particularly in recent years (M. A. P. Meilink-Roelofsz,

S. Arasaratnam, T. Raychaudhuri, A. das Gupta, Om Prakash, Indira Anand *née* Narang, and others), and these are of value in breaking down the vague and fluid notion of 'Asian trade' into more concrete and meaningful concepts. A picture is on the point of emerging, as many-faceted as that which research into commercial history has drawn of Europe. To pedlars should be added merchants conveying goods by sea and middlemen buying and reselling goods in the ports. We see that the markets were connected with one another by regular routes, especially in maritime trade, and that veritable emporia sprang up at the junctions. This had an effect on price-formation.

The Malabar coast, so important in the pepper trade from Asia to Europe, furnishes an example of an Indian trading area in which pedlars are not particularly prominent. Exports played the dominant role in the trade of Malabar, whether they were exports of that country's principal article, pepper, or re-exports of commodities from Indonesia and China. Most of the pepper was produced in small lots by tenant-farmers who had their gardens in the interior, fifty miles or more from the coastal tract. The export trade was concentrated particularly upon the seaports of Calicut and Cochin, where a vigorous merchant class was established and where the European companies had their factories. The seaport merchants, working through agents and using a system of advances, bought up the pepper months before it ripened. The major share of this pepper was not sold to the European companies, in fact, but to northern merchants from Arabia, Gujarat and Sind. It was also via Malabar merchants that the Indonesian commodities imported in bulk to Malabar by the Dutch company were re-sold to the northern traders. The merchants of Malabar varied greatly in wealth and position. Individual or family merchants dominated, and they were free to trade in as many commodities as they pleased; equally, they undertook different kinds of business operations (import, export, retail, freight, credit). The independence of the merchant was limited only by his need for protection. This was usually provided by the local prince. A prosperous trade was as much in the interest of the prince as of the trader, the profit of trade going to the merchant while the prince received the tolls. Cases of oppression do occur, but often a great merchant could stand up to a little king, and emigration was an effective deterrent. As long as Malabar was characterized by small principalities the merchant class remained as above described. But when political conditions changed in the second half of the eighteenth century and the process of centralization began, the merchants' independence came to an end.

If we turn further east, towards Japan and China, it becomes still more difficult to discover pedlars engaged in European commercial intercourse. Foreign trade here was closely supervised and controlled by

the central authorities, partly via their officials and partly through responsible merchant guilds or licensed merchants enjoying the sole right
of conducting business with the outside world. Thus, when Shogun
Tokugawa Iyeyasu promulgated a trade law in 1604 by which the
government superintended and regulated the Portuguese trade, the
Shogunate assisted the powerful Kyoto, Sakai and Nagasaki merchants
dealing in raw silk to organize themselves as a group. This group exclusively bought raw silk imported by the Portuguese at an agreed
price, divided it among the members, and sold it. Europeans called this
system *pancada* or *pancado*. At first *pancada* was applied only to Portuguese ships, but later, when Portuguese trade declined, Chinese and
Dutch ships fell under the system as well. The Nagasaki authorities
often interfered in the silk trade, buying up the major share of the import and disposing of it when raw silk prices rose. In this way they
almost controlled the inland market in silk. The export trade too,
especially that in precious metals and copper, was subjected to a similar
central control, both during the period when Japan was exporting in its
own ships and in the subsequent closed period after 1635, when the
traffic with the outside world was handled by Chinese and Dutch ships.

The Chinese system too featured severe regulation and numerous
restrictions, some of which dated back to the early phase of European
trade with China while others took shape around the middle of the
eighteenth century, when European traffic with China was becoming
very intense. The system, named after the celebrated Co-Hong,
gathered all exports via the European companies into the hands of ten
to thirteen Hong merchants, who acted as a kind of guarantor for the
foreign ships and were responsible for the behaviour of the foreigners.
Similarly, all dues and imposts were paid through the Hong merchants,
and all applications had to be routed via the same channel. The Hong
merchants leased out factory premises to the Europeans, whose activities in Canton were severely restricted. Foreign merchants were forbidden to study the Chinese language or to make their own enquiries
about prices and supplies inland.

The second factor weakening the 'transparency theory' touches on
the matter of monopolization. The new companies are often called
monopolistic or quasi-monopolistic. This is correct on paper in the
sense that they were furnished by their respective governments with a
national monopoly, an exclusive right to trade east of the Cape of Good
Hope. They competed between themselves, however, both in purchases
and in disposing of their wares.

The concentration upon imports was a feature common to all European trade with Asia. The primary aim was not to find new markets for
European products in Asia but to supply Europe with Asian goods.

Secondly, it was not their respective home markets that the companies had in mind in their importing operations but chiefly re-exports, which depended in the end upon fairly precise assessment of the needs of the European market as a whole. Finally, it must be pointed out that the companies were not engaged in this re-export business in their corporate capacities. The trade was left to the private merchants who bought the goods at the company auctions. These fundamental features underline the competitive element. So also does a geographical analysis of the structure and terms of the re-export trade on the European market, where we find supply competition between alternative products, e.g. East Indian and European textiles. We find identical products being supplied by different regions with similar climates, e.g. sugar from Java and Bengal, from Madeira and Sao Tomé, from Brazil and the West Indies. We find supplies of identical products coming from different climatic regions. Tobacco was such a product, being cultivated in tropical, sub-tropical and temperate climates; silk was another, the supplies emanating from China, Persia and Italy; spices from Asia and Africa and America were a third such product; later on there was coffee from Mocca, Java and the West Indies. Metals were independent of climate and came from various regions of the globe: Japanese and West Indian copper was offered on the European market alongside copper from central Europe and Sweden.

Next it needs to be stressed that for a group of merchants to be granted a monopoly of overseas trade was one thing, but for them to maintain it was another. The Dutch company was in a position in this respect to prevent its business rivals from gaining access to Dutch territory, once the competing local companies of the 1590s with government help had been amalgamated in 1602 in the imposing guise of the United East India Company of the Netherlands. But as Dr Violet Barbour has pointed out, the seventeenth-century Amsterdam merchant was an international capitalist, doing business wherever there was business to be done. For many merchants, in any case, patriotism and concepts of economic nationalism were grand but abstract notions. A man who could not find a niche within the framework of his national company would look beyond his national boundaries to the south Netherlands, to France, to Germany and to Scandinavia. There are many instances of individual Dutchmen working against their own national company by placing capital and know-how at the disposal of its business competitors. In doing so they were engaging in a form of interloping between Europe and Asia that weakened or broke the monopoly.

In England, as is well known, this interloping grew to such a scale that periodically we are faced with two or more East India Companies, competing strenuously and furnished with charters, now from the king, now from Parliament. The change of government in 1688 led to a vigorous revival of interloping. The English Company was established in 1698 as a rival to the old East India Company. Although there was agreement as early as 1702 on a merger of the two companies and government sanction for the measure was granted in 1708, the interlopers continued their activities, one reason among others being the high taxes imposed upon East Indian goods, which constituted an invitation to smuggling and thus to interloping as well. A number of enterprises serving the interests of smugglers and interlopers emerged beyond the English frontiers in the first thirty-odd years of the eighteenth century. We see them in Gothenburg, Copenhagen, Altona and Hamburg, but most of all at Ostend, in the south Netherlands, where the Ostend Company, furnished with a charter from the Emperor Charles VI, had many Englishmen in its service.

When the various East India companies are viewed in the broader sort of context sketched out above, i.e. in the framework of the European market, it becomes difficult to sustain the accepted description of them as even quasi-monopolistic, let alone monopolistic, enterprises. This does not, however, preclude monopolistic practice in the re-selling of imports from the east, *viz.* a practice or organization cutting across national frontiers. It has already been pointed out that the companies did not themselves undertake the reselling of the goods imported, whether the small proportion going for local consumption or the larger quantity re-exported abroad. Then how were these re-exports effected? This question must be elucidated both before and after 1600 in order to determine the tenability of the 'transparency' theory. Since the pepper trade plays a part in the theory, the practice in this sector may be examined in a little more detail.

There is scarcely any branch of trade in which the early capitalistic spirit manifested itself more clearly than in the resale of pepper imported into Europe. With both Atlantic and Levant pepper, merchant houses with capital tried to buy up large consignments and to form consortia for the purpose of speculating on the resale of pepper and securing the highest possible profits for themselves. The commodity was well adapted for storage (within certain limits, of course) and could be withheld or placed on sale at the right time and place. A continuous shifting of the constellations accompanying the incessant manipulation of pepper is a constant feature of the scene.

When the Portuguese Crown monopolized the Indies trade in 1505–6, a practice was introduced whereby imports were sold for the king's account en bloc or in large consignments, either at Lisbon or via the factory in the Netherlands. The Italian families of Gualterotti and

Affaitadi dominated the buying of Portuguese imports into Flanders in the early decades of the fifteenth century. Later on the German merchant houses and, more especially, the Portuguese and the Marranos emerged on the scene. The idea of gathering Atlantic and Levant pepper, i.e. both the Portuguese and the Venetian supply, into a single pair of hands, although never brought to fruition, was a persistent one in the sixteenth century. The Venetian senate proposed to the Portuguese king in 1527 that Venice should take over all the pepper imported into Lisbon except for Portugal's own consumption. Philip II of Spain–Portugal offered Venice a contract in 1585 placing the sale of Portuguese imports in Venetian hands.

The Portuguese monopoly was reorganized in 1577. The sale of imported spices was now handled through a 'Europe contract', as it was termed, whereby a firm or consortium pledged itself to accept imports from the East for one to two years at an agreed price and to undertake the marketing of the goods on its own account. The counterpart of this arrangement on the importing side was an 'Asia contract', which was a financing agreement binding the contractors to deliver eastern spices to Casa da India in Lisbon at fixed prices and on their own account. There was no intrinsic reason why the two contracts should not be in the hands of the same consortium, and an Augsburg merchant named Konrad Rot attempted to achieve this in 1578, using Italian and Portuguese firms as his partners. Rot divided up the European pepper market into 'provinces' and entered into price agreements. The headquarters of the Rot cartel was a trading company in Leipzig established for the purpose by August I, elector of Saxony. Sales in the Netherlands, the German Empire, Bohemia, Hungary and Poland were to be handled from here. The remaining European territories were handed over to the consortium's Portuguese and Italian partners. The elector's brother-in-law, Frederik II of Denmark–Norway, was to make ships available for conveying the pepper. This grandiose plan came to nothing, however, partly because of intervention by Hamburg and Magdeburg. Moreover, the fixing of prices was rendered difficult by uncertainty regarding the volume of Levant imports. Finally, Rot proved unable to raise the advance payment of 400,000 florins constituting a condition of the contract with Portugal.

The brief but well-documented involvement of the brothers Philipp Edouard and Octavian Fugger in the international pepper trade sheds light upon conditions in the pepper market in the late sixteenth century. The Fuggers began to interest themselves in the Portuguese contracts in 1585. After profound deliberation they decided to participate in an 'Asia contract' in 1586–91, in association with the house of Welser and the Italian merchant house of Rovalesca. The Fugger brothers found themselves more or less forced to move from the Asia contract into a Europe contract. The Spanish treasury, whose shortage of cash was chronic to the point of its frequently being on the verge of bankruptcy, insisted upon settling the sums due to the Fuggers under the Asia contract with an advance against a Europe contract, adding for good measure a threat to confiscate the Fuggers' funds in Spain–Portugal. The Fuggers then joined a consortium for the Europe contract in 1591. It consisted of Fugger and Welser of Germany, Rovalesca and Giraldo Paris of Italy, Francesco and Pedro Malvenda of Spain, and Andrea and Tomas Ximenes of Portugal. The consortium had representation at many places in Europe but was orientated particularly towards Hamburg. Consignments were carried to that port in Hanseatic bottoms, which collected the pepper from Lisbon on the return voyage after having delivered corn to Spain and Italy. Of the consignments 48 per cent went to Hamburg in 1591, while 23 per cent went to Lübeck (via the Elbe and thence overland to avoid the Sound Tolls) and 28 per cent to Amsterdam. Thus, for a short time Hamburg inherited Antwerp's position upon the European spice market until the lead was assumed by Amsterdam and London. The involvement of the Fuggers in the Europe contract was short-lived. They transferred their share to Ruy Lopez d'Evora, an in-law of Tomas Ximenes, as early as 1592. A contributory factor in this was the fact that the partners in the contract did not comply with the price agreement between them. Ximenes, who was an old hand in the Portuguese pepper trade, perpetrated a dumping operation to get rid of pepper still in stock from one of his previous contracts.

The new northwest European East India companies did not re-export on their own account the pepper they brought to Europe either: they too sold it to private merchant houses and contractors. Here also we find consortia buying up consignments of an order of size not far behind the contracts of the sixteenth century. The Dutch company, for example, sold all its pepper in 1620 to a consortium consisting of Elias Trip, Garriet von Schoonhoven, Jeronimus de Haze and Philippe Calandrini. In 1622 Gert Direksz. Raedt, Cornelis van Campen, Hans Brooers & Co. bought up the whole pepper import of about 10,000 bales. The company promised on that occasion not to offer pepper for sale for a whole year. The same consortium secured the pepper the following year as well. This contract amounted to 4 million florins. It may be noted by way of comparison that the Dutch company's share capital at this stage was 6 million florins. Thus the contract bears witness to the calibre of Dutch capitalism, the more so considering that the parties to it were doing business in other commodities as well.

These great contracts provided excellent opportunities for speculation of the sort that occurred in 1639–40. The events during this year of panics caused the Dutch Company to give up its sales by contract in 1642. Auction sales were introduced as the best means of countering excessive speculation. The English Company too sold its pepper imports by contract in these years except during an early period when the pepper was distributed as dividends to the shareholders in the joint stock. An example of contract sale was the handing over of a big consignment of pepper in 1627 to the famous government war contractor and city financier, Philip Burlamachi & Co. Another was the sale in 1633 of the major portion of the East India Company's pepper to a single contractor, Daniel Harvey, and of the rest to Sir James Campbell and other Eastland merchants for export to the Baltic. Monopolizing tendencies in the onward distribution of pepper on the European market are thus in evidence both before and after 1600. There is nothing to suggest that these tendencies became more powerful after the establishment of the new East India Company about 1600. The market scarcely became more 'transparent' in the short run. Whether it became so in the long run is a question depending upon an analysis of price movements. Such analyses as have been made (van der Wee, Glamann, Posthumus) offer no indication of greater 'transparency' or stability.

The Amsterdam staple market was concerned with other things than pepper and copper. As has been emphasized above in various contexts, it functioned in its heyday primarily as the great corn exchange of Europe. It was ordinary merchants, participating on a massive scale, who were most characteristic of this trade. Only occasionally were attempts made to regulate participation. Towards the end of the seventeenth century, the so-called 'Directorate of the Dutch Baltic Trade' was established. Its life was short and not very brilliant, however. The important Dutch Baltic trade in fact remained without any unifying organization. Similarly, free and individual shipping and commerce prevailed on the Dutch routes to Norway, England, France, the Iberian peninsula, and every territory within these bounds. The Amsterdam market was accordingly characterized by many sellers and many buyers over a wide range of basic commodities (besides corn, commodities like salt, herring, timber and bricks) which indicates that monopolistic and other such speculations were foredoomed to be precarious and short-lived.

In Amsterdam as elsewhere there were merchants and merchants. A commercial aristocracy can be distinguished from the ordinary or average merchant. With the family as the principal unit of enterprise, family ties – especially when reinforced by religion – sometimes sufficed to sustain trade over long distances. This was so, as Professor Kellenbenz has demonstrated on the basis of genealogical material, with the seafaring Jews between the Iberian peninsula and Hamburg, and between Spain and the Levant. The Huguenots of the seventeenth and eighteenth centuries formed a similar family-based network covering large parts of Europe, thereby knitting her markets together. A closer study of the commission trade, so conspicuous in the eighteenth century, would also testify to this. On the other hand, the small- and medium-sized merchants persisted and a certain democratizing trend can be perceived, for example, in the north European trade expansion of the sixteenth century around Antwerp (according to H. van der Wee). Participation in the long-distance trade was no longer the exclusive preserve of those who could afford to travel to the markets or those who were members of the closed guilds (the 'corporate trade'). The small merchant had kept his place in the Hanseatic League, and there was room for him also in the regulated companies. Tensions between big and small enterprise are well known. In England the dissensions between the outports and London are a *leitmotif* of British foreign trade, so are the quarrels between Seville and the smaller cities in Spain.

Socially and politically the status of merchants differed from one country to another. Again Holland (together with the city-states of Italy and Germany) depicts a society where the vocation of merchant was highly regarded and where the mercantile interests succeeded in dominating general economic policy. Here merchants received marks of respect. In Holland the wealthy members of the merchant body were able to marry into the patrician families and the highest offices of the republic. Their children were often brought up to the profession of merchant and carried on the family enterprise. Outside Holland and the city-states, on the European continent, the merchant's place in the social order was lowest in the southern and eastern countries. The new aristocracy created by absolutism as a counter-weight against the old nobility was recruited from middle-class citizens, including merchants who supported the sovereign by lending him money and delivering goods on credit to equip his standing armies and fleets. Thus, creditors of the state played an important part in the introduction of absolutism into Denmark–Norway in 1660. They accepted crown lands as security and became established in government. However, this alliance was not a very stable one. Often the monarch acted according to Schiller's dictum, 'Der Mohr hat seine Arbeit getan! der Mohr kann gehen.' It was only exceptionally that the creditors of the state succeeded in securing a place at the top of society for their descendants, and many of them ended their days in penury.

To conclude our discussion of the various forces at work in forming the markets of international trade, a few remarks will suffice on the conception of the economic function of the state. Again Holland stands out against most other countries in early modern Europe. Here the conception is of business welfare working upwards from the merchant community towards a government with minimum powers. In the absolute states of the continent, we tend rather to find a policy improved by governments in the interests of the state. The role of princely and vested interests in co-determining the policy of the state varied from country to country, but paramount among the interests were those of dynastic power and regard for government revenue. This did not mean, however, that the monarch would never employ his power to promote trade. Often he did so by investing his own resources in it and by coercing noble, ecclesiastical and bourgeois state functionaries into participating. This is particularly true of the furnishing of capital for the risky overseas trading ventures.

In some countries the system of economic nationalism ranged far, depending on the degree of development and the rate of change. It centred around economic development in general and industrial development in particular. Trade regulations were also part of the strategy, but there is a marked difference between the mercantile system that can be observed in the countries in northwestern Europe with their extensive overseas trade and their colonies on the one side, and the more defensive or protectionist system to be found in the countries of northern, central and eastern Europe on the other side. Here the development of production and the nursing of local industries in order to strengthen internal consumption and the local market were in focus. For the cameralists of the German governments and universities of the seventeenth and eighteenth centuries autarchy was the ideal.

Undoubtedly, the market sector of the economy expanded in many, even most, European countries during the period under review, but since the establishing of international markets was not only a question of production costs and demand, but also a matter of transport costs, it was first and foremost the seaports that became identical with these markets. In the corn trade a difference still persisted between the local and regional markets, where prices were determined primarily by the quantities of the harvests, and the international market, where these quantities were secondary to factors such as political (wars, closures of trade routes, governmental regulation of stocks and prices) and monetary ones (concerning quantity and circulation). As to money, it should also be kept in mind that a well-monetized economy in the modern sense of the word never developed. Many of the regulatory efforts centred around the bad repercussions of a more or less confused monetary system. We have mentioned earlier that on the face of it the European monetary system was bi-metallic, but while the countries could get along without gold coins, silver coins were indispensable for a variety of daily transactions, including wage payments where only the smaller denominations of silver would pay.

Perhaps the system was most successful with regard to the institutions and the instruments of the market. Here the national effort succeeded in canalizing foreign trade through distinct points of juncture. Smuggling, it is true, was widespread and bore witness to the incompleteness of the system, but around 1750 several of the European emporia were in charge of and controlling a substantial part of their respective countries' exchange of goods with the world outside, and technically they were better equipped for this task than at any earlier date, with numerous credit institutions, storage and exchange facilities, and fairly uniform laws ruling the usage of bills of exchange and other instruments of credit. On the commodity side, a series of items formerly belonging to the luxury category had turned into articles of mass consumption and were often selected by the governments as the bearers of their new taxes. Finally, the long quest among the poorer countries bordering the European seas for setting up national commercial fleets and thus turning their foreign trade into an active business, not to speak of the positive effects of this on national defence, had met with limited success, thanks to the system of navigation laws with built-in subsidies to national shipowners and manufacturers, with export bounties and other tariff regulations.

In the previous volume of *The Cambridge Economic History of Europe*, Professor Wilson has remarked that in England, to a higher degree than elsewhere, a balance was struck between government and governed. The multifarious motives and ambitions underlying British commercial ideas and policy were perhaps most starkly revealed in the English Navigation Laws which served as a model for other countries. These Laws were being elaborated simultaneously with the growth in the importance of the new colonial territories. Both private and public interests can be detected at work here. To the merchants, the state was undoubtedly a means, not an end. Their appeals to the state were influenced by practical considerations. Much of the contemporary literature in English is written by merchants who identify the national interest with their own. In their eyes, the state was merely a special form – though a very large and powerful one – of corporate economic enterprise. Later on, towards the end of our period, when Joseph Addison was hailing the commonwealth of merchants over his hearty breakfast, his heroes were beginning gradually to feel the system to be somewhat burdensome. They were beginning to favour the liberation of trade and to seek new styles of commercial organization.

CHAPTER V

Monetary, Credit and Banking Systems

I. *Money and Credit in the Local Economy*

(1) REAL COINAGE AND MONEYS OF ACCOUNT

WITH the expansion of the towns in the later Middle Ages, and in response to the needs of their trades and industries, the money economy had everywhere become more pervasive. An essential feature of urban growth, it had also penetrated vigorously the economy of the countryside, disturbing age-old customary routines as it did so. Pure barter did not disappear immediately from the local economy even in the sixteenth and seventeenth centuries. The use of credit facilities in the money sector even enhanced the opportunities for barter transactions in so far as it encouraged barter on an extended time basis.[1] Yet everywhere money was on the march. Rural production, both agricultural and industrial, was increasingly commercialized. Urban industry stimulated internal and external demand through specialization. The expansion of transcontinental and, above all, the Atlantic traffic opened up unprecedented prospects for intra-European distribution of goods. The market, designed to bring supply and demand together more efficiently, catalysed the new impulses of the sixteenth, seventeenth and eighteenth centuries. Urban and rural markets, weekly markets and fairs, multiplied in Europe or intensified their activity, assisting the penetration of the local economy by money and credit in many forms.

First came metallic money. On the local markets most transactions, apart from pure barter, were already valued in money and settled in cash. The increasing use of metallic money in the local economy nevertheless posed serious problems. Usually a real coin with its multiples or divisions would form the basis of the current money of account.[2] The smaller the real divisions, the less was their relative silver content: this content was necessarily less than proportional, because the cost of minting the coins increased more than in proportion. Apart from these deviations, and apart from the seignorage, the circulation value of all these coins was equal to the value of their content. All had a fixed relationship with the current money of account; in other words, they were its basic coins.

[1] See below, pp. 306-7.
[2] H. van Werveke, 'Monnaie de compte et monnaie réelle', *Revue Belge de Philologie et d'Histoire*, XIII (1934), 123–52.

Serious difficulties were caused by repeated increases and decreases in the silver content of the real basic coins, by the introduction of new real basic coins, and by the acceptance of real basic coins originating in other regions. If the authorities reduced the weight of silver in the basic coin – for example the Flemish silver groat – and imposed a new, weaker groat with its divisions and multiples as the basis for the current money of account, they were actually debasing the money of account. If the old, heavier, groats were not allotted a higher money of account rate – and usually they were not – they became officially undervalued. In accordance with Gresham's law they thereupon disappeared from circulation into the royal or seignorial mint, which attracted them by a higher silver price so as to recast them into the new weaker coins at a profit. They were also liable to be drawn off abroad if they continued to be valued here at their actual silver content. It was usually not the man in the street who speculated on these subtle differences in value and profited by them, but the money-changers, merchants, dealers in money and, not least, the authorities.

Sometimes the old heavy basic coin would still remain in circulation after debasement, though only if the official undervaluation was offset by an official or factual increase in the rate of the money of account. Gold coins, which did not serve as standard or basic coin for the current money of account, but were regarded as a special kind of merchandise with a certain money of account value, rose in value upon debasement of the current unit of account. The same applied to the large silver coins, which had become extremely popular since the issue of the *Joachimstaler* in 1519 and were themselves made possible by the increasing production of silver in Central Europe and the massive shipments of silver from the New World. These large silver coins were not yet a standard for the money of account in the beginning of the sixteenth century, so that they too increased in value upon debasement of the moneys of account. (Things changed from the middle of the sixteenth century as the *taler* became more and more a standard multiple for the current money of account.)

The converse situation occurred when the authorities decided to increase the weight of silver in the basic coin and in its multiples and divisions. The money of account, linked to the new, heavier, basic coin, now rose in value. The upward adjustment of the current money of account implied a drop in rate of the gold coins and large silver coins. The old silver basic coin, insofar as it was kept in circulation with its divisions and multiples, had likewise to be reduced in rate. If the authorities kept the old basic coins in circulation they were usually reduced to a rate lower than necessary, the object being that as a result of this official undervaluation they would automatically disappear and make way for the new basic coins. But resistance to a heavier basic coin and, as a result, of a heavier current money of account was usually strong. Not only did force of habit react in the local economy to such a brusque change in the real basic coin and in the value of the unit of account, but the revaluation aggravated the indebtedness of many of those in a small way of business. Moreover, because the new basic coins were not immediately available in sufficient quantities, a period of toleration of the old circulation and the old value of the unit of account often had to be permitted. There ensued a hectic repayment of debts from which only people of substance could profit. Not infrequently such revaluations consequently gave rise to dangerous riots and revolts.

Debasement and revaluation of the current money of account could also be effected by simply raising or lowering the rates, without any issue of new coins. The authorities could raise the rate of the current real silver groat to (for example) 1½ deniers of account, or reduce it to half a denier of account, together with its fractions and multiples. This was an operation that gave rise to confusion and was seldom used. More often the rate of gold or larger silver coins was changed; such measures were debasement or revaluation of the money of account only in terms of the larger coins. Usually these increases in rate were official recognitions of actual debasement of the current money of account, arising from a deterioration of the silver basic coins in circulation, a debasement that had already been attended to in the free market by a rise in the rates of the larger coins. Reductions in the rates for the larger coins mostly represented attempts to avoid such situations; they were doomed to failure unless the cause of the trouble – the deterioration of the silver basic coin in circulation – was eliminated at the same time.

The confusions and strains in the money economy did not originate solely from the debasement and revaluation of the money of account under the influence of the issue of new basic coins, or from the raising or lowering of the rates of the larger coins; they arose also from the duplication of accounting systems used simultaneously in the same place.

When, for example, the monetary system of the Low Countries was reformed under Philip the Good in 1433-4, the Flemish pound groat, based on the Flemish silver groat, was imposed as the standard money of account for the whole of the Netherlands. In Brabant this unit of account took the place of the Brabant pound groat, based of old on the silver Brabant groat. However, the Brabant pound groat continued to be used in Brabant bookkeeping as the current money of account, though in this capacity it had been detached from its original real basic coin and assumed a permanent relation to the Flemish unit of account (*viz.* 1 Flemish pound groat of account = 1·5 Brabant pounds groat of account). From the reform of 1433–4 onwards, the value of the Brabant pound groat was consequently determined by the value of the Flemish unit of account, i.e. indirectly by the silver content of the real Flemish groat. Other things being equal, the same applied to a whole series of other systems of current moneys of account in use in the Netherlands at that time, such as the Artois pound, the Paris pound, the Louvain pound, etc.

In order to escape the confusion caused by the countless debasements of the many systems of current moneys of account, some private institutions or official bodies had successfully adopted real gold coins as the unit of account for their books. These coins naturally had a rate in the current money of account which in turn derived its value from the metal content of the real silver basic coin. Consequently, all real coins and various current moneys of account were converted at this rate into the gold coin used as unit of account in bookkeeping. If the market rate of the gold coin expressed in current money of account remained unchanged, there was no problem. But such stability was exceptional: usually the market rate of the gold coin fluctuated or changed, complicating the conversion operation of the bookkeepers. Not infrequently the gold coin was maintained by the bookkeepers as *unit of account* at its *original* rate in current money of account: the gold coin then became a satellite of the current money of account, bearing a fixed relationship to this money of account, so that the value of the gold coin as a unit of account was determined by the value of the current money of account; this in turn was determined by the metal content of the silver basic coin.

Sometimes the weight of gold in the gold coin introduced as unit of account continued to form the criterion of value of the unit of account. Thus the value of this unit of account became detached from the value of the current money of account; according as the current money of account was debased or revalued in respect of the gold coin in question, the gold coin, used as a unit of account, acquired a higher or lower rate respectively in current money of account. If the real gold coin disappeared from circulation, the gold coin remained in use solely as a unit of account; in other words, this unit of account then represented a certain weight of gold derived from the gold content of the former real gold coin. In some cases it was only to this weight of gold that reference was made, as for the *écu de marc* at the Lyons and Piacenza fairs, which represented 1/65 of the gold mark (on fineness of the *écu*). In Genoa the gold ducat had been put to use as a unit of account with a stable weight of gold from the mid fifteenth century onwards. It was so successful that fixed divisions of account also became desirable. At the time the rate of the gold ducat was 44s of current money of account. On the basis of this rate the pound system was coupled to the ducat as a unit of account in a fixed relation: accounting was then done in pounds of *good money* in accordance with the fixed ratios of 1 pound or 20s or 240d of good money of account = 20/44 ducats of account, and this ducat of account derived its value from the weight of gold in the real ducat. The pound system had thus become a completely dependent satellite of the ducat. In addition, the old pound system naturally remained in use in Genoa as current money of account; it derived its value, as of old, from the metal content of the silver basic coin, which became steadily debased as time went by so that the rate of the ducat in pounds of current money of account steadily increased.[1]

For completeness' sake it should be added here that after the successful distribution of the large silver coins these too sometimes found acceptance as units of account, separately from the current moneys of account. The Dutch bank guilder of the seventeenth century is the most illustrious example of this. It was not, however, to retain its autonomy; gradually it too evolved towards complete dependence on the current guilder (cf. below, pp. 338 ff.).

(2) THE LONG ROAD TOWARDS MONETARY STABILITY

The difficulties which the local economy encountered with the easing of the circulation of money were not confined to problems of debasement or revaluation of its own coinage, or of the diversity of the systems of moneys of account. The authorities might continue to forbid exports of money; gold and silver coins, large and small, went on circulating in great confusion throughout Europe.

Sometimes foreign coins were attracted by the authorities by means of deliberate increases in the rate. Other circumstances could also lead to overvaluation of foreign coinage in a particular area by comparison with the situation in the country of origin. If a country chose to debase its coinage while in the neighbouring country the *rates* of the new, lighter, coins remained those of the older, heavier, ones on account of traditional ties with the current money circulating there, a speculative flow of the newly-issued coins towards the overvaluing country was inevitable. Similar speculative flows developed with the positive explosion of counterfeiting, in the course of the sixteenth and the beginning of the seventeenth century through the success of the large silver coins.[2] Small local lords or imperial cities in the borderland between the

[1] J. Heers, *Gênes au XVe siècle* (Paris, 1971), p. 67.
[2] C. M. Cipolla, *Money, Prices and Civilization in the Mediterranean World* (5th–17th Centuries) (Princeton, 1956), pp. 33–5.

Netherlands and Germany invoked autonomous rights to mint their own coinage, imitated the popular silver *taler* type and issued this imitation at the normal rate, though with a reduction in the silver content. As a result of this reduction higher purchase prices for coin bullion could be offered at the Mint; thus many good silver coins were attracted, while masses of imitation *talers* flooded through Europe on account of overvaluation. Money-changers could make a profit from these speculative manipulations, relying on the ignorance and impotence of the man in the street faced with this hopeless diversity and subtle fraud.

The relation between large and small coins placed further strains on the local economy. The value of the current money of account was usually still determined completely by the metal content of the silver basic coin with its multiples and divisions, i.e. by the whole of the smaller silver coins. In principle, token money, with limited legal validity, did not yet exist in the sixteenth and seventeenth centuries. In practice, however, this function was performed by a series of small coins of domestic or foreign origin, still remaining in circulation from old issues or completely worn away, and known as black money. Such black money could occasionally weaken the position of the current money of account and lead to a rise in the rates of the larger gold and silver coins. Generally, however, the basic silver coin, with its multiples and divisions, was the dominant influence in the monetary life of the local economy. These coins controlled daily circulation because the masses used them intensively as metallic money and as current units of account. If the authorities wished to profit from minting money, as they often did in the sixteenth and seventeenth centuries, they logically concentrated on debasement of the basic coins; after all, quantitatively the operation was worth the trouble. The habit of maintaining the basic coins as the foundation for the current money of account, even if they were new and contained a smaller weight of silver, was so strong among the majority of the population that it could be safely speculated on. But the rates of the large silver and gold coins in current money of account inevitably went up. An analogous upward movement could also occur in the same territory (let us say country A) when the ruler of a neighbouring country (B) carried out a debasing issuing operation in his own territory; when the basic coin in the neighbouring territory B had long had a certain affinity with the current money of account of country A – which was not infrequently the case – the ruler of country B could also count on his new, lighter, basic coin spreading over the frontiers into country A, driving out of circulation the local basic coins. More innocuous, but certainly no less frequent, was the fact of the simple wear of the basic silver coins resulting from their intensive circulation. As the value of the current coin was determined by the metal content of the basic coins, the wear of these coins often resulted in the adjustment, i.e. a factual or official devaluation, of the current money of account and in a rate-increase of the larger coins.

In the world of international trade and finance, men of substance had protected themselves against these threats: from the Middle Ages they had made particular use in their transactions of the stable gold coins and, from the beginning of the modern age, of the large stable silver coins also; they often used these coins as units of account, quite independently of the current money of account, both for their internal bookkeeping and for their local and foreign transactions. The wealthier sections of the population, often enjoying a creditor position, escaped in this way the disastrous consequences of the devaluation of the current money of account; indeed, they might actually profit from it, together with the ruler. Insofar as loans and interest were expressed in these stable units of account, upon devaluation of the current money of account debtors had to tender an increasing number of basic coins in payment, as a result of the increase in rate of which the stable money of account was the subject. And since wages and other costs of production usually lagged behind the devaluation of the current money of account, merchant–entrepreneurs made an extra profit. They paid their workers in debased basic coin, because wages were fixed in current money of account; if they sold the product at the old price in stable units of account, the merchant–entrepreneurs made a larger profit for every product sold; if, thanks to the lower costs, they sold the products at a lower price in stable units of account, sales might well rise and absolute profits be increased.

The gold–silver ratio and the silver–copper ratio likewise led to considerable strains on the local economy during the sixteenth and seventeenth centuries. The enormous but unequal expansion of the production of precious metals in this period widened opportunities for speculating on the difference between the official mint ratios and the market value of precious metals. During the fifteenth century gold was shipped mainly via Portugal and southern Spain from Africa, and during the first half of the sixteenth century from the New World; silver flowed during the fifteenth and early sixteenth centuries into western Europe from Germany, Hungary and Tyrol; masses of silver flowed from the second half of the sixteenth century into Europe from Mexico and Peru, a supply which continued throughout the whole seventeenth century; from the beginning of the eighteenth century gold was increasingly exported to Europe from Brazil; finally, copper flooded Europe in the seventeenth century, especially from Sweden and later from Japan too. These market flows inevitably changed the value ratios between the precious metals: thus the commercial gold–silver ratio evolved from approximately 1:9 to 1:10 in the fifteenth century and gradually to about 1:12 at the end of the sixteenth century, rising to about 1:15 around 1700. In practice the local adjustment to these changes usually lagged behind under the influence of tradition; the observant money-dealer could profit accordingly. The power of the rising mercantilistic states also implied greater intervention in monetary affairs: by proclaiming official money rates, the authorities fixed official gold–silver ratios which, viewed in a European context, were never uniform or in equilibrium with each other. Moreover, the official money of account rates of the different coins in circulation in one and the same country usually proved untenable in the long run, because of the fluctuating character of the market demand for specific coins. In many cases governments deliberately overvalued certain coins by relatively higher rates so as to exert an extra attraction on them: in this way the Dutch Republic favoured silver in the seventeenth century so as to supply the great Amsterdam market in precious metals with white metal urgently needed for export to the Baltic and the Far East. Gold–silver ratios differed markedly from one geographical area to another. In the Middle East, and above all in the Far East, silver was valued much more highly than gold in comparison with western Europe, so that the western merchant had everything to gain from paying for his purchases in the east in silver.

The consequences of speculative movements under the influence of differences in the gold–silver ratios were of great importance to the local economy. If the market price of gold increased and the official or current rates of gold coins lagged behind, gold was undervalued in official or current transactions and tended to disappear from circulation. Silver now circulated more intensively: the large silver coins took the place of the gold coins and the daily transactions in the local economy were well supplied with silver basic coins. But, in the opposite case, the situation was much more serious; not only did the large silver coins disappear but also the whole of the smaller basic coins (which likewise circulated at their intrinsic value): although gold coins replaced the large silver coins they were not capable of assuming the function of the smaller basic coins; the local economy thus suffered an acute shortage of metallic money. Fortunately, the modern age up to the beginning of the eighteenth century was broadly characterized by an increase in the relative market price of gold, so that the general trend favoured the circulation of silver money, including the smaller silver coinage. There were, nevertheless, some periods of obvious stagnation or decline in the market value of gold metal, e.g. the decades before and after 1500 and the beginning of the eighteenth century.

From the macro-economic point of view not all the effects of these contrasts were negative. It was logical that in a still relatively primitive economy the broad masses of the population could have confidence in the medium of exchange only if it was in circulation at its intrinsic value. As long as the smaller basic coins dominated the bulk of the transactions and the current money of account in the local economy, the confidence of the population was vested in the metal content of these smaller coins. Gold coins and large silver coins, being the basis of autonomous units of account, provided stability in high finance and in international transactions. Within the given structures the authorities were thus able to aim at a flexible macro-monetary equilibrium. When economic expansion required an inflationary policy, or when special wartime conditions required additional expenditure, the authorities could expand the volume of the current money of account in a fairly simple fashion by successive debasements of the basic coinage, without fundamentally impairing the stability of high finance and of the international economy. The expansion of the sixteenth century, even more the wars of religion around 1600 and the great period of wars a century later, were partly financed in this way.

A second macro-economic characteristic concerns the irregular but undeniable transition from monetary confusion in the sixteenth century to monetary rehabilitation and stability in the eighteenth century. Many factors played a part in this development. The expansion of the money economy, based on the enormous increase in the production of precious metals from the sixteenth century, gradually brought gold coins, and even more so the large silver coins, within the reach of the middle groups of the population; in other words, these coins came to be used increasingly in the local economy. The need to retain the smaller silver coins as a basis for the current money of account therefore made way for the possibility that this function would be taken over by the larger coins. At the same time, from the sixteenth and above all from the seventeenth century, the acceptance of large silver coins as 'standard coins', i.e. as basic coin for the current money of account, was increasingly advocated. In 1681 the States of Holland, for instance, declared themselves explicitly in favour of this, but it was not until 1694 that the other provinces of the Republic acquiesced. Such acceptance of larger coins as standards for the current money of account (a policy that became increasingly general towards the eighteenth century) formed a milestone in the gradual demotion of the small silver coin to conventional coin, as limited legal tender.

The mass minting of copper coins, viewed in the long term, was also a factor in the transition of the coinage to stability. The rise of copper production in central Europe from the end of the fifteenth century had already opened up prospects for a copper coinage. In the sixteenth century the issues of copper money multiplied: in principle they still remained limited in extent, and consisted only of small coin. The great need for money by the authorities during the wars of religion, and the vigorous expansion of copper production and copper supplies in the course of the seventeenth century, removed all restraints. Spain under-went tremendous copper inflations from 1599 until late in the seven-teenth century; France was taken by surprise by large issues of copper from 1607 to 1621; Germany passed through its notorious *Kipper- und Wipperzeit* from 1621 to 1623, and Sweden was not left untouched either. During this period Spain and Germany even switched com-pletely from a silver to a copper standard; in other words, the value of the current unit of account was determined by the metal content of a whole series of copper coins issued as basic coin. As a result of the gigantic increase in the issue of copper coins, the unit of account de-valued so quickly and alarmingly that economic confidence was destroyed. This in turn psychologically prepared the population for demotion of the smaller coinage to a subsidiary currency and even to the status of token money. Such steps were not taken at once: the population as a whole always wanted to return to the old-style silver standards. (A return to the traditional silver coinage may similarly be observed after the issue of conventional tokens as emergency money in times of siege, e.g. of Haarlem in 1573 and Leiden in 1574.) Temporary paper money issues sometimes went the same way: during the English recoinage of 1696 the government issued certificates against surrender of the old money (which were allowed to circulate without interest as money in anticipation of the issue of the new coinage); in France, John Law, during the second decade of the eighteenth century, made the notes of the Banque Royale legal tender.

As the final important factor in this process of transition, the influence of mercantilist official policy should not be overlooked. For the authorities opted increasingly for a sound and stable money of account, which was regarded as the sign of a flourishing economy. The progress in minting techniques, which reached a climax in the course of the seventeenth century and improved the uniformity of the issues, doubt-less also contributed to the reorganization of the circulation of coinage.

In normal times the authorities therefore concentrated increasingly on keeping the money of account stable. At most, slight adjustments were made if special circumstances – such as changes in the gold–silver ratio or in foreign coin parities – called for counter-measures. During war years, on the other hand, when governments were in urgent need of money, manipulations of the unit of account were more frequent, aiming at extra profit by the devaluation of the current moneys of account. The War of the Spanish Succession was a late and sinister example of this, especially in France. But, regarded generally and in a European context, such deviations no longer formed a main factor in the money economy of the eighteenth century, and monetary stability with gold coins or large silver coins as standards for the current money of account predominated as the major aim of policy.

(3) CONSUMER CREDIT IN THE LOCAL ECONOMY

However important metallic money might be in the local economy of the modern age, it in no way hampered the development of credit. Indeed, the deeper penetration of finance into the local economy caused the need for payments in money to increase more than proportionately to the availability of small metal coinage. A persistent lack of liquid resources was consequently characteristic of the local economy of the sixteenth and seventeenth centuries. On the other hand the expansion of finance in the local economy clearly increased confidence in metallic currency and thus strengthened the basis for an appreciable extension of various forms of credit.

Consumer credit underwent great expansion in the local economy during the period under discussion. Merchants from the town or country regularly bought up agricultural produce from the farmers before it had been harvested against partial or complete cash payment; the rural population was paid cash for linen or cloth that was to be woven later during the winter months. Where the putting-out system occurred in the towns, similar practices were common. Thus farmers and workers received credit guaranteed by their future harvest or future labour output: sometimes merchants supplied the materials and implements themselves. Often the interest charged was so high that personal relations were distorted into complete dependence and arbitrariness. Not only the little man was involved in these credit transactions. In Poland, the Danzig merchants of the sixteenth and seventeenth centuries made similar advances to the landowning nobility of the interior both large and small with a view to future deliveries of grain to Danzig after harvest.

Extension of payment was a much more current form of credit, often even its cornerstone. In the local economy, extension of payment was closely bound up with the development of the retail trade. The tally or, more formally, the current account, kept by the local shopkeeper, craftsman or innkeeper, became a popular form of elementary bookkeeping in town and country. Such accounts often remained open for months and thus favoured mutual 'set-offs'. The shopkeeper would have a current account with the brewer–innkeeper and the latter would keep a reciprocal account with the shopkeeper; periodically the accounts were closed and only the balance was paid in hard cash. Sometimes, even this periodical settlement was not made in cash. It would be settled by an assignment, and thus sometimes made a new set-off possible. If A was in debt to B and was owed money by a third person C, A could ask C to pay the outstanding balance to creditor B for A's account and to reduce A's debt: it was always possible that C was himself owed money by B; subject to that condition a new settlement could be made without the use of liquid assets.

The assignment was a normal way of settling debts in the local economy. It was used not only for the settlement of debts that had been contracted without specific formality, but also made use of credit balances that had been laid down in 'writings obligatory', later known as promissory notes or simply 'notes'. Other early descriptions were 'transferable bonds', 'bills of debt', 'bills obligatory' or (in Fair Courts, for example) *scripta obligatoria*.[1] These special documents were sometimes drawn up officially under a seal, but increasingly they were an informal type of document, an ordinary IOU, drawn up by the debtor or by a third party and signed by the debtor. Often these IOUs were given the clause 'payable to bearer', and thus became transferable, though not negotiable. Backed by confidence in the local economy, these IOUs were already circulating from hand to hand. Thus debts were repaid with credit balances in the form of IOUs; in other words, payment was assigned to a third party by transfer of an IOU. In the course of the seventeenth century the words 'or order' became common in commercial circles of northwest Europe, further legalizing the assignment; in the local economy the usage developed more slowly.

In contrast with northwest Europe, the business world of southwest Europe made little or no use of the 'payable to bearer' clause, so that instruments rarely circulated. On the other hand, private and public deposit or exchange banks were widespread in Italy and Spain during the sixteenth and seventeenth centuries. Accounts preserved from these countries show that many small traders had current accounts with the local banks, so that many payments in current local transactions were also made by transfers from one account to another. Most of the instructions for these payments were oral, but some were in writing: in either case, the debtor assigned payment of the debt to the balance in his current account with the local banks. Such clearing banks were also to be found in northwest Europe, but their clientele was mainly confined to merchants and to noble or patrician families.

[1] For a recent detailed account of their legal character and significance in England see J. Milnes Holden, *The History of Negotiable Instruments in English Law* (London, 1955), especially chaps. III and IV.

Besides extension of payment and the possible resultant set-offs, consumer credit also occurred in the form of ordinary loans at interest. Even in the late Middle Ages, when the church ban on usury still carried great weight, this form of credit had never entirely disappeared. In the modern age there was less hesitation about contravening this prohibition. In 1541 Charles V made loans at interest (with a maximum of 12 per cent) legal for commercial purposes. In England they were allowed as long as the interest rate did not exceed the legal maximum. Nevertheless, the old scruples still remained alive in the local economy; the straightforward loan at interest still incurred considerable odium in daily life until the end of the eighteenth century, certainly in the regions where the Counter-Reformation had triumphed.

Pawnbroking, on the other hand, was a very widespread form of popular consumer credit provision. The Jews, Lombards and Cahorsins had introduced pawnshops throughout Europe in the thirteenth and fourteenth centuries. Strangely enough, the importance of the pawnshops seems to have declined considerably in the fifteenth and early sixteenth centuries. No doubt the high rates of interest charged for this form of credit had given the pawnshops a bad name. The European depression in the fourteenth and fifteenth centuries made it more difficult to sell off pledges and thus sent up interest rates or charges, which brought the poorer borrowers into extremes of misery. The common people came to detest the pawnshops, a fact which did not escape the attention of the authorities. In the fifteenth century, therefore, official measures were regularly taken to restrain the activities of pawnbrokers and to force down the rate of interest. Sometimes these measures even led to complete abolition of the pawnshops.

In Spain the pawnshops in the form of *positos* came under greater municipal supervision from the end of the fifteenth century: they were to be much used in the sixteenth and above all the seventeenth centuries.

The expansion of the European economy from the end of the fifteenth century and the rapid development of the new forms of consumer credit had for a time somewhat lessened the need for the traditional pledge loan. The growth of the retail trade and the related custom of the tally or current account made it possible in a boom period in Europe to bridge temporary income crises in more flexible and less expensive ways within the framework of the local economy. Not until the second half of the sixteenth century, when the price revolution and the wars of religion had seriously begun to undermine once again the income of the lower sections of the population and local depressions started to assume a more severe and more frequent character, did the tally and current account fail fully to absorb the demand for consumer credit. Pledge loans returned more strongly to the fore in northwest Europe, but in a mental climate differing from that of two to three centuries before. Speculating to make a profit from the misery of the population was now condemned more strongly. As a result, pledge loans in these regions also gradually came under complete official supervision, culminating in the founding of public pawnshops directed towards relieving distress and no longer towards making profit.

In the southern Netherlands W. Coberger devised at the beginning of the seventeenth century a complete network of local 'Monts de Piété', under the direction and with the approval of the central government. In the 1620s Olivares vainly tried in Castile to get the approval of the Cortes for an old project dating from the end of the sixteenth century and likewise directed towards the creation of a centralized system of municipal banks and positos. In other European countries a similar evolution was perceptible: the United Provinces introduced municipal pawnshops, chief amongst them the Bank van Leening of Amsterdam (1614). Stockholm followed suit with the Riksens Ständers Bank. Even in towns where public pawnshops were functioning normally, private usurers were not pushed out of business completely. Sometimes private pawnbrokers were able to offer a better service: they could extend the loans over a longer period, they could accept written bonds instead of physical pledges and they could lend more than the relatively small sums to which the municipal pawnshops were restricted.

(4) CREDIT THROUGH ANNUITIES

Although the forms of credit described above were usually intended for consumer credit in the local economy, they were also frequently used for investment purposes. Cash payment in advance against future delivery could be used by the beneficiaries to finance the costs of current production or even invested in expansion.

In the modern age the sale of annuities was to become the most popular and most current form of investment credit at local level, and underwent a tremendous expansion. This was possible only as a result of thorough-going changes in the legal status of medieval cens and annuities during the fifteenth and sixteenth centuries. From the feudal system of charging a cens or annuity on real estate the custom had developed of the landowner assigning a cens or annuity to a third party. This in turn had led to the bail à rente, i.e. the sale of real estate in return for payment of a hereditary annuity, and also to the constitution de rente, i.e. a contract under which the débirentier sold or gave the crédirentier the right to receive out of the income from a specific resource (usually real estate) a periodical annuity (hereditary or on one, two or three lives). The papal bulls *Regimini* (1425 and 1455) permitted *bail à rente* and *constitution de rente* under three restrictive conditions: 1. the annuities created had to be assigned to a specific piece of real estate; 2. it had to be possible to buy them back again if the debtor so desired; 3. they might not represent a higher annual income than 10 per cent of the capital invested.[1]

The annuity system was an ideal way of valorizing the surplus value accruing to real estate in times of expansion of the towns or of agricultural prosperity. Under the influence of the papal bulls, the redeemability clause for annuities on demand by the *débirentier*, which had already occurred in various annuity contracts from the fourteenth century onwards, soon became a universal one. As early as the fifteenth century most towns in the Netherlands ruled that this redeemability was automatically applicable to all annuity contracts. In 1520 an edict of the Emperor Charles made the principle generally applicable to the whole of Brabant, and in 1529 to the whole of Flanders. In 1530, 1548 and 1577 *Reichspolizei-ordnungen* promulgated similar measures for Germany, and in 1533 Henri II did the same for all French towns. As a result both the *bail à rente* and the *constitution de rente* had become instruments of credit particularly suitable for longer-term credit; for only the *débirentier* was permitted to determine repayment and the period of repayment. If the *crédirentier* himself was in need of money, he could not of his own volition regain possession of his capital. In need, he could at most sell his annuity to a third party. Titles to annuities were transferable, but not yet negotiable. In sixteenth-century France the transfer still required a fairly complicated civil procedure. In the Netherlands, on the other hand, transfer was already very simple and became therefore, as at Antwerp, extremely common.

The assignment of an annuity to a given piece of real estate (or sometimes to another source of income) was an essential element of the annuity contract.[2] As was said above, *bail à rente* or *constitution de rente* was very frequently used locally for investment credit in the long or medium term. B. Bennassar and F. Ruiz-Martin have pointed to the great importance of the *censos consignativos* that the Castilian farmers sold through the local notaries in the sixteenth century to help finance land reclamation, the planting of vineyards and olive trees and the building of farmsteads. H. Soly has demonstrated how the urbanization of Antwerp in the sixteenth century was largely financed in this

[1] B. Schnapper, *Les rentes au XVIe siècle. Histoire d'un instrument de crédit* (Paris, 1957), p. 45; Cipolla, *op. cit.*, pp. 35f.
[2] According to B. Schnapper, from the sixteenth century *rentes volantes* also occurred without assignment, but this seems the exception to the rule. Indeed, it was for this very reason that annuities were regarded as 'immovable'.

way: craftsmen or people in a small way of business bought plots of land on a *bail à rente*, laid the foundations for a row of houses and sold annuities on these, with which they financed further building.

Improvement or renovation of farming and building in the towns, the two basic sectors of local investment,[1] were largely buttressed by credit via annuities. They brought long-term or medium-term credit within reach of the smaller businessmen in town and country. This penetration of investment credit within the smaller units of production of the local economy unquestionably helped to stimulate European expansion in the sixteenth century. The drop in the interest rate of perpetual but redeemable annuities (from commonly 10 to 12 per cent in the fifteenth century via 6 per cent in the sixteenth to 3 per cent towards the end of the seventeenth and in the course of the eighteenth century) should not be forgotten in this respect. Yet its influence was not the sole determinant, since during the depression in the seventeenth century many complaints were heard that *bail à rente* or *constitution de rente*, even at the lower interest rates, was no longer being used as much for investment credit but rather to meet operating deficits and to regularize arrears.

Closely connected with the *bail à rente* and with the *constitution de rente* was mortgage credit secured by landed property. According to R. Ashton, many large English landowners made use of this method to improve their farming operations, especially after the middle of the seventeenth century, when the mortgager acquired the right to re-purchase the mortgaged land if desired.[2] In England land banks came into being at the end of the seventeenth century (J. Biscoe, 1695; J. Asgill & N. Barbon, 1695; H. Chamberlen, 1696) for financing agricultural investments.[3] Specific agricultural credit, as organized in England in the course of the seventeenth century, was not a complete novelty to Europe: from the end of the fifteenth century the *arcas de misericordia* in Navarre and the *monte frumentarii* in Italy were already in existence. These were corn banks which lent seed to farmers or provided other aid to agriculture on favourable terms. The Italian *monte-pios*, the Spanish *positos* or other municipal pawnbroking establishments also often performed the function of land banks.

The main intention of the land banks was to supply not long-term credit but floating capital. Even in this respect, their influence remained limited. Normally short-term credit in local farming, industry or trade

---

[1] For the predominant importance of agriculture in the field of capital investment: R. Davis, *The Rise of the Atlantic Economies* (London, 1973), pp. 231–3.

[2] R. Ashton, *The Crown and the Money Market, 1603–1640* (Oxford, 1960), pp. 7–9.

[3] J. K. Horsefield, *British Monetary Experiments, 1650–1710* (London, 1960), pp. 140 f.

was obtained through extension of payment by the suppliers of raw materials or by advance payment by the purchasers. In the putting-out system the farm labourer himself was not infrequently the 'involuntary supplier of short-term capital' when his employer applied the long-pay principle. Sometimes the employer paid his workers in IOUs, vouchers on shops or other tokens which the worker could use for his purchases: in such a situation not only the workers but also the local tradespeople became the employer's bankers.

The appreciable expansion of local consumer and investment credit in the modern age presupposes not only greater confidence but bigger savings and increasing mobility of capital. The upper classes were the biggest savers. A not inconsiderable part was invested in the purchase of annuities through intermediary notaries: the portfolios of rural or urban bourgeoisie, officials and magistracy, clergy and local institutions contained many annuities purchased in town and country. 'La rente décolle', noted E. Le Roy Ladurie of rural France in the sixteenth and seventeenth centuries.

It is striking that the lower middle classes also took an active part in investment in annuities, certainly during boom periods such as the sixteenth century. In Antwerp, of the purchasers of annuities who had their transactions officially entered in the aldermen's register in 1545, 25·15 per cent were craftsmen, 21·19 per cent administrative officials, 16·8 per cent widows, 16·24 per cent merchants (this group also included many small pedlars and hawkers) and 20·62 per cent miscellaneous. In rural districts it became customary to deposit savings with notaries; in the towns potential recipients were money-changers, goldsmith and silversmith bankers or public exchange banks. Not all deposits were used for the local provision of credit, but certainly part – and in times of economic expansion a considerable part – was used thus.

II.   *The World of Trade and Finance*

(1) THE BREAK-THROUGH OF THE LARGE SILVER COINS

In the early modern age international trade still contained many traditional elements. Barter was a regular occurrence; an ideal way of unloading goods that were difficult to sell, provided that the other party was eager for a quick sale of his own goods; in ports where the irregular arrivals of the fleets of sailing vessels could suddenly cause stocks to increase alarmingly, such situations arose frequently. Barter then camouflaged the price and cut the loss. But barter was still used in quite normal conditions. The frequent shortage of hard cash doubtless played a part in the survival of this primitive trading method. In ports and towns where merchants and factors knew each other well and engaged in a trade with little or no specialization, or where ships and convoys of carts speculated on short returns, barter sometimes assured a quicker turnover.

Buying and selling for cash was also common in international trade, though not wholly characteristic of it. Extension of payment was the normal procedure, so normal that the firm of van der Molen, in its correspondence from Antwerp to Italy, would always state the prices of spices in the 1530s and 1540s 'a tempo due fieri', i.e. payable at two fairs or six months. The custom of extension of payment for three or six months on the international markets implied that purchasers paying cash could count on an additional bonus, *viz.* a rebate on the sales price. *A fortiori*, these advantages applied to payment in advance. On the other hand, it was quite usual for the purchaser to pay part of the sum due in cash and to be given an extension for the balance. When payments were assigned to third parties by means of the transfer of commercial instruments to bearer or to order, they were often supplemented in cash, since the respective amounts rarely coincided.

In principle, payments in coin in international trade were made in *large* coins, apart from occasional speculations in the smaller basic coins. Gold *écus* dominated the fairs of Lyons and Besançon-Piacenza. After 1550 the large silver coins came strongly to the fore and dominated European intercontinental trade in the sixteenth and seventeenth centuries. Around 1600 the Spanish *reals* and *piastres* won an international reputation, equalled only by the Dutch silver trade coins, issued in the course of the seventeenth century under the supervision of the Amsterdam Exchange Bank. In Germany the supremacy of the *talers* remained unsurpassed. Not until the eighteenth century did gold acquire a firmer footing again, especially in England, where guineas gained the upper hand.

The international flows of specie throughout the modern age were doubtless strongly influenced by movements of capital and in particular by government transfers. It would, however, be wrong not to recognize the influence of the commercial factor in these flows. The European depression of the fourteenth and fifteenth centuries must also be understood in this light. Papal taxation had caused the church's annual balances north of the Alps to increase greatly in the thirteenth century, this income being spent in Italy or at Avignon. At the same time Italian merchants created debts in the north and credit balances in Italy by their purchases in northwest Europe. The fundamental balance thus attained was completely upset during the fifteenth century when the exports of products from northwest Europe to the south dropped sharply, whereas imports of luxury goods from Italy and the Middle East to the north increased. The negative balance of payments of the north in respect of the south was initially financed by imports of capital by the big Italian firms, which extended their financial investments in the north through local branches, and increasingly by exporting precious metals. The result was a gradual depletion of the reserves of precious metals in northwest Europe, which undermined international trade and hampered international payments. The revival of the fairs north of the Alps in the course of the fifteenth century cannot be isolated from this, for an important function of the fairs was to facilitate and systematize the set-off of international payments and thus effect considerable savings in specie payments.

The intensification of imports of Sudanese gold into Portugal and Castile, the appreciable resumption of central European silver production after 1450, and even more after 1500, likewise affected the orientation of foreign trade and payments. Though northwest Europe was still losing precious metals to Italy and the Middle East, the gradual restructuring of industry in the north led to a much better equilibrium. The cheap, diversified mass products of the countryside and the highly specialized articles of the towns, first directed towards substitution for imports and soon leading to exports, even to the south, had given the industry of northwest Europe new vitality and competitiveness. Thus a larger surplus of exports of English and Dutch manufactured goods directed to the Hanseatic League and central Europe was achieved, balanced by silver imports. The export surplus with the Iberian world was initially covered by gold imports.

The spectacular shipments of gold from the New World in the first half of the sixteenth century accentuated the difference in the gold–silver ratios between Spain and Portugal on the one hand and central Europe on the other. Consequently, the specie flows in settlement of international commercial transactions reflected speculative activities which drained off silver to the Iberian peninsula and gold from there to the northwest and to Italy. Official policy further reinforced the speculative atmosphere by imposing unrealistic gold–silver ratios or by an irresponsible monetary policy, of which the 'Great Debasements' in England were the most notorious example of the sixteenth century. Through the excessive prices for silver bullion offered by the Mint, the 'Great Debasements' attracted a large volume of silver from the continent, but paid a heavy penalty in inflation in England.

Less spectacular changes in the metal content of the basic silver coinage were in themselves often a sufficient incentive for merchants to make commercial payments both at home and abroad in cash, using overvalued coins. An identical opportunity for speculative payments occurred when, under the influence of successful counterfeiting, lighter large coins entered into circulation, when announcements of rate reductions with respect to particular coins were expected, or when such rate reductions had effectively been announced. For governments normally tolerated the older, mostly higher, rates, during a transition period of one or more months. Speculators could put this interlude to good use.

Shipments of silver from Peru and Mexico long dominated European gold–silver ratios. At the same time the price revolution altered the terms of trade in favour of foodstuffs and to the detriment of industrial products, while severe copper inflations manifested themselves in Spain, France, Sweden and, for a shorter period, in Germany too. The effect on commercial specie flows was extremely important. The Dutch, transporting cereals from the Baltic region, were in a privileged position to attract American precious metals from Spain to meet the Spanish trade deficit. The Dutch further strengthened their position during the period of overvaluation of copper when they carried not only Baltic grain but also Swedish copper to Germany, France and (above all) Spain. England, on the other hand, which had specialized in the exporting of industrial specialties, was in an awkward situation. The terms of trade, the stability of the coinage since Elizabeth I, and the devaluation fashionable in many other European countries were all hindrances to English exports: accordingly, to promote sales in Spain and Germany, payments in copper coin were accepted. These were not converted into silver because of the expensive silver premiums, but used to purchase returns in local goods.

Amsterdam was a major centre for the redistribution of commercial silver flows not only to northern Europe but (especially in the seventeenth century) to the Far East. The Portuguese, speculating on the relative high price of silver, had also exported Spanish silver coins to the East Indies as early as the sixteenth century. At first the Dutch also exported many Spanish rials of eight (*reales de a ocho*) to the Levant and the Far East, but from the second quarter of the seventeenth century Holland's own silver trade coins began to gain ground, occupying a strong position in silver exports to the Far East from the second half of the century. Around 1640 the Dutch East India Company was taking out an average of a million guilders in precious metals to the Far East; by 1660 this average had increased to about 1½ million guilders per annum, continuing to climb to a first climax of 5·1 million guilders per annum in 1700 and a second climax of 6·8 to 7·9 million guilders from 1722 to 1728, by this time largely in the form of Dutch *ducatons*. Meanwhile, up to 1668 the Dutch annually exported masses of silver, and from that year gold, from Japan to southern Asia (to an average annual value of 1⅓ million guilders between 1640 and 1680), and the

Spanish also brought large quantities of silver from Acapulco across the Pacific to the Philippines.[1]

(2) THE CLEARING BANK SYSTEM

The progress of financial techniques during the sixteenth century may be discerned in two major directions. First, the thirst for precious metals in the fifteenth century influenced techniques of international payments decisively towards better systems of multilateral clearing. Second, the great expansion in the production of precious metals and in international specie flows during the sixteenth century led gradually to innovations in the field of credit.

In the southern regions of western Europe progress was to a great extent of an institutional nature and related primarily to local and international clearing of payments. Instrumentally, on the other hand, the south remained faithful to the gains of the late Middle Ages. Extension of payment continued to be a frequent form of credit among merchants. The credit could be granted in the shape of an ordinary oral agreement, of a formal document or, more often, of an IOU. However, the words 'payable to X or to bearer' rarely if ever occurred in Italy during the fifteenth and sixteenth centuries. Transfer called for a formal *cessio*, so that circulation was certainly unusual. In Lyons, on the other hand, transfers were much more customary, doubtless reflecting the influence of the north. Extension of payment could also simply be noted in the merchant's books.[2]

Loans at interest, with or without pledge or security, were regularly used for obtaining commercial credit. Great influence was nevertheless exerted by the church's ban on interest (*pecunia pecuniam parere non potest*). Simple loans at interest tended to be restricted in the Catholic south, even in commercial circles, until deep into the modern age. They were replaced ultimately by credit on bills of exchange: this was permitted by the Roman Catholic Church because the *exchange operation* was regarded as the heart of the contract. The bill of exchange consequently developed further during the sixteenth century, especially in

---

[1] K. Glamann, *Dutch-Asiatic Trade, 1620–1740* (Copenhagen–The Hague, 1958), pp. 50–72.

[2] Merchants of any standing in the south had, ever since the Middle Ages, followed the custom of keeping impeccable accounts for their trade. Italy had done really pioneering work in this matter, above all by the introduction of double-entry bookkeeping in the course of the fourteenth century. In 1494 the first clearly set-out manual, the *Summa de Arithmetica*, compiled by the Franciscan Luca Pacioli, had been published in Venice. In south Germany the Italian example developed into a specific technique on account of the great importance attached to entering the quantities dealt in in the books.

the south, but also increasingly in the north, as the dominating commercial instrument of international trade; the time element concealed in the *distancia loci* and in the *cambium-recambium* operation implied provision of credit. Sometimes the exchange contract was a simple camouflage for a loan at interest and a bill of exchange was not even drawn up (so-called dry exchange, or fictitious exchange), however much the church might forbid this practice. Of greater importance in the sixteenth century was the *ricorsa* bill of exchange, which was likewise a concealed form of loan at interest but whose formal exchange contract was accompanied by the issue of a bill of exchange. In addition to the *ricorsa* bill of exchange, *dépôt de foire en foire* and the opening of credit on current account with money-changers/bankers or with merchant bankers were two other very common forms of commercial credit in the course of the sixteenth century. The last two were intimately connected with the fairs and with the clearing banks respectively.

Fairs of exchange and clearing banks were no innovation of the modern age, but they underwent major technical improvements in the south during the fifteenth and sixteenth centuries. The main emphasis of the progress in financial techniques in these regions consequently came to be placed on the institutional plane. R. de Roover has made a distinction for the late Middle Ages between merchant bankers, who as bankers mainly engaged in trading in bills and arbitrage on exchange rates, and the money-changers, who as bankers concentrated on attracting deposits and on the clearing bank system. The distinction was not as sharp as R. de Roover suggests, even during the fifteenth and sixteenth centuries: in practice both financial activities were frequently combined in the same hands, as they were in Florence.

The *banchi di scritto*, which had developed in the late Middle Ages out of money deposits, continued to be a popular medium for commercial payments in the south, including southern Germany, during the fifteenth and sixteenth centuries. Many merchants paid their debts by transfer from one account to another. Normally the instructions for payment would be communicated to the banker orally – in Venice this procedure even remained compulsory – but in the course of time written instruction for transfer also became common: this was really a cheque by which the debtor assigned payment to his current account with the banker. Such assignments did not usually give rise to monetary manipulations but merely to a *scritta in banco*. The same applied also to the payment of bills of exchange, which was usually attended to by transfer from one account to another. It was often already stated on the bill that payment would take place *in banco*; if not, the banker was either informed orally, or written instructions to this effect were drafted. When the beneficiary entered the instructions for payment *in banco* on the back of the bill – and a number of examples of this are known – this might already be described as a certain form of endorsement. On the other hand, the money-changers/bankers also kept current accounts for their local colleagues, so that transfers in favour of a merchant who was the client of another banker could be booked for the time being to this colleague's account. Periodical settlements were then made.

It is generally assumed that the clearing bank system in the south underwent a serious crisis in the course of and especially towards the end of the fifteenth century. This was particularly so in Italy, where numerous dramatic bankruptcies occurred, for example in Venice in the 1490s. This is surprising, especially since so many opportunities for set-off existed in the clearing bank system to deal with the contemporary shortage of precious metals. The probable explanation is that most clearing banks were as yet too small: they operated mainly locally and were little used for interregional or international set-offs. Another important factor was the climate of distrust which the European depression of the fifteenth century had generated. The money-changers/bankers were already freely applying the principle of keeping only fractional cash reserves against deposits, but opportunities for investment were limited and often directed towards medium-term credits of an uncertain nature: public loans often proved difficult to realise, and commercial investments, either by direct participation or in an indirect form by opening credit on current account or by advances on security, increasingly ended in disaster as a result of the European crisis. In these precarious conditions, confidence – the basis of deposit banking – was severely eroded by spasmodic panics.

The strong recovery of foreign trade in the course of the sixteenth century restored confidence and gave new impetus to the clearing bank system in the south. But memories of the difficult years stayed green. As soon as the first great wave of expansion had spent itself and uncertainty periodically emerged again, a movement started in Italy for the foundation of *public* clearing banks. In Genoa the *Casa di San Giorgio*, dating from 1407, had already functioned as a public bank, but had been obliged to abandon the experiment in 1444. In the second half of the sixteenth century, however, development was more general and successful: to quote a few examples, *Tavoli di Palermo* (1552), *Banco di San Paolo* in Turin (1563), *Banco di San Giorgio* in Genoa (1586), *Banco della Piazza di Rialto* in Venice (1587), *Banco di Messina* (1587), *Banco di Sant'Ambrogio* in Milan (1593).

Amongst the most illustrious of the Italian public banks was the *Banco della Piazza di Rialto*, founded by Senate decree of 11 April 1587. This was a continuation of the private clearing banks, which after 1560 had lost the confidence of the Venetian merchants and found themselves in difficulties. The bank was licensed to a private person, but the backing of the Venetian Senate could be clearly felt. In principle, besides transfers from one account to another, withdrawals in cash were permitted. Credit on current accounts was forbidden. Moreover, in 1593 the Senate also obliged the merchants to pay all bills of exchange *per partita di banco*. In 1605-6, all commercial transactions exceeding 100 ducats had to be settled *in banco*. In practice very few cash withdrawals were made in the *Banco della Piazza di Rialto*, and the bulk of the transactions were settled by clearing operations. On the other hand, in the course of time numerous debit balances occurred among the current accounts, not only on a basis of commercial requirements but also for speculative reasons On account of the great confidence placed on them, payments *in banco* soon gained a premium on payments in current coin, so that speculation arose on the fluctuating premium.

More successful even than the Rialto Bank was the *Banco del Giro* of Venice, founded in May 1619. The original purpose of the new foundation was to handle part of Venice's public debt.[1] The bank was to issue interest-bearing obligations (*partite*) on behalf of the state; for its part the government guaranteed the monthly payment of a fixed sum, out of which the bank was to pay the interest due and gradually amortize the principal. The *partite* met with so much success that they soon circulated at a premium and were to remain very popular. The success of the *Banco del Giro* attracted the attention of the merchants, who increasingly placed deposits with it. Transfers from one merchant's account to another and the cashing of cheques now became normal operations of the *Banco del Giro*. So sharp was its competition that it compelled the once illustrious Rialto Bank to close its doors in 1638.

The improvements made by the public clearing bank system were three. The principal was the strengthening of confidence. The clearing bank was either placed under the direct control of the municipality or was linked with a reliable municipal institution of general welfare under indirect official supervision: this basis for confidence was further reinforced by the fact that the whole body of depositors, i.e. the public, were the real owners of the bank; the bank governors performed a managerial function only. Second, set-off operations were centralized, especially in those towns where only one public clearing bank functioned. For example, in Venice, until the second quarter of the seventeenth century still the great commercial centre of the Mediterranean

[1] D. Demarco, 'Quelques moments de l'histoire des banques publiques napolitaines des origines à 1808', *Third International Conference of Economic History, Munich 1965: Proceedings* (Paris–The Hague, 1974), pp. 113–47; L. de Rosa, 'Observations à propos de la relation de M. Demarco sur les banques napolitaines', *ibid.* pp. 165–9.

region, many foreigners had a current account at the local clearing bank, in addition to the Italian merchants. The concentration of payments there thus made an effective multilateral clearing of international payments possible. Finally, the Italian public clearing banks also created money. The Neapolitan public banks, for example, entered the deposits in a *madrefede*, and on the strength of this the clients supplied their creditors with cheques (*polizze*) drawn on the bank, the amount being transferred by the bank to the creditor's account. If the creditor was not a client of the bank, the debtor furnished him with a *fede di credito*, by means of which the latter could pay a third or possibly fourth or fifth person, who had to be a customer of the bank. These *fedi di credito* began to circulate. Since the Italian public clearing banks regularly permitted credit to be opened on current account (and in Naples mortgage or other loans too), the banks actually created money in the form of paper of several kinds.

Public clearing banks were already known in Spain by the beginning of the fifteenth century – Barcelona (1401), Valencia (1407), Palma de Mallorca, Saragossa and others – but they scored no more of a lasting success as commercial institutions in the course of the fifteenth century than did the private money-changers/bankers, who continued to exist side by side with them. On the other hand, the private clearing bank system in Castile enjoyed remarkable prosperity during the same period: here there was definitely no question of a crisis at the end of the fifteenth century. In 1446 an ordinance by Juan II gave official permission for the founding of private deposit and clearing banks in Castile, subject to official agreement and guarantees. During the following years many such clearing banks came into being in Castile: in Burgos, Arande de Duero, Valladolid, Segovia, Madrid, Toledo, Cordoba, Baeza, Seville etc.[1] The surprising prosperity of the Castilian clearing bank system was proof of the economic expansion of this region and of the exceptional importance of its precious metals market, geared to western North Africa. During the first half of the sixteenth century the private deposit and clearing bank system in Castile underwent still further expansion by meshing in with the Castilian fairs. Alas, the private clearing banks in Spain were not to outlive the commercial prosperity of the Castilian fairs: during the second half of the sixteenth century decline was universal.

In 1560 another fruitless attempt was made by government decree to give the *Casa de Contratación* in Seville, which had a monopoly of trade with America, a deposit and clearing bank function: the deposits were to help to finance colonial trade with the aim of further strengthening the bank's funds. In 1595 the government sold private parties a

[1] F. Ruiz-Martin, *La Banca en España hasta 1782* (Madrid, 1970), pp. 13–41.

licence to set up a private deposit and clearing bank monopoly in Seville for ten years, but this too went bankrupt at the beginning of the seventeenth century. Only in eastern Spain did the public clearing banks revive under Italian influence – the *Banca de la Ciudad* in Barcelona (1609), the *Tauli di Canvi* in Valencia (1649) and the former *Tabla de los comunes depositos* in Saragossa.

(3) FROM COMMERCIAL TO FINANCIAL FAIRS

In southern Europe the international commercial fairs formed the second important institutional framework within which progress in payment techniques was made in the fifteenth and sixteenth centuries. At the international fairs in the south the hegemony of the merchant bankers was undisputed. The preponderance of the bill of exchange tied in with this: the trade in bills under the supervision of the merchant bankers had not only international or interregional transfers in view, but increasingly specific credit operations. Moreover, the trade in bills formed the basis for arbitrage on exchange rates, a major financial activity of merchant bankers in the south.

Threatened by increasing insecurity on the continent, by maritime competition and by the gradual reduction in the precious metal reserves, transcontinental commercial transactions during the fourteenth and fifteenth centuries had once again withdrawn largely within the structure of the fairs: there at least some economies of scale could be maintained in the turnover of goods, there the use of precious metals for set-offs of international debts and credits could be kept to a minimum. The vigorous revival of transcontinental trade from the second half of the fifteenth century and the prosperity of the fairs were closely bound up with one another for a long time to come.

The four Geneva fairs, already burgeoning in the course of the fourteenth century as late successors to the Champagne fairs, reached their apogee about the middle of the following century. They formed the new gateway for Italian foreign trade to the European continent. Numerous Italian merchants lived in Geneva. Large firms, such as the Medici bank, had a temporary or permanent branch there. The Geneva trade had lively contacts with France, Catalonia, Switzerland, the hereditary lands of Burgundy (including the Netherlands), the Rhineland, England and southern Germany. The Geneva fairs had also become an important centre of international clearing. As unit of account for commercial transactions the gold mark of 28 ounces troy weight (divided into 64 or 66 *écus*) was used in the last instance, a stable, valuable standard, universally accepted. This considerably eased the international set-off of debits and credits, concentrated during the period of payment of the fairs. Finally, the Geneva fairs enjoyed a busy trade in bills of exchange. These were not simply commercial bills; it may be inferred from the accounts of the Medici bank that arbitrage on exchange rates was also a common activity of the Italian merchant bankers. *Contra-cambium*, the systematic creation of credit bypassing the exchange market, was a regular phenomenon. For all exchange operations, Geneva quoted rates at their local value (fixed exchange), *viz.* the gold mark of 28 ounces troy weight or its division, the *écu*, at 64 or 66 *écus* per mark.[1] The mark thus dominated both commercial settlements and the money and exchange market: a remarkable simplification of payments which added a further dimension to multilateral clearing in international trade and finance. Besides advantages, Geneva had its limitations: payments and set-offs did not yet take place under central direction; no exchange rate was officially fixed either.

At the Castilian fairs a special combination between clearing bank system and fair payments was obtained through the creation of 'fair banks' (*bancos de feria*). The Castilian fairs – Villalon, Rioseco and Medina del Campo – were of older origin, but had clearly gained in importance along with Spanish commercial expansion during the second half of the fifteenth century. Between 1495 and 1505, the May and October fairs of Medina del Campo, the August fair of Rioseco and the Lenten fair of Villalon, with the support of Ferdinand and Isabella, gained the status of fairs of payment (*ferias de pagos*). The Castilian fairs could now join the established system of the European commercial and payment fairs (Lyons, Brabant, Frankfurt-am-Main) and thus enjoy tremendous prosperity during the first half of the sixteenth century.

The *bancos de feria* were peculiar to the fairs of Castile. The money-changers/bankers practising deposit and clearing banking in the towns of Castile designated for each town or group of towns a delegate who was empowered during a given fair to perform banking transactions for his principals and to grant the clients credit up to a certain limit. The significance of these occasional fair banks was initially a regional one; during the period of the fair they not only exchanged coin but also stood surety for purchases on credit or financed by transfer the debts of the hawkers and shopkeepers who were clients of their principals. In the *Libro Mayor* the account of the local money-changers/bankers was debited in the case of such transfers, and the account of the other party, the beneficiary's banker, was credited. The hawkers or shopkeepers, upon their return, repaid the local money-changers/bankers with the proceeds of their sales. These sales were settled in cash or with promissory notes, the latter guaranteed by or assigned to the

[1] This *écu* originated from a real gold coin, the *écu de Savoie*.

coming harvest or sheep-shearing by farmers and shepherds, or assigned to the next payment of salary by officials or of interest by rentiers.

With the internationalization of the Castilian fairs, the *bancos de feria*, especially that of Medina del Campo, acquired a European dimension. In the meantime the regulations had become more strict. The *Rua*, where the bankers held their sessions, was chained off: during a two-hour period in the forenoon and another in the early evening the merchants came to proffer the due promissory notes and bills of exchange to the debtor's banker for registration in the *Libro Mayor* and at the same time indicated their own banker. Payment was then made by debiting the account of the debtor-client and by crediting the account of the creditor-client or of his banker. Every two days the fair bankers met for set-offs and for clearing accounts. Exchange rates were not yet systematically fixed, but a consensus was growing from the mass of new exchange transactions in which the information of the brokers and the arrival of the treasure fleets in Seville naturally played a major role.

The importance of the payments at the fairs of Medina del Campo is clearly illustrated by the size of the accounts of the *bancos de feria*, which in the climacteric around 1530–50 increased broadly to 13,000 to 14,000 folios per fair. In addition to clearing and exchange operations loans were made in the form of deposits or bills of exchange from fair to fair; inland bills of exchange were also common. However, from 1534 measures were taken to limit these forms of credit. At the end of the 1540s bills from fair to fair and other inland bills were forbidden. This handicapped trade in Seville, where dealers were in the habit of issuing *letras de credito* on the Castilian fairs for fitting out the West Indies fleet, on the basis of which the sellers at Medina del Campo could draw bills on Seville.

Through the internationalization of the Castilian fairs the great merchant firms of Burgos were also active at Medina del Campo. Since they controlled the production and exports (above all of wool) of northern Spain, and wielded great financial power founded on marine insurance, they exerted considerable influence on the course of payments and on the fluctuations of the exchange rates. Gradually the power of the great commercial firms of Burgos was to be taken over by the Genoese financiers, who placed the Castilian fairs, together with the Seville banks, at the service of the Habsburg public finances. The commercial fund that nurtured the prosperity of the Castilian exchange and credit market was now quickly drained by the Genoese bankers on behalf of an insatiable exchequer. From the 1550s such developments were heralding the decline of the commercial fairs. Soon afterwards the Atlantic route to northwest Europe became unsafe, and the commercial and financial ties between Seville and Italy were strengthened under the direction of Genoa. Not only did this seal the commercial fate of the Castilian fairs; the fairs of payment at Medina del Campo also gradually withered away. By 1605 they had been completely deserted by the *asentistas*.

The Lyons fairs perfected international payments and transfers by means of a different system, the *virement des parties*. In 1462 the French monarch Louis XI decided to transfer the Geneva fairs to Lyons. In 1484, however, Lyons temporarily lost its fair privilege to Bourges and Troyes, so that it was not until 1494 that its definitive expansion began. The unique success of the Lyons fairs originated in the revival of trans-continental trade between the Atlantic and the Mediterranean worlds, from the territorial ambitions of the French Valois in Italy and from the transition from Tuscan to Genoese hegemony over the international trade and finance of Lyons which was completed in the course of the first half of the sixteenth century. At the Lyons fairs the Tuscan, Milanese and Genoese merchant bankers not only directed an extensive world trade but at the same time centralized their international pay-ments, transfers, exchange and credit operations, so that merchants from France, the Netherlands, the Rhineland and southern Germany were obliged to follow suit. In this way the four Lyons fairs (Epiphany, Low Sunday, the beginning of August and All Saints) gained a double specific function. First of all there were the quarterly commercial fairs, each lasting about a fortnight. Then there were the fairs of *payment*, which lasted about one week. They did not always follow immediately on the commercial fairs, and in this way gradually acquired an indepen-dent status, developing into specific *foires de change* or fairs of exchange, similar to those of Castile.

The regulations of the Lyons fairs of payment were strict.[1] During the first two days the merchants gathered outside the Florentine loggia to hear the public call-over of bills due; bills were accepted, protested or accepted under protest. Everyone entered his accepted debts and claims in a *carnet* and drew up his *bilan des acceptations*, which had force of law among merchants. On the third day a fresh assembly took place (*jour des changes*). The consul of the Florentine 'nation' now announced the date of the next fair of payment at Lyons and the times of payment of the bills concluded in foreign towns and at foreign fairs. After approval by the merchants, the Florentine, Genoese and Lucchese 'nations' consulted on the exchange rates that each would apply to the contracts concluded during the current fair: the averages of these were then announced by the Florentine consul. In emulation of Geneva, Lyons quoted in local value (fixed exchange), *viz.* the gold mark and

---

[1] R. Gascon, *Grand Commerce et vie urbaine au XVIe siècle: Lyon et ses marchands*, 1 (Paris, 1971), 236–79.

its division of account the *écu de marc* at 65 *écus* per mark, so that all debits and credits were expressed in the same unit of account.

In addition to the exchange rates for bills on foreign countries, the rates for the inland bills on the principal centres of the kingdom (*le change intérieur*) were also officially announced; they were expressed in a discount against the *écu de marc*. Finally, although it was not always officially proclaimed, the rate of interest was determined for the *dépôt*, i.e. for the money borrowed at interest from one fair of payment to the next, a form of credit which was very common in Lyons until the papal ban in 1571. The *jours des changes* were then followed by the actual payments: these were made either by set-off (*virement des parties*) or in cash. Every merchant appeared with his *carnet*, in which his credit and debit were noted (*bilan des acceptations*). Debtor and creditor could either offset debits and credits against each other, or they could agree that third parties with debts due to the debtor could pay these to the creditor's account. Once the possibilities of setting-off were exhausted, set-offs in time could be created by new commitments for the next fair of payment, or by new foreign bills. If deficits still remained, the balance was settled in cash, borrowed if necessary from the merchant bankers at the rate of interest laid down for the *dépôt de foire en foire*, which fluctuated around $2\frac{1}{2}$ per cent per quarter between 1540 and 1600.

The success of the Lyons setting-off system consisted in the great volume and in the international nature of the payments concentrated there. But from the second third of the sixteenth century onwards, the French kings increasingly subjected the Lyons money and exchange market to inexhaustible demands for credit. As in Castile, the commercial fund was gradually emptied by excessive government withdrawals. During the 1550s the gap between international trade and the money market was already wide, and commercial transactions severely hampered by the strained situation of public finance. Disaster loomed when the quarterly periods of payment became extremely irregular after 1562. The wars of religion completed the decline of the Lyons fairs. Only the *foires de change* continued to retain some importance in the seventeenth century as financial satellites of Italian and Genoese banking.

The fairs of Besançon and Piacenza were a kind of extension of the Lyons fairs.[1] When the Genoese merchant bankers, through their ties with Seville, with the fairs of Castile and of Lyons, began to strengthen their position in international banking in Europe, the French monarch wanted to harness this rising power under his exclusive control through Lyons. The choice of Besançon was inspired not only by the proximity of Lyons, but also by the possibility of maintaining the *distancia loci* for

[1] J. G. Da Silva, *Banque et crédit en Italie au XVIIe siècle*, 1 (Paris, 1969), 25–281.

the *dépôts de foire en foire*, the usual camouflage for the prohibited loans at interest.

From 1579, when the Genoese had gained indisputable control of the redistribution of American silver throughout Europe, these fairs were held at Piacenza. The Besançon and Piacenza fairs were essentially fairs of payment. They developed into the prototype of the *foires de change*, where the traditional set-off techniques had acquired a high degree of refinement. Ties with the trade in merchandise and precious metals continued to play an important part: the trade with Lyons, Venice, Leghorn and Milan, the shipments of silver from Spain to Genoa and other places under Genoese control, were strongly represented. For all transactions the *scudo di marche* (*écu de marc*) formed the unit of account. It was a fictitious money of account, the value of which was initially determined by taking the average of seven gold coins of reference: the gold *écus* minted in Antwerp, Spain, Florence, Genoa, Naples and Venice (taken in a fixed relation of 101 *écus* to 100 *scudi di marche*) and the French *écu de soleil* (taken in a fixed relation of 100 *écus de soleil* to 103 *scudi di marche*). After 1671 a large Genoese silver coin was also adopted as coin of reference.

Instrumentally the Besançon and Piacenza fairs were dominated by the trade in ordinary and *ricorsa* bills.[1] Insofar as the trade in ordinary bills consisted of *cambium-recambium*, the expenses were incorporated in the re-exchange, so that in fact the interest was accumulated. In the case of the *ricorsa* bill, a camouflaged loan at interest, an agreement was concluded between lender and drawer to name a third party in another place simultaneously as drawee and beneficiary; this third party would not only accept the bill and pay it to himself, but would at the same time draw a new bill on the original drawer in favour of the original lender, all this on the strength of a double instruction (*spaccio*), furnished to the drawee by lender and drawer together with the bill.

The rules for payment were strongly inspired by the customs at Lyons, but with some important technical improvements. First of all there were the ordinary payments. As at Lyons, each of the *banchieri di conto* drew up for himself a balance sheet of acceptance in his *scartafaccio*. On the third day they together fixed the official exchange rates (*conto*). Then came the setting-off of due bills, and more frequently still the conclusion of new exchange contracts between the contracting parties; this was done on the basis of free exchange rates, but the bankers took the official *conto* more or less as their guide. With these bills the original *avanzo* or *mancamento* of the balance sheet of acceptances was quite often eliminated. But not always; for instance a banker could

---

[1] G. Mandich, *Le Pacte de Ricorso et le marché italien des changes au XVIIe siècle* (Paris, 1953), pp. 5–59.

still raise his *avanzo* still further, if he wished to remit extra money to a particular place.

As a result, at Besançon and Piacenza setting-off was obtained not as at Lyons by bilateral or multilateral settlement of due bills (*scontrations*) but more by the mutual drawing and granting of credit by bills drawn on other places. The Genoese solution was in the first place a payment in balance (*pagamento in balancio*); in other words the setting-off for each fair was inherently connected with the existence of an effective money and credit market. If balances still remained, they had to be covered by payment in gold *écus*. On the eighth day every banker had then to be able to submit a perfect balance sheet of payments to the consul.

In addition to the ordinary exchange operations there were regulations for the *ricorsa* bills, which were kept completely outside the balance sheets. The importance of the Besançon and Piacenza fairs consisted above all in the *conto*. The *ricorsa* bills that had been drawn on the fairs always provided that the rate for re-exchange would follow the official *conto*; and since the *conto* at Besançon and Piacenza was always fixed as a function of the rates that had applied at the other fairs, the original lenders were assured of their profit. The impressive stability of the *écu de marc* was an important factor in the successful working of the system. It was of course also common for *ricorsa* bills to be drawn from the Genoese fairs on other fairs; however, to the extent that the *conto* was not as stable there as at Besançon or Piacenza, the risk was greater.

The refinements made in financial techniques by the Genoese fairs were on the plane of control and setting-off of international payments. The Genoese bankers concentrated remittances in their favour at the Besançon fair and later at Piacenza if they wished to use these to purchase bills on other centres where they needed coin; conversely they concentrated *traites* payable by them at the fairs if, by way of set-off, they wished to sell bills on other centres where they had available coin. Arbitrage on the international exchange rates was always available to minimize the cost of international movements of money or to rake in speculative extras. The strong increase in the relative price of gold and the resultant possibilities of speculating on the gold–silver ratios also played a part. For each fair a small group of bankers of world stature accordingly negotiated around 1600 bills of an average value of more than 10 million *écus de marc*, of which about one third was mutually set off in the balance sheets, and the rest by *pagamento in balancio*. This was a remarkable result. The hegemony of Genoese banking over southern Europe led to a strong concentration of international payments and movements of money, thus achieving considerable set-offs. The permanent ties with commerce ensured that great services were rendered to merchants by way of setting-off and paying international commercial debts and achieving international movements of money and specie flows.

A second, technical, characteristic was the strengthening of control. The *banchieri di conto* formed only a limited group: forty to sixty in the heyday of the Genoese fairs at the end of the sixteenth and beginning of the seventeenth century. Only the *banchieri di conto* were allowed to participate in the acceptances, in fixing the *conto* and in negotiating new bills to compensate for *avanci* or *mancamenti*. In this way the setting-off of international payments came under the strict central control of a few Genoese technical bankers and under the authority of the Genoese Republic.

Finally, the Genoese fairs also laid the foundations for the development of a successful and stable money market in southern Europe. The safety of investments was guaranteed by the solid organization of the *foires de change*, by the extension of the practice of the *ricorsa* bill and not least by the stable value of the *écu de marc*. The development of the exchange rates of Besançon and Piacenza is a splendid illustration of this stability. During the inexorable weakening of the current moneys of account throughout Europe at the end of the sixteenth and beginning of the seventeenth century, the *écu de marc* of Besançon and Piacenza remained immovable, offering a safe possibility of investment without spectacular profits but with great stability. Here the south European merchant in need of money found major credit facilities: not only could he utilize the normal credit on bills through the intermediary of the merchant bankers, but in addition *ricorsa* bills drawn on the fairs, a form which facilitated the acquisition of credit in the medium term.

The *foires de change* of Besançon and Piacenza under the direction of the Genoese merchant bankers formed the apogee in the institutional development of banking and credit in southern Europe from the sixteenth to the beginning of the seventeenth century. They were also its finishing point; time would show that the possibilities of further refinement within the structures of the economy of southern Europe were finally exhausted.

(4) MODERN ENDORSEMENT AND DISCOUNT IN ANTWERP

In northwest Europe progress in financial techniques during the sixteenth century lay in the instrumental rather than the institutional field. Important innovations in the circulation of commercial instruments gradually became grouped round Antwerp's world trade and finance. The technical lead of the Italians in financial matters naturally had its influence on developments in northern Europe. Numerous Italian firms were established in Bruges and later in Antwerp. The many contacts with the south, including the Flemish commercial correspondents in Italy and Spain, also furthered the spread of Italian expertise in the north. The publication in Antwerp of J. Ympijn Christoffel's *Nieuwe Instructie...rekeninghe te houden nae die Italiaensche maniere* (1543) was the first indication that Antwerp had become a centre of commercial instruction under clear Italian influence.

The technical financial innovations in northwest Europe did not merely duplicate Italian practice. The progress in financial techniques, above all in Antwerp and later even more so in London, had its own specific nature; it was *sui generis* and formed the immediate basis for the modern discount and issuing banking systems. Indeed, at the beginning of the modern age the institutional and instrumental structure of north-west Europe was far from identical with that of the south. The Brabant fairs (Antwerp and Bergen-op-Zoom) and the Frankfurt *Messen* were no exception to this; they did, however, owe their pronounced expansion from the second half of the fifteenth century to the same commercial and financial circumstances that applied to Lyons and Castile. Moreover, they formed an ideal quarterly exchange point between north, east and south for international payments; but they never grew into real *foires de change* like those of south Europe. By the end of the sixteenth century, as far as periods of payments were concerned, there was in the north no further mention of fairs but merely of quarterly dates of payment.

The deposit and clearance banking system that already seemed well established at Bruges in money-changing circles in the fourteenth century did not expand any further in the north during the fifteenth and sixteenth centuries. On the contrary, the crisis that afflicted the European deposit and clearing bank system in the course of the fifteenth century proved to have inflicted greater damage in the north than in the south. Perhaps this was due to the more recent development and the more limited distribution of the deposit and clearing banks in the north, and to the obstructive policy of the dukes of Burgundy. Owing to their connection with the money-changer's function, the dukes regarded this kind of bank as a threat to their policy of monetary centralization, so that prohibitive ordinances were promulgated *inter alia* in 1433, 1467, 1480, 1488 and 1489. The few deposit and clearing banks once operating in Antwerp and Bergen-op-Zoom had disappeared before the end of the fifteenth century.

No obvious revival of the deposit and clearing banking system in the north followed during the commercial expansion at the beginning of the sixteenth century. In Antwerp, the metropolis of international trade and finance, deposit and clearing banks never took root as typical institutions. Of course, many money-changers or financial brokers gradually emerged as soon as the Antwerp money market gained in European stature, but nowhere were there real clearing banks. Only the slow rise of the *kassiersbedrijf* in Antwerp from the second third of the sixteenth century heralded a change for the future. From this time onwards, foreign trade in the Netherlands acquired a democratic nature, and many smaller domestic merchants began to engage in world trade by means of participations and commission. *Kassiers* (cashkeepers) with a good knowledge of financial techniques now began to keep cash for their merchant clientele, made payments and received money on behalf of their masters. The transition to the deposit and clearing bank system was certainly not difficult, and there are numerous indications that this step was taken more systematically during the last third of the century. But the commercial decline and the political and monetary unrest had already affected the Antwerp economy sufficiently to hamper a complete breakthrough. Not until the seventeenth century in Amsterdam was this cashkeepers' business to attain full development as a private deposit and clearing bank institution.

The bill of exchange was definitely not unknown in the north; on the contrary. But before 1550 the bill of exchange was certainly not yet the characteristic, dominant instrument for foreign trade. Within the Hanseatic League the bill of exchange remained marginal. From the second third of the sixteenth century and definitely from the second half of that century, use of the bill of exchange quickly became general in the north, including the Hanseatic towns and the Baltic. Even then the bill of exchange did not acquire a complete monopoly for foreign trade in the north and for a long time yet it had to face competition from other instruments, especially from promissory notes to bearer, or writings obligatory. Nevertheless, the Antwerp *Costuymen* are clear on the subject. The 1570 version devoted eight articles to writings obligatory and only three to bills; twelve years later (1582) the ratio was 10 to 11; finally, in the 1608 version 'writings obligatory' were given seventeen articles, as against seventy-seven for bills of exchange.

However important the bill of exchange might become for the foreign trade of northwest Europe, arbitrage on exchange rates between different centres and fairs was not an essential activity for firms in the north as it had been for the merchant bankers of the south since the late Middle Ages. In the north, the bill remained first and foremost an instrument for international payments and increasingly for international commercial credit. Arbitrage was not absent from this, but in general it remained subordinate to the commercial objectives of the bill.

The letter (or bill) obligatory, based on extension of payment, had from the late Middle Ages been the characteristic, dominant security in the foreign trade of the north. It continued to hold this position in the fifteenth and sixteenth centuries. The expansion of the Atlantic economy encouraged a wider spread of credit, by extension of payment, and a lengthening of the terms of credit, and moreover intensified the need to accelerate the circulation of money by making use of commercial and credit instruments. To achieve this object the instruments had to be negotiable. As early as the late Middle Ages promissory notes with a bearer's clause were regularly drawn up, but the brisk circulation of such writings obligatory continued to be hampered by the inadequate protection of the bearer. In addition, the deposit from fair to fair enjoyed increasing success in Antwerp from the second third of the sixteenth century. The influence of the Italians residing in Antwerp was obvious in this; the Imperial Edict of 1543, legally permitting loans at interest between merchants provided the maximum of 12 per cent per annum was not exceeded, also encouraged the spread of deposits from fair to fair, and also that of ordinary commercial loans without quarterly dates of payment.

In the budding new trading centres, of which there were so many in the north during the sixteenth century, prosecutions were legion; the merchants' circle was not as closed or intimate as in the traditional centres of the south; unknown, unreliable newcomers kept on turning up. Antwerp was the symbol of the rising commercial city of the north during the sixteenth century. Here for the first time concrete and successful attempts were made to simplify and safeguard the transfer of commercial and credit instruments.

The first step in this direction was the legal protection of the bearer of a writing obligatory with a bearer's clause. To be able to take a defaulting debtor to court the bearer of a writing obligatory, even if it carried a bearer's clause, had first either to obtain an explicit authority from the original creditor – an authority which incidentally could be revoked at any time – or to have an official transfer made by means of a formal *cessio*. A judicial verdict (*turba*) in Antwerp in 1507 granted the bearer of writings obligatory the same rights as the original creditor with regard to the prosecution of an insolvent debtor. Other towns like Bruges, Dordrecht and Utrecht followed Antwerp's example, and in 1537 an Imperial Edict made these more flexible rules of procedure applicable to the whole Netherlands.

The legal guarantees officially granted to the bearer gave a tremendous boost to the circulation from hand to hand of writings obligatory with a bearer's clause in Antwerp. Commercial correspondence and court records of the second and final third of the sixteenth century show that they were often transferred ten or even twenty times. Bills regularly contained the bearer's clause in the north and circulated from hand to hand. The concentration of payments at certain times of the day on the Antwerp Exchange – in 1531 a splendid new building had been opened for this – encouraged the use and circulation of the commercial and credit instruments. In particular the writings obligatory, with their long duration, were extremely suitable for circulation. As a result they functioned not only as a means of payment but furthered the set-off of debits and credits: the writing obligatory regularly circulated until the debtor finally received it himself in payment.

The concentration of payments on the Antwerp Exchange in the course of the sixteenth century also encouraged the international clearing of debits and credits. More than that, the Exchange was a relatively self-contained world of dealers and financiers, within which confidential relationships could systematically develop. Some firms were able to acquire such an image of financial strength and probity on the Exchange that their writings obligatory enjoyed increasing confidence and passed freely and smoothly from hand to hand. The *Fuggerbriefe* were a striking example of this in Antwerp. Thus the way was opened for the transferable promissory notes which were to have such a great future in the England of the seventeenth century.

Antwerp not only paved the way by improving the *legal* protection of bearers of writings obligatory; it also improved *financial* protection. As a result, technical progress gradually evolved from *transferability* to *negotiability*. The legal protection of the bearer contained a deceptive threat: the courts tended to regard all transfers from hand to hand as a *cessio* that relieved the transferring creditor of all responsibility. The greater legal protection of the bearer consequently implied a decrease in his financial security, particularly if he was less acquainted with the debtor. To eliminate this disadvantage, the Antwerp commercial world applied the principle of assignment to the circulation of writings obligatory with a bearer's clause. *Assignment* was an old way of getting third parties to pay debts. Assignment was commonly used in the late Middle Ages in local and commercial economies both in the north and the south; public authorities regularly utilized this technique to refer creditors for payment direct to customs farmers, stewards of estates, municipal treasuries etc. Assignment had an important legal characteristic: the assignor remained responsible for payment by the assignee until the creditor declared that he was entirely satisfied. Applied to the circulation from hand to hand of writings obligatory with a bearer's clause, assignment meant greater financial security for the bearer. In this way the various transferring creditors remained jointly responsible for payment. Antwerp merchant bankers such as Erasmus Schets urged the municipal authorities to persuade the government in Brussels to legalize assignment as financial protection in the transfer of commercial instruments to bearer. This was done by an Imperial Edict of 31 October 1541. Legalization was also closely defined in the Antwerp *Costuymen* compilation of 1608.[1] 'If anyone is referred by his debtor to another, to be paid by him, and so on from hand to hand to four or five persons and more, who all accept the transfer, and if he is not paid by the last one, all those to whom he has been referred have bound themselves to satisfy him.' It was a notable encouragement to a more confident atmosphere amongst businessmen.

Commercial correspondence, accounts, the manuals of business practice and even Tomasso Contarini before the Venetian Senate in 1585 all bear witness to the intensive use of the assignment principle at Antwerp in the circulation of commercial instruments to bearer during the course of the sixteenth century. Antwerp court records also regularly confirm the financial protection of the bearers in the event of assignment. In the Hanseatic towns and in England the writings obligatory likewise circulated with the bearer's clause and assignment was applied to these transfers.

In Antwerp, circulation from hand to hand was particularly intensive. The question of how the connection could be made between *intensive* circulation of instruments and the systematic application of the assignment principle to this therefore became an acute one for the first time in Antwerp. To be able to give concrete shape to the assignment principle in the brisk circulation from hand to hand of commercial instruments to bearer, it was necessary to find an appropriate formula by which the successive assignors remained known. Accounts often served as proof, if required, between merchants. Indications may also be found that in Antwerp an assignment note was attached to the instrument upon transfer. In Rouen and Lisbon, according to G. de Malynes, the assignments were officially noted in a municipal register, but that was a fairly cumbersome procedure.

The *endorsement* of writings obligatory as a designation of assignment occurred little, if at all, in the north during the sixteenth century. It is still unclear why this final step was not taken for writings obligatory in that century. Was it due to the established custom of always noting part-payments on the back of the writing obligatory? In England, in Normandy (Rouen) and in the Netherlands the term *endorsement* was in common use for this kind of entry ('which somme...is endorsed on

---

[1] 'Als ijmant bij sijnen schuldenaer op een anderen wort bewezen, om bij hem betaalt te worden, ende alsoo van handen tot handen voorts tot vier oft vijff persoenen ende meer, die de bewijsinge al aenveerden, indijen hij bij den lesten niet en wort betaelt, heeft tot sijne voldoeninge verbonden alle degene daerop hij bewesen is.' G. De Longé, *Coutumes du Pays et Duché de Brabant. Quartier d'Anvers.* IV: *Coutumes de la ville d'Anvers* (Brussels, 1874), 380, art. 14.

the backside of the bill in thandes of. . .').[1] Not all writings obligatory circulated equally briskly: it was logical that only those signed by trustworthy people passed quickly from hand to hand.

The situation was different with the bill of exchange. From the second half of the sixteenth century the use of bills penetrated international trade in northwest Europe. This breakthrough was largely determined by the broadening of the commercial horizon of the merchants from the northwest and by the multiplication of small foreign traders. However, both circumstances increased the risk of transfers. Payment of bills of exchange *in banco* was uncommon or unknown in the north, on account of the poor development of the clearing bank system in the course of the sixteenth century, so that the custom continued of effecting payment of bills by means of other (due) bills.[2] On the other hand the author of the manual *Tresoir van de Mate*, published in Amsterdam in 1590 (the author was probably an Antwerper), pointed to the risks run by bills of exchange, by reason of the simple bearer's clause (Gerard de Malynes was to stress this disadvantage again in his *Lex Mercatoria* in 1622). Consequently, everything converged here on a further formal development of the assignment, which, for the protection of bearers in the Netherlands, had already been explicitly laid down as a procedure in the edict of 1541 for the transfer of all commercial instruments, and which was already applicable in principle to the transfers from hand to hand of writings obligatory.

The first official formal regulation of the transfer of bills of exchange in the north may be found in the Antwerp *Costuymen* of 1608. So as to increase financial security for bearers, the *avallo* system was made obligatory in the transfer of bills: by this the successive assigning creditors all had to be mentioned by name *in* the bill and thus all remained responsible for ultimate payment to the last bearer. G. de Malynes recommended this system in his *Lex Mercatoria* of 1622 for application in England, but by then it had already been overtaken by events. The *avallo* system had the serious drawback that all the assignors had to be known beforehand; moreover, it was a kind of security bond, thus giving the bearer the right to demand payment from and sue the assignors *before* the principal debtor.

---

[1] J. Peele, *The Pathewaye to Perfectnes in the Accomptes of Debitour and Creditour* (London, 1569).

[2] Examples of these first, still primitive, forms of endorsement, applied to bills and cheques in the south, were found for Venice (1386), Prato (1394–1410), Florence (1430–94), Genoa (1459), Lyons (1519, 1537, 1547), Seville (1537), Medina del Campo (1561ff.). For a survey: R. de Roover, *The Rise and Decline of the Medici Bank (1397–1494)* (Harvard Studies in Business History, No. 21, Cambridge, Mass., 1963), 137–40; H. Lapeyre, 'Las origines del Endoso de letras de cambio en España', *Moneda y Credito: Revista de Economica*, LII (1952).

Antwerp commercial practice therefore evolved more in the direction of maintaining the specific assignment principle. Transfer by assignment was explicitly indicated on the back of the bill at the moment of issue: e.g. 'Received by me underwritten by Mr Robert Rug, whom I have assigned to receive it' (signed by W. Selby) (Antwerp specimen of 20 April 1611).[1] This was the birth of modern endorsement: now bills of exchange became not only more easily transferable, but also negotiable; in other words, the bearer had a greater financial security than the previous bearer, who remained jointly responsible for payment without being a surety in the strictly legal sense.

From the start of the seventeenth century the practice of endorsement developed quickly in Antwerp. R. de Roover and H. Lapeyre have pointed out that traces of modern endorsement may be found in Tuscany as early as the end of the sixteenth century; this may have acted as a model for Antwerp. But as yet bills of exchange were not circulating sufficiently widely in the south to make endorsement generally effective. Moreover, throughout the seventeenth century endorsement met with legislative opposition in Italy. At Antwerp, on the other hand, it was precisely the wide circulation from hand to hand of commercial instruments and of assignment that made the spread of endorsement so rapid and successful. From Antwerp the custom spread to the other commercial centres of northwest Europe. This process of diffusion evidently reached a climax in the second quarter of the seventeenth century. To judge by G. de Malynes's *Lex Mercatoria*, modern endorsement was not yet established in England. On the other hand, J. Marius, in his *Advice concerning Bils of Exchange*, published in England in 1651, could discuss modern endorsement in detail: in his examples Marius makes use of the more modern formula 'A or order', but the original instruction 'A or his assigns' was still of frequent occurrence; another proof of how firmly the negotiability of commercial instruments was rooted in the old technique of assignment.

Not only did Antwerp lay the foundations of modern endorsement, it also played an important part in the origin of modern discount (the surrender of a commercial title to a third party before the due date for a sum lower than the nominal value). The first example of modern discount in Antwerp was found in the Kitson Papers and related to the discounting of a writing obligatory in 1536.[2] It was still an exceptional

---

[1] R. de Roover, *L'évolution de la lettre de change, XIVe–XVIIIe siècles* (Paris, 1953), p. 155.

[2] Accounts by the agent of an English merchant at the fairs of Bergen-op-zoom and Antwerp: MS at the Cambridge University Library.

occurrence. The creditor usually kept the writings obligatory and bills of exchange in his portfolio until the due date. If the creditor suddenly needed cash, he would ask one or more debtors to repay their debt earlier with a *rabat* (rebate): this was still the old procedure that had already been in common use in the Middle Ages (the traditional discount).

The vigorous growth of the Antwerp money market and the intensive circulation of commercial instruments from hand to hand in the course of the sixteenth century were to create the conditions for the spread of modern discount. The money-dealers, *faisant des marchandises d'argent les donnant à gaing et frait*, had acquired an important place for themselves on the Antwerp Exchange, providing credit from fair to fair. It had become customary on the Antwerp Exchange to pay debts by the transfer of due writings obligatory or due bills of exchange, both with a bearer's clause. But during times of *strettezza*, creditors would often opt for cash. The money-dealers profited from this by buying up due commercial instruments, both bills and writings obligatory, for cash at a premium. This was not yet modern discount, but rather a special premium for purchases in hard cash. Nevertheless, payment was also being increasingly made on the Exchange in instruments not yet due, usually writings obligatory to bearer. Once the money-dealers began to buy up these unexpired instruments as well, modern discount was born. The accounts of Antwerp firms and the Antwerp manuals on accounting techniques contain abundant evidence of this modern discount during the second half of the sixteenth century.[1] By the end of that century modern discount was also in use in Hamburg, presumably under the influence of refugee Flemish merchants.

Until that happened, modern discount both in Antwerp and Hamburg still often related to writings obligatory with a bearer's clause and not to bills of exchange. It could hardly have been otherwise: the writings obligatory usually had a long term to run, sometimes up to 12 months or more, so that the need for quick encashment was often quite sharply felt.[2] However, the general introduction of the bill of exchange into northwest Europe was also to foster the discounting of bills. According to the evidence of municipal ordinances between 1560

---

[1] Cashbook of J. Moriel, Antwerp: 14.IX.1567: 'Jay achepté de Mathias Zimmerman une chedulle de Jehan Ployart de £320.—, quy est a payer adi 20 octobre prochain, pour la mesure jay payé comptant £306.—(quoted by J. G. Da Silva, *Banque et crédit en Italie*, p. 531). Examples in manuals on bookkeeping, *inter alia* in V. Mennher, *Praitique brifue pour cyfrer et tenir liures de comptes touchant le principal train de marchandises* (Antwerp, 1550); H. L. V. De Groote, 'De "arithmétique" van Mellema', *Scientiarum Historia*, v (1963).

[2] W. Brulez, *De Firma Della Faille en de internationale handel van Vlaamse firma's in de 16e eeuw* (Brussels, 1959), pp. 403–4.

and 1600, the custom of money-dealers and cashkeepers was to buy up bills for cash at a premium during periods of *strettezza* on the Antwerp Exchange. This had become so common that the distinction between due and unexpired bills no longer remained relevant. In March 1560, the bills of exchange which arrived in Antwerp from Lyons and Besançon for payment at the next fair in May were promptly bought for cash at a premium by the money-dealers. This was already a clear instance of modern discount banking. Until *c.* 1600 it was only an occasional resort, for example when the money market was strained. Not until after 1600 was modern discount in Antwerp to assume a regular character; the spread of endorsement and the permanent prosperity of banking business during the first half of the seventeenth century certainly contributed to this. Modern discount banking had thus become a fact of economic life.

The new Antwerp Exchange, opened in 1531, was originally intended for both commercial and financial transactions. But gradually it developed into a real monetary and financial exchange. Commercial contracts and agreements were increasingly concluded on the 'English Exchange', which opened one hour before the monetary exchange. This gradual separation of trade from finance created a favourable context for the technical development of financial instruments. The Exchange had so powerful an image that in 1571 Thomas Gresham established a similar Exchange in Lombard Street, London, modelled precisely on Antwerp.

The concentration of financial transactions on the Antwerp Exchange also furthered speculation. Speculation was in no way new, even in the northern towns, but on the Antwerp Exchange it acquired a more systematic and organized character, though still closely bound up with the medieval traditions of gambling. Wagers, often connected with the conclusion of commercial or financial transactions, were entered into on the safe return of ships, on the possibility of Philip II visiting the Netherlands, on the sex of children as yet unborn etc. Lotteries, both private and public, were also extremely popular, and were submitted as early as 1524 to imperial approval to prevent abuse.

In this speculative atmosphere transactions in 'futures' gradually developed. First came fixed purchases for future delivery: purchasers bought goods to be paid for later and, speculating on the rise in prices before the due date, sold the goods and pocketed the difference in price; conversely, vendors speculated on a fall in prices (difference dealing). Where prices were subject to considerable fluctuations (such as grain, salt and herring) this form of speculation was common. In addition, *premium transactions* were already popular in Antwerp, for example for the purchase of herrings before they had been caught. The buyer made a contract for future delivery at a fixed price, but with the condition that he could reconsider after two or three months: he could then withdraw from the contract provided that he paid a premium to the vendor (*stellegelt*).[1] Speculators gambled on the rise or fall of the exchange rates at the Castilian or Lyons fairs, reserving the right to pay premiums. The development of marine insurance in Antwerp was likewise closely bound up with speculation. Many merchants, including the smallest ones, participated in marine insurance, speculating on possible profit by pocketing part of the insurance premium. A few specialized insurance firms were already calculating risks on presumptions of probability during the sixteenth century. They were often disappointed.

The danger that this speculative atmosphere would give the Antwerp Exchange a reputation for instability was not imaginary: *per esser la Borsa chomo un bosco*, wrote the Antwerp merchant Daniël van der Molen in 1541. Imperial edicts tried to regulate the financial activities of the Antwerp Exchange from the 1530s and 1540s. Speculation gradually assumed the form of normal trade.

The conclusion is inescapable; the sixteenth century was a time of great financial progress in northwest Europe. It was clearly visible in all the growing commercial centres of the north, but nowhere was renovation so intense as at Antwerp, the great metropolis of trade and finance in the north. The intensified circulation of commercial instruments to bearer opened the way for the later success of promissory notes. Assignment laid the foundations for the later breakthrough of modern endorsement. The development of the cashkeepers' business and the discounting of writings obligatory and of bills of exchange prepared the way for modern discount banking. These were crucial innovations in the field of financial instruments which, backed by the success of the Antwerp Exchange, pointed directly towards further institutional progress in following centuries.

(5) THE INDIAN SUMMER OF THE SOUTH DURING THE SEVENTEENTH CENTURY

The great merchant bankers of the south were increasingly involved during the sixteenth and seventeenth centuries in public finance. Public loans in the form of *asiento* contracts were, however, closely bound up with commercial activities: Portuguese or Italian merchants who had credit balances originating in trade with the Netherlands or Germany made these available to the local representative of the Spanish govern-

---

[1] *Tresoir vande maten, van gewichten, van cooren, lande, vande elle ende natte mate, oock vanden gelde ende wissel* (Amsterdam, 1590), p. 197.

ment, receiving in return specie in Lisbon, Seville, Leghorn or Venice. Foreign trade, international finance, arbitrage and public credit thus spread a wide net of interdependent relations over the economies of southern and northwest Europe.

As long as Genoese high finance was able to maintain its ascendancy in the *asiento* contracts between Spain, Italy and the Netherlands, the fairs of payment (*foires de change*) controlled by Genoa continued to play a leading part in European money movements. An essential aspect of this Genoese financial hegemony was still the integration of Italian foreign trade in the system of the fairs of payment: thus the Genoese had at their disposal a volume of floating commercial capital which helped to absorb the spasmodic development of Spanish government finance. The commercial efflorescence of Venice, the vigorous rise of Leghorn and the growing importance of Naples were still safe guarantees of this system at the beginning of the seventeenth century.

The great Italian depression around 1620 brought about an abrupt change. Foreign trade, including that of Venice, suffered severely, with fatal repercussions on the *foires de change*. In 1622 the Genoese bankers moved their fairs of payment to Novi (on the Ligurian coast), while the Milanese and Tuscan bankers continued to meet at Piacenza, and the Venetian bankers turned to the Verona fairs. A series of secessions followed, which alienated foreign trade from international finance and destroyed the geographical unity of former times. In 1695 came a final attempt at reorganization. The Italian fairs of payment were regrouped at Santa Margharita, Rapallo etc., but by then the heyday of Italian banking was already over. The collapse of Spanish hegemony was another important factor in the decline of Italian banking. The Portuguese merchant bankers, mostly of Jewish origin, strengthened their position in Spain, especially after the amnesty decree of 16 January 1604, which noticeably improved their freedom of movement in the Iberian peninsula. They penetrated the big Andalusian commercial centres, like Seville, Cadiz and San Lucan de Barramuda. They became stewards to the Spanish grandees and financed the development of a sugar empire in Brazil. Through their business relations and weight of numbers in Antwerp, Amsterdam, London and other northern centres, the Portuguese profited especially from the vigorous development which characterized the Atlantic economy in the first half of the seventeenth century. Finally, they found support from Duke Olivares, the leader of Spanish world policy under Philip IV, who was anxious to use their commercial and financial rise to break Genoese control of Spanish government finance. With the *Medio General* of 1627, Olivares's dream came true, and Portuguese merchant bankers came increasingly to the fore in the *asiento* contracts.

In Italy the fairs of payment survived until the mid eighteenth century. The technical refinements introduced during the previous century to absorb the expansion of world trade and international public finance now came to serve a conservative money market geared to Italian requirements. After 1627 the Italian bankers had freed themselves from the grip of Spanish national bankruptcies, and used the fairs of payment solely for arbitrage on international exchange rates in order to finance interregional or international movements of money by the system of *pagamento in balancio*, and to furnish short- or medium-term credits by means of the *ricorsa* bills. The credit function increasingly got the upper hand of the payment function through the *pagamento in balancio* and the *ricorsa* bill.

The Italian fairs of payment thus evolved into institutions aimed at security for the investment of capital. Investments were guaranteed by the system of the *scudi di marche* against possible devaluations of the current money of account,[1] while the control of the exchange rate (*conto*) ensured that interest played a part in exchange operations. Though the interest rate may not have been particularly high, the return was safe. On the other hand, in the long term the purchasing power of the invested capital increased, because from the second quarter of the seventeenth century prices (expressed in *scudi di marche*) declined. Institutions and religious communities, trustees of minors' inheritances and administrators of great fortunes therefore preferred, for safety's sake, to entrust their liquid resources to the merchant bankers active at the fairs of payment.

Meanwhile, a new generation of merchant bankers was developing in Geneva.[2] Here, in this Protestant Rome, numerous Italian refugees had settled in the sixteenth and seventeenth centuries, creating prosperity not only for the silk industry but also for foreign trade. From 1650 the working of precious metals developed into *la grande fabrique*: watchmaking, jewellery and gilding underwent a spectacular expansion. The revocation of the Edict of Nantes in 1685 by Louis XIV brought in a final wave of dynamic immigrants, the French Huguenots,

---

[1] Through the tie with the gold *écus* the value of the *scudi di marche* was self-evidently determined in part by the fluctuations in the world price of gold: this rose until the end of the seventeenth century, after which it grudgingly lost ground to silver (from 1671, in addition to the gold *écus* of Spain, Genoa, Venice, Naples, Florence and Piacenza, the silver *genovina* was therefore also accepted in payment, so that from then on the world price of silver also affected the value of the *scudi di marche*). In addition the *scudi di marche*, as a standard of exchange, were subject to higher or lower valuations in terms of foreign rates of exchange: such fluctuations also reflected domestic or foreign confidence or lack of confidence in the *scudi di marche*. (For further details: J. G. Da Silva, *Banque et crédit en Italie*, pp. 283–398.)

[2] H. Lüthy, *La Banque Protestante en France*. 1: *1685–1730* (Paris, 1959), 37–49.

giving a major fillip to trade and industry. The second rise of banking in Geneva must be considered in the light of this atmosphere of expansion: finance was stimulated by the successes of trade and industry and became in turn the driving force of further growth in both sectors.

In the seventeenth century the new Genevan banking system made its entrée in the European world of finance by way of the Lyons fairs of payment. Though Lyons' world trade had clearly been in decline since the end of the sixteenth century, the city still remained a leading centre of international money and exchange throughout the seventeenth century. The weakened position of Piacenza after 1620 benefited Lyons which again became an essential southern base for the money markets of the north – Amsterdam, Hamburg and London. The world trade of Marseilles, Geneva, Beaucaire and Saint Gallen was financed through the Lyons fairs of payment. The Swiss and Geneva merchant bankers were firmly established in Lyons, linking it with the other international money markets.

After 1685, when the revocation of the Edict of Nantes left a yawning gap in Paris banking, hitherto largely Protestant, the Swiss and Geneva bankers' colonies of Lyons opened branches in Paris. Together with establishments from Paris, the Swiss and Geneva branches in Paris developed into the *Banque protestante*. The Paris banking system of the eighteenth century thus evolved into an internationally oriented *haute finance* of cosmopolitan stature. Characteristic was not only the rapid growth of the number of banks in Paris, but also the geographical spread through branches, agents and correspondents. Banking activity was also different: the traditional arbitrage in international exchange rates remained paramount, but discounting, deposit banking and loans at interest became typical banking phenomena. Finally, banking in Geneva and Paris remained very much a family business: thanks to the prevailing custom of intermarriage the world of the merchant bankers remained closed and homogeneous.

Meanwhile, the French monarchy had dragged the Lyons fairs of payment down with it into the disasters of its war policy. The great financial depression of 1709 was fatal to Lyons. By 1720 the international importance of the fairs of exchange was at an end.

(6) OLD AND NEW IN AMSTERDAM

The ties between Antwerp and Amsterdam were not broken by the Netherlands revolt. Antwerp merchants emigrated in large numbers to Amsterdam, especially after 1585, and through their manifold contacts with those who had remained behind in the south they ensured the lasting importance of Antwerp as a *Dispositionsplatz*. In its turn, Amsterdam foreign trade was enabled to develop in the direction of Spain and Portugal. In 1597 and 1613 new editions of the *Antwerpse Costuymen* were published in Amsterdam. Antwerp exchange law and financial techniques were commonly applied in Amsterdam, as they were in Middelburg and Rotterdam. Oral assignment or assignment by means of circulation from hand to hand of writings obligatory or of bills with a bearer's clause was common in Amsterdam around 1600 (*totten sevenden ende meerdere man*; 'up to seven and more people'). The cash-keepers' business which had originated in Antwerp, and was closely geared to the circulation of commercial instruments, attained its fullest development in Amsterdam. The *kassiers* kept cash for a whole series of merchant clients, who assigned payments to their balances with the cashkeepers. If creditor and debtor happened to be clients of the same cashkeeper, settlement was simple. If not, the cashkeeper paid in cash, or by means of instruments soon becoming due or already due and owed by him or by his clients (in other words, by way of assignment to his own personal claims or to balances claimable by the cashkeeper, for his clients' account). If a merchant customer was short of funds, the cashkeeper would occasionally make an advance on current account or in specie; if the money market was strained, it might happen that the cashkeeper would buy up the claims of his clients in the form of com-mercial instruments for hard cash at a premium. These embryonic forms of clearing, deposit and discount banking, already discernible in Antwerp from the second half of the sixteenth century, developed fur-ther in the commercial towns of the northern Netherlands after 1585. But it was not long before official measures were taken to check the growth of private cashkeeping. From the beginning of the seventeenth century, edicts of the States-General and municipal ordinances of Amsterdam, Middelburg and other places restricted or forbade assign-ments and regulated or prohibited the cashkeepers' business.

The bans had little effect except to provoke violent protests from the merchants (e.g. the protest by 84 Amsterdam merchants in 1608) while oral assignment or assignment by the circulation of instruments from hand to hand and the cashkeepers' business continued to perform an essential function in accelerating the circulation of money. The authori-ties were aware of the importance of this monetary function of cash-keepers and money-changers, but at the same time were convinced that cashkeepers and money-changers were the cause of the instability of the circulating silver medium and of the money of account. Indeed, the rates of the large silver coins always rose beyond the level per-mitted by the official rates, and cashkeepers and money-changers were well placed to isolate the best specie from the current circulation and to sell it back to the merchants at a premium. Cashkeepers and money-changers had been given official permission in 1595 (confirmed by general edicts in 1603 and 1606) to sell good specie in Amsterdam at a premium of not more than 1¼ per cent, but premiums regularly exceeded this maximum.

The failure of the authorities to win effective control over money-changing and cashkeeping led to the alternative of the *Amsterdamsche Wisselbank* (Amsterdam Exchange Bank), which opened on 31 January 1609. Control now made way for substitution: the municipal exchange bank was to take the place of the private money-changers and cash-keepers, both of which professions were for a time officially abolished in 1609. At the same time, the chain payments with instruments or payments by successive oral assignments were to be replaced by one single assignment, *viz.* the one to the Exchange Bank. The new system proved so effective that the English Merchant Adventurers would not set up an establishment anywhere unless a local *Wisselbank* was founded there on the model of the *Amsterdamsche Wisselbank*. This led to the foundation of Exchange Banks in Middelburg (1616), Hamburg (1619), Delft (1621) and Rotterdam (1635).

The Amsterdam Exchange Bank followed the rules of the Venetian *Banco della Piazza di Rialto* as its model. The other exchange banks in the north emulated Amsterdam's example. The city of Amsterdam made itself liable for the deposits, and the account-holder could at all times enjoy the free disposal of his balance, either by transfer to a third party's account or by payment in specie. All the merchant had to do was to hand in personally an assignment note made out in a specific name. If the beneficiary did not have an account with the bank, the sum was debited to the client to whom the receipted assignment note was sent: the beneficiary could then come and collect the sum of money from the bank by means of this note. It was obligatory for merchants to make all bills with a value greater than 600 guilders payable via the bank. All banking services and transfers were performed free of charge (at least until 1683). Overdrawing was forbidden, so that in principle all deposits remained physically present in the bank vaults. Only large gold and silver coins of the correct weight were accepted at their official rate on deposit by the Exchange Bank. All other coins or precious metals deposited were estimated by a bank assayer at their actual bullion value and credited accordingly. When making payment in specie the Exchange Bank undertook to issue only large gold or silver coins of the correct weight (including gold ducats and silver *rijks-daalders* or *leeuwendaalders*; rix dollars and lion dollars) at fixed rates: these became the celebrated 'trade coins' (*negotiepenningen*), intended not only for the domestic market but increasingly for export to the Baltic, the Levant and the Far East.

The concern of the exchange banks always to make available to commerce sound large coins at fixed rates led in the United Provinces to a double system of moneys of account – the Dutch bank guilder and the Dutch current guilder. The reason for this was the decline in the quality of smaller silver coinage and the consequent fall in value of the current money of account. Sound Dutch *rijksdaalders* and *leeuwendaalders* registered by the banks – sometimes at a small premium – paid out at the official rate of 50 *stuivers*, disappeared from daily circulation because they were undervalued and were henceforth dealt in exclusively as trade coins at the official (bank money) rate. The loss in current money of account suffered by a purchaser of trade coins at the bank was accepted as a premium to be paid for obtaining sound export specie.[1]

Meanwhile the lighter *kruisdaalders* and *ducatons* of the southern Netherlands penetrated Holland and filled the gap in Dutch current circulation of large silver coins. The successful penetration of the *kruisdaalders* or *patacons* was due to the fact that they circulated in Holland at a rate of 50 *stuivers*, too high by comparison with the official rates of the better Dutch *rijksdaalders* (which stood also at 50 *stuivers*) but reflecting the real value of Dutch basic silver coinage and of Dutch current money of account. Since they were not at first accepted by the exchange banks as official coins, the *kruisdaalders* or *patacons* kept out of the way of the banks and thus maintained their strong position in current large silver coins circulation. By 1640 the exchange banks were compelled to accept the *patacons* of the southern Netherlands as specie on deposit; soon they too were being sold by the banks as trade coins. The fiction of the official rates, however, continued to be maintained, *viz.* 48 *stuivers* for the *patacons* as against 50 *stuivers* for the superior *rijksdaalders*.[2] An additional argument for maintaining the official rates was the fact that the *patacons* were still effectively circulating in the south for 48 *stuivers*, so that with these rates the unity of the current money of account in the north and south was preserved. A double system of moneys of account came thus into being in the north, *viz.* the Dutch bank guilder and the Dutch current guilder. The bank guilder (of 20 *stuivers*) had consequently become a money of account, whose value was determined fundamentally by the combined silver content

---

[1] If a merchant deposited currently circulating specie in the bank to increase his current bank account, this deposit was evaluated by the bank assayer on its actual bullion value, in proportion to the official precious metal weight of the coins in question.

[2] The official rate of the *patacon* was initially fixed at 47 *stuivers*: this was even a relative undervaluation vis-à-vis the official rate of the *rijksdaalder*, with the obvious intention of keeping the *patacons* out of Holland. The Exchange Bank, which was allowed to give a premium when buying up large species, utilized this right to acquire the *patacons* at 48 *stuivers* (for a time even at 49 *stuivers*).

of the *rijksdaalders, leeuwendaalders, patacons* and *ducatons*.[1] Against this stood the current guilder (of 20 *stuivers*), whose value was basically determined by the metal content of the smaller silver coinage.

This state of affairs changed with the Coinage Ordinance of 1659: henceforth the ratio between bank guilder and current guilder in the north was officially fixed at 48:50 or 100:104$\frac{5}{24}$. Initially the bank guilder, supported by the newly issued lighter large coins, *viz.* the silver ducats and *ryders*, maintained the lead in the valuation of the two systems of moneys of account. But soon the current guilder gained the upper hand and the bank guilder, as a money of account, became simply a satellite of the current guilder; in other words, the metallic value of the bank guilder became dependent on that of the current guilder, the latter money of account being determined by the normally circulating silver coinage.[2] Fortunately, the reorganization of the coinage in the United Provinces was already well advanced by this time: from 1694 the silver guilder and three-guilder piece became the standard coins for current money, so that in the sphere of the money of account the dominance of the current guilder over the bank guilder was no longer a disadvantage.

The Dutch exchange banks were not able to attain their first objective, *viz.* the immediate reorganization of the monetary circulation, by eliminating the rises in the rates of the large coins. But the advent of the bank guilder, even though it evolved after 1659 into a money of account undoubtedly made a major contribution to the stabilization of the Dutch monetary system in the course of the seventeenth century.

More successful in the short term was the influence of the Dutch exchange banks in the field of clearing operations and, for the Amsterdam Exchange Bank in particular, in the field of international payments. The obligation to settle all bills above the value of 600 guilders through the Amsterdam Exchange Bank led most merchants to open an account there. The number of account-holders grew quickly, passing the two thousand mark around 1660. In this way the Amster-

---

[1] For the difference between the two kinds of moneys of account, see above, pp. 290–4.

[2] In 1659 the Republic wanted to eliminate the *patacons* and *ducatons* for good from circulation in the north, and for this purpose issued lighter large coins, the silver ducats and *ryders*, at the same rates as the heavier *patacons* and *ducatons*. The operation succeeded, so that the silver ducats and *ryders* conquered current circulation and gradually also gained the upper hand as trade coins. As their silver content was approximately 5 per cent lighter than that of the *patacons* and *ducatons*, the change meant a devaluation of the bank guilder by about 5 per cent. The undervaluation affected not only the *patacons* and *ducatons* but also the smaller silver coinage, which likewise disappeared from circulation. When the latter, by elimination of the better coins, had adjusted to the new situation, the current circulation, and – connected with this – the current guilder, again set the tone.

dam Exchange Bank grew into the principal banker for regional commerce: all important transactions were settled by transfer from one account to another. The increasing confidence in the stability of the bank guilder and the spectacular expansion of Amsterdam's world trade together gave the Exchange Bank an international dimension. Increasingly, international commercial transactions, even if they had come about outside Amsterdam and without Dutch intervention, were made payable by bills on the Amsterdam Bank. Most large firms of merchants kept guilder balances with the Amsterdam Exchange Bank and settled their international debts with them. In similar fashion international transfers of capital were arranged. Through this concentration of international payments the Amsterdam Exchange Bank grew in the course of the seventeenth century into a central clearing house of world stature, where set-offs were made on a multilateral basis, and where the bank guilder served as convertible key currency.

In addition to the triple monetary function, *viz*. stable bank money, flexible transfers and multilateral clearing of international payments, the Dutch exchange banks also performed an important exchange function in the course of the seventeenth century: they made trade coins (*negotiepenningen*) of guaranteed quality available to the international community of merchants. In the widespread monetary chaos at the end of the sixteenth and beginning of the seventeenth century this certainly acted as an impetus to world trade, especially that part of it which needed to be financed in hard cash. Initially, these trade coins were most successful in financing the Dutch *moedernegotie* with the Baltic; Spanish rials of eight (*reales de a ocho*) still predominated in trade with the Levant and the Far East. But gradually the Dutch *rijksdaalders* and *leeuwendaalders*, the Flemish *patacons* and *ducatons* and finally the Dutch *rijders* and *ducats* penetrated these regions too.

A third function performed by the Dutch exchange banks was the provision of credit. Under its statutes, the Amsterdam Exchange Bank was not allowed to grant credit, but it made a series of exceptions to this rule. In its earliest days it granted several credits to the Provincial States of Holland and to the Count of East Friesland, to a number of masters of the mint and to the Amsterdam *Bank van Leening*, which had been founded in 1614 to grant loans to merchants on guarantee of stocks and other security. But all these credits remained fairly limited. Two other important borrowers were the Dutch East India Company and the Municipal Treasury. From the foundation of the Exchange Bank (*Wisselbank*) the former regularly received large advances (known as *anticipatiepenningen*) for fitting out its fleets. The Municipal Treasury was also the recipient of large credits, especially from the second half of the seventeenth century.

The fourth and last function of the exchange banks consisted in the trade in precious metals. The sale of precious metals to the mints was at first mainly done through the exchange banks. The Amsterdam Exchange Bank had a particularly strong position in this field. The merchants preferred the mediation of the Amsterdam Bank to the direct delivery of precious metal to the Masters of the Mint, since the Bank was always well stocked with various kinds of trade coins and thus could give a more rapid service than the Masters of the Mint. The fact that after 1648, 30 to 50 escorted ships, with specie, precious metals and other goods on board, sailed every year from Cadiz to Amsterdam gives clear proof of the Amsterdam precious metal trade. But even then the private cashkeepers and specie dealers were taking over the job of middleman between merchants and Masters of the Mint in dealings in trade coins.

To give a new impulse to the precious metal trade of the Amsterdam Exchange Bank, a city ordinance of 5 January 1683 allowed the Bank to advance money on the security of specie. The account of the merchant who deposited specie as security was credited with its value, provided that he paid a small custody fee every six months. He was also given a certificate (*recepis*) in his name with a designation of the specie deposited (consequently, there were Dutch ducat notes, French Louis certificates etc.). These were negotiable, and the holder could at all times collect from the Bank without any formality the specie stated on the *recepis*, provided that the custody fee had been paid and that the account of the original depositor was debited for the amount of specie collected or had been settled by repayment of bank money to the extent that the account had meanwhile been completely used for payments.

The new system was a great success. As well as Dutch trade coins, all the large European coins, both gold and silver, were now playing an intensive part in the specie trade of the Amsterdam Exchange Bank. Thus in 1714–15 about one million French *pistoles* were deposited as security in the Bank. Moreover, from 1763 precious metal in bullion form was accepted on deposit as security. An important result of the specie deposits was that merchants no longer withdrew their bank accounts in hard cash; it was now cheaper to buy a *recepis* on the Exchange. From this custom arose the factual inconvertibility of bank money, and hence the danger of greater fluctuations in the rate of bank money as against current money. To avoid this, the Bank management proceeded in the course of the eighteenth century to repurchase bank money when the premium of the bank guilder vis-à-vis the current guilder on the free market fell below $4\frac{1}{4}$ per cent, and to sell bank money when the premium rose above $4\frac{7}{8}$ per cent.

The success of specie deposits as security was of decisive importance to the further expansion of Amsterdam's commerce and finance. It ensured that Amsterdam was to remain during the eighteenth century the principal precious metal and specie market in the world, even for gold from Brazil, which entered Europe via Portugal and London. The Amsterdam Exchange Bank became an enormous storehouse from which all the desired international specie could be obtained immediately and flexibly. The precious metal business further endowed Amsterdam's international exchange business with a special advantage. Amsterdam exchange rates became uncommonly stable: the specie points drew closer together, because in Amsterdam the costs of replacing bills of exchange by a shipment of precious metals in any desired coinage were much reduced. Further, the immediate availability of abundant specie was an ideal condition for the discounting of bills and other credit operations. The vitality of Amsterdam money and credit during the eighteenth century was therefore largely dependent upon the precious metals and specie trade, in which the Amsterdam Exchange Bank was a major participant.

Indeed, during the eighteenth century the specie trade came to be the only major surviving function of the Amsterdam Bank with its vitality intact. Banking functions had passed to the private banks. Permitted to operate again in 1621, the private cashkeepers of Amsterdam began to play an important role from the 1640s, especially with the advent of double money of account. To save the merchants time and trouble, the private cashkeepers became dealers in bank money of account against current money of account,[1] and by this detour, dealers in trade coins (*negotiepenningen*) too. When current money and bank money were linked together in 1659 in a fixed ratio of $100:104\frac{5}{24}$, the specific advantage of the stable bank guilder vis-à-vis the possibly unstable current guilder disappeared and transactions in current money of account gradually began to gain ground. Even bills concluded in current money of account rapidly increased in number. Since the Amsterdam Exchange Bank kept exclusively to the bank guilder,[2] the

[1] J. G. van Dillen, 'Oprichting en functie der Amsterdamsche Wisselbank in de zeventiende eeuw, 1609–1686', *Mensen en Achtergronden. Studies uitgegeven ter gelegenheid van de tachtigste verjaardag van de schrijver* (Groningen, 1964), pp. 336–384. Additional profits from speculation were also possible for the cashkeepers: if the bank money premium was low, it was profitable to buy bank money with current money; if, on the other hand, the bank money premium was a high one, profit could be made by converting bank money into current money.

[2] The exchange banks of Middelburg and Rotterdam had introduced the two money of account systems into their bookkeeping in 1641 and 1645 respectively. Cf. Z. W. Sneller, *Rotterdams Bedrijfsleven in het Verleden* (Amsterdam, 1940), pp. 139–42. Phoonsen also proposed this in 1677 with respect to the Amsterdam Exchange

private cashkeepers came to monopolize cash and exchange transactions in current money of account. In this way the private cashkeepers developed into private deposit and clearing banks for transactions in current money of account. When they also introduced systematic clearing of their mutual accounts in the course of the eighteenth century, the Amsterdam cashkeepers' activities grew into one large banking system for all business transacted in current money of account. The fact that the number of account-holders and the amounts deposited in the Amsterdam Exchange Bank did not increase between 1660 and the introduction of the deposit of specie as security must certainly be ascribed to this momentum of the cashkeeping business.

The cashkeepers also filled a second lacuna of the Amsterdam Exchange Bank: the full-scale provision of credit. While the statutes of the bank forbade the overdrawing of accounts and the prohibition was strictly enforced on its merchant clients, the cashkeepers were already allowing their clients regular credit in current money of account during the seventeenth century. Usually this was book credit, advances on security deposited or discounting of bills; cash credits were also frequent. In the eighteenth century, cashkeepers' promissory notes and receipts (cheques or assignments to a deposit with a given banker) were widespread.

The banking business in Amsterdam was not confined to the *Wisselbank* and the cashkeepers. Many successful private merchants performed financial functions. Jews of German or Polish origin concentrated on the specie trade and were thus money-changers. The Portuguese Jews were specialists in the securities business. Finally, there were great merchant bankers, like the Hopes, Cliffords or Pels, who played a large part in the specie, exchange and securities trade and gradually came to monopolize the issue of international loans.

Whilst one cannot speak of a total separation of functions between the various groups of Amsterdam financiers, it is clear that the great merchant bankers played a predominant role in the arbitrage and exchange business from the seventeenth century onwards. This specialization followed from their commercial activities. The merchant bankers had commercial correspondents all over the world, and the increasing concentration of international payments in Amsterdam meant that these agents acted as Amsterdam correspondents for numerous foreign firms. They not only handled bills between Amsterdam and foreign countries but also exchange operations between various European centres carried on through the Amsterdam exchange market.

Bank, but in vain. Cf. J. G. van Dillen, 'Een boek van Phoonsen over de Amsterdamsche Wisselbank', *Economisch-Historisch Jaarboek*, VII (1921), 30 f.

If an Antwerp merchant wanted to draw a bill on his correspondent in Cadiz and found no takers in Antwerp, he would draw up the bill to the order of his Amsterdam correspondent, and send it to him with the request that he negotiate it by endorsement in favour of a beneficiary in Cadiz. Conversely, a transfer from Cadiz to Antwerp could go via Amsterdam, even if the party concerned was domiciled in London, Paris, or Lyons: the remitter then bought a bill payable in Amsterdam to the order of the Antwerp firm to which he wanted to transfer the money; if the person concerned was a London merchant, the bill was sent there for acceptance; in the process of acceptance the London merchant made the bill payable through his correspondent in Amsterdam or direct at the Amsterdam Exchange Bank. The Antwerp beneficiary endorsed the bill to the order of his Amsterdam correspondent or in the Exchange Bank and asked that the amount be credited to his current account.[1]

It can be inferred from Van Velden's manual (*Fondement van de Wisselhandeling*, Amsterdam, 1629) that during the first half of the seventeenth century the Amsterdam merchant bankers, in addition to trading in bills and making loans at interest, still regularly granted loans in the form of bills at par on Antwerp and Hamburg up to 22–26–30 weeks with a return at 5–7 per cent. Money would be borrowed, e.g. in the form of bills on the next Frankfurt fair, with return at exchange rates fixed in advance, and without any document sent to the Frankfurt fair itself. Inland bills with the rates expressed in a discount against par, already common between Antwerp and Lille in the sixteenth century, received a tremendous fillip in the seventeenth century from the intense traffic in bills between Amsterdam, Antwerp and Lille. Letters of credit were also common: by means of them a merchant could open a credit with his foreign correspondent for the benefit of a third party. Travelling dealers thus no longer needed to carry money with them: with the aid of a letter of credit, Dutch business associates or customers of an Amsterdam banker could draw money in China from correspondents of a merchant banker residing in Canton.

From about 1700 acceptance credit operations became a profitable branch of Amsterdam business. The acceptance banker was prepared to accept bills of exchange which the creditors or commission agents of his client drew on him, on condition that the client ensured that there were sufficient funds in the bank on the due date. Meanwhile the creditor or commission agent could discount the bill and get immediate cash. Gradually it also became the custom for the client himself to draw a bill on his banker and thus acquire the necessary funds by discount,

[1] J. Everaert, *De internationale en koloniale handel der Vlaamse firma's te Cadiz, 1670–1700* (Bruges, 1973), pp. 564–7.

either for cash payment of imports or, in the case of exports, in anticipation of payment by the foreign buyer.

The world position of the Amsterdam bankers ensured that not only
Amsterdam's own foreign trade but soon the international trade of
London, Hamburg and other cities was largely financed by Amsterdam
acceptance credit. This was an important factor in the continuing
prosperity of the Amsterdam money market at a time when the commercial expansion itself was already in the last days of its glory. Nor
did acceptance credit stand alone. The issue of long-term public loans
by the bankers assumed vast proportions in Amsterdam in the course of
the eighteenth century, as did the insurance business and the securities
trade. From the beginning of the seventeenth century a regular securities trade had existed in Amsterdam, dealing in government bonds and
participations in the various chambers of the East India Company
(1602), followed by the shares of the West India Company (1621).
Finally, in 1621 bonds of the East India Company were also on the
market (on printed forms, made out to X or to bearer, and repayable at
short notice). Since 1698 long term bonds were being issued regularly
by the East India Company, bearing annual interest payments.

'Forward business', i.e. buying and selling at a certain moment for
delivery and payment at a later date, was an early phenomenon of the
securities market.[1] Immediately after the foundation of the East India
Company speculation 'for a rise' was already to be observed. In 1607
a group of merchants including Isaac Le Maire, De Moucheron and
others had formed a 'bear consortium' that speculated on the fall of
prices by means of fictitious sales for forward delivery and the systematic spreading of unfavourable rumours. Consequently, an edict of 1610
forbade forward dealings in shares unless one was the material owner of
the stocks dealt in. These prohibitory measures were regularly renewed
(1624, 1639, 1636), but stock jobbery had apparently come to stay.

Such speculative transactions did not inhibit the expansion of normal
business in securities. By 1647 this had already become so important on
the Amsterdam Exchange that the brokerage there was officially
reduced from $\frac{1}{2}$ per cent to $\frac{1}{4}$ per cent. The Spanish and especially
Portuguese Jews were the great specialists in securities. They did not
confine their trade to forward business with fixed purchases, but were
already deeply involved in 'option' transactions. In this gamble, purchasers or potential purchasers of goods or securities had the option of
either honouring the contract concluded or being released from it upon
payment of a *premium* or *sanction*. Lopez de la Vega, an Amsterdam
Portuguese Jew, gives in his *Confusio de Confusiones* (1688) a detailed

[1] M. F. J. Smith, *Tijd-affaires in Effecten aan de Amsterdamsche Beurs* (The Hague,
1919), pp. 21–54.

description of the finesses of the Amsterdam technique in the securities trade. As regards forward business with fixed purchases, de la Vega already mentions, in addition to cash business and buying 'on margin', the carry-over (*Rescounter*) technique, which enabled the parties to speculative deals merely to settle the surpluses every month. For option transactions, printed forms were already in use.

In the eighteenth century the Amsterdam forward business in securities was to increase strongly, quickly assuming international proportions: English stocks had already been traded in during the late seventeenth century, especially under the impetus of the Portuguese Jewish speculators; now securities from other countries also made their way on to the Amsterdam Exchange. Around the middle of the eighteenth century option transactions were organized around four quarterly settlement days and the introduction of share certificates further stimulated trade in these instruments.[1]

What was the real share of Amsterdam in the evolution of the modern money market? The complexity of the Amsterdam money market makes it difficult to give a simple answer. First, however, a distinction must be made between the Amsterdam Exchange Bank and private banking. Contemporaries, including no less a person than Adam Smith, praised the Amsterdam Exchange Bank highly, and rightly so. But in the purely financial field the Bank introduced little that was new, representing as the municipal clearing bank merely a terminus in the centuries-long progress of a financial technique which had been introduced by the Italians in the thirteenth century and had remained under their control ever since. Here Amsterdam imitated the public clearing banks of the south. It followed the principle of a uniform stable money of account system, such as had already been previously introduced by Geneva, Lyons and Piacenza. It adhered to the multilateral clearing system of the Castilian fairs, only refining it further by concentrating all accounts in a single bank. The contribution of the Amsterdam Exchange Bank therefore was to combine the achievements in financial techniques of the past into a balanced whole. Nowhere was there a break with the past; precisely through its continuity with the past the municipal bank clearing system attained a maturity and reliability which astonished the entire mercantile world.

During the second half of the seventeenth century the municipal clearing bank system had already been overtaken as an institution by the economic development of the moment. After 1685 the Amsterdam Exchange Bank no longer derived its vitality from its clearing function

---

[1] Before then transfers of shares had to be noted in a register at the offices of the company in question. From 1720 it had become the custom to give receipts for such transfers, which were then traded in.

but from its trade in precious metals. Despite this change, the Amsterdam money market nevertheless remained vital until almost the end of the eighteenth century. And here the second nuance regarding Amsterdam has to be invoked. The continuing prosperity of the Amsterdam money market was principally due to the progress of the private banks in financial techniques. That the Amsterdam money market remained unusually active until near the end of the eighteenth century was largely due to the creativity and the modernity of the *private* banking system, which from the second half of the seventeenth century played a leading role within the Amsterdam money market. After a severe crisis in the first half of the seventeenth century which severely checked their progress, the Amsterdam bankers, specie dealers, security dealers and merchant bankers made a vigorous comeback, further developing modern deposit, clearing and discount banking, by which they laid a firm foundation for the great prosperity of the Amsterdam money market in the eighteenth century. Tremendous quantities of paper continued to be handled in Amsterdam: bills, shares, government bonds, private bonds and debentures; cheques and even notes were abundant; in the issue of banknotes, however, London had acquired a considerable lead.

One major question remained unanswered. Why, at the beginning of the seventeenth century, did the Dutch commercial towns turn their back on the more modern financial techniques which had come into being in Antwerp in the sixteenth century and which had already been brought to Amsterdam and Middelburg after 1585 by the cashkeepers and merchants who had emigrated from Antwerp? Why did they opt for the more conservative banking system originating in Italy? Were the Antwerp techniques too recent to inspire confidence at a time of constant wartime confusion and monetary chaos? Was the breakthrough of trade from Zeeland and Holland into the Mediterranean and the Levant around 1600 a reason for more direct contact with the Italian banking system, which through its tradition conveyed an impression of greater stability? Certainly the *Casa de Contratación* in Seville and, above all, the public clearing bank of Venice enjoyed an exceptional reputation and prestige among the most influential merchants in the city of Amsterdam around 1600. A final answer to this question has never been given.

(7) THE DEVELOPMENT OF MODERN BANKING IN ENGLAND AND SCOTLAND

England's commercial prosperity in the sixteenth century had laid the foundations for the gradual development of the London money market. The presence of Italian merchant bankers, the active trade of numerous members of the Hanseatic League, the close ties between the Merchant Adventurers and the Netherlands – each had brought contemporary innovations in financial techniques within reach of the London business world. The influence of Antwerp was particularly strong: from 1544 to 1574 Antwerp was the money market *par excellence* for the credit operations of the English Crown: the Royal Exchange, which Thomas Gresham had built in Lombard Street and which was officially opened in January 1571, was modelled entirely on its Antwerp prototype; the generalized use of bills of exchange and the increasing circulation of commercial instruments blended in with similar developments in Antwerp from the second third of the sixteenth century.

In this context, the London money market around 1600 comprised an already active market in commercial instruments, and a range of means by which requirements for non-commercial credit might be met. It also had a wide range of financial instruments at its disposal.[1] Bills of exchange and notes obligatory occupied a privileged position in the business world for the granting of short-term credit: they fitted perfectly into the pattern of the business life of the day dominated as it was by a small circle of dealers and based on mutual confidence. Many types of bond were in use: they were better suited to longer-term loans, since a material collateral was provided and the security was greater than in the case of bills of exchange and writings obligatory, which were based purely and simply on the good reputation of the borrower. The pledge gave even better security, since it offered real estate or personal property as security: in the seventeenth century the long-term loan, secured by a mortgage on land, was also to enjoy increasing success especially after the borrower secured the right of repurchase in the 1640s.

Bills of exchange and writings obligatory with bearer's clause had already been commonly transferable between English merchants in the fifteenth and sixteenth centuries. Under Antwerp's influence, they displayed the first signs of negotiability. According to the Antwerp court records of the mid sixteenth century, it was the custom among English merchants to transfer commercial instruments with bearer's clause to one another in 'final and absolute payment'. True, the principle of transfers of instruments by assignment, whereby the transferring debtor remained liable, was also accepted by the Court of the Merchant Adventurers, but this assignment had to have been expressly provided for and capable of proof by a *contre-obligatie* or by some other form of promise. The special courts that accepted such customs gradually lost

[1] R. Ashton, *The Crown and the Money Market, 1603–1640*, pp. 2-11; J. M. Holden, *The History of Negotiable Instruments in English Law* (London, 1955), pp. 4-29.

their influence: the Staple Courts from the Statutes of 1531 and 1585, the Admiralty Courts from the end of the sixteenth century. The Common Law Courts increasingly dominated commercial jurisdiction from the seventeenth century. This posed special problems. Common law was inimical to the assignment of writings obligatory and declared a transfer of such instruments by assignment legal only if it served the purpose of setting off debts, in other words if the common interest between assignee and assignor had been proven. Only formal writings obligatory were recognized by the Common Law Courts; informal ones were not.[1]

The Common Law Courts were also suspicious of the transferability of bills of exchange, but here they were more prepared to accept the customs of the business world because the bill of exchange was a typical and clearly recognizable commercial instrument. This circumstance not only furthered general acceptance of the bill of exchange in the English business world but also made a major contribution to the transition from transferability to negotiability. In his *Lex Mercatoria* of 1622, in emulation of the *Tresoir van de Mate...vanden Gelde ende Wissel* (Amsterdam, 1590), Gerard de Malynes had already pointed to the disadvantages of the bearer's clause for bills of exchange, which usually had far to travel and were drawn up in a number of copies. On the other hand, the advantages of payments by assignment as applied in the Netherlands were well known. The only difference was that custom among English merchants required explicit proof, which could be given quite simply by replacing the traditional clause 'payable to X or to the bringer thereof' by the clause 'payable to X or his assigns' and by noting the assignments on the back of the bill, the Netherlands practice from the beginning of the seventeenth century.

The transition was also fostered by the expansion and further internationalization of English trade. Before 1600 it affected mainly the transfer of bills obligatory within the limited group of Merchant Adventurers active in the wool and particularly cloth staple markets – men intimately acquainted with one another. Risks were therefore minimal. After 1600 the geographical horizon of commerce widened, the numbers of English merchants so enlarged that increasing unfamiliarity and uncertainty had to be counterbalanced by the introduction of the principle of negotiability in the circulation of bills of exchange.

John Marius's *Advice concerning Bills of Exchange* (1651) demonstrates just how the endorsement of bills of exchange became current in England during the second quarter of the seventeenth century. The

[1] For the legal aspects of this problem see above all: J. M. Holden, *op. cit.*, esp. chapters II–III.

decisive step towards negotiability was taken during the second half of the century: in a judgment of 1699 Chief Justice Holt not only recognized the individual liability of all endorsers for bills of exchange payable to A or his assigns, or payable to A or order, but also accepted for the first time that a 'bona fide holder for value can acquire a good title from a mere finder'.

Marius's book contains other important information on the development of commercial credit during the second quarter of the seventeenth century: the discounting of bills of exchange and the use of inland bills had come to stay in English commercial life. The example of Antwerp discount and the custom of inland bills between Antwerp, Amsterdam and Lille before 1600 were most probably connected with this. In England itself inland bills were already customary at the beginning of the seventeenth century as a means of transferring the local incomes of large landowners to London and, at the same time, of remitting the proceeds of sales by London merchants to inland agents with a view to reprovisioning or settlement.[1]

As against the vigorous expansion of commercial credit on bills of exchange, dominated by the evolution and rapid spread of inland and outland bills, had to be placed the retarded legal development of writings obligatory. The Common Law Courts stubbornly continued to hold that the assignment principle did not apply to writings obligatory, since these served both non-commercial and commercial purposes – so that mercantile custom could not be invoked – and since the endorsement of inland bills could be used as a substitute. In 1653, 1669 and 1672–3 attempts were made in the Lords to make writings obligatory negotiable in principle, i.e. transferable by means of endorsement: on each occasion the effort proved vain. Not until the Promissory Notes Act of 1704 was their legality officially recognized.

Such legal difficulties in no way hampered the further development of the transferability of writings obligatory with bearer's clause. On the contrary, they drove this development in a specific direction. In the circle of London merchants, who had come to know and trust one another, and who also knew the Antwerp and Dutch custom of intense circulation from hand to hand, a new future opened for the transferability of writings obligatory. This transferability was integrated into the rising London banking system, which derived its strength precisely from a position of trust and familiarity and therefore was less hampered by the absence of legal protection.

Ad hoc banking, which attracted mercantile investment in financial transactions at interest, had long been known in England as elsewhere;

[1] A remark by L. Stone, quoted in R. Ashton, *The Crown and the Money Market*, p. 3.

it continued to be very common in the seventeenth century. Money-changers, foreign exchange brokers, scriveners and goldsmiths had also gradually introduced deposit banking proper, in which deposits were received and lent to third parties at interest. Scriveners were already accepting deposits in the sixteenth century and the beginning cf the seventeenth century; more, they were already paying interest on them, which suggests a certain authority to dispose of their deposits. Gold-smiths too were active in this way as early as 1630. But deposit banking business in England did not achieve its real breakthrough until after the 1640s–1650s, under the impulse of the London goldsmiths. From then on the goldsmith bankers systematically accepted from merchants and large landowners deposits on both current account and on term; they lent money at interest by opening credit on current account or by advances, and discounted inland or outland bills and various official securities; in exchange for money deposits on term they issued interest-bearing certificates in the form of simple promissory notes with bearer's clause; they also made the money deposits on call transferable by draw-ing note or cheque. Goldsmiths' notes were not confined to deposit certificates; they were soon issued for the financing of discount business and loans as well. This was deposit, clearing, discount, and issuing banking in the modern sense of the term.

Essentially, the London goldsmiths were elaborating financial func-tions which closely resembled those performed by the cashkeepers of Antwerp and later Amsterdam from the sixteenth and seventeenth centuries. However, there was one important innovation, *viz.* the issue of simple promissory notes with *bearer's* clause, which quickly spread, above all as a result of the negative attitude of the Common Law Courts to the negotiability of writings obligatory. Other special cir-cumstances likewise contributed to the swift success of London deposit banking. England's neutrality during the second half of the Thirty Years War, as a result of which London merchants were able to attract part of the European transit and carrying trade and could institute an English 'Silver Road' via Dover, stimulated feverish financial activity in London in the late 1630s and 1640s. Then came Charles I's closure of the Tower Mint in 1640. Its silver deposits belonging to private persons were converted into a compulsory loan, so that deposits with goldsmith bankers henceforth seemed safer. Finally, government financial needs were also partially responsible for the rise of the gold-smith banks from 1640 to 1672. For as well as commercial bills of exchange the goldsmiths discounted all kinds of public securities assigned to the future income of the Crown. By January 1672 the inflation of public credit became so great that a moratorium had to be declared for the Exchequer. Panic followed. Despite a serious crisis, the

London goldsmiths managed to maintain themselves as general bankers during the following decades. But the institutional structure of London banking was to undergo a thorough change with the decisive innovations which from 1688 were to convert the public finance sector from a floating to a consolidated national debt. A milestone in this transitional process was the foundation of the Bank of England in 1694. In addition to important functions in public finances the Bank of England was granted, under a charter of incorporation, the authority to trade in bullion and bills of exchange, to lend and borrow money and to issue negotiable writings obligatory. At first, notes under Seal were used to make payments from the Bank to the Exchequer. But, increasingly, ordinary banknotes were issued, *viz.* promissory notes with bearer's clause and irregular amounts for paid-in deposits or similar notes with rounded-off amounts for financing discounting operations and loans to private persons and to the government.[1] On the occasion of the re-charter in 1708 the right of issue was more clearly defined as the right to issue banknotes, and the Bank of England was proclaimed the only joint-stock bank of issue. This monopoly of issue was a strong card in the competitive strength of the bank. In Scotland, where the Bank of Scotland had been founded in 1695 as the first joint-stock bank, such a monopoly was granted to a new institution for only 25 years: in 1727 the Royal Bank of Scotland came into being, followed in 1747 by the British Linen Bank, both likewise established as joint-stock banks in Edinburgh.

The successful development of the Bank of England, especially after 1697, was attributable not so much to the growth of its private banking activity as to its close ties with public finance. Technical innovations, by which public loans were assigned funds of perpetual interest as a guarantee, steadily nurtured confidence in English government securities, and issues, short-term and long-term, grew in numbers. Bank of England notes were always issued on the basis of simple convertibility, another factor making for public confidence in the new system. The unique role which the Bank of England assumed in the London money market through its rising prestige and its special relationship with public finances ensured that its bank notes steadily became dominant in the metropolis. D. M. Joslin estimated that the total note issue by the London goldsmith bankers around 1720 was probably only a fraction of that of the Bank of England, with notes to the value of £2,480,000 in circulation.[2]

---

[1] Both kinds of notes were first hand-written but soon appeared in printed form and were further standardized (above all from 1698 to 1699).

[2] D. M. Joslin, 'London private bankers, 1720–1785', *Economic History Review*, 2nd ser., VII (1954–5), 170–85.

In the main the Bank of England remained a government bank and a London bank. Its notes circulated only sporadically and occasionally in Bristol and other large towns. Its rise did not imply the decline of the goldsmith bankers, but it did determine major structural changes in London private banking. The increasing circulation of Exchequer bills, of government's long annuities and ministerial issues, together with the shares or bonds of the commercial joint-stock companies which consolidated the national debt (see section IV), in turn opened up new prospects of profitable operations on the money and capital market for the private bankers, creating a new spectrum of interest-bearing, semiliquid securities from which they could choose their own portfolios, and a new range of sureties for the granting of loans. Fiscal transfers, especially from the provinces to the capital, were often made through the medium of the private bankers. Meanwhile, during the first half of the eighteenth century, discount operations and mortgage loans continued to be concentrated largely in the hands of the London private bankers.

The success of the London private banks is reflected in an increase in their number from about 24 in 1725 to some 51 in 1776, and in the increasing specialization of functions, especially noticeable after 1720. The West End bankers, such as the Hoares, Goslings and Childs, became bankers for the aristocracy and gentry. They collaborated closely with the stewards of the big landowners, kept large cash reserves, invested in shares or government securities for the account of their principals, and managed their personal wealth. They also lent money on mortgage or against a personal bond.

The City bankers, established principally in and around Lombard Street, had a quite different clientele, usually merchants from the City itself or correspondents from home or abroad. Mortgage loans were rarer here; accepting and discounting bills of exchange, making transfers from one account to another, providing advances on current account and other financial services to the merchants – these were the heart of City banking. Relations with the country correspondents turned mainly upon the discounting of inland bills and the remittance of moneys received. These interregional relations were of special importance because after 1750 they opened the way for the rise of country banking, the forerunner of the increasing interregional mobility of capital.

In London, shares of the Bank of England and other joint-stock companies were regularly traded in from the end of the seventeenth century. After the foundation of the South Sea Company in 1711, the proliferation of joint-stock companies was to intensify this trade still further. Forward and premium business encouraged the speculative elements so much that the share business on the Royal Exchange was closed and moved to Jonathan's Coffee House. Yet however strongly the London trade in shares, bonds and public securities developed during the first half of the eighteenth century, the Amsterdam money and capital market still remained dominant.

(8) THE PATTERN OF INVESTMENT IN THE INTERNATIONAL BUSINESS WORLD

The success of commercial and financial capitalism from the sixteenth to the eighteenth centuries may be explained in the first place by the more extensive opportunities for accumulating profits from foreign trade and finance. But the expansion of personal, movable wealth and the greater mobility of capital should not be overlooked.

High profits often led to conspicuous consumption by the great merchants. Inventories upon decease and household records combine to give a vivid picture of the rich *train de vie* they maintained: a splendid town house and a country home, numerous servants, expensive clothing, splendid furniture, objets d'art, patronage of the arts and a preference for costly jewels and silver or gold dinner services. This display of wealth was not just a manifestation of ostentation and self-indulgence; it had also a psychological function: it enhanced the prestige of the merchant and increased confidence in his solvency. Jewels and silver or gold services were potential pledges for loans and were readily convertible into liquid resources.

Much of the merchant's profits was ploughed back into his own firm, in the form of greater liquidity, bigger stocks, larger advances to local producers, more or higher current accounts with commercial correspondents throughout the world, greater participation in international exchange transactions and in transport by sea and by land. This quantitative factor was of vital importance because investment in floating capital occupied a crucial position in the world economy of the sixteenth, seventeenth and eighteenth centuries. But the expansion of world trade was not exclusively determined by this expansion of floating capital. Substantial progress in financial and commercial techniques helped to reduce the capital–output ratio in the field of floating capital. New or improved instruments encouraged the accelerated circulation of money, so that a higher commercial turnover was attained with the same liquidity input. Refinement of the market organization, *inter alia* by the commission business, together with the rationalization of transport, likewise made possible considerable investment savings in floating capital.

Improved commercial and financial techniques also opened new prospects for the merchant for the investment of profits outside his own firm. The spread of ad hoc banking was the first sign of this. Purchases of shares in ships and participations in temporary commercial enterprises of third parties, especially overseas voyages, became popular. Ordinary loans against IOUs, usually short-term or medium-term, were extremely common: the 1572 inventory of Jan Gamel, a successful Antwerp merchant who had retired from active trading, shows that such loans to merchants formed 52·40 per cent of his total fortune. Long-term investments similarly rapidly increased in popularity: they comprised purchases of private life or hereditary annuities (now increasingly redeemable), mortgage loans and, from the seventeenth century, shares and bonds of the great colonial joint-stock companies. A special place in the investment spectrum of the successful merchant was occupied by short- and long-term government loans – perhaps six-monthly loans at interest, perhaps an *asiento*-participation, or a farm of tolls and other taxes, or municipal annuities or annuities issued by regional or administrative bodies, or state annuities, such as the Spanish *juros*, or lottery loans, or shares in the English and French companies to which was entrusted the consolidation of the floating national debts, or government bonds, issued by European powers through the medium of Amsterdam bankers in the course of the eighteenth century. Inventories of eighteenth-century merchants demonstrate impressively how strongly personal, movable wealth spread between 1500 and 1750, how international and diversified personal investments outside one's own firm had become. A special role was played by investments in the insurance business: marine insurance and private and public lotteries, once objects of speculative investment in the sixteenth century, had gradually been converted from the end of the seventeenth century into a normal financial enterprise with the foundation of conventional insurance companies in Holland and England.

Finally, land and houses formed important objects of investment. The motives behind this were highly varied: to some merchants landowning meant the consolidation of acquired wealth, leading to social promotion and ennoblement; others speculated on the direct capital gains that landowning could generate through urbanization and rising agricultural prices, or discovered in such capital appreciation a means of obtaining long-term credit financed by annuities paid for from the profit it afforded; at other times, merchants would speculate also on unusually low prices of land (as many did during the wars of religion), in the expectation that rentals would fall less far and less quickly than land prices. Such investments of the European merchant in real estate cannot simply be dismissed as a *trahison de la bourgeoisie* (F. Braudel).

Investments as described above were not peculiar to the ad hoc banking system. An analogous investment pattern may also be found in deposit banking. For both groups of bankers financial investment was favoured by the increasing geographical mobility of capital. The development of the important European money markets was the decisive factor here.

In this context a fascinating problem presents itself. Why, at a time of strong and persistent commercial expansion, did so many successful merchants turn their backs on commercial investments and increasingly concentrate on financial activities as merchant bankers or traders? Historians have often reproached such merchants for having caused the commercial decline of their country in this way. P. Klein has countered this accusation with regard to eighteenth-century Amsterdam, suggesting that the fossilization of Amsterdam in the course of the eighteenth century was rooted in the structure of Amsterdam world trade as this had been designed by the great pioneers of seventeenth-century Holland; the merchant bankers, by shifting the emphasis to finance, had optimally utilized the opportunities for expansion that were still available in Amsterdam.[1]

The same argument could also be invoked with respect to other financial centres in the sixteenth century. The generalized use of temporary partnerships and of the commission business gave merchants in a small way of business the chance to take part successfully in the expansion of foreign trade. Accordingly, from the second third of the sixteenth century European foreign trade received fresh and special impetus from smaller merchants from the southern Netherlands and the Iberian peninsula, later from the Dutch, English, north Germans and Scandinavians. The large traditional mercantile establishments, with their more rigid system of branch offices and their more capital-intensive structure, were seriously threatened by competition from this new, more flexible organization. In order to save their business the big firms withdrew into finance: a considerable availability of floating capital and an extensive network of branches continued to be essential in this sector and this the big firms had. In other words, the specialization in international finance protected the big firms of merchants against the competition of the smaller ones.

The growing mobility of money capital and the related upsurge of European finance between 1500 and 1750 must also be viewed in the light of monetary, cyclical and political circumstances. The stability of the *Carolus guilder* down to the outbreak of the Netherlands Revolt

---

[1] P. W. Klein, 'Entrepreneurial behaviour and the economic rise and decline of the Netherlands in the 17th and 18th centuries', *Annales Cisalpines d'Histoire Sociale*, 1 (1970), 1–19.

meant great security for the Antwerp money market, just as the bank guilder did for Amsterdam and the pound sterling for London; the stable *écu de marc* and the *scudo di marche* had had the same significance for Lyons and for Piacenza respectively. From the second half of the seventeenth century, Europe's falling trend of agricultural rentals increased the attraction of commercial and financial investments in Amsterdam. Falling prices for foodstuffs and the rising purchasing power of money favoured creditors and stimulated the granting of loans. Finally, commercial transactions were becoming less precarious: the threat of piracy was gradually receding, Atlantic navigation was less of an adventure, more an everyday affair; the risks of transcontinental trade were lessening, marginally after the end of the Wars of Religion, more confidently after the end of the Spanish War of Succession.

Expansion of personal, movable wealth, progress in financial techniques and institutions, and a more favourable psychological climate caused the supply of capital to increase more than proportionally to demand. The interest rate for short-term commercial credits fell in Antwerp from some 14 per cent to 8–10 per cent between 1500 and 1560. During the Wars of Religion the commercial interest rate rose again to 10–12 per cent, but on the Amsterdam money market it crumbled in the course of the seventeenth century. In the 1610s the East India Company was paying the Amsterdam Exchange Bank 6¼ per cent interest for advances received; by the 1620s this had fallen to 5 per cent, from 1653 to 4½ per cent, from 1656 to 4 per cent, from 1685 to 3½ per cent and from 1723 even to 2½ per cent.[1] On the other European money markets the movement of interest rates was also downwards, though money always remained cheaper in Amsterdam than elsewhere. Whilst the European development of interest rates was thus a clear indication of the greatly increased mobility of money capital, Amsterdam's lead demonstrated at the same time that the unification of the international money market was far from perfect.

The slower rise in demand in comparison with supply may be explained largely by the preponderance of the traditional agricultural sector in the European economy.[2] Investment opportunities here still remained limited. Trade and industry needed more money capital, but as long as investment in both sectors was mainly directed towards the provision of floating capital, the opportunities for absorbing financial resources were not inexhaustible. Not until the Industrial Revolution were the relations between agriculture, industry and commerce to

---

[1] J. G. van Dillen, 'Oprichting en functie der Amsterdamsche Wisselbank, in de zeventiende eeuw, 1609–1686', *Mensen en Achtergronden* (Groningen, 1964), p. 376.
[2] R. Davis, *The Rise of the Atlantic Economies* (London, 1973), p. 232.

undergo total change, giving the relation between capital supply and demand an entirely new look.

III.   *The Financing of the Mercantile State*

(1) INERTIA AND MOMENTUM IN THE PUBLIC FINANCES

Control of public finance and taxation were not the exclusive domain of the central governments during the modern age. Towns, provinces, and regions often had considerable autonomy in such matters, which they had retained from the Middle Ages, even in regard to taxes imposed by the central government. There was also a wide diversity of seignorial rights, belonging to private persons or institutions, which as fiscal burdens weighed most heavily on the mass of the peasant population.

Western Europe especially was characterized by a bewildering gap between the growing power of state authority and its inability to substantiate this power financially and fiscally. The development of the national, mercantilist state, especially in its relations with the outside world, created huge new demands for money, but the weight of the medieval institutional and mental structure remained too heavy to allow fundamental reforms in the field of taxation and of public financial control. The great European wars thus placed heavy strains on the public finances. Under the pressure of crisis, measures were often taken purely empirically but later proved to be the source of fundamental innovations.

Originally the ordinary income of the ruler was based on the royal domains and on the seignorial rights bound up with them (*le prince doit vivre du sien*). In France, by the end of the Middle Ages, this income was only a fraction of the total public income. On the other hand, in the Netherlands, where the proximity of numerous towns with large demands for foodstuffs kept prices high for agricultural produce, the income from running the royal domains was still important up to the beginning of the sixteenth century, after which, relatively, it fell quite quickly there too. In less developed economies, such as Poland, the king could still acquire an attractive income by leasing the royal domains to the nobility as late as the end of the sixteenth century; thereafter, the feudalization of the seventeenth century gradually undermined the king's bargaining position, thus inaugurating a period of low rentals and declining royal income. Yet still the public role of the royal domains was not played out. As in the Middle Ages, the central administrations in the sixteenth century still often assigned payments for public purchases or debts to the stewards of the royal domains. When these assignments necessitated payment in advance by the stewards of the revenue owed to the Crown from the proceeds of running the royal domains, the stewards became cheap bankers for the ruler. The same applied to the interest-free advances which, on demand, the stewards had to transfer directly to the central administration. The Emperor Charles V still made regular use of this technique in his Netherlands domains. The royal domains remained important too as a basis for obtaining long-term public credit, forming an excellent 'fund of credit' for the issue of life or hereditary annuities, and particularly suitable as collateral for mortgage credit. Finally, the permanent alienation of royal domains during the sixteenth and seventeenth centuries still continued in times of extraordinary pressure on the public finances. During the Netherlands Revolt Philip II sold off large stretches of his domains. In Stuart England the Corporation of London acquired by the Ditchfield Grant of 1627–8 the authority to sell Crown lands on a large scale towards repayment of the public debt.

In addition to the management of the royal domains, tolls and customs duties had long formed an important source of ordinary public income. The expansion of transcontinental and maritime trade during the sixteenth century reinforced this importance insofar as customs and tolls were adjusted to the fall in the purchasing power of money. Collection of the tolls was often delegated to third parties by means of farming contracts: sometimes a town would farm a toll, as Antwerp did during the sixteenth century with respect to the great Brabant Water Toll; sometimes the toll farmers would form a syndicate, as they did from 1604 for the 'Great Farm of the Customs' in Stuart England. For the ruler, the advantages of farming were manifold. The farming contract, a measure of administrative decentralization, secured the ruler's income and allowed him a flexible measure of repayment of current and even future income, at modest cost. It strengthened the ruler's bargaining position vis-à-vis the great merchants and financiers if further loans were needed. It even brought the smaller saver within the ruler's reach insofar as the farmers divided their farm into shares and marketed these, as they did in England during the seventeenth century.[1]

Among the forms of extraordinary income, import and export duties most resembled simple tolls. In the Netherlands they had already occurred sporadically during the French–Habsburg wars of the mid sixteenth century. The outbreak of the Revolt led to a permanent system of licences and passports which survived the Treaty of Westphalia in 1648, forming the basis for a system of modern import and export duties. Elsewhere the Wars of Religion had led to similar levies, and a triumphant state mercantilism became institutionalized in systems of

[1] R. Ashton, *The Crown and the Money Market*, pp. 79–88.

modern import and export duties. The stagnation (or retarded expansion) of transcontinental trade during the seventeenth century, together with growing protectionism, formed a threat to this source of income, but in the west the expansion of maritime trade compensated for this.

Taxes formed a second considerable source of extraordinary income for the ruler. Originally parliamentary subsidies, permitted only in special or exceptional cases, they were based on the principle of *ubi commune periculum, ibi commune auxilium*. Although the principle was maintained in the modern age, its force lessened as parliamentary powers over the grant of subsidies placed growing obstacles in the way of royal absolutism.

In continental Europe, taxes on consumption – imposts on beer or the *gabelles* on salt – underwent striking increases in the sixteenth and seventeenth centuries. In many European countries they dominated the tax systems by the end of the *Ancien Régime*. Direct taxes also increased. In France the *taille* had become a permanent levy; weighing mainly on the peasant population. In the Netherlands of the sixteenth century taxes on real estate and movable property, such as the hundredth penny, were regularly permitted by the Provincial States. In the Southern Netherlands from the second half of the seventeenth century the twentieth penny, i.e. a 5 per cent levy on immovable income, formed the basis of a permanent direct tax. In England – lightly taxed in Tudor times – the governments of the interregnum borrowed the excise duties from their Dutch enemy. At the Restoration of 1660 many of the innovations of parliamentary government disappeared; excise remained, permanent and growing. Taxes were collected in a great variety of ways, sometimes directly, often through farmers or financiers; sometimes the material outcome of a granted *bede* (request by the ruler for funds) would be distributed among the rural or urban authorities, who in their turn farmed it out. Farmers were usually prepared to grant prepayments or overdrafts, so that current or future tax revenue also became directly available to the authorities. These could immediately dispose of current or future tax income and assign creditors to it for payment.

However vigorous the growth of ordinary and extraordinary public income might be and however considerably its collection gained in regularity, rapidity and 'anticipation' through the intermediary of farmers and financiers, progress remained inadequate fully to satisfy the increasing need for money by the European states. Systematic expansion of public credit was the first real supplementation. Usually these were forms of credit that had already been known in the late Middle Ages but which now increased in importance and technical refinement. For short-term public credit compulsory loans were a frequent resort:

sometimes they were obtained from large mercantile firms – the Fuggers for example – in exchange for certain advantages in both the material and the social sphere, or from towns or institutions which had obligations towards the ruler on account of privileges granted. Voluntary short-term loans from merchants and bankers were even more common: they comprised not only writings obligatory by the ruler and his officials owed to a few large bankers and merchants; institutions which had lent money for the account of the central government also put such writings into circulation. Some of them had already been drawn up in blank to bearer so that they could quickly be negotiated. Particularly in countries where writings obligatory were to bearer or to order, a brisk trade in short-term government securities, concentrated mainly in money markets like Antwerp, Amsterdam and London, developed at quite an early stage. This trade was soon joined by assignments by the authorities to current or future income especially suited to discount operations.

Whilst the *trade* in short-term government securities was more or less confined to the world of bankers, merchants, financiers, civil servants and money-changers, the *effects* of developing long-term public credit reached much larger sections of the population. The sale of hereditary or life annuities, payable out of a public income, enjoyed wide public confidence and was not regarded as conflicting with the church's prohibition on interest. Similar to the annuity contract was the sale of offices, which carried with them annual incomes for the purchaser and possibly for his descendants. The generalized application in the sixteenth century of the 'redeemability clause' to the annuity contract implied an important change: at no time could the purchaser himself change the conditions of the annuity contract, but the monarch acquired the right to repay the loan if it suited his purpose; this made it possible for him to convert public long-term loans raised on costly terms into new loans at lower rates of interest. Further improvements in the seventeenth century enabled the long-term public credit to be taken over by enterprises governed by the articles of association of a limited liability company (like the South Sea Company), until gradually formal long-term public loans became usual.

The reorganization of the public finances was determined not only by the quantitative expansion of the taxing and credit system or by the proliferation or refinement of the forms of taxes or of credit: it was also bound up with a slow but genuine change in the mental attitudes of both authorities and peoples towards taxes and public credit. The growing power of the state strengthened public confidence in government loans, while the authorities became aware of the tremendous potential represented by the savings of the public at large – always pro-

Table 26. *Annual interest (per cent) for short-term loans to the authorities on the money markets of Bruges and Antwerp (five-yearly average) (1401–1570)*

Date	Short-term loans to Burgundian and Habsburg rulers of the Netherlands	Date	Short-term loans to Burgundian and Habsburg rulers of the Netherlands
1401–1405	—	1486–1490	29
1406–1410	32½	1491–1495	27½
1411–1415	32	1496–1500	19⅔
1416–1420	32	1501–1505	—
1421–1425	21	1506–1510	19½
1426–1430	18½	1511–1515	20½
1431–1435	20½	1516–1520	18
1436–1440	20¼	1521–1525	16
1441–1445	18	1526–1530	17½
1446–1450	19¾	1531–1535	14⅞
1451–1455	19¾	1536–1540	15
1456–1460	20	1541–1545	12⅓
1461–1465	19⅔	1546–1550	10½
1466–1470	—	1551–1555	13⅓
1471–1475	—	1556–1560	(12)[a]
1476–1480	18½	1561–1565	(9⅝)[a]
1481–1485	19¼	1566–1570	(11)[a]

[a] No longer fully representative of the market after 1555, because the authorities could then obtain short-term credit through other channels (e.g. *asientos* of Flanders) and the bankruptcy of the Spanish Crown in 1557 had disturbed the relations between the Crown and the money-lenders.

SOURCE: H. van der Wee, *The Growth of the Antwerp Market and the European Economy (Fourteenth–Sixteenth Centuries)*, I, 526.

vided that a climate of confidence could be maintained. The first signs of change were already perceptible from the mid sixteenth century. Despite the catastrophic bankruptcies faced by the great European dynasties, the interest rate did not return to the erratic heights of the fifteenth and early sixteenth centuries; see Table 26 above. During the seventeenth century interest rates for public credit followed a declining trend which was not fundamentally disturbed by the alarming war climate around 1700, bringing fresh, exigent demands for credit. From the symbiosis of quantitative and qualitative progress of the credit system on the one hand and the mental changes of authorities and public on the other, the trade in government securities was gradually enabled to reach full development; this was a crucial innovation in the political and financial history of Europe.

(2) THE DEVELOPMENT OF THE TRADE IN GOVERNMENT SECURITIES

In the towns of northern and southern Europe the sale of life or hereditary annuities by town or ruler was a popular form of public credit in
the late Middle Ages. In a number of Italian and Spanish towns there
developed from this custom a complete system of consolidated municipal debt, whereby trade in municipal securities became quite usual.
Genoa is the best example.[1] A long-term loan issue to the municipality
was always called *Campera*, the shares (*luoghi de la Campera*) each
bearing a nominal value of £100 of Genoese money of account; each
issue also provided for a tax or some other fund of credit from which
the interest and the repayment could be financed. In 1407, with a view
to the reorganization of public debt, a number of *Campere* were combined: this formed the nucleus of the *Casa di San Giorgio*, which
gradually also swallowed up other *Campere*. From 1453 the *Casa di
San Giorgio* also issued new *luoghi* in its own name. The *luoghi* were
entered in the *Cartulario delle Colonne di San Giorgio* with the name of
the owner and could be sold or mortgaged: for example, they were
commonly given as sureties in commercial transactions on credit. The
luoghi were also regularly dealt in on the *Piazza Banchi*: since the market
value was not always identical with the nominal value, and since the
interest rates fluctuated, speculation inevitably developed, and buying
and selling consortia were formed specifically for this purpose. The
luoghi di San Giorgio were highly popular: more than 11,000 names
appear in the registers, including those of many quite humble people –
widows, orphans, and religious communities, both from Genoa itself
and from outside the town. Thus the savings of wide sections of the
population were drawn into the public purse.

Interest was not paid out immediately in coin, but entered in the
registers *delle paghe*. These balances in £ *de paghe* could in turn be dealt
in or mortgaged; each bore the year of registration and had for each
interest year its own market value which might differ from the nominal
value. The £ *de paghe* were commonly used for payments by transfer.
Gradually they were re-absorbed by the *Casa di San Giorgio* because the
farmers of excises and other taxes were allowed to repay their farm
debts to the *Casa di San Giorgio* with these £ *de paghe* at the market
rate. Sometimes the *Casa* would pay out a small remainder in coin at
face value.

From the sixteenth century the papal finances in Rome underwent a
similar development. Credit via bills of exchange had long played a
major role in the transfer to the papal court of income due from the

[1] J. Heers, *Gênes au XVe siècle* (Paris, 1971), pp. 100–42.

entire Christian world. In the sixteenth century this form of credit still remained important. The Fuggers became the bankers of the Church in Germany, Poland, Hungary and Austria charged with remitting the Church's income to Italy: the trade in indulgences was closely linked with this financial cooperation ('Fuggerei, Wucherei'). Ordinary loans at interest by Florentine and later Genoese bankers were likewise common, but the great expansion of the papal credit system, above all after 1526, was in the sphere of long-term annuity credit, which was not forbidden by church law. The Pope sold to a private person or a consortium, for cash, a *Monte*, i.e. a general right to acquire annuities from the proceeds of a given tax. The purchasers split this *Monte* into shares (*luoghi di monte*), which were then sold as annuity certificates among the public at large, inside and outside Rome. The Holy City thus developed into an important market in papal securities which were dealt in from that city over the whole of Italy.[1]

Although the issuing of municipal or papal annuity certificates had developed strongly, their transfer from one owner to another continued to be hampered by the restriction that they were still in the name of a specific person and could only be further traded in with a *cessio* or some equivalent formality. Many certificates consequently remained in the hands of the original owner. This was less true of short-term government securities. These, from the sixteenth century, especially in northern Europe, had usually been drawn up with a bearer's clause and thus opened the way for a real money market in government securities.

The flourishing fairs of Lyons and the activity of the Lucchese and Florentine merchant bankers there (the Bonvisi, Strozzi, Pazzi, Capponi etc.) had early attracted the interest of the kings of France. Commercial expansion and the concentration of international payments had created a liquidity reserve and a credit margin at Lyons too attractive to be disregarded. At the king's request, the great merchant bankers of Lyons put at his disposal the international confidence they had gained on a basis of commerce and finance during the fairs. Initially, this meant short-term loans from fair to fair, occasionally granted when war threatened. By 1522 these had become advances against receipts expected from the sale of the *rentes sur l'hotel de ville de Paris* for the king's account and guaranteed by his income; 1522 marked the birth of a long-term national debt in France. Similar issues of annuities followed shortly, on Paris (1530) and then on Lyons. From 1523 major reforms to simplify and unify the management of public finance were effected: a central and provincial administration was built up within the framework of the *Conseil des Finances* and the *Generalités*.

[1] J. Delumeau, 'Le problème des dettes à Rome au XVIe siècle', *Revue d'histoire moderne et contemporaine*, IV (1957), pp. 5–32.

The interplay of three purely coincidental factors was to give the Lyons market for short-term public credit a further uncovenanted advantage: the appointment of the dynamic Cardinal of Tournon as governor of Lyons in 1536, the increasing need for money by Francis I for the wars against the Habsburgs, and the sudden interest of the south Germans in the person of Hans Kleberg (*der gute Deutsche*) in the great potential of the Lyons money market.[1] Short-term public credit expanded rapidly after 1542. With the aid of Florentine and south German merchant bankers and the manipulations of the astute Imperial agent, Gaspar Ducci, cooperation, and even speculation, came into being between Antwerp and Lyons. In 1548 came a project to found four public banks – in Paris, Lyons, Rouen and Toulouse – with the object of using their deposits for the public credit. Nothing came of it, but royal edicts in 1549, 1556 and 1563 were to found Exchanges after the example of Lyons in Toulouse, Rouen and Paris.

At the death of Francis I in 1547 the royal short-term debt in Lyons stood at £6,860,000 *tournois*. Two thirds of this had already been repaid by 1548, but during the war years of the 1550s the debt rose again, reaching £4,937,000 *tournois* in 1555. The royal bonds contained no bearer's clause, but were transferable by *cessio* before a notary. In spite of this cumbersome procedure, government bonds began to circulate on the Lyons money market. In favourable circumstances they were even negotiated at a premium; in 1550 the premium was up to 1¼ per cent. In times of war and unrest they were disposed of at considerable discounts, as in the autumn of 1551, when there were losses of up to 10 and 12 per cent. In the war years that followed it became increasingly difficult to place short-term loans, even with an increased interest rate of up to 16 per cent p.a. At the Easter market in 1555, therefore, a large-scale repayment scheme (*le Grand Parti*) was devised to deal with the outstanding floating debt, to which a new loan was added, all at 16 per cent p.a. The debt, including compound interest, was to be repaid during the next 41 fairs (10 years), and assignments for this purpose to the *Recettes Générales* of Lyons, Toulouse and Montpellier were granted. Existing bonds were converted into one consolidated public issue. For the payment of interest and redemption sums a new office was created: *le Receveur du don gratuit*.

Le Grand Parti was never put into effect. New short-term loans placed in Lyons caused the floating national debt to soar still higher. On 1 November 1556 a new *Parti* came into being between the king and a consortium of south German and Italian bankers, headed by

[1] R. Ehrenberg, *Das Zeitalter der Fugger*, II, reissue (Hildesheim, 1963), 69–107, 159 f. R. Doucet, 'Le "Grand Parti" de Lyon au XVIe siècle', *Revue historique*, CLXXI (1933), 473–513; CLXXII (1934), 1–43.

G. Obrecht. On the strength of this *Parti*, French royal credit was still able to maintain itself at a time when the Habsburg monarchy was forced to suspend payment (August 1557). By the end of 1557, however, the French monarch, with a floating debt of more than £12,200,000 *tournois*, had to follow the example of Philip II. From 1558 the state bankruptcy became a fact and in April 1559 the king consolidated three quarters of the floating debt by converting it into annuities secured on the city of Lyons and providing for a gradual repayment of the principal (*Le Petit Parti*). Again, it was a failure. Confidence in public finance shrank, and royal bonds were dealt in at discounts of 15 per cent and more. Matters were even worse with the Florentine and south German bankers; confidence in their solvency had practically disappeared, and a flood of bankruptcies in the years to come despatched for ever their financial supremacy in Lyons. The Lyons market in government securities had suffered a severe blow from which it was never completely to recover, the more so since the Genoese bankers had acquired control of European public credit since 1557–8 through the Besançon fairs of payment.

The Habsburg world experienced a similar expansion of the trade in short-term government securities.[1] The spectacular expansion of Imperial sovereignty and its grandiose world policy opened unprecedented horizons for the expansion of public finance. First, it was stimulated by the new *fiscal* opportunities created by the advent of world power: the *Hacienda Real de Castilla* and the *Casa de Contratación de Sevilla* were in the forefront, but the territories of the crown of Aragon, the Italian possessions, from 1528 the alliance with Genoa, not forgetting the wealthy Netherlands, gave it momentum. Secondly, the increasing fiscal income formed a solid public fund for the assignment of new annuity *credit* and of new short-term *loans*. Finally, the impressive private fund of commercial credit that had come into being through the flourishing Castilian and Brabant fairs was gradually incorporated into government finance.

In earlier days Italian and Dutch merchant bankers, including the Frescobaldi, the Gualterotti and Nicolaas van Richterghen, had lent money to the Emperor Maximilian and to the young King Charles I. Such short-term loans were occasional, primitive, and expensive, with interest rates fluctuating around 20 per cent. Rulers preferred to approach the towns, in the first place Antwerp, when they needed credit. Between 1517 and 1521 Charles I made use of Antwerp to sell a large number of redeemable annuities, guaranteed against the *corpus* of the city and with interest and repayment assigned to granted *beeden*

---

[1] R. Carande, *Carlos Quinto y sus banqueros*, 2 vols. (Madrid, 1941–9); R. Ehrenberg, *op. cit.*, II, 25–80, 147–221.

and to domanial income. The issue was made at an interest rate of 6¼ per cent per annum, an attractive rate for the authorities. For the financing of the Imperial election of 1519–20, Charles I made a call on Florentine, Genoese and south German bankers, above all the Fuggers and the Welsers. When war broke out in 1521 the emperor found himself obliged to place new short-term loans at high rates of interest. They were quickly repaid from 1523.

Though such transactions were important, one could not yet speak of a real market in government securities in Antwerp. 1528 was a milestone in its evolution. From that year short-term public loans were a permanent feature at Antwerp. Since the emperor had no normal income in Germany, he used his large liquid resources and credit potential from the south, transferring them through the Antwerp market to their destination. The commercial axis between Antwerp and Medina del Campo thus acquired a financial dimension with which Genoa and Lyons now sought to associate themselves.

The south German merchant bankers proved to be the most interested parties. The houses of Fugger, Welser, Herwart, Höchstetter, Imhof, Tucher etc. redirected their investments towards the public sector. Many had suffered serious damage during the commercial crisis of the 1520s and were pessimistic about the resumption of northern and central European trade. They were correspondingly impressed by the Imperial power, now that the emperor had also assumed control of Italy and brought the German *Bauernkrieg* and the Spanish revolt of the *Comuneros* to a successful conclusion. They lent the emperor short-term money in Antwerp or supplied him with money from Antwerp via the exchange market elsewhere north of the Pyrenees, usually repayable in Medina del Campo or in Seville by means of assignments to Spanish fiscal income or to the expected arrivals of the precious metal fleet. Such assignments were principally made in the form of *libranzas*, i.e. orders to the royal collectors of taxes or toll or domain farmers to pay the banker/creditor. Sometimes the farm would be transferred by the emperor to the bankers for redemption of the debt: thus Jacob Fugger received by the way of repayment the farm of the *Maestrazgos*, the domains belonging to the Military Orders.[1]

Before 1551 permission was granted only rarely for the export of precious metals from Spain (*licencias de sacas*). On the other hand transfers *en masse* via the fairs of payment would have caused the exchange rates to fall disastrously. Merchant bankers therefore bought

[1] F. Ruiz-Martin, 'Credito y Banca. Comercio y Transportes en la Etapa del Capitalismo Mercantil', *Jornados de metodologia aplicada de las Ciencias Historicas 24–27 April 1973, Santiago de Compostella. Ponencias y comunicaciones*, apéndice (Santiago de Compostella, 1973), pp. 7–19.

up merchandise in Spain with a view to exporting it to the rest of Europe. This led to an increase in the purchase prices of goods which rendered commercial profits minimal; but against this could be set the highly attractive proceeds of the financial transactions. Thus the expansion of Iberian–European trade and the augmentation of Habsburg public finance marched together.

Initially the south German merchant bankers held their Spanish assignments until the moment of payment and financed the loans north of the Pyrenees from their own reserves or by raising money from outsiders. From 1536–7, however, the south Germans needed help from Castile. They intensified their purchases of goods in Spain, paid for these purchases with advances obtained on the Castilian fairs and guaranteed by the *libranzas* or other assignments in their possession, and by selling the Spanish goods in western Europe tried to acquire immediate liquid resources in Antwerp or elsewhere. The Fuggers and other firms also began to offer *libranzas* for discounting to the bankers of the fair at Medina del Campo for the account of the private exchange banks in the Castilian towns. If the authorities could not pay the assignments in time (perhaps because the treasure fleet had not arrived on time) the dates of payment at the Castilian fairs were extended. This happened for the first time about 1543; after that extensions were frequent and of longer duration, upsetting the cycle of the fairs of payment. (The commercial fairs remained more regular.)

The fall in the interest rate for short-term public credit to 12 per cent per annum on the Antwerp exchange – temporarily from 1524 and more permanently from the 1530s – gave striking evidence that a new era had dawned (see Table 27). During the war crises, interest rates rose, but the overall trend was downwards: by 1549 a nadir of 8 to 9 per cent was reached. Financial agents were now regularly active for the emperor's and the government's account on the Antwerp money market: Geeraard Sterck from 1528 to 1531, Lazarus Tucher from 1529 to 1541, Gaspar Ducci from 1542 to 1550 and Gaspar Schets from 1552. The loans mostly ran from fair to fair or for a 'double fair', i.e. per three or six months (*deniers prins a fraict et a finance*). Interest rates were now more homogeneous and acquired a specific market character. As most government writings obligatory at Antwerp were drawn up with a bearer's clause (or even issued in blank), they were easily transferable. The opening of the new Exchange in 1531 encouraged such transfers: within the circle of international firms active on the Antwerp Exchange a regular trade in short-term government securities developed, utilizing cash flows from the commodity trade. Letters from the Netherlands government or personal obligations of senior state officials for government account, bonds of the Provincial States or of certain towns and

Table 27. *Annual interest (per cent) for short-term loans to the authorities on the money market of Antwerp (trimestrial averages) (1511–55)*

Date	Winter fair	Easter fair	Whitsun fair	St Bavo fair
1511	20	20	20	20
1512	20	20	20	20
1513	20	20	29	—
1514	—	—	20	—
1515	—	—	20	20
1516	20	18	—	18¾
1517	18	24	20	18
1518	17⅔	15½	—	21
1519	—	21	15½	15
1520	17	16½	13	15¼
1521	—	16⅙	21½	17
1522	20¾	19	19	20⅓
1523	—	20¾	18	15
1524	12½	—	—	12
1525	12	12	12¼	—
1526	12½	12½	—	13
1527	13⅛	18	—	19
1528	16	17½	21⅓	21½
1529	18¼	20⅓	18	21⅓
1530	19	18½	19½	17¾
1531	18½	16¾	18	16⅔
1532	16	15	16	16¾
1533	—	—	—	—
1534	13¾	13½	13¼	13
1535	13¼	12½	13	13
1536	14	14⅓	15–18–20	19
1537	17	14¾	16	13½
1538	12	12½	12	14
1539	12¾	12	16¾	18
1540	19½	16	14⅔	12¼
1541	12	11½	12	12
1542	11½	12	12	12
1543	12	12	12	12
1544	14	15	17	14
1545	12	11	10	11
1546	11	11¼	12	12
1547	12	12	10	10
1548	10	10	10	10
1549	10	10	10	9
1550	10	10	10	11
1551	11	11	11	12
1552	12	13	14–16	14
1553	14	14	14	12
1554	12	14	18–14⅙	14
1555	14	14	14	14–16

SOURCE: H. van der Wee, *The Growth of the Antwerp Market and the European Economy (Fourteenth–Sixteenth Centuries)*, I, 527.

regional bodies, personal obligations of the receivers of the *Recette Generale* (the *Rentmeesterbrieven*), personal obligations of large merchant firms for government account and bonds of the king of Portugal – all circulated on the Antwerp Exchange.

The French and Guelders invasion in 1542 and the war psychosis of the following years opened a new phase of rapidly increasing floating public debts. The Florentine financier, Gaspar Ducci, was active on the Antwerp money market as agent for the emperor and the Brussels government, launching speculations on transfers of money between Lyons and Antwerp in which the south German merchant bankers also participated. From 1544 Stephen Vaughan, governor of the English Merchant Adventurers, concluded short-term loans on the Antwerp money market for the account of Henry VIII. The city of Antwerp borrowed considerable capital on short-term writings obligatory and by the sale of annuities, to pay for the new fortifications ordered by the Emperor Charles. By 1546, the Fuggers held short-term government securities to the value of £1,118,000 Artois, inter alia on the city of Antwerp, the Brussels government, the king of Portugal, the king of England and Gaspar Ducci (the latter for the account of the *Rentmeesters*) at interest rates varying from 11 to 13½ per cent. Against this were set their own borrowings from fair to fair on the Antwerp Exchange for a sum of £661,404 Artois or 110,834 Flemish pounds groat (35 items at interest varying from 8 to 10 per cent).

The savage military conflicts of the 1550s pushed official borrowings to frightening heights. The emperor was so embarrassed for money that during discussions at Innsbruck and Casal de Monferrato in December 1551 he could only persuade the Genoese to extend old loans and grant new ones by allowing them to export precious metals from Spain. On 28 May 1552 an agreement was reached (with difficulty) with Anton Fugger too (the Villach *asiento*). In the Netherlands, the Provincial States of Flanders, Brabant and Holland sold a flood of annuities on behalf of the central government. Vainly the emperor tried to save a hopeless financial situation by unprecedented imports of American silver to Seville, by new taxes, short-term advances on the Castilian fairs and permission for new exports of silver. By 1555 the floating public debt in Spain stood at about £24 million Artois and in the Netherlands at about £6 million Artois. With rising interest rates, this meant a tremendous financial strain: in 1556 it burdened the Netherlands government with £1,357,287 Artois. To make matters worse, a severe famine was foreshadowed in 1556–7, so that the money market was put under pressure by grain speculators.

In June 1557 Philip II issued his first bankruptcy decree: all payments of assignments against official income were suspended and replaced by

5 per cent Spanish state annuities (*juros*). The entire silver cargo arriving with the fleets on 1 July and 26 September of that year in Seville was confiscated. After lengthy discussions, an agreement was arrived at on 14 November 1560 with the Genoese bankers for settlement of their debt. The new decree froze once again the capital of all loans made to the Crown since 1557 and consolidated it by new *juro* certificates at 5 per cent at the *Casa de Contratación* of Seville. The *Casa* thus seemed to be cast for a role as a national Bank of Spain, servicing a national debt; an important innovation indeed. Alas, the experiment was total failure, arrivals of silver shrinking at the very moment when government expenditure was rising. Moreover, the Fuggers and other south German bankers refused to concur in this; not until two years later did they accept a compromise, unfortunately on much less favourable terms. Many went bankrupt. South German banking never recovered from the shock of Spanish state bankruptcy. The supremacy of the Antwerp money market over the Habsburg official finances was likewise góne for ever. Its position had been considerably undermined since the beginning of the 1550s by too great a dependence on Spanish taxes, credits and imports of precious metals.

The revival of Genoese banking was a masterpiece of opportunist strategy. Once Charles V had gained political control of Italy in the 1520s, the Genoese bankers opted decisively for the Habsburgs, allying after 1528 with Seville and Castile, in keeping with the traditional ties between Genoa and Catalonia. To breach the hegemony of the Florentines and Lucchese in Lyons and escape from the political control of the French monarch, they founded in 1534 their own fairs in Besançon, an area beyond the authority of king and emperor. Charles's military campaigns of the 1520s formed the point of departure for the integration of the Italian economy into the Habsburg world complex. The massive state bankruptcies at the end of the 1550s (Habsburg 1557, France 1558 and Portugal 1560) eliminated the south Germans and opened the way for the Genoese to achieve supremacy over world finance. The south Germans had participated to a large extent with their own capital in public financing, unlike the Genoese, who had not committed themselves to the same extent and had participated above all with outsiders' deposits: as a result, the Genoese withstood the crisis much better and at a single stroke reached the rank of the most important government bankers: 'das Zeitalter der Fugger' (R. Ehrenberg) now made way once and for all for 'le siècle des Genois' (F. Braudel).

Other circumstances also favoured the change. After the Treaty of Cateau-Cambrésis in 1559 the emphasis of Spanish world policy shifted to the Mediterranean: here Genoa's location was strategically vital. The

1560s and following years saw a new expansion of Italian trade with the Levant, Spain, Germany and the Netherlands. The result was a fund of credit to which bankers were able to have recourse in order to grant advances to the government. Paradoxically, Genoese dominance was strengthened still more by the new vigour of the Antwerp money market. After the sudden loss of influence by the south German bankers, Antwerp had been compelled to relinquish the monopoly of Habsburg official finance for good, but her position of leading commercial money market in northwest Europe was fully maintained. She derived new strength from the expansion of northern European trade with the south, largely attending to the financial transactions for this until deep into the seventeenth century. From the moment that the Revolt broke out in the Netherlands in 1567-8 and Elizabeth I blockaded the direct shipments of silver from Spain, the Antwerp money and exchange market became a valuable satellite of the Genoese banking system, especially for the financing of the Eighty Years War.

Since the accession of Charles V the *asiento* contracts had occupied an increasingly important place in the credit system of Spanish public finance.[1] The merchant bankers (*asentistas*) sold to the king of Spain, his ministers or to his plenipotentiary in Brussels, bills of exchange issued in Medina del Campo or Madrid and payable outside Spain at fixed times and places at exchange rates fixed above the market rate. Repayment of these advances was secured on Spanish public income, Spanish merchandise and, increasingly, on claims against silver expected from the Indies. Between 1551 and 1560 and above all from 1566, the *asientos* were usually accompanied by licences to export silver from Spain. In addition to these external *asientos* there were internal ones, repayment of which was effected within Spain: these were short-term loans to the Crown, which until the decree of 1575 usually took the form of credits opened in the exchange banks of the Castilian fairs and indicating explicitly the rate of interest (7-8 per cent per annum during the 1560s and 12-16 per cent per annum between 1572 and 1575). The *asiento* contracts were concluded mainly with *consortia* of large merchant bankers; these in turn placed a large part of their contracts with smaller merchants and local financiers by means of indirect participations or deposits. The network of international connections controlled by the big bankers and the confidence they enjoyed enabled them to mobilize credit on behalf of the Crown and realize transfers of capital at regular times and to any place desired in Europe north of the Pyrenees. From 1557-60 the Genoese (Grimaldi, Gentile, Centurione and other families) dominated the *asiento* contracts. Whilst the Genoese before 1557-60

[1] H. Lapeyre, *Simon Ruiz et les asientos de Philippe II* (Paris, 1953); F. Ruiz-Martin, *Lettres marchandes échangées entre Florence et Medina del Campo* (Paris, 1965), pp. xxix-lii.

had based their financial support to the government largely on the participation by minor merchants in the Genoese loans to the ruler or on occasional deposits by outsiders, their promotion to leading bankers of Spanish world policy required a more substantial financial contribution. The Genoese now made a systematic effort to mobilize the savings of the broader sections of the population in Spain and Italy, in the shape of *juros de Castilla*.[1]

Formerly the *asentistas* had regularly received *juros de caucion*: these served solely as a guarantee against the risk that the normal assignments to the fiscal incomes or to the arrivals of treasure fleets in Seville would not be effectively converted into cash. But from the *asiento* of 2 January 1561 the *asentistas* accepted masses of *juros de resguardo*. These were no longer supplied as guarantees but could rather be regarded as temporary advances on encashment of the actual assignments. The *asentistas* were allowed to sell these *juros de resguardo*; they were simply obliged when encashment of the assignments took place to repay the nominal value of the *juros de resguardo* to the government or to offer analogous *juros*. As some *juros* (for instance those of the *Casa de Contratación*) circulated on the market for as little as 50 per cent of the value at which they were issued, speculation was possible: the Genoese received *juros de resguardo* that were still good and which they always could sell at nominal value. When the assignments were cashed they repaid the temporary advances with *juros* which they had bought for less than their nominal value on the market but which they were permitted to offer to the government at their nominal value.

Between 1561 and 1575 *juros de resguardo* were sold profitably through the Genoese bankers, first in Castile itself because the most common (i.e. redeemable) *juros* could be acquired only by subjects of Castile. Soon Castilian corporate bodies – convents, hospitals, chapter-houses and other institutions – also acquired official permission. And when foreigners too were permitted to buy the Spanish *juros*, they penetrated the Netherlands, Germany and Italy, where they became coveted investments in addition to the official annuities on Milan, Naples and Sicily. Confidence in the *juros* grew, causing the interest rate to fall, in spite of the considerable increase in the issues (see Table 28).

The distribution of Europe's precious metals was likewise controlled by the Genoese. The Spanish, Italian and German mercenary armies preferred to be paid in gold, but circulation of current money in Spain and north of the Alps increasingly took the form of silver from the second half of the sixteenth century. Italy still had large reserves of gold, so that Genoese banking became an essential link in war finance, converting silver into gold for the armies' pay. When the *licencias de sacas*

[1] F. Ruiz-Martin, 'Credito y Banca. Comercio y Transportes', pp. 7–19.

13-2

Table 28.　*Total capital and total annual interest yield of the Spanish juros (1504–98)*

Year	Annual outstanding interest in *maravedis*	Interest rate	Capital in *maravedis*	Capital in ducats
1504	112,362,468	[10]	1,123,624,680	2,996,332
1505	109,016,586		1,090,165,860	2,907,108
1515	129,300,000	[9·75]	1,326,153,840	3,536,410
1516	131,103,000		1,344,646,150	3,585,723
1522	137,926,000	[9·50]	1,451,852,631	3,871,607
1523	139,930,000		1,472,947,368	3,927,859
1524	152,515,000		1,605,421,052	4,281,122
1526	186,555,000	[9]	2,072,833,333	3,327,555
1527	185,184,000		2,057,600,000	5,486,933
1529	232,856,000		2,587,288,888	6,899,437
1536	269,530,000	[8]	3,369,125,000	8,984,333
1538	253,143,000		3,164,287,500	8,438,100
1540	266,700,000	[7]	3,810,000,000	10,160,000
1542	273,155,000		3,902,214,285	10,405,904
1545–50	323,689,811	6·25	5,170,180,970	13,811,149
1552	299,580,826	6·09	4,919,225,380	13,117,934
1554	329,329,000		5,407,701,140	14,420,536
1560	550,687,280	6·78	8,122,231,260	21,659,283
1566	790,195,000		11,654,793,510	31,097,449
1573	1,031,892,650		13,219,655,600	40,585,748
1584	1,431,318,546	5·81	24,635,431,000	65,694,482
1598	1,737,860,239	5·79	30,011,857,300	80,039,619

SOURCE: F. Ruiz-Martin, 'Credito y Banca. Comercio y Transportes', p. 14.

made a comeback in 1566 and the English embargo of 1568 put a temporary stop on direct silver shipments to the Netherlands, the increasing importance of the Spain–Genoa silver route again favoured the dominance of Genoa over official Habsburg finance.

The vigorous spread of annuity credit after 1561 and the skilful intervention of the Genoese in the market for *juros* offered no sufficient solution to the increasing demands of public finance. The government therefore continued to have recourse to the Genoese bankers for short-term credits. By 1575 the floating debt had risen again to a total of 15,184,464 ducats. On 1 September 1575 Philip II promulgated an edict under which all *asiento* contracts concluded since 14 November 1560 were declared null and void and the system of the *juros de resguardo* was abolished. The payment of the mercenary armies in the Netherlands, through Genoese aloofness or boycott, became so chaotic that mutiny broke out in Brussels, followed by the plundering of Antwerp (the 'Spanish Fury'). On 5 December 1577 Philip II was obliged to conclude a new agreement with the Genoese bankers: the floating debt was consolidated with the *juros de resguardo* still in Genoese possession as advances, with new *juros* at 3⅓ per cent per annum and a number of other rights; for their part the Genoese agreed to a new *asiento* of 5 million *écus* immediately payable at various centres in Italy.

The crisis of 1575–7 again confirmed the supremacy of the Genoese banks over Spanish public finance.[1] However, the Genoese drew their own conclusions from the events. To strengthen their position they transferred the Besançon fairs of payment in 1578 to Piacenza and organized exports of silver from Spain largely through Genoa. For his part Philip II, after 1575–7, made repeated attempts to smash the Genoese hegemony. Spanish bankers like Simon Ruiz were asked to play a greater part in the *asiento* contracts. From 1579 Francesco de Medici of Florence was also called in. In 1583, Peter van Oudegherste submitted a project for the foundation of a public banking system in Spain. Exports of silver were again forbidden for a time in 1583 and in 1590. Finally, in 1596, Philip II issued an edict that suspended payments relating to the floating debt, followed by a new consolidation with the *Medio General* of 28 November 1597. Genoa reacted to the edict of 1596 by founding a financial company to further the interests of the Genoese bankers and a number of other partners.[2] The company was also given the task of direct supervision of the national accounts of Spain. Genoese dominance seemed re-confirmed in 1618, when a new company, exclusively Genoese, was founded. In reality, such companies betrayed a defensive attitude on the part of the Genoese bankers. Their ranks were closing in concerted efforts to sustain possible blows from the authorities.

The great shift in the world economic situation during the credit crisis of 1619–20 seriously undermined the position of the Genoese. The new Spanish state bankruptcy that followed in 1627 weakened their monopoly once again. Spanish, and above all Portuguese merchant bankers, who were also strongly represented in Antwerp and maintained good relations with Portuguese Jews in Amsterdam, tried with the support of Olivares to take the place of the Genoese. But by now Spanish world policy was already on its last legs. The opening of the 'English Road' via Dover for transfers of silver from Spain to the Netherlands in the mid 1630s led to a change in the organization of

[1] G. J. Da Silva, *Banque et crédit en Italie*, pp. 217–78, 679–91.
[2] F. Ruiz-Martin, 'Formation and Development of "Capitalism"', *Proceedings of the Fourth International Congress of Economic History, Bloomington, 1968* (Paris–The Hague, 1974).

Spanish war financing. The days of the world banking system at the service of Spanish world hegemony were gone for ever.

The age of the Fuggers and the Genoese was one of spectacular growth of public finances. The increase in the need for money multiplied demand and encouraged the search for new techniques. Personal wealth grew more mobile, national debts more organized. Supply responded positively; between 1500 and 1650 the interest rates for short-term and long-term public credit dropped considerably. But the basic structure of public finance was unchanged: the main stress continued to fall on redeemable annuity credit and on short-term advances, both dominated by the merchant bankers. Private banking still dominated public finance: monarchs remained suppliants. No true public credit came into being. Supply and demand steadily grew but, trapped as they were in a framework of still primitive techniques, they led repeatedly to catastrophic state bankruptcies and *moratoria*.

(3) FROM FLOATING TO CONSOLIDATED NATIONAL DEBT

Traditional ideas and techniques continued to set the tone in French public finance during the seventeenth century. Redeemable hereditary or life annuities were still being sold on a large scale by the French king. As soon as a new source of state income came into being, it was capitalized by the sale of annuities, the payment of which was assigned to the new source. For the king, assignment to a specific income had the advantage that the payment of interest could be suspended if for some reason or other the income proved not to be realizable (as repeatedly happened during the Fronde [1648–53]). Moreover, the redeemability clause allowed of extinction or conversion of the public debt. Jean-Baptiste Colbert, who abhorred the annuity system, even worked out in 1663–4 a general extinction plan, under which state annuities would be repurchased on a basis of their market value during the last 25 years. The reaction of the *rentiers* was so violent that concessions had to be granted: the extinction scheme was replaced by a conversion of the public debt into annuities with a reduced yield. Thus the interest rate gradually fell from 7 per cent to 5 per cent and lower: at the end of Louis XIV's reign a capital of some £ two thousand million *tournois* was offset by a service charge of only £86 million *tournois*, representing an overall interest rate of 5·3 per cent.

Apart from his measures for improving the government's budget (with the result that the French budget was in surplus from 1662 to 1671), Colbert also made an attempt to strengthen public finance by founding a *Caisse des Emprunts* in 1674. The new bank accepted deposits from private persons withdrawable at short notice and issued certificates (*promesses*) that were accepted in payment by the authorities and soon became fully negotiable. The intention was to create a system of permanent floating public debt with a minimum liquidity reserve. This system already ran sharply counter to the current practices of the treasury, so that after Colbert's death in 1683, Le Pelletier quickly decided to abolish the *Caisse des Emprunts* and converted the deposits into annuities.

The success of annuities and the drop in the interest rate in seventeenth-century France can also be explained from the demand side. At a time when grain prices showed little or no change and the economic situation was uncertain the annuity, like other immovable assets, represented a safe investment, unlike those in commerce and industry, which were regarded as speculative. Annuities therefore found customers enough, both in the country and in the towns: *la rente domine*. The issue of annuities, however, required elaborate procedures: they had to be registered by the Parlement de Paris and promulgated by royal edict; the sale itself took a considerable time. In order to have liquid resources at their immediate disposal, the French kings therefore had recourse to financiers and bankers. The financiers were those who were directly concerned with public finance. They were first and foremost the royal officials (*officers des finances, intendants, controleurs, receveurs* etc.) and the private financiers. Apart from the organization of the sale of annuities, the collection of almost all other public income, in particular the indirect taxes, was contracted out to the financiers. Four main groups of farms or purchases came particularly to the fore: *partis* (relating to a particular fiscal income), *fermes* (relating to the royal domains), *traites* (relating to occasional instructions, such as supplying a campaigning army), *offices* (relating to a given office). The farms (*fermes*) underwent increasing concentration from the end of the sixteenth century (*bail des cinq grosses fermes*, 1584), so that some contracts demanded enormous investment and were subscribed to only by *consortia* or syndicates of financiers.

The intervention of the financiers provided the French treasury with an accelerated and assured supply of fiscal credit. The financiers themselves were regularly obliged to have recourse to credit from private persons by issuing writings obligatory to bearer (*billets des receveurs de finances, billets des traitants, billets des fermiers généraux* etc.). More specifically, these were promissory notes signed by the financiers concerned, payable on a fixed date, bearing interest and assigned to the income provided for in the contract. Together with promissory notes of the government itself these notes became the subject of lively trade, circulating solely within a limited circle of specialists in public finance.

Many of these dealings in securities related solely to the furnishing of guarantees, and before the founding of the Exchange in Paris in 1724 there was no question of an organized money market. The turnover in securities might increase, but it was accompanied by devaluation and jobbery.

At the beginning of the eighteenth century 'money notes' of a sort joined the securities of the financiers and public bodies. In the recoinage of 1701 temporary certificates were produced to serve as means of payment in commerce in order to bridge the gap between the deposit of the old pieces and minting of the new coins. A flood of such money notes followed (in 1704 bearing interest; from 1706 without interest). By 1707 the total volume amounted to £180 million *tournois* and led to a disastrous fall in value, followed by consolidation in annuity titles. In 1702 the *Caisse des Emprunts* was also refounded, with interest-bearing promissory notes. In 1710 the *Caisse Legendre* developed out of a syndicate of twelve *Receveurs Généraux*, who drew notes on this fund.

The proliferation of securities during the wars of the 1690s and the 1700s involved the merchant bankers deeply in French public finance. The treasury had long made calls on the services of merchant bankers, such as Samuel Bernard, Herwarth etc., to transfer moneys abroad for the account of the French government. Around 1700 the merchant bankers of Paris and Lyons committed themselves even more deeply by agreeing to discount the securities of the authorities and financiers. This discounting was financed not with specie but with bills drawn on their domestic and foreign correspondents. In essence, therefore, they did not lend their own money to the king, but merely the confidence which they enjoyed in the world of international commerce: through this confidence the merchant bankers, with the aid of the bill of exchange, were able to draw heavily on the floating reserve of commercial liquid resources available in Europe. The bankers thus obtained short-term exchange credit for the authorities by bill jobbing *en masse*: this credit was not covered by normal commercial transactions, but was based solely on official promises and assignments, and these were uncertain, particularly during the war. The situation was untenable. In 1709 a severe financial crisis broke: the king granted the merchant bankers a moratorium. In fact it was a moratorium to himself.

By the death of Louis XIV in 1715 French public finances had fallen into impossible chaos. The public debt stood at £3 billion *tournois* of which two thirds consisted of annuities and one third of floating debt; the need for reorganization was thus very urgent. During the Regency various proposals were made and initiatives taken. In 1716 a Secret Committee (*Visa*) was set up; it repudiated dubious creditors and dubious obligations, enforced a reduction of the interest rate of the long-term debt and tried to consolidate the floating debt. Ultimately the project of the Scots banker, John Law, was accepted, the *Système John Law*. It comprised a body of measures for the extinction of the floating debt and for comprehensive monetary and fiscal reform.[1] First, Law proposed the founding of an issuing bank along English and Swedish lines under public control with convertible banknotes that were to take the place of metallic money and which could be used to pay off taxes. On 5 May 1716 Law acquired the permission of the *Conseil des Finances* to found a *Banque Générale* with a capital of £6 million *tournois*; three quarters was to be subscribed in government securities and one quarter in cash: the bank was to accept deposits, perform discount operations and issue notes. In 1717 he founded the *Compagnie d'Occident*, which acquired title to the French territories in the New World for 25 years. Its initial capital was £100 million *tournois*, divided into nominal shares of £500 *tournois*, to be paid up exclusively in government securities, and yielding a fixed interest rate of 4 per cent. By the end of 1718 the whole capital had been subscribed.

In 1718 the *Banque Générale* was converted into the *Banque Royale*, with the issue of new convertible notes bearing the royal seal. Then, from December 1718 the *Compagnie d'Occident* began to swallow up the companies trading with Africa and Asia: a complete monopoly of colonial trade was established. The enterprise acquired a new name, *Compagnie des Indes* (1719), and issued 50,000 new shares. It also acquired monopoly rights to collect taxes for a period of five years. This was an important move: as long as private farmers had collected taxes, they presented the banknotes they received at Law's bank for encashment; the *Compagnie* did not do this, so that pressure on the specie stocks of the bank could now be avoided and the *système Law* increasingly balanced.

Law further proposed in October 1719 that the *Compagnie des Indes* should take over the floating public debt by launching a massive loan to the state at 3 per cent. For this purpose new share issues were launched, to be paid in ten monthly payments in specie, banknotes or government securities. The number of shares ultimately rose to 624,000, and the overall loan to the state to £1,500 million *tournois*. The 3 per cent interest was to be derived provisionally from the proceeds of the farm of the indirect taxes, but Law proposed a fiscal reform in this respect: the levying of taxation ought to be simplified and converted into one single tax on immovables that should amount to 0·5 to 1 per cent, depending on the authorities' requirements.

[1] P. Harsin, 'La Banque et le système de Law', *History of the Principal Public Banks*, collected by J. G. van Dillen (The Hague, 1934), pp. 273–300; H. Lüthy, *La Banque Protestante en France*, pp. 274–428.

Law's system seemed to be crowned with success at the moment when the convertible banknotes of the *Banque Royale* became legal tender and the *Banque Royale* was merged with the *Compagnie des Indes* (1720). The market value of the shares had now risen to £10,000 *tournois* per share, inaugurating a general stock market boom not only in Paris, but in all the important financial centres of Europe. In Paris, the shares of the *Compagnie des Indes* took the place of government securities: thus any creditor of the state became a shareholder of the *Compagnie des Indes*. But now troubles multiplied. The fiscal reforms encountered tremendous resistance; the proceeds of the indirect taxes which had to feed the payment of the farm, out of which the payment of the 3 per cent interest for the big state loan was to be financed, failed to reach expectations; the results of the colonial undertakings were equally unpromising. Distrust grew and soon changed to panic, with the share prices of the *Compagnie des Indes* plummeting to £200 *tournois*. Law fled the country; his system ended in a complete fiasco which inflicted enormous losses on all those who had lent money to the government. The French panic spread to the rest of Europe, generating the first great stock market crash of modern times. In Paris an Enquiry Committee (*Second Visa*) was set up in December 1720; it dissolved the bank and the company, repudiated claims up to £500 million *tournois* and consolidated the remaining paper credits and bank notes presented up to an amount of £640 million *tournois*, with annuities yielding 2–2·5 per cent. Once again, the fragmented group of independent financiers resumed control of French public finance. France remained imprisoned in an antiquated structure. Not until 1776 did the government dare to found a new public issuing bank, the *Caisse d'Escompte*.

Seventeenth-century Swedish public finance likewise laboured under severe pressure from political and military expansion. At first it was vigorously supported by the remarkable growth of copper production at Falun (the *Stora Kopparberg*) and by the introduction by edict of 6 June 1625 of a bimetallic coin standard, based on silver and copper. Silver *talers* were joined by copper *talers* weighing about one kilogram each. From 1644 *ten-taler* pieces (*platmynt*) were put into circulation. Because of the fall in the market price these coins contained 19·7 kilograms of copper each and were unsuitable for normal circulation. This stimulated the issue of banknotes.

With the prospect of being able to obtain extra credits, King Charles X Gustavus had on 30 November 1656 granted Hans Wittmacher (later ennobled under the name of Johan Palmstruck) permission to found a bank in Stockholm to concentrate on exchange and lending operations. In 1661 the Bank of Stockholm acquired the right of note issue for a period of thirty years: thenceforth it issued printed bank-notes, to bearer and without interest. These circulated briskly throughout Sweden and Finland and were commonly used for the payment of salaries and taxes. They were the first modern banknotes in the world. The bank soon made its first mistake: a serious over-issue of notes. When world prices for copper also increased, and the holders of bank-notes consequently displayed a growing preference for a copper coinage, the bank's position became extremely vulnerable. In the summer of 1663 there was a heavy run on the bank, which the government tried in vain to absorb by imposing a compulsory rate for the banknotes. In the autumn the bank failed and was closed by the government in the following year.

At the beginning of the eighteenth century Baron de Goertz in a last attempt to find an immediate solution for Sweden's hopeless financial situation, tried a new expedient; between May 1716 and November 1717 he had 15 million *rixdales* in copper tokens (*myntteckens*) and 3 million *rixdales* in interest-bearing state notes (ranging from 2 to 18 *rixdales* per note) put into circulation. But it was not long before both money substitutes were taken out of circulation at one third of their original value; the Goertz system became a thing of the past.

Between 1544 and 1574 the English Crown had frequently turned to the Antwerp money market for short-term loans guaranteed against bonds of the big English Merchant Companies and later against bonds of the Corporation of London. Transfers of loans to London via the Antwerp exchange market, extensions and repayments required highly skilled debt management of which Sir Thomas Gresham proved himself a true master: Gresham always waited for the right moment, acted with discretion and made skilful use of the Merchant Adventurers and the Staplers to obtain money repayable at imposed rates of exchange.[1] After 1574 no further foreign loans were floated, so that for her short-term borrowings Elizabeth I became mainly dependent on London money-lenders. She did not make excessive use of them. Royal finance continued to be based mainly on feudal income, i.e. on feudal annuities, church income, penalties and tolls. The queen could also regularly count on the subsidies, extraordinary income granted by Parliament in the form of taxation. This prudent system depended on her persistent sense of economy. The Stuarts upset this laboriously constructed equilibrium. Utmost extravagance now became the fashion; all restraints on public expenditure were relaxed. The annual deficit became a permanent feature of the ordinary budget. Debts soared ominously.

[1] R. B. Outhwaite, 'The English Crown and the Antwerp Money Market in the mid-XVIth Century', *Economic History Review*, 2nd ser., XIX (1966), 289–305.

In 1610 Robert Cecil, Earl of Salisbury, in his function of Lord Treasurer, proposed the 'Great Contract', under which the king and Parliament would agree to abolish feudal wardship in exchange for a permanent annual subsidy of £100,000 sterling; other feudal rights would likewise be done away with in exchange for £200,000 sterling per annum; excise duties on foodstuffs, drinks etc., and new tolls, would create supplementary income.[1] Hardly surprisingly, the merchants' opposition to the introduction of the excise duties was so great that Cecil's initiative failed. Public finance headed for catastrophe.

To finance his extravagant spending, the king repeatedly appealed to the goodwill of Parliament: not always with the desired result. In principle new subsidies could be granted only in an emergency (so the argument went); even then specific grievances had to be redressed by the king. Relations became so strained that the king increasingly turned his back on Parliament and sought ways out through his feudal income, his royal prerogatives and short-term borrowings. The 'Great Farm of the Customs', instituted in 1604, fell into the hands of syndicates of merchants possessing ample means who gradually rose to become royal bankers. The king drew on these farmers by means of Exchequer tallies. Originally these were simply receipts for payments to the Exchequer. Later they were issued as cheques drawn on the farmers and assigned to their current or future customs incomes (tallies of *sol*). Sometimes the king also acquired credit by means of overdrafts granted by the farmers to the king (from the reign of Charles I, with interest charged).[2] The king also obtained substantial income from the prerogative rights of the Crown. The sale of royal privileges and concessions (charters, monopolies, patents etc.) enjoyed increasing – and to Parliament ominous – success. The Statute of Monopolies of 1623, by which monopolies could be granted only for a maximum period of 14 years, unless the beneficiaries possessed corporate status, opened the way to systematic sale of these concessions. The sale of offices and exploitation of Crown lands were alternative sources of extraordinary public income. The Royal Contract of 1627/8 authorized the Corporation of London to sell huge areas of royal land in repayment of loans which the Corporation had made for the account of the government.

The Stuarts further made timely use of the concentration of personal wealth in London for short-term borrowings. Members of the nobility and other influential persons at court were suitable sources of this credit, along with fiscal officials and foreign merchants residing in London, such as Philip Burlamachi in the 1620s and Sir Peter van Lore. Sometimes syndicates (like the monopolistic London Society of Soap-

[1] C. Wilson, *England's Apprenticeship, 1603–1763* (London, 1965), pp. 91–3.
[2] R. Ashton, *The Crown and the Money Market*, pp. 47–53.

boilers) were formed to provide royal loans. The Corporation of London was regularly asked to mediate: not infrequently it entrusted the floating of the loan to the livery companies, borrowed direct from the citizenry or approached the City aldermen.

Through the discounting of Exchequer tallies the goldsmith bankers ultimately fell prey to royal finance. Whilst Cromwell was in power this discounting grew, reaching a climax in the early years of Charles II. At the Restoration, king and Parliament had reached an agreement, under which the ancient feudal rights of the Crown were converted into a hereditary income of £1·2 million sterling, to be financed from three large permanent sources of income: the old customs, the excise duties newly instituted on the Dutch pattern, and the hearth tax (1662). The possibility of obtaining extra subsidies from Parliament naturally remained open. The farmers of customs and excise duties still acted as bankers of the Crown by granting advances, but the goldsmiths increasingly dominated short-term public borrowing by means of discount operations: they now discounted not only the royal assignments to the hereditary income but also those to the subsidies granted by Parliament in times of emergency or war.

Parliament's resentment at this controlling position of the goldsmith bankers in the public finances soon made itself felt. When the king sought new additional subsidies during the Dutch War, Sir George Downing, in defiance of Clarendon, introduced a project aimed at eliminating the goldsmiths as Crown bankers. The proposal was approved in 1666: short-term loans were to be floated on the expected proceeds of the subsidy, which had to be paid *direct* by the public to the Exchequer and which would be repaid in chronological order, thanks to numbering of the securities. However, lenders could transfer these new 'orders of payment', as they were called, to third parties; in other words, they could hand them over to bankers by endorsement for discounting. Some orders of payment were clearly specified; they might represent repayment of a loan or payment for goods supplied; others were simply certificates giving the holders the right to payment by the government. From 1667 to 1668 this latter type, assigned to the public income as a whole, circulated in ever-growing quantities and for ever-decreasing fixed amounts: in fact, they already formed a kind of paper money. But such money implied trust among the holders, a trust that was to be fatally undermined by wild over-issue. Orders of payment were submitted for reimbursement with growing urgency, so that by January 1672 the Crown was obliged to grant the Exchequer a moratorium to the amount of £1,173,353 sterling. To Parliament's consternation, the bulk of the orders proved to be held by the goldsmith bankers. Plainly the Downing plan had misfired. Paradoxically, the moratorium achieved Downing's original purpose: the shock caused by the 'Stop of the Exchequer' was so violent that a number of banks came to grief. The grip of the goldsmith bankers on public finance was finally broken.

Whilst the years that followed were relatively quiet, the war climate of the 1690s again confronted public finance with serious problems. In 1688 the English Revolution brought a mixed form of royal-parliamentary government under a Dutch monarch having good connections with Amsterdam: it offered a much firmer basis for confidence in the authorities. The private discounting of official assignments, so popular before 1672, was out of fashion. A crucial change in public finance was foreshadowed: English public credit was gradually developing into a 'National Debt'. In 1692, in emulation of Dutch example, a proposal for launching a tontine loan of £1 million sterling was debated in Parliament. It was adopted in December of that year, receiving royal approval on the following 26 January.[1] The Act had two striking features: the interest was to be paid out of certain new excise duties on beer and liquors, introduced by law, in other words a reliable fund of credit was created *under Parliamentary guarantee*; furthermore, it created *perpetual* (i.e. long-term) annuities, which meant that the annuitant could not demand his capital back, though the government could repay the loan at any time it felt able to do so.

The 1693 loan was no great success, but new principles had been introduced into English public finance with far-reaching consequences. In the 1690s many schemes were proposed and approved for financing the war effort, such as the Million Lottery of 1694, the Malt Lottery of 1697, the Land Banks, the Orphans' Fund Bank etc.[2] One scheme stood head and shoulders above the others on account of its originality and its lasting importance: the proposal of the Scots financier, William Paterson, for the foundation of the Bank of England. Philip Burlamachi and Sir Paul Pindar had already submitted abortive proposals for the foundation of a national bank during the first half of the century, but

[1] Tontine loans, named after Lorenzo Tonti (1630–95), a financial adviser to Cardinal Mazarin, were already in common use in the second half of the seventeenth century in private insurance and in municipal finances in the United Provinces and in France. In return for the capital loaned, annuities were granted, but with the special clause that upon the decease of an annuitant the amount of interest becoming available was added to the annuities of the surviving annuitants. Consequently, the latter enjoyed a steadily increasing interest income until the last surviving annuitant died. In the English loans of 1692–3 creditors were given a choice between a simple annuity at 14 per cent per annum and an annuity at 10 per cent per annum up to 1700 and a tontine arrangement after 1700. Cf. P. G. M. Dickson, *The Financial Revolution in England* (London–New York, 1967), pp. 41–2.

[2] For these projects see Horsefield, *British Monetary Experiments*, pp. 93 f.

politically the time was now ripe for the successful realization of such an idea. In 1694 Paterson proposed a loan of £1,200,000 sterling bearing a fixed interest rate of 8 per cent per annum. To guarantee the payment of this interest Parliament would create a 'perpetual' fund of credit from a new tax on ship's tonnage and on liquors. The subscribers were entitled by a charter of incorporation to perform banking operations, i.e. they could receive deposits, deal in bills of exchange and bullion, lend on security etc. The right to issue banknotes was not clearly specified, but was to be explicitly included in a new charter of 1707. No subscriber was to lend more than a maximum of £20,000 sterling. At least 25 per cent had to be paid up in cash immediately, the rest in instalments.

The proposal was approved by Parliament and aroused great interest: within twelve days the whole loan had been fully subscribed and the first instalment of fully paid capital transferred to the state. The loan was in the form of bills obligatory taken by the Exchequer in exchange for interest-bearing tallies and used for paying creditors. Those who received such bills could present them to the Bank of England: at choice, they could be left on deposit (their certificates were interest-bearing and negotiable, but did not circulate much), or specie and banknotes could be demanded in exchange. The banknotes were usually negotiable 'bearer notes', issued in irregular denominations and soon in printed form. An office was set up in Antwerp to help organize the transfers of money for government account to the Southern Netherlands for financing the war: a clear illustration of how closely the Bank of England was involved with public finance from its very beginnings.

The support given by the Bank of England to the government was not confined to a long-term loan or to cash and transfer functions for government account. It gradually also acquired a leading position in the granting of short-term public credit (see Table 29). Upon the renewal of the Bank's charter in 1707, dealing in Exchequer bills was already stated to be its central task. The Exchequer bill was a short-term, interest-bearing government security, the issue of which had been provided for in the statute of 1696 relating to the founding of Land Banks. The holder could use it to pay his taxes (though in practice during the first months it was refused by the Board of Excise as a means of payment). It could also be submitted to the Bank of England for payment in cash on the due date. The Exchequer bill was intended to be a new, improved, version of the tally and of the order of payment; thanks to Parliament it was under safer control and, through its connection with the Bank of England, rested on a firm institutional basis. Although it was made out to bearer, the Exchequer bill usually circulated from hand to hand by endorsement only. Moreover, it had a

Table 29. *Bank of England financial data,*

Date	14.iii. 1696	10.xi. 1696	25.vi. 1697	31.viii. 1698	31.vii. 1699	31.viii. 1700
LIABILITIES						
(1) Bank bills	1,124	894	956	502	1,198	927
(2) Specie and running cash notes	887	764	982	1,220	504	762
(3) Accomptable notes	—	—	—	20	15	19
(4) Total notes	2,011	1,658	1,938	1,742	1,718	1,709
(5) Deposits and drawing accounts	65[b]	—	—	100	123	100
(6) Foreign exchange	323	300	254	—	—	—
(7) Miscellaneous	13	18	27	56	14	13
(8) Total external liabilities	2,412	1,976	2,219	1,897	1,855	1,822
(9) Internal liabilities[a]	770	1,325	1,243	2,316	2,301	2,300
(10) Total liabilities and assets	3,182	3,301	3,462	4,213	4,155	4,123
ASSETS						
(11) 'Fund of Bank of England'	1,200	1,200	1,200	1,200	1,200	1,200
(12) Interest due	43	50	10	33	2	14
(13) Loans and discounts on other Government Funds	1,567	1,785	1,830	2,401	2,152	2,310
(14) Government account balances	—	—	42	2	2	2
(15) Total Government	2,810	3,035	3,082	3,636	3,356	3,526
(16) Bills discounted and receivable	51	50	40	86	95	173
(17) Personal account balances	64	42	42	37	83	91
(18) Miscellaneous	—	29	3	10[d]	5	5
(19) Total non-Government	115	121	85	133	183	269
(20) Decrease of capital stock	—	—	—	—	18	24
(21) Miscellaneous internal	—	101	18	14	8	4
(22) Cash and bullion	258	45	276	429	590	301
(23) Exchequer bills deducted from both sides						
(24) Cash ratio – gross[f]	10·7	2·3	12·4	22·6	31·8	16·5
(25) Cash ratio – net[g]	12·8	2·7	14·2	23·3	32·0	16·6

[a] Subscriptions, and balances of dividends, salaries, etc.
[b] Discounts.
[c] Exchequer Bills (net holding).
[d] Mainly Foreign Exchange.

formal appearance and clearly retained the character of a short-term loan.
Initially, it had no great success and tallies continued to circulate briskly
as short-term public credit. The Exchequer bill was nevertheless to
develop gradually into the principal instrument of England's floating
debt and was to continue in this capacity throughout the eighteenth
century. The part played by the Bank of England in this was doubtless
essential, since its readiness to convert the bills into cash palpably increased confidence in the new government security.

summary Balance Sheets, 1696–1710 (£ '000)

31.viii. 1701	31.viii. 1702	31.viii. 1703	31.viii. 1704	31.viii. 1705	31.viii. 1706,	31.viii. 1707	31.viii. 1708	31.viii. 1709	31.viii. 1710
891	1,023	900	683	1,029	847	987	920	541	307
741	909	1,168	869	922	773	789	569	673	457
23	102	46	77	51	32	36	30	29	24
1,655	2,034	2,114	1,629	2,002	1,652	1,812	1,519	1,244	787
476	146	227	170	226	198	199	176	171	126
26	—	—	—	—	—	—	—	—	59
34	19	31	11	19	16	17	36	149	22
2,191	2,198	2,372	1,810	2,247	1,866	2,028	1,731	1,564	994
2,287	2,317	2,321	2,291	2,281	2,286	1,713	2,351	4,574	5,211
4,478	4,514	4,693	4,100	4,528	4,152	3,742	4,082	6,138	6,206
1,200	1,200	1,200	1,200	1,200	1,200	1,200	1,200	1,600	1,600
12	6	—	6	—	—	—	—	8	17
2,364	2,024	2,002	1,739	1,677	1,379	888	798	2,467	2,568
						861[e]	1,194[e]	607[e]	498[e]
9	—	—	—	—	—	53	2	33	490
3,585	3,230	3,202	2,945	2,877	2,579	3,002	3,194	4,715	5,173
106	85	75	130	102	161	207	187	245	405
86	24	45	33	21	63	31	106	48	108
66[d]	5	2	8	9	12	9	8	6	194[d]
258	114	122	171	132	236	247	301	299	707
35	145	316	475	673	904	—	—	—	—
4	4	2	2	2	2	16	19	482[e]	28
596	1,021	1,053	507	842	430	475	566	642	296
						1,467	1,570	2,424	3,045
27·2	46·5	44·4	28·0	37·4	23·0	13·6	17·1	16·1	7·3
28·0	47·3	45·0	28·2	37·8	23·2	23·6	33·4	45·4	32·4

e Includes £447,000 'owing from proprietors'.
f Cash and bullion as percentage of gross external liabilities (including all Exchequer Bills).
g Cash and bullion as percentage of notes, deposits and drawing accounts.
SOURCE: J. K. Horsefield, *British Monetary Experiments, 1650–1710*, pp. 264–5.

In 1697 a proposal was adopted for coupling with a new long-term state loan permission to set up an incorporated East India Company as a rival to the old one. Other loans followed in 1709 during the War of Spanish Succession and led to a merger of the two companies into the United East India Company.[1] Finally, in 1710, the South Sea Company received the privilege of trading in Spanish America in return for long-term loans to the state: the Company soon became still more heavily

[1] P. G. M. Dickson, *The Financial Revolution in England*.

involved in government borrowing, when, in June 1711, the new Ministry under Edward Harley, facing depreciation of government short-term paper, consolidated £9 million of floating debt into a unified, permanent and guaranteed fund, which was to be the South Sea Company. In order to make the consolidation operation attractive to the investors, the South Sea Company had to accept the government short-term obligations at face value in exchange for its stock.

The loans of the three big corporations – the Bank of England, the East India Company and the South Sea Company – thus played a crucial role during this period in the transition from floating to consolidated national debt. The loans were perpetual, though redeemable, and consequently formed a strong guarantee for the authorities. The public for its part likewise felt favoured as shareholders of a commercial or financial company, since the latter possessed good assignments for the payment of interest, and could make a profit thanks to commercial or financial privileges and activities; finally, the shares could increase in value.

The English public debt still consisted largely of long-term annuities, some of 6 to 7 per cent running until 1792–1807, others at 9 per cent and running until 1742. In 1717, a first attempt was made to consolidate a part of this long-term debt, mainly the lottery money, into a new fund of stock yielding 5 per cent p.a. and managed by the Bank of England. The shares of the South Sea Company rose feverishly in 1719–20, as a result of the general stock market boom common to Paris, London and Amsterdam, and reconversion of the remaining annuities and other long-term government securities into new shares of the South Sea Company was proposed. The proposal, clearly inspired by the success of John Law's analogous scheme in France, was favourably received by Parliament, and led to the South Sea Act of March 1720. The response was beyond all expectations: about four-fifths of the annuities and still more of the securities were converted by *rentiers* speculating on a further rise in share prices. The speculative expectations were dramatically nipped in the bud by the South Sea Bubble of 1720. Share prices plummeted, but the South Sea Company survived the crisis, thanks in part to the support of the government and the Bank of England. For its part, the Company was compelled to abandon its commercial pretensions and functioned solely as a 'Holding Company for Government Stock'. Consolidated loans now dominated the development of the national debt, which increased from £12·8 million sterling in 1702 to £132·9 million in 1763.[1] The National Debt had acquired a permanent and continuous character, partly on account of the frequency of the wars between 1690 and 1763. The costs

---

[1] C. Wilson, *England's Apprenticeship*, pp. 313–21.

of the wars were partly borne by the greater proceeds from taxation that had become possible through the increasing importance of excise duties. But, more generally, confidence in government grew so strongly that investments in the National Debt could be offered (and sold) at a reduced interest rate. Sir John Barnard fought for a general reduction to 3 per cent, but encountered bitter resistance from the three large corporations and their numerous shareholders, including many members of the middle classes.

The corporations were unable to maintain their monopolistic position with regard to the granting of long-term public credit. Soon they encountered increasing competition from a group of bankers known as the 'underwriters'. When new government loans were issued these 'underwriters' subscribed for large amounts and then placed these with their own clientèle. The position of the underwriters was in turn undermined before the middle of the eighteenth century by the 'open subscription' system, which from 1747 established that direct link between government and individual investors so much desired by George Downing in the 1670s. But the big corporations did not disappear. And the underwriters also continued to be active, in particular the great Dutch merchants and Portuguese Jews residing in London and acting as agents for their Amsterdam principals, who in turn recruited the savings of Dutch private and institutional investors.

The interest of Dutch banking in the English National Debt was particularly lively in the course of the eighteenth century. As early as the 1690s shares of the leading English corporations began to appear on the Amsterdam Exchange. Gradually Dutch merchant bankers, through the intermediary functions of their London agents, also acquired a large share in the English public debt. Soon they were participating through those same agents in the open subscriptions on a large scale.[1] Estimates put Dutch investments abroad at more than 1 thousand million guilders: about one third of this amount was said to have been invested in England, largely in government securities.

The Amsterdam bankers' interest in investments in England's National Debt was stimulated by the increasing solvency of the English government. It was also bound up with the rise of financial capitalism in Amsterdam, from the second half of the seventeenth century, when European mercantilism gradually began to undermine Holland's commercial monopoly.[2] Finally, the opportunities for investing in Dutch

[1] J. De Vries, *De Economische Achteruitgang der Republiek in de Achttiende Eeuw* (Leiden, 1968), pp. 64–6.

[2] P. Klein, *Entrepreneurial Behaviour and the Economic Rise and Decline of the Netherlands*, pp. 1–19.

public finance were too small in comparison to the vast liquid resources available, techniques on the Amsterdam money and capital market, and the international dimension of the Amsterdam banking business. Even within the framework of Dutch public finance the Amsterdam bankers were given little scope. The City of Amsterdam could count on large-scale short-term credit from the Amsterdam Exchange Bank: the Provincial States and the towns could also have recourse to financial aid from the tax collectors and to advances from the farmers of the many taxes on consumption and luxury goods. Farmers and collectors thus often acted as bankers for regional and local authorities.

The tax collectors also played a leading part during the seventeenth century in the initiation of foreign loans on the Amsterdam money and capital market.[1] When foreign rulers were in need of money, the States-General were prepared to grant certain guarantees to subscribers, insofar as a loan concluded in Amsterdam might also promise political advantages for the Province of Holland. Usually the tax collectors were instructed to work out such loans in concrete terms: if the amount of the loan exceeded their own resources, the collectors approached the big Amsterdam merchant bankers with a view to participations and issued personal obligations by agreement. Such loans were not usually concluded for long periods but could become *de facto* long-term loans, such as the loan of 248,000 guilders in 1616 at 7 per cent by the collector of the Amsterdam Admiralty to the elector of Brandenburg, which was not repaid until about 1680.

In the course of the seventeenth century the merchant bankers themselves also made loans direct to rulers. Elias Trip lent to the king of Sweden on the security of Swedish copper, and Jean Deutz (*inter alia*) to the emperor of Austria in 1659 on the pledge of mercury and copper mines. When Emperor Leopold I requested a new loan of 1·5 million guilders in 1695, the firm of Deutz departed from the usual custom of advancing the money itself or of forming a consortium of bankers, on its own or collective responsibility, and raised the money by a public bond issue. The issue of loans in which printed bonds of the same round sum (usually 1,000 guilders) were circulated soon found acceptance. During the eighteenth century such issues became a common formula for long-term loans contracted in Amsterdam by foreign countries.

The Amsterdam merchant bankers became the largest specialists in the issue business. If a European power wanted to raise long-term credit, it approached a celebrated banking firm in Amsterdam with the request that the latter act as 'entrepreneur'. The bank would then organize the issue of the bond loan for the account of the government instructing it. The collaboration of a famous Amsterdam bank not only increased

[1] J. G. van Dillen, *Van Rijkdom en Regenten* (The Hague, 1970), pp. 457–8.

confidence in the loan, but ensured its success among the widest possible public of investors, minimizing costs and interest payments. The bankers Horneca, Fizeaux and Co. and Van Staphorst placed numerous French loans in Amsterdam. Fizeaux and Hasselgreen acted for the Swedes, Pels acted as intermediary for Prussia and Hamburg, the firms of Deutz and later also Goll and Co. represented the emperor of Austria, the Cliffords centred on Danzig and Denmark, and so on. In the second half of the eighteenth century Russia and the young United States were also to make a large call on the services of the Amsterdam bankers.

With the breakthrough of the Amsterdam issue business in the course of the eighteenth century, public finance throughout Europe underwent a thoroughgoing renewal: *floating* national debts were increasingly supplemented by *funded* national debts based on long-term bond loans and financed by international savings. In England, where the parliamentary regime offered the best guarantees for a responsible control of the expansion of the public debt, the solvency of the government stood highest of all: English government bonds thus aroused the greatest interest abroad.

IV.   *Conclusion*

Innovations in public finance exerted a powerful influence on the development of the European economy. The innovations of the sixteenth century gave the royal houses of Europe, and the Habsburg monarchy in particular, a powerful incentive to follow grandiose world policies, but proved inadequate to satisfy the enormous requirements of money and credit that resulted from them. The gulf between need and opportunity induced the authorities to exert irresponsible pressure on the commercial money markets, leading to dislocation of economic expansion and to catastrophic state bankruptcies.

However disruptive the great state bankruptcies might be in the short term on the economy and public finances of Europe, viewed in the long term they nevertheless had important positive effects. State bankruptcies were in essence *moratoria* on payments of the interest on, and repayments of, floating debts: a solution was usually found in the conversion of these short-term loans into state annuities. The episodic state bankruptcies thus formed the first important step in the systematic development of a consolidated, funded national debt, a development that reached a climax during the heyday of national mercantilism. In France, where mercantilism was placed too much at the service of a policy of *military* expansion during the *politique de grandeur* of Louis XIV, the progress in the technique of public finance led to an increase in unproductive state expenditure, contributing little or nothing to the economic development of the country and initiating serious financial crises. In England, on the other hand, where mercantilism was systematically made to serve a policy of *economic* expansion, the reinforcement of financial techniques became a powerful incentive for the development of a modern economy. From the second half of the seventeenth century, and permanently from the beginning of the eighteenth century, floating debts and later the consolidated National Debt made a tangible contribution towards the financing of the commercial, industrial and colonial infrastructure. They were thus a decisive prerequisite for the successful breakthrough of the Machine Age.

In the course of the eighteenth century many other European states similarly put their 'mercantilism' or 'enlightened despotism' consciously at the service of a policy of economic expansion and with this aim in mind also had recourse to the Amsterdam money and capital market. For the modernization of the continental infrastructure and the later success of the Industrial Revolution this development was likewise of crucial importance. In Holland, on the other hand, state mercantilism never took recognizable shape. Thus the remarkable progress in financial techniques characteristic of Amsterdam did not primarily benefit the infrastructure of Holland itself but was put at the disposal of the rest of Europe, together with her large reserves of available capital. Trapped within the limited political and commercial opportunities available after the Revolt, Holland had no option but to sign her own death warrant. Such was the tragedy and ineluctable decline of the Republic during the eighteenth century.

CHAPTER VI

The Nature of Enterprise

A STUDY of the economic processes of any society encompasses a wide variety of topics, all of which are the proper province of the economic historian. Although the rationale of the present study is the same as that of economic history, the history of enterprise gives primary emphasis to only one aspect of economic behaviour: the function of organizing, coordinating, and directing economic agents in the task of producing goods and services. Central to such a study is the entrepreneur. And any true understanding of the historical function of enterprise involves an appreciation of the origins, motives, and opportunities of entrepreneurs; of the techniques at their disposal and the institutions which they create; of the extent to which they innovate, at various levels, in order to attain their ends; of the encouragement which they enjoy, the obstacles which they overcome, and the success which attends their activity.

An examination of the nature of enterprise cannot be confined either to private businessmen or to innovators. Historically, governments have always assumed entrepreneurial functions and organized economic institutions: the early modern State was too important an element in the framework and display of enterprise to be disregarded in a survey such as this.[1] In addition, the approach envisaged here does not presuppose any sharp division between 'creative' and 'routine' enterprise; quite apart from the fact that novelty and tradition are normally intermingled in any branch of entrepreneurial activity, the apparently repetitive aspects of enterprise are frequently as significant, in economic terms, as those which are spectacularly new. This argument is particularly relevant to a period as little susceptible to business change as the one under consideration.

Broadly considered, the entrepreneur has been defined either as an administrator, the agent who makes important decisions for the unit of enterprise, or as the risk-taker and bearer of uncertainty. These views are not necessarily mutually exclusive – the adoption of one or the other depends on the purpose in hand. In the early modern period, before the advent of large-scale enterprise in industrialized economies, risk rather than administration would appear to be the dominant motif of enterprise. But the entrepreneur bore risks primarily in the sense that

---

[1] An area which, in spite of its economic importance, *will* be largely ignored is agriculture. In part this is dictated by precedent, and in part the problems raised by a study of agricultural enterprise, and its quite specific characteristics, argue against its inclusion in a chapter of this nature.

he took the decisions which involved risks for the economic unit as a whole. It was not necessary (as it is by no means necessary in the twentieth century) that he carry the risk of personal monetary loss. For reasons which will be set out in the following pages, uncertainty and insecurity were predominant elements in both the environment and the processes of enterprise. The entrepreneur, therefore, had the task of balancing the reduction of risk and the attainment of desired profit or of other, non-pecuniary, ends. And the means which he adopted – whether they were directed to a re-shaping of his environment or the modification of the structure and policy of the individual enterprise – comprise a large part of the history of enterprise.

The present chapter is designed to illustrate the diverse nature of enterprise in the early modern period. As befits the subject, it will be approached from divergent viewpoints, each emphasizing a different aspect of entrepreneurship. In the main, the principal characteristics of enterprise in international trade and finance and in manufacturing will be examined. In addition to such examples of functional entrepreneurial behaviour, it may also be helpful to deal with the nature of corporate enterprise, with the entrepreneurial role of the aristocracy, and with the degree to which the nature of enterprise in the different European countries varied from one to the other. This approach assumes that the diversity of the subject can only be described in a selective and impressionistic manner. However, before turning to these categories of enterprise, it will be necessary to delineate the general framework – in economic, political, and ideological terms – within which the entrepreneur worked.

I.   *The Framework of Enterprise*

(1) THE ECONOMIC ENVIRONMENT

The processes of economic development after the close of the Middle Ages were slow, hesitant, and extensive. These years were marked by no great technological revolution, no great qualitative shifts in the flow or organization of capital, no dramatic change in the quantity and occupational distribution of the labour force, and – as a consequence – no spectacular overhaulings of economic systems. Yet Europe was undoubtedly richer in 1750 than it had been in 1450, and while total population and production both increased, the wealth of individual nations naturally rose and fell at different rates. In most cases agricultural and industrial production lay at the basis of national prosperity, but it was from commerce, and the allied field of finance, that relative changes in economic power and development seemed most readily to spring. The adulation which contemporaries lavished upon trade reflected the fact that the fortunes of such countries as Spain, Holland, England, and France changed directly with their international economic performance: commerce was a potent factor in European progress or decline, and its varying fortunes the prime determinant of significant enterprise.

The long-term changes in the prosperity of individual European nations have been described elsewhere in these volumes, and there is no need to re-trace them here. Nevertheless, it will be relevant to indicate the factors most important to the pre-industrial economic alignment. These factors were perhaps best exemplified in the contrast between Spain and Holland as early as the sixteenth century.

Spain, a nation of some seven or eight million people, with only rudimentary natural resources and a social and economic system among the most primitive in Europe, nevertheless commanded an empire on the continent and another in America which made her temporarily the envy of far better endowed neighbours. The Low Countries, on the other hand, had commenced the rise to commercial dominance which, while it secured their independence, was based upon geographical position, a relative abundance of liquid capital, and supreme business acumen. In the herring fisheries, in the Baltic trade, in shipbuilding, in the great channels which carried Europe's grain, fish, wine, timber, and naval stores, and in the establishment of entrepôts and processing industries, Holland already posed a rival set of economic realities to Spain's apparent mastery of the bullion trade and political power. The Netherlands exemplified most of the economic characteristics which were to prove the secure bases of long-term enterprise, profit and power. After the mid sixteenth century the lesson was brought home by the crumbling of Spain's economic and political edifice: directed to unproductive ends, manipulated by impecunious and fanatical monarchs, strained by fruitless warfare, and masking a deep aversion to effective enterprise, her apparent economic strength was exposed as a hollow shell. The foundations for economic success lay in production, exports, imports, processing, and re-exports. The Dutch, it is true, lacking a sufficiently broad base on the first score might not, by the eighteenth century, be able to withstand the Anglo-French challenge; but Spain, weak on all counts, could not hope to survive a sixteenth-century inflation.

Coincident with the shift of the European economy's centre of gravity towards the Atlantic, there were irregular expansions and contractions in the economic activity of particular countries. To a considerable extent individual entrepreneurs had to accept such vicissitudes and adapt their enterprise to the provision or destruction of economic opportunity. Yet it was also obvious that national economic destinies were not solely the creatures of impersonal economic forces. Few commonplaces were as widely accepted as the envious deduction that Holland's prosperity was largely due to Dutch enterprise. By contrast, France, a nation of great potential wealth, was held back even in peace by an apparent lack of entrepreneurial spirit. Enterprise both shaped and was shaped by the growth and decline of the different components of the European economy.

The various changes which *trade* has suffered [wrote Defoe], may be attributed to the several turns given to the manufactures by the invention of men; the violent removings of the manufactures, and the markets of them, from one city to another, and from one nation to another, by wars; the convulsions of nations, the fall of old empires and states, and the rise of new ones upon their ruins.[1]

The convulsions to which Defoe referred also served to determine the every-day 'risk environment' of enterprise. The framework of enterprise was rendered insecure by wars and the threat of lawlessness, by currency disturbances and plagues, by arbitrary interferences with business, and by the vicissitudes of natural forces. Prior to the nineteenth century, man's helplessness in the face of nature, and in the face of anarchy created by his fellow men, meant that the management of business enterprise was to a significant degree the victim of chance and fortuitous circumstances.

It was not only natural or man-made disaster which reduced the possibility of rational entrepreneurial planning. The underdeveloped economies of Europe – predominantly agrarian, producing a bare margin above subsistence, backward in both technology and industrialization, bedevilled by a shortage of capital – displayed structural characteristics which were bound to shape the scope and nature of enterprise by the elements of risk which they introduced into economic processes. This was, perhaps, most true of the structure of European markets which were linked by poor means of communication and transport, and which were both limited in size and imperfectly coordinated. As a consequence of the first factor, the commercial entrepreneur, unless he were buying and selling in the same market, constantly had to arrive at decisions and undertake capital investment on the basis of facts which might already be outdated when he studied them, and would very often be irrelevant to the market which his goods ultimately reached. Particularly in commercial enterprise, specific transactions frequently had to be executed beyond the reach of immediate communication. In

[1] Daniel Defoe, *The Complete English Tradesman* (London, 1745), II, 231.

addition, the processes of manufacture and trade were rendered the more insecure by the general absence of large-scale continuous demand or any precise means of coordinating supply and demand. Even the existence of great entrepôts like Antwerp, Amsterdam, London and Hamburg, or periodic inland fairs, could not fully eradicate the risks and adaptations necessitated by the attempt to collate an unsteady demand with a discontinuous supply. Most markets could easily be glutted, and adjustments took place not by the minute higgling familiar to classical economists, but by violent and disturbing swings in price levels.

The industrial entrepreneur, facing somewhat different problems from the merchant, was no less affected by the nature of the economy. In particular, neither existing technology nor potential demand normally justified large-scale units of production, and the possibilities of cost-reduction by an expansion of output were severely limited. Correspondingly, industrial expansion more often took place by a multiplication of units of production and an increase in investment and the demand for labour, than by a relative increase in the allotment of capital and an increase in productivity. In addition, since labour costs were relatively greater than in modern industrial enterprise, manufacturing units tended to be decentralized – especially into rural areas, where raw materials were inexpensive, where living costs, and therefore wages, were low, and where a preponderance of the work force was to be found. Yet in such circumstances the supply of labour was not necessarily elastic. In the absence of a wide choice of consumer goods and a habit of diversified expenditure, a high preference for leisure as against more income might make labour relatively unresponsive to the stimulus of higher wages. Where discontinuity of economic processes did not make for involuntary underemployment, labour psychology could create the voluntary kind. Skilled labour in these respects was marked by the same characteristics as unskilled – with the added feature that shortages of skill were perennial blocks to industrial expansion. In societies with no formal provision for technical education, where industrial techniques might be jealously guarded and communicated only slowly, and where apprenticeship and communal solidarity frequently confined special skills to specific groups, the transfer of particular productive techniques between enterprises, regions, or nations could proceed no faster than the transfer of skilled personnel. This was as true of forge-masters and dyers as it was of master brewers, as true of German miners, Huguenot manufacturers of new draperies, and Italian silk-weavers in the sixteenth century as it was to be of English textile operatives or metal workers in the early stages of the Industrial Revolution. It gave a special economic significance to paternal concepts of industrial organization, to religious persecution, and to subsidized migration.

Another result of the primitive nature of technology and the decentralized character of industrial location was the lack of standardization in manufactured goods. Where the site of production was beyond entrepreneurial oversight, and where an unskilled labour force worked with only primitive mechanical aids, the businessman could never be certain that his products would satisfy such demand as there was. To the risk that there would be no market at all was added the risk that even the market which did exist would reject the goods which he had to offer.

At all levels of economic activity, the supply of capital had a distinctive and crucial role to play in pre-industrial society. Given the nature of technology in manufacturing enterprise and the nature of commercial processes, the availability of liquid or circulating capital was perhaps the principal determinant of the level of non-agricultural activity. More than this, since the mechanisms by which credit could be created were relatively underdeveloped, the supply of capital was to a great degree identified with the supply of money; and an economic system such as that described here must have found that, of all the uncertainties which preyed upon it, the possibility of a shortage of liquid capital was among the most alarming. National attention was therefore sharply focused on monetary flows, entrepreneurial attention on the speed of capital turnover. The scarcity of money was considered a deflationary phenomenon, to be amended at almost any cost, and it was the fear of a shortage of capital which permeated contemporary attitudes towards currency problems. The whole rhythm of economic life – and therefore of entrepreneurial activity – was conditioned by variations in the availability of money, and it is this fact which helps explain the significance of the merchant in the eyes of the State and the community. If merchants did not prosper, Francis Bacon held in his essay on Empire, 'a kingdom may have good limbs, but will have empty veins, and nourish little'. As generator and controller of the most important source of disposable funds, the mercantile capitalists could be the prime mover in many aspects of economic life other than commerce. It is true that to most contemporaries the really important capitalists were overseas merchants: the power and prestige which, among rival commercial nations, Holland derived from an abundance of capital, were paralleled among men of enterprise in nearly every nation by the decisive influence of the great international trader. However, on a slightly lower plane, the domestic wholesaler occupied a strategic position. The influence of both overseas and domestic merchants permeated the economy: it was an age of commercial enterprise.

In the words of a seventeenth-century English writer: 'all other callings receive their vigour, life, strength and increase from the merchant... to whose extravagant and hazardous, as well as prudent and cautious, undertaking this nation chiefly owes all its wealth and glory.'[1]

(2) THE STATE AND ENTERPRISE

So far only the economic aspects of the framework of enterprise have been considered, and it is as well to emphasize that economic institutions and market forces naturally dominated the entrepreneurial scene. However, the ways in which entrepreneurs assumed and performed economic functions were also conditioned by the influence of governments and political institutions.

At the simplest level the State provided, or failed to provide, those elements of security which can be crucial to the continuity and expansion of enterprise. Internal political stability and public order, for example, drastically reduced entrepreneurial risks, but their presence could by no means be taken for granted. The economic strangulation of Antwerp, the religious upheavals in sixteenth-century France, and the ravages of the Thirty Years War illustrate the point. By contrast, England and Holland, taking the period as a whole, exemplify the economic benefits which internal stability could help bring. By the eighteenth century, as men resorted less often to the sword to settle their theological controversies, as warfare became more isolated from the civilian population, and as the growth in income and governmental power decreased the risk of social disturbance, there was a general reduction of this type of insecurity.

Governments could also facilitate entrepreneurial activity by the provision and enforcement of regulations which smoothed the purely mechanical side of enterprise. Thus the rise of the nation state is associated with piecemeal efforts – the extent of which varied between countries – to standardize weights, measures and coinage, to unify the domestic market by eliminating arbitrary local tolls and other barriers to domestic commerce, to establish the hegemony of economic and political power and the uniformity of law, and to favour native as against alien entrepreneurs. Nevertheless, the economic homogeneity towards which such policies pointed was more an ideal than a reality. No government was completely altruistic, and few saw the encouragement of enterprise as an absolute good or distributed their economic favours indiscriminately. As a result, internal barriers to transport and trade were never entirely eliminated; governmental financial necessity – perhaps the principal single motive for economic policy – perpetually

[1] Quoted in E. Lipson, *Economic History of England* (London, 1948), II, 190.

created or maintained privileges for the few (whether native or alien entrepreneurs) which retarded the enterprise of the many; and the vested interests of aristocracy or church, royalty or landed wealth, peasants or craftsmen, were never fully sacrificed to the promotion of business enterprise. In addition, there were some areas where the influence of governments on the climate of enterprise was entirely neutral; in non-European lands, for example the great joint-stock companies were frequently forced to provide their own military, consular and diplomatic services – and in North America in the early seventeenth century they even had to create settled societies and government. Nations differed widely in their efforts to provide a favourable institutional environment for entrepreneurs; but it is probably no coincidence that the countries – Holland and England – whose enterprise led the world were precisely those most free from internal disturbance, most successful in unifying their domestic markets, most sound in the management of their currency, and most energetic in the provision of a legal framework favourable to economic enterprise.

The outstanding characteristic of the State's relationship with the economy was that businessmen and public alike assumed to the point of eliminating controversy that the governments had or could exercise far-reaching economic functions, and that – where official policy was most suitable – enterprise, to be most effective, need not necessarily be free. But in its efforts to control, regulate, encourage or restrain, the State presented entrepreneurs not with any consistent, systematic policy, but with a series of arbitrary measures; measures which, in the nature of the situation, were defended or criticized solely on grounds of expediency. The entrepreneur of the early modern period was forced to be a perennial lobbyist, and government protection could be as effective an entrepreneurial tool as superior productivity or low prices. But the state wielded social as well as economic criteria. In societies with abysmally low standards of living and inefficient police powers, where the maintenance of social stability might be a more important goal than the furtherance of economic progress, the *status quo* had its own justification. It is in the light of the threats posed to public order and the social fabric by high prices, unemployment, and economic change, that we must view official attempts to regulate markets, control middlemen, retard the evolution of a propertyless labour force, restrict labour mobility, and even force owners of capital into unprofitable pursuits. By the late seventeenth and the eighteenth centuries, however, such social policies had declined in importance.

Government policy, of course, was frequently directed in an entirely conscious and positive way to the encouragement of enterprise. There was, for example, the major question of economic nationalism – the aspect of 'mercantilism' which has perhaps received most attention. Unless there were special reasons (such as financial need) to grant privileges to specific groups of alien entrepreneurs, then governments on the whole would tend to favour native as against foreign business- men. This was especially so in the entrepreneurial area where com- petition was most likely: overseas trade. Since all nations recognized international commerce as a major source of wealth, and envisaged only limited economic horizons, the State power was a frequent participant in the processes of international competition – attempting, by differen- tial taxes and subsidies, navigation laws, prohibitions, privileges and the like, to place the native manufacturer, merchant or shipowner in a special position. As the prospects and potentialities of colonial and dis- tant enterprise were opened up, this development became more marked among the seafaring countries; its logical outcome was trade war and colonial war. Dutch commercial and French colonial pretensions kept the English merchants of the seventeenth and eighteenth centuries in a constant state of militant economic nationalism. On another plane, where domestic products suffered in foreign markets by virtue of their poor or varying quality, as did English textiles in the sixteenth and seventeenth centuries, governments might assume the task of imposing and enforcing industrial standards.

There were two areas in which the State could have a more direct and selective effect on enterprise. Firstly, for reasons of trade, strategy, or prestige, governments attempted to create or develop specific lines of enterprise. This especially applied to joint-stock and colonial trading, ship-building, metallurgy, heavy industry, and, for certain nations, luxury goods. The extent to which governments thereby assumed direct or indirect entrepreneurial functions varied both over time and between nations. But it is significant that the economically most advanced nations seem to have made least use of this technique of economic development. Or, to put it another way, the State stepped into the market to provide substitutes for capital principally in situations where capital was in short supply. In a sense, nearly every example of govern- ment-owned or government-stimulated enterprise occurred where private capital was unwilling to assume entrepreneurial risks unaided. The alternative means were broadly state ownership, state subsidy, a guaranteed market, or privileges which acted as substitutes for capital.

The second means by which governments influenced the activity of particular entrepreneurs was by an abdication of the State's privileges or functions. Businessmen found avenues of profit open to them through the economic necessities and financial needs of nation states. But more than the privileges which they could purchase, or the posi- tions of power which they could secure by loans to governments, entrepreneurs discovered possibilities of profit in the fact that the scope and complexity of government tasks expanded at a faster rate than the official mechanism which supplied revenue, administrative skill, goods, and services could be overhauled. As a consequence, until fiscal and administrative reform took place – and in some circumstances even then – private entrepreneurs were enlisted to serve and fulfil the functions of the State, as contractors, tax-farmers, purchasers of offices, wholesalers of land, suppliers of armies, mint-managers, and bureaucrats. It was, in effect, the inefficiency of governments which extended the horizon of the businessman, although at the same time it placed emphasis on a different range of entrepreneurial skills – on the arts of political strategy and bribery, on negotiation and argument. While it largely eliminated one area of risk (the instability of markets and prices and the uncertainty of information) it opened another: the insecurity of dealing with an irresponsible political power whose contractual word was not necessarily its bond.

It is probably easier to exaggerate than to describe accurately the entrepreneurial importance of government activity. Official economic policy was marked by inconsistency, inefficiency, and expediency. The State, in its pursuit of political, religious or financial ends did not hesitate to sacrifice economic interests to its larger goals. Attempts to regulate the whole economy were frequently more optimistic than efficacious, and specific measures designed to help a select group tended as often to hinder as to encourage the totality of enterprise. An entrepreneur, or a group of entrepreneurs, might frequently convince a government by purchase or argument that they merited privileges and/or aid, and successful enterprise, as a consequence, often leaned heavily on State subvention. But to entrepreneurs as a whole, acts of government partook of the arbitrary nature of acts of God – and could be equally disrupting. On the other hand, governments could reduce the risks of investment or strengthen the security environment of enterprise – either for a favoured group of businessmen or for all entrepreneurs. Whether in the last resort this helped many or only a few businessmen, the result was that enterprise perpetually leaned on State aid, and the framework of enterprise is incomprehensible without an understanding of this fact.

(3) IDEOLOGY

The distinction between enterprise and its 'environment' is at its most artificial when the latter is considered in ideological terms. Thus it is obvious that entrepreneurial performance is conditioned by society's attitude towards business, and that social as well as legal sanctions can restrict and mould economic enterprise to conform with accepted behaviour. But the *mechanism* by which such sanctions operate is most frequently the acceptance on the part of the businessman of the doctrines which are supposed to restrict his activity. In the opposite case the encouragement afforded entrepreneurship by a favourable set of social *mores* works not through any artificial stimulant of an otherwise lethargic business group but through the identification of the businessman and society, and the former's wielding of the latter's values. On the other hand there are sufficient historical examples of successful businessmen who succeeded by doing things which society at large frowned upon to make us sceptical of any attempt to place too much emphasis on the primacy of social philosophies *in extenso*. Any discussion of the ideological framework of enterprise must ultimately centre on the ideology of the entrepreneur.

On the surface, the most far-reaching ideological change during these centuries came, of course, with the Reformation. Yet it is difficult to distinguish any clear-cut change in general attitudes towards business enterprise which can be ascribed solely to the influence of reformed religion. The early reformers were themselves as conservative in this respect as most medieval Schoolmen; and, in the realm of practical affairs, the most advanced Protestant centres of capitalism seemed to have viewed entrepreneurial activity in no more favourable a light than that which illuminated Catholic enterprise in medieval Italy, or six-teenth-century Antwerp. In fact, neither school of religious thought had an exclusive monopoly of any economically significant attitude towards business – although as the various branches of Protestant theology evolved and were consciously accepted by entrepreneurs it became clear that certain of them established a closer relationship between some of the values calculated to lead to economic success and the virtues which religion placed in the forefront of its canons of worldly behaviour. What is certain is that, as far as concerned the non-business elements of society, sentiment favourable or antipathetic to business was not based on theological tenets alone; and in many instances they created not one but a variety of attitudes to different types of profit-making enterprise. The extent to which entrepreneurship was accepted or denigrated depended in large part upon economic structures and well-being, geographical position, social stratification, and the like. In a poor community of peasants and artisans – whether Catholic or Protestant – the financier or the middleman could not expect to find the social acceptance which was his due on the commodity or money *bourses* of Antwerp, Amsterdam, Lyons, and Frankfort. Where a rigid social structure, such as that of France or Spain, awarded prestige and status primarily to aristocratic birth or quasi-aristocratic landownership, the

mere merchant or manufacturer could not anticipate as congenial an
ideological environment as in a land which had no great, closed noble
caste, or which, like Holland, was economically committed to international competition. Finally, where a nation like England both contained peasant and handicraft elements and was also dependent upon its
overseas trade, it is not surprising that veneration of the large-scale
merchant and manufacturer should have gone hand in hand with the
denigration of petty usurer and domestic middleman.

It is abundantly clear that the European attitude towards enterprise,
and the attitude of the entrepreneur to his own functions, were sufficiently varied between nations and over time to render any easy
generalization meaningless. Yet, looking at the period as a whole, there
is rather an increasing tendency to accept values which encourage (or
reject sanctions which inhibit) enterprise than any other change. For
European society at large, in its formal profession of theological belief,
there was an undoubted splintering of the official religious hegemony of
the Middle Ages. It was not, however, simply a question of the reduced
power of a religion which had attempted on moral and doctrinal
grounds to restrict the operations of entrepreneurs. Rather, entrepreneurs themselves – or some of them – tended to think in somewhat
different ways about their economic activity. There were, to over-
simplify, two broad developments, each of which had the effect not of
creating a thriving new class of capitalists, but of augmenting the number of entrepreneurs who were not inhibited by other-worldly considerations. First, some businessmen began to accentuate, *in religious
terms*, moral values which were conducive to productivity and the
accumulation of capital. Second, other entrepreneurs, by ignoring or
denying the universal application of traditional moral imperatives,
were able to break through the constraints which a personal ethic might
have imposed on business activity.

That the Protestant ethic, such as it was, could not by itself wholly
account for any quickening of the capitalist spirit is a conclusion which
possibly needs no more labouring. On the other hand, that some of its
attributes pervaded the lives of some men of enterprise is undeniable.
The serious and earnest striving in the affairs of this world, the self-
conscious search for material evidence of moral worth, the worship of
hard work and thrift along with godliness and frugality – these were
elements in Puritanism, and especially in its more Calvinistic branches,
which by the late seventeenth and eighteenth centuries appeared to be
increasingly relevant to the development of business. Either where they
were wholeheartedly endorsed or where they had an indirect effect on
businessmen not entirely dedicated to them, it is possible to speak of a
changing psychology of business. Nevertheless, entrepreneurs who were

not conspicuously attached to the Protestant ethic still managed to undertake successful enterprise and to display qualities of perseverance and economy. In addition, the new religious philosophies, in so far as they were associated with dissent and nonconformity, were more often exemplified in the lower strata of business classes than among the great enterpreneurs.

The 'capitalistic spirit', it is clear, cannot be solely identified with a theological frame of thought. As important as the acceptance of a religious morality favourable to capital accumulation was the evolution or accentuation of an entrepreneurial psychology which by-passed the sanctions of religion in its attitude to wage-costs, prices, competition, and profits. If business were an area of human endeavour not susceptible to the moral dictates of any pulpit, then obviously the scope for purely individual initiative on the part of the entrepreneur was considerably widened. Alternatively, if the businessman successfully sought for the particular balance of religious belief which most readily confirmed the dictates of his own spirit of enterprise, then the same result obtained. In either case the initial process of justification bore little relation to organized religion: it was, for example, on behalf of his own and his children's material interests that Horatio Palavicino advised the Earl of Shrewsbury in 1593 not to 'compt it ill if in the point of profitt a man honestly every waies regard his own commoditie'.[1] The regard for one's 'own commoditie', the self-interest which by the eighteenth century had been incorporated into the powerful and approving body of impersonal economic theory, eroded the link between entrepreneurial activity and non-economic criteria of behaviour. It reinforced a set of attitudes which entailed unlimited enterprise and condoned unlimited acquisition. It lay at the base of the 'spirit of capitalism'. From this viewpoint the dissolution of Catholic hegemony, the splintering of faiths, and the contraction of the area in which religion was generally believed to hold sway – all of which manifested themselves after the fifteenth century – strengthened the evolution of an impersonal attitude towards enterprise. Entrepreneurs could now far more easily envisage their self-imposed tasks in economic terms. On the other hand, it would be wrong to assume that this was a development which was confined to the post-Reformation period. Self-interest, to some degree, is a basic pre-requisite of private entrepreneurship. The rise of economic individualism was far more an accentuation of ancient entrepreneurial characteristics – an accentuation as frequently induced by a favourable economic and social environment as by an intellectual revolution – than a startling efflorescence of new business *mores*. It went hand in hand with the expansion of economic activity, and it would be hazardous to

[1] Quoted in L. Stone, *An Elizabethan: Sir Horatio Palavicino* (Oxford, 1956), p. 40.

attempt a too precise measure of which development produced the other. If the history of capitalistic development in the sixteenth and seventeenth centuries can be interpreted in the light of a breakdown of medieval traditionalism and the formulation of a 'rationalistic economic ethic', then the change was one of degree rather than kind – and it is important to remember that the scope as well as the application of non-traditional ways of thinking about and doing business broadened and increased.

One remarkable feature of entrepreneurial ideology is the fact that in any one economy businessmen fall into different groups (with different attitudes towards enterprise) which are determined to some extent by religion.[1] More than this, there were outstanding examples of religious minorities in northern Europe who were incontrovertibly more success-ful in business activity and therefore, it is assumed, were in securer possession of dynamic values and attitudes to business than the rest of the inhabitants of particular countries. For example, Jews universally, Huguenots in France, and Quakers in England are examples of religious groups which appear to have achieved a level of business development quite out of proportion to their numbers. In each case, there can be little doubt, a specific cast of thought and world outlook contributed both to the willingness to assume entrepreneurial functions and to the aptitudes with which such functions were fulfilled. Nevertheless, such 'ideological' factors cannot be disassociated from the social milieu in which they thrived. Being in a minority can, in some respects, lead to favourable rather than unfavourable results. A heretic can escape many of the limitations as well as the rights of full citizenship. This is not only because in an intolerant society exclusion from some political and social fields may canalize the minority's energies into other areas (e.g. busi-ness). In addition, a minority, by virtue of its position, may well erect formal or informal standards of moral and social values which liberate it from the sanctions of the community at large. Thus French society might impose non-entrepreneurial attitudes upon its members; but the Huguenot businessman presumably never experienced the compul-sion to believe in the criteria of the worthwhile life which the Catholic majority exemplified: the road to business achievement was clear of many an ideological stumbling-block. Finally, and perhaps most im-portant, a religious minority of necessity forms a close social grouping on its own account. As such, its members are linked by far more than a common theological allegiance: intermarriage, education, personal acquaintance, mutual trust, social equality – all act to knit its members

---

[1] There are, of course, a host of other determinants of different entrepreneurial attitudes, among which education and upbringing, social background, and material needs may be mentioned as among the more important.

together, and all are precisely relevant to business activity in an economic environment of the sort already described. In other words, it tended to be as much the social framework as the individual belief of particular minorities which made for entrepreneurial success; because from the social framework businessmen could derive the confidence in subordinates and associates, and the security of financial and functional service, which made the individual enterprise far more effective. It was for this reason that religious minorities tended to be concentrated in particular trades or industries.

As is only logical, the general framework of social thought was most favourable to enterprise in countries where economic activity was at its most sophisticated and virile level. And while a rigid ideology, such as prevailed in Spain, obviously helped retard entrepreneurial development, there were too many other factors at work in the production of strong or weak business systems to put primary emphasis on the ideological. The greatest psychological stimulant to enterprise – although it was often expressed in terms of 'social philosophy' – was in fact the presence of active and dynamic entrepreneurship. And active entrepreneurship was the result, as much as the cause, of a favourable convergence of economic, political, and social factors.

II. *International Enterprise in Trade and Finance*

The intimate connection between finance and trade in the early modern period meant that the financial was frequently indistinguishable from the commercial entrepreneur. In the contemporary vocabulary 'merchant' meant far more a general occupational category than a particular economic function. And international, or at least long-distance, commercial enterprise – because of the strategic role of trade, the potential rewards for the successful trader, and the universal importance of trade as a source of liquid capital – was in the eighteenth as it had been in the fifteenth century the most significant type of economic undertaking.

(1) ECONOMIC RISK AND ORGANIZATION[1]

The trading capitalist, as has already been seen, was normally divided both spatially and intellectually from his markets and, frequently, from his sources of supply: markets and sources of supply fluctuated faster than plans could be changed; and no entrepreneur could be certain that he knew all the economic circumstances which might obtain at that

[1] Corporate enterprise will be separately considered: below, Section IV.

uncertain date when his goods reached their final market. In terms of business needs, the transfer of information was lacking in quality as well as speed; and the institutional provision of information concerning prices, exchange rates, and even 'current news', which developed before the eighteenth century with the growth of printed price-currents, rudimentary newspapers, and the like, was by no means a complete solution to the problem. Price-currents for the major European produce markets (Amsterdam, Frankfort, Nuremberg, Venice, etc.) survive from the late sixteenth century, although only in small numbers, and it is certain that from the early seventeenth century the Amsterdam *Bourse* had a regular weekly publication. London was slower in producing a price-current, as it was slower in attaining importance as an entrepôt; but by 1675 there existed a London price-current listing over 300 articles. Naturally, such publications were of real importance to merchants: they saved a good deal of work and they were probably more accurate than the figures which most merchants or factors would have been able to gather on their own account. Nevertheless, although businessmen on the spot would benefit by being able to deal in a more ordered market, information relevant to *prospective* markets still had to be obtained, and where entrepreneurial decisions were made in other places the price-current would still have to be despatched like any normal business letter. In fact, the most important channel for fact and forecast, for the raw material of business planning, was still the mercantile letter. A businessman's information was still only as good as his correspondence.

Joined to the fact of imperfect communication and slow transportation was the existence of discontinuous and limited markets. And it is these two elements in the economic framework which explain the outstanding characteristics of commercial and financial enterprise: the absence of functional specialization and the need to decentralize the making of entrepreneurial decisions.

Only rarely would a market be sufficiently large and uninterrupted to warrant traders confining their activities to dealings in one commodity or to a single marketing area or even to one mercantile function. By the same token, since the demand for services auxiliary to actual trading was also intermittent, the provision of insurance, transport, storage, exchange, and banking facilities was more often incidental to commercial enterprise than the basis of specialized occupations. Merchants, diversifying investments (and therefore risks), assumed a variety of roles which a more sophisticated economic age would assign to a variety of businessmen. It was, for example, not ignorance of better techniques, but limitations of market structure which for so long kept commercial credit and finance in traders' rather than bankers' hands.

The extent and manner of decentralization offer further evidence of the dominant influence of market risk on commercial enterprise.

The most direct, although in many circumstances the most inefficient, technique was for the trader himself, or one of two partners, to accompany his goods so that at every change in market conditions he could retain entrepreneurial control. Particularly where – as in the trades to Africa and the West Indies – decisions between a variety of goods and a variety of relatively small markets had to be continuously made in the course of one voyage, such 'travelling merchants' might be at an economic advantage. But in order to undertake most sorts of medium- or large-scale business, to secure the benefits of a steady and diversified trade, a system of resident representatives was essential. At the other extreme from the peripatetic entrepreneur, were those rare commercial and financial houses which were sufficiently large to sustain a network of permanent branch houses in separate locations. The most spectacular examples were sixteenth-century enterprises such as the Fugger, the Bonvisi, or the Welser, which spanned the worlds of government finance and extensive trade. And even here, it was probably more the demands of international high finance than the necessities of international trade which induced a widespread branch organization.

For most commercial entrepreneurs the solution to the problems of communication and diversification lay in the employment of factors operating on a commission, or a combination of salaried representatives, apprentices and factors. In the case of apprentices, of course, a double advantage was secured: they could act as personal representatives even while they learned the intricacies of a particular trade and were exercising the responsibilities which might best lead to business maturity. Naturally, however, the importance and routine nature of a particular line of enterprise determined how much entrepreneurial power could be given to a mere trainee. In most instances the entrepreneur would also call upon an experienced businessman, or firm, familiar with the business scene, to undertake commission work. Factorage, however, was rarely undertaken as a specialist task. On the one hand factors and agents traded on their own account as well as on behalf of a principal; on the other they frequently handled the overseas affairs of more than one merchant. In addition, an agent's tasks did not end with the purchase and sale of goods: they extended beyond commodity transactions to include exchange, credit, transportation, and other services. To the extent that a mercantile entrepreneur was himself not a specialist, so his agents assumed a wide range of functions; and these agents, it must be remembered, were often mercantile entrepreneurs in their own right. It was a system of mutual, remunerated service which operated at the highest as well as the lowest levels of commerce, and which was still in the mid eighteenth century, according to Postlethwayt, 'the universal custom of Merchants of the highest credit throughout Europe'.

Commercial enterprise, given the nature of market structures, was continually forced to balance central control and peripheral responsibility; and since available techniques of control were restricted, the mercantile entrepreneur was obliged to allow his representatives to assume an important initiative. From this fact, as from the fact of the personal nature of the markets for goods, capital and auxiliary services, there flowed significant consequences for commercial enterprise. For initiative and informal relationships presupposed trust and confidence. The detection of fraud or the measurement of business efficiency could not be achieved in any systematic way, and the continuity of personal relationships was possibly the most important means of reassuring merchants about the honesty and skill of subordinates or agents. Such knowledge could be gained in the normal course of social and economic activity. In addition, however, entrepreneurs fell back on two social institutions: the family and the religious group frequently provided the operational support to the more formal structure of business enterprise.

It was neither an illogical nepotism nor a bigoted exclusiveness which kept so many commercial and financial partnerships in the hands of one family or members of one religious sect, and which so frequently led entrepreneurs to employ as representatives and agents their relations or their co-religionists. In a business world where the unknown was a credit risk and the entrepreneur's success lay so much in the hands of men beyond his immediate control, the ties of the family, of religion, and of the social community which went with both, were the cement of commercial confidence and commercial organization. The lesson was the same whether exemplified in relationships within the individual enterprise or between different firms which provided commercial services for each other: close personal relationships, whatever their basis, fulfilled economic functions which no others could hope to serve as effectively. Religious minorities illustrated the strength and importance of such entrepreneurial cohesion more than any other; but from the tendency of merchants to employ co-nationals and kinsmen as agents to the fact that the greatest firms of the sixteenth century – the Fugger, the Welser, the Höchstetter – superimposed the partnership on the family, the full range of commercial enterprise exemplified the same situation.

That the most widely used form of entrepreneurial control in commerce was interwoven with qualitative factors of personal relationship is a partial indication of the difficulties involved in the concept of

economic 'rationality'. Broadly speaking, there have been two complementary senses in which the representative entrepreneur of the modern
period has been assumed to be far more rational than his predecessors.
First, it has been held that he broke through the traditional restraints, on
profit-accumulation, innovation, and expansion, which circumscribed
the generality of medieval businessmen. Second, and again in contrast
with medieval enterprise, the modern entrepreneur is supposed to have
used more statistical, quantitative, scientific methods in disposing his
resources and guiding his particular unit of enterprise. From these viewpoints, how rational was the commercial entrepreneur in the early
modern period?

It cannot be denied that in the first sense – acting according to the
dictates of a profit-motive, seeking the most suitable rather than the
most venerable business methods, being unafraid of the implications of
expansion – a significant number of merchants were, indeed, 'rational'
in the three centuries under consideration. Yet it may be doubted if
commercial enterprise as a whole was significantly more rational in its
general outlook than in medieval economies, and if those examples of a
weakening of traditionalism v hich *do* exist reflected a spontaneous
entrepreneurial change rather than a loosening of environmental
restraints upon business activity. For instances of 'objective' and profit-
oriented enterprise abounded in the medieval world, wherever circumstances (e.g. the extent of the market) were propitious; and 'rational'
economic behaviour in the sixteenth, seventeenth and eighteenth centuries was as much a function of expanding economic opportunity as its
cause.

The case against an uncritical acceptance of the concept of 'economic
rationalism' would appear to be even stronger when it comes to the
techniques of individual merchants. For, as has already been shown, the
framework of enterprise – the strong element of uncertainty, the impossibility of direct control, the discontinuity between decisions and
final transactions, the absence of any real pattern in economic processes
– was not such as to allow entrepreneurial problems to be fully, or even
largely, susceptible to scientific analysis. The relevant data were
generally too incomplete and untrustworthy, the entrepreneur was too
remote from any large influence on his environment, and past experience
was too poor a guide to future reality. All this is not to say that entrepreneurs were helpless pawns of their environment, or that haphazard
policies stood as much chance of a successful outcome as those based on
careful reasoning. Clearly, other things being equal, rationality was a
better guide to action than irrationality. But few entrepreneurs could
rely solely on the scientific approach to their problems. In the main,
they would have to employ a piecemeal policy which was based in part

on a pragmatic, empirical approach, and in part on the dictates of an intuitive outlook.

The use of the double-entry method of bookkeeping – the most 'scientific' entrepreneurial tool available – illustrates the point. Perfected in fourteenth-century Italy, and extended by precept and practice, double-entry bookkeeping had permeated north-European sophisticated business procedures by the sixteenth century. In the early years of the century, for example, the great Fugger concern employed the 'Italian method' of accounting in its many branches, each of which submitted annual accounts to the Augsburg head office, where they were combined into a final balance for the entire enterprise. Yet for most merchants double-entry did not so much serve to focus attention on capital and profits (its function in 'rationalistic' business procedure) as to establish greater control or surveillance of transactions internal and external to the firm. Frequently, in fact, the balancing process was merely a device to retain accounting consistency by detecting and eradicating errors[1] rather than a means of measuring the performance of particular parts of the enterprise with a view to future planning. Accounting, in other words, was a control rather than a planning technique.

The effects of competitive insecurity were not limited to the techniques of internal control and organization already considered. The opportunities of monopoly which market imperfections created were merely one part of a business environment which tended to encourage entrepreneurial manipulation of supply and prices. Risk and insecurity naturally produced business techniques designed to reduce their impact by *limiting* competition. The gild and the regulated company were attempts at corporate self-regulation which, lacking the unified action of a single selling organization, nevertheless aimed at controlling competition between the independent entrepreneurs who were members. Looked at from the standpoint of the period as a whole, such institutions declined in relative importance. Either the geographical limits to their power or the very number of entrepreneurs within their compass militated against their restrictive policies: neither organization was able to exercise long-term control of available supplies.[2]

There were, however, more successful – albeit less grandiose – forms of monopoly which smaller combinations were able to undertake. In manufacturing enterprise market control by individuals or primitive cartels depended on either geographical isolation, monopolization of scarce raw materials, or the exercise of privileges; for the single enterprise the last was usually associated with large-scale units and the protec-

---

[1] B. S. Yamey, 'Scientific Bookkeeping and the Rise of Capitalism', *Economic History Review*, new ser., I (1949), 99–113.   [2] Below, pp. 437–9.

tion of their fixed investment.[1] In commercial enterprise, although privileged position – as with joint-stock companies or government creditors – was no less sought after, privately attained monopolies appear to have been more frequent than in industry – in part, presumably, because merchants tended to be nearer markets and purchasers, and so able to concentrate their efforts. The most suitable situation for the earning of a monopoly profit would obviously be one where the supply of the relevant commodities to a particular market could be easily dominated, and where the demand was relatively inelastic. Such a situation could obtain on a minute or a global scale. In local markets throughout the European countryside the unreliability and cost of transport continually opened a range of such possibilities, especially in the supply of foodstuffs – and it was no wonder that municipal and national market regulation was directed in the first instance to the price and supply of victuals. At the other extreme, combination in the great trades of the east, or in their offshoots in Europe's entrepôts, might hope to secure temporary control of the remunerative commerce in spices; or, in marts such as Antwerp, Amsterdam, London, or Hamburg, syndicates of merchants and financiers rang perpetual changes on the idea of cornering silks or dye-stuffs, munitions or copper, sugar or perfume ingredients.

(2) TRADE AND CAPITAL

From the point of view of other economic activity, commercial enterprise was more a source than a user of capital. Even so, it would be misleading to consider the pre-industrial economy as one in which mercantile entrepreneurs were entirely, or even largely, self-financing. First, in large-scale enterprise (and often small) much of the actual capital employed was invested by passive partners or borrowed by the businessman for long periods. Second, the use of credit was universal. In fact, the line between the provision of credit or short-term finance and the supply of medium- or even long-term capital was shadowy. Book credits or notes of hand could run for months or even years; and in the case of an enterprise like the East India Company, its three- or six-month bonds in the late seventeenth century were extended for as long as ten or twelve years, until they assumed all the characteristics of long-term capital loans.

For most of the period the marked feature of the provision of both short- and long-term capital was its informal nature. The seventeenth century, it is true, witnessed the slow growth of purely financial institutions, and by the eighteenth century in advanced commercial centres,

[1] Below, pp. 430–1.

agencies whose specialized function it was to collate the demand for and supply of capital and credit were responding to a variety of needs. Even so, the bulk of capital and credit transactions remained informal and, as a consequence, largely personal in nature. There were two important results of this system. On the one hand, the flow of capital into enterprise was broken up into a heterogeneous series of capital markets, isolated from each other as much by the proclivities of investors and creditors as by difficulties of communication. On the other, the entrepreneur had to rely on a framework of personal relationships to satisfy his needs for capital, in the same measure that he had to rely on a comparable framework for the provision of other business services. Unless entrepreneurial activity were self-financed, its limits were established by the circle of business acquaintances, relatives, and friends, and by the recognized credit-worthiness of the individual entrepreneur. Even joint-stock companies, up to the late seventeenth century, tended to be financed by investors drawn from small and interconnected groups.

The interweaving of financial and commercial enterprise was especially marked in international economic activity where, to take one example, merchants most often turned to other traders for credit facilities, and, to take another, the great 'financiers' either operated in conjunction with an international commodity trade or derived or employed their funds in such commerce. It is indeed difficult to find a financial entrepreneur, from the cosmopolitan houses of Augsburg, Genoa, and Antwerp in the sixteenth century to the City men of eighteenth-century London, who did not have close connections with the physical side of commerce. To the extent that financial enterprise was merely incidental to commerce, its principal characteristics were the same as those of mercantile activity. But the control of capital frequently reflected more specific entrepreneurial tasks. Principal among these was the deriving of profit from loans to the State.

Government finance induced the most spectacular range of international entrepreneurial activity, and the most significant changes of emphasis in that activity. And although loans to governments were most often employed in non-productive uses, they were normally the prelude to an extended chain of economic activity on the part of the creditors. For the financial necessities of states, at least at the beginning of the period, soon outran their long-run as well as their short-run ability to command revenue, and – short of government bankruptcy – either collateral had to be relinquished, or economic privileges had to be awarded to creditors for exploitation. The result was that entrepreneurs who had begun as financiers were soon involved, by choice or necessity, in widespread enterprise which might encompass landownership and management, the production of and trade in minerals, customs administration, or commercial monopolies. It was by such means that Italian and German houses in the early sixteenth century cornered the spice trade between Lisbon and Antwerp; and that the Fugger, in the same period, secured control of the copper production of the Tyrol, Carinthia, and Hungary.

The giants of international enterprise in the sixteenth century were able to eliminate many of the risks which unstable and limited markets imposed on lesser entrepreneurs. Their size, economic power, political prestige, and the market control which these helped produce, all combined to render their immediate environment more secure. But, on the other hand, the nature of the business which they undertook conjured up a host of other risks which could prove no less deadly. Like the Bardi, Peruzzi, or Medici of an earlier era of finance, they were only too susceptible to the vagaries of government default and royal bankruptcy. For the temptation, and sometimes the obligation, to allow their loans to exceed realizable collateral was the most unsound of policies when dealing with sovereign debtors. The Fugger might well have been the wealthiest entrepreneurial family in sixteenth-century Europe, but their capital was to a great extent immobilized in loans to the Hapsburgs and in imperial enterprises. The financial collapse of Spain – a recurring phenomenon – laid bare the weakness of their position.

The sixteenth century, in fact, saw the end of 'heroic' international finance. In part this was due to chastening experiences such as that of the Fugger; in part to the increased ability of nation states to generate current income by taxation; in part to the taming of wilder dynastic ambitions; and in part to the growth of financial institutions, regular syndicates, and formalized, continuous means of raising government loans – all of which tended to replace the spectacular phenomena of massive bargaining by isolated individuals and firms. Some of the characteristics of personal financial enterprise remained constant: economic privilege was still a frequent concomitant of government loans; trade was still an adjunct of international finance; financial enterprise still involved international transfers of money and, therefore, an international organization; and the individual banker of international and clouded reputation was still not unknown. But institutional and impersonal arrangements, which obviously reduced individual risks, increasingly characterized the financial scene – whether in the large-scale corporate form, like the Bank of England, or the syndicate form, like the French *Ferme Générale*, or in the form of organized markets for government securities, in which institutional or private financial intermediaries supplied a diversity of government needs. Such developments in the area of government finance merely reflected the increasing 'institutionalization' of financial enterprise in general.

Even while the organization of large-scale financial enterprise was undergoing a slow change, the relationships between finance and commerce remained close. Economic reality established an intimate bond between the two forms of entrepreneurship and, while each activity lent strength to the other, individual businessmen who combined both functions occupied a position of strategic economic power. Control of trading capital led to extensive participation in government finance, mining, manufacturing, and the domestic land and money markets. The aversion to functional specialization, which was shaped by the nature of markets, was reinforced by the fact that merchants, as already noted, were in dominant possession of all-important liquid capital. The commercial entrepreneur remained an economic 'generalist'.

(3) ENTREPRENEURIAL CHANGE

Broadly considered, the entrepreneurial tasks which faced the mercantile capitalist varied little during the 250 years after the close of the Middle Ages. The pattern of exchange of European goods, for example, did not alter significantly, even though the quantity of goods which moved along its channels increased. By 1750 product-innovation had not progressed sufficiently far to impose any new demands in these respects. There was, of course, a reduction in the natural risks of enterprise. The eighteenth century experienced almost uninterrupted warfare; but compared with the extent of military and economic hostility, and the plagues and religious dissensions of the two previous centuries, there was a greater physical security, a reduction in arbitrary interruptions to trade, by the end of the period. Nevertheless, the most important dislocations and the most ubiquitous elements of risk which could not be satisfactorily provided for, had resided in economic factors: in fluctuation of demand, supply, and therefore price, and in imperfections of the market structure as regards both factors of production and finished goods. In this respect there was no change sufficient to make an appreciable difference to entrepreneurial functions.

The outstanding exception to this generalization lay, of course, in the area served in part by joint-stock enterprise,[1] and therefore came not from within the European economy but from outside it. The introduction of non-European commodities into the European economies naturally presented merchants with new tasks, while the possibility of undertaking commercial transactions outside the economic bounds of the Old World (e.g. the slave trade, the Asiatic carrying trade, intercolonial commerce) presented traders with a new economic environment – in the shaping of which they themselves played an important

[1] See below, pp. 439–47.

part. Initially, the economic exploitation of newly discovered lands or sea routes had been managed or closely and directly regulated by State enterprises. But the Portuguese and Spanish experiments hardly encouraged governments to prevent private entrepreneurs from assuming the tasks and expanding the potentialities of the new trades. The principal distinction between the new and the old commerce appeared to lie in the amounts and the nature of the necessary capital: commerce to Asia, Africa and America demanded heavier and larger capital investments, and this factor, together with the risks involved, stimulated the rise of incorporated enterprises. Moreover, investors secured government privileges in an attempt to protect their fixed-capital investment. Yet joint-stock companies in overseas trade and, more especially, in colonization, had only a limited success. There was, indeed, another range of problems besides those of capital supply. Trading over unprecedented distances, and to lands without the commercial benefits of European social and political systems, merchants found their problems of entrepreneurial control immeasurably enhanced. This was especially so for firms of the size of the largest joint-stock companies which were called on to engender fresh administrative skills. These corporations never resolved their problems fully, and individual as well as corporate enterprise had to adapt its techniques to the new situation. Meanwhile, within Europe the new commodities, in ever-increasing supply, stimulated the development of both entrepôts and processing industries. In each case mercantile skill and mercantile capital helped establish and support a trend.

With the exception of the joint-stock system – and it is well to remember that even incorporated businesses had to face up to new problems with many old techniques – commercial entrepreneurship had to rely largely on traditional tools in dealing with traditional problems. In 1750 as in 1500 the merchant was forced to delegate more responsibility than he wished because communications were too slow. Rudimentary control could be exercised by profit-incentives, accounting, and frequent correspondence. But in the last resort considerable initiative had to be left in the hands of the man on the spot. As a consequence the kinship group still played an all-important role in informal and formal business structures. Merchants still acted as mutual factors and financial agents. And, faced with risk and discontinuous markets, mercantile capitalists still diversified their abilities and their capital into a variety of functions as well as markets. There is evidence that in two respects economic expansion was beginning to have some effect – at least in important centres of commerce. There appears to have been an increase in long-term co-partnerships, and there was some tendency, particularly in the fields of finance and commission agencies, towards a somewhat heightened specialization of function. Even so, neither was sufficient to alter the general nature of commercial enterprise in any drastic way.

(4) ENTREPRENEURIAL SUCCESS

Not surprisingly, the most successful and sophisticated commercial enterprise was centred in the leading port towns of the most successful and sophisticated commercial nations. Yet success was not solely a question of favourable circumstances. The question of what made for success in mercantile enterprise cannot, of course, receive a simple, universally true answer. And while, given the risk environment, sheer luck cannot be ignored, neither can it be always considered a dominant factor: in entrepreneurship, as in invention, chance favours only the mind which prepared. It would, said Postlethwayt, be madness to abandon 'prudence, good sense and education, with intent blindly to pay homage and adoration to so capricious a lady as fortune'.[1] Equally, while a policy of diversification might eliminate a good deal of risk it could not override all market insecurity and there would come a point in diversification when the avoidance of loss might be achieved to the detriment of the securing of profit. Yet the potential ability to take advantage of whatever economic opportunities might arise obviously played an important part in the business careers of merchants. For this a wide-ranging knowledge of commodities and markets, together with a flexibility of approach, was important. The good merchant, wrote Mun, had just this sort of knowledge, 'which is to be as it were a man of all occupations and trades'.[2] On the other hand it took more than technical acquaintance with a variety of commercial areas to enable a merchant to make the most of them: he also had to be in possession of capital or the means to obtain it. Hence, even ancient tradition put great emphasis on the access to capital which the honest apprentice might find in the shape of his master's marriageable daughter (or widow) or his master's confidence and loans. By whatever means it was secured, capital or credit-worthiness could make possible the *calculated* risk, and enable the trader to take quick and more substantial advantage of a change in the entrepreneurial situation.

Capital, where it was judiciously managed, was the best soil in which to breed more capital, but in an economy such as that already described judicious management might involve as much generalized intuition as conscious rationality. As already noted in connection with book-keeping, there was a limit to the extent to which planning – as it is

[1] Malachy Postlethwayt and James Royston, *The British Mercantile Academy* (1750), p. 12.
[2] Thomas Mun, *England's Treasure by Forraign Trade* (1664; 1933 reprint), p. 2.

understood in modern business – was either possible or useful. On the one hand, the quantitative and factual data which must be the raw material of any business plan were unreliable as well as in all too short supply. On the other, the speed with which commercial situations could change, together with the arbitrary reasons for the changes and the relative absence of continuity and routine, meant that the past could not be relied upon as a safe basis for judging the present and that the future was too uncertain to rely upon policies which were long-term or too rigid. The state of communications alone emphasized the significance of a rule-of-the-thumb procedure – but a procedure which was not haphazard and which did rely on certain basic, rationalistic skills. Postlethwayt, in demonstrating the need for a grounding in practical matters, complained that 'Too many, who set out in the capacity of merchants, are apt to flatter themselves they stand in need of little other qualifications than a round capital and an adventurous disposition.'[1] In addition, given the possibility of reducing risks by economic privilege or official aid, access to political power was obviously one of the highroads to financial success. This factor, it is true, accentuated the importance of political skills and friends in high places; but it also underlined the significance of controlling capital with which to purchase the opportunity of accumulating even more wealth. Finally, in this necessarily abbreviated catalogue, the skilled or fortuitous selection and control of effective subordinates clearly played a critical part in the generation of successful commercial firms. Given the possession of basic business aptitudes, the merchant whose kinsmen and acquaintances were most firmly entrenched in entrepreneurial undertakings would obviously enjoy a considerable economic advantage. In other words it was the structure of the enterprise and its relationships with others, as well as the innate abilities and wealth of the entrepreneur, which helped explain the achievement of commercial success.

(5) ENTREPRENEURIAL SUCCESSION

Since perfect occupational mobility has never existed in fact, the question of what factors made for entrepreneurial success cannot be disassociated from questions relating to the social and economic origins and the social and economic aims of entrepreneurs. And these matters were directly related to class patterns and accepted social values in any particular nation, society, or group.

European history is not lacking in examples of businessmen who rose from abject poverty to enviable affluence, or, more often, of 'tradesmen [who] spend one or two hundred pounds a year, whose parents never

[1] Postlethwayt and Royston, *The British Mercantile Academy*, p. 4.

saw forty shillings together of their own in their lives'.[1] But that the
achievement of great mercantile wealth by the sons of poor, non-
commercial families was anything other than exceptional or remarkable
may be doubted. In certain societies – notably England and France –
the tendency of wealthy merchants to establish landed families may well
have reduced the extent to which successful business bred successful
business (the phenomenon was far more common in the Low Countries). But on the whole it was clearly easier for a relatively rich man,
whether from a mercantile or professional or landed family, to become
a wealthy merchant than it was for a relatively poor one. And this was
not solely because of monetary considerations. Education, opportunity,
access to the right strata of society, family friends: all had a role to play.
Being born into a family of agricultural labourers or small farmers or
peasants was a handicap to business mobility not easily overcome. The
same was true, given the criteria of social achievement, of birth into an
established landed family in the case of the eldest son – although junior
members of the family might well have to seek their livelihoods in such
mundane occupations as commercial enterprise. Although occupational
mobility might have been free enough in a horizontal direction, and,
for example in seventeenth-century Bristol, 'a poor shopkeeper that
sells candles will have a bale of stockings or a piece of stuff for Nevis or
Virginia',[2] nevertheless economic mobility upwards assumed a steep
plane. Naturally enough the barriers to occupational mobility varied
between nations and over time. Further, they varied between occupations depending upon the relative esteem and value attached to the
occupation by society at large. This last point was, of course, more
relevant to entry from 'above' than from 'below'. The extent to
which men of aristocratic, landed or professional backgrounds entered
the world of trade clearly depended in large part on the value which
was attached to the commercial life.

Excluding Holland, whose republican leanings and shortage of land
made it a special case, England, of all the important nations with a
variegated social-economic structure, provided the greatest freedom of
entry into the ranks of the commercial class. Thus Defoe, even with
allowance for his economic chauvinism, touched upon an important
truth when he wrote:[3]

As so many of our noble and wealthy families...are raised by, and derive
from trade; so...many of the younger branches of our gentry, and even of

[1] *England's Great Happiness, or a Dialogue between Content and Complaint* (1677), p. 20.
[2] Quoted in Walter E. Minchinton, 'The merchants in England in the eighteenth
century', in *The Entrepreneur, Papers Presented at the Annual Conference of the Economic
History Society...April 1957*, p. 24.
[3] *The Complete English Tradesman*, I, 318 (italics in original).

the nobility itself, have descended again into the spring from whence they flowed, and have become tradesmen; and thence it is, that... our tradesmen in *England* are not, *as it generally is in other countries*, always of the meanest of our people. Nor is trade itself in *England*, as it generally is in other countries, the meanest thing that men can turn their hand to: but, on the contrary, trade is the readiest way for men to raise their fortunes and families; and therefore it is a field for men of figure and of good families to enter upon.

English commercial enterprise therefore benefited more than that of most lands from the influx of educated members of the upper class. In France the process was considerably more difficult, and even though aristocrats were generally more concerned with industrial enterprise than is commonly supposed,[1] the merchant class tended to be more self-generating than in England. In both lands, as in most European societies, there were variations in esteem: wholesaling carrying greater prestige than retailing, and international trade more than domestic. In the Low Countries, the land of 'merchants and mechanics', commercial status was most highly regarded and, possibly, carried with it the greatest satisfactions. Indeed, since entrepreneurs were obviously motivated by far more than the immediate financial rewards of enterprise, it is important to consider the other side of the coin of commercial prestige – the extent to which a merchant could attain social and political prominence in his own country.

Although the reverse is not necessarily true, a society which allows its gentlefolk to become traders will allow, as Defoe pointed out, its traders to become gentlefolk. And in the England of the early modern period – more particularly the seventeenth and eighteenth centuries – wealth was an alternative to birth as a road to social prestige. It was, however, more than a mere question of the purchase of honours or the forging of a family alliance between wealthy bourgeois and impecunious aristocrats. These phenomena were common in France without a commensurate increase in the prestige of trade. Rather, the respect which, in England, was paid to commerce was a *practical* respect and merchants were able to attain a political and social status which in France was denied to them: in their capacity as entrepreneurs they achieved the sort of power which money alone does not necessarily bring. The mercantile aristocracy of London and the provinces had access to government and political office, to social position and influence. Thus France – which laid its honours and offices open to purchase – had little to match the commercial interest in the House of Commons or the national power of the City of London (the Conseil de Commerce was not really the equivalent of either), and little to rival the mercantile oligarchies in local communities.

[1] See below, pp. 449–50.

No matter what prestige was attached to commercial pursuits, there were in most European societies levels of attainment which exceeded it. 'The memory of our richest merchants,' wrote Mun, 'is suddenly extinguished; the son being left rich, scorneth the profession of his father, conceiving more honour to be a gentleman (although but in name) to consume his estate in dark ignorance and excess, than to follow the steps of his father as an industrious merchant to maintain and advance his fortunes.'[1] Yet such cases were most often, perhaps, the inevitable visitation of the sins of the father upon the son, for if we are to believe the gloomy commentaries of commercial pamphleteers, in every important land in Europe except Holland successful merchants tended to channel their gains into non-entrepreneurial pursuits, seeking the rewards of place and prestige. And this, it was held, gave Holland an inevitable economic advantage:

From the moment that a merchant in France has acquired great wealth [wrote Jacques Savary], his children, far from following him in this profession, on the contrary enter public office...whereas in Holland the children of merchants ordinarily follow the profession and the trade of their fathers, and give such considerable sums to their children when they marry that one of these will have greater wealth when he begins trading on his own, than the richest merchant of France will have when he stops trading to establish his family in other professions.[2]

Commercial enterprise, it is clear, was rarely an end in itself. In the Low Countries, the most commercial of societies, a social structure and a set of values were based in large part upon a relative shortage of land, and even the cessation of active commerce on the part of individual merchants might well be followed by diversified mercantile investment and the founding of a financial dynasty. But in England and France entrepreneurial drives had a far more complex character. In the latter, the successful trader appears to have left risk-bearing trade as quickly as possible in order to purchase for himself and his sons the public offices and the lands which could bring a semblance of aristocratic position and a *rentier* income of secure proportions and continuity. In England, the magnet of land and country estate exerted a seemingly irresistible pull upon commercial capital, combining the solidity of preserved capital, the social esteem of squirearchical position, and the satisfaction of founding (it was hoped) a longer line than the insecurities of commerce might support.

[1] Mun, *England's Treasure by Forraign Trade*, pp. 3–4.
[2] Quoted in V. Barbour, *Capitalism in Amsterdam in the Seventeenth Century* (Baltimore, 1950), p. 141. Josiah Child in a memorandum said the same thing more pithily: 'The Dutch master us in trade. We always begin young men here, there it holds from generation.' Quoted in Barbour, *op. cit.*, p. 141.

On the other hand, there was also an economic aspect to the situation: 'when you mount the man upon the pinnacle of his fortunes', wrote Defoe, 'he is past the pinnacle of his *enterprising spirit*; he has nothing to do then but to keep himself where he is.'[1] Given the obvious fact that a merchant did not wish to devote either all his resources or all his lifetime to the pursuit of active international commerce, what investment outlets were available to him? Purely economic considerations dictated that security (of capital and income) should be foremost in his mind. And for most of the period in most economies the safest – and not the least remunerative – investment lay in rural or urban lands and property. It was the natural repository of the merchant's funds 'when he begins to cool in his trading warmth, and has resolved to lay down his business'.[2] Naturally, lands or mortgages were not the only outlet for passive capital; but many of the others (e.g. the money market, ships, early joint-stock companies) carried an element of risk or at least a necessity for management of the variety which such investors might not be willing to assume. In France there were the offices and *rentes*; in Holland, a variegated economy offered some scope for variegated investments. It was not until the eighteenth century that in a country such as England the development of the corporate system and the formalization of public loans began to offer broad-based and important fields for relatively secure capital investment of the rentier type. To some men this appeared to be merely an inefficient waste of resources:

In the good old days of trade, in which our forefathers plodded on, and got estates too, there were no bubbles, no stock-jobbing, no *South Sea* infatuations, no lotteries, no funds, no annuities, no buying of navy-bills, and public securities, no circulating exchequer bills: in a word, trade was a vast great river, and all the money in the kingdom ran down its mighty stream...there were no new canals or side-drains open to abate its waters...and to carry its stream off from the ordinary course.[3]

Whatever the ultimate effects of stock-jobbing and speculation in securities, the fact remained that in most cases commerce (or the varied activities carried on beneath its rubric) by its very nature was not an activity which, when success was once attained, made for entrepreneurial continuity or familial succession. Either other, less enterprising, fields offered more security, or capital accumulation in trade opened doors to more spectacular, more profitable, and more powerful pursuits. Commercial enterprise was thus, frequently, a stopping place in a wealthy entrepreneur's economic journey. Nevertheless, its preeminence in the economies of the early modern period cannot be doubted.

[1] *The Complete English Tradesman*, II, 211–12.
[2] *Ibid.* II, 205.   [3] *Ibid.* II, 234.

III.   *Industrial Enterprise*

In his treatise *Le Parfait Négociant*, Jacques Savary described one essential characteristic of industrial enterprise:

L'ordre est l'ame d'une manufacture, sans quoi il est impossible qu'elle puisse subsister...cet ordre consiste premièrement à tenir des livres tres exacts, & sans confusion, soit pour les matières que l'on fait venir...soit pour celles que l'on donne aux ouvriers pour les manufacturer; des livres de reception d'ouvrages, de teinture, d'envoi; journaux de vente, de caisse, d'extrait, & autres livres necessaires servans aux manufactures.[1]

Three important assumptions are clearly implicit in Savary's description. Each finds some confirmation in the economic history of the period before the Industrial Revolution. First, in context, the passage implies that it was a perfectly normal and anticipated practice for commercial enterpreneurs to invest in and manage manufacturing enterprises. Second, entrepreneurial control was an important prerequisite of economic success in industry. Third, industrial organization was in the main best typified by the 'putting-out' system.

The tendency for mercantile capital to find its way into non-mercantile pursuits has already been referred to. Its movement into industry was a clear reflection of various factors: the trend to diversification, the desire to guard against insecurity (by obtaining outlets for raw materials or sources of supply for trade), the pressure to increase profit margins, and the need to ensure that the products for which there was a demand would in fact be available to the merchant.

Although extensive manufacturing enterprise posed problems of internal control sufficiently like those of commerce to demand the use of accounting techniques, in reality such problems were less insistent than those of long-distance trade. The reason lay in the fact that manufacturing (and mining) undertakings did not have extended lines of internal communication and therefore did not need to decentralize entrepreneurial responsibility to the same degree as commercial firms. Control *was* important in matters pertaining to costs, wastage of raw materials, and the maintenance of quality. Since these, and many other issues, were related to the structure which industrial enterprise assumed, it will be convenient to devote the bulk of this section to that question.

[1] Jacques Savary, *Le Parfait Négociant* (Lyon, 1697), p. 89.

(I) INDUSTRIAL ORGANIZATION

The fundamental division between types of manufacturing and mining units was determined by the nature of capital requirements. Where technological factors meant that workers had to be associated with reasonably expensive items of capital equipment, units of production tended to be concentrated (as will be seen, the resulting *scale* of operations then depended on non-technological factors[1]). On the other hand, where fixed capital was less important there was less need to concentrate the labour force within a workshop. For to do this was to assume overhead costs, administrative burdens, and labour problems, which, given the nature of demand and of the labour market, were rarely justified – especially in view of the limited scope for cost reduction through the sub-division of manufacturing processes. Certainly, there were exceptions to this generalization: a Winchcombe or a Stumpe might temporarily be able to take advantage of a textile boom to create a workshop organization and amaze contemporaries; or, under the non-market stimulus of government aid or aristocratic enterprise, labour and circulating capital might be drawn together in large units of production. But such instances were not representative of the industrial organizations which typified most lines of manufacture. In the main, technology was simple; and where this was so the burden of such overhead costs as existed could be shifted to the labour force. In this case production was organized either by coordinating the activity of workers dispersed in their own homes (the traditional putting-out system), or in small-scale units in which the 'owner' laboured in his home alongside a handful of helpers at most (the 'domestic' system).

It was, again, the nature of the need for capital and the structure of the market which were the dominant – although not the only – factors determining the arrangements of production as between different varieties of the putting-out and the domestic or handicraft systems. Thus a limited and local demand for commodities which could be produced with relatively little fixed or circulating capital would tend to be satisfied by artisan manufacture centred in the homes of independent handicraftsmen, working with a very small number of helpers – who might be employees or members of the family. By contrast, where the production aimed at a long-distance market, or where the supply of raw materials was susceptible to restraint, the possibility of centralized, capitalistic control, through both the power position of trading wealth and the central provision of raw materials and wages, became more apparent. And this tendency was even stronger when the raw materials of production were expensive or the turnover of capital long; for both

[1] Below, pp. 427–31.

situations gave material economic advantages to the capitalistic entrepreneur. There were cases, however, where – as in the eighteenth-
century West Riding textile industry – goods were manufactured for a
sophisticated 'capitalistic' market, but where the cheapness of the
individual article and the speed with which it could be produced meant
that the independent working-producer, even though lacking in capital,
could still hope to survive by turning his small 'stock' quickly and, if
necessary, purchasing the services of capital-intensive processes (e.g.
fulling mills) on a commission basis.

Quite apart from the absence of technological reasons, the putting-
out system was, for many purposes, economically superior to a workshop form of organization. As market insecurity was the dominant
strand in the entrepreneurial environment, so putting-out methods
afforded the most effective scope for entrepreneurial flexibility to meet
the consequent risks. It could adapt to fluctuations in demand quickly,
and with minimum cost to the businessman. By drawing on the labour
of the by-employed and the rural population, through relatively small-
scale units scattered over a wide area, it would tap a responsive and
inexpensive work force. Because of its structure it would allow for
extensive industrial expansion, while, because of the crucial importance
of circulating capital, it allowed for intensive growth in the scale of
operations of the individual entrepreneur. On the other hand, since
business capital was not to any great extent sunk in fixed uses, the entrepreneur could reduce the scope of his operations with relative ease. In
itself, therefore, it was an entrepreneurial adaptation to, and an entrepreneurial tool for, the economic climate of enterprise in underdeveloped regions.

This is not to say that decentralized manufacture had no limitations.
For one thing there was the question of the lack of standardization
already mentioned. But, in contrast with the problem of control in
commerce, the inability to ensure uniformity in the products of an
enterprise was in the main caused not by slow communications but by
the primitive nature of technical processes. Where control problems did
arise they were related to the costs of increased production. For, in the
case of the individual firm, an expansion of output was accompanied
pari passu by an increase in the size of total operations (i.e. labour force,
capital, raw materials) and therefore by at least a proportionate rise in
direct costs. The absence of any commanding tendency towards the
increasing economies of scale in an enterprise based upon putting-out
was indeed accompanied by the *increased* difficulty of controlling the
flow of raw materials, regulating a larger labour force, and coordinating
the greater number of distinct manufacturing units which went to comprise the entrepreneurial unit. In such circumstances it was rare that

expansion came smoothly and homogeneously, for there was a limit to the amount of detailed administration which one entrepreneur could assume. It was more likely to be secured by the retention of professional managers (each in charge of a group of units of production) or by sub-contracting the work to be done to quasi-independent entrepreneurs.

(2) LARGE-SCALE INDUSTRY

The putting-out system, in spite of its limitations, flourished in many lines of industry, and especially in the largest industry of the time: textile production. Nevertheless, it presupposed an inexpensive and easily learned technology. By contrast, there were many commodities in whose production technological requirements played a sufficiently important part to warrant or necessitate centralized manufacturing units. In these lines labour was attracted to the physical means of pro-duction. Clearly, in the mining of natural resources, and the production of metals, ships, glass, flour, beer, sugar, soap, books, paper, and the like, either the nature of the raw materials or the demands of technology exerted a centripetal force on industrial organization. Yet – as with agricultural enterprise, where the small-scale unit exhibited a tenacious longevity – the *relative* significance of fixed capitals did not necessarily mean large-scale operations. The forest glass-blower, the coal mine employing a handful of men, the peasant salt pan, the innkeeper-brewer, the artisan shipbuilder, all represented ubiquitous and signifi-cant forms of enterprise. Heavy industry, as we think of it today, was perhaps less common than tradition would have us believe.

The Industrial Revolution was to demonstrate that mass production depends, among other things, upon a combination of large-scale mar-kets and efficient transport. It was the frequent absence of these factors which limited the development of really large-scale enterprise in the early modern period. The cost of transporting wood-fuel, for example, meant that firms which used it in large quantities were normally forced to avoid concentration by the logic of raw-material costs. Thus, the large enterprise in the English iron industry at best controlled many scattered medium-sized forges and furnaces; and in France, most glass-manufacturing firms were never fully able to eradicate the economic advantages of the small-scale entrepreneur. Even more important than the supply of raw materials, however, were the difficulties in marketing. Over the whole range of manufacturing and extractive industry there were sufficient opportunities of cheap production: rich coal fields and ore beds, coastal transport of raw materials, technological possibilities. The principal limitation to scale was not expensive production but costly marketing. Scattered population and uneven transport – poor by land, and by sea reaching only a limited area – circumscribed even the most efficient entrepreneur. Only special conditions would justify heavy expenditure on overhead capital in the hope of tapping a sufficiently remunerative demand.[1]

Among the special marketing circumstances which provided scope for the realization of the economies of scale might be urban concentration itself. In cities such as London or Paris, a sufficient number of consumers within a small radius might encourage 'heavy' industry – as long as raw material supplies were adequate and cheap. Thus in eighteenth-century England only London brew-houses were able to take advantage of large-scale operations, for beer could only be transported over short distances by land at a reasonable cost. But, on the other hand, where the raw material was itself expensive to transport, or where the metropolitan area's higher prices drove up production costs, large-scale enterprise might prefer other districts: the French Royal Plate Glass Company, for example (producing a product whose transportation cost was low in relation to its price – but using raw materials where the reverse situation obtained), moved soon after its foundation (in 1665) from Saint-Antoine, near Paris, to Tourville in Normandy.

If problems of production costs were not insuperable, then large-scale enterprise would be stimulated by the proximity of water transport leading to profitable markets. The English coal industry was a case in point. Along the Tyne basin, collieries with direct water access to the teeming harbour, and therefore to coastal markets, attained a great size and a high level of investment, whereas inland miners, unless they were immediately on a river leading to urban demand, were circumscribed by rigid transportation costs. In coal mining, more than most industries, of course, transportation costs were a strategic factor, as a French entrepreneur like Christophe Mathieu realized, requesting, in the eighteenth century, an interest-free State loan to build a canal from mine to river.[2] The influence of water transport was not, however, confined to mineral extraction. Both in terms of available raw materials and ultimate distribution, port towns were suited to large-scale processing activities. A great entrepôt such as seventeenth-century Amster-

---

[1] There were, of course, circumstances in which marketing costs were geographically irrelevant because of the natural concentration of raw materials. The possibilities of utilizing massed capital in copper mining, for example, were not limited by any widespread distribution of competing sources of ore; and large-scale operation in Sweden's *Stora Kopparberg* (Great Copper Mountain) or in smelting copper ores in Saxony was facilitated both by the economies of large-scale production and the profitability of capital-control of limited supplies. Similar factors operated with the Fuggers' dominance of Almadén quicksilver mines in the early sixteenth century. But such circumstances were extremely rare.

[2] M. Rouff, *Les Mines de Charbon en France au XVIIIe Siècle* (Paris, 1922), p. 224.

dam, which could supplement abundant supplies of entrepreneurial capital with low-cost stocks of paper, wood, sugar, sand, potash and metals, was the site of large-scale enterprises in printing, saw-milling, ship-building, sugar-refining and glass manufacture.

Enterprise which was able to profit by the use of heavy capital inputs was thus limited to a great extent by fortuitous factors of geography, geology and location. In addition, there were more purely 'economic' factors. The supply of risk capital and willing entrepreneurial skill was equally important. The Swedish metallurgical industry, for example, in the absence of native wealth or skill hinged directly on the willingness of (or incentives to) Dutch and German entrepreneurs to promote iron, munition and copper enterprises. And this also suggests another important reason for the evolution of heavy industry. For the availability of capital, or effective demand, might not merely be a function of market forces: the State had an important role in the creation of concentrated enterprise.

This was especially true of mining and metallurgical industries, since in most European nations, other than England, minerals were not held to be in the undisputed possession of the owners of the soil. The Crown's regalian rights over such natural resources were not only exercised for taxation purposes: they were used to control, by means of concessions, the entrepreneurial exploitation of coal and metals.

Comprehensive government ownership and management was itself quite rare. Where it existed, however, it might be on a very large scale: the Venetian government's shipyard, covering some 60 acres and employing between 1,000 and 2,000 men, was the largest single entrepreneurial unit in early sixteenth-century Europe. To a great extent important State enterprises were largely confined to the manufacture of goods directly of service to war effort: to arsenals and shipyards. In addition, there were instances where an imagined *raison d'état* dictated government promotion for the production of less belligerent goods. France, with its State enterprises of the Gobelins, the Savonnerie and Sèvres, succeeded in providing large-scale units by artificial means, although even here private entrepreneurs organized production on equipment and in buildings owned by the Crown. In Sweden, the strategic importance of copper was utilized by the Crown, which was a substantial owner of the principal mine, and controlled the international marketing of that metal. And in eighteenth-century Germany the State had to undertake or take over businesses which in underdeveloped economies private capital could not sustain but which the governments of Prussia, Austria, Bavaria and Hesse judged to be essential to national welfare.

Yet it did not necessitate outright government ownership to create large-scale State-aided enterprise. In fact most of the latter was provided by a combination of official support and private entrepreneurship. This could be most obviously effected in the fields of the munitions industry, where government demand might provide the secure market without which heavy capital investment could not be justified. Contracts for the supply of gunpowder, which in England during the late sixteenth and early seventeenth centuries were largely confined to the Evelyn family, fostered a growth of large-scale enterprise in Surrey. Contracts for naval iron and anchors helped establish Ambrose Crowley's model works and sustained the score or so forges and foundries which Pierre Babaud de la Chaussade controlled in mid eighteenth-century France.[1] And in early seventeenth-century Sweden, the armament, iron and shipbuilding enterprises of Louis de Geer were directly involved in the supply of goods for government needs. But in most such instances – as in the case of the French king's demand for luxuries from the Royal Plate Glass Company, or the Lourder and Dupont families in the Savonnerie – the contractual basis alone was insufficient to justify large-scale investment and organization. Even in the early modern period the demand for armaments and metals and royal luxuries was not sufficiently steady to eradicate the problems of crippling overheads. Entrepreneurs were forced to lean even more heavily on the State, and to secure from it the direct subsidies, the interest-free loans, the concessions, and the exclusive privileges which they hoped would lighten their own expenditures and increase the market price of their goods. Nowhere was this system of State-encouragement carried as far as in late seventeenth- and eighteenth-century France, where *manufactures royales* and *privilégiés* secured loans and subsidies, honorific titles and practical monopolies, tax-exemptions and labour privileges; and where the government was, in theory at least, sovereign in the industrial field: entrepreneurs seeking the permission to set up factories which so often entailed privileges, coal-mine promoters securing the geographical monopolies without which their investments would have been so much wasted money. With the aid of its monopoly the Royal Plate Glass Company was, in 1750, one of the largest private factories in the world, employing about 1,000 men, and with sales of over 1,000,000 *livres*. Indeed, French industrial firms, like French trading companies, seemed only capable of attaining a large size with the aid of direct or indirect royal subsidies. Yet to a lesser degree, other governments also attempted to provide market-security and capital-substitutes for large-scale industry – especially in the mining and metallurgical fields. In sixteenth-

[1] P. Bamford, 'Entrepreneurship in seventeenth and eighteenth century France', *Explorations in Entrepreneurial History*, IX, 4 (April, 1957), 207 ff.

century England, the Mines Royal and the Mineral and Battery Works, in seventeenth-century Sweden the iron and armaments enterprises of Dutch and German businessmen, in eighteenth-century Berlin the silk-factories, all illustrated this.

It is abundantly clear, then, that large-scale, centralized industrial enterprise needed the presence of exceptional factors before it could be successfully undertaken. In large part, excluding cases of government intervention, these influences were geographical and economic, rather than technological. It was only at the end of the eighteenth and during the nineteenth centuries that improvements in both manufacturing and transportation techniques were so great as to give a resounding competitive advantage to large-scale enterprise. Up to the end of the *ancien régime* even in England – where the existence of rich resources and excellent possibilities of water transport carried heavy industry to its farthest development – other types of organization and small or medium-sized firms were more typical. On the other hand, where the State *did* assume an economic function directed towards the creation of heavy industry, its efforts were obviously circumscribed by economic reality. Although the French government's attitude towards monopolies became more selective and critical in the late eighteenth century, if a particular enterprise needed a continuous monopoly, and this were granted, then clearly the result would be to check, not to expand, the area of large-scale enterprise – if demand could barely justify one firm, let alone two, the effect of such a project was to create infant industries which, precocious as they might have been, would never achieve adulthood until the market situation justified it on purely economic grounds. Meanwhile industrial concessions clashed with each other, and with such other privileges as the rights to establish internal tolls. Yet where State action was directed towards the attraction of indispensable capital or technological or entrepreneurial skill from abroad, then, indeed, it might have a more positive and creative effect in overcoming institutional bottlenecks: especially in an age where international flows of knowledge and industrial capital were only as mobile as movements of personnel. In effect, in such circumstances the State was undertaking part of the capital risks of promotion. And sometimes as in Sweden, or even Germany, this was an important prerequisite of ultimate industrialization.

The slow surge of economic development which lay behind the continuing traditionalistic economic institutions of the period between the fifteenth and eighteenth centuries undoubtedly coincided with an increase in the use of fixed capital in industrial enterprise. The rise in population and even in its urban concentration, the demands of war, the heightened flow of primary goods which needed processing, the increase in wealth and the ultimate hesitant improvement in inland waterways: these factors generated a tendency towards large-scale operation. On the other hand, the nature and cheapness of rural labour supplies, the distribution of natural resources (especially fuel), the costs of marketing, the diversified and fluctuating nature of demand, and the backward technology, all continued to impose strict limits on the individual and aggregate extent of concentrated units of production. It is possible that in many industries characterized by a high input of fixed capital, industrial development proceeded more by an extension and proliferation of units of production below the largest size, than by a growth in the number of industrial giants.

The structural organization of 'heavy' industry was tailored to its needs at the various levels of its operation. At the two extremes of small-scale production and full-blown State enterprise the forms of proprietorship were, of course, straightforward. Whether the former was an independent operation in which the peasant or artisan entrepreneur actually participated or was a minor adjunct to the estates of a land-owner, as a single proprietorship or working partnership it presented few managerial problems of any sophisticated or non-traditional type. State enterprise, under the pressures of size and without the incentives of profit or (frequently) the stimulus of dedicated administrators, often lapsed into spectacular inefficiency. In the middle range – medium- or large-scale private or semi-private undertakings – entrepreneurs on the whole quite naturally adopted forms of organization which would enable them to pool capital most effectively. There were, it is true, industrial enterprises owned by individuals; particularly mining ventures in which the owner of the minerals had been sufficiently wealthy and/or enterprising to undertake their exploitation. This was largely the case in British coal-mining – where nearly all the minority of large collieries which *were* under a single proprietor were in fact owned by the landlord himself. But on the whole large-scale mining and manufacturing, like long-distance trade, was sufficiently demanding of capital and sufficiently risky to produce capital associations. The form of organization most commonly adopted was the partnership.[1] Entrepreneurs could thereby both diversify their own investments and tap resources of passive capital, while at the same time the leading promoters were able to maintain their effective direction of the firm, and, if

[1] Joint-stock organization was relatively rare, and, at least at their inception, even undertakings such as the Mines Royal or the Mineral and Battery Works – although formally incorporated – partook more of the character of contemporary co-partnerships than modern joint-stock companies. The formation of companies apparently increased in the late seventeenth and eighteenth centuries, although partnership remained the predominant mode of organization.

necessary, offer the incentive of a share in the profits to men in possession of scarce technical skills.

Partnerships in mining and metallurgical enterprise assumed standardized forms. They ran for a stipulated term of years and their capital was divided into 'parts' or 'shares'. The number of parts was fixed – but not, in fact, the number of investors: parts frequently could be, and were, divided, either by direct sale or inheritance, into further portions. Many partnerships retained their private character by means of a formal provision that no partner could sell his share without giving at least an option to his co-adventurers, while others had full negotiability for shares at the will of the partner. But nearly all large enterprises eventually encountered the fact if not the problem of a multiplicity of owners. As early as the sixteenth century some silver and copper mines in Saxony and Bohemia had 'parts' running into the hundreds, and although this extreme was unusual, partnerships of any large size normally had to adjust the balance between ownership and management. In most cases, then, minority partners were represented – if at all – by an agent, and the articles of association frequently stipulated a minimum number of parts to be owned for participation in management. The practice of each partner having a single vote irrespective of individual holdings, which was common, for instance, in Liège coal-mining firms did not at all represent the realities of management in industrial partnership at large. Entrepreneurial as well as capital power was concentrated in the hands of the few, and even where the partners were many the frequent provision by which management was to reside in the hands of the partners meeting as a body remained largely a formality.

The position of partners with respect to personal liability and further calls on capital varied. In England, for example, liability of participating partners was unlimited (even the two Elizabethan mining and metallurgical companies imposed calls on shares); but it was, of course, possible to invest in a partnership at a fixed rate of interest with no obligation beyond the amount of the loan. In France, by contrast, there were three main types of organization: the *société en nom collectif*, in which all participants bore full liability, the *société en commandité*, in which the minor (non-managing) partners were financially responsible only to the limit of their share, and the *société anonyme*, which was an even closer approximation to a joint-stock organization with limited liability. The great Anzin mining enterprise and le Creusot were organized on this last basis, although its use was generally rare and limited to the greatest aggregations of capital. It was the *société en commandité* which was easiest to form and provided maximum flexibility for the raising of capital – since small-scale investors could relieve themselves of the onerous duties of management and the hazardous obligation to meet further calls on their capital. To some extent this last result could even be achieved in England: in Northumberland and Durham it was possible, at least in the seventeenth century, to lease or 'farm' a part to another person and thereby to absolve the lessor from any obligation to subscribe further capital.[1]

The influences which, on the side of investment, tended to establish the familiar cleavage between ownership and management, were accentuated by inevitable developments in the field of operational control. For large-scale mining or manufacturing demanded both continuous management and technical expertise for their success – and no matter what the entrepreneurial skills involved in promotion and marshalling of capital, the partners themselves had to fulfil, or had to appoint an agent to carry out, administrative functions of crucial importance to the enterprise. It was, especially, the technical side of business which produced – again at an early stage – the professional manager: men like the scions of the Mathieu family who were concerned with the Anzin firms and ultimately became mine-owners in their own right; or the highly paid clerks and master brewers so essential to London's great brewery partnerships in the eighteenth century; or John Wheeler who, late in the seventeenth century, cemented managerial relationships between three of the interlocking Foley iron partnerships by acting as managing partner for them.[2] Such men complemented entrepreneurial groups like the 'inner rings' of partners in Tyneside collieries or the six men into whose hands the general management of the Anzin colliery was placed upon its formation in 1757.[3] Management was already tending towards that day-to-day administration and control which distinguishes large-scale manufacture from diversified trade.

Partnership in industry, as in trade, could be a flexible means of diversifying capital investment within one general field. More than this, however, it was suited to the task of unifying the entrepreneurial interests of scattered business establishments where geology and problems of transportation enforced a decentralization of manufacturing operations. Thus, at the end of the seventeenth and beginning of the eighteenth centuries, capital of the Foley family, by means of participation in several partnerships, effectively identified the interests of some thirteen furnaces, twenty-nine forges, nine slitting mills, two wireworks, and an anvil works.[4] This system of interlocking partnerships

[1] John U. Nef, *The Rise of the British Coal Industry* (London, 1932), II, 60–1.
[2] B. L. C. Johnson, 'The Foley partnerships: the iron industry at the end of the charcoal era', *Economic History Review*, 2nd ser., IV: 3 (1952), 326–30.
[3] Rouff, *Les Mines de Charbon en France au XVIIIe siècle*, p. 274.
[4] Johnson, 'The Foley partnerships', pp. 324 ff.

was not always a management tool – frequently, as in the case of coal mining, where men often held shares in a group of collieries, it was an investment technique. But where it was, the institutions of family and social and religious groups had a role to play as important as their functions in commerce. The Mathieu family in French coal mining, the Quaker dynasties in London brewing, and the English iron industry, the de Geer, Trip and Momma families in seventeenth-century Swedish iron and copper – all illustrate this. Such groups were the sources of confidence and trust, and therefore of capital as well as administrative talent.

In the generation of successful heavy industry, mercantile capital and capitalists were of supreme significance. From either overseas or domestic commerce investments and entrepreneurs came to control a good deal of Europe's large-scale enterprise in mining, metallurgy, glass, sugar, salt, and so forth. This is not to say that such industries continued to be dominated by commercial enterprise: successful industrial operations of any great size, because of the demands on time and skill, inevitably produced more or less full-time industrial entrepreneurs, and a specialization unfamiliar to most merchants. It is true that commercial capitalists remained active in commerce while still processing the products of their trade in medium-sized establishments. In addition, the strategic importance of marketing, and the control exercised by traders, meant that the predominant entrepreneurs in a local industry such as Tyneside mining were in fact the town merchants. But such a continued ambivalence was not the normal situation. Sir Ambrose Crowley, for example, naturally graduated from his father's iron trade to iron manufacture. When the French commercial bourgeoisie turned to mining it was in conjunction with a move towards the feudalism of estate-ownership, the privilege of the *noblesse de la robe*, and an assumption of the social dignity which was supposed to attach more to the exploitation of the resources of the land than to the exchange of commodities. The English iron masters and brewing dynasties exemplified a comparable dedication, as, in their own way (which, it is true, involved a more speculative diversity), did the Dutch entrepreneurs who embedded themselves in Sweden's finances, landed estates, shipping, iron and copper trades. Wealthy traders, naturally enough, were not the only creative entrepreneurs of industrial expansion. Some men (Abraham Darby is a case in point) rose directly from small-scale to large-scale manufacture. And middle-class wealth – as in the case of the syndicate of four bankers who in 1702 took over the bankrupt Royal Plate Glass Company for a price of almost 2,000,000 livres – had its own entrepreneurial power.

Like most other forms of enterprise, large-scale mining and heavy industry were shot through with incalculable risks. The individual entrepreneur – although, obviously, not the individual firm – could in part hedge the risk by seeking a secure market or diversifying interests and therefore investment. But even so, the commitment to an unknowable future involved in the immobilization of funds in fixed capital carried with it a special and heightened form of uncertainty; and even private individuals stood to lose, and did lose, great sums of money. To a great extent, therefore, entrepreneurs needed strong incentives and much help before they would sink money in some lines of activity. Thus, most of France's really large-scale businesses leaned upon direct or indirect State aid – and in both France and England pecuniary help at the local level was provided for entrepreneurs willing to establish firms.[1] The burden of fixed investment could be lightened by leasing lands, mines and iron works; while, at the same time, any necessary heavy investment in fixed facilities (e.g. mine equipment) might be underwritten by taking a long lease on the premises. Mining – where promoters cannot foresee expenses, let alone income – was especially risky, and it is little wonder that the movement towards private monopoly was strong there. Thus the principal mine-owners of East- and Mid-Lothian met together in 1620 to propound an abortive scheme whereby 'it was proponeit amongis thame that the pryceis of thair collis sould be raised and hichted tuelf pennyes upoun every leade [load]...and that nane of thame sould sell thair coillis chaiper... guhilk propositioun being verry weele lyked of be the haill company, they all applaudit thairunto...'[2] And the colliery entrepreneurs of Languedoc, more than a century later, it was reported, 'ont des conventions entre eux, suivant lesquelles ils vendent tour à tour le charbon à un prix qu'ils ont fixé'.[3] But monopoly was rarely stable, and risks remained high. The conjunction of favourable circumstances was too rare an occurrence for entrepreneurs ever to be certain that they could safely expand into those rosy levels where they could attain spectacular economies of scale. In the structure of industrial enterprise the market continued to play a significant role.

IV. Corporate Enterprise

Although other forms of enterprise were more common, joint-stock organization was the most spectacular and the most novel type of business structure in the early modern period. Since it was a formal

---

[1] See G. Martin, *La Grande Industrie en France sous le règne de Louis XV* (Paris, 1900), pp. 197–8; Nef, *The Rise of the British Coal Industry*, II, 19.
[2] Quoted in Nef, *The Rise of the British Coal Industry*, II, 116.
[3] Quoted in Martin, *La Grande Industrie...Louis XV*, p. 229.

association of men as well as capital, it will be logical to examine in the first instance the two types of permanent business associations whose function was to provide a regulatory framework for the enterprise of individuals: the gild and the regulated company. Each represented attempts by entrepreneurs to shape the immediate framework of their enterprise; neither survived the economic changes which preceded the Industrial Revolution.

The religious and social satisfactions which could be derived from gild membership, and which were so important to medieval entrepreneurs, may still have had some meaning for businessmen in the early modern period. But, in most cases, where gilds had not relapsed into mere organizations of fraternal bonhomie or purely charitable undertakings, their commercial functions were pre-eminent. These functions were on the whole exclusive and restrictive rather than expansive. The economic policy of most gilds, which controlled both the terms of competition and the number of businessmen who *could* compete within one market, was the product of a traditional entrepreneurial outlook. Such organizations embodied the individual's search for security within apparently limited and unelastic markets, where the profits of one entrepreneur might well involve the losses of another, and where local businessmen struggled to preserve a relative balance of supply and demand. The gild, although it might be used in a roughly egalitarian manner among existing members, was also employed as an instrument of industrial and commercial control by small groups of wealthy manufacturers or merchants who, in maintaining their economic dominance of journeymen or small-scale craftsmen or petty traders, ossified an economic structure in their own favour.

Gilds, as institutional adjustments to static or circumscribed markets, designed to guard against the vicissitudes of competition or change, were bound to decline in importance wherever marketing areas or lines of communication were extended. In sixteenth-century England, for example, the development of internal trade and the growing consumption of imported luxuries eroded the economic rationale and the monopoly power of many craft gilds; while, in general, the migration of industry into rural areas, away from the gilds' urban jurisdiction, had the same effect. On the other hand, where gilds managed to retain economic power – as in seventeenth-century Lombardy or eighteenth-century France and Bohemia – they easily degenerated into costly brakes upon economic development or adaptation. Creative entrepreneurial activity in the period was too individualistic, and had too much to lose by indiscriminate association with traditionalistic enterprise, to operate within a gild framework. And the half-hearted attempts by the English and French governments to use gilds to induce coordinated economic growth came to nothing. As entrepreneurial devices of medieval town economies, gilds could not hope to survive the strains of an age of regional, national and rudimentary international economies.

In the case of English enterprise, corporate regulation was also important in the field of overseas trade. 'Companies who trade not by a joint stock, but only are under a government or regulation', as Josiah Child aptly described them, served to provide the State with convenient focuses of mercantile wealth, power, and knowledge which could be called upon for financial aid, diplomatic service, and help in the enforcement of national economic policy. From the viewpoint of entrepreneurs, they served to reduce the insecurities of commerce by providing mutual protection against piracy, representation in foreign lands, and a stable authority overseas. But, as in the case of gilds, their primary function was specifically economic.

By the late sixteenth century mercantile entrepreneurs operating within the framework of regulated companies dominated English overseas trade (even though the prototype of such associations, the Staplers, whose fortunes had been linked to the trade in wool, was then sinking into relative insignificance). The London companies and, to a more limited extent, their branches or the independent groupings in provincial ports, aimed to increase security by preventing excessive competition among members and, for specific channels of trade, eliminating it entirely when it was provoked by non-members ('interlopers'). Bolstered by exclusive privileges, great companies like the Merchant Adventurers, or the Eastland Company, or (at differing times) the Levant and Russia Companies, strove to confine trade to particular 'mart towns' overseas, to limit the times at which goods could be exported and imported, to establish regulations concerning the modes and conditions of sale and purchase by their members, and to exclude from membership retailers, mariners, and the like, who in order to profit by quick returns might be obliged to sell cheap or buy dear. The regulated company was clearly fashioned in an attempt to create a seller's market for exports and a buyer's market for imports. More than this, some companies – notably the Merchant Adventurers – ostensibly attempted to protect the small trader by formally rationing the exports of individuals. But in fact the whole idea of a regulated company dramatized the battle between large- and small-scale entrepreneurs, and tended, if they had any effects at this level, to favour the former at the expense of the latter. This was largely because the rules of a 'well-regulated' company inevitably extended the period of capital turnover and penalized the merchant with only limited supplies of capital or credit.

In spite of their policies, regulated companies were to a great extent not the creators but the creatures of a seller's market. Partaking of the nature of trade associations, they were obliged, like all associations attempting to restrain trade, to be wary of competition, elasticity of demand, and of resentment which could assume a political expression. Ultimately they succumbed to all three. Interlopers competed in and out of mart towns and in and out of 'sailing times'; the expansion of European manufactures (especially of textiles) in the seventeenth century created competition and therefore highly elastic demand; the resentment of outport traders against London control, and of interlopers against company monopolies, found a powerful sounding board in the seventeenth-century House of Commons. The sixteenth and early seventeenth centuries, the golden age of England's predominance in traditional textiles, had nurtured a strong system of regulated companies; but by the late seventeenth century economic reality and political action combined to deprive them of their commercial strength: a new alignment of industrial and commercial powers, while extending the dimensions of competition, had disrupted an old entrepreneurial institution.

While the corporate concept of gild and regulated company declined in importance in the seventeenth century, another adaptation of the medieval inheritance emerged. The joint-stock company, in spite of its relationships to old forms, was at bottom an answer to an entirely new range of entrepreneurial problems. The principal stimulant to corporate enterprise was the need for capital investment of a size and nature which individual entrepreneurs or even highly developed partnerships were unable or unwilling to assume. A fusion of the concept of partnership, with its aggregation of capital, and of incorporation, with its perpetual succession and privileged legal personality, the joint-stock company was a response to the need to draw together and manage capital in long-distance trade, mining and metallurgy, radical innovating projects, and specialized financial business. Rudimentary joint-stock associations had been known among the creditors of medieval Italian cities, and in central-European mining regions. But it was the economic demands of the extension of trade routes, the increasing participation of all the leading European nations in the seventeenth century, and the consequent dramatic changes in the nature of long-distant commercial and colonial enterprise, which really engendered extensive corporate enterprise.

The new trades to non-European lands were, in comparison with more traditional commercial investments, both costly and speculative. The initial outlay for commerce and defence was higher and the period of turnover was much longer, while the risks, of disaster, wastage, and fluctuating markets, were greater. It was therefore natural that entre-

preneurs should wish to continue their practice of diversifying investment by pooling capital. Nevertheless, it was neither the amount of
investment nor the accompanying risks which produced the corporate
form – both problems could easily have been met before the late
seventeenth century by partnerships or syndicates. The corporation had
the advantages of perpetual succession and a clear legal personality: it
could outlast any shifting group of investors, it could own large fixed
assets, and it could be granted exclusive trading rights by the State.
These potentialities proved crucial in the new fields of enterprise opened
up in Africa, Asia and America. For their distinctive feature was the
extent to which they demanded the provision of fixed capital, or 'dead
stock'. Consular, diplomatic and military services, large transports,
depots, and warehouses, a detailed administrative superstructure, community development (in the case of colonial ventures, whole societies)
– all these were necessary, costly, and had to be managed over the long
run. Clearly, no single group would undertake such investment unless
there were provision for its permanent utilization, and unless they could
obtain privileges to ensure that at least no other entrepreneurs of the
same nationality would benefit commercially from facilities the costs of
which they had not borne. Moreover, having joined to provide the
'dead stock', the proprietors would wish to ensure that they all shared
equally in the benefits.

That the new entrepreneurial problems should produce joint-stock
enterprise was not inevitable. In the great days of Portuguese trade to
Asia and Spanish trade to America the State attempted to provide its
own answer – either by monopolistic government enterprise, or inflexible State control and taxation. In addition, of course, a great deal
of Asiatic, American, and African commerce fell into the hands of
interlopers who benefited from other men's investments or merely
assumed some of the very high risks. But in terms of private enterprise
the most significant solution was a joint-stock company – an institution
which could own the common property, could trade as a unit on behalf
of shareholders and divide the proceeds equitably, and which, far more
conveniently than any private group, could secure the requisite monopolistic privileges which would protect the fixed investment.[1] It was a
solution which was, indeed, often arrived at after the inconveniences of
other organizational forms had been experienced: the Dutch (United)

---

[1] It has been argued that after the Monopolies Act (1624) the corporate form of
enterprise was stimulated in England, since private individuals could no longer be
awarded monopolies. It is, of course, true that economic ventures were subsequently
incorporated for this reason, but it would appear that the joint-stock company was
legally and economically more suited to receive privileges quite apart from the 1624
statute – as is demonstrated by its use in many instances prior to that date.

East India Company was formed only after eight years of confused competition between a handful of non-incorporated firms (*vóór-compagnieën*) based on single-venture investment; and in England the East India Company did not become truly permanent until after the mid seventeenth century – for more than fifty years the trade had been managed by 'separate voyages' (1601–12) and 'general voyages', or terminable joint stocks – with resulting accounting problems which were impossible to unravel.[1]

Commerce, in the sixteenth and seventeenth centuries, was the outstanding field for joint-stock enterprise; yet it was not the only one which necessitated heavy capital investment in speculative uses. The formation of companies for the Russia and Guinea trades in the 1550s was soon followed in England by the floating of the Mines Royal and the Mineral and Battery Works. In the English environment mining and metallurgy, as attempted in these two examples, demanded the assumption of high fixed costs and extraordinary risks. The corporate form also helped in the obtaining and wielding of the legal privileges considered so essential to success. Hence in mid sixteenth-century England, following German practice, joint-stock organization was adopted for the mining of silver, copper and lead, as well as the manufacture of iron and brass. Nearly 150 years later, during the joint-stock boom of the 1690s, new copper and lead companies were to repeat the experiment.

In Elizabethan England the commercial application of the technique continued with the Levant trade, and in both England and Holland merchants, contemplating the problems of the rapidly expanding spice trade, formed East India Companies with exclusive privileges. In the first decade of the seventeenth century, as well as later, joint-stock enterprise was the obvious choice for colonial activity – although capital demands were such that most colonial companies, whether private or State-stimulated, eventually failed. In addition to these endeavours, there were experiments with incorporated entrepreneurship in fishing and whaling (e.g. the Dutch *Noordsche* Company, formed by independent firms in 1614 ostensibly to present a united front against English attacks, or the Society of the Fishery of Great Britain and Ireland in the 1630s), and in other works of public development such as water supply and drainage. By the first decades of the seventeenth century this entrepreneurial technique had gone beyond the point of innovation. The way had been prepared for the flotation boom of the last decades of that century.

[1] In 1634, at a meeting of the Company, it was said of the £100,000 debt in India: 'which of these voyages owes it no man can tell'. Eli F. Heckscher, *Mercantilism* (rev. ed., 1955), I, 405.

The private element in joint-stock companies was never entirely divorced, whether by choice or necessity, from some aspect of government activity. The powers which companies could wield, and the strategic importance of their trades, meant that the State was inevitably concerned with their affairs and destinies. In England the companies were largely privately owned, although Elizabeth and the Stuarts invested (more for income than control) in some enterprises. Even so, the connections between corporate and public policy were never remote. On the continent they were even more obvious. The States General, for example, was the catalyst in bringing together, for strategic reasons, the firms which organized the Dutch East India Company. And in Sweden and Denmark trading companies, organized by foreign entrepreneurs on the model of more advanced nations, owed much to the State's desire for sophisticated economic development. There were, indeed, circumstances when a government's wish to see joint-stock companies floated outpaced the willingness of private capital to act on a voluntary basis. Thus, the Dutch West India Company, formed in 1621 largely to exploit (by trade and war) the Spanish possessions in the western hemisphere, was established with half its capital subscribed by the government and the bulk of the remainder produced under official pressure. But it was France which provided the principal example of an attempt to force an entrepreneurial development in which private investors failed to see any substantial profit-making possibilities.

In France the line between formal partnership and the joint-stock was less precise than in most other European jurisdictions, because of the use by entrepreneurs and investors of variations of the *société en nom collectif*, the *société en commandité*, and the *société anonyme*. Yet the really large-scale overseas trading companies in France did not derive from any stimulus of private business. After Henri IV, Richelieu and Mazarin had all attempted to establish an East-Indian trade, it was left to Colbert, in his competitive struggle with Holland, to undertake extensive experiments in the organization of long-distance commerce – in direct imitation of the more spectacular features of Dutch and English enterprise in the Far East. Companies were established for trade with, and sometimes settlement in, the western hemisphere, the Far East, the Levant, the Baltic, and Africa. Formed by State initiative and directed under close government surveillance, these enterprises proved far more a drain on the royal purse than a feather in the royal cap. Over half of the capital of 8,000,000 *livres* of the *Compagnie des Indes Occidentales*, and a similar percentage of the stock of the *Compagnie du Nord*, was subscribed by the king and the public funds. Most of the balance was subscribed only as a result of government pressure on merchant financiers. Such State-induced artificialities were a mockery of commercial effectiveness, and their decline – in the absence of real economic need and efficient entrepreneurial management – was inevitable. Unable to sustain the envisaged competition with Holland, the grandiose experiment demonstrated that it was not alone a shortage of capital which hindered the development of trading companies by French entrepreneurs.

In the late seventeenth and early eighteenth centuries, the characteristics of joint-stock enterprise underwent a change. The great speculative boom in flotations was, indeed, influenced by factors many of which were remote from the aspects of entrepreneurship already considered. Thus, the growth in English incorporation after 1689 was more a reflection of the pressure of capital rendered idle in the normal channels of overseas trade by war,[1] than the appearance of challenges to enterprise which could be met only by corporate organization. Many of the new companies were in fact formed for domestic undertakings, and for the first time a good number of flotations were based not on government charters, but on private articles of association. In addition, much of this activity was centred on the exploitation (or promised exploitation) of new inventions – a fact which might be largely attributed to the promoters' desire to take advantage of a speculative craze, but which, in terms of the necessary fixed capital and the risks of innovation, helps explain why a corporate organization was felt necessary. Whatever the exact mixture of reasons, the preponderance of flotations during the English boom were on a small scale – so small that the absolute size of capital involved could not have been important in the choice of a joint-stock form of enterprise.

At the end of the seventeenth century and the beginning of the next, there was a distinctly new application of the joint-stock principle, which, at least at its inception, was not the result of a mere speculative boom. Its rationale was the marshalling of credit and the servicing of finance which had been traditionally effected within an informal framework. In the fields of banking, insurance, and the management of the national debt such large-scale institutionalization was a complete novelty. In England, the most significant example, was, of course, the Bank of England, which, in return for a loan to the State secured the right to assume financial functions of a size and nature which only a joint-stock company could realistically hope to fulfil. The South Sea Company, on a more grandiose scale, undertook to service the national debt in exchange for extensive commercial privileges. Both firms illustrated the three outstanding characteristics of 'traditional' joint-stock enterprise: a large capital stock involved in long-term tasks, heavy

[1] See K. G. Davies, 'Joint-Stock Investment in the Later Seventeenth Century', *Economic History Review*, 2nd ser., IV (1952), 292.

risks, and the receipt of government concessions. The interrelationship of companies and government finance is, indeed, striking. In addition to the Bank and the South Sea Company, there was the Million Bank (1695), based in part on capital involved in the Million Lottery, insurance companies which loaned money to the government, and the new East India Company (1698) which was based on privileges extended to investors in a £2,000,000 State loan. In France, John Law's system, based on the Company of the Indies, offered a parallel, on an even greater and more complicated scale, to the South Sea Company experiment. In both cases the resulting speculative excesses brought the technique of joint-stock organization into serious disrepute.

Joint-stock companies were a disturbing as well as a new means of enterprise. Corporate monopoly was obviously not a popular device in an age of commercial expansion; and where, as increasingly happened in the late seventeenth century, the corporation was itself monopolized by a small group of entrepreneurs, criticism was bound to be acute. One result was that 'independent' English and Dutch capitalists were the more stimulated to participate in the flotation of ostensibly domestic companies in such underdeveloped lands as Sweden, Denmark, and Brandenburg. Nevertheless, the monopolies were rarely absolute: interlopers and licensed private traders succeeded in establishing a firm foothold in most trading areas. In fact, it is doubtful if a company with nominally exclusive privileges ever really retarded the evolution of a particular field of enterprise. On the other hand, it could be argued that much non-incorporated trade was made possible by the institutional and physical arrangements which companies financed, while the award of monopolistic privileges was a necessary prerequisite for large-scale investment in such commercial innovations.

The joint-stock system demonstrated only a limited ability to carry out the range of entrepreneurial tasks to which it was applied. Adam Smith's verdict that its effective application was largely restricted to routine administration, when considered in the light of the fact that success was normally attended by specific privileges, appears to have been just. There were, in fact, very few large companies which made long-term profits, and from the viewpoint of capital involved or business transacted corporations were unimportant when compared to other forms of entrepreneurial organization. In most cases, once the trade had been established, individuals who wished to invest in the field for which a company had been promoted were able to do so at far less cost, and with much greater flexibility, than the company itself. Joint-stock organization, in the absence of enforceable privileges, was not suited to the long-run needs of most commercial enterprise: its costs were too high, its communications too slow, its processes of formulating and applying policy too cumbersome, and its powers of internal control too limited. In domestic enterprise, too, other organizational forms proved equally adept at raising and managing capital for most purposes. As an entrepreneurial institution the company had to await the later stages of industrialization – with the extensive demand for heavy capital outlays in specific uses, the increased returns to continuous administration, and the mounting pressure of the supply of passive risk capital – before it could register an economic victory.

Even though joint-stock entrepreneurship failed to establish itself on a long-run basis, its significance in the history of enterprise is far greater than that of a mere premature experiment. For an innovation in business technique may point the way to new areas of enterprise, and act as the stimulant for their extensive exploitation, even though other institutions ultimately take over the main burden of enterprise. In this sense, companies – quite apart from those like the East India Companies or the Bank of England which were financially successful – were an important entrepreneurial innovation. They established paths which other entrepreneurs so spectacularly followed and which linked the economies of new worlds and Europe, to the great benefit of the latter. In addition, the attraction which joint-stock organization held for the contemporary entrepreneur, together with the managerial problems which it posed, gave it a particular importance which cannot be measured by its profits.

Joint-stock companies were financed as well as manned by active entrepreneurs. Capital which would not otherwise have gone into productive investment only became important in the eighteenth century,[1] for joint-stock organization derived more from the businessman's desire to use his capital effectively than from a need to tap fresh sources of wealth. And this was reflected in the fact that the cleavage between management and ownership, which is among the most important social results of modern incorporation, was not as great a problem in the early modern period. In Holland small investors certainly complained that an inner ring controlled the East India Company, but even so the real administrators were also heavy investors. And in England, by comparison with the twentieth century, the number of investors was smaller, their holdings proportionately larger, their relationships with management closer, and their own business experience more extensive. Time and again it was a group of active entrepreneurs who felt that there was more to be gained by cooperative than individual enterprise. Time and again they merely succeeded in exchanging one set of risks for another.

[1] This excludes the large amount of capital which was loaned to companies against fixed-interest bonds in the seventeenth century.

Particularly in the English companies there was provision, in the form of the General Court of proprietors, or shareholders, for exposing company policy to general debate to a much greater extent than is possible in the modern Annual Meeting. There were, indeed, important and searching discussions of administration at such gatherings. But in practice, of course, the everyday exercise of entrepreneurial power had to be delegated; and in England, as in Holland, inner rings of dominant individuals naturally evolved with the formal structure of management. The East India Company in 1691, for example, was effectively controlled by eight men, each holding over £10,000 of stock and accounting for more than 25 per cent of the Company's total capital. And this, according to some defenders of the system, was a positive advantage, for 'He that expects all satisfaction to arise from the profit of his own stock is tied with the two great chords which do almost the whole business of the world, viz. Reward by the profit of his own great stock, and fear of great loss if his own stock should miscarry by ill conduct.'[1] But it was not merely the case that large-scale owners became important managers. Partly because wealthy businessmen invested in many companies, and partly because company administration itself became a specialized task, there was a tendency towards the growth of a professional class of corporate managers – a tendency which in no way attained the level of the twentieth century, nor encompassed many managers who were not investors, but which was sufficiently strong to produce such a dedicated entrepreneurial bureaucrat as Sir Thomas Smythe, who in the early seventeenth century was, at varying times, Governor of the Levant, East India, and Russia Companies and Treasurer (an equivalent position) of the Virginia Company.

The directors of joint-stock companies do not appear to merit, at least in comparison with other large-scale enterprise, Adam Smith's dictum that since they were stewards for other people's money, they would be wanting in diligence, and 'Negligence and profusion...must always prevail, more or less, in the management of the affairs of such a company.'[2] The leading administrators of most non-speculative companies appear on the whole to have been businessmen of a high calibre and a firm dedication to their labours. In so far as can be judged, their attendance to their tasks was assiduous – at both centralized committees and sub-committees. 'Negligence and profusion' there may well have been. But it was not necessarily due to any lack of initiative on the part of management. Rather it stemmed from the fact that the joint-stock company, where it was involved in overseas trade, crystallized the

[1] Quoted in Davies, 'Joint-Stock Investment', *Economic History Review*, 2nd ser., IV (1952), 297.
[2] *The Wealth of Nations* (Everyman edition, 1910), II, 229.

very problem – the management of large-scale operations at a distance – which bedevilled commercial enterprise in general. A company necessarily assumed heavy overhead costs and unless it could defeat competition by legal means it might find that it could not justify such expenditures. Like any commercial enterprise, its reliance on subordinates increased with the distance which divided the latter from the base of the enterprise. And where distance, in an age of poor communications, placed such subordinates in positions of irresponsible entrepreneurial power, the best of sedentary managers could do little. Enterprise of the type which the great companies undertook poses organizational problems which only the business of the last 100 years has managed to tackle in any systematic way. The structural defects of joint-stock trade in an age of tedious communication were exposed because, given such large-scale operations, too much discretion had to be left overseas, and unless either market control were effective or the control or cooperation of subordinates could be ensured, the firm was threatened with the financial losses which accompany inefficiency and fixed investment.

V. *Aristocracy and Enterprise*

The decline of the military functions of the feudal warrior class left the European nobility with a structure of ostensible social values which regarded as degrading most economic occupations apart from estate management. It is this factor, together with the tendency of the traditional aristocracy to find itself dependent on others for liquid capital, which has led many students to denigrate the entrepreneurial role of the nobility. Congenital *hubris* or chronic indebtedness, it has been assumed, largely explain a failure to participate in non-agricultural or non-military enterprise. Yet this picture is too stark: social values rarely receive universal acclaim, not all nobles were debtors, and not all debtors borrow merely to consume. Aristocratic enterprise is among the more interesting economic phenomena of pre-industrial Europe. And this is precisely because the upper class of contemporary Europe on the whole judged its own behaviour by criteria which are not generally assumed to encourage the entrepreneurial spirit. Although they were constantly breached, the barriers to aristocratic enterprise were more formidable, if less tangible, than those facing virtually any other social group.

Quite apart from the psychological effects of aristocratic *mores* and the intangible sanctions of society's expectations, there were quite concrete limitations on non-agricultural enterprise at the rarefied levels of contemporary society. There were, for example, the positive attempts by governments and vested economic interests to prevent aristocrats, or even landowners in general, from participating in handicraft manufacture, retailing, or domestic trade. In northern Europe urban commercial capitalists frequently employed non-economic tactics to hinder noble competition. In France, a series of edicts in the sixteenth century forbade all nobles to practise commerce on pain of *dérogeance* – loss of aristocratic status and privileges – and throughout the period the nobility took care to secure formal protection against *dérogeance* whenever it undertook an active entrepreneurial role. But perhaps the greatest obstacles were within rather than outside the aristocracy, whose outlook, activities and interests frequently competed with the expenditure of time, money and skill which successful economic activity entailed. Estate management, attendance at court, the temptations of a life of conspicuous and privileged leisure, political activity, the pursuit of the arts, privileged positions in the army and the Church – all these could be powerful distractions from (and some could prove more lucrative with less effort than) a life of dedicated business zeal.

On the other hand, such limitations were not without their countervaling tendencies: they indicate the possible and not the real hindrances to 'la noblesse commerçante'. Psychological reluctance might be overcome by a modicum of pecuniary need or by a devotion to non-profit-making exercises in national economic development; the opposition of inferior social classes could be dissipated by the application of political power; the French crown from the early seventeenth century, by general laws and in a host of specific exemptions, largely removed the threat of *dérogeance*; there were limits on the number of military and ecclesiastical sinecures, and on the number of younger sons who could fill them; conspicuous consumption sooner or later demanded conspicuous income; some types of entrepreneurial endeavour, especially when successful, were less reprehensible than others. In fact, early modern Europe affords abundant examples of the aristocratic entrepreneur.

Both in direct demesne farming and in the no less enterprising possibilities of the administration of a rent roll, the opportunities for aristocratic agricultural entrepreneurship were extensive. In this regard the Spanish nobility, an urban rentier class given to an indifference to rural life and a devotion to costly splendour, affords a sharp contrast with the English improving landlords or the aristocratic capitalists who exploited the granaries of Europe on the shores of the Baltic. And in northern Europe, especially, it was a short step from production to commerce: in sixteenth-century Denmark the cattle trade was largely in noble hands; the Holstein nobility in the same period, trading in the products of their own estates, had regular Antwerp factors; and the grain stuffs of Prussia and Poland were not all sold direct from the soil to bourgeois merchants.

The value systems which approved of agricultural enterprise by members of the aristocracy were normally sufficiently elastic, as they had been in Rome, to condone the exploitation and even the processing of the non-edible products of the soil by noble estate owners. Aristocratic enterprise was, as a consequence, nowhere more active than in mining and heavy industry. The ownership of natural resources (coal, ores, timber) and the possession of political and social powers, gave quite specific advantages to the nobility in industries which depended so closely on the location of raw materials and, frequently, the securing of government concessions and privileges. The exploitation of coal, iron, lead, copper, timber, and water power could be direct or indirect: i.e., the aristocratic entrepreneur could promote and manage, or merely promote and then lease his productive units to other capitalists. Where the principal motive was the desire to put his estate's natural resources to profitable use the latter course – especially when the furnace or mill was on a relatively small scale – might be more popular. Thus Heinrich Rantzau, the Holstein noble of the sixteenth century, had at one time 39 mills (manufacturing lumber, flour, oil, metals, paper, and powder) on his estates, and most of them were leased out to neighbouring merchants;[1] and French nobles in the eighteenth century frequently obtained industrial concessions which they then sold, leased or even gave away merely in order to provide a market for the charcoal or coal which transportation costs otherwise rendered valueless. In other instances aristocrats retained full entrepreneurial control. Thus in sixteenth-century England the Earl of Shrewsbury had important interests in iron, steel, lead, coal, and glass;[2] in eighteenth-century France the spectacular Anzin firm was a merger, managed by the Duc du Croy, of two rival, aristocratic businesses; and in eighteenth-century Silesia most iron mines and smelters were owned and administered by nobles.[3]

In addition, there were two other forms of estate development which, strictly speaking, fell into neither category of agricultural or industrial enterprise: the reclamation of drowned lands and the improvement of urban real estate. The pioneering enterprise of the nobility in both instances was well illustrated in seventeenth-century England. Both the

[1] See H. Kellenbenz, 'German aristocratic entrepreneurship', *Explorations in Entrepreneurial History*, VI, 2 (December, 1953), 108.

[2] See L. Stone, 'The nobility in business, 1540–1640', *The Entrepreneur: Papers Presented at the Annual Conference of the Economic History Society…April, 1957*, p. 19.

[3] Fritz Redlich, 'European aristocracy and economic development', *Explorations in Entrepreneurial History*, VI, 2 (December, 1953), 85.

Earl of Bedford and the Earl of Clare before the Restoration drew over £2,000 in annual rent from London property which they had improved, and the former organized the syndicate which drained over 300,000 acres of the Great Level. In each case they were only the more spectacular examples of widespread activity.[1]

Although the European aristocracy did not abstain entirely from individualistic trading activities, especially in underdeveloped, primary-producing areas, in the main their principal commercial ventures came through participation in corporate adventures in long-distance trade and colonial development. Willingly, as in England, or to some extent forced, as in France, they contributed capital and prestige to the joint-stock businesses of the seventeenth and eighteenth centuries. It is clear that little real entrepreneurial effort was involved in what was normally a passive investment of money or title. Positive direction was incurred only with very exceptional men or in exceptional circumstances – as with the Puritan peers who were so important to the Massachusetts Bay Company. Yet the assumption of risk in such uncertain ventures, and the encouragement which the peerage gave to them, were themselves entrepreneurial functions of some significance. The concept of national economic development, no less than that of the development of the private agricultural estate, both condoned and encouraged business enterprise by the peerage – and it is possible that in some lines of activity the encouragement which they gave to others, by assuming the difficult and costly tasks of pioneering, was of greater importance than *direct* commercial stimulus of the enterprises which they founded or in which they participated. Particularly in the eighteenth century was this true of industrial activities, and, for example, the basis of linen, cotton, and glass manufacture in Bohemia was laid upon the estates of the eighteenth-century nobility.[2] Along these lines, the enlightened aristocrats who conducted, in conjunction with bourgeois entrepreneurs, industrial as well as agricultural experiments on their estates were of a kind with those government administrators who assumed entrepreneurial functions and were themselves frequently members of the aristocracy.

Naturally enough, the extent to which the nobility assumed the role of entrepreneur varied between the European nations. France, with its *gentilshommes verriers* and constant award of concessions on the one hand, and with its applications of more limiting values and the quest for corporate anonymity on the other, presents the greatest contrasts. Spain, whose nobility more than shared a general aversion to bourgeois striving lay at one end of the international spectrum, and England,

---

[1] Stone, 'The nobility in business', p. 17.
[2] F. Redlich, 'European aristocracy and economic development', p.85.

where there were the fewest emotional or legal obtacles, lay at the other. Entrepreneurial endeavour in England only solidified a relationship with other classes which was the strength of the English social structure; in France the nobility, in so far as it did assume business functions, was sapping both its *raison d'être* and the privileges which set it apart: the capitalistic aristocrat was one of the many anomalies whose problems France could only resolve with the aid of a revolution.

All this is not to say that the entrepreneurial contributions of the European aristocracy will stand comparison with those of some other social groupings. Most nobilities had a basis in land ownership, and where their interests moved towards production their estates could prove a full-time occupation; where income was their concern, the court, politics and the professions could well prove adequate. In addition, even where they were not absolutely averse to non-agricultural enterprise – and this was still very important – it would be hard to disentangle their own efforts from those of the commoners who, as partners, investors, managers, and technicians, were normally to be found in any 'aristocratic' enterprise. Finally, much noble business was a case of businessmen undergoing a metamorphosis into aristocrats, rather than the other way around. In Germany, Scandinavia, France and England the supremely successful entrepreneur frequently looked, either on his own or his children's behalf, to the possession of broad acres and sonorous titles as a reward for his mundane labours. Sometimes, as in Sweden and France, the State – anxious to encourage economic development – wielded ennoblement (of aliens as well as natives) as a tool of economic growth; elsewhere, and France is again a leading instance, wealth could of itself buy aristocratic privileges – in a process which in France did more, through the purchase of offices, to divert capital and skill out of entrepreneurial channels than all the traditional aristocrats did to reverse the flow.

Yet in spite of the relative nature of this importance the aristocratic entrepreneur has escaped much historical attention rightly his due. Land, financial need, and social prominence could be strong incentives to undertake entrepreneurial activity. Enterprise did not necessarily recognize class barriers.

VI. *Nations and Enterprise*

To the contemporary observer the most important dividing lines between different types of entrepreneur frequently coincided not so much with occupational or class boundaries as with national frontiers. And this was not because of any economic chauvinism, for the criterion of entrepreneurial achievement was only rarely insular. In fact, the archetype of the ideal man of business was most generally taken to be the Dutch merchant – the entrepreneur who rained blessings on his otherwise destitute country in measure as he pursued his economic ends. It is, indeed, Holland – the model for all other mercantile nations – which best exemplifies the significance of considering national entrepreneurial types. This is not merely because the Low Countries presented the greatest contrast between limited natural resources and abundant entrepreneurial achievement. The Dutch entrepreneur was distinguished from the businessman of other nations because of a convergence of factors, all in some way associated with Holland *per se*. It was, in other words, the processes as well as the achievements of enterprise which gave Holland its importance and which justify a consideration of enterprise in the light of national characteristics. From one viewpoint the difference between, say, English capitalists and French capitalists was greater than that between merchants and manufacturers or bourgeois and aristocratic entrepreneurs.

The enterprise of a nation was, of course, the compound of a variety of factors. Basic to it was the question of resources and geographical position: the wealth in terms of food, raw materials, population, available capital, and situation vis-à-vis other nations and trade routes. Next came the extent to which, by positive or negative policies, governments provided a favourable or an unfavourable environment for the exploitation of these resources: the extent to which there was a relatively free internal market for the factors of production, the degree to which an expansive overseas trade was facilitated, the absence or presence of non-economic criteria of State policy. In addition, the social structure and ideology were relevant to the creation or continuity of business endeavour: entrepreneurial performance cannot be separated from entrepreneurial motivation and opportunities. Finally, at any given point in time the nature of enterprise was in large part dependent upon the entrepreneurial achievement which had preceded it. Enterprise – in terms of the supply of capital, skill, energy, and motivation – tended quite naturally to feed on itself; and a nation of dynamic entrepreneurs was more likely than any other to produce energetic and successful businessmen.

From these viewpoints the spectrum of enterprise can be illustrated by Holland, England, France, and Sweden.

Holland, the most mercantile and least mercantilist of nations, was proof to all Europe of what enterprise could achieve in the absence of restrictive influences. What the Italian entrepreneur had been to the European economy of the late Middle Ages, the Dutch entrepreneur was in the early modern period. In comparison with France or England the United Provinces were singularly devoid of natural resources; yet Holland's businessmen turned to excellent account her geographical site (with respect both to a continental hinterland and maritime trade routes) and her enforced dependence on the sea and on commerce:

And what are the Dutch but a set of merchants, who take a pride in being such? Let us... bring them back to their primitive condition. We shall find a handful of fishermen, of cheesemongers and soldiers, groping in the dirt of that country, naturally unfit to be inhabited. But that time is over; since the spirit of commerce has spread itself over that little corner of the world, it has assumed another face.[1]

Traders, fishermen and mariners, Dutch entrepreneurs extended their mastery of fishing to encompass the art of efficient and inexpensive ship-building and navigation; with low shipping cost and an unrivalled knowledge of long-distance commerce, they brought under their control the most profitable channels of Europe's carrying trades between the north and south. Logically extending their mercantile and shipping advantages, they participated heavily and successfully in the new trades of the sixteenth and seventeenth centuries. Yet Dutch enterprise did more than carry commodities between other nations or even make Holland the warehouse of Europe. If domestic raw materials were hardly abundant enough for extensive industrial development, then the raw materials or semi-fabricated products of other lands could be made the basis of remunerative processing industries. If home-grown commodities were in short supply, then the Dutch economy, through the agency of its entrepreneurs, could export its own capital as a profitable venture. At the three principal levels of functional enterprise – mercantile, industrial, and financial – Holland had relatively little to learn and much to teach.

The potential entrepreneur in the United Provinces was fortunate in that the political and social framework of enterprise, combined with his economic inheritance, were the most favourable in Europe. Tolerant beyond other nations, free from undue political disturbance and the more rigid aspects of social and aristocratic hierarchy, awarding prestige to (because dependent upon) purely business achievement, and permeated by economic considerations, Dutch society offered the entrepreneur few of the physical or psychological hindrances to expansive economic activity which existed in other countries. To such a great extent a nation of businessmen, it also made those political provisions for entrepreneurial security and freedom which are among the prerequisites of widespread and dynamic business undertakings. The nature

[1] Quoted from the *Memoirs* of the Baron de Polinitz in Malachy Postlethwayt, *Universal Dictionary of Trade and Commerce* (1751–5), I, 546.

of Dutch enterprise was quite naturally conditioned by the social and political implications of the nature of its economy. And from the accumulation of capital and skill which were the concomitants of economic success, each succeeding generation drew support for its own entrepreneurial ventures.

The envy with which all this was viewed in other lands was merely the reflection of another aspect of Dutch enterprise; its contribution to the development of European entrepreneurship. It was, for example, the efforts of Dutch businessmen which laid the successful foundations of the Amsterdam entrepôt; and the Amsterdam commodity market was itself a basis for the proliferation of mercantile enterprise on the part of others. With the possible exception of the trade in joint-stock shares, there were no important business techniques which the Dutch perfected and taught to other nations; but then, as already mentioned, the period as a whole saw no more than the refining of inherited modes of doing business. The greatest contribution which Holland's enterprise made to European entrepreneurs in general[1] was undoubtedly in provoking (on an individual as well as national level) virile competition and a spirit of emulation.

In addition, the vacuum created in other areas by a shortage of risk capital and/or entrepreneurial skill was frequently filled by Dutchmen. Even in such a relatively advanced economy as that of England, Dutch short-term capital in the seventeenth, and long-term capital in the eighteenth century, supplied an important part of the needs of the London investment market. And although Dutch influence on England's industries was limited, specialist entrepreneurs from Holland anticipated extensively in successful land-reclamation projects in the early seventeenth century: in 1630 Cornelius Vermuyden petitioned for the denization of eighteen business associates involved with the drainage of Hatfield Chase.[2] In France, Dutch businessmen, beside their activities in land-drainage, provided their specialist knowledge as well as capital in such industries as textile-manufacture, sugar refining, and paper-making. But the migration of Dutch enterprise was at its most significant where relatively backward economies were concerned. In Sweden, for example, entrepreneurs from Holland, of whom the de Geers were the outstanding examples, were in the seventeenth century the most dynamic element in economic change; partly through their financial connection with the government and partly as a result of investment on its own merits, they were intertwined with finance and

[1] I.e., as distinct from the European economy, which obviously benefited from the efficiency and low costs of Dutch entrepreneurs.

[2] V. Barbour, *Capitalism in Amsterdam in the Seventeenth Century* (Baltimore, 1950), p. 122.

the production of and trade in iron, copper, timber, pitch, tar, and ships. Comparable developments took place in Denmark and Norway; while in Russia Dutch capitalists pioneered the establishment of saw-mills, paper-mills, powder-mills, glass furnaces, and a postal service.[1]

The great period of Dutch entrepreneurial influence naturally coincided with the great period of Dutch enterprise. By the eighteenth century the peak of achievement had been passed: changes in the structure of the European economy began to nullify the advantages which Holland's merchant capitalists had previously enjoyed. Lacking in their own resources, the United Provinces were in the last resort too weak either to counter the rise of better-endowed commercial and colonial nations like England or France, or to compensate for the increasing industrialization of other lands which deprived them of both processing industries and a re-export trade.

English enterprise provides less of a contrast with Dutch than does that of any other European nation. Taking longer to mature, but erected upon a far more secure foundation of domestic wealth, it was ultimately shaped by factors comparable to those which were important to Dutch business. Relatively strong and stable governments, in the late seventeenth and the eighteenth centuries, together with laws and policies which were increasingly favourable to enterprise, ensured a climate of political security. Throughout the period social mobility of both men and ideas prevented the cleavage between business and the rest of society which so restricted the former in other countries. Abundant natural resources and an ideal geographic location made the entre-preneur's task relatively easy, and aided in the accumulation of wealth which was itself a stimulus to further enterprise. Nevertheless, the development of English enterprise, in comparison with that of Dutch, was a slow process. It was not until the latter part of the period, for example, that a relatively free road to entrepreneurship was created by the decline of accepted official views as to the importance of short-term economic stability, and the dangers of uncontrolled industrialization. Tudor England, in its economy and therefore its economic policy, was still sufficiently medieval to substain many barriers to enterprise associ-ated with a traditional society. For English entrepreneurs the seventeenth century was in fact the watershed between the old constraints and new freedoms, which operated in the sphere of ideology as well as law. Thenceforth, businessmen, with almost as much scope for initiative as the Dutch – and far more domestic resources to work with – forged ahead in the battle for entrepreneurial supremacy. Measured in terms of aggregate economic achievement, an increasing independence of foreign supplies of skill and capital, and the extent to which techniques

[1] Barbour, *Capitalism in Amsterdam*, p. 119.

of enterprise were adopted and perfected, English entrepreneurship had won the battle by the eighteenth century.

The influences which conditioned the structure and manifestation of French enterprise differed markedly from the first two cases considered. In economic potential France was far wealthier than Holland and considerably more diversified and self-sufficient than England. In every other respect, however, she offered less scope to enterprise than either. Feudal and particularist survivals obstructed the free flow of goods by means of local tolls, taxes, and trade associations; religious dissension and its concomitant political disturbances reduced the security environment of business; dynastic or non-economic motives shaped a government policy which was at best a burden to the bulk of private enterprise and at worst destructive of it; colonial warfare restricted rather than (as with England) expanded the possibilities of business; and a complex feudal structure and a rigid set of social values combined to restrict entry into the entrepreneurial class, to restrain the effectiveness of entrepreneurial performance, and to facilitate egress from active business. Both because business was not dignified and because quasi-noble office-holding exerted a powerful fascination for men of wealth, business talent and capital were denied to the world of enterprise. The picture can, of course, be overdrawn; aristocratic entrepreneurs and investors *did* exist (especially in occupations related to their estates); men might buy honours and still remain in business; there was a concerted and not entirely unsuccessful attempt to raise the prestige of large-scale merchandising; and there was considerable business achievement in France. But, compared with his counterpart in England or Holland, the French entrepreneur was more bound by tradition, less experimental and creative, less a free agent, more constrained by economic and political structures, more willing to cease the competitive struggle for entrepreneurial profits, and a far less outstanding businessman.

Implicit in the French economic, political, and social situation was the fact that in matters of enterprise the State should assume a far more positive and overt function than in either Holland or England. This factor operated at two related levels. First, since economic difficulty, entrepreneurial weaknesses, and shortages of private venture capital prevented developments which more progressive nations had already undertaken or which the State viewed as necessary to power or glory, the French government was forced to participate in the stimulation and maintenance of specific modes of enterprise. The most spectacular examples were the State-engendered trading companies in the second half of the seventeenth century; the most continuous and ubiquitous examples were the *manufactures royales* and the *manufactures privilégiés* – enterprises which, directly in terms of money or indirectly in terms of privileges, received capital-substitutes from the government. But the French Crown and its ministers proved hardly better as entrepreneurs than the general run of businessmen, and far less astute than the private individuals who had wisely refrained from undertaking such adventures on their own initiative. Even where such large-scale firms continued and expanded (as in the case of some manufacturing enterprises) it was mainly by virtue of their privileged position and a concomitant tax on the economy at large. The second result of the State's more positive role was that French industrial and economic regulation was far more grandiose in design than that of most other lands. Ostensibly it was most often directed to economic development, but in fact the encouragement of private entrepreneurs could never be an end in itself. Vested interests, established businesses or trade associations, local community interests – all might prevent the innovation of new, or the expansion of old, enterprise. In addition, the regulatory power did not always itself know what was best for entrepreneurship and was too often moved by fiscal rather than industrial considerations; while its mere existence imposed a costly burden on the economy and on businessmen. Where the two main elements in official French entrepreneurship were combined in the hands of a statesman like Colbert, with some dedication and ability, then something – albeit much less than he anticipated – could be achieved. But in general State enterprise in France did little to alter the general picture of French entrepreneurship.

Sweden provides yet another national entrepreneurial archetype. From the viewpoint of domestic production, economic structures, and its relationship with the rest of Europe, the Swedish economy was markedly underdeveloped for most of the period. Even with the economic and social progress of the eighteenth century Sweden remained behind Holland, England, and France in most important respects. Intertwined with the general economic situation, as both effect and cause, was the relatively backward nature of Swedish enterprise – the principal concomitant of which was the inevitable and outstanding rôle of alien entrepreneurs in the domestic economy.

In the sixteenth century, Sweden was still, in the words of its economic historian,[1] at a medieval level of economic development. Given the relative unimportance of money, the absence of extended participation in the European economic scene, the political and social structure, and the position of its king, the private entrepreneur in Sweden hardly warrants comparison with the businessmen of central or north-western Europe. Yet these factors were precisely those which help

[1] See Eli F. Heckscher, *An Economic History of Sweden* (Cambridge, Massachusetts, 1954), pp. 61–70.

explain the predominance of State or, more exactly, royal enterprise. Gustavus Vasa (1523–60) has been aptly described as the business manager for the Swedish economy, and his mastery of the basic commodities of trade, together with his economic and political power, justify the phrase. Under his control, Sweden enjoyed unity and relative peace – but it was the unity and peace of a traditional manorial estate. And Gustavus Vasa, when he *did* need the aid of knowledgeable businessmen – as with the development of an iron industry – was forced to turn to aliens, principally to German entrepreneurs and technologists.

For Sweden, the seventeenth century witnessed far more than the *political* participation in Europe's affairs which led to an increasing involvement in the religious and dynastic struggles of northern Europe. Although Sweden hardly increased her negligible role in the Atlantic and Mediterranean trades, which were so much the basis of other nations' prosperity, the expansion in the output and above all the export of iron, copper, and forest products marked a new stage in her economic development and a new set of relationships with other European nations. Even so, the Swedes still displayed an outstanding inability to undertake entrepreneurial tasks. While the State did not relinquish its economic interest (it continued important systems of industrial regulation, participated in the manipulation of production and export, and attempted to stimulate development by means of foreign businessmen), it was in fact alien entrepreneurs who played the most dynamic role in the basic industries. Dutchmen, Germans, and Scots brought business skill, technological expertise, and capital to the profitable tasks of dominating the main arteries of the Swedish economy. It was not until the eighteenth century that the foreign influence underwent an appreciable decline. By that time Sweden was much closer to intimate relationships with other parts of Europe, and the turning of the economy from war to peace, combined with the new concentration of attention upon standards of living, marked the discovery of domestic springs of enterprise – in social and intellectual as well as economic fields.

The lessons which can be drawn from a study of national types of entrepreneurship are crucial to an understanding of at least some of the aspects of enterprise in the early modern period. Primarily, this is because the consideration of the nation as an economic unit focuses attention on the extent to which the convergence of a multiplicity of factors helps determine the nature of the entrepreneur. Social pressures, values, and beliefs, individual psychology, economic opportunity, political constraint or help, national wealth – all these shape the things which businessmen can do. This is not to argue that man is the helpless victim of his circumstances: the creative entrepreneur could still break through the ring of environment; the quiescent businessman could still fail to take advantage of manifest opportunities; the most important component of entrepreneurship was in the last resort the individual's capabilities and drives. But enterprise must on the whole adapt to (or only change very slowly) the reality of economics and society, and the pattern of enterprise is inexplicable without an understanding of the aggregate forces which brought it about. These forces, in their turn, if our interest lies in general rather than functional entrepreneurship, were best exemplified within the unity of nation states.

VII. Conclusion

The characteristics of economic enterprise between the fifteenth and eighteenth centuries bear only an oblique resemblance to those of enterprise in the more recent, industrialized environment. Prior to the type of economic growth associated with industrial revolutions, the very diversity of the businessman's tasks and the special nature of his environment preclude any extensive analysis of the entrepreneur in relation to economic change, innovation and development. Yet the role of enterprise was no less important in an economic environment in which rate of change was slow than it was to be in one where change was very rapid. In each case entrepreneurial activity sustained the framework of economic society. In the early modern period, however, the elements of continuity and diversity were more pronounced than those of creativity and single-minded drive.

The contemporary verdict that of all businessmen the commercial capitalist was the most important is confirmed by the economic history of the period. The merchant, however, did not fulfil a specialist economic function. Rather, his business ability and his resources permeated economic activity at a variety of levels. In the stable nature of his business techniques and the range of his activities were reflected the dominant features of contemporary economic structures. More than this, the roots of enterprise were almost as diverse as its manifestations. Quite apart from the variety of social groups which assumed entrepreneurial functions, and the multiplicity of spheres in which they were carried out, entrepreneurs varied widely according to national origins and social and economic attitudes.

The foregoing examination of the nature of enterprise leads to the conclusion that entrepreneurial problems and the techniques designed to solve those problems were largely derived from the risks of an underdeveloped economy. Without condoning an untenable determinism, it would seem that the environment was a fundamental force in conditioning the nature of enterprise. No doubt this is to be expected where the period under consideration experienced so little economic development, and more weight would have been given to entrepreneurial innovation and spontaneity had the period studied been a more recent one. As it is, the imperfect structure of markets, the rural and scattered distribution of population, the lack of effective techniques of transport and communication, the importance and scarcity of capital flows, and the far-reaching but erratic role of the State were all of substantial significance in determining entrepreneurial organization and performance. Of these factors the most important seems to have been the size, structure, and discontinuity of markets, which fulfilled the predominant function of shaping entrepreneurial organization and performance.

Although, from the viewpoint of its structure and institutions, the economy of the early modern period was relatively stable, the day-to-day environment of the entrepreneur was characterized by an extreme instability which constantly frustrated entrepreneurial expectations. In terms of enterprise this instability induced a strong trend towards decentralization and towards informal and personal devices for ensuring continuity and the reduction of risk. Kinship, religion, and membership of specific social groups came to play an all-important part in the organization of economic activity. Nevertheless, such techniques were never entirely successful – the entrepreneur could rarely approach that control of his environment which they were designed to achieve. The businessman of the early modern period was an 'adventurer' precisely because the risks which he was constantly forced to take were much less calculated than later generations would have found comfortable.

The evolution of modern enterprise can be viewed as a process by which entrepreneurs obtained, both intellectually and physically, an increasing control over their environment. Economic progress takes place only as the product of, and in conjunction with, such increased power. In pre-industrial Europe the limited extent to which economic progress took place is therefore a rough indication of the economic position of the entrepreneur. If convenient, the era can be viewed as one in which the 'pre-conditions' for ultimate development were being created. But this should not be interpreted as a detraction either from the importance of entrepreneurs or from the economic unity of the period. Neither should it be taken to mean that 'capitalism' post-dates the phenomena with which the foregoing pages have been concerned. Capitalism – considered either as a mode of producing and distributing wealth or as a set of assumptions about economic relationships – is older than the sixteenth century. After the mid eighteenth century its achievements were more decisive in measure as its techniques and assumptions were refined and applied more intensively to industrial tasks. But during the intervening generations its bases existed, even if they did not permeate the whole of society. To study enterprise in the early modern period is to examine the groundplan of modern capitalism: in the role of the entrepreneur were foreshadowed his crucial functions at a later date.

CHAPTER VII

The Organization of Industrial Production

I.   *The Sixteenth-Century Prospect*

THE ECONOMIC SITUATION of Europe after 1500 was to favour the growth of industrial production more than at any time since the Black Death. Population growth and the exploitation of Europe's overseas possessions created wider markets and new sources of raw material. The commercial prosperity and the social changes of the sixteenth century led to higher standards of living and a greater measure of comfort – even, for some, of luxury. How far these factors challenged existing European industries and helped to develop new ones is the subject of the following study.

II.   *Definition*

The word 'industry' can bear many meanings and shades of meaning. Its use in this chapter needs some definition: *viz.* the exploitation of raw or semi-finished materials and their processing on a scale so large that the working artisan could not organize production by himself or sell to the consumer. In practice this means we shall be largely discussing those crafts which served more than a purely local market. For the most part it is 'industry' in its 'domestic' or 'putting-out' stage of development that we shall encounter.

III.   *Location*

Many factors contributed to the development of industrial activity in certain areas of Europe in the later Middle Ages. Adequate supplies of raw materials – water, power and fuel as well as the primary product – the presence of an entrepreneurial class and a sufficient supply of cheap labour were all essential. The means of transport in a given area, by land or water, and the policy of the government, regional or municipal, also exerted an important influence on industrial location and progress.

Deposits of a wide variety of raw materials existed in Europe. Almost all the metal ores then known were prospected and mined. The gold deposits in Silesia, Slovakia, Transylvania, Carinthia and the Tyrol may have been modest, but the silver and copper mines of the Harz,

Saxony, Bohemia, Tyrol, Slovakia and Bosnia were most important. In the second half of the sixteenth century the mines of Guadalcanal in Spain were exploited. Important strikes of copper were made at the *Stora Kopparberg* at Falun in Sweden and at Rörås in Norway. Copper was also found in England and in Spain (Rio Tinto). Lead mines were worked in England, the Harz, Carinthia, Silesia and Poland. Calamine, important for the brass industry, was found at the Vieille Montagne between Dinant and Aachen, in the region of Iserlohn and in Upper Silesia. Quicksilver was mined in the Palatinate, and in Bohemia, but the most important strikes were at Idria (in the Habsburg duchy of Crain) and at Almadén in Spanish Estremadura.

Iron deposits were plentiful. As 'bog iron-ore' it was found in many swampy regions of western, central, eastern and northern Europe. In the form of limonite it was found in north Spain, the Island of Elba, the *Massif Central*, Dauphiné, and in many areas along the Franco-German frontier, in eastern central Europe, including the Alps, Carpathians and the Urals, parts of England, Scotland and Sweden.

The location of textile industries was favoured by the existence of sheep breeding and the production of flax and hemp. The high standard of the English cloth industry depended on the quality of English wool; flax growing in Westphalia and upper Germany contributed to the growth of linen weaving in these regions, just as hemp growing did for the hemp industry near the North Sea coast. We say 'favoured': not dictated. The great cloth industry of Leiden flourished on raw materials brought over long distances from east and west. The great bleaching industry of Haarlem bleached mainly coarse linens imported from Westphalia and Silesia.

Many expanding industries required heat and water, even motive power, whether provided by fuel, water or wind, and the availability of these resources influenced the location of user industries.

In some areas of iron mining and metallurgy, deforestation for industrial purposes progressed so far that governments tried to put the brake on further destruction. The pressure on timber supplies also led to a more intensive exploitation of coal deposits, particularly in the Rhineland, England and the south Netherlands. Once mills and hammers became an established part of industrial production, workshops tended to group themselves beside streams and rivers, although in flatter regions, and especially near the coast, the windmill provided an alternative to water power.

A third important influence in determining the location of industry, after raw material supply and power, was the availability of labour. At first the urban gilds controlled the supply of skilled labour (the 'journeymen'), but the development of a putting-out system (*Verlagssystem*) allowed the merchant capitalists to mobilize the unskilled and unorganized workers of the countryside. Rural labour was cheaper and in time might be trained for more skilled work; moreover, idle hands were plentiful in areas where the soil was poor, where sheep or cattle rather than corn crops were raised or where inheritances were fragmented between heirs.

Finally, socio-economic factors might influence the location of an industry: in the south Netherlands, the local nobles patronized the development of rural textile industries to compete with the gild-regimented production of the towns. The attitude of local landowners also influenced the location of mines. In these and in other cases the application of 'mercantilist' ideas by individuals with capital and enterprise at a local level affected the establishment of industries as much as the better-known policies of the governments.

IV. *Organization*

(1) GILDS

The development of many European industries was directly affected by the nature of their organization. Many products were made by small masters, their families, with some journeymen and apprentices organized in craft gilds. Over much of Europe the gilds, concentrated in the towns, organized production and large-scale enterprises were exceptional. But the gilds rarely chose to extend their membership beyond the urban boundary: thus in England most mines were located outside the towns and the miners were not organized in a gild; but in Liège, where the mines were within the town, the reverse was the case. York had ten gilds of specialized iron-workers; the nailers in the villages of Birmingham and Wolverhampton had none. The cloth-workers of London had a powerful corporation but attempts to organize a gild to control the woollen textile industry around Leeds in the late seventeenth century fell flat.

In England, the gilds or 'companies' of London still flourished and retained great power in the sixteenth and even seventeenth century, directing the City's politics and providing its Lord Mayors. Yet already power and wealth were passing from the craft gilds proper to those representative of merchant capitalism. Elsewhere the gilds tended to amalgamate. At Northampton in 1574 seven craft gilds amalgamated into one, and the following year the other town gilds combined into four general 'companies', each including a number of crafts. At Norwich in 1622 all the town's trades were organized into twelve 'grand companies'. Presumably these combined companies were unable to supervise techniques and standards of production as closely as the specialized gilds had done, but they could still exclude outsiders and enforce apprenticeship according to the Statute of 1563.

Practitioners of new trades were not included in this system, but many of them nevertheless developed regular apprenticeship and even obtained charters to enforce it; as did the spectacle-makers, the coach-makers and the gun-makers of London. Elizabeth and the early Stuarts tried to maintain a strict control of the 'companies', and new trades in London were chartered as companies while others received royal permission to separate themselves from existing companies when they became important enough. The haberdashers, who specialized in selling imported felts, received a charter of incorporation in 1604. The clock-makers and the gun-makers separated from the blacksmiths, the tinplate-makers from the iron-mongers. The monopoly granted to the younger companies covered a larger area: some seven to ten miles as opposed to the two to four mile monopoly granted to the older companies.

Yet steadily controls were weakening. Cromwell suspended the apprenticeship statutes in order to help demobilized soldiers to find jobs, and in London the system was further undermined by the Great Fire: Parliament granted freemen's privileges to craftsmen who came to London in order to aid rebuilding. The later spread of the Industrial Revolution was favoured by the fact that only the rump of the once powerful gild and corporation system survived in the eighteenth century.

In France industrial organization took a very different course. The Crown tried to modernize the gilds by edict in 1581, 1597 and 1673. Under Colbert's policies corporations, mostly on the model of those of Paris, were to be created in the provincial towns and even in the open country, so that all craftsmen would be members of a gild. These plans were not altogether realized and in some towns more than half the artisans continued to work without any organization at all.

After the death of Colbert, as the government ran increasingly into debt, its financial interest in the gilds revived. Controls and the super-vision of trade were resurrected in order to raise money from the gilds. Simultaneously, the Crown would grant licences to any 'free masters' who were prepared to pay for their independence of the gilds. Gild power in France as elsewhere was further impaired by the ineluctable spread of the putting-out system.

In Spain the Catholic kings also reorganized the gilds of Catalonia and Valencia and created gilds in Castile. During the sixteenth century a number of new gilds sprang up, the majority during the second half of the century. In Burgos, ten gilds received their *ordenanzas* between 1509 and 1589; in Toledo, six gild privileges were issued, in Zaragoza seven. The same development is to be observed in Barcelona and Valencia. Gilds also appeared in smaller towns. Often the larger towns had more artisans than they could employ, and many urban workers migrated to the small towns and villages. Thus the wool weavers in the tiny Catalan town of Sabadell were numerous enough to establish their own gild in 1558.

At first, gild activity adapted itself to the growth of Spanish industry. Difficulties ensued when decline set in. The gilds became *nuclei* of resistance to change and in the seventeenth century there were moves to do away with them: in 1678 the Cortes of Calatayud demanded their outright abolition. But in many places the gilds continued to flourish. In Madrid the *Cinco Gremios Mayores* ('Five Great Gilds') were created in the seventeenth century and undoubtedly stimulated the city's economic activity. During the eighteenth century, the number of gilds in Spain increased still further, but all were stamped with protectionism and conservatism: what technical and industrial progress there was came from other quarters, especially from the merchant entrepreneurs.

In Portugal the gilds were underpinned by the economic expansion of the sixteenth century. The trend was for the gilds to separate into a number of ever more specialized ones; King John III (1521–57) issued ordinances to regulate the various spheres of gild activity.

The craft gilds of the Netherlands, extremely powerful in the later Middle Ages, lost most of their political and much of their economic importance in the sixteenth and seventeenth centuries. Their protectionism and exclusiveness was undermined most at Amsterdam and the other great ports by capitalist expansion, but inland – for instance at Zutphen – gild power remained formidable.

In central Europe, especially in Germany, the gild system had deeper roots and less flexibility than in the west owing to the relatively high degree of political liberty enjoyed by many of the towns, especially the Imperial free cities, during the later Middle Ages. In the course of the seventeenth and eighteenth centuries many of the new industries which developed through the diversification of production and the rising demand for luxury goods still organized themselves into gilds. Others never did. Increasingly the influence of the gilds was restricted by the ordinances of the emperor and the attitude of the territorial sovereigns, who tended to regard them as centres of opposition to their mercantilist policies. They therefore attempted to suppress them in favour of the 'free masters'. In the eighteenth century the ideological inclination of enlightened despotism was often towards industrial freedom: but as with so many aspirations of the time, this too fell short of realization. Gilds sometimes survived through inefficiency or inertia. When they were swept away, they gave place to state control.

In Scandinavia the medieval gild system had developed in much the same way as on the continent. Crisis came with the Reformation. The leaders of the Reform movement viewed the gilds as supporters of the Roman Catholic order and saw that their properties could with benefit be acquired by secularization and dissolution. Those gilds which were of a religious character therefore disappeared. In Denmark Christian IV (1588–1648) tried to abolish the gild system but it revived after his death, only to give way to the demands of the absolutist system later.

In Italy the organization of trade by the *arti* had been firmly established in most industrial centres during the Middle Ages. After 1500 local rulers used their growing power to deprive the gilds of all authority, restrict their monopolistic tendencies and subordinate them to the state. This happened particularly in Tuscany, in the states under Spanish rule and in Piedmont: the gilds which survived in these states were compelled to defend their privileges vigorously. Elsewhere, however, there was some extension of the crafts. In Rome, population growth brought about economic recovery and (as elsewhere in Europe) led to a differentiation of the existing gilds and the creation of new corporations. In the sixteenth century twenty-three gilds were established, in the seventeenth century twenty-four, and from 1700 to 1760 thirteen more. As in the rest of Europe, while the new trades – printers, barbers, wigmakers – formed new gilds, the older crafts declined and their gilds were obliged to amalgamate.

In Poland, urban development was strongly influenced by the German example with the various crafts organized in gilds. Here, as in Germany, they sought to extend their influence over the surrounding countryside. A few specialized crafts including the *servitoriali* – craftsmen who held their privilege from the king and thus by a legal fiction became members of the royal entourage – remained outside the gild system. It was difficult for the gilds to fight openly against them. Despite decrees of the Sejm (National Assembly) in 1538 and 1552 suppressing the gilds, new ones were constituted in the sixteenth and seventeenth centuries and only a few disappeared (during the disorders of the mid seventeenth century).

The type of exclusive gild which limited the number of masters seldom appeared in Poland: the closed gilds of the bakers, butchers and shoemakers were the exception. High standards were set for those who intended to produce their 'masterpiece', and only the sons and sons-in-law of masters found their path made easy. There were further restrictions to prevent masters from developing their workshops into capitalist enterprises.

Russian craft organization differed radically from that of western and central Europe. There was far less regimentation: in the towns, the crafts were practised freely while many other craftsmen worked on seigneurial and monastic domains. Many of the masters worked without a mate. Apprentices were bound for five years but, except for goldsmiths and silversmiths, they were under no obligation to produce a masterpiece. Often an apprentice would leave his master after a year or two. In the towns, and especially in Moscow, there was much differentiation within each trade – among the bakers, the tanners, the leatherworkers – even among the ikon-painters. Only under Peter the Great were attempts made to introduce full gild organization as part of the tsar's programme of westernization.

In certain parts of eastern and south eastern Europe, although not in the west, Jewish craftsmen entered and formed gilds. The Jews – Sephardic and Ashkenazic – who came to Holland during the seventeenth century, were permitted to cut diamonds, dress tobacco, print and work silk, but the Dutch gilds in other industries refused to admit them. Only in the provincial towns were individual Jews sometimes admitted to the gilds. In Hamburg, Altona, and other German towns Jews were excluded from the gilds, but in Danish Glückstadt Christian IV gave them the right to participate in trade and industry.

In Italy, there were Jewish craft gilds in Rome and in Venice: individual Jewish armourers, goldsmiths and silversmiths worked for the princely courts; pottery, glassmaking and engraving were numbered among the Jewish crafts. Some Jews entered the widespread silk manufacture while in eighteenth century Savoy Jews ran cotton mills. In Leghorn they established silk, cloth and paper industries, soap factories, and most important of all, the coral industry. Italy was also one of the great centres of Hebrew printing. But the specifically Jewish gild (tailors, apothecaries, bakers of *mazot*) seem to have sprung up only in Rome.

In Bohemia and Moravia, Jews took up many trades during the fifteenth and sixteenth centuries. Earlier acts of expulsion were revoked and during the second half of the sixteenth century the position of the Jews improved considerably. They did not, however, gain the right to establish gilds. A royal charter of 1648 paved the way for further expansion of the Jewish trades.

In Poland and Lithuania, where about 300,000 Jews lived at the beginning of the seventeenth century, the first Jewish gilds originated at about this time in Cracow, Lwow and Przemysl, but handicrafts only gained ground among the Jewish community after 1650. In the eighteenth century, Jewish gilds must have been numbered in hundreds; Cracow, Lwow, Brody, Lublin, Posnan, Loszno (Lissa), Vilna and other towns had several – some of them upwards of ten. Several factors account for this – the protection of the Crown, the opposition of the Polish gentry to the gild monopolies, and the existence of a large unorganized labour force among the different ethnic groups in Poland. The Jews filled a gap in the economic structure of these countries and the growing Jewish population itself constituted an inner market of considerable size, serving at the same time the larger demands of Christian consumers. Some crafts certainly served only the internal needs of the Jewish communities, but those which supplied a wider market brought Jews into frequent contact with counts, nobles and others who required luxury goods. Numerically and sociologically the 'depressed crafts' – making and repairing garments especially – were always the most important. Social discrimination against the poorer artisans, coupled with the craft gilds' dependence on the Elders of the community (the *kahal*) sometimes provoked violent clashes.

(2) THE PUTTING-OUT SYSTEM

The craftsman who required a larger market in which to buy his raw materials and to sell his own products needed the services of a merchant who commanded a broader system of commercial contacts. The merchant provided raw wool, cotton, silk or metals and was able to sell the industrial products over a wider area. Often the craftsman fell into partial dependence on the merchant who not only 'put out' his raw materials but also lent his credit and could therefore impose his conditions.

The putting-out system had found a place in the medieval economy, but it expanded with the growth of export industries and especially with the growth of rural industries. In the sixteenth century the 'putting-out system' (*Verlagssystem*) and variants of this system which linked craftsmen to capitalists spread to many branches of production: mining and metallurgy, the manufacture of small articles of metal or wood, textiles, printing, and paper-making. Paper-making was impossible without technical apparatus (a mill) and an organized supply of linen or cotton rags for raw material; a merchant could usually obtain this better than the paper-maker himself. The same was true of the printer and his workshop. In the mining of ferrous and non-ferrous ores, the purchase of pumps, furnaces and other indispensable technical equipment often ran the small workshop into debt, and the help of a merchant was needed. This happened especially when the man who regularly bought the product was an obvious potential source of credit.

The putting-out system used gild craftsmen and free labourers together. In general the rougher work was done in the countryside and the finishing in the towns. Thus in southwestern and eastern England, the putting-out system was extended to the rural population of distant areas, even the labour of Irish rural spinners being drawn upon. Combing was mostly done by gild members, but the yarn went to the weaver who worked along with his family and was paid wages on a piece-work basis. The cloth was then sent to the workshop of the entrepreneur where it was finished ready for sale. Only in rare cases did the clothier sell the cloth as a retailer himself: normally this was done by the draper. Even between clothier and draper, especially in London, there often stood a middleman who provided credit. In Yorkshire the cloth-makers often carried out all the phases of production, except spinning and dyeing, in their own homes.

In the metal industry of Solingen the *Schwertschmied* (swordsmith), the *Härter* (temperer) and the *Reider* (sword furbisher) all participated in the sword-making process, but only the *Reider* was allowed to sell the product and travel with his merchandise. In the same way knife-makers and handle-makers carried out the two basic processes before the knife was finished by the 'finisher', but he it was who became the entrepreneur. A similar process occurred in the small iron industries of Birmingham and Sheffield.

It was unusual for the dependent craftsmen to unite against the entrepreneurs and when they did they faced long odds. In London the felt-hatmakers might try to gain independence from the haberdashers by forming their own company to buy wool and sell their hats, but after some years the venture had to be written off as a failure. Whenever the gilds tried to oppose the entrepreneurs, the latter could always take on non-gildsmen, especially in the rural crafts. In all the textile industries it was of advantage to the entrepreneurs that spinning was an old sideline of peasant life. Weaving also often went on in the peasant's home. The peasantry constituted a much cheaper labour force than the urban craftsmen of the gilds. The growth of the putting-out system involved important displacements of industries into regions where gild restrictions did not exist at all or were at least less onerous – e.g. from the Flemish textile towns into the surrounding rural areas where the lighter cloths were made – Hondschoote, Armentières and Verviers. Similar phenomena may be observed in the English woollen industry and the Italian silk industry.

(3) THE FACTORY

When special knowledge and technical ability were required, the entrepreneur might concentrate the various processes of production under one roof and create a factory. This tendency had been visible in medieval Florence and Flanders, and it became more pronounced after 1500. A famous example, from early sixteenth century England, was

John Winchcombe's factory at Newbury, with (it was said) 200 women carders, 150 children pickers, 200 girl spinners, 200 weavers with 200 boys at the spools, 80 teasers, 50 shearers, 40 dyers and 20 fullers.

Such precocious concentration was exceptional. Neither gild tradition nor state policy favoured factory organization and so until 1750 factories usually grew up primarily to coordinate the initiating or finishing phases of a production process. This system was found, with variations, in all areas of textile production: England, the Netherlands, France, Catalonia, Germany, upper Italy and eastern Europe. The largest factory of the seventeenth and early eighteenth centuries seems to have been the fine textile works of van Robais at Abbéville – favoured by Colbert and a *manufacture royale*. Thousands of male and female workers were employed there, and a large number of them lived and worked in a compound surrounded by a 'wall and ditch'. Even spinning was concentrated within this complex. Other weavers worked in various houses in the town, up to thirty in each house, supervised by workmasters. Otherwise in the seventeenth century it was exceptional to find more than 120 looms concentrated in one silk factory.

Often workers were concentrated under one roof in an orphanage, poorhouse or correction house. The Protestant *ethos* combined with current economic theories to encourage the idea that the unemployed should be put to useful work. We find such welfare institutions used also as 'factories' in Hamburg, Berlin and Copenhagen.

Some processes of textile production were clearly well suited to factory organization, such as cotton-printing, which developed at the end of the seventeenth century in England and Holland and then spread to Switzerland, Augsburg and Saxony. Similarly a factory for lace-making was established in Reims in 1665 which soon employed about 120 female workers. In 1729 a sailcloth factory in Moscow had 1,162 workers. Factories were not of course limited to the textile industry. We find them in many other industries: in metal working, tobacco rolling and, from the beginning of the eighteenth century, in porcelain making. After 1700, factory production gradually spread through other branches of industry.

(4) LARGE-SCALE PRODUCTION EMPLOYING ADVANCED TECHNICAL PLANT

An essential feature of the factory was the concentration of manpower. In certain sectors, for instance in metallurgy and mining, labour concentration was combined with the use of advanced technical apparatus – pumps, furnaces and machines. Thus a thousand or so men worked in the copper mines of Neusohl (Banska Bystrica in Slovakia) during the sixteenth century, and one silver mine in the Tyrol employed nearly 7,000 workers. In 1642 the mining and smelting works of Keswick employed a large body of foreign employees. According to Nef, half the English coal mines in 1700 worked in units of over 100 men, and some of the mines employed 500 to 1,000 workers.

For the conversion of ore to metal a large workshop was built in Stiernsund, Sweden, by the entrepreneur Polhem with 'machines and appliances which will diminish the amount or intensity of heavy manual work'. A worthy precursor of Boulton and Wedgwood, Polhem used 'machines to cut bars, slit railrods, roll iron into sheets, cut cogwheels, hammer pans, shape tinware and make all kinds of household appliances, plowshares, and clock parts'.[1] Considerable technical apparatus was also needed in shipbuilding, for the refining of sugar, the distillation of alcohol and the production of soap, salt, beer, paper, gunpowder and glass. The French Royal Plate Glass Company began with 200 workers, but towards the middle of the eighteenth century it had a thousand or so working in enclosed workshops.

V.   *Technological Progress*

(I) MINING AND METALLURGY

The sixteenth and seventeenth centuries witnessed no spectacular new metallurgical methods (with the possible exception of the Spanish adaptation of the older silver extraction process by mercury amalgam); but the process of mechanization, the rise of capitalist enterprise and the development of printing certainly promoted the diffusion of technical improvements. After 1650, educated men began to take an interest in the basic practical knowledge of the artisan although in fact theoretical science made little advance before 1700.

The earliest comprehensive handbook on metallurgy, the *Pyrotechnia* of Vanoccio Biringuccio, was published in 1540. His description of mining and smelting was soon surpassed by the *De re metallica* of Georgius Agricola (1494–1556) published in 1556, which remained the chief handbook on mining and metallurgy for several succeeding generations. A useful supplement to Agricola's work was published by Lazarus Ercker in 1574: his *Treatise* described the principal types of metallic ores and minerals. Its particular value lay in the instructions he gave on assaying, based on his own experience working in Bohemia. But there was little real progress before Réaumur's essay on the conversion of iron into steel (1722) and the metallurgical handbook of Schlüter (1738).

[1] Herbert Heaton, *Economic History of Europe* (rev. ed., New York, 1948), p. 350.

The improvement of mechanical aids represented the most important advance in mining and in the processing of ores. The use of blast furnaces increased. Mining galleries and shafts, already known by the end of the fifteenth century, were improved; hoists and lifts were used to bring up the ore and the water; water was harnessed to operate pumps. About 1550, at Joachimsthal (Jachymov), at Schwaz and at Kitzbühel in Tyrol, pumps operated by water-power were brought into action; they made it possible to sink shafts to a depth of 886 metres. The demand for mining shafts, hoists, ventilators and other water-powered apparatus acted in turn as a stimulus to the mechanization and expansion of metal production. The capital of the leading German merchants and the privileges bestowed by the princes who owned the mining areas worked to the same end.

Deforestation in England led to experiments to discover a method of smelting iron with coal. Several patents were granted in the seventeenth century, but they proved ineffective. Only in the beginning of the eighteenth century was real progress made.

In 1550 Hans Lobsinger of Nuremberg invented a wooden box-bellow which soon took the place of the old leather model in heating the larger furnaces. Then water wheels were used to drive hammer-forges and rolling-mills, and for wire-drawing. Despite this, good sheet iron was not produced much before 1750.

Steel was produced at first by the direct reduction of the ore. Biringuccio describes how steel was made by simple carbonization and decarbonization. The first account of the fusing of bars of wrought iron with charcoal to produce rough steel is given by Robert Plot in his *Natural History of Staffordshire* (1686). Crucible cast steel was noted by Robert Hooks in his diary in 1675 and two years later Joseph Moxon compared his cast steel to Damascus steel. Only after 1740 did this type of steel gain commercial importance with Huntsman's production.

A method of making brass from copper by a kind of cementation process with calamine and charcoal was already known in the Middle Ages. Biringuccio as well as Ercker described how to make brass and found bronze, important for casting cannon. Savot was the first to write about the production of brass by alloying zinc with copper. The process of alloying copper and lead in order to de-silver copper by liquidation was developed by Nuremberg specialists, and by Johann Thurzo of Cracow, from the beginning of the fifteenth century. It had a decisive effect upon the renaissance of European silver and copper production. Tin and tin alloys were used in plating copper and iron, as solders and for pewter. The addition of bismuth appears in the second half of the sixteenth century. Type-metal was originally rather similar to pewter, but later the harder and cheaper lead antimony alloys came into use.

Lead was used in building, especially in the construction of stained glass windows; at first it was made by casting, later by rolling. The growing demand for sheet metal for roofing was met at first by casting and then also by rolling. De Caus mentioned a hand-operated rolling mill in 1651 and larger mills driven by water- or horse-power were developed during the seventeenth century, especially in England.

Furnaces were used either to reduce ores or to resmelt the metal for alloying and casting. The slow process of replacing open hearths by blast furnaces went on from the fourteenth to the seventeenth century; by 1700 the average size of the furnace was twice that of its mid sixteenth-century predecessor.

Coal mining and metallurgy were both stimulated by the use of coal for smelting. In 1612 and 1613 Simon Sturtevant and John Rovenzon published treatises which advocated the adoption of coal-burning blast furnaces. Their inventions proved unsuccessful, but at the same period coal was successfully substituted for wood in glass-making, and London brewers too began to burn coal. According to J. U. Nef, the discovery of a method of making coke from coal – i.e. how to purge the mineral of some of its impurities – was first made while drying malt for brewing in Derbyshire during the Civil War. Beer which was brewed from malt dried with 'coaks', was found to be sweet and pure. As a result (it was claimed) Derbyshire beer became famous. The repercussions were slowly felt in other industrial processes. Towards the end of the seventeenth century it was possible to substitute coke for charcoal in reverberatory furnaces for the smelting of lead ores and later for tin and copper ores. In 1709, at Broseley in Shropshire, coke was first successfully used to smelt iron, and this method continued until about 1784, when Henry Cort invented his new 'puddling' process for making bar iron from pig iron.

Another serious technical problem was posed by the drainage of mines. At the end of the fifteenth and the beginning of the sixteenth century, when silver was obtained from argentiferous copper ores, mining activity was intensified, especially in central Europe. Here engines driven by horses or hydraulic power were devised to raise the water from the shaft. The high price of silver in Europe, especially before the invasion of American silver, made it profitable to install and use the expensive machinery necessary, but the cost was too high to allow of its use in coal mines. Other and cheaper methods of drainage were therefore sought. The solution was found in the steam engine. Newcomen's invention made it possible to install the first steam engines in Staffordshire about 1712. From here they spread to other parts of the British Isles and then to the Continent.

New methods of transport also aided mining production. During the sixteenth century, wooden rails were used in the Harz in order to transport copper ore. German miners brought the invention to England. Between 1598 and 1606 similar rails were laid from the collieries at Wollaton (near Nottingham) down to the River Trent, as well as from collieries at Brosely to the Severn. The empty coal wagons were hauled back along the rails to the mine by horses. By the eighteenth century, horsedrawn 'railways' were used to haul coal to the rivers and harbours in many parts of Britain.

(2) WINDMILLS

In coastal areas where wind-power was available windmills were used. An older type of windmill with a tower came from the Mediterranean area. The next development was the post-mill, in which the wooden cage was movable. It was already in use in the Middle Ages on the flats which bordered the North Sea. In the Low Countries in the fifteenth century the *wipmolen* was invented, in which only the tower-cap needed to move, and a drawing of its mechanical details was first published in the book of Agostino Ramelli, *Le diverse et artificiose machine* (1588). By that time windmills were widely spread throughout the Netherlands. By means of the windmill the power was increased from ten to thirty horse-power or by twenty to forty per cent. With the advance of metallurgical technique it became possible to cast gears of iron. In 1745 Edmund Lee patented the automatic 'fantail'. The first wind-driven saw-mill was built by Cornelius Cornelisz in Holland in 1592. From the first half of the seventeenth century the saw-mills worked with five and more blades until they were outdated by the new Scandinavian water-mills during the eighteenth century. In the Netherlands, mills were used for many industrial purposes, especially on the Zaan in sawing timber for the shipyards. At one time over 900 were in use there simultaneously.

(3) TOOLS

Throughout this period most of the tools used by farmers and tradesmen were made by village carpenters and blacksmiths. Such improvements as were made originated in tool-making towns – Sheffield in England, Thiers in France, or Solingen and Nuremberg in Germany. Metal tools became popular after 1700 as steel became more common. As the specialization of trades grew – in 1568 the painter Joost Ammann illustrated 90 different trades which were practised in his time, and

Diderot described over 250 in the French *Encyclopédie* – the number of tools which one artisan used likewise increased. But most of the tools used on the farms remained traditional. Progress and invention were slow.

(4) TEXTILE INDUSTRY

The textile industry experienced a series of innovations. In order to make washed wool ready for carding and combing John Kay invented a machine for dressing wool (1733). For carding, handcards of the medieval type were used, but in order to increase output the cards were made larger and handcarding was supplemented by carding machines equipped with carding sticks. Then, in 1748 Daniel Bourn of Leominster patented a carding-machine with a rotary action in which card-covered cylinders driven by hand or by water wheel worked against each other. The same year Lewis Paul designed a rectangular carding-machine and at the same time another with a revolving cylinder. The cylinder-type of Bourn became the prototype of all later roller carding-machines.

The most advanced method of 'braking' (crushing) flax was to be found in Holland, and the Dutch brake was widely used in Europe. In the second half of the seventeenth century, English inventors attempted to mechanize flax-dressing. In 1727 a Scot, David Donald, invented a flax-beating machine driven by water-power. The following year another machine was invented by James Spalding, inspired by a visit to Holland. At the same time machinery for 'scutching' (beating) was introduced. Instead of beating the fibres, a fining mill was used in Holland about 1735. The fibres were then combed or 'hackled', for which Dutch and English combs with long steel teeth were used after the beginning of the eighteenth century. A hemp-stamping (beating) machine was patented in 1721 by Henry Browne.

For spinning, the spindle-and-whorl remained in use, especially for the warp, although in more advanced areas the spinning-wheel was adopted.

The fly-wheel was invented about 1480 and was coupled with the treadle-drive at the beginning of the sixteenth century. The Glockendon Bible of 1524 has an illustration of the mechanism of a foot treadle, but in 1527 the *Garnnahrung* (yarn makers' gild) of Elberfeld prohibited the use of this invention. Master Jurgen, a mason of Brunswick, was reputed to have constructed something better in 1530, and the treadle-wheel spread throughout Europe in numerous forms. After Kay's flying shuttle of 1733 Lewis Paul of Birmingham, in association with John Wyatt, who completed the invention, received a patent in 1738 for 'a system of roller-drafting by means of a series of pairs of rollers'. In 1741 Paul's machine was used at Birmingham, driven by two donkeys. In 1743 at Northampton the same machine was driven by a water wheel.

For weaving, the older looms were supplanted by the horizontal frame-loom or treadle-loom. The draw-loom, which originated in the east for weaving silk, was used in the silk-weaving centres of Italy during the Middle Ages and from there introduced into France. Galantier and Blacho in France, and Joseph Mason in England, improved it. Refinements in the shedding-mechanism were tried out in France. Claude Dangon, a Lyons weaver, invented the lever draw-loom at the beginning of the seventeenth century, which permitted an increase in the number of 'lashes' from 800 to 2,400. An automatic draw-loom which could be used without an assistant was designed by Basile Bouchon in 1725 and improved three years later by Falcon. These looms may not have been successful, but the principles they exemplified were later applied to multi-shuttle looms.

Inventions preparing the way for the power-loom were already adumbrated in the sixteenth century. Anton Möller of Danzig is said to have made such an invention about 1586, but Danzig forbade its use. Power-looms provoked disturbances in Leiden in 1620. Ordinances of 1623 and later regulated and restricted their use. Mechanical or half-mechanical *Bandstühle* (ribbon-looms), began to spread either from the Netherlands or from Switzerland. The bar-loom or Dutch loom-engine was capable of weaving four to six ribbons simultaneously. This number was increased to twelve, then to twenty-four and more. The swivel-loom or 'new Dutch loom' could weave twenty-four ribbons at once. Edicts in many German towns forbade them, but ribbon-mills penetrated the industry at Deutz, Mülheim, Elberfeld, Barmen and Radevormwald. In 1685 an Imperial edict forbade all 'compendious looms' within the Empire, and in 1719, at the urgent request of the Augsburg magistrates, this edict was confirmed. About 1730 Hans Hummel of Basle invented a method of operating the ribbon-loom by water-power: he was prohibited from working with it. A decisive step on the way to an automatic loom was made by John Kay of Bury in 1733 when he patented the flying shuttle which increased the weaver's speed and capacity to weave broader cloths. But the day of automatic weaving had still not arrived.

Instead of fulling by foot-tramping, fulling mills, first illustrated in Italy in 1607, were used from the late Middle Ages onwards. At the beginning of the eighteenth century in Germany and France they were driven by water-mills, in Holland by windmills, and in other places by horses or by hand. Machines for raising the nap on cloth were already in use during the fifteenth century. In England an act of 1551 prohibited the use of such 'gig-mills', but they were still in use at Gloucester in the first half of the seventeenth century. For shearing, the stirrup-grip was used until the end of the seventeenth century when it was replaced by a rotating lever. In 1495 machines for cropping were prohibited in England and a final solution was not found before the end of the eighteenth century.

The Dutch employed the most advanced techniques of bleaching linen and hempen products in the early eighteenth century. The whole process – steeping, washing, bucking (i.e. heating) and watering – required half a year. Instead of the lactic acid of buttermilk for the souring process, diluted sulphuric acid was used in 1756. This innovation halved the time needed for the bleaching process, and Francis Home of Edinburgh introduced it in order to eliminate pressing by foot. Calendering (i.e. smoothing) was used in Paris at the time of Colbert.

Other technological advances marked the steady progress of Europe's textile industries. Florentine workers perfected the art of making coloured and brocaded fabrics in the sixteenth and seventeenth centuries. In England, William Lee, an Elizabethan clergyman, devised the first frame-knitting machine. Lee himself did not find support in England and therefore sought the patronage of Henri IV of France. But the hand-knitters put up such opposition to the knitting machine that it only established itself slowly during the seventeenth century. In England, it contributed notably to the rise of productivity in textiles after the Restoration of 1660. Thus technological progress was not limited by national boundaries. Inventions were spread and applied either by migrants or plagiarists or by both acting in combination.

VI.   *Investment Costs and Financing*

In order to create an industrial plant, capital was indispensable. Workshops, mills, furnaces, forges, had to be built, raw material had to be bought, workers had to be paid. The lone craftsman was in the simplest situation. He had his workshop in his house, generally of a size enabling him to lodge and feed one or two companions and the same number of apprentices. If this was the typical case, there are nevertheless many examples where craftsmen became merchants and industrial entrepreneurs and managed to find the capital necessary to enlarge their enterprise.

Capital was especially needed more in mining and in large-scale metallurgy. In the exploitation of mines, investment costs grew steadily from the end of the fifteenth century. In 1494 Jakob Fugger and Johann Thurzo hired the mines of Neusohl (Banska Bystrica) in Slovakia for 3,000 gold florins annually. With the growing costs entailed by the

Bergwerksverlag, the *Gewerken* had to look for the financial help of merchants. In the beginning of the sixteenth century the advance for one furnace was 500 fl.; by 1525 it had risen to about 2,000. Costs were influenced by the right of the princes over *Wechsel* (preemption). This too, favoured concentration in the hands of the big merchants, because only they were able to provide the advances demanded by the princes. In 1557 the Manlich of Augsburg engaged themselves to advance 300,000 fl. to the counts of Mansfeld in order to get their mines on lease.

Especially costly was the construction of *Saigerhütten*. A plant which yielded 7,000 centner of copper a year consisted of '8 Schmelzöfen, 10 Saigeröfen, 3 Garherden, 3 Treibherden und 2 Dörröfen'.[1] The construction of the Hütte Leutenberg took several years and the costs were more than 3,000 fl. Whereas the Company of the Hütten Schwarza and Mansfeld had enough capital with their 6,000 fl. in 1472, and the company of Arnstadt commanded 31,500 fl. in 1502, the capital of the Steinacher Gesellschaft in 1554 rose to more than 236,000 fl.

In the textile industry, too, costs grew with the rise of the factory system. In the fifteenth century the Medicis had two *botteghe di lana* and one *bottega di seta* working partly on the putting-out basis with a capital between 4,000 and 6,000 fl. In 1579, Henry Cramer, the wealthiest Leipzig merchant, established a factory on his demesne, Meuselwitz, with the help of specialists from the Netherlands; it consisted of 'eine Walkmühle, ein Wirkhaus, eine Färberei und eine Wohnkolonie'.[2] The biggest German linen firm in the beginning of the seventeenth century, Viatis and Peller at Nürnberg, worked with a capital of about one million florins. It occupied, on the basis of the putting-out system, about 2,000 weavers with their *Gesellen* and apprentices. In 1710 the factory van Robais at Abbéville worked with 100 looms representing a capital of 500,000 livres. Some years later the Count Waldstein established a factory at Oberleutensdorf for 10 looms. The whole installation cost 5,000 fl., each loom cost 20 fl., a spinning wheel 37 kr., a press of wool 170, a press of iron 250 fl.[3] Two last examples from England: around 1760, the Spitalfields brewery of Truman, Hanbury and Buxton worked with £130,000, £70,000 of which represented good debts, £24,000 the value of the material in storage, e.g. vats, barley, hops and beer. The buildings, tools, and leasing of public houses were put at £30,000 or one tenth of the capital. Lombe's silk mill needed an investment of about £30,000.

Where business was run on the basis of the putting-out system, costs

---

[1] J. Strieder, *Studien zur Geschichte kapitalistischer Organisationsformen* (Munich–Leipzig, 1925), p. 47.

[2] Forberger, *Die Manufaktur in Sachsen*, p. 20.

[3] Freudenberger, *The Waldstein Woollen Mill*, p. 381.

for the technical installation tended to remain low. The central nucleus consisted mostly only of the office and the warehouses. The important cost factors were the stocks of raw material and manufactures, and the time lag between the beginning of production and the return of receipts.

How were entrepreneurs able to find the capital necessary for their investments? In the case of mining and *Saigerhütten*, a *Verlag* of big merchants was the solution. Often industrialists formed a company with a merchant. Such was the case of the Medici; other examples can be quoted from eighteenth-century France. The Bavarian experience of the early factory phase shows that only one-third of all entrepreneurs were by origin craftsmen or specialized workers. Usually these could establish a factory only where they had made a good marriage or came into money by inheritance, or when they could find a capitalist partner. Whereas in eastern Europe the nobility was more active, in Bavaria most factories were founded by *Verleger*, and in Saxony textile merchants took over the foundation of mills. Where mercantilist policy predominated, the role of state help – subventions, prizes or loans – was of great importance. Private credit was given not only by merchant bankers but by charitable foundations too. The institution of *jernkontoret*, in Sweden, took over production from the *brukspatroner* and gave them the credit they needed from time to time.

VII.   *The Role of Government*

Economic policy in the period 1500–1750 was consciously influenced by mercantilist theories and programmes, but these were not always identical in different countries. Mercantilism in France was different from mercantilism in central and eastern Europe; and systematic mercantilist policies appeared in France much earlier than elsewhere in continental Europe.

In England, Tudor and early Stuart policy favoured the creation and expansion of industries of a luxury or military character, such as fine paper, silk, glass, canvas or gunpowder. Wool exports were restricted by a growing number of ordinances designed to favour the domestic textile industry. Under James I they were prohibited altogether. Scotland was somewhat behind with this policy of export control, but followed England in developing her own industry. In 1681 Scotland also prohibited the export of yarn and unfulled cloth and the import of woollen goods and other textiles; in the same year the privileged woollen factory of Newmills was founded near Haddington, west of Edinburgh. Between 1683 and 1704 eight more organized factories followed. One of the consequences of the Union between England and Scotland (1707) was that Scotland became unable to compete, and Newmills and the other factories were driven to the wall.

Until the late seventeenth century England exported mostly unfinished cloth. The trade was a monopoly entrusted by charter to the Merchant Adventurers' Company. Seeing an opportunity to present private benefit in the guise of the public interest, Alderman Cokayne (with the support of James I) organized a scheme under which the export of 'white' cloth would be prohibited. Unemployment would be reduced and the value of England's export trade much increased by developing the export of dyed, finished cloth (1614). Too few of the necessary skills were available: the Dutch (whose interests were most adversely affected) took retaliatory measures. Cokayne's ambitious scheme had to be abandoned, leaving only a disastrous aftermath of depression and unemployment in its wake for many years.

The first attempts to stimulate French industries by government action were made in the reign of Henri IV, under the influence of Barthélemy de Laffemas. Colbert continued the process more systematically: in order to coordinate industrial activity, he re-created in 1664 the *Conseil de Commerce* first established by de Laffemas over sixty years before, which dealt not only with questions of trade but also with technology, innovations and factories. In 1669 Bellinzani was named inspector-general of factories.

All French factories were to a greater or lesser extent dependent on state aid. The state itself owned some, such as the *tapisseries* of Paris and Beauvais and the arsenals of Brest, Toulon and Rochefort. Others were accorded the right to mark their products with the 'Arms of His Majesty'. Specialists were brought in from abroad – Italians to make mirror glass, laces and other luxury goods; miners, founders, and brickmakers from Sweden and Germany; and clothmakers from Holland such as van Robais. Rigid measures were taken against the flight of French specialist artisans and in 1682 those who tried to emigrate were threatened with death.

Colbert also tried to stimulate entrepreneurial activity in France. In 1665 he sent two master clothmakers from Paris to Bourges with orders to improve the statutes of the clothmakers in that town. Thanks to the initiative of the local *intendant*, a factory producing stockings and woollen caps was founded at Poitiers and another at Chatellerault for leather working. Others were established in hospitals, for instance at Bordeaux, to weave stockings, card wool and make lace. Soldiers' barracks were also used partly as factories. Entrepreneurs intending to establish a factory received interest-free loans, workshops, and means of production. Factory workers were exempted from paying the *taille* and relieved of the obligations of serving in the militia and billeting soldiers. Often towns and the provincial estates were obliged to help, and the factory might receive monopoly privileges in the locality. This policy was dropped after Colbert's death and the Revocation of the Edict of Nantes in 1685 did much damage in the industrial field. Nevertheless the state continued to give encouragement, especially until 1750, through privileges and premiums designed to help private entrepreneurs.

The establishment of the Bourbon dynasty in Spain led to attempts by the government to stimulate industry after the French example, especially the textile industry. The first steps were taken in the years 1717–19. Royal *cédulas* (edicts) prohibited the sale of silk and other textiles from Asia (as in contemporary France and England) and the importation of ready-made clothing and decreed the use of national manufactures for the equipment of the army. In the late 1720s new measures of protectionism followed. In 1726 it was determined by decree that Spaniards should wear only silk and cloth produced in Spain. In October 1742 the prohibition on importing cotton textiles was lifted, but at the insistence of the producers of Barcelona it was re-imposed in December the following year. The most interesting state creations were the royal factories (*manufacturas reales*), the product of collaboration between the Royal Treasury and the Castilian nobility. As in France, many of the factories had a decidedly luxury character, providing objects to adorn the royal palace in Madrid – such as the tapestry-works of Madrid and the crystal-factory of San Ildefonso. Others were intended to shore up private enterprises against threatened ruin (the silk factories of Murcia and the cloth factories of Ezcaray), while yet others were harnessed to the military programme of the monarchy. Some were intended to stimulate techniques which were in decay, such as the silk works of Talavera de la Reina, and the cloth factories of Guadalajara, San Fernando, Brihuega and La Granja.

Another field of action for the mercantilistic policy of the government was the privileged companies, some founded to stimulate overseas trade, others to promote industrial production. In 1746 the *Compañía de Zarza la Mayor* was floated with a capital of 21 million *reales*[1] to manufacture woollen and silk articles in Estremadura, Valencia and Toledo, for export to Portugal. A year later, in 1747, companies were founded at Granada and Seville with the similar intention of producing silk textiles for export to America. The Company soon ran into difficulties and was amalgamated with that of *Zarza la Mayor* into the *Compañía de Estremadura*, which in turn merged with a *Compañía de Comercio y Fabrica de Toledo* founded in 1748. Even this giant company soon found it difficult to keep its head above water.

[1] 1 silver *real* was worth 4s 4½d.

At the same time the important Madrid gilds, the *Cinco Gremios Mayores*[1] were active in the American trade and worked to stimulate the export industries. Thus in 1748 the gild of drapers established a separate company to encourage the manufacture of Spanish cloths. This was only one move towards the combination of the industrial activities of the capital with those of other commercial networks, especially Cadiz, in order to gain a foothold in the American trade.

The Empire evolved a remarkably active industrial policy from the sixteenth century onwards in both the independent territories and the Imperial free cities (*Reichsstädte*). Mining and metallurgy in Saxony developed under the active patronage of Duke George and later of the Elector Augustus, and in the Harz thanks to the energies of Duke Julius of Brunswick-Wolfenbüttel. In southern Germany Duke Frederick of Württemberg was a typical mercantilist prince: he encouraged the Urach linen-production and the Calw cloth-printing factory. Immigrants introduced new industries to the Imperial cities of Frankfurt and Hamburg, on the estates of the count of Hanau and the Elector Palatine. In the aftermath of the Thirty Years War, mercantilist ideas stimulated industrial progress in many other places. The Great Elector of Brandenburg encouraged linen-weaving in Westphalia, Huguenot exiles contributed to the rise of silk-weaving and other luxury trades in his towns of Spandau and Magdeburg, and in the territories of the Margraves of Ansbach and Bayreuth at Erlangen and Schwabach.

In Denmark the first phase of state industrial policy began with Christian IV, who tried to turn his capital Copenhagen and his new town of Glückstadt on the lower Elbe into industrial centres. His efforts and those of his successors met with little success. Denmark's domestic market was too small and its products could not compete with western and central European production in foreign markets.

In Sweden the government's attempts to regulate the location of metal industries were likewise unsuccessful. During the minority of Queen Christina, the government tried to move the iron foundries from Bergslagen to other provinces – especially Värmland – but the increased costs of transport there defeated this exercise in industrial planning.

Industrial development in Russia was almost inconceivable without state initiative, but this was not provided with any show of determination before Peter the Great. The governments of Portugal, and the Italian states similarly failed to formulate a positive industrial policy much before 1750. In Austria, despite the propaganda and efforts of men such as Becher or Hörnigk, industrial policy was not really successful before Maria Theresa.

[1] Literally = the five greater gilds.

VIII.   *Private Entrepreneurship and the Labour Force*

(I) ENTREPRENEURSHIP

The leading figure of industrial progress was the entrepreneur. He appeared in several guises. The most important was that of the merchant, able to furnish the craftsmen and other workers with raw materials and capital, and to command a good market for their products.

In the sixteenth century an outstanding group of entrepreneurs throve in south Germany, beginning with the Fuggers who exploited the copper mines of Tyrol and Slovakia, the gold mines of Silesia, the lead mines of Carinthia and the quicksilver mines of Almadén in Spain. Among their Augsburg rivals were the Gossenprot, Paumgartner, and Höchstetter. The last, followed later by the Paumgartner, exploited the quicksilver mines of Idria. The Höchstetter were also active in the English copper industry. Nuremberg merchants exploited the iron mines of the upper Palatinate, the copper mines of Thuringia (Mansfeld) and Bohemia (Kuttenberg or Kutna Hora) and the tin and silver mines of Saxony. The most important capitalists here were the Fürer, the Nuremberg branch of the Welser, and the Pfinzing. They were rivalled by later groups of entrepreneurs from Leipzig and other Saxon towns. In the Rhineland, the Aachen families of Wolff and van Richterghen were outstanding entrepreneurs in the calamine and copper industry. (The latter were related to the Schetz who played a prominent role in the financial and commercial life of Antwerp.)

Merchants from Liège and Luxemburg were active in the industry of the Hunsrück and the Lahn area in the first half of the seventeenth century. At the same time emigrants from the Aachen region developed significantly the existing metallurgical industries in Sweden and around Hamburg and Lübeck. The meteoric rise of the Swedish copper, brass, and iron industry in the seventeenth century was in fact principally the work of those entrepreneurs of the Netherlands who had emigrated from Liège and Namur to Holland and thence to Sweden.

The outstanding figure amongst these Liégeois was Louis de Geer, simultaneously merchant, arms manufacturer, factory owner and the modernizer of Swedish iron production. He was involved in all kinds of manufacture, producing brass, steel, bricks, wire, paper, textiles and even ships in his own shipyards. There were other Walloons in Sweden, such as the De Besche and De Rees. After 1650 the Momma brothers built up a large concern of iron and copper mining in Norrbotten, Kengis and Svappavaara, but alas their end was bankruptcy.

In Russia the outstanding group of merchant entrepreneurs were

Netherlanders – the Marselis – who combined their Russian interests with a prominent place in the mining industry of Norway. Another group active in Denmark and Norway was represented by the Portuguese bankers Teixeira and Nunes Henriques of Hamburg and Amsterdam. In Russia, of course, there were also native merchant industrialists, of whom the Stroganov are the best known example.

Noblemen and even princes took a personal interest in industrial activity or were prepared to act as its patrons. The most famous Protestant examples in the sixteenth century were Duke Julius of Brunswick-Wolfenbüttel and Henry Rantzau, Statthalter of the king of Denmark in Schleswig and Holstein. On the Catholic side, Count Waldstein in Bohemia established a woollen industry around his seigneurial residence, and in the late sixteenth and early seventeenth century leading nobles in Poland encouraged mining and metallurgy on their domains. From the end of the seventeenth century a number of magnates of the Habsburg monarchy actively promoted industrial enterprise, especially in textile manufacture, using their serfs as cheap labour. In Scandinavia Ulrik Frederik Gyldenlöve, half-brother of King Christian V of Denmark and governor of Norway, owned saw-mills; Joachim Irgens, courtier of King Christian IV, developed copper-mining in Norway; Claude Roquette, Queen Christina's tailor, patronized the porcelain industry. Many other court favourites and state officials during the phase of absolutism and mercantilism used their favour with princes for industrial purposes or were even entrusted by the princes with the execution of their industrial projects.

From the end of the fifteenth century, marching in step with the development of mining and metallurgy, a new class of ironmasters appeared. They included many men of peasant origin who prospered as *Reidemeister* in Germany or *brukspatroner* in Sweden. In textile production, by contrast, entrepreneurial activity was often the monopoly of the dyers or, in the putting-out system, of the 'middlemen'. Generally, economic development justified contemporary belief that mercantile capital was gradually taking control of the industrial crafts.

From the fifteenth century a high percentage of emigrants made a career in industrial entrepreneurship. First among them came the Sephardic Jews who modernized the textile industry of Salonica in the course of the sixteenth century. Later came the Netherlanders who fled to central and northern Europe, the Italians who went to Switzerland, and the wave of Huguenot *émigrés* who left France for England, the Netherlands and Prussia after the Revocation of the Edict of Nantes in 1685. Groups of Calvinists or Lutherans moved into industrial activity in such places as Krefeld, Mülheim or Elberfeld-Barmen. Many specialists seized the opportunities offered by Swedish industrialization; from

Austria came the brothers Geijer in the reign of Gustavus Adolphus, specialists in the latest German iron techniques. One of their descendants took over one of Sweden's most important iron works, Uddeholm. Christopher Polhem, who came to Sweden via Pomerania, was also probably of Austrian extraction. From Aachen and its region came specialists in brass manufacture. The *vallonsmidet*[1] process was brought over by Walloons who came to Sweden from Liège and Namur at the request of Louis de Geer, familiar with the most recent techniques of iron working. At the same time a new type of furnace, called 'French', was also imported into Sweden.[2] From Austria or south eastern Germany came smiths, who introduced *tysksmide*.[3] One of the most famous iron works, at Eskilstuna, was founded by a Dutchman whose family originally came from Aachen, Reinhold Rademacher. A new method of refining copper (*garmakeriet*) was introduced by Govert Silent who immigrated from the south Netherlands. The influx of these cosmopolitan specialists and entrepreneurs, with their technical skills, innovations, and their capital for investment, was of primary importance for the efficient exploitation of Sweden's vast mineral resources. Seventeenth-century Sweden provides the classic example of the role of immigrant entrepreneurs in the development of a potentially rich but still backward economy. To a lesser extent, Russia after 1650, first with Vinius and later with the foreign experts invited by Peter the Great, is another illustration of similar development.

(2) THE LABOUR FORCE

Even in the Middle Ages industry had drawn on sources of labour lying outside the gilds, especially in mining, metallurgy and the textile industry. With the sustained industrial development after 1500 the differentiation of labour intensified. In mining, many of the *Gewerken*[4] in the Alps, central Germany and the Carpathians lacked the capital to install new mechanical techniques and of necessity had to rely on wage-workers. With the capitalist expansion of mining and metallurgy in the sixteenth century a hierarchy began to develop from the *Obersteiger*[5] and the *Schichtmeister*[6] through the various *Steiger*,[7] *Hauer*[8] and *Knechte*[9] to the *Jungen*[10] and female workers. Their functions varied – from highly skilled miners and smelters on the one hand, craftsmen such as smiths or

---

[1] Literally: the Walloon smithy.
[2] Other Walloons were the Gauffin, Hybinette, Sporrong, Lemoine, Guillaume (Gilljam): Heckscher, *Svenskt arbete och liv*, pp. 131f.

[3] The German smithy.   [4] Member of a mining corporation.
[5] Foreman of a mine.   [6] Master of a shift.   [7] Foremen.
[8] Miners.   [9] Journeymen.   [10] Boys.

carpenters to unskilled workers and horse drivers on the other. The differentiation of labour in the textile industry was even more marked: in the wool factory of Linz in Upper Austria the hierarchy ran from the cleaning, carding and spinning of the wool, to weaving, fulling, dyeing or bleaching. A hierarchy easily developed in enterprises where up to a hundred and more people were often working under one roof in a factory; under the putting-out system most employees worked in their own homes. The staff of such enterprises was engaged by skilled masters, and under them worked a growing number of untrained employees – often women and children – occupied in diverse ancillary services. Many women worked in the textile industry, and certain branches, such as silk spinning, bone-lace making and the linen industry, were almost exclusively the preserve of women. Women were also employed in the Alpine and Swedish mines and, during the sixteenth century, in arms factories too. Children were widely employed in the printing trade and later in cotton printing, in many of the auxiliary services of mining and metallurgy and, naturally, in domestic industries in their own homes.

Many of these 'industrial' workers remained essentially peasants: for them and their families, industrial wages brought in merely a supplementary (though important) income. Some processes of the mining and metal industry were only active in seasons when agricultural activity was slack. In mining and metallurgy as well as in glass-making a part of wages was paid in the form of land which could be cultivated by the workers. Workers had also to accept some of their pay in merchandise, the *Pfennwert*, and some in housing. Wages in cash were paid in various ways: the *Gesindeverhältnis*[1] which included subsistence (the medieval form) was gradually replaced by agreed wages (the *Gedinge*). At Bleiberg (Carinthia) the work schedule prescribed six and a half shifts weekly, each shift lasting nine hours – in all a $58\frac{1}{2}$-hour week. The industrial stress was enlivened however by frequent holidays. Only 245 days in each year seem to have been active workdays.[2] Medieval habits died hard.

In such industries, free and unfree existed side by side. In mining and glass-making the free workers represented an unstable element, miners are found migrating, in the sixteenth century, from Saxony to Bohemia, and from Germany to Sweden, England, Spain and to America. Unfree workers were those incarcerated in the houses of correction and on the demesnes of the magnates in Bohemia, Moravia and Russia. Elsewhere,

[1] Conditions of a servant.
[2] H. Wiessner, *Geschichte des Kärntner Bergbaus, II. Geschichte des Kärntner Buntmetallbergbaues mit besonderer Berücksichtigung des Blei- und Zinkbergbaues* in: *Archiv für vaterländische Geschichte und Topographie 36/37* (Klagenfurt, 1951), p. 275.

freer workers might organize themselves into associations parallel to the *Gesellenverbände*[1] or even organize strikes. The Tyrolese and the Styrian *Knappen*[2] joined the Peasants' War of 1525 and there were numerous strikes among the Leiden woollen workers in the seventeenth century.

In England small masters such as the sawyers and feltmakers began to appreciate that their interests coincided with those of the journeymen, combining to form associations which aroused the suspicion of Parliament. Wheelwrights and tailors formed similar organizations. At Newcastle there was a shoemakers' society in 1719 which arranged sickness and death benefits. About 1721 many associations of this kind existed in Sheffield. In 1726 Parliament found it advisable to pass a law against 'unlawful clubs and societies among wool workers in the West Country' and in 1749 it extended the law against combinations of workers in the silk, flax, iron, leather and some other trades.

In Spain, bad working conditions, low wages, and the suppression of the *fiestas* contributed to deep social discontent. In 1730 a *huelga* (strike) occurred in the cloth factory of Guadalajara, the first in Bourbon Spain.

IX.   *Production*

(1) MINING AND METALLURGY

The imports of gold from the New World removed most of the incentives for exploring the deposits within Europe. Goldmining in the Reichenstein in Silesia and in the Harz declined in favour of exploiting ores containing copper, lead, zinc and arsenic. The mining of precious metals had flourished in Carinthia, and especially near Obervellach: here the first goldmines were organized in small units, with numerous peasants, burghers and nobles among the share-holders. The situation changed round the middle of the sixteenth century with the intervention of substantial capitalists such as Hans Rosenberger from Augsburg, the brothers Weitmoser from Gastein (in 1571) and the *Wielandsche Gewerken*.[3] They rationalized mining by closing down unprofitable small mines and intensifying the exploitation of good ones – but to such an extent that their resources were soon exhausted. All that was gold did not glitter. The new phase of European gold mining was not to begin until the gold strikes in the Urals, made in 1745.

Copper and silver were mined in the Harz around Goslar, in the county of Mansfeld, around Salzburg, and in Saxony, Bohemia, Tyrol, and Slovakia. In the upper Harz, by the side of the old mines of Goslar and Clausthal, new ones were opened shortly after 1500 at St Andreasberg.

[1] Unions of journeymen.   [2] Miners.
[3] Members of a corporation organized by the Wieland family.

The Mansfeld mines, where production reached its zenith between 1521 and 1537, were of great importance. In the Erzgebirge, another important area of silver mining, production expanded rapidly after 1470, attracting entrepreneurs from Freiberg, Leipzig, Magdeburg and Erfurt, and capital from most of south Germany and especially from Nuremberg. The most important mining centres were Schneeberg, St Annaberg, Buchholz and Marienberg. Saxon production diminished temporarily at the end of the twenties when many of the miners emigrated to Joachimsthal, but rose again thereafter to reach its summit in 1533. The mines of St Annaberg and Marienberg attained their maximum output in the years before 1560; after 1577 production diminished considerably.

About 1540 the summit of European silver production as a whole was reached with an annual output of c. 65,000 kg, of which Germany herself mined about 16,000; silver production in the Tyrol, Bohemia and Slovakia was also mostly in the hands of south German capitalists. After 1551 the volume of silver imported from America rivalled and eventually far surpassed German production.

In Norway some silver was mined in Telemark in the first half of the sixteenth century, but the seam was soon exhausted. In 1624 a silver mine was opened by the Crown near Kongsberg; the output was small, and in 1627 a private company took over control. Production in some years rose to 2,000 kg, and in 1661 the Crown once again resumed control of the mine.

Sweden possessed silver mines near Sala with a modest output during the reign of Gustavus Vasa; in Russia, towards the close of the sixteenth century, German miners opened up a silver mine near the Gylma, a river flowing to the Petchora. In Spain the silver mines of Guadalcanal were in production towards the end of the reign of Charles V, while in Greece Jews exploited the silver mine of Sidrocopso near Salonica; labour was provided by a mixed force of Albanians, Greeks, Serbs, Turks, Circassians and Jews. Its annual output in the sixteenth century was worth between one and two million ducats.

Copper was worked in *Saigerhütten*[1] which were built at a number of sites in Thuringia (Leuthenberg, Gräfenthal, Arnstadt, Luderstadt and Steinach) and near Nuremberg (Enzendorf); the Fuggers processed copper at Hohenkirchen and Fuggerau (Carinthia). South German capital played an important part in numerous copper companies of which the biggest, financed by entrepreneurs from Nuremberg, were the *Saigerhandelsgesellschaften* of the foundries of Arnstadt and of Steinach, which disposed respectively of a capital of 100,000 and more than 230,000 fl. South German entrepreneurs also exploited the copper

[1] Refining works.

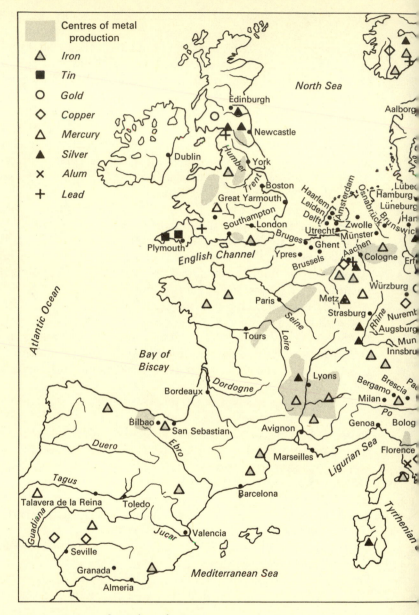

Fig. 7. Centres of metal production.

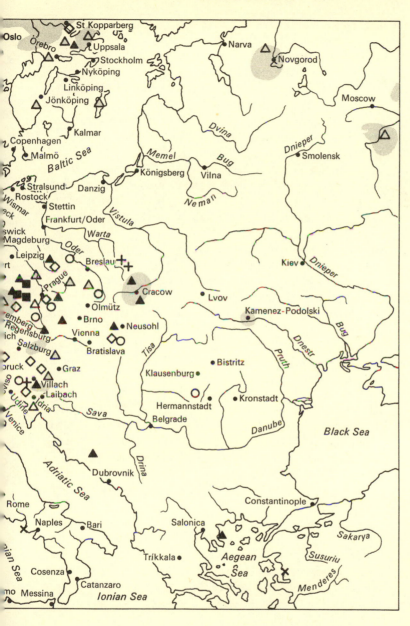

mines of Kuttenberg (Kutna Hora), Tyrol, Salzburg and Slovakia (Neusohl (Banska Bystrica), Libethen). Including the mines of Norway, England and the Alsace, total production may have been some 6,000 tons a year during the sixteenth century.

The silver of the Erzgebirge was mined from a base of lead–silver. Indeed in the Harz, in upper Silesia (near Tarnowice), and on the northern border of the Eifel, lead production was more important although Germany as a whole produced so little lead that it had to be imported from England, Carinthia and Poland.

Round 1500, Carinthia possessed several lead mines around Windisch-Bleiberg, at the west side of the Petzen and around Bleiberg. Silver and lead ores were found around Rübland on the north side of the Bleiberger Erzberg and in the area of Kreuzen-Stockenboi; lead and zinc in the area of Raibl.

The lead mines of the Bleiberg near Villach are the best known. The Fuggers, needing lead for their copper and silver mining in Slovakia, Tyrol and the valley of Lavant, opened mines at Bleiberg in 1495 and in the same year built a *Saigerhütte* near Markt Arnoldstein. Here they ran into competition from the Emperor Maximilian who also needed lead for his copper mines in the Tyrol. The dispute was settled when the Fuggers took over the Tyrol mines themselves. Within ten years the *Saigerhütte* was able to send to Venice about 50,000 centners of copper and 22,000 marks of silver.

The mines' shares were widely held by a varied collection of owners: burghers of Villach and the agents of the monastery of Milstatt rubbed shoulders with merchants from the south German towns such as the Ungelter of Augsburg and Virgil Fröschlmoser of Gastein. In time the small local share-holders made way for larger capitalists who began to rationalize mining. Thus by 1585 the Fuggers owned ninety-three mines but were only working twenty-six; the Lentners owned eighty-six but only worked eighteen.

After the middle of the sixteenth century Carinthian lead mining began to decline. In 1546 the Fuggers retired from mining in Slovakia although they held on in Carinthia: between 1553 and 1563 the yearly production there was about 10,000 centners of lead, falling to about 5,000 during the last quarter of the century. In 1570 they sold the works of Fuggerau to the Abbot of Arnoldstein and most of the miners were thrown out of work.

In Poland lead with a considerable mixture of silver was mined with the aid of apparatus for pumping shafts dry. Technical invention after 1450 enabled miners to reach deposits as far down as forty or fifty metres below ground-level. Sometimes special shafts were sunk to drain off the water. This Polish mining activity was concentrated in

Silesia and the Cracow district. The region of Tarnowskie Gory, where
a complete mining town was founded, was of special importance;
during the 1530s output rose to 2,900 tons of lead containing silver.
More than twenty other mining centres developed in the southern area
of the deposits in the Malopolska province. Olkusz, which at first was
the most important centre, ran into difficulties after 1470, but overcame
them in part by the beginning of the sixteenth century. Here in the
1530s ores especially rich in silver content were discovered. Lead from
these Polish mines was used for extracting silver from black copper in
Slovakia, partly in Kuttenberg (Kutna Hora), and Joachimsthal
(Jachymov). Polish lead was also a familiar product on the markets of
central Europe.

Technical progress and investment made necessary by expansion
inevitably demanded outside capital. Burghers from Cracow and
Breslau (Wroclaw) built metal-works, organized drainage, bought
shares or established their own mining companies. Members of the
nobility and clergy also participated. The *verlagssystem* spread: capitalists lent money to the miner at interest for the exploitation of his mines.
Thanks to this influx of merchant capital mining enterprises were partly
transformed into *consortia* of businessmen closely associated with production. On the other hand the process of mining steadily became
rationalized because the bigger enterprises could supervise the entire
industry from the mining of ore right through to the sale of the finished
product. In Olkusz at the end of the fifteenth century, the Morstyn, the
Thurzo and Salomon functioned as active entrepreneurs in this way; at
the beginning of the sixteenth century the Ber, Kauffman and Boner
followed, and the Fugger collaborated with the Thurzo. But this
process did not result in any kind of centralized manufacture. Only part
of the total process, mainly metal working, was centralized and used
hired labour: mining itself often remained in the hands of small producers who functioned more or less independently or on a family basis.

By the middle of the sixteenth century, mining in Silesia and around
Cracow was stagnant, especially at Olkusz. The abandonment of some
mines seems to have been connected more with technical difficulties
than with a shortage of ore. Drainage by horse power was so costly that
it took much of the profit out of mining. In the flat terrain around
Olkusz in the Malopolska province and in Upper Silesia, long 'galleries'
were necessary if mining was to continue. These demanded large-scale
investment which was not available until the second half of the century.
Meanwhile growing competition came from other centres of European
production such as England, the Harz and Carinthia.

Thanks to the existence of the calamine deposits of the Altenberg
(Vieille Montagne), Aachen developed a flourishing brass production

after about 1450. Copper was brought from Mansfeld and other places. Production at Aachen and Stolberg enjoyed excellent opportunities of export through Antwerp, the entrepôt for trade with the colonial empires of Spain and Portugal. From 1493 the Altenberg mines were farmed by Peter Wolf, an Aachen citizen who was related to the leading Aachen family, the van Richterghen. Nikolaus van Richterghen, the son of the mayor of Aachen, moved to Antwerp. After his death (1511), his son-in-law, Erasmus Schetz, from a family which originated in Limburg, assumed control of the enterprise in collaboration with the families Vleminck and Proenen. As successor to the van Richterghen business, Schetz took over the mines of Altenberg, controlling the calamine trade through Aachen. His sons continued the business (in collaboration for some years with the Vleminck) until 1579.

The religious troubles which followed disturbed mining in the Altenberg as well as brass production at Aachen. In 1611 the Brussels government took over direct control of the mines, although from 1621 until 1648 they were farmed out to an Aachen citizen, Johann Stuppart. About 1645 a record annual level of production, 50,000 centners, was reached. The apogee of the Aachen copper industry lasted until the end of the sixteenth century, when religious tensions and the conflict between the entrepreneurs (the *Kupfermeister*)[1] and the restrictive practices of the gilds impeded any further rise in production which technological progress might have produced. Many of the copper masters emigrated to Stolberg in the duchy of Juliers where they suffered none of the gild restrictions which complicated life at Aachen. Production in Stolberg rose during the Thirty Years War and by 1648 there were sixty-five furnaces at work. Nevertheless, down to the middle of the seventeenth century the Aachen *Kupfermeisterzunft*[2] continued to conclude contracts involving the production of 100,000 centners and more within ten years. Only in the second half of the century did Stolberg production overtake that of Aachen. In a contract of 1669 the Aachen copper masters undertook to produce 50,000 centners over 10 years, but the Stolberg masters agreed in the same year to provide 60,000 centners in only five years. From 1730 Aachen's annual production fell to between 15,000 and 20,000 centners a year.

Swedish copper production grew after 1550 and continued to rise into the early seventeenth century. The expansion was linked with the great demand for copper in Spain as the Spanish monetary system moved over to a pure copper standard. When Sweden had to pay the second 'Älvsborg ransom' the Swedish Crown alienated the whole of its copper production to a group of merchants who sold it in the markets of western, northern and central Europe. The demands of these

---

[1] Copper masters.   [2] Gild of Copper Masters.

new markets greatly stimulated copper production, and the principal mine of Falun was extended. Its maximum production was reached about 1650. The importance of copper in the financing of the so-called Swedish *Stormaktstid* (Imperial era) lay in the fact that the Crown itself took a leading part in production and that mining was concentrated in one place – Falun and the Stora Kopparberg. In order to facilitate the sale of copper, the government created copper companies – first in the time of Gustavus Adolphus and again during the minority of Queen Christina – which, it was hoped, would manage the exploitation and sale of copper better than the Crown or the small operators of the Stora Kopparberg could do. The first Royal Company did not function at all well, and came to an early end. The second company was a failure from the start and again only lasted for a few years. As a consequence of the troubles of the Thirty Years War, which disrupted Slovakian copper mining, Swedish copper sold by Louis de Geer and a group of Netherlands entrepreneurs including the Trips, dominated most of the European market. In 1650, Swedish copper production broke all records with an output of 3,000 tons. The long-term annual average was smaller – perhaps 2,100 tons – and after 1661–5 annual production fell below 2,000 tons. Only one other country produced as much copper as Sweden: Japan. But in the seventeenth century only small quantities of Japanese copper penetrated to Europe.

In 1690, Charles XI sent one of Sweden's most famous metallurgists, Erik Odhelius, on a fact-finding mission. He was to observe the other copper-mining areas of Europe and to locate the most promising markets available. Odhelius's report made it clear that although Sweden's copper production was in decline, it was still much higher than that of her European rivals, accounting for nearly half of Europe's total copper production. Between 1716 to 1720, however, it sank below 1,000 tons, and it continued at this new lower level throughout the eighteenth century.

The Danish–Norwegian kingdom had copper deposits too, though less abundant than Sweden's. The first known copper mine in production was at Sundsberg in Selford, for which Bishop Mogens of Hamar received a privilege in 1524. At the Reformation the king appropriated it and brought in Saxon miners.

In 1632 rich copper deposits were found near Kvikne. They were exploited by a mine run by royal officials. Other mines were developed, at Lökken in the Ork valley and especially at Röros, which was chartered in 1646. Norwegian copper-mining was at first under royal supervision but financed by foreigners; later on, the Hamburg and Amsterdam bankers, Teixeira and Nunes Henriques, took over the direct exploitation of the mines themselves.

In Russia copper was found in Siberia. In 1574 the Stroganov were granted the privilege to exploit it but it was only in the first half of the eighteenth century that copper exploitation acquired real importance. Between 1722 and 1724 four works were established in the Urals.

In England, two great companies were chartered in 1568 to exploit the copper mines, principally in the north and south west; the Mines Royal and the Mineral and Battery Works. German capitalists and specialists developed the new industries in the Newlands valley near Keswick, but their productivity proved to be poor. Tin ore was exploited in the Mendips. The Mineral and Battery Works produced brass and iron wire at Tintern; then, after 1580, they smelted Devon and Cornish copper ore at Neath. These companies resumed their activity after the Civil War, but lost their monopolies in 1689 when copper and zinc mining was thrown open to private enterprise.

Tin production in Saxony was important. In contrast to silver and copper, it did not require so much business capital because tin for the most part was dug in *Tagebau* in so-called *Seifen* (shallow, open-work diggings). The centre of Saxon tin-mining was Altenberg, where exploitation had begun before the middle of the fifteenth century. Other tin mines lay in the Fichtelgebirge. For some time Bohemia was the largest producer. Tin was important as a material in the manufacture of household ware and for the sheet metal industry which was centred in the Upper Palatinate, especially in Amberg, Sulzbach and Wunsievel. The raw sheets were mostly transported to Nuremberg and distributed from there to the various manufacturers. Entrepreneurs from Nuremberg and the upper Palatinate began to produce 'white-sheet' in the Erzgebirge. Tin and copper were combined in the alloy known as bronze. In the sixteenth century many workshops developed the technique of casting bells and cannon from bronze. The most important ones were to be found in the Southern Netherlands at Malines, Namur and Liège, in Germany at Nuremberg, in Tyrol at Innsbruck, and in Italy at Brescia. After the separation of the northern Netherlands the Dutch began to cast bronze cannon. Only in the seventeenth century did iron-cast cannons, in the sixteenth century a speciality of the English, begin to replace bronze.

In 1490, quicksilver was discovered at Idria, but it was not until the beginning of the sixteenth century that the extensive deposits which made the place famous were discovered. The Venetians were the first to exploit the mines, but they were soon expelled by the emperor, who began to work the deposits on his own account. He in turn was persuaded to lease a part to a consortium of native capitalists, mostly nobles, such as Auersberg, Lamberg, Dietrichstein and Rauber. The third *Gewerkschaft* of Idria was founded in 1520 and also consisted of nobles, together with some city merchants. In 1523 a new mine was granted to the Count of Ortenburg, Gabriel de Salamanca, but soon the other *Gewerkschäfte* joined him to form a cartel for the sale of quicksilver. The Augsburg merchant Höchstetter was one of Salamanca's partners. Towards the end of the twenties Höchstetter went bankrupt: it became difficult to find a market for quicksilver.

In 1539 another Augsburg merchant, Hans Paumgartner, concluded a new sales contract; mining reached a new level of prosperity after 1550, partly as a consequence of the destruction of the Almadén mines in 1550 by fire and partly through the new amalgamation process which made quicksilver necessary for the mining of silver in Spanish America. After the reconstruction of Almadén the Fuggers, who administered the lands of the Military Order of Calatrava to which Almadén belonged, intensified exploitation. Idrian production came into the hands of the Augsburg firm of Haug, Langnauer and Company for a time, but they went bankrupt in 1574. Thereafter the Idria mines came under the direct control of the archduke.

During the first half of the sixteenth century when cobalt began to be used to produce blue dye and *Blauschmelz* (blue glaze), mills were built in Schneeberg, Oberschlema and Pfannenstiel to manufacture these dyes. They were exported to Nuremberg, Hamburg and Holland and influenced the development of the blue Delft tiles.

(2) IRON

The English iron industry was a typical rural industry of the sixteenth century, reaching 'from the Lake District iron works of the Abbots of Furness to those of the Sussex Weald'.[1] There was some concentration of production, as at Sheffield and Birmingham where smiths, cutlers, lorimers and nailers worked together, but hundreds of industrial peasant nailers and scythe-makers plied their trade throughout Worcestershire, Staffordshire and the Forest of Dean. In Scotland the monopolistic policies of the small towns seem to have favoured a greater concentration of industry and trade in the hands of the craftsmen and merchants living there.

The technical progress made in the late Middle Ages – especially the discovery of methods of casting iron by means of a blast furnace and the value of water-powered hammerworks – accounts for the expansion of the metal industry in many regions rich in water and woods, especially when iron ores were found there as well. Thus in the Weald of Sussex iron-masters established their works in early Tudor times, subsequently

[1] J. Clapham, *A Concise Economic History of Britain from the Earliest Times to 1750* (Cambridge, 1937).

attracting the participation of members of the gentry and nobility, even of Queen Elizabeth herself, in joint-ownership.

Furnaces were also built in other regions. When wood and iron ore became scarcer, new centres of production were prospected in the north and northwest of the country. Bolder entrepreneurs did not hesitate to set up their works as far away as the west coast of Scotland in order to secure their fuel supply. The limited availability of charcoal stimulated 'projectors' to experiment with coal, found in considerable deposits near Durham and in south Nottinghamshire. One such 'projector' was Dudley, the author of *Metallum Martis*, published in 1665, although it was not until about 1708 that Abraham Darby, a Quaker, discovered practicable methods of feeding his furnaces at Coalbrookdale in Shropshire with coked coal. But Darby's innovation spread only slowly, and Swedish and Russian charcoal-iron continued to be imported. Darby's process seems to have caught on only in the region of Shropshire and Wrexham. He was in fact one of a group of Quakers, including Rawlinson and Lloyd, who in the early eighteenth century initiated important technical improvements, used mineral coal and deployed large-scale capital investment in iron manufacture. Thanks to their action the iron industry, so important for English exports, began to concentrate round Birmingham and Sheffield. Near Birmingham the villages of Dudley, Wednesbury, and Wolverhampton were active centres of production which grew later into towns. Meanwhile the industry spread northwards from Lancashire and Cumberland into the Scottish Highlands, attracted by the abundant supplies of wood. Many rural communities produced ironware for a local market. Even during the eighteenth century, and especially in Scotland, most metal-working remained in the hands of smiths living in the countryside. In the region of Birmingham and Sheffield, production was increasingly controlled by merchant capital, so that although some urban workers were still organized in gilds, a growing proportion of labour, especially in rural areas outside the older centres of production, worked outside any formal regulation (or protection) of gild or municipality.

In Spain the sixteenth century saw iron exploitation increase in Vizcaya, centring on Somorrostro. Part of the iron produced was exported to France and England; part was used in Spain to make the famous Basque steel used in shipbuilding. On the other side of the peninsula, the *fargues* (smithies) of the Catalan Pyrenees were in decay partly because the French established forges around Foix, and supplied them with bar iron smuggled out of Spain. In Castile, Toledo especially retained its ancient fame as a centre of the weapon industry.

Private metallurgical industry was generally concentrated in the north of Spain. Modern iron-works with blast furnaces were established in Asturias with the assistance of two Flemish specialists, Jean Curtius and Georges de Brande. In 1755 their owner, Olivares, received a royal monopoly for the exclusive supply of cannon and iron shot to the army. From 1711 to 1718 the annual export to England was 1,500 *toneladas*, rising to 1,770 *toneladas* from 1729 to 1735. Thereafter production and exports declined in the face of competition from superior ironware from Sweden and Russia.

In France, metal was worked in Dauphiné, Franche Comté, Nivernais, Champagne and Lorraine. Knives were made around Thiers, needles in the region of Laigle. During the ministry of Colbert the metal industries of St Etienne and Forez made progress. From the coast shipbuilding and armaments stimulated the iron industry. In the neighbouring bishopric of Liège the discovery of iron ore in the region between the Sambre and the Meuse, rich in timber, in the valley of Hoyaux and in the marquisate of Franchemont, enabled the rural workers to begin mining and forging. Many, probably most, were still agricultural workers. By 1740, some 1,000 smiths were at work in the principality of Liège. Production was directed by merchants who furnished the smiths with their iron; the smiths received wages on a piece-work system.

In Germany, too, growing markets and technical progress gave the mining industry a considerable fillip. Iron was produced in many regions, giving rise in turn to industries making a wide variety of iron products. In the Saar, ore was dug in open-cast strikes until the eighteenth century. A lively iron industry sprang up in the Hunsrück and in the Eifel region around Düren. On the right bank of the Rhine the counties of Siegen, Dillenburg and Sayn were most important: in 1563 round Siegen alone the industry reached its peak with 32 active foundries (*Hütten*). Genuine blast-furnace foundries began earlier here than in the region of Dillenburg, where they were only built before the end of the sixteenth century.

In Nassau-Weilburg, Solms, Hesse and in the territories of Wittgenstein, iron ore was mined and worked. From the foundries at Haina in Hesse, iron working spread into Waldeck and the Sauerland. The partition of Hesse after the death of Landgrave Philip encouraged the foundation of other ironworks.

In the Westphalian Mark, wire was made at Altena, Lüdenscheid, and Iserlohn. After Sweden curtailed the export of *osmund* (bar iron), iron was imported from the Siegerland and the first blast-furnace foundry was established at Sundwig about the middle of the sixteenth century. Production was specialized very early in the Mark: Lüdenscheid, where most of the *osmund* hammers were found, produced the unfinished articles; more delicate articles were made at Altena, while Iserlohn concentrated on turning out fine wire. The manufacture of swords and daggers at Solingen in the county of Berg was important, not least in creating a demand for iron from the Siegerland.

Thuringia's iron-works were concentrated in the country of Schmalkalden. The ore of this region contained manganese and was therefore well suited to the manufacture of steel. It had long been famous as a producer of excellent knives and scissors. Suhl, a village in southern Thuringia which became a town in 1527, was famous for a race of craftsmen who specialized in making muskets. From 1530 these were produced by a system of manufacture based on a carefully organized division of labour.

Harz iron was worked in the county of Stolberg and in the lordship of Blankenburg-Elbingerode. At the end of the fifteenth century Elizabeth, Countess of Stolberg, had founded the iron industry of Gittelde and Grund near the Iberg, rich in iron ore. In the 1520s immigrant miners from Joachimstal struck iron at Andreasberg and the mining towns of Wildemann (1529), Zellerfeld and Lauthenthal (1532) sprang up. Duke Julius of Braunschweig, who ruled from 1568, did much to encourage mines and foundries: a man gifted with the qualities of both organizer and merchant, he saw how mining in the Oberharz could be modernized.

By the second half of the sixteenth century, twenty-six iron forge hammers were at work in Schwarzenberg and Krottendorf in the Saxon mountains. They sent their crude iron to Annaberg, Zwickau and Schneeberg for further processing and manufacture. Weapons were a speciality of the industries of the coastal region between Hamburg and Lübeck.

The most important iron-mining area of southern Germany was the region of Amberg and Sulzbach in the upper Palatinate. Of the 30,000 tons of iron which Germany produced annually, 10,000 came from this area. Industrial development was far advanced: mines went down to depths of 100–200 metres and in the fifteenth century two hundred iron hammers were at work. Towards the end of the sixteenth century the number dwindled but the region remained important.

Patricians and merchants from Amberg, Sulzbach, Nuremberg and Regensburg stepped in as entrepreneurs, following the unsuccessful attempts of the towns to manage the mines themselves. Plants to process the iron were established in Nuremberg, Regensburg and Ulm, partly employing Styrian steel. Iron industries producing for export existed at Schwäbisch Gmünd, Rottweil and Wangen (Allgäu).

It is astonishing how widely iron was mined and worked in central Europe. The industry was in fact one of the main supports of the flourishing German economy in early modern times. If the annual production of Europe as a whole in the first half of the sixteenth century is estimated at 60,000–100,000 tons, Germany accounted for a main part.

In Austria also the sixteenth century saw the rise of a relatively advanced iron industry. Here the unit of production was larger and the technology superior to the simpler, peasant iron industry centred round Hüttenberg in Carinthia. Styria borrowed some of its innovations from Brescia (see below), and a variety of hammers was used to turn out a wide range of iron products – soft iron, steel, bar iron, rod iron, plate and wire. The entire system called for an increasing volume of capital, which was provided by the capitalist iron merchants of Leoben and Steyr. The Styrian industry was in fact dominated by Steyr capital by the mid sixteenth century.

Only one large enterprise existed in the region of the eastern Alps: the *Waffenschmiede* (armour works) of the Pögl family at Thörl (near Aflenz) in the region of Bruck and Leoben. Sebastian Pögl was one of the most active gun-founders for the Emperor Maximilian. He was at once industrial entrepreneur and merchant and after his death (about 1528) his son, Sebald, continued the enterprise. A centre for the production of scythes was Kirchdorf-Micheldorf with an output of about 800,000 scythes in 36 smithies towards 1670.

On the southern fringe of the Alps iron production was concentrated in the region of Brescia and Bergamo and on the isle of Elba. The centre of arms manufacture, the Bresciano Gardone (Val Trompia) reached its zenith of technology and production in the mid sixteenth century. In the first half of the eighteenth century after a century of decline there still existed, in the Bresciano and the Bergamasco, several small enterprises. But in general north Italian mining and metallurgy, which earlier had instructed central and east Europe, remained the most retarded sector of industry throughout the eighteenth century.

In eastern central Europe iron was produced in Moravia, in the Zips and in Slovakia. In Bohemia the mines and forges of Brdy suffered during the Thirty Years War, but afterwards their production recovered. In the Balkans only the mines of Samokov in Bulgaria were of any importance. In Transylvania too the Habsburgs established a few iron-works. In Poland a few minor *Rennfeuer* iron-works existed – a hammer and a smithy driven by water-power. Free entrepreneurs from the towns and even men of peasant origin hired these works from the local landowner. Often they also ran a mill and a farm and therefore had free workers whom they were able to pay in part with small gifts of land. The number of workers could rise to as many as 30 and the specialization of the labour force was highly developed. In the course of the sixteenth century, iron production came to be concentrated in the region between Wielun and Olkusz, lying in the hills around Cracow and Censochova – with thirty-five works in 1577 – and in the hills north of Kielce, with sixty-four works.

Towards the close of the century *Stücköfen* and blast furnaces were introduced, mostly prompted by the needs of war. Stefan Bathory gave a franchise to Georg Langner to install a 'hammer-forge' near Stuhm in 1577. In 1598 the brothers Cacci from Bergamo established iron-works on the estates of the bishop of Cracow near Kielce and in the first half of the seventeenth century at least two blast furnaces were working there. In 1620 the Crown Grand Marshal Mikolaj Wolski established two furnaces at Panki and Lazioc near Censtochova. A blast furnace was also built at Halicz by Andrzej Potocki and probably another existed among the eighteen forges of the Ataman Stanislaw Koniecpolski in the Teterew in the Ukraine. But the demobilization of the Polish army and the economic and political decline of Poland in the second half of the seventeenth century left these iron-works in ruins.

In Russia, iron craftsmanship was in decay from the end of the Middle Ages: iron was imported through Novgorod and was worked in the villages of the hinterland. Ivan the Terrible tried to stimulate mining and iron production with the help of western immigrants, and in the 1550s craftsmen and miners were attracted from England, while in 1554 Hans Stitte from Goslar brought German iron-masters to Russia. In 1558 the tsar gave a privilege to the Stroganov family allowing them to exploit the iron deposits of the Kama region and in 1574 they received the right to mine iron and other metals in Siberia. Lack of capital and technical specialists seems to have impeded its exploitation. In 1569 a so-called 'English Company' received the right to mine iron and to establish works on the border of the Wytchegda. Other concessions were granted on the borders of the Sotchuna. In 1628 German prospectors discovered iron deposits in the region of Irbit and established the first blast furnace in Tula. In 1632 the Dutchman Vinius received the monopoly of iron-working and a cash grant on condition that he should live in Tula and teach the Russians how to work iron. Vinius developed the Tula or Gorodisce works. Two of them had blast furnaces and two were forges. During the 1650s more plants were established on the Skniga near Kašira: the entrepreneurs were the Netherlanders Marselis and Akkema. Netherlanders also hired the smelting-works of the *boyar* Miroslavskij and built another blast furnace on the Ugodka. Hans Kilburger, a German, worked yet another near Moscow. Thus, Russian iron production bore the clear stamp of immigrant enterprise and technology. With the aid of its west European specialists, Russia could even rival Swedish production by the late seventeenth century.

Peter the Great established a large number of iron-works in the Urals and in Siberia, as in 1697 at Vierkotur and Tobolsk in Siberia and, between 1699 and 1701, at Neviansk and Kamensk in the central Urals. In 1693 a new plant was established at Katchinsky near Tula, while that of Olonetz was re-established in 1703. In 1705 yet another works was founded at Sestrabesk near St Petersburg. Production developed so satisfactorily that after 1716 Russia began to export iron. When the war with Sweden was over Peter turned his attentions to the increase of exports. Thanks to the initiative of the Demidov and the state officials Tatichev and Hennin, between 1722 and 1724 five new works were created in the Urals, four of them producing copper. The Demidov themselves established four works between 1716 and 1725, including one in the basin of Kuznetz. In Siberia, partly with the labour of Swedish prisoners of war, a steel works was established at Irkutsk. Finally there were thirty-eight foundries in the 'government' of Kazan, the same number in the 'government' of St Petersburg, thirty-nine in that of Moscow and seventy on the Volga and the Oka. No precise production figures have survived, but in 1718 the total production seems to have reached something more than 25,000 tons.

Though numerous, these Russian works were ill-provided with tools and specialists and the quality of production necessarily remained low. Until 1730, government initiative predominated, but the subsequent expansion of private enterprise was favoured by the discovery of the rich deposits of Blagoletz in 1735. A German, Schönburg, was nominated Director of Mines. A commision, instituted by him, advocated the transfer of all works on private demesnes to private entrepreneurs. In 1739 the works of Blagoletz were taken over by a company to which Schönburg, the brothers Biron and a Polish merchant belonged. The other iron works of the Urals came into the hands of master smiths or of foreigners. After the disappearance of Biron, the old system of state control was re-established for a time, but in 1754 the state-controlled works were again sold. Until 1750 the annual export of Russian iron exceeded 19,000 tons.

In Norway iron mining began in the 1540s in the region of Oslo and Skien. Here the works of Baerum, Hakadal and Fossum prospered. Other iron-works were to be found in Barbu near Arendal (the later iron-works of Nes), on Hadeland, at Eidsvoll and Eiker. Most were run ostensibly for royal profit but output and profits alike seem to have been small and the royal interest dwindled. From 1624 a private iron company with Danish capital took over iron mining in Norway, and during the 1630s privileges were granted to other entrepreneurs.

Blast furnaces to produce iron from iron ores were introduced in Sweden, as in other countries, in the middle of the fifteenth century.

Some progress was made in raising the quality of wrought iron, especially by the German smiths called in by Gustav Vasa. *Osmund* (a Swedish form of malleable iron) already known in the Middle Ages, seems to have been produced in quantity only after 1540. At the end of the sixteenth century a Dutchman, William van Wijk, introduced new techniques from the Netherlands; at first in the employment of Duke Charles, he later moved into the services of King John III. Most notably at Dannemora, the so-called 'French furnaces' superseded the *mull-timmershytta*,[1] and the production of *vallonjärn*[2] began, becoming the basis of steel production. In rivalry with the iron industry of Uppland (especially Dannemora where most iron was produced), Duke Charles endeavoured to develop an iron industry in Värmland on his own estates, but Värmland did not achieve pre-eminence before the first half of the seventeenth century.

Until 1600 more *osmund* than bar-iron was exported, reflecting the fact that only half as much bar-iron as *osmund* was produced. In the course of the seventeenth century Swedish *osmund* lost its earlier importance, although small individual factories continued to produce it.

The export values of Swedish iron were always higher than those of copper. The proportion was about 50:30 and together they represented about four-fifths of Sweden's total exports: as the export of copper went down, that of iron rose. At the beginning of the *Frihetstid*[3] the export of iron represented about three-quarters of the total value whereas copper was down to a tenth. In 1720 Sweden produced 32,600 tons of iron, rising to 51,000 tons in 1739. By the middle of the century Swedish production may have represented 35 per cent of Europe's total output of bar-iron. The most important market was England: at the end of the reign of Charles XII over 80 per cent of English iron imports came from Sweden, representing about 40 per cent of the iron which England needed in that time. But even this 40 per cent was only about 4 per cent of England's total imports of all kinds: the new 'Iron Age' had not yet begun. Sweden's importance as an iron producer lay in the allied facts that she had huge forests which could furnish fuel; that her iron ore was purer than that of any other country; and, finally, that her production techniques were among the best in Europe. When Colbert wanted to modernize French iron-working and cannon-production he chose immigrant Swedish smiths to provide the technical assistance. English iron-masters tried to copy Swedish methods. Until the eighteenth century steel represented only a small part of Swedish

[1] A foundry working by the combination of earth and wood.
[2] Cf. p. 488. *Vallonjärn* was a new kind of iron produced according to methods first developed in the bishopric of Liège and Namur.
[3] The liberal period beginning after the death of Charles XII.

production – perhaps 10 to 12 per cent of Sweden's total iron exports.

In the course of this remarkable expansion, Värmland became the most important Swedish iron province. Statistics of the tax on the forges in 1695 shows that 22 per cent of the total iron production came from Värmland, 17 per cent from Närke, 16 per cent from Västmanland, 14 per cent from Uppland, 7½ per cent from Dalarna and 6 per cent from Gästrikland. Göteborg acted as entrepôt for the export of Värmland's iron.

The iron-works of this period (*bruk*) required a large stock of capital. They were directed by *brukspatroner* – men regarded as the equals of noblemen, and set apart from the *bergsmänner* (miners) who were regarded as mere peasants. Capital for the *bruks* came from merchants, some of them foreigners who bought Swedish iron from export houses generally in Stockholm or Göteborg, paid a part in advance or else provided continuous credit. As they extended credit to the iron-works, these in turn allowed credit to their workers, to the coal-working peasants and the carters. Some of the *bruks* produced cannon and other ordnance to serve the needs of the Swedish army, but small arms were also exported. Others, like Christopher Polhem[1] at Stjärnsund, operated a workshop which turned out household and agricultural articles.

(3) GLASS AND MINERALS

Venetian glass manufacturing, the most celebrated in Europe, was concentrated on the island of Murano where the register of 1604 mentioned 173 families specializing in it. Production was highly diversified – from bottles to precious vases, mirrors and window glass. In spite of attempts by the Republic to maintain a monopoly based on technological secrecy, Venetian glassmaking techniques spread to western, central and northern Europe after 1550.

The number of French glassworks has been estimated, surely optimistically, at 2,000 or more. Most of them were probably short-lived. Large sheets of clear glass were cast for the first time in Normandy. A Norman glassmaker, Lucas de Nehou, introduced the method in the St Gobain works in the second half of the seventeenth century. In the Low Countries the bishopric of Liège had a well developed *verrerie* and in Germany glassmaking was practised in the Black Forest, in Thuringia, in Hesse, the Weserbergland, and the Harz, as well as in the Erzgebirge. Scarcity of wood limited the number of glassworks in any one region. The mountains of east Bavaria, one of the most important centres of production, had four glassworks in the fifteenth

[1] See also p. 488.

century and ten in the sixteenth, but only five new factories were added in the seventeenth. In the first half of the eighteenth century four more works were built. Bohemia gradually took the lead as the principal glass producer, and Bohemian crystal came to be imitated even in Italy. In 1739 Braiti, who introduced Bohemian crystal glassmaking to the Venetians, was granted the right to establish a furnace not on Murano but in Venice itself. The mirror-factory which was established at Erlangen by Freyesleben in 1744 also worked with Bohemian glass. Many mercantilist programmes put glass high on the list of favoured luxury products. The St Gobain glassworks near Paris and the establishment of Peter the Great are the tangible consequences of such policies.

Sultan Selim I profited from his victory over the Persians by obliging Persian ceramicists to settle in Istanbul (and Iznik) in 1514; hence a rapidly successful *fayence*[1] industry in Turkey. The wave of new buildings which arose in the capital, Istanbul, encouraged the expansion of the production of glazed tiles. Moorish Spain too had an old tradition of lustrous ceramics, but this decayed after the conquest of Granada and the final expulsion of the Moors at the beginning of the seventeenth century. Thereafter lustrous ceramics were manufactured primarily in Valencia. Simple household ware was made in Talavera de la Reina in Castile from the end of the sixteenth until the eighteenth century. Dominated at first by the influence of Italian *fayence*, it later took to imitating east Asiatic motifs. In 1726/7 the count of Aranda founded the factory of Alcora where production soon rivalled the workshops of Talavera. In southern Spain the production of *azulejos* (blue ware) was widely diffused, the most important centre being Seville, while Valencia predominated in pottery and lustre ware. Here, as well as around Seville, many workshops were set up outside the town, the most famous being in Manises and Paterna. In Portugal too, the production of *azulejos* was widespread.

The earliest Italian centres for the production of *majolica* – Florence and Faenza – were joined by Caffagiolo and Castel Durante, and, for a short time, by Siena. The Casa Pirota of Faenza became the most renowned. In 1528 the greatest master of Castel Durante, Nicola Pellipario, followed his son Guido Fontana to Urbino which, with its istoriati-painting, became a famous centre of ceramics.

Venetian ceramics were so renowned that in 1520 Alfonso I of Este at Ferrara ordered forty-two jars for his pharmacy, the making of which was supervised by Titian. The best-known Venetian master of the second half of the century was Maestro Domenico.

The ornamental ware, *bianco di Faenza*, in the second half of the

---

[1] *Fayence, faenza, majolica* (from Majorca) and *aardewerk* (Dutch) were all local forms of earthenware as distinguished from later forms of translucent porcelain.

century inaugurated a new type of pottery, and was acclaimed at the courts of France and Bavaria. The thriving commerce of the Faenza and Urbino ceramicists led other towns such as Turin, Genoa, Savona, Albissola and Castelli, and then towns in France and Bohemia to imitate their production. On the mainland of Venetia, especially at Padua, Ottoman ceramics were imitated. Towards the end of the seventeenth century majolica ware enjoyed a late revival at Castelle in the Abruzzi and San Quirico, Bassano and Siena became centres of the Castelli ware. Only when porcelain was invented, and with it the new fashion for *chinoiseries*, did majolica production atrophy.

Meanwhile new techniques of ceramics spread to the countries north of the Alps. From the end of the seventeenth century, Delft ware, a kind of *fayence* suitable for the painting of Asian motifs, flourished in the Netherlands. In France ceramics were produced at Rouen and Paris (St Cloud and Sèvres). The real 'Chinese' hard porcelain was independently invented by a Saxon, Johann Friedrich Böttger, and provided the basis for the establishment of the Meissen porcelain factory in 1705. From then onwards it became a matter of aristocratic etiquette for the German princes to imitate Meissen porcelain in the factories on their own estates. With the rise of tobacco-smoking, a special industry to make clay-pipes grew up, centred on Gouda in Holland, where 374 pipe-makers lived in 1751.

House-building in Europe created a brisk demand for supplies of stones and bricks, especially after 1400 as wooden construction was overtaken by stone-built houses on a large scale. In mountainous regions there was no lack of specialized stone-industries – such as the quarries of Carrara in Italy or the quarries of Bentheim, the Weserbergland and the Baumberge in Germany. The production of mill-stones was an old export industry of the region around Andernach. The lime-trade of Helgoland, Segeberg with its famous *Kalkberg*, and of the isle of Gotland, which exported limestone and sandstone as well, was important to the building industry. On the great plains, in Lombardy, the Netherlands and northern Germany, bricks provided a substitute for stone. Brickmaking was a widespread industry in Gelderland and Overijssel. Part of its output was exported to the Baltic region; even more to England. Brick production was also stimulated by the improved techniques of siege warfare which made it necessary to repair decayed town walls – often building in brick rather than stone – and to construct new citadels within key-towns. Over large areas of France, Belgium and western Germany quarried slate was used for covering roofs.

(4) CHEMICAL INDUSTRIES

Many branches of industrial production depended upon chemical processes. Bleaching and dyeing, tanning and papermaking were among them. Some metal working – the cementation of lead with copper ore, and the elimination of cinnabar from quicksilver ore – also embodied chemical knowledge. The manufacture of glass, soap, gunpowder, paints, varnishes, glues and sugar all depended on essentially chemical reactions and processes.

Venice, Marseilles, and Seville were major centres of soapmaking, all three cities enjoying a good supply of olive oil. Sulphur from Iceland, Sweden or Sicily, and saltpetre, which came from the Baltic, were necessary for producing gunpowder, and powder-mills were established at places where transport was easy and water supply plentiful, as in the neighbourhood of Hamburg, Lübeck or Nuremberg.

(5) WOOD AND COAL

Wood was a vital commodity in all branches of industry, for mining as well as for finishing processes. It was used in huge quantities for firing the furnaces. In iron-producing regions such as the Siegerland, special *Hauberggenossenschaften*[1] existed in order to cut the young trees at an age of about 15–20 years and burn them to charcoal, which was sold as far as the Sauerland and the Mark. In the regions of oak woods, especially in the Ardennes and in northwest Germany, the bark was used for dressing leather. For glassmaking and for dyeing, wood was burned to potash in the Bayerischer Wald and on the southern shores of the Baltic.

Two commodities necessary for shipbuilding and ship-fitting were tar and pitch, and during the sixteenth and seventeenth centuries production of these developed on a large scale in Sweden and Finland; they were joined in the eighteenth century by Russia and, on a smaller scale, by Norway. The Netherlands and other parts of western Europe created an insatiable demand for timber for both housebuilding and shipbuilding. During the sixteenth and seventeenth centuries tree trunks began to be floated down the Rhine, the Danube and other rivers. Timber from the Baltic and Scandinavia was particularly important, and from the sixteenth century onwards a special timber-processing industry developed, with water-mills for sawing the trunks into beams and boards. In the Netherlands, especially on the Zaan (Zaandam was famous as the 'village of carpenters' visited by Peter the Great), and near Rotterdam and Amsterdam, the great sawmills were a familiar sight.

[1] Associations for timber production.

In central Europe the provision of combustible materials to the various industries was already creating difficulties by 1500. Governments were obliged to place restrictions on the felling of trees and woods for the forges and foundries. At the same time serious efforts were made to replace charcoal by coal, even in the Harz and the Erzgebirge. From the thirteenth to the middle of the sixteenth centuries only the coal mines of the region of Liège and Aachen seem to have been intensively exploited. Then the movement gathered pace rapidly. During the first half of the sixteenth century the output of coal in the Liège region tripled or quadrupled in response to the need to furnish fuel for the factories working iron and other metals in and around Liège, and Liège coal began to vie with coal from the Tyne for export markets. In the Aachen region as well as in the Ruhr, coal was widely used for industrial purposes.

From the reign of Elizabeth I England steadily moved into first place as the largest producer of coal. By the early seventeenth century coal was being widely used in the south Midlands, Yorkshire and south Lancashire, the region of Bristol and the Forest of Dean, especially in the manufacture of glass, bricks, tiles, the extraction of salt, soap-boiling and many other processes where heat was necessary. The expansion of the manufacture of alum on the Yorkshire coast depended on a supply of coal. The coal trade from Newcastle increased in spectacular fashion. In 1563/4 about 33,000 tons of coal were shipped; by 1634 shipments had risen to 452,000 tons. The coal production of Sunderland furnished an additional 69,000 tons. Between a quarter and a third of these exports went to London. In 1580 London's import of 'sea-coal' had been less than 15,000 tons; after the Civil War it had risen to about 323,000 tons.

Coal was also mined in southern Scotland, Wales and other parts of England. Production approached two million tons annually – about five times as much as the total produced by the rest of the world. About the turn of the seventeenth century Savery and Newcomen made their steam-pumping inventions (1698 and 1710–12), and Newcomen's coal-fired steam-engine was first put to work in 1712 near Dudley Castle in order to pump water from the coal-pits. Within a short period these machines were introduced into mines in many parts of England and on the continent too. Their swift adoption testifies to the high development of the coal mines of the region of Liège, Mons and Charleroi: the first of Newcomen's pump-designs, first used in England in 1705, was established near Liège by 1720, in the region of Charleroi in 1725, and near Mons in 1734.

(6) TEXTILES

(i) *The British Isles*

Manufacture was traditionally concentrated in old towns like Coventry, but already in the high Middle Ages a good part of the weaving and finishing processes had migrated to the country. There were two techniques of manufacture: 'worsted' fabrics were made with combed wool, being neither fulled nor raised; true 'woollens' were fulled, raised and sheared. During the sixteenth century, worsted fabrics and woollens were both in decay in areas such as Suffolk and Kent, but three regions – the West Country, the north and East Anglia – specialized in their production. In the west, and especially in the southern Cotswolds, broadcloths, kerseys and other cheaper grades of cloth were manufactured. Kerseys were also made in the West Riding of Yorkshire, particularly around Leeds. In Westmorland the famous 'kendals' were made. Professor Eleanor Carus-Wilson has stressed that it was the use of water-power which gave England's rural cloth production its superiority over that of the Netherlands.[1] Flemish and Brabant cloth workers who emigrated to England brought with them the techniques of making the 'new draperies' – light fabrics of the worsted type – which took root in Norfolk, Essex and Suffolk and made them the centre of the revived cloth industry. In Essex, 'bays' were manufactured at Colchester, Braintree and Docking. Norwich 'stuffs' could be fine worsted or combined with silk or cotton; Devon concentrated on serge. While exports of conventional woollens declined in the second half of the sixteenth century, those of the new light worsteds steadily rose.

A second branch of the English textile industry was based on the combined use of cotton and flax to make fustians, bombazines and inkles. It was younger than the wool industry and grew up in the sixteenth century, probably stimulated by refugee weavers. These new processes took root in the countryside in the same way as the wool industry, especially in Lancashire, round Bolton and Manchester, and in parts of Dorset, Cheshire and Derbyshire. Mercers or linendrapers brought the raw material – cotton – from the Turkey merchants of London. Much of this new production was organized on the putting-out system, but many independent masters in the countryside also employed their own workers. Only slowly, towards 1750, did dependence on the merchant living in the town become universal.

Ireland produced friezes and other cheap goods which found a

---

[1] E. Carus-Wilson, 'The Woollen Industry', in *The Cambridge Economic History* II, 409 f.

market in the American plantations and the Levant, but after the
passing of an Act of Parliament in 1699 they could only be exported
through England. From the early eighteenth century the manufacture
of many types of cotton goods sprang up in Spitalfields and Lancashire.
Rough cotton checks were followed and paralleled by calico for
printing.

In Scotland and Ireland the linen trade developed strongly in the
countryside in the course of the eighteenth century, until it was producing high quality products able to rival those of continental manufacturers. The majority of the Irish linen-weavers were small tenants
who because of the inadequate size of their holding were obliged to eke
out a living by some domestic industrial activity. The low wages for
which they worked contributed to the stiff competition the Irish linen
industry offered to other, older-established centres of production in
Germany and the Low Countries.

In Scotland the Board of Trustees for Manufactures, operating after
1727, did much to promote the expansion of the local linen industry.
Large quantities of yarn were exported to Ireland and England. Coarse
Scotch linen was in demand for the plantations, and Fife, Perth and
Glasgow became leading production centres. The Bounty Act of 1742
aimed to stimulate exports, and in 1746 the British Linen Company
was incorporated with the same object. In 1741 4,858,190 yards of linen
were stamped – more than double the production of 1728 – and in 1750
total output reached 7,752,540 yards.

Stocking knitting was widespread in the seventeenth and eighteenth
centuries in more backward regions, such as the north Yorkshire dales
and the hinterland of Aberdeen, and the village knitting industry was a
familiar sight in parts of Dorset and Somerset.

Before 1500 London virtually monopolized the English silk manufacture and long remained its principal centre. Here the 'throwsters'
who twisted the fibres for the warp were incorporated in 1629, and
skilled Huguenot immigrants supplied a further stimulus in 1685.
Outside the London area, offshoots began to flourish in Kent, Essex and
(for ribbons) in Coventry. After Lombe's invention, silk-throwing
moved to places where water-power was available; manual throwing,
however, continued in Spitalfields.

(ii) *The Low Countries*

During the Middle Ages the southern Netherlands had become one of
the two most highly industrialized regions of Europe. Textile production was concentrated in Flanders, Hainault, Brabant and the valley
of the Meuse. Early activity was predominantly urban, but the expansion of the market and the conservatism of the gilds acted as pressures on

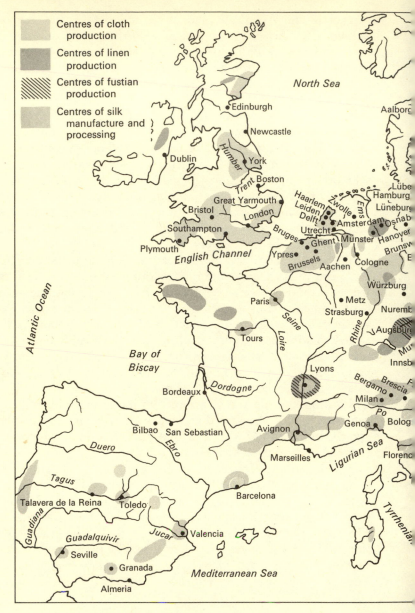

Fig. 8. Centres of textile production.

industry to migrate and settle in the countryside. The religious and political troubles of the sixteenth century generated further pressures leading to the migration of merchants and artisans to England, the northern Netherlands and to Germany. When the tumults calmed down, the manufacture of *lakens* (broadcloths) recovered in the villages around Lille, and in the region of Nieuwkerke and Ypres the textile industry maintained itself into the eighteenth century.

Cotton manufacture and mixed textiles survived the devastation of its centre, Hondschoote, in 1582, and developed in the region of Bruges and in small towns such as Poperinghe. The flax industry maintained a steady expansion, and found good markets in the Iberian ports in place of the old outlets of central Flanders (Tielt, Roselaare, Itzegem and Eeklo). The peasant producers mostly furnished their yarn and linen to Bruges, Ghent, Oudenaarde or Courtrai. After the wars of 1689–1713, production recovered again. By 1765 the magistrates of Ghent estimated the total Flemish linen production at 100,000 pieces – probably a good deal below the true output – noting with satisfaction that the greater part of their output was exported to France, England or Germany. Throughout the seventeenth century the linen production of the southern Netherlands was totally dependent on the bleacheries of the north Netherlands, at Haarlem especially, but in 1700, a big bleachery was opened at Borgerhout, just outside Antwerp. Others followed.

Another trade which employed as much labour in the towns as in the countryside was lace-making. The finer pieces were worked in the town, while the female population of the countryside produced the coarser articles which were sold in the country or exported to Spain and Spanish America.

The loss of the Spanish Netherlands was the gain of the lands of the bishop of Liège: confronted with the difficulties of exporting to Belgium, the Liégeois drapery of Verviers looked for export markets to the east. It was fortunate that in the country of Herve (Entre-Vesdre-et-Meuse) the transition from arable farming to cattle-breeding freed surplus labour for industry. The Verviers drapery was thereby enabled to capture and maintain, within the next two centuries, a leading place in the European textile industry with an annual production of about 22,000 pieces. During the later seventeenth and eighteenth centuries, though many workers were certainly attracted to the Leiden textile industries, the regions of Liège and of Limburg enjoyed a decisive advantage in their lower wages and in the protectionist policies of the prince-bishop. In the mid eighteenth century, 25,000 artisans were estimated to be working in the drapery of the Vesdre.

The eastern Netherlands also produced linen, woven in Kampen, Deventer and Zutphen, partly for export through Deventer. These centres were joined later by the region of Twenthe, which imported flax from the Overkwartier of Guelders, the Rhineland and Westphalia. Venlo and Maastricht combined linen with their older cloth-industry, and exported to southern Germany as well as Westphalia. In Zeeland and Holland the cloth *drapery* developed into a leading export industry with special centres in Amsterdam, Leiden, Gouda and Haarlem, using English, Scotch and Spanish wool as raw material. For dyeing, *meekrap* (madder) and *waid* (woad) were used. *Meekrap* (a red dye) was cultivated chiefly in Zeeland, but it was also imported from other areas, such as southern France. *Waid* (a blue dye) was imported from Limburg and Jülich, indigo and other dyes from overseas. The industries therefore were heavily dependent on international trading channels.

Its technology and enterprise revivified by the immigration from the South Netherlands, the Leiden textile industry enjoyed growing prosperity from the end of the sixteenth century. By 1600 the annual output of Leiden rose to 40,000–50,000 pieces and reached a peak of 144,000 in 1664. Initially it preserved its former character of a town trade and only later were parts of the process put out to villages in Brabant. The bleaching industry of Haarlem likewise retained a markedly urban character.

Other textile manufacturers diversified the already varied industrial economy of the Low Countries. In the south, tapestry making was concentrated in Brussels, Bruges, Antwerp and other Flemish and Brabant towns. In the north, Amsterdam developed silk weaving, while outside Utrecht Jakob van Mollen established his silk mill in 1689.

(iii) *France*

In France textile industries were widespread in the countryside, but production was less buoyant than in England and the Netherlands. In the course of the sixteenth century expansion was most characteristic of the established regions of drapery: in Poitou and Picardy, round Orleans, in Berry and the Languedoc – everywhere based on the putting-out system. Later the Beauce, Sologne and Gâtenais developed their own industry. A new worsted textile branch, the *sayetterie*, began to flourish at Amiens and its *plat-pays* in the later sixteenth century and centres of cloth manufacture developed at Louviers, Sedan, Elbeuf, Abbeville. Flax and canvas-weaving were widely practised in Brittany, Normandy, lower Maine and Burgundy. Cotton manufacture took root in the region of Lyons, later spread to Normandy, the Vosges, and the Orléanais.

Lace was a speciality of the Bourbonnais, Auvergne, Velay, Alençon and parts of Normandy. Silk was woven and spun in Touraine, lower Languedoc, in the region of Nîmes, in Vivarais, and in Provence.

Lyons was the busiest silk-weaving centre north of the Alps. Henri IV and his mercantilist *valet de chambre*, Laffemas, paid special attention to measures encouraging silk cultivation and weaving, and Colbert's even more ambitious programme of industrial expansion favoured imitations of the Netherlands tapestry manufactures – the famous *gobelins*.

(iv) *Spain*

During the first half of the sixteenth century Spain exported a good deal of its wool to Flanders and to Italy. The rest was worked in the country itself especially in and around Segovia, Cuenca, Córdoba, Baeza and Ubeda. The production of cloth before 1548 already exceeded 3,000 pieces. Demand in Spain and the Indies grew, while the export of wool to the Netherlands declined with the troubles of the sixties. Between 1584 and 1589 the annual production of Segovia averaged between 12,500 and 13,049 pieces, rising to a peak of over 16,000. The improved market in Spain and the Indies continued to expand (according to Ruiz-Martin) until 1590. The example of Juan de Villa Ximena illustrates the concentration of production after 1570: Villa Ximena had more than 100 employees in his factory and occupied a further 1,000 people as spinners within a radius of 15 leagues.[1]

A structural crisis struck Spain's woollen production in 1586 and afterwards, but real decadence did not set in before 1650. In Cuenca production was already declining at the end of the sixteenth century, but at Córdoba, Baeza and Ubeda output actually increased. Here the entrepreneurial centre was Córdoba, which had a high percentage of new Christian population. At its peak in 1580 and 1581 the production of Córdoba cloth exceeded 18,000 pieces; at Ubeda and Baeza it never exceeded 8,000. This level was sustained until 1585, when regression set in even faster than in Castile. Was this because capital at Seville was orientated more towards commerce than towards industry?[2] Whatever the reasons, the seventeenth century saw the cloth industries of Spain in ruins. Efforts to revive the cloth industries of Segovia and Valladolid in 1733 and 1737 were unsuccessful; on the other hand the production of Béjar grew, thanks to the protection given by the Duke of Béjar to Flemish specialists. In 1744, 145 looms were at work there.

The cotton industry enjoyed the patronage of the Bourbon government. This certainly helped to create internal and colonial markets, but cannot by itself account for the rise of the cotton industry in Catalonia.

---

[1] Felipe Ruiz-Martin, 'Rasgos estructurales de Castilla en tiempo de Carlos V', in *Moneda y Credito*, xcvi (Madrid, 1966), 91 ff.

[2] See e.g. Ruiz-Martin, 'La empresa capitalista y la indústria textil castellana durante los siglos XVI y XVII', in *Third International Conference of Economic History at Munich 1965, Communications*.

Here the commercial enterprise of those groups which were interested in exporting textiles in return for imports of colonial products was of crucial importance. Like contemporary governments in France and England, Philip V prohibited the importation and sale of silks and other textiles from China and other parts of Asia in 1717 and 1718. The prohibition was re-enacted in 1728 and extended to colonial linen and all cotton textiles coming from Asia or imitated in Europe. This protection encouraged immigrant French entrepreneurs to establish workshops in Barcelona and thence the manufacture of cottons spread all over Catalonia. In the 1730s we find in Barcelona the factory of Esteban Canals making 'Indian textiles'. In the next few years others followed, some of them situated outside Barcelona. Not all of them prospered: Campans and Company at Mataro, for example, went bankrupt for lack of technicians and adequate organization, though in 1760 10,000 Spanish workers were said to be still engaged in cotton production.

The manufacture of hats from Peruvian *vicuña* wool seems to have developed during the first half of the eighteenth century. A royal decree of 1758 ordered that half of all cargoes of hats going to America had to be of Spanish origin. Hat making flourished in Madrid, in some towns of Old Castile (Valladolid, Zamora) and in the coastal regions of Barcelona, Valencia, Seville, San Lucar de Barrameda and Coruña. One of the most important establishments was the factory of San Fernando near Madrid.

In contrast to Spain's burgeoning wool production in the sixteenth century there was a marked depression in the production of linen and hemp products (like sailcloth), essential for fitting out ships and for the American market.

The sixteenth century boom in silk spinning and weaving in the kingdom of Granada, was the work of entrepreneurs from Genoa, Toledo and elsewhere. The industry reached its apogee as early as 1546; about 1550 production was said to have reached 135,000 lb made by 40,000 people living in 335 towns and villages. The silk weavers of Valencia survived and even grew in numbers into the eighteenth century, while those of Toledo, Barcelona and Granada diminished: in 1724 Valencia had 2,400 looms and 3,400 in 1750; Granada's 1,000 looms of 1724 had dwindled to 200 in 1750. Murcia too decayed little by little. The silk industry in Catalonia and Seville was more or less moribund. Ambitious projects to establish great new factories in Talavera de la Reina and Madrid (1719-35), made little headway. Economic recovery in Spain was uphill work.

(v) *Germany*

The old centres of wool weaving were concentrated in the lower Rhine region: at Aachen, Düren, Münstereifel and Cologne. Parallel to the rise of woollen drapery in the bishopric of Liège during the first half of the eighteenth century, drapery production in Monschau spread into the countryside. A second cloth region extended from the middle Rhine to Hesse. Cloth was also made in various imperial towns of Swabia and in Nuremberg; in Bavaria the centre was Munich where 120 *loderer* (cloth masters) employed some 3,000 spinners in the town and the neighbouring country in 1608. Brunswick, Stendal and Salzwedel in the Altmark, Kottbus in the Lausitz, and Görlitz in Silesia, were famous cloth-making centres. As in England and France, it was Netherlands emigrants who brought the technique of the 'new draperies' to Germany as well as the arts of making lace, carpets, and the embroidery of silk and stockings. These and other textile industries were to be found in Wesel, Bremen, Hamburg, Frankfurt, Frankenthal, Gera and Meuselwitz and later Krefeld.

At Calw in southern Germany a *Zeughandlungskompagnie* developed in a region poor in soil but with a long-established tradition of sheep farming. Here, towards the end of the sixteenth century, far-sighted dyers introduced the putting-out system into the cloth manufacture. The early seventeenth century saw 500–600 clothmakers at work. In 1622 fifteen entrepreneurs agreed to amalgamate into a single company, and although the Thirty Years War caused a temporary disruption, the project was resumed again in 1650.

Flax spinning made substantial progress in Westphalia, lower Saxony, Swabia and east Germany, drawing its raw material supplies from a belt of lands near the north German coast where hemp too was grown. Coesfeld, Münster, Bielefeld, Minden and Herford were the putting-out centres of Westphalia, and it was also there that the institutions of supervision called *Leggen* (displays or inspections) were concentrated.[1] The *Leggen*, at first an urban institution, were later adopted by the territorial sovereigns throughout their territories. The first, in 1650, was organized by the Brandenburg government for the county of Tecklenburg. Others followed at Ibbenbüren, Lengerich and Westerkappeln. Osnabrück's linen industry enjoyed privileges dating from 1634 which were renewed after the war by the emperor.

In the county of Ravensberg the Great Elector tried to organize the *Leggezwang*[2] according to the Osnabrück system. In 1669 three *Leggen* were established for the *Löwend*[3] produced in the country. After the

[1] Literally, the bleaching ground.
[2] Obligation to present the linen wares at the display.   [3] Raw linen.

decree of 1718 which permitted free weaving in the countryside, peasant weaving of *klare Leinwand*[1] forged ahead; weaving in the towns (Bielefeld, Herford) declined – a parallel perhaps with developments in the woollen cloth industry in England.

The county of Lippe, in the seventeenth century, had *Leggen* in the towns of Lemgo, Salzufflen, Detmold, Blomberg and Horn. During the Thirty Years War they were destroyed and the countrypeople took up linen-trading themselves. Only in 1663 did Count Hermann Adolf order that all the towns should reintroduce the old *Legge* system, restricting the trade in linen to native merchants. The private *Leggen* were thereupon re-established: but this concession to private individuals failed to bring about any expansion of production.

Crucial to the quality of linen manufacture was the bleaching process. As with so many 'finishing' processes – dyeing, sugar refining, tobacco-cutting, to name only a few – the Dutch had effectively captured it along with the supply of much of the output of raw German linens. Local attempts to develop the necessary techniques in Germany nevertheless continued. In 1719 a bleaching works was established in the county of Ravensburg (Bielefeld) on the model of Warendorf at Milse. Bleachers were given grants in order to study the bleaching techniques employed in Holland and Ireland.

The part of Swabia famous for linens stretched from Lake Constance and the *Schwäbische Alb* to the Danube and Lech. Constance lost its predominance in cloths to St Gallen and the 'Great Company' of Ravensburg fell into decline. The towns of the Allgäu district maintained their reputation, especially for the production of fustians: Ulm, Biberach, Augsburg, Memmingen and Kaufbeuren. Then, towards the end of the sixteenth century, fustians went into decline and were replaced by linens, which commanded a wide overseas market. In the sixteenth century some 450 linen weavers working in surrounding towns and rural districts delivered their products to the *Schau*[2] at Ulm. Besides the linens of Ulm and Württemberg, Bavarian and Silesian linen was bleached here. Linen production was important in the Allgäu too: in 1610 5,000 pieces of bleached linen came on the market of Leutkirch. In 1612 Augsburg, the most important centre, had 3,024 weavers; but half a century later only 735 were left.

New production centres arose in competition with the earlier ones. In the first half of the sixteenth century fustian production was in full swing on the Fugger estates at Weissenhorn – almost at the gates of Ulm. In Württemberg, at the close of the century, Duke Friedrich I organized a weavers' gild at Urach and built a separate suburb for its members. To Urach he also granted the monopoly of bleaching in

[1] Fine linen.   [2] The same as *Legge* = display or inspection.

Württemberg. In 1600 a company was founded to handle linen trading, but it suffered losses during the Thirty Years War. In the eastern areas of central Germany, linen production advanced steadily. West Saxony first, then the remoter eastern districts of Lusatia and Silesia were concerned in this expanding production. Immigrant Swabian weavers helped to adapt the local craft to Swabian techniques, and dyed linens were encouraged at the expense of bleached linens. Despite this, most of the products were sent to south Germany to be dyed at Nuremberg. Low wages kept down the local consumption of this comparatively costly product.

Production was everywhere organized on the base of the putting-out system, usually through the collective delivery contract – i.e. purchase through a gild. An idea of the level of the production may be gathered from the fact that the great south German companies commanded capital of over 800,000 fl., while that of the Viatis and Peller of Nuremberg brought up the total capital fund to about one million fl. In west Saxony, east Saxony, upper and lower Lusatia and part of Silesia, 3,755 masters were at work, operating one or more looms apiece. If we include the weavers of the Bohemian towns – 630 masters – a yearly linen production to the value of 630,000–750,000 *thaler* was reached, not counting the linen produced by the villages and the coarser types of linen, nor the cotton goods and cloths which were produced in Thuringia, the county of Henneberg, the Meininger Oberland and in Vogtland.

Meanwhile Silesian linen production enjoyed an extraordinary development centred on Hirschberg and Jauer. In 1748/9 Silesia exported linen worth about 3½ million *thaler*. It was a heavy loss for the Habsburg economy when Frederick II of Prussia conquered the country.

Thanks to the privileges granted by the Duke of Berg in 1527 and the quality of the water of the river Wupper, Elberfeld and Barmen became centres for the trade in linen yarn which was brought from spinning centres as far off as Hesse-Kassel, Bielefeld-Minden, the country of Lippe, Paderborn, Göttingen-Hanover, Hildesheim and Braunschweig; after being bleached it was sold at Antwerp, later in Amsterdam, and in various German marts such as Cologne, Frankfurt, Bremen and Leipzig.

Meanwhile the weaving of linen ribbons grew. The Netherlands invention of the *Bandstuhl* (ribbon-loom) allowed the weaving of ribbons in several 'chains'. Cotton and silk were used as the new raw materials and from the end of the seventeenth century dyeing began. The invention of the *Riemengang*[1] by Johann Heinrich Borkenmühl of

[1] *Riemengang*: mechanically driven machinery for making round or flat straps, boot laces, shoe strings, etc.; a sort of braiding machine.

Barmen allowed an increased output of the famous Barmen products. Weaving was organized as a domestic industry in the Mark, but in the Wuppertal alone there were 300 linen weavers in 1740, and from 1738 the government allowed them to organize a gild.

In Wesel, Cologne, Frankfurt and Hamburg the Netherlands emigrants of the sixteenth century gave an important stimulus to silk-working. At Cologne in 1605 the manufacture of 'pasmentry' (braid) was organized into a gild which soon numbered 2,600 masters. Towards the middle of the seventeenth century Regensburg, Nuremberg, Frankfurt, Hanau, Strassburg and Hamburg forbade the use of ribbon mills, suggesting that in these towns some kind of silk industry was in existence. The restrictive policy enforced in Cologne drove entrepreneurs to emigrate to Deutz and Mülheim on the other side of the Rhine in the duchy of Berg. It was Cologne merchants who organized a general putting-out system there. Other techniques followed. Christoph Andreae and his sons established their own bleaching-works. Soon they were employing some 600 men handling various kinds of silk and cotton.

The most important centre of silk weaving in the Rhineland was Krefeld with a Protestant population partly made up of immigrants. During the eighteenth century the town supported a very active group of entrepreneurs, headed by the von der Leyen brothers, so highly regarded by Frederick the Great. In the Kurmark, in Berlin, Potsdam, Frankfurt-on-the-Oder and Köpenick too, sizeable quantities of silk were woven.

A cotton industry developed in Swabia, especially in Augsburg, where cotton printing began towards the end of the seventeenth century. In Thuringia and Saxony, Gera, Greiz and Chemnitz were cotton-producing centres.

(vi) *Switzerland*

Towards the end of the Middle Ages, Swiss linen was produced chiefly in the region of St Gallen. Through its *Schau*, which was famous throughout Switzerland and around Lake Constance, St Gallen was able to control production beyond the borders of its small territory. Rural textile activity gradually developed to a point where, by the beginning of the eighteenth century, it was much more important than the production of the town of St Gallen itself. At the same time other trading centres sprang up – Herisau, Trogen, Rorschach, Arbon and Hauptwil, each with its own *Schau*, and possessing the advantage of a cheaper labour force. By 1600 other linen manufacturing centres developed in central Switzerland, in the four *Landgerichte*, the Aargau, Canton Luzern and the *Landvogtei* of Willisau.

In Canton Zürich, thanks to the immigration of exiles from Locarno, wool weaving, dyeing and fulling flourished. A woollen textile industry based on the putting-out system gradually spread all over the Canton and into those of Zug, Luzern, Glarus and the *Freie Ämter*, even into the valley of Töss and the Thurgau. Spinning and weaving were carried on in the country, combing was concentrated in the town; the *Appretur* (finishing) was reserved to the craft gild in Zürich. Cotton working had already spread from the northeast of Switzerland to Zürich during the fifteenth century. The earliest fabrics were mixtures (*Barchent* or *Schürlitz*), but by the end of the century pure cotton articles were being produced.

Spinning and weaving offered the peasantry new opportunities of gainful employment. The new textile industry could expand freely because it was not subjected to the restrictions of a gild. Production was organized by *Verleger* in the town, but there were also rural craftsmen called *Tüchler* who developed into a kind of rural entrepreneur. It was urban policy, reinforced after 1662, that rural products should be brought exclusively to the Zürich market. By means of the putting-out system, spinning spread widely within the Catholic cantons. Another centre of the putting-out system grew up near Zürich in Winterthur. Spinning also spread to Unteraargau and the countryside around Luzern. Geneva and Neufchâtel began to produce printed cotton *indiennes* and from there the industry spread into the countryside.

Meanwhile several centres of the cotton industry sprang up in eastern Switzerland. For St Gallen and its small territory opportunities were restricted by its reliance on labour which was politically dependent on other seigneurs – in the county of Appenzell, in the territory of the Abbot of St Gallen, in the region of Toggenburg, in the valley of the Rhine and in the Thurgau. Glarus, parts of the Vorarlberg, southern Swabia, and the Graubünden were included in this manufacturing region. In all this area, at the beginning of the eighteenth century, about 80,000 or 100,000 people were employed in the textile industry, a third of them in embroidering. Production was organized in several different systems but the putting-out system predominated. In general, spinning and weaving were carried out by rural part-time workers; spinning prevailed in the poorer regions.

During the eighteenth century the Canton of Glarus, the Landvogtei of Werdenberg, Wartau, Utznach and Gaster developed into a second major area of cotton spinning and in time entrepreneurs appeared here too. By the middle of the eighteenth century cotton production was Switzerland's most important industry.

Silk had been woven in Zürich since the Middle Ages. After some hesitation during the fifteenth century, production recovered with the immigration of refugees from Locarno in 1555 and the silk-industry was thereafter able to develop free from gild control. It remained nevertheless a commercial monopoly of the citizens of Zürich who organized silk-weaving on the putting-out system. Silk twist was likewise a Zürich monopoly but rural labour was used for spooling and reeling the twisted silk.

'Pasmentry' was introduced into Basle in the third quarter of the sixteenth century by immigrants from Locarno and by Huguenots. This was the only Basle industry which successfully maintained its stand against gild organization. In 1612 it was finally confirmed as a 'free' trade, and henceforth enjoyed a golden age of prosperity while other branches of weaving were stunted by the restrictions imposed by the gilds.

Basle's policy of limiting freedom to weave to the *bourgeoisie* led many of the foreigners who did not become freemen of Basle to settle in the countryside in order to work for a *Verleger* of the town. The same phenomenon occurred in the region of Zürich. At first the urban gild members produced work superior in quality to that of rural producers. Then in the 1660s the invention of the *Kunststuhl*[1] and its widespread adoption towards the end of the century took away the advantage of the 'pasmentry' craftsmen; they, too, could be replaced by unskilled labour. The weaving of silk ribbons became more and more a domestic side-line in the Basle region. Many of the rural weavers worked with looms hired from a Basle *Verleger* or from a *Verleger* living in the Aargau or elsewhere. In the course of the eighteenth century the Basle *Verleger* came to monopolize manufacture and the possession of *Bandstühle* (ribbon-looms).

Another branch of textiles which took root in the Basle region after 1550 was embroidery. Knitted hose for men were made there too, as production spread from the canton and the territory of the bishop of Basle to Aargau, and later to the territory of Schaffhausen, cantons Zürich, Luzern and Solothurn. Hand embroidery and *Wirkerei*[2] were important in the sixteenth century, especially in the German part of Canton Bern; lace-making developed around Neufchâtel.

(vii) *Austria, Bohemia and Moravia*

In the second half of the seventeenth century upper Austria still held the advantage over Bavaria in linen-weaving. In 1713 there were still 83 gilds of urban linen-weavers, as well as rural craftsmen. Bavarian production then began to improve in quality, and after 1730 the printed *Ober-Österreichische Leinwand Beschau- und Bleicherordnung* faced strong competition from the new Bavarian products.

[1] A type of mechanical loom. [2] *Wirken*: a kind of weaving.

Lack of adequate raw materials accounts for the failure of wool production to gain ground, despite the *Wollzeugfabrik* established at Linz in 1672 by Christian Sind. Foreign specialists were employed at this factory and the labour force was widely drawn from Austria and Bohemia. In order to compete with imported foreign articles the factory was obliged to expand its repertoire of products to thirty in 1730. By 1735 10,000 to 12,000 spinners were busy for the Linz enterprise. Its heyday came under Maria Theresa in 1748 when it manufactured 11,763 pieces of cloth (*Wollzeug*). But there were also other smaller enterprises. Thus the abbot of Kremsmünster established a wool factory about 1749 which employed some 600 spinners. Another was established at Steyr. In lower Austria at Schwechat a cotton factory was built in the 1730s.

Other centres of textile production were located in Bohemia and Moravia. Here the factory age began as early as the second half of the seventeenth century and underwent a visible intensification after the beginning of the eighteenth century. Apart from foreign entrepreneurs, landowning nobles were active largely because they disposed of a cheap labour force in their peasants, widely subject to *robota* (forced labour) and organized in factories based on more or less centralized production. Such were the enterprises of the Waldstein at Oberleutensdorf, the Kaunitz at Slavkov and Drisanov, the Gallas at Hrádek, the Harrach at Namest (on the Man) and at Janovici, the Haugwitz at Potstein and Namest (on the Oslau), and Duke Francis of Lorraine at Kladrub. Profiting by the old Bohemian and Moravian clothmaking tradition, the local bourgeoisie also began to establish factories after the beginning of the eighteenth century, such as those at Planic, České Lípě and Tachov. A cotton industry was also built up after 1650, the principal factory being that built by Textor at Prague in 1752.

In Slovakia in 1725 a group of merchants established a cloth factory at Banska Bystrica, employing specialists from Saxony and Silesia, but after some years the enterprise was forced to close down. A cotton factory at Sastin fared better: it was founded in 1736 by Francis of Lorraine and employed over 10,000 people.

Austria's silk industry, at Vienna and Graz, was an old craft organization. Under the stimulus of the mercantilist publicist J. J. Becher, and employing a staff of trained silk workers from France, Holland and the Netherlands, a new silk-works was developed at Waldersdorf, a domain of Count Sinzendorf. Like most of Becher's experiments it did not last long, but the workers who had migrated to Austria remained and formed a pool of skilled labour with whose aid silk manufacture developed elsewhere. In 1702, twenty silk manufacturers of Vienna were still paying taxes. The silk 'masters' in 1710 were granted the privilege of joining a *Bruderschaft* (fraternity) which at that time was limited to only twenty-four to thirty members with six looms each. In 1717 Francois Dunant, a taffeta manufacturer from Geneva, was granted permission to settle at Vienna with sixteen workers; even though fifteen more joined him later his enterprise enjoyed no great success. In 1727 there were about thirty enterprises producing silk products of one kind or another at Vienna, and in other parts of Austria silk stockings, silk ribbons and *Dünntuche* (finery) were manufactured in some quantities.

Further afield, at Avio and Roveredo there were several workshops which made *Seidenzeug* (silkstuff) and stockings. *Seidentüchel* (silk cloths) were made at Gradisca and Horizia, in Graz and its suburb Muhr-Vorstadt. Other workshops were located further north; in 1725 eleven members of the Austrian nobility formed a company to build a silk mill under French masters who were to train native workers. But the forty-two looms of 1729 dwindled to twenty-five by 1732. Native production was apparently not able to hold foreign imports in check. Lack of capital, lack of quality and high production costs similarly prevented the Prague silk enterprises from being fully competitive. Few of the measures taken by the government to increase silk production were successful until the second half of the century. An exception to the general rule was the manufacture of 'pasmentry'. In 1736 there were in Vienna twenty-two lacemakers, nineteen *Decretists* and eighteen *Stohrer*.[1] Gabriel Garlipp, who had a privileged factory in the Josefsstadt, exported silk ribbons worth 'many thousands of guilders'.

(viii) *Italy*

In Italy the textile industry was highly developed in many areas, but fell into almost universal decline during the seventeenth century. In Venice the woollen industry at the beginning of that century had a production of over 28,000 cloths annually; by 1700 it had fallen to about 2,000. Between 60 and 70 firms were operating in Milan about 1600 with an annual production of some 15,000 woollen cloths. By 1640 the annual output had fallen to about 3,000 cloths and in 1709 produced little more than 1,000 cloths. In Como in 1600 about 60 firms produced 8,000 to 10,000 pieces a year, but by the eighteenth century woollen cloth production had almost ceased. In Florence towards the end of the sixteenth century some 120 firms produced perhaps 14,000 cloths annually. By 1627 the 62 remaining firms had a yearly production of no more than 8,000 cloths. This decline continued. Cloth production, it is true, was spreading to other places: it increased at Treviso, Padua and Bergamo, at Tremezzo, Menaggio, Bellagio and in the Valtelline.

[1] Garment makers who worked in a customer's house.

If the serge industry disappeared from Cremona, 'it developed at Monticelli, Busseto, Parma and in the Duchy of Mantua. Moreover the eighteenth century saw a measure of recovery. In Ormea (Piedmont) the Marquess Ferrero founded a wool factory in 1724 with the assistance of an Englishman named Coward. In 1753 30 looms were at work there. In the rest of the country production was on a small scale, mostly to satisfy purely local demand. The general decline of the old urban centres does not seem to have been compensated for by new growth.

In Venice the decline of the wool gild continued; its production was only about 2,000 pieces by the middle of the eighteenth century. The same was true of the *università dei drappieri* which specialized in dyeing, and the *arte dei berettieri* which produced the red 'fez'. On the other hand, the cloth-factory established by Gentili in 1727 employed about 1,000 persons in 1763. At the beginning of the eighteenth century the *università laniera* of Padua, organized on a putting-out system, produced well over 3,000 pieces, but later its production also declined. The *arte minore* produced stockings, berets, gloves and light cloths also. Free entrepreneurship characterized the textile industry of Schio around Vicenza. Sponsored by Niccolo Tron, an enterprise was opened in 1738 with 44 looms and quickly came to employ 500 persons. Kay's invention was used in Italy for the first time at this factory. It produced *londrine*[1] and imitated the cloths of Carcassonne. Verona kept only the remnants of its cloth-making tradition; its maximum production (in 1725) was only 744 cloths. The manufacture of stockings had long been one of the strongest branches of Veronese industry. In the Bergamasco in its prime, some 80,000 persons were occupied in wool production, but here too the eighteenth century was a time of decline. Tuscany too preserved only a fragment of its glorious tradition: Prato, called the *Schio della Toscana* by Caizzi,[2] had a thriving industry, based on the putting-out system in the valley of the Bisenzio. In 1738/9 the *lanaioli* (clothmakers) of Prato produced about 2,000 pieces and finished more than 15,000 pieces which came from the whole Grand Duchy; in Florence 11 *lanaioli* produced 4,000 pieces. As a whole, the Grand Duchy had – excluding those of the capital – 177 enterprises in 34 places.

Production of linen was widespread in Italy as a domestic industry. In Piedmont, a linen factory was built at Vercelli which in 1757 had 60 looms. Others worked outside the town. In all, almost 500 persons were employed. In Lombardy the old rural centres of Busto and Gallarate continued to produce linen, fustians and bombasines. Codogno and Cremona were also centres of the linen industry, but more important was the production of the Veneto. At Tolmezzo the factory

[1] From Londra = London.
[2] Caizzi, *Storia dell' industria italiana* (Turin, 1965), p. 118.

of Giacomo Linussio produced about 25,000–30,000 pieces. At Cividale Lorenzo Foramiti, who set up his factory in 1744, quickly achieved an output of 20,000 pieces.

Silk production was already highly developed in the Genoese Republic toward the end of the sixteenth century when some 18,000 looms were at work. By the beginning of the seventeenth century the number had fallen to 3,000 and in 1675 only about 2,500 were left. In 1635 Pavia counted 25 master silk-weavers; by 1700 only 10 remained. At Como, production with some 30 silk-looms remained pretty steady into the eighteenth century. Generally, the eighteenth century was to witness a remarkable growth of silk production especially in Piedmont, Lombardy and the Veneto, as entrepreneurs responded to the opportunity of the international market.

Piedmont around 1750 could boast workshops for extracting the silk from the cocoons with up to 60, 80 and even 100 *fornelli* (ovens) at Casalborgone, Caselle and Caraglio. Again, concentration characterized the *filatoio*, the mill which wound the silk thread. In 1730 126 *filatoi* were working in the territory of the king of Sardinia, with a cluster around Racconigi. In Lombardy Milan was a centre for the manufacture of the *filati*,[1] in the Brianza 13 small towns possessed in all 48 mills in 1750. Bergamo and its *contado* (county) possessed about 60 and from there much worked silk was exported to northern Europe.

Silk spinning and weaving did not advance at the same pace. In the old centres, such as Milan, Venice, Bologna and Florence, labouring under the traditional regulations of the *arti*, industry was unable to compete with foreign production. By contrast, in the mid eighteenth century Piedmont possessed 1,510 looms, 1,150 of them installed in Turin in small workshops. In Vigevano at the same time there were 976 looms, and the recovery of the Milanese industry was only just beginning.

Venetian silk weaving preserved its privileged position – albeit in decline – and in 1730 at least 3,000 looms were still at work, though the looms making silk stockings sank from 300 at the beginning of the century to 100 in 1741. On the other hand production rose in Padua and Vicenza. In Padua, Jewish merchants began to produce silk *cordelle*[2] in the middle of the seventeenth century, and Christians followed suit. In Vicenza silk weaving provided a welcome substitute for the decaying wool industry and rivalled Venice itself. The silk industry of the Genoese republic retained a good part of its ancient prosperity, reflected in the high export figures just after 1750. The Republic of Lucca which had 1,244 looms in 1700 suffered from the import restrictions imposed by Austria and Prussia just after the middle of the century. In Florence,

[1] The product of the *filatoio* = the thread.   [2] Ribbons.

where at the time of Cosimo de Medici 7,000 looms were at work, there was some decline but not of disastrous dimensions, and with the middle of the eighteenth century recovery began. In the south, Catanzaro during the seventeenth century possessed up to 1,000 looms; by 1700 only 400 remained. Naples and S. Leucio manufactured silk, and in Sicily, Catania, Messina and Palermo tried to ensure the survival of some production by means of special privileges. Like most textile industries, silk was especially sensitive to fluctuations in demand and the rise of competition – especially overseas.

(ix) Southeast Europe

The dynamic centre of the textile industry in the European part of the Ottoman Empire was Salonica, with its strong Jewish settlement partly composed of emigrants from Spain and Portugal. These Jewish emigrants played a considerable role in the development of the textile industry in the first half of the sixteenth century. This was also aided by the rural economy of the Salonican hinterland which concentrated on pastoral farming and produced wool. The standard cloth was the heavy *aba*. A lighter, cheaper product, the *sobremano*, was made in Plevna. According to Hans Dernschwam, the factor of the Fuggers who travelled in Turkey from 1533 to 1535, the products of Jewish weavers in Salonica were sold throughout Turkey. The Turkish army itself wore uniforms of Salonica cloth, made by capitalist clothiers who bought their raw material from the Macedonian peasants and sold it to the craftsmen on credit. At a later stage the capitalists began to concentrate production in their own workshops and tried to monopolize the provisioning of the army. Synagogues operated textile workshops to raise money for their welfare work.

After 1600, competition from abroad, especially from Venice and Ancona and later from England and France, brought about the decline of the Salonican industry. During the eighteenth century Dutch, Austrian and Saxon cloths also invaded the Ottoman market: the Turkish government permitted free importation of these foreign textiles. Attempts like that by a Minister of State, Rami Effendi, to set up a textile factory in Constantinople with the help of Salonican Jews came to nothing.

The products of one branch of Salonican industry – *manteros* and carpets – found a wide market. A Turkish traveller, Mustafa ben Abdulla Hadschi Halfa, who visited Salonica in the seventeenth century, called the multicoloured carpets made in Salonica 'world-famous'. Salonican silk thread was exported to Ancona and Venice.

Jews also manufactured textiles in other Balkan cities, such as Plevna, Scopie, Edirne (Adrianople), Veria, Larissa and Tricala. Under the influence of the Sephardic immigration, a division of labour similar to that at Salonica developed at Tricala, which had three fulling mills. On the island of Rhodes, the textile industry was largely a Jewish development and two textile mills which belonged to the Sultan were leased to Jewish entrepreneurs: shifts, trousers, cloaks, silk wrappers and buttons were exported to Anatolia, Egypt and other parts. In Moldavia and Wallachia Jewish artisans and manufacturers were an essential element in industry during the eighteenth century.

(x) *Russia*

The fortunes of early industrial experiments in Russia were, to say the least, fluctuating. Towards 1500 an Italian immigrant tried to introduce the manufacture of silk; in 1625, a Dutch immigrant made another attempt: neither was successful. The 'factory' stage makes an uncertain appearance after 1650. Imitating royal patrons of industry in the west, Tsar Alexis began the cultivation of the cotton plant and mulberry tree. In 1681 a velvet factory was established, but was typically short-lived. In 1684 a Dutchman established a woollen cloth factory at Moscow. But the lack of qualified workers, the absence of a home market and shortage of capital, all hampered industrialization. With Peter the Great came a new surge of interest in industry. Foreign specialists were attracted from western Europe, many of them French or Dutch. Sizeable factories equipped with up to 500 looms were established. In 1702 a factory was built in Moscow to make sail linen, and in 1705 factories for cloth followed. When Peter died about ten cloth factories were in existence, about the same number of linen factories and half a dozen for the production of silk articles. The most important were to be found at Moscow and St Petersburg, but there were others at Voroneš, Kasan and Asov. 'Pasmentry', hose, hats and tapestries were also manufactured. Russian cloths never attained the quality of the west European articles, although the English were able to re-export some to the colonies. Then, towards the middle of the century, a new phase began. English specialists arrived, bringing the modern machines of England; Collins and Chamberlain established an *indienne* factory at Petersburg, and they were joined by Germans and other foreigners active in cloth and silk production. Silk working especially spread widely throughout the country. The Frenchman Verdier's silk factory at Saratov was a characteristic example of Russian dependence on imported skill.

(xi) *Scandinavia*

In Scandinavia textile production played a modest role. The manufacture of cloth and silk articles was closely dependent on mercantilist policies of state encouragement, mainly in Copenhagen, under

Christian IV, Frederick IV and Christian VI. By 1738 14 wool factories with 36 looms and 373 workers were at work in Copenhagen, besides some smaller enterprises. In all 1,524 people were employed. In Norway Jörgen thor Möhlens' enterprises at Sydnes (near Bergen) only lasted a short time. Lack of capital, and of a sufficient internal market, hampered the sound development of production, which depended essentially on government protection.

Mercantilist protectionism in favour of Swedish textile manufacture began under Charles XI. The results – at Stockholm and Norrköping – were flourishing centres of wool manufacture. Among those who established the textile industry around the capital was Peter Speet, an immigrant from Lübeck who established a factory at Norrköping. The most important entrepreneur was Alströmer, who made Alingsås into the third Swedish textile centre.

(7) TRANSPORT INDUSTRIES: SHIPBUILDING

The building of large ships, merchant or warlike, in England was concentrated round the port of London and in or near other smaller ports – Southampton, Dover, Boston, Hull, Newcastle and Bristol especially. Many smaller ports round the English coast built boats, but only a few had shipwrights' gilds. From 1550 onwards overseas expansion, the whaling and Newfoundland fishing and the rise of coal transport along the coast and to the continent all helped to stimulate the building of a growing merchant marine. By 1630 it had grown from about 50,000 tons to 115,000 tons; England now had between 300 and 400 colliers, and 145 ships with 200 or more tons. After a peak in the eighties (340,000 tons) came a pause; only after the wars of the mid eighteenth century the mercantile marine and the Royal Navy alike grew rapidly again. In 1751 English merchant shipping reached 421,000 tons. About 1760, the first date for which evidence survives, Great Britain had 7,081 ships with a total tonnage of 486,740 tons: about one ship in every seven was Scottish.

Round about 1680 it seems likely that at least a quarter of the English mercantile marine was built outside England, mostly in Holland, the flyboat being superior to the English defensible ship in hull and masting. Dutch design had raised the tonnage and lowered building and running costs of the merchant ship. But English shipbuilders, especially of the northeast at Whitby and Scarborough, were already beginning to copy and develop Dutch models; thus began the age of the great sailing ships of 400 and more tons. During the eighteenth century the shipbuilding activity of the American colonies became increasingly important.

The seventeenth century witnessed some decline in shipbuilding in the East Anglian ports (like Ipswich), perhaps in fear of competition from Dutch ships taken as prizes. The northeastern ports specialized in their pinks and flyboats. For the great, strongly built ships for the Levant, East India, West India trades, London stood unchallenged. There was a remarkable concentration of shipbuilding activity in the yard of Henry Johnson at Blackwall in the seventeenth century, and later in the Royal Yards. In design there was no particular progress, except that from the late eighteenth century ships were sheathed with copper.

In the course of the sixteenth century, the Dutch had become the leading shipbuilding nation. Dutch yards were equipped with wind-driven saw-mills and large cranes. Thanks to their large mercantile fleet the Dutch could command supplies of cheaper raw materials; timber, hemp, flax and pitch could be imported in bulk, mostly from the Baltic. The Dutch paid higher wages than their competitors, but their market was large, both in the Netherlands and elsewhere. They built the *fluitschip*, or 'flute', with light simple rigging, and without forecastle or round-house for guns. It was especially suited for long-distance voyages and its tonnage varied between 200 and 500 tons. When war or piracy threatened, the 'flutes' sailed in convoy.

Dutch shipbuilding was concentrated primarily on the river Zaan. Towards the end of the seventeenth century there were about 60 wharfs building ships for ocean-going trade and indeed Dutch-built ships were sold all over the world. Even the trade of the old Baltic ports such as Lübeck and Königsberg was carried on the so-called flyboats. The pre-eminence of Holland began to fade slowly after the beginning of the eighteenth century, but over 300 ships still lay in the Zaandam yards in 1707 and Amsterdam in 1736 still numbered about 2,000 ships' carpenters. In the South Netherlands, Dunkirk became a shipbuilding centre. France had her own shipbuilding industry at many places on the Atlantic and Mediterranean coasts, especially in Normandy (e.g. Dieppe) and Brittany. Shipyards at la Rochelle, Nantes, Bordeaux and Bayonne built for the Atlantic trades. But until the period of Colbert, France – like England – still bought many ships from the Dutch Republic or from Sweden. Only during the eighteenth century did shipbuilding on the Atlantic coast, stimulated by the growth of French overseas trade, raise the standards of the Dutch.

At the end of the Middle Ages the best *astilleros* (shipyards) in Spain were to be found on the Cantabrian coast at Santander, Pasajes, Renteria and Santona. From the time of the Catholic Kings, shipbuilding prospered in the numerous *rias* of Galicia, like the Cantabrian hinterland a country rich in woodland. With the rise of the American trade, shipbuilding developed at Seville as well as at Cadiz. After the defeat of the Armada, a phase of decline set in and during the War of the Spanish Succession Spain was virtually without a navy. Philip V and Ferdinand VI set about re-creating it. The *astilleros* of Coruña, Pontevedra, Rivadeo, Noya and others were still using old-fashioned methods and antiquated equipment: but the foundation of the arsenals of la Grana, near Ferrol, in 1727, inaugurated a new phase. Patino, chief minister of Philip V, encouraged factories making *jarcia* (rigging) and decreed a new organization for sailors. The ancient naval base of Santander was moved to la Grana, but progress was hampered by structural crises and it was not before the middle of the century, when the shipwrights of la Grana were moved to Ferrol, that substantial progress in shipbuilding was made – and this with the help of foreign technicians: in 1749 the first British experts arrived at Ferrol.

In Portugal, overseas expansion brought about the creation of several shipbuilding centres near the ports, Lisbon becoming the most important. Here towards the middle of the sixteenth century more than 400 specialists were employed. But steadily ships built overseas began to compete with Portuguese, first in East Africa and India, then after 1650 in Brazil.

Genoa and Venice had long been the principal Italian shipbuilders. The Genoese furnished their galleys to the Spanish Armada for the wars against the Barbary pirates and the Turks. The *Darsena* of Venice was famous for its galleys. But the growing scarcity of timber and conservatism among the shipwrights contributed to the decline of Venetian shipbuilding during the sixteenth century. After the last galleys had disappeared from the route to the North Sea each year saw the building of a few great carracks of 600 and even 1,000 tons or more. But after 1600, only the naval arsenal continued the old galley-building tradition.

Along the North Sea and the Baltic coasts shipbuilders were active in many ports: Emden, Bremen, Hamburg, Lübeck, Rostock, Wismar and Danzig, to name only a few. Among the Hanse towns, Lübeck and Danzig maintained a leading position. Between 1560 and 1800 some 2,450 ships of about 150,000 lasts are estimated to have been built in Lübeck. The peak years – from 1590 to about 1646 – were those when Lübeck's trade with Spain and Portugal was most prosperous. About 800 ships were built at Lübeck, among them 136 large vessels of between 150 and 300 lasts. After the Twelve Years Truce in 1609, when the Dutch established a virtual hegemony of the Iberian trade and pushed the Hansards away into the local trades of the North Sea and Baltic, fewer large ships were built. When war broke out again on the expiry of the Truce in 1621 the Hansards' trade to the Iberian peninsula recovered, and there was a new demand for larger ships more suited to the convoys essential for safe trading. The *fluit* which the Dutch had begun to build from 1595 was not adopted at Lübeck until 1615.

Copious supplies of local timber, pitch, tar, hemp, and iron as well as copper and brass (in Sweden especially) made the Scandinavian shipyards formidable competitors, especially from the seventeenth century. Until that time shipbuilding in Norway was hampered by such curious antiquities as the edict that ships could only be built with special permission from the king. In Denmark Christian IV tried to simulate shipbuilding by patronizing *defensionsskibe*, armed vessels which could be used in case of war. He met with little success. Danish shipbuilding prospered most when the great powers were at war and the Danish Crown was able to take advantage of its neutrality. The same was true of Norway: a real shipbuilding industry seems to have started there in the 1630s and 1640s, when Norwegian trade with England began to flourish. From about 1629, *defensionsskibe* were laid down in Norwegian ports, and shipbuilding was taken up in the remoter areas, especially in the coastal district of Vestfold-Agder.

Swedish shipbuilding centred on Stockholm and Göteborg. Peasant shipbuilding flourished in Halland and other coast regions. This was still more the case in the Finnish Skärgård and Österbotten. Towards the end of the seventeenth and in the first half of the eighteenth century ships were built at Kokkola, and to a lesser extent at Pietarsaari and other places. Shipbuilding was the most important industry of the towns of Österbotten, which sold its ships to Sweden. Meanwhile shipyards also developed in Åbo (1732), Turku, Helsinki (1745) and Loviisa.

Peter the Great's passionate interest in shipbuilding is legendary. It made St Petersburg a centre of Russian shipbuilding based on the Dutch models with which he had become familiar during his stay at the Zandam yards.

Overland traffic

The development of overland traffic using carts and waggons brought into being a special profession of cartwrights. The farmer's two-wheeled cart was generally made by a rustic carpenter, but now the needs of the growing overland trade and the itinerant courts encouraged specialists to establish their own workshops. There was an important advance towards the end of the sixteenth century, when princes and nobles took to travelling in carriages instead of on horseback. The development of the coach made carriage-building a specialized luxury industry. The *carosse*, a highly ornamented coach, made its appearance after 1660, and its trappings came to reflect changes in style as much as the *boiseries* of domestic interiors. Specialized *menuisier*, *carossier* and *sellier* workshops combined to build the coronation *carosse* of Charles

XII of Sweden in 1696. In the overcrowded streets of Regency Paris (1715–21) the *berline*, more practical than the big *carosse*, gained in popularity and the output of specialized workshops rose visibly.

(8) PRINTING AND PAPERMAKING

Printing from movable type was a Mainz invention and German printers at first maintained a monopoly of this new art which was soon developed by enterprising merchants into an industry. Printing presses were established by Germans as far afield as Valencia, Naples, Budapest, Stockholm and Westminster. In southern Germany, Nuremberg, Basle, Augsburg and Strassburg, centres of international banking and trade, also developed into centres of printing; among the Hanse towns, Cologne and Lübeck, and in the Netherlands, Bruges, had important and renowned printing presses. The heyday of the early Strassburg firms continued until the middle of the sixteenth century, thanks to their role in propagating the literature of the Lutheran Reformation. The Amerbach and Froben press at Basle became standard-bearers of humanism. The Augsburg printers quickly learned to combine letter-press and illustration. The most active business was that of Anton Koberger (1445–1513) at Nuremberg: at his zenith, Koberger was employing 24 presses operated by over 100 compositors, proof-readers, pressmen, illuminators, and binders. Koberger went into partnership with printer-publishers at Basle, Strassburg, and Lyons in order to increase his output and selling. His print-catalogue contains more than 200 titles.

Venice became the metropolis of Italian printing. By 1500, some 150 presses were at work, many of them short-lived. Throughout the century the greatest name was that of Manutius, especially in printing the texts of ancient authors, while Francesco Marcolini and Gabriele Giolito de Ferrari specialized in Italian literature. In France the Paris printers were rivalled only by the Estiennes of Lyons. Robert Estienne and his son Henri were the most eminent scholar-printers of their century, and the uninterrupted tradition of the Estienne printing-house ended only in 1674.

In Spain in 1502 Jacob Cromberger founded the most important press in Seville, and his son Juan obtained an exclusive privilege for printing in Mexico.

The free development of printing in England was stifled by the Stationers' Company, the organ of the printer-publishers, which received a royal charter in 1557. Such restrictions were common in Europe: in seventeenth-century France, in order to facilitate state control, the number of licensed printers was arbitrarily restricted to thirty-six in Paris, eighteen in Lyons and Rouen and twelve in Bordeaux.

Decisive moves towards book production on an industrial scale were made in the Netherlands, first by Christopher Plantin, who settled at Antwerp in 1549, then by the Elzevir press at Leiden. Plantin used twenty-two presses. After Plantin's death, the Moretus family kept the firm for eight generations. From Plantin's Antwerp workshop came Louis Elzevir who concentrated on the commercial aspects of printing and publishing including wholesale, retail, and second-hand book-selling on a broad international basis. But the pace of printing techno-logy was leisurely and until the end of the eighteenth century only small technical innovations were achieved.

In response to the printers' needs, the practice of making paper from cotton or linen rags spread widely over Europe during the late middle ages. Portugal established its first papermill in 1441 in Leiria; another followed at Batalha in 1514 and a third near Alcobaça. In 1537 this mill was granted monopoly status, but in 1565 a privilege was issued for the construction of a new papermill at Alenquer. Paper production then remained static, only increasing at the beginning of the eighteenth century with the construction of an important new mill at Louisa. Spanish papermills in the sixteenth and seventeenth centuries were concentrated especially in Catalonia. The rising demand for paper led to new establishments in the eighteenth century.

French papermills were established in Brittany, Dauphiné, Provence and in the southwest, but in general they were on a small scale. In the Champagne and the Auvergne, especially at Ambert and Thiers, paper was produced for export.

From the beginning, Italy and Germany were leading papermakers. The region around Milan, Genoa and Venice developed paper produc-tion as an export industry. Papermills flourished in Tuscany, in Riviera di Salo and in the kingdom of Naples. The general malaise afflicted Italian papermaking during the seventeenth and eighteenth century, but left the small papermills of the Ligurian coast at work, and in the Veneto the Remondini of Bassano had a large enterprise occupying (in 1767) about 2,400 people.

By 1500 about fifty papermills existed in Germany, with special concentrations at Ravensburg (with five and later six works) and Basle. Others took root in Swabia, Bavaria, the Rhineland and northern Germany – wherever waterpower, capital from a *Verleger* and supplies of raw material were available. Papermaking flourished in the region of Düren, where from the second half of the sixteenth century eight mills were established. Others followed in the next few decades. East of Cologne, papermills worked in the region of Bergisch Gladbach. The industry began to flourish in the Netherlands after 1600, at first near Dordrecht and in the Veluwe, in north Holland, especially on the Zaan.

Here towards the middle of the eighteenth century about 130 people (mostly women) were at work. With the invention of the *Hollander* (a rag-pulping machine) the Dutch became the leading paper manufacturers.

The scarcity of raw material limited the size of each mill as well as the number of mills which could operate in any region. In upper Austria (ob der Enns) there was economic elbow-room only for about four or five mills to function; their production in 1693 was 3,873 reams, about a quarter of the output of lower Austria. Towards 1767 thirty-two papermills were working in Saxony; Franconia (Ansbach and Bayreuth) had about fourteen by 1700.

It was a common feature of mercantilist programmes to insist on the use of locally made paper. The first Russian papermill was built at Moscow in 1576 and a second in 1640. A new phase began under Peter I when several more were established at Moscow, Petersburg and Duderow. In Denmark a corresponding phase began under Frederik II, in Norway under Christian V. But, in general, these northerly countries (like England) always had to import some – especially better quality – paper from abroad.

(9) FOOD AND DRINK

The trades which provided food largely retained their traditional organization. Bakers and butchers in the towns kept their gilds. In the countryside the peasant household (like the noble and middle-class household) often baked its own bread, killed its own animals and grew its own vegetables. Moves towards mass production appeared first in response to the need to provide food and drink for armies and fleets. In Lisbon entrepreneurs built great ovens to bake ship's biscuits in the valley of the Zebro.

Population growth after 1450 provided the spur to a search for new fishing grounds. In the North Sea, from Heligoland to Iceland, German and Dutch clashed with Norwegian and English fishermen. From Bergen, with financial help from Germany, and later with money and new methods from the Dutch, the 'Nordland' fishing was organized. The Newfoundland banks began to attract Normans, Bretons, Spaniards, Portuguese and English people from the end of the Middle Ages.

The Dutch, the first to industrialize herring fishing, defended their important national industry with warships against English interlopers and Dunkirk corsairs. Enkhuizen, Delft, Rotterdam, Schiedam and Brielle, grouped in the organization called the *Groote Visscherij*, had a virtual monopoly. The ports of Holland, Zealand and Friesland together may have deployed as many as 2,000 drifters. The coastal villages such as Vlaardingen and Delftshaven also participated, and Dutch herrings found a market in many parts of Europe. The wars of the second half of the seventeenth century did great damage to the industry, and only a few centres like Vlaardingen survived intact into the eighteenth century.

In the later Middle Ages the Portuguese and Basques were active in whale-fishing. When the whales inconveniently migrated to northern waters the whalers followed. Here they met the Dutch as rivals. Dutch whaling expanded rapidly during the Twelve Years Truce (1609–21). In 1616 Amsterdam and other Holland ports organized (on the lines of the East India Company) the *Noordsche Compagnie*. Zealand entrepreneurs joined them in 1622, forming a single large enterprise, which organized whaling as a virtual monopoly. The major problem was to obtain trained pilots and harpooners. From the second half of the seventeenth century Germans from the North Sea ports competed with the Dutch, profiting from the latter's wars. The products of whaling-blubber and whalebone were in demand in many branches of industry. Train-oil factories were established either near the fishing places or in the home ports.

Consumption of beer, brewed from barley with hops as a preservative, increased greatly during the sixteenth century as population grew and living standards rose. Breweries, representing aggregations of fixed capital almost unique in manufacturing industry, scattered over northern Germany and the Netherlands. In Germany the most important places were Hamburg, Bremen, Brunswick, Einbeck, Rostock and Zerbst. Their output of hopped beer could be kept, barrelled and widely distributed, both overseas and throughout the hinterland. Brewing was widespread in the Netherlands towns, especially round ports and corn markets. By 1748, the province of Holland alone counted more than 100 breweries employing about 1,200 workers. In Scandinavia only Denmark had a major brewing enterprise: the Royal Brewery at Copenhagen. Towards 1640 its thirty-five employees were producing 20,000 barrels annually. There was always rivalry between this enterprise and the Copenhagen Brewers' Gild which was only ended in 1739 when the gild took over the brewing house.

In England the largest concentration of breweries was in London. In England and Wales, in 1700, there were 'common brewers' who brewed only for sale to publicans and private customers: 174 had breweries in London. In addition there were said to be over 39,000 'brewing victuallers' – innkeepers who brewed mainly for their own retail trade. Demographic growth, the expansion of overseas trade, and technical innovations greatly stimulated brewing in the following half century. By 1750 there were 996 breweries and 48,421 'brewing victuallers'.

In the course of the seventeenth and eighteenth centuries spirits – notably brandy and gin – became serious rivals of beer. The brandy industry developed in wine regions such as Bordeaux and Cognac, Andalusia and Catalonia; distilleries, on the other hand, sprang up in countries which commanded supplies of suitable grain, like the Netherlands and north Germany, Amsterdam boasted over 400 distilleries in 1663. The prohibition on imports of French and other foreign products helped to raise the Dutch output of spirits. Schiedam, where production of spirits began about 1630, developed into the main distilling centre because it commanded a cheap labour force; in 1711 it had eighty-five distilleries. Rotterdam (with fifty distilleries by 1650) and Weesp were also centres of brandy production. In Germany, distilleries flourished in Westphalia and in Schleswig, centred on Flensburg. Ålborg was the most important Danish centre.

Everywhere brewing and distilling were 'capital-intensive' industries employing costly fixed plant. Many of the early centres retained their reputation into the present century – e.g. Schiedam, Copenhagen, Ålborg, London.

Salt

Salt was essential to life as well as luxury, and drying-pans were found all along the coasts of Europe from the shores of the north Frisian Islands and the western coast of Schleswig to the shores of the Mediterranean. Everywhere it was essential not only to flavour and embellish but to preserve through the long winters the never adequate supply of meat and fish.

In the north Netherlands sea-salt was refined at Rotterdam, Edam and Dordrecht. In France salt-pans were situated in the Bay of Bourgneuf, south of the mouth of the Loire, in Bourin, Beauvoir, La Barre de Monts, in the south of the Isle of Noirmoutier, on the shore of the Isle of Oléron and in Brouage. Provence produced sea-salt, too. On the Portuguese coast the most important centres were at Setubal, Aveiro, and Alcacer do Sal, while Spain relied on the salt-driers on the coasts of Andalusia and the Isle of Ibiza.

Sea-salt or salt from brine springs was cheaper than salt raised from mines; it was therefore imported in increasing quantities through the north European ports for the refineries which ringed the ports. German princes set up and operated their own refineries: the Electors of Brandenburg and Saxony, the emperor in Silesia and the counts of Schauenburg on the Weser. Salt-mines were exploited in many parts of Europe from the Baltic coast to south Germany and east to Poland, Transylvania and Russia where the Stroganov family controlled a large proportion of the salt-pans. The salt of Lorraine, of Salins in Burgundy and Moutiers-en-Tarentaise in Savoy found a wide market. Lüneburg possessed the largest German salt mine. Its peak of production was reached in the sixteenth century, when 30,000 tons were raised and 500 people employed. But this was exceptional and generally the unit of production remained small.

In the eastern Alps the Dukes, later Electors, of Bavaria possessed Reichenhall which produced about 9,000 tons in the beginning of the sixteenth century, from 1619 the production of Traunstein was added which reached a fourth of that of Reichenhall. The archbishop of Salzburg had the salt-pans of Hallein and until 1556 those of Schellenberg (Stift Berchtesgaden) with a total production of about 21,400 tons, but because the market of the Habsburg estates was closed and in the west Bavaria dominated with its production, Salzburg had to cease production, remaining dependent on the policy of Bavaria. The Habsburg princes from Maximilian I and Ferdinand I built up a monopoly in their territories as far as the Bohemian countries for the production of Hallstatt, Hall/Tirol and Aussee. Their output rose from 26,595 tons about 1520 to 51,224 in 1618; in 1660 it was at 36,445 and rose again to 47,345 tons by 1700.

Sugar

Before the Ottoman advance and the overseas expansion of Spain and Portugal, European sugar production was concentrated round the Mediterranean – in the lower valley of the Nile, Syria, Rhodes, Cyprus, Sicily, and on the Mediterranean coast of Spain. Some was produced in Crete and Malta. The conquests of the Ottoman Turks destroyed a good part of the production of the eastern Mediterranean: after conquering Egypt in 1517, in 1522 they became masters of Rhodes, and in 1571 they overran the greater part of Cyprus. When Ulrich Kraft from Ulm visited the islands about 1575 he found that the fields were wasted, and the factories abandoned. Thus within half a century the three most important medieval sugar producers – Syria, Egypt and Cyprus – had virtually disappeared from the market. The competition of sugar from Madeira, the Canaries and South America had likewise squeezed out the producers of Sicily, Calabria, Valencia and Majorca. Throughout the sixteenth century increasing supplies arrived in Europe from Madeira and S. Tomé, from the Canaries, the West Indies, Mexico and Brazil. Moroccan production also expanded after 1519. These imports of raw sugar brought into being a widespread European refining industry. The first refineries were established in important entrepôts such as Seville, Lisbon and Antwerp, where the first *suyker-siedere* or *suyker bakkers* are recorded soon after 1500. In 1536 the number of these small refineries rose to nineteen. Emigrants from the troubles at Antwerp (1566–86) brought their knowledge of refining sugar to Amsterdam as they brought so much else in the way of technology. By 1605 Amsterdam had three refineries.

Venice also became a centre of sugar-refining during the first half of the sixteenth century. Some of its sugar came from the Mediterranean; the rest from Lisbon. Genoa imported sugar from Barcelona, Granada and Valencia, but its sugar refineries could not compete with those of Venice. For sugar-refining was a highly competitive affair, as England found when her first two refineries opened in 1544. They could not compete with Antwerp either on quality or price. London's sugar production, like that of Amsterdam, increased only after the fall of Antwerp (1585). About 1620 a refinery was established in Liverpool by a London sugar merchant. The Navigation Acts of 1651 and 1660 favoured the production of English refineries fed from the colonies. Outside London, refineries were established in Bristol, Greenock, and Glasgow, and Dutch and German sugar boilers were much in demand. By 1688 England had fifty refineries and they exported a good part of their production to Germany and Scandinavia. By 1750 the number of refineries had grown to 120 and English sugar consumption had increased over the half century by nearly five-fold to over one million cwt.[1] Sugar was one of those re-export trades so important to England's expanding overseas trade from the Restoration onwards.

The first German refinery was built in Augsburg in 1573 by the patrician Leonhard Roth, though in Nuremberg the profession of *Zuckerbäcker* was already in existence during the fourteenth century. Hamburg built its first refinery in 1585, Dresden in 1587. Thanks again to the immigration of Netherlands refugees, sugar-refining became a leading industry in Hamburg.

In Venice, sugar-refining maintained itself throughout the seventeenth and eighteenth centuries, supplying even the Turkish markets. Collaboration with Spain gave the Genoese refineries a large share of the Spanish market. In Spain itself sugar-cane planting and refining declined especially after the expulsion of the Moorish population in 1609–11.

A French refinery was established in 1653 at Orleans by the Dutchman Vanderberg; in 1662 two existed at Rouen. Under the protection afforded by the mercantilistic policy of Colbert, refineries were soon operating at Dunkirk, Nantes, Bordeaux, La Rochelle, Rouen and elsewhere. Nantes had five in 1671. In 1674 the merchant house of Maurelles opened the *Raffinerie Royale* at Marseilles. In order to protect

[1] MacCulloch, *A Statistical Account of the British Empire* (2nd ed., London, 1839), has higher figures: for 1734, 940,800 cwt (instead of 650,747 as Reed gives) and 1,000,000 (instead of 807,471) for 1755.

French domestic production, her colonies were forbidden in 1669 to produce white sugar. By 1700 export bonuses had helped to make sugar France's most important export, and there were large refineries at Marseilles, Nantes, Angers, Orleans and Saumur, occupying 'many thousands' of people. Marseilles expanded its production during the first half of the eighteenth century; the four refineries of 1728 had risen to fourteen by 1755. Orleans had twelve in 1770. About 1700 France consumed 200,000 cwt, and even larger amounts were exported.

Dutch sugar-refining rose rapidly after 1609 and the armistice with Spain. The number of refineries in operation seems to have increased to over 110. In 1661 Amsterdam alone had sixty refineries supplying the greater part of Europe with sugar. Decline set in after 1650. By 1681, the number of refineries had fallen to twenty, processing about 8,000 cwt a year; but during the first half of the eighteenth century production rose again and the number of refineries had recovered to ninety-five by 1762.

Hamburg, as the leading port, was the biggest centre of German sugar-refining. By the second half of the seventeenth century more than thirty refineries were at work and by 1700 Hamburg sugar dominated the Scandinavian and Baltic markets. Around 1690 some 8,000 people in Hamburg derived a living from producing and trading in sugar. In 1750 there were 365 refineries, although only a few employed as many as twenty to forty men. Some eighty to one hundred plants employed only between five and twelve people. The largest refinery produced up to 6,000 cwt of sugar and 12,000 cwt of syrup a year. Like brewing, sugar-refining was capital-intensive.

The sugar consumption of Europe as a whole was estimated for 1730 at 1,500,000 cwt, and for 1756 at 2,500,000. About a third of this was consumed in England. The rapid increase in consumption during the second half of the eighteenth century is indeed astonishing, and can only be understood in conjunction with the growing consumption of other overseas products, such as cocoa, tea and coffee, all of which were sweetened with sugar.

Tobacco

With the growing imports of tobacco from America, special industries began to develop in the European markets during the seventeenth century to prepare tobacco for smoking, snuff-taking and chewing. The north Netherlands especially became a centre of tobacco-working. In the region of Amersfoort, in the provinces of Gelderland and Overijssel, tobacco was cultivated and mixed with imported leaf from Spain, Portugal, England or overseas. Amsterdam added tobacco trading and manufacturing to its increasingly diversified business and Dutch techniques of cutting, rolling and packing spread to most of the other European tobacco factories, such as those of Cologne.

Luxury products

Werner Sombart first underlined – perhaps too strongly – the interrelation between the human desire for luxury and the growth and expansion of industry during the phase of early capitalism. Certainly some industries were specially geared to the luxury demand of the upper classes – e.g. silk-weaving, lace-making and mirror and porcelain manufacture. Goldsmiths in cities like Paris and London expanded their workshops into factories. The cutting and polishing of precious stones (a craft already practised in Venice and the Netherlands) increased with the imports of gems from India. About 1530 a German, Jorge Hervart, founded a diamond workshop north of Lisbon. Imports from Lisbon turned Antwerp into the leading centre of the diamond trade, with a special *diemantensnydernatie* formed in 1584. Benefiting by Antwerp's troubles Frankfurt successfully intruded on the business. By 1613 it numbered 51 masters – rather less than one third of the 164 masters still active at Antwerp. Others were active at Brussels, Mechelin and Liège. Venice, with 186 diamond polishers at work, was probably still the largest diamond centre. Then, towards the middle of the seventeenth century the processes of diamond working were improved. Amsterdam became the principal centre of diamond working, employing in the eighteenth century about 600 families.

Generally speaking, the seventeenth century saw production for luxury purposes becoming a specialized group of industries, distinct from production for the mass market. The specialized production of velvet in Genoa, Venice, Florence, Valencia, Toledo and Seville in the sixteenth century, and the weaving of fine cloths in northern France and England are examples of this specialization. (A reverse aspect of the same process was the development, from the second half of the seventeenth and beginning of the eighteenth centuries, of a ready-made clothing industry in the big cities, quite distinct from the production of quality goods.)

The cartwright, the upholsterer, and the saddler combined to build the *carosse*. In the workshops of London or Paris the shell of the coach was made up with leather covering and upholstery; to this the wood carver, the wheelmaker, the founder, the leatherworker, the smith and the harness-maker added their refinements. The coach builder needed considerable working capital - the more so since aristocratic clients were notoriously bad payers.

The making of furniture and furnishings also lent itself to specialization for the luxury market. Even in sixteenth-century Augsburg, the maker of *furnehm Arbeit*[1] stood in contrast to the maker of *gemeinem Handwerk*.[2] During the seventeenth century, and favoured by the needs of the king or his government, large-scale enterprises developed, such as the *Manufacture Royale des Gobelins* in the epoch of Colbert. Here everything necessary for the equipment of royal or noble palaces was made. Famous artists, painters, sculptors and engravers were commissioned to prepare patterns and designs. Modelled on the lines of Gobelins a whole new industry of luxury furniture arose, the most famous *atelier* being that of Charles Boule and his four sons, which flourished between 1672 and 1731. In England Sheraton and Chippendale produced for a similar market. 'Passmenters', owners of gold and silver factories, and the makers of luxury soaps, especially at Marseilles, developed their enterprises in a similar way. The fact that this was the Age of Elegance was stamped on a sizeable sector of the European and overseas economies.

X. *Industrial Production: Expansion and Crisis*

We have spoken of technology as one of the decisive factors affecting productivity of the industrial process, but on the other side industrial production encountered obstacles from time to time in the limited scope of the markets. This can be seen in the Middle Ages and it remained a factor in the development of our period.

Concerning the periodization of development in industrial production we may set a first phase from the end of the fifteenth until the beginning of the seventeenth century – generally a long period of expansion and economic growth. In Europe there was a demographic increase which ended with the crisis of wars, pestilence and other difficulties after about 1620. Until this date there was an expansion of inland trade as well as of overseas trade. Overseas trade affected particularly the production of copper, brass and bronze, thanks to the demands made by the navigational enterprises of the Spanish and the Portuguese in Africa, America and East India. But we should not exaggerate the importance of overseas trade; it was still Europe which dominated by its own inherent potentialities, and by the increase of inter-European trade. In the industrial sector there was marked progress, thanks to technological improvements introduced after the second half of the fifteenth century, thanks also to collaboration between governments (Habsburg, Saxony, Mansfeld) and the great merchants who were able to invest their capital in mines, in the trades in non-ferrous metals, and in textiles. Until the middle of the seven-

---

[1] High-quality furniture.   [2] Furniture for common people.

teenth century, apart from silver and gold, copper and its associates, brass and bronze dominate the international metal market. But soon production and markets were in conflict. The most interesting parameter is copper. The first copper market crisis occurs at the end of the fifteenth century. It can be observed especially at Venice, where Tyrol and Slovak copper were in rivalry. Another crisis follows in the fifteen-twenties and lasts until the forties, when Mansfeld copper dominates the market. In order to surmount the difficulties caused by overproduction, the Nuremberg merchant Christoph Fürer tried to form a producers' syndicate. It was not successful, and in the mid-forties Anton Fugger left the 'Ungarische Handlung' because of market difficulties. Once more copper dominates the international market from the end of the sixteenth century. Swedish export begins to grow, the great merchants of Hamburg and Amsterdam during the increase of the two cities are merchants of copper, from Sweden, from Mansfeld, from Bohemia and Slovakia. Mineral deposits form the basis of the dominant copper, brass and bronze industry of Germany and the Netherlands. It serves as a substitute for silver money nearly everywhere; it is exported to Poland, Russia, and Spain. This copper inflation penetrates to the 'calada' of Bohemia (1623) up to the Spanish edict of 1626. From that moment growing difficulties arise. Copper supplies were amassing in the ports of the Swedish market and Swedish policy during its continental intervention was to dominate the international copper market with the collaboration of the big Netherlands and Hamburg merchants.

In the textile markets, a considerable expansion and crisis may also be discerned. The phase of high quality cloth was passing. Instead there was a growing interest in kerseys, bays, says, *Zeuge* – products of the 'New Draperies'. The English themselves in part surmounted the crises with the help of Netherlands immigrants and new markets for the new textiles in central and eastern Europe. On the Continent, losses of production in Belgium and Germany were compensated by the transfer of production to new regions such as the north of France (in the region of Valenciennes and Amiens), the northern Netherlands and Switzerland, where the centres of immigration became the homes of the new draperies. There was a growing production through most of the sixteenth century at Ragusa, at Salonica, in Transylvania, Moravia, Lusatia and Silesia and the new output found markets partly in east Europe.

There was growth also in the production of linen, as of fustians, in Switzerland, in south Germany and particularly in the middle east of Germany and the realm of the Bohemian Crown. This growth was assisted by the migration of industrial activity from town to country. The process began in the Middle Ages and continued during the sixteenth century, lasting and intensifying until the beginning of the seventeenth century. The same phenomenon can be observed in the metallurgical industries of the bishopric of Liège, the Aachen region and Westphalia. One of the first consequences of the expansion of rural industries in Switzerland was the decline in the supply of mercenaries (*Reislaufen*): growing textile production and its influences on other economic sectors caught up with demographic pressures.

A second phase begins with the growing economic difficulties of the 1620s. Much has been written about this 'crisis of the seventeenth century', but we have to ask what precisely the word 'crisis' means. War crisis? Demographic crisis? Social crisis? Crisis of ideas? Economic crisis? The word 'crisis' is too ambiguous to explain adequately all the facts in the different economic sectors and the changes experienced. In explaining the development of industries during this phase we first have to consider the demographic facts. Demographic losses through war should not be overemphasized; nevertheless there was a diminution of population – in Germany e.g. about a third – but this was the result of other factors as well, particularly epidemics.

Let us add what we know about international commerce. There was a diminution of regular Spanish and Portuguese voyages to their colonies in the *carrera de Indias* and the East Indies. On the other hand there was an increase in Dutch, English, French, Danish and Swedish enterprises to India, Africa, the Antilles and Brazil. Overall, the result was to enlarge the Atlantic traffic. For the situation in Europe we have the indices of the Registers through the Danish Sound. Taking the average of 60–75 lasts (or 120–50 tons) for each ship passing the Sound, we can see that the year 1620 with 5,241 passages represents the close of a particularly active phase. With the spread of the Thirty Years War fluctuations mark an irregular but, in its totality, important contribution to the main economy of northwest Europe. Through the Sound flowed raw materials from the Baltic, the North Sea gathered materials from Norway, from Archangel, the Mediterranean and the Atlantic: we have to see this flow of raw materials in combination with industrial activity, especially in the Dutch Republic.

The wars themselves usually had a stimulating influence on industrial production. J. U. Nef underlines this fact, particularly for armaments. The industrialization of Sweden was influenced by the necessities of military intervention on the Continent. In 1620 Sweden exported about 7,000 tons of *osmund* and hammered iron. With the help of emigrant specialists from Belgium and Germany, production of iron rose, especially during the thirties when there was increased demand from the Dutch. In 1641 Swedish iron exports stood at 15,000 tons. The culmination of Swedish production of copper came towards the mid seventeenth century, just after the end of the Thirty Years War and the Eighty Years War in the Netherlands. These wars had likewise stimulated metallurgical production in the Netherlands, especially in the Belgian and German enterprises around Liège and Aachen, in the Hunsrück, the Siegerland, in the county of Berg, in the Mark and the region around Nuremberg.

The Peace of Westphalia ended the Thirty Years War and the Eighty Years War in the Netherlands. A second phase of wars ended with the treaties of 1659 and 1660, only to give way to another which continued until the Great Northern War.

Once again, we must not exaggerate the demographic losses by these wars; there were also deadly epidemics – the typhus in Denmark and Schleswig towards the end of the fifties, the great famine in Finland at the end of the century, and renewed plague in the first and second decade of the eighteenth century. It is difficult to judge the extent to which domestic markets were influenced by the demographic crises that followed. The demographic curve rose decisively only with the third and fourth decades of the eighteenth century. In the colonies there was a new rise of the Indian population in America during the seventeenth century. With the expansion of the plantation economy came the steady immigration of negro slaves needing more cloths and tools. Besides the Spanish and the Portuguese, the enterprises of the English and French, and the privileged companies in the other trading countries also contributed to the growth of the volume of transatlantic commerce, and in this way stimulated European industrial production.

For Europe let us look once again at the Customs Registers of the Danish Sound. For several decades the curve of ship passages through the Sound fluctuated with the wars. In 1672 the slump cut the number of passages to 1783; the peak numbers during the second part of the seventeenth century came in 1693, with 4,689 passages. The Great Northern War caused passages to drop to 1,413 and 1,091 in 1710 and in 1717, but during the last years of the war traffic reached a new peak of 5,242 passages in the second decade and 5,370 passages in 1740. In general, the volume of traffic reached at the beginning of the seventeenth century was regained in the second decade of the eighteenth century. What the Baltic trade lost during the years of depression was partly compensated by larger exchanges with Norway, the Archangel route and the Mediterranean. And we must not forget transcontinental trade. A certain parameter is given by the customs revenues of Hamburg, which were very sensitive to effects of war. The war year 1673/4, for example, trebled Hamburg's revenues as compared with those of 1586.

How to judge the influence of the vicissitudes of these decades on European industries? If agrarian history points to recession and demography has its examples of stagnation, how to characterize the pace of industrial production? While English overseas trade shows a net expansion after 1700 the figures available for the production sectors of metallurgy and textiles show a general tendency towards recovery, but not yet clear growth. Unmistakable growth can be seen in English production in some sectors after 1720, but in general there were still too many handicaps, especially in metallurgy, in spite of the economic shifts in favour of Russia, rich in iron and forests. The signals were nevertheless set at ready as the coking processes developed in England. But growth was far from constant, even in England. The example of the Swedish *brukspatroner* shows how the competition of Russian iron obliged them to look for additional markets in the Mediterranean and in the Levant. State protectionism contributed to the diffusion of the copper and brass industries. We have a similar impression in the European textile sector, where displacements were common. Old centres lost, Leiden fell from its dominant position, the era of 'cottons' began, 'new draperies' were produced in town and country, stimulated by the innovating activity of emigrants and state protectionism. This applied especially in southeast, east and north Europe, though the products of the frontier regions of the Continent were only adequate for local markets; in quality they could not compete with the west. (Danzig was one of the few frontier posts which could compete with the metallurgical products of the west.) Thus the European economy preserved the structure which it had already begun to assume during the Middle Ages: the west and parts of the centre of the Continent continued to function as a dominant area, while the frontier regions remained producers of raw material and food and provided markets for industrial products. This was a structure which was to survive even the Industrial Revolution.

XI.   *Conclusion*

We have tried to follow the development of European industrial production from the turn of the fifteenth century until the first half of the eighteenth century. We have found it necessary to include the whole Continent as far north as Scandinavia, as far east as the Balkans and the Urals. When these are included, the interdependencies between the active centres in the west and middle of Europe and these distant regions become more clear. These interdependencies were a decisive element in the industrial process during the whole period treated here. As purveyors of raw material and food and as markets for manufactures the border regions performed the function of supplementing the domestic potentialities of the economically innovatory and decisive areas of the west. In spite of the efforts of the governments of these distant regions they were never wholly able to abandon their 'supplementary' character. As far as overseas markets were concerned, they remained in a secondary position until the eighteenth century.

Most striking is the complexity of the factors which influenced the forward pace of different industries. Advantages of location, legal conditions, the organization of labour, technological progress, the costs of investment, government bounties, the initiative of entrepreneurs, the skills of the workers, the possibilities and limits of the markets, the influence of population movements, the effects of wars and other catastrophes – all these worked together, making any neat and tidy analysis virtually impossible.

The other striking impression is the dynamism which steadily propelled economic development forward. If stagnation afflicted one sector, new growth took place in another. These shifts represented a constant but multiform element. The expansion of rural industries served as a counterweight to restrictions imposed by the towns. Displacements occurred not only between different industries but from one region to another. The impression remains that the conjunctural 'valley' of the seventeenth century contains important advances which foreshadow the progress which was to mark the eighteenth century, giving it the role of an introduction to 'Industrial Revolution', to the 'take-off' of industrialization. But this phase of transition must not be regarded as a direct or unimpeded line of growth. There were still too many retarding factors. Viewing the push and pull of economic life, the economist as well as the historian can see more clearly than ever that a posterior phase can only be comprehended by the given facts of an anterior phase, that history is always the perspective of the whole past.

CHAPTER VIII

Government and Society

I. The Military–Bureaucratic Monarchies and the 'Société d'Ordres'

SINCE THE DAYS when the interest of historians was principally focused on forms of government 'the age of absolutism' has been a label commonly attached to the period of European history between 1660 and 1789. There had, of course, been absolute monarchies before this period and some outlasted it. Even during it other forms of government continued to exist in some territories. In the early years of Louis XIV's personal rule, however, when France dominated Europe in the arts of peace as well as in those of war, and threatened to dominate the colonized world, French absolutism seemed the most successful form of government and many rulers in consequence were tempted to imitate it.

Absolutism is a term which was invented at the beginning of the nineteenth century and is used to describe a particular form of autocracy. Though this autocracy functioned differently in different countries, it showed certain similar characteristics, and was imposed on similar kinds of societies, in all the places where it was adopted. The present account, however, will be concerned with it primarily in the three major military powers (France and the Hohenzollern and Habsburg dominions) which had come to dominate the European scene by the middle of the eighteenth century. The omission of the lesser states can be justified on several grounds: that they played a smaller part in European history and are thus of smaller interest; that they tended to imitate their more powerful neighbours; that the social and political arrangements which were the objects of their emulation were to a greater or less extent a response to the needs of war, from which they themselves were largely or wholly exempt. The omission of the major powers (Britain and Russia) on the western and eastern peripheries of Europe is dictated by the fact that each diverged markedly from the common pattern. The British did so because they were economically, socially and politically more advanced; the Russians because they were in every respect more backward.

The countries where absolutism established itself all consisted of communities, or collections of communities, in which the large majority of the inhabitants – upwards of 80 per cent – earned their living from the land and by more or less primitive forms of agriculture that over large parts of Europe had not changed significantly since the early Middle Ages. The kind of society which developed on these foundations was one to which there was never any exact parallel in the Anglo-Saxon world and for which in consequence there is no name in English. The French, however, call it the *société d'ordres* and the Germans the *Ständegesellschaft*.

In the eighteenth century this society was being eroded, though to a greater extent in the west than in central Europe, by the development of trade and manufactures, and the rise in agricultural rents, which occurred throughout the greater part of the century. This growth in prosperity, as contemporaries often complained, increasingly made the possession of money, rather than birth or occupation, the ultimate determinant of social status. By 1789, nevertheless, the relationships of the *société d'ordres* were still embodied in the law and, though to a greater or less extent in different countries and among different groups, accepted as natural by most people.

The essential characteristics of this society may be described by saying that it was particularist, corporative, hierarchical, and privileged in the sense in which the term 'privilege' was always used until the prophets of the French Enlightenment began to give it its modern meaning of an undeserved advantage. Society was particularist in the sense that the loyalty of most people, including the upper classes, was primarily to an individual, the reigning prince, whom they could identify in person, and to the locality of which they had immediate knowledge, rather than to the state or the nation.

In the eighteenth century large parts of Europe – Italy and most of what later became the German empire – were composed of small or very small principalities and imperial cities. Even, however, in the countries that were major military powers, the monarchs had accumulated their various territories piecemeal over the centuries, some of them in the recent past, and by 1789 had only imperfectly succeeded in creating administrative unity or national consciousness.

National consciousness was strongest in France, but even there was far from general, as can be seen, for example, by the continual insistence of the Pays d'États on their special laws and customs. In Prussia it was a great deal weaker. Frederick the Great used to complain that his army officers persisted in referring to themselves as men of the Mark, of Pomerania etc., and would not accustom themselves to the common name of Prussians. Though in the speech he delivered to them before the battle of Leuthen in 1757 he began: 'When you consider that you are Prussians...' ('Wenn Sie...bedenken daß Sie Preußen sind'),[1] this was a way of looking at things that was still being repudiated over half

---

[1] *Oeuvres de Frédéric le Grand*, ed. J. D. E. Preuss (Berlin, 1851), XXVII, 262.

a century later by the leaders of the opposition against Hardenberg.[1] In the Habsburg dominions at Maria Theresa's accession in 1740 there was nothing in the way of a central administration, let alone a nation. A central administration only began to come into existence after 1748, and then only in the so-called German hereditary lands of Austria and Bohemia.

In general, in fact, though national consciousness existed to some degree in the west it hardly did so elsewhere. Nor was it taken into account in international relations. Provinces changed hands after every war, and without any significant protests from the inhabitants – a state of affairs that was only possible because it was generally accepted that territories acquired by conquest or the provisions of peace treaties should be allowed to keep their liberties.

Society was corporative in the sense that most public activities were discharged by corporations, or groups of one kind or another – the gilds, for example, the chartered trading companies, the village communities which regulated agricultural activities where the open-field system still prevailed – of which membership was compulsory for those who wished to engage in the activities in question. Not surprisingly in these conditions the ruler looked on his subjects not as a collection of individuals but as a collection of groups. The French kings habitually referred to the 'corps', or the 'corps et communités', of which their kingdom was composed. These were natural arrangements in communities where on the one hand the individual was too weak to stand on his own feet, but where, on the other hand, the state was too weak to protect him.

The corollary of these corporative arrangements was privilege in the medieval sense of the term. All the various groups of which society was composed – for the purposes of trade, commerce, agriculture, administration, fighting, the pursuit of knowledge, the service of God – had their privileges (their *privilèges* in France, their *Privilegien* in Germany). By privilege was meant the special rights, guaranteed by law, sometimes to individuals as such, but usually to the members of groups, in order (theoretically at least) that the group might fulfil its functions. At a time when the state was too weak to discharge even the minimal tasks of keeping the peace and collecting the taxes by means of its own paid servants, the functions which the various groups were expected to fulfil

---

[1] See F. Meusel, *Friedrich August Ludwig von der Marwitz* (Berlin, 1908–13), Vol. III, p. 686. Marwitz, famous for having attempted (wholly without success) to instigate a revolt against Hardenberg, and for the vigour with which he expressed the reactionary opinions of a section of the Prussian nobility, referred on one occasion to the 'tolle Idee, aus einem so zusammengesetzten Staat, wie der preußische ist, alle Abgeornete in eine einzige Versammlung zu vereinigen.'

were commonly of both a public and a private nature, as for example in the notorious case of the French tax farm, which collected the indirect taxes and managed the royal monopolies of salt and tobacco, but was a private company working for profit.

Since in the *société d'ordres* people could not conceive of any relationship except that of command and obedience, the privileged were graded into hierarchies. Society, it was believed, not only was, but ought to be, based on inequality before the law. On state occasions, such as the meeting of the States General in France, or the swearing of allegiance which took place in the various Prussian provinces on the accession of a new king, the whole community was represented by the heads of the most important groups, whose positions in the ceremony were determined by a long-established order of precedence. State occasions of this sort were, however, rare. The relationships of daily life were governed by the hierarchy which prevailed within the individual groups, starting with the family, where the wife was subordinated in law to the husband, the children to the parents and the younger sons to the eldest. Saint Simon once said that equality among nobles would be insupportable. The ducs et pairs and the princes of the blood in France had not only greater prestige, but particular legal rights, which distinguished them from lesser nobles. Even the village had its hierarchy. In the serf-owning areas of Prussia and the Habsburg dominions, for example, the peasants were graded into categories sanctioned by law or custom – full peasants, half peasants, quarter peasants – according to the number of beasts they owned for ploughing; below them were large numbers of agricultural workers, who were not, strictly speaking, peasants (*Bauer*) at all, but were given various designations, such as *Häusler* or *Innleute*, because they did not own sufficient land in the common fields to support a plough team.

Privilege, in fact, involved both the absence of any distinction in law between a person in his private and his public capacity, and what the Germans call a *Zersplitterung des Rechts* – a state of affairs in which royal edicts had to take into account the particular legal privileges of every town, province, or 'Land', as well as the similar privileges of estates and other corporate bodies; so that it was rarely if ever possible to speak of a 'loi Commun' in the sense in which Sieyès used that term, that is, a law which applied to everyone.

All these attributes of society in the seventeenth and eighteenth centuries were very old. They dated far back into the Middle Ages and some even into the feudal era. The form of government known as absolutism was, on the other hand, relatively new since it reached its prime in France only in the reign of Louis XIV, and in central Europe not till fifty to a hundred years later.

It was distinguished from earlier types of monarchy because, in Professor Mousnier's words, the king was held to share his power with no one,[1] and exercised it through a standing army, and through royal officials, in the capital and the provinces, who are commonly described as constituting a bureaucracy. As in other forms of autocracy, the absolute monarch was above the law, that is, he alone had the right to issue or abrogate laws and to dispense particular groups or individuals from their operation. Opposition to the royal policy had no recognized channels of expression, apart from the negative rights of protest which belonged to the French parlements and which were comparable to those exercised by the English parliament under the Tudors and early Stuarts.

The parlements had a power to obstruct the royal wishes which in the eighteenth century was without parallel in the other European autocracies; for they not only possessed a long tradition of opposing the Crown, which even Louis XIV had been unable to destroy; they were corporations with a strong esprit de corps fostered by their being continuously in session for a large part of the year. In France they kept alive the medieval tradition of a monarchy limited by 'fundamental law', which in fact meant existing custom, and by Montesquieu's 'pouvoirs intermédiaires'.[2] Though they claimed the right to refuse to register royal edicts which they held to be unconstitutional, this right was never recognized by the king or his council. The doctrine of absolutism which was propounded in these circles, and which endured until the Revolution, was that which Louis XVI expressed in 1787 in his reply to the Duke of Orléans's assertion that to raise a loan without the consent of the parlements was illegal. 'Si...c'est légal parce que je le veux.'[3]

Like all other forms of government, absolutism depended for its efficient functioning, and ultimately for its existence, on the active support of some sections of the population and the acquiescence of the others. Since, however, by definition, the absolute monarchs did not seek to gain this consensus by allowing their subjects, or any groups among them, the right to participate in the formulation of policy, the consensus, in so far as it existed, was won by other means. The absolute monarchs exploited the belief in hereditary, autocratic, power which was natural to the societies of the time. They were careful (or if they were successful they were careful) not to come into serious collision with the most powerful groups in the community. Frederick the Great,

[1] Mousnier and Hartung, 'Quelques problèmes concernant la monarchie absolue', in Relazioni del X Congresso di Scienze Storiche. Storia Moderna, IV (Florence, 1955).

[2] See Michel Antoine, Le Conseil du Roi Sous le Règne de Louis XV (Paris, 1970), Book III, Chapter II, pp. 571–98.

[3] J. Égret, La Pré-Révolution Française 1787–1788 (Paris, 1962), p. 191.

for example, though he frequently pronounced serfdom to be a disgrace to humanity did not touch it on the private estates, among other reasons for fear of offending the nobility.

Finally the absolute monarchs used the weapons employed by all autocracies to suppress opposition or the threat of it. They were the originators of the standing army and the secret police. As far as seemed necessary and possible they exercised a censorship over the press. They regularly threw people into prison without trial and kept them there indefinitely. In the continental absolutisms before the Revolution, in other words, most, and generally all, of the civil liberties were unrecognized.

In all these respects the absolute monarchs were autocrats like other autocrats. But absolutism nevertheless had its peculiar features which distinguished it from other forms of autocracy. The absolute monarchs did not gain their power, like Napoleon and many later dictators, by military *coups d'état*. Nor did they gain it as the charismatic leaders of popular movements. They owed their position to their birth. Absolutism, that is, did not come in by revolution but, on the contrary, was only built up slowly and left many links with the past intact.

In the major continental countries, as in Tudor England, the absolute monarchs left a great number of medieval institutions standing, though the further east one goes the less true this generalization becomes. Their characteristic procedure was to impose new institutions on the old ones as, for example, the French kings created the intendants, and the Prussian kings the Kriegskommissarien, to control and to a greater or lesser extent to usurp, the functions of the existing local authorities.[1]

Similarly though the absolute monarchs were determined to suffer no interference from their over-mighty subjects, in general (Joseph II was an exception) they had no idea of revolutionizing existing social relations or the distribution of property. The fact that they owed their power to their birth meant that a considerable degree of conservatism was built into their policies. Broadly speaking they accepted the society they had inherited and interfered with it only in so far as this seemed necessary to the achievement of the particular policies they had in mind. In so doing, however, they effected great changes.

Their first preoccupation was always war. We commonly judge the predilections of an individual by the way he spends his money. If we apply this test to the absolute monarchs in the eighteenth century the conclusion is very clear. Even in peace all of them appear to have spent upwards of 70 per cent of their annual revenues on war purposes – that is, on the upkeep of their armed forces, on servicing the debt accumulated in past wars or, as in Prussia where there was no mechanism for

---

[1] See particularly O. Hinze, *Staat und Verfassung* (Göttingen, 1962), pp. 242 ff.

borrowing from the public, in putting aside large sums every year for accumulation in the so-called war chest.

The need to defend or expand their trade and territories made it necessary for the absolute monarchs to increase their resources of men and money, and their achievements were a by-product of this necessity. If the rulers were to be masters in their own dominions, and equipped for the tasks of defence and aggrandisement, they needed armies under their own control, staffed by native officers (or officers who at least became the subjects of the rulers they served) and with a high proportion of native troops. The advent of the standing army meant taxing the population directly on a permanent basis. The old medieval notion that the king should 'live of his own' became impracticable. Everywhere the standing armies gave rise to new methods of taxation and heavier taxes, as the opponents of the Stuarts in Britain continually pointed out in their diatribes against 'arbitrary power'.

The need for standing armies, and for the taxes to pay for them, involved an expansion of state activity which increased more or less uninterruptedly in every continental absolutism throughout the period under discussion, and led to a continuous growth in the size of royal bureaucracies. Civilian officials were not only needed to meet, or to help in meeting, the armies' immediate requirements – for weapons, for uniforms, for food and lodging, for fodder for the animals, for transport, for hospitals and so on – they were also needed to direct or control the civilian activities on which the efficiency and strength of armies depended. In every major continental power some system of conscription had to be introduced, even though in France it only extended as far as the creation of a militia for use in garrison duties and to supplement the field armies in time of war.

Since the sums that could be raised in taxes (and in the more developed communities by loans from the wealthier classes) turned not only on the power of the administration to levy tribute, but also on the amount of available wealth, the requirements of the fighting services gave rise to the need to supervise on a national basis, if not to control, all the workings of the economy. In every major continental power – first in France, next in Prussia, finally in the Habsburg dominions (and also, for that matter, in Russia, and to a considerable extent even in Britain as well) – it was the demands of war and the economic policies and administrative changes to which they led, that gradually transformed the medieval monarchs, who were merely landlords like other landlords though with more extensive rights of overlordship, into the heads of states.

This process proceeded differently, and was justified in different terms, in France and in central Europe. In France the king was seen as

God's representative on earth. At his coronation he was anointed with holy oil, and his authority was thus sacred in a particular sense that distinguished him from the other 'powers that be' which were also assumed to be ordained of God. 'Le titre de Christ', Bossuet went so far as to say, 'est donné aux rois, et on les voit partout appelés les Christs, ou les oints du Seigneur.'[1] To attack the monarch's person was sacrilege. 'La majesté est l'image de la grandeur de Dieu dans le prince...c'est l'image de Dieu qui, assis sur son trône au plus haut des cieux, fait aller toute la nature.'

In central Europe, where absolutism reached its prime at a later date, and contemporaneously with the acceptance of the German Enlightenment, the monarchs were not credited with these semi-divine attributes. Their power was seen as an expression of natural law, as then understood, and in consequence as being part of the natural order of things which God had created. God, however, was assumed not to have prescribed any particular form of government, and the monarch was held to derive his authority from a contract made with his people.

This belief, which was an essential part of the creed of the so-called 'enlightened despots' (a term which was invented in the nineteenth century), did not, however, diminish the monarch's right to unquestioning obedience either in his own eyes or in those of his subjects. The enlightened despots prided themselves on being the first servants of the state, but by this they did not mean that they need take their subjects' wishes into account. They meant only that they should subordinate their dynastic interests, and their personal pleasures and predilections, to the interests of the state (as they interpreted them). In practice the monarchs to whom the attribute of enlightened is most commonly applied, particularly Joseph II and Frederick the Great, ruling as they did over communities where manners were more primitive and invasion and dismemberment much more immediate dangers than in France, were far more autocratic and ruthless than their French counterparts.

Absolutism in central Europe was both more recent than in France and, when reasons of state seemed to demand that it should be so, less tolerant of vested interests. Tocqueville maintained – in a judgment that modern scholars would not dispute – 'Au moment où la Révolution survint, on n'avait encore presque rien détruit du vieil édifice administratif de la France; on en avait, pour ainsi dire, bâti un autre en sous-oeuvre.'[2] Without many qualifications this could not be said of

---

[1] 'Politique Tirée des Propres Paroles de l'Écriture Sainte', in *Textes Choisis et Commentés*, ed. H. Brémont (Paris, 1913), II, 106.

[2] Alexis de Tocqueville, 'L'Ancien Régime et la Révolution' in *Oeuvres Complètes*, ed. J. P. Mayer (Paris, 1952), II, 127.

either the Hohenzollern dominions or the hereditary lands of the house of Habsburg; for the Hohenzollerns had no administrative arrangements that were common to all their provinces before the reign of Frederick William I, and even in the Austrian and Bohemian lands there were none until after the middle of the eighteenth century. When the task of state-building began in this part of Europe it often involved curtailing the powers of medieval institutions to an extent that had not seemed practicable in France.

In France, for example, Louis XIV's attempts to reduce the liberties of the French towns were largely nullified for various reasons, particularly the sale of offices, which were bought by the town oligarchies. 'Les grandes villes', in Professor Goubert's words, 'surtout marchandes, continuèrent à avoir une réelle politique, des intérêts puissants, des représentants même auprès du Roi, au Conseil du Commerce...en droit comme en fait à peu près toutes les villes restèrent privilegiées... elles sauvegardèrent souvent une réelle autonomie culturelle...'[1] In Prussia, by contrast, Frederick William I began, and Frederick the Great completed, the total destruction of urban independence. The Prussian towns, it is true, continued to remain privileged in the sense of possessing particular legal rights, for example the immunity from conscription for military service, which Frederick the Great distributed liberally to various categories of town-dwellers and in a number of cases to town communities as a whole. All urban financial affairs, however, and a large range of other activities – the construction of buildings, for example, the establishing of manufactures, the drawing up of regulations for the conduct of trade and production, the keeping of statistics relating to the population, the number of houses, the space available for billeting troops and other matters of concern to the government – were subject to the control of Commissars, known as *Steuerräte*, who carried out their duties in accordance with regulations applicable throughout all the Hohenzollern dominions.[2]

Tocqueville maintained that the revolution which occurred in France in 1789 was the outcome of a European movement that sooner or later was bound to change the structure of government and society in every country, but did not do so in Germany in the eighteenth century because what he called 'feudal' institutions had retained a greater vitality there. It is indeed true that in the Habsburg dominions until 1781 and in Prussia until 1807 the bulk of the peasantry were serfs who were bound to the soil. (Even after they had been granted their personal freedom the land-holding serfs remained, until the middle of the nineteenth century, subject to the servile obligations attached to the land.)

---

[1] Pierre Goubert, *L'Ancien Régime*, II *Les Pouvoirs* (Paris, 1973), 81.
[2] See G. Schmoller, *Deutsches Städtewesen* (Berlin, 1922), p. 375.

In general throughout the eighteenth century the barriers dividing the various estates from each other could be crossed much less easily than in France. While, however, in central Europe society was in most respects more primitive, and the *société d'ordres* subject to less erosion, the machinery of state, which was of a more recent construction, was in a number of ways more modern than the French, and in Prussia, where the small size of the population diminished administrative difficulties, was very greatly more efficient.

Particularly in her financial administration, in the structure of her bureaucracy, and in the relative incorruptibility of her civil servants Prussia by 1789 was in advance of France. In the eighteenth century the Prussian system of taxation was the admiration of Europe, though only because it was more intelligently administered and not because it was less bedevilled by privilege than the systems elsewhere. On the other hand the insistence at every level of administration on the meticulous keeping of accounts, and the determination shown by Frederick William I and Frederick the Great to adjust ends to means, as far as possible in their foreign as well as their domestic policies, made Prussia unique among the European autocracies in the eighteenth century, and prevented the waste of resources which distinguished, particularly, the French administration.

The Prussian bureaucracy at the beginning of the nineteenth century was a favourite target for the abuse of Stein, Schön, Humboldt and many other reformers for whom it epitomized the 'mechanischer Staat', that bugbear of the German romantics. Its defects have been made familiar by the writings of these men as well as by modern historians. The part it played in shaping the destiny of Prussia, for better and for worse, is nevertheless beyond dispute.

In the eighteenth century, as one American authority noted: 'in the Prussian bureaucratic mechanism authority was more effectively centralised than in France, just as there was a greater degree of uniformity in the application of administrative maxims'. Without any legal rights, continuously spied upon, liable to indefinite imprisonment without cause shown, and to the 'preposterous and degrading tyranny of incompetent superiors', the psychology of the Prussian bureaucrat 'had to be that of surrender'.[1] By the beginning of the nineteenth century there had nevertheless emerged from this system, by a process that seems never to have been adequately explained, a body of educated and highly intelligent men, from whom Stein was able to choose his collaborators, and Hardenberg to build up his brains-trust, and of whom Friederich von Raumer (who had no love for the state service,

---

[1] Walter L. Dorn, 'The Prussian Bureaucracy in the Eighteenth Century', *Political Science Quarterly*, XLVI, XLVII (1931, 1932), esp. XLVI, 407.

which he left early for the academic life) could write in the following terms when, as a very young man, he was Chef de Cabinet to Hardenberg:

In our state neither the nobility, nor the bourgeoisie nor the peasants nor the provinces constitute effective units...There are no forces, still less counterforces. No constitution in the true sense of the word unites the various parts (of the monarchy). The officials in the various territories have hitherto up to a certain point been a substitute for representation and even for a constitution itself. Only in these great bodies is there firmness and cohesion. If they are disrupted I foresee that nothing will remain in our state except isolated groups and individuals.[1]

In the eighteenth century the concept of the state played a much larger part in political thinking in Prussia than in the other principal autocracies, and the influence of the state was much more widespread and powerful. Everywhere, nevertheless, the bureaucracies which the absolute monarchs developed or created played, to a greater or less extent, a similar role in promoting unification, centralization and national consciousness.

A limit was nevertheless set to this process by the nature of the bureaucratic monarchies themselves. The absolute monarchs, it was said, were not in general revolutionaries and could hardly have been so, given the hereditary nature of their office and its privileges, and the climate of opinion in which absolutism developed and reached its prime. The principal members of the royal bureaucracies, for reasons that must be discussed later, were all or for the greater part noblemen. They and the monarchs were thus attached by ties of interest and inheritance to the *société d'ordres*.

On the other hand, as wealth, education, and the costs of war and administration all increased in the course of the eighteenth century, this form of society, and the kind of autocracy superimposed on it, came to seem inappropriate to the needs of the times, and particularly to the needs of war with its insatiable demands for men and money, which required that more wealth should be created and existing wealth used more efficiently. The arguments, moreover, which could be brought against the existing order on the grounds of expediency, were reinforced, and indeed often suggested, by the prophets of the French Enlightenment speaking in the name of social justice and humanity.

Absolutism as it operated in the eighteenth century, allowing the monarch as it did to interfere arbitrarily in the course of administration, and, if he so chose, without regard to the opinions of the ministers concerned, came to seem incompatible with justice and orderly govern-

[1] Quoted by E. von Meier, *Die Reform der Verwaltungsorganisation unter Stein und Hardenberg*, 2nd ed. (Munich–Leipzig, 1912).

ment. The innumerable privileges of groups and localities were seen to complicate the tasks of administration, to frustrate the attempts to devise more rational systems of taxation, to impede economic growth and, because of the dissensions they caused, to be responsible for the lack of any sense of common interest among the members of the population. As Dupont de Nemours put it in his 'Mémoire sur les Municipalités'[1] – a summary of his and Turgot's views intended for but never presented to Louis XVI – the French nation 'est une société composée de différents ordres mal unis, et d'un peuple dont les membres ont entre eux que très peu de liens sociaux'. The result, he concluded, was a 'désunion qui décuple les travaux de Vos serviteurs et de Votre Majesté et qui diminue nécessairement et prodigieusement Votre puissance'.

However unwilling the leading members of the administrations in the various autocracies might be to overturn the existing order, they were not deaf to the teachings of the French Enlightenment or to the practical needs of the times, and it was from their ranks that the first protests came. In any given country, however, their discontent seems to have been more or less proportionate to the extent of the success or failure in war and diplomacy. In France and the Habsburg dominions, whose international position in the second half of the eighteenth century was declining or precarious, the protests were loudest, and in the Habsburg dominions were led against the *société d'ordres* by the monarch himself. In Prussia, on the other hand, which was the most successful of the military monarchies, there reigned in government circles during the last twenty years of Frederick the Great's life a mood of the utmost complacency, which received an annual demonstration in the lecture which Ewald Graf von Herzberg, Frederick's most trusted minister, delivered to the Berlin Academy of Sciences on the occasion of the king's birthday.[2] This mood, however, was gradually undermined, and finally destroyed, by the decline in Prussia's international prestige which began in 1793 and culminated in the debacles of Jena and Auerstädt. It was then that Stein and Hardenberg embarked on their programmes of reform.

Round about the end of the eighteenth century, in fact, the *société d'ordres* and the form of autocracy which had been superimposed on it, were called in question in all the major continental countries, and everywhere the problem of how much should be reformed divided the members of the ruling groups against each other, and often, particularly in France, in their own minds.

[1] Printed in G. Schelle, *Oeuvres de Turgot* (Paris, 1913–23), IV, 568.
[2] *Dissertations lues dans les séances publiques de l'Académie des Sciences et Belles-Lettres de Berlin dans les années 1780, 1781, 1782 à 1787 par M. de Herzberg* (Berlin, 1787).

In France the disputes which arose whenever a reforming minister attempted to modernize the existing social or administrative structure proved insoluble. They led to a paralysis of government, to the summoning of the States General and to revolution. In the Habsburg dominions most of Joseph II's schemes for reform had to be abandoned. Only in Prussia, where the state was strongest, was it possible to avoid the scylla and charybdis of revolution on the one hand and political and social stagnation on the other; so that Madame de Staël, when she went to Germany at the beginning of the nineteenth century, could say that the 'vraie capitale' was no longer Vienna but Berlin.[1] The Prussian reformers, it is true, did not succeed in limiting the powers of the autocrat by means of a constitution or in dismantling completely the *société d'ordres*, but they nevertheless removed, by means of changes considerably more radical than is sometimes admitted, all the obstacles which the old social and political order had come by the end of the eighteenth century to place in the way of economic development and the growth of military power.

II. *The Monarchs and their Nobility*

When the monarchs had been struggling to establish their absolute power, their principal opponents had been the heads of the great noble houses, who had aspired to control policy and dominate local government. In the end the monarchs achieved their object and excluded their former over-mighty subjects from office, or retained only those among them whom they could trust. They promoted to high positions men of inferior birth whom they could make and unmake and who, being parvenus, were in general both subservient and ruthless, and could be relied upon to enforce the royal will. This state of affairs for a long time fostered the legend that absolutism in its hey-day mobilized the bourgeoisie to defeat the nobility.

This legend misrepresents the nature of the societies in which absolutism developed. They were all overwhelmingly agrarian societies in which the business communities had little or no prestige or class consciousness. In his study of Beauvais between 1600 and 1730 Professor Goubert argued that in this town there was 'pas de culture, pas d'idéal, pas de programme, pas de revendications qui soient commune à toute la bourgeoisie – il faudra attendre les années 1760 pour constater l'apparition de quelque chose qui ressemble à cette conscience de classe et qui annonce les temps nouveaux'.[2] Another twenty years had to pass

---

[1] Madame de Staël, *De l'Allemagne*, ed. Comtesse de Pange (Paris, 1958), I, 240.
[2] P. Goubert, *Beauvais et le Beauvaisis de 1600 à 1730* (Paris, 1960), p. 348.

before, even in France, it was possible to speak, in Professor Égret's words, of 'le réveil du tiers état'.[1] In central Europe, where the urban communities were fewer and smaller than in France, and the mentality of their members more than proportionately servile, it was necessary to wait a great deal longer still.

Some absolute monarchs did, it is true, promote to high positions men of non-noble birth, though in France this was rarely if ever necessary. When Turenne heard in 1661 that Louis XIV's principal advisers were Fouquet, Lionne and Le Tellier he is said to have asked 's'il se pourrait bien faire que trois bourgeois eussent la principale part dans le gouvernement de l'état'.[2] What he meant, nevertheless, was not what in the twentieth century might be supposed. Fouquet, Lionne and Le Tellier all came from established noble families. Fouquet indeed at this time was a marquis, living in his chateau of Vaux-le-Vicomte in a grandeur that excited Louis XIV's envy. He and his two colleagues, however, were by profession and family tradition men of the robe – pen-pushers or *Federfüchser* as Turenne's German counterparts later expressed it. Turenne, on the other hand, was a Maréchal de France, the grandson on his mother's side of William I of Orange, who taught him the art of war, and descended, on the side of his father, the Duc de Bouillon, from the famous Constable Montmorency. The scion of distinguished military families, and himself one of Louis' most famous generals, he ended his life appropriately on the battlefield at the age of 64. To him as to Saint Simon and to many other court families the men of the robe were by definition bourgeois even if they had titles dating back several generations.

This point of view continued to be expressed up to the Revolution by people who prided themselves on their distinguished ancestry, and was no doubt responsible for Tocqueville's assertion that the government in France under the ancien régime was in the hands of bourgeois. In fact, however, there was throughout the eighteenth century, apart from Necker, who was a protestant foreigner, no minister, intendant, or high official of any kind who was not a noble. That these officials continued in certain circles to be described as bourgeois, even when they came from well-established noble families, was an expression of the belief which persisted, though to a diminishing extent, until 1789, that work in an office was beneath the dignity of a gentleman.

Had the nobility in the various continental countries constituted the kind of social class that was constituted by the British aristocracy, whose members were few and more or less constant in number, and who shared comparable incomes and styles of life, the arguments about who

[1] Jean Égret, *La Pré-Révolution Française 1787–1788* (Paris, 1962), Chapter VII, V.
[2] F. Bluche, *Les Magistrats du Parlement de Paris au XVIIIe siècle* (Paris, 1960), p. 304.

should be reckoned a nobleman and who a bourgeois, which bedevilled French social life in the eighteenth century, and later the writing of French history, would not have arisen. The English model had, however, no counterpart in the major continental countries.

In these countries the nobility was an order or estate, defined, like other groups in the *société d'ordres*, in terms of its rights in law. In the period here under discussion it was never, in any sense of the word, a social class. Because entry into it was comparatively easy in France, and also in the Habsburg dominions in the second half of the eighteenth century, and even in Prussia was far from impossible, and because all the children of a man possessing hereditary nobility were themselves noble, the nobility in every country was a very numerous group which included people who pursued a variety of different professions, and were separated from each other by greatly varying degrees of wealth or poverty. In France at the top of the income scale came the princes of the blood, the non-royal dukes, and the ennobled *fermiers généraux*. The average fortune left by each of the *fermiers généraux* who died between 1751 and 1775 has been estimated at 3·9 million livres (say £170,000 in the English currency of the time).[1] A number of the dukes enjoyed incomes equivalent to £26,000 a year or more.[2] The richest man in France, the Duc d'Orléans (the future Philippe Égalité) is estimated to have had, on the eve of the Revolution, an annual gross income of approximately 10 million livres, or, roughly, £440,000 in English money.[3] At the bottom of the scale came the destitute. Jean Meyer found that in one district in Brittany a third of the nobility was reduced to beggary and believed that a similar noble proletariat existed in other parts of France.[4] It seems likely that judged by any other standard than that of destitution a considerable proportion of the French nobility was very poor. From such evidence as is available it seems probable that similar, perhaps even worse, conditions prevailed among the nobility in the other major European countries.

On the other hand in France in the eighteenth century the richest individuals were always nobles, and the nobility the richest group in any community;[5] and there seems no reason to doubt that a similar state of affairs prevailed elsewhere. In these circumstances, though noble status

---

[1] Yves Durand, *Les Fermiers généraux au dixhuitième siècle* (Paris, 1971), pp. 132 f.

[2] H. Carré, *La Noblesse de France et l'opinion publique au XVIIIᵉ siècle* (Paris, 1920), pp. 41 f.

[3] B. Hyslop, *L'Apanage de Philippe Égalité, Duc d'Orléans* (Paris, 1965).

[4] Jean Meyer, *La Noblesse Bretonne* (Paris, 1972), p. 35.

[5] See particularly G. Lefebvre, *Études Orléanaises* (Paris, 1962), p. 172; R. Forster, *The Nobility of Toulouse in the Eighteenth Century* (Baltimore, 1960); Jean Sentou, *Fortunes et groupes sociaux à Toulouse sous la révolution* (Paris, 1969); A. Daumard and F. Furet, *Structures et relations sociales à Paris au milieu du XVIIIᵉ siècle* (Paris, 1961).

was not in itself a sign of prestige, and became increasingly less of one, there could be no prestige without it. In France until the Revolution to become a noble was the goal of every ambitious bourgeois and its attainment was greatly facilitated by the Crown's perennial shortage of money, caused principally by its numerous wars. Louis XIV sold titles of nobility in very large numbers (500 for example in March 1696 alone) and permitted many other people to acquire them by the purchase of offices to which they were attached.

Necker, in his *De l'Administration des Finances*, which he wrote in 1785, estimated that, apart from offices conferring only personal nobility, there were nearly 3,000 others which conferred hereditary nobility either immediately or after a lapse of time.[1] These offices were for the greater part in the parlements and other sovereign courts, particularly the cour des aides, and in the central financial administration; but there were also, Necker calculated, 900 holders of the office of king's secretary, the duties of which were minimal, and which throughout the greater part of the eighteenth century was the means of acquiring noble status most favoured by prosperous financiers, men of letters (Voltaire, for example, acquired nobility by this means) and successful commoners in general. All these offices became on purchase the personal property of their purchasers, who were at liberty to bequeath them to their heirs or to sell them on the market at the current price, which varied in accordance with the demand for them.

The practice of selling offices, which Louis XIV did not invent, but which assumed larger proportions in his reign than in the reigns of any of his predecessors, was at once a testimony to the Crown's need for money, to the prestige attached to noble status and, as the tasks assumed by the central government increased, to the necessity of tapping new sources of ability.

Louis XIV's fault in the eyes of the great noble families was thus not that he despised the order of nobility as such (only too obviously, as the etiquette insisted on at his court demonstrates, he did no such thing) but that he debased it because, for financial reasons, he created nobles wholesale, and because, in the interests of efficiency and to maintain an unchallengeable authority, he disrupted the noble hierarchy; for he excluded the princes of the blood and the ducs et pairs from his council and appointed in their stead men who, though always nobles at the time they assumed office, and commonly by inheritance, were of inferior noble status and generally came from the robe.

In France, in Professor Bluche's words, the sale of offices was the 'mécanisme d'ascension sociale', and some such mechanism became necessary in the countries of central Europe when they, too, aspired to

[1] Jacques Necker, *Oeuvres Complètes* (Paris, 1821), v, 365 ff.

the position of major military powers. Maria Theresa sold titles according to a tariff – 250 florins for a marquisate, 200 for an earldom and so
on.[1] Joseph II, in all respects less moderate, appears to have sold them
for the highest sum the purchaser could be induced to pay.[2] Even
Frederick William I of Prussia sold offices, though not on a hereditary
basis or with titles attached to them.

In the poverty-stricken dominions of the Hohenzollerns at Frederick
William's accession in 1713, the bulk of the nobles appear to have
deserved the description of 'stupid oxen', which their monarch applied
to them, and it seems clear that it was necessity that drove him to
employ bourgeois, many of whom were foreigners, in large numbers –
indeed in numbers larger, it has been claimed, than in any subsequent
period before the nineteen twenties.[3] As the head of one of the Boards
of War and Domains, Kammerdirektor Hille, whom the king appointed
to instruct the future Frederick II in cameralistics, said to his august
pupil when the latter complained that bourgeois were set above
noblemen: 'The world is indeed upside-down. How else should the
princes, who are not very intelligent, or who preoccupy themselves
with trifles, find sensible men to carry out their orders?'[4]

Frederick William I, a barbarian who in his childhood had shown
every sign of being educationally subnormal (by the time he was nine
it had proved impossible to teach him to count up to ten, or to learn the
alphabet), and who throughout his life was subject to psychopathic fits
of rage, was in no position to pose as the arbiter of manners after the
fashion of Louis XIV. The crude types of bourgeois, such as Johann
Andreas Kraut, whom he entrusted with important affairs of state, were
sometimes his personal friends. His Huguenot tutor, however, had
brought him up to believe that though the government employed
people who were not noblemen and who were of more value to it than
many nobles, nevertheless 'when a nobleman and a bourgeois had equal
deserts [gleiche Verdienste besässen] the nobleman was always to be
preferred to the bourgeois for both civilian and military offices'.[5] These
were the principles on which Frederick William acted. In spite of the
many bourgeois whom he promoted to high offices, the highest offices
in the civil service, and a fortiori in the army, were reserved for the
members of the old noble families whom he could trust.

There thus emerged during his reign, as in the early days of every

[1] I. Vianello, *Il Settecento Milanese* (Milan, 1934), p. 64.
[2] T. C. W. Blanning, *Joseph II and Enlightened Despotism* (London, 1970), p. 52.
[3] H. Rosenberg, *Bureaucracy, Aristocracy and Autocracy. The Prussian Experience*
(Cambridge, Mass., 1958), p. 67.
[4] F. Mehring, *Die Lessinglegende* (1953 edition), p. 150.
[5] C. Hinrichs, *Friedrich Wilhelm I* (Hamburg, 1941), p. 70.

bureaucratic absolutism, two separate hierarchies, a hierarchy based on birth and landed property, and a hierarchy based on function. The first determined social prestige and prevailed at court; the second governed relationships in the armies and the civil administrations. This was, however, commonly an unstable state of affairs. The old families resented their exclusion from power and the discipline which the new bureaucracies attempted to enforce on them. The parvenus were humiliated by the consciousness of their inferior birth, and while ruthless in the exercise of power developed an insatiable appetite for land and titles. This combination of circumstances promoted an unwillingness to accept authority on the one hand, and a violence in its exercise on the other, which in the course of time came to seem an impediment to efficiency.

Throughout the period under discussion the land employed the overwhelming mass of the population. Its possession thus conferred an amount of power over human beings obtainable in no other way. When combined with noble birth, which symbolized a hereditary right to rule – at a time when only inherited power appeared legitimate – it was the principal source of prestige. No government which on the one hand aroused the hostility of the landowners, or on the other failed to satisfy its principal servants, could hope to enforce its policies effectively. These were facts which Joseph II refused to recognize, but to which the French government came to accommodate itself (though to a diminishing extent in the second half of the eighteenth century) and on which Frederick the Great based his policy.

Both Frederick William I and Louis XIV, through the agency of their parvenu ministers, pushed their arbitrary power near to the limits of their nobility's endurance. The cost of Louis XIV's wars, and the means by which he financed them, combined with the natural calamities that afflicted France during his reign, greatly diminished the incomes, or means of subsistence, of all classes of his subjects apart from the financiers in the Crown's service. Frederick William's attempts to reclaim crown lands on an enormous scale are said to have driven the landowners to the verge of revolt. The activities of his recruiting sergeants, before the introduction of the form of conscription known as the canton system, caused the flight of whole villages.[1] In Prussia in his day, as in France under Louis XIV, there were cases when landlords and peasants combined together to resist the exactions of the royal officials. These experiences had a sobering effect. Louis XIV died lamenting that he had loved war too much. Frederick William admitted that he must 'soutenieren' his servants if he wished himself to be 'souteniert'.

In the course of the eighteenth century (except in the Habsburg

[1] O. Büsch, *Militärsystem und Sozialleben im alten Preußen* (Berlin, 1962), p. 16.

dominions, where things proceeded in the inverse order and absolutism progressed from the moderate policies of Maria Theresa to the revolutionary ones of Joseph II) the turbulence of the earlier reigns gave way, as the new bureaucracies became established, to more orderly procedures, and a compromise was reached between the monarchs and the great noble families. The standing armies and the royal officials in the provinces made revolts on the part of the nobility impossible. The new bureaucracies afforded growing opportunities for the exercise of power and the accumulation of wealth. These facts, together with the growth of education, made the tasks of the pen-pusher appear more respectable. The courts (except in Prussia where during the eighteenth century this institution can hardly be said to have existed) became not only the centres of fashion but the principal source of patronage. As one French writer put it: the French king was 'le premier des seigneurs de France mais surtout le grand patron des bureaux de Versailles'.[1] As a result of this combination of circumstances the distinguished noble families, with the monarch's approval, integrated themselves into the machinery of state.

They did so in increasing numbers. In 1758 the Duc de Belle-Isle (perhaps unduly sensitive on this subject because he was the direct descendant of that Fouquet whom a hundred years earlier Turenne had called a bourgeois), when offered the post of secretary of state for war, immediately turned it down. As his predecessor in the office, Cardinal Bernis, put it: 'Il était encore dans la vieille erreur q'un duc et pair et un maréchal de France ne pouvait sans déroger être secrétaire d'état.'[2] In the end, however, after considerable argument, Belle-Isle was persuaded to yield, and during the remaining thirty years of the ancien régime many other dukes followed his example. The members of distinguished court families in this period usually held the offices of secretary of state for war and for the navy. The office of contrôleur général, on the other hand, which was the most important in the kingdom, and included the responsibility for financial affairs, continued to be held by members of the robe. Comparable developments occurred in Prussia, where the bourgeois who had held the higher posts under Frederick William I were replaced under Frederick the Great, except in the administration of justice, by nobles.

In these ways the gulf between the hierarchies of birth and function was bridged and there emerged first in France and then in Prussia (but not, it seems, in the hereditary lands of the house of Habsburg where the bureaucracy was too recent a creation) a ruling élite, which cut

[1] F. Furet, 'Le Catéchisme de la Révolution Française' in *Annales, E.S.C.*, March–April, 1971.
[2] Michel Antoine, *Le Conseil du Roi sous le règne de Louis XV*, pp. 211–12.

across the divisions of the *société d'ordres*, and of whose members some came from old noble families distinguished before the days of absolutism, and others had risen to power by various different routes.

In France, as has been shown, the principal means of ascent was the purchase of office. The ambitious and able members of enterprising families from all the humbler walks of life, including the prosperous peasantry, bought and then sold one office after another until in two or more generations they were able to buy the office of maître de requêtes which provided one of the best tickets of entry to the competition for the highest posts – the intendances, the secretaryships of state and the contrôle général – which were not for sale but were, as far as circumstances permitted, awarded according to merit.

In Prussia, where the purchase of nobility, of hereditary office and, after the middle of the eighteenth century, of office of any kind was not permitted, things proceeded differently. One of the principal means of rising to a high position in the state and society was provided by the army. The army played a much more important part in Prussian life than in the life of any other country because of its enormous size in relation to the population. Whereas the peace-time strength of the French army at the end of the ancien régime was about 170,000 men out of a population of 26 million, the Prussian army at the same date was approximately 200,000 men out of a population of 5½ million; and though a high proportion – up to 50 per cent – of the troops were mercenaries, all the officers were Prussian by birth or adoption. At the end of the eighteenth century 68 per cent of all adult nobles in the Kurmark and 60 per cent in the province of East Prussia were or had been serving officers.[1]

In France service in the army was a way of losing money because of the cost of equipment, of buying a commission, and of the style of life an officer had to maintain. In Prussia, by contrast, for any man after he had reached the rank of company commander and possessed the necessary acumen, it was the principal road to affluence because of the permitted (but also the illegitimate) traffic in mercenaries. These opportunities were not so exclusively confined to nobles as Frederick the Great's notorious contempt for bourgeois might suggest; for a non-commissioned officer could win promotion, and with it noble status, in reward for distinguished service; and it was possible to obtain a commission by faking a title. This, it appears, was not uncommonly done – Gneisenau and Yorck von Wartenburg are examples – particularly by men from other parts of Germany. The procedure was one to which the military establishment was prepared to shut an eye in the case of talented soldiers; and once a parvenu thus equipped made a successful

[1] O. Büsch, *Militärsystem und Sozialleben im alten Preußen*, p. 95.

military career, and married a wife rich enough to enable him to buy a Rittergut, or noble estate, his social position and the future of his children were assured.[1]

For talented civilian commoners the way to promotion lay through the universities, the state examinations, and the patronage (often only to be had in return for services rendered) of some established bureaucratic dynasty. The outstandingly successful – commonly the sons of pastors, doctors, university professors, sometimes merchants, occasionally even free peasants[2] – were rewarded, like their counterparts in the army, with the grant of nobility.

Whatever the means of achieving a position of power and prestige, however, all those who achieved it were distinguished by the possession of an income that was large or at least substantial by the prevailing standards. In France and Prussia (though on a different scale in the two countries) wealth was not only the reward of success but to some extent, and increasingly, a prerequisite of attaining it. In France the purchase of a civilian office or a commission in the army was beyond the means of most nobles. In Prussia, too, many nobles could not afford the cost of life in the army until they reached the rank of captain, or the long unpaid apprenticeship in the civil service. The position in fact was that which Tocqueville described when he said: 'la séparation durable de la noblesse et de la richesse est une chimère qui aboutit toujours après un certain temps à la destruction de la première ou à l'amalgame des deux'.[3]

It was this amalgam that distinguished the new ruling élites in the second half of the eighteenth century, and that gave rise among those who observed it to the belief, according to whether the observer's inclinations were radical or conservative, that it must be either recognized or abolished by means of changes in the law. Turgot said in 1776 that the cause of the privileged was no longer the cause of the distinguished families against the *roturiers*, but the cause of the rich against the poor.[4] Diatribes against the power of money to disrupt the old relationships became a commonplace in France in the second half of the eighteenth century, and also began to be heard in Prussia, as the profits from trade, manufactures and finance increased, and as the rise in agricultural rents led to speculation in land, to frequent changes in the ownership of

[1] See P. Paret, *Yorck and the Era of Prussian Reform 1807 to 1815* (Princeton, 1966), Ch. II, 'The Frederician Age'.

[2] Christian von Rother (1788–1849), head of the Seihandlung, is an example of a man who rose from the peasantry to this high position (see *Forschungen zur Brandenburgischen und Preußischen Geschichte*, vol. 46, 1934).

[3] Quoted by Lefebvre in his introduction to Tocqueville's 'Ancien Régime', in *Oeuvres*, ed. J. P. Mayer, II, 21.

[4] Turgot, *Oeuvres*, ed. Schelle (Paris, 1913–23), V, 188.

noble estates and hence to the disruption, it was complained, of the patriarchal relationship between the landlord and his peasants.[1]

All this is not to say, however, as was often said at the time and later, that money alone procured entry into the ruling élites. It was in fact never more than a sine qua non, providing the basis for a common culture, shared by the educated members of the nobility and the upper bourgeoisie to which Tocqueville testified when he said: 'L'éducation et la manière de vivre avaient déjà mis entre ces deux hommes (the bourgeois and the noble) mille...ressemblances. Le bourgeois avait autant de lumières que le noble, et, ce qu'il faut bien remarquer, ses lumières avaient été puisées précisément au même foyer.'[2] In the diary of Graf Lehndorf (a Prussian noble whom an injury in childhood had precluded from a military career and whom Frederick the Great appointed gentleman in waiting to his wife), it is possible to trace as early as the seventeen-fifties a growing, and somewhat astonished, awareness that one could live among the rich bourgeoisie 'als wäre man bei den vornehmsten Leute'.[3] Among the members of the ruling élites, however, ancient lineage, when combined with wealth, still remained the principal source of power and prestige, even though it had increasingly to compete with distinction of intellect and notable service to the state on the part of the recently ennobled or, in Prussia, even sometimes of those who still remained commoners.

Already, in fact, by the end of the eighteenth century, there had begun to emerge in both France and Prussia,[4] though hardly it would seem in the hereditary lands of the house of Habsburg, the genesis of that society described by A. J. Tudesq in his Grands Notables en France 1840–1849 – a society in which the members of the ruling groups were for the greater part landowners (land being still the principal source of wealth) and came from substantial, though not necessarily noble, families; for only a substantial family background seemed capable of producing that 'épanouissement de la personalité individuelle' on which Turgot in France and Stein and Wilhelm von Humboldt in Prussia placed their hopes.

[1] See Martini, 'Die Adelsfrage in Preußen vor 1806', in Vierteljahrschrift für Sozial- und Wirtschaftsgeschichte (1938), Beiheft 35.   [2] Tocqueville, in Oeuvres, II, 146.
[3] Dreißig Jahre am Hofe Friedrichs des Grossen, ed. K. A. Schmidt-Lötzen (Gotha, 1907), p. 441.
[4] Rosenberg pointed this out in his Bureaucracy, Aristocracy and Autocracy, the Prussian Experience. It is confirmed by many contemporary writings. Lehndorf, for example, who had an insatiable curiosity about the incomes and the origins of the Prussian grandees with whom he associated, noted that a considerable number had risen from the bourgeoisie and been granted titles for various reasons. He also noted a very large number of marriages between Prussian noblemen and women from the bourgeoisie. The mother of Friedrich von der Marwitz's first wife was a bourgeoise, as was Bismarck's mother.

This kind of society was, however, plainly incompatible with the *société d'ordres*, with its large numbers of more or less ignorant and poverty-stricken, though nevertheless privileged, nobility. In the age of absolutism the great expansion in state activity, and the economic growth which the state had set itself to promote, had widened the gap between wealth and poverty in every group, and particularly in the estate of the nobility. In France those nobles who could not afford to buy themselves a commission in one of the fighting services, or some civilian office, saw themselves doomed to economic stagnation if not decline. Retail trade was closed to them by law and in any case was incompatible with their pride. The money-making activities in which it was possible for them to engage without dérogeance – particularly overseas trade, industry and finance – all required capital which *ex hypothesi* they lacked. Only very exceptional individuals among those born into genteel poverty could escape from these restrictions.

In Prussia, where the general poverty was greater, and tradition stronger, the position of that 'great mass of poor, landless and indebted noblemen, uneducated, needy and presumptuous',[1] as Stein described them, appears to have been even more deplorable than in France. One of them, after describing how he was physically unfitted for army life, and was unable to afford the training, and the long period without payment, necessary for success in the bureaucracy, concluded that it would not be strange if nobles in his circumstances shot themselves or threw themselves out of windows.[2]

In France long before the end of the eighteenth century the difference in income between the rich and the poor nobles had become far too great to permit a common way of life or even any sense of common purpose. Arthur Young discovered to his amazement that not even the Revolution was capable of uniting the nobility in self-defence.[3] As a contemporary biographer of General Charette, one of the leaders of the Vendée revolt, put it when speaking of Charette's relations with the emigrés whom he despised:

Loin de trouver parmi ces hommes déjà presque égaux par la naissance cette égalité qu'établit toujours la même fortune, il vit que toute l'etiquette et tous les vices de la Cour de Versailles avaient été transplantés à Coblenz.... Quelle figure pouvait d'ailleurs faire Charette avec...sa physionomie dure et farouche et sa manière un peu sauvage au milieu des courtisans qui se piquaient de pousser au dernier point la galanterie, les grâces, la politesse?[4]

[1] Gerhard Ritter, *Stein*, 3rd ed. (Stuttgart, 1958), p. 285.
[2] *Briefe eines schlesischen Grafen an einen kurländischen Edelmann* (Altona, 1795).
[3] Arthur Young, *Travels in France*, ed. C. Maxwell (Cambridge, 1929), pp. 180–90.
[4] J. Meyer, *La Noblesse Bretonne*, p. 248.

The existence of the large number of poor nobles raised great difficulties for the monarchs and their ministers who still believed in the *société d'ordres*. In France and Prussia, though not in the hereditary lands of the house of Habsburg where the standing army was a creation of the second half of the eighteenth century and had little appeal for the nobility, it was common to invoke the myth that a nation's greatness turned on the military virtues, that these were the nobleman's prerogative, and that the rights of birth must in consequence be protected against the eroding power of money. The desire to maintain what the French military reformers of the second half of the eighteenth century described as the 'armée pure et dure' provided the mainspring of Frederick the Great's social and economic policy, driving him into many actions which cramped economic development, for example his refusal to allow commoners to buy noble land. Similar motives in France inspired the notorious loi Ségur of 1781 which permitted the sale of commissions in most regiments only to people who could show four generations of nobility on the father's side, and which has been shown to have been directed not against the bourgeoisie, but against the sons of rich and recently ennobled families who drove up the price of commissions and with whom the poor nobility could not compete.[1]

Such measures expressed the view of conservatives who wished to preserve the nobility as a privileged order and hence the whole *société d'ordres* of which it formed an integral part. Many radical ministers, however, in France in the second half of the eighteenth century, and in Prussia after 1806, and the Emperor Joseph II in the Habsburg dominions, had no patience with this attitude. Stein described the poor nobles, for whose benefit institutions were continually being founded, as a burden on the state. He would have abolished their privileges, and Turgot and Necker would have liked to do the same. Such people, and their point of view was widespread, did not want to do away with nobility as such, but only with nobility as an order or estate. They would have welcomed a nobility on the British model, according to which titles were associated with landed wealth, were granted only for outstanding service, and carried no legally guaranteed social privileges.

Sooner or later the conflicting views about the rights and functions of the nobility came to divide the governments in every country and the minds of individual noblemen. Among the monarchs in the major powers at the end of the eighteenth century, only Frederick the Great was determined to bolster up the existing society at all costs, notwithstanding his theoretical objections to it. The attitudes of Louis XV and Louis XVI were always ambivalent. They veered first to one side and then to the other according to which groups of ministers or courtiers

[1] F. Furet, 'Le Catéchisme de la Révolution Française', *Annales*, 1971, p. 275.

gained their ear. Only the Habsburgs Joseph and Leopold would have liked to see the old order go. They lacked, however, any significant degree of support among either the nobility or the bourgeoisie, and did not possess a bureaucracy sufficiently powerful to effect such reforms as the Prussian bureaucracy was able to introduce under the leadership first of Stein and then of Hardenberg.

III. *Mercantilism and the Bourgeoisie*

Before the last quarter of the eighteenth century, the monarchs were unable to conceive of a society in which the order or estate of the nobility did not play the dominant part. They nevertheless felt obliged to promote trade and manufactures, and in consequence the growth of a bourgeoisie, in order to provide themselves with the resources needed to meet the continually increasing demands of war. They deliberately embarked on the task of increasing wealth by means of the policies commonly described as mercantilist.

Mercantilism as practised on the continent of Europe was an essential concomitant of absolutism and developed in every state *pari passu* with the growth in the monarch's power. Though increasingly discredited in France from the middle of the eighteenth century, when many other aspects of absolutism also came under attack, it reached its golden age in Prussia under Frederick the Great and in the hereditary lands of the house of Habsburg under Maria Theresa and Joseph II. Essentially a response to the needs of war, it was enforced by the autocratic methods characteristic of absolutism, and on the assumption that the needs of the state were paramount and individual interests of no account.

The nature of mercantilism has been discussed in an earlier volume, and no more need be said about it here than is necessary to describe and account for its social consequences. Everywhere the mercantilists were moved by the ambition to increase the wealth of their states at the expense of the wealth of other states. Just as power is by definition relative, so in the pursuit of wealth, on which power was seen to depend, the objective was relative not absolute. As Locke once put it: 'Riches do not consist in having more gold and silver, but in having more in proportion than the rest of the world or than one's neighbours...who sharing the gold and silver of the world in less proportion want the means of plenty and power and so are the poorer.'[1] Though the mercantilists did not believe, as this quotation might suggest, that wealth consisted in the possession of the precious metals, they accepted Locke's principle that the purpose in seeking it was to be richer than

[1] E. F. Heckscher, *Mercantilism*, Engl. trans. (London, 1935), II, 23.

one's rivals. Mercantilism, in consequence, meant economic warfare which the belligerents waged by methods designed to make their own states as nearly as possible self-sufficing and to force other states into economic dependence on them. These objectives involved on the one hand building up one's own industries and curtailing or prohibiting imports; on the other hand monopolizing as far as possible the sources of raw materials, transport and technical skill. They were objectives avowedly pursued with a view to power politics, and, particularly in Prussia, even when it was apparent that they obstructed economic growth. In December 1769, for example, the Hamburgers, whose entrepôt trade between western and central Europe the Prussians had long been trying to destroy, pointed out to the Prussian government the economic advantages that Prussia herself would reap from a liberalization of trade. The Prussians did not deny the argument. Mindful, however, of their successes in dominating states such as Saxony, which were economically and culturally more advanced, but militarily impotent, they pointed out that for them it was not the welfare of the human race that was at issue but their own military power.[1]

Mercantilists, it was shown in the previous volume, were always vitally concerned to create a favourable balance of trade, and were so of necessity, since in the absence of adequate credit facilities and paper currencies governments needed supplies of bullion for the purposes of domestic trade, in order to make possible the payment of taxes, the hiring of mercenaries, and the purchase abroad of such essential commodities as they could not produce themselves. The relative importance, nevertheless, which mercantilists attached to foreign trade, industry and agriculture varied from time to time and from country to country.

Colbert's principal biographer said of him that 'so highly did he esteem manufacturing enterprises that it is hard to tell whether they or commercial ventures were nearer to his heart'.[2] He showed, however, very little interest in agriculture because, it has been suggested, he looked on it as a lost cause.[3] In central Europe the cameralist tradition always recognized that agriculture provided the population with its principal means of livelihood, though the governments increasingly (to judge by the numbers of edicts issued on the subject) paid more attention to manufacturers. Foreign trade, on the other hand, generally seemed of secondary importance, except in so far as it was necessary to build up stocks of bullion.

---

[1] *Quellen zur Geschichte von Hamburgs Handel und Schiffahrt im 17., 18. und 19. Jahrhundert*, ed. E. Baasch (Hamburg, 1910), pp. 171 ff.

[2] C. W. Cole, *Colbert and a Century of French Mercantilism* (New York, 1939), II, 133.   [3] W. Naudé, *Getreidehandelspolitik* (Berlin, 1896), I, 34 ff.

In the west one spoke of 'the noble profession of the merchant who deserves all favour as being the best and most profitable member of the commonwealth'.[1] 'Commerce', it was said in France in the reign of Louis XIV, 'provides the riches of towns and of the state.'[2] In the eighteenth century, before the physiocrats came to power, it was believed in French government circles that a large colonial trade was the essential basis of a great power – a view that derived support from the fact that when French overseas trade collapsed in war, so did the ability of the French government to borrow, and hence to finance its war effort. As Choiseul put it to his Austrian allies in 1759: 'L'interruption du commerce, suite de la perte des colonies a anéanti le crédit et conduit à une espèce de banqueroute...ce n'est pas tout d'avoir du courage; il faut avoir le moyen de le soutenir.'[3] French economic development came to conform to this point of view. Overseas trade increased rapidly, particularly between 1763 and the middle seventies, but was not accompanied by a comparable increase in manufactures, since the expanding trades were largely re-export trades in colonial produce.[4] In Prussia, by contrast, though the unfavourable balance of trade which had characterized the reign of Frederick William I was reversed, and though the number of people employed in manufacture increased, the volume of foreign trade would appear to have declined.[5]

In the more primitive communities under the rule of the Habsburgs and the Hohenzollerns western attitudes to trade were inappropriate. The settlement and exploitation of overseas territories were no tasks for the rulers of these sparsely populated areas which were themselves urgently in need of immigrants. The 75 per cent or more of the governments' revenues that were absorbed by the armies left nothing over for navies on whose protection the colonial trades depended. Frederick abandoned the colonial projects he had at one time cherished on the principle, as he put it, that 'Qui trop embrasse, mal étreint.'[6] The capital for investment, which until late in the eighteenth century in central Europe only governments could accumulate, was spent by the rulers in their own territories – in developing technical skills which had been destroyed during the Thirty Years War, and in rehabilitating areas such as East Prussia, which at the beginning of the eighteenth century lost half its population through plague and famine, and Hungary where the expulsion of the Turks left huge areas uncultivated. In

[1] Heckscher, *Mercantilism*, II, 282.

[2] L. Rothkrug, *Opposition to Louis XIV* (Princeton, 1965), p. 225.

[3] R. Waddington, *La Guerre de Sept Ans* (Paris, 1899), III, 445.

[4] E. Labrousse, *La Crise de l'économie française à la fin de l'ancien régime* (Paris, 1943), p. xxxvii.

[5] A. Zottmann, *Die Wirtschaftspolitik Friedrichs des Großen* (Vienna and Leipzig, 1937), p. 66.   [6] R. Koser, *König Friedrich der Große* (Stuttgart, 1893), I, 456.

this part of Europe the merchant, in so far as he was merely a trader, was associated with the importation of luxury goods which drained the state of bullion, and was seen as a social nuisance. Frederick the Great expressed the typical attitude when he said: 'I remain firmly on the side of industry, for at all costs I must give my people work, and it is clear that a manufacturer can employ 2,000 hands when a trader [*Handelsmann*] can barely employ 20.'[1] The type of business man whom Frederick encouraged (while nevertheless despising him) was the entrepreneur who gave employment, and increased technical knowledge and the numbers of skilled workers.

Notwithstanding, nevertheless, the different order of priorities adopted by mercantilists in France and in central Europe, economic policy in these two areas was plainly inspired by aims that were more similar than different. In both it was a response to the decline brought about by civil war (in France by the Fronde; in central Europe by the Thirty Years War). In both it was based on the assumption that the interests of the state, as interpreted by the monarch, took precedence over every other consideration and justified an unlimited degree of government interference. In both it was inspired by the conscious desire to bring the economies of the countries concerned up to the level of the most advanced contemporary models, so that it may be seen as a means of overcoming economic backwardness. In both it deliberately set out to combat idleness; to inculcate habits of orderliness and industry; to encourage inventiveness and to break the bondage to tradition.

How far the mercantilists succeeded in promoting economic development has long been a matter of debate. Colbert plainly achieved his objects well enough during his lifetime (whether or not because of his attempts to foster industry) to permit France to maintain a larger army and navy than any state had hitherto possessed, and to threaten Europe, and indeed the world, with French domination. During the heyday of mercantilism in central Europe, the Habsburgs built up a standing army larger than the French, and seemed to Frederick the Great a more formidable military power. Frederick himself during the Seven Years War, with a population of less than five million, and aided only by plunder from Saxony and other conquered territories, and by British subsidies which accounted for some 20 per cent of his war expenditure,[2] achieved the remarkable feat of defending his territories against enemies whose combined populations amounted to about 100 million. In the twenty-three years that intervened between the peace of

[1] K. Hinze, *Die Arbeiterfrage zu Beginn des modernen Kapitalismus in Brandenburg-Preussen* (2nd ed., Berlin, 1963), p. 74.

[2] See W. O. Henderson, *Studies in the Economic Policy of Frederick the Great* (London, 1963), p. 39.

Hubertusberg in 1763 and his death, he more than made good the damage which the war had caused, while continuing to maintain his army at a figure equivalent to 4 per cent of his population although, in Adam Smith's judgment, 1 per cent was as much as any state could afford. Even in the other powers, whose monarchs and ministers were less dedicated to militarism, mercantilist policies permitted an increase in the armed forces, and a mobilization of resources for war, on a hitherto unparalleled scale.

As a result, much wealth was destroyed. The last years of Louis XIV's reign were years of economic calamity. Colbert's schemes of empire were in ruins and his navy annihilated. Most foreign trades were at a standstill and agriculture greatly impoverished. Quesnay estimated the loss of population at 4½ million souls, or nearly 20 per cent of the figure at Louis' accession.[1] If we may believe Professor Goubert, who puts the loss at '2 to 3 million at least' for the years 1689–97[2] – that is, before the famine and epidemics at the end of the reign – this figure would not be impossible. In the famous judgment of Fénelon, which modern research has not modified, France at Louis' death seemed like 'un grand hôpital désolé et sans provision'.[3]

Many of these disasters, however, were due to Louis' violations of Colbert's principles, as well as to the natural calamities and falling prices for which he was not responsible, though his policies greatly exacerbated their results. In the more favourable economic climate that prevailed throughout most of the eighteenth century, as well as because of more rational policies and practices, no reign in any major country had such calamitous social consequences. War was waged on a larger scale, and became more expensive. It was, however, less continuous and directed to more limited objectives. In the second half of the century national income appears to have increased in all the three states here under consideration.

In none, however, was it as large as in Britain which had never known mercantilism on the continental model. This fact led Heckscher, who measured the achievements of Colbert's system by British standards, to pronounce French mercantilism a failure, and there were many Frenchmen even in Louis' own day who shared this view. Mirabeau passed a similar judgment on Prussia and found supporters among the Prussians after Frederick's death. In modern times judgments have tended to follow national patterns. To the British, at one extreme, who

---

[1] *Hommes*, printed in *François Quesnay et la Physiocratie* (Institut National d'Études Démographiques, Paris, 1958), II, 513.

[2] P. Goubert, *Louis Quatorze et vingt millions de français* (Paris, 1966), p. 170.

[3] Quoted by E. Lavisse, *Histoire de France depuis les origines jusqu'à la Révolution* (Paris, 1908), VIII (i), 272.

attributed their successes in the eighteenth century and their industrial revolution to the relative freedom of their economy from government control, the innumerable regulations and continuous government interference which characterized continental mercantilism, have usually seemed repulsive. To the Germans, at the other extreme, they have always seemed the means by which Prussia, in Frederick the Great's words, was lifted 'out of the dust', and which permitted Germany as a whole to make good the damage done by the Thirty Years War. The Germans, nevertheless, do not see the essential achievements of mercantilism in the wealth which was created during the period when mercantilist policies prevailed. This was indeed only small, for, as in France, many of the new industries foundered, and by the end of the eighteenth century central Europe was still an overwhelmingly agricultural area with a largely unreformed agriculture. They see these achievements as consisting primarily in the social habits which mercantilism engendered. In Professor Lütge's judgment, the mercantilists educated people to approach economic problems rationally; they instilled a new ethos of work; they produced a *Verbürgerlichung* of society.[1]

If these aspects have not been so strongly stressed in France it is because mercantilist policies, which were alien to the traditions of the monarchy and the nobility, were pursued less purposefully. The desire of the monarchs for a magnificent court and of all such nobles as could afford it for a magnificent style of life; the love of war and conquest and the determination to pursue them regardless of the cost; the power of ancient institutions, particularly the parlements, to defend ancient customs – all these made France a relatively unfavourable soil for Colbert's gospel, which was more honoured in central Europe.

Mercantilism logically involved some degree of state planning which was impossible without the collection of statistics and the willingness of governments to live within their means. 'Trade', Colbert said, 'is the source of public finance and public finance is the vital nerve of war.'[2] These were principles which Louis XIV and his two successors were never willing to accept. 'In regard to expenditures', Colbert wrote to Louis XIV in 1680, 'I beg Your Majesty to permit me only to say to him, that in war as in peace he has never consulted the amount of money available, in determining his expenditures, a thing which is so extraordinary that assuredly there is no precedent in it.'[3] However extraordinary this may have seemed to Colbert, it seemed natural to the Bourbons until the Revolution. Its results were fiscalism (or the attempt

[1] F. Lütge, *Deutsche Sozial- und Wirtschaftsgeschichte* (3rd ed., Berlin, 1966), p. 403.
[2] Heckscher, *Mercantilism*, II, 17.
[3] Cole, *Colbert and a Century of French Mercantilism*, I, 311–12.

to raise money by any means that were to hand regardless of the social and economic consequences), corruption and the perversion of justice; it precluded the rational use of resources and the rational prosecution of foreign relations and war; it impeded economic growth and frustrated all attempts at reform.

In spite, nevertheless, of the failures of Louis XIV's reign, and the obstacles with which mercantilism had to contend in France afterwards, Colbert nursed up a class of merchants into self-consciousness, and his visions of France as a great naval and imperial power were realized, if somewhat precariously, in the eighteenth century. Throughout the greater part of this century France led the world in the luxury industries and in various forms of technical invention. Though the figures are too uncertain to make it possible to estimate the proportion of the French population, compared with the populations of other nations, that lived in towns, France certainly had many more and larger towns than the other major continental powers. Paris in 1789, with a population of about 600,000, was the largest city in the world after London, more than three times the size of Vienna and nearly four times that of Berlin.

These facts could not fail to be significant, and in France the growth of trade in the eighteenth century has commonly been adduced to support the thesis that in the age of mercantilism the French bourgeoisie gradually achieved a degree of wealth which exceeded that of the nobility. As Mathiez put it in his *Révolution Française*, 'La bourgeoisie possédait certainement la majeure partie de la fortune Française. Elle progressait sans cesse, tandis que les ordres privilégiés se ruinaient.'[1] As Lefebvre put it in his *Quatre-Vingt-Neuf*: '...la renaissance du commerce et de l'industrie avait créé, chemin faisant, une forme nouvelle de la richesse, la richesse mobilière, et une nouvelle classe, la bourgeoisie... La structure légale du pays leur [the nobility] conservait le premier rang, mais, dans la réalité, la puissance économique, la capacité, les perspectives d'avenir passaient aux mains de la bourgeoisie.'[2]

For fifty years these judgments have provided the accepted interpretation of French social development in the eighteenth century and of the causes of the Revolution. They have, however, recently been subjected to increasing criticism, and can no longer be believed. In France, it was said earlier, all the available evidence goes to show that in the eighteenth century the richest people were still nobles and the nobility still the richest group in the community.[3] It was not in fact the bourgeoisie that was getting richer at the expense of the nobility, but the more favoured sections of the nobility that were getting richer at the expense of the bourgeoisie, because the successful bourgeois bought

---

[1] *La Révolution Française* (Paris, 1933), I, 13.
[2] G. Lefebvre, *Quatre-Vingt-Neuf* (Paris, 1939), p. 5.   [3] See p. 564, n. 5 above.

themselves titles, and married their daughters into noble families, which had no objection to a parvenue if her dowry were large enough.[1]

Lefebvre's belief that the eighteenth century saw the rise of a class of capitalist bourgeois has been shown by Professor G. V. Taylor to be largely unwarranted.[2] Professor Taylor estimated that at the end of the Ancien Régime only about 20 per cent of the wealth in private hands in France was industrial and commercial wealth. The remaining 80 per cent was what he called 'proprietary wealth', by which he meant wealth that was non-capitalist in function and consisted in investments in land, urban property, annuities and so-called 'venal' offices, or offices purchased on a hereditary basis. This form of wealth yielded small but fairly constant returns which varied between 1 per cent and 5 per cent and which were realized not by entrepreneurial effort, which was thought degrading, but by 'mere ownership and the passage of calendar intervals'.

'Proprietary wealth' was the form of wealth that was preferred by the bulk of the bourgeoisie and of the nobility alike because it provided the stable fortune necessary for gentility. On the other hand, in the small industrial and commercial sector many members of the nobility, and particularly of the court nobility, were investing in various lucrative but more or less risky enterprises such as ship-owning, the slave trade, mining and metallurgy.

This analysis, together with the accumulating evidence about the distribution of wealth between the nobility and the bourgeoisie, disposes of the belief that the eighteenth century saw the development in France of a class of bourgeois capitalists rich and self-confident enough to aspire to take over the control of the state. It does not, however, preclude but, on the contrary, to some extent supports the view that sections of the nobility were adopting bourgeois ideas and practices, or, as the Germans would say, were becoming *verbürgerlicht*.

Verbürgerlichung or *embourgeoisement*, and its opposite, *Feudalisierung* or *Aristokratisierung*, are processes which the English-speaking peoples so long ignored that they have not even words for them. Since they postulate ways of behaving and attitudes of mind peculiar respectively to nobles and bourgeois, they have seemed dangerous concepts to English and American historians because of the difficulties of giving them a clear meaning. Professor Hexter, in a famous essay in which he castigated the writers on Tudor England for speaking of the rise of the middle classes without attempting to define them, himself defined the bourgeois as follows: 'In this paper the middle class is Seyssel's estat

[1] See J. Sentou, *Fortunes et groupes sociaux à Toulouse sous la Révolution*, p. 472.
[2] G. V. Taylor, 'Non-capitalist wealth and the origins of the French Revolution', *American Historical Review*, vol. 121 (Jan. 1967).

moyen – merchants, financiers, industrialists, the town rich, the bourgeoisie.' In defence of his definition he said that he had been 'impelled to this draconian measure by the conviction that otherwise the middle class becomes so fluid, indeed so ethereal, as to defy attempts to say anything about it'.[1]

Professor Hexter's definition precludes, as he doubtless intended, the possibility of embourgeoisement because it recognizes no attribute peculiar to the bourgeois, apart from that of function. Sombart, on the other hand, whose classic *Der Bourgeois* appeared at the beginning of the present century, and who profoundly influenced all subsequent German thinking, defined the bourgeois not in terms of function but of the attitudes of mind which pursuing his functions bred in him. To Sombart the bourgeois seemed essentially a psychological phenomenon ('ein Mensch von ganz besonderer Seelenbeschaffenheit') whose ideals he deduced from the memoirs of merchants, from the mottos hung above the desks in counting-houses, and from such works as *The Way to Wealth*, first published in 1758, which went into 146 editions in English, French, German and Italian.

Sombart saw the eighteenth-century bourgeois, whose prototype he found in Benjamin Franklin,[2] as preeminently distinguished by the capacity to think in terms of figures and by the habit of rational calculation, particularly in matters of money. These were people, he said, who believed in relating ends to means; who saw idleness as a sin and planned the use of their time as carefully as they planned their expenditure. (It was Franklin who coined the phrase 'Time is money.') They conceived the idea of saving; in business affairs they believed in reliability, in honesty, and in the keeping of bargains. In private life they preached living 'correctly'. Moderation seemed to them the cardinal virtue.

Whatever the judgment on Sombart's analysis of the spirit of capitalism, of which he saw the point of view typified by Benjamin Franklin as an essential component, it is plain that this point of view became widely prevalent in what is commonly referred to as the age of bourgeois civilization, whose prerequisites were described by Adam Smith when he said,

Commerce and manufactures can seldom flourish in any state which does not enjoy a regular administration of justice, in which the people do not feel themselves secure in the possession of their property, in which the faith of

---

[1] 'The myth of the middle class in Tudor England' (in *Reappraisals in History*, Aberdeen, 1961), p. 75.

[2] To be exact, Sombart saw Benjamin Franklin as typical of 'der Bürger', whom he distinguished from the industrial capitalist or 'der Bourgeois'.

contracts is not supported by law, and in which the authority of the state is not supposed to be regularly employed in enforcing the payment of debts from all those who are able to pay.[1]

The rule of law (in the sense of law administered by professional judges who are irremovable by the government and to whose judgments the government itself is subject); equality before the law (in the sense that no person, in his private capacity, has a legal claim to privileges by virtue of birth, status, race or religion); the sanctity of private property; freedom of enterprise from corporate or state ownership or direction; the civil liberties and (at least in the west) representative government, were the distinguishing features of bourgeois government and society. All of them were absent in France before the Revolution, but the need for them was increasingly stressed in governing circles in the last four or five decades of the Ancien Régime.

The attempts of Machault d'Arnouville, Terray, Turgot, Calonne, Necker and others to rationalize the system of direct taxation by reducing or abolishing the nobility's tax privileges; the attempts to do away, at the expense of the privileges of provinces and towns, with the internal tolls and customs barriers and the multiplicity of different tariffs; the attempts to free manufactures from the control of the gilds, and agriculture from what were known as the 'servitudes collectives' required by the open-field system; Necker's attempts to reduce the number of venal offices in the central financial administration and to replace their owners by paid servants of the state, and Maupeou's similar attempts in the sphere of justice; the repeated assertions of successive *contrôleurs généraux* that bankruptcy (in former ages the accepted means by which the Crown extricated itself from its financial difficulties) was both dishonest and economically disastrous; the protests against arbitrary imprisonment made by Malesherbe when he was president of the Cours des Aides; the desire for some form of popular representation expressed in Turgot's and Dupont de Nemours' *Mémoire sur les Municipalités* and in the various schemes for setting up provincial assemblies – all these attempts at reform illustrate the truth of Tocqueville's assertion that the rulers of France in the second half of the eighteenth century held views very different from those of their predecessors, and demonstrate the extent to which embourgeoisement had proceeded in governing circles.

This process of embourgeoisement was doubtless furthered by contacts between officials and the business world which mercantilist policies made necessary, and of which the careers of Trudaine, Roland, and other government officials concerned with manufactures are an illustration. The pursuit, however, by ministers of bourgeois objectives

[1] *The Wealth of Nations*, ed. E. Cannan (Methuen, London, 1950).

was not the result of pressures brought to bear on them by traders and manufacturers, but was the product of their own experience in the service of the state – an experience which increasingly demonstrated that the continued existence of the *société d'ordres* was incompatible with efficiency and the maintenance of national prestige.

On the other hand embourgeoisement plainly did not go far enough in France to allow the projected reforms to be translated into practice. Attachment to the old order was deeply entrenched in certain key institutions, notably the parlements, and was indeed in varying degrees widely diffused throughout the population. The monarchs, in spite of yielding temporarily to the persuasions of reforming ministers, remained staunch in its defence. The opposite process of *Feudalisierung*, by which men of bourgeois origins accepted aristocratic values, had long been at work. The parvenus, and most conspicuously the *fermiers généraux*, who in the course of the eighteenth century had infiltrated the establishment from below, imitated the ways of life of the grand seigneur. Though bourgeois ideas gained an increasingly wide currency, and were paid lip-service by much of the fashionable world, they did not eradicate, even among those who professed them, a belief in the old standards. Apart from Turgot, who appears to have foreseen and welcomed the prospect of revolution,[1] though he was not prepared himself to take any action to further it, even the reformers who advocated the most drastic changes preached at the same time, as did Calonne and Necker, the dangers of breaking too radically with tradition. There were thus no revolutionaries in France before the outbreak of the Revolution which, as Tocqueville said 'a pris,...le monde à l'improviste' even though the causes that produced it had been at work for a long time.[2]

In central Europe as in France, though to a much greater extent, it was the state that was the principal agent of embourgeoisement. The work of rehabilitation and development in which the Hohenzollerns engaged throughout the eighteenth century, and the Habsburgs in the second half of it, increased the scope and number of bourgeois activities. The first newspapers in Prussia, for example, were set up by Frederick the Great for the purposes of combating foreign propaganda. As a result a class of journalists developed. The founding of schools and universities, particularly remarkable in the Habsburg dominions, and the respect for knowledge inculcated by the Berlin Academy of Sciences, gave the learned professions a new importance and increased their numbers. The continual expansion of armies and bureaucracies; the government

[1] See Turgot's letter to Hume of 3 July 1768, quoted in L. B. Bongie, *David Hume. Prophet of Counter-Revolution* (Oxford, 1965), pp. 50–1.
[2] *Oeuvres Complètes*, p. 96.

sponsored schemes for the improvement of transport and agriculture, and for the creation of new industries and credit facilities, provided new opportunities for the employment of bourgeois and a greater demand for education. The towns increased in size. The population of Berlin is estimated to have been about 147,000 at Frederick the Great's death in 1786, and thus represented a slightly higher proportion of the total population than did Paris at the same date. Admittedly in Berlin the soldiers and their families quartered in the city accounted for nearly 97,000 people. Of these, however, some 61,000 were employed in manufactures, that is in civilian occupations, though they lived under military discipline.[1]

Mercantilism in the Hohenzollern and Habsburg dominions, as in the west, though it stood for state control, never stood for state ownership except when (as happened, it is true, not infrequently in Prussia) the entrepreneurs went bankrupt or for other reasons proved themselves incompetent. The rulers were anxious to develop initiative within the limits of the policies they had laid down (no man, for example, could ever win the favour of Frederick the Great unless, whatever his essential activities, he agreed to promote manufactures). The rulers saw that initiative must be suitably rewarded. As in France, the big rewards went to the men who engaged in financial operations on behalf of the Crown. J. A. Kraut, for example, who in the reign of Frederick William I was responsible for collecting the Kontribution (the Prussian equivalent of the Taille) and for paying the proceeds in bullion to the government; who administered the finances of the army and other departments of state; who, for the purposes of paying the army, introduced the bill of exchange into Prussia, and who died in the possession of a large fortune, the extent of which it has never been possible to assess.[2] During the Seven Years War many more and apparently larger fortunes were accumulated. Daniel Itzig, who had a finger in many pies, but who, together with his partners Ephraim and Isaac, was notorious for carrying through the debasement of the Prussian coinage in 1759, died worth approximately a million taler. (At this time there were about 10 taler to the £-sterling.) H. C. Schimmelmann, an army contractor, who started life as an apprentice to a silk merchant in Stettin, left at the lowest estimate three million taler, and at the highest estimate fourteen million.[3]

Frederick the Great, in fact, for all his parsimony, careful accounting and conviction that riches were demoralizing, was, like the French kings, unable to develop his economy, or conduct his wars, without

[1] K. Hinze, *Die Arbeiterfrage zu Beginn des modernen Kapitalismus*, p. 171.
[2] H. Rachel and P. Wallich, *Berliner Großkaufleute und Kapitalisten* (Berlin, 1938), II, 134ff.   [3] *Ibid.* p. 437.

allowing huge fortunes to be accumulated by such of his subjects as combined a spirit of enterprise with subservience to the royal wishes. This was part of the social pattern of the times – a pattern that was broadly similar in the western and central European absolutisms, but nevertheless showed significant differences in different countries.

In Prussia and the hereditary lands of the house of Habsburg trade and manufactures were less developed than in France, and the towns were fewer and smaller, although it would appear that the proportion of the population living in towns of over 20,000 inhabitants at the end of the eighteenth century was much the same in Prussia as in France.[1] Even in the absence of any reliable figures, however, it does not seem possible to doubt that the merchant and manufacturing communities in central Europe at this time were much less wealthy and technically advanced than their French counterparts.

This fact nevertheless may not have the significance that is attributed to it by those who argue that the absence of revolutionary movements of any significance in this part of Europe before the middle of the nineteenth century must be accounted for by the primitiveness of the economies which had not as yet produced a capitalist bourgeoisie. Even in France at the end of the Ancien Régime the capitalist bourgeoisie was still very small and in any case its members bore no responsibility for the Revolution. As is now a platitude, the Revolution was started by the revolt of the parlements (by what Mathiez called 'la révolte nobiliaire') against the government's attempts at reform, and was followed by the revolt of the third estate. Among the members of this estate, however, who were elected to the States General, only 13 per cent were merchants and manufacturers.[2] The remainder were minor officials, lawyers and members of the liberal professions. This kind of bourgeoisie undoubtedly existed in Prussia. It is unlikely that it was less educated, or formed a smaller proportion of the population than it did in France, and it was in some ways more influential.

In France the Enlightenment, however bourgeois its social and political ideas, found its first apostles and a large number even of its prophets, among the ruling groups of nobles. There was no parallel to this state of affairs in central Europe and particularly not in Prussia, the centre from which the early German Enlightenment spread to the Habsburg dominions. Christian Garve, a professor in Breslau whom his fellow academics looked on, not without reason, as superficial, but

---

[1] See the figures in the German sources already quoted, in R. Mols, *Introduction à la Démographie Historique des Villes d'Europe du XIVᵉ au XVIIIᵉ siècle* (Louvain, 1955), vol. II, and in Reinhard and Armengaud, *Histoire générale de la population mondiale* (Paris, 1961).

[2] A. Cobban, *The Myth of the French Revolution* (London, 1955).

who had on occasion a sharp eye for the distinguishing characteristics of different social classes, observed in 1802 that in Prussia it was the bourgeoisie which had educated the nobility in knowledge and taste.[1] This would seem beyond dispute. The prophets of the early German Enlightenment, Thomasius and Christian Wolff; the outstanding figure of the later Enlightenment, Lessing; the famous writers of the classical age of German literature; the university professors, some of whom, notably Kant, achieved international reputations at the end of the eighteenth century, and at whose feet sat the young noblemen destined for a career in the bureaucracy, and, in Königsberg, also the local gentry and officers from the garrison – all these men were almost without exception bourgeois. Commonly they did not even come from well-to-do families – Goethe is the outstanding exception – but were, like Lessing, the sons of parsons or like Kant of artisans. Most of them suffered extreme privation before they achieved fame.

'Among us Germans', Garve said, 'the barrier between the noble and the non-noble is the strongest and the hardest to overcome.'[2] It had been greatly strengthened during Frederick the Great's *Heldenzeit* or heroic age by the premium that was then set on physical courage and honour as interpreted in military circles. Frederick, who despised bourgeois hardly less than he despised Jews, although he was prepared to make exceptions in both cases, persistently maintained that courage and a sense of honour were virtues which bourgeois naturally lacked. Garve, whom Frederick always summoned to see him when he went to Silesia, and who was acutely conscious of being a bourgeois himself, wrote in 1798 that the king always spoke as if he were unaware of the multitude of sins that mere physical courage could conceal, and that in any event if the bourgeois in general lacked this quality it was because they were denied the opportunity to develop it.[3]

What was commonly referred to as *Adelsdünkel*, or aristocratic arrogance, was bitterly resented in many bourgeois circles at the end of the eighteenth century. Bismarck said that as a boy at school he had suffered from the hatred of the nobility which he saw as a legacy from the period before the reforms of Stein and Hardenberg.[4] Even in the eighteenth century, however, the noble's arrogance had been accompanied by many bourgeois attitudes inculcated into him not only by an education and culture that were exclusively bourgeois, but by the habits of careful accounting, of thrift, of saving, of hard work, and of

[1] Christian Garve, *Versuche über verschiedene Gegenstände aus der Moral, der Literatur und dem gesellschaftlichen Leben* (Breslau, 1802), I, 306–7.   [2] *Op. cit.*, p. 305.
[3] Garve, *Fragmente zur Schilderung des Geistes, des Charakters und die Regierung Friedrichs des Zweyten* (Breslau, 1798), Part II, pp. 155ff.
[4] *Gedanken und Erinnerungen* (1928 edition), p. 49.

contempt for the patterns of aristocratic behaviour prevalent elsewhere, which had characterized not only the civil but the military organization in Prussia since the reign of Frederick William I.

If it was the bourgeois who, in the second half of the eighteenth century, educated the nobility in learning and taste, the army was the school where Frederick William I's 'stupid oxen' first learned those habits of rational calculation which Sombart saw as typical of the bourgeois. The company commander in the Prussian army was required to render a strict account of the sums which the government put at his disposal. The quality and equipment of his men were subject to strict examination at the annual reviews; but within these limits he ran the affairs of his company, including in peace the hiring of mercenaries, as a private undertaking. He was in fact an entrepreneur who, if he were skilful, could make a large profit, but if he were incompetent ended up bankrupt and in disgrace. Many men made considerable fortunes by these means, and by virtue of the high pay, the perquisites and, in the case of successful generals, the large gifts, enjoyed by officers above the rank of captain.[1]

The army officers invested their wealth in land. Whereas in France land was seen primarily as a symbol of social prestige which was not expected to yield more than a moderate return, the Junkers in the eighteenth century, according to Professor Büsch, ran their estates for profit, and the profits were sometimes very large. After the creation of Frederick the Great's *Landschaften*, or credit institutes, a huge speculation in noble estates developed. This involved highly risky transactions, which, with the fall in land values and the French invasion at the beginning of the nineteenth century, drove many landowners bankrupt.

From such modern historical works as have been devoted to the Prussian Junkers, from the memoirs which a number of them began to write at the turn of the eighteenth century, and from the evidence collected by the novelist Fontane for whom they exercised a fascination, the Prussian soldier-farmers of the end of the eighteenth century emerge (to quote a phrase which Fontane put into the mouth of a Polish noble) as 'pirates who pursued their avocations on land',[2] but who nevertheless combined with these predatory qualities the interest in and the capacity to absorb technical details, and the attitudes to the spending and saving of money characteristic of Sombart's bourgeois.

In France the monarchs and the court families retained until the Revolution the love of magnificence and, to a greater or less extent, the ways of life which Sombart saw as typical of the seigneur. Indeed the French economy, which Quesnay indicted as a consuming not an

---

[1] Büsch, *Militärsystem und Sozialleben im alten Preußen*, Part II.
[2] Bninski in *Vor dem Sturm* (4th edition), p. 510.

investing one, may be said to have conformed to this pattern. In the Habsburg dominions, where the state was a more recent creation than in Prussia, and where the great noble families were much richer, and less willing to assimilate the ennobled bourgeois,[1] 'the persistent adherence to quasi-feudal values, including its consumption patterns', persisted throughout the nineteenth century.[2]

In Prussia, on the other hand, as Delbrück observed in his life of Gneisenau, there was never 'an aristocracy in the true sense of the word'.[3] To Thomas Mann 'das Deutsche und das Bürgerliche das ist eins' ('The German and the bourgeois are one and the same').[4] This was true in some senses even in Prussia in the eighteenth century, though not altogether in the sense which Thomas Mann had in mind. The Prussians in consequence in the nineteenth century made the transition to a capitalist society more successfully than did the Austrians, or even the French, their revolution notwithstanding.

IV. The Social and Political Gospels of the German and French Enlightenment

The term Enlightenment has been interpreted differently not only in different countries but within the same country by different people. A German historian, Paul Schwarz, for example, writing in 1925 on the reaction in Prussia under Frederick the Great's successor, Frederick William II, pointed to the number of works bearing, like Kant's, the title 'Was ist Aufklärung?', and noted some ten more or less incompatible definitions produced in the seventeen-eighties in Prussia alone. This state of affairs, in which everyone claimed to be enlightened, but few could agree on what enlightenment meant, seemed to Schwarz to be epitomized in a sketch which was made by the popular illustrator, Daniel Chodowiecki, and reproduced in the Göttingen pocket diary for 1792. It portrayed a hilly landscape with a man on foot, a man on horseback and a coach, all facing towards the rising sun. It was designed to illustrate enlightenment. It could, however, as Schwarz observed, hardly have been less illuminating and might equally well have borne the title 'The Stage-coach at Sunrise'.[5] It was nevertheless a testimony

[1] See H. N. von Preradovich, *Die Führungsschichten in Österreich und Preußen* (Wiesbaden, 1955).

[2] N. T. Gross, *The Industrial Revolution in the Habsburg Monarchy, 1750–1914* (Fontana Economic History of Europe, London, 1972), p. 28.

[3] Pertz and Delbrück, *Das Leben des Feldmarschalls Grafen Neithardt von Gneisenau* (Berlin, 1864–80), v, 12. [4] *Betrachtungen eines Unpolitischen* (1929 edition), p. 80.

[5] Paul Schwartz, *Der erste Kulturkampf in Preußen im Kirche und Schule 1788–1798* (Berlin, 1925), p. 1.

to the widespread conviction among the educated classes that they lived in an age of progress. A similar conviction, notwithstanding the doubts expressed by many of the Philosophes, developed in large parts of Europe during the second half of the eighteenth century and found its supreme expression in France in the debates of the Constituent Assembly.

The belief in progress which prevailed generally in educated circles, however great the misgivings about the chances of achieving it felt by some of the more sophisticated intellectuals, and however variously the term itself could be interpreted, was a consequence of the growing prosperity experienced throughout most of the eighteenth century, and of that sense of having become 'enlightened' which d'Alembert expressed in 1759 when he said:

If one examines carefully the mid-point of the century in which we live, the events which excite us or at any rate which occupy our minds, our customs, our achievements and even our diversions, it is not difficult to see that in some respects a very remarkable change in our ideas is taking place...The discovery and application of a new method of philosophising, the kind of enthusiasms which accompany discoveries, a certain exaltation which the spectacle of the universe produces in us – all these causes have brought about a lively fermentation in our minds. Spreading through nature in all directions like a river which has burst its dams, this fermentation has swept with a sort of violence everything along with it which stood in its way...Thus, from the principles of the secular sciences to the foundations of religious revelation, from metaphysics to matters of taste, from music to morals, from the scholastic disputes of theologians to matters of trade, from natural law to the arbitrary laws of nations, – everything has been discussed or analysed – the fruit or sequel of this general effervescence of minds has been to cast new light on some matters and new shadows on others, just as the effect of the ebb and flow of the tides is to leave some things on the shore and wash others away.[1]

From the enthusiasm and fermentation of minds of which d'Alembert spoke there emerged the ideas in whose name absolutism and the *société d'ordres* were destroyed in France. In the works of the great French Philosophes of the eighteenth century are to be found the genesis of most of the theories relating to society and government which have been elaborated in western Europe since their day, apart from those commonly described as fascist. Since, however, the Philosophes did not produce, or aim at producing, a programme of social and political reform, they postulated as desirable conditions, notably liberty and equality, which, however defined, proved incompatible one with

[1] Quoted by Cassirer, *The Philosophy of the Enlightenment* (Eng. trans., Princeton, 1951), p. 3.

another in eighteenth-century circumstances as well as commonly in the circumstances of succeeding centuries.

The attempts to find a common denominator for the beliefs of the Philosophes, and to see the Enlightenment as a 'European phenomenon whose apostles constituted a family of intellectuals united by a single line of thinking',[1] has long preoccupied scholars, sometimes with unfortunate results. This is not a task that can be undertaken here. The present account can only be concerned with the enlightened ideas that were accepted by rulers, or by their ministers and officials, or which gained a hold in wide sections of the reading public.

The Enlightenment in this sense, understood as a movement for social and political change, showed marked differences in the west and in central Europe, because material conditions differed in these two areas, because the French had a much older and more sophisticated intellectual tradition than had the central Europeans, and because any attempt to translate a philosophy into action involves compromises which necessarily take a different form in different places, and which, if successful, themselves breed attitudes which distinguish one from another the communities which adopt them. In both France and central Europe, nevertheless, the thinking of all who professed to be enlightened proceeded from certain common assumptions of which the most important was that which Frederick the Great expressed when he said: 'La raison terrassa la superstition. On prit un dégóùt pour les fables qu'on avait crues.'

Whatever else it may or may not have stood for, the Enlightment everywhere, in popular estimation as well as in the estimation of its major prophets, was essentially hostile to 'superstition', that is to beliefs, and particularly to beliefs inculcated by the churches whether catholic or protestant, that were accepted blindly as matters of faith or tradition, and whose holders were impervious to rational argument.

In France the apostles of the Enlightenment were for the greater part deists, or even atheists, for whom the catholic church was the embodiment of superstition, and for long the principal target for an attack which Voltaire urged his friends to pursue with the injunction 'Quoi que vous fassiez écrasez l'infâme.' In central Europe, on the other hand, except for the free-thinking which flourished in Berlin and was encouraged by Frederick the Great, himself a deist, the apostles of the Enlightenment generally remained christians (even Joseph II was a believing catholic) and, in contradistinction to their contemporaries in France, were greatly preoccupied by religious questions. Everywhere, nevertheless, whatever their attitudes to religion, the apostles of

[1] P. Gay, *The Enlightenment: an Interpretation.* 1 *The Rise of Modern Paganism* (Weidenfield & Nicolson, London, 1967), 12.

the Enlightenment preached the secularization of government and society.

In Prussia, where the population was predominantly Lutheran though the dynasty was Calvinist and where (as Svarez, the principal author of the *Allgemeines Landrecht*, put it) the law looked on the members of the church as officials of state,[1] this task was a great deal easier than in the catholic dominions of the house of Habsburg, where the church was vastly richer and more powerful even than it was in France. In the second half of the eighteenth century it was subjected to an attack, begun by Maria Theresa and pursued on a much larger scale by Joseph II, to which there was no parallel anywhere before the French Revolution. The church was ousted from its control of the schools and the universities, and from the guardianship of morals which it exercised through the censorship. All the monasteries belonging to the contemplative orders were dissolved and the estates of the bishops secularized, their holders being granted a salary by the state. Civil rights, hitherto confined to catholics, were extended to the members of other confessions, including Jews. Various practices held to be 'superstitious' were forbidden. Parish priests were instructed to inculcate into their flocks the civic virtues, including those, such as the employment of new agricultural techniques, which promoted economic development.[2]

Jospeh II's attempts not only to nationalize the church but to rationalize its practices, were largely unsuccessful because they encountered an impassioned opposition from the mass of his subjects and found few supporters in any class of the population. They were nevertheless typical of a point of view which found a wide response in educated circles in both France and Prussia, and which Groethysen and Lüthy (who attributed its origins not, like Max Weber, to calvinist dogma but to the nature of calvinist discipline) saw, in Groethysen's words, as 'one of the most momentous revolutions in human values known to history'.[3]

Groethysen traced the course of this revolution by examining the sermons which were preached in France in the century before the Revolution and which, since of necessity they had to take the opinions of the audience into account, afforded an indication of public opinion. He emphasized that in the age of Enlightenment the educated classes came to speak a language wholly different from that of their forefathers

[1] 'Wenn man bedenke daß das Gesetz die Geistlichen als Beamten des Staates betrachtet.' Quoted in A. Stölzel, *Carl Gottlieb Svarez* (Berlin, 1885), p. 185.

[2] For a good summary of Maria Theresa's and Joseph II's ecclesiastical policy, see Blanning, *Joseph II and Enlightened Despotism*.

[3] B. Groethuysen, *Die Entstehung der bürgerlichen Welt- und Lebensanschauung* (Halle, 1927), I, 12.

and to endow the key concepts of religious discourse – God, man, death – with a new significance.

In the pre-enlightened ages the world of faith was the only world of which the christian was conscious. The teaching of the church dominated his entire view of life and the universe. Children, as Bossuet said, learned the church's language as they learned to talk, without knowing how. What the christian understood of life on earth he understood only in relation to the hereafter. Death and eternity, in Bossuet's vision, reduced all earthly power to nothingness. Man was seen as by nature sinful, and God as just. God's justice was, however, a mystery, inexplicable (since, for example, it decreed that the sins of the fathers should be visited on the children) in terms of human reason.

The attitude of the Enlightenment to these beliefs was expressed by Voltaire's famous words when he said of Pascal: 'J'ose prendre le parti de l'humanité contre ce misanthrope sublime',[1] and when he proclaimed that man was not born wicked but only became so in the same way as he became ill. The thinking of all those who claimed to be enlightened was concerned, even when they remained believing christians, with improving the conditions of life on earth. Religion, whatever importance might continue to be attached to it, was relegated to the sphere of private life. It no longer seemed proper that the churches should dictate to governments, should lay down, as for example in the laws relating to usury, how business affairs should be conducted, or should prescribe the subjects which the young should study. For faith as the guiding principle of life the apostles of the Enlightenment substituted reason.

Reason is a term which is capable of – and indeed in the eighteenth century was given – different meanings. It was invoked on behalf of many different and mutually exclusive courses of action. In a social or political context it nevertheless always involved for its apostles a refusal to sanction practices or institutions merely because they were old; a deliberate relating of ends to means as distinct from blind adherence to tradition, and a belief in the right of the individual to doubt and question. It was thus potentially an instrument of revolution although it was by no means necessarily so in practice.

In practice the enlightened in every country held a number of assumptions in common about the nature of government and society. All believed that the object of rulers should be to promote the greatest happiness of the greatest number of their subjects, though happiness and the conditions necessary to it were understood differently. All believed in religious toleration and (though within greatly varying limits) in free discussion. All condemned arbitrary power and thought that rulers and their officials should be bound by the law. All believed that the law

[1] *Ibid.* I, 347.

should be clear and precise, and uniform throughout the dominions or any given ruler, and that it derived its sanction from the state, as distinct from custom. All prized orderly government and the progress of knowledge and the arts – a progress which everywhere was contrasted with the state of affairs which had prevailed in what the French habitually referred to as 'les siècles gothiques et barbares'. Agreement, however, on these broad generalizations left scope for many differences.

In the German-speaking world the man who exercised the greatest influence on social and political thinking between the second and the seventh decades of the eighteenth century was Christian Wolff, who personified the *Aufklärung* to his own generation and was always portrayed in contemporary engravings against the background of a rising sun. He was the pupil of Leibnitz and to the best of his comprehension (which, however, it appears, was highy inadequate)[1] popularized and systematized his master's ideas for the benefit of a wide public. Like Descartes and Leibnitz, Wolff remained a believing christian, but nevertheless denied the right of the churches to control or limit intellectual speculation. He accepted Leibnitz's belief in natural laws which he assumed that God had created but had then left to operate in accordance with their own logic. He compared God to a clock maker and the universe to a clock which functioned with perfect precision according to ascertainable mechanical principles. 'Since God', he said, 'who represents the highest form of reason, can never act except in accordance with reason, or lay his wisdom aside, it is not possible that he should bring anything about by miracles that can happen naturally.'[2] To Wolff what was natural meant what was in the nature of things. He held that the task of the philosopher was to discover not only the principles which determined the workings of the material universe, but also those on which government and society should be organized so as to permit man to progress towards perfection (*Vollkommenheit*), or the realization of his true nature. Whether the subject was the material universe or human affairs, Wolff assumed the task of understanding to consist, as in mathematics, in deductions by strict processes of logic from propositions which he assumed to be self-evident without empirical investigation. He had the contempt for empirical investigation which Voltaire attributed to Descartes, and required of the students of his *Politik* only that they should have a proper grounding in methods of thinking, which he assumed could best be acquired by a

[1] The judgment of L. W. Beck (*Early German Philosophy* (Harvard U.P., 1969), p. 267) was that it is 'positively painful to see how little Wolff profited from his reading of Descartes, Leibnitz and Locke'.
[2] *Deutsche Literatur*, ed. F. Bruggemann. II, *Reihe Aufklärung. Das Weltbild der deutschen Aufklärung* (Leipzig, 1930), II.

study of his own works on logic, metaphysics, morals, and the physical sciences.

In 1706, when he was 27, Wolff became a professor in Halle, the capital of the duchy of Magdeburg, which had been a Prussian province since 1680. He remained there until 1723, when Frederick William I gave him 48 hours to leave the country, under pain of death, because of accusations (at the time unsubstantiated and later proved false) which were brought against him by the religious sect of the Pietists who enjoyed the royal favour. From Halle Wolff removed himself to Marburg, and resisted the efforts which Frederick William made to get him back, once it emerged that many foreign students had left Halle with him and thus deprived the Prussian government of much needed foreign currency. He only returned to Prussia in 1740, when his disciple Frederick the Great acceded to the throne and recalled him in order to demonstrate the triumph of reason over 'barbarism, ignorance and superstition'.[1]

Though Wolff refused a seat in the Berlin Academy of Sciences in order to resume his teaching, he was by this time an old man whose task was already accomplished. In the thirty-six years of his teaching life he had educated throughout central Europe not only several generations of scholars but a broad middle class of pastors, school teachers and government servants. In the hereditary lands of the house of Habsburg his doctrines inspired the first promoters of the catholic Enlightenment, which, like the Enlightenment in the protestant parts of Germany, also stood for the secularization of knowledge. 'From Halle and Leipzig [where Gottsched carried on his work] the German Enlightenment', it has been said, 'started out on its triumphal progress.'[2] The sons of Maria Theresa were brought up on Wolff's philosophy. He profoundly influenced the thinking of Frederick the Great, who once wrote to Voltaire that his 'façon de raisoner...est applicable à toute sorte de sujets. Elle peut être d'un grand usage à un politique qui sait s'en servir. J'ose même dire qu'elle est applicable à tous les cas de la vie privée.'[3] To Voltaire, who professed to detest all system-builders, these sentiments were anathema. In the end he convinced Frederick the Great that Christian Wolff was just another German pedant, as indeed he was. Henceforward Frederick neglected him. Nevertheless, Wolff's *Weltanschauung*, which (as a German student of his political ideas once expressed it) perfectly epitomized the Prussian spirit, made a far deeper impression on Frederick than did Voltaire's.[4]

[1] W. Frauendienst, *Christian Wolff als Staatsdenker* (Historische Studien, 171, Berlin, 1927), p. 5.   [2] E. Winter, *Der Josefinismus* (Berlin, 1962), p. 31.
[3] Frauendienst, *Christian Wolff*, p. 58.   [4] *Ibid.* p. 64.

Wolff's belief that reason could provide the answer to every problem and that he himself was endowed with it in the highest degree, concealed from him how deeply his thinking was influenced by the Prussia of his day. Notwithstanding his unfortunate experience of its methods of government he produced in his *Politik* a philosophical justification of them. Like the Cameralists, whose beliefs he incorporated within his general philosophical system, he held that the state had come into existence through a contract between the ruler and his subjects, the subjects having pledged themselves to unqualified obedience in return for the material and moral conditions necessary to enable them 'to walk in the ways of natural law'.

Believing that natural law prescribed no particular form of state or religious belief, Wolff preached religious toleration but held absolutism to be the best form of government. He saw the state as the source of all rights and its power as unlimited in scope. He believed that the ruler should be the first servant of the state in the sense that he should operate the state machine in accordance with the dictates of reason as expounded by the philosophers. This doctrine of enlightened absolutism postulated that the ruler should have no interests other than those of the state, and that he should always act rationally, that is, that he should never give way to whims or passions and never make arbitrary judgments, but that he should abide by his own laws and dispense an even-handed justice.

Wolff's philosophy embodied doctrines which the Cameralists had long preached. The Cameralists were a group of people concerned with promoting 'Cameralistic studies', that is, in the words of their principal representative, Justi, with studying 'all the contrivances of the great housekeeping of the state'.[1] They were university professors all of whom had held government office at various periods of their lives. Justi, for example, who began life as a soldier, was employed for some time in the Austrian administration before Maria Theresa appointed him to a professorship in Vienna which required him to lecture to candidates for the bureaucracy on trade, commerce, taxation and manufactures. When he moved to Berlin in 1760 he was employed in the mines department until Frederick the Great threw him into prison for some undisclosed offence.[2]

As servants of the state either in an administrative capacity, or as the instructors of young men hoping to graduate from the universities into the state service, the Cameralists were concerned with questions of economics, but from a strictly practical point of view. They preached the doctrines of mercantilism already described (to the Germans,

[1] A. W. Small, *The Cameralists* (Chicago, 1909), p. 304.   [2] *Ibid.*

Cameralism and mercantilism are more or less synonymous terms), and in the process of so doing justified the absolute power of the monarch and the paramountcy of the state, the belief in which was necessary to the enforcement of mercantilist policies.

To the Germans mercantilism seems an integral part of the Enlightenment because of the rational and secular nature of its thinking. Heckscher, too, stressed that this was among its distinguishing characteristics. The mercantilists, he said, believed in relating ends to means and 'were obviously anxious to find reasonable grounds for every position they adopted'.[1] To readers unfamiliar with the mental attitudes and practices in vogue before their day, this may sound less of a tribute than Heckscher intended. The mercantilist doctrines described earlier were designed to educate societies in which superstition and blind worship of tradition still governed most peoples' lives; in which a Prussian gild could issue an ordinance laying down that no artisan 'shall conceive, invent, or use anything new';[2] in which the blacksmith's apprentice, when his bellows failed to work, assumed them to be bewitched instead of looking to see if they had a hole in them; in which begging was an honourable profession encouraged by the churches, and in which even war, as one enlightened German once put it, 'was still not a science'.[3]

The Cameralism or mercantilism of central Europe was distinguished from its French counterpart because the study of its doctrines constituted an academic discipline which was obligatory for all the holders of administrative posts, and because the rulers themselves were its most receptive students. Its doctrines, which formed part of a philosophy claiming to provide a comprehensive explanation of the universe, were the official doctrines of the state, and in Prussia penetrated wide circles of the population through the pastors, the schools and the universities which were subjected to strict state control.

The Prussia of Frederick the Great was long seen as the enlightened state *par excellence*. The legend to this effect grew up in Frederick's lifetime and endured until the first world war. As Dilthey put it in 1901: 'Kein anderer deutscher Staat war mit den Ideen der Aufklärung so tief verwachsen.' ('No other German state was so deeply impregnated with the ideas of the Enlightenment.')[4] What he meant was that in no other German state had the belief in reason, understood as a body

[1] Heckscher, *Mercantilism*, II, 308.

[2] Lütge, *Deutsche Sozial- und Wirtschaftsgeschiche*, p. 360.

[3] J. H. Eberhard, 'Über die Zeichen der Aufklärung eine Nation', in *Literarische Chronik* (Bern, 1786), II, 164.

[4] W. Dilthey, 'Die Deutsche Aufklärung im Staat und in der Akademie Friedrichs des Großen', in *Deutsche Rundschau*, 107 (1901), 21.

of principles evolved by a process of inexorable logic, taken such deep root. The Prussian state, Dilthey said, was seen not as the product of historical development, but as a machine.

The simile of the machine was indeed one which Frederick the Great himself applied to his administration and the same idea was commonly attributed, and with even greater justice, to Joseph II. It involved the belief, which found its supreme expression in the Prussian army, but was also, as the reformers after 1806 continually insisted, exemplified in Frederick's mercantilist policies, that in pursuit of aims held to be desirable on rational grounds human beings could be treated as automata from whom a blind obedience was to be expected. Stein's one-time friend and collaborator, Theodor von Schön, who was born in 1773, described the famous edict of October 1807, which granted personal freedom to the serfs and threw open the trades and professions to everyone, regardless of birth or status, as the Habeas Corpus of Prussian history. This was the first time, he said, that the ideas of freedom and humanity had found any recognition in Prussian history.[1]

In the legend of Prussian Enlightenment these ideas, which belonged to the age of romanticism, found no place. Enlightened Prussia was held to stand for hard work, for thrift, for order, for incorruptibility, for the rational relating of ends to means and, above all, for justice and the rule of law, for religious toleration and freedom of discussion, and for economic and intellectual progress under the tutelage of a state guided by reason.

Like other legends this legend by no means altogether corresponded to the facts. Notably freedom of discussion, as Wilhelm von Humboldt was well aware, meant merely the freedom to speculate on literary, philosophical and religious questions. It was not extended to cover criticism of the social or political order which no one, apart from Lessing, seems to have wished to criticize during Frederick's lifetime. The much-vaunted Prussian justice and observance of the rule of law deserved their reputation only in relation to the cases – and not invariably even to them – in which the Crown and its officials were not parties. The so-called *Kabinettsjustiz* – the justice exercised by the king in his cabinet either personally or by means of ad hoc commissions – and the *Machtspruch*, or judgments given by people in authority other than by due process of law, were commonly resorted to in Frederick's day and to an even greater extent under his successor.

It can hardly be denied, however, that even in these matters Frederick acted more in accordance with generally accepted enlightened prin-

[1] 'Selbstbiographie', part 1 in *Aus den Papieren des Ministers Theodor von Schön* (Halle, 1875), I, 43.

ciples than did the rulers in the other major continental countries,[1] and that however extensively the *Kabinettsjustiz* and the *Machtspruch* were employed, their employment was neither so extensive nor so arbitrary as to destroy among the educated public, or even among many of those who, like Svarez, were in a position to know, the belief, widely prevalent indeed throughout Europe, that Prussia in Frederick's day was distinguished by its respect for law and justice.[2]

When, notwithstanding this and the other indubitably enlightened policies which Frederick pursued, Prussia's claim to enlightenment was rejected by many Frenchmen, in the eighteenth century and afterwards, this was because French standards were different from those that prevailed in central Europe. Though Voltaire, in defiance of his principles, could never restrain his admiration for Frederick the Great's military achievements, Diderot, on seeing Frederick's portrait by Van Loo, observed that it showed 'quelque chose de la bouche du tigre'.[3] He pronounced the principles of enlightened monarchy to be the 'maximes d'un tyrant'. 'Qu'est-ce qui characterise le despote?' he asked, 'Est-ce la bonté ou la méchanceté? Nullement. Ces deux notions n'entrent seulement pas dans sa définition; c'est l'étendu et non l'usage de l'autorité qu'il s'arroge.'[4] Rousseau, d'Alembert, Mirabeau and many others shared these views, seeing Prussia as a typical example of the poverty and oppression characteristic of despotically ruled states.

When in the eighteen-fifties Tocqueville was collecting material for his *Ancien Régime et la Révolution*, he made incursions into German history and studied the *Allgemeines Landrecht*, whose compilation had been begun under Frederick the Great but which was first published in

[1] For a justification of this point of view, see O. Hinze, *Die Entwicklung Preußens zum Rechtstaat*, in *Forschungen zur Brandenburgischen und Preussischen Geschichte*, vol. 32 (Munich and Leipiz, 1920). For a detailed exposition of the arbitrary features of Prussian justice see U. J. Heuer, *Allgemeines Landrecht und Klassenkampf* (Deutscher Zentralverlag) (East Berlin, 1960), pp. 64 ff.

[2] Svarez made an eloquent defence of the respect shown for justice under Frederick the Great in his *Vorträge über Recht und Staat* (edited H. Conrad and G. Kleinheyer, Cologne, 1960), pp. 609–10. These were lectures which Svarez delivered to the future Frederick William III when he was crown prince, in 1791–2. There is no reason why Svarez should have stressed the point unless he had believed in it. Madame de Staël noted (*De l'Allemagne*, p. 225) that 'Le gouvernement de Frédéric étoit fondé sur la force militaire et la Justice Civile', and said (p. 227) that she had not encountered in the whole of Prussia a single individual who complained of arbitrary actions. As Wilhelm von Humboldt, however, observed in effect in 1792 ('Ideen zu einem Versuch die Grenzen der Wirksamkeit des Staates zu bestimmen', *Gesammelte Schriften*, ed. A. Leitzmann (Berlin, 1903), I, 234), governments (and he must have had the Prussian government in mind) could do a lot by means of brainwashing.

[3] Quoted by S. Skalweit, *Frankreich und Friedrich der Große. Der Aufstieg Preußens in der öffentlichen Meinung des 'Ancien Régimes'* (Bonn, 1952), p. 115.

[4] *Ibid.* p. 116.

1794. He pointed out that this extraordinary document, which is indeed the best testimony to what Enlightenment did and did not mean in Prussia, was not only a civil and criminal code, but in effect, as Svarez had intended, a constitution, for it set out in precise detail the relationships of the various classes of the population to each other and to the state. Tocqueville noted that it gave expression to many of the principles laid down in the Declaration of the Rights of Man, but that 'sous cette tête toute moderne nous allons voir apparaître un corps tout gothiqe', for the *Allgemeines Landrecht* gave legal sanction to absolutism, to serfdom, and to all the various rights and obligations belonging to the different Stände or estates. In its modern conception of the omnipotent state, and of a law that was clear, precise and binding throughout the Hohenzollern dominions, combined with its recognition of autocracy and of a medieval social structure, it appeared to Tocqueville 'un être monstrueux qui semble une transition d'une création à une autre'.[1]

The pursuit of enlightened policies in the Habsburg dominions proceeded in a fashion very different from the Prussian. Joseph II was in all respects more radical than Frederick, particularly in relation to the serfs and to privilege, of which something must be said later. Convinced of the need to modernize immediately the administration and the social structure in his various territories, but lacking the support of any class in the population, or even of any substantial group in his bureaucracy, his policies necessarily failed. In the process of trying to enforce them, however, he had recourse to arbitrary actions, and to the use of the secret police, on a scale that to contemporary Prussians,[2] not to mention contemporary Frenchmen, ruled him out of the category of enlightened.

Whatever, indeed, the attempt to put the gospel of the Enlightenment into practice came to involve in central Europe, it is plain that by French standards enlightened autocracy, whether or not it is pejoratively described as despotism, came to seem a contradiction in terms; for essentially the French Enlightenment stood for liberal principles with which autocracy was by its nature incompatible, and was particularly so in the eighteenth century in central Europe, where the rulers were primarily concerned with modernizing communities economically and culturally backward by western standards.

Enlightenment as understood in central Europe provided absolutism with its justification and its ideology, and the monarchs attempted to enforce it from above. In France, on the other hand, where absolute government was older, and much more inefficient and corrupt at least

[1] Tocqueville, *Oeuvres Complètes*, footnote entitled 'Code de Grand Frédéric', p. 268.
[2] See Svarez, *Vorträge über Recht und Staat*, p. 614, for an indictment of Joseph II.

than in Prussia, but where the standard of life was higher and educated society much more sophisticated, the social and political ideas of the Enlightenment were an attack not only on the *société d'ordres*, as to a greater or less extent they were in central Europe, but also (even though this was not explicitly stated) on absolutism itself.

The French Philosophes reacted with the same, and indeed with a greater degree of passion against the disorderliness, the irrationality, the superstition and the reverence for tradition which had been the targets of enlightened attack in central Europe. Like the Cartesians in France and Christian Wolff in Germany they were worshippers at the shrine of 'reason'. They nevertheless interpreted reason in a new sense and made it serve new purposes.

Voltaire held Leibnitz up to ridicule in his *Candide* and said of Descartes: 'il était le plus grand géométricien de son siècle; mais...ne fit guère que des romans de philosophie. Un homme qui dédaigna les expériences, qui ne cita jamais Galilée, qui voulait bâtir sans matériaux, ne pouvait élever qu'un édifice imaginaire.'[1] To the Philosophes reason did not mean, as it did to Descartes, that 'clear and distinct' apprehension of universal principles deduced logically from *a priori* assumptions;[2] it meant the scientific method as the Philosophes believed it to have been applied by Newton. The Philosophes stressed the importance of observation and experiment, and continually abused the philosophers who built systems on unverified hypotheses. The first sentence of Newton's *Opticks* ran: 'My design in this book is not to explain the properties of light by hypotheses but to propose and prove them by reason and experiment.'[3] They held that questions which could not be answered by such methods were questions it was profitless to ask.

It has often been pointed out that the Philosophes not only failed to abide by their own principles, but were unaware of their implications. Many of them – d'Alembert, Maupertuis, and the Physiocrats for example – were themselves system-builders, and though these new systems were less all-embracing than the old ones there were more of them, since the Philosophes concerned themselves with many matters – notably economics and criminology in the fields of the social sciences – which had never previously been examined in a systematic way. In the process of their system-building, moreover, they inevitably had recourse to hypotheses, without which no systems can be constructed, and many of these seemed to later generations as implausible, and as unrelated to reality, as the ones against which they themselves had

[1] *Siècle de Louis XIV*, ed. René Groos (Paris, 1947), II, 107.
[2] *Discours sur la Méthode*, ed. Gilbert Gadoffre (Manchester U.P., 1964), p. 37.
[3] Gerd Buchdahl, *The Image of Newton and Locke in the Age of Reason* (Sheed and Ward, 1961), p. 13.

complained. For the purposes of the present argument, however, it is not so much the nature of their thinking that is significant as the conclusions about society and government to which it led them.

These conclusions emerged to a large extent incidentally, as a by-product of their essential preoccupations, which in the main were with mathematics, the natural sciences, philosophy and the arts. The leading Philosophes became increasingly conscious of the complexities of the material universe and human society, and of the limitations of the human intellect. They were professional writers and scholars, without experience of government or political ambitions, and with the anarchic attitudes common among societies of intellectuals. Though often asked for their advice, particularly by foreign governments, they did not see it as their essential task, nor were they equipped, to draw up practicable schemes of reform. They were all aristocrats, or the protégés of aristocrats, and being thus associates of the Establishment could not easily contemplate a total reversal of the existing order of things. Yet they nevertheless lived at a time when their nation's position in the world was rapidly declining and its institutions patently failing to work. As a result of this combination of circumstances they held the whole social and political order up to ridicule, and pronounced it to be rotten, while ignoring the possibility of revolution.

They differed greatly amongst themselves and many different social and political creeds later derived nourishment from their writings. They nevertheless shared certain attitudes, of which the most important was an individualism hostile alike to the bureaucratic state and the corporative organization of society. Obsessed, unlike their western predecessors in the age of mercantilism, with the possibilities of human progress (whether or not they were personally optimistic), they saw the individual as its agent. They saw happiness as the *summum bonum*, and its promotion as the ultimate test of the rightness of all human action. They were however largely, if not primarily, preoccupied with the happiness of the individual – 'le bonheur individuel', or happiness as an individual state of mind – as distinct from 'le bonheur commun' or 'collectif', that is, the well-being of the community.[1]

This, too, however, was a common subject of discussion and its realization seemed dependent on changing man's environment. What changes, precisely, were necessary was a matter of continual dispute. Here again, however, there was a certain measure of agreement that was later crystallized in the revolutionary slogans of liberty, equality and fraternity. Different Philosophes interpreted these terms differently. Liberty, nevertheless, whatever else it may have included, always meant

[1] See R. Mauzi, *L'Idée du bonheur au XVIIIe siècle* (Paris, 1960), and review by L. Trénard in *Annales historiques de la révolution française*, vol. 35 (1963).

the civil liberties – freedom of speech, freedom of the press, freedom of worship, freedom of association, freedom from arbitrary arrest, the right to a fair trial. Though equality was often extended to cover a more equal distribution of wealth, it always meant equality before the law in the sense defined earlier. Fraternity was not a current term before the Revolution but the notion of it nevertheless greatly preoccupied the Philosophes. Its significance is nowhere brought out better than in Turgot's and Dupont de Nemours' 'Mémoire sur les municipalités' of 1775. The purpose of this remarkable document was to demand that the tasks of levying the taxes, and determining their incidence, should, together with various functions of local government, be handed over to bodies elected locally. This was advocated on the grounds that only by such means would it be possible to overcome the conviction, prevalent in all sections of the population, that the government was the enemy of the people – a conviction that, in Turgot's view, had not only caused a general obstructiveness towards government regulations, but had completely destroyed all sense of public obligation, and even all sense of obligation to one's neighbour, so great was every man's desire to transfer to other shoulders the intolerable burdens of taxation which the government placed on him.

In this 'Mémoire' Turgot and Dupont de Nemours outlined their vision of a nation united by a common purpose, and expressed their awareness of the atomization of society for which (like Tocqueville and many other observers before and after them) they held absolutism combined with medieval privilege to be responsible. Here are set out the first tentative proposals for government based on consent, though (if one excludes Rousseau's *Contrat Social*, which was little read before the Revolution) this never formed a part of the Philosophes' creed, and the demand for representative government did not find expression till late into the eighties.

Mercantilism obviously could not survive in this atmosphere, though it was not the people commonly described as the Philosophes who launched the first attack on it, but the so-called *philosophes économistes*, or Physiocrats. The founder of physiocracy was Louis XV's doctor, Quesnay, who developed his opinions piece-meal in various articles for the *Encyclopédie*, and in his famous *Tableau Économique* of 1758. His system was first presented to the public as a coherent whole in 1767 by his disciple Mercier de la Rivière under the title *L'ordre naturel et essentiel des sociétés politiques*, a work which Adam Smith pronounced to be 'the most distinct and best account of this doctrine'.[1]

The Physiocrats discredited themselves in the eyes of most other Philosophes by their doctrinaire attitude (they were the one group of

[1] Quoted by H. Higgs, *The Physiocrats* (London, 1897), p. 2.

French thinkers in the age of Enlightenment who formed, as it was said, a 'sect' or party, threshing out their ideas among themselves and then presenting them to the public as indisputable truths) and by the palpable absurdity of some of their conclusions; for they insisted that the land was the source of all wealth; that the problems of taxation could be solved by abolishing all taxes apart from a tax on land (their so-called *impôt unique* which Voltaire described as the *impôt inique*) and that their programme could be translated into action by means of what they called 'le despotisme légal', the nature of which is epitomized in a conversation allegedly held between Quesnay and the Dauphin. 'What', the Dauphin is supposed to have asked, 'would you do if you were king?'

'Nothing.'

'Then who would govern?'

'The law.'[1]

This doctrine made the Physiocrats look ridiculous to a generation of Frenchmen which was becoming increasingly suspicious both of autocracy and of theories of natural law. Notwithstanding their aberrations, however, Adam Smith said of them that 'their system with all its imperfections, is perhaps the nearest approximation to the truth that has yet been published on the subject'. The Physiocrats are commonly reckoned as the fathers of the science of economics. Their merits and defects as economists are irrelevant to this account, which can only be concerned with the social implications of their doctrines. These, however, could hardly be overestimated.

The Physiocrats argued that increases in wealth could only come from investment, and thus condemned as disastrous the unproductive expenditure on courts, militarism and conspicuous consumption. They stressed the need to give the individual the incentive to produce and assumed, among other things, that he must be freed from the burdens of excessive taxation, from the restrictions imposed by the communal system of agriculture, by the communal control exercised by the guilds, and by state regulation of trade and industry. They maintained that the individual must possess his property in full ownership and dispose of it as he chose, and that he understood his own interests better than did any of the paternalistic authorities who had hitherto presumed to dictate to him. They concluded – and by this means appeared to bridge the gulf between the needs of the individual and those of the community – that (in Mercier de la Rivière's words) 'chacun de nous...à la faveur de cette pleine et entière liberté...augmente ainsi la somme du bonheur commun en augmentant celui qui lui est personnel'.

---

[1] Quoted by Higgs, *op. cit.*, p. 45.

'Propriété, sureté, liberté', Mercier de la Rivière wrote in capital letters, 'voila ce que nous cherchons.' In his summary of Quesnay's economic doctrines, which Dupont de Nemours summarized later in an even more simple form, he provided the reading public with a justification in terms of economics for the liberty and equality before the law which the Philosophes had proclaimed in the name of humanity and social justice.

V.   *The Physiocrats and the Peasants*

Civilization in the age of absolutism rested on a peasant base. The peasants formed the overwhelming majority of every population and the bulk of the revenues of every state was derived from the land. In this period of European history, famous for the increase in trade and manufactures, and for the efforts of governments to promote them, agriculture by comparison made little progress over most of the continent of Europe. It was only after the beginning of the eighteenth century in France and Prussia, and at a considerably later date in various other parts of central, not to mention eastern, Europe, that society began to escape from what Professor Goubert has called the 'mécanisme régulier des catastrophes démographiques'[1] – the periodic recurrence of bad harvests followed by epidemics (or of epidemics followed by bad harvests) which in the worst-afflicted districts could cause the death of a quarter, a third, or even on occasions of half of the population, as happened, for example, in the province of East Prussia between 1708 and 1711, when out of 600,000 inhabitants 250,000 died from starvation and disease.[2]

These catastrophes were the product of many causes – social, economic and political – besides the natural ones immediately responsible for them. The most obvious were the primitive implements and organization of agricultural production, and the lack of adequate means of transport. Agricultural production was still based on the open-field system, still concentrated primarily on the growth of cereals, and was subjected to what French agronomists in the eighteenth century described as 'le cercle vicieux de la jachère' – the vicious circle of the fallow land, in accordance with which the amount of land that was devoted to grain crops left an inadequate amount available for pasturing livestock. There was in consequence shortage of manure and this perpetuated the wasteful recourse to the fallow. The inadequate transport facilities meant that it was difficult or impossible in times of

[1] P. Goubert, *L'Ancien Régime*. 1 *La Société* (Paris, 1969), ch. 11.
[2] Döhnhoff, *Namen die keiner mehr nennt* (Mönchen-Gladbach, 1962), p. 108.

local scarcity to move grain from the surplus to the deficit areas. In France a bad harvest or the threat of one led to hoarding, speculation and panic purchases. It drove up the price of grain by a proportion far higher than that by which the yield of the harvest fell short of normal, and to a level which the poor could not afford. This was a state of affairs that could have been remedied by holding stocks of grain. The administrative difficulties, however, in the way of such a policy were very great, and continually defeated the French government in the period under discussion. In the eighteenth century they appear to have been overcome only by the Prussian government in the reigns of Frederick William I and Frederick the Great.

Even when, for reasons that are still a matter of debate, famine and epidemics ceased in many parts of Europe to be regular occurrences, and to take their toll in the lives of men and animals, the French peasants, in Professor Labrousse's words, merely exchanged a sentence of death for under-employment and starvation wages. Turgot, when he was Intendant in the Limousin between 1761 and 1774, wrote that in his *généralité* (which admittedly was among the poorest, but where he judged that conditions were little worse than in four-sevenths of France) the peasant was reduced 'à la plus profonde misère'.[1]

It is not possible to sink lower while remaining alive, and in each of the major European powers, apart from certain fortunate categories of peasants and certain exceptional districts, this seems to have been the usual state of affairs. So widespread a phenomenon, plainly, cannot be explained in terms of the actions of individual governments, or even of whether the peasant was bond or free; for, since serfdom is a legal and not an economic category, and varied greatly in its onerousness, the serf did not necessarily suffer a greater degree of material deprivation than did the free peasants.

In France in the period under discussion the great majority of peasants were personally free in the sense that they were at liberty to move about at will (though very few in fact left the places where they were born before the second half of the eighteenth century) and that no legal provisions prevented them from engaging in what work they chose, or from mortgaging, selling or bequeathing their land as they saw fit.

It is commonly estimated that the peasants owned about 35 per cent of the cultivated land of France. They constituted, however, some 80 per cent or more of the population, and few of them owned enough land to support a family – an increasing number owned none at all – so that most peasants augmented their means of livelihood, or supported themselves entirely, as day-labourers, domestic servants, share-croppers or (though more rarely) tenant farmers.

[1] *Oeuvres*, II, 452.

Ownership, moreover, did not mean what it means today, since the so-called *propriétaire*, or peasant proprietor, was burdened with many obligations which prevented him from cultivating his property and disposing of its produce as he chose. Wherever the open-field system still prevailed, as it did over the greater part of France, the peasant proprietor (like other proprietors including the seigneurs) was subject to the so-called *servitudes collectives* – or decisions imposed on him by the village community – for example as to the crops he might grow and the times at which he might sow and harvest – which were a necessary consequence of the communal system of agriculture. Together with other proprietors he was required to surrender annually a proportion of his crops to meet the *dîme* or tithe imposed by the church, although this proportion was in general considerably less than a tenth. To the seigneur – and the principle of 'nulle terre sans seigneur' still generally prevailed – he owed feudal dues which varied very greatly from district to district but which involved payments in money or kind, often substantial, and other obligations, impossible to assess in money terms but highly vexatious or damaging, such as the obligation to grind his corn in the seigneur's mill and to allow the seigneur hunting rights over his land.

In addition to these obligations imposed on him because of the communal system of agriculture and by the landlords lay and ecclesiastical, the French peasant also owed obligations to the state in the form of taxes, and of personal services – notably those known as the *corvée royale* or compulsory unpaid labour on the roads, and to provide transport for the army.

Numerous attempts were made at the time and afterwards to estimate the proportion of the land-holding peasant's gross or net produce that was taken from him by these various exactions. Many of the exactions, however, defy measurement, and in any case conditions varied so greatly from one part of France and one category of peasants to another that no general estimates could have any claim to accuracy. It is nevertheless plain that the exactions in total were not only often, if not commonly, very heavy; they rank high among the causes that made for inefficient agriculture.

In 1776, Boncerf, in a famous work called *Les Inconvénients des Droits Féodaux*, pointed out that the feudal dues were the cause of innumerable law-suits, which descended from father to son and 'dévorent les seigneurs, les vassaux et les terres'.[1] He maintained that the sums which the seigneurs expended in the attempt to exact their dues were larger than those which the dues brought in. Turgot, when he was Intendant in the Limousin, bombarded the Contrôle Général with memoranda to

---

[1] Boncerf, *Les Inconvénients des Droits Féodaux* (London, 1776), p. 17.

demonstrate the disastrous effects of the irrational system of taxation from which the peasants were the principal sufferers, and the losses which the *corvée*, with its requisitioning of men and oxen, inflicted on agriculture and on the individual peasant. He stressed the cost which the state incurred in pursuing and imprisoning the defaulters, and the 'complication extrême' in which the Intendance became entangled in its attempts to enforce a system which, if it were merely to work with the minimum show of fairness, must involve a huge number of investigations and calculations, and at its best could not avoid creating injustices and ill-will, and resulting in shoddy work.[1] He proposed to replace the *corvée* by free, paid labour, which he assumed would ensure that supply and demand were brought effortlessly into harmony to the benefit of all concerned.

In central Europe, as in France, the peasant was burdened by obligations to the village community, to the landlords and to the state. These obligations, however, varied very greatly from one country, and even from one district, to another. They were moreover of a different kind on the one hand, in those parts of western Europe where the relationships of the *société d'ordres* were still enforced by law, and, on the other hand, in eastern and much of central Europe.

In France, where the bulk of the land was divided into seigneuries, or fiefs, the seigneur's estate commonly consisted of two parts. In one part (the *domaine proche*) the seigneur cultivated the land himself with paid labour, or let it out to share-croppers or tenant farmers. The other part (the *domaine utile* or *mouvance*) consisted of peasant properties from which he claimed feudal dues.[2] Similar arrangements prevailed in much of western Germany, for example in Baden, Württemberg and the Rhineland,[3] and are known in German by the term *Grundherrschaft*. The position of the French, German and other European peasants living under *Grundherrschaft* may be described as something in between the freedom on the one hand which they acquired in France during the Revolution, and in central Europe in the course of the nineteenth century and, on the other hand, the kind of serfdom enforced under what is known as *Gutsherrschaft* (from *Gut*, meaning an estate, and *Herrschaft* meaning lordship or dominion).

Gutsherrschaft prevailed in Poland and Russia, in various parts of the hereditary lands of the house of Habsburg – notably in Hungary, Bohemia, Moravia and Austrian Silesia – and, to a large extent, in the Hohenzollern territories east of the Elbe. Here a landlord's estate was

---

[1] Turgot, *Oeuvres*, II, 213.
[2] A. Soboul, *La France à la veille de la révolution*.
[3] See J. Kulischer, *Allgemeine Wirtschaftsgeschichte* (Munich, 1958), II, 88. Lütge, *Deutsche Sozial- und Wirtschaftsgeschichte*, pp. 120 ff.

managed as a single enterprise by the lord himself or his bailiff, and was worked by the compulsory labour of the peasants living on it, who were, as the saying went, 'an die Scholle gebunden', or tied to the soil.

In the eighteenth century it began commonly to be said that the peasants under *Gutsherrschaft* were little better than slaves. They were known as the *Untertanen*, or subjects of the landlords – a term which exactly described their condition except when they were conscripted into the army. A large serf estate was a kingdom in miniature, with its own administration, justice and police. It might contain many thousands of subjects whose needs the estate was presumed to meet (the serf might not buy or sell outside it without permission) while producing a surplus for sale in home or foreign markets for the benefit of the landlord.

The population of a large estate comprised many different categories of serfs, ranging from those who owned no land, or only small plots or gardens, to those with considerable holdings and a team or teams of oxen. The landholding serfs held their land under various conditions prescribed by manorial custom or by written agreements, which the manorial authorities manipulated to their advantage. The serf rarely had security of tenure (the most numerous category of landholding serfs in Prussia, the so-called *Lassiten*, could be turned off their holdings with six months' notice; their counterparts in Bohemia, though commonly life-tenants, could be turned out at will). The landholding serf was obliged to provide the landlord with free labour (if he preferred this to a money rent, as in the period under discussion he commonly did) and to the free use of his carts and animals, for periods of time which the landlords were continually tempted to increase. All serfs, whether they held land or not, were subject to the personal obligations of serfdom. Being bound by law to the soil, if they left the manor without permission they committed a criminal offence, which deprived them of all standing in society and all right to protection and placed them in the position of outlaws. They were forced to do the work assigned to them by the manorial authorities; they might not marry without permission; the most resented of all the obligations of serfdom forced them, if required, to give their children into domestic service in the lord's household for a term of years limited by laws more honoured in the breach than the observance.

The investigations conducted by Maria Theresa's officials after the War of the Austrian Succession revealed that these arrangements had often led to the grossest abuses and cruelties. Scandals were brought to light no less horrifying than those with which readers of Russian history are familiar. Conditions in the Prussian provinces east of the Elbe were shown to be not incomparable when the emancipation of the serfs was first seriously considered there after 1806. Stein in a famous phrase once compared the estates of the Mecklenburg junkers to the 'den of a beast of prey which lays waste everything around it and surrounds itself with the silence of the grave'.[1] Though the law in central Europe allowed the serf rights which he did not possess in Russia, these seem to have been virtually impossible to enforce. Except that in the Habsburg dominions, and in Prussia after the Seven Years War, the serf was rarely if ever sold as an individual, but only with the estate to which he belonged, it does not seem that he had any more protection than in Russia against landlords and bailiffs who, for whatever reasons, were unable or unwilling to treat him with such consideration as the current morality and sense of the expedient required.

These did not, in any case, demand much. The prevailing standards appear to have been those which Richelieu expressed when he said in his *Testament Politique* that the peasants should be compared to mules

qui, étant accoutumés à la charge, se gâtent par un long repos plus que par le travail. Mais ainsi que ce travail doit être modéré, et qu'il faut que la charge de ces animaux soit proportionée à leurs forces, il en est de même des subsides à l'égard des peuples; s'ils n'étaient modérés, lors même qu'ils seraient utiles au public, ils ne laisseraient pas d'être injustes.[2]

These were the ideals, which the mercantilists inherited, of a society which accepted social relationships as static and saw every estate or *Stand* as having its appropriate functions and standards of living. Justi expressed essentially the same point of view as Richelieu when he said that 'the domestic security of a state consists in such a well-ordered constitution that the parts of the civic body are held in the appropriate correlation and the consequent repose'.[3]

As in other periods, however, so in the period under discussion, many causes combined to prevent the professed standards from being observed. Sometimes, as in France under Louis XIV, a major cause of the peasants' misery was an irrational, self-defeating policy of aggression that ruined the country by war; sometimes, as in the hereditary lands of the house of Habsburg, it was the lack of adequate machinery – indeed before the middle of the century of any machinery at all – for curbing the landlords' exactions. Before the Physiocrats' ideas gained general currency, the Prussian government showed more concern for agriculture, and for the peasants' welfare, than did the governments of the other major continental countries. In the second half of the eighteenth century the Prussians boasted, apparently with justice, that the royal

[1] Ritter, *Stein*, p. 70.
[2] *Oeuvres du Cardinal de Richelieu*, ed. R. Gaucheron (Paris, 1933), p. 102.
[3] Small, *The Cameralists*, pp. 334–5.

stock policy, which kept grain prices stable, protected the peasants from the famines which decimated other parts of central Europe and from the local shortages that were common in France throughout the century. The huge demands of Frederick's army, however, as well as the attempt to build up manufactures often at the expense of agriculture, seem calculated to have reduced the peasant's standard of living to subsistence level, even if it had proved possible (which Frederick believed it was not) to remove the control over his destinies from the hands of the serf-owners.

In the second half of the eighteenth century the results of government action (or inaction) disadvantageous to the interests of a peasantry too ignorant and lacking in organization to resist successfully, were intensified by economic change. The great growth in population, which towards the end of the century became apparent even in central Europe, and which was unaccompanied by a proportionate rise in production and employment, depressed the peasant's standard of life. The increase in foreign trade, including trade in agricultural products, and the growing desire among those landowners in a position to do so to extract a profit from their estates, led everywhere to attempts to insist on a more rigorous exaction of feudal dues.

Speaking of the French peasants at the end of the eighteenth century, Tocqueville said that civilization seemed to turn against them alone. This was not wholly true. The picture which Professor Labrousse drew of the French economy between the beginning of the 1730s and the end of the 1770s, at a time of rising prices and growing prosperity, shows that the beneficiaries of these fortunate circumstances were the manufacturers, merchants and financiers and, in the countryside, those who produced for the market and let out land for rent. The share-croppers, and the landowners (including many nobles) who engaged in subsistence agriculture, did not benefit; nor did those who lived from wages in either town or country; for though wage rates and employment rose, neither rose fast enough to keep pace with the increase in population, and average real wages fell. In France in the eighteenth century (and it is plain that things were moving in the same direction in central Europe) the peasants were not the only sufferers in an economy that brought increasing wealth or affluence to only a small proportion of the community. As in the less favourable economic climate that had prevailed at the end of the seventeenth century, however, they were the most numerous class of sufferers; and in the second half of the eighteenth century their sufferings increasingly came to pose serious social and political problems. The growing disparity between the wealth of the wealthy few, which the existing tax systems were incapable of tapping, and the poverty of the many poor who had no wealth to tax; the rise in population which was a contributory cause of peasant unrest; the growing need of the state for tax-payers, of the armies for healthy recruits, of the entrepreneurs and the civil and military authorities for technical skill, which the ignorant and impoverished mass of the population could not supply in sufficient quantities – all these causes combined to make the peasant question a matter of immediate government concern.

It was round about the middle of the eighteenth century that the English example and the gospel of the Physiocrats began to turn all the old ideas upside down. The Physiocrats preached that the wealth of nations was to be increased not by trying to destroy one's neighbours' trade but by division of labour and cooperation between nations. In domestic affairs they held out the hope of increasing production, in the first place agricultural production, not indeed on a limitless scale (although it has been claimed that even this possibility was implicit in their doctrines[1]) but at least to an extent unimaginable by previous generations.

The essence of the Physiocrats' doctrine was expressed in Quesnay's maxim: 'Pauvres paysans, pauvre royaume.'[2] Quesnay spoke on behalf of his own kind, for though he died a wealthy noble with a hereditary title and several seigneuries, he was born a peasant – the eighth of thirteen children brought up in a two-roomed cottage. His parents, nevertheless, counted as relatively prosperous by the standards of the times, since they owned cows and horses, and land the proceeds of which, when eked out by the profits of a small shop, enabled them to support their family and two servants.[3] They belonged, in fact, to the class of substantial peasants known as 'laboureurs'. To Quesnay the future of France lay in the hands of such people and particularly with such of them as rented land from the larger landowners.

Quesnay attributed the disastrous condition of French agriculture to the shortage of prosperous tenant farmers and the wide prevalence of *métayage*, or share-cropping, which he saw as both the result and the cause of poverty, dooming the land to inefficient cultivation, and to a yield far lower than that in the so-called 'pays de grande culture' where farms were leased for a money rent. Quesnay believed that the prosperous tenant farmer, if he were to replace the *métayer*, would give employment to the surplus agricultural population which could not find work in the districts where *métayage* prevailed; that the growth in

[1] M. Moës, 'Y a-t-il une theorie de la croissance chez François Quesnay?', *Revue d'Histoire Économique et Sociale*, XL (1962).

[2] Quesnay, *François Quesnay et la Physiocratie*, II, 973.

[3] *Ibid.* I. Jacqueline Hecht, 'La Vie de François Quesnay', in *François Quesnay et la Physiocratie* (Paris, 1958).

employment and prosperity on the land would stimulate trade and industry, and that as a result of these transformations the landlords' rents and the state's tax-revenue would increase. He constructed his system in order to demonstrate these points and to show the conditions that would be necessary if his vision were to achieve substance.

He started from the assumption that

il faut des richesses pour produire des richesses; un laboureur dont la fortune est détruite par la grêle, ou par une mortalité de bestiaux, ou par des impositions, ou par d'autres causes, ne peut plus continuer de faire des dépenses qu'exige la culture...l'indigence dans lequel il est tombé le retient nécessairement dans l'indigence et dans l'impuissance d'exercer sa profession et d'y établir ses enfants.[1]

'Les dépenses qu'exige la culture': this seemed the crucial point. If they could be met Quesnay assumed a threefold increase in agricultural production. Failure to meet them seemed to him to portend a decline in every sphere of national activity. From these conclusions he derived his famous concept of 'le produit net', which he appears never to have entirely clarified, but by which, broadly speaking, he seems to have meant what was left over after the necessary costs of cultivation had been met, including the costs of allowing the cultivator some never clearly specified level of reward for his labours. 'Le produit net' was a term which entered the vocabulary of ministers and officials all over Europe, and which even Figaro, in Beaumarchais's version of his activities, had learned to use. It carried with it the implication that to tax the cultivator beyond the point at which he could meet the necessary costs of production was national suicide.

On the basis of these assumptions the Physiocrats reached the conclusions described earlier about the ways in which government and society should be changed. Their demands for economic freedom challenged the assumptions on which the absolute, mercantilist monarchy and the corporative society alike rested. Their insistence that the taxes and dues demanded from the *laboureur* must not be so heavy that he could not meet the necessary costs of cultivation was an indictment of the French government's tax policies. It was also an indictment of the French nobles' material privileges, which Quesnay saw as merely the result of a 'cupidité ignorante',[2] since the noble was the first to suffer from his tenants' poverty. A fortiori it was an indictment of serfdom, 'cette tyrannie féodale...qui n'est pas moins contraire à la domination du Souverain que désavantageuse à la prospérité d'un État'.[3] The Physiocrats saw all expenditure on war, except for purposes of self-defence, and the conspicuous consumption for which the courts until

---

[1] *Ibid.* II, 540.   [2] *Ibid.* p. 981.   [3] *Ibid.* p. 567.

their day had set the model (except in Prussia since the accession of Frederick William I) as disastrous and self-defeating in countries where agriculture was starved of capital. They reversed the order of priorities to which all governments had hitherto subscribed; for though they saw the small class of prosperous landholding peasants as the class to be encouraged, the condition of the peasantry in general was their principal concern. As Quesnay put it: 'La consommation qui se fait par des sujets est la source des revenus...ce sont...les gains et les dépenses du peuple qui font la richesse du soverain.'[1] The home market thus took precedence over the foreign market with which the mercantilists had been principally preoccupied; the goods for mass consumption took precedence over the luxury industries on which the mercantilists had principally concentrated; 'the people', whom Richelieu had compared to beasts of burden deserving only the consideration which an intelligent farmer gives to his animals, were made to appear as the most important section of the community.

It was one thing, however, to enunciate these principles and quite another to translate them into practice; nor did the Physiocrats, typical of the French Enlightenment as they were, ever consider the practical obstacles which the attempts to give effect to them were likely to encounter; for the personal emancipation of the peasant, and the freeing of peasant land from the obligations imposed on it, struck at the roots of the *société d'ordres*.

In the major continental countries the Physiocrats' gospel appealed most strongly to the governments that found themselves in difficulties. During Frederick the Great's lifetime it had only a limited appeal in Prussia where the existing social arrangements appeared sanctified by success, and where the measures for agricultural reform which Frederick sponsored left serfdom untouched on the private estates. (Even on the royal estates the peasants were not given their personal freedom until 1804.) To the French, on the other hand, who were increasingly unable to sustain their international position for lack of money for their armed forces, and to the Habsburgs who were in a similar situation, the increase in national wealth which acceptance of the Physiocrats' gospel offered seemed to hold out the only hope of salvation.

In Hungary and the hereditary lands of Austria and Bohemia at Maria Theresa's accession, no one could lay the miseries of the peasants at the door of the state, which was powerless to intervene in their affairs. Maria Theresa inherited a collection of medieval monarchies, duchies and other overlordships, in which the ruler was expected to live of his own, and direct taxation was granted by the various Estates only in emergencies, and then in grossly inadequate amounts. In the perennial

[1] *Ibid.* p. 460.

struggle between the monarchs and the landowners over the fruits of the peasants' labour, the monarchs, from lack of a royal bureaucracy, came off worst in the Habsburg dominions. In 1741, when the Prussian victory at Mollwitz convinced all the states of Europe that the Habsburg inheritance was ripe for partition, Maria Theresa, from all her vast dominions, had only been able to muster 16,000 ill-clothed and ill-equipped men to oppose the 24,000 Prussians. Prince Esterhazy's palace at Esterhaza in the Burgenland, meanwhile, seemed to foreign visitors comparable only to Versailles.

It was as a remedy for this state of affairs that the Habsburgs adopted the gospel of the German Enlightenment but mixed it with physiocracy. The reforms for which Maria Theresa is principally famous broke the power of the estates in the Austrian and Bohemian lands, laid the foundations of a royal bureaucracy, and subjected the various provinces of Austria and Bohemia to a single administration. Her work in these respects was comparable to that which had been started in Prussia nearly a century earlier and completed by Frederick William I.

While this work was in progress, however, a number of her ministers and officials, educated in cameralist principles, diluted by physiocratic ideas which reached them not only from France but from Italy, began to take a serious interest in the condition of the peasants. Having reached the edge of the abyss in 1741, and living in continual fear of doing so again, the Austrians were less disposed than the other major powers to treat this problem with caution, particularly after the great Bohemian famine of 1770. This famine, and the epidemics which accompanied it, is estimated to have caused the death of 250,000 people or 10 per cent of the population of the province.[1] It was followed, in 1775, by a peasant revolt (more or less contemporaneous with the great Pugachev revolt in Russia) when 15,000 peasants marched on Prague, having burned all the chateaux en route. These calamities and various misfortunes associated with them – the poor physique of the army conscripts, the limits set on economic expansion by the poverty and ignorance of the mass of the population – were laid at the door of the miserable agriculture for which serfdom was held responsible.

A great number of edicts was issued in Maria Theresa's reign to regulate the relations of master and man and to protect the peasant from exploitation. The *Hauptpatent* of 1771 and the *Robotpatent* of 1775 relating to the Bohemian lands were veritable industrial codes, laying down in minute detail which categories of peasants could be required to perform what labour services, and for what length of time, and requiring that all peasants should keep a tally, and all landlords a

[1] W. E. Wright, *Serf, Seigneur and Sovereign. Agrarian Reform in Eighteenth Century Bohemia* (Minneapolis, 1966), p. 44.

register, in which every labour service rendered should be recorded.[1]

These edicts inevitably remained a dead letter. The impossibility of working to rule on a farm; the landlords' conviction that the peasants were their property, to be used for their convenience; the cunning obstructiveness which the peasants developed in response – all this would have made the regulations extremely difficult to enforce even if a body of royal inspectors had been domiciled in every manor. As things were, the officials of Maria Theresa's newly-established bureaucracy either would not or could not stand up to the landlords. In his classic account of Bohemian serfdom, Grünberg said of Maria Theresa's attempt to protect the peasants on the private estates: 'If we ask what changes Maria Theresa brought about in the institution of serfdom... the answer is none at all.'[2] Serfdom as it operated under *Gutsherrschaft* in fact was an institution, as Frederick the Great realized, which was largely beyond the power of the government to control. It had either to be tolerated or abolished.

Joseph II in consequence decided to abolish it, as indeed his mother had succeeded in doing on a number of the Crown's Bohemian estates, where the problems were nevertheless very different, and where the successes claimed for the operation at the time must remain dubious for lack of reliable evidence. The ends which Joseph hoped to achieve, and the means he adopted, have been variously, though never altogether convincingly, described, and are obscure in a number of respects. His principal object appears to have been to create a class of prosperous hereditary tenant farmers. (His regulations as finally formulated did little for the *Innleute*, *Häusler* and other landless serfs who constituted the majority.) For this purpose he had not only to give the serfs their personal freedom; he had to ensure that the landholding serfs had sufficient land, sufficiently unencumbered with dues and taxes.

Joseph set the serfs free in 1781. His law of 1789 attempted at one and the same time to impose an equal rate of tax on all holders of land, and to prevent the landlord from making undue demands on the peasant. The landholding peasant was freed from the obligation to render labour services; it was laid down as a principle that the total sum which he paid in rent and taxes should never exceed 30 per cent of the gross yield of his holding (an assessment of the net yield having proved impracticable).[3]

It need hardly be said that the attempt to translate these principles into practice faced the recently established Habsburg bureaucracy with

[1] C. Grünberg, *Die Bauernbefreiung* (Leipzig, 1893–4), I, 175 ff. and 222 ff.
[2] *Ibid.* I, 275.
[3] R. Rozdolski, *Die große Steuer- und Agrarreform Josefs II* (Warsaw, 1961), p. 118.

herculean tasks, including the task of surveying all the land in Hungary, Austria and Bohemia at a time when there were very few trained surveyors. It has recently been maintained that the survey was accomplished by rough and ready methods with a greater degree of accuracy than might be imagined possible.[1] The fact nevertheless remains that Joseph's attempted agrarian reforms were totally impracticable. He appears to have supposed that by depriving the landlords of their free labour, thus increasing the time available to the peasants to cultivate their holdings, he would force the landlords to let out their demesne and enable the peasants to rent it, since his reforms would make the peasants more prosperous. He evidently believed, in accordance with physiocratic principles, that not only the peasants would benefit from these arrangements, but that the landlords would receive more in rent than the value of the produce the manor had yielded when it had been operated by serf labour. In fact, however, as even his admirers do not attempt to deny, his proposals (whether or not they could have worked in any circumstances) faced many, if not most, landowners with ruin during the period of the changeover, for which he made no provision.

Joseph was prepared to act more despotically than any of his fellow despots. He has been acclaimed as the inventor of the secret police in its modern form, for in his reign this organization, reporting to him directly and not, as in Maria Theresa's day, to the *Hofkanzlei*,[2] became the most powerful body of men in the state. His autocratic powers, however, could not save him. Unlike Peter the Great, to whom his principal biographer, Mitrofanov, found him in many ways comparable, he made no attempt to build up a body of convinced and resolute supporters. He had inadequate military force at his disposal because his army was engaged in an unsuccessful war with the Turks. Virtually his entire bureaucracy turned against him, though many of them were convinced of the need to lighten the serfs' burdens. By 1790, when he died, the Hungarian nobility was in open revolt, and the nobility in Austria and Bohemia on the verge of it. Because he had held out hopes to the peasants which it had been impossible to fulfil, peasant unrest had been continuous throughout his reign and had often had to be put down by force. His heir and brother Leopold, who sympathized with his objectives but not with his methods, spoke of the 'heillose Verwirrung und Unordnung'[3] which he encountered when he came to Vienna to take up his inheritance.

Joseph's schemes thus collapsed in ruins, but remain a testimony to the revolutionary implications of the Physiocrats' gospel – implications

[1] *Ibid.* p. 41.
[2] D. Silagi, *Jakobiner in der Habsburger-Monarchie* (Vienna and Munich, 1962), pp. 49 ff.   [3] A. Wandruszka, *Leopold II* (Vienna and Munich, 1965), II, 252.

which the *Hofkanzlei* in Vienna epitomized in January 1789 when it said of his proposed agrarian and tax reforms:

they will completely revolutionize the whole order of things in the German hereditary lands. They will change the position of every individual, lord and serf, the value of each man's possessions, and hence the extent of his productive capacity, taken in relation to himself, to others and to the state. They will greatly diminish the national wealth since the peasant's gains will not be proportionate to the landlord's losses.[1]

In France a whole succession of Contrôleurs Généraux from Turgot's day onwards, whether or not they counted themselves Physiocrats, attempted to improve peasant conditions on physiocratic lines. These attempts have not appeared revolutionary only because the government withdrew its measures when faced with opposition, as for example in the case of the edicts to free the grain trade and to abolish the *corvée*. Its plans to reduce the arbitrariness of the *taille* were conspicuously successful in one or two districts, but these were too few to be significant.[2] Its attempts to lighten the burden of the direct taxes that fell on the peasants, by transferring a part of it to the nobles, were foredoomed to failure, notwithstanding the energy with which they were pursued, because, apart from any other reasons, the nobles constituted only between 1 and 2 per cent of the population and no government in Europe at this time was capable of operating a tax-system that could tap the wealth of the rich landlords without driving the poorer ones bankrupt. The attempts to foster an agricultural revolution on the English model by encouraging the landowners to enclose found little favour among the seigneurs, were resisted by the landholding peasants, and thus foundered on the rock of the conservatism of these two classes which the government could see no means of overcoming.[3]

Lefebvre often claimed that failure to solve the peasant problem doomed France to revolution and this seems beyond dispute. Poor peasants, as Quesnay said, meant a poor kingdom – in France a kingdom too poor to maintain its status as a great power in the face of British competition. It was this state of affairs, to which the ruling classes could not reconcile themselves, but on the remedies for which they could not agree, that led to the collapse of authority and the summoning of the States General. The collapse of authority gave the peasants their chance. Though driven desperate by a series of bad harvests, like the peasants in other countries, they could have done nothing against the power of the

---

[1] Rozdolski, *Die große Steuer- und Agrarreform Josefs II*, p. 114.
[2] See M. Marion, *Les Impôts Directs sous l'Ancien Régime* (Paris, 1910), *passim*.
[3] See Marc Bloch, 'La Lutte pour l'Individualisme Agraire', *Annales d'Histoire Économique et Sociale* (Paris, 1930), *passim*.

state if it had been resolutely directed against them. When it disintegrated they rose over the greater part of France, burned the chateaux and the manorial records and put the landlords and the local authorities to flight. These events were the necessary prelude to the major social revolution which followed.

A comparable situation did not exist in either of the other major continental absolutisms. In the hereditary lands of the house of Habsburg, though the peasants in the eighteenth century had shown a rebelliousness not paralleled in France before the eve of the Revolution, the ruling classes remained united. Admittedly from Maria Theresa's day onwards divisions had developed between the bureaucracy and the majority of the landlords over the question of agrarian reform. These differences, however, disappeared before the fear of chaos which Joseph's actions had conjured up, and which the French Revolution reinforced. The beliefs of the Philosophes in liberty, equality and fraternity found no substantial body of supporters. Leopold was forced to revoke most of Joseph's reforms. This seemed to him *reculer pour mieux sauter*. He was profoundly convinced, like his brother, of the need to modernize the social structure of his dominions in the interests of economic development. But unlike his brother he did not believe that this objective could be achieved by direct action from above. He hoped to create a body of opinion in favour of it by devious means, such as surreptitiously inciting the servile Hungarian bourgeoisie to protest against the domination of the landlords.[1] He died, however, after he had reigned for only two years and was succeeded by a reactionary.

At the end of the eighteenth century Prussia was the only one of the major powers here under discussion which was not shaken by revolutionary disturbances. There were isolated peasant revolts in Frederick the Great's reign, though only, apparently, on a small scale. Others, inspired by the French example, broke out after his death, particularly in Silesia. They were, however, easily suppressed by military force. As Czybulka put it in one of the best accounts of peasant conditions in Prussia in the eighteenth century: the ruling classes 'showed all the qualities needed by a minority if it is to defend a position based on the oppression of the majority'.[2] Tocqueville's belief that the peasants were more discontented in France than under the so-called 'feudal' arrangements of *Gutsherrschaft* was patently untrue in relation to the hereditary lands of the Habsburgs, and is not supported by the facts even in Prussia.

After Frederick's death, however, some Prussian landowners and many members of the Prussian bureaucracy became increasingly

---

[1] Silagi, *Jakobiner in der Habsburger-Monarchie*, pp. 87ff.
[2] Czybulka, *Die Lage der ländlichen Klassen Ostdeutschlands im 18. Jahrhundert* (Brunswick, 1949), p. 85.

convinced of the economic arguments against serfdom. The gospel of the Physiocrats, as amended by Adam Smith, entered Prussia via the University of Königsberg. At the end of the eighteenth century and the beginning of the nineteenth Adam Smith, indeed, found his most fervent admirers among Prussian professors and civil servants who referred to him as 'the divine Smith' ('der göttliche Smith'),[1] made pilgrimages to his tomb, and saw him (in the words of Alexander von der Marwitz in 1811) as 'together with Napoleon the mightiest monarch in Europe'.[2]

The consequences of this attitude found expression in Prussia, among other things, in an agricultural revolution more complete than that achieved in any other continental state, France included, in the first half of the nineteenth century.[3] This story, however, belongs to a period later than the one considered here; for just as absolutism developed, reached its prime and fell into decay at different dates in different countries (though always earlier in western than in central Europe), so also did the *société d'ordres* on which it had been superimposed, and with which its fate was to a greater or less extent linked.

In his *Ancien Régime et la Revolution*, first published in 1856, Tocqueville maintained that the French Revolution had only brought about by violence changes that sooner or later were bound to come everywhere. He may or may not have been right in supposing that even without the Revolution 'le vieil édifice social n'en serait pas moins tombé partout, ici plus tôt, la plus tard';[4] it is, however, true that in the second half of the eighteenth century the increase in trade and manufactures and in the prosperity of the professional and propertied classes, together with the growth of education, of sophistication in matters of government, and of visions of new freedoms and new possibilities of creating wealth, combined to make the privileges and obligations of the *société d'ordres* seem everywhere and increasingly a source of injustice and inefficiency.

In this situation the most fundamental and the most difficult of the tasks to be undertaken was that of freeing the land, and the people who lived from it and who formed the vast majority of every population, from the multiplicity of restrictions to which the *société d'ordres* had subjected them – restrictions imposed by the *servitudes collectives* and other obligations to the community; by the dues and services owed to the landlords; by the personal servitude of the peasants in the areas of

---

[1] See Bodelschwingh, *Leben des Freiherrn von Vincke* (Berlin, 1853), p. 96.

[2] Rahel Varnhagen von Ense, *Briefwechsel mit Alexander von der Marwitz* (Munich, 1966), p. 93.

[3] See Lütge, *Deutsche Sozial- und Wirtschaftsgeschichte*, pp. 436 ff. and B. Gebhardt, *Handbuch der deutschen Geschichte* (9th ed., Stuttgart, 1970), pp. 384 ff.

[4] Alexis de Tocqueville, *Oeuvres Complètes*, ed. J. P. Mayer, II, 96.

Gutsherrschaft, and by the obligations which also fell on the landlords in these areas and which made it possible to speak of freeing the landlord as well as the peasant.[1]

Nearly half a century before it occurred to Tocqueville to see these various forms of emancipation as inevitable, the same idea had occurred to Theodor von Schön, who presided over the implementation of the agrarian reforms in East and West Prussia after the Napoleonic wars, but who as early as 1811 had said: 'Our times have this in common with the Revolution that they demand changes in the nature of the ownership of land. These are changes which no human power can arrest.'[2]

[1] A. Wald, 'Die Bauernbefreiung...eine Befreiung der Herrn', *Hist. Vierteljahrschrift* (1933).

[2] Quoted by E. W. Mayer in *Das Retablissement Ost- und Westpreussens unter der Mitwirkung und Leitung Theodors von Schön* (Jena, 1916), p. 42.

Bibliographies

EDITORS' NOTE

In accordance with the established practice of the Cambridge series of histories, the bibliographies printed below are selective and incomplete. Their purpose is not to list all the publications bearing directly or indirectly on the subject, but to enable the readers to study some of the topics in greater detail. As a rule, books and articles superseded by later publications have not been included, and references to general treatises indirectly relevant to the subject-matter of individual chapters have been reduced to the minimum. As most of the chapters are not new pieces of research, but summaries and interpretations of knowledge already available in secondary literature, references to original sources have either been left out altogether or have been confined to the principal and most essential classes of evidence.

Within the limits set by these general principles, the individual contributors were given the freedom of composing and arranging bibliographies as they thought best. The 'layout' of the bibliographical lists, therefore, varies from chapter to chapter.

CHAPTER I

The Historical Study of Economic Growth and Decline in Early Modern History

ASHTON, T. S. *The Industrial Revolution*. London, 1954.
 Economic Fluctuations in England 1700–1800. Oxford, 1959.
ASHTON, T. S. and SCHUMPETER, ELIZABETH BOODY. *English Overseas Trade Statistics 1697–1808*. Oxford, 1960.
BAILYN, B. *The New England Merchants in the Seventeenth Century*. New York, 1955.
BENNASSAR, B. *Recherches sur les grandes épidémies dans le nord de l'Espagne à la fin du XVIᵉ siècle*. Paris, 1969.
BEVERIDGE, WILLIAM (1st Baron). *Prices and Wages from the Twelfth to the Nineteenth Century*. London, 1965.
BLOCH, MARC. 'Pour une histoire comparée des sociétés européennes.' *Revue de Synthèse Historique*, XLVI, 1928.
BOGUCKA, MARIA. 'The monetary crisis in XVIIth century Poland and its social and psychological consequences.' *Journal of European Economic History*, IV: 1, 1975.
BOXER, C. R. *The Dutch Seaborne Empire 1600–1800*. New York, 1965.
BRAUDEL, F. *Capitalism and Material Life 1400–1800*. Trans. by M. Kochan. London, 1973.
BROWN, H. PHELPS and HOPKINS, S. 'Seven centuries of the prices of consumables, compared with builders' wage-rates.' *Economica*, 1956.
CIPOLLA, CARLO. *Public Health and the Medical Profession in the Renaissance*. Cambridge, 1976.
 The Economic Decline of Empires. London, 1970.
CLAPHAM, SIR J. H. 'Economic history as a discipline.' *Encyclopaedia of the Social Sciences*, Vol. 5. New York, 1930.
CLARK, G. N. *The Wealth of England 1496–1760*. London, 1946.
COLEMAN, D. C. 'Eli Heckscher and the idea of mercantilism.' *Scandinavian Economic History Review*, V: 1, 1957.
 'An innovation and its diffusion: the "New Draperies".' *Economic History Review*, 1969.
 The Rise of the British Paper Industry 1495–1850. 1958.
CUNNINGHAM, W. *The Growth of English Industry and Commerce*. 5th ed. Cambridge, 1922.
DAVIES, N. Z. 'The rites of violence: religious riots in 16th century France.' *Past and Present*, May 1973.
DAVIS, RALPH. *The Rise of the Atlantic Economies*. 1973.
DECHESNE, L. *Histoire économique et sociale de la Belgique*. Paris–Liege, 1932.
DUBY, GEORGE. *Early Growth of the European Economy*. London, 1974.
ELLIOTT, J. H. 'The decline of Spain.' *Past and Present*, 1961.
FELIX, D. 'Profit inflation and industrial growth: the historic record and contemporary analogies.' *Quarterly Journal of Economics*, 1956.
FLINN, MICHAEL. 'The stabilisation of mortality in pre-industrial western Europe.' *Journal of European Economic History*, III: 2, 1974.
FLOUD, R. (ed.). *Essays in Quantitative Economic History*. Oxford, 1974.
FOGEL, R. W. and ENGERMAN, S. L. *The Reinterpretation of American Economic History*. New York, 1971.
GLAMANN, K. *European Trade 1500–1750* (Fontana Economic History, ed. C. M. Cipolla). London, 1971.
GORSKI, KAROL. 'La Mentalité Polonaise du XVI–XVIIIᵉ siècle.' (Paper as yet unpublished, in preparation for the International Congress at Los Angeles 1975 and read in preliminary form to the *Istituto Internazionale di Storia Economica Francesco Datini*, Prato, Italy, May, 1974.)
GOUBERT, P. 'Historical demography and the re-interpretation of early modern French history: a research review.' *Journal of Interdisciplinary History*, I, 1970–1.
 'Les Fondements démographiques.' In F. Braudel and E. Labrousse (eds.), *Histoire économique et sociale de la France*, II, Paris, 1970.

GRIFFITHS, G. TALBOT. *Population Problems of the Age of Malthus*. Cambridge, 1926.
HALE, J. R. *Renaissance Europe 1480–1520*. London, 1971.
HAMILTON, E. J. 'American treasure and the rise of capitalism.' *Economica*, VII, 1929.
  'The decline of Spain.' *Economic History Review*, VIII, 1938.
  'Profit, inflation and the industrial revolution 1751–1800.' *Quarterly Journal of Economics*, LVI, 1942.
HAMMARSTRÖM, INGRID. 'The price revolution of the sixteenth century: some Swedish evidence.' *Scandinavian Economic History Review*, 1957.
HARPER, L. A. *The English Navigation Laws*. New York, 1939.
HECKSCHER, E. 'A plea for theory in economic history.' *Economic History* (Supplement to the *Economic Journal*, I, 1926–9).
  Mercantilism. 2 vols. Trans. by M. Schapiro. London, 1931. Rev. ed. 1955, edited by E. F. Söderlund.
HICKS, J. R. *A Theory of Economic History*. Oxford, 1969.
HOFFMANN, W. *British Industry 1700–1950*. Trans. by W. H. Chaloner and W. O. Henderson. 1955.
HOUTTE, J. A. VAN. *Economische en sociale geschiedenis van de lage landen*. Ziest, Antwerp, 1964.
JONES, E. L. 'Institutional determinism and the rise of the western world.' *Economic Enquiry*, XII: 1, 1974.
KEYNES, J. M. *Treatise on Money*, II (London, 1930), 152–63.
KING, GREGORY. 'Natural and Political Observations,' 1696 (reprinted in J. H. Hollander (ed.), *Two Tracts by Gregory King* (Baltimore, 1936), pp. 54–6).
LABROUSSE, C. E. *Esquisse du mouvement des prix et des revenus en France au XVIIIe siècle*. Paris, 1933.
LANE, F. C. and RIEMERSMA, J. C. (eds.). *Enterprise and Secular Change*. Homewood, Ill., 1953.
LE ROY LADURIE, E. *Les Paysans de Languedoc*. Paris, 1966.
MACZAK, ANTONI. 'Money and society in Poland–Lithuania of the 16th–17th centuries.' (Paper, to be published, read to the *Istituto Francesco Datini* at Prato, Italy.)
  'Progress and under-development in the eyes of Renaissance and Baroque man.' *Studia Historiae Oeconomicae*, IX, Poznan, 1974.
MADDALENA, A. DE. *Rural Europe 1500–1750* (Fontana Economic History, ed. C. M. Cipolla). London, 1970.
MAKKAI, L. 'The Hungarian Puritans and the English Revolution.' *Acta Historica*, V: 1–2, Budapest, 1958.
MATHIAS, P. *The Brewing Industry in England 1700–1830*. Cambridge, 1959.
MEREDITH, H. O. *Outlines of the Economic History of England*. 1927.
MEUVRET, J. 'Les crises de subsistances et la démographie de la France d'ancien régime.' *Population*, I, 1946.
  Études d'histoire économique; recueil d'articles. Paris, 1971.
MOLS, R. *Introduction à la démographie historique des villes d'Europe du XIVe au XVIIIe siècle*. Louvain, 1955.
NADAL, J. 'La revolución de los precios españoles en el siglo XVI.' *Hispania*, 1959.
NEF, J. U. 'Prices and industrial capitalism 1940–1640.' *Economic History Review*, VII, 1937.
NORTH, D. C. and THOMAS, R. P. *The Rise of the Western World: A New Economic History*. New York and Cambridge, 1973.
OGG, DAVID. *England in the Reigns of James the Second and William the Third*. Oxford, 1955.
PARKER, N. G. *The Army of Flanders and the Spanish Road 1567–1659*. Cambridge, 1972.
PIKE, RUTH. *Aristocrats & Traders: Sevillian Society in the Sixteenth Century*. New York, 1972.
PIRENNE, H. 'The place of the Netherlands in the economic history of medieval Europe.' *English Historical Review*, II, 1929.
POSTAN, M. M. *The Historical Method in Social Science*. Cambridge, 1939.
  'Sir John Clapham: the economic historian.' *University of Leeds Review*, XVII: 1, 1974.
POSTHUMUS, N. W. *Inquiry into the History of Prices in Holland*. 2 vols. Leiden, 1971.
PULLAN, B. *Rich and Poor in Renaissance Venice*. Oxford, 1971.
  Crisis and Change in the Venetian Economy in the Sixteenth & Seventeenth Centuries. London, 1968.

RENIER, G. *The Dutch Nation*. London, 1944.

ROGERS, J. E. THOROLD. *History of Agriculture and Prices*. 6 vols. Oxford, 1866–87.

ROPER, H. R. TREVOR. *The Gentry 1540–1640*. Supplement to the *Economic History Review*, London, 1953.
Religion, the Reformation and Social Change. London, 1967.

ROSTOW, W. W. *The Stages of Economic Growth*. Cambridge, 1960.

SCHMOLLER, GUSTAV. 'Volkswirtschaft, Volkswirtchaftslehre und -methode.' *Handwörterbuch der Staatswissenschaften*, VIII, 1911.

SELLA, D. 'Industrial production in 17th-century Italy: a reappraisal.' *Explorations in Entrepreneurial History*, 1969.

SIMIAND, F. 'La Causalité en histoire.' *Bulletin de la Société Français de Philosophie*, VI, 1906.

SPIETHOFF, A. 'Anschauliche und reine Volkswirtschaftliche Theorie und ihr Verhältnis zueinander.' *Festgabe für Alfred Weber*, Heidelberg, 1948.

STOLS, E. *De Spaanse Brabanders*. Brussels, 1971.

SUPPLE, B. E. *Commercial Crisis and Change in England 1600–1642*. Cambridge, 1959.

TAWNEY, R. H. *Religion and the Rise of Capitalism*. London, 1926.

THIRSK, JOAN. 'Industries in the countryside.' In *Essays in the Economic and Social History of Tudor and Stuart England*, ed. F. J. Fisher, Cambridge, 1961.
'Seventeenth century agriculture in England.' *Agricultural History Review*, 1970.
English Peasant Farming. London, 1957.
(ed.). *Agrarian History of England and Wales 1500–1640*, Vol. IV, Cambridge, 1967.

TOOKE, T. and NEWMARCH, W. A. *A History of Prices and the State of the Circulation 1792–1856*. (Ed. with intro. by T. E. Gregory.) Reprinted London, 1928.

UYTVEN, R. VAN. 'Politique monétaire et conjoncture dans les Pays Bas du XIVe au XVIe siècle.' Paper read to the Annual Conference of the Istituto Francesco Datini at Prato, Italy; to be published shortly.

UZTARIZ, GIERONYMO DE. *The Theory and Practice of Commerce and Maritime Affairs*. (Trans. by J. Kippax.) London, 1751.

VERLINDEN, C., CRAEYBECK, J. and SCHOLLIERS, E. 'Mouvement des prix et des salaires en Belgique au XVIe siècle.' *Annales*, X, 1955.

VICENS VIVES, JAIME. *An Economic History of Spain*. Princeton, New Jersey, 1969.

VILAR, JEAN. 'L'Espagne au temps de Philippe II.' *Ages d'Or et Réalités*, Paris, 1965.
'Docteurs et marchands: l'école de Tolède 1615–1630.' *Ve Congrés International d'Histoire Economique*, 1970.

VRIES, JAN DE. *The Dutch Rural Economy in the Golden Age 1500–1700*. New Haven, Yale University Press, 1974.

WEBER, MAX. *The Protestant Ethic and the Spirit of Capitalism*. English trans. 1930.
Gesammelte Aufsätze zur Wissenschaftslehre. Tübingen, 1922.

WEISSER, M. 'The decline of Castile revisited: the case of Toledo.' *Journal of European Economic History*, II: 2, 1973.

WIEBE, G. *Zur Geschichte der Preisrevolution des 16. und 17. Jahrhunderts*. Leipzig, 1895.

WILSON, CHARLES. *Economic History and the Historian – Collected Essays*. London, 1969.
The Dutch Republic and the Civilisation of the Seventeenth Century. London, 1969.
England's Apprenticeship. London, 1965.
'Transport as a factor in the history of economic development.' *Journal of European Economic History*, II: 2, 1973.
'Taxation and the decline of empire.' In *Economic History and the Historian*, 1969.

WOUDE, A. M. VAN DER. 'The A.A.G. Bijdragen and the study of Dutch rural history.' *Journal of European Economic History*, IV: 1, 1975.

CHAPTER II

Agriculture in the Vital Revolution

The number of books and articles covering this period is extremely large. The appended bibliography is by no means complete, but it does contain those writings which are of particular importance for this chapter. For information on demographic history and on prices the reader is referred to the bibliographies of the chapters concerned.

ABEL, W. 'Wandlungen des Fleischverbrauchs und der Fleischversorgung in Deutschland seit dem ausgehenden Mittelalter.' *Berichte über Landwirtschaft*, N.F., XXII, 1938.
Agrarkrisen und Agrarkonjunktur. Eine Geschichte der Land- und Ernährungswirtschaft Mitteleuropas seit dem hohen Mittelalter. Revised ed., Hamburg, 1966.
Geschichte der deutschen Landwirtschaft vom frühen Mittelalter bis zum 19. Jahrhundert. Deutsche Agrargeschichte, II, Stuttgart, 1962.
ACHILLES, W. 'Getreidepreise und Getreidehandelsbeziehungen europäischer Räume im 16. und 17. Jahrhundert.' *Zeitschrift für Agrargeschichte und Agrarsoziologie*, VII, 1959.
Vermögensverhältnisse braunschweigischer Bauernhöfe im 17. und 18. Jahrhundert. Stuttgart, 1965.
Actes du colloque sur la forêt, Besançon 21–22 octobre 1966. 1967.
ADEN, O. *Entwicklung und Wechsellagen ausgewählter Gewerbe in Ostfries – von der Mitte des 18. bis zum Ausgang des 19. Jahrhundert*. Aurich, 1964.
ANDERSON, C. A. 'Patterns and variability in the distribution and diffusion of schooling.' *Education and Economic Development*, 1966.
ANDERSON, R. H. 'Graindrills through thirty-nine centuries.' *Agricultural History*, X, 1936.
APPOLIS, E. *Un pays languedocien au milieu du XVIIIᵉ siècle, le diocèse civil de Lodève*. 1951.
ARENDS, FR. *Ostfriesland und Jever in geographischer, statistischer und besonders landwirthschaftlicher Hinsicht*. 3 vols., 1818–20.
ARNIM, V. VON. *Krisen und Konjunkturen der Landwirtschaft in Schleswig-Holstein vom 16. bis zum 18. Jahrhundert*. Neumünster, 1957.
ASHLEY, W. 'The English improvers.' *Mélanges d'histoire offerts à Henri Pirenne*, I, 1926.
ASHTON, T. S. *An Economic History of England. The Eighteenth Century*. London, 1955.
Economic Fluctuations in England, 1700–1800. Oxford, 1959.
AUBIN, G. *Zur Geschichte des gutsherrlich-bäuerlichen Verhältnisses in Ostpreussen*. 1910.
AUGÉ-LARIBÉ, M. *La Révolution agricole*. Paris, 1955.
AYMARD, M. 'En Sicile: dîmes et comptabilités agricoles.' *Études rurales*, XXXV, 1969.
BACKHAUS, A. *Entwicklung der Landwirtschaft auf den gräflich Stolberg-Wernigerödischen Domänen*. Jena, 1888.
BAEHREL, R. *Une Croissance: la Basse-Provence rurale*. Paris, 1961.
BAIROCH, P. 'Le rôle de l'agriculture dans la création de la sidérurgie moderne.' *Revue d'histoire économique et sociale*, XLIV, 1966.
BAMFORD, P. W. *Forests and French Sea Power, 1660–1789*. Toronto, 1956.
BARANOWSKI, B. et al. *Histoire de l'économie rurale en Pologne jusqu'à 1864*. Warsaw, 1966.
BARRY, J. P. and LE ROY LADURIE, E. 'Histoire agricole et phytogéographie.' *Annales*, XVII, 1962.
BAUDUIN, H. O. J. H. and JANSEN, J. C. G. M. 'Aspecten van de Limburgse landbouwgeschiedenis.' *Studies over de sociaal-economische geschiedenis van Limburg*, XIV, 1969.
BECHTEL, H. *Wirtschaftsgeschichte Deutschlands*. 3 vols., Munich, 1951–6.
BENNASSAR, B. 'L'alimentation d'une ville espagnole au XVIᵉ siècle.' *Annales*, XVI, 1961.
BENNETT, M. K. 'British wheat yield per acre for seven centuries.' *Economic History*, III, 1935.
BENTZIEN, U. 'Pferde und Ochsen als Spannvieh in der mecklenburgischen Landwirtschaft vor dem Dreissigjährigen Krieg.' *Zeitschrift für Agrargeschichte und Agrarsoziologie*, XII, 1964.

BERESFORD, M. W. 'The commissioners of enclosure.' *Economic History Review*, XVI, 1946.
The Lost Villages of England. London, 1954.
BERTHOLD, R. 'Wachstumsprobleme der landwirtschaftlichen Nutzfläche im Spätfeudalismus (zirka 1500 bis 1800).' *Jahrbuch für Wirtschaftsgeschichte*, II–III, 1964.
'Die Leistungsfähigkeit der Getreidewirtschaft im spätfeudalen Deutschland (1500–1800).' *Acta musaeorum agriculturae*, 1966.
BEST, H. 'Rural economy in Yorkshire in 1641.' *Publications of the Surtees Society*, XXXIII, 1857.
BEVERIDGE, W. H. 'Weather and harvest cycles.' *The Economic Journal*, XXXI, 1921.
Prices and Wages in England from the Twelfth to the Nineteenth Century. London, 1965.
BEZARD, Y. *La vie rurale dans le sud de la région parisienne de 1450 à 1560*. Paris, 1929.
BLASCHKE, K. 'Soziale Gliederung und Entwicklung der sächsischen Landbevölkerung im 16. bis 18. Jahrhundert.' *Zeitschrift für Agrargeschichte und Agrarsoziologie*, IV, 1956.
Bevölkerungsgeschichte von Sachsen bis zur industriellen Revolution. Weimar, 1967.
BLINK, H. *Geschiedenis van den boerenstand en den landbouw in Nederland*. II, 1904.
BLOCH, M. *Les Caractères originaux de l'histoire rurale française*. 2 vols., Paris, 1952–6.
BLUM, J. 'The rise of serfdom in Eastern Europe.' *The American Historical Review*, LXII, 1957.
'Russian agriculture in the last 150 years of serfdom.' *Agricultural History*, XXXIV, 1960.
Lord and Peasant in Russia from the Ninth to the Nineteenth Century. Princeton, 1961.
BOEKEL, P. N. *De zuivelexport van Nederland tot 1813*. 1929.
BOELCKE, W. *Bauer und Gutsherr in der Oberlausitz*. Bautzen, 1957.
'Wandlungen der dörflichen Sozialstruktur während Mittelalter und Neuzeit.' *Wege und Forschungen der Agrargeschichte*, 1967.
BOERENDONK, M. J. *Historische studiën over den Zeeuwschen landbouw*. 1935.
BOG, I. *Die bäuerliche Wirtschaft im Zeitalter des Dreissigjährigen Krieges*. 1952.
BÖHME, O. *Entwicklung der Landwirtschaft auf den königlich sächsischen Domänen*. 1890.
BONDOIS, P. M. 'La protection du troupeau français au XVIIIe siècle. L'épizootie de 1763.' *Revue d'histoire économique et sociale*, XX, 1932.
BONENFANT, P. *Le Problème du paupérisme en Belgique à la fin de l'ancien régime*. Brussels, 1934.
BOURDE, A. J. *The Influence of England on the French Agronomes*. Cambridge, 1953.
Agronomie et agronomes en France au 18e siècle. 3 vols., Paris, 1967.
BRAUDEL, F. *La Méditerranée et le monde méditerranéen à l'époque de Philippe II*. 2 vols., Paris, 1966.
and SPOONER, F. 'Prices in Europe from 1450 to 1750.' *The Cambridge Economic History of Europe*, IV, 1967.
BRAURE, M. *Lille et la Flandre wallonne au XVIIIe siècle*. 2 vols., 1932.
BROADBENT, L. 'Potatoes and weather.' *Quarterly Journal of the Royal Meteorological Society*, LXXV, 1949.
BROLIN, P. E. 'Omdömen om skördarna i Sverige under 1700-talet och början av 1800-talet.' *Statistisk Tidskrift*, N.F., III, 1954.
BROOKS, C. E. P. *Climate Through the Ages*. Rev. 2nd ed., London, 1949.
BRUNT, D. 'Climatic cycles.' *The Geographical Journal*, LXXXIX, 1937.
BUBLOT, G. *La Production agricole belge, étude économique séculaire, 1846–1955*. Louvain, 1957.
BUCHINSKY, I. E. 'Climatic fluctuations in the arid zone of the Ukraine.' *Arid Zone Research*, XX, 1963.
BULFERETTI, L. *Agricoltura, industria e commercio in Piemonte nel secolo XVIII*. 1963.
BULL, E. *Vergleichende Studien über die Kulturverhältnisse des Bauerntums*. Oslo, 1930.
BUREMA, L. *De voeding in Nederland van de middeleeuwen tot de twintigste eeuw*. 1953.
BUSCH-ZANTNER, R. *Agrarverfassung, Gesellschaft und Siedlung in Südosteuropa*. Leipzig, 1938.
BUTTRESS, F. A. and DENNIS, R. W. G. 'The early history of cereal seed treatment in England.' *Agricultural History*, XXI, 1947.
CAROSELLI, M. R. *Critica alla mezzadria di un vescovo del '700*. Milan, 1963.

CHAMBERS, J. D. 'Enclosure and labour supply in the industrial revolution.' *Economic History Review*, 2nd ser., V, 1953.
  The Vale of Trent, 1670–1800. London, 1957.
  and MINGAY, G. E. *The Agricultural Revolution, 1750–1880.* London, 1966.
CHATELAIN, A. 'La lente progression de la faux.' *Annales*, XI, 1956.
CHAYANOV, A. V. *The Theory of Peasant Economy.* Homewood, Ill., 1966.
CHEVALLAZ, G. A. *Aspects de l'agriculture vaudoise à la fin de l'ancien régime.* 1949.
CIPOLLA, C. M. 'Comment s'est perdue la propriété ecclésiastique dans l'Italie du nord entre le XIe et le XVIe siècle.' *Annales*, II, 1947.'
CLAPHAM, J. H. 'The growth of an agrarian proletariat, 1688–1832.' *The Cambridge Historical Journal*, I, 1923.
CLAY, C. 'Marriage, inheritance and the rise of large estates in England, 1660–1815.' *Economic History Review*, 2nd ser., XXI, 1968.
COLEMAN, D. C. 'Labour in the English economy of the seventeenth century.' *Economic History Review*, 2nd ser., VIII, 1956.
CONFINO, M. *Domaines et seigneurs en Russie vers la fin du XVIIIe siècle.* Paris, 1963.
CONNELL, K. H. *The Population of Ireland, 1750–1845.* Oxford, 1950.
CONZE, W. *Agrarverfassung und Bevölkerung in Litauen und Weissrussland.* 1940.
COO, J. DE. *De boer in de kunst van de 9e tot de 19e eeuw.* 1945.
COOPER, J. P. 'The social distribution of land and men in England, 1436–1750.' *Economic History Review*, 2nd ser., XX, 1967.
CORNWALL, J. 'Farming in Sussex, 1560–1640.' *Sussex Archaeological Collections*, XCII, 1954.
CROESEN, V. R. Y. 'Tabakscultuur in Nederland.' *Agronomisch-historisch Jaarboek*, I, 1940.
DAUZAT, A. *La Vie rurale en France des origines à nos jours.* Paris, 1946.
DAVIES, A. 'The new agriculture in lower Normandy, 1750–1789.' *Transactions of the Royal Historical Society*, 5th ser., VIII, 1958.
DAVIES, C. S. *The Agricultural History of Cheshire, 1750–1850.* Manchester, 1960.
DEBIEN, G. 'Land clearings and artificial meadows in eighteenth-century Poitou.' *Agricultural History*, XIX, 1945.
  En Haut-Poitou, défricheurs au travail, XVe–XVIIIe siècles. Paris, 1952.
DEBUS, A. G. 'Palissy, Plat and English agricultural chemistry in the 16th and 17th centuries.' *Archives internationales d'histoire des sciences*, XXI, 1968.
DEFOE, D. *A Tour through England and Wales.* 2 vols., 1948.
DEFOURNEAUX, M. 'Le problème de la terre en Andalousie au XVIIIe siècle et les projets de réforme agraire.' *Revue historique*, CCXVII, 1957.
DEINUM, B. *Climate, Nitrogen and Grass.* 1966.
DELASPRE, J. 'La naissance d'un paysage rural au XVIIIe siècle sur les hauts plateaux de l'est du Cantal et du nord de la Margeride.' *Revue de géographie alpine*, XL, 1952.
DELATTE, I. *Les Classes rurales dans la principauté de Liège au XVIIIe siècle.* 1945.
  'L'évolution de la structure agraire en Belgique de 1575 à 1850.' *Annales du XXXIIIe congrès, fédération archéologique et historique de Belgique*, II, 1951.
DEVÈZE, M. *La Vie de la forêt française au XVIe siècle.* 2 vols., Paris, 1961.
  Histoire des forêts. Paris, 1965.
DEWEZ, W. J. 'De landbouw in Brabants Westhoek in het midden van de achttiende eeuw.' *Agronomisch-historische bijdragen*, IV, 1958.
DION, R. *Histoire de la vigne et du vin en France.* Paris, 1959.
DOD, J. P. 'The state of agriculture in Shropshire, 1775–1825.' *Transactions of the Shropshire Archaeological Society*, LV, 1954.
DOORMAN, G. *Octrooien voor uitvindingen in de Nederlanden uit de 16e–18e eeuw.* 1940.
DOROŠENKO, V. V. *Očerki agrarnoj istorii Latvii v XVI veke.* 1960.
DOVRING, F. 'The transformation of European agriculture.' *The Cambridge Economic History of Europe*, VI: 2, Cambridge, 1965.
DUHAMEL DU MONCEAU, H. L. *Traité de la culture des terres.* 6 vols., Paris, 1753–61.
DUNSDORFS, E. *Der grosse schwedische Kataster in Livland, 1681–1710.* Stockholm, 1950.
DUPAQUIER, J. *La Propriété et l'exploitation foncières à la fin de l'ancien régime dans le Gâtinais septentrional.* Paris, 1956.
  'Etat présent des recherches sur la répartition de la propriété foncière à la fin de l'ancien régime.' *Troisième conférence international d'histoire économique*, I, 1968.

EASTON, C. *Les Hivers dans l'Europe occidentale*. Leyden, 1928.

EMERY, F. V. 'West Glamorgan farming circa 1580–1620.' *The National Library of Wales Journal*, IX–X, 1955–7.

ENEQUIST, G. *Nedre Luledalens byar*. 1937.

ENJALBERT, H. 'Le commerce de Bordeaux et la vie économique dans le bassin aquitain au XVIIᵉ siècle.' *Annales du Midi*, LXII, 1950.

ENNO VAN GELDER, H. A. *Nederlandse dorpen in de 16e eeuw*. 1953.

ERCEG, I. 'Die Theresianischen Reformen in Kroatien.' *Wege und Forschungen der Agrargeschichte*, 1967.

ERNLE, LORD. *English Farming, Past and Present*. 6th ed., London, 1961.

EUVERTE, G. *Les Climats et l'agriculture*. 1959.

EVERDINGEN, E. VAN. 'Enkele opmerkingen over het verband tusschen het weer en de tarwe oogst.' *Landbouwkundig tijdschrift*, LV, 1943.

EVERSLEY, D. E. C. 'The home market and economic growth in England, 1750–80.' *Land, Labour and Population in the Industrial Revolution*, 1967.

FABER, J. A. 'Bildtboer met ploeg en pen.' *Estrikken*, XXXI, 1960.
'Cattle-plague in the Netherlands during the eighteenth century.' *Mededelingen van de Landbouwhogeschool*, LXII, 1962.
'The decline of the Baltic grain-trade in the second half of the 17th century.' *Acta historiae neerlandica*, I, 1966.

FEEKES, W. 'Invloed van het klimaat op de groei en de kwaliteit van tarwe.' *Landbouwkundig tijdschrift*, L, 1938.

FEIGL, H. *Die niederösterreichische Grundherrschaft vom ausgehenden Mittelalter bis zu den Theresianisch-Josephinischen Reformen*. 1964.

FESTY, O. *L'agriculture pendant la révolution française*. Paris, 1947.

FISHER, F. J. 'The development of the London food market, 1540–1640.' *Economic History Review*, V, 1935.

FLATRÈS, P. *Géographie rurale de quatre contrées celtiques: Irlande, Galles, Cornwall et Man*. 1957.

FLINN, M. W. 'Agricultural productivity and economic growth in England 1700–1760: a comment.' *Journal of Economic History*, XXVI, 1966.

FOJTÍK, J. 'Naturálne dávky zo zivočíšnej produkcie na Trenčianskom panstve v 17. a 18. storočí.' *Agrikultúra*, VII, 1968.

FORSTER, R. 'The noble as landlord in the region of Toulouse at the end of the old regime.' *Journal of Economic History*, XVII, 1957.
'Obstacles to agricultural growth in eighteenth-century France.' *The American Historical Review*, LXXV, 1970.

FRANKLIN, T. B. *A History of Scottish Farming*. London, 1952.

FRANZ, G. *Der deutsche Bauernkrieg*. Munich, 1956.
Der dreissigjährige Krieg und das deutsche Volk. Stuttgart, 1961.
Quellen zur Geschichte des deutschen Bauernstandes in der Neuzeit. Munich, 1963.
Geschichte des Bauernstandes vom frühen Mittelalter bis zum 19. Jahrhundert. Deutsche Agrargeschichte, IV, 1970.

FRAUENDORFER, S. VON. *Ideengeschichte der Agrarwirtschaft und Agrarpolitik im deutschen Sprachgebiet*. I, 1957.

FREESE, J. C. *OstFriess- und Harrlingerland*. I, 1796.

FUSSELL, G. E. 'The size of English cattle in the eighteenth century.' *Agricultural History*, III, 1929.
Robert Loder's Farm Accounts, 1610–1620. London, 1936.
The Old English Farming Books, 1523 to 1730. London, 1947.
The English Rural Labourer. London, 1949.
More Old English Farming Books, 1731 to 1793. London, 1950.
The Farmer's Tools, from A.D. 1500–1900. London, 1952.
'Low Countries' influence on English farming.' *English Historical Review*, LXXIV, 1959.
Farming Technique from Prehistoric to Modern Times. London, 1965.
The English Dairy Farmer, 1500–1900. London, 1966.
'Science and practice in eighteenth-century British agriculture.' *Agricultural History*, XLIII, 1969.

Fussing, H. H. 'Gessingholm, 1609–1663, en landbrugshistorisk studie.' *Historisk tidsskrift*, tiende raekke, x, 1934–6.
  Stiernholm len, 1603–1661, studier i krongodsets forvaltning. Copenhagen, 1951.
Gaetani d'Aragona, G. *Evoluzione agricola e incremento demografico nel Mezzogiorno anteriormente all'Unità (1500–1860).* n.d.
Gagliardo, J. G. 'Moralism, rural ideology and the German peasant in the late eighteenth century.' *Agricultural History*, xlii, 1968.
Garcia–Badell y Abadia, G. *Introducción a la historia de la agricultura española.* 1963.
Gay, F. 'Production, prix et rentabilité de la terre en Berry au XVIIIe siècle.' *Revue d'histoire économique et sociale*, xxxvi, 1958.
Génicot, L. 'Crisis, from the middle ages to modern times.' *The Cambridge Economic History of Europe*, i, Cambridge, 1966.
Gilboy, E. W. *Wages in Eighteenth Century England.* Cambridge, Mass., 1934.
Giralt Raventos, E. 'En torno al precio del trigo en Barcelona durante el siglo XVI.' *Hispania*, lxx, 1958.
Gissel, S. *Landgilde og udsaed på Sjaelland i de store mageskifters tidsalder.* Copenhagen, 1968.
Goblet d'Alviella, F. *Histoire des bois et forêts de Belgique.* 4 vols., 1927–30.
Goehrke, C. *Die Wüstungen in der Moskauer Rus'.* Wiesbaden, 1968.
Goertz–Wrisberg, W. *Die Entwicklung der Landwirthschaft auf den Goertz-Wrisbergischen Gütern in der Provinz Hannover.* Jena, 1880.
Gorce, R. de la. 'L'homme et la nature dans le pays de "Thiérache".' *Revue du Nord*, xl, 1958
Goubert, P. 'Les techniques agricoles dans les pays picards aux XVIIe et XVIIIe siècles.' *Revue d'histoire économique et sociale*, xxxv, 1957.
  Beauvais et le Beauvaisis de 1600 à 1730. 2 vols., Paris, 1960.
Gould, J. D. 'Mr Beresford and the lost villages: a comment.' *The Agricultural History Review*, iii, 1955.
  'Agricultural fluctuations and the English economy in the eighteenth century.' *Journal of Economic History*, xxii, 1962.
Goy, J. and Head-Koenig, A. L. 'Une expérience: les revenus décimaux en France méditerranéenne (XVIe–XVIIIe siècles).' *Études rurales*, xxxvi, 1969.
Gras, N. S. B. *The Evolution of the English Corn Market from the Twelfth to the Eighteenth Century.* Cambridge, Mass., 1915.
Grigg, D. *The Agricultural Revolution in South Lincolnshire.* Cambridge, 1966.
Griziotti-Kretschmann, J. *Il problema del trend secolare nelle fluttuazioni dei prezzi.* Pavia, 1935.
Gstirner, A. 'Die Schwaighöfe im ehemaligen Herzogtume Steiermark.' *Zeitschrift des historischen Vereins für Steiermark*, xxxi, 1937.
Habakkuk, H. J. 'Economic functions of English landowners in the seventeenth and eighteenth centuries.' *Explorations in Entrepreneurial History*, vi, 1953.
  'The English land market in the eighteenth century.' *Britain and the Netherlands*, 1960.
Handley, J. E. *Scottish Farming in the Eighteenth Century*, London, 1953.
  The Agricultural Revolution in Scotland. Glasgow, 1963.
Hanssen, G. *Agrarhistorische Abhandlungen.* 2 vols., Leipzig, 1880–4.
Hart, M. L. 't. 'De invloed van de weersomstandigheden op de kwaliteit van grashooi en kuilgras.' *Landbouwkundig tijdschrift*, lxxii, 1960.
  'Het verband tussen wintermelk aflevering, ruwvoeder kwaliteit en weersomstandigheden in het zomerhalfjaar.' *Landbouwkundig tijdschrift*, lxxii, 1960.
Hauser, A. *Schweizerische Wirtschafts- und Sozialgeschichte.* 1961.
Haushofer, H. 'Das kaiserliche Pflügen.' *Wege und Forschungen der Agrargeschichte*, 1967.
Haussherr, H. *Wirtschaftsgeschichte der Neuzeit.* Cologne, 1954.
Havinden, M. A. 'Agricultural progress in open-field Oxfordshire.' *The Agricultural History Review*, ix, 1961.
  Household and Farm Inventories in Oxfordshire, 1550–1590. London, 1965.
Heaton, H. *Economic History of Europe.* Rev. ed., New York, 1948.
Heckscher, E. F. *Sveriges ekonomiska historia från Gustav Vasa.* 4 vols., Stockholm, 1935–49.

'Swedish population trends before the industrial revolution.' *Economic History Review*, 2nd ser., II, 1950.

An Economic History of Sweden. Cambridge, Mass., 1954.

HEDEMANN, P. VON. 'Hemmelmarck, eine Gutswirtschaft des vorigen Jahrhunderts.' *Zeitschrift für schleswig-holsteinische Geschichte*, XXX, 1900.

HEISIG, J. *Die historische Entwickelung der landwirtschaftlichen Verhältnisse auf den reichs-gräflich-freistandesherrlich-Schaffgotschischen Güterkomplexen in preussisch Schlesien*. Jena, 1884.

HEITZ, G. 'Zur Diskussion über Gutsherrschaft und Bauernlegen in Mecklenburg.' *Zeitschrift für Geschichtswissenschaft*, V, 1957.

'Über den Teilbetriebscharakter der gutsherrlichen Eigenwirtschaft in Scharbow (Mecklenburg) im 17. und 18. Jahrhundert.' *Wissenschaftlich Zeitschrift der Universität Rostock*, VIII, 1958/9.

HELLEINER, K. F. 'The population of Europe from the Black Death to the end of the vital revolution.' *The Cambridge Economic History of Europe*, IV, Cambridge, 1967.

HÉMARDINQUER, J. J. 'Faut-il "démythifier" le porc familial d'Ancien Régime?' *Annales*, XXV, 1970.

HENNING, F. W. *Herrschaft und Bauernuntertänigkeit*. Würzburg, 1964.

Dienste und Abgaben der Bauern im 18. Jahrhundert. Stuttgart, 1969.

Bauernwirtschaft und Bauerneinkommen in Ostpreussen im 18. Jahrhundert. Berlin, 1970.

HINTON, R. W. K. *The Port Books of Boston, 1601–1640*. 1956.

HOBSBAWM, E. J. 'The general crisis of the European economy in the 17th century.' *Past and Present*, V–VI, 1954.

HORVÁTH, P. 'K dejinàm pestovania obilnín na Slovensku v 16.–18. storočí.' *Agrikultúra*, I, 1962.

HOSKINS, W. G. *Studies in Leicestershire Agrarian History*. Leicester, 1949.

Essays in Leicestershire History. Liverpool, 1950.

'The Leicestershire farmer in the seventeenth century.' *Agricultural History*, XXV, 1951.

'English agriculture in the 17th and 18th centuries.' *Relazioni del X congresso internazionale di scienze storiche*, IV, 1955.

'English provincial towns in the early sixteenth century.' *Transactions of the Royal Historical Society*, 5th ser., VI, 1956.

The Midland Peasant. London, 1957.

'Harvest fluctuations and English economic history, 1480–1619.' *The Agricultural History Review*, XII, 1964.

'Harvest fluctuations and English economic history, 1620–1759.' *The Agricultural History Review*, XVI, 1968.

HOSZOWSKI, S. 'The Polish Baltic trade in the 15th–18th centuries.' *Poland at the XIth International Congress of Historical Sciences*, 1960.

HOTTENGER, G. 'La Lorraine agricole au lendemain de la révolution.' *Mémoires de l'académie de Stanislas*, CLXXV, 1925.

HOURS, H. *La Lutte contre les épizooties et l'école vétérinaire de Lyon au XVIIIe siècle*. 1957.

HOUTTE, H. VAN. 'Avant Malthus. La théorie de la population et le mouvement en faveur de la petite culture dans les Pays-Bas à la fin de l'ancien régime.' *Mélanges d'histoire offerts à Charles Moeller*, II, 1914.

Histoire économique de la Belgique à la fin de l'ancien régime. Ghent, 1920.

HOUTTE, J. A. VAN. *Schets van een economische geschiedenis van België*. Louvain, 1943.

Economische en sociale geschiedenis van de Lage Landen. Zeist, 1964.

HOWELLS, B. E. 'Pembrokeshire farming circa 1580–1620.' *The National Library of Wales Journal*, IX, 1955–6.

HROCH, M. and PETRAŇ, J. 'Europejska gospodarka i polityka XVI i XVII wieku: kryzys czy regres?' *Przegląd historyczny*, LV, 1963.

HUNT, H. G. 'Aspects de la révolution agraire en Angleterre au XVIIIe siècle.' *Annales*, XI, 1956.

'The chronology of parliamentary enclosure in Leicestershire.' *Economic History Review*, 2nd ser., X, 1957.

HYAMS, E. *Dionysus, a Social History of the Wine Vine*. London, 1965.

ILZHÖFER, H. 'Die Deckung des Vitaminenbedarfes in früheren Jahrhunderten.' *Archiv für Hygiene und Bakteriologie*, CXXVII, 1942.

IMBERCIADORI, I. *Campagna toscana nel' 700 dalla reggenza alla restaurazione, 1737–1811.* 1953.

IMBERT, G. *Des mouvements de longue durée Kondratieff.* Aix-en-Provence, 1959.

INDOVA, E. I. *Dvorcovoe hozjajstvo v Rossii; pervaja polovina XVIII veka.* Moscow, 1964.

JACOBEIT, W. *Schafhaltung und Schäfer in Zentraleuropa bis zum Beginn des 20. Jahrhunderts.* 1961.

JANOUŠEK, E. 'Die Arbeitsprodiktivität auf dem tschechischen feudalen Grossgrundbesitz im 18. Jahrhundert.' *Acta musaeorum agriculturae*, I–II, 1966.
Historický vývoj produktivity práce v zemědělství v období pobělohorském. 1967.

JANSEN, J. C. G. M. 'Landbouw rond Maastricht (1610–1865).' *Studies over de sociaal-economische geschiedenis van Limburg*, XIII, 1968.

JIRLOW, R. and POEL, J. M. G. VAN DER. *De inheemse Nederlandse ploegen.* 1968.

JOHN, A. H. 'The course of agricultural change, 1660–1760.' *Studies in the Industrial Revolution*, 1960.
'Aspects of English economic growth in the first half of the eighteenth century.' *Economica*, XXVIII, 1961.
'Agricultural productivity and economic growth in England, 1700–1760.' *Journal of Economic History*, XXV, 1965.

JOHNSEN, O. A. *Norwegische Wirtschaftsgeschichte.* Oslo, 1939.

JONES, E. L. 'Agricultural conditions and changes in Herefordshire, 1660–1815.' *Transactions of the Woolhope Naturalists' Field Club*, XXXVII, 1961.
Seasons and Prices. The Role of the Weather in English Agricultural History. London, 1964.
'Agriculture and economic growth in England, 1660–1750: agricultural change.' *Journal of Economic History*, XXV, 1965.
Agriculture and Economic Growth in England, 1650–1815. London, 1967.
'Le origini agricole dell'industria.' *Studi storici*, IX, 1968.

JORDAN, W. *Viehseuchen im bayerisch-schwäbischen Voralpengebiet während des 17., 18. und 19. Jahrhunderts.* 1951.

JUILLARD, E. *La Vie rurale dans la plaine de Basse-Alsace.* Paris, 1953.

KAHAN, A. 'The "hereditary workers". Hypothesis and the development of a factory labor force in eighteenth- and nineteenth-century Russia.' *Education and Economic Development*, 1966.
'Natural calamities and their effect upon the food supply in Russia.' *Jahrbücher für Geschichte Osteuropas*, N.F., XVI, 1968.

KAHK, J. *Krest'janskoe dviženie i krest'janskij vopros v Estonii. V konce 18. i v pervoj četverti 19. veka.* 1962.

KENYON, G. H. 'Kirdford inventories, 1611 to 1776.' *Sussex Archaeological Collections*, XCIII, 1955.

KERHOUEL, M. *Les Mouvements de longue durée des prix.* Paris, 1935.

KERRIDGE, E. W. 'The notebook of a Wiltshire farmer in the early seventeenth century.' *The Wiltshire Archaeological and Natural History Magazine*, LIV, 1952.
'The movement of rent, 1540–1640.' *Economic History Review*, 2nd ser., VI, 1953.
'Turnip husbandry in High Suffolk.' *Economic History Review*, 2nd ser., VIII, 1956.
The Agricultural Revolution. London, 1967.
'Arthur Young and William Marshall.' *History Studies*, I, 1968.
Agrarian Problems in the Sixteenth Century and After. London, 1969.

KIESEWETTER, H. C. P. *Praktisch ökonomische Bemerkungen auf einer Reise durch Hollstein, Schleswig, Dithmarsen . . . 1807.*

KIRILLY, Z. and KISS, I. N. 'Production de céréales et exploitations paysannes en Hongrie aux XVIe et XVIIe siècles.' *Annales*, XXIII, 1968.
et al. 'Production et productivité agricoles en Hongrie à l'époque du féodalisme tardif (1550–1850).' *Nouvelles études historiques p.p. la Commission Nationale des Historiens Hongrois*, I, 1965.

KISS, I. N. 'Nagybirtokok árutermelése és külkereskedelme a XVII. századi Magyarországon.' *Magyar Mezögazdasági Múzeum közleményei*, 1968.

KIUS, O. 'Die thüringische Landwirthschaft im 16. Jahrhundert.' *Jahrbücher für National-ökonomie und Statistik*, III, 1864.

KLEIN, E. *Die historischen Pflüge der Hohenheimer Sammlung landwirtschaftlicher Geräte und Maschinen*. Stuttgart, 1967.

KLEIN, J. *The Mesta, a Study in Spanish Economic History, 1273–1836*. Cambridge, Mass., 1920.

KLIMA, A. 'Industrial development in Bohemia, 1648–1781.' *Past and Present*, XI, 1957.

KÖTZSCHKE, R. and EBERT, W. *Geschichte der ostdeutschen Kolonisation*. Leipzig, 1937.

KOHT, H. 'Self-assertion of the farming class.' *Mélanges d'histoire offerts à Henri Pirenne*, I, 1926.

KOK, J. *Grepen uit het verleden van de landbouw in de Groninger veenkoloniën.* 1948.

KONDRATIEFF, N. D. 'Die langen Wellen der Konjunktur.' *Archiv für Sozialwissenschaft und Sozialpolitik*, LVI, 1926.

KOPPE, W. 'Wie und mit welcher Ergebnissen wurden Ackerbau und Viehzucht vor gut 300 Jahren in Cismar und Körnik betrieben?' *Jahrbuch für den Kreis Oldenburg/Holstein*, 1958.

KRZYMOWSKI, R. *Geschichte der deutschen Landwirtschaft*. 1951.

KULCZYKOWSKI, M. 'En Pologne au XVIIIᵉ siècle: Industrie paysanne et formation du marché national.' *Annales*, XXIV, 1969.

KULISCHER, J. *Allgemeine Wirtschaftsgeschichte*. II, 1929.
'Das Aufkommen der landwirtschaftlichen Maschinen um die Wende des 18. und in der ersten Hälfte des 19. Jahrhunderts.' *Jahrbücher für Nationalökonomie und Statistik*, CXXXIX, 1933, II.

KUSKE, B. *Wirtschaftsgeschichte Westfalens*. Münster, 1949.

LABRIJN, A. *Het klimaat van Nederland gedurende de laatste twee en een halve eeuw*. 1945.
'Verandert ons klimaat?' *Hemel en dampkring*, XLVIII, 1950.

LABROUSSE, C. E. *Esquisse du mouvement des prix et des revenus en France au XVIIIᵉ siècle*. Paris, 1932.
'Comment contrôler les mercuriales?' *Annales d'histoire sociale*, II, 1940.
La crise de l'économie française à la fin de l'ancien régime et au début de la révolution. I, Paris, 1943.

LADEWIG PETERSEN, E. 'La crise de noblesse danoise entre 1580 et 1660.' *Annales*, XXIII, 1968.
'The Danish cattle trade during the sixteenth and seventeenth centuries.' *The Scandinavian Economic History Review*, XVIII, 1970.

LAFARGE, R. *L'agriculture en Limousin au XVIIIᵉ siècle et l'intendance de Turgot*. 1902.

LAMB, H. H. 'Climatic change within historical time as seen in circulation maps and diagrams.' *Annals of the New York Academy of Sciences*, XCV, 1961.
'On the nature of certain climatic epochs which differed from the modern (1900–39) normal.' *Arid Zone Research*, XX, 1963.

LAMBERT, A. M. 'The agriculture of Oxfordshire at the end of the eighteenth century.' *Agricultural History*, XXIX, 1955.

Landbouwgeschiedenis, 1960.

LANGE, G. *Die Entwickelung der landwirtschaftlichen Verhältnisse, insbesondere der Viehzucht, auf dem Rittergute Bersdorf in Schlesien von 1770 bis zur Gegenwart*. 1907.

LASLETT, P. 'The study of the social structure from listings of inhabitants.' *An Introduction to English Historical Demography*. London, 1966.

LAVROVSKY, V. M. 'Parliamentary enclosures in the county of Suffolk.' *Economic History Review*, VII, 1936.

LECCE, M. 'I redditi di un fondo agricolo mezzadrile nel XVIII secolo.' *Archivio storico italiano*, CXVIII, 1960.

LECLERC DE MONTLINOT, C. 'Mémoire sur la culture flamande en 1776.' *Le théâtre d'agriculture et mesnage des champs*, I, 1804.

LEFEBVRE, G. *Questions agraires au temps de la Terreur*. Paris, 1954.
Etudes sur la Révolution française. Paris, 1954.
Les Paysans du Nord pendant la Révolution française. Lille, 1959.
Etudes orléanaises. 2 vols., Paris, 1962–3.

LEFEBVRE, L. *Les Droits d'usage dans la forêt d'Ardenne, 1754–1795*. 1942.

LEHMANN, R. *Die Verhältnisse der niederlausitzischen Herrschafts- und Gutsbauern in der Zeit vom Dreissigjährigen Kriege bis zu den preussischen Reformen*. Cologne, 1956.

LENNARD, R. V. 'English agriculture under Charles II.' *Economic History Review*, IV, 1932.

LENSKI, G. *Power and Privilege, a Theory of Social Stratification*. New York, 1966.

LÉON, P. et al. *Structures économiques et problèmes sociaux du monde rural dans la France du Sud-Est*. 1966.

LEONHARD, R. *Agrarpolitik und Agrarreform in Spanien unter Carl III*. 1919.

LEQUEUX, A. 'L'accourtillage en Thiérache aux XVIIe et XVIIIe siècles.' *Mémoires de la société d'histoire du droit des pays flamands, picards et wallons*, II, 1939.

LE ROY LADURIE, E. 'Histoire et climat.' *Annales*, XIV, 1959.
'Climat et récoltes aux XVIIe et XVIIIe siècles.' *Annales*, XV, 1960.
'Aspects historiques de la nouvelle climatologie.' *Revue historique*, LXXXV, 1961.
Les Paysans de Languedoc. 2 vols., Paris, 1966.
Histoire du climat depuis l'an mil. Paris, 1967.
'Les comptes fantastiques de Gregory King.' *Annales*, XXIII, 1968.
'Dîmes et produit net agricole (XVe–XVIIIe siècle).' *Annales*, XXIV, 1969.

LESKIEWICZOWA, J. *Dobra osieckie w okresie gospodarki folwarczno-pańszczyźnianej XVI–XIX w.* Warsaw, 1957.
Zarys historii gospodarstwa wiejskiego w Polsce. 2 vols., Warsaw, 1964.
Materialy konferencji w Rogowie, 16–18 Wrzesnia 1964. Warsaw, 1966.

LIIV, O. *Die wirtschaftliche Lage des estnischen Gebietes am Ausgang des XVII. Jahrhunderts*. 1935.

LINDEMANS, P. *Geschiedenis van de landbouw in België*. 2 vols., 1952.

LIVET, G. *L'intendance d'Alsace sous Louis XIV, 1648–1715*. Paris, 1956.

LIZERAND, G. *Le Régime rural de l'ancienne France*. 1942.

LODGE, E. C. *The Accountbook of a Kentish Estate, 1616–1704*. London, 1927.

LOM, F. 'Vyvoj osevních ploch obilnin a sklizní od 16. století v Čechách.' *Sborník československé akademie zemědělských věd, Historie a musejnictvi*, II (XXX), 1957.

LOPEZ, R. S. 'The origin of the Merino sheep.' *The Joshua Starr Memorial Volume, Jewish Social Studies*, V, 1953.

LUNDEN, K. 'Agrartilhøve ca. 1600–1720.' *Historisk tidsskrift* (Oslo), 1969.

LÜTGE, F. *Die bayerische Grundherrschaft*. Stuttgart, 1949.
Deutsche Sozial- und Wirtschaftsgeschichte. Berlin, 1952.
Die mitteldeutsche Grundherrschaft und ihre Auflösung. Stuttgart, 1957.
Strukturelle und konjunkturelle Wandlungen in der deutschen Wirtschaft vor Ausbruch des Dreissigjährigen Krieges. Munich, 1958.
Geschichte der deutschen Agrarverfassung vom frühen Mittelalter bis zum 19. Jahrhundert. Deutsche Agrargeschichte, III, Stuttgart, 1967.
'Die Robot-Abolition und Kaiser Joseph II.' *Wege und Forschungen der Agrargeschichte*, 1967.

LUTTERLOH, E. O. *Dienste und Abgaben der Bauern des Herzogtums Braunschweig-Wolfenbüttel in der Mitte des 18. Jahrhunderts*. 1969.

LYASHCHENKO, P. *History of the National Economy of Russia to the 1917 Revolution*. New York, 1949.

McCOURT, D. 'Infield and outfield in Ireland.' *Economic History Review*, 2nd ser., VII, 1955.

McNEILL, W. H. *Europe's Steppe Frontier, 1500–1800*. Chicago, 1964.

MĄCZAK, A. *Gospodarstwo chłopskie na Zuławach Malborskich w początkach XVII wieku*. Warsaw, 1962.
'Export of grain and the problem of distribution of national income in Poland in the years 1550–1650.' *Acta Poloniae historica*, XVIII, 1968.

MADDALENA, A. DE. 'Il mondo rurale italiano nel cinque e nel seicento.' *Rivista storica italiana*, LXXVI, 1964.

MALOWIST, M. 'A certain trade technique in the Baltic countries in the 15th–17th centuries.' *Poland at the XIth International Congress of Historical Sciences*, 1960.
'Les produits des pays de la Baltique dans le commerce international au XVIe siècle.' *Revue du Nord*, CLXVI, 1960.

MANDROU, R. *Classes et luttes de classes en France au début du XVIIe siècle*. Paris, 1965.

Man'kov, A. G. *Razvitie krepostnogo prava v Rossii vo vtoroj polovine XVII veka.* Moscow, 1962.

Manley, G. 'The extent of the fluctuations shown during the "instrumental" period in relation to post-glacial events in N.W. Europe.' *Quarterly Journal of the Royal Meteorological Society,* LXXV, 1949.

'On British climatic fluctuations since Queen Elizabeth's day.' *Weather,* V, 1950.

'Climatic variation.' *Quarterly Journal of the Royal Meteorological Society,* LXXIX, 1953.

'Late and postglacial climatic fluctuations and their relationship to those shown by the instrumental record of the past 300 years.' *Annals of the New York Academy of Sciences,* XCV, 1961.

Mantel, K. 'Bedeutung und Aufgaben der Forstgeschichte.' *Zeitschrift für Agrargeschichte und Agrarsoziologie,* III, 1955.

Marion, M. 'L'agriculture et les classes rurales aux XVIIᵉ et XVIIIᵉ siècles.' *Revue des cours et conférences,* XXVIII, 1926–7.

Marshall, W. *The Rural Economy of Glocestershire.* 2 vols., Edinburgh, 1789.

The Rural Economy of the Midland Counties. 2 vols., London, 1796.

The Rural Economy of the West of England. 2 vols., London, 1796.

The Rural Economy of Yorkshire. 2 vols., London, 1796.

The Rural Economy of the Southern Counties. 2 vols., London, 1798.

Martens van Sevenhoven, A. H. 'Geldersche pachtcontracten uit de 16e eeuw.' *Verslagen en mededeelingen oud-vaderlandsch recht,* IX: 5, 1942.

Martin, J. M., 'The cost of parliamentary enclosure in Warwickshire.' *University of Birmingham Historical Journal,* IX, 1964.

Masefield, G. B. 'Crops and livestock.' *The Cambridge Economic History of Europe,* IV, Cambridge, 1967.

Massé, P. *Varennes et ses maîtres.* Paris, 1956.

Mathias, P. 'Agriculture and the brewing and distilling industries in the eighteenth century.' *Economic History Review,* 2nd ser., V, 1952.

'The social structure in the eighteenth century: a calculation by Joseph Massie.' *Economic History Review,* 2nd ser., X, 1957.

Mavor, J. *An Economic History of Russia.* 2 vols., London, 1965.

Medinger, W. *Wirtschaftsgeschichte der Domäne Lobositz.* 1903.

Meuvret, J. 'Les crises de subsistances et la démographie de la France de l'ancien régime.' *Population,* I, 1946.

'Agronomie et jardinage au XVIᵉ et au XVIIᵉ siècle.' *Hommage à Lucien Febvre,* II, 1953.

Relazioni del X congresso internazionale di scienze storiche, IV, 1955.

Minchinton, W. E. 'Agricultural returns and the government during the Napoleonic wars.' *The Agricultural History Review,* I, 1953.

Mingay, G. E. 'The agricultural depression, 1730–1750.' *Economic History Review,* 2nd ser., VIII, 1956.

English Landed Society in the Eighteenth Century. 1963.

'The agricultural revolution in English history: a reconsideration.' *Agricultural History,* XXXVII, 1963.

'The eighteenth-century land steward.' *Land, Labour and Population in the Industrial Revolution,* London, 1967.

Enclosure and the Small Farmer in the Age of the Industrial Revolution. London, 1968.

Mireaux, E. *Une Province française au temps du grand roi, la Brie.* 1958.

Morineau, M. 'Y a-t-il eu une révolution agricole en France au XVIIIᵉ siècle?' *Revue historique,* CCXXXIX, 1968.

'D'Amsterdam à Séville: de quelle réalité l'histoire des prix est-elle le miroir?' *Annales,* XXIII, 1968.

'Histoire sans frontière: prix et "révolution agricole".' *Annales,* XXIV, 1969.

'La pomme de terre au XVIIIᵉ siècle.' *Annales,* XXV, 1970.

Mousnier, R. *Progrès scientifique et technique au XVIIIᵉ siècle.* Paris, 1958.

Fureurs Paysannes. Paris, 1967.

Müller, H. H. *Märkische Landwirtschaft vor den Agrarreformen von 1807.* Berlin, 1967.

Müller-Wille, W. *Die Ackerfluren im Landesteil Birkenfeld und ihre Wandlungen seit dem 17. und 18. Jahrhundert.* 1936.

MULLETT, C. F. 'The cattle distemper in mid-eighteenth century England.' *Agricultural History*, XX, 1946.

MUSSET, R. *Le Bas-Maine*. Paris, 1917.

NABHOLZ, H. *et al.* 'Der schweizerische Bauernkrieg.' *Geschichte der Schweiz*, II, Zurich, 1938.

NAUDÉ, W. *Die Getriedehandelspolitik der europäischen Staaten vom 13. bis zum 18. Jahrhundert*. Berlin, 1896.

und SKALWEIT, A. *Die Getriedehandelspolitik und Kriegsmagazinverwaltung Preussens, 1740–1756*. Getreidehandelspolitik, III, Berlin, 1910.

NEDELEC, Y. 'Le couchage des terres dans le pays d'Auge au XVIIIe siècle.' *Revue historique de droit français et étranger*, 4me série XXXVII, 1959.

NICHTWEISS, J. *Das Bauernlegen in Mecklenburg*. Berlin, 1954.

'Einige Bemerkungen zum Artikel von G. Heitz.' *Zeitschrift für Geschichtswissenschaft*, V, 1957.

NIELSEN, A. *Die Entstehung der deutschen Kameralwissenschaft im 17. Jahrhundert*. 1911. *Dänische Wirtschaftsgeschichte*. Jena, 1933.

NOU, J. *Studies in the Development of Agricultural Economics in Europe*. 1967.

OCHMAŃSKI, J. 'La situation économico-sociale et la lutte de classe des paysans dans les domaines royaux de Kobryń.' *Roczniki dziejów społecznych i gospodarczych*, XIX, 1957.

'Gospodarka folwarczna w dobrach hospodarskich na Kobryńszczyźnie.' *Kwartalnik historii kultury materialnej*, VI, 1958.

Wiedza rolnicza w Polsce od 16. do połowi 18. wieku. Warsaw, 1965.

OGRIZKO, Z. A. 'Zernovoe chozjaístvo polonikov troice-gledenskogo monastyrja v XVII veke.' *Materialy po istorii sel'skogo chozjaístva i krestjanstva SSSR*, IV, 1960.

OJA, A. *Länsi-suomen maatalous isonvihan aikana* (*Agriculture in Western Finland in 1719*). 1956.

OLAGÜE, I. 'Les changements de climat dans l'histoire.' *Cahiers d'histoire mondiale*, VII, 1963.

OLIMPIA DA ROCHA GIL, M. *Arroteias no vale do Mondego durante o seculo XVI. Ensaio de historia agraria*. 1965.

OLIVER, J. 'The weather and farming in the mid-eighteenth century in Anglesey.' *The National Library of Wales Journal*, X: 3, 1957.

OLSEN, E. *Danmarks økonomiske historier siden 1750*. Copenhagen, 1962.

OLSEN, G. 'Studier i Danmarks kornavl og kornhandelspolitik i tiden 1610–1660.' *Historisk tidsskrift*, tiende raekke VII, 1942–4.

Hovedgård og bondegård. Studier over stordriftens udvickling i Danmark i tiden 1525–1774. Copenhagen, 1957.

OLSEN, M. *Farms and Fanes of Ancient Norway*. Oslo, 1928.

OOSTEN SLINGELAND, J. F. VAN. *De Sijsselt; een bijdrage tot de kennis van de Veluwse bosgeschiedenis*. 1958.

ORDISH, G. *Untaken Harvest. Man's Loss of Crops from Pest, Weed and Disease*. London, 1952.

ORWIN, C. STEWART. *A History of English Farming*. London, 1949.

and ORWIN, C. SUSAN. *The Open Fields*. Oxford, 1967.

PAAUW, F. VAN DER. 'Ritmische opbrengstschommelingen en hun oorzaak.' *Landbouwkundig tijdschrift*, LXXIII, 1961.

'Ritmische variaties van bemestingseffecten in de loop van de jaren onder invloed van het weersverloop.' *Landbouwkundig tijdschrift*, LXXIII, 1961.

'Periodic fluctuations of soil fertility, crop yields and of responses to fertilization effected by alternating periods of low or high rainfall.' *Plant and Soil*, XVII, 1962.

'Het weer en de vruchtbaarheid van de grond.' *Landbouwkundig tijdschrift*, LXXIX, 1967.

PACH, Z. P. *Die ungarische Agrarentwicklung im 16.–17. Jahrhundert*. Budapest, 1964.

PANE, L. DAL. 'Per la storia dei libretti colonici.' *Studi in onore di Amintore Fanfani*, V, 1962.

PARAIN, C. 'Les anciennes techniques agricoles.' *Revue de synthèse*, 3rd ser., VII, 1957.

PARKER, R. A. C. 'Coke of Norfolk and the agrarian revolution.' *Economic History Review*, 2nd ser., VIII, 1955.

PETERS, J. 'Ostelbische Landarmut.' *Jahrbuch für Wirtschaftsgeschichte*, II, 1970.

PETRÁŇ, J. *Zemědělská výroba v Čechách v druké polovině 16. a počátkem 17. století*. 1963.

PLAISSE, A. *La Baronie de Neubourg, essai d'histoire agraire, économique et sociale*. Paris, 1961.

PLUMB, J. H. 'Sir Robert Walpole and Norfolk husbandry.' *Economic History Review*, 2nd ser., V, 1952.

POCHILEWICZ, D. L. 'W sprawie kryzysu i upadku gospodarki obszarniczej rzeczypospolitej w drugiej połowie XVII i pierwszej połowie XVIII wieku.' *Kwartalnik historyczny*, LXV, 1958.

POEL, J. M. G. VAN DER. 'De landbouw-enquête van 1800.' *Historia agriculturae*, I–III, 1953–6.

Het dorsen in het verleden. 1955.

'Beschrijving der boerderijen op de kleilanden in Friesland door Dirk Fontein te Salvert, 1779.' *Historia agriculturae*, IV, 1957.

Oude Nederlandse ploegen. 1967.

POITRINEAU, A. *La Vie rurale en Basse-Auvergne au XVIIIᵉ siècle (1726–1789)*. 2 vols., Paris, 1965.

PONI, C. *Gli aratri e l'economia agraria nel Bolognese dal XVII al XIX secolo*. Bologna, 1963.

PONSOT, P. 'En Andalousie occidentale: les fluctuations de la production du blé sous l'Ancien Régime.' *Études rurales*, vol. 34, 1969.

PORISINI, G. *La proprietà terriera nel Comune di Ravenna dalla metà del secolo XVI ai giorni nostri*. Milan, 1963.

PORSCHNEW, B. F. *Die Volksaufstände in Frankreich vor der Fronde, 1623–1648*. 1954.

PRANDOTA, W. 'Produkcja rolnicza w folwarkach starostwa Sochaczewskiego w XVI i XVII wieku.' *Studia z dziejów gospodarstwa wiejskiego*, II, 1959.

PUNDT, A. G. 'French agriculture and the industrial crisis of 1788.' *The Journal of Political Economy*, XLIX, 1941.

QUESNAY, F. *Oeuvres économiques et philosophiques*. Frankfurt, 1888.

RAMMELAERE, C. DE. 'De beroepsstructuur van de plattelandse bevolking in Zuidoost-Vlaanderen gedurende de 18e eeuw.' *Tijdschrift voor sociale wetenschappen*, IV, 1959.

RAPPARD, W. E. *Le Facteur économique dans l'avènement de la démocratie moderne en Suisse*. I. *L'agriculture à la fin de l'ancien régime*. 1912.

RAVEAU, P. *L'agriculture et les classes paysannes. La transformation de la propriété dans le Haut Poitou au XVIᵉ siècle*. Paris, 1926.

RECHT, P. *Les Biens communaux et leur partage à la fin du XVIIIᵉ siècle. Contribution à l'étude de l'histoire agraire et du droit rural de la Belgique*. 1950.

REZNIKOV, F. I. 'Zemledelie v basseíne severnoí dviny v XVII–XVIII vekach.' *Materialy po istorii sel'skogo chozjaistva i krestjanstva SSSR*, IV, 1960.

RICCHIONI, V. *Studi storici di economia dell'agricoltura meridionale*. 1952.

RICHES, N. *The Agricultural Revolution in Norfolk*. London, 1937.

RIEMANN, F. K. *Ackerbau und Viehhaltung im vorindustriellen Deutschland*. 1953.

RIGAUDIÈRE, A. 'La Haute-Auvergne face à l'agriculture nouvelle au XVIIIᵉ siècle.' In A. Rigaudière *et al.*, *Études d'histoire économique rurale au XVIIIᵉ siècle*, 1965.

ROESSINGH, H. K. 'Beroep en bedrijf op de Veluwe in het midden van de achttiende eeuw.' *A.A.G. Bijdragen*, XIII, 1965.

'Hoe functioneerde een dorp in het midden van de 18de eeuw?' *Spiegel historiael*, II, 1967.

ROGERS, J. E. T. *A History of Agriculture and Prices in England*. 8 vols., London, 1866–1902.

ROMANI, M. *L'agricoltura in Lombardia dal periodo delle riforme al 1859. Struttura, organizzazione sociale e tecnica*. Milan, 1957.

'I rendimenti dei terreni in Lombardia dal periodo delle riforme al 1859.' *Studi in onore di Amintore Fanfani*, V, 1962.

ROMANO, R. 'Tra XVI e XVII secolo. Una crisi economica: 1619–1622.' *Rivista storica italiana*, LXXIV, 1962.

RÖSSLER, H. 'Über die Wirkungen von 1525.' *Wege und Forschungen der Agrargeschichte*, 1967.

ROSTOW, W. W. 'Business cycles, harvests and politics, 1790–1850.' *Journal of Economic History*, I, 1941.

ROTELLI, C. *La distribuzione delle proprietà terriera e delle colture ad Imola nel XVII e XVIII secolo*. Milan, 1966.
'Produzione e produttività dei terreni di una famiglia nobile imolese del 700.' *Rivista di storia dell'agricoltura*, VI, 1966.
L'economia agraria di Chieri attraverso i catasti dei secoli XIV–XVI. Milan, 1967.
'Rendimenti e produzione agricola nell'Imolese dal XVI al XIX secolo.' *Rivista storica italiana*, LXXIX, 1967.
ROTHERT, H. 'Ist die Kiefer von altersher in Westfalen heimisch?' *Westfälische Forschungen*, IX, 1956.
ROUPNEL, G. *Histoire de la campagne française*. Paris, 1955.
La ville et la campagne au XVIIe siècle. Paris, 1955.
RÓŻYCKA, M. 'Struktura wysiewów i wysokość plonow w drugiej połowie XVIII wieku w kluczu spatowskim. *Studia z dziejów gospodarstwa wiejskiego*, IV, 1961.
RUWET, J. *L'agriculture et les classes rurales au pays de Herve sous l'ancien régime*. Liège, 1943.
'Prix, production et bénefices agricoles. Le pays de Liège au XVIIIe siècle.' *Bijdragen tot de prijzengeschiedenis*, II, 1957.
et al. *Marché des céréales à Ruremonde, Luxembourg, Namur et Diest aux XVIIe et XVIIIe siècles*. Louvain, 1966.
RYCHLIKOWA, I. 'Prukcja zbożowa wielkiej Własnosci w Małopolsce w latach 1764–1805.' *Studia z dziejow gospodarstwa wiejskiego*, IX: 1, 1967.
RYDER, M. L. 'The animal remains found at Kirkstall Abbey.' *The Agricultural History Review*, VII, 1959.
SAALFELD, D. *Bauernwirtschaft und Gutsbetrieb in der vorindustriellen Zeit*. Stuttgart, 1960.
'Die Produktion und Intensität der Landwirtschaft in Deutschland und angrenzenden Gebieten um 1800.' *Zeitschrift für Agrargeschichte und Agrarsoziologie*, XV, 1967.
SABBE, E. *De Belgische vlasnijverheid*. I, Bruges, 1943.
SAFRONOV, F. G. 'Technika zemledelija lensko–ilimskich i angarskich krest'jan v XVII veke.' *Materialy po istorii sel'skogo chozjaistva i krestjanstva SSSR*, III, 1959.
SAINT JACOB, P. DE. *Les Paysans de la Bourgogne du Nord au dernier siècle de l'ancien régime*. Paris, 1960.
SALAMAN, R. N. *The History and Social Influence of the Potato*. Cambridge, 1949.
SALOMON, N. *La Campagne de Nouvelle Castille à la fin du XVIe siècle d'après les Relaciones Typográficas*. Paris, 1964.
SALTMARSH, J. and DARBY, H. C. 'The infield–outfield system on a Norfolk manor.' *Economic History*, III, 1935.
SANGERS, W. J. *De ontwikkeling van de Nederlandse tuinbouw*. 2 vols., 1952–3.
ŠČEPETOV, K. N. 'Sel'skoe chozjastvo v votčinach iosifo-volokolamskogo monastyrja v konce XVI veka.' *Istoričeskie zapiski*, XVIII, 1946.
SCHIFF, O. 'Die deutschen Bauernaufstände von 1525 bis 1789.' *Historische Zeitschrift*, CXXX, 1924.
SCHIFFERS, H. 'Landschaftlicher und landwirtschaftlicher Strukturwandel im Eupener Ländchen vom Mittelalter bis zur Neuzeit.' *Zeitschrift des Eupener Geschichtsvereins*, II, 1952.
SCHMIDT, G. C. L. *Der schweizer Bauer im Zeitalter des Frühkapitalismus*. 2 vols., 1932.
SCHMIEDECKE, A. *Johann Christian Schubart, Edler von Kleefeld*. 1956.
SCHMITZ, H. J. *Faktoren der Preisbildung für Getreide und Wein in der Zeit von 800 bis 1350*. Stuttgart, 1968.
SCHOLLIERS, E. *De levenstandaard in de XVe en XVIe eeuw te Antwerpen*. 1960.
SCHOVE, D. J. 'European raininess since A.D. 1700.' *Quarterly Journal of the Royal Meteorological Society*, LXXV, 1949.
'European temperatures A.D. 1500–1900.' *Quarterly Journal of the Royal Meteorological Society*, LXXV, 1949.
'Solar cycles and the spectrum of time since 200 BC.' *Annals of the New York Academy of Sciences*, XCV, 1961.
SCHRÖDER-LEMBKE, G. 'Die Hausväterliteratur als agrargeschichtliche Quelle.' *Zeitschrift für Agrargeschichte und Agrarsoziologie*, I, 1953.
'Entstehung und Verbreitung der Mehrfelderwirtschaft in Nordostdeutschland.' *Zeitschrift für Agrareschichte und Agrarsoziologie*, II, 1954.

Die Einführung des Kleebaues in Deutschland vor dem Auftreten Schubarts von dem Klee-felde. 1954.

'Die mecklenburgische Koppelwirtschaft.' *Zeitschrift für Agrargeschichte und Agrar-soziologie*, IV, 1956.

'Wesen und Verbreitung der Zweifelderwirtschaft im Rheingebiet.' *Zeitschrift für Agrargeschichte und Agrarsoziologie*, VII, 1959.

Martin Grosser, Anleitung zu der Landwirtschaft. Abraham von Thumbshirn, Oeconomia. Zwei frühe deutsche Landwirtschaftsschriften. Stuttgart, 1965.

'Die Genesis des Colerschen Hausbuches und die Frage seines Quellenwertes.' *Wege und Forschungen der Agrargeschichte*, 1967.

SCHWABE, A. *Grundriss der Agrargeschichte Lettlands*. 1928.

SCHWERZ, J. N. *Anleitung zur Kentniss der belgischen Landwirtschaft*. 3 vols., 1807–11.

Beschreibung der Landwirthschaft im Nieder-Elsass. 1816.

Beschreibung und Resultate der Fellenbergischen Landwirthschaft zu Hofwyl. 1816.

Beobachtungen über den Ackerbau der Pfälzer. 1816.

Beschreibung der Landwirthschaft in Westfalen und Rheinpreussen. 1836.

SÉE, H. *Les Classes rurales en Bretagne du XVIᵉ siècle à la révolution*. Paris, 1906.

Esquisse d'une histoire du régime agraire en Europe aux XVIIIᵉ et XIXᵉ siècles. Paris, 1921.

La France économique et sociale au XVIIIᵉ siècle. Paris, 1952.

Histoire économique de la France. I, Paris, 1948.

SEEBOHM, M. E. *The Evolution of the English Farm*. London, 1952.

SERENI, E. *Storia del paesaggio agrario italiano*. Bari, 1962.

'Agricoltura e sviluppo del capitalismo. I problemi teoretici e metodologici.' *Studi storici*, IX, 1968.

SERRES, O. DE. *Le Théâtre d'agriculture et mesnage des champs*. 2 vols., Paris, 1804.

SEVRIN, R. 'Les cultures industrielles et fourragères dans le Hainaut occidental avant le XIXᵉ siècle.' *Annales du XXXIIIᵉ congrès de la fédération archéologique et historique de Belgique*, II, 1951.

SIEGRIST, J. J. 'Beiträge zur Verfassungs- und Wirtschaftsgeschichte der Herrschaft Hallwil.' *Argovia*, LXIV, 1952.

Die Gemeinde Unterkulm und das Kirchspiel Kulm. 1957.

SILBERT, A. *Le Portugal méditerranéen à la fin de l'ancien régime*. 2 vols., Paris, 1966.

SILVA, J. GENTIL DA. *En Espagne, développement économique, subsistence, déclin*. 1965.

'L'autoconsommation au Portugal (XIVᵉ–XXᵉ siècle).' *Annales*, XXIV, 1969.

SIMIAND, F. *Recherches anciennes et nouvelles sur le mouvement général des prix du XVIᵉ au XIXᵉ siècle*. Paris, 1932.

Les Fluctuations économiques à longue durée et la crise mondiale. Paris, 1932.

SIROL, J. *Le Rôle de l'agriculture dans les fluctuations économiques*. 1942.

SJOERDS, F. *Algemene beschrijving van oud en nieuw Friesland*. Leeuwarden, I, 1765.

SKEEL, C. 'The cattle trade between Wales and England from the fifteenth to the nine-teenth centuries.' *Transactions of the Royal Historical Society*, fourth ser., IX, 1926.

SLICHER VAN BATH, B. H. *Mensch en land in de middeleeuwen*. 2 vols., 1945.

Een samenleving onder spanning. Geschiedenis van het platteland in Overijssel. 1957.

'Een Fries landbouwbedrijf in de tweede helft van de zestiende eeuw.' *Agronomisch-historische bijdragen*, IV, 1958.

The Agrarian History of Western Europe, A.D. 500–1850. London, 1963.

'The yields of different crops (mainly cereals) in relation to the seed, c. 810–1820.' *Acta historiae Neerlandica*, II, 1967.

'Yield ratios, 810–1820.' *A.A.G. Bijdragen*, X, 1963.

'Les problèmes fondamentaux de la société pré-industrielle en Europe occidentale.' *A.A.G. Bijdragen*, XII, 1965.

'Eighteenth-century agriculture on the continent of Europe: evolution or revolu-tion?' *Agricultural history*, XLIII, 1969.

'Constante, fluctuerende en variabele factoren in de productie en consumptie van agrarische goederen in de pre-industriële maatschappij.' *A.A.G. Bijdragen*, XV, 1970.

'Vrijheid en lijfeigenschap in agrarisch Europa (16e–18e eeuw).' *A.A.G. Bijdragen*, XV, 1970.

'Twee sociale stratificatie's in de agrarische maatschappij in de pre-industriële tijd.' *A.A.G. Bijdragen*, XV, 1970.

SMIRNOV, I. I. *et al. Krestjanskie vojny v Rossi 17.–18. vekov.* Moscow, 1966.

SMITH, A. *The Wealth of Nations.* London, 1776.

SMITH, R. E. F. *A Model of Production and Consumption on the Russian Farm, 15th–17th Centuries.* 1964.

The Enserfment of the Russian Peasantry. Cambridge, 1968.

SOBOUL, A. 'The French rural community in the eighteenth and nineteenth centuries.' *Past and Present*, X, 1956.

'La communauté rurale (XVIIIᵉ–XIXᵉ siècle).' *Revue de synthèse*, 3ᵉ série, 1957.

Les Campagnes montpelliéraines à la fin de l'ancien régime. Paris, 1958.

ŠOŁTA, J. *Die Ertragsentwicklung in der Landwirtschaft des Klosters Marienstern.* Bautzen, 1958.

SOMEŞAN, L. *Alter und Entwicklung der rumänischen Landwirtschaft in Siebenbürgen.* 1941.

SOOM, A. *Der Herrenhof in Estland im 17. Jahrhundert.* Lund, 1954.

'Gutswirtschaft in Livland am Ausgang des 16. Jahrhunderts.' *Zeitschrift für Ostforschung*, V, 1956.

SOREAU, E. *L'agriculture du XVIIᵉ siècle à la fin du XVIIIᵉ.* Paris, 1952.

SPAHR VAN DER HOEK, J. J. and POSTMA, O. *Geschiedenis van de Friese landbouw.* 2 vols., 1952.

SPEYBROECK, L. VAN. 'De wijziging van het landschapsbeeld en van het leven van den mensch in het Land van Waas in de 18e eeuw.' *Annalen van de oudheidkundige kring van het Land van Waas*, LV, 1947.

ŠPIESZ, A. 'Die neuzeitliche Agrarentwicklung in der Tschechoslowakei. Gutsherrschaft oder Wirtschaftsherrschaft?' *Zeitschrift für bayerische Landesgeschichte*, vol. 32, 1969.

'Czechoslovakia's place in the agrarian development of middle and east Europe of modern times.' *Studia historica Slovaca*, VI, 1969.

SPRUNCK, A. 'Les derniers temps de l'ancien régime dans le Luxembourg wallon.' *Annales de l'institut archéologique du Luxembourg*, LXXXIII, 1952.

ŠRENIOWSKI, S. 'W kwestii plonów v ustroju folwarczno-pańszczyźnianym Polski XVI–XVIII w.' *Roczniki dziejów społecznych i gospodarczych*, XIV, 1952.

'Oznaki regresu ekonomicznego w utroju folwarczno-pańszczyźnianym w Polsce od schyłku XVI w.' *Kwartalnik historyczny*, LXI, 1954.

STARK, W. 'Niedergang und Ende des landwirtschaftlichen Grossbetriebs in den böhmischen Ländern.' *Jahrbücher für Nationalökonomie und Statistik*, CXLVI, 1937.

'Die Abhängigkeitsverhältnisse der gutsherrlichen Bauern Böhmens im 17. und 18. Jahrhundert.' *Jahrbücher für Nationalökonomie und Statistik*, CLXIV, 1952.

STAVENHAGEN, R. *Les Classes sociales dans les sociétés agraires.* 1969.

STEGENGA, T. *et al.* 'De invloed van milieuveranderingen op de melkproduktie per koe per jaar van 1933 tot 1960.' *Landbouwkundig tijdschrift*, LXXIX, 1967.

STEINBERG, S. H. 'The Thirty Years' War: a new interpretation.' *History*, XXXII, 1947.

STOIANOVICH, T. 'Le Maïs.' *Annales*, VI, 1951.

STOLDT, P. H. *Bauer und Herzog. Die Amtsbauern des Herzogtums Sachsen-Lauenburg bis 1689.* 1966.

STOLZ, O. 'Zur Geschichte des Getreidebaues und seines Rückganges im Bregenzerwald.' *Vierteljahresschrift für Geschichte und Landeskunde Vorarlbergs*, VII, 1923.

'"Der rechte Kreis", eine dreijährige Fruchtfolge mit Flurzwang im Pustertal nach Belegen des 16. bis 18. Jahrhunderts.' *Vierteljahrschrift für Sozial- und Wirtschaftsgeschichte*, XXV, 1932.

Die Schwaighöfe in Tirol. 1930.

STONE, L. 'Literacy and education in England, 1640–1900.' *Past and Present*, XLII, 1969.

SZCZYGIELSKI, W. 'Próba ustalenia wysokości plonów w królewszczyznach powiatu wieluńskiego w latach 1564–1661.' *Studia z dziejów gospodarstwa wiejskiego*, IV, 1961.

'Wysokość plonów w dobrach przygodzkich w drugiej połowie XVIII wieku.' *Studia z dziejów gospodarstwa wiejskiego*, IV, 1961.

'Le rendement de la production agricole en Pologne du XVIᵉ au XVIIIᵉ siècle sur le fond européen.' *Ergon*, V, 1966; *Kwartalnik historii kultury materialnej*, XIV, 1966.

SZKURŁATOWSKI, Z. 'Wysokość plonów w folwarkach klucza Luboradz na Śląsku w drugiej połowie XVIII i na początku XIX wieku.' *Acta universitatis Wratislaviensis*, XXXVII; *Historia*, X, 1965.

TATE, W. E. 'Opposition to parliamentary enclosure in eighteenth-century England.' *Agricultural History*, XIX, 1945.

'Members of Parliament and their personal relations to enclosure.' *Agricultural History*, XXIII, 1949.

THIRION, L. 'La commune de Clermont-sur-Berwinne. Contribution à l'étude du paysage rural au pays de Herve.' *Bulletin de la société belge d'études géographiques*, XV, 1946.

THIRSK, J. 'The Isle of Axholme before Vermuyden.' *The Agricultural History Review*, I, 1953.

'Agrarian history, 1540–1950.' *The Victoria History of the County of Leicester*, II, 1954.

English Peasant Farming: the Agrarian History of Lincolnshire from Tudor to Recent Times. London, 1957.

(ed.). *The Agrarian History of England and Wales.* IV, *1500–1640.* Cambridge, 1967.

THOMAS, D. S. *Social and Economic Aspects of Swedish Population Movements, 1750–1933.* 1941.

THÜNEN, J. H. VON. *Der isolierte Staat in Beziehung auf Landwirthschaft und National-ökonomie.* I, Rostock, 1842.

TITOW, J. 'Evidence of weather in the account rolls of the bishopric of Winchester, 1209–1350.' *The Economic History Review*, 2nd ser., XII, 1959–60.

TOPOLSKA, M. B. 'Dobra Szkłowskie na Białorusi wschodniej w XVII i XVIII wieku.' *Studia z dziejów gospodarstwa wiejskiego*, XI: 3, 1969.

TOPOLSKI, J. 'O literaturze i praktyce rolniczej w Polsce na przełomie XVI i XVII wieku.' *Roczniki dziejów społecznych i gospodarczych*, XIV, 1952.

'La regression économique en Pologne du XVIe au XVIIIe siècle.' *Acta Poloniae historica*, VII, 1962.

TOUTAIN, J. C. *Le Produit de l'agriculture française de 1700 à 1958.* 2 vols., Paris, 1961.

La Population de la France de 1700 à 1959. Paris, 1963.

TROW-SMITH, R. *A History of British Livestock Husbandry to 1700.* London, 1957.

A History of British Livestock Husbandry, 1700–1900. London, 1959.

TUMA, E. H. *Twenty-six Centuries of Agrarian Reform.* Berkeley, 1965.

USHER, A. P. 'The application of the quantitative method to economic history.' *The Journal of Political Economy*, XL, 1932.

A History of Mechanical Inventions. Cambridge, Mass., 1954.

UTTERSTRÖM, G. 'Climatic fluctuations and population problems in early modern history.' *The Scandinavian Economic History Review*, III, 1955.

Jordbrukets arbetare. Levnadsvillkor och arbetsliv på landsbygden från frihetstiden till mitten av 1800-talet. I, 1957.

'Population and agriculture in Sweden.' *The Scandinavian Economic History Review*, IX, 1961.

VANDENBROEKE, C. 'Aardappelteelt en aardappelverbruik in de 17e en 18e eeuw.' *Tijdschrift voor geschiedenis*, LXXXII, 1968.

VARGA, J. *Typen und Probleme des bäuerlichen Grundbesitz in Ungarn, 1767–1849.* Budapest, 1965.

VENARD, M. *Bourgeois et paysans au XVIIe siècle.* Paris, 1957.

VERHULST, A. *Histoire du paysage rural en Flandre de l'époque romaine au XVIIIe siècle.* Brussels, 1966.

VERVELDE, G. J. *De ongewisheid van de oogst.* 1962.

VICENS VIVES, J. *Historia económica de España.* 1959.

VILAR, P. 'Géographie et histoire statistique, histoire sociale et techniques de production; quelques points d'histoire de la viticulture méditerranéenne.' *Hommage à Lucien Febvre*, I, Paris, 1953.

Villages désertés et histoire économique. Paris, 1965.

VOGT, J. 'Zur historischen Bodenerosion in Mitteldeutschland.' *Petermann's Mitteilungen*, 1958.

VOLLRATH, P. *Landwirtschaftliches Beratungs- und Bildungswesen in Schleswig-Holstein in der Zeit von 1750 bis 1850.* Neumünster, 1957.

VOOYS, A. C. DE. 'De verspreiding van de aardappelteelt in ons land in de 18e eeuw.' *Geografisch tijdschrift*, VII, 1954.

WÄCHTER, H. H. *Ostpreussische Domänenvorwerke im 16. und 17. Jahrhundert*. Würzburg, 1958.

WALTER, G. *Histoire des paysans de France*. Paris, 1963.

WARNER, C. K. (ed.). *Agrarian Conditions in Modern European History*. New York, 1966

WARREN, G. F. 'The agricultural depression.' *The Quarterly Journal of Economics*, XXXVIII, 1923/4.

WASCHINSKI, E. *Währung, Preisentwicklung und Kaufkraft des Geldes in Schleswig-Holstein von 1226–1864*. 2 vols., Neumünster, 1952–9.

WAWRZYŃCZYK, A. 'Problem spadku wydajności dóbr Pabianice w drugiej połowie XVI w.' *Studia z dziejów gospodarstwa wiejskiego*, XII: 2, 1970.

WAWRZYŃCZYKOWA, A. 'Próba ustalenia wysokości plonów w dobrach Pabianice w drugiej połowie XVI w.' *Studia z dziejów gospodarstwa wiejskiego*, II, 1959.

'Proba ustalenia wysokósci plonu w królewszczyznach województwa sandomierskiego w drugiej połowie XVI i początkach XVII wieku.' *Studia z dziejów gospodarstwa wiejskiego*, I, 1957.

'Problem wysokósci plonów w królewszczyznach mazowieckich w drugiej połowie XVI i pierwszej ćwierci XVII w.' *Studia z dziejów gospodarstwa wiejskiego*, IV, 1961.

Gospodarstwo chłopskie w dobrach królewskich na Mazoïwszu w XVI i na początku XVII w. 1962.

WEE, H. VAN DER. *The Growth of the Antwerp Market and the European Economy*. 3 vols., The Hague, 1963.

WELLMANN, I. 'Földmüvelési rendszerek Magyarországon a XVIII. században.' *Agrártörténeti szemle*, 1961.

'Pest megye viszálya Pest városával piacra vitt paraszti termelvények körül az 1730-as évekken.' *Magyar mezögazdasági múzeum közleményei*, 1965–6.

'Határhasználat az Alföld északnyugati peremén a XVIII. század elsö felében.' *Agrártörténeti szemle*, 1967.

'Esquisse d'une histoire rurale de la Hongrie depuis la première moitié du XVIIIᵉ siècle jusqu'au milieu du XIXᵉ siècle.' *Annales*, XXIII, 1968.

WESTIN, J. *Kulturgeografiska studier inom Nätra-, Näske- och Utbyårnas flodområden samt angränsande Kusttrakter*. 1930.

(WESTON, SIR RICHARD.) *A Discourse of Husbandrie used in Brabant and Flanders*. 1652.

WIARDA, D. *Die geschichtliche Entwickelung der wirthschaftlichen Verhältnisse Ostfrieslands*. Jena, 1880.

WIATROWSKI, L. 'Gospodarstwo wiejskiew dobrach Pszczyńskich od połowy XVII do początku XIX wieku.' *Acta universitatis Wratislaviensis*, XXXVIII; *Historia*, XI, 1965.

WIEMANN, H. 'Rechnungen des Klosters Meerhusen um 1600.' *Jahrbuch der Gesellschaft für bildende Kunst und vaterländische Altertümer zu Emden*, XLIII, 1963.

WIESE, H. and BÖLTS, J. *Rinderhandel und Rinderhaltung im nordwesteuropäischen Küstengebiet vom 15. bis zum 19. Jahrhundert*. Stuttgart, 1966.

WIESSNER, H. *Sachinhalt und wirtschaftliche Bedeutung der Weistümer im deutschen Kulturgebiet*. 1934.

WILSON, C. *England's Apprenticeship, 1603–1763*. London, 1965.

The Dutch Republic. London, 1969.

WINKLER, K. *Landwirtschaft und Agrarverfassung im Fürstentum Osnabrück nach dem Dreissigjährigen Kriege*. Stuttgart, 1959.

WINTERWERBER, P. *Die geschichtliche Entwicklung der Flurverfassung und der Grundbesitzverhältnisse im Kreis St. Goarshausen*. 1955.

WISWE, H. 'Grangien niedersächsischer Zisterzienserklöster. Entstehung und Bewirtschaftung spätmittelalterlich-frühneuzeitlicher landwirtschaftlicher Grossbetriebe.' *Braunschweigisches Jahrbuch*, XXXIV, 1953.

WOLF, I. A. 'Das Entstehen von Wüstungen durch Bauernlegen.' *Zeitschrift für Geschichtswissenschaft*, V, 1957.

WOPFNER, H. 'Beobachtungen über den Rückgang der Siedlung.' *Tiroler Heimat*, III, 1923.

WOUDE, A. M. VAN DER. 'De consumptie van graan, vlees en boter in Holland op het einde van de achttiende eeuw.' *A.A.G. Bijdragen*, IX, 1963.

WRIGHT, W. E. *Serf, Seigneur and Sovereign. Agrarian Reform in Eighteenth Century Bohemia*. Minneapolis, 1966.

WYCZAŃSKI, A. 'Le niveau de la récolte des céréales en Pologne du XVIe au XVIIIe siècle.' *Contributions, communications, première conférence internationale d'histoire économique*, 1960.

'Plony zbóż w folwarkach królewskich województwa lubelskiego w 1564 roku.' *Studia z dziejów gospodarstwa wiejskiego*, IV, 1961.

'Tentative estimate of Polish rye trade in the sixteenth century.' *Acta Poloniae historica*, IV, 1961.

'En Pologne. 1. L'économie du domaine nobiliaire moyen (1500–1580).' *Annales*, XVIII, 1963.

Studia nad gospodarka starostwa Korczyńskiego, 1500–1660. Warsaw, 1964.

YELLING, J. 'The combination and rotation of crops in East Worcestershire, 1540–1660.' *The Agricultural History Review*, XVII, 1969.

YOUINGS, J. A. 'The terms of the disposal of the Devon monastic lands, 1536–1558.' *The English Historical Review*, LXIX, 1954.

YOUNG, A. *A Six Weeks Tour through the Southern Counties of England and Wales*. London, 1768.

A Six Months Tour through the North of England. 4 vols., London, 1770.

The Farmer's Tour through the East of England. 4 vols., London, 1771.

A Tour in Ireland. London, 1780.

Travels during the Years 1787, 1788 and 1789: undertaken more particularly with a view of ascertaining the cultivation, wealth, resources and national prosperity of the kingdom of France. Bury St Edmunds, 1794.

General View of the Agriculture of the County of Suffolk. London, 1794.

General View of the Agriculture of the County of Lincoln. London, 1799.

General View of the Agriculture of the County of Sussex. London, 1808.

ZABINSKI, Z. 'L'indice biologique du pouvoir d'achat de la monnaie.' *Annales*, XXIII, 1968.

ZANETTI, D. 'Contribution à l'étude des structures économiques: L'approvisionnement de Pavie au XVIe siècle.' *Annales*, XVIII, 1963.

Problemi alimentari di una economia preindustriale: cereali a Pavia dal 1398 al 1700. Turin, 1964.

ZANGHERI, R. 'Ricerca storica e ricerca economica: agricoltura e sviluppo del capitalismo.' *Studi storici*, VII, 1966.

ZANINELLI, S. *Una grande azienda agricola della pianura irrigua lombarda nei secoli XVIII e XIX*. Milan, 1964.

ZIJP, A. 'Hoofdstukken uit de economische en sociale geschiedenis van de polder Zijpe in de 17e en 18e eeuw.' *Tijdschrift voor geschiedenis*, LXX, 1957.

ZUCCHINI, M. *L'agricoltura ferrarese attraverso i secoli*. 1967.

ŻYTKOWICZ, L. 'Ze studiów nad wysokością plonów w Polsce od XVI do XVIII wieku.' *Kwartalnik historii kultury materialnej*, XIV, 1966.

'An investigation into agricultural production in Masovia in the first half of the 17th century.' *Acta Poloniae historica*, XVIII, 1968.

'Studia nad wydajnością gospodarstwa wiejskiego na Mazowszu w XVII wieku.' *Studia z dziejów gospodarstwa wiejskiego*, XI: 1, 1969.

'Plony zbóż w Polsce, Czechach, na Węgrzech i Słowacji w XVI–XVIII w.' *Kwartalnik historii kultury materialnej*, XVIII, 1970.

CHAPTER III

The European Fisheries in Early Modern History

Certain aspects of the European fisheries dealt with above are summaries of the contributor's own work in progress on the fisheries of Europe from 1500 to the advent of steam fishing.

MANUSCRIPT SOURCES

Archives Nationales, Paris
  Archive de la Marine B_2 B_3
  AP. 127
Algemene Rijksarchief, The Hague
  Archief van de Groote Visscherij
Norfolk Record Office, Norwich
  Great Yarmouth Corporation Manuscripts
Public Record Office, London
  C.O. 194; 390
  E.190
Scottish Record Office
  Customs Records
National Library of Scotland
  Sir Robert Sibbald, Discourses on Trade. 1693. MS. 33.5.16.

SELECT PRINTED WORKS

BANG, N. E. and KORST, K. *Tabeller over Skibsfart og Varetransport.* 6 vols., Copenhagen, 1906–33, 1930–53.

BEAUJON, A. *History of the Dutch Sea Fisheries: Their Progress, Decline and Revival.* International Fisheries Exhibition Literature, IX: Prize Essays, Pt II, London, 1883.

DALGARD, S. *Dansk-Norsk Hvalfangst 1615–1660.* Copenhagen, 1962.

DARDEL, E. *La Pêche Harenguière en France.* Paris, 1941.

FULTON, T. W. *The Sovereignty of the Seas.* London, 1912.

GELDER, H. E. VAN. 'Gegevens betreffende de haringvisscherij op het einde de 16e eeuw.' *Bijdragen en Mededeelingen van het Historisch Genootschap.* XXXII, 1911.

GENTLEMAN, T. *England's Way to Win Wealth.* London, 1614.

HAHN, L. *Ostfrieslands Heringsfischereien.* Oldenburg, 1941.

HEMARDINQUIER, J. J. (ed.). 'Pour une histoire de l'alimentation.' *Cahiers des Annales,* XXVIII, Paris, 1970.

INNIS, H. A. *The Cod Fisheries.* Toronto, 1954.

'The Rise and Fall of the Spanish Fishery in Newfoundland.' *Transactions of the Royal Society of Canada,* 1931.

International Fisheries Exhibition Literature. IX: II. London, 1884.

JENKINS, J. T. *The Herring and the Herring Fisheries.* London, 1928.

A History of the Whale Fisheries. London, 1921.

JUDAH, C. B. *The North American Fisheries and British Policy to 1713.* Urbana, 1933.

KRANENBURGH, H. A. H. *De Zeevisscherij van Holland in den Tijd der Republiek.* Amsterdam, 1946.

LA MORANDIÈRE, CH. DE. *Histoire de la Pêche Française de la Morue dans l'Amérique Septentrionale. Des origines à 1789.* 3 vols., Paris, 1962.

LOUNSBURY, R. G. *The British Fishery in Newfoundland 1634–1763.* New Haven, Connecticut, 1934.

LYTHE, S. G. E. *The Economy of Scotland in its European Setting 1550–1625.* London, 1960.

ØSTENSJØ, R. 'The Spring Herring Fishery and the Industrial Revolution in West Norway in the 19th Century.' *Scandinavian Economic History Review,* XI, 1963, 135–55.

SEYMENS, M. *Een korte beschrijving van de haringvisscherije in Hollandt.* Amsterdam, 1640.

SIMON, THOMAS H. *Onze IJslandvaarders in de 17e en 18e eeuw.* Amsterdam, 1937.

SMITH, H. D. 'The Historical Geography of Trade in the Shetland Islands 1550–1914.' Unpublished Ph.D. thesis, Aberdeen, 1972.

STEEN, S. and BUGGE, A. *Det Norske Folks Liv og Historie.* Oslo, 1932–3.

TOMFOHRDE, T. 'Die Heringsfischereiperiode an der Bohus-Len-Kuste van 1559–1589.' *Archiv für Fischereigeschichte,* III, 1914.

WATJEN, H. 'Zur Statistik der holländischen Heringfischerei im 17. und 18. Jahrhundert.' *Hansische Geschichtsblätter,* Lubach, 1910.

ZORGDRAGER, C. G. *Bloeyende Opkomst der aloude en hedendaagsche Groenlandsche Visscherij.* Amsterdam, 1720.

CHAPTER IV

The Changing Patterns of Trade

ABEL, WILHELM. *Agrarkrisen und Agrarkonjunktur. Eine Geschichte der Land- und Ernährungswirtschaft Mitteleuropas seit dem hohen Mittelalter.* Hamburg–Berlin, 1966.

ACHILLES, W. 'Getreidepreise und Getreidehandelsbeziehungen europäischer Räume im 16. und 17. Jahrhundert.' *Zeitschrift für Agrargeschichte und Agrarsoziologie,* VII, 1959.

AMBURGER, ERIK. *Die Familie Marselis. Studien zur russischen Wirtschaftsgeschichte.* Giessner Abhandlungen zur Agrar- und Wirtschaftsforschung des europäischen Ostens, IV, Giessen, 1957.

ANAND, INDIRA (NÉE NARANG). 'India's Overseas Trade, 1715–1725.' Unpubl. thesis, Delhi School of Economics, 1969.

ARASARATNAM, SINNAPPAH. *Dutch Power in Ceylon, 1658–1687.* Amsterdam, 1958.

ARUP, ERIK. *Studier i engelsk og tysk handels historie. En undersøgelse af kommissionshandelens praksis og theori i engelsk og tysk handelsliv 1350–1850.* Copenhagen, 1907.

Les Aspects Internationaux de la Découverte Océanique aux XVe et XVIe Siècles. Paris, S.E.V.P.E.N., 1966.

ÅSTRÖM, SVEN-ERIK. 'The English Navigation Laws and the Baltic Trade, 1660–1700.' *Scand. Econ. Hist. Rev.,* VIII, 1960.

From Stockholm to St Petersburg. Commercial Factors in the Political Relations between England and Sweden 1675–1700. Studia Historica, publ. by the Finnish Historical Society, II, Helsinki, 1962.

From Cloth to Iron. The Anglo-Baltic Trade in the Late Seventeenth Century. Part I, *The Growth, Structure and Organization of the Trade.* Societas Scientiarum Fennica. Commentationes Humanarum Litterarum, XXXIII: 1, Helsinki, 1963.

ATTMAN, ARTUR. *The Russian and Polish Markets in International Trade, 1500–1650.* Publications of the Institute of Economic History of Gothenburg University, XXVI, Göteborg, 1973.

BANG, N. *Tabeller over Skibsfart og Varetransport gennem Øresund 1497–1660.* 3 vols., Copenhagen, 1906–22.

and KORST, K. *Tabeller over Skibsfart og Varetransport gennem Øresund 1661–1783 og gennem Storebaelt 1701–1748.* 3 vols, Copenhagen, 1930–45.

BARBOUR, VIOLET. *Capitalism in Amsterdam in the Seventeenth Century.* The Johns Hopkins University Studies in Historical and Political Science, Ser. LXVII: 1, Baltimore, 1950.

'Dutch and English Merchant Shipping in the Seventeenth Century.' *Economic History Review,* II, 1929–30.

BASTIN, JOHN. *The Changing Balance of the Early Southeast Asian Pepper Trade.* Papers on Southeast Asian Subjects, No. 1, Department of History, University of Malaya in Kuala Lumpur, 1960.

BERGIER, JEAN-FRANÇOIS. *Genève et l'économie européenne de la Renaissance.* Collection Affaires et Gens d'Affaires, Paris, S.E.V.P.E.N., 1963.

BERRILL, K. 'International Trade and the Rate of Economic Growth.' *Economic History Review,* 2nd ser., XII, 1960.

BEUTIN, LUDWIG. *Der deutsche Seehandel im Mittelmeergebiet bis zu den napoleonischen Kriegen.* Neue Folge der Abh. zur Verkehrs- und Seegeschichte, ed. Dietrich Schäfer, 1, Neumünster, 1933.

BLITZ, RUDOLPH C. 'Mercantilist Policies and the Pattern of World Trade, 1500–1750.' *Journal of Economic History,* XVII, 1967.

BOG, INGOMAR. *Der Reichsmerkantilismus. Studien zur Wirtschaftspolitik des Heiligen Römischen Reiches im 17. und 18. Jahrhundert.* Stuttgart, 1959.

'Türkenkrieg und Agrarwirtschaft.' In O. Pickl (ed.), *Die wirtschaftlichen Auswirkungen der Türkenkriege,* 1971.

(ed.). *Der Aussenhandel Ostmitteleuropas 1450–1650. Die ostmitteleuropäischen Volkswirtschaften in ihren Beziehungen zu Mitteleuropa.* Cologne–Vienna, 1971.

BOGUCKA, MARIA. 'Die Bedeutung des Ostseehandels für die Aussenhandelsbilanz Polens in der ersten Hälfte des 17. Jahrhunderts.' In I. Bog (ed.), *Der Aussenhandel Ostmitteleuropas,* 1971.

BRAKEL, S. VAN. 'De Directie van den Oosterschen handel en reederijen te Amsterdam.' *Bijdragen v. Vaderl. Geschiedenis en Oudheidkunde,* 4. R. IX, 1910.

BRAUDEL, FERNAND. *La Méditerrannée et le monde méditerranéen à l'époque de Philippe II.* I–II, rev. ed., Librairie Armand Colin, Paris, 1966.

BRAUNSTEIN, PHILIPPE. 'Venedig und der Türke (1480–1570).' In O. Pickl (ed.), *Die wirtschaftlichen Auswirkungen der Türkenkriege,* 1971.

BRULEZ, WILFRIED. *De Firma della Faille en de Internationale Handel van Vlaamse Firma's in de 16e Eeuw.* In Verhandelingen van de Koninklijke Vlaamse Academie voor Wetenschappen, Letteren en Schone Kunsten van België, Klasse der Letteren No. 35, Brussels, 1959.

CERNOVODEANU, PAUL. *England's Trade Policy in the Levant 1660–1714.* Bibliotheca Historica Romaniae, Economic History Section, Studies, XLI: 2, Bucharest, 1972.

CHAUDHURI, K. N. 'The East India Company and the Export of Treasure in the Early Seventeenth Century.' *Economic History Review,* 2nd Ser., XVI, 1963.

The English East India Company. The Study of an Early Joint-Stock Company 1600–1640. London, 1965.

'Treasure and Trade Balance: The East India Company's Export Trade, 1660–1720.' *Economic History Review,* 2nd Ser., XXI, 1968.

CHAUNU, H. and P. *Séville et l'Atlantique 1504–1650.* I–V, Series Ports-Routes-Trafics, No. VI, Paris, S.E.V.P.E.N., 1959.

CHAUNU, PIERRE. *Les Philippines et le Pacifique des Ibériques (XVIème, XVIIème, XVIIIème siècles). Introduction Méthodologique et Indices d'Activité.* Series Ports-Routes-Trafics, No. XI, Paris, S.E.V.P.E.N., 1960.

CHRISTENSEN, AKSEL E. *Dutch Trade to the Baltic around 1600. Studies in the Sound Toll Register and Dutch Shipping Records.* Copenhagen–The Hague, 1941.

CIPOLLA, CARLO M. *Money, Prices, and Civilization in the Mediterranean World: Fifth to Seventeenth Century.* London, 1956.

'Per una Storia della Produttività nei Secoli del Medioevo e del Rinascimento.' *Prato Conference Papers,* 1971 (mimeographed).

Città, mercanti, dottrine nell'economia europea dal IV al XVIII secolo. Saggi in memoria di Gino Luzzatto. Biblioteca della Rivista Economia e Storia, XI, Milan, 1964.

COORNAERT, E. *Les François et le commerce international à Anvers: fin du XVe–XVIe siècle.* 2 vols., Paris, 1961.

CRAEYBECKX, J. 'Les François et Anvers au XVIe siècle.' *Annales E.S.C.,* XVI, 1962.

Un grand commerce d'importation: les vins de France aux anciens Pays Bas, XIIIe–XVIe siècles. Paris, S.E.V.P.E.N., 1958.

DAS GUPTA, ASHIN. *Malabar in Asian Trade, 1740–1800.* Cambridge South Asian Studies, Cambridge, 1967.

DAVIS, RALPH. 'English Foreign Trade, 1660–1700'. *Economic History Review,* 2nd Ser., VII, 1954.

'English Foreign Trade, 1700–1774.' *Economic History Review,* 2nd Ser., XV, 1962.

The Rise of the English Shipping Industry in the Seventeenth and Eighteenth Centuries. London, 1962.

DELAFOSSE, MARCEL and LAVEAU, CLAUDE. *Le commerce du sel de Brouage aux XVIIe et XVIIIe siècles.* Cahiers des Annales, Paris: Colin, 1960.

DERMIGNY, LOUIS. *La Chine et l'Occident. Le Commerce à Canton au XVIIIe siècle, 1719–1833.* Series Ports-Routes-Trafics, XVIII, 4 vols., Paris, 1964.

DILLEN, J. G. VAN. 'Amsterdam als wereldmarkt der edele metalen in de 17de en 18de eeuw.' *De Economist,* LXXII, 1923.

Van Rijkdom en Regenten. Handboek tot de Economische en Sociale Geschiedenis van Nederland tijdens de Republiek. 's-Gravenhage, 1970.

ELLEHØJ, SVEND. 'Christian IV's tidsalder.' *Politikens Danmarkshistorie*, VII, Politikens Forlag, Copenhagen, 1964.

EMBER, GYÖZÖ. 'Ungarns Aussenhandel mit dem Westen um die Mitte des XVI. Jahrhunderts.' In I. Bog (ed.), *Der Aussenhandel Ostmitteleuropas*, 1971.

FABER, J. A. *Drie Eeuwen Friesland, Economische en sociale ontwikkelingen van 1500 tot 1800*, I–II. *A.A.G. Bijdragen*, XVII, Wageningen, 1972.

'Het probleem van de dalende graanaanvoer uit de Oostzeelanden in de tweede helft van de zeventiende eeuw.' *A.A.G. Bijdragen*, IX, 1963.

FARNIE, D. A. 'The Commercial Empire of the Atlantic, 1607–1783.' *Economic History Review*, 2nd Ser., XV, 1962.

FISHER, F. J. 'The 16th and 17th Centuries: the Dark Ages in English Economic History.' *Economica*, N.S., XXIV, 1957.

FISHER, H. E. S. *The Portugal Trade. A Study of Anglo-Portuguese Commerce 1700–1770.* London, 1971.

FRIIS, ASTRID. *Alderman Cockayne's Project and the Cloth Trade. The Commercial Policy of England in its Main Aspects 1603–1625.* Copenhagen–London, 1927.

FÜGEDI, ERIK. 'Der Aussenhandel Ungarns am Anfang des 16. Jahrhunderts.' In I. Bog (ed.), *Der Aussenhandel Ostmitteleuropas*, 1971.

GERSCHENKRON, ALEXANDER. *Europe in the Russian Mirror. Four Lectures in Economic History.* Cambridge, 1970.

GLAMANN, KRISTOF. *Bryggeriets historie i Danmark indtil slutningen af det 19. århundrede.* Copenhagen, 1962.

'The Danish East India Company.' In Michel Mollat (ed.), *Sociétés et Compagnies de Commerce en Orient et dans l'Océan Indien*, Paris, S.E.V.P.E.N., 1970.

Dutch-Asiatic Trade, 1620–1740. Copenhagen–The Hague, 1958.

'The Dutch East India Company's Trade in Japanese Copper 1645–1736.' *Scandinavian Economic History Review*, I, 1953.

Otto Thott's Uforgribelige Tanker om Kommerciens Tilstand. Et nationaløkonomisk Programskrift fra 1735. Københavns Universitets Fond til Tilvejebringelse af Læremidler, 1966.

'Studie i Asiatisk Kompagnis økonomiske historie 1732–1772.' *Historisk Tidsskrift* II: 11, 1947–9.

GOUBERT, PIERRE. *Beauvais et les Beauvaisis de 1600 à 1730. Contribution à l'Histoire Sociale de la France du XVIIe siècle.* Paris, S.E.V.P.E.N., 1960.

GOULD, J. D. *The Great Debasement. Currency and Economy in Mid-Tudor England.* Oxford, 1970.

HAMMARSTRÖM, INGRID. *Finansförvaltning och varuhandel 1504–1540. Studier i de yngre Sturarnas och Gustav Vasas Statshushållning.* Uppsala, 1956.

HASAN, AZIZA. 'The Silver Currency Output of the Mughal Empire and Prices in India during the 16th and 17th Centuries.' *The Indian Economic and Social History Review*, VI, 1969.

HECKSCHER, ELI F. *Merkantilismen. Ett led i den ekonomiska politikens historia.* I–II, Stockholm, 1931.

HICKS, JOHN. *A Theory of Economic History.* Oxford, 1969.

HILDEBRAND, K.-G. 'Salt and Cloth in Swedish Economic History.' *Scandinavian Economic History Review*, II, 1954.

HILDEBRANDT, REINHARD. *Die 'Georg Fuggerischen Erben'. Kaufmännische Tätigkeit und sozialer Status 1555–1600.* Schriften zur Wirtschafts- und Sozialgeschichte, VI, Berlin, 1966.

HINTON, R. W. K. *The Eastland Trade and the Common Wealth in the Seventeenth Century.* Cambridge, 1959.

HOSZOWSKI, S. 'The Polish Baltic Trade in the 15th–18th Centuries.' *Poland at the 11th International Congress of Historical Sciences in Stockholm*, Warsaw, 1960.

HOUTTE, J. A. VAN. 'Anvers aux XVe et XVIe siècles: avènement et apogée.' *Annales E.S.C.*, XVI, 1961.

Economische en Sociale Geschiedenis van de Lage Landen. Antwerp–Zeist, 1964.

HROCH, MIROSLAV. 'Die Rolle des zentraleuropäischen Handels im Ausgleich der Handelsbilanz zwischen Ost- und Westeuropa 1550–1650.' In I. Bog (ed.), *Der Aussenhandel Ostmitteleuropas*, 1971.

HUHNHÄUSER, A. 'Rostocks Seehandel von 1635–1648.' *Beiträge zur Geschichte der Stadt Rostock*, VIII, Rostock, 1914.

JEANNIN, PIERRE. 'Les comptes du Sund comme source pour la construction d'indices généraux de l'activité économique en Europe (XVIe–XVIIe siècles).' *Révue historique*, CCXXXI, 1964.

Les Marchands au XVIe Siècle. Collections Microcosme *Le Temps qui court*, Editions du Seuil, Paris, 1957.

'Les relations économiques des villes de la Baltique avec Anvers, XVIe siècle.' *Vierteljahrschrift für Sozial- und Wirtschaftsgeschichte*, XLIII, 1956.

KELLENBENZ, HERMANN. 'Der kontinentale Handel zwischen Ost- und Westeuropa vom 15. Jahrhundert bis zum Beginn des Eisenbahnzeitalters.' *V. Int. Kongress der ökonomischen Geschichte, Leningrad, August 1970* (mimeographed).

'Der Pfeffermarkt um 1600 und die Hansestädte.' *Hansische Geschichtsblätter*, LXXIV, 1956.

Sephardim an der unteren Elbe. Ihre wirtschaftliche und politische Bedeutung vom Ende des 16. bis zum Beginn des 18. Jahrhunderts. Vierteljahrschrift für Sozial- und Wirtschaftsgeschichte, Beiheft 40, Wiesbaden, 1958.

Südosteuropa im Rahmen der europäischen Gesamtwirtschaft.' In O. Pickl (ed.), *Die wirtschaftlichen Auswirkungen der Türkenkriege*, 1971.

Unternehmerkräfte im Hamburger-, Portugal- und Spanienhandel, 1590–1625. Veröffentlgn. d. wirtschaftsgeschl. Forschungsstelle, X, 1954.

KERNKAMP, J. H. '"Straatfahrt": Niederländische Pionierarbeit im Mittelmeergebiet.' *Jahrbücher für Nationalökonomie und Statistik*, CLXXVIII, 1965.

KHAN, S. A. *The East India Trade in the 17th Century*. Oxford, 1923.

KIRCHNER, WALTHER. *Commercial Relations between Russia and Europe 1400 to 1800, Collected Essays*. Indiana University Publications, Russian and East European Series, XXXIII, Bloomington, Indiana, 1966.

KLAVEREN, JACOB VAN. *Europäische Wirtschaftsgeschichte Spaniens im 16. und 17. Jahrhundert*. Forschungen zur Sozial- und Wirtschaftsgeschichte, Stuttgart, 1960.

'Fiskalismus–Merkantilismus–Korruption.' *Vierteljahrschrift für Sozial- und Wirtschaftsgeschichte*, XLVII, 1960.

KLEIN, P. W. (ed.). *Van stapelmarkt tot welvaartsstaat*. Universitaire Pers Rotterdam, 1970.

De Trippen in de 17e eeuw. Een studie over het ondernemersgedrap op de Hollandse stapelmarkt. Assen, 1965.

KOBATA, A. 'The Production and Uses of Gold and Silver in Sixteenth- and Seventeenth-Century Japan.' *Economic History Review*, 2nd Ser., XVIII, 1965.

KOOY, T. P. VAN DER. *Hollands stapelmarkt en haar verval*. Amsterdam, 1931.

KRANNHALS, DITLEV. *Danzig und der Weichselhandel in seiner Blütezeit vom 16. zum 17. Jahrhundert*. Leipzig, 1942.

KULA, WITOLD. *Théorie Economique du Système Féodal. Pour un modèle de l'économie polonaise 16e–18e siècles*. Civilisations et Sociétés, XV, Paris, 1970.

KUMLIEN, K. *Sverige och hanseaterna. Studier i svensk politik och utrikeshandel*. Kungl. Vitterhets Historia och Antikvitets Akademiens Handlingar, LXXXVI, Stockholm, 1953.

KUSKE, BRUNO. 'Die wirtschaftliche und soziale Verflechtung zwischen Deutschland und den Niederlanden bis zum 18. Jahrhundert.' *Köln, der Rhein und das Reich*, Cologne–Graz, 1956.

LANE, F. C. *Venice and History. The Collected Papers of Frederic C. Lane*. The Johns Hopkins Press, Baltimore, 1966.

LE ROY LADURIE, E. *Les Paysans de Languedoc*. Paris, S.E.V.P.E.N., 1966.

LEUR, J. C. VAN. *Indonesian Trade and Society. Essays in Asian and Economic History*. Selected Studies on Indonesia by Dutch Scholars, I. Bandung, The Hague, 1955.

LÜTGE, F. *Struktur-Wandlungen im ostdeutschen und osteuropäischen Fernhandel des 14. bis 16. Jahrhunderts*. In Bayer. Akademie d. Wissenschaften, Philos.-Hist. Klasse, Sitzungsberichte, 1, Munich, 1964.

Mączak, Antoni. 'Der polnische Getreideexport und das Problem der Handelsbilanz (1557–1647).' In I. Bog (ed.), *Der Aussenhandel Ostmitteleuropas*, 1971.

Magalhães-Godinho, Vitorino. *L'Économie de l'Empire Portugais aux XVe et XVIe Siècles*. Paris, S.E.V.P.E.N., 1969.

Makkai, László. 'Der ungarische Viehhandel 1550–1650.' In I. Bog (ed.), *Der Aussenhandel Ostmitteleuropas*, 1971.

Malowist, M. 'Un essai d'histoire comparée: les mouvements d'expansion en Europe aux XVe et XVIe siècles.' *Annales E.S.C.*, xvii, 1962.

'The Problem of the Inequality of Economic Development in Europe in the Later Middle Ages.' *Economic History Review*, 2nd Ser., xix, 1966.

'Les produits des pays de la Baltique dans le commerce international au XVIe siècle.' *Revue du Nord*, xlii, 1960.

Mauro, Frédéric. *Le Portugal et l'Atlantique au XVIIe siècle (1570–1670)*. Ports-Routes-Trafics, No. 10, Paris, S.E.V.P.E.N., 1960.

'Towards an International Model: European Overseas Expansion between 1500 and 1800.' *Economic History Review*, 2nd Ser., xiv, 1961.

Meilink-Roelofsz, M. A. P. *Asian Trade and European Influence in the Indonesian Archipelago between 1500 and about 1630*. The Hague, 1962.

Melis, Federigo. *Documenti per la storia economica dei secoli XIII–XVI*. Istituto Internazionale di Storia Economica 'F. Datini'. Firenze, 1972.

Michelsen, L. 'Het Kapitalisme te Antwerpen in de XVIIde en XVIIIde Eeuwen.' *Nederlandsche Historiebladen*, ii, 1939.

Minchinton, W. E. (ed.). *The Growth of English Overseas Trade in the 17th and 18th Centuries*. 'Editor's Introduction', London, 1969.

Mollat, Michel (ed.). *Le Rôle du Sel dans l'Histoire*. Publications de la Faculté des Lettres et Sciences Humaines de Paris-Sorbonne, Série 'Recherches', xxxvii, Paris, 1968.

Mols, R. *Introduction à la démographie historique des villes d'Europe du XIVe au XVIIIe siècles*. 2 vols., Gembloux–Louvain, 1954–6.

Naudé, W. *Die Getreidehandelspolitik der europäischen Staaten vom 13. bis zum 18. Jahrhundert*. Berlin, 1896.

North, D. C. and Thomas, R. B. 'An Economic Theory of the Growth of the Western World.' *Economic History Review*, 2nd Ser., xxii, 1970.

Odén, Birgitta. *Kopparhandel och statsmonopol. Studier i svensk handelshistoria under senare 1500-talet*. Kungl. Vitterhets Historia och Antikvitets Akademiens Handlingar, Historiska Serien, v, Stockholm, 1960.

Rikets uppbörd och utgift. Statsfinanser och finansförvaltning under senare 1500-talet. Bibliotheca Historica Lundensis, i, Lund, 1955.

Öhberg, Arne. 'Russia and the World Market in the Seventeenth Century.' *Scandinavian Economic History Review*, iii, 1955.

Pach, Zsigmond P. 'The role of East Central Europe in international trade (16th and 17th centuries).' *Études historiques publiées à l'occasion du XIIIe Congrès International des Sciences Historiques*, i, Budapest, 1970.

Die Ungarische Agrarentwicklung im 16.–17. Jahrhundert. 1964.

Parry, J. H. *The Age of Reconnaissance*. 2nd ed., London, 1966.

Pedersen, E. Ladewig. *The Crisis of the Danish Nobility 1580–1660*. Odense, 1967.

Pickl, Othmar. 'Die Auswirkungen der Türkenkriege auf den Handel zwischen Ungarn und Italien im 16. Jahrhundert.' *Die wirtschaftlichen Auswirkungen der Türkenkriege*, Grazer Forschungen zur Wirtschafts- und Sozialgeschichte, i, Graz, 1971.

'Der Handel Wiens und Wiener Neustadts mit Böhmen, Mähren, Schlesien und Ungarn in der ersten Hälfte des 16. Jahrhunderts (mit einem Exkurs über den Ochsenhandel von Ungarn nach Venedig im letzten Viertel des 16. Jahrhunderts).' In I. Bog (ed.), *Der Aussenhandel Ostmitteleuropas*, 1971.

(ed.). *Die wirtschaftlichen Auswirkungen der Türkenkriege*. Grazer Forschungen zur Wirtschafts- und Sozialgeschichte, i, Graz, 1971.

Posthumus, N. W. *Nederlandsche Prijsgeschiedenis*. i, Leiden, 1943.

De Oosterse Handel te Amsterdam. Het oudst bewaarde koopmansboek van een Amsterdamse vennootschap betreffende de handel op de Oostzee 1485–1490. Leiden, 1953.

PRAKASH, OM. 'The Dutch East India Company and the Economy of Bengal, 1650–1717.' Unpublished thesis, Delhi School of Economics, 1967.

PRICE, JACOB M. *The Tobacco Adventure to Russia. Enterprise, Politics and Diplomacy in the Quest for a Northern Market for English Colonial Tobacco 1676–1722.* Transactions of the American Philosophical Society, LI: 1, Philadelphia, 1961.

RABE, HANNAH. 'Aktienkapital und Handelsinvestitionen im Überseehandel des 17. Jahrhunderts.' *Vierteljahrschrift für Sozial- und Wirtschaftsgeschichte*, XLIX, 1962.

RAMSEY, G. D. *English Foreign Trade During the Centuries of Emergence.* London, 1957.

RAU, VIRGINIA. *A exploração e o commercio do sal de Setúbal.* Lisbon, 1951.

RAYCHAUDHURI, TAPAN. *Jan Company in Coromandel 1605–1690. A Study in the Inter-relations of European Commerce and Traditional Economics.* Verhandelingen van het Koninklijk Instituut voor Taal-, Land- en Volkenkunde, deel 38, The Hague, 1962.

ROOVER, RAYMOND DE. *L'Évolution de la Lettre de Change, XIVe–XVIIIe Siècles.* Affaires et Gens d'Affaires, no. IV, École des Hautes Études – VIe Section, Paris, 1953.

RUIZ-MARTIN, F. *Lettres marchandes échangées entre Florence et Medina del Campo.* Affaires et Gens d'Affaires, No. 27, Paris, S.E.V.P.E.N., 1965.

SAMSONOWICZ, HENRYK. 'Les foires en Pologne au XVe et XVIe siècles sur la toile de fond de la situation économique en Europe.' In I. Bog (ed.), *Der Aussenhandel Ostmitteleuropas*, 1971.

SCHOLLIERS, E. *Loonarbeid en honger. De levensstandaard in de XVe en XVIe eeuw te Antwerpen.* Antwerp, 1960.

SILVA, J. GENTIL DA. *Stratégie des Affaires à Lisbonne entre 1595 et 1607. Lettres Marchandes des Rodriques d'Evora et Veiga.* Paris, S.E.V.P.E.N., 1956.

'Trafics du Nord, marchés du Mezzogiorno, finances gênoises: recherches et documents sur la conjoncture à la fin du XVIème siècle.' *Revue du Nord*, April–June 1959.

SLICHER VAN BATH, B. H. 'Die europäischen Agrarverhältnisse im 17. und der ersten Hälfte des 18. Jahrhunderts.' *A.A.G. Bijdragen*, XIII, 1965.

'Les problèmes fondamentaux de la société pré-industrielle en Europe occidentale. Une orientation et un programme.' *A.A.G. Bijdragen*, XII, 1965.

SMOUT, T. C. 'Scottish Commercial Factors in the Baltic at the End of the Seventeenth Century.' *Scottish Historical Review*, XXXIX, 1960.

Scottish Trade on the Eve of Union, 1660–1707. Edinburgh, 1963.

Sociétés et Compagnies de Commerce en Orient et dans l'Océan Indien. Paris, S.E.V.P.E.N., 1972.

SOMBART, WERNER. *Der moderne Kapitalismus.* I–III, 1927–8.

SOOM, ARNOLD. 'Der Kampf der baltischen Städte gegen das Fremdkapital im 17. Jahrhundert.' *Vierteljahrschrift für Sozial- und Wirtschaftsgeschichte*, XLIX, 1962.

SPERLING, J. 'The International Payments Mechanism in the Seventeenth and Eighteenth Centuries.' *Economic History Review*, 2nd Ser., XIV, 1962.

SPOONER, F. C. *L'Économie Mondiale et les Frappes Monétaires en France, 1493–1680.* Series Monnaie, Prix, Conjoncture, IV, Paris, 1956.

STEENSGAARD, NIELS. *Carracks, Caravans and Companies: The structural crisis in the European–Asian trade in the early 17th century.* Scandinavian Institute of Asian Studies Monograph Series, No. 17, Studentlitteratur, Lund, 1973.

SUPPLE, B. E. *Commercial Crisis and Change in England 1600–1642. A Study in the Instability of a Mercantile Economy.* Cambridge, 1959.

TOPOLSKI, JERZY. 'La Regression économique en Pologne du XVIe au XVIIIe siècle.' *Acta Poloniae Historica*, VII, 1962.

TVEITE, STEIN. *Engelsk-norsk trelasthandel 1640–1710.* Bergen–Oslo, 1961.

UNGER, W. S. 'Trade through the Sound in the Seventeenth and Eighteenth Centuries.' *Economic History Review*, 2nd Ser., XII, 1959.

VINER, JACOB. *Studies in the Theory of International Trade.* Reprinted, London, 1964.

VLACHOVIČ, JOZEF. 'Produktion und Handel mit ungarischem Kupfer im 16. und im ersten Viertel des 17. Jahrhunderts.' In I. Bog (ed.), *Der Aussenhandel Ostmitteleuropas*, 1971.

VOGEL, WALTHER. 'Handelskonjunkturen und Wirtschaftskrisen in ihrer Auswirkung auf den Seehandel der Hansestädte 1560–1806.' *Hansische Geschichtsblätter*, LXXIV, 1956.

VRIES, J. DE. *De Economische Achteruitgang der Republiek in de Achtiende Eeuw*. Amsterdam, 1959.

WEBER, MAX. *Wirtschaftsgeschichte. Abriss der universalen Sozial- und Wirtschaftsgeschichte*. Ed. S. Helmann and M. Palyi, 3rd ed. rev. J. Winckelmann, Berlin, 1958.

WEE, HERMAN VAN DER. 'Een dynamisch Model voor de seculaire Ontwikkeling van de Wereldhandel en de Welvaart (12e–18e eeuw).' *Historische Aspecten van Economische Groei*, Antwerp–Utrecht, 1972.

The Growth of the Antwerp Market and the European Economy. I–III, The Hague, 1963.

'Typologie des crises et changements de structure aux Pays-Bas (XVe–XVIe siècles).' *Annales E.S.C.*, XIX, 1963.

WIESE, HEINZ. 'Die Fleischversorgung der nordwesteuropäischen Grosstädte von XV. bis XIX. Jahrhundert unter besonderer Berücksichtigung des internationalen Rinderhandels.' *Jahrbücher für Nationalökonomie und Statistik*, CLXXIX, 1966.

and BÖLTS. *Rinderhandel und Rinderhaltung im nordwesteuropäischen Küstengebiet vom 15. bis zum 19. Jahrhundert*. 1966.

WILLAN, T. S. *Studies in Elizabethan Foreign Trade*. Manchester, 1959.

WILSON, CHARLES. 'Cloth Production and International Competition in the Seventeenth Century.' *Economic History Review*, 2nd Ser., XIII, 1960.

England's Apprenticeship, 1603–1763. London, 1965.

Profit and Power. A Study of England and the Dutch Wars. London, 1957.

WOLÁNSKI, MARIAN. 'Schlesiens Stellung im Osthandel vom 15. bis zum 17. Jahrhundert.' In I. Bog (ed.), *Der Aussenhandel Ostmitteleuropas*, 1971.

WYCZAŃSKI, ANDRZEJ. 'La base intérieure de l'exportation polonaise des céréales dans la seconde moitié du XVIe siècle.' In I. Bog (ed.), *Der Aussenhandel Ostmitteleuropas*, 1971.

CHAPTER V

Monetary, Credit and Banking Systems

SOURCES

AMZALAK, M. B. *O economista Isaac de Pinto, o seu 'Tratado da circulação e do credito', e outros escritos económicos* (1771). Lisbon, 1960.

BALDASSERONI, COMTE P. *Leggi e costumi del cambio che si osservano nelle principali piazze di Europa e singularmente in quella di Livorno*. Pescia, 1784.

BARRÊME, F. *Le Livre des monnoyes étrangères ou le grand banquier de France. Dédié a Monsieur Colbert*. Paris, 1685.

BELLONI, C. *Dizionario storico dei banchieri italiani*. Florence, 1951.

BIGWOOD, G. and GRUNZWEIG, A. (eds.). *Les Livres des comptes des Gallerani*. 2 vols. Brussels, 1961.

BLOK, P. J. (ed.). *Relazioni Veneziane. Venetiaansche berichten over de Vereenigde Nederlanden van 1600–1795*. The Hague, 1909.

BOISGUILLEBERT. P. DE. *Dissertation sur la nature des richesses, de l'argent et des tributs*. Ed. E. Daire. Paris, 1843.

BORLANDI, F. *El libro di mercatantie et usanze de' paesi*. Turin, 1936.

BOYER, C. *Briefve méthode et instruction pour tenir livres de raison par parties doubles, en laquelle se voit la plus grande partie des négoces que faict Lyon en toutes les principales villes d'Europe*. Lyons, 1627.

BRANTS, V. (ed.). *Les Ordonnances monétaires du XVIIIe siècle. Albert et Isabelle, 1598–1621 . . .* Brussels, 1914.

BUONINSEGNI, T. *Trattato dei cambi*. Florence, 1573.

Capitoli delle fieri di qualsivoglia sorte di mercanzia nella città di Piacenza rinovati 1685. Piacenza, n.d.

CASSANDRO, G. *Un trattato inedito e la dottrina dei cambi nel cinquecento*. Naples, 1962.

CHAPPUZEAU, S. *Lyon dans son lustre*. Lyons, 1656.

CHAUNU, H. and P. *Séville et l'Atlantique (1504–1650)*. 8 vols. Paris, 1955–60.

CLEIRAC, E. *Usance du négoce ou commerce de la Banque des lettres de change*. Paris, 1659.

COPPI, A. *Discorso sulle finanze dello Stato Pontificio dal secolo XVI al principio del XIX.* Rome, 1855.

DAVENANT, C. *Discourses on the Public Revenues and other Trade of England* . . . 2 vols. London, 1698.

DENUCÉ, J. *Inventaire des Affaitadi, banquiers italiens à Anvers de l'année 1568.* Antwerp–Paris, 1934.

Koopmansleerboeken van de XVIe en XVIIe eeuwen in handschrift. (Verhandelingen van de Koninklijke Vlaamsche Academie voor Wetenschappen, Letteren en schoone Kunsten van België. Klasse der Letteren, III, no. 2.) Antwerp–Brussels–Ghent–Louvain, 1941.

DILLEN, J. G. VAN. *Bronnen tot de Geschiedenis der Wisselbanken: Amsterdam, Middelburg, Delft, Rotterdam.* (Rijksgeschiedkundige Publicatiën, no. 59–60.) 2 vols. The Hague, 1925.

DUTOT. *Réflexions politiques sur les finances et le commerce.* Integral edition by Paul Harsin. 2 vols. Paris, 1935.

FERRARA, F. 'Documenti per servire alla storia dei banchi veneziani.' *Archivio veneto,* 1871.

FISHER, F. J. (ed.). *Calendar of the Manuscripts of the Right Honourable Lord Sackville of Knole, Sevenoaks, Kent.* II (Great Britain Historical Manuscripts Commission), London, 1966.

GIRAUDEAU. *Le Guide des Banquiers de l'Europe.* Paris, 1727.

GUERAUD, J. *La Chronique lyonnaise de Jehan Gueraud, 1536–1562, publiée avec une introduction et une table par Jean Tricou.* Lyons, 1929.

GUICCIARDINI, L. *Description de tout le Pays-Bas.* Antwerp, 1567.

HARSIN, P. (ed.). *Oeuvres complètes de John Law (avec préface de P. Harsin).* 3 vols. Paris, 1934.

HEERS, J. *Le Livre de comptes de Giovanni Piccamiglio, homme d'affaires génois 1456–1459.* Paris, 1959.

HOC, M. (ed.). *Placards monétaires de Philippe II (1555–1598), des archiducs Albert et Isabelle (1598–1621), de Philippe IV (1621–1665) et de Charles II (1665–1700).* 3 vols. Brussels, 1934.

IRSON, C. *Pratique générale et méthodique des changes étrangers.* Paris, 1687.

KLARWILL, V. *Fugger–Zeitungen: Ungedruckte Briefe an das Haus Fugger aus den Jahren 1568–1605.* Vienna–Leipzig–Munich, 1923.

LA PORTE, SIEUR DE. *Le Guide des négocians et teneurs de livres.* Paris, 1685.

LAFFEMAS, B. DE. *Les Trésors et richesses pour mettre l'Estat en splendeur.* Paris, 1598.

Advertissement et réponse aux marchands et autres, où il est touché des changes, banquiers et banque-routiers. Paris, 1600.

LAMEERE, J. P. A. (ed.). *Recueil des ordonnances des Pays-Bas, 1506–1555.* 2nd Ser. 6 vols. Brussels, 1893–1922.

LAPEYRE, H. *Documents pour servir à l'histoire des foires de Lyon. Extrait de Homenaje à D. Ramon Carande.* Madrid, 1963.

LE BRANCHU, J. Y. (ed.). *Ecrits notables sur la monnaie (XVIe siècle: de Copernic à Davanzati).* 2 vols. Paris, 1934.

LE GENDRE, F. *L'arithmétique en sa perfection.* Paris, 1663.

LE MOINE DE LESPINE, SIEUR. *Le Négoce d'Amsterdam ou traité de sa banque.* Amsterdam, 1694.

LECOUREUR, J. *Traité de la pratique des billets entre négocians.* Louvain, 1682.

LEFÉVRE, J. (ed.). *Correspondance de Philippe II sur les affaires des Pays-Bas (1577–1591).* VII, Brussels, 1940.

LUYPAERT-DE COMBELE, O. 'Een onuitgegeven Spaanse memorie over theorie en praktijk van het krediet in de 16e eeuw.' *Bulletin de la commission royale d'histoire,* CXXVI, 1960.

MALYNES, G. *Consuetudo vel lex mercatoria, or the Ancient Law-Merchant* . . . London, 1622.

MARECHAL, M. *Traicté des changes et rechanges licites et illicites et moyens de pourvoir aux fraudes des banque-routes.* Paris, 1625.

MARIUS, J. *Advice concerning Bills of Exchange.* 4th ed. 1651.

MATTHEWS, G. T. *News and Rumor in Renaissance Europe. The Fugger News-letters.* New York, 1959.

MENNHER, V. *Praitique brifue pour cyfrer et tenir liures de comptes touchant le principal train de marchandises.* Antwerp, 1550.

MISSELDEN, E. *Free trade, or the Meanes to make Trade florish*. London, 1622.

MOLLAT, M. and FAVREAU, R. *Comptes généraux de l'État bourguignon entre 1414 et 1420*. (Recueil des Historiens de la France, directed by R. Fawtier, Documents Financiers, V: 1.) Paris, 1965.

MÜLLER, K. O. *Welthandelsbräuche (1480–1540)*. Reprinted Wiesbaden, 1962.

MUN, T. *England's Treasure by Forraign Trade or The Ballance of our Forraign Trade in The Rule of our Treasure*. Edited by his son John Mun. London, 1664.

PEELE, J. *The Pathewaye to Perfectnes in the Accomptes of Debitour and Creditour*. London, 1569.

PEGOLOTTI, F. B. *Pratica della mercatura*. Lisbon–Lucca, 1766.

PERI, G. D. *Il negotiante di . . . diviso in quattro parti (1638, 1647, 1651, 1672–1673)*. Venice, 1682.

PHOONSEN, J. *Wisselstijl tot Amsterdam*. Amsterdam, 1711.

Les loix et les coutumes du change des principales places de l'Europe . . . Amsterdam, 1715.

PINTO, I. DE. *Traité de la circulation et du credit . . .* Amsterdam, 1771.

POSTHUMUS, N. W. *Inquiry into the History of Prices in Holland*. I. Leyden, 1946.

Privilèges des Foires de Lyon, octroyez par les roys très-chrestiens aux marchands français et estrangers y négocians sous lesdits privilèges ou residans en ladite ville. Lyons, 1649.

REATZ, C. F. *Ordonnances du duc d'Albe sur les assurances maritimes de 1569, 1570, 1571* (Compte-rendu des séances de la Commission royale d'histoire, 9th Ser., V). Brussels, 1878.

Recueil des Edits, Déclarations, Arrests et Règlements du Roy, au sujet des Lettres, Billets de Change et Billets payables au Porteur et concernant les Faillites et Banqueroutes. Depuis 1684 jusqu'à present. Rouen, 1718.

RICARD, J.-P. *Le Négoce d'Amsterdam*. Amsterdam, 1722.

RICARD, S. *Le Nouveau Négociant contenant les réductions toutes faites des mesures, poids et monnoyes de France*. Bordeaux, 1686.

ROSA, L. DE. *I cambi esteri del Regno di Napoli dal 1591 al 1707*. Naples, 1945.

RUIZ-MARTIN, F. *Lettres marchandes échangées entre Florence et Medina del Campo*. Paris, 1965.

SACCIA, S. *Tractatus de commerciis et cambio*. Frankfurt-on-Mainz, 1648.

SAVARY, J. *La Théorie et pratique des nombres méthodiquement proposée dans l'usage des financiers*. Paris, 1644.

Le Parfait Négociant, ou instruction générale pour ce qui regarde le commerce . . . Paris, 1675.

SAVARY DES BRUSLONS, J. *Dictionnaire universel du commerce*. 5 vols. Copenhagen, 1759–65.

SEGARD, R. *La Pratique des changes contenante la façon de prester et changer licitement avec l'extrait des décisions de la roue de Gênes*. Lille, 1613.

SILVA, JOSÉ GENTIL DA. *Marchandises et finances*. II–III. *Lettres de Lisbonne, 1563–1578*. 2 vols. Paris, 1959 and 1961.

STOURM, R. *Bibliographie historique des finances de la France au XVIIIe siècle*. Paris, 1895.

STRIEDER, J. *Die Inventar der Firma Fugger aus dem Jahre 1527*. (Zeitschrift für die gesamte Staatswissenschaft, Suppl. XVII.) Tübingen, 1905.

TAWNEY, R. H. and POWER, E. (eds.). *Tudor Economic Documents, being selected Documents illustrating the Economic and Social History of Tudor England*. 3 vols. London–New York–Toronto, 1951.

TERLINDEN, C. *Liste chronologique provisoire des édits et ordonnances des Pays-Bas. Règne de Philippe II (1555–98)*. Brussels, 1912.

TERLINDEN, C. and BOLSÉE, J. (eds.). *Recueil des ordonnances des Pays-Bas*. Brussels, 1957.

Tresoir vande maten, van gewichte van coren, vande elle ende natte mate, oock vanden gelde ende wissel. Amsterdam, 1590.

TURRI, RAPHAËL DE. *Tractatus de cambiis*. Genoa, 1641.

UZZANO, G. A. DA. *La pratica della mercatura (1442)*. Lisbon–Lucca, 1766.

VASQUEZ DE PRADA, V. *Lettres Marchandes d'Anvers*. II–IV. Paris, n.d.

VERCAUTEREN, E. 'Note sur les opérations financières de Charles Quint dans les Pays-Bas en 1523.' *Revue historique*, CLXXI, 1958.

VILLALON, C. DE. *Provechoso tratado de marcaderes y reprovacion de usura*. (Photographic reproduction of the edition of 1546.) Valladolid, 1945.

WHEELER, J. *A Treatise of Commerce*. 1st ed. Middelbourg and London, 1601 (reprinted, New York, 1931).

WILSON, T. *A Discourse upon Usury*. Edited and with an Introduction by R. H. Tawney. London, 1962.

STUDIES

AMSTAD, R. *Des Conceptions monétaires et bancaires en France et de la pratique des banques à Lyon de 1660 à 1720*. Basle, 1949.

ANDREADES, A. *Essai sur la fondation et l'histoire de la Banque d'Angleterre (1694–1844)*. Paris, 1901.

ANDRIANI, G. *Le fiere di cambio genovesi*. Genoa–Sampiedarena, 1931.

ARMINJON, P. and CARREY, P. *La Lettre de change et le billet à ordre*. Paris, 1938.

ARNOULD, M. A. 'L'impôt sur le capital en Belgique au XVIe siècle.' *Le Hainaut économique*, I, 1946.

'L'Incidence de l'impôt sur les finances d'un village à l'époque bourguignonne: Beussoit-sur-Haine, 1400–1555.' *Contributions à l'histoire économique et sociale*, I. Brussels, 1962.

'L'Impôt dans l'histoire des peuples.' *L'Impôt dans le cadre de la ville et de l'Etat. Colloque International, Spa 6–9 Septembre 1964. Actes*. (Collection d'Histoire, XIII.) Brussels, 1966.

'Prolégomènes à l'étude des finances publiques des Pays-Bas espagnols.' *Recherches sur l'histoire des finances publiques en Belgique*. (*Acta Historica Bruxellensia*, II.) Brussels, 1970.

ASHLEY, M. *Financial and Commercial Policy under the Cromwellian Protectorate*. London, 1962.

ASHTON, R. *The Crown and the Money Market, 1603–1640*. Oxford, 1960.

BABBIERI, G. *Origini del capitalismo lombardo*. Milan, 1961.

BADALO-DULONG, C. *Banquier du roi. Barthélemy Hervart, 1606–1676*. Paris, 1951.

BAETENS, R. 'Een Antwerps handelshuis uit de XVIIe eeuw. De firma Van Colen.' *Tijdschrift voor Geschiedenis*. 1960.

BARATIER, E. and REYNAUD, F. *Histoire du commerce de Marseille*. II: *1291–1480*. Paris, 1951.

BARBOUR, V. *Capitalism in Amsterdam in the 17th Century*. Ann Arbor, 1963.

BARTIER, J. *Légistes et gens de finances au XVe siècle. Les conseillers des ducs de Bourgogne, Philippe le Bon et Charles le Téméraire*. (Mémoires de l'Académie Royale de Belgique. Classe des lettres, no. 50.) Brussels, 1955.

BARUCHELLO, M. *Livorno e il suo porto*. Livorno, 1932.

BASAS FERNANDEZ, M. 'Burgos en el comercio lanero del siglo XVI.' *Moneda y crédito*, LXXVII, 1961.

BENASSI, U. 'Per la storia delle fiere dei cambi.' *Bolletino storico piacentino*, X, 1915.

BENNASSAR, B. 'En Vieille-Castille, les ventes de rentes perpétuelles. Première moitié du XVIe siècle.' *Annales: E., S., C.*, 1960.

Valladolid au siècle d'or. Une ville de Castille et sa campagne au XVIe siècle. Paris–The Hague, 1967.

BERGIER, J.-F. *Genève et l'économie européenne de la Renaissance*. Paris, 1963.

Zu den Anfängen des Kapitalismus: das Beispiel Genf. (Kölner Vorträge zur Sozial- und Wirtschaftsgeschichte, XX.) Cologne, 1972.

'La dynamique de la banque privée.' *Quarta Settimana di Studio: Credito, Banche e Investimenti, Secoli XIII–XX. Prato, 14–21 Aprile 1972*. Xerox copy.

BIGWOOD, G. *Le régime juridique et économique du commerce de l'argent dans la Belgique du Moyen Age*. (Académie royale de Belgique, Classe des lettres et sciences morales et politiques. Mémoires, 2nd Ser., XIV.) 2 vols. Brussels, 1921–2.

BISSCHOP, W. R. *The Rise of the London Money Market, 1640–1826*. (3rd ed.) London, 1968.

De opkomst der Londensche geldmarkt, 1640–1826. The Hague, 1896.

BLOCH, M. 'Le problème de l'or au Moyen Age.' *Annales d'histoire économique et sociale*, 1933.

'Les mutations monétaires.' *Annales: E., S., C.*, 1953.

Esquisse d'une histoire monétaire de l'Europe. Paris, 1954.

BOGUCKA, M. 'Les dernières recherches sur l'histoire de la Baltique.' *Acta Poloniae Historica*, VII, 1962.

Handel zagraniczny Gdańska w pierwszej Polowie XVII wieku. Wrocław–Warsaw–Cracow, 1970.

'L'emploi des lettres de change et le développement du crédit à Gdansk, au cours de la première moitié du XVIIe siècle' (in Polish). *Roczniki Dziejów Spolecznych I Gospodarczych*, XXXIII, 1972.

'Amsterdam and the Baltic in the First Half of the Seventeenth Century.' *Economic History Review*, 2nd Ser., XXVI, 1973.

BONZON, A. 'La Banque à Lyon aux XVI, XVII et XVIIIe siècles.' *Revue d'histoire de Lyon*, I–II, 1902–3.

BOREL, F. *Les foires de Genève au XVe siècle.* Geneva–Paris, 1892.

BOSHER, J. F. *French Finances, 1770–1795. From Businesses to Bureaucracy.* Cambridge, 1970.

BOUVIER, J. and GERMAIN-MARTIN, H. *Finances et financiers de l'Ancien Régime. (Que sais-je?)* 2nd ed., Paris, 1969.

BRAAMCAMP FREIRE, A. *Noticias da Feitoria de Flandres* (Arquivo Historico Português). Lisbon, 1920.

BRAUDEL, F. *La Méditerranée et le monde méditerranéen à l'époque de Philippe II.* Paris, 1949.

'En relisant Earl J. Hamilton. De l'Histoire d'Espagne à l'Histoire des prix.' *Annales d'histoire sociale*, 1951.

'Le pacte de ricorsa au service du roi d'Espagne et de ses prêteurs à la fin du XVIe siècle.' *Studi in onore di Armando Sapori*, II. Milan, 1957.

and LABROUSSE, E. *Histoire économique et sociale de la France.* II. *1660–1789.* Paris, 1970.

and ROMANO, R. *Navires et marchandises à l'entrée du port de Livourne (1547–1611).* Paris, 1951.

and SPOONER, F. 'Prices in Europe from 1450 to 1750.' *The Cambridge Economic History of Europe.* IV. *The Economy of expanding Europe in the sixteenth and seventeenth centuries.* Ed. by E. E. Rich and C. H. Wilson. Cambridge, 1967.

and SILVA, JOSÉ GENTIL DA. 'Réalités économiques et prises de conscience: quelques témoignages sur le XVIe siècle.' *Annales: E, S., C.,* 1959.

and JEANNIN, P., MEUVRET, J., ROMANO, R. 'Le déclin de Venise au XVIIe siècle. Aspetti e cause della decadenza economica veneziana nel secolo XVII.' *Civiltà veneziana. Studi,* 9. Venice–Rome, n.d.

BRESARD, M. *Les foires de Lyon au XVe et XVIe siècles.* Paris, 1914.

BRIDREY, E. *La théorie de la monnaie au XIVe siècle. Nicole Oresme, étude d'histoire des doctrines et des faits économiques.* Paris, 1906.

BRISMAN, S. 'Den Palmstruchska Banken (1657–1668).' *Sveriges Riksbank, 1668–1918,* edited by C. Hallendorff, I. Stockholm, 1918.

BRULEZ, W. 'Les difficultés financières de la ville de Saint-Omer dans le troisième quart du XVIe siècle.' *Revue du Nord,* 1952.

'De wisselkoersen te Antwerpen in het laatste kwart van de 16e eeuw.' *Bijdragen voor de Geschiedenis der Nederlanden,* XI, 1956.

De Firma Della Faille en de internationale handel van Vlaamse firma's in de 16e eeuw. (Koninklijke Vlaamse Academie. Klasse der Letteren. Verhandelingen, no. 35.) Brussels, 1959.

'The Balance of Trade of the Netherlands.' *Acta Historiae Neerlandica,* IV, Leyden, 1970.

BUCKLEY, H. 'Sir Thomas Gresham and the Foreign Exchanges.' *The Economic Journal,* XXXIV, 1924.

BUIST, M. G. *At Spes Non Fracta: Hope & Co., 1770–1817, Merchant Bankers and Diplomats at Work.* The Hague, Nijhoff, 1974, VIII, 716f.

BUYTEN, L. VAN. 'Politieke en administratief-technische aspecten van het stedelijk financiewezen in de Zuidelijke Nederlanden tijdens de XVIIe en XVIIIe eeuw.' *Handelingen van het 41ste Congres van de federatie van de Kringen voor Oudheidkunde en Geschiedenis van België, Mechelen, 3–6 november 1970.* Vol. II. Malines, 1971.

CAHN, J. 'Der Strassburger Stadtwechsel. Ein Beitrag zur Geschichte der ältesten Banken in Deutschland.' *Zeitschrift für die Geschichte des Oberrheins,* XIV, 1899.

CAILLET, L. *Note sur le mode de paiement des tailles royales à Lyon et la circulation des monnaies étrangères dans cette ville sous Charles VII et Louis XI.* Châlon-sur-Saône, 1908.

Etude sur les relations de la commune de Lyon avec Charles VII et Louis XI (1417–1483). Lyons–Paris, 1909.

'Lyon et les Lucquois.' *Revue d'histoire de Lyon*, VIII, 1909.

CAIMATI, R. 'L'attività bancaria a Siena nel seicento attraverso la ricostruzione e l'analisi statistica di cento bilanci del Monte dei Paschi di Siena.' *Archivi Storici delle Aziende di Credito*, I. Rome, 1956.

CALDERON QUIJANO, J. A. *El Banco de San Carlos y las comunidades de Indios de Nueva España*. Madrid, 1963.

CARANDE, R. *Carlos V y sus banqueros*. 2 vols. Madrid, 1941–9.

El credito de Castilla en el precio de la politica imperial. Madrid, 1949.

'Das Westindische Gold und die Kreditpolitik Karls V.' *Spanische Forschungen des Görresgesellschaft*, I, 10. Münster (Westphalia), 1955.

CARRERA, PUJAL, J. *Historia de la economia española*. 5 vols. Barcelona, 1943–7.

CARRIÈRE, C. *Négociants Marseillais au XVIIIe siècle. Contribution à l'étude des économies maritimes*. 2 vols. Marseilles, 1973.

CASTELOT, E. 'Les bourses financières d'Anvers et de Lyon au XVIe siècle.' *Journal des Economistes*, XXXII, 1898.

CASTILLO, A. 'Dans la Monarchie Espagnole du XVIIe siècle: les banquiers Portugais et le circuit d'Amsterdam.' *Annales: E., S., C.*, XIX, 1964.

'Population et "richesse" en Castille durant la seconde moitié du XVIe siècle.' *Annales: E., S., C.*, XX, 1965.

CAUWÈS, P. 'Les commencements du crédit public en France; les rentes sur l'Hôtel de Ville au XVIe siècle.' *Revue d'économie politique*, IX–X, 1895–6.

CHABOD, F. *Note e documenti per la storia economica – finanziaria dell'Impero di Carlo V*. Padua, 1937.

CHAMBERLAND, A. 'Le budget de l'Epargne en 1607 d'après des documents inédits.' *Revue Henri IV*, II: 5, 1908.

CHANDLER, G. *Four centuries of Banking as illustrated by the Bankers, Customers and Staff associated with the constituent Banks of Martins Bank Limited*. I. *The Grasshopper and the Liver Bird. Liverpool and London*. London, 1964.

Charles Quint et son temps. (Colloques internationaux du Centre National de la Recherche scientifique. Sciences humaines, Paris 30 septembre – 3 octobre 1958.) Paris, 1959.

CHARLETY, S. 'Le voyage de Louis XIII à Lyon en 1622. Etude sur les relations de Lyon et du pouvoir central au début du XVIIe siècle (1592–1622).' *Revue d'histoire moderne et contemporaine*, II, 1900–1.

Histoire de Lyon. Depuis les origines jusqu'à nos jours. Lyons, 1903.

CHARPIN-FEUGEROLLES, COMTE DE. *Les Florentins à Lyon*. Lyons, 1889.

CHAUDHURI, K. N. 'The East India Company and the Export of Treasure in the early Seventeenth Century.' *Economic History Review*, 2nd Ser., XVI, 1963.

CHAUNU, P. 'Séville et la "Belgique", 1555–1648.' *Revue du Nord*, XXXXII, 1960.

CIPOLLA, C. M. *Studi di Storia della moneta*. I. *I movimenti dei cambi in Italia dal secolo XIII al XV*. (Pubblicazioni della Università di Pavia. Studi nelle Scienze Giuridiche e Soziale, no. 101.) Pavia, 1948.

'Note sulla storia del saggio d'interesse. Corso, dividendi e sconto dei divendi del banco di S. Giorgio nel sec. XVI.' *Economia internazionale*, V, 1952.

Mouvements monétaires dans l'état de Milan (1850–1700). Paris, 1952.

Money, Prices and Civilization in the Mediterranean World (Fifth to Seventeenth Centuries). Princeton, 1956.

Le avventure della lira. Milan, 1958.

'Aspetti e problemi nell'economia milanese e lombarda nei secoli XVI, XVII.' *Storia di Milano*, XI. *Il declino spagnolo, 1630–1706*. Milan, 1958.

CLAPHAM, J. *The Bank of England. A History. 1694–1914*. 2 vols. Cambridge, 1944.

CLARK, G. N. *The Seventeenth Century*. 2nd ed., Oxford, 1960.

CLERJON, P. *Histoire de Lyon depuis sa fondation jusqu'à nos jours*. 7 vols. Lyons, 1829–45.

COLE, C. W. *Colbert and a Century of French Mercantilism*. 2 vols. New York, 1939.

COORNAERT, E. 'La genèse du système capitaliste: grand capitalisme et économie traditionnelle à Anvers au XVIe siècle.' *Annales d'histoire économique et sociale*, VIII, 1936.

'Caractères et mouvements des foires internationales au Moyen-Âge et au XVIe siècle.' *Studi in onore di Armando Sapori*, I. Milan, 1957.

Les Français et le commerce international à Anvers (fin XVe et XVIe siècles). 2 vols. Paris, 1961.

COUDY, J. 'La "Tontine Royale" sous le règne de Louis XIV.' *Revue historique de droit français et étranger*, XXI, 1957.

COURTOIS, A. *Histoire des banques en France*, 2nd ed., Paris, 1881.

COZZI, G. *Il doge Nicolò Contarini. Ricerche sul patriziato veneziano agli inizi del seicento.* Venice–Rome, 1958.

CRAEYBECKX, J. 'Aperçu sur l'histoire des impôts en Flandre et au Brabant au cours du XVIe siècle.' *Nord*, XXIX, 1947.

'La portée fiscale et politique du 100e denier du duc d'Albe.' *Recherches sur l'histoire des finances publiques en Belgique*, I. Brussels, 1967.

CUNEO, C. *Memorie sopra l'antico debito publico. Mutui, Compere e banca di S. Giorgio in Genova.* Genoa, 1842.

CUSUMANO, V. *Storia dei Banchi della Sicilia.* I. *Banchi privati.* Rome, 1887.

DAHLGREN, W. *Louis de Geer, hans Lif och Verk.* 2 vols. Uppsala, 1923.

DAIRE, E. *Economistes français du siècle.* Paris, 1843.

DAVIS, R. *The Rise of the Atlantic Economies.* (World Economic History. General Editor, C. Wilson.) London, 1973.

DELUMEAU, J. 'Le problème des dettes à Rome au XVIe siècle.' *Revue d'histoire moderne et contemporaine*, IV, 1957.

Vie économique et sociale de Rome, dans la seconde moitié du XVIe siècle. 2 vols. Paris, 1959.

L'alun de Rome. XVe–XIXe siècle. Paris, 1962.

DEMARCO, D. 'Quelques moments de l'histoire des banques publiques napolitaines des origines à 1808.' *Third International Conference of Economic History, Munich 1965: Proceedings.* Paris–The Hague, 1974.

DENUCÉ, J. 'De Beurs van Antwerpen. Oorsprong en eerste ontwikkeling.' *Antwerpsch Archievenblad*, 2nd Ser., VI, 1931.

Italiaansche koopmansgeslachten te Antwerpen in de XVIe–XVIIIe eeuwen. Malines–Amsterdam, 1934.

De Hanze en de Antwerpsche handelscompagnieën op de Oostzee-landen. Antwerp, 1938.

DESPY, G., *et al. Recherches sur l'histoire des finances publiques en Belgique.* (Acta Historica Bruxellensia: travaux de l'Institut d'Histoire de l'Université libre de Bruxelles, II.) Brussels, 1970.

DEYON, P. *Le mercantilisme.* Paris, 1969.

DICKSON, P. G. M. *The Financial Revolution in England. A Study in the Development of Public Credit, 1688–1756.* London–New York, 1967.

DIETZ, A. *Frankfurter Handelsgeschichte.* 4 vols. Frankfurt, 1910–21.

DIETZ, F. C. 'The Receipts and Issues of the Exchequer during the Reign of James I and Charles I.' *Smith College Studies in History*, XIII: 4. Northampton, 1928.

English Public Finance, 1485–1641, 2 vols. 2nd ed., London, 1964.

DILIS, É. 'Les courtiers anversois.' *Annales de l'Académie royale d'archéologie de Belgique*, 6th ser., 1910.

DILLEN, J. G. VAN. 'Een boek van Phoonsen over de Amsterdamsche Wisselbank.' *Economisch-Historisch Jaarboek*, VII. The Hague, 1921.

'Amsterdam als wereldmarkt der edele metalen in de 17e en 18e eeuw.' *De Economist*, II, 1923.

'Amsterdam marché monétaire des métaux précieux au XVIIe et XVIIIe siècles.' *Revue historique*, CLII, 1926.

'La Banque d'Amsterdam.' *Revue d'histoire moderne*, XV, 1928.

'De Girobanken van Genua, Venetië en Hamburg.' *Tijdschrift voor Geschiedenis*, XLII, 1927.

(ed.). *History of the Principal Public Banks, accompanied by Extensive Bibliographies of the History of Banking and Credit in eleven European Countries.* (Contribution to the history of banking.) The Hague, 1934.

'De opstand en het Amerikaanse zilver.' *Tijdschrift voor Geschiedenis*, LXXIII, 1960.

Mensen en achtergronden. Studies uitgegeven ter gelegenheid van de tachtigste verjaardag van de schrijver. (Historische Studies uitgegeven vanwege het instituut voor geschiedenis der rijksuniversiteit te Utrecht, no. 19.) Groningen, 1964.

Van Rijkdom en Regenten. Handboek tot de Economische en ·Sociale Geschiedenis van Nederland tijdens de Republiek. The Hague, 1970.

DOMINGUEZ ORTIZ, A. *Politica y hacienda de Felipe IV.* Madrid, 1960.

DONNET, F. *Coup d'oeil sur l'histoire financière d'Anvers au cours des siècles.* Antwerp, 1927.

DOUCET, R. 'Les finances de la France en 1614.' *Revue d'histoire économique et sociale*, XVIII: 2, 1930.

'Le "Grand Parti" de Lyon au XVIe siècle.' *Revue historique*, CLXXI, CLXXII, 1933–4.

Finances municipales et crédit public à Lyon au XVIe siècle. Paris, 1937.

'La Banque en France au XVIe siècle.' *Revue d'histoire économique et sociale*, XXIX: II, 1951.

DUBY, G. *L'économie rurale et la vie des campagnes dans l'Occident médiéval (France, Angleterre, Empire, IXe–XVe siècles). Essai de synthèse et perspectives de recherches.* 2 vols. Paris, 1962.

EHRENBERG, R. *Hamburg und England im Zeitalter der Königin Elisabeth.* Jena, 1896.

Das Zeitalter der Fugger. Geldkapital und Kreditverkehr im 16. Jahrhundert. 2 vols. 2nd ed.. Hildesheim, 1963.

EINAUDI, L. 'Teoria della moneta immaginaria nel tempo di Carlomagno alla rivoluzione francese.' *Rivista di storia economica*, I: I, 1936.

EMMANUELLI, R. *Gênes et l'Espagne dans la guerre de Corse, 1559–1569.* Paris, 1964.

ENDEMANN, W. *Studien in der romanisch-kantonistischen Wirtschafts- und Rechtslehre bis gegen Ende des siebzehnten Jahrhunderts.* 2 vols. Berlin, 1874–83.

ENNO VAN GELDER, H. *Munthervorming tijdens de Republiek, 1659–1694.* Amsterdam, 1949.

ESPEJO, C. and PAZ, J. *Las antiquas ferias de Medina del Campo.* Valladolid, 1908.

ESPINAS, G. *Les finances de la commune de Douai des origines au XVe siècle.* Paris, 1902.

EVERAERT, J. *De internationale en koloniale handel der Vlaamse firma's te Cadiz, 1670–1700.* Bruges, 1973.

FAVREAU, R. 'Les changeurs du royaume sous le règne de Louis XI.' *Bibliothèque de l'Ecole des Chartes*, CXXII, 1964.

FEAVEARYEAR, A. *The Pound Sterling. A History of English Money.* (2nd ed., rev. by E. Victor Morgan.) Oxford, 1963.

FELLONI, G. *Gli investimenti finanziari genovesi in Europa tra il Seicento e la Restaurazione.* Milan, 1971.

FILANGIERI, R. *I banchi di Napoli dalle origini alla costituzione del Banco delle Due Sicilie (1539–1808).* Naples, 1940.

FOURNIAL, É. 'Réalités monétaires et réalités économiques.' *Annales: E., S., C.*, 1958.

FOURQUIN, G. *Histoire économique de l'Occident médiéval.* Paris, 1969.

FRIEDMANN, E. *Der mittelalterliche Welthandel von Florenz in seiner geographischen Ausdehnung (nach der Pratica della Mercatura des Balducci Pegolotti).* Abhandlungen der K.K. geograph. Gesellschaft in Wien, X: 7, 1912.

FRIIS, A. 'An Inquiry into the Relations between Economic and Financial Factors in the Sixteenth and Seventeenth Centuries. I. The two Crises in the Netherlands in 1557.' *The Scandinavian Economic History Review*, I: 2, 1953.

FRIIS, A. and GLAMANN, K. *A History of Prices and Wages in Denmark (1660–1800).* I. London, New York, Toronto, 1958.

FUCHS, R. *Der Bancho Publico zu Nürnberg.* (Nürnberger Abhandlungen zu den Wirtschafts- und Sozialwissenschaften, no. 6.) Berlin, 1955.

GANDILHON, R. *Politique économique de Louis XI.* Rennes, 1940.

GASCON, R. F. 'Nationalisme économique et géographie des Foires. La querelle des Foires de Lyon (1484–1494).' *Cahiers d'histoire publiés par les universités de Clermont–Lyon–Grenoble*, III, 1956.

'Les Italiens dans la renaissance économique lyonnaise au XVIe siècle.' *Revue des études italiennes*, V, 1958.

'Quelques aspects du rôle des Italiens dans la crise des foires de Lyon du dernier tiers du XVIe siècle.' *Cahiers d'histoire*, V, 1960.

Grand commerce et vie urbaine au XVIe siècle: Lyon et ses marchands. 2 vols. Paris, 1971.

GASKIN, M. *The Scottish Banks. A Modern Survey.* London, 1965.

GENEVET, A. *Histoire de la Compagnie des Agents de change de Lyon depuis les origines jusqu'à l'établissement du Parquet en 1845.* Lyons, 1890.

GIESEKING, H. 'Das Bankwesen in Genua und die Bank von S. Giorgio.' *History of the principal Public Banks,* edited by J. G. van Dillen. The Hague, 1934.

GIOFFRE, D. *Gênes et les foires de change. De Lyon à Besançon.* Paris, 1960.

GIRARD, A. 'La guerre monétaire, XIVe–XVe siècles.' *Annales d'histoire sociale,* XX: III–IV, 1940.

GIRY, D. *A la recherche des traditions bancaires de l'Occident méditerranéen.* Montreal, 1965.

GLAMANN, K. *Dutch-Asiatic Trade, 1620–1740.* Copenhagen–The Hague, 1958.

'European Trade, 1500–1750.' *The Fontana Economic History of Europe,* II. London, 1974.

GODDING, P. *Le droit foncier à Bruxelles au Moyen-Age.* (Etudes d'histoire et d'ethnologie juridiques, no. 1.) Brussels, 1960.

GOLDSCHMIDT, L. *Universalgeschichte des Handelsrechts.* 3rd ed., Stuttgart, 1891.

GOMEL, C. *Les causes financières de la Révolution française.* 2 vols. Paris, 1892 and 1893.

GORIS, J. A. *Etude sur les colonies marchandes méridionales (Portugais, Espagnols, Italiens) à Anvers de 1477 à 1567. Contribution à l'histoire des débuts du capitalisme moderne.* Louvain, 1925.

GOUBERT, P. *Beauvais et la Beauvaisis de 1600 à 1730. Contribution à l'histoire sociale de la France au XVIIe siècle.* Paris, 1960.

GREPPI, E. 'Il Banco di S. Ambrogio.' *Archivio storico lombardo,* X, 1883.

GRICE-HUTCHINSON, M. *The School of Salamanca. Readings in Spanish Monetary Theory, 1544–1605.* Oxford, 1952.

GROOTE, H. L. V. DE. 'Zestiende-eeuwse Antwerpse boekhoudingen en cijfermeesters.' *Scientiarum Historia,* II–III, 1960–1.

'De "arithmétique" van Mellema.' *Scientiarum Historia,* V, 1963.

'De Zestiende-eeuwse Antwerpse schoolmeesters.' *Bijdragen tot de Geschiedenis inzonderheid van het oud Hertogdom Brabant (Antwerpen),* 3rd ser., XIX–XX, 1967–8.

'De zestiende-eeuwse Nederlandse drukken over boekhouden en handelsrekenen hoofdzakelijk in betrekking met Antwerpen.' *De Gulden Passer,* XXXXIX, 1971.

GROSSMANN, J. *Die Amsterdamer Börse vor zweihundert Jahren (1672–1673). Nach den Akten des Wiener Staats-Archiven.* The Hague, 1876.

GUILLON, A. *Essai historique sur la législation française des faillites et banqueroutes avant 1673.* Paris, 1903.

HAEBLER, K. 'Die Finanzdekrete Philip's II und die Fugger.' *Deutsche Zeitschrift für Geschichtswissenschaft,* XI, 1894.

HAMILTON, E. J. 'American Treasure and the Rise of Capitalism (1500–1700).' *Economica,* Nov. 1929.

American Treasure and the Price Revolution in Spain, 1501–1650. Cambridge, Mass., 1934.

War and Prices in Spain, 1651–1800. Cambridge, Mass., 1947.

'Origin and Growth of the National Debt in Western Europe.' *The American Economic Review,* XXXVII, 1947.

'Plans for a National Bank in Spain, 1701–1783.' *The Journal of Political Economy,* LVII, 1949.

'Spanish Banking Schemes before 1700.' *The Journal of Political Economy,* LVII, 1949.

HANAUER, ABBÉ A.-C. *Etudes économiques sur l'Alsace ancienne et moderne.* 2 vols. Paris, 1876–8.

HANKE, L. 'El otro tesoro de las Indias durante la época de Carlos V.' *Revista del Instituto de Historia del Derecho,* 1959.

HARSIN, P. *Les doctrines monétaires et financières en France du XVIe au XVIIIe siècle.* Paris, 1928.

Crédit public et Banque d'Etat en France du XVIe au XVIIIe siècles. Paris, 1933.

'La Banque et le système de Law.' *History of the Principal Public Banks, accompanied by Extensive Bibliographies of the History of Banking and Credit in eleven European Countries,* collected by J. G. van Dillen. The Hague, 1934.

'La Finance et l'Etat jusqu'au système de Law.' *Histoire économique et sociale de la France.* II. *1660–1789.* Edited by E. Labrousse *et al.* Paris, 1970.

Recueil d'études. Liège, 1970.

HARSIN, P., *et al. Finances publiques de l'Ancien Régime. Finances publiques contemporains. Processus de mutation, continuités et ruptures.* (Colloque international de Spa, 16–19 septembre 1971: Actes.) Brussels, 1972.

HAUSER, H. 'Reflexions sur l'histoire des banques à l'époque moderne de la fin du XVe siècle à la fin du XVIIIe siècle.' *Annales d'histoire économique et sociale,* I, 1929.

'The European Financial Crisis of 1557.' *Journal of Economic and Business History,* 1929–30.

La modernité du XVIe siècle. Paris, 1930.

Les débuts du capitalisme. New ed., Paris, 1931.

'La crise de 1557–1559 et le bouleversement des fortunes.' *Mélanges Abel Lefranc.* Paris, 1936.

and RENAUDET, A. *Les débuts de l'age moderne.* 4th ed., Paris, 1956.

HECKSCHER, E. F. 'Natural and Money Economy as illustrated from Swedish History in the Sixteenth Century.' *Journal of Economic and Business History,* 1931.

'The Bank of Sweden in its Connection with the Bank of Amsterdam.' *History of the Principal Public Banks,* edited by J. G. van Dillen. The Hague, 1934.

Sveriges Ekonomiska Historia. Stockholm, 1935.

An Economic History of Sweden. Cambridge, Mass., 1954.

HEERS, J. *Gênes au XVe siècle. Activité économique et problèmes sociaux.* Paris, 1961.

HILL, C. *Puritanism and Revolution. Studies in Interpretation of the English Revolution of the 17th Century.* London, 1962.

HINTON, R. W. K. 'The Mercantile System in the Time of Thomas Mun.' *Economic History Review,* 2nd ser., VII: 3, 1955.

The Eastland Trade and the Common Weal in the Seventeenth Century. Cambridge, 1959.

HOBSBAWM, E. 'The Crisis of the 17th Century.' *Past and Present,* 1954.

HOLDEN, J. M. *The History of Negotiable Instruments in English Law.* London, 1955.

HOMER, S. *A History of Interest Rates.* New Brunswick, New Jersey, 1963.

HORSEFIELD, J. K. 'The cash ratio in English Banks before 1800.' *The Journal of Political Economy,* LVII, 1949.

British Monetary Experiments, 1650–1710. London, 1960.

HOUTTE, J. A. VAN. 'Anvers aux XVe et XVIe siècles. Expansion et apogée.' *Annales: E., S., C.,* XVI, 1961.

'Declin et survivance d'Anvers (1550–1700).' *Studi in onore di Amintore Fanfani,* v. Milan, 1962.

IMBERT, G. *Des mouvements de longue durée Kondratieff.* Aix-en-Provence, 1959.

ISAAC, J. 'Le Cardinal de Tournon lieutenant général du Roi.' *Revue d'Histoire de Lyon,* XII, 1913.

JACQUETON, G. 'Le trésor de l'Epargne sous François Ier (1523–1547).' *Revue historique,* LV–LVI, 1894.

JANNET, C. *Le crédit populaire et les banques en Italie du XVe au XVIIIe siècle.* Paris, 1885.

JANSSENS, V. 'Het ontstaan van de dubbele koers courant geld-wisselgeld in het geldwezen der Zuidelijke Nederlanden.' *Bijdragen voor de Geschiedenis der Nederlanden,* IX, 1954.

Het geldwezen der Oostenrijkse Nederlanden. (Koninklijke Vlaamse Academie, Klasse der Letteren, no. 29.) Brussels, 1957.

JASSEMIN, H. 'La Chambre des comptes et la gestion des deniers publics au XVe siècle.' *Bibliothèque de l'Ecole des Chartes,* LXXXXIII, 1932.

JEANNIN, P. 'Anvers et la Baltique au XVIe siècle.' *Revue du Nord,* XXXVII, 1955.

'Les relations économiques des villes de la Baltique avec Anvers au XVIe siècle.' *Vierteljahrschrift für Sozial- und Wirtschaftsgeschichte,* XXXXIII, 1956.

Les Marchands au XVIe siècle. Paris, 1957.

L'Europe du Nord-Ouest et du Nord aux XVIIe et XVIIIe siècles. Paris, 1969.

JENNINGS, R. M. and TROUT, A. P. 'Internal Control: Public Finance in 17th Century France.' *The Journal of European Economic History,* I, 1972.

JOSLIN, D. M. 'London Private Bankers, 1720–1785.' *Economic History Review,* 2nd ser., VII, 1954–5.

KELLENBENZ, H. 'Les foires de Lyon dans la politique de Charles V.' *Cahiers d'histoire,* v, 1960.

Die Fuggersche Maestrazgpacht, 1525–1542. Tübingen, 1967.

KERNKAMP, J. H. *De handel op den Vijand 1572–1609.* 2 vols. Utrecht–The Hague, 1931 and 1934.

KERR, A. W. *History of Banking in Scotland.* 3rd ed., London, 1918.

KLEIN, P. W. *De Trippen in de 17e eeuw. Een studie over het ondernemersgedrag op de Hollandse stapelmarkt.* Assen, 1965.

Kapitaal en stagnatie tijdens het Hollandse Vroegkapitalisme. Rotterdam, 1967.

'Entrepreneurial Behaviour and the Economic Rise and Decline of the Netherlands in the 17th and 18th Centuries.' *Annales Cisalpines d'Histoire Sociale,* I, 1970.

KLEINCLAUSZ, A. *Histoire de Lyon.* 3 vols. Lyons, 1939–48.

KOENIGSBERGER, H. G. and MOSSE, G. L. *Europe in the Sixteenth Century.* London, 1971.

KOPF, W. *Beiträge zur Geschichte der Messen von Lyon, mit besonderer Berücksichtigung des Anteils der oberdeutschen Städte im 16. Jahrhundert.* Ulm, 1910.

LABROUSSE, E. 'Recherche sur l'histoire des prix en France de 1500 à 1800.' *Revue d'économie politique,* 1939.

LAFAURIE, J. 'Les "Billets de Monoye" et les "Billets de l'Estat", 1701–1716. Essai de catalogues des "Billets de Monoye". Les "Billets de l'Estat".' *Bulletin de la société d'étude pour l'histoire du papier-monnaie,* V, 1950.

'Les billets des Banques de Law. I. La Banque Générale (1716–1718); II. La Banque Royale (1719–1720).' *Bulletin de la société d'étude pour l'histoire du papier-monnaie,* VII, 1952.

LANDES, D. G. 'Vieille Banque et Banque nouvelle: la révolution financière du XIXe siècle.' *Revue d'histoire moderne et contemporaine,* III, 1956.

LANDRY, A. *Essai économique sur les mutations des monnaies dans l'ancienne France de Philippe le Bel à Charles VII.* (Bibliothèque de l'école des hautes études: sciences historiques et philologiques, no. 185.) Paris, 1910.

LAPERCHE, A. *Essai sur le prêt à intérêt au XVIe siècle.* Rennes, 1902.

LAPEYRE, H. 'Las origines del Endoso de letras de cambio en España.' *Moneda y Credito: Revista de Economica,* LII, 1955.

Simon Ruiz et les asientos de Philippe II. Paris, 1953.

Une Famille de marchands: les Ruiz. Paris, 1955.

'La banque, les changes et le crédit au XVIe siècle.' *Revue d'histoire moderne et contemporaine,* III, 1956.

'Une lettre de change endossée en 1430.' *Annales: E., S., C.,* 1958.

'Banque et crédit en Italie du XVIe siècle au XVIIIe siècle.' *Revue d'histoire moderne et contemporaine,* VIII, 1961.

'Alphonse V et ses banquiers.' *Le Moyen Age,* 1961.

LATTES, A. *Il diritto commerciale nella legislazione statutaria delle città italiane.* Milan, 1884.

'Genova nella storia del diritto cambiario italiano.' *Rivista di diritto commerciale,* I, 1915.

LATTES, E. *La libertà delle banche à Venezia dal secolo XIII al XVII.* Milan, 1869.

LAURENT, H. *La loi de Gresham au Moyen Age. Essai sur la circulation monétaire entre la Flandre et le Brabant à la fin du XIVe siècle.* Paris, 1933.

LAWSON, W. J. *The History of Banking, with a comprehensive Account of the Origin, Rise and Progress of the Banks of England, Ireland and Scotland.* London, 1850.

LEGIER, H. J. 'L'Eglise et l'économie médiévale. Un exemple: la monnaie ecclésiastique de Lyon et ses vicissitudes.' *Annales: E., S., C.,* 1957.

'Réalités monétaires, réalités économiques, réalités historiques.' *Annales: E., S., C.,* 1959.

LEJEUNE, J. *La formation du capitalisme moderne dans la principauté de Liège au XVIe siècle.* (Bibliothèque de la Faculté de Philosophie et Lettres de l'Université de Liège, LXXXVII.) Paris, 1939.

LESAGE, G. L. 'La circulation monétaire en France dans la seconde moitié du XVe siècle.' *Annales: E., S., C.,* III, 1948.

LESCURE, J. 'Esquisse de l'évolution du change et des théories relatives au change.' *Revue d'histoire économique et sociale,* 1910.

LEVASSEUR, E. 'Foires et marchés en France pendant la royauté féodale (XIIIe, XIVe et XVe siècles).' *Revue d'histoire économique et sociale,* 1910.

LEVY-BRUHL, H. *Histoire de la lettre de change en France aux XVIIe et XVIIIe siècles.* Paris, 1933.

Lièvre, L. *La Monnaie et les changes en Bourgogne sous les ducs Valois.* Dijon, 1929.

Lodolini, A. 'I Monti camerali nel sistema della finanza pontificia.' *Archivi storici delle aziende di credito,* I. Rome, 1956.

Lonchay, H. 'Recherches sur l'origine et la valeur des Ducats et des Ecus espagnols.' *Bulletin de l'Académie Royale de Belgique, Classe des Lettres,* no. 11, 1906.
'Etude sur les emprunts des souverains belges aux XVIe et XVIIe siècles.' *Bulletin de l'Académie Royale de Belgique. Classe des Lettres,* 1907.

Longé, G. de (ed.). *Coutumes du Pays et Duché de Brabant. Quartier d'Anvers.* Vol. IV: *Coutumes de la ville d'Anvers.* Brussels, 1874.

Lopez, R. S. and Miskimin, H. A. 'The Economic Depression of the Renaissance.' *Economic History Review,* 2nd ser., XIV–XV, 1962–3.

Lopez Yepes, J. *Historia de los Montes de Piedad en España. El Monte de Piedad de Madrid en el siglo XVIII.* 2 vols. Madrid, 1971.

Lüthy, H. *La Banque Protestante en France de la Révocation de l'Edit de Nantes à la Révolution.* 2 vols. Paris, 1959–61.

Luzzato, G. 'Les banques publiques de Venise. Siècles XVI–XVIII.' *Studi di storia economica veneziana.* Padua, 1954.
'L'oro e l'argento nella politica monetaria veneziana dei sec. XIII–XV.' *Studi di storia economica veneziana.* Padua, 1954.
An Economic History of Italy from the Fall of the Roman Empire to the Beginning of the Sixteenth Century. London, 1961.

Maddalena, A. de. *Prezzi e aspetti di mercato a Milano durante il seculo XVII.* Milan, 1949.
'Les hommes d'affaires lombards sur les foires de Bisenzone 1579–1619.' *Annales: E., S., C.,* 1967.

Magelhães-Godinho, V. *L'économie de l'empire portugais aux XVe et XVIe siècles.* Paris, 1969.

Malowist, M. 'Les mouvements d'expansion en Europe aux XVe et XVIe siècles.' *Annales: E., S., C.,* 1962.

Mandich, G. 'Delle fiere genovesi di cambi particolarmente studiate come mercati periodici del credito.' *Rivista di storia economica,* IV, 1939.
'Di una tentata speculazione cambiaria in Venezia nel 1636.' *Rivista di storia economica,* VII, 1942.
Le Pacte de Ricorsa et le marché italien des changes au XVIIe siècle. Paris, 1953.

Mandrou, R. *Introduction à la France moderne. Essai de psychologie historique.* Paris, 1961.
La France aux XVIIe et XVIIIe siècles. Paris, 1967.

Maréchal, J. 'Bruges, centre du commerce de l'argent aux derniers siècles du Moyen Age.' *La Revue de la Banque,* 1950.
'Le départ de Bruges des marchands étrangers (XVe et XVIe siècles).' *Annales de la Société d'émulation de Bruges,* LXXXVIII, 1951.

Marengo, E., Manfroni, C. and Pessagno, G. *Il Banco di San Giorgio.* Genoa, 1911.

Marion, M. *Histoire financière de la France depuis 1715.* I. *1715–1785.* Paris, 1914.

Marques, A. H. de Oliveira. 'Notas para a história da feitoria portuguesa na Flandres, no seculo XV.' *Studi in onore di Amintore Fanfani,* II. Milan, 1962.

Martin, G. 'La monnaie et le crédit privé en France aux XVIe et XVIIe siècles; les faits et les théories (1550–1664).' *Revue d'histoire des doctrines économiques,* II, 1909.
L'histoire du crédit en France sous le règne de Louis XIV. I. *Le Crédit public.* Paris, 1913.

Mateu y Llopis, F. *La moneda española.* (Breve historia monetaria de España.) Barcelona, 1946.

Matthews, G. T. *The Royal General Farms in Eighteenth Century France.* New York, 1958.

Mauro, F. *Le Portugal et l'Atlantique au XVIIe siècle, 1570–1670. Etude économique.* Paris, 1960.
'Marchands et marchands-banquiers portugais au XVIIe siècle.' *Revista portuegesa de historia,* IX, 1961.
Le XVIe siècle européen: aspects économiques. Paris, 1970.

Mees, W. C. *Proeve eener Geschiedenis van het Bankwezen in Nederland gedurende den tijd der Republiek.* Rotterdam, 1838.

MELIS, F. 'Di alcune girate cambiarie dell' inizio del cinquecento rinvenute a Firenze.' *Moneta e credito. Rivista trimestriel della Banca Nazionale del Lavoro*, 1953.

Aspetti della vita economica medievale (Studi nell'archivio Datini di Prato). 1. Siena, 1962.

'Motivi di storia bancaria senese: dai banchieri privati alla banca publica.' *Note Economiche*, nos. 5–6, 1972.

MERTENS, J. E. *La naissance et le développement de l'étalon-or, 1696–1922. Les faits et les théories. Essai de synthèse économique et sociologique*. Paris, 1944.

MERTENS, L. *Les Changes et les fonds publics à Anvers depuis le XVIe siècle jusqu'à 1792*. Antwerp, 1894.

MEUVRET, J. 'Circulation monétaire et utilisation économique de la monnaie dans la France du XVIe et XVIIe siècles.' *Etudes d'histoire moderne et contemporaine*, I, 1947.

'Manuels et traités à l'usage des négociants aux premières époques de l'âge moderne.' *Revue d'histoire moderne et contemporaine*, V, 1953.

'Circuits d'échanges et travail rural dans la France du XVIIe siècle.' *Studi in onore di Armando Sapori*, II. Milan, 1957.

'Vers une économie historique; Monnaie et vie économique en France de 1493 à 1680.' *Annales: E., S., C.*, XV, 1960.

Etudes d'histoire économique. Recueil d'articles. Paris, 1971.

'Les Français et l'Argent.' *La France et les Français*, Paris, 1972.

MICHIELSEN, A. *De evolutie van de handelsorganisatie in België sedert het begin der 18e eeuw*. (Bibliotheek van de Handelshoogeschool. Instituut voor handels- en economische wetenschappen. Universiteit te Leuven.) Turnhout, 1938.

MICHIELSEN, L. 'Het kapitalisme te Antwerpen in de XVIIe en XVIIIe eeuw.' *Nederlandsche Historiebladen*, 1939.

MISKIMIN, H. A. 'Le problème de l'argent au Moyen-Age.' *Annales: E., S., C.*, 1962.

MOLLAT, M. 'Recherches sur les finances des Ducs Valois de Bourgogne.' *Revue historique*, CCXIX, 1958.

MORINEAU, M. 'D'Amsterdam à Séville.' *Annales: E., S., C.*, XXIII, 1968.

MOUSNIER, R. *La Vénalité des offices en France sous Henry IV et Louis XIII*. Rouen, 1945.

'L'évolution des finances publiques en France et en Angleterre pendant les guerres de la Ligue d'Augsbourg et de la Succession d'Espagne.' *Revue historique*, 1950.

NATALIS DE WAILLY. *Mémoire sur les variations de la livre tournois depuis le règne de Saint-Louis jusqu'à l'établissement de la monnaie décimale*. Paris, 1857.

NIELSEN, A. *Dänische Wirtschaftsgeschichte*. Jena, 1933.

NORDMANN, C. J. *La Crise du Nord au début du XVIIIe siècle*. Paris, 1962.

'Monnaies et finances suédoises au XVIIe siècle.' *Revue du nord*, CLXXXIII, 1964.

OLDEWELT, W. F. H. 'Twee eeuwen Amsterdamse faillissementen en het verloop van de conjunctuur, 1638 tot 1838.' *Tijdschrift voor Geschiedenis*, LXXV: 4, 1962.

OUTHWAITHE, R. B. 'The Trials of Foreign Borrowing. The English Crown and the Antwerp Money Market in the mid-XVIth Century.' *Economic History Review*, 2nd ser., XIX, 1966.

PAMPALONI, G. 'Cenni storici sul monte di Pietà di Firenze.' *Archivi storici delle aziende di credito*, I, Rome, 1956.

PARKER, G. *The Army of Flanders and the Spanish Road, 1567–1659*. Cambridge, 1972.

'The Emergence of Modern Finance in Europe, 1500–1730.' *The Fontana Economic History of Europe*, II. London, 1974.

PERROY, E. 'A l'origine d'une économie contractée: les crises du XIVe siècle.' *Annales: E., S., C.*, 1949.

PIKE, R. *Enterprise and Adventure: The Genoese in Sevilla*. Ithaca (New York), 1966.

PIRENNE, H. 'L'Instruction des marchands au Moyen-Age.' *Annales d'histoire économique et sociale*, 1929.

Histoire économique et sociale du Moyen-Age. New edition, revised and completed by Hans van Werveke, Paris, 1969.

PLATBARZDTS, A. *Sveriges första Banksedlar (1661–1668)*. Stockholm, 1960.

POHL, H. *Die Portugiesen in Antwerpen, 1567–1648*. (Habilitationsschrift der Hohen Wirtschafts- und Sozialwissenschaftlichen Fakultät der Universität zu Köln.) Cologne, 1968.

'Die kastilischen Staatsfinanzen am Ende des 15. Jahrhunderts.' *Offentliche Finanzen und privates Kapital in Späten Mittelalter und in der ersten Hälfte des 19. Jahrhunderts.* (Forschungen zur Sozial- und Wirtschaftsgeschichte, XVI.) Stuttgart, 1971.

'Zur Bedeutung Antwerpens als Kredietplatz im beginnenden 17. Jahrhundert.' *Die Stadt in der Europäischen Geschichte. Festschrift Edith Ennen.* Bonn, 1972.

POLIAKOV, L. *Le Commerce de l'argent chez les Juifs d'Italie du XIIIe au XVIIe siècles.* Paris, 1965.

PÖLNITZ, G. VON. *Jakob Fugger. Kaiser, Kirche und Kapital in der Oberdeutschen Renaissance.* Tübingen, 1949.

Fugger und Hanse. Ein hundertjähriges Ringen um Ostsee und Nordsee. Tübingen, 1953.

Anton Fugger. I. 1493–1535. Tübingen, 1958.

PONTI, E. *Il Banco di Santo Spirito fondato da S.S. Paolo V con breve del 13 décembre 1605.* Rome, 1941.

POSTAN, M. M. 'The Rise of a Money Economy.' *Economic History Review,* 2nd ser., XIV, 1944–5.

The Medieval Economy and Society. An Economic History of Britain, 1100–1500. London, 1972.

Medieval Trade and Finance. Cambridge, 1973.

POSTAN, M. M., RICH, E. E. and MILLER, E. (eds.). *The Cambridge Economic History of Europe.* III. *Economic Organization and Policies in the Middle Ages.* Cambridge, 1963.

POWEL, E. T. *The Evolution of the Money Market (1385–1915). An Historical and Analytical Study of the Rise and Development of Finances as a Centralized, Co-ordinated Force.* London, 1915.

PRATO, G. *Problemi monetari e bancari nei secoli XVII e XVIII.* Turin, 1916.

PRESSNELL, L. S. 'Public Monies and the Development of English Banking.' *Economic History Review,* 2nd ser., V, 1952.

(ed.). *The Country Banks.* Oxford, 1956.

PUSCH, G. *Staatliche Münz- und Geldpolitik in den Niederlanden unter den Burgundischen und Habsburgischen Herrschern, besonders unter Kaiser Karl V.* Munich, 1932.

RAMSAY, G. D. *English Overseas Trade during the Centuries of Emergence.* London, 1957.

RAMSEY, P. 'Some Tudor Merchants' Accounts.' *Studies in the History of Accounting,* eds. A. C. Littleton and B. S. Yamey, London, 1956.

Tudor Economic Problems. (Men and Ideas Series, no. 1.) London, 1963.

(ed.). *The Price Revolution in Sixteenth-Century England.* London, 1971.

REDLICH, F. *Die Deutsche Inflation des frühen 17. Jahrhunderts in der Zeitgenössischen Literatur: die Kipper und Wipper.* (Forschungen zur internationalen Sozial- und Wirtschaftsgeschichte, edited by Hermann Kellenbenz.) Cologne–Vienna, 1972.

REMOND, A. 'Economie dirigée, et travaux publics sous Colbert.' *Revue d'histoire économique et sociale,* 1959.

RENOUARD, Y. *Les Relations des Papes d'Avignon et des compagnies commerciales et bancaires de 1316 à 1378.* Paris, 1941.

Les Hommes d'affaires italiens du Moyen Age. Paris, 1949.

RICARDS, R. D. *The Early History of Banking in England.* London, 1929.

'The First Fifty Years of the Bank of England (1694–1744).' *History of the Principal Public Banks accompanied by Extensive Bibliographies of the History of Banking and Credit in eleven European Countries.* Collected by J. G. van Dillen. The Hague, 1934.

RICHET, D. 'Le cours officiel des monnaies étrangères circulant en France au XVIe siècle.' *Revue historique,* CCXXV, 1961.

ROBERTS, M. *Gustavus Adolphus. A History of Sweden.* 2 vols. London, 1958.

ROBINSON, W. C. 'Money, Population and Economic Change in Late Medieval Europe.' *Economic History Review,* 2nd ser., 1959.

RODRIGEZ Y FERNANDEZ, I. *Historia de Medina del Campo.* Madrid, 1903–4.

ROGERS, J. E. THOROLD. *The First Nine Years of the Bank of England.* Oxford, 1887.

ROMANO, R. 'Banchieri genovesi alla Corte di Filippo II.' *Rivista storica italiana,* LXI, 1949.

'Trà XVI e XVII secolo. Una crisi economica: 1619–1622.' *Rivista storica italiana,* LXXIV, 1962.

'Le marchand italien entre Moyen Age et Renaissance.' *Odrodzenie i Reformäcja w Polsce,* VIII, 1963.

ROOVER, FLORENCE EDLER DE. 'The Effects of the Financial Measures of Charles V on the Commerce of Antwerp, 1539–42.' *Revue Belge de Philologie et d'Histoire*, XVI, 1937.

ROOVER, R. DE. *The Medici Bank. Its Organization, Management, Operations and Decline.* New York–London, 1948.

Money, Banking and Credit in Medieval Bruges. Italian Merchant-Bankers, Lombards and Money-Changers. A Study in the Origins of Banking. Cambridge, Mass., 1948.

Gresham on Foreign Exchange. An Essay on Early English Mercantilism with the Text of Sir Thomas Gresham's Memorandum for the Understanding of the Exchange. Cambridge, Mass., 1949.

'Anvers comme marché monétaire au XVIe siècle.' *Revue Belge de Philologie et d'Histoire*, XXXI/IV, 1953.

L'évolution de la lettre de change, XIVe–XVIIIe siècles. Paris, 1953.

'The Origins of Discounting.' *South African Bankers' Journal*, 1956.

'Cambium ad Venetias: Contribution to the History of Foreign Exchange.' *Studi in onore di Armando Sapori*, I. Milan, 1957.

'La balance commerciale entre les Pays-Bas et l'Italie au XVe siècle.' *Revue Belge de Philologie et d'Histoire*, XXXVII, 1959.

The Rise and Decline of the Medici Bank, 1397–1494. (Harvard Studies in Business History, No. 21.) Cambridge, Mass., 1963.

San Bernardino of Siena and Sant'Antonio of Florence. The Two Great Economic Thinkers of the Middle Ages. Boston, Mass., 1967.

'Early Banking before 1500 and the Development of Capitalism.' *Revue Internationale d'Histoire de la Banque*, 1971.

ROOVER, R. DE and SARDY, H. *The Bruges Money Market around 1400. With a Statistical Supplement.* (Verhandelingen van de Koninklijke Vlaamse Academie voor Wetenschappen, Letteren en Schone Kunsten van België, Klasse der Letteren, no. 63.) Brussels, 1968.

RÖRIG, F. *The Medieval Town.* London, 1967.

ROSA, L. DE. 'Observations à propos de la relation de M. Demarco sur les banques napolitaines.' *Third International Conference of Economic History, Munich, 1965: Proceedings.* Paris–The Hague, 1974.

ROUCHE, ABBÉ A. 'La nation florentine à Lyon, au commencement du XVe siècle.' *Revue d'histoire de Lyon*, XI, 1912.

RUIZ-MARTIN, F. 'Las finanzas españolas durante el Reinado de Felipe II (Alternativas de participación que se ofrecieron para Francia).' *Cuadernos de Historia*, II, 1968.

La Banca en España hasta 1782. Madrid, 1970.

'Credito y Banca. Comercio y transportes en la etapa del capitalismo mercantil.' *Jornados de metodologia aplicada de las Ciencias Historicas 24–27 April 1973, Santiago de Compostella. Ponencias y comunicaciones, apéndice.* Santiago de Compostella, 1973.

RUTENBURG, V. *Statuti di Monte di Pieta, 1463–1499.* 'Gubbio'. Moscow–Leningrad, 1965.

RUWET, J. 'Un aspect de la politique monétaire liègeoise au XVIe siècle: le change. *Scrinium Lovaniense.* (Mélanges historiques Etienne Van Cauwenbergh. Université de Louvain. Receuil de travaux d'histoire et de philologie, 4th ser., fasc. 24.) Louvain, 1961.

SAINT-GERMAIN, J. *Samuel Bernard, le banquier des rois.* Paris, 1960.

SAMSONOWICZ, H. 'La structure du commerce de Gdansk dans la première moitié du XVe siècle.' *Przeglad historyczny*, LIII: 4, 1961.

SÁNCHEZ SARTO, M. 'Les banques publiques en Espagne jusqu'à 1815.' *History of the Principal Public Banks accompanied by Extensive Bibliographies of the History of Banking and Credit in eleven European Countries.* Collected by J. G. van Dillen. The Hague, 1934.

SAPORI, A. *Studi di storia economica medievale.* Florence, 1947.

'La Banca Medici.' *Moneta e credito*, VIII, 1949.

Le Marchand Italien au Moyen-Age. Paris, 1952.

SARDELLA, P. *Nouvelles et spéculations à Venise au début du XVIe siècle.* (Cahiers des Annales, no. 1.) Paris, 1950.

SAUTIJN KLUIT, W. P. 'De Amsterdamsche Prijs-courantiers in de 17de en 18de eeuw.' *Bijdragen voor Vaderlandsche geschiedenis en Oudheidkunde*, 1875.

SAYERS, R. S. *Banking in Western Europe*. Oxford, 1963.

SAYOUS, A. E. 'La spéculation dans les Pays-Bas au XVIe siècle.' *Journal des économistes*, 5th ser., XLVI, 1901.

'Observations d'écrivains du XVIe siècle sur les changes et notamment sur l'influence de la disparité du pouvoir d'achat des monnaies.' *Revue économique internationale*, 1928.

'Les placements de fortune à Genève depuis le XVe siècle jusqu'à la fin du XVIIIe.' *Revue économique internationale*, 1935.

Les Origines du marché à terme sur marchandises. Les origines de la bourse en valeurs. Brussels, 1936.

'La genèse du système capitaliste: la pratique des affaires et leur mentalité dans l'Espagne du XVIe siècle.' *Annales d'histoire économique et sociale*, VIII, 1936.

'L'affaire de Law et les Genevois.' *Revue d'histoire suisse*, XVII, 1937.

'Die grossen Händler und Kapitalisten in Amsterdam gegen das Ende des sechzehnten und während des siebzehnten Jahrhunderts.' *Weltwirtschaftliches Archiv*, XXXXVI–XXXXVII, 1937–8.

'Augsbourg au temps des grandes faillites.' *Annales d'histoire économique et sociale*, 1938.

'La crise financière de 1709 à Lyon et à Genève.' *Revue d'histoire économique et sociale*, 1938.

SCHÄFER, E. *El Consejo real y supremo de las Indias*. 2 vols. Seville, 1935 and 1947.

SCHANZ, G. *Englische Handelspolitik gegen Ende des Mittelalters, mit besonderer Berücksichtigung des Zeitalters der beiden ersten Tudors, Heinrich VII und Heinrich VIII*. 2 vols. Leipzig, 1881.

SCHICK, L. *Un grand homme d'affaires au début du XVIe siècle: Jacob Fugger*. (Affaires et gens d'affaires, no. 11.) Paris, 1957.

SCHNAPPER, B. 'Les baux à vie (Xe au XVIe siècle).' *Revue historique de droit français et étranger*, 1957.

Les Rentes au XVIe siècle. Histoire d'un instrument de crédit. Paris, 1957.

SCHNEE, H. *Die Hoffinanz und der moderne Staat*. 4 vols. Berlin–Munich, 1958–63.

SCHULTE, A. *Geschichte der grossen Ravensburger Handelsgesellschaft, 1380–1530*. 3 vols. Stuttgart–Berlin, 1923.

SCOVILLE, W. C. *The Persecution of Huguenots and French Economic Development 1680–1720*. Berkeley and Los Angeles, 1960.

SÉE, H. *Histoire économique de la France*. 2 vols. Paris, 1948.

Les Origines du capitalisme moderne (Esquisse historique). 6th ed., Paris, 1951.

SENTENACH, N. 'El maravedi, su grandeza y decadencia.' *Revista de Archivos, Bibliotecas y Museos*, XII, 1905.

SHAPIRO, S. 'The Structure of English Banking and the Industrial Revolution.' *Third International Conference of Economic History, Munich 1965: Proceedings*. Paris–The Hague, 1974.

SHAW, W. A. *Histoire de la monnaie, 1252–1894*. Paris, 1896.

SIEVEKING, H. *Genueser Finanzwesen mit besonderer Berücksichtigung der Casa di S. Giorgio*. 2 vols. Freiburg–Tübingen, 1898–1900.

'Die Hamburger Bank, 1615–1875.' *Festschrift von Melle*, 1933.

SILVA, JOSÉ GENTIL DA. *Stratégie des affaires à Lisbonne entre 1595 et 1607. Lettres marchandes des Rodrigues d'Evora et Veiga*. Paris, 1956.

'Capitaux et marchandises, échanges et finances entre XVIe et XVIIIe siècle.' *Annales: E., S., C.*, 1957.

'Le sconto à Gênes. A propos d'un croquis.' *Annales: E., S., C.*, 1958.

'Trafics du Nord, marchés du "Mezzogiorno" finances génoises: recherches et documents sur la conjoncture à la fin du XVIe siècle.' *Revue du Nord*, CLXII, 1959.

'L'histoire des changes: les foires de "Bisenzone" de 1606 à 1650.' *Annales: E., S., C.*, 1962.

En Espagne: développement économique, subsistance, déclin. Paris, 1965.

Banque et crédit en Italie au XVIIe siècle. 2 vols. Paris, 1969.

'Fructification du capital et dynamique sociale dans les sociétés commerciales (XVI–XVII siècles).' *Third International Conference of Economic History, Munich 1965: Proceedings*. Paris–The Hague, 1974.

SMEDT, H. DE. *Antwerpen en de opbloei van de Vlaamse verrehandel tijdens de 16e eeuw. Rijkdom en inkomen van de Antwerpse koopman Jan Gamel volgens zijn staat van goed, 1572.* (Licentieverhandeling: Wijsb. & Letteren. Afd. Moderne Geschiedenis, Univ. Leuven, 1970.) Louvain, 1970.

SMEDT, O. DE. 'De keizerlijke verordeningen van 1537 en 1539 op de obligaties en wisselbrieven.' *Nederlandsche Historiebladen*, III, 1940.

De Engelse Natie te Antwerpen in de XVIe eeuw (1496–1582). 2 vols. Antwerp, 1950–4.

SMIT, H. J. *De opkomst van den handel van Amsterdam.* Amsterdam, 1914.

SMITH, A. *An Inquiry into the Nature and Causes of the Wealth of Nations.* 2 vols. London, 1925.

SMITH, M. F. J. *Tijd-affaires in Effecten aan de Amsterdamsche Beurs.* The Hague, 1919.

SNELLER, Z. W. 'Het wisselaarsbedrijf in Nederland vóór de oprichting der Stedelijke Wisselbanken.' *Tijdschrift voor Geschiedenis*, XXXXIX, 1934.

Rotterdams bedrijfsleven in het verleden. Amsterdam, 1940.

SOLY, H. 'Grondspeculatie en kapitalisme te Antwerpen in de 16e eeuw.' *Economisch en Sociaal Tijdschrift*, XXVII, 1973.

'Het "verraad" der 16de-eeuwse burgerij: een mythe?' *Tijdschrif tvoor Geschiedenis*, LXXXVI, 1973.

SOMBART, W. *Der moderne Kapitalismus.* 6 vols. Munich, 1921–8.

SOMMA, C. DE. 'L'attività bancaria della confraternità dello Spirito Santo dalle origini alla crisi monetaria del 1622. Contributo alla storia dei banchi publici napolitani.' *Archivi storici delle aziende di credito*, I. Rome, 1956.

SORESINA, A. *Il Banco Giro di Venezia.* Venice, 1889.

SPERLING, J. 'The International Payments Mechanism in the 17th and 18th Centuries.' *Economic History Review*, XIV, 1962.

SPOONER, F. C. *L'économie mondiale et les frappes monétaires en France 1493–1680.* Paris, 1956.

SPUFFORD, P. *Monetary Problems and Policies in the Burgundian Netherlands, 1433–1496.* Leiden, 1970.

STEFANO, M. DE. *Banchi e vicende monetarie nel Regno di Napoli. 1600–1625.* Livorno, 1940.

STELLA, A. 'La crisi economica veneziana nella seconda metà del secolo XVI.' *Archivio veneto*, LVII–LIX, 1956.

STEVELINCK, E. *La comptabilité à travers les âges.* (Catalogue d'une exposition organisée à l'occasion du premier symposium international des historiens de la comptabilité, Bruxelles, 3 octobre – 8 novembre 1970.) Brussels, 1970.

STONE, L. *The Crisis of the Aristocracy, 1558–1641.* Oxford, 1965.

STRIEDER, J. *Zur Genesis des modernen Kapitalismus. Forschungen zur Entstehung der grossen bürgerlichen Kapitalvermögen zu Ausgang des Mittelalters und zu Beginn der Neuzeit, zunächst in Augsburg.* Leipzig, 1904.

Studien zur Geschichte kapitalistischer Organisationsformen: Monopole, Kartelle und Aktiengesellschaften im Mittelalter und zur Beginn der Neuzeit. Munich–Leipzig, 1914.

STROMER, W. VON. 'Das Schriftwesen der Nürnberger Wirtschaft vom 14. bis zum 16. Jahrhundert. Zur Geschichte oberdeutscher Handelsbücher.' *Beiträge zur Wirtschaftsgeschichte Nürnbergs*, II. Nürnberg, 1967.

Oberdeutsche Hochfinanz, 1350–1450. 3 vols. Wiesbaden, 1970.

Sveriques Riksbank, 1668–1224. Stockholm, 1931.

TANGELDER, F. B. M. *Muntheer en muntmeester. Een studie over het Berghse muntprivilege in de tweede helft der zestiende eeuw.* Arnhem, 1955.

TAWNEY, R. H. *Religion and the Rise of Capitalism.* London, 1926.

TAYLOR, H. 'Trade, Neutrality and the "English Road", 1630–1648.' *Economic History Review*, 2nd ser., XXV, 1972.

TAYLOR, R. E. 'Luca Pacioli.' *Studies in the History of Accounting.* Eds. A. C. Littleton and B. S. Jamey. London, 1956.

TOPOLSKI, J. 'La régression économique en Pologne du XVIe au XVIIIe siècle.' *Acta Poloniae Historica*, VII, 1962.

TOUSSAINT, P. *Les Foires de Chalon-sur-Saône des origines au XVIe siècle.* (Collections d'études sur l'histoire du droit et des institutions de la Bourgogne, XXII.) Dijon, 1910.

TREVOR-ROPER, H. R. 'The General Crisis of the Seventeenth Century.' *Past and Present*, XVI, 1959.

ULLOA, M. *La Hacienda Real de Castilla en el reinado de Felipe II*. Rome, 1963.

USHER, A. P. 'The Primitive Banks of Deposits, 1200–1600.' *Economic History Review*, IV, 1934.

The Early History of Deposit Banking in Mediterranean Europe. I. The Structure and Functions of the Early Credit System. Banking in Catalonia: 1240–1723. Cambridge, Mass., 1943.

VAESEN, J. *La Jurisdiction commerciale à Lyon sous l'ancien régime. Etude historique sur la conservation des privilèges royaux des Foires de Lyon (1463–1795)*. Lyons, 1879.

VAZQUEZ DE PRADA, V. *Lettres marchandes d'Anvers*. I–IV. Paris, n.d.

VERCAUTEREN, F. 'Note sur les opérations de Charles Quint dans les Pays-Bas en 1523.' *Revue historique*, CLXXII, 1933.

VERLINDEN, C. 'De zeeverzekeringen der Spaanse kooplui in de Nederlanden gedurende de XVI eeuw.' *Bijdragen voor de Geschiedenis der Nederlanden*, II, 1948.

'En Flandre sous Philippe II: durée de la crise économique.' *Annales: E., S., C.*, VII, 1952.

VIAL, E. 'Jean Cleberger. Ses origines. Sa vie.' *Revue d'histoire de Lyon*, XI–XIII, 1912–14.

VIARD, J. 'La Chambre des comptes sous le règne de Philippe VI de Valois.' *Bibliothèque de l'Ecole des Chartes*, LXXXXIII, 1932.

VIGNE, M. *La Banque à Lyon du XVe au XVIIIe siècle*. Lyons–Paris, 1903.

VILAR, P. 'Problems of the Formation of Capitalism.' *Past and Present*, 1956.

La Catalogne dans l'Espagne moderne. Recherches sur les fondements économiques des structures nationales. 3 vols. Paris, 1962.

VILLERS, R. 'Réflexions sur les finances publiques en Europe aux XVIIe–XVIIIe siècles.' *Annales de l'Université de Paris*, 1962.

VRANKRIJKER, A. C. J. DE. *Geschiedenis van de belastingen*. Bussum, 1969.

VRIES, J. DE. *De economische achteruitgang der Republiek in de achttiende eeuw*. Leiden, 1968.

VUHRER, A. *Histoire de la dette publique en France*. Paris, 1886.

VUITRY, A. *Le Désordre des finances et les excès de la spéculation à la fin du règne de Louis XIV et au commencement du règne de Louis XV*. Paris, 1885.

WASCHINSKI, E. 'Zwischenstaatliche Wechselkurse aus dem letzten Viertel des 16. und im ersten Drittel des 18. Jahrhunderts.' *Vierteljahrschrift für Sozial- und Wirtschaftsgeschichte*, XXXVII, 1960.

WEE, H. VAN DER. 'Sporen van disconto te Antwerpen tijdens de 16e eeuw.' *Bijdragen voor de geschiedenis der Nederlanden*, X, 1955.

'Het geld in de XVIIe en XVIIIe eeuw.' *Bijdragen voor de geschiedenis der Nederlanden*, XIII, 1959.

The Growth of the Antwerp Market and the European Economy (Fourteenth–Sixteenth Centuries). 3 vols. The Hague, 1963.

Anvers et les innovations de la technique financière aux XVIe et XVIIe siècles. *Annales: E., S., C.*, XXII, 1967.

Historische aspecten van de economische groei. Tien studies over de economische ontwikkeling van West-Europa en van de Nederlanden in het bijzonder (12e–19e eeuw). Antwerp–Utrecht, 1972.

and VAN CAUWENBERGHE, E. 'Histoire agraire et finances publiques en Flandre du XIVe au XVIIe siècle.' *Annales: E., S., C.*, XXVIII, 1973.

WERVEKE, H. VAN. 'Monnaie de compte et monnaie réelle.' *Revue Belge de Philologie et d'Histoire*, XIII, 1934.

'Les origines des bourses commerciales. Faut-il abandonner la thèse Guicciardini–Ehrenberg?' *Revue Belge de Philologie et d'Histoire*, XV, 1936.

Miscellanea Mediaevalia. Ghent, 1968.

WESTERMANN, E. *Das Eislebener Garkupfer und seine Bedeutung für den europäischen Kupfermarkt. 1460–1560*. Cologne–Vienna, 1971.

WILSON, C. *Anglo-Dutch Commerce and Finance in the Eighteenth Century*. Cambridge, 1941.

Mercantilism. (Pamphlet of the Historical Association, G. 37.) London, 1958.

'The Other Face of Mercantilism.' *Transactions of the Royal Historical Society*, 5th ser., 1959.

England's Apprenticeship, 1603–1763. London, 1965.

WILSON, J. S. G. *French Banking Structure and Credit Policy*. London, 1957.

WITTROCK, G. *Karl XI: s. förmyndares finanspolitik, 1661–1667*. Uppsala, 1914.

Svenska Handelskompaniet och Kopparhandeln under Gustaf II Adolf. Uppsala, 1919.

WOLFF, P. *Commerce et marchands de Toulouse (vers 1350, vers 1450)*. Paris, 1945.

'Le problème des Cahorsins.' *Annales du Midi*, LXII, 1950.

WOLONTIS, J. *Kopparmyntningen i Sverige, 1624–1714*. Helsingfors, 1936.

WYCZANSKI, A. 'En Pologne. L'économie du domaine nobiliaire moyen (1500–1580).' *Annales: E., S., C.*, 1963.

ZARB, M. 'Aperçu des relations ayant existé entre la Provence et Genève au cours des XVe et XVIe siècles.' *Provence historique*, VI, 1956.

ZELLER, G. 'Deux capitalistes strasbourgeois au XVIe siècle.' *Etudes d'histoire moderne et contemporaine*, I, 1947.

ZERBI, T. *Le origini della partita doppia. Gestioni aziendali e situazioni di mercato nei secoli XIV e XV*. Milan, 1952.

ZORN, W. 'Grundzüge der Augsburger Handelsgeschichte 1648–1806.' *Vierteljahrschrift für Sozial- und Wirtschaftsgeschichte*, XXXXIII, 1956.

CHAPTER VI

The Nature of Enterprise

In light of the scope of this Chapter's subject-matter, and the extent to which it overlaps with that of other Chapters in volumes IV and V, it is not thought appropriate to include a bibliography aiming at systematic coverage of the areas involved. Instead, the list which follows is designed as a selective and relatively brief introduction to the topics discussed in the Chapter. It should be used in conjunction with the bibliographies relating to other Chapters.

I. THE FRAMEWORK OF ENTERPRISE

BRAUDEL, F. *La Méditerranée et le monde méditerranéen a l'époque de Philippe II*. Paris, 1949.

CHAUNU, H. and CHAUNU, P. *Séville et l'Atlantique, 1504–1650*. 3 vols. Paris, 1956.

CHRISTENSEN, A. E. *Dutch Trade to the Baltic c. 1600*. Copenhagen, 1941.

COLE, C. W. *Colbert and a Century of French Mercantilism*. 2 vols. New York, 1939.

French Mercantilism, 1683–1700. New York, 1943.

COLEMAN, D. C. 'Eli Heckscher and the idea of mercantilism.' *Scandinavian Economic History Review*, 1957.

DOBB, MAURICE. *Studies in the Development of Capitalism*. London, 1946.

GRAS, N. S. B. *Business and Capitalism*. New York, 1939.

HAUSER, H. 'Les Origines du capitalisme moderne en France.' *Revue d'économie politique*, 1902.

HECKSCHER, E. *Mercantilism*. 2 vols. Revised edition, 1955.

JUDGES, A. V. 'The idea of the mercantile state.' *Transactions of the Royal Historical Society*, 1939.

MARSHALL, T. H. 'Capitalism and the decline of the English gilds.' *Cambridge Historical Journal*, 1929.

REDLICH, FRITZ. *The German Military Entrepreneur and his Work Force: A Study in European Economic and Social History*. 2 vols. Wiesbaden, 1964.

ROBERTSON, H. M. *Aspects of the Rise of Economic Individualism*. Cambridge, 1933.

SAMUELSSON, K. *Religion and Economic Action*. London, 1961.

SAYOUS, ANDRÉ E. 'The bourgeoisie of Geneva in the age of the Reformation.' *Economic History Review*, 1936.

'La Genèse du système capitaliste: La Pratique des affairs et leur mentalité dans l'Espagne du XVIe siècle.' *Annales d'Histoire Economique et Sociale*, 1936.

SÉE, H. 'Dans quelle mesure Puritains et Juifs ont-ils contribué au progrès du capitalisme moderne?' *Revue historique*, V, 1927.

'Le capitalisme commercial en France au XVIIe siècle.' *Revue d'histoire économique*, 1924.
The Origins of Modern Capitalism, 1927.
SOMBART, WERNER. *The Jews and Modern Capitalism*. London, 1913.
The Quintessence of Capitalism. London, 1915.
STRIEDER, JACOB. 'Origin and evolution of early European capitalism.' *Journal of Economic and Business History*, 1929.
SUPPLE, B. E. 'The great capitalist man-hunt.' *Business History*, 1963.
TAWNEY, R. H. *Religion and the Rise of Capitalism*. London, 1926.
'Modern capitalism.' *Economic History Review*, 1933.
TROELTSCH, E. *The Social Teaching of the Christian Churches*. 2 vols. London, 1931.
UNWIN, GEORGE. *The Gilds and Companies of London*. London, 1908.
'The Merchant Adventurers' Company in the reign of Elizabeth.' In *Studies in Economic History: The Collected Papers of George Unwin*. Edited by R. H. Tawney. London, 1927.
WEBER, MAX. *The Protestant Ethic and the Spirit of Capitalism*. London, 1930.

II. INTERNATIONAL ENTERPRISE IN TRADE AND FINANCE

ASHTON, ROBERT. *The Crown and the Money Market, 1603–1640*. Oxford, 1960.
BARBOUR, V. *Capitalism in Amsterdam in the Seventeenth Century*. Baltimore, 1950.
BRAUDEL, F. and ROMANO, R. *Navires et merchandises à l'éntree du port de Livourne (1547–1611)*. Paris, 1951.
CASTILLO, A. 'Dans la monarchie espagnole du XVIIe siecle: les banquiers portugais et le circuit d'Amsterdam.' *Annales*, 1964.
COLEMAN, D. C. *Sir John Banks, Baronet and Businessman: A Study of Business, Politics and Society in Later Stuart England*. Oxford, 1963.
DEFOE, DANIEL. *The Complete English Tradesman*. London, 1745.
DICKSON, P. G. M. *The Sun Insurance Office, 1710–1960: The History of two and a half Centuries of British Insurance*. London, 1960.
The Financial Revolution in England: A Study in the Development of Public Credit, 1688–1756. London, 1967.
EHRENBERG, RICHARD. *Capital & Finance in the Age of the Renaissance: A study of the Fuggers and their connections*. New York, 1928.
GOUGH, J. W. *Sir Hugh Myddelton: Entrepreneur and Engineer*. Oxford, 1964.
HOUTTE, J. A. VAN. 'Anvers aux XVe et XVIe siècles.' *Annales*, 1961.
JEANNIN, P. 'Le cuivre, les Fuggers et la Hanse.' *Annales*, 1955.
KELLENBENZ, H. 'Les Fuggers et le marché internationale du poivre c. 1600.' *Annales*, 1956.
KLARWILL, VICTOR VON (ed.). *The Fugger News-Letters*. London, 1924.
LAPEYRE, HENRI. *Une Famille de marchands: les Ruiz. Contribution à l'étude du commerce entre la France et l'Espagne au temps de Philippe II*. Paris, 1955.
LOPEZ, R. 'Le marchand génois.' *Annales*, 1958.
LÜTHY, HERBERT. *La Banque Protestante en France de la Révocation de l'Edit de Nantes à la Révolution*. 2 vols. Paris, 1959.
McGRATH, P. V. *Merchants and Merchandise in seventeenth-century Bristol*. Bristol, 1955.
MATTHEWS, GEORGE T. *The Royal General Farms in Eighteenth-Century France*. New York, 1958.
MINCHINTON, W. E. 'The merchants in England in the eighteenth century.' *Explorations in Entrepreneurial History*, 1957–8.
MORET, MICHELE. *Aspects de la société marchande de Séville au début du XVIIe siècle*. Paris, 1967.
PELLET, JEAN. *Commerçant de Gros, 1694–1722: contribution a l'étude du négoce Bordelais du XVIIIe siècle*. Paris, 1967.
SAVARY, J. *Le Parfait Négociant*. Lyons, 1675.
SAYOUS, ANDRÉ E. 'Le Rôle d'Amsterdam dans l'histoire du capitalisme commercial.' *Revue Historique*, 1938.
SCHICK, LEON. *Un grand homme d'affaires au début du XVIe siècle: Jacob Fugger*. Paris, 1957.
SÉE, H. 'Le Commerce des Hollandaise à Nantes pendant la minorité de Louis XIV.' *Tidjschrift voor geschiedenis*, 1926.

SILVA, J. GENTIL DA. *Stratégie des affaires à Lisbonne entre 1595 et 1607: Lettres marchandes des Rodrigues d'Evora et Veiga*. Paris, 1956.

STONE, LAWRENCE. *An Elizabethan: Sir Horatio Palavicino*. Oxford, 1956.

STRIEDER, JACOB. *Jacob Fugger the Rich: Merchant and Banker of Augsburg, 1459–1525*. New York, 1931.

TAWNEY, R. H. *Lionel Cranfield: Business and Politics under James I*. Cambridge, 1958.

UPTON, ANTHONY F. *Sir Arthur Ingram, c. 1565–1642: A Study of the Origin of an English Landed Family*. London, 1961.

WILSON, C. H. *Anglo-Dutch Commerce and Finance in the Eighteenth Century*. Cambridge, 1941.

YAMEY, B. S. 'Scientific bookkeeping and the rise of capitalism.' *Economic History Review*. New Series, I, 1949.

III. INDUSTRIAL ENTERPRISE

BAMFORD, P. 'Entrepreneurship in seventeenth and eighteenth century France.' *Explorations in Entrepreneurial History*, IX: 4, April, 1957.

BOISSONADE, P. *Le Socialisme de l'état, l'industrie et les classes industrielles pendant les deux premières siècles de l'ère moderne*. Paris, 1927.
  Colbert, le triomphe de l'étatisme, la fondation de la suprématie industrielle de la France, 1661–1683. Paris, 1932.

BONDOIS, P. M. *Le développement de la grande industrie en France au XVIIe et XVIIIe siècles*. Paris, 1898.

COLEMAN, D. C. *The British Paper Industry, 1495–1860: A study in industrial growth*. Oxford, 1958.

DONALD, M. B. *Elizabethan Copper: The History of the Company of Mines Royal, 1568–1605*. London, 1955.
  Elizabethan Monopolies: The History of the Company of Mineral and Battery Works from 1565 to 1604. Edinburgh and London, 1961.

DOWNES, R. L. 'The Stour partnership, 1726–36: a note on landed capital in the iron industry.' *Economic History Review*, 1950.

GILLE, BERTRAND. *Les Origines de la grande industrie métallurgique en France*. Paris, 1947.

JOHNSON, B. L. C. 'The Foley partnerships: the iron industry at the end of the charcoal era.' *Economic History Review*, 2nd ser., IV: 3, 1952.

MARTIN, G. *La Grande Industrie en France sous le règne de Louis XV*. Paris, 1900.

NEF, J. U. 'The progress of technology and the growth of large-scale industry in Great Britain, 1540–1640.' *Economic History Review*, 1935.
  The Rise of the British Coal Industry. London, 1932.
  Industry and Government in France and England, 1540–1640. Chicago, 1940.

RAMSEY, G. D. *The Wiltshire Woollen Industry in the Sixteenth and Seventeenth Centuries*. Oxford, 1943.

REMOND, A. *John Holker, manufacturier et grand fonctionnaire en France au XVIIIe siècle*. Paris, 1946.

ROUFF, M. *Les Mines de Charbon en France au XVIIIe siècle*. Paris, 1922.

SCOVILLE, W. C. *Capitalism and French Glassmaking, 1640–1789*. California, 1950.

SÉE, H. 'Remarques sur l'évolution du capitalisme et les origines de la grand industrie.' *La Revue de Synthèse Historique*, 1924.
  'Remarques sur le caractère de l'industrie rurale en France et les causes de son extension au XVIIIe siècle.' *Revue historique*, 1923.

UNWIN, GEORGE. 'The history of the cloth industry in Suffolk.' In *Studies in Economic History: The Collected Papers of George Unwin*. Edited by R. H. Tawney. London, 1927.

WADSWORTH, A. P. and MANN, J. DE L. *The Cotton Trade and Industrial Lancashire, 1600–1780*. Manchester, 1931.

ZELLER, G. 'L'industrie en France avant Colbert.' *Revue d'histoire économique et sociale*, 1950.

IV. Corporate Enterprise

BONNASSIEUX, PIERRE. *Les Grandes Compagnies de commerce*. Paris, 1892.
BOISSONADE and CHARLIOT, P. 'Colbert et la Compagnie de Commerce du Nord.' *Revue d'histoire économique et sociale*, 1928 and 1929.
CHAUDHURI, K. N. *The English East India Company: The Study of an Early Joint-Stock Company, 1600–1640*. London, 1965.
DAVIES, K. G. *The Royal African Company*. London, 1957.
HARSIN, P. 'La création de la Compagnie d'Occident.' *Revue d'histoire économique et sociale*, 1956.
HUSSEY, ROLAND D. *The Caracas Company, 1728–1784: A Study in the History of Spanish Monopolistic Trade*. Cambridge, Mass., 1934.
RABB, THEODORE K. *Enterprise and Empire: Merchant and Gentry Investment in the expansion of England, 1575–1630*. Cambridge, Mass., 1967.
RICH, E. E. *The History of the Hudson's Bay Company, 1670–1870*. 2 vols. London, 1958–9.
SCOTT, W. R. *The Constitution and Finance of English, Scottish and Irish Joint-Stock Companies to 1720*. 3 vols. Cambridge, 1910–12.
SMITH, R. S. *The Spanish Guild Merchant*. Durham, N.C., 1940.
WILLAN, T. S. *The Early History of the Russia Company*. Manchester, 1956.
WOOD, A. C. *A History of the Levant Company*. Oxford, 1935.

V. Aristocracy and Enterprise

FREUDENBERGER, H. *The Waldstein Woollen Mill: Noble Entrepreneurship in Eighteenth Century Bohemia*. Cambridge, Mass., 1962.
HABAKKUK, H. J. 'Economic function of English landowners.' *Explorations in Entrepreneurial History*, 1953–4.
KONETZKE, RICHARD. 'Entrepreneurial activities of Spanish and Portuguese noblemen.' *Explorations in Entrepreneurial History*, 1953–4.
OHLIN, PER GORAN. 'Entrepreneurial activities of the Swedish aristocracy.' *Explorations in Entrepreneurial History*, 1953–4.
REDLICH, F. 'European aristocracy and economic development.' *Explorations in Entrepreneurial History*, VI: 2, December, 1953.
STONE, LAWRENCE. *The Crisis of the Aristocracy, 1558–1641*. Oxford, 1965.

CHAPTER VII

The Organization of Industrial Production

AMBURGER, ERIK. *Die Familie Marselis*. Giessen, 1957.
ANDERSON, R. and R. C. *The Sailing Ship*. London, 1926.
ASTEN, HERBERT VON. 'Wolfgang Wilhelm und Philipp Wilhelm von Pfalz-Neuburg und der Aufbau des Montangewerbes in den Herzogtümern Jülich und Berg.' *Annal. d. Histor. Ver. f.d. Niederrhein*, CLXI, 1959.
AUBIN, HERMANN. *Das westfälische Leinengewerbe im Rahmen der deutschen und europäischen Leinwanderzeugung*. Dortmund, 1964.
AUBIN, H. and KUNTZE, A. *Leinenerzeugung und Leinenabsatz im östlichen Mitteldeutschland zur Zeit der Zunftkäufe*. Stuttgart, 1940.
BARKHAUSEN, ERNST. 'Die staatliche Wirtschaftslenkung in freies Unternehmertum.' *Vierteljahrschrift für Sozial- und Wirtschaftsgeschichte*, XLV, 1958.
BLAICH, FRITZ. *Die Wirtschaftspolitik des Reichstages im Heiligen Romischen Reich*. Stuttgart, 1970.
BODMER, WALTER. *Die Entwicklung der schweizerischen Textilwirtschaft im Rahmen der übrigen Industrien und Wirtschaftszweige (Schweizerische Industriegeschichte)*. Zurich, 1960.
BOG, INGOMAR. *Der Reichsmerkantilismus*. Stuttgart, 1959.
BRAUDEL, FERNAND. *Civilisation matérielle et capitalisme (XVe–XVIIIe siècles)*. I, Paris, 1967.

BRAUDEL, FERNAND and SPOONER, FRANK. 'Prices in Europe from 1450 to 1750.' *The Cambridge Economic History of Europe*, IV, Cambridge, 1966.

BRAUDEL, F., SPOONER, F. C., PORTAL, R., ASHTON, T. S., LEUILLIOT, P. and VIDALENC, J. 'Commerce et industrie en Europe du XVIe au XVIIe siècle.' *Relazioni V, Xe Congresso Internazionale di Scienze Storiche*, Rome, 4–11 September 1955; Florence, 1955.

BULFERETTI, LUIGI and CONSTANTINI, CLAUDIO. *Industria e commercio in Liguria nell'età del risorgimento*. Milan, 1966.

BURWASH, H. D. *English Merchant Shipping, 1460–1540*. Toronto, 1947.

CAIZZI, B. *Storia dell'industria italiana dal XVIII s. ai giorni nostri*. Turin, 1965.
    Industria e commercio della Repubblica Veneta nel XVIII secolo. Milan, 1965.
    Industria, commercio e banca in Lombardia nel XVIII secolo. Milan, 1968.

CAMPBELL, R. H. *Scotland since 1707, the Rise of an Industrial Society*. Oxford, 1955.

CHRISTENSEN, A. E. *Tiden intil ca 1730*. Industriens Historie i Danmark. Copenhagen, 1943.

CIPOLLA, CARLO M. 'The decline of Italy, the case of a fully matured economy.' *Economic History Review*, 2nd ser., V, 1952.

CLOWES, G. S. LAIRD. *Sailing Ships, their History and Development*. London, 1932.

CONRAD, GILL. *The Rise of the Irish Linen Industry*. 1925.

COORNAERT, E. *Un Centre industriel d'autrefois, la draperie-sayetterie d'Hondschoote (XIVe–XVIIIe siècles)*. Paris, 1930.

DAVIS, G. W. *The Early English Cotton Industry*. Manchester–London, 1920.

DAVIS, RALPH. *The Rise of the English Shipping Industry in the Seventeenth and Eighteenth Centuries*. Newton Abbot, 2nd ed., 1972.

DICKINSON, H. W. *A Short History of the Steam Engine*. London, 1963.

DONALD, M. B. *Elizabethan Copper. The History of the Company of the Mines Royal*. London, 1955.

ENDREI, WALTER. *L'évolution des techniques du filage et du tissage du Moyen Age à la révolution industrielle*. Paris, 1968.

ERCEG, IVAN. 'Organisation und Produktion des Tuches in Dubrovnik-Ragusa in XV. und XVI. Jahrhundert.' *Secunda Settimana di Studio, Produzione, commercio e consumo dei panni di lana XII–XVII secoli*, Prato, 10–16 April, 1970.

FANFANI, AMINTORE. *Storia del lavoro in Italia*. Milan, 1959.

FISCHER, FRANZ. *Die blauen Sensen, Sozial und Wirtschaftsgeschichte der Sensenschmiedezunft zu Kirchdorf-Micheldorf bis zur Mitte des 18. Jahrhunderts*. Graz–Cologne, 1966.

FISHER, F. J. 'Commercial trends and policy in sixteenth century England.' *Economic History Review*, X, 1940.

FLANAGAN, J. F. 'Figured fabrics.' *A History of Technology*, III, Oxford, 1957.

FORBERGER, RUDOLF. *Die Manufaktur in Sachsen vom Ende des 16. bis zum Anfang des 19. Jahrhunderts*. Berlin, 1958.

FREUDENBERGER, HERMANN. *The Waldstein Woollen Mill. Noble Entrepreneurship in Eighteenth Century Bohemia*. Cambridge, Mass., 1963.
    'Three mercantilistic protofactories.' *The Business History Review*, XI, 1966.

FRITZ, SVEN. *Studier i svenskt Bankväsen, 1772–1789*. Stockholm, 1967.

FURGER, FRIDOLIN. *Zum Verlagssystem als Organisationsform des Frühkapitalismus im Textilgewerbe*. Stuttgart, 1927.

GARDLUND, T. 'Manufakturdiskonten och fabrikatindustrins finansering.' *Studier tillägnadè Eli F. Heckscher*. Uppsala, 1944.

GILLE, B. *Les origines de la grande industrie metallurgique en France*. Paris, 1949.
    Histoire économique et sociale de la Russie du Moyen Age au XXe siècle. Paris, 1949.

GOLDENBERG, S. 'Commercio, produzione e consumo dei panni di lana nei paesi romani (XIV–XVII sec.).' *Secunda Settimana di Studio*. Prato, 1970.

HALL, A. R. 'Scientific method and the progress of techniques.' *The Cambridge Economic History of Europe*, IV, Cambridge, 1965.

HAMILTON, HENRY. *The Industrial Revolution in Scotland*. New ed. London, 1966.

HAUSER, HENRI. *La Pensée et l'action économique du Cardinal Richelieu*. Paris, 1944.

HASSINGER, HERBERT. *Johann Joachim Becher*. Vienna, 1956.
    'Der Stand der Manufakturen in den deutschen Erbländern.' *Die wirtschaftliche Situation in Deutschland und Österreich um die Wende vom 18. zum 19. Jahrhundert*, ed. F. Lütge, Stuttgart, 1964.

HEATON, HERBERT. *Economic History of Europe*. Rev. ed., New York, 1948, esp. ch. XVII: 'Industrial and commercial organisation: 1500–1750.'

HECKSCHER, ELI F. *Svenskt arbete och liv. Från medeltiden til nutiden*. Stockholm, 1941.

HEITZ, GERHARD. *Ländliche Leinenproduktion in Sachsen, 1470–1555*. Berlin, 1961.

HOFFMANN, ALFRED. *Wirtschaftsgeschichte Oberösterreichs*. I, Salzburg, 1952.

HUSA, VACLAV, PETRAN, JOSEF and SUBTOVA, ALENA. *Homo Faber*. Prague, 1967.

HUTCHINS, J. G. B. *The American Maritime Industries and Public Policy, 1789–1914*. Cambridge, Mass., 1941.

KELLENBENZ, HERMANN. 'Die Unternehmertätigkeit der verschiedenen Stände während des Übergangs zur Neuzeit.' *Vierteljahrschrift für Sozial- und Wirtschaftsgeschichte*, XLIV, 1957.

'Industries rurales en l'Occident de la fin du Moyen Age au XVIIIe siècle.' *Annales, E.S.C.*, XVIII, 1963.

'Standewesen und Merkantilismus in Schleswig-Holstein und Skandinavien.' *Vierteljahrschrift für Sozial- und Wirtschaftsgeschichte*, L, 1964.

'Probleme der Merkantilismusforschung.' *XIIe Congrès International des Sciences Historiques, Rapports IV*, Vienna, 1965.

'Ländliches Gewerbe und bäuerliches Unternehmertum in Westeuropa vom Spätmittelalter bis ins 18. Jahrhundert.' *Deuxième Conférence Internationale d'Histoire Economique à Aix-en-Provence, Second International Conference of Economic History 1962* (= Ecole Pratique des Hautes Etudes/Sorbonne, Sixième Section – Sciences Economiques et Sociales, Congrès et Colloques VIII), The Hague–Paris, 1965.

'Les Industries dans l'Europe moderne (1500–1750).' *Industrialisation en Europe au XIXe siècle, cartographie et typologie*. Lyons, 7–10 October 1970. Colloques Internationaux du Centre National de la Recherche Scientifique, Sciences Humaines, No. 540, Paris, 1970.

'Die Aachener Kupfermeister.' *Zeitschrift des Aachener Geschichtsvereins*, LXXX, 1970.

'Rural Industries from the End of the Middle Ages to the Eighteenth Century.' In Peter Earle (ed.), *Essays in European Economic History 1500–1800*. Oxford, 1974.

Wolltuchproduktion und Tuchhandel. Secunda Settimana di Studio. Prato, 1970.

KELLENBENZ, H. (ed.). *Kupferproduktion in Europa*. (Contributions by P. JEANNIN, P. BRAUNSTEIN, K. GLAMANN, H. POHL, S. TVEITE, J. VLACHOVIČ, J. JANAČEK, O. PICKL and F. TREMEL.) Cologne, 1976.

KIRCHGÄSSNER, BERNHARD. *Merkantilistische Wirtschaftspolitik und fürstliches Unternehmertum. Die dritte Kurfürstliche Hauptstadt Frankenthal*. Speier, 1968.

KLEIN, P. W. *De Trippen*. Assen, 1965.

KLIMA, ARNOŠT. *Manufakturni obdobi v Čechách (Die Manufakturperiode in Böhmen)*. Prague, 1955.

KRÜGER, HORST. *Zur Geschichte der Manufakturen und der Manufakturarbeiter in Preussen. Die mittleren Provinzen in der zweiten Hälfte des 18. Jahrhunderts*. Berlin, 1958.

KULA, WITOLD. *Szkice o manufakturach w Polsce w VIII Wieku*. Warsaw, 1956.

'Die Meissner Porzellan-Manufaktur in der sächsischen Manufakturgeschichte.' *250 Jahre staatliche Porzellan-Manufaktur*. Meissen, 1960.

LANDES, DAVID. *The Rise of Capitalism*. New York, 1966.

LEBRUN, PIERRE. *L'Industrie de la laine à Verviers pendant le XVIIIe et au debut du XIXe siècle*. Liège, 1948.

LENTZE, HANS. 'Nürnbergs Gewerbeverfassung des Spätmittelalters im Rahmen der deutschen Entwicklung.' *Beiträge zur Wirtschaftsgeschichte Nürnbergs*, II, Nuremberg, 1967.

LÉON, P. *Economies et societés préindustrielles*. II *1650–1780, Les Origines d'une accélération de l'histoire*. Paris, 1970.

'L'industrialisation en France en tant que facteur de la croissance économique du début du XVIIe siècle à nos jours.' *Première Conférence Internationale d'Hist. Econ., Stockholm*. The Hague–Paris, 1960.

LEWIS, M. A. *The Navy of Britain*. London, 1948.

LIVI, C., SELLA, D. and TUCCI, U. 'Un problème d'histoire: La décadence économique de Venise.' *La decadenza economica veneziana nel secolo XVII*, Venice–Rome, 1961.

MADDALENA, A. DE. 'L'industria tessile a Mantova nel 500 e all'inizio del 600.' *Studi in onore di Amintore Fontani*. IV, Milan, 1962.

MATHIAS, PETER. *The First Industrial Nation, an Economic History of Britain 1700–1914.* London, 1969.

MAURO, FRÉDÉRIC. *Histoire générale du travail, La prérévolution du travail.* Paris, n.d.

MOLENDA, DANUTA. *Gornictwo kruszowe vo krenie zloz slasko-krakowskich do polowy XVI wieku.* Wroclaw–Warsaw–Cracow, 1963.

NANCE, R. MORTON. 'The ship of the Renaissance.' *Mariner's Mirror*, XLI, 1955.

NEF, J. U. 'Coal mining and utilization.' *A History of Technology*, III, Oxford, 1957.
The Conquest of the Material World. Chicago–London, 1964.
'Silver production in central Europe 1450–1618.' *Journal of Political Economy*, CLIX.

NORBERG, JAMES. 'A note on knitting and knitted fabrics.' *A History of Technology*, III, Oxford, 1957.

PATTERSON, R. 'Spinning and weaving.' *A History of Technology*, III, Oxford, 1957.

PEYER, H. C. *Leinwandgewerbe und Fernhandel der Stadt St. Gallen von den Anfängen bis 1520.* 2 vols., St Gallen, 1959/60.

PICKL, OTHMAR. 'Die Salzproduktion im Ostalpenraum am Beginn der Neuzeit.' *Österreichisches Montanwesen, Produktion, Verteilung, Sozialformen*, ed. M. Mitterauer, Vienna, 1974.

PÖLNITZ, GÖTZ FREIHERR VON. *Jakob Fugger.* 2 vols., Tübingen, 1949–51.
Anton Fugger. I–III (III: 1), Tübingen, 1957–71.

PORTAL, ROGER. *L'Oural au XVIIᵉ siècle.* Paris, 1950.

RAMSAY, G. D. *The Wiltshire Woollen Industry in the Sixteenth and Seventeenth Centuries.* London, 1965.

REDLICH, FRITZ. 'Der deutsche fürstliche Unternehmer, eine typische Erscheinung des 16. Jahrhunderts.' *Tradition*, 1958.

RESS, F. M. *Geschichte und wirtschaftliche Bedeutung der oberpfälzischen Eisenindutrie.* Regensburg, 1950.

REUTER, ORTULF. 'Die Manufaktur im Fränkischen Raum. Eine Untersuchung groß-gewerblicher Anfänge in den Fürstentümern Ansbach und Bayreuth als Beitrage zur Gewerbegeschichte des 18. und beginnenden 19. Jahrhunderts.' Dissertation, Munich–Stuttgart, 1961.

ROOVER, RAYMUND DE. *The Medici Bank.* Cambridge, Mass., 1963.

RUIZ-MARTIN, F. *Lettres marchandes échangées entre Florence et Medina del Campo.* Paris, 1965.
Un testimonio literario sobre las manufacturas de paños en Segovia por 1625. Valladolid, 1966.
'Rasgos estructurales de Castilla en tiempo de Carlos V.' *Moneda y Credito*, XCVI, 1960.

SCHICK, LÉON. *Un Grand Homme d'affaires au début du XVIᵉ siècle: Jacob Fugger.* Paris, 1957.

SCHIWANK, HANS. 'Die Technik im Zeitalter des Barock.' *Die Technik der Neuzeit* (ed. Friedrich Klemm), Potsdam, 1941.

SCHMITZ, EDITH. *Leinengewerbe und Leinenhandel in Nordwestdeutschland (1650–1850).* Cologne, 1957.

SCHREMMER, ECKART. *Die Wirtschaft Bayerns – vom hohen Mittelalter bis zum Beginn der Industrialisierung – Bergbau, Gewerbe, Handel.* Munich–Leipzig, 1914.

SCHUBERT, H. R. *History of the British Iron and Steel Industry from c. 450 B.C. to A.D. 1775.* London, 1957.

SCHULTE, FRITZ. *Die Entwicklung der gewerblichen Wirtschaft in Rheinland-Westfalen im 18. Jahrhundert.* Cologne, 1959.

SCHUMPETER, ELIZABETH BOODY. *English Overseas Trade Statistics 1600–1808.* Oxford, 1960.

SÉE, H. *Französische Wirtschaftsgeschichte.* I, Jena, 1933.

SELLA, DOMENICO. *European Industries 1500–1700.* The Fontana Economic History of Europe, II: 5, London, 1970.
'Les Mouvements longs de l'industrie lainière à Venise aux XVIᵉ et XVIIᵉ siècles.' *Annales*, 1957. (Repr.: 'La industria della lana in Venezia nel secoli sedecesimo e diciassettesimo.' *Storia dell'economia italiana*, I (Turin, 1959).)

SINGER, CHARLES, HOLMYARD, E. J., HALL, A. R. and WILLIAMS, TREVOR. *A History of Technology*. II, III, Oxford, 1957.
SLAWINGER, GERHARD. *Die Manufaktur in Kurbayern. Die Anfänge der großgewerblichen Entwicklung in der Übergangsepoche vom Merkantilismus zum Liberalismus.* Stuttgart, 1966.
SMITH, CYRIL STANLEY. 'Metallurgy and assaying.' *A History of Technology*, III, Oxford, 1957.
SOMBART, WERNER. *Der moderne Kapitalismus.* I/II, Munich–Leipzig, 1925.
SPIESZ, ANTON. *Manufacturne obdobie na Slovensku, 1725–1825.* Bratislava, 1961.
'Die Manufaktur im östlichen Europa.' *Kölner Vorträge zur Sozial- und Wirtschaftsgeschichte*, Heft 2, ed. H. Kellenbenz, Cologne, 1969.
SPOONER, FRANK C. *L'économie modiale et les frappes monétaires en France, 1493–1680.* Paris, 1956.
SPRANDEL, R. *Das Eisengewerbe im Mittelalter.* Stuttgart, 1968.
STRIEDER, JAKOB. *Studien zur Geschichte kapitalistischer Organisationsformen. Monopole, Kartelle und Aktiengesellschaften im Mittelalter und zu Beginn der Neuzeit.* Munich–Leipzig, 1914.
'Die deutsche Montan- und Metallindustrie im Zeitalter der Fugger.' *Das reiche Augsburg*, ed. Deininger, Munich, 1938.
TREMEL, F. *Der Frühkapitalismus in Innerösterreich.* Graz, 1954.
USHER, A. P. *A History of Mechanical Inventions.* Rev. ed. Oxford, 1954.
VICENS VIVES, JAIME. *An Economic History of Spain.* Princeton, New Jersey, 1969.
WADSWORTH, A. P. and MANN, J. DE L. *Cotton Trade and Industrial Lancashire, 1600–1780.* Manchester, 1965.
WAILES, REX. 'Windmills.' *A History of Technology*, III, Oxford, 1957.
WESTERMANN, EKKEHARD. *Das Eislebener Garkupfer und seine Bedeutung für den europäischen Kupfermarkt 1460–1560.* Cologne–Vienna, 1971.
WHITE, LYNN. *Medieval Technology and Social Change.* Oxford, 1975.
WILSON, C. H. *Profit and Power.* London, 1957.
WISCHNITZER, MARK. *A History of Jewish Crafts and Guilds.* New York, 1965.
YERNAUX, JEAN. *La métallurgie liégeoise et son expansion au XVIIᵉ siècle.* Liège, 1939.
ZORN, W. *Handels- und Industriegeschichte Bayrisch-Schwabens 1648–1870.* N.p., 1961.

CHAPTER VIII

Government and Society

This bibliography makes no claim to comprehensiveness, but is merely a list of the books which the writer has referred to in the above chapter, or has found useful to an understanding of the subjects discussed.

Useful general surveys of the period covered by this account are to be found in the relevant volumes of the two following series: *The Rise of Modern Europe*, ed. by W. L. Langer, and the *Library of European Civilisation*, ed. by G. Barraclough.

Allgemeines Landrecht. 1974.
ANER, K. *Der Aufklärer Friedrich Nicolai.* Giessen, 1912.
ANTOINE, M. *Le Conseil du Roi sous le règne de Louis XV.* Paris, 1970.
ARENDT, H. *Rahel Varnhagen.* Munich, 1959.
BAASCH, E. (ed.). *Quellen zur Geschichte von Hamburgs Handel und Schiffahrt im 17., 18. und 19. Jahrhundert.* Hamburg, 1910.
BAUMGART, P. 'Absoluter Staat und Judenemanzipation.' *Jahrbuch für die Geschichte Mittel- und Ostdeutschlands*, XIII–XIV, 1965.
BECK, L. W. *Early German Philosophy.* Harvard, 1969.
BESENVAL, BARON DE. *Mémoires.* Ed. Ségur, Paris, 1805.
BLANNING, T. C. W. *Joseph II and Enlightened Despotism.* Longman, London, 1970.
Reform and Revolution in Mainz. Cambridge, 1974.
BLOCH, M. 'La Lutte pour l'Individualisme Agraire.' *Annales d'Histoire Economique et Sociale (E.S.C.)*, vol. 2, 1930.
Les Caractères originaux de l'histoire rurale française. 2 vols. Paris, 1964.
BLUCHE, F. *Les Magistrats du Parlement de Paris au XVIIIᵉ siècle.* Paris, 1960.

BODELSCHWINGH. *Leben des Freiherrn von Vincke*. Berlin, 1853.

BONCERF. *Les Inconvénients des Droits Féodaux*. London, 1776.

BOSHER, J. F. *The Single Duty Project*. London, 1964.

French Finances 1770–1795. Cambridge, 1970.

BOSSUET, J.-B. 'Politique tirée des propres paroles de L'Ecriture Sainte.' H. Brémont, *Textes Choisis et Commentés*, II, Paris, 1913.

BRUGGEMANN, F. *Das Weltbild der deutschen Aufklärung*. II. *Reihe Aufklärung*. Leipzig, 1930.

BRUNSCHWIG, H. *Société et Romanticisme en Prusse au XVIIIe siècle*. Paris, 1973.

BÜSCH, O. *Militärsystem und Sozialleben im alten Preußen*. Berlin, 1962.

CARRÉ, H. *La Noblesse de France et l'opinion publique au XVIIIe siècle*. Paris, 1920.

CASSIRER, E. *Philosophy of the Enlightenment*. Trans. F. A. Koelln and J. P. Pettigrove, Princeton, 1951.

COBBAN, A. *The Myth of the French Revolution*. London, 1955.

COLE, C. W. *Colbert and a Century of French Mercantilism*. 2 vols. New York, 1939.

DAKIN, D. *Turgot and the Ancien Régime in France*. Methuen, London, 1939.

DARDEL, E. *Commerce, industrie et navigation à Rouen et au Havre au XVIIIe siècle*. Rouen, 1966.

DARNTON, R. 'Literary Low Life in Pre-revolutionary France.' *Past and Present*, LI, May 1971.

DAUMARD, A. and FURET, F. *Structures et relations sociales à Paris au milieu du XVIIIe siècle*. Paris, 1961.

DEMETER, K. *Das deutsche Offizierskorps in Gesellschaft und Staat 1650–1945*. Frankfurt a/M, 1965.

DILTHEY, W. 'Die deutsche Aufklärung im Staat und in der Akademie Freidrichs des Großen.' *Deutsche Rundschau*, CVII, 1901.

DÖHNOFF, M. *Namen die Keiner Mehr Nennt*. Mönchen-Gladbach, 1962.

DORN, W. L. 'The Prussian Bureaucracy in the eighteenth century.' *Political Science Quarterly*, XLVI, XLVII, 1931, 1932.

DUCLOS, C. P. *Considérations sur les Moeurs*. Ed. F. C. Green, Cambridge, 1939.

DUPONT DE NEMOURS, P. 'De l'Origine et des Progrès d'une Science Nouvelle, 1768.' *Collections des Economistes et des Reformateurs Sociaux de la France*. Paris, 1910.

DURAND, Y. *Les Fermiers Généraux au XVIIIe Siècle*. Paris, 1971.

EBERTY, F. *Jugenderinnerungen eines alten Berliners*. Berlin, 1878.

EBERHARD, J. H. 'Über die Zeichen der Aufklärung einer Nation.' *Literarische Chronik*, II, Bern, 1786.

ÉGRET, J. *La Pré-Révolution Française, 1787–1788*. Paris, 1962.

Louis XV et l'opposition parlementaire. Paris, 1970.

FLAMMERMONT, J. *Le Chancelier Maupeou et les parlements*. Paris, 1883.

FONTANE, T. *Wanderungen durch die Mark*. 4 vols.

Vor dem Sturm.

Der Stechlin.

FORSTER, R. *The Nobility of Toulouse in the Eighteenth Century*. Baltimore, 1960.

FRAUENDIENST, W. *Christian Wolff als Staatsdenker*. Berlin, 1927.

FREYMARK, H. *Die Reform der preußischen Handels und Zollpolitik*. Jena, 1898.

GARVE, C. *Fragmente zur Schilderung des Geistes, des Charakters und die Regierung Friedrichs des Zweyten*. Breslau, 1798.

Versuche über verschiedene Gegenstände aus der Moral, der Literatur und dem Gesellschaftlichen Leben. Breslau, 1802.

Über den Charakter der Bauern und über ihr Verhältniss gegen die Gutsherrn und gegen die Regierung. Breslau, 1796.

GAY, P. *Voltaire's Politics*. Princeton, 1959.

The Enlightenment: An Interpretation. I *The Rise of Modern Paganism*. Weidenfeld & Nicolson, London, 1967.

II *The Science of Freedom*. New York, 1969.

GÖRLITZ, W. *Die Junker*. Glucksburg, 1957.

GOUBERT, P. *Familles marchandes sous l'Ancien Régime*. Paris, 1959.

Beauvais et le Beauvaisis. Paris, 1960.

Louis XIV et vingt millions de Français. Paris, 1966.
L'Ancien Régime. I *La Société.* Paris, 1969.
II *Les Pouvoirs.* Paris, 1973.
GROETHUYSEN, B. *Die Entstehung der bürgerlichen Welt- und Lebensanschauung.* 2 vols. Halle/Saale, 1927–31.
GROSCLAUDE, P. *Malesherbes témoin et interprète de son temps.* Paris, 1961.
GROSS, N. T. *The Industrial Revolution in the Habsburg Monarchy, 1750–1914.* (Fontana Economic History of Europe.) Collins, London, 1972.
GRÜNBERG, C. *Die Bauernbefreiung und die Auflösung des gutsherrlichen Verhältnissen in Böhmen, Mähren und Schlesien.* Leipzig, 1893–4.
HAUSSHERR, H. *Hardenberg.* I *1750–1800.* Cologne–Graz, 1963.
HECKSCHER, E. *Mercantilism.* Trans. M. Schapiro. 2 vols. (Rev. ed. London, 1955.)
HENDERSON, W. O. *The State and the Industrial Revolution in Prussia 1740–1870. Studies in the Economic Policy of Frederick the Great.* London, 1963.
HEROLD, C. *Mistress of an Age. A Life of Madame de Staël.* London, 1959.
HEUER, U. J. *Allgemeines Landrecht und Klassenkampf.* [East] Berlin, 1960.
HIGGS, H. *The Physiocrats.* London, 1897.
HINRICHS, C. *Friedrich Wilhelm I. Jugend und Aufstieg.* Hamburg, 1941.
HINZE, K. *Die Arbeiterfrage zu Beginn des modernen Kapitalismus in Brandenburg-Preußen.* 2nd ed., Berlin, 1963.
HINZE, O. *Regierung und Verwaltung.* Gottingen, 1967.
Staat und Verfassung. Göttingen, 1962.
KANT, E. *Was ist Aufklärung?*
KNAPP, G. F. *Die Bauernbefreiung und der Ursprung der Landarbeiter in den älteren Teilen Preußens.* 2nd ed., Munich, 1927.
KOSELLECK, R. *Preußen zwischen Reform und Revolution.* Stuttgart, 1967.
KOSER, R. *König Friedrich der Große.* 2 vols. Stuttgart, 1893–1903.
KULISCHER, J. *Allgemeine Wirtschaftsgeschichte.* 2 vols. 2nd ed., Munich, 1958.
LABROUSSE, E. *La Crise de l'économie française à la fin de l'ancien régime.* Paris, 1943.
LACOUR-GAYET, R. *Calonne.* Paris, 1963.
LAVISSE, E. *Histoire de France depuis les origines jusqu'à la révolution.* VIII–IX. Paris, 1906–10.
LEFEBVRE, G. *Quatre-Vingt-Neuf.* Paris, 1939. (Translated by R. R. Palmer under the title *The Coming of the French Revolution,* Princeton, N.J., 1967.)
La Grande Peur. Paris, no date. (Translated by J. White, London, 1973.)
Etudes sur la révolution français. 2nd ed. Paris, 1963.
Etudes Orléanaises. Paris, 1962.
LEHNDORF, GRAF. *Dreißig Jahre am Hofe Friedrichs des Großen.* Ed. K. A. Schmidt-Lötzen. Gotha, 1907.
LÜTGE, F. *Deutsche Sozial- und Wirtschaftsgeschichte.* 3rd ed. Berlin, 1966.
Geschichte der deutschen Agrarverfassung. Stuttgart, 1963.
LÜTHY, H. *La Banque Protestante en France.* 2 vols. Paris, 1959–61.
Le Passé Présent: combats d'idées de Calvin à Rousseau. Monaco, 1965.
MANUEL, F. E. *The Prophets of Paris.* New York, 1965.
MARION, M. *Dictionnaire des institutions de la France aux XVIIᵉ et XVIIIᵉ siècles.* 2nd ed. Paris, 1968.
MARTINI, F. 'Die Adelsfrage in Preußen vor 1806.' *Vierteljahrschrift für Sozial- und Wirtschaftsgeschichte.* 1938, Beiheft 35.
MATTHEWS, G. T. *The Royal General Farms in Eighteenth-Century France.* Columbia, 1958.
MAUZI, R. *L'Idée du bonheur au XVIIIᵉ siècle.* Paris, 1960.
MAY, G. *Madame Roland.* Columbia, 1970.
MAYER, E. W. *Das Retablissement Ost- und Westpreussens unter der Mitwirkung und Leitung Theodors von Schön.* Jena, 1916.
MEIER, E. VON. *Die Reform der Verwaltungsorganisation unter Stein und Hardenberg.* 2nd ed., Munich–Leipzig, 1912.
MEINECKE, F. *Idee der Staatsräson.* Ed. W. Hofer. 2nd ed., Munich 1960. (Translated by D. Scott under the title *Machiavellism,* London, 1957.)
MERCIER DE LA RIVIÈRE. *L'Ordre naturel et essentiel des sociétés politiques.* Paris–London, 1767.

MEUSEL, F. *Friedrich August Ludwig von der Marwitz.* 3 vols. Berlin, 1908–13.

MEYER, J. *La Noblesse Bretonne au XVIIIe siècle.* Paris, 1972.

MITROFANOV, P. VON. *Joseph II, seine politische und kulturelle Tätigkeit.* Vienna, 1910.

MOLS, R. *Introduction à la démographie historique des villes d'Europe du XIVe au XVIIIe siècle.* Louvain, 1955.

MONTESQUIEU, BARON DE. *De l'esprit des lois.*

MORNET, D. *Les Origines intellectuelles de la révolution française 1715–1787.* 5th ed., Paris, 1954.

MOUSNIER, R. *La Venalité des offices sous Henry IV et Louis XIII.* Rouen, 1945.

MOUSNIER, R. and HARTUNG. 'Quelques problèmes concernant la monarchie absolue.' *Relazioni del X Congresso Internationale di Scienze Storiche. Storia Moderna,* IV, Florence, 1955.

NAUDÉ, W. *Getreidehandelspolitik.* Berlin, 1896.

NECKER, J. 'De l'Administration des Finances.' *Oeuvres Complètes,* ed. Baron de Staël, V, Paris, 1821.

OLIVIER-MARTIN, J. M. *L'Organisation corporative de la France d'ancien régime.* Paris, 1938.

PARET, P. *Yorck and the Era of Prussian Reform 1807 to 1815.* Princeton, 1966.

PARISET, F. G. (ed.). *Bordeaux au XVIIIe siècle.* Bordeaux, 1968.

PRERADOVICH, H. N. VON. *Die Führungsschichten in Österreich und Preußen.* Wiesbaden, 1955.

QUESNAY, F. *François Quesnay et la Physiocratie.* I *Études, Biographie.* II *Textes Annotés.* Published by l'Institut National d'Etudes Démographiques. Paris, 1958.

RACHEL, H. and WALLICH, P. *Berliner Großkaufleute und Kapitalisten.* II, Berlin, 1938.

RAUMER, F. VON. *Lebenserinnerungen und Briefwechsel.* Berlin, 1861.

REINHARD, M. *Le Grand Carnot.* 2 vols. Paris, 1950–2.

REINHARD, M. and ARMENGAUD, A. *Histoire générale de la population mondiale.* Paris, 1961.

RITTER, G. *Stein.* 3rd ed., Stuttgart, 1958.

Friedrich der Große: ein historisches Profil. Leipzig, 1936. (Translated by P. Paret, London, 1968.)

ROSENBERG, H. *Bureaucracy, Aristocracy and Autocracy. The Prussian Experience 1660–1815.* Cambridge, Mass., 1958.

ROZDOLSKI, R. *Die große Steuer- und Agrarreform Josefs II.* Warsaw, 1961.

SAINT JACOB, P. DE. *Les Paysans de la Bourgogne du Nord au dernier siècle de l'ancien régime.* Paris, 1960.

SCHMOLLER, G. *Deutsches Städtewesen.* Berlin, 1922.

SCHÖN, T. VON. *Aus den Papieren des Ministers Theodor von Schön.* 6 vols. Halle, 1875–83.

SCHWARTZ, P. *Der erste Kulturkampf in Preußen 1788–1798.* Berlin, 1925.

SÉGUR, COMTE DE. *Mémoires, souvenirs et anecdotes.* Paris, 1825.

SÉNAC DE MEILHAN, G. *Considérations sur les richesses et le luxe.* 1787.

Des Principes et des causes de la révolution en France. 1790.

SILAGI, D. *Jakobiner in der Habsburger-Monarchie. Ein Beitrag zur Geschichte des aufgeklärten Absolutismus in Österreich.* Vienna–Munich, 1962.

Ungarn und der geheime Mitarbeiterkreis Kaiser Leopolds II. Munich, 1961.

SKALWEIT, S. *Frankreich und Friedrich der Große.* Bonn, 1952.

SMALL, A. W. *The Cameralists.* 2nd ed., New York, 1909.

SMITH, A. *The Wealth of Nations.* Ed. E. Cannan, Methuen, London, 1950.

SOBOUL, A. *La France à la veille de la Révolution.* Paris, 1966.

SOMBART, W. *Der Bourgeois.* Leipzig, 1913. (Translated by M. Epstein under the title *Quintessence of Capitalism.* London, 1915.)

STAËL, MADAME DE. *De l'Allemagne.* Ed. Comtesse de Pange. 2 vols., Paris, 1958.

STEIN, R. *Die Umwandlung der Agrarverfassung Ostpreußens.* Jena, 1918.

STÖLZEL, A. *Carl Gottlieb Svarez.* Berlin, 1885.

SVAREZ, C. G. *Vorträge über Recht und Staat.* Ed. H. Conrad and G. Kleinheyer, Cologne, 1960.

TAYLOR, G. V. 'Non-capitalist wealth and the origins of the French Revolution.' *Am. Hist. Review,* CXXI, Jan. 1967.

TOCQUEVILLE, A. DE. *Oeuvres Complètes.* Ed. J. P. Mayer, II, Paris, 1952.

TUDESQ, A. J. *Les Grandes Notables en France 1840–1849.* Paris, 1964.

Vergleichende Enzyklopedie. Sowjetsystem und demokratische Gesellschaft. 1 (article on absolutism), Freiburg, 1966.

VOLTAIRE. *Dictionnaire Philosophique.*
  Lettres Philosophiques.
  L'Ingénu.
  Siècle de Louis XIV.
  Candide.

WANDRUSZKA, A. *Leopold II.* 2 vols. Vienna and Munich, 1965.

WANGERMANN, E. *The Austrian Achievement 1700–1800.* Thames and Hudson, London, 1973.

WINTER, E. *Der Josefinismus. Die Geschichte des österreichischen Reformkatholizismus 1740–1848.* Berlin, 1962.

WILSON, A. M. *Diderot: The Testing Years 1713–59.* New York, 1957.

ZELLER, G. *Aspects de la politique française sous l'ancien régime.* Paris, 1964.

INDEX

Aachen, 490, 546; brass industry, 244, 486, 494–5; calamine from, 463, 484; coal mines, 509; copper, 484, 494, (gild of copper masters) 494; emigrants from, in Sweden, 484; wool weaving, 518

Abbeville, textile factory at, 471, 515

Abel, Wilhelm: on cattle and grain prices, 233; on grain prices, 43, 200, 223; *Agrarkrisen und Agrarkonjunctur...*, 43

Aberdeen, 141; salmon exports, 147; stocking knitting, 511

Aberdovey fish market, 142; fisheries, 143

absolutism, 549–61, 566, 595, 599, 604, 619; enlightened absolutism, 595–600; and mercantilism, 573, 596; ministers and office-holders under, 561–2, 564–73; Philosophe view of, 602; Physiocrat challenge to, 612; private fortunes under, 585

English, 554, 555; French, 549, 552–62, 564, 566, 573, 582–3, (end of) 589, 600, (and the French Revolution) 618; Hapsburg dominions, 554–7, 561, 566, 573, 618; Prussian, 552–60, 566, 573, 583–5, 618; Russian, 555

Acapulco, silver from, 257, 310

Accademia dei Georgofili (Florence, 1753), 103

accounting and book-keeping, 296, 310n2, 330, 417, 418, 441; a bourgeois habit, 586; in commerce and industry, 424; double-entry, 412; duplication of systems, 292–4; by enlightened despots, 558, 584; in farming, 102; by shopkeepers, 300–1

Achilles, Walter, on corn prices and corn trade, 220, 223, 229

Addison, Joseph, Secretary of State, 185, 186, 193, 202, 289

Adolf, Count Hermann, restores *Leggen* system to linen trade, 519

Adriatic, 206, 270

Adrichem, Claes Adriaensz van, Delft merchant, 226

Affaitadi, Italian merchants, 283–4

Africa, 409, 440, 442, 543, 545; exports of copper to, 244, (of *lakens*) 254; gold shipments from, 257, 260, 264, 296; slave trade, 212–13; spices from, 282

East, 532

North, 250, 314

northwest, 136

South, 210

Age of Elegance, 543

agrarian history, 42–4

Agricola, George, *De re metallica* (1556), 472

agricultural revolution, 42, 617; a misnomer, 71, 72, 81; in Prussia, 619

agricultural societies, 103; and absolutist monarchies, 549–50

agriculture

credit for, 305–6

depression in, 200

enterprise in, 393n, 448–50

equipment, 56, 103, 96–100, 103, 604

expansion and regression, 8, 66, 69, 99, 104, 604, (table) 55–6; changes during, 74–9, 97, 100; and serfdom, 119–20; yield ratios, 82

government regulations, 74–5, 107–8, 112, 220

improvements in, 44, 52, 81–2, 305

a lost cause, 574; its inefficiency, 606; shortage of capital, 613

monocultural, 10, 68, 96

open-field system, 551, 582, 603–4, 606

Physiocrat view of, 611–12

predominance of before 1800, 44–5, 357; critical importance of, 28, 38

prices, 69–71, 106

reforms, 616, 617, 620

risks of, 59, 60, 65–6

rotation of crops, 24, 56, 66, 69, 71–4, 82; and manuring, 94–5

tillage systems, 72–5, 95

see also arable farming; cattle; crops; dairy produce; farming; grain; stock farming

Akkema, Netherlands iron entrepreneur in Russia, 502

Alba, Duke of, 152

Albania, 221, 489
Albertus Magnus, *Historia Naturalis*, 73
Ålborg, 512, 538
alcoholic drinks, 201–2; aquavit, 199, 201–2; brandy and gin, 538; *see also* beer; distilleries; wine
Alembert, Jean le Rondd', on 'enlightenment', 589, 598, 600
Alexis, Tsar, 529
Alfonso I, of Este, his pharmacy, 506
Allgemeines Landrecht, 591, 598, 599–600
alloys, 473–4; *see also* brass industry; bronze
Alps, 67, 242; iron industry, 501
Alsace: agriculture, 71, 88, 93, 102; copper mines, 492
Alströmer, Swedish entrepreneur, 530
Altena, 499
Altona, 283, 468
alum, 207, 490, 509
Amerbach press, Basle, 534
America, 67, 543; discovery of, 7; mining immigrants, 487; silver from, 212, 260, 264, 320, 489; spices, 214, 282; trade with, 212, 314, 440, 483, 531, (in hats) 517, (in Irish frieses) 510–11; *see also* New England; New World; North America; South America; United States of America
American historians, 580
American Indians, 546
Amiens: herring consignments, 167; worsted industry, 515, 544
Ammann, Joost, painter, 474
Amsterdam
    banking: *Bank van Leening*, 303, 340; clearing bank system, 324, 343, 345–7, 390; Exchange Bank, *see* Amsterdam Exchange Bank; issue business, 355, 391; merchant bankers, 344, 390, 495
    barometer of world prices, 214; holds key to international payments system, 261
    decline of, 356
    distilleries, 538
    as entrêpot, 397, 408, 413, 428–9, 454, 520
    finance: bills of exchange, 264; cash-keeping, 336, 342, 343, 347, 351; financial capitalism, 389; financial techniques, 335–7, 346–7; financiers, 343; forward business, 345

gilds, 466
imports of cattle, 200; import and export tolls, 274
as international trading mart, 268, 273–5, 276, 340
markets: cattle, 216, 236; copper, 241, 244, 248–9, (staple market) 245–7, 273, 544; cowry, 213; grain market of the world, 188, 215, 222–3, 224, 227–31, 274, 276, 286, (mechanism) 276–7, (wheat prices) 70; local grain market, 231; pepper, 285; precious metals, 260, 297, 309; textiles, 253, 515
merchants, 286–7, 544; protest against banking edicts, 336
money and capital market, 335, 345, 354, 357, 361, 390, 392; money and credit, 342–7; specie accepted for security, 341
port of, 537
Portuguese Jews in, 333, 375
protectionist policy, 273
securities trade, 345
shipbuilding, 531
silk-weaving, 515
staple market, 28, 286
stock market boom (1720), 388
sugar refineries, 540, 541
ties with Antwerp, 335–6; with England, 384
tobacco trading and manufacture, 541
trade: with the Baltic, 276; with the Levant and Far East, 337; with Spain and Portugal, 335–6; trade coins, 337
Amsterdam Admiralty, 390
Amsterdam Corn Exchange, 223, 276; quotations on, 228
Amsterdam Exchange (Bourse), 223, 343, 345–6, 389; exchange rates, 342; weekly price sheet, 408
Amsterdam Exchange Bank, 307, 337, 343, 390; Adam Smith on, 346; loans to East India Company, 357; trade in precious metals, 346–7
Amsterdam silver fleet, 260
Anand, Indira (*née* Narang), 280
Andalusia: agricultural system, 68, 72; brandy industry, 538; corn exports, 221; overseas trade, 206; Portuguese Jews in, 333; salt-drying, 538

Andreae, Christoph, and sons, bleaching-works, 521

Andreasberg, 488, 500

Anglo-Saxons, 550

animal husbandry, 89–93; animal fodder, 555; and the international market, 188; switch from/to arable farming, 74–5, 101, 231; *see also* cattle; stock farming

animal traction, 46, 82, 90, 93, 96, 97–8, 100, 220, (as criterion of agricultural classes) 126–7, 552, 611; cows, 46, 90, 93; donkeys, 477; horses, 46, 91, 93, 96–100; mules, 260; oxen, 46, 90, 93, 96–9

annuities, 303–6, 353, 355, 359, 361, 423

investment in, 580

perpetual, 384

as public credit, 363, 364, 366, 374, 370; English, 388; French, 376–8, 380

redeemability, 361, 366, 376

Spanish state annuities (*juros*), 371, 373–5; others, 391

Ansbach, 536; Margrave of, 483

Antwerp, 84, 217, 365, 414, 484, 514; annuities, 304, 306; banking system, 323–4; bills of exchange, 330–1; cashkeepers, 351; cattle imports, 200; coins, 320; copper market, 218, 244, 275; *Costuymen*, 324, 327, 328, 336; credit for rulers, 366–72; decline of, 324, 399; diamond trade, 542; emigrants from, 347, 539–40; English office in, 385; as entrepôt, 397, 413, 449, 494, 539; fairs, 323, 329n; financial techniques, 322–32, 347, 350; Fuggers in, 275; grain trade, 222–3; growth of, 190–1; influence in London, 348, 350, 351; interest rates, 357, 362, 368–70; Italian influence, 323–2, 325; marine insurance, 332; merchants, 344, 355, (merchant capitalism) 218; money market, 330, 357, 361, 368–72; Portuguese merchant bankers in, 333, 375, (Portuguese factory) 244; printing presses, 535; spice market, 285, 415; sugar refining, 539, 540; textile market, 520, (collapse of) 254, (staple for English cloth) 269, (tapestry making) 515; ties with Amsterdam, 335–6; as trading centre, 214, 215, 221, 275, 325, (the metro-polis of trade and finance) 332; the 'troubles' of 1566–86, 539, 542, (the 'Spanish Fury') 375, (conquest by Parma) 218, 540; urbanization, 304–5

Antwerp Exchange, 326, 330, 368; exchange market, transfer of loans to London, 381; modelled on Royal Exchange, London, 348; separation of trade from financial transactions, 331; speculation on, 331–2

Anzin mining enterprise, 433, 434, 439

apprenticeship, 465, 468

Apulia, grain from, 207

aquavit, 199, 201–2; mash from, fed to cows, 202

arable acreage and population changes, 131–2

arable farming, 8; shifts: among grains, 101; from/to industrial crops, 101; from/to livestock breeding, 56, 75–5, 90, 94, 101, 231, 515; from/to pasture farming, 74–5, 76; from/to wine-growing, 75–6, 77, 101; *see also* agriculture; crops; grain

Aragon, kingdom of, 366

Aranda, Count of, founder of Alcora ceramic factory, 506

Arasaratnam, S., 280

arbitrage, 315–16, 321, 324, 333, 334, (in Paris banking) 335; arbitrage and exchange business, 343

Archangel, 217, 262, 545, 546; corn shipments from, 229; staple town for Muscovy Company, 270

Arctic trade route, 217, 262

aristocracy, 400, 403, 542; British, 562–3, 572; commercial, 287–8; Elizabethan, 14; Philosophe, 601

and the bourgeoisie, 583; and business enterprise, 420–4, 425, 448–51; in the cattle trade, 238; entrepreneurial role of, 394, 447–51

see also nobility

armaments: demand for, 430; enterprises in, 431, 505, 545; export of, to east, 210, 255; manufacturers of, 484; munitions business, 245, 430; weapon industry, 498–9, 500, (royal monopoly for) 499, (and royal bureaucracies) 555

armourers, 468; cannon, bronze, 207, 242, 243, 473, 496, iron, 243, 496, armaments, armourers (*cont.*) 504, (cannon-founding) 240; fortifications, 370, 507; gun-makers, 465, 501; muskets, 500; navy armaments, 243, 430; saltpetre and gunpowder, 265, 430, 472, 480, 508; swordsmiths, 470

Armenians, 256, 259

armies: commissions in, 568, 569, 571, 572; conscription, 555, 557, 566, 608, 614; cost of, 575; and education, 583, ('stupid oxen' educated by) 587; mercenary, 373, 374-5, 545, 574, 587; nobility and, 566, 567, 568-72, 587; proper size for, 577; standing armies, 553, 554-5, 567, 572, 576; transport for, 606; victualling of, 234, 536, 555; *see also* Prussia

Arnoldstein, Abbot of, buys *Fuggerau* works, 492

Arnouville, Machault d', 582

Arnstadt Company, 479

arsenals, 481, 532

artisans, 15, 127, 131, 469, 481; artisan production distinguished from industrial, 462

Artois: corn from, 222; progressive farming, 71, 94, 100

Artois pound, 293

Asgill, J. & N. Barbon land bank (1695), 305

Ashton, R., *The Crown and the Money Market* (1973), 305, 350n, 359n, 382n

Ashton, T. S., 8, 13, 64, 112

Asia
and balance of trade, 256-7
carrying trade, 416
ceramics, Asiatic motifs for, 506, 507
copper market in, 246, 249
European trade with, 211
flow of precious metals to, 213, 257
imports from, 281-2; pepper, 280, ('Asia Contract' for) 284-5; spices, 214, 282; textiles, 250-2, (restrictions on) 482, 517
joint-stock and interloper enterprise in, 440
pedlars and merchants, 279-80
see also China; East Indies; India; Japan

asiento contracts, 213, 332-3, 355, 362; in Spanish credit system, 372-5

assaying, 472

assignment, *see* credit; financial techniques

associations for timber cutting, 508

Atlantic: coastal trade, 209-10, 290; economy, expansion of, 325, (shift of European centre of gravity to) 395; navigation, 357; oceanic trade, 211-13, 458, 545, (ships for) 531; pepper trade, 283-4; route to north-west Europe, 317, 318; tuna fishing, 138

Atlantic seaboard, 17-18

Attman, A., on the Russian market in Polish politics, 228, 261, 262, 263

Auersberg, noble entrepreneur, 496

Augsburg, 477; corn, traffic in, 220; cotton printing, 471, 521; entrepreneurs, 414, 479, 484, 492; farming, 71; Fuggers at, 217; furniture making, 542-3; international banking and trade, 534; linen production, 519, (fustian) 512; printing, 534; sugar refining, 540

August I, Elector of Saxony, 284

Augustus, Elector of Saxony, 483

Aurangzeb, death of, 252

Austria
farming: arable and cattle, 76, 100; farm households, 125; imports of oxen, 234
immigrants, 524
iron: deposits, 490-1; industry, 501; iron specialists and smiths in Sweden, 486
nobility: participation in industry, 525; oppose reforms, 616
paper making, 536
peasants, 117; peasant revolts, 108, 122
seignorial rights, 116
serfdom, 118
state enterprise, 429, 483
textiles, 523-5; cotton, 524; linen, 523; pasmentry and lace, 525; silk, 524-5, (foreign specialists in) 524, (import restrictions on foreign) 527; woollens, 524, (exports of cloth) 528
war of the Austrian Succession, 608; war with Turks, 120

Austria, Emperor of, 390, 391; *see also* Joseph II; Leopold I; Maria Theresa

autocracies, *see* absolutism; monarchy

Auvergne, 126, 535; lace, 515

Aveiro, 157, 538
Avignon, 217, 307

Babaud de la Chaussade, Pierre, entrepreneur, 430
Bacon, Francis, 398
Baerum, Hakadal and Fossum, iron-works, 503
Baeza, 314, 516
bakers, bakeries, 45, 132, 180; gilds, 467, 468, 536
Bakewell, Robert, 93
balance of payments, 17, 30–1, 75; balance-of-payments men, 30, 36; negative balance, financed by exports of precious metals, 308
balance of trade, 18, 194, 256–64
    balance estimates for eastern Europe, 262–3; for England, 261, 263; for Holland, 263–4
    imbalance of trade with East, 256–7, 258, 261, 264
    and mercantilism, 193, 574, 575
    transit imbalance in Baltic, 261–3; deficit divided between Holland and England, 264
Balkan countries, 91, 547; iron mines, 501; Jewish textile manufacturers in, 528–9
Baltic commerce, 263–4, 272; Amsterdam's key position in, 261, 274, ('mother trade' of the Dutch) 276; trade coins for, 340; trading companies in, 442
Baltic corn trade, 222–3, 225–32, (value of) 233; demand for Baltic corn, 201, 231; exported to Amsterdam, 197, (Low Countries) 88, (Mediterranean) 208, (Sweden) 64; grain fleet, 10, 24; the granary of northern Europe, 214, 448; participation of nobility in, 271; the 'root of all other trades', 276
Baltic ports, 217; states, 53, 55, 98
Baltic region, 214–15
    balance of trade, 261–4; preponderance of exports, 262; flow of precious metals through, 262–3
    bills of exchange, 264
    Eastland Company in, 270
    exports: potash, 508; saltpetre, 508; tar and pitch, 531; timber, 508
    herring fishery, 135, 149, 164; salt

herrings from, 215; fish imports, 147–8, 154, 155, 177, 183
    imports: bricks, 507; cloth, 255; Dutch, 184; salt, 209; sugar, 541
    poor harvests (1622–24), 228
    shipbuilding, 532
    Swedish conquests in, 228–30; effect of wars on, 254
Bang, Nina, and Knud Korst, edition of Sound Toll Registers, 226–7
Bank of England, 352–4, 415; financial data (table), 386–7; foundation (1694), 352, 384–5, (charters) 385; as a joint-stock enterprise, 443–4, 445; note issue, 352, 385; and public finance, 352, 384–6, 388
banks and banking
    ad hoc banking, 355, 356
    clearing bank system, 310–15, 323–4, 328, 346–7; private banks, 310–12, 314–15, 347, 353; public banks, 312–14, 315, 346
    country banking, 353
    deposit banks, 301, 312, 335, 336, 343, 347, 351, 356; banchi di scritto, 311
    exchange banks, 301, 337–43, 368, 380–1; overdrawing forbidden, 337, 343; as clearing houses, 340
    family banking, 335
    issuing banks, 323, 351
    joint-stock enterprise in, 443–4
banking business: cheque payments, 311, 313, 343, 347; debit balances, 313; discount, 347, 351; international payments clearance, 314; management of government loans, 313; withdrawals of cash, 313
bankers, see fairs: fair banks; merchant bankers; underwriters
    bank governors, 313
banknotes, 347, 352–3, 380–1, 385; bank money, 341; paper money, 314
bankruptcies of Europe's dynasties, 362, 366, 371, 391
Barback, R. H., 179
Barbary pirates, 532
barbers, 132, 467
Barbon, N., see Asgill, J.
Barbour, Dr Violet, 282, 422 n, 454
Barcelona, 217, 260, 540; banking, 314, (Banca de la Ciudad) 315; gilds, 466; textiles, 482, ('Indian textiles') 517

Bardi, house of, 415
barley, 23, 56, 58, 59; for breweries, 57, 219; harvesting, 97, 98; in Norfolk rotation system, 73; production and consumption, 87; yield ratios, 80–1, 87, 95
Barmen: linen yarn trade, 520–1; ribbon-mills, 477; Elberfeld-Barmen, 485
Barnard, Sir John, 389
barter, 306–7
Basle, 477; braid making, 523; deaths from famine, 9; papermaking, 535; printing, 534
Basque fishermen, 157–8, 159, 164, 177; whale fishers, 168, 172, 537; Port aux Basques, 156
Basque steel, 498
Bassano, 507, 535
Batavia, 210, 247, 248, 258
Bathory, Stefan, 502
Bauernlegen, 111, 112
Bavaria, 69, 429; ceramics, 507; entre-preneurs, 480; glassworks, 505–6; papermaking, 535; peasant revolts, 108; textiles, 518, 519, 523
Bavaria, Dukes of, their salt mines, 539
Bayonne, 531
Bayreuth, 536; Margrave of, 483
beans, 23, 59, 78
Beauce, 222, 514
Beaumarchais, Pierre Augustin Caron de, 'Figaro', 612
Beauvais, Goubert's study of, 20, 61, 196, 561; *tapisseries*, 481
Becher, J. J., mercantilist publicist, 465, 524
Bedford, Earl of, improving landlord, 450
beer, 198, 199, 201, 427, 537; brewed from coke-dried malt, 474; competition from other beverages, 201–2, 538; consumption in north Europe, 219–20; exports, 274; tax on, 360; *see also* brewing
bees, 90
Behrens, Betty, 21
Béjar, Duke of, aid to cloth industry, 516
Belgium, 514, 544; agricultural classes, 127; arable and cattle farming, 76, and wine growing, 77; corn from, 222; emigrants from, in Sweden, 545; farm administration, 107; landholding

and farming methods, 75, (a 'Mal-thusian universe') 187; *see also* Netherlands: southern
Belle Isle, 156
Belle-Isle, Duc de, 567
Bellinzani, inspector-general of factories in France, 481
bells, 242, 496
Below, Georg von, 42
Bengal, 248; investment in, 259; silks, 251, 252; sugar from, 214, 282
Bennassar, B., 304
Ber, mining entrepreneurs, 493
Berg, Duchy of, 500, 521, 546; Duke of, grants privileges to linen towns, 520
Bergamo, 490; iron, 501, 502; silk, 512, 527; woollens, 525, 526
Bergen-op-Zoom: clearing banks, 323; English cloth trade centre at, 269; fairs, 323, 329n; fish staple, 154, 164, 182, ('Nordland' fishing) 136, 536
Berlin, 579, 595; the 'new capital' of Germany, 561; free-thinkers, 590; population, 584; silk-factories, 431, 521; 'welfare' factories, 471
Berlin Academy of Sciences, 560, 583
Bernard, Samuel, French merchant banker, 378
Bernis, Cardinal, 567
Besançon fairs, 307, 319–22, 366, 371; exchange rates, 322; *foire de change*, 322; rules for payment, 320–1; trans-ferred to Piacenza, 375
Beukelsz, William, invention for pre-serving fish, 180–1
Beveridge, Sir William, 11
Bideford, 136, 160
Bielefeld, 518, 520
bills of exchange, 261, 264, 313, 344, 347–50, 504; as credit, 310–11, 324, 350; endorsement of, 329, 349–50; at fairs, 315–17, 318–19; in France, 378; on London money market, 348–50; in the north, 324, 328–32; in papal finance, 363–4, (credit on, allowed by Church) 310–11; and precious metals business, 342; *ricorsa* bills, 320–2, 334; in Spain, 372
bimetallism, 192, 245–6, 288, 380
Biringuccio, Vanoccio, *Pyrotechnia* (1540), 472, 473

Birmingham iron industry, 470, 497, 498; nailers, 464; technical advances, 476–7

Biron brothers, in Russia, 503

birth control, 25

birth-rate, 54

Biscay whale, 168

Biscoe, J., his land bank (1695), 305

Bismarck, Prince, 586

Blacho, and draw-loom, 477

Black Sea, 206–7, 217; fishing grounds, 136

blacksmiths, 132, 180, 475, 596; gilds, 465; see also smiths

Blake, Admiral Robert, 179

bleaching, 487, 514, 515; advanced techniques in, 478, 519; bleaching grounds, 518n; chemical processes in, 508

Bleiberg lead mines, 492

Bloch, Marc, 2, 42, 126

Bluche, F., 562n, 564

Bodin, Jean, 30

Bog, Ingomar, 199–200

Bogucka, Maria, 261

Bohemia, 472, 539, 551, 557; agricultural classes, 127; ceramics, 507; copper mines, 433, 463, 484, 488, 544, (technical advances in mining) 473, (immigration of miners) 487; 'factory age' in, 524; famine, 614; gilds, 468; glass manufacture, 450, (crystal glass) 506; iron industry, 501; nobles and landlords, 115, 116, 485, 524, 616; peasant misery, 613, (revolts) 122, 614, (Gutsherrschaft and the peasant) 607; reforms, 614–15; serfdom, 117–18, 119–21, 615, (land-holding serfs) 608; silver mines, 488, 489; textiles: (cloth exports) 204, 219, (linen) 250, 450, 544, (factories) 524; tin mines, 496; trade balance, 263; villeinage, 115–16, (unfree labour) 487, 524

Boncerf, Les Inconvénients de Droits Féodaux (1776), 606

bonds: bond issues for long-term credit, 390–1; fixed-interest bonds, 445n; as security for short-term loans, 381; see also under government finance

Boner, mining entrepreneurs, 493

Bonvisi, house of, entrepreneurs in government finance, 409

book production, 534, 535

Boot, Adriaen, land reclamation, 68

Bordeaux: brandy industry, 538; cloth staple, 269; fishing fleet, 159; hospital factories, 481; printing, 534; shipyards, 531; sugar refinery, 540; wine exports, 75, 198

Borkenmühl, Johann Heinrich, inventor of the braiding machine, 520–1

Bossuet, Jacques Bénigne, 556, 592

Boston, Lincs., 164, 510, 530

Böttger, Johann Friedrich, invention of hard porcelain, 507

Bouchon, Basile, automatic draw-loom invention, 477

Boule, Charles, and sons, luxury furniture atelier, 543

Boulogne, 108, 153

Boulton, Mathew, 472

Bouniatian's formula, 51

bounties and subsidies, 30, 289; Bounty Acts (England), 171, 183, 511; export bounties, 231, 541; subsidies: (for capital-intensive industries) 430, (for royal income in England) 381–3, (British subsidy to Prussia) 576

Bourbon, 107

Bourbon dynasty: in Spain, 482, 488, (patrons of cotton industry) 516; in France, 578; see also under individual monarchs

bourgeoisie
distinguishing features, 582, 586–7; Sombart's definition, 581
embourgeoisement, 580–4
military careers for, 568
purchase of nobility by, 564, 580; nobles of the robe regarded as, 562; comparative wealth of nobles and, 579–80; nobles and, in the Enlightenment, 585–8
as state officials, 565, 567
textile factories established by, 524; weaving restricted to, in Basle, 523
upper bourgeoisie, 570

Bourges, clothmaking, 481; fair, 318

Bourn, Daniel, carding-machine patented by, 476

Brabant: annuity contracts, 304; fairs, 218, 316, 323, 366; farming: (intensive) 71, 73, 76, 77, 103, (buckwheat) 231, (plough) 99, (yield ratios of cereals) 81; grain consumption, 78, 83–4, (corn imports) 274, (merchants in

Brabant (*cont.*)
corn trade) 222; metals market, 218; population, 224; textiles, 203, 514, 515, (cloth-workers in England) 510, (tapestries) 515
Brabant pound groat, 292–3
Brabant Water Toll, 359
braid (pasmentry), 520–1, 523, 525, 529; braiding machine (*Riemengang*), 520; gild of braidmasters, 521; a 'free trade' in Switzerland, 523
Braiti, crystal glass works in Venice, 506
Brakel, S. van, 226
Brandenburg: land-ownership, 111; serfdom, 115, 117; stock-raising, 233, 235
Brandenburg, Electors of, 390, 483, 538
brass industry, 243, 463, 484, 493–4, 547; brass wire, 496; manufacture, 241, 441, 473, 486, (for household articles) 243, (for ships) 533, 543
Braudel, Fernand P.: on capitalism and material life, 140n; on the Mediterranean world, 20, 31, 32, 206, 220, 371; on prices in Europe, 44, 189, 197; *trahison de la bourgeoisie*, 355
Braunschweig, *see* Brunswick
Braunschweig, Julius, Duke of, 483, 485, 500
Braunstein, Ph., 208
Brazil, 545; gold from, 212, 260, 264, 296, 342; plantation-type colony, 211; shipbuilding, 532; slave trade, 212, 214; sugar from, 212, 214, 282, 333, 539
Bremen, 169, 520; breweries, 198, 537; fish imports, 180; shipbuilding, 532; textiles, 518
Brescia iron industry, 501
Breslau, 219, 263
Brest, 225, 481
brewing: brewers, 132, 180, (family role) 435, ('common' brewers and brewing victuallers) 537, (gilds) 537; capital investment in, 12, 27, 537, (large-scale operations) 428, 434, 538; copper for, 242; grain for, 24, 45, 57; technical apparatus, 472; transport needs, 39; use of coal and coke, 474; *see also* beer
brick industry, 484, 507, 509
Brighton, 136, 174

Brill, 148, 152
Bristol, 160, 353, 509; seamen, 155; a shopkeeper, 420; shipbuilding, 530; sugar refinery, 540
Britain: and absolutist régimes, 549, 617, (freedom from government regulation) 578; aristocracy in, 562–3, 572; coalmining, 432; commercial policy, 289; early industrialization in, 8, 577–8; navy, 200; shipbuilding experts from, 532; subsidies to Prussia, 576; *see also* England; Scotland; Wales
British fishing zones off New England, 156
British Linen Company, 511
Brittany; fisheries: (pilchard) 166, (Nordland fishing) 536, (subsistence fishermen) 140, 141; flax and canvas-weaving, 515; noble beggars, 563; paper mills, 535; peasant revolts, 108; shipbuilding, 531
Brolin, P. E., 64
bronze: casting, 241, 496, (for armaments) 242–3, 496; founding, 473; increased demand for, 543; *see also* armaments
Brooers, Hans & Co., pepper consortium, 285
Broseley coke works, 474
Browne, Henry, hemp-stamping machine, 476
Bruges: Baltic traffic to, 273, 275, (staple for Hanseatic League) 273, 275; clearing-bank system, 323; financial techniques, 325; foreign trade, 221; herring fisheries, 155; interest for short-term loans, 362; Italian firms in, 322; overtaken by Antwerp, 215, 275; printing, 534; textiles, 512, 514, (tapestries) 515
Brunswick, 476, 520; agricultural classes, 127, 128; breweries, 537; buckwheat, 231; cloth-making, 518; family holdings, 46; metals, 490–1; ploughing, 98
Brunswick-Wolfenbüttel, Julius, Duke of, 483, 485, 500
Brussels, 370, 372; diamond trade, 542; tapestries, 515
Bryan, William Jennings, 20
Bublot, G., 97
Bucharest, 219

buckwheat, 59; increasing cultivation of, 45, 56, 78–9, 201, 231; Polish preference for, 87
Budapest, 217, 534
Bug, 217, 225
Bulgaria, 68, 219; iron mines, 501
bullion: demand for, 574; deposits of, as security, 341; exports of, 210, 259, 264; inflow of, 265; trade in, 352
bullionists, 29–30, 193
bureaucracy: and absolutism, 553–5, 567, 583, (Prussian) 558–9, 566, 571, 573, 618; in the Enlightenments, 586, 601, (Hapsburg) 614, 615, 616
burgher enterprise, 488, 492, 493; see also bourgeoisie; enterprise
Burgos: clearing banks, 314; gilds, 465; merchant firms, 317
Burgundy, 68, 315; agricultural classes, 128; enclosures, 112; farming, 76, 90, (farm households) 125; flax and canvas-weaving, 515; grain consumption, 84; salt exports, 538–9; subleasing, 107
Burgundy, Dukes of, 323, 362
Burlamachi, Philip, government war contractor, 286; in London, 382, 384
Busch, O., 587
business enterprise, 12, 396, 400, 439; and religion, 403–7
business technique, 445, 454, 459
businessmen, 431, 561, 576; as adventurers, 460; and aristocrats, 451
butchers, 132, 180; gilds, 467, 536
Buttstädt cattle fair, 235

cabbages, 23, 78
Cabot, John, 155
Cacci brothers, iron-works, 502
Cadiz, 333, 483; shipbuilding, 531; silver supplies from, 261, 341
Cahorsin pawnshops, 302
Caizzi, B., Storia dell'industria italiana, 526
Calais fisheries, 153, 182, 183; the red herring, 154
calamine, 473, 484, 493, 494
Calandrini, Philippe, member of pepper consortium, 285
Calatrava, Military Order of, 497
calico (muslins, shades): demand for, 250; 'the Indian craze', 250–1; legislation against imports of, 251

calico-printing works in Europe, 251; in England, 511
Calicut, 280
Calonne, Charles-Alexandre de, 582, 583
Calvin, John, and usury, 14
Calvinism, 14–16; and business enterprise, 406–7; Hohenzollern, 591
Calvinist emigrants, 485
Calw, cloth company, 518
Camden, William, antiquarian, 142
cameralists, 288, 595, 614; view of government, 595–6
Campans and Company, cotton manufacturers, 517
Campbell, Sir James, Eastland merchant, 286
Campen, Cornelis van, pepper consortium, 285
Canada, 184
canals, 24, 155, 428
Canals, Estaban, factory for 'Indian textiles', 517
Canaries, sugar from, 539
Canton, 211, 281
canvas, 218, 249, 480, 515; duckweavers, 180; sailcloth, 471, 517, 529; sailmakers, 180
Cape route, 32, 209, 281; opening of, 210
capital; accumulation of, 419, 423, 454, (and moral values) 404–5; aggregation of, 439, (in breweries) 537; availability of, 418, 429; control of, 414; credit and, 413–14; export of, 453; movements, 261, 307, 372; supply of, 357, 398, 452; transfers, 340; turnover, 276, 398, 425, 438; wars and, 183
capital: circulating (liquid), 192, 395, 398, 407, 447, (and industrial organization) 425–6; entrepreneurial, 429; fixed, 12, 427, 431, (demand for, and corporate enterprise) 436, 440, 441; floating, 305, 333, 354, 356, 357; mercantile, 12, 424, 485; overhead, 428; risk, 429, 431, 445, 454; working, 542
capital-intensive enterprise, 67, 356, 426, 432; in agriculture, 68, 82; in textiles, 520
capital investment: in agriculture, 66, 68, 100, 104–5, 123, 124; in fisheries, 153, 168, 181; in industry, 478–80,

capital investment (*cont.*)
  493; in mining, 489, 498; in overseas trade, 417; and corporate enterprise, 439; heavy investment, 429, 441, 486, 498; shortages of investment capital, 396, 575

capital-substitutes, 430, 457

capitalism: Dutch, 285, 389; financial, 354; and gilds, 467; industrial, 12; and luxury, 542; mercantile, 12, 197, 218; modern, 11, (early modern) 460–1; and Protestantism, 403–6; Sombart on, 581; Tawney on, 14

capitalists: aristocratic, 448, 451; bourgeois, 580, 585; and Calvinists, 15; clothiers, 528; commercial, 435, 459; financiers, 241; international, 282; iron merchants, 501; mercantile, 398, 416–18, 435, 464, (loans to miners) 493; trading, 407, (and their market) 407–9

  capitalist enterprise, 472; society, 588

  capitalistic outlook, 101, 283; production, 183, 279, 488, 492

carding, 252, 487; carding machines, 476

Carinthia: copper from, 415, 489, 493; gold deposits, 462, (organization of gold mines) 488; lead mines, 463, 484, 492, (lead exports) 492; peasant iron industry, 501; working hours, 487

carpenters, 131, 132, 180, 475, 487; ship's carpenters, 531; village cartmakers, 533; 'village' of (Zaandam), 508

carriages and coaches, 533–4; ancillary crafts, 542; *berline*, 533; *carosse*, 533, 542; carriage-building, 533; coachmakers, 465

carrying trade, 215, 351, 453; Asiatic, 416; ships for, 24, 208

cartels, 412, 497

carting, 75, 127; carters, 505; cartwrights, 132, 533, 542; wheelwrights, 488, 542

carts and wagons, 533; for copper transport, 242; seignorial rights over, 608; for silver transport, 260; two-wheeled carts, 533

Carus-Wilson, Eleanor, 161, 164, 510

Cary, John, *A Discourse concerning the East India Trade* (1699), 250–1

Casa da India (Lisbon), 244, 284

Casa de Contratación (Seville), 314

cashkeepers (*kassiers*), 324, 331, 332, 336–7, 342–3, 347, 351; promissory notes, 343

Casimir IV, of Poland, 271

Castel Durante, *majolica*, 506

Castile: banking: (clearing banks) 314, (exchange banks) 368, 372, (government withdrawals of cash) 319; exchange and credit market, 317; fairs, 314, 316–18, 323, 346, 366, 368, 370, (speculation at) 332; farmers, 126, 304; fish consumption, 178; gilds, 465–6; gold imports, 308; grain from, 221; *Hacienda Real de Castilla*, 366; *juros*, sale of, 373; nobility, and royal factories, 482; precious metals market, 314; textiles, 516

Catalonia: brandy industry, 538; cotton industry, 516–17; gilds, 465–6; intensive farming, 71, 102; papermills, 535; silk industry, 517; smithies, 498; ties with Geneva, 315; ties with Genoa, 371

Catherine II, of Russia, 121

Catholic Enlightenment, 594

Catholics: enterprise, 403; and gilds, 467; noble entrepreneurs, 485

Cats, Jacob, money-lender, 68

cattle: dairy, 91, 92; for draught, 90, 93; for meat, 92–3, 200; numbers, 89–90, 129; production, 92; 'transhumance' feeding, 91

  cattle trade, 232–40, (long-distance) 91–2, 233; cattle fleets, 237; cattle-plague, 234, 238; drove roads, 200, 232, 234–5; duties on, 235–6, 238; fattening areas, 233–5; markets, 216, 233–6, 237, 267; ordinances on, 236; profits from, 239; rights of nobility in, 233, 236, 237, 238, 240; stock-rearing areas, 233–5; value of cattle, 233; volume of trade, 236, 237; *see also* animal husbandry; ox trade; stock farming

Caus, Isaac de, 474

causality in history, 15, 43

Cavalini, Tadeo, improvements in agricultural machinery, 99

Cecil, Robert, Lord Salisbury, the 'Great Contract', 382

Cecil, William, Lord Burghley, his 'fish days', 178

Centurione, Genoese merchant banker, 372

ceramics, 506–7; *azulejos*, 506; clay pipes, 507; for dairy use, 99; faience, majolica, 506–8; for kitchen and table use, 203; lustre-ware, 506; porcelain, 507, 542, (factories for) 471, 485; tiles, 506, 509

  Chinese, 203, 507; Delft, 27; French, 429, 507; German, 507; Holland, 507; Italian, 507–8; Netherlands, 507; Portugal, 506; Saxony, 507; Spain, 506; Turkish, 506; Venice, 32, 507

cereals: cereal farming, 24, 604, (yield ratios and manuring) 95; imports into villages, 132; prices, fluctuations in, 82; *see also* corn; crops; grain

Ceylon, 210, 248, 259

Chamberlen, H., his land bank (1696), 305

Chamberlin, establishes *indienne* factory in Russia, 529

Chambers, J. D., 8, 112

Champagne: animal husbandry, 89–90; fairs, 315; land erosion, 69; metal working, 499; papermaking, 535

charcoal, 473, 474, 498, 508; replaced by coal, 509

Charette, General, 571

charitable foundations, and credit, 480

Charles I, of England: closes Tower Mint, 351; extravagance, 382; hostility to Dutch fishing, 147, 179

Charles II, of England, 155, 383

Charles V, Emperor (formerly Charles I, King of the Romans), 20, 271, 304, 372, 489; Imperial election, 367; loans to, 366, (legalizes interest on loans) 302, 325; political control of Italy, 371; royal finance, 359, 367; wars, 370, 371

Charles VI, Emperor, 283

Charles X, of Sweden: financial policy, 380; wars against Poland, 230

Charles XI, of Sweden: state enterprise in textiles, 530

Charles XII, of Sweden, 504; his coronation coach, 533–4

Charles, Duke, of Sweden, 504

Chaudhuri, Dr K. N., 250, 260

chemical industries, 508

Chemnitz, 217, 521

Child, Sir Josiah, Chairman of East India Company, 251

Child, house of, London bankers, 353

children in industry, 471, 487

China: carrying trade, 281; ceramics from, 203, (hard paste porcelain) 507; gold coins from, 258; merchant bankers in, 344; northeast passage to, 254; organization of foreign trade, 281; production of precious metals, 257; ratios of gold and silver, 257; silks from, 208, 214, 252, 282, (imports forbidden in Spain, France, England) 211; tea trade, 211

'Chinese fashion' in Europe, 250; *chinoiseries*, 507

Chippendale, Thomas, furniture for the luxury market, 543

Chodowiecki, Daniel, 587

Christensen, Aksel E., *Dutch Trade to the Baltic*, 226, 227–8, 261, 262

Christian IV, of Denmark, 467, 468, 485; industrial policy, 483, 529–30

Christian V, of Denmark, 485, 536

Christian VI, of Denmark, 530

Christian Socialists, 18

Christina, Queen of Sweden, 483, 485, 495

Christoffel, J. Ympijn, *Nieuve Instructe... rekeninghe te houden nae die Italiaenische maniere* (1543), 323

Church and clergy: and the Enlightenment, 590–4; exemption from taxes, 108; and fish on Fridays, 175–6; land owned by, 109–10, (sale of, in Protestant countries) 110–11, (confiscated in France in 1789) 113; participation in industry, 493; village ministers, 132

Cipolla, Carlo, 10, 32, 34, 189; *The Economic Decline of Empires*, 36, 38; *Money, Prices and Civilization in the Mediterranean World*, 294n, 304

Clapham, Sir John, 3–4, 11, 112, 497n; on empty boxes, 4; the 'statistical' sense, 37; 'Economic History as a Discipline' (1930), 3; *The Economic Development of France and Germany 1815–1914* (1928), 9

Clare, Earl of, improving landlord, 450

Clarendon, Edward Hyde, Earl of, 383

Clark, Sir George, 14, 134

Clifford, Dutch banking house, 27, 343, 391

climatic zones of Europe, 60–1; history of climate, 135; weather and climate, 57–65

clock- and watchmaking, 132, 334, 472, 593; gilds, 465

cloth: Austrian, 524, 528; Bohemian, 524; Dutch, 255, 528; English, 253–4, 255, 510, 542; Flemish, 254; French, 255–6, 515, 542; German, 483, 518, 528; Hungary, 254; Indian, 250; Italian, 255, 525–6; Low Countries, 514; Moravian, 524; Russian, 529; Salonica, 528; Scandinavia, 529; Silesia, 254; Slovakia, 524; Spain, 482, 516; Swiss, 522
    bays, 510, 545; broadcloth, 510, 514; kerseys, 510, 544; lakens, 254; says, 510; serge, 13, 25, 253, 510; stuffs, 510; for plantation negroes, 213, 546; see also worsteds

cloth industry: centres of production, 512–13; cloth masters, 518; factories, 482, 524, 526, 529, (cloth-printing factory) 483; gilds, 464, 483; government regulations, 480, 482; Jews in, 468; labour costs, 26; New Draperies, 253–4, 544; rural cloth production, 510

cloth trade, 204–5, 212, 214, 218, 219, 249, 265, 274; cloth routes, 249, 255, 271; competition for export markets, 253–6; slump in traditional cloth, 254, 544; staples, 349; see also textiles and under individual countries

clothing, 250–1, 254; garment workers, 469, 525; gloves, 526; hats, 470, 517, 526, 529; ready-made clothing industry, 482, 542; shoemakers, 467; trousers, 529; woollen cap and stocking factory, 481; see also stockings; tailors

clover, 23, 73, 74

coal: coke from, 474; as substitute for wood in smelting, 473, 474, 498, 509

coal mines, 427, 449, 463; large-scale production in, 472, 509; partnerships in coalmining, 434–6; rails and horse-drawn wagons used in, 475, and steam-pumping, 509

Coalbrookdale, 498

cobalt, 497

Coberger, W., 'Monts de Piété', 303

Cochin, 280

cocoa, 541

cod: catches, 165, (catching seasons) 139; dried, 176; fishing grounds, 136; green cod, 159, 161; habits of, 138; low cost of cod fishing, 140; see also fisheries

Coen, Jan Pietersz, governor-general in the Netherlands, 246

coffee, 199, 201; imports, 211, 214, 282; and sugar, 541

Cognac, 538

coins: in the monetary system, 290–4; coinage ordinances, 339; counterfeiting, 294–5, 309; foreign coins, 294, 295, 299; large and small, 295, 297; stability of, and money markets, 356–7; trade coins, 337, 338, 340–1
    bank guilder, 357
    Carolus guilder, 356
    dollars, rix and lion, 64
    écu de marc, 293, 319, 320–2, 357; gold écu, 307, 316, 320–1, 334n; de Savoie, 316n; de soleil, 320
    Joachimstaler, 291
    scudo di marche, 357
    see also debasement; gold coins; silver coins

Cokayne, Alderman, 481

coke, 474, 498

Colbert, Jean-Baptiste
    economic management of France, 41, 457, 482; Conseil de Commerce, 481; fisheries, 181; gilds, 465; metals, 499; mines, 504; public finance, 376–7; shipbuilding, 531; sugar refineries, 540; textiles, 471, (gobelins) 516, 543; trading companies, 442
    his mercantilism, 17, 574, 576, 578–9; differing views of, 17, 18–19; ruined by Louis XIV's wars, 577

Colchester, 253, 510

Coleman, Donald, 40, 140

Collins, English textile specialist in Russia, 529

Cologne, 218, 236, 490, 520; printing, 534; restrictive practices, 521; textiles, 512, (braidmakers' gild) 521, (silk-working) 521, (wool-weaving) 518; tobacco factories, 542

colonial trade, 35, 191, 211, 288, 314, 401, 494

colonial trade (*cont.*)
 exports and imports, 8, 212–14, 540–1;
  silks and linens from colonies prohibited, 517
 French view of, 575
 joint-stock enterprise in, 440, 441;
  aristocratic, 450
 monopolies, 379
 re-exports of colonial produce, 184,
  212, 455, 575; re-exports to colonies,
  529
 inter-colonial commerce, 416
 see also America; Brazil; New England;
  Newfoundland; North America;
  West Indies
colonies, 211–13
 advantage of colonial nations, 455
 colonial settlements (New England,
  Newfoundland), 158–9, 160, 211,
  212, 546
 mixed forms (America, Mexico, Peru),
  211
 plantation type (Brazil, southern states
  of North America, West Indies), 191,
  211, 546; coarse linen for, 204–5, 213,
  511; slave labour for, 191, 212, 213
 shipbuilding in the colonies, 530
Columbus, Christopher, 155
Comans, Jérome de, 68
Commendom, Cardinal, 225
commerce, 323–4, 356–7, 395–9, 407–11,
 417–23, 438, 447; crisis of 1520s, 367;
 government policy on, 273, 288, 289;
 joint-stock enterprise in, 439–41, 443,
 444; long-distance, 442, 453; transatlantic, 546
 Dutch, 215, 401; English, 420–3, 441;
  French, 442, (nobles forbidden to take
  part in) 448; Holland, 453; interlopers, 440; international, 378, 401,
  407–23, 545; Italian, 208; Low
  Countries, 395, 421, 422; north
  European, 448; Spanish, 517
commercial correspondents, 323, 343, 354,
 408
commercial crops, *see* crops, industrial
commission business, 354, 356
common land, 42, 108, 112, 113; common
 fields, 552
common law ('loi Commun'), 552
Common Law Courts, 349, 350, 351
Como, textiles, 255, 525, 527

Compagnie des Indes Occidentales, 442–3
Compagnie du Nord, 442–3
Compañía de Estramadura, 482
Compañía de Zarza la Mayor, 482
companies: chartered, 465, 468, 551; industrial, 480; limited liability, 361;
 livery, 464; regulated, 270, 412,
 437–9; town, 464–5; *see also* joint-
 stock companies; *individual companies*
company administration, 446–7; company organization in textiles, 518,
 520, 525, in fishing, 537
Company of the Hütter Schwarza and
 Mansfeld, 479
competition, 412, 454; and commercial
 enterprise, 437–9; Dutch and English
 27, 28, 153; Dutch and Hanseatics,
 215; Holland and France, 442–3;
 Venice against Dutch and English, 33
 in fisheries, 153, 155, 168, 175, 177; in
 grain trade, 222; in mining, 493; in
 sugar refining, 540; in textiles,
 527–8
Comte, Auguste, 1
conjoncture, 6, 10, 19, 20, 230, 436; the
 17th century a conjunctural 'valley',
 548
Conrad, J. E. C., 44
Considerations on the East India Trade
 (1707), 178–9
consortium: of bankers, 365, 372, 390;
 'bear', 345; of financiers, 377; for
 mining, 493; in papal finance, 364;
 in pepper trade, 284–5; for quicksilver mining, 496
conspicuous consumption, 30, 203–4, 354,
 448, 603, 612; leisure, 448
Constantinople (Istanbul), 206, 208, 219;
 cattle exports to, 234; grain exports
 to, 119, 234; Persian ceramicists in,
 506; staple city for Levant Company,
 270
consumer credit, 300–3
consumption, 195, 196–202, 588; government attempt to regulate, 199; taxes
 on, 360
 consumption of: barley, 87; beer,
 219–20; dairy products, 84, 201; fish,
 172–8, 180; grain, 83–9; meat,
 84–5, 92–3, 200–1, 536; rice, 201,
 230; rye, 84, 87–8; sugar, 202, 540,
 541; wheat, 84; *see also* diet

Contarini, Tomasso, 327
contract between monarch and people, 556; *contrat social*, 602
contractors for land reclamation, 67–8
convoys for: cattle fleet, 237; fishing fleets, 134, 152, 155, 158, 181–2; merchant fleets, 531, 533; precious metals fleet, 341; silver carts, 260
coopers, 75, 132, 180
Copenhagen, 483; Brewers' Gild, 537, (Royal Brewery) 537; cattle exports, 239; interlopers, 283; milk yield of cows, 202; tea trade, 211; 'welfare' factories, 471; wool factories, 529–30
copper: for cannon founding, 207, 242–3, 245, 473; for sheathing ships, 531, 533; as a substitute for silver, 544; other uses, 99, 242, 309
   coinage, 29, 240, 243, 245–6, 298–9, 381, (*taler*) 380; as standard of value, 299, 495; in Spain, 299, 495; silver and copper bimetallism in Sweden, 380
   industry, 484, 544, 547; copper-working industries, 244, 245
   inflation, 243, 299, 309, 544; in Germany, 299, 309; in Spain, 29, 243, 245, 246, 299, 309, 544; in Sweden, 299, 309
   market, 244, 246, 247, 248; crises in, 544; Amsterdam market, 241, 244; Antwerp, 218, 244, 275; in Asia, 246, 249; in Germany, 244; staples, 245–6, 272
   mines, 462–3, 484, 488–91; mining, 241, 428n, 433; joint-stock organization for, 441
   ore, 240–1, 242, 449, 488, 508; smelting, 428n; transport for, 242, 243–4; refining, 486, 489
   production, 489–91, 494–6; annual production, 492, 495; companies for, 489; European, 245, 249, 296, 380, 473; fluctuations in, 189; Fugger control of, 244–5, 415, 484, 489; overseas, 246–9, 258, 296; and power politics, 241, 246, 249; regulation of output, 244
   production in: Aachen, 484, 494; Alsace, 492; central Europe, 215, 240, 242–4, 282, 298–9, 488, 492, 544; England, 463, 496; Germany,

207, 489; Hungary (Neusohl), 189, 214, 219, 241–4, 275, 415, 471, 492; Japan, 214, 246–9, 258, 282, 296, 495; Norway, 248, 463, 492, 495; Russia, 496, 503; Slovakia, 495, 544; Spain, 463, 489; Sweden, 189, 214, 242, 244–5, 249, 272–3, 282, 296, 380, 463, 494–6, 504, 544–6; Thuringia (Mansfeld), 189, 242, 244, 489, 544; Tyrol, 189, 242–4, 415, 484, 488, 492, 544; West Indies, 214, 246, 282
   'copper purchase', 242
   trade, 207, 208, 214, 215, 218, 240–9, 263, 281, 282, 413; involvement of Swedish Crown in, 272–3, 495
coral industry, 468
Cordoba, 314, 516
corn
   banks, 305
   corn-crop acreage, proportion to total arable, 88–9; shifts from corn to other crops, 220–1, 230–1
   Exchange, *see* Amsterdam Corn Exchange
   fluctuations in supplies, 220–2, 230; corn crises, 228
   government regulations, 220, 231; Turkish embargo on export, 221
   harvests, 186
   imports and exports, *see* grain
   prices, 74, 223, 229, 271; and deliveries, 229–30; and transport, 220
   production, 45–6, 56–7, 60; and consumption, 83–9, 201, 231; improved implements and, 96; in overseas possessions, 221
   trade, 215, 216, 218, 219–32, 271; ancillary employments, 225; Baltic trade, 222, 223, 226, 227–9, 230–1, 276; decline in after 1650, 230, 232; east–west orientation, 223, 227, 230, 231; government concern with, 265; link with salt trade, 209, 210; local trade, 231–2
   value of, shipped through Baltic, 91
   yields of, and manuring, 95; and sowing in drills, 99
   see also crops; grain
Coromandel coast, 248, 259, 260
corporate enterprise, 436–47
corporate system, 423; of society, 550, 551–2, 612

corvée, 606–7, 617

cottage industries, 28, 46, 77; cottage weavers, 77, 132

cottars, 126–8, 130; cottar farming, 131

cotton: 'era of', 547; growing, 68, 529; imports, 250; manufacture, 515, (and aristocratic enterprise) 450; mills, 468; printing, 471, 487, 521, 522; for ribbon weaving, 520

goods: from Asia, 250, 251; checks, 512; Indian, for household uses, 205; mixtures, 253, 510, 522; rags, for paper, 469, 535; *see also* calico; textiles

industry: Austria, 524; England, 510, 511, (cotton printing) 471; France, 515; Germany, 521; Holland, cotton-printing, 471; Prague, 524; Switzerland, 522

Coward, helps found Italian wool factory, 526

cows: age of, 93; as criterion for peasant classification, 127; dairy products from, 91; fed on mash, 202; grazing land needed for, 94–5; live and dead weight, 92; for traction, 46, 90, 93; *see also* cattle; milk

Cracow, 217, 219, 225, 275; burghers, 493; Jewish gilds, 468; lead mining, 491, 493, (lead alloys) 502, (stagnation in mining) 493

Cracow, bishop of, 502

crafts, 469, 485; craft organization, 524, (in Russia) 467–8

craftsmen, 469, 478, 497, 500; in the hierarchy of labour, 486–7; lists of, 132, 180; and machines, 523

bakers, 45, 132, 180; blacksmiths, 132, 180, 475, 596; carpenters, 16, 131, 132, 180, 475, 487, 508, 531; cart-makers, cartwrights, 132, 533, 542; coachbuilders, 465; diamond cutters, 468, 542; dyers, 485, 518; felt-workers, 470, 488; masons, 16, 476; nailers, 464; painters, 132, 468, 508; plasterers, 131, 132; rope makers, 45, 180; sailmakers, 180; shoemakers, 488, (clogmakers) 132; smiths, 24, 497–8, 499, 501, 503; tailors, 132, 485, 488; wheelwrights, 542; wood-carvers, 542

Cramer, Henry, Leipzig merchant, 479

credit: acceptance credit, 344–5, 353; by assignment, 301–2, 304, 311, 326–9, 332, 336–7, 361; and capital, 413–14; through cashkeepers, 343; consumer credit, 300–3; extension of payments, 300–1, 306, 310, 324–5; for industry, 469, 480, (for ironworking) 505; in-land and outland bills, 350, 353; IOUs, 301, 306, 310, 355; at international fairs, 319, 322, 337, 364; 'payable to bearer' clause, 301, 310; by pledge, 348; public, 333, 359, 360–2, 363–9, 372, 376, (by over-drafts) 382, (by open subscription) 389, (short-term) 385–6; and the staple market, 268, 289; *see also* annuities; bills of exchange; loans

credit balances, 307, 332

credit crisis of 1619–20, 375

credit, letters of, 344

credit weapon, 278

Cremona, 526

Crete, 68, 207, 539

Cromberger, Jacob and Juan, Seville printers, 534

Cromwell, Oliver, 179, 383, 465

crops: cropping variability, 59; labour-intensive crops, 89; specialization in Holland, 23, 24; yields, 23–4

cereal: barley, 23, 56, 58, 59, 73, 80–1, 87, 95; buckwheat, 45, 56, 78–9, 201, 231; maize, 10, 34, 46, 78–9; oats, 23, 56, 58, 59, 73, 80; rye, 58, 59, 72, 80–1, 87; wheat, 57–8, 59, 60, 61–2, 73, 80–1, 87, 95

fodder, 57, 69, 96, (in Norfolk rotation) 72, (for production of manure) 71, 90, 94; clover, 23, 73, 74; grass (hay), 23, 58; spurrey, 73; turnips, 73; vetch, 57, 73

food, 10, 59, (Holland peasant production of) 23–4; beans, 23, 59, 78; cabbages, 23, 78, 89; carrots, 78; peas, 59; potatoes, 10, 46, 58, 59, 78–9, 83, 96; rice, 10, 33–4, 46, (cultivation in Italy) 33–4, 78, (in south Europe) 46

industrial, 23, 77, 95, 231; colza, 56; cotton, 68, 529; flax, 23, 27, 46, 56, 73, 77, 89, 95; hemp, 23, 77, 89, 265, 463, 518; hops, 23, 56, 77, 95, 265, 274; madder, 23, 56, 77; oil-bearing

crops: industrial (*cont.*)
  seeds, 23, 77; rape, 23, 89; saffron, 77;
  tobacco, 23, 95; weld, 77; woad, 77,
  515
Crowley, Ambrose, model iron works,
  430, 435
Crown lands, 107, 109; income from,
  358, 382, 429; sale of, 111, 359, 382;
  as security for loans, 287, 358–9
Crown mineral rights, 429, 479
Croy, Duc du, manager of Anzin merger,
  449
Culley brothers, English stockbreeders, 93
Cunningham, William, 5; *Alien Immigrants in England*, 40; *The Growth of
  English Industry and Commerce*, 2–3
Curtius, John, mining specialist, 499
customs and excise, 25, 179, 181, 582; as
  source of public revenue, 238, 260,
  359–60, 382, 383, 389; customs posts,
  235; customs records, 134, 216, 225,
  226, 235–6, 237, 240, 263; see also
  Danish Sound Tolls
Cyprus, 68, 207, 539
Czechoslovakia: fishing revenues, 175;
  yield ratios of grain, 80–1
Czybulka, on peasant conditions in
  Prussia, 618

dairy produce, 23, 56, 74, 90–1; as an
  alternative to stock-breeding, 237;
  consumption of, 84, 201; utensils for
  the dairy, 99; see also milk
Dangon, Claude, lever draw-loom, 477
Danish Asiatic Company, 261
Danish 'compartment' for cattle-trade,
  236
Danish Sound, 222, 272; figures for fish
  traffic, 177; tolls, 266, 285; register of
  tolls, 134, 215, 223, 226–7, 235,
  261–2, 545, 546
Danube, 217
Danzig: Amsterdam and Antwerp connections, 222–4, 226; blockade of,
  228; comes under Polish suzerainty,
  271; exchange rates, 223; forbids
  power-loom, 477; international trade,
  (in copper) 244, 275, (grain) 188,
  221, 225, 227–31, 264, 271, 275,
  (salt) 210, (wines) 198; merchants,
  215, 300; metallurgy, 547; shipbuilding, 224, 532; staple for cloth,

269, (for Eastland Company) 270;
  staple rights, 271; and Swedish wars,
  230, 231; trade balance, 262; see also
  Hanse towns
Darby, Abraham, 435, 498
Dardel, E., 134, 174
das Gupta, A., 280
Datini, Francesco, wool merchant, 208
Dauphiné, 463, 499, 535
Davis, Lance, 41
Davis, Ralph, 39–40, 357n
De Besche, Walloon entrepreneur, 484
de Brande, Georges, mining specialist, 499
De Moucheron, merchant, 345
De Rees, Walloon entrepreneurs, 484
debasement of coinage, 20, 258, 291–5,
  298, 584; the 'Great Debasements',
  308
Dechesne, L., 5
Declaration of the Rights of Man, 599
Defoe, Daniel, *The Complete English
  Tradesman* (1745), 396, 420–1, 423
deforestation, 463, 473
Delbrück, Hans, *Life* of Gneisenau, 588
Delft, 180; ceramics, 27, 497, 507; exchange bank, 337; fisheries, 148, 536
Delftshaven fishing fleet, 150–2, 180, 536
demand: changes in, 210–11; colonial, 8,
  516; and the demographic curve, 30;
  domestic, 8, 18, 25; effective, 429;
  elasticity of, 186, 200, 250, 413, 439;
  fluctuations in, 426, 432; international,
  25; market, 12
  demand for: cloth, 516; copper, 494–5,
  543; corn, 188; fish, 175–8; paper,
  535; timber, 508
demesne land, 114–16, 118–23, 487
Demidov, Russian entrepreneurs, 503
demography, and economic history, 4,
  6–9, 14, 17, 19, 21–2, 30, 38, 43, 82,
  123, 196; and breweries, 537
  demographic catastrophes, 604; crises,
  546; exhaustion, 25–6; pressure, 545;
  upswing, 31, 543, 546
Denmark
  agriculture: convertible husbandry, 73,
    74; threshing, 100; yield ratios of
    cereals, 80
  breweries, 537; distilleries, 538
  cattle: exports, 91, 200, 233, 235–40,
    448; change from beef to dairy farm-
    ing, 237; horses, 93

Denmark (*cont.*)
enterprise: aristocratic, 448; Dutch, 455; Portuguese, 485; overseas, 545; state, 442, 483, 529–30
fisheries: legislation on, 155, 164, 182; merchants, 147; whaling fleets, 171
gilds, 467; Jews in, 468
liquidity crisis, 236
nobility, in cattle trade, 237, 238, 240
papermills, 536
shipbuilding, 533
transoceanic trade, 210, 216
typhus, 546
war, civil, 238; with Sweden, 238
Denmark, kings of, 260, 485; Crown revenues, 266; *see also* Christian IV, V, VI, Frederick II, IV
Denmark–Norway, 287, 495; Danish capital in Norwegian mining, 503
depressions, 53
after 1350, 121
14th and 15th centuries, 307, 312, 323
16th century, 242; in textiles, 254, 517
17th century, 43, 54, 105, 108, 228, 305, 333, 535, 543; a grain crisis, 53; the lessors' heyday, 106–7; analysis of, 545–6
of 1672, 546
Derbyshire: beer, 474; New Draperies, 510
Dernschwam, Hans, factor of the Fuggers, 528
Descartes, René, 600; Cartesians, 600
Deutz, 477, 521
Deutz, John, banker, 390, 391
devaluation and revaluation, 20, 292, 296, 299–300
Devon serges, 13, 25, 253, 510
d'Evora, Ruy Lopez, merchant, 285
diamonds, diamond-cutting, 468, 542
Diderot, Denis, 598; *Encyclopédie*, 76
Dieppe: fishermen, 139–40, 153–4, 164, 174; herrings, 136, 173, 174; shipbuilding, 531
diet, 197–8; impact of trade-routes on, 202
diet of: farmers, 126; the poor, 173, 176; upper class, 173, 176, 195
elements of diet: animal protein, 132; beer and wine, 220, 537; bread and corn, 48, 173, 187, 201, 220, 536, (maize) 230, (other food crops) 78–9; dairy products, 84, 201; dog's flesh,

35; eggs, 84; fish, 84, 141, 172–3, 175, 180; meat, 84–5, 92–3, 173, 200–1, 211, 536; vegetables, 201, 536
see also consumption; food
Dietrichstein, noble entrepreneur, 496
Dillen, J. G. van, 260, 342n, 343n, 357n, 390n
Dilthey, W., 596
Dircsz, Reyer, Amsterdam merchant, 226
discounting, *see* financial techniques
Dissenters, 15
distilleries: capital investment in, 27, 538; copper for, 242; grain for, 24, 45; technical apparatus, 472; transport needs, 39
products: aquavit, 199, 201–2, (mash from, fed to cows) 202; brandy, 538; gin, 201, 538
diversified economies, 53, 515; trend to diversification, 424; a means of hedging risks, 436
diversification in: capital investment, 434, 440; farming, 123; mercantile markets, 418; production, 466, 475
Domenico, Maestro, Venetian ceramics master, 506
domestic industries, 511
domestic servants, 605, 611; seignorial rights over, 608
Donald, David, flax-beating machine, 476
donkey-power, 477
Dopsch, Alfons, 42
Dordrecht, 49, 325, 538
Dover, 182, 351, 375; shipbuilding, 530
Dovring, F., 44
Downing, Sir George, 25; project for short-term loans, 383–4
drainage and irrigation, 67–9, 441, 450; of mines, 474–5, 492, 493; machinery for, 473–4, 492
drapers, 470; gilds, 483; production, 514–15, 518
drovers, 235; drove roads, *see under* cattle trade
Duby, Georges, 3
Ducci, Gaspar, Florentine banker, 365, 368, 370
Dudley, 498; coal mines, 509
Dunant, François, taffeta manufacturer, 525
Dunbar, 139, 147
Dunkirk, free port, 274; corsairs, 536;

Dunkirk (*cont.*)
    fishing fleet, 149, 159, 164, 182; fishing grounds, 136; shipbuilding, 531; sugar refinery, 540
Dupont de Nemours, P., 'Memoire sur les Municipalités', 560, 582, 602; on Quesnay, 604
Dupont family, 430
Düren, 499, 518, 535
Durkheim, Emile, 2
Dutch
    archives, 226
    banking, 27; exchange banks, 339–42
    bronze cannon casting, 496
    capitalism, 285, 455; investment abroad, 389
    carrying trade, 209–10, 275, 309, 453; Mediterranean, 232, 256; in the Sound, 227
    coins, 307, 338–9, (ducatoons) 264, (guilders) 294, 338, (rix-dollars) 264, 338; coinage ordinance, 339
    copper market, 245; investment in copper, 246
    emigrants, 529
    enterprise, 396, 452, (overseas) 545; entrepreneurs, 245, 275–6, 429, 431, 435, 452, 453, 486, (outside Holland) 435, 454–5
    excise duties, 383
    exports, 184, 274, (*lakens*) 254, 528, (ships) 531, (silver coins) 309; export surplus, 308
    fabrics, 222
    factories, in Firando, 246–7; in India, 248, 259
    financial instruments, 350; public finance, 389–90
    finishing processes, 519
    fisheries: buss herring fishery – *Groote Visscherij*, 140, 142–3, 148–53, 536–7; capital outlay, 153; collegiate organization, 148, 149, 152, 174; decline, 149, 183; fish curing on board, 142, 143, 148, 152–3; fishermen in the Shetlands, 142; free trade in, 175; joint-stock financing of, 174–5; markets for, 177–8, (in the Baltic) 148, 149, 177, 184; *Ventjagers*, 149, 152, 177; warships for defence of, 536
    fisheries, other: coastal herring fishery,

153, 183; cod fleet, 165; whale fishery, 168–71, 537
    gilds, 468
    iron imports, 545
    looms, 477
    machinery, innovations in manufacturing technique, 476–8
    merchants, 272, 356, 452; merchant bankers, 366, 389, (cattle exporters) 240
    money lenders, 68
    paper manufacture, 536
    peasant agriculture, 23, 28
    pioneering in sea-routes, 215, 218; pre-eminence in transoceanic trade, 210, 215, 532
    shipbuilding, 530, 531, 533; *fluitschip*, 24; grain ships, 45; manure barges, 24; mercantile fleets, 10, 24, 39, 531, 533
    society, 453
    spirits, 538
    staple market, 276–8
    sugar refining, 541; boilers, 540
    taxes, 25–6, 40–1, 390
    tobacco industry, 542
    towns, 275–6
    traders, 246, 249
    treat, 199
    wars, 27, 147, 179, 383
    see also Holland
Dutch East India Company, 200, 209, 440–1, 442
    amalgamated into United East India Company (1602), 282
    Asiatic trade, 256–7, 258–9; competition for textile market, 251–2; factories in Asia, 248, 249; Japanese trade, 246–9, 258
    exports of silver and gold, 309; imports, 211, 280, (of copper) 246–9, (cowries) 213
    loans from Amsterdam Exchange Bank, 340
    spice profits, 249; pepper sales, 285–6
Dutch-Hanseatic copper company, 249
'Dutch linen', 253
Dutch provinces, 69, 71
Dutch Republic, 16, 21, 35, 545; commercial capital, 216; currency policy, 298, 339; grain imports, 75; immigration policy, 18, 26, 40; international

Dutch Republic (*cont.*)
exchange economy, 22, 25, 27; merchant rulers, 14; silver requirements, 297; and Spain, 25; taxation, 25–6, 40–1; Treasury loans, 340

Dutch West India Company, 442

dyeing industry, 45, 487, 519, 522, 526; chemical processes in, 508; potash for, 508

dye-producing plants, 23, 24, 77, 89; madder, 515; meekrap, 515; woad, 499, 515

dyers, 485, 518

East Anglia (eastern England), 8, 15, 25, 91
'Agricultural Revolution' in, 42; arable and cattle farming, 76; intensive cultivation, 71, 102; land reclamation, 68

fishermen, 139, 143, (ancillary crafts) 180; cod fishery, 161, 166, 177, 182; herring, 166

migrants from Netherlands, 253, 510

money wages replace 'doles', 183

see also Norfolk; Norwich; Yarmouth

East Friesland: farming, 76; fishery, 143, 155; land reclamation, 69, 71; yield ratios of cereals, 80, 82; *see also* Friesland

East Friesland, Count of, 340

East India companies, 209, 283–9, 441, 445

East India Company (1600), 254, 441; Asiatic trade, 256–7; China sailings, 252, (imports) 203; competition with Dutch Company, 251; gold and silver from Amsterdam, 260–1, and loans, 357; India trade, 205, 259, (monopoly of, lost) 252; interlopers, 282–3; loans to government, 388; merged in United East India Company (1709), 387; pepper contracts, 286; re-export trade, 261; reorganized (1698), 444, 445–6; shares in, 345, 413; silk and calico imports, 250–2

East India House, attacked by weavers, 251

East Indies (East India), 191, 543, 545; ships for trade with, 531; silver, demand for, 264, 309; sugar from, 248; textiles from, 211, 282; *see also* India

Eastland Company, 438; merchants, 286

Edinburgh, 141, 478; woollen factory, 480–1, 512

education: educated classes in the Enlightenment, 591–4; and farming, 102–3; in mercantilist states, 578, 583–4, 586–7, 596; as a path to promotion, 569; and technology, 472

Égret, J., 553n, 562

Egypt, 529, 539

Ehrenberg, R., 365n, 366n, 371

Eislebener, copper wire, 241

Elba, island of, 463, 502

Elbe, 216; cattle market, 235, 236, 237, 238, 239; cloth market, 269

Elberfeld, 475, 477

Elbing, 270, 271

Elizabeth I, of England, 381, 509; blockade of silver ships, 372, 374; investment in companies, 442, 498; stabilization of coinage, 309

Elizabeth, Countess of Stolberg, 500

Elliott, J. H., 30

Elzevir, Louis, international bookseller, 535
Elzevir press, 535

Ember, Gy., Hungarian historian, 234, 263

embroidery, 518, 522, 523

Emden, 171, 532; cloth staple, 269

emigration, *see* immigration; migration

enclosures, 16, 74, 101, 110, 111–12, 617; Acts of Parliament for, 112; peasant revolts against, 108, 112

endorsement, *see* financial techniques

England
absolutism, 554, 555

agriculture: advanced stage of, 34, 49, 71, 72, 73, 81, 611, 617; agricultural classes, 127; arable and cattle farming, 76; corn production and consumption, 83, 84–6, 88–9, (bounties on export) 74–5, 231; cereals, 176, (yield ratios on) 80–2, 95; credit for, 305; farming and education, 102–3; improving landlords, 448, 450; ploughing, 98, 99; stock-farming, 89, 91, 93, (inoculation against cattle-plague) 65

artillery, 243, 448–51

asiento contracts, 213

balance of trade, 261; in the Baltic, 263–4, 275; in east Europe, 262; deficit paid with bills of exchange, 264

England (cont.)
banking, 347–54; banknotes, 76, 347; Land Banks, 305, 384, 385; private, 352–3; underwriters, 389; West End and City, 353; see also Bank of England
brass and iron wire, 496
breweries, 479, 537; brewing dynasties, 435
carrying trade, 210, 215, 256, 309, 351
class and commerce, 420–2, 451, 455
cloth trade, 254, 463, 469–70, 481, 528; staples for, in Europe, 269–70
coal industry, 428; mines, 463, 472, 498; mining, 432, 435, (horse-drawn railways for) 475, (steam engine) 475, (large-scale production) 472; output, 509, (use of, for iron smelting) 473, (for industries) 509, (coked coal) 498, 547; coal transport, 530; colliers, 530
colonization, 211, 212, 289
copper mines, 463, 490, 492, 496; copper industry, 484
cottage industries, 28
craftsmen in Russia, 502
crisis and change, 12
customs records, 134
deforestation, 473
emigration, 18
enterprise, 400, 455; aristocracy and, 448–51; commercial, 421; corporate, 438, (regulated companies) 439, (joint stock) 441–6; government aid to, 431; local aid to, 436; overseas, 545, 546; partnerships in, 433–5
excise duties, 383, 384, 389
exports, 498; corn, 216, 221, 229; export surplus, 308; lead, 492; refined sugar, 540; textiles, 203, 204, 210, 219, 222, 254–6, 510; wool, 274
financial techniques, 392; assignment, 327, 328, 348–50; bills of exchange, 348–50, 385; discount, 353; endorsement, 327–8, 329, 349–50; interest on loans, 302; mortgage credit, 348, 353; promissory notes, 326, 351, (Act for) 350
fisheries, 135; companies for, 153, 168, 170–1, 179; competition with Dutch, 153, 179; fish consumption, 172–3, 176; government attitude to, 178–9; hosting system, 174; legisla-

tion relating to, 147, 176, 179; markets, 142, 175; technique, 160, 175; value of nets, 140
cod: Iceland fishery, 161, 164, 166, 176; Newfoundland, 138–9, 155, 159, 160–1, 162–3, 166; North Sea, 164, 166, 176, 183, (convoys for) 158; sack ship, 158, 160
East Anglia: coastal fishery, 139, 143, 166, 180; cod fishing, 139, 161, 166; doles replaced by money wages, 183
freshwater fish, 141, 175
herring, 142–3; north Yorkshire coast, 143; Yarmouth, 138, 139, 141, 143–6, 155, 164
mackerel, 138–9, 144–6, 166–8
pilchards, 166, 179
preserving industry, 153, 181; smoked 'red' herrings, 143, 154, 173, 176, 178; wind-dried cod, 176
whale: New England, 172; Spitzbergen, 138, 168, 170–2
gentry, decline of, 14
gilds, 464–5; decay of, 437
government: and industry, 480–1; laws against combinations of workmen, 488; protectionist legislation, 231; and trading companies, 283
Great Debasements, 308
guineas, 307
and the Hanseatic League, 224, 348
immigration, 40, 487, 510, 514, 518, 544; Huguenots, 485
imports: bricks, 507; grain, 223; linen, 514; paper, 536; Spanish wool, 255; Swedish iron, 504
industrial revolution, 36, 392, 465
insurance companies, 355
inventions and technical advance, 80, 473–8; opposition to machines, 477, 478
investment, 423; Dutch investment in, 27; investment costs, 479; problem of raising capital, 153; stock shares, 346, (trading in, on Amsterdam Exchange) 345, 346
iron industry, 427, 434, 435, 497–8; iron-cast cannon, 243; iron deposits, 463, 490; iron masters, 435, 504
land: enclosure of common land, 16, revolts against, 108, 112; ownership,

England (*cont.*)

106, 110–11, 422–3; reclamation, 69, 454

lead, 207, 441, 449, 463, 474, 490, 492

lottery schemes, 384

mass production, 28

meat consumption, 92

mercantilism, 392

merchant companies, 381, 389; merchant marine, 530; merchants, 289, 349, 356, (as government bankers) 382, (status of) 420–2

mining and metallurgy, 472, 493, 496, 547; German specialists in, 496

mortality from famine, 9

Navigation Laws, 289

overseas trade, 540, 547; dependence on, 404

population, 83, 85

printing, and the Stationers' Company, 534

public finance, 381–91; Exchequer Bills, 353; Exchequer crisis, 351, (moratorium on) 383–4; the Great Contract, 382; the 'Great Farm of Customs', 359, 382; government bonds, 391; National Debt, 352, 353, 355, (and the Bank of England) 384–7, 388–9, 391, (investments in) 389; tontine loan, 384; Tower mint closed, 351; war finance, 383–5, 389

putting-out system, 469–70, 510

re-exports, 212, 250

Royal Contract, 382

royal finance, 351, 359, 381–3

Royal Navy, 530

salt monopolies, 181

shipbuilding, 530–1

stability, 34–5, 399, 455; of pound sterling, 357

Statute of Apprentices, 465

Statute of Monopolies, 382, 440n

sugar refining, 540; sugar consumption, 540, 541

taxation, 360, 383, 385

textiles, 13, 249–55, 547, (types of cloth and areas of production) 510–11; golden age of, 439; import prohibitions, 251, 254, 517; 'Indian craze' in, 250–1; masters, 510; specialists in Russia, 529; workshops and factories, 470–1, (water-power for) 510, 511

bays, 510, 544; bombazines, 510; broadcloth, 510; calico-printing, 251; cotton and flax mixtures, 510, 511; cotton-printing, 471; fine cloth, 542; fustians, 510, 544; kendals, 510; kerseys, 510, 544; 'New Draperies', 253, 510, 544; serge, 13, 25, 253, 510; silks, 511; stuffs, 510; woollen cloth, 254, 510; worsteds, 254, 510

tin, 207, 496

tobacco, 541

toolmaking, 475

transoceanic trade, 210, 218

wars: Anglo-Dutch (1665–7), 238; Civil, 496; with Spain, 157, 255

weather, 62–3

wool, 463; exports, 480, 515; woollen industry, 470; woolworkers' associations, 488

zinc, 496

see also Britain; London

England's Great Happiness (1677), 420

English Company, The, 283, 502

'English Exchange' in Antwerp, 331

English Fishery Company, 138

English historians, 580

English Muscovy Company, 168, 270

English Revolution (1688), 384

English 'Silver Road', 351, 375

Enkhuizen, 148, 152, 180, 183; in the Great Fisheries, 136, 536

Enlightenment, the, 588, 590–1, 597–8; in central Europe, 590, 598, 599–600; enlightened despots, 31, 556; French, 550, 559, 560, 585, 589–600; German, 556, 586, 588–600; in Hapsburg dominions, 591, 594, 599; in Prussia, 588, 590, 592–600

Ens, Jan van, land reclamation, 68

enterprise, 404, 452, 459–61; 'risk environment', 393–4, 396–8, 409, 411, 415–18, 426; role of the State in, 399–402, 425, 429–32, 442, 452, 455, (government ownership) 429, 432, (state-aided enterprise) 430–2

agricultural, 393n, 448–9, 450; aristocratic, 394, 425, 447–51; business, 400, (and religion) 403–7, 410; colonial, 401, 439, 441, 450; commercial, 396–7, 398–9, 407–11, 413, 417, 420–3, 435, 439, 441–2, 444, 447, 517, and financial, 414–15, 416;

enterprise (*cont.*)

corporate, 394, 417, 436–47, 493, (gild) 437–8, (regulated companies) 438–9, (joint-stock) 439–47; financial, 414–16, 443–4, 453, 571, and commercial, 414–15, (and trade) 407–24; industrial, 424–36, 450, 453, 454–5, (large-scale) 427–36, 493, 543; international, 407–23, 444–5; manufacturing, 412, 424, 435, 441; mercantile, 409, 453, 454; mining, 435–6, 441, 449; overseas, 401, 440, 545, 546

Dutch, 435, 442, 444, 452–5; English, 400, 420–1, 427–8, 430–6, 438–9, 441–4, 450–2, 455–6, 546; French, 428–30, 433–6, 442–4, 450–2, 456–7, 546; German, 429, 431, 451; Italian, 452; Spanish, 450; Swedish, 429, 431, 435, 442, 451–2, 457–8; Venetian, 429

entrepôts, 395, 417, 505, 539; or staples, 268; *see also* Amsterdam; Antwerp; Hamburg; London

entrepreneurs, 402, 438, 458–9; definitions, 393–4; industrial, 397–8, 435–6, 501, 576, (emigrants as) 487–8; Jewish, 529; in mining, 489, (*Kupfermeister*) 494; in putting-out system, 426, 470, 486; in textiles, 470, 517, (free entrepreneurship) 526

entrepreneurial control, 424; innovations, 445; skills, 402, 429, 434; succession, 419–23

Éon, Jean, 30

Ercker, Lazarus, treatise on metallic ores and minerals (1574), 472, 473

Erfurt, 71, 217, 489

Ernle, Lord, 112

Erzgebirge: glass making, 505; silver mining, 489, 492, ('white-sheet' metal) 496, (fuel for mining) 509

Eskiltuna iron works, 486

Essex, 71, 510

Esterhazy, Prince, 614

Esthonia, 61, 118, 120

Estienne, Robert and Henri, scholar-printers, 534

Estienne printing-house, 534

Europe: balance of trade with Asia, 256–7, 281; differential rates of progress in, 36–7, 71, 113–14, 126; the European economy, 302, 305, 445, 455; power politics, 241, 391

zones: climatic, 60–1; of production, 80–1, 216–17; static and dynamic, 186; stock rearing, 233, (cattle trails) 200; trading compartments, 217–18, 233–4, (overland trade routes) 190–1, (zones) 205–6, 209, 210, 214

Europe, central and east: absolutism, 552, 556–7, 558; agricultural character of, 121–2, 567, 578, (low grain yields) 80–1, 121, 126, (famines) 610; economic backwardness, 118, 576, (in towns) 122, 562; effect of wars on, 120, 254–5, (peasant wars) 122; embourgeoisement, 583–4; emigrants to, 485; gilds, 466, 468; serfdom, 113–23; trade balances, 262–3

Evelyn family, gunpowder contracts, 430

Exchanges, 331, 365

Amsterdam, 223, 343, 345–6, 389; exchange rates, 223, 342; weekly price sheet, 408

Antwerp, 326, 330–2, 348, 368, 381

London, 331, 348, 353–4

Lyons exchange market, 319, 335; Exchange, 365

Paris, 378

Rouen, Toulouse, 365

exchange rates, 223, 342, 372; rates at fairs, 315–22, 334, 344; gambling in, 332; exchange rates quoted, Danzig, Middelburg, Rouen, Seville, 223

Exchequer Bills, 353, 385–6, 423

Exchequer tallies, 382–3

Exeter, 160, 253

export: export dealers, 277; as a market function, 277, 280; surplus, 256, 262, 264, 308

Faber, J. A., 191, 231

factories, 431, 470–1, 481–3; 'welfare' factories, 471; privileged factories, 480, 482, 525

for: arsenals, 481; breweries, 479; luxury goods, 481, 482, 542–3; textiles, 471, 479, 480, 481, 482, 483, 529

in: Asia, 251, 281; Austria, 525; Bavaria, 480; England, 471, 479, 542; Firando, 246–7; France, 430, 471, 479, 481–2, 542, 543; Germany, 479, 483; Russia, 529; Scotland, 480–1; South America, 211; Spain, 482

factory workers, privileges for, 481–2

Faënza, 506, 507

fairs

  cattle, 235

  commercial and financial, 315–22; fairs of exchange (*foires de change*), 318–20, 322–3, 333; fairs of payment (*ferias de pagos*), 316, 318, 320, 366, 368, (Italian) 333–4; fair banks, 316, 317; bills of exchange at, 331; deposit from fair to fair, 311, 325; short-term loans from fair to fair, 364–6, 370; specie payments and, 308

  for individual fairs, see Besançon; Brabant; Castile; Champagne; Frankfurt; Geneva; Genoa, Lyons; Piacenza

Falcon, his improvements to draw loom, 477

Falkenberg, von, Swedish Crown agent in Amsterdam, 247

family and kinship: in diamond working, 542; hierarchy in, 552; in mining enterprise, 493; partnerships, 410, 417, 434, 435, 460; *see also* farms

famines, 21, 22; famine crises, 9–10; 16th century, 370; 17th century, 230, 546; 18th century, 132, 575, 577, 610, 614

farmers: credit arrangements for, 300, 304; progressive, 100–4, 106; tenant, 605, 607, 615, (Quesnay's regard for) 611–12; *see also* land; peasant farmers

farming: extensive, 67; and fluctuations in prices, 124–30; intensive, 57, 71–4, 102–3; size of farms and productivity, 46, 96–7, 100; *see also* agriculture; cattle; dairy produce

farms: demesne, 448; experimental, 103; family, 125–30; farm accounts, 100–2, (receipts and expenditures) 104–8; farm inventories, 99; farm tools, 475–6; small, 55, 56, 112–13, 124, 139

fashion, 250–2, 567

feltworkers, 470, 488; felts, 465

Fénélon, François de Salignac de la Mothe, 577

Ferdinand I, Emperor, 539

Ferdinand VI, of Spain, 532

Ferrero, Marquis, wool factory, 526

Ferrol, shipbuilding, 532

feudalism: feudal dues, 606–7, 610, (income) 381–3; feudal era, survivals of, 552, (institutions) 557; *Feudalisierung*, 583

financial techniques, 310; in south Europe, 311, 315, 320, 321–2; in the northwest, 322–4, 346–7, 352; institutional, 310, 311, 315, 322, 323, 346, 352, 357, *and see* banks *and* credit *and* fairs of payment; instrumental, 322–3, 327–32, 336–7, 346, (in England) 348–50; in international business, 354–5, 357; in public finance, 362, 376, 391–2

  assignment, 301–2, 326–7, 332; of annuities, 304; for bills of exchange, 328–9; for commercial payments, 311; to Exchange Banks, 337; of promissory notes, 316–17, 343; in public finance, 361, 358–9; of writings obligatory, 336. In England, 348–50, 383–4; France, 376; Spain, 368, 373

  bearer's clause, 325–8, 336; for annuity contracts, 364; in England, 348–52; on government instruments, 368; for IOUs, 301

  bills of exchange, *see* bills of exchange

  cashkeepers (*kassiersbedrijf*), 324, 332, 336–7, 342–3, 347, 351; promissory notes issued by, 343

  discounting, 323, 329–31, 332, 335; of bills, 342, 343; at commercial fairs, 368; of securities, 378. In England, 353, 383–4

  endorsement, 312, 331, 332; for negotiation of bills, 344; in transfer by assignment, 329; of writings obligatory, 327–8. In England, 383

  negotiability and transferability, 301; by assignment, 329; in public finance, 361, 365. In Antwerp, 325–6, 348; in England, 348–9, 385

  promissory notes, 301, 332; to bearer, 324, with bearer's clause, 325, 351, 352; at Castile fairs of payment, 316–17; interest-bearing, 377, 378; transferable, 326

  writings obligatory, 301, 324; assignment applied to, 326, 329, 336; with bearer's clause, 325, 330, (legal protection for bearer) 325, 330, (financial protection) 326–7; discounting of, 329–30; endorsement, 327–8, 329; negotiability, 351, in public finance, 361, 368, 370; transfers, 328–9. In England, 348–50 financiers: on the Antwerp Exchange, 326; in capital-intensive enterprise, 67, in international, 414; and needs of rulers, 359, (in France) 377–8; rewards of, 584, 610; short-term trade in government securities, 361; as tax collectors, 360

Finland: bank-notes, 381; famine, 546; farm animals, 89–90; shipbuilding, 533; tar and pitch from, 508

fiscalism, 578–9

fish: consumption, 172–8, 180, (tables) 173; days, 175–6, 178; fairs, 142, 148; markets, 172–8; merchants, 173–4; ponds, 176; trade, 161, 219, (long-distance) 184, (in salt-fish) 207, 214, 215

Fisher, F. J., 34

Fisher, H. A. L., 41

fisheries, 133–84; capital equipment for, 134; duties on, 174; financing of, 133, 157, 174–5, 183; fluctuations in catch, 135–40, 161, 166, 176, (decrease after 1689) 182–3, (recovery after 1750) 183–4; government regulations of, 148, 155, 164, 176, 177, 178–82; history of, 134–5; population and, 536; skill and knowledge in, 171–2; strategic importance of, 178–9; structure of, 134, 140–2, 157, 159, 161, 183. coastal fisheries, 139, 140, 141, 153, 172, 181, 183; commercial, 142, 172, 176; deep-water, 139; freshwater, 141, 175

catch: cod, 136, 155–66; Iceland, 135, 138, 140, 142, 155, 157, 158, 161, 164–6, 176, 178, 180, 182; New-foundland, 134–5, 138, 142, 155–7, 158–61, 166, 177–8, 536, (hostilities between rival fleets) 157–8, (markets in Europe for) 161, 177, 212, (salt cod) 196; North Sea, 135, 138, 139, 155, 157, 158, 164, 166, 176, 178, 180
herring, 133, 134, 135, 142–55, 176, 215; Baltic, 135, 149, 164, (salt herring) 215; Channel, 139, 143, 153, 154; East Friesland and Hamburg, 155; North Sea, 135, 139, 144–5, 208, 215, 274; Norwegian coast, 154; Scottish coast, 147, 149; Yarmouth, 138, 139, 141, 153, 154, 155; Zuider Zee, 153, 155

pilchard and mackerel, 138, 139, 142, 144–6, 166–8
whale fishery, 168–72, 537, (industrial products from) 171, 537; Biscay, 168; New England, 172; Spitzbergen, 168–71
other fisheries (tuna, whitefish), 136, 138, 139, 140, 141, 166

markets, 161, 172–8; Baltic, 177; French, 177; Italian, 177, 178; London, 161, 174, 175; monastic houses, 176; Paris, 173–4; Rouen, 153, 174, 177; Scotland, 142; Spain, 178; West Indies, 161

preserving industry, 133, 159, 172, 177; salt for, 154, 158, 159, 179, 180–1
cod: dried (la pêche sedentaire), 158, 159, 161; green salted (la pêche errante), 159; lightly salted and wind-dried (stockfish), 157, 161, 164, 177
herring: buss curing on board (salt white herring), 143, 148, 152–3, 177; smoked ('red herring' or bokking), 143, 153, 154, 176, 177; glut of, 178
mackerel: pickled, 168

fishing, trades ancillary to, 180

fishing boats, 143, 158; five-man cobbles, 143; herring buss, Dutch 'factory' ship, 148; ownership of, 175; sack ship, 158, 160, 162–3; ventjagers, 149, 152

fishing companies, 441

fishing equipment
drogue sail, 164
hake nets, 140; herring nets, 140, 180; mackerel nets, 140; seine nets, 175; stationary nets, 141; trawl nets, 139
lines, 139, 158; lines and nets, 140; multi-hook line, 160

fishing fleets: in times of war, 133–4, 154, 160–1; convoys for, 134, 152, 155, 158, 181–2
Basque fleet, 158
Bruges, 155
Delftshaven, 150–2
Dutch, 138, 178; whaling fleet, 169–70; bay fleet, 181; taxed by James I, 179
English, 138, 158, 160, 179; Great Yarmouth, 144–6, 164
French, 138, 153–4, 158; Dunkirk, 148, 164
Swedish, 165

fishing ports, 139–40, 159, 182, 184

Fishmongers' Company, 141, 176

Flanders, Flemish, 45, 91, 362; agricultural classes, 128; annuity contracts, 304, 370; artillery, 243; coins, silver groat, 291, 292–3, 340; commercial correspondents, 323; factories, 470; fishing boats, 148; grain consumption, 78, 83–4, (exports) 221–2, (imports) 222, 274; intensive farming, 71, 72, 73, 74, 103–4, (plough) 99, (small holdings) 126, (yield ratio of cereals) 81; mining specialists, 499; population, 224; ports, 260; refugee merchants, 330; textiles, 511–14, (exports) 203, 204, 254, (cloth imports forbidden) 269, (cloth workers in England) 510, (cloth workers in Spain) 516, (linen production) 514, (Spanish wool imports) 255, 516, (tapestries) 515, (textile towns) 470; trade with Italy, 275

flax: as a crop, 23, 27, 46, 56, 77, 89; in 'Land van Waas' system, 73; manuring, 95; and location of linen industry, 463

flax industry, 514, 515; spinning, 518; weaving, 515; flax-dressing machines, 476

trade in, 214, 217, 488, 531

fleets: commercial, 289; mercantile, 10, 24; mercantile marine: (Dutch) 531, (English) 530–1; precious metals fleet, 260, 367; see also fishing fleets; navies; shipbuilding

Flinn, Michael, 9

Florence, 32, 221, 328n; banking system, 311, (bankers) 364, 365–7; ceramics, majolica, 506; coins, 320, 334n; factories, 470; textiles: (cloth) 255, 525, (brocaded fabrics) 478, (silks) 527, (velvet) 542

Florentine 'nation' at Lyons fair, 318

flying shuttle, 476, 477

fly-wheel, 476

fodder crops, see crops

Foley iron partnerships, 434

Fondaco dei Tedeschi, 208

Fontane, T., novelist, 587

food, 195–201; and festivals, 196; government policy and, 187, 197; imports and exports, 206; long-distance carriage, 200; prices, 125–6, 178, 309, 357; production, 90–1, 126, 182–3, 231, 536, 538; regional specialities, 198; supplies, 216; trade, 218

bread, 48, 173, 187, 201, 536; cheese, butter, milk, 84, 201; fish, 133, 141–2, 147, 157, 161, 172–3; meat, 84–5, 92–3, 200–1, 536, (beef, pork, mutton) 92, 201

see also crops: food; diet; pepper; salt; spice

Foramiti, Lorenzo, linen factory, 527

foreign trade, 185; bills of exchange for, 324; depression in (1620), 333; foreign money trade, 263; government policy towards, 192–3, 265–7, 272, 289, 401; market system in, 289; municipal charters and, 270; peasants and, 610; role in developing capitalism, 354; small merchants in, 356; in textiles, 204; foreign traders, 328; see also commerce; markets; staple markets; trade flows

forges, 498, 499, 502, 505; hammer forges, 473; see also blacksmiths; smiths

Formosa, 258

foundries, 499; fuel problem, 509

Fouquet, minister of Louis XIV, 562, 567

Fowler, Robert, English stockbreeder, 93

France

absolutism, 549, 552–62, 564, 566, 573, 582–3, 589, 600

agriculture, 611; open-field system, 606

annuities, 304, 306, 364, 376–8, 380

army, 568, 569, 571, 576, 611; cost of commissions, 568, 569, 571, 572

banking: Banque Générale (Banque Royale), 379–80; Caisse d'Escompte, 380

ceramics, porcelain factories, 429, 507

coal mining, 435

colonies, 380, 541, 575

Constituent Assembly, 589

Dutch businessmen, 454

enterprise, 456–7

famine and disease, 577, control of, 604, 605, 610

fisheries, 134, 138, 139, 147; dole system, 183; duties on, 174; fishing zones off New England, 156; government attitude to, 180, regulations for, 177, 181; hosting system, 173–4;

France: fisheries (*cont.*)

markets, 174, 177; fish prices, 183; salt for, 181; in times of war, 154, 158, 177, 181–2

cod: Iceland, 164; Newfoundland, 157, 158–60, 161, (structural changes) 159, (technique) 160; North Sea, 164

herring: Dieppe, 139, 142, 153–4, 183; Boulogne, 153

mackerel, 139

whale, 168

white fish, 139, 140

fish preserving industry: curing, 154, 174, (the red herring) 154; drying, 158; drying and salting (green cod), 159; pickling, 168

fishing ports: Boulogne, 153; Calais, 183; Dieppe: (coastal) 139, 140, 141, 143, 154, (deepwater) 139, 153–4; Dunkirk, 164

fiscalism, 578–9

forges and foundries, 430

iron deposits, 490

luxury goods, preeminence in, 579; royal demand for, 430

mercantilism, 391–2, 573–80, 582–3, 585, 587–8

monarchy, 551, 553–7, 560–1, 583; royal monopolies, 552; *manufactures royales et privilégiés*, 430, 455

navy, 576, 577

nobility, 562–4, 567–8, 570–2, 610, 612; and the Crown, 566–7, 583; in enterprise, 450–1, 456

overseas trade, 546, 575

parlements, 377, 583

partnerships, 433, 442; companies, 444

peasants, 605–7, 609, 617, 618; and seigneur, 606–7; and taxation, 606, 612

Physiocrats, 613

public (royal) finance, 300, 319, 358, 364–6, 376–80, 391–2; state bankruptcy (1558), 371, (1709), 378; and war policy, 335, 378

secret committee on public debt (1715), 378–9; Law's project, 379–80; panic starts stock-market crash, 380

sale of offices, 451, 456

servitudes collectives, 606

state enterprise, 429, 430, 456–7; aid to large-scale enterprise, 430, 436, 442–3, 456

taxation: *gabelle*, 181, 360; on land and produce, 108; peasant taxes, 606; proposal for single tax on immovables, 379; *taille*, 360; inequity of system, 610–11; Physiocrat view of, 612

farming of indirect taxes, 377, 379–80, 552; fortunes made by *fermiers généraux*, 464

textiles, 512, 515–16; factories, 471, 479, 481; putting-out system, 515

cloth, 255–6, 481, 515, 542; New Draperies, 544; worsteds (*sayetterie*), 515

cotton, 515, (French cotton entrepreneurs in Spain) 517; flax and canvas-weaving, 515; lace, 483, 515; silk weaving and spinning, 515–16, (Van Robais' silk factory) 471, 479, (Asian imports forbidden) 482, 517; stocking and wool caps factory, 481; tapestry, 516, (*Manufacture Royale des Gobelins*) 429, 543

towns, 579

wars, 335, 555, 575, 578; French–Hapsburg, 359, 365; Fronde, 576; Louis XIV's wars of aggression, 238, 564, 577, 609, (cost of) 566

Colbert's views of, 578–9; Physiocrat view, 612; 'military virtues', 572; secretary of state for war, 567

wealth and poverty, 610–11

see also French

Francis I, of France, 365

Frankfurt am Main, 217, 225, 263, 408, 521; cattle imports, 200, 236; copper imports, 242, 244, 245; diamond trade, 542; fairs, 38, 46, 72, 269, 316, 323, 344; textiles, 518, 521

Franklin, Benjamin, 581

Frederick I, Duke of Württemberg, 483; enterprise in textiles, 519–20

Frederick II, of Denmark-Norway, 284, 536

Frederick IV, of Denmark, 530

Frederick II (the Great), of Prussia, 565, 570, 618; administrative machine, 597; colonial projects, 575; credit institutes, 587; 'enlightened autocracy', 556, 558, 560, 567, 595–9, (a disciple of reason) 590; grain stocks, 605; mercantilist policy, 573, 576, 578, 584–5, 597; and the nobility,

Frederick II (*cont.*)
553–4, (bolsters up existing society) 572; policy of peasant protection, 117; not interested in Physiocrats, 613; attitude to serfdom, 615; his wars, 576–7, 610, (conquest of Silesia) 520, (battle speech) 550, ('armée pure et dure') 572, (heroic age of) 586

Frederick William I, of Prussia, 557, 613; balance of trade, 575; bourgeois ministers, 565–6, 567; financial administration, 558; grain stocks, 605; reforms, 614

Frederick William II, of Prussia, 588

Frederick William III, of Prussia, 598n

free trade, 175, 574; in corn, 222

freight market, 210; rates, 239, (maritime rates) 223; *see also* carrying trade

French Flanders, 71, 76, 222

French furnace, 486, 504; forges, 498

French Revolution, 116, 553, 554, 578, 620; causes, 561, 579, 585, 617, 619; effect on distribution of land, 110, 113; and the nobility, 451, 563, 571, (seigneurial rights abolished) 113; and the reformers, 583; Tocqueville on, 556, 557, 562

French Royal Plate Glass Company, 428, 430, 435, 472

Frescobaldi, merchant bankers, 366

Freyesleben, mirror factory, 506

Friesland, 191–2
farming: arable and pasture, 66, 78, (intensive) 71, (improvements) 81, (use of manure) 74–5; dairy farming, 34, 99
fisheries, 172, 178, 536
grain consumption, 84; imports, 24
'pasturing' zone for cattle, 234; cattle market, 239
see also East Friesland

Friis, Astrid, 238

Froben press, Basle, 534

Fröschlmoser, Virgil, south German merchant, 492

Fugger (House of), 16th-century mercantile dynasty, 410; 'age' of, 371, 376; in Antwerp, 275; at Castilian fairs, 368; Church bankers, 364; fustian production, 519; Italian book-keeping, 412; mining enterprise, 493, (copper) 245, 415, 484, 489, 492, (gold) 484, (lead) 484, 492, (quicksilver) 428n, 484, 497, (silver) 492; public finance and trade, 361, 367, 370, 409, (effect on, of state bankruptcies) 371, 415; spice and pepper interests, 208; transit trade between Mediterranean and Continent, 217

Fugger, Anton, 370, 544

Fugger, Jakob: buys up Tyrol copper output, 244; loans to Emperor, 367; hires Neusohl copper mines, 478

Fugger, Octavian, activities in pepper trade, 284–5

Fugger, Philipp Edouard, activities in pepper trade, 284–5

Fuggerbriefe, 222, 326

fulling, 487, 510, 522; technological progress in, 477, 478; fulling mills, 529

fur trade, 212, 214, 217, 263

Fürer (Saxon entrepreneurs), 484

Fürer, Christoph, 544

furnaces, 471, 473–4, 486, 494, 504; blast furnace, 497, 498, 499, 502, 503; fuel for, 509

furniture, 542–3

fustians, 510, 512–13, 519, 526, 544

futures, speculation in, 331–2

Galantier, and draw-loom, 477

Gallas, Bohemian nobles, 524

Gamel, Jan, Antwerp merchant, 355

Gamron, Dutch factories at, 259

Garlipp, Gabriel, his privileged ribbon factory, 525

Garve, Christian, professor at Breslau, 585–6

Geer, de, Dutch entrepreneur family in Sweden, 435, 454

Geer, Louis de, Dutch entrepreneur in Sweden, 246, 247; armament, iron and shipbuilding enterprises, 430, 484, 486, 495

Geiger brothers, specialists in iron technique, 486

Gelderland, Guelders, 507, 515

Geneva, 217; banking system, 334–5, 346; fairs, 315–16, (transferred to Lyons) 318; foreign trade, 334, 335; French Huguenots in, 334–5; Italian merchants in, 315, (refugees) 334; merchant bankers, 334, 335; printed cottons, 522; silk production, 527, (taffeta) 525

Genicot, L., 44, 126
Genoa, 217, 328n, 414
  age of, 371, 376
  banking, 319, 321–2, 371–6
    Banco di San Giorgio, 312, 363
    merchant bankers, 318, 319–20, 322; control of American silver shipments, 320, of *asiento* contracts, 372–3, of European public credit, 366, of precious metals, 373–4; financial hegemony, 333; in international banking, 319; management of Hapsburg finances, 317–18, 371–5, (loans to rulers) 367, 370, 372–3; sale of *juros*, 373, 374
  ceramics, 507
  corn supplies for, 221
  entrepreneurs in silk industry, 517
  fairs, 321–2; 'Genoese nation' at fairs, 318
  gold ducat, 293–4, *écu*, 320, 334n
  municipal finance, 363
  papermaking, 535
  shipbuilding, 532
  sugar refineries, 540, 541
  ties with Catalonia, 371
  velvet, 542
Gentile, Genoese merchant, 372
Gentleman, T., *England's Way to Win Wealth* (1614), 143n
George, Duke of Saxony, 483
Gera, 518, 521
German Empire, 550
German princes, operation of salt refineries, 538–9
Germany, 27, 91, 260, 364
  agriculture: arable and cattle farming, 76, and wine-growing, 77; corn production, 89; enclosures, 116; farming incomes, 104, services due, 106; manure yields, 94
  annuity contracts, 304
  artillery, 243
  brickmaking, 507
  coins, taler, 291, 292, 307
  copper, brass and bronze industry, 544; copper imports, 244; merchants, 249; *Kipper-und-Wipperzeit* (copper inflation), 299, 309
  emigration, 18, 545; of miners, 487
  entrepreneurs, 245, 429, 431, 458; joint-stock enterprise, 441; aristocracy and,

451, 500; spice trade, 415; state enterprise, 429, 431
  fisheries, 536; whaling fleet, 171
  gilds, 466, 467, 519–21
  glassmaking, 505
  grain consumption, 84
  immigration, 514
  imports: cattle, 234, 235; copper, 244; fish, 161, 180; lead, 492; sugar, 540
  iron mining and industry, 490–1, 499, 500–1; peasant ironmasters, 485
  juros, sale of, 373
  land reclamation, 67, 69, 90, 111
  meat consumption, 92
  mercantilism, 578; merchants, 269–70, 473, (cattle merchants) 240, (status of) 287
  mercenary army, 373; food for, 200
  mines and minerals, 490–1, 540; silver mines, 296, 489; miners, 475, 486–7, 489
  papermaking, 535
  population, 545
  porcelain factories, 507
  printing, invention of, 534; printing presses in Europe, 534
  putting-out system, 518
  social stratification: bourgeoisie, 588; feudal institutions, 557; hierarchies and privileges, 551, 552; nobles and non-nobles, 586; villeinage, 116
  specialists in: France, 481; Russia, 489, 502, 529; Sweden, 482, 504, 545
  stone quarries, 507
  sugar boilers and refineries, 540
  textiles: areas and types of production, 518–21; cloth and woollen goods, 518; cotton, 521; flax and linen, 463, 479, 518–21, (export of linen) 519; silk, 521 bleaching, 519, 521; fulling mills, 477; government regulation of industry, 519; *Leggen* system of inspection, 518; new textile machinery, 477, 520
  wars: Thirty Years War, effects of, 68, 111, 545, 578; peasant wars, 367; religious, 218
Germany, east: agricultural classes, 127, 128–30, (serfdom) 115, 117–20, (working day on a farm) 98; flax and hemp, 518, (linen) 520, 544; landed gentry, 116

Germany, north: agriculture, intensive, 71, 72–3, 74; beer consumption, 201; breweries, 537; brickmaking, 507; cattle imports, 236; distilleries, 538; grain imports, 88; horses, 93; linen manufacture, 249–50, 253; merchants, 356; salt from, 215

Germany, south: banking system, 311, 371, (merchant bankers) 365–8, 370–2; book-keeping, 310n; cattle imports, 233; copper and silver mines, 207, (capital for) 489, (market) 244; entrepreneurs, 484, 488, 492; foreign trade, 218, 224; government encouragement for industry, 483; iron industry, 500; merchants, 318, 492, (in Antwerp) 275, (in Venice) 208, (Geneva contacts) 315; peasant revolts, 108; smiths, 486; textiles: (cloth) 518, (linen) 249, 544, (imports of linen) 515, (textile companies) 520; urbanization, 66

Germany, west: crops: buckwheat, 79, rye, 72; *Grundherrschaft* and the peasant, 607

Gerschenkron, Alexander, 265

Ghent, 222, 514

Gilbert, Sir Humphrey, 159

gilds, 39, 412, 464–9
    artisan, 33; closed, 467; craft, 464, 522
    collective delivery contract, 520; control lost to merchant capital, 464, 466, 498; and factories, 471; 'masterpiece', 467, 468; mercantilist view of, 466, 596; Physiocrat view, 603; putting-out system and, 463–4, 465, 469–70; take-over operations by, 537
    individual gilds: apothecaries, 468; bakers, 467, 468, 536; butchers, 467, 536; clothworkers, 464; drapers, 483; Five Great Gilds of Madrid, 466, 483; ironmongers, 465; ironworkers, 464, 498; Jewish gilds, 468–9; leather workers, 468; linen-weavers, 523; shipwrights, 530; silversmiths, 468; tailors, 468; weavers, 466, 519, 521, 522; yarnmakers, 476
    see also companies

Giolito de Ferrari, Gabriele, Venetian printer, 534

Glamann, Kristof, 21, 286, 310n

glass: crystal glass, 482, 506; forest glass-blowers, 427; glaziers, 132; mirror glass, 481, 506; sheet glass, 505; spectacles, 465

Bohemian, 450, 506; English, 449, 480; French Royal Plate Glass Company, 428, 430, 435, 472; German, 505; Low Countries, 505; Russian, 455; Venetian, 32, 208

manufacture, 429, 435; aristocratic interest in, 449, 450; chemical processes in, 508; furnaces, 455, (coal used in) 474; government support for, 480; large- and small-scale, 427; potash for, 508; technical apparatus, 472; wages, 487

Glockenden Bible, 476

Gneisenau, Field-Marshal Grafen Neithardt von, 588; his army commission, 568

Gobelins tapestry industry, 429; *Manufacture Royale des Gobelins*, 543

Goertz, Baron de, 381

Goethe, Johann Wolfgang von, 586

gold: export boom (1670), 258; gold dinner-services, 354; gold and silver factories, 543; gold–silver ratios, 257–8, 260, 264, 296–7, 299, 308; mines, European, 484, (organization) 488; payments in: (army) 260, 373, (for corn) 260, (international trade) 307, 308, 309; price fluctuations, 261, 264, 297
    from: Africa, 264, 296; Brazil, 212, 260, 264; the East, 257–8; Europe, 462, 488, 490–1; Japan, 258; New World, 308, 488; Sudan, 308

gold coins: in the monetary system, 291–5, 297–8, 300; demand for, 259; regarded as merchandise, 291
    gold ducats, 259, (as negotiating money) 260, 264, (as unit of account) 293–4, (as trade coin) 337; gold mark, 293; guinea, 307; *koubangs*, export of, 258; 'pagodas', 259

goldsmiths, 306, 468, 542; 'masterpiece', 468; workshops and factories, 542

goldsmith bankers, 351, 353

gold-standard areas, 259

Goll and Co., bankers, 391

Gorski, Karol, 15

Goslar, 488, 502

Gosling, London bankers, 353

Gossenprot, Augsburg entrepreneurs, 484

Göteborg (Gothenburg), 211, 283; Swedish entrepôt for iron, 505; shipbuilding, 533

Gottorp, customs registers for cattle movements, 235–6

Goubert, P., 9, 557, 577, 604; study of Beauvais, 20, 61, 196, 561

Gouda: clay pipes, 507; drapery, 515

Gould, J. D., 64

government finance

bonds: in Amsterdam securities trade, 345, 347, 355; on Antwerp Exchange, 468, 470; Dutch investment in, 216; on Lyons money market, 365, 366; royal bonds, 366, 367; Venetian, 313

securities: trade in, 362, 363–76; in Antwerp, 361, 367; English, 352, 353, (Exchequer Bills) 385–6, (Dutch investment in) 389; long-term, 388–9; in Lyons, 366; municipal, 363; organized markets for, 415; short-term, 361, 364, 366, 368, (held by Fuggers) 370

see also annuities; asiento; loans; taxation

grain

cargoes, 45

cultivation, 59–62; minimum and maximum yields, 60; effect of war on, 75

for distilling, 538

future deliveries in, 300, 331–2

imports and exports, 24, 118–19, 188, 207, 229–30, 264; value of, compared with cattle, 233

from: the Baltic, 24, 64, 88, 177, 208, 214, 221–2, 229; north Europe, 221–2; Poland, 86, 88, 275

to: Low Countries, 88; Mediterranean, 61, 207, 208, 221; north Netherlands, 24; Sweden, 64

Dutch dependence on imports, 75; English export bounty, 74; Spanish export embargo, 74

industrial uses of, 55, 85, 86, 88

markets, see Amsterdam

and other food crops, 78–9

prices: fluctuations in, 43, 44, 47–54, 55, 78, 79, 82, 111; and annuities, 377; and farmers, 123; and serfdom, 118–20; and weather conditions, 63–5

primacy of in agriculture, 53, 66

production and consumption, 83–9; grain-producing countries and serfdom, 121–3

reserves, 10, 605, 609–10

see also cereals; corn; crops

Granada, 486, 506, 540; silk industry, 517

grass (hay), 23, 58; and arable land, 94–5, 111, 113; grassland, 89, 94; haymaking, 98

Great Level, drainage of, 450

Great Northern War (1563–70), 238, 546

Great Yarmouth, see Yarmouth

Greece, 69, 219; silver mines, 489

Greenland Company, 171

Greenland whaling, see Spitzbergen

Gresham, Sir Thomas: establishes London Exchange (1571), 331, 348; management of public debt, 381

Gresham's law, 290

Gresley, Sir Thomas, 93

Griffiths, Talbot, 7

Grimaldi, Genoese merchant banker, 372

Griziotti-Kretschmann, Madame, 43

Groethysen, B., 591

Groningen, 24, 76; tillage systems, 72

Groote Visscherij, see Dutch fisheries

growth, distinguished from expansion, 22, and decline of national economies, 21, 23, 36–7, 38

in: Dutch Republic, 23–6, 28, 35; England, 34–5; Friesland, 191–2; Holland, 23–8, 396; Italy, 32–4, 36; Netherlands, 22; Spain, 28–32, 35, 36

Grünberg, C., 615

Grundherrschaft and Gutsherrschaft, 607–8, 618, 620

Gualterotti, Italian Portuguese merchant bankers, 283–4, 366

Guelders, Gelderland, 507, 515

Guicciardini, L., Italian historian, 24, 276

Guinea, trade with, 441

guinea, English coin, 307

guinee, textile for plantation slaves, 205, 213

Gujarat, 259, 280

Gustav Vasa, King of Sweden, 204, 272, 489, 504; 'business manager' of Swedish economy, 458

Gustavus Adolphus, King of Sweden, 228–9, 241, 486, 495; introduces bimetallic standard, 245–6

Gutsherrschaft and *Grundherrschaft*, 607–8, 618, 620
Gyldenlove, Ulrik Frederick, governor of Norway, 485

Haarlem, 253; bleaching industry, 463; siege of, 299; textiles, 512, 515
haberdashers, 465, 470
Habsburg hereditary dominions: absolutism, 556–7, 561, 566, 573, 618; Catholic Church in, 591, (medieval monasteries) 613–14; feudal elements, 588; German Enlightenment, 599, 614; *Gutsherrschaft*, 607–8; landlords' exactions, 609; mercantilism, 573, 575, 584, 585; nobility, 563, 567; peasants, and agrarian reform, 618; Philosophe reforms not adopted, 618; Physiocrats and, 613; schools and universities, 583; standing army, 572, 576; *see also* Austria; Germany
Habsburg monarchy: autocracy, 549–61; bankruptcies, 366; bureaucracy, 615–16; collaboration with merchants, 543; establishment of iron-works, 501; loans to, 362, 415; loss of Silesia, 520; magnates of, 485; and the new order, 573, 583; and peasants, 117; adopt Physiocracy, 614; public finances, 317, 366, 371, 372, and world policy, 366, 368, 371, 391; salt monopolies, 539; wars, 359, 365; *see also* Charles V; Joseph II; Maria Theresa; Maximilian; Philip II
Hakluyt, Richard, 157
Hale, J. R., 39
Halland: kale, 198; shipbuilding, 533
Hamburg, Hanse town, 283, 500, 508; banking families, 485, 495; breweries, 537; Canton trade, 211; copper market, 244, 245, 273, 275, 544; customs revenues, 546; discount practice, 330; English cloth staple, 269, 270; as entrepôt, 397, 413, 574; exchange bank, 337; grain exports, 229; herring fishery, 143, 155, 177; imports: (blue dye) 497, (cattle) 200, 216, 236; industries, 483, (metallurgical) 484, (textiles) 518, 521; international trade, 198, 214, 215–16, 267, 274, 345; Jewish craftsmen, 468; loans in Amsterdam, 391; money

market, 335; paper trade, 284, 285; refugees in, 330; salt route, 215; shipbuilding, 532; sugar refineries, 540, 541; welfare factories, 471; whaling port, 169–70, 171
Hamilton, E. J., 11, 28–9, 157, 178
hammers, 501; hammer-forge, 502; iron forge hammers, 500; *osmund* hammers, 499; water-powered, 497
Hammerström, Ingrid, 30
Hammond, J. L. and Barbara, 112
Hanau, 521
Hanau, Counts of, 483
Hanover, 84, 520
Hanse towns: boycott of Flanders, 224, 275; cod fisheries, 161, 164, 177, 182; competition with Dutch, 215–16, 274–5, (with English) 224, 254, 269, 275, (with south German merchants) 275; corn trade, 227; decline of, 216, 222; financial techniques: (bill of exchange) 324, (writings obligatory) 327; merchants, 142, 147, 209, 218, 222; printing presses, 534; shipbuilding, 532; *see also* Danzig; Hamburg; Lübeck
Hanseatic League, 273, 275, 285, 324
Hardenberg, Friedrich von, Prussian reformer, 551, 558–9, 560, 573, 586
Harley, Edward, and the South Sea Bubble, 388
Harper, L. A., 39–40
Harrach, Bohemian noble entrepreneur, 524
harvests, 34, 48, 59–61, 187; and payments in kind, 105; periodic bad, 604–5, 617; relation to grain prices and population, 54, 65, 123
Harvey, Daniel, contractor, 286
Harz: glass-making, 505; gold mines, 488; iron industry, 500; lead production, 463, 492; silver and copper mines, 462–3, 488, 493, (coal for) 509, (government aid to) 483, (wooden rails for) 475
Hasan, Aziz, 213
Hasselgreen, banker, 391
Hatfield Chase, 454
hats, hatmaking, 529; berets and fezzes, 526; felt hats, 470; Peruvian wool hats, 517
Haug, Langnauer and Company, of Augsburg, 497

Haugwitz, Bohemian noble entrepreneur, 524

hay, *see* grass

Haze, Jeronimus de, pepper consortium, 285

Hecksher, Eli, 2, 195, 261, 457n, 596; *Mercantilism*, 2, 573n, 577, 578n

Helleiner, Karl F., 8–9, 44, 83

Hemmema, Rienck, progressive Friesland farmer, 100–1

hemp, 23, 265, 463, 518; bleaching, 478; dressers, 180; machines for stamping, 474; products from, 517; profitability, 24, 77; for ships, 531, 533; trade in, 214, 217

Hennin, Russian state official, 504

Henning, F. W., 45

Henri II, of France, 304

Henri IV, of France, 442, 478, 481, 516

Henriques, Nunes, banker, 485, 495

Henry VIII, of England, 370

Heresbach, *Rei rusticae libri quattuor* (1570), 195

herring: catching seasons, 138, 139, 142, 143; consignments, 167; consumption, 173; fishing grounds, 136; fluctuations in shoals, 176; future deliveries in, 331–2; industrialization of herring fisheries, 536; salted herring, 179, 198, 208; trade in, 536–7; wars fought over, 179, 536; *see also* fisheries; red herrings

Hervart, Jorge, his diamond workshop, 542

Herwart, merchant banker, 367, 378

Herzberg, Graf Ewald von, 560

Hesse, 429, 499, 505, 518

Hesse-Kassel, 520

Hexter, Jack H., 580–1

Hicks, Sir John, 4

Hildebrand, K.-G., 204

Hille, Prussian Kammerdirektor, 565

Hitchcock, R., *A Political Plat for the honour of the Prince* (1580), 179

Hoare, London bankers, 353

Hoch, Mirslaw, 217

Höchstetter, Augsburg entrepreneurs and merchant bankers, 367, 410, 484, 497

Hoeufft, Jan, money-lender, 68

Hogguer Horneca, Dutch banking house, 27

Hohenkirchen smelting works, 242

Hohenzollern, House of: *Gutsherrschaft* in territory of, 607–8; mercantilism under, 575, 583, 584; and Prussian autocracy, 549–61, 565, 599; *see also* Frederick II; Frederick William I, II; Prussia

Holland
  agriculture, 23–4, 40–1; intensive farming, 71, 73, 103; peasant efficiency, 23; yield ratios of cereals, 81
  balance of trade, 263–4
  bleaching technique, 478, 519
  breweries, 537
  capital, availability of, 153, 398
  cattle imports, 91, 237, 240; import duty, 238
  clay pipe industry, 507
  commerce, dependence on, 453; loses European monopoly in, 389; transoceanic trade, 210, 347
  competition, 404
  corn trade, 224, 232
  currency policy, 298, 338–9
  dairy farming, 66; methods, 99
  economic growth, 23–8, 396
  enterprise, leaders in, 400, 420, 422, 452
  exports: bullion, 264; silver coins, 309; cloth draperies, 515
  fisheries, 134, 155, 178, 180, 183; dependence of prosperity on, 184; fishing boats, 148, 536; fish consumption, 175
  government attitudes to economic affairs, 273–4, 287–8; loans from Exchange Bank, 340
  grain: consumption, 84; imports, 55, 222, 229, 264; ships, 221
  immigration, 23, 484
  insurance companies, 355
  Jewish craftsmen in, 468
  joint-stock enterprise, 441, 446
  manufactures, 224; innovations in technique, 476
  merchant status, 287; a mercantile, not mercantilist state, 392, 452
  paper-making, 535–6
  peasant ownership, 23
  population, 84, 180, 216, 224; maintained by immigration, 23, 25
  re-exports of colonial goods, 212
  shipbuilding, 24, 531
  stability, 399

Holland (*cont.*)
textiles, 203; cotton printing, 471; clothmakers in France, 481; silk-workers in Austria, 524
the warehouse of Europe, 453
windmills, 477, 531; wind-driven saw-mills, 475
see also Amsterdam; Dutch
Hollander, rag-pulping machine, 536
Holt, Chief Justice, 350
Home, Francis, Scottish bleaching inventor, 478
Hondschoote, 470, 514
Hong merchants, 281
Hooks, Robert, diary (1675), 473
Hope, Dutch banking house, 27, 343
Hopkins, Sheila, 11
hops, 23, 56, 77, 95, 265, 274; trade in, 218
Horneca, Fizeaux and Co., Dutch bankers, 391
Hörnigk, mercantilist publicist, 483
Horsefield, J. K., 387
horses: age of, 93; as criterion of peasant classification, 126–7, 129; as draught animals, 46, 91, 93, 96, 99–100, (for harrowing) 98, (ploughing) 97–8, (threshing) 98, 100; food for, 220; harness makers, 542, (lorimers) 497; hides, 90; horse-drawn hoe, 99; horse-drivers, 487; horse-power in mining and industry, 474–5, 493; manure from, 90; numbers of, 89–90, 131
hostmen, 173–4
household utensils, 168, 202–3; copper, 203, 242; crockery and porcelain, 203; glass, 505, 506; iron, 203, 472; tin, 472, 496
housing, 132, 507; billets for troops, 555, 557; financing, 304–5; materials for, 186, 507, 508; palaces, 543; as wages, 487
Houtte, J. A. van, 32
Hove, Willem van den, money-lender, 68
Hroch, M., 261
Huguenots, 287
business success as a group, 406
Huguenot tutor of Frederick William I, 565
in: Basle, 523; England, 485, 512; Geneva, 334–5; Montpellier, 15
silk-weaving, 483, 512

skills of, an advantage to receiving country, 40
Huhnhäuser, A., 226
Hull, 168, 255, 530
Humboldt, Wilhelm von, 558, 570, 597, 598n
Hume, David, 18–19
Hummel, Hans, ribbon-loom invention, 476
Hungary, 195, 364
balance of trade, 263
bourgeoisie, 618
cattle exports, 200, 214, 219, 233–4; cattle-plague, 65; ox trade, 116, 218, 263; stock-farming, 91; Turkish embargo on, 219
conquest of, 120, 121; expulsion of Turks, 575–6
copper production, 189, 241–2, 243–5, 275, 415; decline in, 263
nobles: opposition to reforms, 616; seignorial rights, 116
peasant misery, 613; peasants and free-holders, 117, and *Gutsherrschaft*, 607
serfdom, 118, 119–21
silver from, 296
textiles, 254
yield ratios of cereals, 80–1
Hunsrück, 484, 499
Hunt, H. G., 112
Huntsman, Benjamin, steel production, 473
Huygens, Constantijn, money-lender, 68

Iberian trade, 210, 356, 368, 514, 532; *see also* Portugal; Spain
Iceland: cod fisheries, 135, 136, 138, 140, 142, 155, 157, 158, 161, 164–6, 176, 178, 180, 182, (dried fish) 196, (Yarmouth boats bound for) 144–6; sulphur from, 508
Idria, quicksilver from, 463, 484, 491, 496–7
Imhof, south German merchant banker, 367
immigration
areas in need of, 575
Dutch liberal policy, 18, 23, 26; English, 40
entrepreneurial immigrants, 485–6, 502, 517

immigration (*cont.*)
  immigrant merchants, 77; miners, 500;
    smiths, 504
  and transfer of technical skills, 40;
    through French Huguenots, 334–5,
    483; Italian refugees in Geneva, 334;
    south Netherlands refugees, in tex-
    tiles, 515, 518, 544, 547, in sugar
    refining, 539–40; Swabian weavers,
    520; textile workers from Locarno,
    522, 523
  see also migration
Imperial free cities, 466, 483
Improvers in the Knowledge of Agri-
    culture, Society of (Edinburgh, 1723),
    103
India: copper for, 243; Dutch: (trade with)
    210, (factories in) 248, 249; gems
    from, 542; gold and silver shipments
    to, 259, (gold–silver ratios) 257,
    259–60, (policy on gold and silver
    coinage) 259; Indians in Leghorn,
    256; interlopers, 252; prices, and in-
    flux of silver, 213; shipbuilding, 532;
    textiles: (calicoes and muslins) 203,
    205, 208, 213, (silks) 250–2, ('Indian
    textiles' made in Spain) 517, (the
    Indian craze in) 250–1
indiennes (muslins) from Switzerland, 522;
    from Russia, 529
Indonesia, 280
industrial revolution, 35, 36, 357–8, 427,
    445, 459, 547, 548, 578
industrialization, 431, 548; British, 8, 28;
    Dutch, 27–8, 224, 455, (of herring
    fishery) 536; Russian, 529; Swedish,
    485, 545
industry: definition, 462; location, 462–4,
    548; organization, 425–72, (collective
    delivery contract) 520, (domestic
    system) 425, 521, 526, ('industrial
    codes') 614, (workshops) 463, 469, 472,
    528, *and see* factories *and* putting-out
    system; regulation of: (by gilds)
    464–9, (by government) 399, 401,
    578, 603; shifts between agriculture
    and, 55
  capital-intensive, 538, 541; heavy, 427–
    36, (aristocratic enterprise in) 449;
    labour-intensive, 27; rural, 469, 548
  *see also under individual industries and
    countries*

inflation, 11, 20, 243, 308; credit inflation
    in England, 351; and deflation in
    Spain, 29; the 'great inflation', 30,
    38; *see also* copper: inflation
Innis, H. A., 160
innkeepers, 132, 300, 537; public houses in
    London, 479
insurance, 268, 345, 384n, 408; insurance
    companies, 355, 443, 444; marine
    insurance, 317, 332, 355
interest: Church ban on, 302, 310, 316,
    592; legalized by Charles V (1541),
    302; loans at interest, 302, 310, 325;
    promissory notes, interest-bearing,
    377, 378; *see also* rate of interest; usury
interlopers, 213–14, 438, 439, 444; in
    Eastern textile trade, 252; ports of,
    275; and smugglers, 282–3; in tea
    trade, 211; in whale trade, 168, 170;
    warships used against, 536
international exchange economy, 22, 186,
    354; role of staples in, 273
international finance, 356, 333: 'heroic'
    period of, 415; indistinguishable
    from trade, 407, 414–16; payments
    system, 261, 314, 326, 328, 335, 343,
    (through exchange banks) 339–40,
    342, (at fairs) 315–22, 323, 364; role of
    enterprise in, 394, 407; stability of,
    298
international trade, 190, 296; export
    surpluses, 256; payments system,
    306–10, 345; strategic importance,
    407; *see also* commerce; foreign trade
intuition, 14, 19, 412, 418; historical in-
    stinct, 37
investment, 13, 312, 322, 423; in agri-
    culture, 305, 357; in annuities, 303–6,
    355, 377; aristocratic, 450; in coal-
    mines, 428; through corporate enter-
    prise, 440–7; Dutch, 24, 27; at fairs
    of payment, 332, 334; in financial
    transactions, 350–1, 355–7, (in floating
    capital) 354, 357, (government issues)
    355; in fisheries, 161, 166, 175; in-
    vestment costs of industry, 478–80,
    548; in land, 45, 355, 423; in mines,
    441, 543; Physiocrat view of, 603;
    in *rentes*, 423; in ships and overseas
    voyages, 355; in town buildings, 305;
    see also capital; government bonds;
    securities; speculation

Ireland
    arable and cattle farming, 76; temporary cultivation, 72
    bleaching technique, 519
    fishing, 139, 140, 143, 166; fish exports, 177
    food crises, 10
    potatoes, 79
    textiles, 203; frieses, 510–11, (export limitation, 511); linen, 250, 511; Irish spinners, 470, (weavers) 511; yarn imports, 511
Irgens, Joachim, 485
iron: for agricultural implements, 98–9; for armaments, 501, (iron-cast cannon) 243, 496, 499, (muskets) 500; gears for windmills, 475; naval iron and anchors, 430, 533; needles, 499; table and kitchen utensils, 203, 243; wire, 499–501
iron industry, 497–505; areas of production, 490–1; coal and coke for smelting, 473, 498; entrepreneurial activity, 427, 449, 458, 486, 498; gilds, 464, 465, 498; joint-stock organization, 441; new 'Iron Age', 504; peasant iron industry, 501
    bar iron, 498, 504, (puddling process for) 474; cast iron, 497; *osmund* iron, 504; sheet iron, 473; *vallonjärn*, 504; wrought iron, 504
    production in: Austria, 501; Balkans, 501; Bohemia, 501; Brescia, 501; Bulgaria, 501; England, 427, 434, 435, 490, 497–8; France, 490; Germany, 490–1, 499, 500–1; Liège, 499, 504n, 546; Norway, 503; Poland, 501–2; Russia, 502–3; Scotland, 463, 497, 498; Silesia, 449; Slovakia, 501; Spain, 463, 490, 498–9; Sweden, 463, 503–5; Thuringia, 500
iron merchants, 501
iron mines, 484, 490–1; deposits, 463; ore, 504
iron trade, 214, 263
ironmasters, 485, 497, 502, 504
ironmongers, 24
Italy
    abandoned villages, 68, 69
    agriculture, 32–4; arable and cattle farming, 76; crops, 73, (rice and maize) 78, 201, 230; farming incomes, 104; threshing block, 100; yield ratios of cereals, 80–1
    asiento contracts, 333
    balance of trade, 307–8
    banking system, 310, 319, 347; deposit or exchange banks, 301; land banks (*monte frumentarii*), 305; public clearing banks, 312–14; merchant bankers, 316, 334, 371, (loans to rulers) 332–3, 365–6
    bronze casting, 496
    cattle imports, 219
    ceramics, 506–7
    commercial empire, 208
    depression (1620), 333, 535
    emigrants from, 485
    entrepreneurs, 452; in spice trade, 415
    experts in French industry, 481
    fairs of payment, 333–4
    financial technique, lead in, 322–3; double entry, 310, 412; opposition to endorsement, 329
    fish consumption, 173, 177, 178; imports, 207
    foreign trade, 315, 372; with Flanders, 275
    gilds, 467; Jews in, 468
    gold reserves, 373
    government enterprise, 483
    grain supplies for, 223, 285; shortages, 219, 221–2
    health measures, 17
    joint-stock enterprise, 439
    juros, 373
    land ownership, 34
    luxury goods, 542
    mercenary army, 373
    merchant status, 287
    montepios (pawnshops), 305
    municipal finance, 363
    papermaking, 535
    Physiocrats, 614
    population, 34
    printing, 534
    progress and decline, 32–4, 35
    savings, 373
    shipbuilding, 532
    Spanish-ruled states, 467
    textiles: areas and types of production, 525–8; fulling mills, 477; imports of English cloth, 269, of Spanish wool, 255, 516; putting-out system, 526

Italy: textiles (*cont.*)
　　cloth industry, 207; linen, 526–7; serge, 526; silks, 214, 255, 282, 470, 477, 527–8, (emigrant silk manufacturers in Russia) 525–6; woollens, 525–6
　　ties with Antwerp, 322, with Bruges, 322, with Iberian peninsula, 208
Italy, north, 66–7, 107; agriculture, 33–4; cattle imports, 234; foreign trade, 218; grain shortage, 197; mining and metallurgy, 490–1, 501
Italy, south, olive oil exports, 207
Itzig, Daniel, Ephraim and Isaac, debasement of Prussian coinage, 584
Ivan IV, the Terrible, Czar of Russia, 118, 502

James I, of England, 176, 179, 480, 481
Jansz, Dirk, progressive Friesland farmer, 100–1
Japan
　　copper from, 214, 246–9, 258, 281, 282, 296, 495; embargo on exports, 248
　　foreign trade, 280–1
　　gold and silver from, 257–8, 309, (gold coins) 258; export of silver prohibited (1668), 258
　　textiles from, 203; silk trade, 281
Java, 210; coffee and sugar from, 214, 282
Jeannin, Pierre, 209, 215, 230
Jews, 586; business success as a group, 406; community in Leghorn, 256; in the Enlightenment, 591; gilds, 468–9; merchant bankers, 71; merchants, 219; mine owners, 489; money-changers, 343; and pawn shops, 302; Portuguese, 256, 333, 343, 346, 375, 389; seafaring, 286–7; Spanish, 15, 256, (amnesty in Spain in 1604) 333; silk ribbon production, 527; textile manufacture in the Balkans, 528–9, (Sephardic emigrants, in textile industry) 485, 529
Joachimsthal (Jachymov), 493; immigrant miners, 489, 500; pumps operated by water-power, 473
John III, of Portugal, 466
John III, of Sweden, 504
John, A. H., 250
Johnson, Henry, shipyard owner, 531
joint-stock companies, 439–47; as an entrepreneurial innovation, 416, 436–7, 445; directors, 446; investors in, 414, 440, 444, 445; limitations of, 444–5; pepper distributed as dividends, 286; privileges for, 413, 440, 441, 444; proprietors and management, 446; relations with government, 401, 442–4
　　banks, 352, 443, (shares in) 353–4; colonial, 355, 417, 441; commerce, 441, 442, 444; finance, 443–4; fisheries, 174–5, 441; manufacture, 432n, 441; mining, 432n, 441; for new inventions, 443; overseas establishments, 400, 417, 446–7; water supply and drainage, 441
　　see also company administration, *separate companies*
Jonathan's Coffee House, 354
Jones, E. L., 4, 39, 41n
Joseph II, of Austria
　　his Christian faith, 590; attacks power of Church, 591
　　as enlightened despot, 554, 556, 566, 597; revolutionary policies, 567, 572, 573; sets serfs free, 615–17; reforms abandoned, 561, 618
　　mercantilism under, 573
　　sale of offices, 565
　　secret police, 616
Joslin, D. M., 352
journeymen, 463, 488
Juan II, of Spain, 35
Judah, C. B., 160
Junkers, 35, 609
Jurgen, Master, mason, 476
juros, see annuities
Justi, J. H. G. von, German cameralist, 595, 609
Jutland, ox-trade, 52, 91, 200, 216, 233, 235, 236–7, 238, 268

Kant, Immanuel, 586, 588
Kauffman, mining entrepreneurs, 493
Kaunitz, noble family, textile factories, 524
Kay, John, flying shuttle, 476, 477, 526
Kellenbenz, Hermann, 12, 13, 21, 36, 286, 449n
Kerhuel, M., 43
Keymor, John, 134
Keynes, J. M., 17

Khan, S. A., 250

Kilburger, Hans, German mining entrepreneur, 502

King, Gregory: corn yields, 83; 'Gregory King's law', 51, 133; stock figures, 89; taxation figures, 40

Kirchdorf-Micheldorf, scythes manufacture, 501

Kitson Papers, 329

Klaveren, Jacob van, 279

Kleberg, Hans, south German merchant banker, 365

Klein, P. W., 246, 273, 277–8, 356, 389n

Klippehäfen, interlopers' ports, 275

knitting: frame-knitting machine, 478; *see also* stocking-knitting

knives and scissors, 470, 499, 500; cutlers, 497; handle-makers, 470

Koberger, Anton, printer-publisher, 534

Kohlbrugge, J. H. F., 26

Kondratieff, N. D., 97

Koniecpolski, Stanislaw, his forges, 502

Kongsberg (Norway), silver mines, 260, 489

Königsberg (Kaliningrad), 228, staple town for Eastland Company, 270, for Teutonic Knights, 275; balance of trade, 262; and the Enlightenment, 586; rye and wheat shipments from, 227, 229, (Dutch flyboats for) 531, (wheat prices) 70; University of, 619

Kooy, Dr van der, 276–7

Korst, Knud, *see* Bang, Nina

Köstner, Johann, Danzig merchant, 229–30

Kraft, Ulrich, visit to Cyprus and Rhodes, 539

Krakow, *see* Cracow

Kranenburgh, H. A. H., 134, 148, 149

Kraut, Johann Andreas, minister of Frederick William I, 565, 584

Krefeld, 485, 518, 521

Kremsmünster, Abbot of, establishes wool factory, 524

Krottendorf, 500

Kula, Witold, 187

Kuske, Bruno, 205

Kyoto, 281

la Morandière, Ch. de, 134

La Rochelle, 159, 531, 540

la Vega, Lopez de, *Confusio de Confusiones* (1688), 345–6

labour, 486–88; casual, 129, (seasonal) 487; child labour, 471, 487; day labour, 100, 126–8, 130, 198, 605; differentiation (specialization), 486–7, 501; division of, 500, 610; in factories, 471; family labour, 96, 98, 128; free labour, 501, (and gildsmen) 469–70, 463–4, and unfree labour, 487–8; hours of: (in farming) 93, 97–8, (in industry) 487; as proportion of production costs, 192, 397; and serfdom, 120; supplies of: (for farming) 97, (for industry) 397–8, 425, 432, 514; (for New England colonies) 160, (for plantations) 212–13; unskilled, and machines, 523; women: (in farming) 101, (in industry) 101, 471, 486–7, 514, 536; workers and employers, 101–2; workmen's associations, 488; *see also* wages

Labrousse, Ernest, 2, 43, 605, 610

lace, 481, 542; bone-lace, 487; French, 515; Swiss, 523; technique transferred by Netherlands emigrants, 518; Viennese, 525

Laffemas, Barthélemy de, *valet de chambre* of Henri IV, 481, 516

Lamberg, noble entrepreneur, 496

Lancashire, 509, 510

Lancisi, Giovanni, 65

land: demesne, 114–16, 118–23, 487; erosion of, 69; investment in, 45, 106, 355, 423, 580, 587; mortgages on, 305; Physiocrat view of, 603; restrictions on, 619–20; and the *société d'ordres*, 549–50; speculation in, 569; state revenue from, 604; as wages, 487, 501

land banks, 305–6, 384, 385; *Landschaften*, 587

land reclamation, 22, 56, 66–71, 454; by the aristocracy, 449–50; Dutch enterprise, in England, 454; financing of, 304; in Germany, 111; speculation in, 106; and stock farming, 90–1

land tenure
copyhold, 114
customary, 14
freeholders, 14
leasehold, 114; contracts, 100, 106, 110; long leases, 74; short, 106; shared, 105

land tenure (*cont.*)
  serf tenure, 608
  tenant farmers, 109, 608
landed interest, 271, 400, 448–51, 464
landownership, 109–13, 414
  distribution of land, by families, 127–8
  effect on, of enclosures, 110, 111–12; of war, 110–11
  and farm management, 107; progressive farming, 102–4
  in Italy, 33–4
  landed farmers, 55
  land-holding serfs, 557, 608
  owner-occupiers, 109
  peasant proprietors, 605–6
  political power based on, 566, 570
  smallholdings, 109, 111
  as status symbol, 51, 106, 355, 403–4, 422, 435, 451, 587; as a disability, 420
Lane, Frederick C., 32, 265, 279
Langner, Georg, hammer-forge, 502
Languedoc
  agriculture: agricultural classes, 127; farm households, 125; intensive farming, 171; literacy among farmers, 102; real wages, 106; smallholdings, table, 128; yield ratios of cereals, 80
  colliery entrepreneurs, 436
  grain consumption, 84
  olive trees, 58
  peasant revolts, 108
  silk manufacture, 515
Lapeyre, H., 328n, 329, 372n
Law, John, 299; 'system' for extinguishing French floating debt, 379–80, 388
le Creusot, partnership firm, 433
Le Maire, Isaac, merchant, 73, 345
le Pecq, 167, 174
Le Pelletier, 377
Le Roy Ladurie, E., 15, 17, 20, 21, 161, 187, 306
Le Tellier, minister of Louis XIV, 562
lead mines, 219, 463, 484, 490–3; aristocratic enterprise in, 449; joint-stock organization for, 441; lead–silver mines, 492–3; production methods, 474, 492, 508
  in: Carinthia, 463, 484, 491, 492; England, 207, 441, 449, 463, 474, 490, 492; Harz, 463, 488, 490–1, 492; Poland, 463, 491, 492–3; Silesia, 463, 488, 491, 492–3

leases: of looms, 523; for manufacturing premises, 436; for mines and iron works, 436, 449; *see also* land tenure
leather industries, 207, 208, 488, 542; bark for, 508; factories, 481; harness-makers, 343; hides and skins, 8; leather workers' gilds, 468
Lee, Edmund, inventor of 'fantail' windmill, 475
Lee, William, knitting machine inventor, 478
Leeds, 464, 510
Lefebvre, Georges, 2, 563n, 617; *Quatre-Vingt-Neuf*, 579, 580
Leggen system of inspection, 518–19
Leghorn: cosmopolitan character, 256, 333; a free port, 256; gilds and Jewish craftsmen, 468; grain port, 221; red herrings, 154, 178; trade, 320
Lehndorf, Graf, diary of, 570
Leibnitz, Gottfried Wilhelm, 600
Leiden: printing presses, 535; siege of, 299; textiles, 513, 514, 516, 547, (camlets) 254, (cloth industry) 463, ('New Draperies') 253, 515, (strikes among woollen workers) 488; decline of, 36
Leipzig, 217, 481, 484, 489, 520; bills of exchange, 264; fairs, 263
Lemberg (Lwow), 217, 468–9
Lent, and demand for fish, 175–7, 183, 196
Leopold I, Emperor, 121; loans to, 390
Leopold II, Emperor, rescinds reforms of Joseph II, 616, 618
Leslau customs registers, 225
Lessing, Gotthold Ephraim, 586, 597
Leur, J. C. van, 278–81
Levant, 206; company trade with, 441, 442; copper for, 243; Dutch traffic in, 254, 347; export of silver coins to, 309; Italian trade in, 372; ships for Levant trade, 531; spice trade, 209, (pepper) 283–4; Swedish iron, market for, 547; textile imports, 254, 255–6, (English cloth) 222, 269, (Indian cloth) 250, (Irish frieses) 511; trade coins for, 340
Levant Company, 270, 446
Levy, Hermann, 112
Leyen, von der, brothers, silk-weaving entrepreneurs, 521

liberty, equality, fraternity, 589–90, 601–2, 604, 618

Libro Mayer, 316–17

Liège, 222, 484; bronze casting, 496; coal mines, 433, 509, (coal exports) 509; diamond trade, 542; smiths from, 486

Liège, bishopric of: drapery exports, 514, 518; glass works, 505; iron ore, 499, (production) 504n, 546; metallurgical industries, 545; protectionist policy of prince-bishop, 514

Lille: inland bills, 344; manufacture of broadcloth, 514

Limburg, 222, 515

lime trade, 507

linen production, 479, 511–14, 517–21, 523, (technology) 476; aristocratic enterprise in, 450, 483; bleaching for, 253, 478, 514, 519; canvas, 218, 249, 480, 515; dyed linen, 520; government aid to, 511, 519; privileges for, 518; putting-out system, 479, 520; as a rural craft, 203, 249, 511, 514, 521, 523; sailcloth, 471, 517, 529; women in, 487

Austria, 523; Bavaria, 523; Bohemia, 520; colonial, 517; 'Dutch', 253; Germany, 249–50, 253, 479, 483, 518–21; Ireland, 250, 511; Italy, 526–7; Low Countries, 514; Russia, 529; Saxony, 250, 520; Scotland, 511; Silesia, 250, 520; Swabia, 519–20; Switzerland, 521

linen rags, for paper-making, 469, 535

linen ribbons, 520–1

linen trade, 218, 249–50, 511, 514, 520

linen-weavers' gilds, 523

linen yarn, 520

Linussio, Giacomo, linen factory, 527

Linz, woollen factory, 524

Lionne, minister of Louis XIV, 562

Lippe, 519, 520

Lipson, E., 5, 399n

liquidity reserve, 364, 377, 378

Lisbon, 136; assignment, 327; cloth staple, 269; Danzig trade route, 210, 275; diamond exports, 542; ovens for ship's biscuit, 536; sailings from, 212, 214; salt and spices from, 275, 415; shipbuilding, 532; silver supplies from, 261, 333; sugar refining, 539, (exports) 499

Lithuania, 225; Jewish gilds, 468–9

Liverpool, sugar refinery, 540

Lloyd, Edward, Quaker iron manufacturer, 498

loans

private: arrangements for, at fairs, 317; loans at interest, 302, 310, 325; state loans, interest-free, for industry, 430, 480

public: *asiento* contracts, 332–3; Bank of England loan to State, 443; compulsory loans, 360–1; consolidated, 388; financing of, 352, 363, 365; as investment, 312, 423; long-term loans, 345, 361, 363, 376, 387, (subscribed by underwriters) 389; Paterson's proposed loan, 385; short-term loans, 364–7, 370, 372, 376, (Stuart borrowings) 382–3, (tables of interest on) 362, 369; *see also* credit; financial techniques

Lobsinger, Hans, wooden box bellow, 473

Locatelli, Joseph, improved agricultural machinery, 99

Locke, John, 573

Loder, Robert, progressive English farmer, 95, 98, 100–2

Lombardy, 206; brickmaking, 507; gilds, 437; pawnshops, 302; textiles, 526, 527

Lombe, Thomas, silk mill, 479, 511

London, 71, 414; Antwerp, influence of, 348; Asian textile market, 252; brew-houses, 428, 434, 435, 474, 537; cloth exports from, 254–5; coachbuilding, 542; depression years, 255; Dutch capital in, 454; as entrepôt, 397, 413; Exchange, foundation of (1571), 331, 348, (trade in shares) 353–4; financial techniques, 323, 348–52; fish market, 161, 175, (fishing ships sail from) 160, 164, 168, 170; foreign merchants in, 348, 382; gilds and companies, 464–5, 470, (regulated companies) 438, 439; gold shipments to, 342; goldsmiths, 542, (as bankers) 351–3, 383–4; Great Fire of, 465; improvements in real estate, 450; international trade, 214, 345; investment market, 454; merchants, 350, (mercantile aristocracy) 421; moneylenders, 381; money market, 335, 347–8, 352–3, 357, 361;

London (*cont.*)
and outposts, 287; population, 67,
579; Portuguese in, 333, 389; price-
current list, 408; sea-coal from
Newcastle, 509; shipbuilding, 530,
531; silk manufacture, 511; spice
trade, 285; Turkey merchants, 510;
weather, 60; West Indian merchants,
205

London, Corporation of: bonds issued by,
381; livery companies and, 464; royal
loans, 383; sale of Crown lands by,
359, 382

London Society of Soapboilers, 382–3

londrine, Italian cloth, 526

looms: Bandstuhl (ribbon loom), 477,
520; concentration of, in factories,
479; draw looms, 477; hire of, 523;
innovations in, 477; *Kunstsfuhl*, 523;
multi-shuttle, 477; numbers, (Austria)
525, (Italy) 527–8, (Spain) 517; power
loom, 477; *see also* weavers; weaving

Lorraine, 69, 500; salt exports, 538

Lorraine, Francis, Duke of, textile factory,
524

lotteries, 384, 388

Louis XI, of France, 318

Louis XIV, of France, 376, 565, 575, 579;
his 'bourgeois' advisers, 562; edict
on Dutch fisheries, 148, 181; Edict of
Nantes, revocation of, 334; and
French absolutism, 549, 552, 553,
557; *politique de grandeur*, 391; sale of
offices and titles, 564; wars, 238, 564,
(cost of) 566, 577, 578, 609

Louis XV, of France, 572, 602

Louis XVI, of France, 553, 560, 572; as
Dauphin, 603

Lourder family, 430

Low Countries: animal husbandry, 93,
(sale of manures) 95; cereal crops,
78–9, (yield ratios) 80–2, (corn production and consumption) 88–9;
commercial dominance, 395; currency reform, 292–3; entrepreneurial
activity, 452; farming and education,
102–3; farming incomes, 104; glassmaking, 506; herring fishery, 135,
148, (fishermen) 147; land reclamation, 67–8; merchant status, 420, 421,
423; population, 88; rural non-
agricultural classes, 131; textiles,
511–15, (English competition) 254,
511, (move from urban to rural
centres) 511–12, (broadcloths (lakens),
cotton, lace, linen) 514, (cloth
drapery, silk, tapestry) 515; villeinage,
116; windmills, 475; *see also* Dutch;
Flanders; Holland; Netherlands

Lowestoft, 155, 174, 183

Lübeck, 271, 274, 500, 508, 530; Amsterdam, rivalry, 273; Antwerp, rivalry,
275; cattle imports, 236; copper
market, 244–5, 272–3; Dutch ships
for, 531; grain trade, 215, 216, 222;
metallurgical industry, 484; pepper
trade, 285; shipbuilding, 532–3; trade
with Spain and Portugal, 532; *see also*
Hanse towns

Lublin, 225; Jewish gilds, 468; printing,
534

Lucca, 527; Lucchese bankers, 364,
('nation' at Lyons fair) 318, 371

Lusatia: linen production, 520, 544; serfdom, 117, 119, 121, (peasant wars)
122; yield ratios of rye, 62

Lütge, F., 578

Lutheran emigrants, 485

Lutheran Prussia, 593

Lüthy, H., 334n, 379n, 591

luxury goods, 542–3; demand for, 466,
469, 542, (and inflation) 30; government encouragement of, 401, 430,
481; luxury industries, 579, 613;
merchant consumption of, 354; and
prices of necessaries, 13; reduced to
mass consumption level, 212, 289;
specialization in, 542; trade in, 437
diamonds and precious stones, 542;
furniture, 542–3; glass, 506; textiles,
203–4, 255, 542; travelling coaches,
533, 542
French, 430, 481; German, 483; Italian,
308, 542; Oriental, 210, 308; Spanish,
482; role of Vienna in, 219

Luzern, textiles, 521, 522, 523

Lwow (Lemberg), 217, 468–9

Lyons, 328n, 367; clearing banks, 310,
346, (merchant bankers) 364, 378;
cotton manufacture, 515, (fustian)
512; fairs of payment, 293, 307, 316,
323, 335, 371, (rules for payment)
318–19, 320–1, (speculation on exchange rates) 332, (loans to rulers)

Lyons (*cont.*)
364, 365–6; international trade, 320; money and exchange market, 319, 335, 357, 365, 370; printing and publishing, 534; silk-weaving, 477, 516; veterinary school, 66
Lythe, S. G. E., 147

Maastricht, 73, 514
Macedonia, 219, 528
machines: for mining, 473–4, 492; for processing of metals, 472, 497, 501; in textile manufacture, 476–8; steam engine, 474–5
for processes: beating, stamping, 476; braiding, 520; carding, 476; cropping, shearing, 478; flying shuttle, 476, 477; fly-wheel, treadle wheel, 476; frame for knitting, 478
see also furnaces; hammers; looms; mills; pumps
mackerel, 136, 144–6, 166–8; catching seasons, 138, 139, 142; consignment of, 167; consumption, 173; fishing grounds, 136, 138, 139; 'stinking mackerel', 168; *see also* fisheries
Maçzak, A., 261
Maddalena, Aldo de, 33–4
madder, 23, 56, 77
Madeira, 221; sugar from, 214, 282, 539
Madrid: bills of exchange, 372; clearing bank, 314; gilds, 466, 483; hat-making, 517; tapestry works, 482
Magdeburg, 483, 489
maize, 10; introduction of, 34, 46, 78–9; consumption, 201, 230
Majorca, 244, 539
Malabar, pepper trade, 280
Malesherbe, Chrétien Guillaume, 582
Malowist, M., 261
Malthus, T. R., 7, 86, 187
Malvenda, Francesco and Pedro, 285
Malynes, G. de, *Lex Mercatoria* (1622), 327, 328, 329, 349
management: aristocratic, 449; entrepreneurial, 443; in industry, 434; and ownership, 445–6; managers, 427, 434, 446–7
Manchester, 6, 510
Manila, 214, 257
Manley, Gordon, 62
manorial system, 113, 115–16

Mansfeld, copper and silver mines, 479, 488–9, 494, 544
Mansfeld, Counts of, 479, 543
Mantoux, Paul, 112
manure, 64; manure barges, 24; night-soil, 24; pigeon manure, 95; production of, 90, 604; trade in, 95
manuring, 56, 59, 66, 94–5; methods of, 94; and yield ratios of cereals, 82, 95
Manutius, Aldus, Venetian printer, 534
Marcolini, Francesco, Venetian printer, 534
Maria Theresa, Empress of Austria: Austria at her succession, 551, 613–14; bureaucracy, 595; industrial policy, 483, 524; mercantilism under, 573; moderate reforms, 567, 614, (attacks power of Church) 591, (attempt to relieve peasants) 608, 614–15, 618; sale of offices, 565
Marienburg, 275, 489
mariners, 180, 438, 453
Marius, J., *Advice concerning Bils of Exchange* (1651), 329, 349, 350
Mark, The (region), 508, 546; men of, 550; weaving, 521; wire-making, 499–500
market organization, 265–89, 290, 416, 425, 460; and commission business, 354; control of, 412–13, 447; institutions and instruments of market, 289; Physiocrat view of, 613; role of the State in, 287–9; strategic importance of, 435, 436; theories of market structure, 276–83, 287
markets: international, 188, 214, 267, 275, 282, 287–9, 407–9, (Amsterdam the centre of) 276–7; local, 187–8, 267, 276, 452; mass, 542; overseas, 548; pedlar, 278–81; in the pattern of consumption, 262; permanent and sporadic, 278; seasonal, 276; world, 276; *see also* fairs; money market; staple market; *and see under particular commodities*
marling, 74
Marseilles, 67, 206, 217; soapmaking, 508, 543; sugar refineries (*Raffinerie Royale*), 540–1; world trade, 335
Marselis, Netherlands entrepreneurs, 485, 503
Marshall, William, 43–4

Marwitz, Alexander von der, on Adam Smith, 619

Marxism, 5–6, 18, 114

Mason, Joseph, and draw-loom, 477

mass consumption, 212, 289, 613; mass market, 542; mass production, 28, 427, (for victualling armies and fleets) 538

Massachusetts Bay Company, 450

masters: ceramics, majolica master, 506; copper, 494; in diamond trade, 542; iron masters, 485, 497, 502, 504; in textile factories, 487, 510, 518, 520, (silk-masters' fraternity) 524–5; masterpiece, 467, 468

Mathieu, Christophe, French coal-mining entrepreneur, 428, 434, 435

Mathiez, Albert, *La Révolution Française*, 579

Maupeou, R. N. C. de, 582

Maupertuis, P. L. M. de, 600

Maurelles, merchant house of, 540

Maximilian, Archduke, 20

Maximilian, Emperor, 501; his copper mines, 244, 492; loans to, 366; salt monopolies, 539; war finance, 241

Mazarin, Cardinal, 442

meat: carriage of, 200; consumption, 84–5, 92–3, 173, 200–1, 211, 536; production, 90–1, 231

Mecklenburg, 73, 117, 121

Medici, Cosimo de, 528

Medici, house of, 415, 480; silk and wool workshops, 479

Medici bank, 315, 316

medicine: army hospitals, 555; in France and Switzerland, 17; medical care in villages, 132; midwives, 132; quarantine regulations, 10, 17; surgeons, apothecaries, 132, (apothecaries' gild) 468; jars for a princely pharmacy, 506

Medina del Campo: Antwerp and, 367; bills of exchange, 372; endorsement, 328n; fairs, 316–18, 368, (*banco de feria*) 317–18

Mediterranean region: alum from, 207, 490–1; cloth trade, 255, 256; Dutch traffic in, 232, 254; fisheries, 136, 166, (demand for fish) 178; grain supplies, 220–2, 228, 260; and Levant Company, 270; monocultures in, 68; naval wars, 219; sugar from, 214,

539, 540; as a trading region, 206–9, 458, 546, (decay of) 191

Meilink-Roelofsz, N. A. P., 279

Meissen porcelain factory, 507

Melis, Federigo, 208

mercantilism: and absolutism, 573, 596; balance of payments (trade), 17, 30, 256, 574; and the bourgeoisie, 573–88; Cameralism and, 595–6; and the Dutch, 25, 273, 389–90, 392; economic expansion, 392, 576, (economic nationalism) 391, 401, 573–4; gilds and, 466; historians' views on, 2, 16–19, 39, 577–8, 596; industry and trade, preoccupation with, 19, 108, 574, 578, 584; legislation, 18, 179; and location of industry, 464; monetary policy, 297, 299; Physiocrat challenge to, 602, 612–13; and protectionism, distinction between, 288; state mercantilism, 358, 359–60, 485, 573, 584, (financing of) 358–92, (progress in public finance) 391–2, (planning) 578, (programmes) 30, 506, 536, (tariffs and subsidies) 30, 209–10; and war, 577

English, 18, 179, 392, 480–1, 577–8; central European, 575–7, 596; French, 18, 391–2, 480, 481, 576–8, 579; German, 483, 578, 596; Prussian, 583–4, 596–7; Scandinavian, 209, 483; Scottish, 183; Spanish, 30, 482–3

mercenaries, *see* armies

Merchant Adventurers: Antwerp, activity in, 218, 370; and bills of exchange, 349; English cloth market in Europe, 269–70, 438, 481; exchange banks, operations through, 337; Hamburg, headquarters at, 216; Hanse, rivalry with, 254, 269; loans to government, 370, 381; Netherlands, ties with, 348

merchant bankers: arbitrage and exchange business, 343; in clearing-bank system, 311; at commercial and financial fairs, 315–16, 318–19, 322, 334, 367–8; international loans, 343; in public finance, 332–5, 364–73, 376, 378

merchant firms, 317

merchants: among Calvinists, 14–16, 406–7; aspirations to nobility, 355, 422, 435, 569, (rivalry with noble traders) 271; conspicuous consumption by,

merchants (*cont.*)
354; diversification of roles, 408–
9, 459; entrepreneurship, 409–13,
416–18, 484–6, (the good merchant)
418–19, 452; financiers and, 317, 356,
414, 442; function of, in society,
192–3, 398–9, 407, 459; inventories
of, 354, 355; land purchases by, 106,
355, 420, 423; loans to rulers, 241–2,
287, 359–61, 479; loans to consumers, 300; merchants and pedlars,
279–81; overseas merchants, 398, 416,
438–9; status of, 18–19, 286–7, 325,
403–4, 420–2, 575; 'travelling' merchants, 409

Mercier de la Rivière, *L'Ordre naturel et
essentiel des sociétés politiques* (1767),
602, 603–4

mercury, *see* quicksilver

Meredith, H. O., 5

Messina, Banco di, 312

Messina silk trade, 312

metallurgical industry, 401, 429, 433, 435,
463, 545; capital investment in, 478–
9; labour force, 486–7; production,
488–97, 546; putting-out system, 469,
470

metallurgy, 472–5, 485, 486, 580

metals, 427, 429, 490–1; metalworking,
469, 471, 493, 499, 508; metal market,
544; metal tools, 475
bismuth, 473; manganese, 500; *see also*
copper; gold; iron; lead; quicksilver;
silver; tin

métayage, *see* share-cropping

Meuvret, J., 9

Mexico: colonization, 211; drainage
operations, 68; printing in, 534;
silver from, 296, 309; sugar, 539

Meyer, Jean, 563

Middelburg: Antwerp financial techniques in, 336, 347; English cloth
trade centred on, 269; exchange bank,
337, 342n, (exchange rates) 223

middle classes: definition, 580–1; clothing,
204; in Dutch Republic, 22, 27–8,
(Friesland) 192; gold and silver coins,
use of, 298; middle-class wealth, 435,
(comfort) 27; and the 'new' aristocracy, 287; purchase of annuities,
306; shareholders in National Debt,
389; *see also* bourgeoisie

Middle East: caravan trade, 278; luxury
goods from, 308; silver preferred to
gold, 297

middlemen: in Asian trade, 280; in cloth
trade, 470; in farming, 107; between
merchants and masters of the mint,
341; social acceptance of, 403–4; in
textiles, 485

migration, 10, 40; from country to town,
23–4, 437; of Dutch enterprise, 454;
of industry from town to country,
470, 523, 544–5; of miners, 487;
subsidized, 398; of textile merchants
and artisans, 253, 514, 518; *see also*
immigration

Milan, 32, 217, 320; Banco di Sant'
Ambrogio, 312, (merchant bankers)
318, 333; *juros* sold in, 373; paper-
making, 535; textiles, 255, 525, (silk
thread) 527

Military Order of Calatrava, 497

milk, 23, 84, 90, 91, 237; milk yields, 34,
49, 58, 92, 96, (on aquavit mash)
202; milk churn, 96, 98, 99

millers, 132

Million Bank, 444; Lottery, 444

mills: aristocratic, 449; peasant, 501;
seignorial rights over, 108, 606; water
mills, 96, 463, 508; windmills, 96,
463, 475, 477, 485, 533
dye-mills, 497; fining, 476; flour, 45;
fulling, 426, 477, 529; gig-mills, 477;
oil, 45; paper, 469, 535–6; powder,
455, 508; ribbon mills prohibited,
521; rolling mills, 473; sawmills, 475,
485, 531; winnowing, 99

Mineral and Battery Works, English
Chartered Company, 431, 432n, 433,
441, 496

Mines Royal, English Chartered Company,
431, 432n, 433, 441, 496

mining, 424–5, 428–32, 462–3, 484–5,
488–97; aristocratic enterprise in,
449, 485, 580; capital investment, 12,
435–6, 478–9, 493; and Crown rights
over minerals, 429; drainage, 474–5;
gilds, 494; labour differentiation, 486,
(free labour) 486–8, (women workers)
487; management, 434–6; mining
companies, 241, 431, 441, 493–4,
(shares in) 492; partnerships, 433;
putting-out system, 427, 469; ration-

mining (*cont.*)
  alization, 493; technology, 471–5, 499, 500, 504; *see also under separate minerals*
mints, 299, 341
Mirabeau, Honoré, Comte de, 577, 598
Miroslavskij, *boyar*, 503
mirrors, 506, 542
Mitrofanov, P. von, 616
Mocca, coffee from, 214, 282
Mogens, Bishop of Hamar, copper mine, 495
Mogul emperor, 259
Moldavia, 217; cattle exports, 234; corn exports, 119; Jewish artisans and manufacturers, 529; serfdom, 118
Mollen, Jakob van, silk mill, 515
Möller, Anton, power-loom, 477
Mollwitz, battle of, 614
Mols, Father, 224
Momma family partnership, 435; bankruptcy, 484
monasteries, 176–7, 492
money: circulation of, 267, 325, 333, 336, 354; depreciation, 105, 119, 322; the 'Great Debasement', 308; in the local economy, 290–300; power of, 569–70, 572; purchasing power, 357, 359; 'sound' and 'easy', 20; as status determinant, 550; monetary system, 192, 288–9, (of account) 290–300, 322, 334, 336, 343, 346, 363, (double system) 338, 342, (unit of account) 291–6, 298–9, 315–16, 318–20; 'black' money, 295; 'negotiating money', 260, 264; paper money, 299, 314, 378; token, 295, 299, 306, 381; *see also* coins; banknotes
money-changers, 291, 295, 306, 323–4, 336–7, 343, 351, 361; as bankers, 311–12, 314, 316
money dealers, 297, 326, 330–1
money market: Amsterdam, role in, 346–7, 354, (in government securities) 364, (Amsterdam market) 335, 346–7, 354, 357, 361; Antwerp, 324, 330, 357, 361, 372; Hamburg, 335; Italian, 334; international, 357; London, 335, 347–8, 352–3, 357, 361; Lyons, 319, 335, 357, 365, 370
Monnet, M., 17
monopolies, 277–8, 281, 412–13, 430–1;

colonial, 379; corporate, 439, 444; gilds, 437, 465, 467, 468; in government enterprise, 440; royal, 552; Statute of (Britain), 382; towns, 497
in bank issue, 352; bleaching, 519; copper, 244, 246, 249, 272–3, 278; fisheries, 171; fur, 263; mining, 436; navigation, 211; paper, 535; pepper, 284, 286; salt, 181, 539, 552; silk, 523; spice, 278; textile imports, 251; tobacco, 552
Monson, Sir William, 134
Montesquieu, 553
Moors, expulsion from Spain, 29, 506, 540
Moravia: iron industry, 501; Jews and gilds, 468; peasants and *Gutsherrschaft*, 607; serfdom, 117, 118, (unfree labour) 487; textiles, 219, 524, 544
Moretus family, publishers, 535
Moriel, J., his cashbook (1567), 330n
Morocco: ceramics, 506; crops, 68, 221; sugar from, 539
Morstyn, mining entrepreneurs, 493
mortality rates, 1, 22, 23, 26, 64, 125
mortgage loans, 305, 314, 353, 355, 359, 363
Moscow: cloth factories, 529, (sailcloth) 471, 529; gilds, 468; iron production, 502, 503; paper mills, 536
Mousnier, Roland, 97, 553
Moxon, Joseph, 473
Muilman, Dutch banking house, 27
Mülheim, 477, 485, 521
Mun, Thomas, *England's Treasure by Foreign Trade*, 30, 256, 418
Munich, 200, 518
munitions industry, 413, 429, 430–1; *see also* armaments
Muscovy Company, *see* English Muscovy Company
Mustafa ben Abdulla Hadschi Halfa, Turkish traveller, 528

nails and nailers, 464, 501
Namur: bronze casting, 496; corn from, 222; emigrants from, 484, (smiths) 486; tillage system, 72
Nantes: beer and wine, 198; fishing port, 159; shipyards, 531; sugar refinery, 540, 541
Nantes, Revocation of Edict of (1685), 334, 335, 482, 485

Naples, 67; banking, 314; coins, 320, 334n; finance, 333, 373; monoculture, 68; papermaking, 535; printing press, 534; silk manufacture, 528

Napoleon, 554, 620

Nashe, Thomas, *Nashes Lenten Stuffe*, 172

national (public) debt: from floating to consolidated, 376–92; England, 352, 353, 355, 384–9, (Paterson's scheme) 384–5, (investment in) 389–91, (joint-stock principle applied to) 443–4; France, 364–6, 376–8, (Law's consolidation scheme) 379–80; Spain, 371, 374–5

natural law, 556, 593, 595, 603

natural resources, 452–3, 449, 455; *see also* raw materials

Navarre, land banks (*arcas de misericordia*), 305

navies, 575; copper for, 531, 533; food for, 538; iron for, 430, 533; English, 178; French, 576, 577; Spanish Armada, 531–2; Swedish, 443; *see also* fleets; ships

navigation laws, 273, 289, 401; Navigation Acts (England), 40, 289, 540

Necker, Jacques, French finance minister, 562, 564, 572, 582, 583; *De l'Administration des Finances* (1785), 564

Nef, John U., 11, 434n, 470, 545

Negroes, export of African slaves to New World, 212–13, 546

Nehou, Lucas de, sheet glassmaker, 505

net makers and net tanners, 180; nets, *see* fishing equipment

Netherlands: annuity contracts, 304; *asiento* contracts, 333; assignment, 327–8, 349; Baltic trade, 227–8, 275–6; book production, 535; breweries, 537; brickmaking, 507; cattle imports, 235, 236, 239; ceramics, 507; coin and bullion shipments to India, 259; copper industry, 244, 245, 544, (imports of Japanese copper) 246–9, (copper market) 245, 247, 248–9; craft gilds, 466; distilleries, 538; emigration, 484, 485, 521, 540, ('new draperies' transmitted by) 518, 544; enterprise, the home of, 395, (entrepreneurs in Russia) 485, 502, (in Sweden) 495; farming, (arable and cattle) 76, 78, (farm administration)
107, (manure yields) 94, (tillage systems) 72; foreign trade, 47, 218, 324; grain imports, 188, 227; import and export duties, 359; *juros*, 373; landownership, 110, 116, (reclamation) 68, 69–71, 90; mercenary armies, 374–5; merchants, 318, 544; metallurgical production, 546; mining technique, 504; money of account, 292–3, ('negotiating' money) 260; monopolies, 277–8; papermaking, 535–6; population, 216, 223–4; Portuguese factory, 263; precious stones, cutting and polishing, 542; printing, 534; public finance, 358, 370; saw mills, 508; silver shipments to, 375; taxation, 108, 360; textiles, 510, (factory system) 471, (imports of Spanish wool) 255, 516, (innovations in manufacture) 477, 520, (the 'New Draperies') 252–3, 254, (tapestries) 516; timber imports, 508; transit trade in corn, 222; 'troubles of the sixties', 236, 514, 516, (Spanish war in) 32, 149; windmills, 475; *see also* Dutch; Flanders; Holland; Low Countries; United Provinces

eastern Netherlands: agricultural classes, 127; linen and cloth production, 514–15; rye cultivation, 72; seignorial services, 106; villeinage, 116

northern Netherlands (after 1585): banking, 336, (edicts on) 336, 337; bleacheries, 514; farming, (agrarian economy) 21–2, (literacy among farmers) 102, (threshing block) 100; immigration, 514; price inflation, 11; sea-salt refineries, 538; textiles, 544; tobacco industry, 541; growth and decline, 23; *see also* Amsterdam; Holland; Dutch Republic

southern (Austrian) Netherlands: bleachery, 514; bronze-casting, 496; coal mines, 463; emigration, 18, 486, 514, 515; food exports, 24; industrialization, 511; land reclamation, 69; merchants, 356; pledge loans (*Monts de Piété*), 303; ploughing, 99; recovery after 1579, 32; shipbuilding, 531; Spanish armies in, 260, (coins) 338; taxation, 360; textiles, 464, 511–14

Netherlands, Revolt of, 356–7, 359, 372, 392

Neufchâtel, 522, 523

Neusohl (Banska Bystrica), copper mines, 189, 219, 241, 242, 245, 471, 491, 492; cost of hiring, 478–9

'New Draperies', 26, 222, 252–4, 397, 544, 547

New England: Anglo-French rivalry, 158–60; colonization, 160, 211, 212, 546; exports to, 212; fishing industry, 178, 184, (British and French zones) 156; see also North America

'new husbandry', 73–4

New World: colonization, 211–13; copper for, 244; linen for, 250; precious metals from, 212, 257, (gold) 296, 308, (silver) 291; skins from, 208–9; stimulus to, from fisheries, 184; see also America; South America

Newbury, Winchcombe's factory at, 471

Newcastle-upon-Tyne, 255; sea-coal from, 509; shipbuilding, 530; shoemakers' society, 488

Newcomen, Henry, invention of steam engine, 474; his pump design used in France, 509

Newfoundland: Anglo-French rivalry, 158–60; fishing settlements, 158, 160, 168; cod fisheries, 134–5, 138, 142, 155–7, 158–61, 166, 177–8, 536, (hostilities between rival fleets) 157–8, (markets in Europe for cod) 161, 177, 212, (declining yield) 182, (salt cod) 196; whale fisheries, 168, 184

Newmarch, William, with Thomas Tooke, History of Prices (1886–7), 10

newspapers, 583

Newton, Sir Isaac, 261, 600

nobility: army as entry to, 566–72, (commissions the preserve of) 572; and the bourgeoisie, 562–4, 570, 579; in cattle trade, 238, 271, (special privileges) 233, 236, 237; clothing for, 204; in corn trade, 271; and the Enlightenment, 585–6; as entrepreneurs, 487, 524, (in industrial companies) 479, (in mining) 493, 496–7, 498, 500; (as ironmasters (brukspatroner)) 504–5, (patronage of textile trades) 464; exemption from taxation, 108; governments and, 448, (kings and) 554, 559,

564, 566; hierarchies in, 552, 564, 566, 567; investments in gold mines, 488; investments in industry and commerce, 580; landed property, 109–10; loans to, on future grain deliveries, 300; luxuries for, 219, 542, (carriages for long-distance travel) 533; men of the robe, 562, 567; noble and non-noble, 586; as office-holders, 562, 567, (development of a ruling élite), 567–8, 569, 570; as a privileged estate, 563, 572, 582, 612; Prussian nobles, 559, 565; rich and poor, 563, 571–2; rights and functions, 572–3; sale of titles to, 564, 568; and serfdom, 120–1; attitudes to trade, 18, 420–2, 451; West End banks for, 353; see also aristocracy

Noordsche Compagnie, 170, 441, 537

'Nordland' fishing, 536

Norfolk: farming, (crop rotation) 72, ('Norfolk system' of tillage) 73, (Norfolk plough) 98, (working day on a farm) 98; 'peddars', 174; stuffs, 13, 510

Normandy: fishing, 141, 154, 159, 177, 536; flax and canvas-weaving, 515; sheet-glass manufacture, 428, 505; shipbuilding, 531

North, Douglass, 4

North, Dudley, 214

North America: demand for consumption goods, 212; fisheries, 135, 175, 178, (fish market) 161; investment in, 27; joint-stock enterprise in, 400; labour shortage, 96; plantations in southern states, 211, (slaves for) 212–13, (linen cloth for) 204; see also New England; Newfoundland

North Sea fisheries, see fisheries

North Sea zone, 80–1, 545; cattle trails, 234; colonial trade, 191; hemp cultivation, 463; shipbuilding, 532; windmills, 475

Northampton, 464, 477

Northampton, Earl of, 176

Norway: copper from, 248, 463, 485, 492; customs revenues, 260; farming, 76; fish consumption, 175; fisheries, 140, 154–5, 164, 165, 176, 183, 536; foreign enterprise in, 455, 485; iron production, 503; mining, 485, (silver

Norway (*cont.*)
  mines) 489; papermaking, 536; seaborne trade, 192, 545, 546, (with England) 533; shipbuilding, 533; tar and pitch from, 508
Norwich, 253; gilds, 464
Novgorod, 217, 274, 502
Novi, fairs of payment, 333
Nuremberg, 473, 508, 546; bell-casting, 496; capital from, 489; cattle plague, 234; copper, (imports) 242, 244, 245, (production) 489, (small ware manufacture) 203; dye works, 520, (blue dye imports) 497; English cloth staple, 269; entrepreneurs, 484, (patrician) 500; iron-processing, 500; price currents for, 408; printing, 534; sheet-metal industry, 496; textiles, 479, 517, 521; toolmaking, 475; *Zuckerbäcker*, 540

oats, 23, 56, 58, 59, 73, 80; threshing, 97; for horses and humans, 220
Oberleutensdorf textile factory, 479
Obrecht, G., banker, 365-6
Oder, 217, 225
Odhelius, Erik, 495
offices, sale of, 361; Austrian Empire, 565; England, 382; France, 422, 451, 564, 568, 569, 580, (attempt to abolish) 582; Prussia, with a difference, 565, 568
Ogg, David, 15
oil: oil-bearing seeds, 23, 77; oil production, 224, (lamp oil) 274, (train oil) 162-3, 168, 171, 537; *see also* olives
Ökonomische und gemeinnützige Gesellschaft des Kantons Bern (1759), 103
oligopoly in copper, 244
Olivares, Duke, 303, 333, 375, 500
olives: cultivation, 22, 58, 68, 220, 221, (financing of) 304; olive oil, 199, (trade in) 207, 219, (for soap) 508
Olkusz, 493, 502
Orkneys, 147, 153
Orléans, 515, 540, 541; herring consignments, 167
Orléans, Duc d', 553, 563
Ortiz, Luis, *Memorial against the Flight of Money from this Realm* (1558), 30
Osnabrück, *Leggeszwang* system, 518

Ostend, 211; fishing fleet, 149, 182
Ostend Company, 252, 283
Ottoborn, Marc, 220
Ottoman Empire: ceramics, 507; conquest of south Hungary, 118, 120, 121; sugar supplies cut off by, 539; textile industry, 528; trade with Europe, 218-19; *see also* Turkey
outport traders, 439
Overijssel: agriculture, (agricultural classes) 129-30, (non-agricultural) 131-2, (literacy among farmers) 102, (numbers of animals) 90, (population) 45, (population growth and animal farming) 131, (small holdings) 125; brickmaking, 507; tobacco industry, 541
overseas trade: capital needs for, 288, 571; competition in, 401; companies for, 442-3, (privileged) 482; government policy on, 452; overseas distribution of beer, 537; stimulus to copper production, 543; stimulus to shipbuilding, 530, 531, 532; *see also* enterprise; foreign trade; merchants
oxen: as draught animals, 46, 90, 93, 96, 97, (for ploughing) 97-8, 99, (area worked by, in a day) 98; for East India Company ships, 200; numbers of, 90, (weight) 92; ownership, and peasant classification, 126-7; trade in, 52, 91-2, 214, 216, 234-40, 263, (rights of nobility in) 237, 238, (transport) 200; *see also* cattle trade
Oxenstierna, Axel, 228

Pach, Zs. P., 119, 263
Pacioli, Luca, *Summa de Arithmetica* (1494), 310n
Padua: ceramics, 507; grain consumption, 84; textiles, 525, 526, (silk ribbons (*cordella*)) 527
paints, painters, 132, 508; ikon-painters, 468
Palatinate: intensive farming, 71, 102, (manuring) 94; iron mines, 484, 500; quicksilver, 463; sheet metal, 496
Palatinate, Elector of, 483
Palavicino, Horatio, 405
Palermo: *Tavoli di Palermo*, public clearing bank, 312; privileged silk production, 528
pancada, 281

papacy: ban on interest, 319; papal finances, 363–4, (taxation) 307; *Regimini* (papal bulls of 1425, 1455), 304

paper, 429; fine paper, 480

paper mills, 535–6

paper money, 299, 383, 574; *see also* banknotes

papermaking, 535–6; capital-intensive, 27; chemical processes in, 508; Dutch enterprise in, 454, 455; a large-scale industry, 427; Jews in, 468; protective tariffs on, 40; putting-out system, 469; technical apparatus for, 472

Paris: annuities, 364; banking, 335, (*Banque protestante*) 335, (merchant bankers) 378; calendering, 478; ceramics, 507; coachbuilding, 542, (the *berline*) 534; Exchange, 378; fish market, 173–4, (consignments to) 167; glass works, 428; goldsmiths, 542; paris pound, 293; population, 67, 579; printing, 534; stock-market boom, 388; *tapisseries*, 481; trade with Angers, 223

Paris, Giraldo, merchant, 285

Parker, N. G., 32

Parkhurst, Anthony, 157

Parma, 526

Parma, Duke of, conquest of Antwerp (1585), 218

partnerships, 356, 417, 432–6, 440; personal liability, 433; shares in, 433; *société en nom collectif, société en commandité, société anonyme*, 433

Pascal, Blaise, 592

pasmentry, *see* braid

'passmenters', 543

patents, 473, 476

Paterson, William, plan for the Bank of England, 384–5

Patino, chief minister of Philip V of Spain, 532

Paul, Lewis, textile machines, 476–7

Paumgartner, Augsburg entrepreneurs, 484

Paumgartner, Hans, 497

Pavia, 32, 527

pawnbrokers, 14, 302–3; '*monts de piété*' and *positos*, 303, 305

payment in kind, 105, 124, 125; in industry, 487; obligatory, 114; payment in cloth, 204; land as wages, 487, 501; pepper as dividends, 286

peasant farmers, 6, 16, 21–2, 23, 28; ownership of land, 23, 113, 605–6, (abolition of peasant land in Poland), 271

peasant wars and revolts, 108, 122; in Austria, unrest under Joseph II, 616; in Bohemia (1775), 614; in England, against enclosures, 108, 112; in France (1789), 617–18; in Hungary (1514), 118, 120; in Russia, (1670–1) 122, (1773–5) 122, 614; in Spain, revolt of *Comuneros* (1520s), 367; in Switzerland (1652–3), 108; in lands of Teutonic Knights (1525), 120, 245, 488

peasantry: absolutism based on, 604; bond and free, 605; and cattle trade, 233, 238; credit for peasant coal workers, 504; and food production, 536; *Grundherrschaft* and *Gutsherrschaft*, 607–8, 618, 620; hierarchy of, 552, 611; as industrial labour, 470, 487, (nailers and scythe-makers) 497; as ironmasters, 485, 501; landlords and, 568, 570; their miserable lot, 605–11; obligations to the State, 606–7, 612; obstacles to reform, 613–16, 617; from peasant to noble, 568, 569, 611; Physiocrat view of, 611–20; ('poor peasants, poor kingdom') 611, 617; in Prussia, 559, 609–10; shareholders in gold mines, 488; under *société d'ordres* and *servitudes collectives*, 619, (and seignorial rights) 358, 606, 607; in textiles, ('forced' labour) 524, (spinners) 470, 522, (yarn-weavers) 519, 522, (yarn and linen producers) 514

peat, 24, 192; salt from burning peat, 181

'peddars' (of herrings), 174; pedlars (hucksters), 203, 306; pedlar market in Asia, 278–81; peddling, 193

Pedersen, Professor Ladewig, 236

Peele, J., *The Pathewaye to Perfectnes in the Accomptes of Debitour and Creditour* (1569), 328n

Pelham, Sir William, 35

Pellipario, Guido Fontano, majolica manufacturer, 506

Pellipario, Nicola, majolica master, 506

Pels, Dutch banking house, 27, 343, 391

pepper, 208, 210; distributed as dividends, 286; pepper trade, 280, 283–6

'period-hunters' and climatic change, 62
periodization in industrial production, 543–7
'Periwig Period', 26, 38
Perroux, François, 205
Persia: ceramics, 506; copper sales to, 248; Dutch trade, 210; East European trade, 217; flow of precious metals to, 259; Persians in Leghorn, 256; silks from, 208, 214, 282
Peru: colonization, 211; silver from, 296, 309; wool from, 517
Peruzzi, banking house, 415
Peter the Great, of Russia: demesne system, 121; glass factory, 506; iron works, 503; shipbuilding, 533, (visit to 'village of carpenters') 508; textiles, 529; westernization policy, 468, 483, 486, 616
Peto, merchant bankers, 71
pewter, 473, 474
Phelps Brown, Henry, 11
Philip I (the Handsome), of Spain, 222
Philip II, of Spain, 331; bankruptcies, 366, 370–1, (edicts on finance) 374–5, (monetary policy) 20; and the pepper trade, 284; sale of domains, 359
Philip III (the Good), of Spain, 292
Philip IV, of Spain, 333
Philip V, of Spain: prohibits imports of Eastern textiles, 517; rebuilds navy, 532
Philip, Landgrave of Hesse, 499
Philip of Cleves, 20
Philippines, 214, 310
Philosophes, 589, 590, 600–2; 'liberty, equality and fraternity', 600, 602, 604, 618
Phinzing, Saxon entrepreneur, 484
Physikalische (Naturforschende) Gesellschaft of Zürich (1747), 103
Physiocrats, 575, 604–20; challenge to mercantilism, 18, 612–13; in France, 613, 617–18; in Hapsburg dominions, 615–17, 618; in Prussia, 613, 618–20; Adam Smith on, 604, 619; Quesnay on, 611–13
Piacenza, fair of payment, 319; foires de change at, 322, (exchange rates) 322; gold écus at, 293, 307, 322, 334n, 357; rules for payment, 320–1; Besançon fairs transferred to, 375; decline of, 335

Picardy, 141, 154, 222; textiles, 515
Piedmont: gilds, 467; silk workshops, 527; wool and linen factories, 526
pigs: and cottar farming, 131; numbers of, 89–90, 93, 131, (live and dead weight) 92; pork meat, 92, 93, 195
Pike, Ruth, 15
pilchards (sardines): catching seasons, 138, 142, (equipment for) 172; export of, 166; fishing grounds for, 136, 166
Pindar, Sir Paul, 384
Pirenne, Henri, 23
plague, 8, 22, 416; 16th century, 31, 33; 17th century, 69, 230, 543; 18th century, 118, 120, 546, 575
  epidemics and population, 120, 545, 546, 577, 604, 614; typhus, 546; other demographic catastrophes, 548
planning, 17, 418–19; by bourgeoisie, 581; by farmers, 100–1; by mercantilist states, 578; planned market transactions, 278
plant growth, 57–63; diseases, 65
plantations, see colonies
Plantin, Christopher, publisher, 535
plasterers, 131, 132
Plot, Robert, Natural History of Staffordshire (1686), 473
Plotzk, 217, 225
ploughs: Norfolk, 98; foot, and wheel-carriage, 99
ploughing, deep, 96, 97–8; area ploughed in a day, 97–8
Plymouth, 160, 490
Po Valley, 71, 102
Pögl, Sebald and Sebastian, gun-founders, 501
Pögl armour works, 501
Poitiers, 481, 515
Poland, 259, 364; agricultural classes, 127; balance of trade, 263, 264; copper imports, 544; corn, production and consumption, 83, 86–8, (exports) 87–8, 119, 188, 216, 220, 224–5, 449, (nobility and the corn trade) 271, (wheat yields) 61, (yield ratios of cereals) 80–1; currency devaluation, 20; deserted villages, 69; decline of, 502; fish consumption, 173; food crises, 10; gilds, 467, (Jewish) 468–9; iron works, 501–2; lead mines, 463, 492–3, (exports) 492, 493; nobility,

Poland (*cont.*)
(in farming) 117, (in industry) 485;
peasants and *Gutsherrschaft*, 607–8;
peasant revolts, 122; population, 86;
price controls, 187; relations with
Danzig, 271; serfdom, 115–16, 118–
21; stockfarming, 91, 233, 234,
(advantages to nobles) 238, (exports
of cattle and skins) 208, 218, 235,
(Thirty Years War and) 263; textiles,
25; 'trading compartment', 217, 219;
war, effect on Poland, 68, 263, 502;
war with Prussia, 275; war with
Sweden, 68, 118, 120, 228–9, 230
Poland, king of, 228; and craft gilds, 467;
royal income, 358
polders, 67–8, 69; speculation in, 106
Polhem, Christopher, Swedish entrepreneur, 472, 486, 505
Pomerania (Prussian): cattle exports, 233,
235; 'men of', in army of Frederick
the Great, 550
Pomerania (Swedish), 486; rural stratification, 129; serfs, 117, 121
Pontoise, 167, 174
poor relief, 111, 179; 'welfare' factories,
471
population: changes in, and social stratification, 123–32; and fisheries, 135,
184; and grain supplies, 47, 208, 216,
220, 223, 230–1, (grain prices) 50,
51, 54, 64, 65, 69; and industrial
growth, 8; and intensive agriculture,
103; Malthusian view of, 187; movements of, 5, 6, 459; statistics, 557;
and stock farming, 91, 216
periods of increase, 8, 10, 66, 127, 128,
130, 148, 536, 610–11; periods of stagnation, 22, 231; periods of decrease,
123, 216; depopulation, (through
disease) 9, 575, 604, 614, (famine)
575, 604, (war) 9, 111, 120, 545, 577
see also demography
porcelain: Chinese, 507; Meissen, 507;
St Cloud, 507; Sèvres, 429, 507; *see
also* ceramics
Portugal
ceramics, 506
copper imports, 244
Dutch investment in, 27
emigration, 18; of Jews, 528
fisheries, (cod) 157–8, 177–8, 536,

(pilchards) 166, (sardine) 172, (whale)
537, (drying industry) 157, (salt for)
180–1, (salt-on-salt method) 181;
dried fish trade, 207; fish consumption, 175, 178, (preference for dried
fish) 157, 177, 207, (imports) 177
gilds, 466
global commerce, 205; overseas enterprise, 546; pioneer of trans-oceanic
trade, 210; trade to Asia, 440;
voyages to New World, 543, 545
gold shipments to, 296, 308, 342
grain: maize, 78, 201, 230; shift to
cultivation of olives, 221
merchants, 332–3
merchant bankers, 333, 373
paper mills, 535
pepper trade, 283–5
raw silk from Japan, 281
salt-drying, 538; salt exports, 209
shipbuilding, 532
silver coins, export of, 309
slave trade, 212–13
spice trade, 218
State bankruptcy, 371; enterprise, 417,
440, 483
see also Iberian trade
Portugal, king of: colonial empire, 494;
Fuggers and, 370; monopoly of
Indies trade, 283–4
postal service, 455
Postan, M. M., 4, 6, 38, 164n
Posthumus, N. W., 11, 253, 277, 286
Postlethwayt, Malachy (with James Royston), *The British Mercantile Academy*
(1750), 410, 418, 419, 453n
potash, 214, 271, 429, 508
potatoes, 10, 46, 58, 59; as an alternative
to grain, 78–9, 83, 96
Potocki, Andrzej, blast furnace inventor,
502
Prague, 524, 525, 614
Prakash, Om, 280
Prato, clothmaking, 526
precious metals: and balance of trade,
256–8, 261–4, 308, 315; demand for,
in India, 259; distribution in Europe,
373; jewellery and *la granele fabrique*,
334, 542; market, 314, (Amsterdam
the world market) 260–1, 297, 342;
and monetary stability, 298; shortage
of, 264, 312; speculation in, 296–7;

precious metals (*cont.*)

    trade in, 281, 320, 342, 347, (export permits for) 367, 370, (sale of, to mints) 341; transport for, 259, 260, 341, (fleet) 260, 367; *see also* gold; silver

Price, J. M., 261

price currents, printed sheets, 408

prices: differentials, 10, 75; history, 10–11, 14; of necessities, 13, 33; and polder-making, 69–70; and production, in local, interregional and international markets, 50, 64–5, 105, 187, 188, 288; and wages, 2, 3, 10–11, 13, 20, 49, 52–4, 55, 610

    fish prices, 157, 176, 177, 178; fall in after 1650, 183

    grain prices, fluctuations in, 6, 13, 43, 44, 47–54, 55, 101; and population, 44, 50, 51, 54, 69, 123–5; and serfdom, 118–20; and weather conditions, 63–5

        periods of rising prices, 30, 53, 55, 64, 69–70, 78, 79, 119, 121, 123, 611; of falling prices, 55–6, 63, 64, 69–70, 79, 121, 123, 577

    price ratios, 44, 51, 53–4, 65, 66, 69, 100–1; long-term changes in, 123–4

    price revolution, 7, 302, 309

princes: carriages for, 533; control of trade, 266–7, 272, 288; as entrepreneurs, 485, 495, 500, 516, (in salt-mining) 538–9; in the hierarchy of nobility, 552, 563, 564; and merchants, 280, 287, 479; their palaces, 543; in the particularist society, 550–1; and porcelain, 507

printing, 27, 429, 534–5; ancillary occupations, 534; book production, 535; censorship, 554, (restrictions) 534–5; letter-press and illustration, 534; presses, 534; printers, 467; putting-out system, 469; technical improvements, 472, 534; type metal, 473–4

    presses: England, 534; France, 534; Germany, 534; in Hebrew, 468; Netherlands, 436; Spain, 534; Venice, 32, 534

privilege: legal and social, 569, 582, 602; privileged towns, 557; society based on, 550–2

privileges, economic: for government creditors, 414, 415; and entrepre-neurial success, 419, 430, 440; for joint-stock companies, 444, 482, 546; in mining, 473, 495, 503; in paper-making, 535; in printing, 534; in textiles, 518, 528

processing industries, 417, 431, 453, 455; 'finishing' in textiles, 519; iron, 500; ores, 473; timber, 508

production, 488–543; costs, 428, (overheads) 425, 430, 447; diversification, 22, 466, 475, (specialization) 499; *le produit net*, 612; regions of, 216–18, 242; units of, 425, 427, 432, (in mining) 501

production and consumption, 13, 45, 47–8, 193–4; constant and variable factors of, 48–50

    producers and consumers, 6, 44, 47, 48; adaptability, 78; social stratification of, 123–5; consumer taste, 250

    see also consumption

productivity, 188–9, 397: in agriculture, 46–7, 54; in copper, 189; and the markets, 543–5; and morals, 404; unproductive expenditure, 603

Proenen, entrepreneur, 494

profits, 11–13; profit motive, 411, 417, 432, 446, (aristocratic) 449; unprofitable enterprises, 442; religion and profit-making, 403

    in specific activities: of army commanders, 587; cattle trade, 233, 238, 239, (losses) 237; copper trade, 246, 249; cloves, 249; from devaluation, 296, 299–300; farming, 100, 101, 104, 119, (from specialized crops) 24; fisheries, 177, 181, 183; foreign investment, 27; investment in industry, 424, in land, 587; joint-stock enterprise, 444; landownership, 26, 610; from loans to Governments, 318, 414–15; merchants' profits, 354–5; money dealers' profits, 297; pepper trade, 283; as state functionaries, 402; from tax-farming, 552

progress, and the Enlightenment, 589, 593; Philosophe belief in, 601

promissory notes, *see* financial techniques

protectionism: and mercantilism, 273, 288, 360, 540; protective legislation, 231, 517, (tariffs) 40; *see also* navigation laws protectionism (*cont.*)

in Amsterdam, 273; Liège, 514; Spain, 482

in copper and textiles, 547

Protestants: and business enterprise, 403–5; and fish consumption, 175–6; Protestant ethic, 14, 15, 40, (workshops for the poor) 471; Protestant nobles in enterprise, 485; Protestant immigrants in Germany, 521

Provence, 515, 535, 538

Prussia

absolutism, 552–60, 566, 573, 583–5, 618

agricultural reforms, 613, 619, 620

army, 555, 597, 614; road to affluence, 568, 569; size of, 570; speech to, 550; terms for sale of commissions, 572; the company commander, 587

balance of trade, 575

bourgeois and noble, 570, 585–6

bureaucracy, 558–9, 573, 583; royal officials, 566, 584

control of famine and disease, 604; grain stocks policy, 605, 610

debasement of coinage, 584

decline and debacle, 560

education, 596

the Enlightenment in, 588, 591, 594–9

foreign trade, 575

golden age of, 573

grain consumption, 84; trade, 449

hierarchy, 552

immigration, 40, 485

import restrictions, 527

Junkers, 587

justice, 597–8

kings and peasants, 117; peasant revolts, 618

loans raised in Amsterdam, 391

mercantilism, 573–8, 583–5, 596

newspapers, 583

nobility, a privileged estate, 271, 551n, 572–3; purchase of, forbidden, 568; entry *via* the army, 563, 568; in offices of state, 567; a ruling élite, 567–8, 569, 570; wealth and poverty among, 571

power politics, 574; power of money, 569–70

reclamation of land, 69

reformers, 560–1, 614

serfs, 118, 120, 557, 608–10, 615, 618–20;

edict of freedom, 597; Physiocrat view accepted, 619

the State: a machine, 597; its efficiency, 558, 561; avoids revolution, 618; has no extravagant Court, 613; lacks national consciousness, 550; State enterprise, 429

stock-raising, 233

taxation, 558

towns, 585; privileged, 557

transition to capitalist society, 588

war with Poland, 275; battle of Leuthen, 550; war chest, 554–5

Prussia, East: agrarian reforms, 620; deaths from plague and famine, 575, 604

Puckle, J., *England's Path to Wealth and Honour* (1700), 180

Pugachyov, Yemelyan, leader of peasant revolt in Russia, 122

Pullan, B., 32

pulses, alternative to grain as food crop, 78, 89, 96

pumps, 471, 492; pumpmakers, 180; steam pumping, 509; water power, 473

Puritans, 404, 450

putting-out system, 424, 425–6, 462, 463–4, 469–70, 479–80, 487; in textiles, 485, 510, 515, 518, 520, 522, 526; in other industries, 469

Quakers, 406, 498

quantitative measurement, 2, 15, 37, 40–1, 354, 361; in business, 419; in commercial statistics, 194; in copper imports, 247; in corn trade, 223, 226; and economic rationality, 411; Gregory King's tax rates, 40; of landownership, 109; records for, in fishing industry, 134, 135, 142; Usher on secular trends, 43

quarantine, 10, 17

Quesnay, François, 577, 587, 603, 604; founder of physiocracy, 602; his doctrine, 'pauvres paysans, pauvre royaume', 611–13, 617; *Tableau économique* (1758), 602

quicksilver: mines, 428n, 463, 484, 490–1, 496–7; in mining of silver, 497; processing of, 508

Rademacher, Reinhold, 486

Raedt *et al.*, pepper consortium, 285

Ragusa (Dubrovnik), 218–19, 544

Raleigh, Sir Walter, 178

Ramelli, Agostino, *Le diverse et artificiose machine* (1588), 475

Rami Effendi, Ottoman Minister of State, 528

Rantzau, Heinrich, Holstein noble, 449, 485

Rapallo, 333

Rastell, John, fishing expedition to New-foundland (1517), 157

rate of interest, 13; on annuities, 305, 367, 376, (*juros*) 374; in credit trans-actions, 300, 362, 363; Dutch low rate, 175, 181; at Italian fairs of pay-ment, 334; in pawnbroking, 302; for short-term loans to authorities, 362, 365, 367, 368–70, 376; variations in, 357; *see also* interest; usury

rational thought: eighteenth-century poli-cies, 577; bourgeois calculation, 581, 587

rationalization of mining, 488, 492, 493

Ratzeburg, 89, 90

Rau, Virginia, 209

Rauber, noble entrepreneur, 496

Raumer, Friederich von, 558–9

Ravensburg, 518; bleaching works, 519; 'Great Company' of, 519; paper works, 535

raw materials, 452; and costs of industry, 480; flow of, through Danish Sound, 545; location of industry determined by, 462–4; mercantilist view of, 574; noble ownership of, 449; and organization of industry, 424, 425–8, 536; producing regions of Europe, 547

Rawlinson, Thomas, Quaker iron manu-facturer, 498

Raychaudhuri, Tapan, 191, 280

Razin, Stepan, leader of peasant revolt in Russia, 122

Réaumur, René-Antoine Ferchault de, essay on conversion of iron into steel (1722), 472

red herrings, 143, 154, 173, 176, 178

re-exports (entrepôt trade): of Baltic corn, 225; colonial produce, 184, 212, 455, 575; Indian textiles, 251; pepper, 283–6; Russian cloth, 529; salt, 181, 212; sugar, 540

Dutch, 395, 455; East India Company (English), 261, 283; on the European market, 282

Reformation, the: and business enterprise, 403, 405; effect on fishing industry, 175–7; and gilds, 467; land redistri-bution, 110–11, 495; printing and, 534

Regensburg: 'great trading company' of, 217–18; iron processing, 500; silk industry, 500

regulated companies, *see* companies

Reims: herring consignments, 167; lace factory, 471

religion: as basis for partnerships, 410, 435, 460; and the Enlightenment, 590–7; and gilds, 437; wars of, *see* wars

Remondini, paper enterprise of Bassano, 535

Rendsborg, customs registers for cattle movements, 235–6

Renier, Gustaf, 14

rentiers, 20, 376, 388, 422, 448

rents, 14, 55, 105, 124, 126, 610; rent roll, 448

fall in, 357; rise, 550, 569; speculation on, 355, 569

retail trade: in books, 535; forbidden to nobles, 448, 571; status of, 421; use of tally or current account, 300–1, 302; retailers, 438, 470, (shopkeepers) 420

Reyersz, Symon, Amsterdam merchant, 226

Rhine, river system, 217

Rhineland, 66, 318; coal, 463; fish supplies for, 177; flax, 515; intensive farming, 71, 80; merchants, 484; paper mills, 535; silk-weaving, 521; wool-weav-ing, 518; trade, 276, 315

Rhodes: sugar from, 539; textile mills, 529

ribbon-weaving, 520–1, 523; ribbon-loom, 477, 520; silk ribbons, 525, (*cordelle*) 527

Ribe cattle trade, 237

rice, 10; consumption, 201, 230; cultiva-tion, (Italy) 33–4, 78, (southern Europe) 46; imports from North America, 78

rich and poor, 569, 610; rich and richer, 573–4

Richelieu, Cardinal Armand Jean Duplessis, duc de, 442, 613; *Testament Politique*, 609

Richterghen, Nicolaas (Nikolaus) van, merchant banker, 366, 494

Richterghen, van, Aachen family of entrepreneurs, 484

Riemann, F. K., 44

Riemengang, braiding machine, 520

Riga: corn shipments from, 227, 228, 229; trade balance, 262

river systems and trade routes, 217

Robais, van, textile factory at Abbeville, 471, 479, 481

Rode, Steffen, Danish merchant, 237, 239

Rogers, J. E. Thorold, 10, 44, 141

Roland, French government official, 582

Rome, 67, 221, 222; Jewish craft gilds in, 468

roofing: lead for, 474; slates for, 507; roofers, 131, 132, 242

Roover, R. de, 311, 328n, 329

rope-makers, 45, 180

Roquette, Claude, royal tailor, 485

Rosenberger, Hans, Augsburg capitalist, 488

Rostock: breweries, 537; shipbuilding, 532; Toll Registers, 226

Rot, Konrad, Augsburg pepper merchant, 284

rotation of crops, 24, 56, 66, 69, 71–4, 82, (and manuring) 94–5; 'convertible husbandry', 73, 74; Norfolk system, 73

Roth, Leonhard, patrician entrepreneur, 540

Rother, Christian von, from peasant to noble, 569n

Rotterdam, 508; distilleries, 538; diverse economy, 180; exchange bank, 336, 337, 342n; fisheries, 136, 148, 536; salt refining, 538

Rouen: assignment, 327; ceramics, 507; Exchange, 365, (exchange rates) 223; fish market, 153, 174, 177, (port for Newfoundland fleet) 159; printing, 534; sugar refineries, 540

Rousseau, Jean-Jacques, 598; *Contrat social*, 602

Rovalesca, Italian merchant house, 284–5

Rovenzon, John, treatise on blast furnaces (1613), 474

Royal Exchange, London, 331, 348, 354

Royston, James, *see* Postlethwayt, Malachy

Rufz, Felipe, merchant house, 208

Ruiz, Simon, 372n, 375

Ruiz-Martin, Felipe, 208, 304, 314n, 367n, 373n, 374, 375n, 516

rural entrepreneurs, 522

rural industries, 469, 548, (iron-mining) 450, 497, 499, (textiles) 510, 519, 521–3

rural population: classification systems 126–30; rural proletariat, 55

Russia: absolutism, 549, 555; balance of trade, 262, 363; bullion payments, 264; caviare trade, 200; copper production, 496, 503, imports, 544; Dutch enterprise in, 455, 529, investment in, 27; economic growth, 547; enterprise: State, 483, 503, 529, private, 484–5, 503, immigrant, 486, 529; exports, 503, (corn) 228, (ironware) 499, (skins) 208, 217, (tar and pitch) 508; farming households, 125, (small holdings) 126, (stock farming) 91, 233, (working day on a farm) 98, (yield ratios of cereals) 80–1; foreign capital and specialists in, 502, 503, 529, (German miners) 489; fur trade, 263; gilds, 467–8; imports, 502; industrialization, problem of, 529; iron industry, 502–3, (charcoal-iron) 498; loans on Amsterdam, 391; paper mills, 536; peasants and freeholders, 117, (and *Gutsherrschaft*) 607–8, (peasant revolts) 122, 614; production, 503; salt mines, 538, trade, 210; serfdom, 114–15, 118–21, 609, (unfree labour) 487; shipbuilding, 533; silver mines, 489; taxation, 125; textiles, 529, (for rich and poor) 204; trade with western Europe, 272

Russia and Muscovy Company, 270, 441, 446

rye, 58, 59; calorific value, 78; continuous rye cultivation, 72; exports, 86–8, 227; food for servants, 101, (rye bread) 219; harvesting, 98; production and consumption, 84, 87–8; yield ratios, 80–1, 87, (and serfdom) 121–2

Saigerhütte (refining works), 489, 492

sailcloth, 471, 517, 529; sailmakers, 180

St Cloud porcelain factory, 507
St Gallen, 335, 521, 522
St Germain en Laye, 167, 174
St Gobain glass works, 505, 506
Saint Jacob, P. de, 107
St Petersburg, 503, 529, 536; shipbuilding, 533
Saint-Simon, Louis de Rouvray, duc de, 552, 562
Salamanca, Gabriel de, Count of Ortenburg, mining entrepreneur, 497
salmon, 136, 147, 183
Saloman, mining entrepreneur, 493
Salonika, 219; textiles: carpets and silk thread, 528; division of labour, 529; heavy and light cloths, 528, 544; Jewish enterprise in, 485, 528
salt: drying, 538; duties on (*gabelle*), 179, 209–10, 360; extraction of, 509; future deliveries in, 331–2; fish-preserving, 153, 154, 180–1; monopolies on, 181, 539, 552; salt ships, 209–10; salt mines, 538–9; salt pans, 538–9; sea-salt, 538; strategic value of, 265
salt trade, 209–10, 214, 219, 271; large-scale enterprise in, 435; Dutch, 274; French, 154, 209; Portuguese, 209, 275; Russian, 210
Salzburg, silver and copper mines, 488, 492
Salzburg, Archbishop of, his salt pans, 539
Samsonowicz, H., 261
San Fernando hat factory, 517
San Lucan de Barramuda, 333, 517
Santa Margharita, 333
Santander, 531, 532
Sao Tomé, sugar from, 214, 282, 539
Saragossa, banking in, 314, 315
sardines and sprats, *see* pilchards
Sardinia, 27, 527
Sauerland, 499, 508
Savary, Jacques, *Le Parfait Négociant*, 422, 424
Savery, Thomas, steam-pump, 509
savings, 13, 359, 361; a bourgeois idea, 581; deposit savings, 306; Dutch, 27, 389; and the public purse, 363, 373
Savonnerie, French State enterprise, 429, 430
Savot, Louis, writer on brass production, 473

Savoy, 468, 539
sawmills, 485; water-driven, 508; wind-powered, 475, 531
sawyers, 180, 429, 455, 488, 508
Saxony
 agriculture: classes, 127, 128; cultivation of flax, 518; land erosion, 69; manuring, 94
 ceramics: hard porcelain, 507
 merchants, 480
 mining and metallurgy, 483, 500; copper mines, 433, 463, 488–9, (smelting) 428n; silver mines, 463, 484, 488–9; tin, 484, 496; miners, 495, (emigration of) 485
 paper mills, 536
 princes and peasants, 117; dominated by Prussia, 574, 576
 trade routes, 217
Saxony, Electors of: collaboration with merchants, 543; operation of salt mines, 538
Scandinavia
 breweries, 537
 Dutch investment in, 27
 entrepreneurs and aristocrats, 451, 486
 farming, 9, 49; stock farming, 91; yield ratios of cereals, 80–1
 fisheries, 161
 gilds, 467
 Hanseatic traders in, 215; rivalry with League, 224, 275
 mercantilist policy, 209–10, 529–30
 merchants, 356
 shipyards, 533
 sugar imports, 540, 541
 textiles, 529–30
 timber from, 508
 water mills, 475
 see also Denmark; Norway; Sweden
Scania: herring fishery, 135, 136, 149, 154, 176, 274; herring fair, 142; ox trade, 16, 233, 238, 240
Schauenburg, Counts of, salt-refineries operated by, 538
Scheldt, blockade of (1585), 218, 275
Schets, Gaspar, imperial agent, 368
Schetz, Antwerp financiers, 484
Schetz, Erasmus, merchant banker, 326, 494
Schiedam, 148, 149, 180; distilleries, 538; included in the Great Fisheries, 536

Schiller, Johann von, 287

Schimmelmann, H. C., army contractor, 584

Schleswig-Holstein: cattle exports, 91, 216, 233, 235, 237, (ox breeding) 52; distilleries, 538; land reclamation, 69; princes and industry, 485; tillage systems, 72; wheat yields, 61, 62, 73, 80, 81; typhus, 546

Schlüter, Christoph Andreas, handbook on metallurgy (1738), 472

Schmoller, Gustav, 1, 557n

Schnapper, B., 304

Schneeberg, 489, 500

Scholliers, E., 201

Schön, Theodor von, 588, 597, 620

Schönburg, German Director of Mines in Russia, 503

Schoonhoven, Garriet von, pepper consortium, 285

Schumpeter, Elizabeth B., 8

Schumpeter, J., theory of monopoly, 277

Schwartz, Paul, 588

Schwarzenberg, 500

Scotland
  banking: Bank of Scotland (1695), 352; British Linen Bank (1747), 352; Royal Bank of Scotland (1727), 352
  Bounty Act (1742), 511
  coal mines, 509; mine owners of Lothian, 436
  entrepreneurs, Scots in Sweden, 458
  farming: arable, 78; extensive stock-farming, 91; land administration – tacksmen, 107; tillage systems, 72
  fisheries, 153; bounty on, 179, 183; exports, 147–8, 149, 177, 183; fish markets, 142; increased production in 18th century, 183; salt for preserving, 181
      cod, 164, 165, (and ling) 142; herring, 139, 141, 142–3, 147–8, 153, 177; salmon, 147, 183; whitefish, 141
      consumption of fish, 147, 175; fishing communities, 140–1
  food crises, 10
  freight market, 210
  industrial innovations, 476
  iron deposits, 463; iron industry, 497, 498
  manufactures, Board of Trustees for, 511
  salt, for English cod trade, 181

shipbuilding, 530

silver and gold, 490

stocking-knitting, 511

sugar refineries, 540

textiles: linen, 511; woollens, 480–1; export of raw wool, 514, (forbidden) 253, 480; factories, 480–1

Union with England (1707), 481

see also Britain

scythes, 98, 497, 501

securities: trade, 343, 345–6, 353–4, 362, 363, (in France) 377–8; forward business in, 345–6, 353–4, (edict (1610) on) 345; 'option' transactions, 345, 346; papal securities, 364; security dealers, 347; see also under government finance

Segovia, 314, 516

seigneuries, 607; seigneurs, 522; seignorial rights, 108, 358, 606–9, (abolished in France (1789)) 113

Selim I, Sultan, 506

Sella, Domenico, 32

Serbia, 219, 489

serfdom, 113–23; under Gutsherrschaft, 607–8, 615, 620; limitations set to (Robot-patente), 117, 614; mercantilist attitude to, 609; Physiocrats' indictment of, 612, 619; poor agriculture attributed to, 614, 616; restrictions and obligations, 608–9; serfs and free peasants, 605, (as cheap labour) 485; serfdom and villeinage, 114–16
  abolition of, 117, 557, 615–16; in Hapsburg dominions, 552, 557, (under Joseph II) 599, 615–16; in Poland, 20; in Prussia, 552, 554, 557, 616; in central and eastern Europe generally, 113–14

serge, see textile products

Serra, Antonio, 30

servitudes collectives, 606, 619

Seville, 31, 287; blue ware (azulejos), 506; clearing banks, 314, 317; commerce, predominance of, 516; endorsement, 328n; exchange rates, 223; hats, 517; Italy, ties with, 317–18; Portuguese Jews in, 15, 333; printing, 534; shipbuilding, 531; silk industry, 517; silver shipments from America, 206, 212, 333, (treasure fleets sail to) 317, 367, 371, 373, (mule-trains leave

Seville (*cont.*)
from) 260; soapmaking, 508; sugar refining, 539; trade with America (*Casa de Contratación*), 214, 314, 347, 366, 371, 373

Sèvres, porcelain industry, 429, 507

Seyssel, Claudius, 580–1

share-cropping (*métayage*), 605, 607, 610, 611

sheep: numbers of, 90, 131, (preferred in extensive farming) 91; mutton, 92; other products, 91, 92; wool from, 91, 92, 93; and location of woollen industry, 463

sheep-farming, 56, 128, 518

sheet-metal industry, 496; 'white-sheet', 496

Sheffield, 470, 475; iron production, 497, 498; workers' associations, 488

Sheraton, Thomas, furniture for the luxury market, 543

Shetlands, 136; fishermen, 140, 161, 164; fish markets, 142; exports of fish, 183

shipbuilding, 530–1; ancillary industries, 180, 532; Basque steel for, 498; copper for, 242, 533; equipment, 531 (technical apparatus) 472; large-scale and artisan, 427; State concern with, 401; tar and pitch for, 508, 531, 532; wood for, 475, 508, 531, 532, 533

shipbuilding in American colonies, 530; Danzig, 224–5, 532; Dutch, 39, 453, 530, 531; England, 530, 531; France, 500, 531; Genoa, 532; Portugal, 532; Russia, 533; Scotland, 530; south Netherlands, 531; Spain, 531–2; Sweden, 430, 484, 531, 533; Venice, 32, 429, 532; others, 532–3

shipping trade, 209; shippers, 75; *see also* carrying trade

ships: carracks, 532; colliers, 530; *fluitschip*, 531, 533; flyboat, 530, 531; galleys, 532; pinks, 531; sailing ships over 400 tons, 530–1

investment in, 580; shares in, 355 *see also* fleets; navies

shipwrights, 180, 532; gilds, 530

Shrewsbury, Earl of, 449

Siberia, 217, 502, 503

Sicily: annuities on, 373; fish and salt from, 207, 222; grain from, 207, 222, (yield ratios) 80; monocultures, 68;

privileged silk manufacture, 528; sugar production, 539; sulphur from, 508

Siebengebirge, 217, 219

Siegerland, 500, 508

Siena ceramics, 506, 507

Sieyès, Abbé, 552

Silent, Govert, copper refinery, 486

Silesia
cattle exports, 234
conquest of, by Frederick II of Prussia, 520
gold deposits, 462, 484, 488
iron mines, 449
lead mines, 463, 492, 493
manuring, 94
peasants: classification of groups, 127; *Gutsherrschaft*, 607; peasant revolts, 122
salt refinery, 538
serf labour, limited by *Robot-patente*, 117
textiles, 203, 544; cloth-making, 518, (specialists in Slovakia) 524; linens, 463, 519, (dyed) 520, (exports) 204, 219, 250, 520; competition with English textiles, 254
trade routes, 217

silk industry: centres of manufacturing and processing, 512–13; factories and mills, 431, 471, 479, 482, 515, 527; gilds, 468, 523, (fraternities) 525; government concern with, 431, 480, 482, 488, 525; (imports from China and Asia forbidden) 482, 517; putting-out system, 523; silk-masters, 524; silk-weavers, 483, 515–16, 527; spinning, 487; thread-winding, 527, (twisting) 523; throwing, Lombe's invention, 511; weaving, 515–17, 521, 523, 527–8, (draw loom) 477

Asian, 250; Austrian, 524; Bengali, 251; Berlin, 431; Chinese, 252; Dutch, 515; French, 471, 481, 516–17; Italian, 255, 477, 527, 542, Venetian, 32, 527; Prague, 525; Russia, 529; Spain, 482; Zürich, 522–3

silk products: embroidery, 518; flowered silk, 251; ribbons, 520–1, 525, 527; stockings, 525, 527; taffeta, 525; silk and woollen mixtures, 253, (and camelhair) 254; wrappers and buttons, 529

silk trade, 207, 214, 219, 281, 282, 413;
  East India Companies in, 251
silver
  from America, 30, 213, 260, 264, 291,
    296, 309, 320, 489; impact on Spain,
    11, 28–9, 31, (her wars financed by)
    241, 260, 308; imports to Seville,
    370, 371; shipments from Spain to
    Netherlands blockaded by Elizabeth I,
    372, 374
  from eastern countries, 257–8; from
    Europe, 30, 218, 241, 291, 296, 308,
    473, 490–1; obtained from copper
    ores, 474, from lead, 492–3
  exports, 208, 375; to Asia, 257, 258, 259;
    shipments between European coun-
    tries, 320, 375; licences to export, 372
  market, 241, at Amsterdam, 309; compe-
    tition with copper, 245; demand for
    silver, 259, 264; price changes, 259,
    261, 264, 474; effect of purchases on
    exchange rates, 261; silver crises, 264
  mines, 462–3; large-scale production in,
    472; shares in, 433; technical processes
    in, 472, 497
  transport of, 260; silver routes, 374
  value ratios: with gold, 257–8, 260, 264,
    296–7, 299, 308; with copper, 296
silver coins, 290–303; used for negotiating
    money, 260; silver content of basic
    coins, 290–5, 339; changes in metal
    content, 308–9
  exports of, 308, 309; to Baltic, 297; to
    India, 259, 264
  large coins, 291–2, 294–5, 296–7, 336;
    as standard coin, 298, 300; in inter-
    national trade, 307; in banking, 337–9,
    341
  types: Brabant silver groat, 292, 293,
    Flemish groat, 291, 292, 293; duca-
    toon, 260, 264; *Joachimstaler*, 291;
    rix-dollars, 259, 264; *taler*, 295, 380
silver standard (silver–copper), 259, 299;
  silver–copper ratio, 296
silversmiths, 468; gild, 468; dinner services
  in silver, 354
Simiand, François, 2, 7, 11, 43, 97
Sind, 280
Sind, Christian, woollen entrepreneur, 524
Sinzendorf, Count, silk-works, 524
Skaw, 270, 275
skills: and enterprise, 452, 454, 548; trans-

fer of, 397, 431, (through migration)
  18, 40, 486, 502, 504, 515, 518, 524,
  528, 529
skins, trade in, 207, 208–9, 217, 219
slate, 507
Slav countries, 117
slave trade, 205, 212–13, 416; investment
  in, 580; slave-traders, 205
Slicher van Bath, B. H., 6, 21, 23, 188, 223
Slovakia: copper mines, 462–3, 478, 484,
  488, 492, 495, 544, (large-scale production in) 471, (Fuggers retire from)
  492; iron industry, 501; silver mines,
  488, 489, 492; textiles, 524
smelting, 486, 502
Smeth, de, Dutch banking house, 27
Smith, Adam
  Prussian admiration for, 619
  views on: Amsterdam Exchange Bank,
    74, 346; army, correct size for, 577;
    commerce and the rule of law, 581–2;
    consumption, 195; the Dutch, 26;
    fishing bounty, 179, 183; joint-stock
    companies, 444, 446; mercantilism,
    18–19; Physiocrats, 602, 603, 619;
    ratios of precious metals, 257, 260
  Wealth of Nations, its intellectual pa-
    ternity, 18–19
smiths and smithies, 24; in iron industry,
  497–8, 499, 501; master smiths, 503;
  tysksmide (German smithy), 486;
  vallonsmidet (Walloon smithy), 486;
  see also blacksmiths
Smolensk, 217, 262, 263
smuggling, 283, 289
Smythe, Sir Thomas, governor of various
  trading companies, 446
soap, 171; exports, 274; luxury soaps, 543;
  production, 224, 427, (factories) 468,
  (technical apparatus) 472, (processes)
  508, 509
London Society of Soapboilers, 382–3
Savonnerie, 429, 430
Soboul, A., 126
social structure, 452, 550, 609, 618
  class patterns: and business enterprise,
    400, 419–23, 464; in enlightened
    Prussia, 599; hierarchies in, 550–2;
    emergence of new patterns, 570–1
  social stratification, 54, 55, 77; relation
    to prices and population changes, 123–
    32

Société d'agriculture, du commerce et des arts (Rennes, 1757), 103

société d'ordres (Ständegesellschaft), 550–2, 558, 559–61, 563, 568, 571–2, 583, 607; end of, 589, 600, 613, 619

société en commandité, 433–4, 442

Société libre d'économie de Saint-Petersbourg (1765), 103

Society of Dublin (1736), 103

Society of the Fishery of Great Britain and Ireland, 441

soil conditions, 59–60, 100, 125

Solingen, 470, 475, 500

Soly, H., 304

Sombart, Werner, 542, 581; Der Bourgeois, 581, 587

South America: factory system in, 211; linen exports to, 204; sugar from, 539; see also America; Brazil; Mexico; New World; Peru

South Sea Act (1720), 388

South Sea Company (1711), 353, 361, 443–4; English whaling revived by, 171; loans to State, 387–8; South Sea Bubble, 388, 422

Southampton, 160, 530

Spain
    Armada, 531–2
    asiento contract, 333
    banking: clearing banks, 314–15; deposit and exchange banks, 301; bankers, 375; merchant bankers, 375
    brigandage, 16
    ceramics, azulejos, 506
    colonial empire, 442, 494; navigation to New World, 543, 545; overseas enterprise, 546; state control of sea routes, 417
    copper: mines, 463, 489–90; imports, 241, 244, 245, 544; coinage, 29, 245, 246, 299; standard adopted, 494; inflation, 243, 309, 544
    decline, 28–32, 35, 38, 517; end of Spanish hegemony in Europe, 205; end of her world policy, 375
    deserted villages, 68, 69
    edicts (1626), 544
    emigration, 18; of Jews, 528
    expulsion of Moriscoes, 29
    farming: arable and cattle, 76; extensive stock farming, 91; grain supplies for, 221, 223, 285; maize cultivation, 78,

201, 230; yield ratios of cereals, 80–1; wine-growing, 77
    fisheries, 134–5; cod, 157–8, 177, 536; fish consumption, 172, 175, 177, 178, salt fish, 207; imports, 177, 207; salt for preserving, 180–1; 'salt-on-salt' method, 181; 'protection' licences for fishing-boats, 181–2; whale fishery, see Basque
    food crises, 18
    gilds, 465–6
    gold: shipments from Africa, 297; gold écu, 320, 334n; gold–silver ratios, 308
    Holland, contrast with, 395
    immigration, 487
    iron deposits, 463, 490; iron industry, 498–9; exports, 498, 499; Flemish experts in, 499
    leather industries, 207, 208; skin imports, 208
    mercenary army, 373, 374–5
    and the Netherlands, 25, 32, 149, and see Netherlands, Revolt of
    nobility, 448, 450
    olive oil exports, 207
    paper mills, 535
    pawnshops (positos), 302
    population, 29, 30, 31
    Portuguese Jews in, 333
    printing, 534
    public finance: annuities, 371; assignments, 367–8; bankruptcies, 29, 334, 362, 371, 375, 415; floating debt, 370–1, 374, 375; Genoese control of, 333, 375; licences for exports of precious metals, 367, 370; loans from foreign merchants, 332–3; taxation, 31; war financing, 376
    quicksilver, 484
    revolt of Comuneros, 367
    salt, 180–1; salt-drying, 538; exports, 209
    shipbuilding, 531–2; reorganization of navy, 532
    silver: mines, 463, 489, (extraction techniques) 472; shipments from New World, 28–31; exports, 320, 375; transport for, 260
    social structure, 403–4
    State enterprise: trade with Asia, 440; royal factories, 482; monopolies, 499
    sugar canes and refineries, 539, 540

Spain (*cont.*)
  taxation, 29, 31, 32, 367
  textiles: areas and types of production,
    516–17; exports of, in return for
    colonial products, 517; government
    aid to, 482–3; imports from China
    and Asia forbidden, 517
      cottons, 516, 517; hats, 517; linen
    and hemp products, 517, (imports)
    250; wool, 517, (exports) 515, 516,
    (woollen cloth) 516, (factory) 488
  tobacco exports, 541
  Treasury, 285
  working conditions, 488
Spalding, James, flax-beating machine, 476
Spanish Netherlands: fisheries, 143, 177;
  tillage systems, 74; *see also* Netherlands, southern
specie: international flow of, 307–9, 310,
  322; payments in, 308, 333, 337; as
  security for loans, 338, 341–3; specie
  market, 342
speculation: and banking technique, 313;
  and pawnbroking, 303; on Antwerp
  Exchange, 331–2, 365, 370; in coins,
  291, 294–5, 307, 309; in corn, 197,
  220, 232, 370, 605; in forward business, 345–6, 353–4; in gold–silver
  ratios, 321; in insurance business,
  355; in land, 67–8, 355, 569; in *luoghi*,
  363; in pepper, 283, 285–6; on
  precious metals, 296–7, 308; speculative investment, 377, 441, 443, 444,
  587, (South Sea Bubble) 388; speculative long-distance trades, 439
Specz, Mÿnheer, Dutch resident at
  Firando, 246
Speenhamland system, 7
Speet, Peter, textile entrepreneur in
  Sweden, 530
Sperling, J., 261
spice trade, 207, 209, 218, 219, 243, 307;
  Asian and American, 214, 282; companies for, 441; European spice
  market, 285, (cornered by Italians
  and Germans) 415; Fuggers' concern
  with, 208; Lisbon supplies, 275;
  monopolies, 413; shift from Levant
  trade to East Indies, 209; *see also*
  pepper
spices, in the diet, 199, 202, 210–11
Spiethoff, Artur, 1

spinning: peasant spinning, 522; putting-
  out system in, 522; spinning-wheel,
  476, 479
  cotton, 522; flax, 518; linen-spinning
  centres, 520; silk, 515, 517, 527;
  thread- and twine-spinners, 180;
  wool, 487, 518, 522, 524
Spitzbergen (Greenland), fisheries, 138,
  158, 168; Dutch vessels sailing to,
  169–71
Spooner, F., 44, 189, 197
Spreull, John, on Yarmouth cod fishermen, 141
Staël, Madame de, 561, 598n
Staphorst, Van, Dutch banker, 391
Staple Courts, 78, 349; Staplers, 381,
  438
staple markets, 268–74; Amsterdam as,
  273–4, 278, 286; cloth staples, 269–70,
  349; corn staple, 276; importing/
  exporting and storage facilities, 276–7,
  278, 279, 289; for internal trade, 270,
  (in Poland) 271, (in Sweden) 272;
  wool staple, 349
State, concept of, 287–8, 289, 400–1, 559;
  bankruptcies, 371, 391; enterprise,
  417, 555, 571, (loans to entrepreneurs)
  428, 480; gilds and, 467; planning,
  578
Stationers' Company, 534
steam engine, 474–5
steel: Basque, 499; Damascas, 473; iron
  for, 504; Styrian, 500
  steel production, 449, 473, 484, 500,
  501; steel combing teeth, 476
Steensgaard, Dr Niels, 278–9
Stein, Heinrich Friedrich Karl, Prussian
  reformer, 558, 560, 570, 572, 573,
  586, 597; on junkers, 609
Steinacher Gesellschaft, 479
Sterck, Geeraard, imperial agent, 368
Stettin, 222, 225, 243
Stitte, Hans, German entrepreneur in
  Russia, 502
stock farming, 8, 89–93; extensive and
  intensive, 90–1; shifts from arable to,
  74–6, (conflicts of interest between)
  90, 92; stall feeding, 71, 94; stock-
  breeders, 93; stock prices, 52;
  supplying the meat market, 92–3;
  transhumance, 91; *see also* animal
  husbandry; cattle; oxen

stock market: boom and crash (1720), 380, 388; stockjobbing, 345, 423; *see also* securities; South Sea Company

stockfish (poor John, Iceland cod), 155, 157, 161, 164, 166n, 177, 182

Stockholm: Bank of, 380–1, (Riksens Ständers Bank) 303; copper market, 272; printing press, 534; shipbuilding, 533; wool manufacture, 530

stockings: knitting, 511, 518, 523; silk stockings, 525, 527; woollen, 526, 529; India stockings, 251

Stolberg, 494, 500

Stols, E., 32

stone: for building, 507; mill-stones, 507; quarries, 507

Stone, Lawrence, 12, 13, 350n, 405n, 449n

storage, 276–7, 278, 279, 289; of grain, 10, 605, 609–10

Strassburg, 521, 534

strikes, 488

Stroganov, Russian merchant entrepreneurs, 485, 496, 502; control of salt-pans, 538

Stuart kings: extravagance, 381–3, 555; industrial policy, 480; investments, 442; parliaments, 553; *see also* James I; Charles I; Charles II

stuffs, 253, 510

Stumpe, textile innovations, 425

Sturtevant, Simon, treatise on coal-burning furnaces (1612), 474

Styria, 488; steel, 500, 501

Sudan, gold from, 308

Suffolk, 71, 174, 510

sugar, 539–42; areas of production, 68, 212, 214, 219, 539; consumption, 202, 540, 541, (from luxury to mass consumption) 212; refining, 27, 435, (Dutch) 39, 429, 454, 519, (Spanish) 539–40, (Venetian) 32, 540, (chemical processes in) 508, (technical apparatus for) 472; *suyker bakkers*, 539–40; *Zuckerbäcker*, 540

sugar trade, 206, 413; sugar used for ballast, 248; sugar empire in Brazil, 333

sulphur, 508; sulphuric acid for bleaching, 478

sunspot cycles, 62–3

Supple, Barry, 12, 193

supply and demand, 2, 8, 30, 50, 194, 376; of capital, 357–8; entrepreneurial

problem of, 397, 416, 437; in European copper market, 244; of labour, 607

Surat, 248, 259

Sussex, 99, 497

Svarez, Carl Gottlieb, lectures to the Crown Prince, 598n; *Allgemeines Landrecht*, 591, 598

Swabia: paper mill, 535; textiles, 518, 519, 521, (techniques in linen-weaving) 520

Sweden
 agriculture: agricultural classes, 128; arable and cattle farming, 76; temporary cultivation, 72; threshing block, 100; wheat yields, 61, 62, 64, 80
 alliance with States General of the Netherlands (1614), 245
 aristocratic diet, 195
 artillery, 243
 Bank of Stockholm, 380–1; banknotes, 380–1
 climate, 63
 coins, 380
 control of Baltic trade, 228–9, 230
 copper from, 189, 214, 242, 244–6, 272–3, 282, 296, 380, 390, 458, 463, 494–5, 504, 545–6; international market dominated by, 544; revenues from copper royalties, 272, 429, 495
  copper inflation, 299, 309; copper and silver bimetallism, 380; 'Great Copper Mountain', 428n
 Crown trade staples, 272
 enterprise: credit for industry, 480; large-scale production, 472; overseas, 540; trading companies, 442
  alien entrepreneurs, 457–8, (Dutch) 435, 444, 454, 458; aristocratic, 451; peasant, 485; royal, 458; State, 429, 430, 431, 483, 529
 fishing fleet, 165
 food, 198
 foreign trade, 271–2
 forest products, 458
 Frihetstid (liberal period), 504
 herring fishery, 138n, 155; fish consumption, 173; the farmer's herring, 198
 industrialization, 485, 545; industrial experts in France, 481
 iron: deposits, 463; industry, 458, 483, 484, 486, 502, 503–5; capital for,

Sweden: iron (*cont.*)
505; emigrant specialists in, 545; exports, 499, 504–5, 545; hierarchy in iron-works, 505; production techniques, 504; Russian competition, 547; charcoal-iron, 498
mining and metallurgical immigrants, 484, 486, 487; industry, 429, 472, 484
navy, 243
public finance, 380–1, 390; loans in Amsterdam, 391
shipbuilding, 430, 484, 533; ships sold to France, 531
silver mines, 489
sulphur, 508
tar and pitch from, 508
taxation, 505
textiles, 530; cloth imports, 204
wars: Polish, 68, 118, 120, 228, 229–30; with Russia, 503
Swedish Copper Company, 245, 249
Swedish territories, 121; *see also* Pomerania
Switzerland
agriculture: agricultural classes, 127, 128; arable and cattle farming, 76, (and wine-growing) 77; farm households, 125; manure yields, 94; ploughing, 97–8; seigneurial labour, 523; yield ratios of cereals, 80–1
famine crises, 10
Geneva trade, 315
gilds, 522, 523
health measures, 17
immigration, 485, 522, 523
mercenary soldiers, 545
merchant bankers, 335
peasant revolts, 108
putting-out system, 522
textiles, 544; cotton, 522, (cotton printing) 471, 522; embroidery, 522, 523; *Kunststuhl* (mechanical loom), 523; lace, 523; linen, 521; pasmentry, 523; silk, 522–3; stocking-knitting, 523; woollens, 522
Syria, sugar from, 539

taille, 617
tailors, 132, 488; Jewish gilds, 468
Talavera de la Reina, 482, 517; ceramics, 506
tanning and tanners, 468, 508

tar and pitch, 214, 265, 271; for shipbuilding, 508, 531, 533
Tarello, Camillo, inventor of farm machinery, 99
tariffs, 39, 186, 194, 289; on fish, 174; French, 582; protective, 40; Scandinavian, 209; *see also* customs; tolls
Tarnowskie Gory, mining town, 493
Tatichev, Russian state official, 503
Tavernier, Jean Baptiste, *Les Six Voyages* (1678), 259
Tawney, R. H., 5; *Religion and the Rise of Capitalism* (1926), 14
taxation, 5, 358, 360, 361–2, 415, 617
burden of, 602; on agriculture, 107–8; on peasants, 606–7, 610; exemption of nobility, 108, 582
farming of, 355, 359, 360, 402; in England, 359, 360, 383; France, 377, 379, 552; Germany, 367; Italy, 363; Spain, 367; United Provinces, 390
through foreign trade, 265–6, 289, 401
Physiocrat view of, 603, 612
Prussian system, 558
reforms, 615, 617
and standing armies, 554–5
tax registers, 129
taxes: *corvée*, 607; direct, 360; drainage and land tax, 26; on fish landings, 181; on food, 253; on forges, 505; *gabelle* (salt tax), 149, 181; on houses, 125; indirect, 25; in kind, 241; ship tax, 385; Tenth Penny, 25; *see also* customs; tariffs; tithes; tolls
Taylor, G. V., 580
tea, 199, 201; and sugar, 541; tea trade, 211
technology, 433, 472–8, 611; technological factors in industrial organization, 425–7, 543; backward technology in large-scale industry, 432; improvements, 543, 548
in bleaching, 478, 519; brewing, 537; brass manufacture, 486; business management, 434; iron techniques, 486; mining and manufacture, 434, 458, 472–5, 486, 492, 493, 497, 498, (in Swedish mining) 504; polder-making, 67, 68; textiles, 476–7, 510, 518
Teixeira, Portuguese banker, 485, 495
Terray, Joseph Marie, 582
Teutonic Knights, 118, 271, 275; defeat at Tannenberg, 120

textile industry, 13, 203–5, 510–30, 544–5
    aristocratic enterprise in, 450, 485, 524, 525
    centres of production, 512–13
    factories, 470–1, 479, 524, 526–7, 529; privileged, 480; state-owned, 481; factory system, 479; East India Company factories in India, 251
    gilds, 469–70, 511, 523; cloth-workers', 464; drapers', 483; linen weavers', 519, 521, 523; wool, 522, 526; wool weavers', 466; collective delivery, 520
    government aid to, 480–3, 485, 516, 525, 530, 547; restrictions and prohibitions, 251, 253, 477, 478, 480, 482, 511, 517, 519, 521, 527
    inspection (*Leggen*), 518, 519
    investment costs, 479
    labour, 514, 522, 523, 524; hierarchy of, 487; strikes, 488; wages, 511, 514, 520, (paid in cloth) 204
    location, 463
    machines and technology, 476–8, 520, 523; opposition to, 476, 477, 478
    masters, 525; independent masters, 510
    mills, 480; cotton, 468; fulling, 477; gig-mills, 477; ribbon, 477; silk, 479, 515, 527
    monopolies, 255, 519–20, 523
    peasant producers, 514; weavers, 519, 522
    power for: donkey, 477; water, 476, 477, 510, 511; wind, 477
    putting-out system, 12, 427, 469–70, 479, 510, 515, 518, 520, 523, 526
    rural (cottage) industries, 55, 128, 203, 469, 521; *lakens* and lace, 514; linen and canvas, 249, 520; ribbon-weaving, 523; spinning and weaving, 77, 470, 522
    workshops, 425, 470, 527
    working-producer, 426, 470
textile products: class distinctions in, 204–5; bombazines, 526; broadcloth, 510, 514; brocades, 204, 255, 478; camlets, 254; carpets, 528; clothing, 481, 526, 529, 542, (for armies) 528; frieses, 512–13; fustians, 510, 519, 526, 544; guinees, 205; household linen, 205; kerseys and bays, 510, 544; *lakens*, 254; New Draperies, 26, 222, 252–3, 254, 510, 544, 547; satin, 255; says and

Zeuge, 544; serge, 13, 25, 253, 510, 526; stuffs, 253, 510; taffeta, 525; tapestry, 429, 516, 543; velvet, 204, 255, 529, 542; worsteds, 253, 254, 510, 515; *see also* braid; calico; canvas; cloth; cotton; linen production; ribbon-weaving; silk industry; stockings; woollen industry
textile trade, 203–5, 219, 249–56
    booms, 425, 517; depressions, 254, 255, 517
    East India Companies trade, 250–2
    fashion and, 250–1
    imports from Asia, 250–2; exports to Africa, Levant, West Indies, 254, 516, 529; exports to America, 204–5, 511, 514, 517; legislative restrictions on, 251, 253, 511, 517, 527
    markets: European, 250, 514, 516, 520, 526, 530, 544, 547; colonial, 516–17; Levantine, 255–6, 528; competition for, 251, 253, 254, 524, 528
    pedlars' traffic in, 203
    see also under separate countries and textiles
Thiers, 475, 499, 535
third estate, 562, 585; *see also* bourgeoisie
Thirty Years War, 231, 351, 399, 483; damage to Germany, 230, 578
    effect on: agriculture, 68, 69, 71, 73, 108, 110–11; cattle trade, 236, 237, 263; copper industry, 189, 245, 249, 494, 495; economic policy, 576; international commerce, 545–6; iron industry, 501; serfdom, 118, 120; technical skills, 575; textiles, 518, 519, 520
Thomas, R. P., 4
Thrace, 68, 219
threshing, 97–8; threshing blocks, 99–100
Thünen, J. H. von, 44, 205; concentric circles, 91, 92
Thuringia: copper production, 189, 241, 242, 244–5, 484, 489; cotton, 521; glassmaking, 505; iron-works, 500; land erosion, 69; trade routes, 217
Thurzo, House of, mining entrepreneurs, 493
Thurzo, Johann, alloy processing, 473; hires Neusohl copper mines, 478
tillage systems, 72; convertible husbandry, 72, 73, 74, 75; extensive and intensive, 95; infield–outfield, 72; 'Land van Herve', 74–5; 'Norfolk' system, 73;

tillage systems (*cont.*)
> temporary cultivation (*Feldgraswirt-schaft*), 72, 74, 75; *see also* rotation of crops

timber, wood, 429, 508–9; and aristocratic enterprise, 449; for charcoal and potash, 508, 509; deforestation, 463; fuel for mining, 497, 498; for furnaces, 508, 509; for glassmaking, 505; for shipbuilding, 531–3; strategic value of, 265; Swedish timber-forests, 504, 533; timber-felling, 128; timber-processing industry, 508; trade in, 214, 271; wood products, craftsmen in, 180

tin: mines, 484, 490–1, 496; production, 496; trade in, 207, 243; tin alloys, 473, 496; tinplate, 465, 473; tinware, 472, 496
> Bohemia, 496; England, 207, 496; Saxony, 484, 496

Tinto, 198; Rio Tinto copper mines, 463

tithes, 47, 79, 105, 126, 606; in secular hands, 107; paid in copper, 241

Titian (Tiziano Vecelli), 506

Titow, J., 59–60

tobacco, 541–2; cultivation in Europe, 23, 242, (manure for), 95; gilds, 468; imports from Brazil, 212; from America, 541; market in, 214, 282; tobacco pipes, 507
> processing, 45; cutting, 519, 541; rolling, 471, 542; factories for, 471, 542

Tocqueville, Alexis de: *Ancien Régime et la Révolution*, 556, 557, 562, 569, 570, 582, 583, 598, 602, 610, 618, 619–20

Tokugawa Iyeyasu, Shogun of Japan, 281

Toldsted, cattle customs register, 240

Toledo: clearing bank, 314; entrepreneurs in Granada, 517; gilds, 465; textiles, 482, (velvet) 542; weapons industry, 498; decline of, 29, 31–2, 36

tolls, 39, 209–10; on cattle, 235–6, 238; as Crown revenue, 241, 266, 273, 280, 359; farming of, 355, 359; feudal, in France, 456; import and export, Amsterdam, 274; internal, 431, 582; *see also* Danish Sound tolls

Tonkin, 246, 257

Tonti, Lorenzo, 384n

tontine loans, 384

Tooke, Thomas, and William Newmarch, *History of Prices* (1838–57), 10

tools, 475–6, 546; *see also* crafts; machines

Toulouse Exchange, 365

Tournon, Cardinal of, governor of Lyons, 365

towns: citadels and city walls, 507; credit for rulers, 366–7; enterprise in ceramics, 507; liberties and privileges, 361, 557, 582, (Frederick II's policy) 557; mart towns, 438, 439, 520; mining towns, 493, 498, 500; municipal finance, 358, 363, 364, 370, (toll-farming contracts) 359; restrictive practices, 497, 548; size of, 130, 579, 585; townspeople, land owned by, 109–10; urban occupations, 132; urban real estate, improvements of, 305, 449–50, (investment in) 580; *see also* staple markets; urbanization

trade cycle, 243

trade flows, trade routes, 205–64; and trade compartments, 216–18, 233–4, 236, 242, 266, 268; and staple markets, 268–70, 276; assigned to regulated companies, 270; Amsterdam the focal point of north Europe, 274–7; impact on diet, 202

traders, licensed, 444

trades: connected with coachbuilding, 542; connected with fishing, 180; connected with international trade, 190; food trades, 536; new trades, 467, 475–6

transport
> costs of, 190, 209, 220, 239, 288, 413, 428, 440, 449
> and industrial enterprise, 427–9, 455
> lack of, and 'demographical catastrophes', 604–5
> and migration, 10
> for copper, 242, 243, 247, 272; food, 24, 200, 206, 212; precious metals, 260; sugar as ballast, 248; salt ships, 209–10; tea cargoes, 211; treasure fleet, 317, 368, 373
> carriage by water, 8, 24, 39, 190, 191, 200, 220, 428, 431, 432; barges, 24, 191, 220; canals, 24, 428; merchant fleets, 10, 24, 206, 221, 530; river traffic, 216, 217, 219, 225; seaborne, 190, 223, 275, 417

transport (*cont.*)
overland transport: carts and wagons, 220, 242, 533; coaches and carriages, 533–4; horseback, 220, 533, horse and cart, 260, (horse-drawn railways) 475; mule-trains, 260; pack animals, 190

transport industries, 530–4; shipbuilding, 530–3; wheeled vehicles, 533–4

Transylvania, 462, 501, 544

Transylvanus, Maximilian, 271

treadle-wheel, 476

treaties: Cateau-Cambrésis (1559), 371; Twelve Years Truce (1609), 532, 537; Westphalia (1648), 359

Tresoir Van de Mate (1590), 328, 332n, 349

Trevor-Roper, H. R., 14

Trip, Amsterdam family firm of money-lenders, 68, 435; as arms merchants, 247; copper investments, 246, 247, 249, 495

Trip, Elias: pepper consortium, 285; Swedish Crown debt to, 249, 390

Tron, Niccolo, textile entrepreneur, 526

Troyes, 167, 318

Trudaine, French government official, 582

Truman, Hanbury and Buxton, Spital-fields brewery, 479

Tucher, House of, south German merchant bankers, 367

Tucher, Lazarus, imperial agent, 368

Tudesq, A. J., *Grands Notables en France 1840–1849*, 570

Tudor monarchs, 41, 480, 553, 554, 580; *see also* Henry VIII; Elizabeth I

Tula blast furnace, 502

tuna fish, 136, 138, 207

Turenne, Henri de la Tour d'Auvergne, Vicomte de, marshal of France, 562, 567

Turgot, Anne-Robert-Jacques, Baron de l'Aulne, 560, 569, 570, 572, 582, 583; on the state of the peasants, 605, 606–7; 'Mémoire sur les municipa-lités', 602

Turin: Banco di San Paolo, 312; ceramics, 507; silk looms, 527

Turkey (Turkish regions), 263, 489; exports, 219, (of grain) 221, (embargo on) 221; faience industry, 506; imports of sugar, 540; wars, 68, 199–200, 532, 616, (cloth for army) 528, (victualling requirements) 200, 234, (Turks expelled from Hungary) 575; *see also* Ottoman Empire

Turkey, Sultan of, leases textile mills to Jews, 529

Turkey merchants, 510

Turkish yarn (camelhair), 254

turnips, 73

Tuscany: clothmaking, 526; endorse-ment, 329; gilds, 467; merchant bankers, 318, 333; paper mills, 535

Tuscany, Grand Duke of, 221

Tyneside collieries, 434, 435

Tyrol: bronze-casting workshops, 496; copper mines, 484, 488, 492, (pro-duction) 189, 243–4, 415, 544; gold deposits, 462; silver mines, 296, 462–3, 488, 489, 492, (large-scale production in) 472, 473

Ukraine, 502

Ulm, 500, 519

underdeveloped countries, 186, 396, 426; in Baltic states, 53; regions in Italy, 34; influence on enterprise, 450, 459

underwriters, 389

unemployment, 16, 22, 400, 481; of agri-cultural workers, 611; Dutch, 27–8

'Ungarische Handlung', 544

Ungelter, South German merchants, 492

United East India Company of the Netherlands (1602), 282, 387; *see also* Dutch East India Company

United Provinces, 18; coinage, 339; in-surance, 384n; moneys of account, 338; pawnshops, 303; population, 88; ships passing through the Sound, 227; decline, 455; *see also* Dutch; Fries-land; Holland; Overijssel; Utrecht

United States of America: loans on Amsterdam, 391; monetary policy, 19; plough, 99; *see also* America; Colonies; New England; North America

Unwin, George, 5

Urach, weavers' gild, 519–20

Urals, 488, 547

urbanization, 66–7; and consumption patterns, 201, 202; financing of, in Antwerp, 304–5; in Flanders, 224; in Holland, 23, 224; and large-scale industry, 428

Urbino, ceramics, 506, 507
Usher, A. P., 43
usury: and Calvinism, 14; Church ban on, 302, 310, 592; *see also* interest; rate of interest
utensils: for the dairy, 99; the kitchen, 242; the table, 202–3; exports to the colonies, 212
Utrecht, 24, 325, 512, 514
Uytven, R. van, 20
Uztariz, Geronymus de, 31

Valckenburgh, van, money-lenders, 68
Valencia, 217; banking, 314; gilds, 465–6; hat-making, 517; lustre ceramics, 506; printing press, 534; sugar from, 539, 540; Tauli di Canvi, clearing bank, 315; textiles, 482, (silk weavers) 517, (velvet) 542
Valladolid, 136; clearing bank, 314; cloth industry, 516; fish consumption, 172; grain consumption, 84; hat-making, 517
Valois, 222
Valois kings of France, 318, 319–20; *see also* Francis I, Louis XI
van der Molen, Antwerp merchants, 307
van der Molen, Daniël, 332
Van Loo, J. B., painter, 598
van Lore, Sir Peter, London merchant, 382
Vanderberg, Dutch entrepreneur in France, 540
Värmland, Swedish iron province, 505, 506
Vauban, Sébastien le Prestre, 182
Vaughan, Stephen, governor of Merchant Adventurers, 370
Velden, Van, *Fondement van de Wissel-handeling* (1629), 344
velvet, 204; Italian, 255, 453; Russian, 529; Spanish, 542
Venice
    banking, 311–13, 333; Banco della Piazza di Rialto, 312–13, 337, 347; Banco del Giro, 313
    cattle imports, 200, 234,
    ceramics, 506
    coins, 320, 334n
    copper market, 243–4, 544
    endorsement, 328n
    financial policy of Senate, 312–13, 327
    foreign trade, 320, 333; and the Cape route, 32, 209
    galley-building, 532; government-owned shipyard, 429
    glass manufacture, 208, 505, 506
    grain consumption, 220, 221–2
    Jewish craft gilds, 468
    papermaking, 535
    precious stones and diamond-working, 542
    price currents for, 408
    printing, 534
    quicksilver works, 496
    red herrings, 178
    soapmaking, 508
    South German merchants in, 208
    spice trade, 207; pepper, 284
    sugar-refining, 32, 540
    textiles, 512–13; cloth industry, 255, 525, (exports) 528; wool gild, 526; silk industry, 526, (stockings) 526, (imports of silk thread) 528; velvets, 542
Verdier, silk factory in Russia established by, 529
Verlinden, Charles, 32
Vermuyden, Cornelius, land reclamation, 68, 454
Verona: fairs, 333; stocking manufacture, 526
Versailles, 614
Verviers, 470; drapery, 514
Viatis and Peller, Nuremberg linen firm, 479, 520
Vicens Vives, Jaime, 29, 31
Vicenza, 526, 527
Vienna, 561, 579; cattle for, 200; luxury goods, and the Court, 219; textiles, (lace and pasmentry) 525, (silk industry) 524–5; University of, 595
Vilar, Jean, 31
villages: abandoned, 56, 68, 69; corporative nature of, 551, 606, 607; hierarchy in, 552; knitting industry, 511; textile industries, 514; 'village of carpenters', 508; village trades, 132
villeinage, 42, 114–16, 121, 271
vine (grapes): cultivation, 22, 58, (at expense of corn) 220, 221, (labour-intensive) 89, (a monoculture) 68; financing of vineyards, 304; grape-picking, 63; *see also* wine
Vinius, entrepreneur in Russia, 486, 502

Virginia Company, 446
Vistula corn route, 225, 231, 271
Vleminck, entrepreneurs, 494
Voetius, Gisbert, 14
Voltaire, F. M. A. de, 564, 590, 592, 603; admiration for Frederick the Great, 598; *Candide*, 600
Vondel, Joost van den, Dutch poet, 260
Vries, Jan de, 23, 389n; *The Dutch Rural Economy in the Golden Age, 1500–1700*, 22, 26n, 28

wages: agricultural, 48–9, 101–2, (starvation wages) 605; fall in real wages (1730–70), 610; and grain prices, 52–4, 55; industrial, 487; and profits, 296; in rural areas, 397; skilled and unskilled, 52, 55; for smiths, 500; in shipbuilding, 531; in textiles, 511, 514, 520, 524, (paid in cloth) 204, (piece-work rates) 470; wage-earners, 20, ('golden age for') 106
Waldstein, Count, his woollen industry, 479, 485, 524
Wales: animal husbandry, 91; breweries, 537; coal mines, 510; corn production and consumption, 83, 85; herring-fishing, 142; population, 85
Wallachia: cattle exports, 234; grain exports, 119; Jewish artisans and manufacturers, 529; serfdom, 118; trade routes, 217
Wallenstein, General A. W. E. von, 236
Walloons: clothmaking, 254; entrepreneurs in Sweden, 484; smithies, 486
war, 254, 358, 401, 416, 560; and absolute monarchy, 549, 554–5, 559, 573; depopulation through, 9, 111, 120, 545, 577; economic warfare, 574; financing of, 107–8, 298, 299–30, 359–60, 365, 367, 368, 370, 372, 373–6, 378, 383, 384, 388–9, 576; fishing in wartime, 152, 154, 181–2, 536–7; Physiocrats on, 612–13; prisoners of war, 503
wars
   Austrian Succession, 608
   Dutch–English, 147, 179, 383
   Eighty Years War, 69, 181, 372, 546; Twelve Years Truce (1609–21), 532, 537; renewed war, 532–3
   French–Hapsburg wars, 359, 365
   Fronde, 576

Great Northern War, 238, 546
Hussite War, 120
Imperial wars, 367, 370
Louis XIV's wars of aggression, 238, 564, 566, 577, 609
Nine Years War (1688–97), 75
Prussia–Poland, 275
Russian, 120, 503
Seven Years War (1756–63), 576, 577, 609
Spanish Succession (1702–13), 75, 300, 387, 532; end of, 357
Swedish–Polish (1655–60), 68, 118, 120, 228, 229–30, 503
Turkish, 68, 118, 199–200, 532, 616
Wars of Religion, 15, 218, 298, 302, 319, 355, 357, 359, 494, 514; end of, 357
battles: Auerstädt (1806), 560; Jena (1806), 560; Leuthen (1757), 550; Mollwitz (1741), 614; Tannenburg (1410), 118, 120; White Mountain (1620), 118, 120
sieges: Haarlem (1573), 299; Leiden (1574), 299; siege warfare, 507
treaties, 521; Cateau-Cambrésis (1559), 371; Westphalia, 546
see also Netherlands, Revolt of; French Revolution; peasant wars; Thirty Years War
wasteland, 67, 111, 131; under *Feldgraswirtschaft* system, 74; as grazing for cattle, 89, 90
water mills: for casting, 474; drainage, 474; mining, 473, 497, 501; paper-making, 535; textiles, 476–7, 510, 511
water power, 449, 462, 463, 508
water supply, public works in, 441
water transport, *see* transport
Watson, Robert, *History of the Reign of Philip III* (1783), 29
wax, trade in, 217, 219
Way to Wealth, The (1758), 581
wealth: accumulation of, 455; distribution of, 602; mercantilist view of, 573–4; of nations, 452; Physiocrat view of, 603, 611, 613; and poverty, 571, 610; for taxation, 555; war needs and, 559
weather and climate, 57–65
weavers: action against calico imports, 251; cottage, 77, 132, 523; peasant, 522; gilds, 466, 519, 521, 522, 523,

weavers (*cont.*)
(fraternities of master weavers) 525;
in hierarchy of textile workers, 487;
immigrants, 520, 521, 522; limitations
on freedom to weave, 523, (free
weavers) 519; outwork weavers, 28;
refugee, 520
canvas, 515; linen, 520, 523; silk, 515–16,
517, 520, 523, 527–8, (fraternities)
525; wool, 518, 522
weaving: as a domestic industry, 521; in
factories, 479; putting-out system,
470, 523; technological progress, 475,
(draw-loom, power loom) 475, (ribbon loom) 520–1, 523; a village trade,
132
Weber, Max, 1, 591; Weber–Tawney
thesis, 14
Wedel cattle fair, 235, 267–8
Wedgwood, Josiah, 472
Wee, Hermann van der, 190–1, 218,
286–7, 362, 369
Weissenberg customs registers, 225
Weisser, Michael, 31
Weitmoser brothers, mining enterprise,
488
welfare: Jewish, 528; sickness benefit,
488; welfare factories, 471
Welser, German merchant house, 284–5,
367, 409, 410, 484
Wesel, 518, 521
Weserbergland, 505, 507
West India Company, 73, 213, 442; shares
in, 345
West Indies: coffee from, 214, 282; copper
from, 214, 282; Dutch exports to,
254; fleet, 531; market for fish, 161,
178; plantation colonies, 211, (limited
colonial activity) 191; slave trade,
212; Spanish textiles for, 516; sugar
from, 214, 282; West India trade,
205, 409
Wester, English stockbreeder, 93
Westermann, Dr, 241
Westminster, 534
Weston, Sir Richard, 73; travels through
Flanders, 103–4
Westphalia: distilleries, 538; flax-growing,
463, 515, 518; iron-working, 499;
linen-weaving, 483; *Leggen* system of
inspection, 518
Westphalia, Peace of (1648), 546
whales, 136, 138; whaling companies, 441,

537; whale bone, 171, 537; meat,
171; oil (train oil), 162–3, 168, 171,
537; *see also* fisheries
wheat, 23; demand for, 232; consumption, 84; trade in, 87, 227; wheat
bread, 219; *see also* corn; grain
cultivation, 57–8, 59, 60; in Norfolk
rotation, 73; minimal and maximal
yields, 60; yield ratios, 61–2, 73,
80–1, 87, effect of manuring on, 95;
reaping, 98; threshing, 97, 98
Wheeler, John, managing partner in
Foley iron partnership, 434
wheelwrights, 488, 542
Whitby, 136, 164, 530
White Mountain, Battle of, 118, 120
whitefish industry, 138, 139, 140, 166;
fishing grounds, 136; dried whitefish,
141
wholesalers: domestic, 398; of land, 402;
wholesale trade, 193
Wiebe, Georg, 10–11
Wieland corporation (*Wielandsche Gewerken*), 488
Wiese, Heinz, customs data on cattle
movements, 235–6, 238–9
Wijk, William van, Dutch mining expert,
504
Wildervanck, family firm of money-
lenders, 68
William of Orange, 148, 562
Wilson, Charles, 253, 261, 289, 382n,
388n; *The Dutch Republic*, 68; 'Taxation and the decline of empires', 41
Winchcombe, John, textile innovations,
425; his factory at Newbury, 471
windmills, 96, 463, 475; in Holland, 475,
477, 531; in Netherlands, 475
wine, 198, 199; exports, 75, 212
wine-growing, 52, 56; switch between
arable farming and, 75–6, 77; as a
secondary occupation, 127
wire, 484, 496, 499–500; wire-drawing,
473
Witt, Johan de, 180
Wittmacher, Hans (Johan Palmstruck),
foundation of Bank of Stockholm,
380
Wloclawek (Leslau) customs registers, 225
woad, 77, 515
Wolfe, Captain James, 159
Wolff, Aachen family of entrepreneurs,
484

Wolff, Christian, 586, 600; the triumph of reason, 593–4; doctrine of enlightened absolutism, 595

Wolff, Thomasius, 586

Wolski, Crown Grand Marshal Mikolaj, 502

Wolverhampton, 464, 498

women and girls: in farming, 101; in industry, 101, 471, 486–7, 536, (women's 'preserves') 487, 514; noble entrepreneurs, 500; see also Elizabeth I; Christina of Sweden; Maria Theresa

woodcarvers, 542; see also carpenters; timber

wool, 8, 56, 524, 528; English, changes in quality, 255; English and Scotch, 515; Peruvian, 517; Spanish, 253–4, 317, 515, 516; trade in, 219, 349, 516; restrictions on export, 253

woollen industry, 524, 525, 530; carding, 252, 476, 487; combing, 252, 253, 470, 510, 522; factories, 524, 526, 529; gilds, 464, 470, 522, 526; hierarchy of labour in, 487; New Draperies, 252; putting-out system, 522; spinning, 487, 518, 522, 524; weaving, 487, 518, 522; woollen products, (hats) 517, 526, (stockings) 526

woollen textiles: bays, 510; greinen (camlet), 254; kendals, kerseys, 510; sayetterie, 515; stuffs, 253, 510; worsteds, 253, 254, 510, 515; see also cloth

workers' associations, 488

workshops: for conversion of ore to metal, 472; Jewish textiles, 528; plate glass, 472; printer's workshop, 469; silk, 525; technical equipment for, 469, 472; water power for, 463

Worlidge, John, improved agricultural machinery, 99

worsteds, 253, 254; distinguished from pure 'woollens', 510; exports, 510; greinen (camlet), 254; sayetterie, 515; stuffs, 510

Wrigley, E. A., 20

writings obligatory, see financial techniques

Württemberg, weavers' gild, 519

Würzburg, 71, 220, 492

Wyatt, John, patent roller-drafting machine, 476

Wyczański, Andrzej, 83, 86, 188

Ximena, Juan de Villa, cloth factory, 516

Ximenes, Andrea, of Portugal, 285

Ximenes, Tomas, of Portugal, 285

Yarmouth
deep-water cod fishermen, 139, 141, 164; their drogue sail, 164
excise drawback on beer, 179
fish dinners, 172
'free fair', 142, 148
herring fishery, 136, 138, 155, season for, 139; French fishing fleet at, 153; herring and mackerel fleets (1581–1714), 144–6; hostmen, 174; nets lost in a storm, 140
    fish curing, 174, (attempt to copy Dutch method) 152–3; red herrings, 154, 176–7, 178
interlopers in the whaling trade, 168
merchants, 180
trades other than fishing, 184

yarnmakers' gild, 476

yield ratios, of seed sown to quantity harvested, 46–7, 49, 56, 73, 79–82, 83, 85–7; effect of climate on, 61–2, 63–4; in east and west Europe, 126; population and, 82; yield–price ratios of grain, 50–1

Yorck von Wartenburg, H. D. L., his army commission, 568

Yorkshire: iron-workers' gilds of York, 464; textiles, 13, 25, 426, (cloth) 470, 512, (kerseys) 510, (knitting) 511

Young, Arthur, 44, 571; Travels in France, 571n

Zaan river, 531; paper mills on, 535

Zaandam, 'village of carpenters', 508; shipbuilding yards, 531, (Peter the Great at) 533

Zamora, hat-making at, 517

Zealand: draperies, 515; farming, (intensive) 71, 81, (madder crop) 515, (ploughs) 99, (wheat) 70; fisheries, 147, 148–9, 182, 536; international trade, 274, 347; merchants, 222

Zerbst, breweries, 537

zinc, 473, 488, 492, 496

Zürich: refugees from Locarno, 523; textiles, (cotton) 522, (silk) 522–3, (woollens) 522

Zuyder Zee herring fishery, 153